AMERICA ON WHEELS

Southeast

ALABAMA, GEORGIA, KENTUCKY, MISSISSIPPI, NORTH CAROLINA, SOUTH CAROLINA, AND TENNESSEE

MACMILLAN • USA

Frommer's America on Wheels: Southeast

Regional Editor: Bob Sehlinger, Menasha Ridge Press
Associate Regional Editor: Holly Brown
Assistant Regional Editor: Robert Clay White
Inspections Coordinator: Laura Van Zee

Contributors: Nicole Blouin, Tommy Brown, Gentry Edwards, Carol Gallant, Christine Harmel, Scott Holt, Mike Jones, Jane Kapp, Tina Kapp, Shane Kennedy, Dave McCrary, Marc Molina, Amy Persons, Carol Thalimer, Dan Thalimer, Jane Wilkins, Bill Woolston, Budd Zehmer.

Frommer's America on Wheels Staff
Project Director: Gretchen Henderson
Senior Editor: Christopher Hollander
Database Editor: Melissa Klurman
Assistant Editor: Marian Cole

Design by Michele Laseau
Driving the State maps by Raffaele DeGennaro

Macmillan Travel
A Simon & Schuster Macmillan Company
1633 Broadway
New York, NY 10019-6785

Find us online at **http://www.mcp.com/mgr/travel** or on America Online at keyword SuperLibrary.

MACMILLAN is a registered trademark of Macmillan, Inc.

Manufactured in the United States of America

ISSN: 1082-085X
ISBN: 0-02-860933-6

SPECIAL SALES
Bulk purchases (10+ copies) of Frommer's and selected Macmillan travel guides are available to corporations, organizations, mail-order catalogs, institutions, and charities at special discounts, and can be customized to suit individual needs. For more information write to Special Sales, Macmillan General Reference, 1633 Broadway, New York, NY 10019.

Contents

Mississippi

North Carolina

South Carolina

Tennessee

Introduction

America on Wheels introduces a brand-new lodgings rating system—one that factors in the latest trends in travel preferences, technologies, and amenities and is based on thorough inspections by experienced travel professionals. We rate establishments from one to five flags, plus a unique rating we call Ultra, a special award reserved for only a handful of outstanding properties in each category. Our restaurant selections represent the ethnic diversity of today's dining scene and are categorized with symbols according to their special features, ambience, and services available. In addition, the series provides in-depth sightseeing information, including driving tours and best-of-the-state highlights.

State Introductions

Coverage of each state in the *America on Wheels* series begins with background information that will help familiarize you with your destination. Included is a summary of the state's history and an overview of its geography, followed by practical tips that we hope you will find useful in planning your trip—what kind of weather to expect, what to pack, sources of information within the state, driving rules and regulations, and other essentials.

The "Best of the State" section provides you with a rundown of the top sights and attractions and the most popular festivals and special events around the state. It also includes information on spectator sports and an A-to-Z list of recreational activities available to you.

Driving Tours

The scenic driving tours included guide you along some of the most popular sightseeing routes. Every tour is keyed to a map and includes mileage information and precise directions, refreshment stops, and, for longer tours, recommended places to stay.

The Listings

The city-by-city listings of lodgings, dining establishments, and attractions together make up the bulk of the book. Cities are organized alphabetically within each state. You will find a brief description or "profile" for most cities, including a source to contact for additional information. Any listings will follow.

TYPES OF LODGINGS

Here's how we define the lodging categories used in *America on Wheels*.

Hotel

A hotel usually has three or more floors with elevators. It may or may not have parking, but if it does, entry to the guest rooms is likely to be through the lobby rather than directly from the parking lot. A range of lodgings is available (such as standard rooms, deluxe rooms, and suites), and a range of services is available (such as bellhops, room service, and a concierge). Many hotels have a restaurant or coffee shop open for breakfast, lunch, and dinner; they may have a cocktail lounge/bar. Recreational facilities may be available (such as a swimming pool, fitness center, and tennis courts).

Motel

A motel usually has one to three floors, and many of the guest rooms have doors facing the parking lot or outdoor corridors. A motel may only have a small, serviceable lobby and usually offers only limited services; the nearest restaurant may be down the street. A motel is most likely to be located alongside a highway or in a resort area.

Inn

An inn is a small-scale hotel or lodge, usually in an older building that may or may not have been designed for lodgings, and it is often located in scenic surroundings. An inn should have a warm, welcoming atmosphere, with a more homelike quality to its furnishings and facilities. The guest rooms may be individually decorated in a style appropriate to the inn's age and location, and the rooms may or may not have telephones, televisions, or private bathrooms. An inn usually has a lounge or sitting room for guests (with parlor games and perhaps a television) and a small dining room that may or may not be open to the public. Breakfast, however, is almost always served.

Lodge

A lodge is essentially a small hotel in a rural, remote, or mountainous location. The atmosphere, service, and furniture may be more casual than you'd find in a regular hotel, and there may not be televisions or telephones in every guest room. The facilities usually include a coffee shop or restaurant, bar or cocktail lounge, games room, and indoor or outdoor swimming pool or hot tub. In ski areas, the lounge usually has a fireplace and facilities for storing ski gear.

Resort

A resort usually has more extensive facilities and recreational activities than a hotel, and offers three meals a day. The atmosphere is generally more informal than at comparable hotels.

HOW THE LODGINGS ARE RATED

Every hotel, motel, resort, inn, and lodge rated in this series has been subjected to a thorough hands-on inspection by our team of accomplished travel professionals. We ask the kinds of questions that readers would ask if they could inspect the rooms in advance for themselves (How good is the sound-proofing? How firm is the bed? What condition are the room furnishings in?). Then all of the inspection reports are reviewed by regional editors who are experts on their territories. The top-rated properties are then rechecked by a special consultant who has been reviewing and critiquing luxury hotels around the world for almost 25 years. *Establishments are not charged to be included in our series.*

Our ratings are based on *average* guest rooms—not lavish suites or concierge floors—so they're not artificially high. Therefore, in some cases a hotel rated four flags may indeed have individual rooms or suites that might fall into the five-flag category; conversely, a four-flag hotel may have a few rooms in its lowest price range that might otherwise warrant three flags.

The detailed ratings vary by category of lodgings

—for example, the criteria imposed on a hotel are more rigorous than those for a motel—and some features that are considered essential in, for example, a four-flag city hotel are relaxed for a resort that offers alternative attractions, sporting facilities, and/or beautiful and spacious grounds. Likewise, amenities such as telephones and televisions—essential in hotels and motels—are not required in inns, whose guests are often seeking peace and quiet. Instead, the criteria take into account such features as individually decorated rooms and complimentary afternoon tea.

There are, of course, several basic attributes that apply to all lodgings across the board: the cleanliness and maintenance of the building as a whole; the housekeeping in individual rooms; safety, both indoors and out; the quality and practicality of the furnishings; the quality and availability of the amenities; the caliber of the facilities; the extent and/or condition of the grounds; the ambience and cleanliness in the dining rooms; and the caliber and professionalism of the service in relation to the rates and types of lodging. Since the *America on Wheels* rating system is highly rigorous, just because a property has garnered only one flag does not mean it is inadequate or substandard.

WHAT THE INDIVIDUAL RATINGS MEAN

🏳 **One Flag**

These properties have met or surpassed the minimum requirements of cleanliness, safety, convenience, and amenities. The staff may be limited, but guests can generally expect a friendly, hospitable greeting. Rooms will have basic amenities, such as air conditioning or heating where appropriate, telephones, and televisions. The bathrooms may have only showers rather than tubs, and just one towel for each guest, but showers and towels must be clean. The one-flag properties are by no means places to avoid, since they can represent exceptional value.

🏳🏳 **Two Flags**

In addition to having all of the basic attributes of one-flag lodgings, these properties will have some extra amenities, such as bellhops to help with the luggage, ice buckets in each room, and better-quality furnishings. Some extra services may include availability of cribs and irons, and wake-up service.

🏳🏳🏳 **Three Flags**

These properties have all the basics noted above but also offer a more generous complement of amenities, such as firmer beds, larger desks, more drawer space, extra blankets and pillows, cable or satellite TV, alarm clock/radios, room service (although hours may be limited), and dry cleaning and/or laundry services.

≣≣≣ Four Flags

This is the realm of luxury, with refinements in amenities, furnishings, and service—such as larger rooms, more dependable soundproofing, two telephones per room, in-room movies, in-room safes, thick towels, hair dryers, twice-daily maid service, turndown service, concierge service, and 24-hour room service.

≣≣≣≣ Five Flags

These properties have everything the four-flag properties have, plus a more personal level of service and more sumptuous amenities, among them bathrobes, superior linens, and blackout drapes for lightproofing. Facilities normally include a business center and fitness center. Generally speaking, guests pay handsomely to stay in these properties.

⬧ Ultra

This crème-de-la-crème rating is reserved for those rare hotels and resorts, possibly also motels and inns, that are truly outstanding in every or almost every department—places with a "grand hotel" presence, an almost flawless level of service, and a standard of dining equal to that of the finest restaurants.

UNRATED

In the few cases where an inspector was not able to make a detailed inspection, the property is listed as unrated. Also, in some cases where a property was in the process of changing owners or managers, or if the property was undergoing the kind of major renovations that made formal evaluation impossible, then, again, it is listed as unrated.

TYPES OF DINING

Restaurant

A restaurant serves complete meals and almost always offers seating.

Refreshment Stop

A refreshment stop serves drinks and/or snacks only (such as an ice cream parlor, bakery, or coffee bar) and may or may not have seating available.

HOW THE RESTAURANTS WERE EVALUATED

All of the restaurants reviewed in this series have

been through the kind of thorough inspection described above for lodgings. Our inspectors have evaluated everything from freshness of ingredients to noise level and spacing of tables.

Unique to the *America on Wheels* series are the easy-to-read symbols that identify a restaurant's special features, its ambience, and special services. (See the inside front cover for the key to all symbols.) With them you can determine at a glance whether a place is a local favorite, offers exceptional value, or is "worth a splurge."

HOW TO READ THE LISTINGS

LODGINGS

Introductory Information

The rating is followed by the establishment's name, address, neighborhood (if applicable), telephone number(s), and fax number (if there is one). Where appropriate, location information is provided. In the resort listings, the acreage of the property is indicated. Also included are our inspector's comments, which provide some description and discuss any outstanding features or special information about the establishment. You can also find out whether an inn is unsuitable for children, and if so, up to what age.

Rooms

Specifies the number and type of accommodations available. If a hotel has an "executive level," this will be noted here. (This level, sometimes called a "concierge floor," is a special area of a hotel. Usually priced higher than standard rooms, accommodations at this level are often larger and have additional amenities and services such as daily newspaper delivery and nightly turndown service. Guests staying in these rooms often have access to a private lounge where complimentary breakfasts or snacks may be served.) Check-in/check-out times will also appear in this section, followed by information on the establishment's smoking policy ("No smoking" for properties that are entirely nonsmoking, and "Nonsmoking rms avail" for those that permit smoking in some areas but have rooms available for nonsmokers). This information may be followed by comments, if the inspector noted anything in particular about the guest rooms, such as their size, decor, furnishings, or window views.

Amenities

If the following amenities are available in the majority of the guest rooms, they are indicated by symbols (see inside front cover for key) or included in a list: telephone, alarm clock, coffeemaker, hair dryer, air conditioning, TV (including cable or satellite hook-up, free or pay movies), refrigerator, dataport (for fax/modem communication), VCR, CD/tape player, voice mail, in-room safe, and bathrobes. If some or all rooms have minibars, terraces, fireplaces, or whirlpools, that will be indicated here. Because travelers usually expect air conditioning, telephones, and televisions in their guest rooms, we specifically note when those amenities are not available. If any additional amenities are available in the majority of the guest rooms, or if amenities are outstanding in any way, the inspector's comments will provide some elaboration at the end of this section.

Services

If the following services are available, they are indicated by symbols (see inside front cover for key) or included in a list: room service (24-hour or limited), concierge, valet parking, airport transportation, dry cleaning/laundry, cribs available, pets allowed (call ahead before bringing your pet; an establishment that accepts pets may nevertheless place restrictions on the types or size of pets allowed, or may require a deposit and/or charge a fee), twice-daily maid service, car-rental desk, social director, masseur, children's program, babysitting (that is, the establishment can put you in touch with local babysitters and/or agencies), and afternoon tea and/or wine or sherry served. If the establishment offers any special services, or if the inspector has commented on the quality of services offered, that information will appear at the end of this section. Please note that there may be a fee for some services.

Facilities

If the following facilities are on the premises, they are indicated by symbols (see inside front cover for key) or included in a list: pool(s), bike rentals, boat rentals (may include canoes, kayaks, sailboats, powerboats, jet-skis, paddleboats), fishing, golf course (with number of holes), horseback riding, jogging path/parcourse (fitness trail), unlighted tennis courts (number available), lighted tennis courts (number available), waterskiing, windsurfing, fitness center, meeting facilities (and number of people this space can accommodate), business center, restaurant(s), bar(s), beach(es), lifeguard (for beach, not pool), basketball, volleyball, board surfing, games room, lawn games, racquetball, snorkeling, squash, spa, sauna, steam room, whirlpool, beauty salon, day-care center, playground, washer/dryer, and guest lounge (for inns only). If cross-country and downhill skiing facilities are located within 10 miles of the property, then that is indicated by symbols here as well. Our "Accessible for People With Disabilities" symbol appears where establishments claim to have guest rooms with such accessibility. If an establishment has additional facilities that are worth noting, or if the inspector has commented about the facilities, that information appears at the end of this section.

Rates

If the establishment's rates vary throughout the year, then the rates given are for the peak season. The rates listed are EP (no meals included), unless otherwise noted. We'll tell you if there is a charge for an extra person to stay in a room; if children stay free, and if so, up to what age; if there are minimum stay requirements; and if AP (three meals) and/or MAP (breakfast and dinner) rates are also available. The parking rates (if the establishment has parking) are followed by any comments the inspector has provided about rates.

If the establishment has a seasonal closing, this information will be stated. A list of credit cards accepted ends the listing.

DINING

Introductory Information

If a restaurant is a local favorite, an exceptional value (one with a high quality-to-price ratio for the area), or "worth a splurge" (more expensive by area standards, but well worth it), the appropriate symbol will appear at the beginning of the listing (see inside front cover for key to symbols). Then the establishment's name, address, neighborhood (if applicable), and telephone number are listed, followed by location information when appropriate. The type of cuisine appears in boldface type and is followed by our inspectors' comments on everything from decor and ambience to menu highlights.

The "FYI" Heading

"For your information," this section tells you the reservations policy ("recommended," "accepted," or "not accepted"), and whether there is live entertainment, a children's menu, or a dress code (jacket required or other policy). If the restaurant does not have a full bar, you can find out what the liquor policy is ("beer and wine only," "beer only," "wine only," "BYO," or "no liquor license"). This is also

where you can check to see if there's a no-smoking policy for the entire restaurant (please note that smoking policies are in flux throughout the country; if smoking—or avoiding smokers—is important to you, it's a good idea to call ahead to verify the policy). If the restaurant is part of a group or chain, address and phone information will be provided for additional locations in the area. This section does not appear in Refreshment Stop listings.

Hours of Operation

Under the "Open" heading, "Peak" indicates that the hours listed are for high season only (dates in parentheses); otherwise, the hours listed apply year-round. If an establishment has a seasonal closing, that information will follow. It's a good idea to call ahead to confirm the hours of operation, especially in the off-season.

Prices

Prices given are for dinner main courses (unless otherwise noted). If a prix-fixe dinner is offered throughout dinner hours, that price is listed here, too. This section ends with a list of credit cards accepted. Refreshment Stop listings do not include prices.

Symbols

The symbols that fall at the end of many restaurant listings can help you find restaurants with the features that are important to you. If a restaurant has romantic ambience, historic ambience, outdoor dining, a fireplace, a view, delivery service, early-bird specials, valet parking, or is family-oriented, open 24 hours, or accessible to people with disabilities (meaning it has a level entrance or an access ramp, a doorway at least 36 inches wide, and restrooms that are on the same floor as the dining room, with doorways at least 36 inches wide and properly outfitted stalls), then these symbols will appear (see inside front cover for key to symbols).

ATTRACTIONS

Introductory Information

The name, street address, neighborhood (if located in a major city), and telephone number are followed by a brief rundown of the attraction's high points and key attributes so you can quickly determine if it's worth a full day of exploration or just a brief detour.

Hours of Operation & Admission

Service information includes hours of operation ("Peak" indicates that the hours listed are for high season only) and the cost of admission. The cost is

ABBREVIATIONS	
A/C	air conditioning
AE	American Express (charge card)
AP	American Plan (rates include breakfast, lunch, and dinner)
avail	available
BB	Bed-and-Breakfast Plan (rates include full breakfast)
bkfst	breakfast
BYO	bring your own (beer or wine)
CC	credit cards
CI	check-in time
CO	check-out time
CP	Continental Plan (rates include continental breakfast)
ctr	center
D	double (indicates room rate for two people in one room (one or two beds))
DC	Diners Club (credit card)
DISC	Discover (credit card)
EC	EuroCard (credit card)
effic	efficiency (unit with cooking facilities)
ER	En Route (credit card)
info	information
int'l	international
JCB	Japanese Credit Bureau (credit card)
ltd	limited
MAP	Modified American Plan (rates include breakfast and dinner)
MC	MasterCard (credit card)
Mem Day	Memorial Day
mi	mile(s)
min	minimum
MM	mile marker
refrig	refrigerator
rms	rooms
S	single (indicates room rate for one person)
satel	satellite
stes	suites (rooms with separate living and sleeping areas)
svce	service
tel	telephone
V	Visa (credit card)
w/	with
wknds	weekends

indicated by one to four dollar signs (see inside front cover for key to symbols). It's a good idea to call ahead to confirm the hours.

SPECIAL INFORMATION

DISABLED TRAVELER INFORMATION

The Americans with Disabilities Act (ADA) of 1990 required that all public facilities and commercial establishments be made accessible to disabled persons by January 26, 1992. Any property opened after that date must be built in accordance with the ADA Accessible Guidelines. Note, however, that not all establishments have completed their renovations to conform with the law; be sure to call ahead to determine if your specific needs can be met.

TAXES

State and city taxes vary widely and are not included in the prices in this book. Always ask about the taxes when you are making your reservations. State sales tax is given under "Essentials" in the introduction to each state.

A DISCLAIMER

Readers are advised that prices fluctuate in the course of time, and travel information changes under the impact of the varied and volatile factors that affect the travel industry. The publisher cannot be held responsible for the experiences of readers while traveling. Readers are invited to send ideas, comments, and suggestions for future editions to: *America on Wheels,* Macmillan Travel, 1633 Broadway, New York, NY 10019-6785.

TOLL-FREE NUMBERS/WORLD WIDE WEB SITES

The following toll-free telephone numbers and URLs for World Wide Web sites were accurate at press time; *America on Wheels* cannot be held responsible for any number or address that has changed. The "TDD" numbers are answered by a telecommunications service for the deaf and hard-of-hearing. Be sure to dial "1" before each number.

LODGINGS

Best Western International, Inc
800/528-1234 North America
800/528-2222 TDD

Budgetel Inns
800/4-BUDGET Continental USA and Canada

Budget Host
800/BUD-HOST Continental USA

Clarion Hotels
800/CLARION Continental USA and Canada
800/228-3323 TDD
http://www.hotelchoice.com/cgi-bin/res/
webres?clarion.html

Comfort Inns
800/228-5150 Continental USA and Canada
800/228-3323 TDD
http://www.hotelchoice.com/cgi-bin/res/
webres?comfort.html

Courtyard by Marriott
800/321-2211 Continental USA and Canada
800/228-7014 TDD
http://www.marriott.com/lodging/courtyar.html

Days Inn
800/325-2525 Continental USA and Canada
800/325-3297 TDD
http://www.daysinn.com/daysinn.html

DoubleTree Hotels
800/222-TREE Continental USA and Canada
800/528-9898 TDD

Drury Inn
800/325-8300 Continental USA and Canada
800/325-0583 TDD

Econo Lodges
800/55-ECONO Continental USA and Canada
800/228-3323 TDD
http://www.hotelchoice.com/cgi-bin/res/
webres?econo.html

Embassy Suites
800/362-2779 Continental USA and Canada
800/458-4708 TDD
http://www.embassy-suites.com

Exel Inns of America
800/356-8013 Continental USA and Canada

Fairfield Inn by Marriott
800/228-2800 Continental USA and Canada
800/228-7014 TDD
http://www.marriott.com/lodging/fairf.html

Fairmont Hotels
800/527-4727 Continental USA

Forte Hotels
800/225-5843 Continental USA and Canada

Four Seasons Hotels
800/332-3442 Continental USA
800/268-6282 Canada

Friendship Inns
800/453-4511 Continental USA
800/228-3323 TDD
http://www.hotelchoice.com/cgi-bin/res/
webres?friendship.html

Guest Quarters Suites
800/424-2900 Continental USA

Hampton Inn
800/HAMPTON Continental USA and Canada
800/451-HTDD TDD
http://www.hampton-inn.com

Hilton Hotels Corporation
800/HILTONS Continental USA and Canada
800/368-1133 TDD
http://www.hilton.com

Holiday Inn
800/HOLIDAY Continental USA and Canada
800/238-5544 TDD
http://www.holiday-inn.com

Howard Johnson
800/654-2000 Continental USA and Canada
800/654-8442 TDD
http://www.hojo.com/hojo.html

Hyatt Hotels and Resorts
800/228-9000 Continental USA and Canada
800/228-9548 TDD
http://www.hyatt.com

Inns of America
800/826-0778 Continental USA and Canada

Intercontinental Hotels
800/327-0200 Continental USA and Canada

ITT Sheraton
800/325-3535 Continental USA and Canada
800/325-1717 TDD

La Quinta Motor Inns, Inc
800/531-5900 Continental USA and Canada
800/426-3101 TDD

Loews Hotels
800/223-0888 Continental USA and Canada
http://www.loewshotels.com

Marriott Hotels
800/228-9290 Continental USA and Canada
800/228-7014 TDD
http://www.marriott.com/MainPage.html

Master Hosts Inns
800/251-1962 Continental USA and Canada

Meridien
800/543-4300 Continental USA and Canada

Omni Hotels
800/843-6664 Continental USA and Canada

Park Inns International
800/437-PARK Continental USA and Canada
http://www.p-inns.com/parkinn.html

Quality Inns
800/228-5151 Continental USA and Canada
800/228-3323 TDD
http://www.hotelchoice.com/cgi-bin/res/
webres?quality.html

Radisson Hotels International
800/333-3333 Continental USA and Canada

Ramada
800/2-RAMADA Continental USA and Canada
http://www.ramada.com/ramada.html

Red Carpet Inns
800/251-1962 Continental USA and Canada

Red Lion Hotels and Inns
800/547-8010 Continental USA and Canada

Red Roof Inns
800/843-7663 Continental USA and Canada
800/843-9999 TDD
http://www.redroof.com

Renaissance Hotels International
800/HOTELS-1 Continental USA and Canada
800/833-4747 TDD

Residence Inn by Marriott
800/331-3131 Continental USA and Canada
800/228-7014 TDD
http://www.marriott.com/lodging/resinn.html

Resinter
800/221-4542 Continental USA and Canada

Ritz-Carlton
800/241-3333 Continental USA and Canada

Rodeway Inns
800/228-2000 Continental USA and Canada
800/228-3323 TDD
http://www.hotelchoice.com/cgi-bin/res/
webres?rodeway.html

Scottish Inns
800/251-1962 Continental USA and Canada

Shilo Inns
800/222-2244 Continental USA and Canada

Signature Inns
800/822-5252 Continental USA and Canada

Super 8 Motels
800/800-8000 Continental USA and Canada
800/533-6634 TDD
http://www.super8motels.com/super8.html

Susse Chalet Motor Lodges & Inns
800/258-1980 Continental USA and Canada

Travelodge
800/255-3050 Continental USA and Canada

Vagabond Hotels Inc
800/522-1555 Continental USA and Canada

Westin Hotels and Resorts
800/228-3000 Continental USA and Canada
800/254-5440 TDD
http://www.westin.com

Wyndham Hotels and Resorts
800/822-4200 Continental USA and Canada

CAR RENTAL AGENCIES

Advantage Rent-A-Car
800/777-5500 Continental USA and Canada

Airways Rent A Car
800/952-9200 Continental USA

Alamo Rent A Car
800/327-9633 Continental USA and Canada
http://www.goalamo.com

Allstate Car Rental
800/634-6186 Continental USA and Canada

Avis
800/331-1212 Continental USA
800/TRY-AVIS Canada
800/331-2323 TDD
http://www.avis.com

Budget Rent A Car
800/527-0700 Continental USA and Canada
800/826-5510 TDD

Dollar Rent A Car
800/800-4000 Continental USA and Canada

Enterprise Rent-A-Car
800/325-8007 Continental USA and Canada

Hertz
800/654-3131 Continental USA and Canada
800/654-2280 TDD

National Car Rental
800/CAR-RENT Continental USA and Canada
800/328-6323 TDD
http://www.nationalcar.com

Payless Car Rental
800/PAYLESS Continental USA and Canada

Rent-A-Wreck
800/535-1391 Continental USA

Sears Rent A Car
800/527-0770 Continental USA and Canada

Thrifty Rent-A-Car
800/367-2277 Continental USA and Canada
800/358-5856 TDD

U-Save Auto Rental of America
800/272-USAV Continental USA and Canada

Value Rent-A Car
800/327-2501 Continental USA and Canada
http://www.go-value.com

AIRLINES

American Airlines
800/433-7300 Continental USA and Western Canada
800/543-1586 TDD
http://www.americanair.com/aahome/aahome.html

Canadian Airlines International
800/426-7000 Continental USA and Canada
http://www.cdair.ca

Continental Airlines
800/525-0280 Continental USA
800/343-9195 TDD
http://www.flycontinental.com

Delta Air Lines
800/221-1212 Continental USA
800/831-4488 TDD
http://www.delta-air.com

Northwest Airlines
800/225-2525 Continental USA and Canada
http://www.nwa.com

Southwest Airlines
800/435-9792 Continental USA and Canada
http://iflyswa.com

Trans World Airlines
800/221-2000 Continental USA
http://www2.twa.com/TWA/Airlines/home/
home.html

United Airlines
800/241-6522 Continental USA and Canada
http://www.ual.com

USAir
800/428-4322 Continental USA and Canada
http://www.usair.com

TRAIN

Amtrak
800/USA-RAIL Continental USA
http://amtrak.com

BUS

Greyhound
800/231-2222 Continental USA
http://greyhound.com

The Top-Rated Lodgings

ULTRA

The Cloister, Sea Island, GA

FIVE FLAGS

The Ritz-Carlton Buckhead, Atlanta, GA

FOUR FLAGS

Atlanta Hilton & Towers, Atlanta, GA
Brookstown Inn, Winston-Salem, NC
The Brown Hotel, Louisville, KY
Callaway Gardens Resort, Pine Mountain, GA
Château Elan Resort, Braselton, GA
Crystal Sands Crowne Plaza Resort, Hilton Head Island, SC
DoubleTree Guest Suites, Lexington, KY
1884 Paxton House, Thomasville, GA
Eseeola Lodge, Linville, NC
Evergreen Conference Center & Resort, Stone Mountain, GA
Fearrington House Inn, Pittsboro, NC
The Gastonian, Savannah, GA
The Grand Hotel, Atlanta, GA
The Greystone Inn, Lake Toxaway, NC
Grove Park Inn Resort, Asheville, NC
Hilton Greensboro, Greensboro, NC
Hotel Nikko, Atlanta, GA
Hound Ears Lodge, Blowing Rock, NC
Huntsville Hilton Inn, Huntsville, AL
Hyatt Regency, Hilton Head Island, SC
Innisfree Inn, Glenville, NC
Jasmine House, Charleston, SC
John Rutledge House Inn, Charleston, SC
The Kehoe House, Savannah, GA
Kiawah Island Resort, Kiawah Island, SC
Loew's Vanderbilt Plaza Hotel, Nashville, TN
Marriott's Grand Hotel, Point Clear, AL

Marriott's Griffin Gate Resort, Lexington, KY
Mills House Hotel, Charleston, SC
Opryland Hotel, Nashville, TN
Orient Express Charleston Place, Charleston, SC
The Park—A Bissell Hotel, Charlotte, NC
The Peabody, Memphis, TN
Pinehurst Resort and Country Club, Pinehurst, NC
Presidents' Quarters, Savannah, GA
Renaissance Nashville Hotel, Nashville, TN
Renaissance Pineisle Resort, Lake Lanier Islands, GA
Renaissance Waverly Hotel, Atlanta, GA
Rhett House Inn, Beaufort, SC
Richmond Hill Inn, Asheville, NC
The Ritz-Carlton, Atlanta, GA
The Seelbach, Louisville, KY
Sheraton Music City, Nashville, TN
Swissôtel, Atlanta, GA
The Tutwiler Grand Heritage Hotel, Birmingham, AL
Vendue Inn, Charleston, SC
The Victoria Inn, Anniston, AL
Washington Duke Inn & Golf Club, Durham, NC
The Westin Resort, Hilton Head Island, SC
Whitney Hotel, Columbia, SC
Windsor Hotel, Americus, GA

ALABAMA

The Heart of Dixie

In order to understand the depth and pervasiveness of the Southern hospitality visitors to Alabama receive, it's necessary to understand the character and diversity of the state's citizens. As early as the 16th century, the French controlled the territory. (Their use of the *dix* (ten) monetary note led to the region being called the "land of dix" or "Dixie.") Many 18th- and 19th-century settlers—both lowly farmers and wealthy planters—came from North and South Carolina. During the early years of this century, steel workers came from the North and Europe to join blacks and poor white workers in creating thriving industrial centers. In the post–World War II years, Alabama's fledgling rocket research industry brought still another group of settlers, as the Germanic influence of Wernher Von Braun and his team of scientists has given north Alabama a distinctive Alpine flavor. This history of coming from other places is probably the reason Alabamians have such an unbridled interest in where you came from and who "your people" are.

The antebellum planter aristocracy's interest in education resulted in the formation of educational institutions, the proliferation of libraries and museums, and the creation of archives. The University of Alabama opened in 1831 and the rudiments of a public school system were in place by 1852. The Alabama Department of Archives and History was the first such department established in the United States. Montgomery's Alabama Shakespeare Festival offers world-class productions year-round, and the Montgomery Museum of Fine Arts and the Birmingham Museum of Art are among the finest in the South.

Even though they were denied the benefits of these cultural activities, the isolated, rural lives of African Americans resulted in rich oral traditions and culture. An abundant vein of folklore permeates close-knit African American communities, in particular, where storytelling is an art. W C Handy,

considered the Father of the Blues, was born in Florence in northwest Alabama. The state has also spawned a significant number of jazz greats.

It seems incongruous that the "cradle of the Confederacy" could—100 years later—give birth to the modern civil right movement, or that stately antebellum homes could sit almost within sight of ultramodern Saturn rockets. But Alabama is, and always has been, a state of great contrasts. The variety of its culture today makes it an ideal place to "stop and sit for a spell."

A Brief History

The First Inhabitants   Archeological excavations indicate that Alabama was inhabited as early as 10,000 BC, although the recorded history of the area begins with the Choctaw and Albaamo peoples. (*Alba* means "dense vegetation" and *amo* means "to clear," so the name *Alabama* means "thicket clearers.") Other tribes included the Chickasaw, Cherokee, and Upper Creek or Muskogee. Several dozen large ceremonial mounds that snake across the river valleys are visible remnants of their occupancy.

Fight for Control   Like most of the Southern states, Alabama has spent time under five flags. Spanish explorers made brief forays into the territory in 1519 and 1528, but it wasn't until 1540 that a European traveled extensively in Alabama. Although Hernando de Soto's search for gold was futile, he left behind detailed descriptions of the areas he visited and the Native Americans he met. All his encounters weren't peaceful. A fierce battle with Chief Tuscaloosa's tribe resulted in the deaths of several thousand Native Americans—the single bloodiest battle between whites and natives in what was to become the United States. In 1559 the Spanish erected a fort in Mobile Bay.

The French came in to Alabama in 1702 when LaSieur de Bienville established Mobile and Port Dauphin on Dauphin Island. Alabama came under British rule with the Treaty of Paris in 1763, and so it remained until the colonists' victory over the British at Yorktown in 1781. In 1814—after Andrew Jackson's army defeated the Red Stick band of the Creeks in the Battle of Horseshoe Bend—the Creek, Chickasaw, Choctaw, and Cherokee tribes were forced to cede most of their land to the whites and not long afterward they were forcibly removed to the West. The Alabama Territory was created in 1817 and it became a state in 1819.

Civil War   The first African slaves on the North American continent were unloaded off ships at Port Dauphin in 1719. By the 1830s, cotton grown in the Black Belt (so named because of the region's rich, black soil) was firmly established as the economic backbone of the state, and a plantation society based on slavery arose. Although other segments of the economy—based on railroading; mining of coal and iron ore; manufacturing steel, gin-milling machinery, and textiles—were firmly in place by the 1850s, questions about states' rights versus federal rights with regard to the slavery issue fanned the flames of dissension.

Alabama seceded from the Union in January 1861, the fourth state to do so. Jefferson Davis was inaugurated as president of the Confederacy at the new capital in Montgomery; five months later, the capital was moved to Richmond. Huntsville and the northern part of the state were occupied early in the war on by Union forces, and a huge naval battle over Mobile was won by the Union.

Reconstruction & Rebirth   The Reconstruction period that followed the bloody conflict saw the state legislature controlled by Southern white scalawags, Northern white carpetbaggers, and newly freed slaves—although the former slaves never gained as much power here as they did in South Carolina, Mississippi, and Louisiana. Reaction to Reconstruction led to the ascendance of the Ku Klux Klan and in 1875 to the reemergence of a white-controlled legislature and the effective disenfranchisement of African Americans.

Fun Facts

- The "Yellowhammer State" got its nickname from the yellow-trimmed uniforms that the state's Confederate soldiers wore during the Civil War. They reminded people of a bird called the yellowhammer, which has yellow patches under its wing.
- Mobile has been celebrating Mardi Gras every year since 1703—even longer than New Orleans.
- Most likely the world's first and only monument to an insect—the boll weevil—was dedicated by the citizens of Enterprise in 1919. The prodigiously pesky weevil, which wreaks havoc on cotton plants, had forced farmers to diversify their crops, a step that eventually led to greater prosperity for the region.
- In 1953, Alabama established the country's first statewide educational television network.
- In 1860, nearly half the population of Alabama was of African descent.

Rigid racial segregation under Jim Crow laws endured until the mid-1950s, when Rosa Parks' refusal to give up her seat on a Montgomery bus gave birth to a bus boycott led by the young Dr Martin Luther King Jr. The state received much unwanted international attention for its brutal response to the bus boycott, the Freedom Riders, and Dr King's Freedom March from Selma to Montgomery: Snarling police dogs, swinging billy clubs, and unmerciful torrents of water blasting from fire hoses "greeted" protesters. Federal troops were sent into the state after four small African American girls were killed in a church bombing. Despite the trauma and violence experienced in the quest for racial equality, today's African Americans have made tremendous strides in modern Alabama society.

Heavy industry became a player in Alabama's economy early in this century, but cotton still remained the state's chief product until the entire 1915 crop was decimated by the boll weevil. Forced to diversify its agricultural base, the state now depends on forestry, dairy and beef cattle, peanuts, soybeans, and corn, in addition to cotton. The George C Marshall Space Flight Center in Huntsville has been instrumental in bringing the aerospace industry to Alabama.

DRIVING DISTANCES

Birmingham

90 mi NW of Montgomery
101 mi S of Huntsville
119 mi SE of Florence
150 mi W of Atlanta, GA
231 mi E of Jackson, MS
241 mi NE of Mobile

Huntsville

61 mi SW of Chattanooga, TN
101 mi N of Birmingham
103 mi S of Nashville, TN
180 mi NW of Atlanta, GA
191 mi N of Montgomery
282 mi E of Florence

Mobile

49 mi W of Pensacola, FL
70 mi E of Gulfport, MS
144 mi E of New Orleans, LA
174 mi SW of Montgomery
241 mi SW of Birmingham
266 mi S of Tuscaloosa

A Closer Look

GEOGRAPHY

Most of Alabama is flat and barely above sea level, although the terrain rises sharply in the northeast corner of the state. But the state is laced with 26 major rivers, which together provide more than 1,600 miles of navigable waterways in addition to the vast water area of Mobile Bay. One of these rivers, the mighty **Tennessee,** cuts across most of northern Alabama south of the border with Tennessee. The Tennessee River Valley's rich soil allows farmers to grow corn, cotton, and hay, while the river provides water transportation and hydroelectric power. Flor-

ence, Decatur, and Huntsville (the "space city") all lie along the river.

Extending from the northeastern corner of the state and running southwest, the **Cumberland Plateau** (also known as the Appalachian Plateau) varies from flat to rolling, with elevations varying between 500 feet and 1,800 feet. The sandy soils here were not conducive to agriculture until the development of commercial fertilizers. Guntersville and Scottsboro lie further north along the plateau.

The **Appalachian Ridge and Valley Region,** the state's only mountainous region, traces a northeast-to-southwest path parallel to the Cumberland Plateau. The serendipitous proximity of coal, iron ore, and limestone—the three basic minerals used in making iron and steel—made this region a center of iron and steel production. The largest cities in the region are Birmingham (the largest steel-producing center in the South), Gadsden, and Anniston.

A half-circle-shaped region in east-central Alabama, called the **Piedmont,** is characterized by low hills and ridges separated by sandy valleys and covered by forests. Although the clay soils have been badly eroded, the presence of coal, iron ore, limestone, and marble, as well as the production of electric power and textiles, make this area an important manufacturing region. The highest point in Alabama—2,407-foot **Cheaha Mountain**—is in the Piedmont.

Alabama's largest region, the **East Gulf Coastal Plain** covers the southern two-thirds of the state and has several distinct sections. In the extreme southwest is the low, swampy area of the **Mobile River Delta,** while wiry grass and pine forests characterize the southeast. The remainder of this region consists of low, rolling hills covered by pine forests, which stretch almost to the Tennessee border in western Alabama. Extending across central Alabama into Mississippi is the slim band of rolling prairie known as the **Black Belt,** noted for its sticky black-clay soil. In the 19th century, this was the area of huge cotton plantations, but today is more noted for raising livestock. Camden and Selma are the chief cities of this region.

Alabama's coastline consists of a mere 53 miles on the Gulf of Mexico, but when bays and inlets are accounted for the total extends to 607 miles. **Mobile Bay,** an important harbor, is the chief feature of this region. Dauphin Island, Alabama's largest coastal island, lies across the entrance to Mobile Bay. Other bays include Mississippi Sound (west of Mobile Bay) and Perdido Bay (on the Alabama-Florida border).

CLIMATE

For the most part, Alabama enjoys a moderate climate year-round, although extreme northeast Alabama experiences some cold weather and even snow in the winter. Spring arrives early, however, with warm temperatures arriving as early as March. The area from Birmingham northward experiences summer temperatures in the high 80s and low 90s; the southern part of the state can get even hotter (although Gulf breezes do provide some relief). Autumn is delightful throughout the state.

AVG MONTHLY TEMPS (°F) & RAINFALL (IN)		
	Birmingham	Mobile
Jan	43/5.0	51/4.6
Feb	46/4.6	54/4.9
Mar	54/6.6	60/6.5
Apr	63/6.3	68/6.4
May	70/3.8	75/5.5
June	77/3.2	81/5.1
July	81/4.2	82/7.7
Aug	80/3.9	82/6.8
Sept	74/4.6	78/6.6
Oct	63/2.8	69/2.6
Nov	52/3.5	59/3.7
Dec	45/4.8	53/5.4

WHAT TO PACK

Alabama enjoys such a temperate climate that it's easy to pack for a trip almost any time of year. Cool cottons are appropriate most of the time and it's always a good idea to pack layers for the occasional hot or cool spell. Pack a sweater or jacket for cool evenings in the mountains or along the breezy shore; you'll rarely need a heavy coat. A hat, gloves, and boots are necessary only occasionally in higher elevations. Although Alabamians dress casually, you'll want to pack something dressier for upscale restaurants and resorts or for a special night out on the town.

TOURIST INFORMATION

For information about Alabama, contact the **Alabama Bureau of Tourism and Travel,** PO Box 4309, Montgomery, AL 36103-4309 (tel toll free 800/ALABAMA). The Governor's Correspondence Office maintains a Web page (http://alaweb.asc.edu)

with general information about the state. To find out how to obtain tourist information for individual cities and parks in Alabama, look under specific cities in the listings section of this book.

DRIVING RULES AND REGULATIONS

The minimum age is 16 to obtain a driver's license. Alabama's maximum speed limit is 65 mph on specified rural interstates and 55 mph on open highways unless otherwise marked. Alabama permits right turns on red, unless a sign forbidding such turns is posted. All front-seat passengers must be restrained by a seat belt. In both front and back seats, children under six must occupy federally approved safety restraints (child safety seats for children three and under; four- and five-year-olds may use seat belts). Motorcyclists are required to wear helmets.

RENTING A CAR

All the national car rental companies have offices throughout Alabama. Minimum age requirements to rent a car vary between 21 and 25, depending on the company. Most companies sell collision damage waiver protection, but check your own insurance policy or the credit card that you will use to see if you are already covered.

- **Alamo** (tel toll free 800/327-9633)
- **Avis** (tel 800/831-2847)
- **Budget** (tel 800/527-0700)
- **Dollar** (tel 800/800-4000)
- **Hertz** (tel 800/654-3131)
- **National** (tel 800/227-7368)
- **Thrifty** (tel 800/367-2277)

ESSENTIALS

Area Code: Alabama has two area codes. The northern third (including Birmingham, Huntsville, and Florence) uses the **205** area code, while the southern section (including Montgomery and Mobile) uses **334.**

Emergencies: Call 911 from anywhere in the state

Road Info: Call the state patrol at 334/270-1122.

Smoking: Smoking laws are determined on a local basis or by individual businesses. Many restaurants maintain a nonsmoking section and a few are even smoke-free. Larger hotels and chains often offer nonsmoking rooms.

Taxes: Alabama's sales tax is 4%, although many counties and localities impose an additional amount.

Time Zone: Alabama is in the Central time zone, and daylight saving time is observed statewide.

Best of the State
WHAT TO SEE AND DO

Below is a general overview of some of the top sights and attractions in Alabama. To find out more detailed information, look under "Attractions" under individual cities in the listings portion of this book.

National Parks Alabama boasts several parks and refuges operated by the National Park Service. The spot where Andrew Jackson defeated the Creeks is enshrined at the **Horseshoe Bend National Military Park** in Dadeville, where interpretive markers describe the battle along a three-mile route. In addition to a museum with a slide presentation about the battle, exhibits, and an electronic map, the park offers picnicking, a boat ramp, and five miles of hiking trails. Visitors can observe the flights of migratory waterfowl from September through May at the **Wheeler National Wildlife Refuge** in Decatur and examine displays of native animals at Givens Wildlife Interpretive Center. The marshes, forests, and uplands of the **Eufaula National Wildlife Refuge,** bordering the Walter F George Reservoir on the Chattahoochee River, provide a winter habitat for waterfowl, birds of prey, songbirds, and other migrant birds.

State Parks From the grandeur of the mountainous north to the sun-kissed Gulf beaches, Alabama's 24 state parks offer something for everyone. All but a few of the parks offer camping; the seven resort parks have a lodge and/or cabins and a wide array of activities such as boating, fishing, tennis, hiking, and even golf. Call Alabama State Parks (tel 334/242-3334) for more information.

Natural Wonders Alabama's varied topography —particularly in the northern regions—is filled with natural phenomena. Prehistoric relics are contained in the cave shelter at Bridgeport's **Russell Cave National Monument.** At the site you can enjoy hiking and horseback trails, an Indian Garden, and living history demonstrations, or perhaps ride the 130-year-old free ferry across the Tennessee River. **Cherokee Rock Village,** near Centre, is composed of enormous boulders of all shapes and sizes—some as large as 200 feet tall. Hike through heavy woods to the spectacular double sandstone **Natural Bridge** near Double Springs. The 60-foot-high and 148-foot-long bridge is the longest natural span east of the Rockies. The **Sipsey Wilderness,** also near Double Springs, features gorges, canyons, stands of virgin timber, exotic plants, and rare birds and animals. **DeSoto Falls,** in DeSoto Falls State Park, plunges 100 feet from a mile-long lake into a deep pool. **Little River Canyon,** near Fort Payne, is one of the deepest canyons east of the Mississippi. Little River, which formed the gorge over thousands of years, is the only river in the country that forms, runs its entire course, and ends on top of a mountain. Numerous overlooks along the gorge permit different views of its rugged scenery. **Noccalula Falls,** located in the park of the same name in Gadsden, plummets 90 feet over a Lookout Mountain ledge into a lush ravine. **Rock Bridge Canyon,** near Hodges, provides a panorama of natural bridges, waterfalls, and beautiful rock formations. **Dismals Canyon,** in the northwestern part of the state, is famous as the home of mysterious twinkle-in-the-dark worms called Dismalites. The canyon also contains exotic plants, natural bridges, strange rock formations, plunging waterfalls, and a limestone pool.

Dramatically lit underground lakes and towering stalagmites make **Sequoyah Caverns,** north of Valley Head, resemble an underground palace. Tour the onyx caves of **DeSoto Caverns,** near Childersburg, and see not only spectacular underground formations, but also a Laser, Sound, Light, and Water Show in the cave. Also on the grounds are a prehistoric burial ground and a Confederate gunpowder mining center.

Manmade Wonders Alabama and Georgia were the homes of an ancient civilization of mound builders. The **Indian Mound** at Florence is the largest domiciliary mound in the Tennessee Valley. A museum there houses a large collection of Native American relics from the Paleolithic period. **Moundville Archaeological Park,** at Moundville, has 20 platform mounds on 320 acres as well as a museum, reconstructed Native American village and temple, and nature trails. Birmingham's *Vulcan*—a colossal 55-foot-tall statue honoring the god of the forge—is the largest iron statue in the world. Visitors can ride an elevator to an all-weather observatory for breathtaking panoramas of the gardens and Birmingham's skyline.

The **Tennessee Valley Authority** (TVA) was created in 1933 to reshape the unruly Tennessee River in hopes of economically transforming the surrounding valley. Gigantic dams regulate water turned by huge turbines to create abundant, pollution-free electricity, control periodic flooding, provide jobs, and create innumerable recreational opportunities.

Family Favorites Families can experience more than 60 hands-on space and science exhibits at the **US Space and Rocket Center/NASA Visitor Center** in Huntsville. See a full-size space shuttle, a *Saturn V* moon rocket, and the NASA Marshall Space Flight Center.

Alabama's climate is ideal for water theme parks and there are several from which to choose. Named for the ducks that come each winter to the adjacent Wheeler National Wildlife Refuge in Decatur, 750-acre **Point Mallard Park** features an aquatic center with a wave pool, an Olympic-size diving pool, water slides, and two kiddie pools; an ice rink (winter only), 18-hole golf course, hiking and biking trails, and a 175-site campground are also available. **Goose Pond Recreation Complex,** south of Scottsboro, is bounded on three sides by the Guntersville Reservoir of the Tennessee River. In addition to 116 campsites and several cottages, the park features an 18-hole golf course, Olympic-size pool, an amphitheater, two-mile hiking trail, marina, bait and tackle shop, and pontoon boat rentals. **Water World** in Dothan features a wave pool, three flume rides, a 400-foot water slide, and kiddie play area. **Waterville, USA** in Gulf Shores contains a 25,000-square-foot wave pool, seven water slides, 825 feet of white-water rafting, body flumes, a kiddie area, and a

dive shop. **Styx River Water World** in Robertsdale has speedboats, water slides, and bumper boats.

The **Talladega Superspeedway** and the **International Motorsports Hall of Fame and Museum,** both in Talladega, pay homage to the fast-paced sport of auto racing. At the museum, you can see more than 100 racing vehicles and memorabilia from 1902 to the present, and even experience the thrill of competition by trying out the Richard Petty Single Seat Race Car Simulator. A special museum just for kids, the **Children's Hands-On Museum** of Tuscaloosa, includes a miniature planetarium; a mock-up of a Choctaw village; Images (a light and color experience); Grandma's Attic (where children can dress up in old-fashioned costumes); and child-size replicas of a TV studio, hospital, bank, general store, and print shop.

Beaches Dauphin Island, on the west side of Mobile Bay, is a family-oriented beach community that retains the charm of 25 years ago. Three communities draw sun worshipers to the east side of Mobile Bay and on eastward to Florida. The hotels, restaurants, and attractions at **Gulf Shores** are family oriented, while the more upscale resort community of **Orange Beach** is home to the largest charter fishing fleet on the Gulf of Mexico. Next door **Perdido Pass,** Alabama's Gateway to the Gulf, connects 380,000 acres of backwater bays and bayous to the Gulf of Mexico. **Gulf State Park** features 2½ miles of beach, a beach pavilion, an 825-foot fishing pier, sailboat charters, a hotel, and campsites.

Historic Sites Although Alabama lost many of its treasures during the Civil War, it did not suffer as much destruction as some of the other Southern states. Many antebellum structures remain, the most magnificent of which is the **State Capitol** in Montgomery. **Gaineswood** mansion in Demopolis is an architectural masterpiece that took 17 years to complete. The 20-room Greek Revival home boasts galleried rooms flooded with light from glass ceiling domes. In Eutaw, Greek Revival **Kirkwood,** with its oversized belvedere, is the most photographed home in Alabama. An outstanding example of neoclassical architecture, **Sturdivant Hall** in Selma is a 10-room mansion filled with antiques and surrounded by formal gardens of native flowers, trees, and shrubs.

In addition to its surviving antebellum structures, Alabama has a wealth of late-Victorian edifices. The Old Town Historic District in Selma contains more than 1,200 such buildings. Decatur boasts two historic neighborhoods: **Albany** and **Old Decatur,** as does Huntsville: **Twickenham** and **Old Town.** Talladega's most impressive homes are found in the **Silk Stocking District,** so named because the ladies who lived there were the only ones in town who could afford silk stockings.

Alabama's first permanent capital, **Old Cahaba** was established at a strategic location at the confluence of the Cahaba and Alabama Rivers. Almost nothing of the once-thriving town remains at what is now the **Old Cahawba Archaeological Park,** south of Selma. The interpretive park features a welcome center, descriptive signs, the remains of old streets, and hiking trails. Picturesque ruins of a later Capitol building remain in **Capitol Park** behind the Old Tavern Museum in Tuscaloosa.

Museums   Many of Alabama's museums relate local or state history, but there is something to satisfy your curiosity on almost any subject. Because so much of the civil rights movement took place in Alabama, several museums are devoted to that struggle. The **Birmingham Civil Rights Institute** is a state-of-the-art facility that houses exhibits relating to historical events from the post–World War II era to the present. The museum is the centerpiece of a Civil Rights District that includes Kelly Ingram Park, the Alabama Jazz Hall of Fame, and the 16th Street Baptist Church. The **National Voting Rights Museum,** in Selma at the foot of the Edmund Pettus Bridge, chronicles the history of the voting rights movement.

Old Alabama Town in Montgomery contains three square blocks of houses and commercial structures depicting 19th-century life in central Alabama. Just a few of the buildings include the Lucas Tavern, Ordeman-Shaw Townhouse, Rose-Morris Craft House, Alabama Pharmaceutical Association Drugstore Museum, and a working cotton gin. **Landmark Park** near Dothan depicts the natural and cultural heritage of the Wiregrass region through a living history town and farmstead, a rustic interpretive center, a planetarium, and several nature trails. A state that thrived with the Golden Age of the railroads in the last quarter of the 19th century, Alabama is graced by several railroad museums: **Albertville Train Depot Museum, North Alabama Railroad Museum** in Chase, **Depot Museum** in Fort Payne, **Huntsville Depot Museum, Stevenson Depot Museum, Old Depot Museum** in Selma, and the Depot Museum in Enterprise—all of which pay

homage to the Iron Horse.

One of the most outstanding natural history museums in the Southeast, the **Anniston Museum of Natural History** contains displays ranging from dinosaurs and fossils to North American mammals. A turn-of-the-century set of dioramas includes 400 species of birds—many of which are now extinct or endangered. Other unusual displays include two Egyptian mummies and a walk-through replica of an Alabama cave. Both the **Birmingham Museum of Art** and the **Montgomery Museum of Fine Arts** house exceptional collections. The museum in Birmingham is noted for its accumulations of 18th-century French decorative arts and the largest assemblage of Wedgwood outside England as well as its multilevel outdoor sculpture garden, while the museum in Montgomery is renowned for the Blount Collection of American art. The **Fine Arts Museum of the South** (FAMOS) in Mobile contains more than 4,500 works spanning 2,000 years of culture.

Football fans, especially University of Alabama enthusiasts, will enjoy the **Paul W Bryant Museum** on the campus of the university in Tuscaloosa. The museum chronicles the history of the university's football team with special emphasis on the tenure of Coach Bryant. Memorabilia highlighting the careers of other Alabama sports figures such as Heisman Trophy winner Pat Sullivan and boxer Joe Louis is displayed at the **Alabama Sports Hall of Fame** in Birmingham.

Gardens   Alabama's climate is ideal for year-round blooms. The queen of gardens in Alabama is **Bellingrath Gardens and Home** at Theodore, not far southwest of Mobile. Breathtaking in any season, the 65-acre garden along the Oies River showcases flowers, sculpture, lakes, and waterfowl. The predominant floral seasons are azaleas in the spring, roses in the summer, cascading chrysanthemums in the fall, and poinsettias at Christmas. Not to be outdone, the **Mobile Botanical Gardens** feature collections of holly, ferns, rhododendron, wildflowers, and herbs as well as trees and greenhouse plants. A fragrance and texture garden is designed for the visually impaired. **Birmingham Botanical Gardens,** encompassing 68 acres, contains thousands of flowers, trees, and shrubs, as well as 230 species of native birds. Featured gardens include rose, Japanese, wildflower, camellia, iris, lily, and vegetable collections. In addition, the garden boasts a fine selection of sculpture and one of the largest glass conservatories in the Southeast. A serene haven within the city, the 112-acre **Huntsville/Madison County Botanical Garden** is a blend of woodland paths, grassy meadows, floral collections, and seasonal colors. Brilliant blossoms form a vibrant background for 17 acres of Greek art, fountains, and a replica of Olympic temple ruins at **Jasmine Hill Gardens and Outdoor Museum** near Montgomery.

Parks & Zoos   One of the largest zoos in the Southeast, the **Birmingham Zoo** is home to more than 800 rare and exotic animals. Along with the zoo's new cheetah display, visitors can see exhibits devoted to predators and social animals. The **Montgomery Zoo** features more than 800 animals in natural, barrier-free environments representing five continents. **Zooland Animal Park** in Gulf Shores features 200 animals in natural habitats visible from meandering paths and elevated observation decks. The **Animal House Zoological Park,** near Moulton, features everything from African lions to crocodiles and red-ruffed lemurs. The park is particularly noted for its collection of African and Asian antelope. A 538-acre urban forest, Birmingham's **Ruffner Mountain Nature Center** features native plants and animals amid unusual geological formations and free-flowing springs crisscrossed by seven miles of hiking trails.

EVENTS AND FESTIVALS

- **Mardi Gras,** Mobile. Two weeks of parades, balls, carnival, other events. February or March. Call toll free 800/566-2453.
- **Azalea Trail and Festival,** Mobile. Driving tours of 27-mile trail of flamboyant blossoms, historic home tours, runs and walks. March to May. Call toll free 800/566-2453.
- **Eufaula Pilgrimage Tour of Homes and Antiques Show,** Eufaula. Antebellum homes, antiques show, candlelight tours, arts and crafts. Early April. Call 334/687-6664.
- **Dauphin Island Race,** Dauphin Island to Mobile. This 37-year-old event regularly draws 300 sailboats. Fish fry, bands, and dancing. April. Call 334/434-7304.
- **Blessing of the Fleet,** Bayou La Batre. Land and water parades, contests, entertainment, seafood. Late May. Call 334/824-2415.
- **City Stages,** Birmingham. National music acts, dancing, food. Mid-June. Call 205/251-1272.
- **Spirit of Freedom Festival,** Florence. Live enter-

tainment, fireworks, picnic. July 4. Call 205/383-2525.
- **W C Handy Music Festival,** Florence. Jazz, blues, 5K run, Century Bike Ride, parade. Early August. Call toll free 800/47-BLUES.
- **Anniston Museum Day,** Anniston. Music, comedy, magicians, live animal presentations, crafts. Mid-August. Call 205/237-6766.
- **International Cityfest,** Tuscaloosa. German food, wines, beer, oompah band, arts and crafts. Late September. Call toll free 800/538-8696.
- **Madison Street Festival,** Madison. Craftspeople, old-time demonstrations, square dancing, vocal groups. Late September. Call 205/772-0535.

SPECTATOR SPORTS

Auto Racing   The world's fastest speedway, the Talladega Superspeedway (tel 205/362-9064), hosts two NASCAR Winston Cup events: the Winston 500 on the first Sunday in May and the DieHard 500 in late July.

Baseball   Although Alabama has no major league teams, it does have several minor league teams. The **Birmingham Barons** (tel 205/988-3200) play at Hoover Metropolitan Stadium; the **Huntsville Stars** play at Joe W Davis Stadium (tel 205/882-2562); and the **Mobile Baysharks** (tel 334/342-SHARK) play at Eddie Stanky Field.

College Basketball   Alabama has no NBA teams; however, basketball fever runs high when its two major college basketball teams meet. Both are members of the Southeast Conference and are perennial rivals for the state bragging rights. The **University of Alabama Crimson Tide** play at Coleman Coliseum in Tuscaloosa (tel 205/384-3600), and the **Auburn University Tigers** (also known as the War Eagles) play at Beard-Eaves Memorial Coliseum in Auburn (tel 334/844-9800).

College Football   Both of Alabama's major colleges have impressive football teams. Each is often included in the nation's Top Ten teams and the fervor of their respective fans is legendary. The **University of Alabama Crimson Tide** play at Bryant-Denny Stadium in Tuscaloosa (tel 205/384-3600) and the **Auburn University Tigers** (also known as the War Eagles) play at Jordan Hare Stadium in Auburn (tel 334/844-9800).

Hockey   Amazingly enough, Alabama does have

two professional hockey teams: the **Birmingham Bulls** (tel 205/458-8833), who play at the Birmingham/Jefferson Civic Center; and the **Mobile Mystics** (tel 334/434-7932), who play at the Mobile Civic Center.

Horse Racing   Alabama is one of the few Southern states with thoroughbred horse racing. Simulcast horse racing is broadcast year-round and live horse racing occurs seasonally at the **Birmingham Race Course,** 1000 John Rogers Dr (tel toll free 800/998-UBET).

Greyhound Racing   Live greyhound racing is offered year-round at the **Birmingham Race Course** (tel toll free 800/998-UBET). Thirteen races per evening are offered at **Greenetrack** in Eutaw (tel toll free 800/633-5942). **VictoryLand**, in Montgomery (tel toll free 800/688-2946), seats 1,000 in the clubhouse and 400 in the grandstand. The $25,000 Port City Puppy Classic is the premier event at the **Mobile Greyhound Park** (tel 334/653-5000), a multimillion dollar facility with touch-screen betting machines.

ACTIVITIES A TO Z

Bicycling   Mountain biking is growing in popularity in Alabama. Three well-liked locations for cyclists are the Bartrum Trail in Tuskegee National Forest, Oak Mountain State Park, and Monte Sano State Park. For more information contact **Cahaba Cycles** in Birmingham (tel toll free 800/846-9829) or **Cycle Escape** in Montgomery (tel 334/277-5572).

Climbing   One of the deepest gorges east of the Mississippi, Little River Canyon near Fort Payne is one of the best places to climb in the Southeast. Contact **Adams Outdoors** (tel 205/845-2988) or **DeSoto State Park** (tel 205/845-0051). To get in shape and practice before you go, you can use the inside climbing wall at **Alabama Outdoors Outfitters** (tel 205/870-1919).

Fishing   From the surf of the Gulf of Mexico to the icy streams in the northern Alabama mountains, the state offers myriad fishing opportunities. The best source of fishing information is *Fish Alabama,* available from the **Alabama Bureau of Tourism and Travel** (tel toll free 800/ALABAMA). It lists 39 premier fishing areas and gives licensing information as well as creel limits and fresh and saltwater records. If you are in or near Eufaula, the staff at

Tom Mann's Fish World on US 431 (tel 334/687-3655) can supply you with advice and/or equipment.

Golf   The state-created Robert Trent Jones Golf Trail is a system of seven exceptional public courses stretching from Mobile on the Gulf Coast to Huntsville in the northeastern mountains. With a total of 18 courses offering 324 holes, this 342-mile trail has made Alabama a world-class golfing destination. The courses are strategically located around the state and each one has unique architecture; they offer golfers the experience of all types of topography, scenery, and vegetation. Although the layouts of the courses are vastly different, the clubs all have spacious, well-appointed clubhouses with displays of antique golf memorabilia; full-service pro shops with snack bar, dining facilities, and locker rooms; and low greens and cart fees. Facilities are no more than 15 minutes off an interstate, no more than two hours from each other, and located close to cities or towns with a wide variety of attractions and comfortable accommodations. Call the **SunBelt Golf Corporation** (tel toll free 800/949-4444) for more information.

Alabama has many other golf courses open to public play or which have reciprocal arrangements with various country clubs around the country. For more information, consult *Golf Alabama,* available from the **Alabama Bureau of Tourism and Travel** (tel toll free 800/ALABAMA).

Horseback Riding   Trails rides and hayrides of varying lengths are offered at the Shady Grove Dude and Guest Ranch (tel 205/634-4344), Alabama's only dude ranch, located near Mentone on the Lookout Mountain Parkway. A lodge, farmhouse, and bunkhouse are available for overnight stays. Horse and mule riding are offered at the **Wheeler National Wildlife Refuge** in Decatur (tel 205/350-6639). On the Gulf Coast near Fort Morgan, you can ride on the beach with **Horseback Beach Rides,** Gulf Shores (tel 334/943-6674). **Oak Mountain State Park,** Birmingham (tel 205/663-6783); **Buck's Pocket State Park,** Grove Oak (tel 205/659-2000); the **Shoal Creek Ranch District** of the Talladega National Forest, Heflin (tel 205/463-2272), and **Owl Creek Horse Camp** in the Bankhead National Forest, Houston (tel 205/489-5111) have bridle trails but do not rent horses.

Skiing   Believe it or not, Alabama does offer snow skiing. **Cloudmont Ski and Golf Resort** near Mento-

SELECTED PARKS & RECREATION AREAS

- **Russell Cave National Monument,** Rte 1, Box 175, Bridgeport, AL 35740 (tel 205/495-2672)
- **Eufaula National Wildlife Refuge,** Rte 2, Box 97-B, Eufaula, AL 36027 (tel 334/687-4065)
- **Wheeler National Wildlife Refuge,** Box 1643, Decatur, AL 35602 (tel 205/350-6639)
- **Horseshoe Bend National Military Park,** Rte 1, Box 103, Daviston, AL 36256 (tel 205/234-7111)
- **Blue Springs State Park,** Rte 1, Box 132, Clio, AL 36017 (tel 334/397-8703)
- **Buck's Pocket State Park,** Rte 1, Box 36, Grove Oak, AL 35975 (tel 205/659-2000)
- **Cheaha State Park,** Rte 1, Box 77-H, Delta, AL 36258 (tel 205/488-5111)
- **Chewacla State Park,** PO Box 447, Auburn, AL 36831 (tel 334/887-5621)
- **Claude D Kelley State Park,** Rte 2, Box 77, Atmore, AL 36502 (tel 334/862-2511)
- **DeSoto State Park,** Rte 1, Box 210, Fort Payne, AL 35967 (tel 205/845-0051)
- **Florala State Park,** PO Box 322, Florala, AL 36442-0322 (tel 334/858-6425)
- **Gulf State Park,** 20115 AL 135, Gulf Shores, AL 36542 (tel 334/948-7275)
- **Joe Wheeler State Park,** Rte 4, Box 369-A, Rossville, AL 35652 (tel 205/247-5466)
- **Lake Guntersville State Park,** PO Box 7966, Guntersville, AL 35976-9126 (tel 205/571-5444)
- **Lakepoint Resort State Park,** Rte 2, Box 94, Eufaula, AL 36027-9202 (tel 334/687-6676)
- **Monte Sano State Park,** 5105 Nolen Ave, Huntsville, AL 35801 (tel 205/534-3757)
- **Oak Mountain State Park,** PO Box 278, Pelham, AL 35124 (tel 205/620-2520)
- **Rickwood Caverns State Park,** Rte 3, Box 357, Warrior, AL (tel 205/647-9692)
- **Roland Cooper State Park,** 49 Deer Run Dr, Camden, AL 36726 (tel 334/682-4838)
- **Wind Creek State Park,** Rte 2, Box 145, Alexander City, AL 35010 (tel 334/329-0845)

ne (tel 205/634-4344) is not only one of the nation's southernmost ski resorts; it also offers challenging mountain golf. As long as nighttime temperatures are cold enough to make snow, guests may choose between both sports.

White-Water Rafting   Exciting opportunities for white-water adventures abound in northwest Alabama on the Upper and Lower Factory Falls on the Bear Creek Canoe Run. In fact, Lower Factory Falls is Class VI in difficulty (for experts only). You can kayak on the Coosa River in Wetumpka when there are recreational releases by Alabama Power Company. For more information on white-water sports, contact the **Birmingham Canoe Club** (tel 205/870-4022), **Friends of Locust Fork** (tel 205/647-8835), or the **Cahaba River Society** (tel 205/322-5326).

ALONG THE ALABAMA

Start	Montgomery
Finish	Mobile
Distance	200 miles
Time	2–3 days
Highlights	Alabama State Capitol, Civil War sites, civil rights sites, historic structures, art and history museums, Alabama Shakespeare Festival, lost towns, gristmill, World War II battleship and submarine, ornate ironwork, Mardi Gras memorabilia

Stretching through south-central Alabama, the Alabama River flows alongside some of the most historically significant and picturesque sites in the state. The river begins near Montgomery ("the cradle of the Confederacy") and meanders west to Selma (one of the birthplaces of the civil rights movement), then swings south past the ruins of Old Cahaba, the first capital of Alabama. Next, the Alabama wanders through the Black Belt (with its rich soil, restored antebellum homes, and other reminders of the old South) before emptying into Mobile Bay.

Although the end points of this tour are marked by two modern cities, most of the route is lined with small towns. The people of this region are proud of their vibrant history, so much so that nearly every town or crossroads boasts a historic house or a local history museum. This is an itinerary characterized by a leisurely pace of life and sedate recreational activities such as fishing and flat-water paddling. Food options in the area range from down-home country cooking to gourmet cuisine, while accommodations include a converted historic railroad station in Montgomery, antebellum homes in Selma, and modern high-rise hotels in Mobile.

For additional information on lodgings, dining, and attractions in the region covered by the tour, look under specific cities in the listings portion of this chapter.

I-65 (from either the north or south) and I-85 (from the east) both give easy access to the starting point:

1. **Montgomery,** capital of Alabama and birthplace of the Confederacy and the modern civil rights movement. In 1861, delegates from the seceding states met in the Senate chamber of the **Capitol,** Bainbridge St at Dexter Ave, to form the Confederate States of America. In 1954, nearly a century later, seamstress Rosa Parks stepped onto a bus across the street from the Capitol; her simple refusal to yield her seat in the front of the bus to a white man led to her arrest and a 1½-year bus boycott led by Dr Martin Luther King Jr. It was on the steps of the Capitol that the famous Selma-to-Montgomery march came to an end in 1965. One of the most elegant capitol buildings in the country, the imposing Greek Revival structure has been restored to its Civil War–era appearance.

Within walking distance of the Capitol are several other important sites. **Dexter Avenue King Memorial Baptist Church,** 454 Dexter Ave, was King's first pastorate and the site of many rallies during the bus boycott. A huge mural in the church depicts scenes from King's life. Just across a side street from the Capitol is the **First White House of the Confederacy,** 644 Washington Ave, where President Jefferson Davis and his family lived until the Confederacy's seat of government was moved to Richmond, VA. A block and a half down Washington Ave is the stunning **Civil Rights Memorial,** located on the grounds of the Southern Poverty Law Center, 400 Washington Ave. Designed by the creator of the Vietnam Veterans Memorial in Washington, the memorial honors all those—both black and white—who died in the struggle for justice.

After wandering through the Capitol district, you may wish to stop by the restored 1850s residence that now houses the **Montgomery Visitor Center,** 401 Madison Ave. Just behind the visitor center stretches **Old Alabama Town,** centered on 310 N Hull St. The complex consists of three square blocks of houses and businesses that depict central Alabama life in the 19th century. Among the structures open to visitors are the Rose-Morris Craft House, the Alabama Pharmaceutical Association Drugstore Museum, and a turn-of-the-century cotton gin.

Two stars in Montgomery's cultural firmament are the **Montgomery Museum of Fine Arts,** One

Take a Break

Although the decor is an afterthought, folks flock to the downtown **Farmer's Market Cafeteria,** 315 N McDonough St (tel 334/262-9163), for the huge servings of fried chicken, catfish, country-fried steak, and tender vegetables. Entrees are $6 to $8.

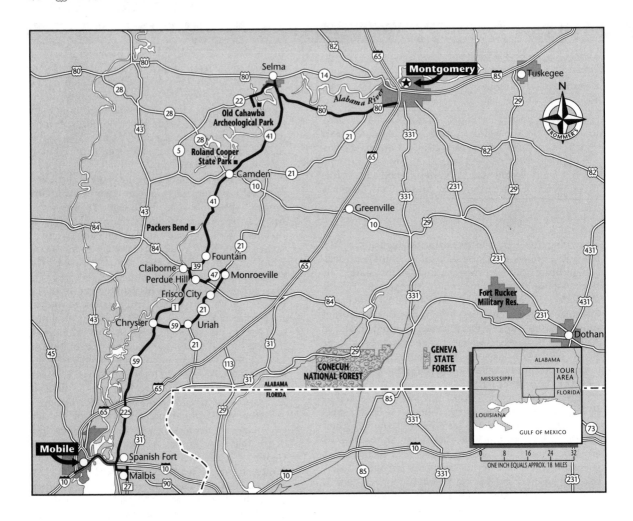

Museum Dr, and the **Alabama Shakespeare Festival,** One Festival Dr, both in Blount Park. The museum's permanent collection emphasizes American art from the 18th century to the 20th century, while world-class classical and contemporary theater productions are presented year-round at the Shakespeare Festival.

From Montgomery, take US 80/AL 8 west for 68 miles to the next stop:

2. **Selma,** site of one of the last great Civil War battles and the point of origin for Dr King's march to Montgomery. The town was laid out by William Rufus King, a US senator and later vice president under Franklin Pierce. The best place to get a complete picture of Selma's history is at the **Old Depot Museum,** 4 Martin Luther King St. Located in a grand Romanesque railroad station built in 1891, the interpretive museum includes rooms devoted to the Civil War, African American heritage, and the struggle for voting rights; other rooms depict a turn-of-the-century schoolroom and a 19th-century medical office.

While in town, you can drive through the **Old Town** historic district of 1,200 buildings dating from the 1820s; particularly noteworthy is **Sturdivant Hall,** 713 Mabry St, an outstanding example of neoclassical architecture furnished with opulent period pieces. Next door is **Heritage Village,** five relocated historic structures incorporating a doctor's office, a lawyer's office, a servant house, and even a pigeon coop.

Historic Water Avenue, which runs parallel to the Alabama River, is a restored 19th-century commercial district of shops, restaurants, and several small waterfront pocket parks. The **National Voting Rights Museum** is located at 1012 Water Ave at the foot of the Edmund Pettus Bridge, where civil rights marchers were met with violence when they first attempted to march to Montgomery. From there you can walk through the civil rights district on **Martin Luther King Street,** where plaques explain milestones in the battle for equality.

Take a Break

Major Grumbles, 1 Grumbles Alley (tel 334/872-2006), is located in an old warehouse in the Water Avenue district overlooking the river. The menu offers a variety of salads, sandwiches, and light entrees (such as flounder amandine) for lunch; heartier meals such as shrimp and scallops marinara, baby-back ribs, and New York strip are features at dinner. Entrees cost $9 to $14.

If you decide to spend the night in Selma, an outstanding and moderately priced choice is **Grace Hall,** 506 Lauderdale St (tel 334/875-5744). Several of the guest rooms are located in the former servants' quarters of the 1857 mansion, and the grounds include a New Orleans–style courtyard and a walled Williamsburg English garden.

Take AL 22 W southwest for 10 miles, then turn right on a county road (no number) marked TO CAHABA to:

3. **Old Cahawba Archaeological Park,** 17 First South St, site of Alabama's first permanent capital at the confluence of the Cahaba and Alabama Rivers. The park contains a welcome center and a few surviving structures, as well as interpretive signs and hiking trails.

    Return to Selma and take AL 41 southwest for 37 miles to:

4. **Camden,** located at a bend in the Alabama River where, when cotton was king, its strategic location made it one of 50 steamboat landings along the river. The gracious Old South town is distinguished by its delicate ironwork staircases and white clapboard churches. Because the Civil War essentially ended with the burning of Selma, Camden's structures were spared; as a result, the Wilcox County area has more surviving antebellum structures than almost any other area in Alabama.

    One of the most important structures in Camden is the **Wilcox Female Institute,** 301 Broad St, built in 1850. One of the first schools for girls in the state, the Wilcox Female Institute attracted students from all over the South. Today the graceful two-story brick building operates as a museum.

    Pick up a guide for the **Camden Cemetery Tour** from the Wilcox Development Council, 110 Court St. Located just outside the gates on Broad Street is the **Confederate Memorial.** Efforts to raise funds for the monument—the second to be built in the state—began in 1866. Notable Camden citizens buried in the cemetery include Emmett Kilpatrick (a presidential interpreter and Red Cross official during World War I); Alexander Bragg (brother of Confederate Gen Braxton Bragg and the architect who designed many of Camden's antebellum homes); and Benjamin Meek Miller and Arthur Pendleton Bagby (both governors of Alabama). A pile of bricks marks the common grave of victims of the *Orline St John,* a riverboat destroyed by fire in 1850.

    Just west of town is **Roland Cooper State Park,** 49 Deer Run Dr. This riverside park offers boat launching ramps, public campgrounds, rental cabins, a country store, hiking trails, and a nine-hole golf course.

    Take AL 41 north for 5 miles, then the Haines Island Ferry—one of Alabama's two free ferries—to:

5. **Packers Bend,** a historic African American community noted for the magnificent quilts produced by many of its denizens. These colorful bed coverings are so prized that they've been displayed at the Smithsonian and many folk art museums. If you're interested in purchasing a quilt, look for the brightly hued spreads hanging on clotheslines outside the small cottages.

    Return to AL 41 and advance south to Fountain, where you will turn southwest on County 39 and drive 53 miles to:

6. **Claiborne/Perdue Hill.** Claiborne, which early writers described as an enchanting community situated on a level plateau high above the river, is now a lost town identified only by its cemetery. Established in 1813, Claiborne was not only the chief cotton port on the Alabama River, it was also a thriving county seat and was once under consideration to become the state capital. Unfortunately, population attrition from diseases—in addition to the economic calamity of being bypassed by the developing railroads—spelled doom for the town. Although two architectural remnants of Claiborne survive, they have been moved 2 miles east on AL 12 to Perdue Hill.

    The **Masonic Lodge,** constructed between 1823 and 1827, is the oldest documented public building in Alabama. When it was located in Claiborne, the building also served as the county courthouse. In 1825, the Marquis de Lafayette gave a speech here. When Claiborne declined, the lodge was moved to Perdue Hill in 1884, after which it served as the town hall, a school, and a church. Today the

Masonic Lodge houses a collection of photographs of steamboats that once plied the river.

Next door is the **William Barrett Travis Cottage.** Travis, who died while serving as a commander at the Alamo, lived in the small house and operated his law office from it. Meticulously restored, the interior features the original chair rail, wainscoting, paneled doors, and other architectural details that are quite elegant for so early a structure.

Continue east for 15 miles on AL 12 to:

7. **Monroeville,** home of novelist Harper Lee. Once you reach Monroeville, head for the downtown square. The focal point of the community is the **Monroe County Museum,** located in the upstairs of the imposing, red brick 1903 courthouse. Changing exhibits in the courtroom (used as the model for the trial scene in Lee's much-celebrated novel *To Kill a Mockingbird*) illustrate Monroe County's colorful past and dramatic presentations of Lee's work are given here annually. Downstairs, the **Chamber of Commerce** dispenses information.

Take AL 21 north out of town and stop at **Rikard's Mill,** an 1845 water-powered gristmill situated in a recreational park in the piney woods along Flat Creek. Now serving as a living history museum, the board-and-batten mill grinds grain for sale—you can even bring your own to be ground. A bridge on the property has been enclosed to create the **Covered Bridge Gift Shop.**

Return to Monroeville. From there, you have two choices: You can take AL 21 and AL 59 southwest passing through the turn-of-the-century towns of Frisco City and Uriah; or, you can return via AL 12 to Perdue Hill and turn south on County Rd 1. Either route meanders for nearly 60 miles through cotton and cattle country before reaching Chrysler, where you will turn south on AL 225 to:

8. **Malbis,** founded as a Greek colony in 1906. Visit the **Malbis Greek Orthodox Church,** County Rd 27 off US 90. This million-dollar church—magnificently adorned with marble, mosaics, murals, and stunning stained-glass windows—is all the more remarkable when you consider that all the construction was financed by the 50 original members of the congregation.

Retrace County Rd 27 and US 90 to I-10 and proceed 6 miles to Spanish Fort, site of the:

9. USS *Alabama* **Battleship Memorial Park,** 2703 Battleship Pkwy. Visitors who tour the battleship learn how the vessel won nine battle stars in World War II without ever taking a hit—earning it the sobriquet Lucky Lady. Also in the park are the World War II submarine USS *Drum,* a Mach 3 A-12

Blackbird supersecret spy plane and 17 other aircraft, and weaponry from all branches of the military.

Continue on I-10 west for 13 miles to:

10. **Mobile,** an important port and the birthplace of Mardi Gras in America. The visitor center at **Fort Condé,** 150 South Royal St, is a good spot to begin your tour. Built of solid brick between 1724 and 1735, the fort served as French headquarters in the early years of colonization. In later years, however, the fort housed British, Spanish, and American troops. Guides costumed to represent the French period not only give tours, but also fire replicas of period rifles and cannons.

Take a Break

Savor a mixture of Creole and Continental cuisine at the intimate **Malaga Restaurant,** 359 Church St (tel 334/438-4701), located in the former carriage house of the historic Malaga Inn. French doors open into the lush courtyard and overlook the sparkling pool. Dinner entrees include roast duck, walnut snapper with summer relish, and grilled scallops with orange Pernod and braised leeks; lighter fare is served for lunch. Dinner entrees cost $16 to $20.

Mobile's history may also be traced at the **Museum of the City of Mobile,** 355 Government St. This beautifully restored 19th-century Italianate townhouse contains gowns worn by Mardi Gras queens, other Mardi Gras costumes and float designs, and various horse-drawn carriages.

Among the historic homes in Mobile are the **Bragg-Mitchell Mansion,** 1906 Springhill Ave, one of the grandest and most photographed structures on the Gulf Coast; **Carlen House Museum,** 54 S Carlen St, a Creole cottage; **Condé-Charlotte Museum House,** 104 Theatre St, the city's first official jail; **Oakleigh Historic Complex,** 350 Oakleigh Place, an 1833 home featuring outstanding collections of silver, china, jewelry, and kitchen implements; and the **Richards DAR House,** 256 N Joachim St, an 1860 Italianate house with a curved cantilevered staircase.

If your schedule allows, you might want to spend an extra day or two just exploring the small towns around Mobile Bay. On the west side of the bay are the **Bellingrath Gardens and Home;** the charming fishing village of **Bayou La Batre;** and **Dauphin Island,** home of **Fort Gaines.** Around the east side of the bay are the villages of **Daphne, Fairhope,** and **Point Clear,** (home of the **Marriott Grand Hotel**), as well as historic **Fort Morgan.**

From Mobile, you could extend your Alabama River Basin exploration by taking I-10 west to Mississippi's Gulf Coast, or take I-10 east into the Florida panhandle.

Alabama Listings

Anniston

See also Oxford

"The Model City of the South," founded in 1872 by progressive industrialist Samuel Noble, who contributed the 1881 Romantic Romanesque church. Site of museum of natural history and US Army museums. **Information:** Calhoun County Convention & Visitors Bureau, 1330 Quinard Ave, PO Box 1087, Anniston, 36202 (tel 205/237-3536).

MOTELS 🏨

🏳🏳 Hampton Inn
1600 AL 21 S, Oxford, 36203; tel 205/835-1492 or toll free 800/HAMPTON; fax 205/835-0636. Exit 185 off I-20. Located near the Museum of Natural History and Silver Lakes Golf Course; and only 12 miles to the Talladega Speedway and International Motorsports Hall of Fame. **Rooms:** 129 rms. CI open/CO noon. Nonsmoking rms avail. **Amenities:** 🛁 🐾 📺 A/C, cable TV w/movies, dataport. **Services:** 🚐 🛝 🛎 **Facilities:** 🛗 🏊 ☕ **Rates (CP):** $44–$51 S; $55–$59 D. Extra person $8. Children under age 18 stay free. Min stay special events. Parking: Outdoor, free. Senior and government rates avail. AE, CB, DC, DISC, MC, V.

🏳🏳🏳 Ramada Inn
300 Quintard Ave, 36201; tel 205/237-9777 or toll free 800/272-6232; fax 205/231-1090. Exit 185 off I-20. Conveniently located near area attractions such as the Women's Air Corp Museum, Fort McClellan, and the Museum of Natural History. **Rooms:** 97 rms and stes. CI 4pm/CO noon. Nonsmoking rms avail. **Amenities:** 🛁 🐾 📺 A/C, cable TV w/movies. **Services:** ✕ 🛝 🛎 🛗 Guest passes to local YMCA. **Facilities:** 🛗 🏊 ☕ 1 restaurant (see "Restaurants" below), 1 bar (w/entertainment). **Rates (CP):** $45–$50 S; $53–$60 D; $80–$90 ste. Extra person $6. Children under age 18 stay free. Min stay special events. Parking: Outdoor, free. Golf package avail. AE, CB, DC, DISC, MC, V.

🏳 Super 8 Motel
6220 McClellan Blvd, 36201; tel 205/820-1000 or toll free 800/533-3770; fax 205/820-1000. 12 mi N of I-20. Located right off AL 21, close to area shopping and movie theaters. **Rooms:** 44 rms. CI open/CO noon. Nonsmoking rms avail.

All rooms on ground level. **Amenities:** 🛁 A/C, cable TV w/movies, refrig. **Services:** 🛎 **Facilities:** 🛗 ☕ Washer/dryer. **Rates (CP):** $37 S; $45 D. Extra person $4. Children under age 11 stay free. Min stay special events. Parking: Outdoor, free. AE, DC, DISC, MC, V.

INN

🏛🏛🏛🏛 The Victoria Inn
1604 Quintard Ave, 36202 (Downtown); tel 205/236-0503 or toll free 800/260-8781; fax 205/236-1138. Between 16th and 17th Sts. 3 acres. This gracious inn offers luxurious accommodations, elegant dining, and well-organized business gatherings. Museums, shopping, and fine restaurants are nearby. **Rooms:** 47 rms and stes; 1 cottage/villa. CI 3pm/CO noon. Nonsmoking rms avail. **Amenities:** 🛁 🐾 A/C, cable TV w/movies, dataport. Some units w/whirlpools. **Services:** ✕ 🆅🅿 🛝 🛎 Guest passes to YMCA. **Facilities:** 🛗 🍽 ☕ 1 restaurant (bkfst and dinner only; see "Restaurants" below), 1 bar (w/entertainment), guest lounge w/TV. **Rates (CP):** $64–$74 S or D; $85–$105 ste; $135–$150 cottage/villa. Extra person $10. Children under age 12 stay free. Min stay special events. Higher rates for special events/hols. Parking: Outdoor, free. Romantic and Robert Trent Jones Golf Trail packages avail. AE, DC, DISC, MC, V.

RESTAURANTS 🍴

Pinoccio's Steer & Stein
In Ramada Inn, 300 Quintard Ave; tel 205/237-9777. **American.** A comfortable, family-oriented spot specializing in steak, catfish, and ribs. Lunch buffet. **FYI:** Reservations accepted. Children's menu. Dress code. **Open:** Breakfast daily 6–11am; lunch daily 11am–1:30pm; dinner Sun–Thurs 5–8:30pm, Fri–Sat 5–9:30pm. **Prices:** Main courses $8–$20. AE, DC, DISC, MC, V. 🅿 ♿

⭐ Top O' the River
3220 McClellan Blvd; tel 205/238-0097. 1 mi S of Fort McClellan. **Seafood/Steak.** An Old South atmosphere reigns at this large, family-style eatery. Fresh local catfish and steak are popular entree options. **FYI:** Reservations accepted. Children's menu. Dress code. Additional location: 500 Rain-

bow Dr, Gadsden (tel 547-9817). **Open:** Mon–Fri 5–9pm, Sat 4:30–10pm, Sun noon–9pm. **Prices:** Main courses $9–$15. AE, CB, DC, DISC, MC, V.

♥ Victoria Inn Restaurant

1604 Quintard Ave; tel 205/236-0503. **Seafood/Steak.** A local landmark with an antique and old-lace atmosphere. You might start off with crab cakes or mustard quail before moving on to pumpkinseed-crusted salmon, double-cut lamb chop, or seafood Cajun pasta. Delicious pecan pie and pumpkinseed cheesecake can round out the meal. Outdoor dining available on the sun porch. **FYI:** Reservations recommended. Guitar/piano. Dress code. **Open:** Mon–Thurs 6–9pm, Fri–Sat 6–10pm. **Prices:** Main courses $14–$18. AE, DC, DISC, MC, V.

ATTRACTION

Fort McClellan

AL 21; tel 205/848-5575. Houses the US Army Military Police and Chemical Regiments. Tours include the Women's Army Corps Museum, where uniforms, photographs, and archives trace the WACs from their inception in 1942 to the present. **Open:** Mon–Fri 8am–4pm. **Free**

Athens

Originally named "Athenson" when it was founded in 1818, this town features Greek Revival homes along its tree-lined streets. Home to Athens State College; hosts the flagship convention of Old Time Southern Fiddlers in October. **Information:** Athens–Limestone County Chamber of Commerce, 101 S Beaty St, PO Box 150, Athens, 35611 (tel 205/232-2600).

MOTELS

≡ Best Western Inn

Jct I-65/US 72, PO Box 816, 35611; tel 205/233-4030 or toll free 800/321-0122; fax 205/233-4554. Comfortable accommodations with easy access from I-65. Centrally located between attractions like the Helen Keller home and the Space and Rocket Center in Huntsville. **Rooms:** 88 rms and effic. CI 2pm/CO noon. Nonsmoking rms avail. **Amenities:** A/C, cable TV w/movies, dataport. **Services:** **Facilities:** Rates (CP): $35–$39 S; $40–$51 D; $38–$53 effic. Extra person $4. Children under age 12 stay free. Parking: Outdoor, free. AE, CB, DC, DISC, MC, V.

≡≡ Bomar Inn

Jct US 31/72, PO Box 1125, 35611; tel 205/232-6944 or toll free 800/824-6834; fax 205/232-8019. Good for business travelers. Located near area shopping, Athens State College, and attractions such as the Helen Keller birthplace in Florence, and the Space and Rocket Center in Huntsville. **Rooms:** 80 rms. CI 3pm/CO noon. Nonsmoking rms avail. **Amenities:** A/C, cable TV w/movies. **Services:** X

Facilities: 1 restaurant. **Rates:** $33–$35 S; $38–$42 D. Extra person $5. Children under age 12 stay free. Parking: Outdoor, free. AE, CB, DC, DISC, EC, JCB, MC, V.

≡≡ Hampton Inn

1488 Thrasher Blvd, 35611; tel 205/232-0030 or toll free 800/HAMPTON; fax 205/233-7006. At jct US 72 and I-65. This is a good stopping point for long distance travelers on their way to Florida. Frequented by businesspeople, and only three miles from downtown Athens. **Rooms:** 56 rms. CI noon/CO 11am. Nonsmoking rms avail. **Amenities:** A/C, cable TV, refrig, dataport, VCR. Some units w/whirlpools. **Services:** **Facilities:** Whirlpool. Free passes to a local fitness center. **Rates (CP):** Peak (May–Sept) $50–$70 S or D. Extra person $5. Children under age 18 stay free. Lower rates off-season. Parking: Outdoor, free. AE, CB, DC, DISC, MC, V.

Auburn

Founded in 1856, the town's historic district reflects revivalist architectural styles from the 1850s to the early 1900s. Home to Auburn University. **Information:** Auburn/Opelika Convention & Visitors Bureau, 714 E Glenn Ave, PO Box 2216, Auburn, 26831 (tel 334/887-8747).

HOTELS

≡≡≡ Auburn University Hotel

241 S College St, 36830; tel 334/821-8200 or toll free 800/2-AUBURN; fax 334/826-8755. Handsome six-story property located across the street from Auburn campus. **Rooms:** 248 rms and stes. Executive level. CI 3pm/CO noon. Nonsmoking rms avail. **Amenities:** A/C, satel TV w/movies, dataport, VCR. **Services:** X **Facilities:** 2 restaurants (see "Restaurants" below), 1 bar. **Rates:** $75 S; $85 D; $165–$275 ste. Extra person $10. Children under age 12 stay free. Min stay wknds and special events. Parking: Outdoor, free. Golf and romance packages avail. Higher rates on football weekends. AE, CB, DC, DISC, MC, V.

≡≡ Hampton Inn

2430 S College St, 36830; tel 334/821-4111 or toll free 800/HAMPTON; fax 334/821-2146. Exit 51 off I-85. Located within five miles of Auburn University and local shopping and movie theaters, and next door to a softball facility. Near Robert Trent Jones Golf Course. **Rooms:** 105 rms. CI 4pm/CO 11am. Nonsmoking rms avail. **Amenities:** A/C, cable TV w/movies. **Services:** **Facilities:** Auburn Links Golf Course discount avail. **Rates (CP):** $45–$48 S; $51–$54 D. Extra person $6. Children under age 18 stay free. Min stay wknds and special events. Parking: Outdoor, free. AE, DC, DISC, MC, V.

≣≣≣ Quality Inn University Center

1577 S College St, PO Box 3467, 36830; tel 334/821-7001 or toll free 800/AUBURN-3; fax 334/821-7001. 1 mi N off I-85 on US 29. Very popular with visitors to Auburn University and Jordan Hare Football Stadium, which are less than a mile away. **Rooms:** 122 rms and stes. CI 1pm/CO 11am. Nonsmoking rms avail. **Amenities:** 📺 A/C, cable TV w/movies. **Services:** ✗ ⊷ ⊷ **Facilities:** 🛐 🏋 🔲 ⅃ 1 restaurant, 1 bar. **Rates (CP):** $59–$74 S or D; $84–$99 ste. Extra person $5. Children under age 18 stay free. Min stay wknds. Parking: Outdoor, free. Golf discounts to guests. Camp War Eagle discounts. AE, DC, DISC, JCB, MC, V.

RESTAURANTS 🍴

Ivy's

In Auburn University Hotel & Conference Center, 241 S College St; tel 334/821-8200. **Eclectic.** Offers everything from deli sandwiches and a salad bar to steak and seafood dinner entrees, all in a comfortable and welcoming atmosphere. **FYI:** Reservations recommended. Children's menu. Dress code. No smoking. **Open:** Daily 6am–11pm. **Prices:** Main courses $10–$15. AE, CB, DC, DISC, MC, V. ❤ &.

⑤ ★ Niffer's Place

1151 Opelika Hwy; tel 334/821-3118. 5 mi E of Auburn University. **American/Burgers.** Locally owned and operated, Niffers specializes in burgers, fiery chicken wings, and salads. It is located close to the Auburn location of the Robert Trent Jones Golf Trail. **FYI:** Reservations accepted. Children's menu. Dress code. Beer and wine only. Additional location: 405 College Ave, Clemson (tel 803/653-7522). **Open:** Mon–Thurs 11am–10:30pm, Fri–Sat 11am–11pm. **Prices:** Main courses $5–$13. AE, DISC, MC, V. 🍜 🖼 &.

ATTRACTION 🏛

Auburn University

S College St; tel 334/844-9999. Founded in 1856 by the Methodist Church, this is one of the nation's earliest land-grant schools and one of the first to admit women. Walking tours of the campus available; self-guiding tour maps in Samford Hall. **Open:** Daily 24 hours. **Free**

Bessemer

Noted for homes dating as far back as 1817, all on the National Register of Historic Places. Named for the inventor of the steel-making process; America's leading manufacturer of ductile iron pipe. **Information:** Bessemer Area Chamber of Commerce, 321 N 18th St, PO Box 648, Bessemer, 35021 (tel 205/425-3253).

MOTEL 🏨

≣≣ Econo Lodge

1021 9th Ave SW, 35023; tel 205/424-9780 or toll free 800/523-2399; fax 205/424-9780 ext 191. Exit 108 off I-20/59. Popular with budget-minded golfers—the local golf course is right next door. **Rooms:** 158 rms. CI 2pm/CO noon. Nonsmoking rms avail. **Amenities:** 📺 A/C, cable TV, refrig. **Services:** ⊠ ⊷ **Facilities:** 🛐 🔲 1 restaurant (bkfst and dinner only), 1 bar (w/entertainment), washer/dryer. **Rates:** $36–$39 S; $39–$45 D. Extra person $5. Children under age 16 stay free. Parking: Outdoor, free. AE, CB, DC, DISC, MC, V.

RESTAURANTS 🍴

★ Bob Sykes Bar-B-Que

1724 9th Ave; tel 205/426-1400. At 18th St. **Barbecue.** Highly acclaimed for barbecue and fresh homemade pies, this place offers hearty fare in a fast-food atmosphere. Family-owned and -operated since 1958. **FYI:** Reservations not accepted. Dress code. No liquor license. **Open:** Mon–Thurs 10am–10pm, Fri–Sat 10am–11pm. **Prices:** Main courses $5–$7. DISC, MC, V. 🖼 &.

★ The Bright Star

304 N 19th St (Downtown); tel 205/424-9444. At 3rd Ave N. **American/Greek.** Opened in 1907 and expanded to its original location in 1915, The Bright Star is an Alabama favorite. Ceiling fans, tile floors, and mirrored and marbled walls create a pleasing atmosphere. Fresh seafood, vegetables, and fine steaks predominate on the menu. **FYI:** Reservations accepted. Children's menu. Dress code. **Open:** Mon–Sat 11am–10pm, Sun 11am–9pm. **Prices:** Main courses $10–$18. AE, DC, DISC, MC, V. ◼ &.

Birmingham

See also Sterett

The largest city in Alabama and the leading iron and steel center in the South. Connected by canal with the Gulf of Mexico, it is the site of the Civil Rights Institute, several colleges and cultural institutions, and the Alabama Sports Hall of Fame. **Information:** Greater Birmingham Convention & Visitors Bureau, 2200 9th Ave N, Birmingham, 35203 (tel 205/458-8086).

PUBLIC TRANSPORTATION

Metro Area Express (MAX) buses serve the city. Fare is 80¢; transfers are 15¢. Exact change required. Call 205/521-0101 for more information.

HOTELS 🏨

≣ Amad Inn

300 10th St N, 35203 (Downtown); tel 205/328-8560 or toll free 800/272-6232; fax 205/323-5841. Exit 260 off I-65.

Clean, comfortable property. **Rooms:** 185 rms. CI 3pm/CO noon. Nonsmoking rms avail. **Amenities:** 🔒 ⚙ 🍴 A/C, cable TV, dataport. **Services:** 🚐 🛎 ♻ **Facilities:** 🛗 ⛱ 150 ⚖ **Rates (CP):** $55 S; $60 D. Extra person $5. Children under age 16 stay free. Parking: Outdoor, free. AE, CB, DC, DISC, JCB, MC, V.

≣≣ Best Western Medical Center

800 11th St S, 35205; tel 205/933-1900 or toll free 800/528-1234; fax 205/933-8476. University Blvd exit off I-65. Comfortable, family-friendly accommodations near the UAB campus, Legion Field, and UAB Medical Center Complex. **Rooms:** 189 rms. CI 2pm/CO noon. Nonsmoking rms avail. **Amenities:** 🔒 ⛱ A/C, satel TV w/movies, dataport. **Services:** 🛎 **Facilities:** 🛗 20 ⚖ 1 bar, washer/dryer. **Rates:** $40 S; $44 D. Extra person $5. Children under age 12 stay free. Min stay special events. Parking: Outdoor, free. AE, DC, DISC, MC, V.

≣≣≣ Courtyard by Marriott Homewood

500 Shades Creek Pkwy, 35209; tel 205/879-0400 or toll free 800/321-2211; fax 205/879-6324. Proximity to area shopping and restaurants and easy access to I-65 make this property a convenient place for an overnight stay. Attractively landscaped grounds, spacious accommodations. **Rooms:** 140 rms and stes. CI 4pm/CO noon. Nonsmoking rms avail. **Amenities:** 🔒 ⛱ A/C, satel TV w/movies, dataport, voice mail. All units w/terraces. **Services:** ✕ 🖼 🛎 **Facilities:** 🛗 🏊 25 ⚖ 1 restaurant (bkfst only), 1 bar, whirlpool, washer/dryer. **Rates:** $78 S; $88 D; $98 ste. Extra person $10. Children under age 18 stay free. Parking: Outdoor, free. AE, DC, DISC, MC, V.

≣≣≣ Courtyard by Marriott Hoover

1824 Montgomery Hwy S, 35244; tel 205/988-5000 or toll free 800/321-2211; fax 205/988-4659. Exit 13 off I-459 S. Well-kept and modern-looking property, with rooms surrounding a central courtyard. **Rooms:** 153 rms and stes. CI 4pm/CO noon. Nonsmoking rms avail. **Amenities:** 🔒 ⛱ A/C, cable TV w/movies, dataport. Some units w/terraces. **Services:** 🖼 🛎 **Facilities:** 🛗 🏊 25 ⚖ 1 restaurant (bkfst only), 1 bar, whirlpool, washer/dryer. **Rates:** $78–$88 S or D; $88–$98 ste. Extra person $10. Children under age 18 stay free. Parking: Outdoor, free. AE, DC, DISC, MC, V.

≣≣ Days Inn Birmingham North

616 Decatur Hwy, PO Box 476, Fultondale, 35068; tel 205/849-0111 or toll free 800/325-2525; fax 205/849-9367. Exit 266 off I-65. A basic chain hotel, 20 minutes from the airport and downtown. **Rooms:** 98 rms. CI open/CO noon. Nonsmoking rms avail. **Amenities:** 🔒 ⛱ A/C, satel TV w/movies, in-rm safe. **Services:** ✕ 🖼 🛎 ♻ **Facilities:** 🛗 200 ⚖ 1 restaurant (bkfst and dinner only), 1 bar. **Rates:** $51–$59 S; $56–$105 D. Extra person $6. Children under age 12 stay free. Parking: Outdoor, free. AE, CB, DC, DISC, MC, V.

≣≣≣ Embassy Suites

2300 Woodcrest Place, 35209; tel 205/879-7400 or toll free 800/433-4600; fax 205/870-4523. All the rooms in this sleek, modern downtown property open onto a wonderfully landscaped lobby decorated with waterfalls, plants, and comfortable furniture. **Rooms:** 242 stes. Executive level. CI 3pm/CO noon. Nonsmoking rms avail. Nice, spacious rooms. **Amenities:** 🔒 ⛱ 📺 A/C, cable TV w/movies, refrig, dataport, VCR, voice mail. All units w/terraces. **Services:** ✕ 🚐 🖼 🛎 **Facilities:** 🛗 300 ⚖ 1 restaurant (lunch and dinner only), 1 bar, sauna, steam rm, whirlpool, washer/dryer. **Rates:** $118–$199 ste. Extra person $10. Children under age 12 stay free. Parking: Outdoor, free. AE, CB, DC, DISC, JCB, MC, V.

≣ Hampton Inn

3910 Kilgore Memorial Dr, 35210; tel 205/956-4100 or toll free 800/HAMPTON; fax 205/956-0906. Exit 133 off I-20. A well-kept property offering comfortable accommodations with few frills. **Rooms:** 70 rms. CI 2pm/CO noon. Nonsmoking rms avail. **Amenities:** 🔒 ⛱ A/C, satel TV w/movies. **Services:** 🛎 **Facilities:** 🛗 25 ⚖ **Rates (CP):** $56–$58 S; $61–$63 D. Children under age 18 stay free. Parking: Outdoor, free. AE, DC, DISC, MC, V.

≣≣ Hampton Inn Colonnade

3400 Colonnade Pkwy, 35243; tel 205/967-0002 or toll free 800/861-7168; fax 205/969-0901. Off US 280. A sparkling new hotel located in a beautiful office park. Large lobby and sitting area. A movie theater, restaurants, and shopping are all within walking distance. **Rooms:** 93 rms. CI noon/CO noon. Nonsmoking rms avail. Rooms are larger than at the average Hampton. **Amenities:** 🔒 ⛱ A/C, cable TV w/movies, dataport. King rooms avail. **Services:** 🖼 🛎 Babysitting. Nearby Ruby Tuesday's restaurant will bill deliveries to room. **Facilities:** 🛗 65 ⚖ 10 minutes to Eagle Point Golf Course. **Rates (CP):** $57–$66 D. Extra person $9. Children under age 18 stay free. Parking: Outdoor, free. AE, CB, DC, DISC, MC, V.

≣ Hampton Inn Mountain Brook

2731 US 280, 35233; tel 205/870-7822 or toll free 800/HAMPTON; fax 205/871-7610. Five-story chain hotel, popular with families. **Rooms:** 131 rms. CI 1pm/CO noon. Nonsmoking rms avail. **Amenities:** 🔒 ⛱ A/C, satel TV w/movies, dataport. **Services:** 🖼 🛎 ♻ Babysitting. Complimentary passes to Sportslife fitness center. **Facilities:** 🛗 15 ⚖ **Rates (CP):** $52–$61 S; $58–$69 D. Extra person $9. Children under age 18 stay free. Parking: Outdoor, free. AE, CB, DC, DISC, MC, V.

≣≣≣ Holiday Inn Homewood

260 Oxmoor Rd, 35209; tel 205/942-2041 or toll free 800/HOLIDAY; fax 205/290-9309. Exit 256 off I-65. One of the nicest Holiday Inns around, close to all attractions. **Rooms:** 193 rms and stes. CI 3pm/CO 11am. Nonsmoking rms avail. Rooms are extremely homey. **Amenities:** 🔒 ⛱ 📺 🍴 A/C, cable TV w/movies, dataport. **Services:** ✕ 🚐 🖼 🛎 **Facilities:** 🛗 🏊 300 💻 ⚖ 1 restaurant, 1 bar (w/entertain-

ment), washer/dryer. Local fitness center offers access to guests. **Rates:** $72 S or D; $125 ste. Children under age 19 stay free. Min stay special events. Parking: Outdoor, free. Golf packages avail. AE, CB, DC, DISC, JCB, MC, V.

Holiday Inn Redmont
2101 5th Ave N, 35203 (Downtown); tel 205/324-2101 or toll free 800/HOLIDAY; fax 205/324-2101. At 21st St. This historic landmark (built in 1925, it's one of the city's oldest hotels) still offers some of the most comfortable rooms in town. **Rooms:** 112 rms and stes. Executive level. CI 3pm/CO noon. Nonsmoking rms avail. **Amenities:** A/C, cable TV w/movies, refrig, dataport. **Services:** Guest passes to local YMCA. **Facilities:** 1 restaurant, 1 bar. **Rates:** $89–$99 S or D; $114–$159 ste. Extra person $10. Children under age 18 stay free. Min stay special events. Parking: Indoor/outdoor, free. Golf and honeymoon packages avail. AE, CB, DC, DISC, JCB, MC, V.

UNRATED Inn Towne Lodge
400 Beacon Pkwy W, 35209; tel 205/942-2031 or toll free 800/347-2031; fax 205/942-7280. Exit 256 off I-65. Basic accommodations that are conveniently located. **Rooms:** 193 rms and stes. CI 3pm/CO noon. Nonsmoking rms avail. **Amenities:** A/C, cable TV w/movies, refrig. **Services:** **Facilities:** 1 bar (w/entertainment), whirlpool, washer/dryer. **Rates:** $65 S or D; $90–$120 ste. Extra person $10. Children under age 18 stay free. Parking: Outdoor, free. AE, DISC, MC, V.

La Quinta Motor Inn
905 11th Court W, 35204; tel 205/324-4510 or toll free 800/531-5900; fax 205/252-7972. Exit 123 off I-20 W. A very basic three-story chain hotel, with easy access to I-20 and most area attractions. **Rooms:** 106 rms. CI 3pm/CO noon. Nonsmoking rms avail. **Amenities:** A/C, satel TV w/movies. **Services:** **Facilities:** Washer/dryer. **Rates (CP):** $52–$65 S; $59–$72 D. Extra person $7. Children under age 18 stay free. Min stay special events. Parking: Outdoor, free. AE, DC, DISC, MC, V.

The Mountain Brook Inn
2800 US 280, 35223; tel 205/870-3100 or toll free 800/523-7771; fax 205/870-5938. An exceptionally comfortable and homey property, the Mountain Brook Inn caters to families. **Rooms:** 162 rms and stes. CI 3pm/CO noon. Nonsmoking rms avail. **Amenities:** A/C, cable TV, dataport. Some units w/fireplaces. **Services:** Nintendo available for fee. **Facilities:** 1 restaurant, 1 bar (w/entertainment). **Rates:** $89 S; $99 D; $165 ste. Extra person $10. Children under age 16 stay free. Min stay special events. Parking: Outdoor, free. AE, DC, DISC, MC, V.

The Parliament House
420 20th St S, 35233 (Downtown); tel 205/322-7000 or toll free 800/579-KING; fax 205/322-3046. At 5th Ave. A recently renovated property offering convenience and com-

fort to its guests. **Rooms:** 223 rms and stes. Executive level. CI 3pm/CO 11am. Nonsmoking rms avail. Rooms are clean and comfortable. **Amenities:** A/C, cable TV w/movies, refrig, dataport, voice mail, in-rm safe. Some units w/terraces. **Services:** **Facilities:** 1 restaurant, 2 bars (1 w/entertainment), spa. **Rates (CP):** $60–$80 S or D; $120 ste. Children under age 18 stay free. Min stay special events. Parking: Indoor, free. AE, DC, DISC, MC, V.

The Pickwick Hotel
1023 20th St S, 35205; tel 205/933-9555 or toll free 800/255-7304; fax 205/933-6918. An art deco–style property, located in the heart of Five Points South. Easy accessibility to shopping and restaurants. **Rooms:** 63 rms and stes. CI 2pm/CO noon. Nonsmoking rms avail. Rooms are nice and clean. **Amenities:** A/C, cable TV w/movies, dataport. Some rooms have refrigerators. **Services:** **Facilities:** On-site drugstore and beauty salon. **Rates (BB):** $109 S; $119 D; $139 ste. Extra person $10. Children under age 18 stay free. Min stay special events. Parking: Indoor, free. Honeymoon and weekend packages avail. AE, DC, DISC, MC, V.

UNRATED Radisson Hotel
808 20th St S, 35205; tel 205/933-9000 or toll free 800/333-3333; fax 205/933-0920. At 8th Ave. A modern establishment, conveniently located near all of downtown Birmingham's sights and activities. **Rooms:** 298 rms and stes. CI 3pm/CO noon. Nonsmoking rms avail. **Amenities:** A/C, cable TV. Some units w/terraces. Suites have wet bars. **Services:** **Facilities:** 1 restaurant, 1 bar, sauna. **Rates:** $89 S; $99 D; $150 ste. Extra person $10. Children under age 12 stay free. Min stay wknds and special events. Parking: Indoor, free. AE, DC, DISC, MC, V.

UNRATED Ramada Inn Airport
5216 Airport Hwy, 35212; tel 205/591-7900 or toll free 800/228-2828; fax 205/592-6476. Airport Hwy exit off I-59/20. An average Ramada Inn, offering comfortable rooms and few surprises. **Rooms:** 192 rms and stes. Executive level. CI 3pm/CO noon. Nonsmoking rms avail. **Amenities:** A/C, cable TV w/movies. **Services:** Pets allowed with a $25 charge. **Facilities:** 1 restaurant, 1 bar (w/entertainment). **Rates:** Peak (Mar–Aug) $55–$69 S; $63–$77 D; $85 ste. Extra person $8. Children under age 17 stay free. Min stay special events. Lower rates off-season. Parking: Outdoor, free. B&B and golf packages avail. AE, DC, DISC, JCB, MC, V.

Rime Garden Suites
5320 Beacon Dr, 35210; tel 205/951-1200 or toll free 800/772-7463; fax 205/951-1692. Exit 133 off I-20. With its roomy accommodations and home-away-from-home atmosphere, this hotel is best suited for extended stays. **Rooms:** 134 stes. CI 3pm/CO noon. Nonsmoking rms avail.

Apartmentlike suites, with full kitchen facilities. **Amenities:** 🔒 🅰 🖵 A/C, satel TV w/movies, refrig. All units w/terraces. **Services:** ✗ 🚐 🖾 🍴 **Facilities:** 🖼 🔲 ⅃ 1 restaurant, 1 bar, washer/dryer. **Rates (CP):** $70–$140 ste. Extra person $10. Children under age 12 stay free. Min stay special events. Parking: Outdoor, free. AE, DC, DISC, MC, V.

🏨🏨🏨 Sheraton Civic Center Hotel

2101 Civic Center Blvd, 35203 (Downtown); tel 205/324-5000 or toll free 800/325-3535; fax 205/307-3045. The largest hotel in Alabama, this modern-looking property is very popular with convention-goers and business travelers due to its connection to the Civic Center. **Rooms:** 770 rms and stes. Executive level. CI 3pm/CO noon. Nonsmoking rms avail. **Amenities:** 🔒 🅰 🖵 🍴 A/C, satel TV w/movies, dataport, voice mail. Some units w/whirlpools. **Services:** ✗ 🕾 �📠 🚐 🖾 🍴 **Facilities:** 🖼 🔲 💻 ⅃ 2 restaurants, 1 bar (w/entertainment), sauna, steam rm, whirlpool, washer/dryer. **Rates:** $115 S; $125 D; $199–$750 ste. Extra person $15. Children under age 18 stay free. Parking: Indoor/outdoor, $3/day. AE, CB, DC, DISC, JCB, MC, V.

🏨🏨🏨 Sheraton Perimeter Park South

8 Perimeter Dr, 35243; tel 205/967-2700 or toll free 800/325-3535, 800/268-9393 in Canada; fax 205/972-8603. At jct I-459/US 280 E. A mid-rise hotel catering mainly to business travelers. Although there's shopping and recreation nearby, this hotel is quite far from downtown. **Rooms:** 200 rms and stes. Executive level. CI 3pm/CO noon. Nonsmoking rms avail. **Amenities:** 🔒 🅰 🖵 A/C, cable TV w/movies, dataport, voice mail. **Services:** ✗ 🕾 🚐 🖾 🍴 Local transportation provided. **Facilities:** 🖼 🔲 💻 🍴 1 restaurant, 1 bar. **Rates:** $99–$114 S or D; $500 ste. Extra person $10. Children under age 12 stay free. Min stay special events. Parking: Outdoor, free. Golf and honeymoon packages avail. AE, DC, DISC, MC, V.

🏨🏨🏨🏨 The Tutwiler Grand Heritage Hotel

Park Place at 21st St N, 35203 (Downtown); tel 205/322-2100 or toll free 800/845-1787; fax 205/325-1183. A landmark hotel originally built as luxury apartments in 1913, the Tutwiler now offers European-style elegance and old-world charm to its guests. The lobby practically gleams, with its brass fixtures and chandeliers. **Rooms:** 147 rms and stes. Executive level. CI 3pm/CO noon. Nonsmoking rms avail. **Amenities:** 🔒 🅰 🍴 A/C, cable TV, bathrobes. Some units w/terraces. Complimentary newspaper. Fresh flowers in rooms. **Services:** 🍴 🕾 📠 🚐 🖾 ⅃ 🛎 Social director. VCRs available upon request. Turndown service with chocolates. Guest passes to local YMCA. 24-hour security. **Facilities:** 🔲 🍴 1 restaurant (see "Restaurants" below), 1 bar, beauty salon. On-site florist. **Rates:** Peak (Nov–mid-Jan/late May–Aug) $70–$130 S or D; $110–$170 ste. Extra person $15. Children under age 15 stay free. Lower rates off-season. Parking: Indoor/outdoor, $5/day. Honeymoon packages avail. AE, CB, DC, DISC, MC, V.

UNRATED Wynfrey Hotel

1000 Riverchase Galleria, 35244; tel 205/987-1600 or toll free 800/476-7006; fax 205/987-0454. This elegant 15-floor establishment is the anchor of a downtown shopping mall with over 200 stores. The lobby's Italian marble floors are covered with colorful Oriental carpets, and the brass escalators gleam. **Rooms:** 330 rms and stes. Executive level. CI 3pm/CO 11am. Nonsmoking rms avail. Rooms are richly decorated in either traditional English Chippendale or French Regency furnishings. **Amenities:** 🔒 🖵 🍴 A/C, cable TV w/movies. 1 unit w/minibar, 1 w/terrace, 1 w/whirlpool. **Services:** 🍴 🕾 📠 🚐 🖾 ⅃ **Facilities:** 🖼 🔲 🔲 🍴 2 restaurants, 1 bar (w/entertainment), spa, washer/dryer. **Rates:** $131–$162 S; $141–$172 D; $205–$770 ste. Children under age 17 stay free. Parking: Indoor/outdoor, $4/day. Reunion, honeymoon, and getaway packages avail. AE, DC, DISC, MC, V.

MOTELS

🏨 Best Western Civic Center Inn

2230 Civic Center Blvd, 35203 (Downtown); tel 205/328-6320 or toll free 800/636-4669; fax 205/328-6681. At 23rd St N. Equally popular with vacationers and business travelers, this property offers clean and comfortable accommodations. **Rooms:** 240 rms and stes. CI 3pm/CO noon. Nonsmoking rms avail. **Amenities:** 🔒 A/C, cable TV w/movies. **Services:** 🖾 ⅃ **Facilities:** 🖼 🔲 🍴 Washer/dryer. **Rates (CP):** $42–$50 S or D. Extra person $7. Min stay special events. Parking: Outdoor, free. AE, CB, DC, DISC, MC, V.

🏨 Fairfield Inn by Marriott

155 Vulcan Rd, 35209; tel 205/945-9600 or toll free 800/228-2800; fax 205/945-9600. Exit 256 W off I-65. Basic budget accommodations. **Rooms:** 132 rms. CI 3pm/CO noon. Nonsmoking rms avail. Rooms are clean and comfortable. **Amenities:** 🔒 🅰 A/C, satel TV w/movies, dataport. **Services:** 🖾 ⅃ **Facilities:** 🖼 🍴 **Rates (CP):** $50–$54 S; $57–$60 D. Children under age 19 stay free. Parking: Outdoor, free. AE, DC, DISC, MC, V.

🏨🏨 Motel Birmingham

7905 Crestwood Blvd, 35210; tel 205/956-4440 or toll free 800/338-9275; fax 205/956-3011. Exit 132 off I-20. Although this humble property has been in business for over 40 years, it has been well kept and is still a good choice. **Rooms:** 242 rms, stes, and effic. CI 3pm/CO noon. Nonsmoking rms avail. **Amenities:** 🔒 🖵 A/C, cable TV w/movies, dataport. Some units w/terraces. **Services:** 🚐 🖾 ⅃ 🛎 Guest privileges at local fitness center, with free transportation. **Facilities:** 🖼 🔲 🍴 Playground. **Rates (CP):** $53 S or D; $125 ste; $125 effic. Extra person $5. Children under age 21 stay free. Parking: Outdoor, free. AE, DC, DISC, MC, V.

🏨 Villager Lodge

1313 3rd Ave N, 35203 (Downtown); tel 205/323-8806 or toll free 800/328-7829; fax 205/323-5591. At 13th St.

Conveniently located two blocks from I-65, the Villager is adequate for the interstate traveler. **Rooms:** 150 rms. CI open/CO 11am. **Amenities:** ☎ A/C, cable TV w/movies, in-rm safe. **Services:** ✕ 🚗 ⌒ **Facilities:** ⛱ 1 restaurant, 1 bar (w/entertainment), washer/dryer. **Rates:** $30 S; $36 D. Children under age 12 stay free. Parking: Outdoor, free. AE, DC, DISC, MC, V.

RESTAURANTS 🍽

Ali Baba Persian Restaurant
In Centre at Riverchase, 110 Centre at Riverchase; tel 205/823-2222. Off I-459. **Persian.** Menu specialties include ground meat and lamb dishes and eggplant stews, all served with hot steamed basmati rice. An appetizer plate of fresh basil, walnuts, feta, radishes, and pita-type bread is particularly interesting. Food is prepared to the diner's taste, by a personable, knowledgeable staff. The daily lunch buffet is popular with businesspeople in the area. Adjacent Middle Eastern market. **FYI:** Reservations accepted. Children's menu. Dress code. **Open:** Lunch Tues–Sun 11am–2:30pm; dinner Tues–Sun 5–10pm. **Prices:** Main courses $9–$15. AE, DC, DISC, MC, V. ♿

♟ Arman's at Parklane
2117 Cahaba Rd; tel 205/871-5551. At 21st Ave. **Italian.** Once a neighborhood market, this property has been renovated into a classic upscale dining establishment with refinished hardwood floors, high ceilings, simple yet elegant wood furniture, and an open kitchen. Locals love the salmon with lemon-dill sauce and asparagus, and the veal medallions. **FYI:** Reservations recommended. Dress code. **Open:** Mon–Wed 5–10pm, Thurs–Sat 5–11pm, Sun 5–9pm. **Prices:** Main courses $16–$25. AE, MC, V. ♥ VP ♿

Asahi
In 280 Station, 444 Cahaba Park Circle (Inverness); tel 205/991-5542. **Japanese.** Locally owned and operated eatery offering teppanyaki dining as well as full service dining at the sushi bar. Families and couples will enjoy the great show put on by the teppanyaki chefs. Sushi, sashimi, and tempura are attractively presented, and there's a good selection of Japanese beer. **FYI:** Reservations accepted. Children's menu. Dress code. **Open:** Sun–Thurs 5–10pm, Fri–Sat 5–11pm. **Prices:** Main courses $10–$20. AE, DC, DISC, MC, V. ♿

Bombay Cafe
2839 7th Ave S (Lakeview District); tel 205/322-1930. At 29 St S. **Continental/Seafood.** Large plate-glass windows in the front of the dimly lit dining room allow guests to watch passersby. Tables are spaced far enough apart to provide privacy. Intricate, beautifully presented entrees include snapper en papillote (with béchamel sauce, oysters, and crabmeat). Perfect for business lunches or a quiet dinner for two. **FYI:** Reservations accepted. Dress code. **Open:** Mon–Thurs 6–10pm, Fri–Sat 6–11pm. **Prices:** Main courses $15–$22. AE, MC, V. ♥ VP ♿

♟ Bottega
2240 Highland Ave; tel 205/939-1000. **Italian/Mediterranean.** Owned and operated by chef Frank Stitt, this eatery is upscale without being pretentious. The exquisite food featured includes chicken scaloppine and homemade pastas. Bottega Cafe, next door, offers more casual dining that appeals to a younger and hipper crowd. Gourmet pizzas and unique pasta dishes are the specialties here. Bottega's attractive outdoor patio features wrought-iron and brightly colored table umbrellas. **FYI:** Reservations recommended. Dress code. **Open:** Mon–Sat 11am–10pm. Closed 4th of July week. **Prices:** Main courses $10–$20. AE, MC, V. ♥ 🍽 ♿

★ Browdy's of Mountain Brook
In Mountain Brook Village, 2713 Culver Rd; tel 205/879-8585. **Southern.** A family business for 75 years, Browdy's offers catering, counter sales of specialty food items, a meat market, and a bakery, in addition to its restaurant. The meat-and-three special at lunch is a local favorite with businesspeople. Kosher sandwiches, ribs, and beef brisket are popular options. **FYI:** Reservations not accepted. Children's menu. Dress code. Beer and wine only. **Open:** Mon 11am–2:30pm, Tues–Sun 11am–8:30pm. **Prices:** Main courses $5–$13. AE, DISC, MC, V. 👪 ♿

Christian's
In the Tutwiler Grand Heritage Hotel, Park Place at 21st St N (Downtown); tel 205/939-1000. **Continental.** Fine dining in a beautiful yet comfortable atmosphere. Hearty, classic entrees focus on seafood, beef, veal, chicken, and other basic fare. Extensive wine list. **FYI:** Reservations recommended. Dress code. **Open:** Breakfast Mon–Sat 6:30–10:30am; lunch Mon–Sat 11:30am–2pm; dinner Mon–Sat 5:30–10:30pm. **Prices:** Main courses $18–$24. AE, DC, DISC, MC, V. ♥ 🍽 VP ♿

Cosmo's Pizza
In Pickwick Place, 2012 Magnolia Ave; tel 205/930-9971. At 20th St. **Pizza.** The art deco decor is carried out via a pastel color scheme and lots of neon, while a big glass window up front lets diners watch the scene on Magnolia Avenue. Dough and sauces are prepared fresh daily, and the trendy toppings include pesto, sun-dried tomatoes, and Italian sausage. The antipasto platter and alligator medallion appetizers are wonderful. **FYI:** Reservations not accepted. Dress code. **Open:** Mon–Thurs 11am–11pm, Fri–Sat 11am–midnight, Sun noon–10pm. **Prices:** Main courses $6–$19. AE, MC, V.

★ Fish Market Restaurant
611 21st St S; tel 205/322-3330. Between 6th and 9th Aves. **Seafood.** A combination market/restaurant offering some of the freshest seafood on the Gulf Coast. There's not much atmosphere here, but owner-chef George Sarris makes up for it with the quality of his food. Blackened redfish, Caribbean crabmeat salad, and raw oysters on the half shell are among Sarris's specialties. **FYI:** Reservations not accepted. Children's menu. Dress code. Additional location: Riverchase

Shopping Center (tel 823-3474). **Open:** Mon–Thurs 10am–9pm, Fri–Sat 10am–10pm. **Prices:** Main courses $6–$15. AE, MC, V. 🎬 🚼

♟ Highlands: A Bar and Grill

2011 11th Ave (Five Points South); tel 205/939-1400. **Southern.** Nationally recognized chef Frank Stitt serves creative and innovative dishes like grilled salmon, fillet of sole with wine sauce, and quail with raspberry sauce. The light and airy dining room has a peach-and-white color scheme, with lots of flowers and artwork. **FYI:** Reservations recommended. Dress code. **Open:** Lunch Thurs–Fri 11am–2pm; dinner Tues–Thurs 6–10pm, Fri–Sat 6–10:30pm. Closed Aug 27–Sept 5. **Prices:** Main courses $15–$21. AE, MC, V. ♥

★ John's

112 21st St N (Downtown); tel 205/322-6014. Between 1st Ave N and 2nd Ave N. **Seafood.** Located in the heart of downtown Birmingham for over 50 years. It caters to businesspeople during lunch, and other locals and families at dinner. Greek-style seafood dishes are especially popular. Shredded cabbage slaw with John's secret dressing (sold in grocery stores throughout the area) is locally famous. **FYI:** Reservations accepted. Children's menu. Dress code. **Open:** Mon–Sat 11am–10pm. Closed 4th of July week. **Prices:** Main courses $10–$16. AE, CB, DC, DISC, MC, V. ♿

Klingler's European Bakery & Deli

621 Montgomery Hwy; tel 205/823-4560. **German.** Klingler's has delighted the Birmingham area with European-style baked goods (prepared fresh daily) since 1982. This family-owned and -operated eatery is one of the only local places to serve Hungarian goulash, a wide variety of German sausages, specialty tortes, and cooked red cabbage. **FYI:** Reservations not accepted. Dress code. Beer and wine only. No smoking. **Open:** Mon–Sat 7am–6pm, Sun 9am–2pm. **Prices:** Main courses $5–$9. DISC, MC, V. 🚼 ♿

La Paz

99 Euclid Ave; tel 205/879-2225. At Oak and Church Sts. **Mexican.** A loud, action-oriented spot, popular with families and young people from the neighborhood. For starters, there's an interesting variety of "dips for chips." The spicy seafood dishes; selections with shredded pork, almonds, and raisins; and unique vegetarian dishes make this menu stand out above others in town. Great margaritas. **FYI:** Reservations not accepted. Dress code. **Open:** Sun–Thurs 5–10pm, Fri–Sat 5–11pm. **Prices:** Main courses $6–$14. AE, DISC, MC, V. 🍴 ♿

Magic City Brewery

420 21st St S; tel 205/328-BREW. At 5th Ave. **Pizza/Pub.** Birmingham's first "brew-pub" (since Prohibition) is located in the Old Historic Automotive District right across from the original Schillenger brewery. Old beer vats are on display in the center of the restaurant, and the menu is filled with standard pub fare: beer cheese soup, cheesy artichoke dip, gourmet pizzas, and various chicken dishes. **FYI:** Reserva-

tions accepted. Blues/jazz/rock. Children's menu. Dress code. **Open:** Mon–Thurs 11am–10pm, Fri–Sat 11am–11pm. **Prices:** Main courses $9–$16. AE, DC, DISC, MC, V. 🎬 ♿

The Meadowlark

County Rd 66, Alabaster; tel 205/663-3141. **American/Continental.** Originally a family farm house, The Meadowlark is now comfortably renovated into a fine dining establishment. This family-owned and -operated spot offers classic beef, chicken, and seafood entrees in a comfortable atmosphere. **FYI:** Reservations accepted. Children's menu. Dress code. **Open:** Wed–Sat 5–10:30pm. Closed July 1–14. **Prices:** Main courses $21–$50. DISC, MC, V. ♥ VP ♿

Merrit House Restaurant

2220 Highland Ave; tel 205/933-1200. At 11th Court S. **Continental/Creole.** Located in a multistory, white-columned antebellum-style house, this restaurant offers fine dining and lots of atmosphere. Most of the repeat customers come for the Cajun- and Creole-style seafood dishes and luscious, homemade desserts. **FYI:** Reservations accepted. Children's menu. Dress code. **Open:** Lunch Mon–Fri 11am–2pm; dinner Mon–Sat 5–10pm. **Prices:** Main courses $16–$22. AE, DC, DISC, MC, V. ♥ VP ♿

Ming's Cuisine

514 Cahaba Park Circle; tel 205/991-3803. **Chinese/Seafood.** A humble storefront establishment providing a surprisingly quiet and cool respite from the suburban bustle outside its doors. The entranceway is designed around a reflecting pool and fountain. Ming's has a large menu and offers some selections not usually found in local Chinese restaurants. **FYI:** Reservations accepted. Dress code. **Open:** Lunch daily 11am–2:30pm; dinner Sun–Thurs 4:30–9:30pm, Fri–Sat 4:30–10:30pm. **Prices:** Main courses $7–$26. AE, MC, V. ♿

★ Ollie's B-B-Q

515 University Blvd; tel 205/324-9485. Off I-65. **Barbecue.** In business since 1926, this barbecue spot has been owned and operated by the same family for four generations. The uniquely tangy barbecue sauce is vinegar-based, and the homemade salad dressings are delicious. Many famous celebrities and state officials have dined at Ollie's over the years. **FYI:** Reservations not accepted. Children's menu. Dress code. No liquor license. **Open:** Mon 10am–3pm, Tues–Sat 10am–8pm. Closed Sept 1–7. **Prices:** Main courses $5–$7. DISC, MC, V. 🎬 🚼 ♿

★ The Original Whistle Stop Cafe—Irondale Cafe

1906 1st Ave N (Irondale); tel 205/956-5258. At 19th St N. **Soul/Southern.** The true home of *Fried Green Tomatoes*. (The Ironside was the inspiration for the fictional Whistle Stop Cafe made famous by the popular book and movie.) The best bets are the simplest: vegetable plates, meat-and-three, deli sandwiches. Everything is served cafeteria-style. Souvenirs—such as cookbooks and famous batter mixes—are sold in the adjacent market. **FYI:** Reservations not accepted. Dress code.

No liquor license. **Open:** Lunch Sun–Fri 10:45am–2:30pm; dinner Tues–Fri 4:30–8pm. Closed July 1–7. **Prices:** Main courses $5–$12. No CC. 🍴 🖼️ ⚫

Ralph & Kacoo's
3500 Grandview Pkwy; tel 205/967-4087. Off I-459. **Cajun/ Seafood.** Locals familiar with the original Ralph & Kacoo's (in New Orleans) flock to this bustling and colorful branch for a variety of Cajun seafood, pasta, and Angus beef dishes. The large bar and distinctive appetizers are popular with the after-work crowd. Jazz brunch every Sunday. **FYI:** Reservations not accepted. Jazz. Children's menu. Dress code. **Open:** Mon–Thurs 11am–10pm, Fri–Sat 11am–10:30pm, Sun 11am–9pm. **Prices:** Main courses $13–$18. AE, MC, V. ⚫

Rossi's
2737 US 280; tel 205/879-2111. **Italian.** Traditional Italian fare, prime rib, and seafood are served in this large, dark, and quiet dining room. Rossi's is popular with businesspeople, families, and couples. **FYI:** Reservations accepted. Dress code. **Open:** Lunch Mon–Fri 11am–2pm; dinner Mon–Thurs 4:30–10pm, Fri–Sat 4:30–11pm. **Prices:** Main courses $12–$18. AE, MC, V. ⚫ 🆅🅿 ⚫

★ Taj India
2226 Highland Ave S; tel 205/939-3805. At 22nd St S. **Indian.** A favorite of hip neighborhood locals. The small dining room is quiet and features modest Indian art. The popular, moderately priced lunch buffet is usually heavy on vegetable and chicken dishes, but the extensive dinner menu offers an ethnic eating adventure. The tandoori meats and breads are especially good. Indian beers are not available (due to state law), but the wine list is well considered. **FYI:** Reservations accepted. Dress code. **Open:** Lunch Mon–Fri 11am–2pm, Sat–Sun 11:30am–2:30pm; dinner Mon–Sat 5:30–10pm, Sun 5:30–9pm. **Prices:** Main courses $9–$17. AE, DISC, MC, V. ⚫ ⚫

ATTRACTIONS 🏛️

Arlington
331 Cotton Ave; tel 205/780-5656. This fine example of Greek Revival architecture was built in the 1840s by Judge William S Mudd, one of the founders of Birmingham. Today, the beautifully restored and furnished house boasts a collection of 19th-century decorative arts and antiques, as well as displays of Civil War memorabilia. **Open:** Tues–Sat 10am–4pm, Sun 1–4pm. Closed some hols. **$**

Birmingham Museum of Art
2000 8th Ave N; tel 205/254-2566. The BMA houses a permanent collection of over 15,000 paintings, sculptures, drawings, and textiles, from ancient to modern times. Highlights include works by European legends such as Rembrandt, Monet, and Gainsborough, plus American masterpieces by John Singer Sargent, Robert Motherwell, and Frank Lloyd Wright. There's also a strong collection of Western art by Frederic Remington and others, plus the largest collection of Wedgwood china outside England. **Open:** Tues–Sat 10am–5pm. Closed some hols. **Free**

Alabama Sports Hall of Fame
2150 Civic Center Blvd; tel 205/323-6665. A high-tech, three-story museum housing over 4,500 pieces of memorabilia associated with over 170 of Alabama's sports heroes, including Jesse Owens, Willie Mays, and legendary University of Alabama football coach Bear Bryant. Included in the displays are two Heisman trophies, three World Series trophies, and the winners' trophy from Super Bowl XXV. **Open:** Mon–Fri 9am–5pm, Sun 1–5pm. Closed some hols. **$$**

Birmingham Civil Rights Institute
520 16th St N; tel 205/328-9696. Permanent exhibit galleries are arranged in a chronological fashion, beginning with a film covering the history of Birmingham from its founding to the 1920s. The Barriers Gallery depicts the quality of life for Birmingham's black residents under segregation (1920–1954) and includes replicas of a segregated streetcar and other public facilities. A video jukebox highlights musicians of the era. The Movement Gallery features 16 exhibits and 4 multimedia presentations on the Montgomery bus boycott, the Freedom Riders, Martin Luther King Jr, and the 1963 March on Washington. Other galleries focus on the international scope of the civil rights movement. The institute also includes touring exhibits, and an oral history project documenting the movement in Birmingham. **Open:** Tues–Sat 10am–6pm, Sun 1–5pm. Closed some hols. **Free**

Southern Museum of Flight
4343 73rd St N; tel 205/833-8226. Airplanes, flight instruments, and other items relating to aviation history are on display here. There are also exhibits containing memorabilia of famous pilots, including a propeller used by Baron Von Richtofen (better known as the Red Baron). **Open:** Tues–Sat 9:30am–4:30pm, Sun 1–4:30pm. Closed some hols. **$**

Red Mountain Museum
2230 22nd St S; tel 205/933-4153. Architecturally unique museum carved into the side of Birmingham's Red Mountain, with a focus on natural history. Interactive, hands-on exhibits on geology and weather; fossil collection includes a 14-foot prehistoric lizard. Picnic area. **Open:** Mon–Fri 9am–5pm, Sat 10am–4pm, Sun 1–4pm. Closed some hols. **$**

Discovery Place
1320 22nd St; tel 205/939-1176. A children's museum with hands-on exhibits exploring the worlds of health, science, communication, and energy. Discovery Place houses the only solar telescope in the country open to the public. Combination ticket with Red Mountain Museum (see above). **Open:** Oct–Aug, Mon–Fri 9am–3pm, Sat 10am–4pm, Sun 1–4pm. Closed some hols. **$**

Birmingham Botanical Gardens
2612 Lane Park Rd; tel 205/879-1227. Peace and tranquillity—the foundation of Japanese gardens—can be found

throughout Birmingham Botanical Gardens. The 67½-acre site sits on a former Native American campground and features an Irish rose garden, a floral clock, the largest clearspan greenhouse in the Southeast, and a bird sanctuary containing more than 230 species. **Open:** Gardens, daily sunrise–sunset; Garden Center, daily 8am–5pm. **Free**

Birmingham Zoo
2630 Cahaba Rd; tel 205/879-0408. More than 750 animals are in residence here, including rare Siberian tigers and the world's only self-sustaining colony of golden spider monkeys in captivity. A miniature train traverses the wooded, parklike setting. **Open:** Daily 9am–5pm. Closed some hols. **$$**

Legion Field
400 Graymont Ave W; tel 205/254-2391. Home games of the University of Alabama at Birmingham's football team are played at this stadium. The Iron Bowl, a legendary football showdown between the University of Alabama and Auburn University, is held here every other year on the last weekend in November. **$$$$**

Clanton

Located in the Alabama highlands country, Clanton is the self-proclaimed Peach Capital of the World—with a water tower shaped like a peach to prove it. **Information:** Chilton County Chamber of Commerce, PO Box 66, Clanton, 35045 (tel 205/755-2400).

HOTEL 🛏

⊨⊨⊨ Holiday Inn
I-65 and US 31, PO Box 2010, 35045; tel 205/755-0510 or toll free 800/HOLIDAY; fax 205/755-0510 ext 116. Exit 205 off I-65. Nice two-story property, popular with fishing enthusiasts (Lay Lake and Lake Mitchell are both nearby). **Rooms:** 100 rms. CI 2pm/CO noon. Nonsmoking rms avail. **Amenities:** 🛁 ♨ A/C, satel TV w/movies, dataport. **Services:** ✕ 🚐 🖎 🖵 ♿ **Facilities:** 🔧 125 & 1 restaurant, 1 bar. **Rates (BB):** $44–$51 S; $44–$55 D. Extra person $5. Children under age 19 stay free. Parking: Outdoor, free. AE, DC, DISC, MC, V.

REFRESHMENT STOP 🗋

★ Peach Park
Exit 205 off I-65; tel 205/755-2065. **Desserts.** Owned and operated by Gray & Sons Farms, Peach Park is famous for its delicious Chilton County peaches. Visitors can choose from a wide variety of fresh produce and fresh baked goods, or enjoy fresh homemade ice cream while relaxing in the gardens. **Open:** Daily 8am–9pm. Closed Dec 23–Mem Day. MC, V. 🚢 👪 ♿

Cullman

Prosperous farm town and light manufacturing center, founded by a German refugee responsible for immigration of 20,000 Germans to the town. Home to the Ave Marie Grotto, "Jerusalem in Miniature," on the National Register of Historic Places. The longest covered wooden bridge in the state is nearby. **Information:** Cullman Area Chamber of Commerce, 211 2nd Ave NE, PO Box 1104, Cullman, 35056 (tel 205/734-0454).

HOTEL 🛏

⊨⊨⊨ Ramada Inn
I-65 and AL 69 W, PO Box 1204, 35056; tel 205/734-8484 or toll free 800/2-RAMADA; fax 205/739-4126. Exit 304 off I-65 and AL 69. Located near Looney's Tavern (offering reenactments of the Civil War) and the Cullman County Museum. This Ramada is halfway between Birmingham and Huntsville, and 50 miles from the Boaz Outlets. **Rooms:** 126 rms and stes. CI noon/CO noon. Nonsmoking rms avail. **Amenities:** 🛁 ♨ 🖭 A/C, cable TV w/movies. **Services:** ✕ 🖎 🖵 ♿ **Facilities:** 🔧 200 & 1 restaurant, whirlpool, washer/dryer. **Rates (CP):** $48 S; $52 D; $100 ste. Extra person $5. Children under age 18 stay free. Parking: Outdoor, free. Golf package with Cullman Municipal Golf Course AE, DC, DISC, MC, V.

MOTEL

UNRATED Howard Johnson Lodge
I-65 and US 278 W, PO Box 267, 35056; tel 205/737-7275 or toll free 800/446-4656; fax 205/734-8336. Exit 308. Property was undergoing renovation at time of inspection. **Rooms:** 97 rms. CI noon/CO noon. Nonsmoking rms avail. **Amenities:** 🛁 ♨ A/C, cable TV w/movies. Sega games available. **Services:** 🖵 ♿ Nonrefundable $5 pet fee. **Facilities:** 🔧 100 & 1 restaurant. Jerry's Family Restaurant offers 10% discount. **Rates:** $40–$79 S; $42–$89 D. Extra person $5. Children under age 18 stay free. Parking: Outdoor, free. AE, DC, DISC, MC, V.

RESTAURANT 🍴

★ Johnny's Bar-B-Q
1401 4th St SW; tel 205/734-8539. Exit 308 off I-65. **Barbecue/Seafood.** Specializes in barbecue pork and chicken, seafood, and their famous Bar-B-Que baked potato. **FYI:** Reservations not accepted. Children's menu. Dress code. No liquor license. No smoking. **Open:** Tues–Sat 10am–9pm. Closed 4th of July week. **Prices:** Main courses $5–$11. No CC. 👪

ATTRACTIONS 🏛

Cullman County Museum
211 2nd Ave NE; tel 205/739-1258. A local museum filled with memorabilia from Cullman's past, including Native

American artifacts; 19th-century tools, farm implements, household items, and clothing; children's dolls, toys, baby carriages, and doll houses; and photos documenting the history of Cullman County. There's even a re-creation of the town's Main St as it looked a century ago, complete with shops, a doctor's office, and a beer wagon. The building itself is a replica of the home of the town's founder, Col John G Cullman, who encouraged his fellow Germans to settle in what he called "the garden spot of America." **Open:** Mon–Wed and Fri 9am–noon and 1–4pm, Sun 1:30–4:30pm, Sat by appointment. Closed some hols. **$**

Ave Maria Grotto at St Bernard Abbey

1600 St Bernard Dr SE; tel 205/734-4110. These miniature versions of world-famous buildings and Biblical stories are the work of one man—Brother Joseph Zoettl, a Benedictine monk. Nestled along a two-block-long hillside are miniatures of the Temple of Jerusalem, St Peter's Basilica, Noah's Ark, the Hanging Gardens of Babylon, the Pantheon, the Roman Coliseum, the Leaning Tower of Pisa, the Statue of Liberty, the Alamo, and over a hundred more structures. Brother Joseph used materials from all over the world in building his miniatures—old bird cages, cold-cream jars, and fishnet floats, all covered with discarded glass, stones, and brick. **Open:** Daily 7am–sunset. Closed Dec 25. **$$**

Decatur

Busy railroad, market, and industrial center on the banks of the Tennessee River, named for naval hero Commodore Stephen Decatur. **Information:** Decatur Convention & Visitors Bureau, 719 6th Ave SE, PO Box 2349, Decatur, 35602 (tel 205/350-2028).

HOTELS 🏨

≣≣≣ Amberley Suite Hotel

807 Bank St NE, 35601; tel 205/355-6800 or toll free 800/288-7332; fax 205/350-0965. At Church St. Located in Historic Old Decatur, near the Tennessee River. Shopping and restaurants are nearby. **Rooms:** 110 rms and stes. Executive level. CI 1pm/CO noon. Nonsmoking rms avail. **Amenities:** 🛁 🔥 📺 🍽 A/C, cable TV w/movies, dataport. 1 unit w/whirlpool. **Services:** ✗ 🚗 🖼 🔂 **Facilities:** 🏋 🎱 🛗 🖥 👤 1 restaurant, 1 bar, sauna, steam rm, whirlpool, washer/dryer. **Rates:** $67 S; $70 D; $75–$100 ste. Extra person $10. Children under age 18 stay free. Parking: Outdoor, free. Honeymoon package avail (includes champagne, dinner, movie). AE, DC, DISC, MC, V.

≣≣≣ Holiday Inn Downtown

11061 6th Ave, 35601; tel 205/355-3150 or toll free 800/553-3150; fax 205/350-5262. S end of Tennessee River bridge. Five-story stucco building, with a high-rise tower, a low-rise wing, and a central Holidome with rooms facing the pool. **Rooms:** 225 rms and stes. CI 2pm/CO noon. Non-smoking rms avail. **Amenities:** 🛁 🔥 📺 A/C, satel TV w/movies. **Services:** ✗ 🚗 🖼 🔂 🍽 **Facilities:** 🏋 🎱 👤 1 restaurant, 1 bar, games rm, whirlpool, washer/dryer. Guest privileges at local fitness center. **Rates:** $65–$79 S or D; $90–$130 ste. Extra person $8. Children under age 18 stay free. Parking: Outdoor, free. Golf packages avail. AE, DC, DISC, MC, V.

MOTELS

≣≣≣ Days Inn Decatur

810 6th Ave NE, PO Box 2063, 35602; tel 205/355-3520 or toll free 800/DAYS-INN; fax 205/355-7213. At Church St. Conveniently located, average chain motel. **Rooms:** 117 rms. CI 2pm/CO 11am. Nonsmoking rms avail. **Amenities:** 🛁 🔥 📺 A/C, cable TV w/movies, in-rm safe. **Services:** ✗ 🔂 🍽 Nonrefundable $10 pet fee. Guests receive discounts at local attractions. **Facilities:** 🏋 🎱 1 restaurant, 1 bar. Room key may be used as pass at nearby Gold's Gym. **Rates:** $47–$53 S; $45–$51 D. Extra person $5. Children under age 17 stay free. Parking: Outdoor, free. AE, DC, DISC, MC, V.

≣≣ Ramada Limited

1317 AL 67 E, 35603; tel 205/353-0333 or toll free 800/579-5464; fax 205/351-6285. A handsome establishment, with a nice picnic and gazebo area. Centrally located for surrounding attractions. **Rooms:** 84 rms. CI noon/CO noon. Nonsmoking rms avail. **Amenities:** 🛁 🔥 📺 A/C, cable TV w/movies. **Services:** 🖼 🔂 🍽 **Facilities:** 🏋 🛝 👤 Playground, washer/dryer. **Rates (CP):** Peak (May–Sept) $44 S; $49–$54 D. Extra person $5. Children under age 18 stay free. Lower rates off-season. Parking: Outdoor, free. AE, DC, DISC, JCB, MC, V.

RESTAURANT 🍽

❦ ✹ Simp McGhee's

725 Bank St; tel 205/353-6284. At Lafayette St. **Cajun/Seafood.** Housed in a restored turn-of-the-century building that is listed on the National Register of Historic Places. The downstairs dining area has a pub atmosphere while the upstairs offers comfortable fine dining with linens and silver. The kitchen specializes in fresh seafood: Cajun shrimp, filet gumbo, catch of the day. Steak, chicken, and pasta entrees also available. **FYI:** Reservations not accepted. Dress code. **Open:** Mon–Sat 5–9pm. **Prices:** Main courses $14–$20. AE, DC, DISC, MC, V. ❤ 🍴 👤

ATTRACTIONS 🏛

The Old State Bank

925 Bank St NE; tel 205/350-5060. This architecturally impressive building, combining elements of federal and Greek Revival styles, started life in 1833 as a branch of the first state bank in Alabama. It has since been a Union Army hospital, a boardinghouse, a town hall, and an American

Legion building. Today, the bank houses exhibits on the history of Decatur and of Alabama as a whole. **Open:** Mon–Fri 9:30am–noon and 1:30–4:30pm. Closed some hols. **Free**

Point Mallard Park

1800 Point Mallard Dr; tel 205/350-3000 or toll free 800/669-WAVE. Activities from golf to swimming to ice skating are available at this 750-acre family park. The J Gilmer Blackburn Aquatic Center (open May through Labor Day only) features the Squirt Factory, the Duck Pond, and the Three Flume Tube ride, as well as America's first wave pool. Other highlights include a rustic 175-site campground, hiking and biking trails, and an indoor recreation center with basketball and racquetball courts. **$$**

Demopolis

French refugees founded a colony here in 1817 on bluff above the Tombigbee River. Situated in the historic plantations region, Demopolis offers "Bluff Hall" on the limestone bluffs, and "Gainswood," a 20-room Greek Revival mansion with original furnishings. **Information:** Demopolis Area Chamber of Commerce, 102 E Washington, PO Box 667, Demopolis, 36732 (tel 334/289-0270).

MOTELS 🏨

🚩 Best Western Mint Sunrise

1034 US 80, 36732; tel 334/289-5772 or toll free 800/528-1234; fax 334/289-5772. Bare-bones accommodations, popular with vacationing families. **Rooms:** 70 rms and effic. CI noon/CO 11am. Nonsmoking rms avail. **Amenities:** 🅃 🅰 🆅🅿 A/C, cable TV w/movies, dataport. **Services:** 🆅🅿 ⬜ ↩ **Facilities:** 🄵 🔤 ⬜20⬜ 🅰 Picnic area. **Rates (CP):** $40 S; $44 D; $44 effic. Extra person $2. Children under age 12 stay free. Parking: Outdoor, free. AE, DC, DISC, MC, V.

🚩🚩 Riverview Inn Demopolis Yacht Basin

1301 N Walnut, PO Box 1024, 36732; tel 334/289-0690; fax 334/289-0690. A unique, privately owned property overlooking the Demopolis Yacht Basin and marina. A quiet, comfortable place to stay. **Rooms:** 25 rms. CI open/CO 11am. Nonsmoking rms avail. **Amenities:** 🅃 🅰 A/C, cable TV w/movies. **Services:** ↩ 🄰 **Facilities:** 🔲 🄰⬛8⬛ ⬜25⬜ 1 restaurant (lunch and dinner only; see "Restaurants" below), 1 bar, washer/dryer. Covered parking and boat docking available. Restaurant overlooks the water. **Rates:** $34 S; $37 D. Extra person $3. Children under age 3 stay free. Min stay special events. Parking: Indoor/outdoor, free. AE, DC, DISC, MC, V.

RESTAURANT 🍴

★ Jolly Roger's

In Demopolis Yacht Basin; tel 334/289-8103. **Seafood.** A waterside establishment overlooking the Tombigbee waterway. Seafood (available broiled or fried) is as fresh as it can

be. The crab claws are a favorite among the locals. **FYI:** Reservations accepted. Dress code. **Open:** Tues–Thurs 11am–9pm, Fri–Sat 11am–10pm. **Prices:** Main courses $8–$13. No CC. 🏞

ATTRACTION 🏛

Bluff Hall

405 N Commissioners Ave; tel 334/289-1666. A fine example of an antebellum Greek Revival house, built in 1832. Owned by Francis Strother Lyon during the Civil War, the house received many prominent Confederate officers and political leaders, including Jefferson Davis. The mansion is filled with Empire and Early Victorian antiques, and a collection of period clothing is also on display. An adjacent craft shop sells handwoven baskets, old-fashioned dolls, and historical photos. **Open:** Tues–Sat 10am–5pm, Sun 2–5pm. Closed some hols. **$**

Dothan

Wiregrass region's chief trade center. The National Peanut Festival and an annual peanut recipe cook-off—including such original goodies as peanut pie—pay tribute to the region's most successful crop. **Information:** Dothan Area Convention & Visitors Bureau, 3311 Ross Clark Circle, PO Box 8765, Dothan, 36304 (tel 334/794-6622).

HOTELS 🏨

🚩🚩 Comfort Inn

3593 Ross Clark Circle NW, PO Box 9311, 36304; tel 334/793-9090 or toll free 800/474-7298; fax 334/793-4367. Off US 231 S. Located near the Northside Shopping Mall and theaters. Area attractions include the Wiregrass Museum of Art, Adventure Land Theme Park, Fort Rucker Aviation Museum, Landmark Park, Robert Trent Jones Golf, and the Civic Center and Opera House. **Rooms:** 122 rms. CI 2pm/CO 1pm. Nonsmoking rms avail. **Amenities:** 🅃 🅰 🆅 🅰 A/C, cable TV w/movies, dataport. Some units w/whirlpools. **Services:** ⬜ ↩ 🄰 **Facilities:** 🄵 🔤 ⬜50⬜ 🅰 **Rates (CP):** $53–$80 S; $61–$85 D. Extra person $5. Children under age 18 stay free. Parking: Outdoor, free. Robert Trent Jones Golf Trail package avail. AE, DC, DISC, JCB, MC, V.

🚩🚩🚩 Holiday Inn West

3053 Ross Clark Circle SW, 36301; tel 334/794-6601 or toll free 800/HOLIDAY; fax 334/794-6601. Off US 231 bypass. Located near shopping, theaters, restaurants, and area attractions such as Water World and Westgate Softball Complex. **Rooms:** 102 rms. CI noon/CO noon. Nonsmoking rms avail. **Amenities:** 🅃 🅰 A/C, cable TV w/movies. **Services:** ✗ ⬜ ↩ **Facilities:** 🄵 ⬜40⬜ 🅰 1 restaurant (bkfst and dinner only), 1 bar. **Rates:** $49–$64 S or D. Extra person $5. Children under age 12 stay free. Parking: Outdoor, free. AE, DC, DISC, MC, V.

MOTELS

〓〓 Days Inn

2841 Ross Clark Circle SW, 36301; tel 334/793-2550 or toll free 800/544-1448; fax 334/793-7962. Off US 231 bypass. Near shopping and restaurants. Water World, Adventure Land, Landmark Park, and the Air Museum at Fort Rucker are also nearby. **Rooms:** 120 rms. CI 10am/CO noon. Nonsmoking rms avail. **Amenities:** 🛏 🕭 📺 A/C, cable TV w/movies. **Services:** 🖼 🖐 🖐 **Facilities:** 🖼 ㅊ Volleyball. Texaco gas pumps on property (24 hours). **Rates:** $38 S; $42 D. Extra person $5. Children under age 12 stay free. Parking: Outdoor, free. AE, DC, DISC, MC, V.

〓〓 Hampton Inn

3071 Ross Clark Circle SW, 36301; tel 334/671-3700 or toll free 800/HAMPTON; fax 334/671-3700 ext 182. Off US 231 bypass. Located near area attractions such as the Westgate Softball Complex, Water World, Robert Trent Jones Golf Trail. **Rooms:** 113 rms. CI 3pm/CO noon. Nonsmoking rms avail. **Amenities:** 🛏 🕭 A/C, cable TV w/movies. **Services:** 🖼 🖐 🖐 **Facilities:** 🖼 🔲 ㅊ Guest may use passes to local fitness center. **Rates (CP):** $49–$56 S or D. Extra person $5. Children under age 18 stay free. Parking: Outdoor, free. Robert Trent Jones Golf Trail package avail. AE, DC, DISC, MC, V.

〓〓〓 Holiday Inn South

2195 Ross Clark Circle SE, 36301; tel 334/794-8711 or toll free 800/777-6611; fax 334/671-3781. Off US 231. Area attractions include Water World, Landmark Park, Adventure Land, and the Wiregrass Museum of Art. Shopping and restaurants also nearby. **Rooms:** 144 rms and stes. CI 3pm/CO noon. Nonsmoking rms avail. **Amenities:** 🛏 🕭 A/C, cable TV w/movies, dataport. **Services:** ✗ 🖼 🖐 🖐 **Facilities:** 🖼 🔲 ㅊ 1 restaurant, 1 bar (w/entertainment). **Rates (BB):** $45–$52 S; $45–$58 D; $64 ste. Extra person $6. Children under age 12 stay free. Parking: Outdoor, free. AE, DC, DISC, MC, V.

〓〓 Olympia Spa Resort

AL 231 S, PO Box 6108, 36301; tel 334/677-3321; fax 334/677-3321. 200 acres. This resort is near theaters, shopping malls, and recreational facilities, and only 70 miles north of Panama City. **Rooms:** 96 rms. CI 1pm/CO noon. Nonsmoking rms avail. **Amenities:** 🛏 🕭 📺 🍴 A/C, cable TV w/movies. **Services:** ✗ 🚗 🖼 🖐 🖐 Catering services and banquet facilities available. **Facilities:** 🖼 ▶18 🔲 1 restaurant, 1 bar, spa, sauna, steam rm, whirlpool. 19th Hole Sports Lounge. Natural Hot Mineral Springs located on premises. **Rates:** Peak (Mar–May) $40 S or D. Children under age 18 stay free. Lower rates off-season. Parking: Outdoor, free. Golf packages avail. AE, CB, DC, DISC, MC, V.

〓〓〓 Ramada Inn

3011 Ross Clark Circle, 36301; tel 334/792-0031 or toll free 800/272-6232; fax 334/794-3134. Off US 231. Located near Water World, the Robert Trent Jones Golf Complex, and the Wiregrass Museum of Art. **Rooms:** 158 rms and stes. CI 3pm/CO noon. Nonsmoking rms avail. **Amenities:** 🛏 A/C, cable TV w/movies. Safe-deposit box available. **Services:** ✗ 🚗 🖼 🖐 🖐 **Facilities:** 🖼 🔲 ㅊ 1 restaurant, 1 bar (w/entertainment). Use of local fitness center. Trader Bob's Bar features Wed night comedy shows. **Rates:** Peak (Mar–Aug) $50 S; $56 D; $68 ste. Extra person $6. Children under age 18 stay free. Lower rates off-season. Parking: Outdoor, free. AE, CB, DC, DISC, JCB, MC, V.

RESTAURANT 🍴

★ Old Mill Restaurant

2501 Murphy Mill Rd; tel 334/794-8530. **Seafood/Steak.** Locally owned and operated, this family-friendly place is known for its seafood selections and fast service. **FYI:** Reservations accepted. Dress code. **Open:** Mon–Sat 5–10pm. **Prices:** Main courses $7–$19. AE, MC, V. 🖼 ㅊ

ATTRACTIONS 🏛

Wiregrass Museum of Art

126 N College St; tel 334/794-3871. The permanent collection at the Wiregrass includes contemporary paintings, sculpture, pastels, decorative arts, and multimedia installations. The hands-on ARTventures gallery for children and their parents provides a variety of sensory activities. **Open:** Tues–Sat 10am–5pm, Sun 1–5pm. Closed some hols. **Free**

Landmark Park

AL 431 N; tel 334/794-3452. A 60-acre park built to preserve the natural and cultural heritage of the Wiregrass region of southeast Alabama. Historical exhibits include a one-room schoolhouse, a late 19th-century church, and an 1890s farm complete with farmhouse, smokehouse, and farm animals. An elevated boardwalk winds its way through the surrounding woods. Nature trails, wildlife exhibits, picnic area, and the Starlab Planetarium round out the activities. (Small additional fee for the planetarium.) **Open:** Mon–Sat 9am–5pm, Sun noon–5pm. Closed some hols. **$**

Eufaula

Its location on a bluff above the Chattahoochee River made this town an important trade cotton embarkation point. As a result, there are many interesting structures here, including the Shorter Mansion (the visitors center for the town), one of the Alabama's finest neoclassical mansions. Eufaula National Wildlife Refuge, which borders on the Chattahoochee River, includes alligators, egrets, and deer. **Information:** Eufaula/Barbour County Tourism Council, 102 N Orange Ave, PO Box 1055, Eufaula, 36072 (tel 334/687-5283).

MOTELS

≣≣ Best Western Eufaula Inn

1337 AL 431 S, 36027; tel 334/687-3900 or toll free 800/528-1234; fax 334/687-6870. This spotless establishment is located within two miles of Eufaula's historic district and is surrounded by shopping and restaurants. **Rooms:** 42 rms. CI 11am/CO 11am. Nonsmoking rms avail. **Amenities:** A/C, cable TV w/movies. Some units w/whirlpools. **Services:** **Facilities:** **Rates (CP):** $42–$46 S; $44–$60 D. Extra person $4. Children under age 12 stay free. Parking: Outdoor, free. AE, CB, DC, DISC, MC, V.

≣≣≣ Holiday Inn

US 82 at Riverside Dr, PO Box 725, 36027; tel 334/687-2021 or toll free 800/HOLIDAY; fax 334/687-2021 ext 4. Overlooks Lake Eufaula and is close to many antebellum homes. **Rooms:** 96 rms. CI noon/CO noon. Nonsmoking rms avail. **Amenities:** A/C, cable TV w/movies, dataport. **Services:** **Facilities:** 1 restaurant, 1 bar. **Rates:** $44 S; $49–$56 D. Extra person $5. Children under age 19 stay free. Min stay special events. Parking: Outdoor, free. Golf package with Red Eagle Golf Course avail. AE, CB, DC, DISC, JCB, MC, V.

RESORT

≣≣≣ Lakepoint Resort

AL 431 N, PO Box 267, 36072; tel 334/687-8011 or toll free 800/544-5253; fax 334/687-3273. 7 mi N of Eufaula. 45,000 acres. Offers easy access from US 82. Within 5–10 miles of the Shorter Mansion, Fendall Hall, historic antebellum homes of Eufaula, Tom Mann's Fish World, and Eufaula National Wildlife Refuge. **Rooms:** 101 rms and stes; 22 cottages/villas. CI 1pm/CO 11am. Nonsmoking rms avail. **Amenities:** A/C, satel TV. All units w/terraces, some w/fireplaces. **Services:** Pontoon and fishing boats may be rented. **Facilities:** 1 restaurant (*see* "Restaurants" below), 1 bar, 1 beach (lake shore), games rm, playground, washer/dryer. Marina offers covered and uncovered boat slips for rent; gasoline island, and snack store. **Rates:** Peak (Mar–Oct) $44–$49 S; $49–$58 D; $116 ste; $68–$124 cottage/villa. Extra person $5. Children under age 12 stay free. Min stay wknds and special events. Lower rates off-season. Parking: Outdoor, free. Golf and winter getaway packages avail. AE, MC, V.

RESTAURANT

Lakepoint Resort Restaurant

In Lakepoint Resort, PO Box 267; tel 334/687-8011. **Regional American.** A wide selection at each meal is offered here, and the restaurant specializes in hearty and filling food. The wide windows overlook Lake Eufaula. **FYI:** Reservations accepted. Dress code. **Open:** Sun–Thurs 7am–9pm, Fri–Sat 7am–10pm. **Prices:** Main courses $7–$15. AE, MC, V.

ATTRACTION

Eufaula National Wildlife Refuge

Old AL 165; tel 334/687-4065. Established in 1964 to provide feeding and resting habitat for migratory waterfowl, the refuge is home to thousands of geese, eagles, ospreys, egrets, gulls, mourning doves, and many other varieties of birds. The "Wildspread Wildlife Drive" self-guided auto tour (pick up guide at refuge headquarters) provides an excellent overview. The refuge also offers opportunities for fishing, hunting, boating, and hiking, and the adjacent **Lake Point Resort State Park** offers swimming, camping, and a golf course. **Open:** Daily sunrise–sunset. **Free**

Evergreen

County seat of Conecuh County, a largely rural area with vast forests. An active arts and crafts community draws artists from throughout the South for Heritage Day in November. **Information:** Evergreen/Conecuh County Area Chamber of Commerce, 100 Depot Sq, Evergreen, 36401 (tel 334/578-1707).

MOTEL

≣ Comfort Inn

Bates Rd, PO Box 564, 36401; tel 334/578-4701 or toll free 800/424-4777; fax 334/578-3180. Exit 96 off I-65. A basic chain motel, convenient to all major attractions. **Rooms:** 58 rms. CI 11am/CO 11am. Nonsmoking rms avail. Rooms are well maintained. King-size rooms available. **Amenities:** A/C, cable TV w/movies. **Services:** **Facilities:** **Rates:** $30–$45 S; $36–$52 D. Extra person $5. Parking: Outdoor, free. AE, JCB, MC, V.

ATTRACTION

Conecuh National Forest

AL 137, Andalusia; tel 334/222-2555. Located along the Alabama/Florida border, this 84,000-acre park is made up of two distinct recreation areas. **Open Pond Recreation Area** (south of AL 24) is open year-round, and offers camping, picnicking, fishing, and boating. **Blue Lake Recreation Area** (north of AL 24) offers swimming and fishing, and is open March 15–October 31. In all, the forest boasts more than 50 miles of streams, 2 lakes, and 4 ponds for fishing (ask at the district ranger's office in Andalusia about license requirements). Horseback riding, hiking, and primitive camping (except during winter hunting season) are also available. **Open:** Daily sunrise–sunset. **Free**

Florence

Birthplace of the "Father of the Blues," W C Handy; his original log cabin home is a museum. The town is also the site of the largest Native American mound (43 feet high) on the

Tennessee River. Alabama's official Renaissance Faire is held in October. **Information:** Shoals Chamber of Commerce, 104 S Pine St, Florence, 35630 (tel 205/383-4704).

MOTELS

≣≣≣ Best Western Executive Inn

504 S Court St, 35630; tel 205/766-2331 or toll free 800/528-1234; fax 205/766-3567. N end of O'Neal Bridge. Located in downtown Florence and near area attractions such as Ivy Green, Alabama Music Hall of Fame, W C Handy Home and Museum, Pope's Tavern, and Indian Mound and Museum. **Rooms:** 120 rms and stes. CI noon/CO noon. Nonsmoking rms avail. **Amenities:** 🛏 A/C, cable TV w/movies, dataport. **Services:** ✗ ☎ 🍴 Facilities: 🔶 150 ⅙ 1 restaurant (*see* "Restaurants" below), 1 bar, whirlpool, washer/dryer. **Rates (CP):** $49–$54 S or D; $75–$95 ste. Extra person $5. Children under age 12 stay free. Parking: Outdoor, free. Weekly and monthly rates avail. AE, DC, DISC, MC, V.

≣≣ Comfort Inn

400 S Court St, 35630; tel 205/760-8888 or toll free 800/760-8888; fax 205/766-1681. At Hicks Dr. Located in downtown Florence and near area attractions such as Renaissance Tower, Wilson Dam, W C Handy birthplace, Pope's Tavern. Convenient to shopping and restaurants. **Rooms:** 85 rms and stes. CI noon/CO noon. Nonsmoking rms avail. **Amenities:** 🛏 🍴 A/C, cable TV w/movies. Some units w/whirlpools. **Services:** ☎ 🍴 Facilities: 🔶 125 **Rates (CP):** $44 S; $49 D; $60–$98 ste. Extra person $5. Children under age 18 stay free. Parking: Outdoor, free. AE, DISC, JCB, MC, V.

≣ Days Inn of Florence

1915 Florence Blvd, 35630; tel 205/766-2620 or toll free 800/325-2525; fax 205/766-2620 ext 185. Off US 72. A single-story property located near the TVA reservation, the University of North Alabama, and Regency Square Mall. **Rooms:** 82 rms. CI noon/CO noon. Nonsmoking rms avail. **Amenities:** 🛏 A/C, cable TV w/movies. **Services:** 🍴 Facilities: 🔶 50 ⅙ **Rates:** $40 S; $45–$47 D. Extra person $5. Children under age 12 stay free. Parking: Outdoor, free. AE, DC, DISC, MC, V.

RESTAURANTS

★ Dale's Restaurant

1001 Mitchell Blvd; tel 205/766-4961. **Seafood/Steak.** Home of "world-famous" Dale's steak sauce. In business since 1962, they offer steak, seafood, and chicken entrees and a comfortable, elegant atmosphere. **FYI:** Reservations accepted. Children's menu. Dress code. **Open:** Mon–Sat 5–10pm. **Prices:** Main courses $10–$21. AE, CB, DC, MC, V.

★ Renaissance Grille

In Renaissance Tower, 1 Hightower Place; tel 205/718-0092. **Seafood/Steak.** Specialties—including pork tenderloin, ribs,

and creative salads—served in an elegant dining room with gorgeous views of the Tennessee River. **FYI:** Reservations accepted. Piano. Children's menu. Dress code. **Open:** Sun–Thurs 11am–10pm, Fri–Sat 11am–11pm. **Prices:** Main courses $7–$18. AE, CB, DC, DISC, MC, V.

ATTRACTIONS

W C Handy Home and Museum

620 W College St; tel 205/760-6434. Birthplace of W C Handy, commonly known as the "Father of the Blues." His piano and trumpet are on display, as are original manuscripts and citations from his admirers, including George Gershwin and Louis Armstrong. **Open:** Tues–Sat 10am–4pm. Closed some hols. **$**

Indian Mound and Museum

S Court St; tel 205/760-6427. One of the largest Indian mounds in the Tennessee River Valley, the pre-Columbian mound measures 43 feet high. The museum is filled with Native American artifacts, some dating back more than 10,000 years. **Open:** Tues–Sat 10am–4pm. Closed some hols. **$**

Fort Payne

Site of the deepest gorge east of the Rocky Mountains, with the only river in the country that forms and flows on top of a mountain. A large country music concert, "Alabama June Jam," is held here. **Information:** Fort Payne Chamber of Commerce, 300 Gault Ave N, PO Box 125, Fort Payne, 35967 (tel 205/845-2741).

MOTEL

≣ Quality Inn

I-59 and AL 35, PO Box 655, 35967; tel 205/845-4013 or toll free 800/228-5151. An engaging, two-story motel offering a picnic area, a playground, and a wonderful, Olympic-size swimming pool. Near DeSoto State Park and Little River Canyon. **Rooms:** 79 rms. CI 2pm/CO 11am. Nonsmoking rms avail. **Amenities:** 🛏 A/C, cable TV w/movies. **Services:** ☎ 🍴 Facilities: 🔶 80 ⅙ Washer/dryer. **Rates (CP):** $37–$44 S; $42–$49 D. Extra person $5. Children under age 16 stay free. Parking: Outdoor, free. AE, CB, DC, DISC, MC, V.

LODGE

≣≣≣ DeSoto State Park Lodge

Rte 1, PO Box 205, 35967; tel 205/845-5380 or toll free 800/568-8840; fax 205/845-3224. 5,000 acres. A surprisingly plush state park lodge, offering many of the amenities of any chain hotel with the added bonus of park activities—and the great outdoors—just outside your room. **Rooms:** 25 rms; 22 cottages/villas. CI 4pm/CO 11am. Nonsmoking rms avail. **Amenities:** 🛏 🍴 A/C, cable TV w/movies, refrig. All units w/terraces, some w/fireplaces. **Facilities:** 🔶 🎾 🏊 🍴1 100 ⅙

1 restaurant, basketball, volleyball, lawn games, playground, washer/dryer. Country-style front porch, with rocking chairs. **Rates:** Peak (Mar–Nov) $44–$49 S or D; $56–$68 cottage/villa. Extra person $5. Children under age 12 stay free. Min stay peak. Lower rates off-season. Parking: Outdoor, free. AE, MC, V.

ATTRACTION 🏛

DeSoto State Park

County Rd 89 off DeSoto Pkwy; tel 205/845-0051. Encompassing three distinct areas spread out over 5,067 mountainous acres, DeSoto State Park offers a wide range of recreational activities. Swimming, fishing, and boating are available at DeSoto Lake, while sections of the Little River offer challenging white-water thrills. There are seven hiking trails, several picnic areas, and a swimming pool (open Memorial Day to Labor Day only), and guided nature walks are offered in the summer. The park also boasts 15 waterfalls, including 100-foot-tall De Soto Falls. Motorists may wish to follow the 22-mile Little River Canyon Scenic Drive. **Open:** Daily 7am–sunset. **$**

Gadsden

Home to park featuring caverns, a 200-year-old homestead, and a zoo. The world's largest tire factory is here. The start of Lookout Mountain Parkway to Chattanooga, one of America's most colorful 100-mile scenic drives. **Information:** Gadsden-Etowah Chamber of Commerce, One Commerce Sq, PO Box 185, Gadsden, 35902 (tel 205/543-3472).

HOTEL 🏨

📶📶 Hampton Inn

129 River Rd, 35901; tel 205/546-2337 or toll free 800/426-7866; fax 205/547-5124. Exit 4B off I-759. Relatively new place across the street from the Gadsden Mall. **Rooms:** 66 rms and stes. CI 2pm/CO 11am. Nonsmoking rms avail. **Amenities:** 🛏 📺 A/C, cable TV w/movies. **Services:** 🍴 **Facilities:** 🛋 🔳 ⅃ **Rates (CP):** $56–$61 S; $60–$67 D; $120 ste. Extra person $6. Children under age 18 stay free. Min stay special events. Parking: Outdoor, free. AE, CB, DC, DISC, JCB, MC, V.

MOTELS

📶📶 Days Inn Gadsden

1600 Rainbow Dr, 35901; tel 205/543-1105 or toll free 800/329-7466; fax 205/543-1105 ext 301. Exit 4A off I-759 on the Coosa River. Near DeSoto State Park and Little River Canyon—a good choice for outdoors enthusiasts. **Rooms:** 102 rms and stes. CI 2pm/CO 11am. Nonsmoking rms avail. **Amenities:** 🛏 🌊 A/C, cable TV w/movies. **Services:** 🍴 ⅃ **Facilities:** 🛋 💯 ⅃ **Rates (CP):** $46–$58 S or D; $66–$140

ste. Extra person $4. Children under age 18 stay free. Min stay special events. Parking: Outdoor, free. AE, CB, DC, DISC, JCB, MC, V.

📶📶 Holiday Inn Express

801 Cleveland Ave, Attalla, 35954; tel 205/538-7861 or toll free 800/HOLIDAY; fax 205/538-1010. Exit 183 off I-59. Recently remodeled and conveniently located, this motel offers basic accommodations in the business district, just off I-59. **Rooms:** 143 rms. CI 1pm/CO noon. Nonsmoking rms avail. **Amenities:** 🛏 🌊 A/C, cable TV w/movies, dataport. **Services:** 🛎 ⅃ 🍴 **Facilities:** 🛋 🔳 ⅃ Washer/dryer. **Rates (CP):** $52–$58 S or D. Extra person $6. Children under age 19 stay free. Min stay special events. Parking: Outdoor, free. AE, CB, DC, DISC, ER, JCB, MC, V.

ATTRACTION 🏛

Center for Cultural Arts

5th and Broad Sts; tel 205/543-2787. Home to a variety of visual, musical, and theatrical presentations, including the Gadsden Symphony. The Center's second floor features the world's largest site- and date-specific model railroad, consisting of six trains traveling through a miniature version of Gadsden in the 1940s and early 1950s. At Imagination Place, children can "try on" various careers in a child-sized city complete with a post office, hospital, supermarket, and radio station. **Open:** Mon and Wed–Sat 9am–6pm, Tues 9am–9pm, Sun 1–5pm. Closed some hols. **$**

Gulf Shores

See also Orange Beach

Gulf Coast resort community with sugar-white sand beaches and a fishing pier extending into the Gulf of Mexico. Site of Gulf Coast Mardi Gras Parade. Dauphin Island, three miles offshore, was named by early French inhabitants as "Massacre Island" for the mysterious pile of human bones they discovered. The name was soon changed to honor King Louis XIV's son, the dauphin of France. Six different flags have flown here, providing a dramatic history. **Information:** Alabama Gulf Coast Chamber of Commerce, 3150 Gulf Shores Pkwy, PO Drawer 3869, Gulf Shores, 36547 (tel 334/968-5332).

HOTELS 🏨

UNRATED Best Western on the Beach

337 E Beach Blvd, PO Box 481, 36547; tel 334/948-2711 or toll free 800/788-4557; fax 334/948-7339. Located in the heart of Gulf Shores, this very well-maintained hotel is always in great demand. Wonderful view of the beach and close to all major sights and activities. **Rooms:** 114 rms and stes; 4 cottages/villas. CI 3pm/CO 11am. Nonsmoking rms avail. **Amenities:** 🛏 🌊 📺 🍴 A/C, cable TV. All units w/terraces, 1 w/whirlpool. **Services:** ⅃ Babysitting. **Facilities:** 🛋 🏊 💯

& 1 restaurant, 1 beach (ocean), whirlpool. **Rates:** Peak (May–Oct) $179 S or D; $225 ste; $225 cottage/villa. Extra person $10. Children under age 18 stay free. Min stay wknds and special events. Lower rates off-season. Parking: Outdoor, free. AE, CB, DC, DISC, MC, V.

☰☰☰ Lighthouse Resort Motel
455 E Beach Blvd, PO Box 233, 36547; tel 334/948-6188; fax 334/948-6100. Off US 182 E. A relaxed atmosphere for enjoying all the fun of the Gulf Coast. Nearby, you'll find challenging golf courses and recreational facilities. **Rooms:** 200 rms, stes, and effic; 3 cottages/villas. CI 3pm/CO 11am. Rooms are average in size, and comfortable. Most enjoy a breathtaking view of the beach. **Amenities:** 🛁 🖵 A/C, cable TV w/movies, refrig. Some units w/terraces. **Services:** 🛏 🖐 **Facilities:** 🏊 & 1 beach (ocean), volleyball, games rm, whirlpool, washer/dryer. **Rates:** Peak (May–Labor Day) $64–$94 S; $68–$86 D; $87–$135 ste; $71–$135 effic; $110 cottage/villa. Children under age 18 stay free. Min stay wknds and special events. Lower rates off-season. Parking: Outdoor, free. AE, DC, DISC, MC, V.

UNRATED Quality Inn Beachside
931 W Beach Blvd, PO Box 1013, 36547; tel 334/948-6874 or toll free 800/844-6913; fax 334/948-5232. Off I-59 S. A Quality Inn that really lives up to its name. Two pools and a beach location means guests are never more than a few steps away from water. Minutes away from deep-sea fishing, golf, tennis, and shopping. **Rooms:** 158 rms and stes. CI 4pm/CO 11am. Nonsmoking rms avail. Rooms offer breathtaking views of the Gulf. **Amenities:** 🛁 🕭 🖵 A/C, cable TV w/movies. All units w/terraces. Some rooms have refrigerators. **Services:** ✗ 🖾 🖐 **Facilities:** 🏊 🛆 🖺 250 & 1 restaurant (see "Restaurants" below), 1 bar (w/entertainment), 1 beach (ocean), volleyball, games rm, whirlpool, washer/dryer. **Rates:** Peak (May–Sept 4) $105–$137 S or D; $139–$215 ste. Extra person $6. Children under age 18 stay free. Min stay wknds and special events. Lower rates off-season. Parking: Outdoor, free. AE, DC, DISC, MC, V.

RESORT

☰☰ Gulf State Park Resort Hotel
21250 E Beach Blvd, PO Box 437, 36547; tel 334/948-4853 or toll free 800/544-4853; fax 334/948-5998. 6,000 acres. A family-friendly beachside resort, convenient to sightseeing, Zooland, Fort Meyers, and major shopping areas. Dated facilities could use some upgrading. **Rooms:** 144 rms, stes, and effic. CI 4pm/CO 11am. Nonsmoking rms avail. Rooms are large, comfortable, and exceptionally clean. **Amenities:** 🛁 A/C, cable TV. All units w/terraces. Suites have refrigerators. **Services:** 🖐 **Facilities:** 🏊 🛆 🖺 ▶18 🏊2 600 & 1 restaurant, 1 bar, 1 beach (ocean), lifeguard, volleyball, games rm, lawn games. **Rates:** Peak (May–Sept 4) $99 S or D; $205 ste; $105 effic. Extra person $6. Children under age 12

stay free. Min stay wknds and special events. Lower rates off-season. Parking: Outdoor, free. Golf, getaway, and honeymoon packages avail. AE, MC, V.

RESTAURANTS 🍴

★ Original Oyster House
In Bayou Village Shopping Center, 701 Gulf Shores Pkwy; tel 334/948-2445. **Seafood.** A humble storefront serving up some of the best oysters on the half shell to be had on the Gulf Coast. Seafood gumbo (with four or five types of seafood—whatever is freshest) makes a great starter, and there are fried and broiled seafood entrees as well. **FYI:** Reservations not accepted. Children's menu. Dress code. **Open:** Daily 11am–10pm. **Prices:** Main courses $12–$15. CB, DC, DISC, MC, V. 🖼

Pompano's Restaurant
In Quality Inn Beachside, 921 W Beach Blvd; tel 334/948-6874 ext 100. **Seafood.** A comfortable, family-friendly eatery with fabulous shoreline views of the Gulf of Mexico. Specializes in seafood dishes. **FYI:** Reservations accepted. Singer. Children's menu. Dress code. **Open:** Peak (May–Sept) breakfast daily 7–11am; dinner daily 5–9pm. **Prices:** Main courses $11–$17. AE, DC, DISC, MC, V. ♥ 🖼 🖼 &

ATTRACTIONS 🖼

Fort Morgan
AL 180; tel 334/540-7125. Located 22 mi W of Gulf Shores. Completed in 1834, this was one of the last Confederate forts to fall to Union forces. It was here in 1864 that Admiral David Farragut issued his now-famous command during the Battle of Mobile Bay: "Damn the torpedoes! Full speed ahead!" Today, the museum contains a variety of weapons, uniforms, and artifacts that chronicle the fort's importance from the War of 1812 through World War II. **Open:** Mon–Fri 8am–5pm, Sat–Sun 9am–5pm. Closed some hols. **$**

Fort Gaines Historic Site
E Bienville Blvd, Dauphin Island; tel 334/861-6992. Located 20 mi W of Gulf Shores. One of the fortifications that guarded Mobile Bay during the Civil War. The three-week siege of the Battle of Mobile Bay resulted in the capture of Fort Gaines by Union forces, and the ultimate defeat of the Confederate fleet. Today, visitors can touch the battlements and cannons, and explore the tunnels and bastions used by the Confederate Army. The fort also hosts Civil War reenactments and other special events; call ahead for schedule. **Open:** Daily 9am–5pm. Closed some hols. **$**

Bon Secour National Wildlife Refuge
AL 180 at MM 13; tel 334/540-7720. The 6,200-acre refuge protects and preserves the plants and animals of the Gulf Coast, including the endangered Alabama beach mouse and loggerhead sea turtle, as well as wildflowers such as scarlet

red basil and goldenrod. Popular recreational activities at the refuge include hiking, fishing, and nature study. **Open:** Mon–Fri 8am–4:30pm. Closed some hols. **Free**

Gulf State Park
AL 135; tel 334/948-7275. Popular Gulf Coast park boasts 6,000 acres of land with 2½ miles of beaches. Located on the four preserved stretches of sand are a public pavilion, an 825-foot fishing pier, and a resort complex with lodging, dining, and convention facilities. Inland, 500-acre Lake Shelby hosts fishing enthusiasts, boaters, skiers, and swimmers. Additional park facilities include an 18-hole golf course, tennis courts, playgrounds, and a marina. **Open:** Daily sunrise–sunset. **$**

Guntersville

Incorporated as Marshall in 1838 and given its present name in 1848, after settler John Gunter. **Information:** Lake Guntersville Chamber of Commerce, 200 Gunter Ave, PO Box 577, Guntersville, 35976 (tel 205/582-3612).

HOTEL 🏨

≡≡≡ Holiday Inn
2140 Gunter Ave, 35976; tel 205/582-2220 or toll free 800/HOLIDAY; fax 205/582-2059. Popular with fishing enthusiasts, due to its location overlooking Lake Guntersville. Close to area shopping and eateries, and only 14 miles to the Boaz Shopping Outlet Center. **Rooms:** 100 rms and effic. CI 3pm/CO 11am. Nonsmoking rms avail. Energy Saver System in rooms to help conserve energy. **Amenities:** 🛏 ⚒ 🖭 A/C, cable TV w/movies, dataport, in-rm safe. **Services:** ✗ 🖼 ↩ ⟡ **Facilities:** 🔁 🏋 📅 ⅄ 1 restaurant, 1 bar, washer/dryer. Boat slip located behind hotel. **Rates:** $52 S or D; $56–$60 effic. Extra person $6. Children under age 19 stay free. Min stay special events. Parking: Outdoor, free. AE, CB, DC, DISC, JCB, MC, V.

LODGE

≡≡≡ Lake Guntersville State Park Lodge
1155 Lodge Dr, 35976; tel 205/571-5440 or toll free 800/LGVILLE; fax 205/571-5459. 6 mi NE of Guntersville off AL 227. 5,909 acres. Nestled at the base of the Appalachian Mountains, this 20-year-old complex is constructed with dark-stained beams of laminated Alabama pine. Marshall county rock is prominent in the seven large fireplaces. **Rooms:** 100 rms and stes; 35 cottages/villas. CI 4pm/CO 11am. Nonsmoking rms avail. Average, motel-style rooms. Some rooms have magnificent views of lake and surrounding forest. Chalets and cottages also available. **Amenities:** 🛏 ⚒ A/C, satel TV. All units w/terraces, some w/fireplaces. **Services:** ↩ **Facilities:** 🔁 🏊 ▶₁₈ 🏋 🔵 📞₆₀₀ ⅄ 2 restaurants (*see* "Restaurants" below), 1 beach (lake shore), basketball, volleyball, sauna, playground, washer/dryer. **Rates:** Peak (Mar–Oct) $54–$58 S; $56–$60 D; $98 ste; $98 cottage/villa. Extra person $5. Children under age 12 stay free. Min stay. Lower rates off-season. Parking: Outdoor, free. AE, MC, V.

RESTAURANT 🍴

Chandelier Dining Room
In Lake Guntersville State Park Lodge, 1155 Lodge Dr; tel 205/571-5448. **Seafood/Southern.** Named for the massive wrought-iron chandeliers that hang in the dining room, this elegant dining room offers gorgeous lake views and plush surroundings. The menu features many seafood dishes—seafood divan, fried catfish—in addition to chicken and steak. **FYI:** Reservations not accepted. Children's menu. Dress code. No liquor license. **Open:** Sun–Thurs 2–9pm, Fri–Sat 2–10pm. **Prices:** Main courses $7–$15. AE, MC, V. ♥ ⛰ 👥 ⅄

Hamilton

This agricultural town in the highlands—originally called Toll Gate, as it was once a stop for stage coaches—sits astride the historic Military Road, a passage carved out of wilderness 150 years ago by soldiers returning to their homes after their victory over the British at New Orleans. **Information:** Hamilton Area Chamber of Commerce, PO Box 1168, Hamilton, 35570 (tel 205/921-7786).

HOTEL 🏨

UNRATED Best Western
US 43 S, PO Box R1 Bx 591A, 35570; tel 205/921-7831; fax 205/921-7831 ext 601. A convenient, comfortable, two-story property with few frills. Near shopping and movie theater. **Rooms:** 80 rms and stes. CI noon/CO noon. Nonsmoking rms avail. **Amenities:** 🛏 ⚒ A/C, cable TV w/movies, dataport. **Services:** ✗ 🖼 ↩ **Facilities:** 🔁 📅 ⅄ 1 restaurant, washer/dryer. **Rates:** $51–$56 S; $54 D. Extra person $5. Children under age 19 stay free. Parking: Outdoor, free. AE, DC, DISC, MC, V.

Huntsville

The birthplace of Alabama in 1819. Today it is the space capital of America, with NASA's Marshall Space Flight Center and the US Space and Rocket Center, the largest space museum on earth, located here. The once-thriving antebellum market town emerged from the Civil War with its plantation townhomes and historic areas intact, and remained primarily a textile town until 1950, when a team of German scientists arrived to develop rockets at Redstone Arsenal. **Information:** Huntsville–Madison County Convention & Visitors Bureau, 700 Monroe St, Huntsville, 35801 (tel 205/551-2230).

HOTELS 🏨

☰☰☰ Amberley Suite Hotel

4880 University Dr W, 35816; tel 205/837-4070 or toll free 800/456-1578; fax 205/837-4535. Off US 431. A recently renovated hotel close to the US Space and Rocket Center, Madison Square Mall, and many restaurants. **Rooms:** 169 rms and stes. CI 2pm/CO noon. Nonsmoking rms avail. **Amenities:** 🏨 ⚐ 🖭 ☏ A/C, cable TV w/movies, refrig, dataport, voice mail. Some units w/terraces, some w/whirlpools. **Services:** 🚗 🖼 ⊄ Babysitting. **Facilities:** 🔟 ₩ 🔟 ₺ 1 restaurant (bkfst and lunch only), 1 bar, spa, sauna, whirlpool. **Rates:** $40–$71 S; $40–$86 D; $40–$86 ste. Extra person $6. Children under age 18 stay free. Parking: Outdoor, free. AE, CB, DC, DISC, MC, V.

☰☰ Courtyard by Marriott

4804 University Dr, 35816; tel 205/837-1400 or toll free 800/321-2211; fax 205/837-3582. Off US 72 E. Conveniently located near the US Space and Rocket Center and Huntsville Int'l Airport. Popular for extended stays. **Rooms:** 149 rms and stes. CI 4pm/CO noon. Nonsmoking rms avail. **Amenities:** 🏨 ⚐ A/C, satel TV w/movies, dataport. All units w/terraces. Refrigerators in suites. **Services:** 🖼 ⊄ Babysitting. Meals can be ordered from local Fridays restaurant and billed to your room. **Facilities:** 🔟 ₩ 🔟 ₺ 1 restaurant (bkfst only), 1 bar, whirlpool, washer/dryer. **Rates:** $62 S; $69 ste. Extra person $10. Children under age 12 stay free. Parking: Outdoor, free. AE, CB, DC, DISC, MC, V.

☰☰ Executive Lodge Suite Hotel

1535 Sparkman Dr, 35816; tel 205/830-8600 or toll free 800/248-4722; fax 205/830-8899. Off I-565. Attractive, all-suite property. **Rooms:** 313 stes. CI 3pm/CO noon. Nonsmoking rms avail. **Amenities:** 🏨 ⚐ 🖭 A/C, satel TV w/movies, refrig. Some units w/terraces, some w/fireplaces, some w/whirlpools. **Services:** 🚗 🖼 ⊄ 🐶 **Facilities:** 🔟 🔟 ₺ Washer/dryer. Guests are provided passes to a local fitness center. **Rates (CP):** $50–$70 ste. Parking: Outdoor, free. Robert Trent Jones Golf Trail packages avail. AE, DC, DISC, MC, V.

☰☰☰ Holiday Inn Airport

9035 AL 20 W, PO Box 6290, 35824; tel 205/772-7170 or toll free 800/826-9563; fax 205/464-0762. Off I-565 W. Near the US Space and Rocket Center. **Rooms:** 171 rms and stes. CI 2pm/CO 11am. Nonsmoking rms avail. **Amenities:** 🏨 ⚐ 🖭 A/C, cable TV w/movies, dataport, voice mail. Some units w/whirlpools. **Services:** ✗ 🚗 🖼 ⊄ Passes to local fitness center. **Facilities:** 🔟 🔟 ₺ 1 restaurant, 1 bar (w/entertainment), whirlpool. **Rates:** $62 S or D; $125 ste. Extra person $7. Children under age 19 stay free. Min stay special events. Parking: Outdoor, free. Hampton Cove Golf Course, US Space and Rocket Center packages avail. AE, CB, DC, DISC, JCB, MC, V.

☰☰☰ Howard Johnson Park Square Inn

8721 AL 20 W, PO Box 520, Madison, 35758 (Airport); tel 205/772-8855 or toll free 800/882-3067; fax 205/464-0783. 3 mi E of Huntsville International Airport. Centrally located, well-kept chain hotel. Good for all types of travelers. **Rooms:** 140 rms and stes. Executive level. CI noon/CO noon. Nonsmoking rms avail. **Amenities:** 🏨 ⚐ ☏ A/C, cable TV w/movies. Some units w/terraces, some w/whirlpools. Sega games available on request. **Services:** ✗ 🚗 🖼 ⊄ 🐶 Pets under 10 lbs allowed with $50 security deposit. **Facilities:** 🔟 ₩ 🔟 ₺ 1 restaurant, 1 bar, whirlpool. Special discount offered at local fitness center. **Rates (BB):** $51 S or D; $95–$105 ste. Extra person $5. Children under age 12 stay free. Parking: Outdoor, free. Honeymoon and holiday packages avail. AE, CB, DC, DISC, MC, V.

☰☰☰☰ Huntsville Hilton Inn

401 Williams Ave, 35801; tel 205/533-1400 or toll free 800/544-3197; fax 205/533-1400. Across from Von Braun Civic Center. A four-story property close to the historic district. Lobby decor includes Oriental rugs, antique furniture, and a grand piano. Very popular with the businesspeople. **Rooms:** 277 rms and stes. Executive level. CI 2pm/CO noon. Nonsmoking rms avail. **Amenities:** 🏨 ⚐ 🖭 A/C, cable TV w/movies. Suites and executive-level rooms have wet bars. **Services:** ✗ 🚗 🖼 ⊄ 🐶 **Facilities:** 🔟 ₩ 🔟 ₺ 1 restaurant, 1 bar (w/entertainment), whirlpool. Live music and jazz in piano bar; comedy club operates Thurs–Sat. **Rates (CP):** Peak (Feb–Sept) $69–$109 S; $79–$119 D; $125–$250 ste. Extra person $10. Children under age 12 stay free. Lower rates off-season. Parking: Outdoor, free. Honeymoon, romance, and golf packages avail. AE, CB, DC, DISC, MC, V.

☰☰☰ Huntsville Marriott

5 Tranquility Base, 35805; tel 205/830-2222 or toll free 800/228-9290; fax 205/895-0904. Take exit for US Space and Rocket Center off I-565. A lively, attractive chain hotel, with an excellent location next to the US Space and Rocket Center. **Rooms:** 290 rms and stes. Executive level. CI 3pm/CO noon. Nonsmoking rms avail. **Amenities:** 🏨 ⚐ A/C, satel TV w/movies, dataport. Some units w/terraces. **Services:** ✗ 🚗 🖼 ⊄ 🐶 **Facilities:** 🔟 ₩ 🔟 ₺ 2 restaurants, 1 bar (w/entertainment), sauna, whirlpool, playground. **Rates (BB):** $58–$120 S or D; $225–$275 ste. Parking: Outdoor, free. Honeymoon package avail. AE, CB, DC, DISC, JCB, MC, V.

☰☰☰ Radisson Suite Hotel

6000 Memorial Pkwy S, 35802; tel 205/882-9400 or toll free 800/333-3333; fax 205/882-9684. South Parkway close to Redstone Arsenal. Located at the gate of NASA's Marshall Space Flight Center. **Rooms:** 153 stes and effic. Executive level. CI 3pm/CO noon. Nonsmoking rms avail. **Amenities:** 🏨 ⚐ 🖭 ☏ A/C, satel TV w/movies, refrig, dataport. Some units w/whirlpools. Complimentary coffee in rooms. **Services:** ✗ 🚗 🖼 ⊄ 🐶 $100 pet deposit. Transportation provided to various points around Huntsville. **Facilities:** 🔟

1 restaurant, 1 bar, whirlpool, washer/dryer. **Rates:** $87–$97 ste; $175–$200 effic. Extra person $10. Children under age 18 stay free. **Parking:** Outdoor, free. AE, CB, DC, DISC, EC, ER, JCB, MC, V.

Residence Inn by Marriott
4020 Independence Dr, 35816; tel 205/837-8907 or toll free 800/331-3131; fax 205/837-5435. Off US 72 E. A very homey atmosphere prevails at this apartment-style hotel. Comfortable, safe, and close to shopping and restaurants. **Rooms:** 112 stes. CI 4pm/CO noon. Nonsmoking rms avail. **Amenities:** A/C, cable TV, refrig. All units w/terraces, all w/fireplaces. **Services:** Evening social held daily 5–7pm. **Facilities:** Basketball, whirlpool, washer/dryer. Access to local health club. Picnic tables. **Rates (CP):** $80–$100 ste. **Parking:** Outdoor, free. AE, DC, DISC, MC, V.

Sheraton Inn Huntsville Airport
1000 Glen Hearn Blvd, PO Box 20068, 35824; tel 205/772-9661 or toll free 800/241-7873; fax 205/464-9116. Classy, service-oriented hotel catering to business travelers and families. **Rooms:** 146 rms and stes. Executive level. CI 1pm/CO noon. Nonsmoking rms avail. **Amenities:** A/C, cable TV w/movies, dataport. Some units w/whirlpools. **Services:** Car-rental desk. Discounted tickets to area attractions. **Facilities:** 1 restaurant, 1 bar, volleyball, sauna. Complimentary use of Jetplex Municipal Golf Course. **Rates:** $79–$99 S or D; $109–$259 ste. **Parking:** Outdoor, free. Robert Trent Jones Golf Trail packages avail. AE, DC, DISC, JCB, MC, V.

MOTELS

Hampton Inn
4815 University Dr, 35816; tel 205/830-9400 or toll free 800/426-7866; fax 205/830-0978. Off US 72 W. Average chain property, located near the US Space and Rocket Center, Madison Square Mall, and the University of Alabama at Huntsville. **Rooms:** 164 rms and stes. CI 2pm/CO noon. Nonsmoking rms avail. **Amenities:** A/C, cable TV w/movies, voice mail. Some units w/whirlpools. **Services:** **Facilities:** Whirlpool. Passes to local fitness center. **Rates (CP):** $48 S; $50–$58 D; $65 ste. Extra person $5. Children under age 18 stay free. **Parking:** Outdoor, free. AE, DC, DISC, MC, V.

Ho Jo Inn
4404 University Dr, 35816; tel 205/837-3250 or toll free 800/446-4656; fax 205/837-3250 ext 7160. Off US 72. Part of Howard Johnson's line of budget properties. Expect the basics, and not much more. **Rooms:** 120 rms. CI open/CO noon. Nonsmoking rms avail. **Amenities:** A/C, cable TV w/movies. **Services:** **Facilities:** **Rates (CP):** $37–$90 S or D. Extra person $5. Children under age 18 stay free. **Parking:** Outdoor, free. AE, CB, DC, DISC, MC, V.

Holiday Inn Express
3808 University Dr, 35816; tel 205/721-1000 or toll free 800/345-7720; fax 205/721-1000 ext 301. At Jordan Lane. Remodeled two years ago into an Express, this property shares some facilities with the Holiday Inn Space Center next door. **Rooms:** 62 rms. CI 2pm/CO noon. Nonsmoking rms avail. **Amenities:** A/C, satel TV w/movies, dataport. **Services:** **Facilities:** Games rm, washer/dryer. **Rates (CP):** $55 S or D. Extra person $8. Children under age 19 stay free. **Parking:** Outdoor, free. AE, CB, DC, DISC, JCB, MC, V.

La Quinta Motor Inn Research Park
4870 University Dr NW, 35816; tel 205/830-2070 or toll free 800/531-5900; fax 205/830-4412. At corner of Wynn. Only five minutes away from the US Space and Rocket Center and the University of Alabama at Huntsville. **Rooms:** 130 rms and effic. CI 1pm/CO noon. Nonsmoking rms avail. **Amenities:** A/C, satel TV w/movies, dataport. **Services:** **Facilities:** Washer/dryer. Passes to local health club. **Rates (CP):** $50–$57 S or D; $66 ste. Extra person $6. Children under age 18 stay free. **Parking:** Outdoor, free. AE, CB, DC, DISC, MC, V.

Ramada Inn
3502 Memorial Pkwy SW, 35801; tel 205/881-6120 or toll free 800/272-6232; fax 205/881-6120 ext 300. South of Joe Davis Stadium. Basic, chain motel–style accommodations, convenient to the airport and shopping. **Rooms:** 105 rms. CI 1pm/CO 11am. Nonsmoking rms avail. **Amenities:** A/C, cable TV w/movies. **Services:** **Facilities:** 1 restaurant, 1 bar. A covered deck overlooks the pool. **Rates:** $40–$45 S or D. Extra person $7. **Parking:** Outdoor, free. AE, CB, DC, DISC, JCB, MC, V.

RESTAURANTS

Cafe Berlin
In Westbury Square Shopping Center, 975 Airport Rd; tel 205/880-9920. **German.** Elegant, European-style cafe offering traditional favorites—Wiener schnitzel, jaeger schnitzel, sauerbraten—in addition to several American options. Salads are very popular. Extensive selection of gourmet desserts ranges from cheesecake to praline torte. **FYI:** Reservations accepted. Dress code. **Open:** Sun–Thurs 11am–9pm, Fri–Sat 11am–10pm. **Prices:** Main courses $7–$15. Lunch main courses $6–$9. AE, DISC, MC, V.

Kountry Kitchen
128 South Side Sq (Historic District); tel 205/533-1915. **Southern.** Hearty portions of down-home food. You might try their homemade biscuit breakfast, or a vegetable plate for lunch. **FYI:** Reservations not accepted. Dress code. No liquor license. No smoking. **Open:** Breakfast Mon–Fri 7:30–10:30am; lunch Mon–Fri 11am–2pm. **Prices:** Lunch main courses $4–$6. No CC.

★ **The Mill Bakery, Eatery & Brewery**
2003 Whitesburg Dr; tel 205/534-4455. Across from Huntsville Hospital. **Deli.** The Mill is known for its extensive line of baked goods made daily from scratch on the premises. Entrees on offer include Colorado calzone and Thai pasta. **FYI:** Reservations not accepted. Bands. Children's menu. Dress code. Additional location: 311 Jordan Lane (tel 837-8555). **Open:** Sun–Thurs 6:30am–10pm, Fri–Sat 6:30am–midnight. **Prices:** Main courses $4–$8. AE, MC, V. ▦ 🎦 ⴟ

Richard's on the Square
109 North Side Sq; tel 205/534-8633. Across from Madison County Courthouse. **Eclectic.** Located in a renovated turn-of-the-century warehouse with an elegant but comfortable atmosphere. The weekend menu changes each week but usually includes grilled salmon, fillet of beef, veal marsala, and vegetarian pasta selections. On weekday evenings, Richard's offers ten specialties for less than $10 each, including pepper-sliced roast beef, pecan trout, and crawfish cakes. A variety of excellent sandwiches are offered at lunch. **FYI:** Reservations recommended. Piano. Dress code. **Open:** Lunch Tues–Fri 11am–2pm; dinner Tues–Fri 5:30–10pm, Sat 6–11pm. **Prices:** Main courses $13–$17. MC, V. ♥ ▦ ⴟ

ATTRACTIONS 📷

US Space and Rocket Center
Exit 15 off I-565; tel 205/837-3400 or toll free 800/63-SPACE. The world's largest space museum and site of the US Space Camp. Exhibits include a life-size replica of a lunar crater, simulated test flights into space, a simulated launching ramp, and a collection of more than 1,500 rockets and lunar modules. Admission price also includes an Omnimax movie and a tour of NASA's Marshall Space Flight Center. **Open:** Mem Day–Labor Day, daily 9am–6pm; Labor Day–Mem Day, daily 9am–5pm. Closed some hols. $$$$

Burritt Museum and Park
3101 Burritt Dr; tel 205/536-2882. The museum is housed in an 11-room mansion (built circa 1935) and includes antique furnishings, geological and mineral displays, and paintings by local artists. The 167-acre park is traversed by nature trails and offers picnic facilities. Special events include folk festivals, the Alabama Indian Heritage Festival, and a Candlelight Christmas celebration held the first Saturday in December. **Open:** Museum, Mar–Nov, Tues–Sat 10am–5pm, Sun noon–5pm; grounds, daily 7am–sunset. **Free**

Alabama Constitution Village
109 Gates Ave; tel 205/535-6565 or toll free 800/678-1819. This "living history museum" is located on the site where Alabama was granted statehood in 1819, and everything here is meant to recapture that year in Alabama history. The Village is very much a "hands-on" experience. Guests can visit a cabinetmaker's shop where they are invited to help with the lathe, a spinning wheel where they can touch the cotton boll, and a typical town home of the period filled with the

smell of real bread being baked for dinner. There's also a Confectionery Shop that offers unique souvenirs and Alabama crafts. **Open:** Mar–Dec 20, Mon–Sat 9am–5pm. Closed Thanksgiving. $$$

Jasper

In coal-rich Walker county, settled in 1815 and named for Sgt William Jasper, a Revolutionary War soldier. Heritage Day in May features the Northwest Alabama Grand Master Fiddling championship. **Information:** Chamber of Commerce of Walker County, 1707 2nd Ave, PO Box 972, Jasper, 35501 (tel 205/384-4571).

HOTEL 🏨

🛏 **Jasper Inn**
1400 US 78W, 35501; tel 205/221-3050 or toll free 800/554-0238; fax 205/221-3050 ext 508. Very basic accommodations. **Rooms:** 153 rms. CI 2pm/CO noon. Nonsmoking rms avail. Rooms are clean and neat, but the decor is slightly dated. **Amenities:** 🛁 A/C, satel TV, dataport. **Services:** ⬜ 🍴 **Facilities:** 🛗 🏊75 ⴟ 1 restaurant (lunch and dinner only). **Rates:** $34–$38 S; $42–$44 D. Extra person $6. Children under age 12 stay free. Parking: Outdoor, free. Higher rates for poolside rooms in summer months. AE, CB, DC, DISC, MC, V.

Mentone

Its name means "musical mountain," and this historic community atop Lookout Mountain is known for its crafts, recreation, and festivals, including the Gospel Music Festival.

INN 🏨

🛏🛏🛏 **Mentone Inn**
AL 117, PO Box 290, 35984; tel 205/634-4836 or toll free 800/455-7570. 3 acres. Originally constructed in 1927, this quaint inn features nicely redecorated rooms and a big front porch. **Rooms:** 11 rms. CI noon/CO 11am. No smoking. **Amenities:** 🛁 A/C. No phone or TV. Three rooms have showers; the rest have clawfoot tubs. **Services:** 🍴 Afternoon tea served. **Facilities:** 🚲 1 restaurant, whirlpool, guest lounge w/TV. **Rates (BB):** $60–$125 S or D. Extra person $7. Parking: Outdoor, free. AE, MC, V.

RESTAURANT 🍴

★ **Log Cabin Deli**
AL 117 (Downtown); tel 205/634-4560. **Southern.** Housed in an authentic 1896 log cabin, this down-home spot serves up hearty country-style food. Country ham, chicken-fried steak, barbecue chicken, pinto beans, and an unusual dish called chile corn pone (a layer of cornbread topped with homemade chili and sour cream) keep customers happy. **FYI:**

Reservations not accepted. Children's menu. Dress code. No liquor license. **Open:** Tues–Sat 11am–9pm, Sun 11am–7pm. **Prices:** Main courses $3–$8. No CC. ▆

Mobile

See also Gulf Shores, Point Clear

Mobile was founded in 1710 and was capital of French Louisiana from 1710 to 1719. A shipbuilding center, Mobile is noted for antebellum houses, annual Mardi Gras (celebrated here since the 18th century), and Azalea Trail Festival. There are many museums; it is also the site of the USS *Alabama* Memorial. **Information:** Mobile Convention & Visitors Bureau Corp, One S Water St, PO Box 204, Mobile, 36601 (tel 334/415-2000).

HOTELS 🏨

☰☰☰ Adam's Mark Riverview Plaza Hotel

64 S Water St, 36602; tel 334/438-4000 or toll free 800/444-2326; fax 334/415-3060. Off I-10. This hotel overlooks the Port of Mobile and Historic Fort Condé and is within close walking distance of numerous businesses, shopping, and entertainment. **Rooms:** 375 rms and stes. Executive level. CI 3pm/CO noon. Nonsmoking rms avail. Extremely comfortable rooms, with key-card access. **Amenities:** 🛎 🅟 A/C, satel TV w/movies, dataport, voice mail. Some units w/minibars. **Services:** 🍽 VP 🚗 🖼 🗘 Shoe-shine services. Safe-deposit boxes and security storage available. **Facilities:** 🖼 🛄 2000 🔥 1 restaurant (*see* "Restaurants" below), 2 bars (1 w/entertainment), sauna, whirlpool. Terrific outdoor pool with sun deck. **Rates:** $98 S or D; $150 ste. Children under age 18 stay free. Min stay special events. Parking: Indoor, $5/day. AE, CB, DC, DISC, JCB, MC, V.

☰☰ Best Suites

150 Beltline Hwy S, 36608; tel 334/343-4949 or toll free 800/237-8466; fax 334/343-4949. Nice and clean accommodations with a convenient location. **Rooms:** 94 stes. CI open/CO 1pm. Nonsmoking rms avail. **Amenities:** 🛎 🅟 A/C, cable TV w/movies, refrig, dataport, VCR. Some units w/whirlpools. **Services:** 🖼 🗘 🖼 Movies for rent. Full breakfast and cocktails. **Facilities:** 🖼 🛄 60 🔥 Whirlpool, washer/dryer. **Rates (BB):** $62–$110 ste. Extra person $10. Children under age 18 stay free. Parking: Outdoor, free. Weekly and monthly rates avail. AE, DC, DISC, MC, V.

☰☰☰ Best Western Battleship Inn

2701 Battleship Pkwy, PO Box 110, 36610; tel 334/432-2703 or toll free 800/528-1234; fax 334/432-6111. Exit 27 off I-10. A nice hotel, just 300 feet away from the USS *Alabama*. **Rooms:** 100 rms. CI 2pm/CO noon. Nonsmoking rms avail. Rooms are clean and comfortable. **Amenities:** 🛎 A/C, satel TV w/movies. **Services:** ✗ 🖼 🗘 🖼 Harbor cruises available.

Facilities: 🖼 1 restaurant (*see* "Restaurants" below), 1 bar. **Rates:** $56 S; $61 D. Extra person $5. Children under age 12 stay free. Parking: Outdoor, free. AE, DC, DISC, MC, V.

☰☰☰ Clarion Hotel

3101 Airport Blvd, 36606; tel 334/476-6400 or toll free 800/CLARION; fax 334/476-9360. Located across the street from the downtown historic district and major shopping area. **Rooms:** 250 rms, stes, and effic. CI 3pm/CO noon. Nonsmoking rms avail. Gold rooms are like homes away from home. **Amenities:** 🛎 🅟 🖼 A/C, satel TV w/movies, dataport. Safe-deposit boxes. **Services:** ✗ 🚗 🖼 🗘 🖼 Babysitting. **Facilities:** 🖼 750 🔥 1 restaurant, 1 bar, whirlpool, washer/dryer. Guests receive free access (and transportation) to the Riviera Fitness Center. **Rates:** $79–$99 S or D; $179–$249 ste; $250 effic. Extra person $10. Children under age 18 stay free. Parking: Outdoor, free. AE, CB, DC, DISC, MC, V.

☰☰☰ Courtyard by Marriott

1000 S Beltline Hwy, 36609; tel 334/344-5200 or toll free 800/321-2211; fax 334/341-0300. Conveniently located to shopping, restaurants, and all major sights of interest, this recently opened hotel is sure to please. **Rooms:** 78 rms, stes, and effic. CI 4pm/CO noon. Nonsmoking rms avail. Excellent housekeeping. **Amenities:** 🛎 🅟 🖼 🍴 A/C, cable TV w/movies, dataport. Some units w/terraces, some w/whirlpools. **Services:** 🖼 🗘 Babysitting. **Facilities:** 🖼 🛄 40 🔥 1 restaurant (bkfst only), 1 bar, sauna, washer/dryer. **Rates:** $73 S; $83 D; $99–$109 ste; $100 effic. Children under age 18 stay free. Parking: Outdoor, free. Golf packages avail. AE, CB, DC, DISC, MC, V.

☰☰ Hampton Inn

930 S Beltline Hwy, 36609; tel 334/344-4942 or toll free 800/426-7866; fax 334/341-4520. Exit 3B off I-65. Spacious accommodations; great for families. **Rooms:** 118 rms. CI 2pm/CO noon. Nonsmoking rms avail. **Amenities:** 🛎 🅟 A/C, cable TV w/movies, dataport. **Services:** 🖼 🗘 **Facilities:** 🖼 20 🔥 **Rates (CP):** $42 S; $52 D. Extra person $5. Children under age 18 stay free. Parking: Outdoor, free. AE, DC, DISC, MC, V.

☰☰☰ Holiday Inn Downtown

301 Government St, 36602; tel 334/694-0100 or toll free 800/692-6662; fax 334/694-0160. At Jackson St. A standard chain hotel, located in the heart of the historic district. Easy access to I-10. **Rooms:** 213 rms and stes. CI 3pm/CO noon. Nonsmoking rms avail. Housekeeping standards are above average. **Amenities:** 🛎 🅟 🖼 A/C, cable TV w/movies. **Services:** 🍽 🖼 🗘 🖼 **Facilities:** 🖼 500 🔥 2 restaurants, 2 bars (1 w/entertainment), beauty salon, washer/dryer. On-site clothing store and travel agency. **Rates:** $64 S; $72 D; $80–$160 ste. Extra person $8. Children under age 12 stay free. Min stay special events. Parking: Indoor/outdoor, $4/day. Rates increase during Mardi Gras. AE, DC, DISC, MC, V.

Holiday Inn Express
255 Church St, 36602; tel 334/433-6923 or toll free 800/HOLIDAY; fax 334/433-8869. At Jackson. A conveniently located hotel, completely renovated in 1992. **Rooms:** 131 rms and stes. CI 2pm/CO noon. Nonsmoking rms avail. Nice, comfortable rooms feature key-card access. **Amenities:** 🕾 👁 🖂 A/C, cable TV w/movies. **Services:** 🖂 🖵 **Facilities:** 🔾 🗔 30 ᴧ Washer/dryer. **Rates (CP):** $49 S or D; $64 ste. Extra person $5. Children under age 19 stay free. Min stay special events. Parking: Outdoor, free. AE, CB, DC, DISC, JCB, MC, V.

Holiday Inn I-65
850 S Beltline Hwy, PO Box 16646, 36616; tel 334/342-3220 or toll free 800/HOLIDAY; fax 334/342-8919. Airport Blvd (exit 3B) off I-65. Renovated in 1995. Suitable for all travelers. **Rooms:** 200 rms. CI 2pm/CO noon. Nonsmoking rms avail. Rooms are average in size and comfort. **Amenities:** 🕾 🖂 A/C, cable TV w/movies, dataport. **Services:** ✗ 🚗 🖂 🖵 🕭 **Facilities:** 🔾 🖳 200 ᴧ 1 restaurant (bkfst and dinner only), 1 bar, whirlpool, washer/dryer. **Rates (BB):** $61 S; $68 D. Extra person $6. Children under age 12 stay free. Min stay special events. Parking: Outdoor, free. AE, DC, DISC, MC, V.

Howard Johnson Lodge
3132 Government Blvd, 36606; tel 334/471-2402 or toll free 800/535-8029; fax 334/471-9912. Off I-65. Basic, chain hotel–style accommodations, conveniently located to all major attractions. **Rooms:** 159 rms. CI 2pm/CO noon. Nonsmoking rms avail. **Amenities:** 🕾 A/C, cable TV w/movies, dataport. All units w/terraces. **Services:** ✗ 🚗 🖂 🖵 🕭 Safe-deposit boxes available upon request. **Facilities:** 🔾 🖳 100 ᴧ 1 restaurant, 1 bar, whirlpool. **Rates:** $45–$60 S; $49–$65 D. Extra person $5. Children under age 18 stay free. Parking: Outdoor, free. AE, DC, DISC, MC, V.

Radisson Admiral Semmes Hotel
251 Government St, 36602; tel 334/432-8000 or toll free 800/333-3333; fax 334/432-8000 ext 7111. At Joachim St. This quaint but beautifully restored hotel is located right off Government Street in the beautiful downtown historic district. Within easy view of all Mardi Gras parades and a short drive from some of the most beautiful beaches in the world. **Rooms:** 170 rms and stes. CI 3pm/CO 11am. Nonsmoking rms avail. Rooms are large, well-decorated, and have nice views. Keyless entry offers better security. **Amenities:** 🕾 👁 🖂 🗨 A/C, cable TV w/movies, dataport, VCR, in-rm safe. Some units w/minibars. Some rooms have refrigerators. **Services:** ✗ VP 🖂 🖵 🕭 Babysitting. **Facilities:** 🔾 🖳 500 ᴧ 1 restaurant, 1 bar (w/entertainment), whirlpool. Large banquet facilities. Guests may use local YMCA. **Rates:** Peak (Feb–Mardi Gras) $140 S; $150 D; $175–$350 ste. Extra person $10. Children under age 18 stay free. Min stay special events. Lower rates off-season. Parking: Indoor/outdoor, $4/day. Romance/honeymoon packages avail. AE, CB, DC, DISC, MC, V.

Ramada Conference Center
600 S Beltline Hwy, 36608; tel 334/344-8030 or toll free 800/752-0398; fax 334/344-8055. Exit 3B W off I-65. Conveniently located hotel made up of a Tower section (with indoor access, more in-room amenities, and a fourth-floor executive level) and a Wing section (with parking lot access, more reminiscent of a motel). **Rooms:** 236 rms and stes. Executive level. CI 3pm/CO 1pm. Nonsmoking rms avail. Tower rooms are large and sophisticated; wing rooms are average but well kept. **Amenities:** 🕾 👁 🖂 A/C, cable TV w/movies, dataport, voice mail. **Services:** ✗ 🚗 🖂 🖵 Babysitting. **Facilities:** 🔾 ▶3 🔳 🍴 400 ᴧ 1 restaurant, 2 bars (w/entertainment), whirlpool. **Rates:** $69–$79 S; $89 D; $150 ste. Extra person $10. Children under age 18 stay free. Parking: Outdoor, free. Honeymoon and golf packages avail. AE, DC, DISC, JCB, MC, V.

MOTELS

Gone With the Wind Motel
1705 Dauphin Island Pkwy, 36605; tel 334/471-6114; fax 334/476-6189. Exit 22 off I-10. Easily accessible from all major highways, this motel is great for someone just passing through. **Rooms:** 150 rms. CI 2pm/CO noon. Nonsmoking rms avail. **Amenities:** 🕾 A/C, satel TV w/movies. **Services:** 🖵 **Facilities:** 🔾 200 ᴧ **Rates (CP):** $38 S; $45 D. Extra person $7. Children under age 12 stay free. Parking: Outdoor, free. AE, DC, DISC, MC, V.

La Quinta Motor Inn
816 S Beltline Hwy, 36609; tel 334/343-4051 or toll free 800/531-5900; fax 334/343-2897. Exit 3B off I-65. Basic two-story chain motel, located along a major chain-motel strip. **Rooms:** 122 rms. CI 3pm/CO noon. Nonsmoking rms avail. **Amenities:** 🕾 👁 A/C, satel TV w/movies, dataport. **Services:** 🖂 🖵 🕭 Pets accepted; call for more info. **Facilities:** 🔾 25 ᴧ **Rates (CP):** $51–$58 S; $59–$66 D. Extra person $8. Children under age 18 stay free. Parking: Outdoor, free. Golf packages avail. AE, DC, DISC, MC, V.

INN

Malaga Inn
359 Church St, 36602; tel 334/438-4701 or toll free 800/235-1586; fax 334/438-4701 ext 123. At Claiborne. An exquisite property housed in a pair of restored 1860s townhouses. The gorgeous European Courtyard (with garden and fountain) is breathtaking. **Rooms:** 40 rms and stes. CI 2pm/CO 11am. Nonsmoking rms avail. Each room is individually decorated (some with period antiques) and extremely comfortable. **Amenities:** 🕾 👁 A/C, cable TV w/movies. Some units w/terraces. **Services:** ✗ 🖂 🖵 **Facilities:** 🔾 ᴧ 1 restaurant (bkfst and dinner only; see "Restaurants" below), 1 bar, guest lounge. **Rates:** $72 S; $79 D; $125 ste. Extra person $5. Children under age 18 stay free. Min stay special events. Higher rates for special events/hols. Parking: Outdoor, free. AE, DISC, MC, V.

RESTAURANTS

Almost Six Cafe
6½ N Jackson St; tel 334/438-3447. At Dauphin St. **Eclectic/Seafood.** Housed in a recently restored 150-year-old building, this classy dining room features a New Orleans-style atmosphere and menu with a contemporary twist. Diners can sit in the historic interior or in the courtyard as they enjoy specialties such as garlic veal cutlet, chicken marsala, and New York strip. The grilled snapper—served under a delicious basil-tomato sauce—is a standout. **FYI:** Reservations not accepted. Dress code. **Open:** Mon–Thurs 6–10pm, Fri–Sat 6–11pm. **Prices:** Main courses $11–$18. AE, MC, V. ▉

The Captain's Table
In Best Western Battleship Inn, 2701 Battleship Pkwy; tel 334/433-3790. **Seafood/Steak.** Affiliated with the Best Western Inn next door, the Captains Table offers basic steak and seafood entrees amid great views of the Gulf. **FYI:** Reservations not accepted. Children's menu. Dress code. **Open:** Mon–Sat 6am–11pm, Sun 6am–10pm. **Prices:** Main courses $10–$22. AE, MC, V.

♣ ★ La Louisiana
2400 Airport Blvd; tel 334/476-8130. 1½ mi off I-65. **Eclectic.** Nice, casual, and elegant dining, with a touch of Cajun spice. Fresh seafood is prepared with okra and various peppery spices; there are also a few Italian dishes, made with homemade pasta. **FYI:** Reservations recommended. Dress code. **Open:** Mon–Sat 5–10pm. Closed July. **Prices:** Main courses $12–$20. AE, DC, DISC, MC, V. ♥ ▉

Mayme's
In Malaga Inn, 359 Church St; tel 334/433-5858. At Claiborne St. **Cajun/Seafood.** This restaurant in the downtown historic district offers a comfortable yet elegant atmosphere. The menu has a strong Creole accent, with specialties such as snapper Brennan—served with crabmeat, mushrooms, and wine sauce. **FYI:** Reservations accepted. Jazz. Children's menu. Dress code. **Open:** Mon–Sat 6–10pm. **Prices:** Main courses $16–$18. AE, DISC, MC, V. ♥ ▉

♣ Pillars
1757 Government St; tel 334/478-6341. At Houston St. **New American/Seafood.** Housed within one of Mobile's finest restored mansions, with wide verandas and 18th- and 19th-century antiques. The menu highlights fresh Gulf Coast seafood; lamb, veal, and beef entrees are also available. Baking is done on premises. **FYI:** Reservations recommended. Dress code. **Open:** Mon–Sat 5–10pm. **Prices:** Main courses $14–$20. AE, DC, DISC, MC, V. ♥ ♿

★ Port City Brewery
225 Dauphin St; tel 334/438-BREW. At Joachim. **Burgers/Pizza.** One of Alabama's original brew pubs—established in 1890 and refurbished in 1994. Handcrafted beer is brewed on site. Typical pub menu is served, with an emphasis on gourmet pizzas and burgers. **FYI:** Reservations not accepted. Jazz/rock. Children's menu. Dress code. **Open:** Mon–Wed 11am–midnight, Thurs–Sat 11am–2am. **Prices:** Main courses $6–$14. AE, MC, V. ▉ ♿

Riverview Cafe & Grill
In Adam's Mark Riverview Plaza Hotel, 64 Water St; tel 334/438-4000. **Seafood.** Gulf Coast seafood specialties served in a comfortable dining room with fantastic views of the Port City. **FYI:** Reservations accepted. Piano. Children's menu. Dress code. **Open:** Breakfast Mon–Sat 6:30am–2pm; dinner Sun–Thurs 5:30–10pm, Fri–Sat 5:30–11pm; brunch Sun 11am–2pm. **Prices:** Main courses $9–$20. AE, DISC, MC, V. ♥ ▲ ♿

★ Rousso's Restaurant
166 S Royal St; tel 334/433-3322. Next to Fort Condé Welcome Center. **Seafood.** Dark but attractive decor consisting of fishnets, nautical paintings, and Old Mobile brick and cedar walls. Seafood specialties include crab claws; chicken and steak also available. **FYI:** Reservations accepted. Children's menu. Dress code. **Open:** Mon–Sat 11am–10pm, Sun 11:30am–9pm. **Prices:** Main courses $8–$18. AE, MC, V. ▉ ▦ ♿

★ Trattoria at Broad
908 Government St; tel 334/433-6922. At Broad St. **Italian.** A relatively new and very popular eatery specializing in a wide variety of Italian dishes using fish, meat, veal, or duck. Scaloppine of duck is highly recommended. The Trattoria also caters to vegetarians. **FYI:** Reservations accepted. Dress code. **Open:** Lunch Mon–Fri 11am–2:30pm; dinner Mon–Sat 5–9:30pm. **Prices:** Main courses $8–$16. AE, MC, V. ▲ ▦ ♿

ⓢ Weichman's All Seasons
168 S Beltline Hwy; tel 334/344-3961. Exit 3-B off I-65. **Seafood/Steak.** Fresh Gulf Coast seafood, thick steaks, and other gourmet specialties, served in an elegant atmosphere. They have one of the most extensive wine lists in the state. **FYI:** Reservations accepted. Children's menu. Dress code. **Open:** Lunch Sun–Fri 11am–3pm; dinner daily 5–9pm. **Prices:** Main courses $8–$21. AE, MC, V. ▦ ♿

ATTRACTIONS

Oakleigh Period Museum House
350 Oakleigh Place; tel 334/432-1281. Built in 1833 by Mobile merchant James W Roper, this impressive Greek Revival mansion is beautifully furnished with fine period collections of furniture, portraits, silver, china, jewelry, kitchen implements, and toys. Guided tours available. **Open:** Mon–Fri 10am–4pm, Sun 2–4pm. Closed some hols. $

Bellingrath Gardens and Home
12401 Bellingrath Gardens Rd; tel 334/973-2217 or toll free 800/247-8420. Located 10 mi S of Mobile. The gardens encompass 65 landscaped acres in the midst of a 905-acre semitropical forest. The azalea garden contains over 250,000 azalea plants, some of which were brought from France in

1754. Other specialty gardens feature Oriental, American, rose, and bridal themes. Bellingrath House, built for Mobile's first Coca-Cola bottler, is an opulent antebellum beauty furnished with American, French, and Irish crystal; Georgian silver; European porcelains; Baccarat chandeliers; Aubusson rugs; and an inlaid chess table that once belonged to Queen Victoria. The *Southern Belle* riverboat offers scenic cruises along the "River of Birds." Combination gardens/cruise admission is available. **Open:** Daily 8am–sunset. **$$$**

Carlen House

54 S Carlen St; tel 344/470-7768. An authentic 19th-century Gulf Coast Creole cottage, containing period furnishings, tools, clothing, toiletries, and table settings. Guided tours available by appointment. **Open:** Tues–Sat 10am–5pm, Sun 1–5pm. Closed some hols. **Free**

Museum of the City of Mobile

355 Government St; tel 334/434-7569. Visitors to this multimedia museum can travel back to colonial Mobile, relive the drama of the Battle of Mobile Bay during the Civil War, and share in the city's remarkable development into a commercial and maritime center. The museum's 100,000 artifacts include an array of Mardi Gras regalia. Guided tours are available. **Open:** Tues–Sat 10am–5pm, Sun 1–5pm. Closed some hols. **Free**

Phoenix Fire Museum

203 S Claiborne St; tel 334/434-7554. A unique collection of authentic turn-of-the-century steam engines, fire alarms, fireman's helmets, and other fire-fighting equipment and mementos, housed in the former home of Phoenix Volunteer Fire Company No 6. **Open:** Tues–Sat 10am–5pm, Sun 1–5pm. Closed some hols. **Free**

Fort Condé

150 S Royal St; tel 205/434-7304. Originally called Fort Louis de la Louisiane, the fort served for nearly a century as headquarters for French, British, and Spanish forces. Restored to its 18th-century appearance, the building now houses a museum with artifacts from the original fort. Costumed guides are available to demonstrate period artillery as well as describe the history of the fort. Fort Condé serves as the official welcome center for the city of Mobile, and maintains information about local historic homes and other sites. **Open:** Daily 8am–5pm. Closed some hols. **Free**

Malbis Memorial Church

29300 CR 27, Daphne; tel 334/626-3050. Located 10 mi E of Mobile. This magnificent Greek Orthodox church was the dream of one man—Greek immigrant and ex-monk Jason Malbis. Soon before his death in 1942, Mr Malbis declared his wish that his land be used for a church and, more than twenty years and $1 million later, his dream finally became reality. The structure, based on a Byzantine church in Athens, is considered one of the finest examples of the neo-Byzantine style in the United States. Master painters and artisans came from Greece to paint the interior murals and panels, and the

marble used for the interior was all quarried in Greece. Mosaics grace the pediments over the front doors, rose windows illuminate the transept, and red-marble columns line the nave. Self-guided tour booklets available. **Open:** Daily 9am–noon, 2–5pm. Closed Dec 25. **Free**

USS *Alabama* Battleship Memorial Park

2703 Battleship Pkwy; tel 334/433-2703 or toll free 800/426-4929. During World War II, this 42,500-ton battleship saw over three years of active duty without a single casualty or any significant damage. Today, the *Alabama* welcomes more than 300,000 visitors per year, who can take a self-guided tour of the ship or check out the collections of military aircraft, submarines, tanks, and artillery. There's a picnic area, and scenic Mobile Harbor cruises are available for an additional fee. **Open:** Daily 8:30am–sunset. Closed Dec 25. **$$$**

Wildland Expeditions

7536 Tung Ave N, Theodore; tel 334/460-8206. Capt Gene Burrell, the proprietor of Wildland Expeditions, promises "the adventure of a lifetime" to all nature lovers who accompany him on his swamp tour. His custom-built 25-foot boat, the *Gator Bait,* allows passengers the opportunity to experience firsthand the lush vegetation, unique wildlife, and endangered species of the delicate ecosystem of the Alabama Delta. Tours include informative tidbits from Capt Gene about the geological, biological, Native American, and Civil War history of the area. Tours take a little over two hours, including rest stops. **Open:** Tues–Sat tours at 9am and 2pm. Closed some hols. **$$$$**

Montgomery

A major agricultural center and once referred to as the "Cradle of the Confederacy," Montgomery, Alabama's capital, was capital of the Confederacy following the formation of the Confederate States of America in 1857. The old state capitol, where Jefferson Davis was inaugurated as President of the Confederacy, has been restored, as well as many antebellum homes. Site of a civil rights memorial honoring 40 Americans who died during the black civil rights movement in the 1960s. Alabama Shakespeare Festival (on the outskirts of town) presents classic and contemporary productions 10 months per year. **Information:** Montgomery Area Convention & Visitors Bureau, 401 Madison Ave, PO Box 79, Montgomery, 36101 (tel 334/240-9455).

HOTELS 🏨

≡≡ Comfort Suites

5924 Monticello Dr, 36117; tel 334/272-1013; fax 334/260-0425. Exit 6 off I-85. Located near area attractions such as the Shakespeare Festival, the zoo, the State Capitol, the Civil Rights Monument, and downtown, this property welcomes its guests with manicured grounds and a spacious, well-decorated lobby. A great value considering its quality and size. **Rooms:** 49 stes. CI open/CO noon. Nonsmoking rms avail. Very spacious and clean. **Amenities:** 🔒 🛁 📺 A/C, cable TV w/movies. Some units w/whirlpools. **Services:** ✗ 🍽 🛎 **Facilities:** 🏋 [27] & **Rates (BB):** $64–$77 ste. Parking: Outdoor, free. AE, DC, DISC, MC, V.

≣≣≣ Courtyard by Marriott
5555 Carmichael Rd, 36117; tel 334/272-5533 or toll free 800/321-2211; fax 334/279-0853. Exit 6 off I-85. Modern, well-kept property. Popular with business travelers. **Rooms:** 363 rms and stes. CI 3pm/CO noon. Nonsmoking rms avail. **Amenities:** 🔒 🛁 📺 A/C, cable TV w/movies, voice mail. Some units w/terraces. Refrigerators in suites. **Services:** ✗ 🛎 🍽 **Facilities:** 🏋 🏊 [75] & 1 restaurant (bkfst and dinner only), 1 bar, whirlpool, washer/dryer. **Rates:** $79 S; $89 D; $99–$109 ste. Extra person $10. Children under age 18 stay free. Parking: Outdoor, free. AE, DC, DISC, MC, V.

≣≣ Fairfield Inn by Marriott
5601 Carmichael Rd, 36117; tel 334/270-0007 or toll free 800/228-2800; fax 334/270-0007. Exit 6 off I-85. Located near area bowling lanes, shopping, and restaurants; close to Shakespeare Festival, Historic Downtown, and Victory Land Dog Track. **Rooms:** 133 rms. CI 3pm/CO noon. Nonsmoking rms avail. **Amenities:** 🔒 🛁 A/C, cable TV w/movies, dataport. **Services:** 🛎 🍽 **Facilities:** 🏋 [15] & Guests may use fitness center at adjacent Courtyard by Marriott. **Rates (CP):** $49–$56 S or D. Children under age 18 stay free. Parking: Outdoor, free. AE, DC, DISC, MC, V.

≣≣≣ Holiday Inn
1100 W South Blvd, 36105; tel 334/281-1660 or toll free 800/HOLIDAY; fax 334/281-1660 ext 102. Exit 168 off I-65. A top-notch Holiday Inn located near the state capitol. **Rooms:** 150 rms. CI 2pm/CO noon. Nonsmoking rms avail. **Amenities:** 🔒 🛁 🍴 A/C, cable TV w/movies, dataport. **Services:** ✗ 🚐 🛎 🍽 🍴 **Facilities:** 🏋 [300] & 1 restaurant, 1 bar, washer/dryer. Kids under 12 eat free in hotel restaurant. **Rates:** $48–$59 S or D. Extra person $5. Children under age 18 stay free. Parking: Indoor/outdoor, free. AE, DC, DISC, MC, V.

≣≣ Holiday Inn Downtown
120 Madison Ave, 36104; tel 334/264-2231 or toll free 800/HOLIDAY; fax 334/263-3179. At Lawrence and Perry Sts. Basic accommodations; fine for families looking for a convenient, downtown location. **Rooms:** 189 rms and stes. CI 2pm/CO noon. Nonsmoking rms avail. **Amenities:** 🔒 📺 A/C, cable TV w/movies, voice mail. **Services:** ✗ 🚐 🛎 🍽 🍴 **Facilities:** 🏋 🏊 🖥 & 2 restaurants, 2 bars (1 w/entertainment), whirlpool. Hank's Restaurant memorializes country music star and Montgomery native Hank Williams. **Rates:** $68 S or D; $120 ste. Extra person $5. Children under age 18 stay free. Parking: Indoor/outdoor, free. Honeymoon package avail. AE, DC, DISC, MC, V.

≣≣≣ Riverfront Inn
200 Coosa St, 36104; tel 334/834-4300; fax 334/265-5500. At Tallapoosa St. Listed on the National Register of Historic Places. Originally a Western Railway depot, this property was restored as a unique hotel in the early 1980s. Located on the Alabama River, near the State Capitol, the Civic Center, and Montgomery's Old Alabama Town. Popular with business travelers. **Rooms:** 130 rms. CI 3pm/CO noon. Nonsmoking rms avail. Reproduction Victorian furnishings. **Amenities:** 🔒 🛁 A/C, cable TV w/movies. Complimentary morning coffee and newspaper on request. **Services:** 🍽 **Facilities:** 🏋 [80] & 1 restaurant, games rm. **Rates (CP):** $55 S; $61 D. Parking: Outdoor, free. AE, DC, DISC, MC, V.

≣≣≣ State House Inn
924 Madison Ave, 36104 (Downtown); tel 334/265-0741 or toll free 800/552-7099; fax 334/834-6126. Located in the heart of downtown Montgomery, just a block away from the State Capitol. The charming lobby features terra-cotta tiles and a mauve-and-gray color scheme. **Rooms:** 168 rms and stes. CI 3pm/CO noon. Nonsmoking rms avail. **Amenities:** 🔒 🛁 🍴 A/C, cable TV w/movies. **Services:** ✗ 🛎 🍽 🍴 **Facilities:** 🏋 [150] & 1 restaurant, 1 bar (w/entertainment), washer/dryer. **Rates (CP):** $50 S; $56 D; $85 ste. Extra person $6. Children under age 18 stay free. Parking: Outdoor, free. AE, DC, DISC, MC, V.

MOTELS

≣≣ Best Western Montgomery Lodge
977 W South Blvd, 36105; tel 334/288-5740 or toll free 800/528-1234; fax 334/288-5740 ext 154. Exit 168 off I-65. A two-story property on the outskirts of town. **Rooms:** 100 rms. CI 11am/CO 11am. Nonsmoking rms avail. Nice decor. **Amenities:** 🔒 🛁 📺 A/C, cable TV w/movies. Most rooms have recliners. **Services:** 🛎 🍽 🍴 **Facilities:** 🏋 [200] 1 restaurant (dinner only), 1 bar, washer/dryer. **Rates:** $35–$48 S or D. Extra person $3. Children under age 12 stay free. Parking: Outdoor, free. AE, CB, DC, DISC, MC, V.

≣≣ Days Inn Airport
1150 W South Blvd, 36105; tel 334/281-8000 or toll free 800/239-3986; fax 334/284-6540. Exit 168 off I-65. Easy access to I-65. Near the Alabama Shakespeare Festival, Donnelly Field Municipal Airport, Lagoon Park, Maxwell Air Force Base, and Montgomery Zoo. **Rooms:** 126 rms and effic. CI 3pm/CO noon. Nonsmoking rms avail. **Amenities:** 🔒 🛁 A/C, cable TV w/movies. **Services:** 🍽 🍴 **Facilities:** 🏋 [150] **Rates (CP):** $35 S; $40 D; $45 effic. Extra person $5. Children under age 12 stay free. Parking: Outdoor, free. AE, DC, DISC, MC, V.

≣ Days Inn Montgomery
2625 Zelda Rd, 36107; tel 334/269-9611 or toll free 800/325-2525; fax 334/269-9611 ext 286. Exit 3 off I-85. Rather average-looking chain motel. **Rooms:** 120 rms. CI 2pm/CO noon. Nonsmoking rms avail. **Amenities:** 🔒 A/C, cable TV w/movies. **Services:** 🍽 🍴 **Facilities:** 🏋 🏊 [60] & Washer/

dryer. Courtyard with gazebo and picnic area with grills. Adjacent restaurant open 24 hours. **Rates (CP):** $45 S; $49 D. Extra person $5. Children under age 18 stay free. Parking: Outdoor, free. AE, DC, DISC, MC, V.

≡≡ La Quinta Motor Inn
1280 East Blvd, 36117; tel 334/271-1620 or toll free 800/531-5900; fax 334/244-7919. Above-average establishment offering good value. **Rooms:** 130 rms. CI noon/CO noon. Nonsmoking rms avail. **Amenities:** 🛁 ☿ A/C, cable TV w/movies, dataport. Complimentary coffee in rooms. **Services:** 🖐 🔄 **Facilities:** 🛗 🚸 ㅊ **Rates (CP):** $52–$59 S; $59–$66 D. Extra person $7. Children under age 18 stay free. Parking: Outdoor, free. AE, DC, DISC, MC, V.

RESTAURANTS 🍴

⑤ ✹ Chappy's Deli
In Perry Hill Place, 1611 Perry Hill Rd; tel 334/279-7477. Off I-85. **Deli.** Chappy's serves a traditional breakfast, offering Belgian waffles, eggs, french toast, bagels, pancakes, and omelettes. Its lunch menu offers a wide variety of deli specialties (both hot and cold) and many healthy substitute dishes for those trying to stay fit. Some examples are their turkey burger, veggie burger, and salad plates. **FYI:** Reservations not accepted. Children's menu. Dress code. Beer and wine only. **Open:** Mon–Sat 7am–9pm. **Prices:** Main courses $4–$5. AE, MC, V. 🚸 ㅊ

✹ Chris' Hot Dog Stand
138 Dexter Ave; tel 334/265-6850. At N Lawrence. **Burgers/Hotdogs.** A Montgomery tradition since 1917; the son of the original Mr Chris now operates the property. The vinyl-and-chrome decor has not changed much since the 1950s, and neither has Mr Chris's secret sauce (a blend of onions, peppers, and spices). Also housed in the restaurant are a game room and gift shop. **FYI:** Reservations not accepted. Dress code. Beer and wine only. **Open:** Mon–Thurs 8:30am–7pm, Fri 8:30am–8pm, Sat 10am–7pm. **Prices:** Lunch main courses $1–$3. No CC.

✹ Farmer's Market Cafeteria
315 N McDonough St; tel 334/262-9163. At Columbus St. **Southern.** Frequented by many state and local government officials, the Farmer's Market is known for its Southern-style vegetables, baby back ribs, fried chicken, and catfish. Breakfast consists of bacon, sausage, biscuits, and other classic fare. The rather spare dining area is decorated with photos of historical sports events and famous Alabama athletes and officials. **FYI:** Reservations not accepted. Dress code. No liquor license. Additional location: State Market Cafe (tel 271-1885). **Open:** Mon–Fri 5am–2pm. **Prices:** Lunch main courses $4–$7. No CC. ■ 🚸 ㅊ

✹ Green Lantern
5725 Troy Hwy; tel 334/288-9947. **Steak.** A local institution for over six decades, this out-of-the-way place is locally famous for its cheese biscuits. The menu—which is recited by the waitstaff, since it is not printed—consists of steak, fried chicken, and other hearty fare. **FYI:** Reservations accepted. Children's menu. Dress code. Beer and wine only. BYO. **Open:** Mon–Sat 5–10pm. **Prices:** Main courses $8–$25. AE, MC, V. 🚸

Partridge Pine Restaurant
7906 Old Carter Hill Rd, Pike Road; tel 334/284-0512. 12 mi S of Montgomery Mall. **Barbecue/Soul/Southern.** Housed in a log cabin with beveled glass doors, exposed brick, and dramatic wallpaper. Butter-pecan chicken, blackened tuna or pork chops, snapper in Creole butter sauce. **FYI:** Reservations accepted. Children's menu. Dress code. No smoking. **Open:** Tues–Thurs 11am–9pm, Fri–Sat 11am–9:30pm, Sun 11am–2pm. **Prices:** Main courses $9–$19. MC, V. ⛰ 🚸 ㅊ

♣ Sahara Restaurant
511 E Edgemont Rd; tel 334/262-1215. At Norman Bridge Rd. **Seafood/Steak.** In business for 42 years, this establishment offers many fine dining options. Fresh flounder, seafood gumbo, and chargrilled steak are among the menu's highlights. **FYI:** Reservations accepted. Children's menu. Dress code. **Open:** Mon–Sat 11am–10pm. **Prices:** Main courses $10–$20. MC, V. ♥ ㅊ

Sassafras Tearoom
532 Clay St; tel 334/265-7277. At Whitman. **Eclectic/Health/Spa.** Located near the Civic Center and Old Alabama Town, this establishment offers a lovely Victorian atmosphere and updated Southern cuisine. Chicken salad is a favorite, and all the desserts are homemade. While there, browse through the various rooms filled with antiques (most of which are for sale) and enjoy the panoramic view of the Alabama River. **FYI:** Reservations accepted. Dress code. Wine only. No smoking. **Open:** Mon–Fri 11am–2pm. **Prices:** Lunch main courses $4–$6. MC, V. ■ ⛰

TP Crockmier's Restaurant
5620 Calmar Dr; tel 334/277-1840. Off I-85. **Seafood/Steak.** A family-oriented eatery with a basic sports motif. Menu specialty is prime rib. **FYI:** Reservations accepted. Guitar/rock/singer. Children's menu. Dress code. **Open:** Tues–Sun 11am–11pm. **Prices:** Main courses $11–$16. AE, MC, V. ♥ ㅊ

♣ Vintage Year
405 Cloverdale Rd; tel 334/264-8463. At Norman Bridge Rd. **Eclectic.** Specializes in seafood prepared with an Italian accent, as snapper, tuna, and salmon are grilled and served up with pasta and various sauces and spices. Upscale, chic dining room is frequented by many visiting celebrities and politicians. **FYI:** Reservations recommended. Dress code. **Open:** Tues–Sat 6–10pm. Closed 1st week of July and Jan. **Prices:** Main courses $12–$18. AE, MC, V. ♥

✹ Wesley's Fine Food & Spirits
In Cloverdale Plaza, 1061 Woodley Rd; tel 334/834-2500. **International.** A comfortable hangout catering to the stu-

dents at nearby Huntingdon College. They offer a wide range of foods, from wood-fired oven pizzas to roasted chicken and grilled steaks. They have a large bar and many local bands play here regularly. **FYI:** Reservations accepted. Guitar/rock/singer. Dress code. **Open:** Mon–Thurs 5:30–10pm, Fri–Sat 5:30–11pm, Sun 11am–10pm. **Prices:** Main courses $10–$19. AE, MC, V. ♥ ⴵ

ATTRACTIONS 📷

Alabama State Capitol

Bainbridge St at Dexter Ave; tel 334/242-3184. Built in 1851 in a colonial style, the building features a 97-foot white dome, and resembles the US Capitol in Washington, DC. For a short while during the beginning of the Civil War, this building served as the capitol of the Confederacy. Special points of interest inside the capitol building include a bronze star on the floor of the west portico where Jefferson Davis stood to take the oath of office, and the three-story, self-supporting double spiral staircase. **Open:** Mon–Sat 9am–4pm, Sun noon–4pm. Closed some hols. **Free**

First White House of the Confederacy

644 Washington Ave; tel 334/242-1861. President of the Confederacy Jefferson Davis and his wife moved into this fine Italianate house in 1861, after the Provisional Confederate Congress authorized funds for an Executive Mansion. The white frame home was the seat of the Confederate government from March until May 1861, when the Provisional Congress voted to move the permanent capital to Richmond, VA. Today, the house is filled with 19th-century antiques, Davis family heirlooms and portraits, and Civil War memorabilia. **Open:** Mon–Fri 8am–4:30pm. Closed some hols. **Free**

Scott and Zelda Fitzgerald Museum

919 Felder Ave; tel 334/264-4222. F Scott and Zelda Fitzgerald came to Montgomery in 1931, after several years as Parisian expatriates. During the couple's two-year stay in this house, Scott worked on his novel *Tender is the Night* and Zelda began what was to be her only novel, *Save Me the Waltz*. The house is now maintained as a museum and arts center, featuring nine of Zelda's original paintings, as well as books and memorabilia belonging to the couple. Half-hour video presentation. **Open:** Wed–Fri 10am–2pm, Sat–Sun 1–5pm. Closed some hols. **Free**

Montgomery Museum of Fine Arts

1 Museum Dr; tel 334/244-5700. Nestled in the Wynton M Blount Cultural Park, the MMFA boasts a wide selection of paintings, etchings, engravings, and prints. The museum is especially rich in works by Southern artists, including Montgomery native Zelda Sayre Fitzgerald. The Blount Collection traces the evolution of American art from the 18th century to the present, with representative works by Sargent, Copley, Hopper, and many others. European masters represented include Dürer, Matisse, and Rembrandt. **Open:** Tues–Wed, Fri–Sat 10am–5pm, Thurs 10am–9pm, Sun noon–5pm. Closed some hols. **Free**

Dexter Avenue King Memorial Baptist Church

454 Dexter Ave; tel 334/263-3970. The Rev Dr Martin Luther King Jr was the pastor here from 1954–60, during which time he became a prominent leader in the civil rights movement. A large detailed mural in the basement of the church depicts scenes from Dr King's life and his nonviolent crusade for equal rights. Guided tours Mon–Thurs at 10am and 2pm, Fri at 10am, Sat 10am–2pm. Donations accepted.

Muscle Shoals

Named for the shallow waters where mussels are harvested. Home of the Alabama Music Hall of Fame.

MOTEL 🏨

🏳🏳 Days Inn

2700 Woodward Ave, 35661; tel 205/383-3000 or toll free 800/579-5464; fax 205/383-3000. Off US 43. Near area attractions such as the birthplace of Helen Keller, the University of North Alabama, TVA park, and the Alabama Music Hall of Fame, plus shopping and restaurants. **Rooms:** 79 rms. CI 11am/CO noon. Nonsmoking rms avail. **Amenities:** 🛉 ⴵ A/C, cable TV w/movies. **Services:** ⬛ ⬛ ⬛ **Facilities:** 🔲 🔳 ⴵ 1 bar (w/entertainment), washer/dryer. **Rates (CP):** $42 S; $48 D. Extra person $5. Children under age 18 stay free. Parking: Outdoor, free. Family Fun rates avail. AE, DC, DISC, MC, V.

Opelika

Located in plantation country. The restored historic downtown area and residential historic district invites strolls. **Information:** Opelika Chamber of Commerce, 601 Ave A, PO Box 2366, Opelika, 36803 (tel 334/745-4861).

MOTELS 🏨

🏳🏳 Best Western Mariner Inn

1002 Columbus Pkwy, 36801; tel 334/749-1461 or toll free 800/528-1234; fax 334/749-1468. Exit 62 off I-85 and US 280. Basic, centrally located lodgings. **Rooms:** 100 rms. CI open/CO 11am. Nonsmoking rms avail. **Amenities:** 🛉 🔳 A/C, cable TV w/movies. **Services:** ⬛ Complimentary coffee in lobby. **Facilities:** 🔲 ⴵ 1 bar (w/entertainment), spa, whirlpool. Hideaway Lounge has live bands on weekends. **Rates:** $28 S; $30 D. Extra person $5. Children under age 12 stay free. Min stay wknds and special events. Parking: Outdoor, free. AE, CB, DC, DISC, MC, V.

🏳🏳🏳 Holiday Inn Opelika

1102 Columbus Pkwy, 36801; tel 334/745-6331 or toll free 800/HOLIDAY; fax 334/749-3933. Exit 62 off I-85. Conveniently located near Surfside Water Park, Robert Trent Jones Golf Course (15 minutes), and outlet shopping center. **Rooms:** 119 rms. CI 1pm/CO noon. Nonsmoking rms avail.

Amenities: 🏨 ⚲ ⚑ A/C, cable TV w/movies, dataport. **Services:** ✗ 🚗 🖥 🛏 🗂 **Facilities:** 🛗 🖥 🛗250 ⛳ 1 restaurant, 1 bar (w/entertainment). Banquet facilities available. **Rates:** $45 S; $50 D. Extra person $5. Children under age 18 stay free. Min stay wknds and special events. Parking: Outdoor, free. Robert Trent Jones Golf Trail packages avail. AE, CB, DC, DISC, JCB, MC, V.

Orange Beach

This resort community has the largest charter fishing fleet on the Gulf of Mexico and is known for the plentiful red snapper caught here. Perdido Pass connects 380,000 acres of backwater bays, bayous, and tributaries with the Gulf.

HOTELS 🏨

◫◫ Days Inn
US 182 E, PO Box 1003, 36561; tel 334/981-9888 or toll free 800/207-6160; fax 334/981-9254. Standard chain accommodations in a convenient location. **Rooms:** 94 rms and effic. CI 4pm/CO 11am. Nonsmoking rms avail. Rooms are comfortable. **Amenities:** 🏨 A/C, cable TV, refrig. Some units w/terraces. **Services:** 🗂 **Facilities:** 🛗 🛗100 ⛳ 1 beach (ocean), washer/dryer. **Rates (CP):** Peak (May–Sept) $139 S; $149 D; $139 effic. Extra person $6. Children under age 18 stay free. Min stay wknds and special events. Lower rates off-season. Parking: Outdoor, free. AE, DC, DISC, MC, V.

UNRATED Hampton Inn Beachfront Resort
22988 Perdido Beach Blvd, 36561; tel 334/981-6242 or toll free 800/981-6242; fax 334/981-6309. Best suited for the outdoors lover, this property is located right on the Gulf of Mexico. Championship golf courses are nearby, and Gulf State Park is just a mile away. **Rooms:** 98 rms. CI 4pm/CO 11am. Nonsmoking rms avail. **Amenities:** 🏨 ⚲ 📺 A/C, cable TV w/movies, refrig. Some units w/terraces. **Services:** 🗂 **Facilities:** 🛗 🛗150 ⛳ 1 beach (ocean), washer/dryer. Indoor atrium. **Rates (CP):** Peak (May–Sept) $115–$140 S or D. Extra person $10. Children under age 18 stay free. Min stay special events. Lower rates off-season. Parking: Indoor/outdoor, free. AE, DC, DISC, MC, V.

◫◫◫ Island House Hotel
26650 Perdido Beach Blvd, PO Box 280, 36561; tel 334/981-6100 or toll free 800/264-2642; fax 334/981-6543. A beachfront hideaway with 336 feet of private beach. Directly across from a marina. **Rooms:** 161 rms and stes. Executive level. CI 3pm/CO 11am. Nonsmoking rms avail. **Amenities:** 🏨 ⚲ 📺 ⚑ A/C, cable TV w/movies, dataport, in-rm safe. All units w/terraces, some w/whirlpools. **Services:** ✗ 🗂 Children's program, babysitting. Beach cabana and chair rentals available. **Facilities:** 🛗 🚲 ⚠ 🛗100 ⛳ 1 restaurant, 2 bars, 1 beach (ocean), volleyball, games rm, washer/dryer. **Rates:**

Peak (May–Sept) $129–$148 S or D; $246–$278 ste. Extra person $10. Min stay peak and special events. Lower rates off-season. Parking: Outdoor, free. AE, MC, V.

INN

UNRATED The Original Romar House
23500 Perdido Beach Blvd, 36561; tel 334/981-6156 or toll free 800/487-6627. Established in 1924, this is Alabama's first seaside bed & breakfast. Wonderful views and a charming historic atmosphere predominate. Unsuitable for children under 12. **Rooms:** 6 rms. CI 4pm/CO 11am. No smoking. Art deco–style rooms are furnished with period antiques and feature luxurious appointments such as stained-glass windows and marble tiles. **Amenities:** ⚲ A/C. No phone or TV. **Services:** Wine/sherry served. Complimentary wine and cheese. Full Southern-style breakfast includes biscuits, eggs, grits, and homemade muffins. **Facilities:** 🚲 🛗15 1 bar, 1 beach (ocean), whirlpool, guest lounge w/TV. Whirlpool, hammock, deck. **Rates (BB):** Peak (May–Labor Day) $120 S or D. Extra person $10. Min stay wknds and special events. Lower rates off-season. Higher rates for special events/hols. Parking: Outdoor, free. MC, V.

RESORT

◫◫◫ Perdido Beach Resort
27200 Perdido Beach Blvd, 36561; tel 334/981-9811 or toll free 800/634-8001; fax 334/634-5672. Located on the shores of the Gulf of Mexico, this beach resort offers nearby shopping, restaurants, championship golf courses, deep-sea fishing, sailing, and motor boating. Rooms are situated in two stucco-and-tile towers. **Rooms:** 345 rms and stes. CI 4pm/CO noon. Nonsmoking rms avail. Rooms have Mediterranean-style decor, and all have views of the Gulf. **Amenities:** 🏨 ⚲ A/C, satel TV w/movies. All units w/terraces. **Services:** ✗ 🖥 VP 🚗 🛏 🗂 Social director, children's program. **Facilities:** 🛗 ⚠ ⚲ 🍴 🖥 🛗1000 ⛳ 2 restaurants (see "Restaurants" below), 3 bars (w/entertainment), 1 beach (ocean), volleyball, games rm, spa, sauna, steam rm, whirlpool, playground. **Rates:** Peak (May–Sept) $69–$155 S or D; $125–$295 ste. Extra person $10. Children under age 18 stay free. Min stay peak, wknds, and special events. Lower rates off-season. Parking: Indoor/outdoor, free. Golf and romance packages avail. AE, CB, DC, DISC, JCB, MC, V.

RESTAURANTS 🍴

Dempsey's Restaurant
182 Gulf Beach Hwy; tel 334/981-6800. **Seafood.** A tropical-style dining room dominated by a dramatic indoor waterfall. The menu brings together fresh Gulf seafood with the culinary influence of New Orleans. All-you-can-eat dinner buffet with up to 40 items. **FYI:** Reservations not accepted. Children's menu. Dress code. **Open:** Daily 11am–10pm. **Prices:** Main courses $10–$16. AE, CB, DC, DISC, MC, V. ⛳

Hazel's Family Restaurant
In Gulf View Square Shopping Center, AL 182; tel 334/981-4628. **Seafood.** Three outstanding buffets a day are served in this friendly eatery. Fresh Gulf Coast seafood is a specialty. **FYI:** Reservations not accepted. Children's menu. Dress code. **Open:** Daily 6am–10pm. **Prices:** Main courses $7–$19. AE, DC, DISC, MC, V. 👥 ♿

★ **Live Bait**
24281 Perdido Beach Blvd; tel 334/981-6677. **Regional American/Seafood.** Diners are seated at wooden tables (decorated with brightly painted fish) with views of swampy marshland and the occasional alligator. The menu lists standard fried seafood fare: shrimp, oyster, and crawfish po' boys. Seafood spud is a delicious alternative. A family atmosphere predominates at lunch and dinner, while young partiers tend to fill the place after 10pm. **FYI:** Reservations not accepted. Jazz/rock/singer. Children's menu. Dress code. **Open:** Lunch daily 11:30am–3:30pm; dinner daily 4:30–10pm. **Prices:** Main courses $7–$17. MC, V. 🖼 👥

The Outrigger Restaurant
27500 Perdido Beach Blvd; tel 334/981-6700. **Seafood.** The dining room at this relatively new place displays photographs from Hurricane Frederick. The menu offers a variety of seafood dishes, and there are great views of the Gulf of Mexico. **FYI:** Reservations not accepted. Children's menu. Dress code. **Open:** Daily 11am–8pm. **Prices:** Main courses $13–$17. AE, DC, DISC, MC, V. 🖼 👥 ♿

♣ **Voyagers**
In Perdido Beach Resort; tel 334/981-9811. **Continental/Creole.** Beautiful views of the Gulf of Mexico and the surrounding sugar-white beaches make a perfect backdrop for this elegant cuisine. The menu emphasizes fresh local seafood and classic continental preparation, with just a touch of Creole spice. Typical offerings: soft-shell crab served with Creole sauce Choron, trout with meunière sauce, praline soufflé. **FYI:** Reservations recommended. Dress code. **Open:** Daily 5–11pm. **Prices:** Main courses $15–$25. AE, DC, DISC, MC, V. ♥ 🖼 VP ♿

★ **Zeke's Landing Restaurant and Oyster Bar**
26619 Perdido Beach Blvd; tel 334/981-4001. **Seafood.** The large, light-wood dining room overlooks Zeke's Landing Marina. Predictably, the menu is heavy on seafood—broiled, baked, sautéed, and fried. But they also offer unusual seafood sandwiches and salads, plus some impressive steaks. **FYI:** Reservations not accepted. Jazz. Dress code. **Open:** Peak (May–Aug) Sun–Thurs 11am–10pm, Fri–Sat 11am–11pm. **Prices:** Main courses $12–$28. AE, DC, DISC, MC, V. 🖼 👥 ♿

Point Clear

In the Gulf Coast delta region, this town offers lavish day cruises to Bellingrath Gardens and Sand Island. Punta Clara Kitchen, which operates out of a Victorian home, makes candies and confections daily for the public.

RESORT 🏨

═ ═ ═ Marriott's Grand Hotel

1 Grand Blvd, 36564; tel 334/928-9201 or toll free 800/544-9933; fax 334/928-1149. 550 acres. A wonderful resort overlooking beautiful Mobile Bay. With its multitude of activities, you'll never be bored. But if you do want to get away, the hotel is close to Gulf Coast beaches, antebellum home tours, and the greyhound dog track. **Rooms:** 306 rms and stes; 8 cottages/villas. CI 4pm/CO noon. Nonsmoking rms avail. Rooms are large, exquisitely decorated, and very comfortable. **Amenities:** 🛏 🍷 🖥 A/C, cable TV w/movies, dataport, bathrobes. Some units w/terraces. **Services:** 🍽 VP 🛎 👔 Social director, children's program, babysitting. **Facilities:** 🏌 🚲 ⛳ 🎾 ▶36 🎣 🏊 ◀6 🏐 🚤 1300 ♿ 2 restaurants, 3 bars (2 w/entertainment), volleyball, games rm, lawn games, sauna, steam rm, whirlpool, beauty salon, playground, washer/dryer. **Rates:** Peak (Mar–Oct) $200–$220 S or D; $210 ste; $190 cottage/villa. Min stay special events. Lower rates off-season. MAP rates avail. Parking: Outdoor, free. AE, CB, DC, DISC, MC, V.

Rogersville

A small southern crossroads town, rural and pretty, in the Alabama highlands. Several antique shops are in town.

LODGE 🏨

═ ═ ═ Joe Wheeler State Park Lodge

US 72, Drawer K, 35652; tel 205/247-5461 or toll free 800/544-5639; fax 205/247-5471. 2,550 acres. An exceptionally well-kept lodge, housed in a striking three-story building of redwood and stone. More amenities than most lodges of its type. **Rooms:** 75 rms, stes, and effic. CI 3pm/CO 11am. Nonsmoking rms avail. All rooms have views of the lake. **Amenities:** 🛏 A/C, satel TV. All units w/terraces. **Services:** 👔 **Facilities:** 🏌 ⛳ ▶18 🎾 🏐 🛶 600 ♿ 1 restaurant, 1 beach (lake shore), basketball, volleyball, playground. **Rates:** Peak (Apr–Nov) $59 S; $66 D; $99–$114 ste; $76 effic. Extra person $5. Children under age 12 stay free. Min stay wknds and special events. Lower rates off-season. Parking: Outdoor, free. Winter getaway packages avail. AE, MC, V.

Scottsboro

Seat of Jackson County, in northeast Alabama. Its peninsula park and recreation complex is bounded on three sides by

Guntersville Reservoir and the Tennessee River. **Information:** Scottsboro–Jackson County Chamber of Commerce, 407 E Willow St, PO Box 973, Scottsboro, 35768 (tel 334/875-7241).

MOTEL

≡≡ Days Inn

1106 John T Reid Pkwy, PO Box 518, 35768; tel 205/574-1212 or toll free 800/579-KING; fax 205/574-1212. At jct US 72 and US 35. A quiet, small, two-story motel. **Rooms:** 84 rms and stes. CI 1pm/CO 11am. Nonsmoking rms avail. **Amenities:** A/C, cable TV w/movies, dataport. **Services:** **Facilities:** Playground, washer/dryer. Goose Pond Colony Golf Course and Marina is five miles away. **Rates (CP):** $35–$39 S; $35–$42 D; $40–$44 ste. Extra person $5. Children under age 18 stay free. Parking: Outdoor, free. AE, CB, DC, DISC, JCB, MC, V.

ATTRACTION

Russell Cave National Monument

Bridgeport. Located 30 mi NE of Scottsboro. Archeological evidence indicates that as long ago as 6500 BC, early Native Americans occupied Russell Cave. The lives of those formerly nomadic people who stumbled upon the cave changed in many ways: They no longer had to build shelters; they had a constant supply of running water during the winter; and the nearby woods provided ample food supply. Native Americans still used the cave, as a hunting campsite, for thousands of years after they had started to live in villages. This fascinating history is illustrated in exhibits at the park's **visitors center**, and at the cave itself. Visitors can learn about the archeological excavations that revealed the cave's history and can see demonstrations of corn grinding, flint flaking (for fashioning stone tools), and the use of the *atlatl* (throwing stick).

For further information about the monument, contact Superintendent, RR 1, Box 209, Bridgeport, AL 35740 (tel 205/495-2672). **Open:** Daily 8am–5pm. Closed Dec 25.

Selma

Offers pre–Civil War grace and civil rights history. Selma has a restored historic district and offers tours of its beautiful antebellum homes in the spring. It was the site of the first African Methodist Episcopal church (founded in 1867), which served as headquarters for much of the civil rights movement. The bridge to Montgomery stretching across the Alabama River serves as a silent reminder of the peaceful civil rights marches led by a young Dr Martin Luther King Jr. **Information:** Selma Convention & Visitors Bureau, 513 Lauderdale St, PO Drawer D, Selma, 36702 (tel 334/875-7241).

MOTEL

≡ Best Western Selma

1915 W Highland Ave, 36701; tel 334/872-1900 or toll free 800/528-1234; fax 334/872-6635. A low-rise white stucco building housing bare-bones accommodations. **Rooms:** 51 rms and effic. CI 2pm/CO 11am. Nonsmoking rms avail. Some rooms have kitchenettes. **Amenities:** A/C, cable TV w/movies, dataport. **Services:** **Facilities:** Washer/dryer. **Rates (CP):** $45 S; $55 D; $60 effic. Extra person $5. Children under age 12 stay free. Parking: Outdoor, free. AE, DC, DISC, MC, V.

RESTAURANT

★ Tally-Ho

507 Magnum Ave; tel 334/872-1390. At Summerfield Rd. **American/Steak.** Visitors enter this fine dining establishment through the remains of an old log cabin. Once inside, they can sit at the oyster bar or enjoy the fresh seafood specialties in the main dining area. Catering and banquet facilities available. **FYI:** Reservations accepted. Children's menu. Dress code. **Open:** Mon–Sat 5–10pm. **Prices:** Main courses $12–$16. AE, DC, DISC, MC, V.

Sheffield

See also Muscle Shoals

Located on bluffs overlooking the Tennessee River. Home to industries and historic water tower and cemeteries.

HOTELS

≡≡≡ Holiday Inn Sheffield

4900 Hatch Blvd, 35660; tel 205/381-4710 or toll free 800/465-4329; fax 205/381-4710 ext 403. At jct US 43/72. Convenient to movie theaters, Southgate Mall, Ivy Green, Pope's Tavern. **Rooms:** 204 rms and stes. CI noon/CO noon. Nonsmoking rms avail. **Amenities:** A/C, satel TV w/movies. Some units w/terraces. **Services:** Shuttle service to area malls. **Facilities:** 1 restaurant (*see* "Restaurants" below), 1 bar (w/entertainment), whirlpool. **Rates:** $69–$72 S or D; $125–$281 ste. Parking: Outdoor, free. AE, CB, DC, DISC, JCB, MC, V.

≡≡≡ Ramada Inn Convention Center

4205 Hatch Blvd, 35660; tel 205/381-3743 or toll free 800/272-6232; fax 205/381-2838. Off US 72. Suitable for all travelers and near shopping, movie theaters, and area attractions such as the Helen Keller home and Pope's Tavern. **Rooms:** 150 rms and stes. CI open/CO noon. Nonsmoking rms avail. **Amenities:** A/C, satel TV w/movies. Some units w/whirlpools. **Services:** Weekend security patrol. **Facilities:** 1 restaurant, 1 bar (w/entertainment), whirlpool. Guests can receive Gold's Gym passes. Bar has acoustic bands during the week. **Rates (CP):** $57 S;

$55 D; $125–$175 ste. Extra person $7. Children under age 21 stay free. Parking: Outdoor, free. AE, CB, DC, DISC, JCB, MC, V.

RESTAURANT 🍽

⑤ Palm Court

In Holiday Inn Sheffield, 4900 Hatch Blvd; tel 205/381-4710. **Eclectic.** Comfortable dining room most popular for its country-style breakfast buffet of eggs, grits, bacon, sausage, flapjacks, french toast, assorted fruits and fruit juices, and various yogurts. The chicken finger platter is a lunch favorite, while swordfish steak is a fine dinner choice. Nightly specials include a complimentary glass of wine. **FYI:** Reservations accepted. Children's menu. Dress code. **Open:** Breakfast daily 6:30am–2pm; lunch daily 11am–2pm; dinner daily 5:30–10pm. **Prices:** Main courses $10–$15. AE, CB, DC, DISC, MC, V. 📷 &

Sterett

Home to one of state's "newest" old covered bridges in wooded conference center and span Lake Lauralee.

RESORT 🏨

⊨⊨⊨ Twin Pines Resort & Conference Center

1200 Twin Pines Rd, 35147; tel 205/672-7575; fax 205/672-7575. 200 acres. Rustic elegance in a spectacular outdoor setting. Attractions include an authentic moonshine still, wildlife, recreation, country-style meals, and excellent meeting rooms. **Rooms:** 46 rms and stes. CI 3pm/CO noon. Nonsmoking rms avail. **Amenities:** 🔒 ⚷ 📺 🗤 A/C, TV, refrig. All units w/terraces, some w/fireplaces. **Services:** ⇥ **Facilities:** ⚠ 🖼 🖼 ⚓2 110 & 1 restaurant, 1 beach (lake shore), basketball, volleyball, games rm, playground. Bob Saunders Family Covered Bridge and 46-acre Lake Lauralee are both on the property. **Rates:** $75–$110 S or D; $120–$152 ste. Extra person $10. Children under age 6 stay free. Parking: Outdoor, free. Getaway package avail. AE, DISC, MC, V.

Sylacauga

Famous for the marble quarried nearby and used in building the US Supreme Court. Nearby in Childersburg is DeSoto Caverns Park. **Information:** Sylacauga Chamber of Commerce, 17 W Fort Williams St, PO Box 185, Sylacauga, 35150 (tel 205/249-0308).

MOTEL 🏨

⊨ Super 8 Motel

40770 US 280, PO Box 828, 35150; tel 205/249-4321 or toll free 800/800-8000; fax 205/245-7473. Basic, no-frills atmosphere. **Rooms:** 44 rms and effic. CI 1pm/CO 11am. Non-

smoking rms avail. **Amenities:** 🔒 A/C, cable TV w/movies. **Facilities:** 🖼 & 1 bar. **Rates:** $34–$57 S or D; $37–$61 effic. Extra person $4. Children under age 12 stay free. Min stay special events. Parking: Outdoor, free. Rates increase on Race weekends. AE, DISC, MC, V.

ATTRACTION 🏛

DeSoto Caverns Park

5181 DeSoto Caverns Pkwy, Childersburg; tel 205/378-7252. Located 10 mi NW of Sylacauga. These onyx caves, considered sacred by the Creek tribe, were rediscovered in 1540 by Hernando De Soto. The caverns were later used by the Confederate Army to store equipment and supplies. Their most spectacular natural feature is the Onyx Cathedral, where dramatically lit stalactites hang from a cavern roof higher than a 12-story building. Visitors can pan for gems, visit a Confederate gunpowder mine, or stop by the "Prohibition Moonshine Speakeasy." **Open:** Mon–Sat 9am–5pm, Sun 12:30–5pm. Closed some hols. $$$$

Troy

Commercial city southeast of Montgomery; the seat of Pike County and home of Troy State University. **Information:** Pike County Chamber of Commerce, 246 US 231 N, Troy, 36081 (tel 334/566-2294).

MOTELS 🏨

⊨⊨ Econo Lodge

1013 US 231, PO Box 1086, 36081; tel 334/566-4960 or toll free 800/553-2666; fax 334/566-5858. A comfortable, dependable chain motel. Near Troy State University and Pike Pioneer Museum. **Rooms:** 69 rms. CI open/CO 11am. Nonsmoking rms avail. **Amenities:** 🔒 ⚷ A/C, cable TV w/movies. **Services:** ⊠ ⇥ ⇔ **Facilities:** 🖼 & **Rates (CP):** $36 S; $41 D. Extra person $5. Children under age 16 stay free. Min stay special events. Parking: Outdoor, free. AE, DC, DISC, MC, V.

⊨⊨⊨ Holiday Inn

Jct US 231/US 29, PO Box 564, 36081; tel 334/566-1150 or toll free 800/HOLIDAY; fax 334/566-7666. Convenient to area attractions such as the Pioneer Museum and L&L Lake, and close to Troy State University. **Rooms:** 98 rms. CI 1pm/CO noon. Nonsmoking rms avail. **Amenities:** 🔒 ⚷ A/C, cable TV w/movies, dataport. **Services:** ✗ 📷 ⊠ ⇥ ⇔ Pets under 10 lbs only. **Facilities:** 🖼 300 & 1 restaurant, 1 bar, washer/dryer. **Rates (CP):** $45–$47 S; $51–$53 D. Extra person $6. Children under age 19 stay free. Min stay special events. Parking: Outdoor, free. AE, DC, DISC, MC, V.

RESTAURANTS ▯▯▯

★ **Mossy Grove Schoolhouse Restaurant**
Elba Hwy; tel 334/566-4921. **Seafood/Steak/Southern.**
Originally a schoolhouse built in 1856, this eatery is decorated with period antiques and old school equipment (a blackboard, school desks). Rib eye and charbroiled shrimp are among the kitchen's specialties. **FYI:** Reservations accepted. Children's menu. Dress code. Beer and wine only. No smoking. **Open:** Tues–Sat 5–9pm. **Prices:** Main courses $5–$15. MC, V. ▮ ▥ ႕

★ **The Pines Restaurant**
1044 Elm St; tel 334/566-5382. Off George Wallace Dr. **Seafood/Steak.** Nestled in a wooded area overlooking Crowes Lake, The Pines specializes in steak and seafood dishes and offers a comfortable dining atmosphere for couples and families. **FYI:** Reservations accepted. Children's menu. Dress code. **Open:** Tues–Sat 5–9pm. **Prices:** Main courses $7–$14. AE, DISC, MC, V. ▱ ▥ ႕

Tuscaloosa

Established in 1816 on the elevated left bank of the Black Warrior River, it preserves an Old South atmosphere. Towering oaks shade all sections, giving Tuscaloosa the moniker "Druid City." The state capital from 1826 to 1846, the city is named in memory of Tushkalusa, the Choctaw chief who opposed the conquistador Hernando De Soto. The University of Alabama located is here, as is the museum for the winningest college football coach in history, Paul "Bear" Bryant. South of the city in Moundville are 20 prehistoric platform mounds, a reconstructed Native American village, nature trails, and a branch of the Museum of Natural History at the University of Alabama. **Information:** Chamber of Commerce of West Alabama, 2200 University Blvd, PO Box 020410, Tuscaloosa, 35402 (tel 205/391-0559).

HOTELS 🏨

▤▤ Hampton Inn
600 Harper Lee Dr, 35404; tel 205/553-9800 or toll free 800/HAMPTON. 3 mi N of exit 73. New establishment located near the University of Alabama campus. **Rooms:** 102 rms. CI 3pm/CO noon. Nonsmoking rms avail. **Amenities:** 🛏 ⓐ ▤ ¶ A/C, cable TV w/movies, dataport, voice mail. **Services:** ▱ ↺ **Facilities:** ᵹ ႕ **Rates (CP):** Peak (Sept–Nov) $56 S; $62 D. Children under age 18 stay free. Min stay special events. Lower rates off-season. Parking: Outdoor, free. Rates increase over Alabama football season weekends. AE, CB, DC, DISC, MC, V.

▤▤▤ Sheraton Capstone Inn
320 Paul Bryant Dr, 35401; tel 205/752-3200 or toll free 800/477-2262; fax 205/759-9314. Comfortable lodgings located on the University of Alabama campus. An obvious choice for 'Bama football fans—the Paul "Bear" Bryant

Museum is across the street. **Rooms:** 152 rms. CI 3pm/CO noon. Nonsmoking rms avail. **Amenities:** 🛏 ⓐ ▤ A/C, cable TV w/movies, dataport. In-room Lodgenet channel offers movies and Nintendo games. Refrigerators in suites. **Services:** ✕ 🚐 ▱ ↺ Babysitting. **Facilities:** ᵹ ⸩1000⸨ ▯ ႕ 1 restaurant, 1 bar. **Rates:** $89 S or D. Extra person $5. Children under age 18 stay free. Parking: Outdoor, free. Honeymoon package (including gift basket, chilled champagne, and dinner and breakfast for two) avail. AE, DC, DISC, MC, V.

MOTELS

▤▤ Best Western Park Plaza
3801 McFarland Blvd, 35405; tel 205/556-9690 or toll free 800/235-7282; fax 205/556-9690. Near shopping, a movie theater, and the University of Alabama campus, this simple property is suitable for all travelers. **Rooms:** 120 rms. CI 1pm/CO noon. Nonsmoking rms avail. **Amenities:** 🛏 ⓐ ▤ A/C, cable TV w/movies, dataport. Some rooms have mini-refrigerators. **Services:** ▱ ↺ Nearby O'Charley's Restaurant will bill deliveries to room. **Facilities:** ᵹ ⸩40⸨ ႕ **Rates (CP):** $52–$65 S; $60–$70 D. Extra person $4. Children under age 12 stay free. Min stay peak. Parking: Outdoor, free. Higher rates during football weekends and graduation. AE, DC, DISC, MC, V.

▤ Holiday Inn of Tuscaloosa
3920 McFarland Blvd E, PO Box 5265, 35405; tel 205/553-1550 or toll free 800/322-3489; fax 205/553-1550. At jct I-59/US 82. An older motel, popular with University of Alabama football fans and alumni. Sufficient for an overnight stay. **Rooms:** 166 rms. CI 3pm/CO noon. Nonsmoking rms avail. Rooms are a little worn, and the decor is dated. **Amenities:** 🛏 ⓐ A/C, cable TV w/movies. **Services:** ✕ ▱ Security guard on weekends only. **Facilities:** ᵹ ႕ 1 restaurant, 1 bar, playground, washer/dryer. **Rates:** $55 S or D. Parking: Outdoor, free. AE, DC, DISC, MC, V.

▤▤ La Quinta Motor Inn
4122 McFarland Blvd E, 35405; tel 205/349-3270 or toll free 800/531-5900. Exit 73 off I-20/59. Located near shopping malls and movie theaters. **Rooms:** 122 rms. CI 3pm/CO noon. Nonsmoking rms avail. **Amenities:** 🛏 ⓐ A/C, cable TV w/movies. **Services:** ▱ ↺ ➿ **Facilities:** ᵹ ⸩30⸨ ႕ **Rates (CP):** $51–$58 S or D. Extra person $5. Children under age 18 stay free. Parking: Outdoor, free. AE, CB, DC, DISC, MC, V.

▤▤ Ramada Inn
631 Skyland Blvd E, 35405; tel 205/759-4431 or toll free 800/228-2828. Off I-20/59. Comfortable accommodations attracting many visitors to the University. **Rooms:** 108 rms and stes. CI 3pm/CO noon. Nonsmoking rms avail. **Amenities:** 🛏 ⓐ A/C, cable TV w/movies. **Services:** ⦿ ▱ ↺ ➿ Babysitting. **Facilities:** ᵹ ⸩200⸨ ႕ 1 restaurant, 1 bar (w/entertainment), games rm, washer/dryer. **Rates:** $45–$75

S or D; $100–$150 ste. Extra person $8. Children under age 12 stay free. Parking: Outdoor, free. AE, CB, DC, DISC, JCB, MC, V.

RESTAURANTS 🍽

★ Bob Baumhower's "Wings" Sports Grille

500 Harper Lee Dr; tel 205/556-5658. 3 mi N off I-20/59. **Eclectic.** A popular hangout for the college crowd, noted for their buffalo wings with varying degrees of "heat"—from plain to "911." The collegiate decor features the Tide with photos, videos, TV screens. **FYI:** Reservations not accepted. Children's menu. Dress code. Additional location: Lakeshore Blvd Wildwood Shopping Center, Birmingham (tel 290-9464). **Open:** Sun–Thurs 11am–10pm, Fri–Sat 11am–11pm. **Prices:** Main courses $6–$15. DISC, MC, V. ▮ 🏮 &

★ Capstone Grille

1006 7th Ave; tel 205/345-1708. At Paul Bryant Dr. **International.** Only one block from the University of Alabama campus, the Capstone caters to a young, lively, college crowd. The menu offers everything from steaks and chicken to pasta and burgers. Chicken Florentine is a good bet. **FYI:** Reservations not accepted. Children's menu. Dress code. **Open:** Lunch Mon–Fri 11am–2pm, Sat–Sun 11am–3pm; dinner Mon–Thurs 5–10pm, Fri–Sat 5–11pm, Sun 5–9pm; brunch Sat–Sun 11am–3pm. Closed Dec 20–Jan 3. **Prices:** Main courses $5–$15. AE, MC, V. ♥ 🍽 🏮

Cypress Inn

501 Rice Mine Rd; tel 205/345-6963. **American/Southern.** Rustic decor, with cypress-wood paneling and furniture, sets the tone at this riverside restaurant. Predictably, the menu emphasizes fresh fish, especially catfish, although steak and chicken are also available. Desserts are prepared on site. **FYI:** Reservations accepted. Children's menu. Dress code. **Open:** Lunch Sun–Fri 11am–2pm; dinner Mon–Sun 5:30–9:30pm. **Prices:** Main courses $10–$16. AE, DISC, MC, V. ♥ 🏔 &

★ Dreamland Barbeque

5535 15th Ave E; tel 205/758-8135. **Barbecue.** The decor is not pretty—just old license plates and autographed photos of famous customers—but people really come here for the ribs. The menu is short and simple—ribs and white bread, with beer by the can and soft drinks. **FYI:** Reservations not accepted. Additional locations: 14th Ave S & 15th St, Birmingham (tel 933-2133); Old Shell Rd, Mobile (tel 334/479-9898). **Open:** Mon–Thurs 10am–9pm, Fri–Sat 10am–10pm. **Prices:** Main courses $4–$14. MC, V. ▮ &

The Globe

430 Main Ave; tel 205/391-0949. **Eclectic/International.** Housed in a restored general store in historic Northport, the Globe offers creative cuisine like sautéed shrimp tortellini, tandoori chicken, quesadillas, and pan-seared orange roughy with juniper-berry sauce. The gourmet pizzas are also a tasty option. The decor aims to recreate the Globe Theater of Shakespeare's day, with a pub-style bar and scenes from the Bard's works lining the dark walls. The Globe, Etc, located across the street, offers gourmet foods for takeout. **FYI:** Reservations not accepted. Guitar. Children's menu. Dress code. **Open:** Lunch Tues–Sat 11am–3pm; dinner Tue–Thurs 5–10pm, Fri–Sat 5–11pm. **Prices:** Main courses $6–$15. AE, DISC, MC, V. ▮ &

♟ Kozy's Fine Dining

3510 Pelham Loop Rd; tel 205/556-0665. **Regional American/Continental.** Elegant dining in a nostalgic 1940s setting, featuring photos of actors and musicians from the era and a jukebox stocked with oldies. Dishes include pesto-parsley chicken topped with two jumbo shrimp, and roast duck. **FYI:** Reservations recommended. Dress code. **Open:** Mon–Thurs 5–10pm, Fri–Sat 5–11pm. **Prices:** Main courses $14–$19. AE, MC, V. ♥

ATTRACTION 📷

Moundville Archaeological Park

AL 69 S, Moundville; tel 205/371-2572. Located 15 mi S of Tuscaloosa. This park preserves 317 acres of what was one of the most powerful prehistoric Native American communities in the southeast. From AD 1100–1500 (known as the Mississippian Era), when Europe was in the middle of its Dark Ages, a cultural and economic center was flourishing here. Temples, council houses, and homes of the nobility were built on top of huge earthen mounds, some of which still survive. A museum houses archeological artifacts and exhibits explaining the lifestyle of the natives; recreational facilities include a campground, a boardwalk nature trail, and a picnic area. **Open:** Daily 9am–5pm. Closed some hols. **$$**

Tuscumbia

Manufacturing city, named for a Cherokee chief, located on the Tennessee River 10 miles from Wilson Dam. Site of Ivy Green, Helen Keller's childhood home. **Information:** Colbert County Tourism, PO Box 440, Tuscumbia, 25674 (tel 205/383-0783).

MOTEL 🏨

≡≡ Key West Inn

1800 US 72 W, 35674; tel 205/383-0700 or toll free 800/833-0555; fax 205/383-3191. At US 43. Comfortable accommodations located near area attractions such as the Helen Keller birthplace, the Alabama Music Hall of Fame, Renaissance Tower, and Wilson Dam. **Rooms:** 41 rms. CI 2pm/CO noon. Nonsmoking rms avail. **Amenities:** 🛁 A/C, cable TV w/movies. **Services:** 🛎 🧺 🛗 Resident manager present 24 hours. Discounts provided to local area attractions. **Facilities:** 🅿️ & Washer/dryer. **Rates (CP):** $42–$47 S; $47–$52 D. Extra person $5. Children under age 18 stay free. Parking: Outdoor, free. AE, CB, DC, DISC, MC, V.

ATTRACTIONS 📷

Ivy Green/Birthplace of Helen Keller

300 W North Commons; tel 205/383-4066. Helen Keller was born in the small cottage here, east of the main house, in 1880. At the age of 19 months, she was struck with an illness that left her blind and deaf. Her dedicated parents, Capt Arthur and Kate Adams Keller, took Helen to various doctors and specialists but no one was able to pierce her isolation until a young teacher named Anne Sullivan taught the girl to use sign language by sticking her hand under a water pump. The Kellers' house is located on a 640-acre tract filled with magnolias, mimosa, honeysuckle, and the eponymous ivy. The main house, birthplace cottage, and carriage house are decorated with Keller family furniture and contain hundreds of Helen's personal mementos and books, including her complete library of Braille books and her Braille typewriter. The well pump, site of Helen's epiphany, is still in its original location.

Playwright William Gibson's *The Miracle Worker,* the basis for the 1962 film of the same name, is performed on the grounds every weekend from late June through late July. Call for schedule and fee information. **Open:** Mon–Sat 8:30am–4pm, Sun 1–4pm. Closed some hols. **$**

Alabama Music Hall of Fame

US 72 W; tel 205/381-4417 or toll free 800/239-2643. Exhibits here honor the state's musical achievers, from Hank Williams to Nat "King" Cole to Lionel Richie. Visitors can see Elvis Presley's original recording contract, board the tour bus of the group Alabama, and hear music from the world's largest guitar. There's even a recording studio where guests are invited to record their own "hit." **Open:** Mon–Sat 9am–5pm, Sun 1–5pm. Closed some hols. **$$$**

Tuskegee

For lodgings and dining, see Auburn, Opelika

Incorporated in 1820, this city 38 miles east of Montgomery is home to Tuskegee Institute, founded by Booker T Washington in 1881 and the place where George Washington Carver conducted his famous experiments. **Information:** Macon County Chamber of Commerce, PO Box 338, Tuskegee, 36083 (tel 334/727-6619).

RESTAURANT 🍽

★ Thomas Reed's Chitlin House—Chicken Coop

527 Old Montgomery Rd; tel 334/727-3841. At Franklin Rd. **Soul/Southern.** Down-home cooking in a very casual eatery near Tuskegee University. Students and locals flock here for authentic Southern-style yams, string beans, macaroni and cheese, cabbage, and fried and baked chicken. **FYI:** Reservations not accepted. Dress code. No liquor license. Additional location: 101 E Southside (tel 727-3901). **Open:** Mon–Fri 9am–5pm. **Prices:** Main courses $3–$7. No CC. 👥

Leader of the New South

Georgia presents an intriguing blend of history, high culture, and that famous Southern hospitality. The strong points of this modern Sun Belt state, with its idyllic year-round climate, go far beyond the moonlight and magnolias of *Gone with the Wind*. Stretching from the golden beaches of the Atlantic Ocean to the foothills of the Appalachians, the Peach State includes glitzy, sophisticated Atlanta as well as numerous small towns that retain much of their turn-of-the-century charm.

Spectacular natural and manmade wonders pop up unexpectedly in every section of the state. Water lovers and sun worshipers flock to Georgia's fabled barrier islands and recreational lakes, while outdoor sports abound along the state's network of rivers and hiking trails. National parks and forests and 40 state parks provide recreational activities, lodges, cabins, and campgrounds. Family diversions range from amusement parks and miniature golf complexes to game ranches. History buffs can visit the homes of two former presidents, the birthplace of Martin Luther King Jr, or Civil War battlefields, and the gracious homes of Savannah are attracting more visitors than ever due to the 1994 bestseller *Midnight in the Garden of Good and Evil*.

Atlanta's Hartsfield International Airport, well known for being one of the busiest air traffic hubs in the country, has airport shops that used to trade on this notoriety by selling T-shirts that read "I died and went to heaven and had to change planes in Atlanta." But for those arriving in the Peach State not for a change of planes but rather a change of scenery, there is much here to surprise and delight even the most jaded traveler.

A Brief History

Mound Builders Heaps of shells found on Cumberland Island indicate that the area now known as Georgia was inhabited 4,000 years ago by Native Americans who

STATE STATS

CAPITAL
Atlanta

AREA
58,910 square miles

BORDERS
Alabama, Florida,
North Carolina,
South Carolina,
Tennessee, Atlantic Ocean

POPULATION
7,055,336 (1994 estimate)

ENTERED UNION
January 2, 1788 (4th state)

NICKNAMES
Empire State of the South,
Peach State

STATE FLOWER
Cherokee rose

STATE BIRD
Brown thrasher

FAMOUS NATIVES
James Brown, Jimmy Carter,
Ray Charles,
Flannery O'Connor,
Jackie Robinson

called the island *Missoe,* or sassafras. Similar excavations on St Catherine's Island have revealed human remains, household items, weapons, and religious items. In northwest Georgia, Spanish explorer Hernando de Soto encountered a Mississippian civilization of mound-building Native Americans during his expedition through the Southeast in 1540. The Mississippian culture eventually declined as a result of wars with the Cherokee and Creek and other tribes, and the introduction of European diseases.

Colonial Years During the 16th century, England, Spain, and France battled for control of Georgia and the rest of the New World. Spanish soldiers and missionaries occupied the barrier islands off the Atlantic Coast in the 1520s, and a brief period of French control followed in 1562. The Spanish, who were searching for gold, used the barrier islands off the Georgia coast to protect Florida from incursions by the English, who had formed a permanent colony at Savannah in 1738. In fact, if the English hadn't defeated the Spanish on nearby St Simons Island in 1742, might Georgians be speaking Spanish today?

Trail of Tears At the beginning of the 18th century, the Five Civilized Tribes of the Southeast included the Creek, Cherokee, Chickasaw, Choctaw, and Seminole tribes. By 1650, the Cherokee Nation, largest of the five tribes, controlled 40,000 square miles of territory and had a population of 22,500. (The capital of the nation was established at New Echota, near present-day Calhoun.) When gold was discovered in 1838 near contemporary Dahlonega, prospectors pressured the state legislature into rescinding Cherokee sovereignty and confiscating their lands. US and Georgia troops rounded up 15,000 Cherokees and herded them along the 2,000-mile Trail of Tears to reservations in Oklahoma. (In a sad footnote to the shameful affair, the gold was soon depleted and the prospectors moved on to richer veins in California.)

War is Hell Only a few years later, another tragic episode marked Georgia forever. The Civil War, also known as the War Between the States or "the War of Northern Aggression," nearly destroyed the quiet state. Much of the intense action took place in the northwestern corner of Georgia, where one of the most significant Confederate victories of the war occurred at a tiny place called Chickamauga. But the Confederate failure to take quick advantage of the conquest resulted in a catastrophic defeat at Chattanooga and opened up north Georgia to Union Gen William Tecumseh Sherman and his troops. Then followed one of the darkest periods in the state's history—Sherman's infamous march to the sea in which his troops cut a 60-mile-wide swath through central Georgia from Atlanta to Savannah, destroying nearly everything in their path.

The New South Georgia's economy picked up after surviving enormous deprivation during the Civil War and Reconstruction period, and it has never looked back. The state's economic life has always prospered from one transportation system or another. Beginning as an important seaport in the early 1700s, the state's transportation focus soon shifted to take advantage of river access into the interior. Atlanta was originally known as Terminus due to its role as a railroad hub; today, the state is an important air crossroads.

Another primary source of income revolves around agriculture. At first cotton was king, but that crop was supplanted by pecans, peaches, peanuts, and sweet Vidalia onions. (In recent years the state has developed a burgeoning kiwi fruit industry.) Despite the continued importance of these traditional sources of income, Georgia's current economy relies on services, finance, tourism, and even an emerging music and movie industry.

A New South leader in race relations, Atlanta—described in the 1960s as "the city too busy to hate"—integrated early and peacefully. The state's large and active African American middle class has led the way in the fight for racial equality, and Georgia is home to prestigious (and historically black) colleges like Spelman and Morehouse. African

Fun Facts

• Scarlet O'Hara's plantation "Tara," as featured in Margaret Mitchell's *Gone with the Wind,* is the most often sought tourist attraction in Georgia. Much to many tourists' dismay, Tara is Mitchell's purely fictional creation.

• Macon, GA has some 100,000 cherry trees—more than Washington, DC.

• The lost Confederate Treasury, monies hidden by Confederate sympathizers at the end of the Civil War, is rumored to be buried somewhere in Lincoln or Wilkes County.

• Atlanta's MARTA is the only subway system in the entire South.

• Stone Mountain in Atlanta is the world's largest-known isolated granite boulder. It is 825 feet high.

Americans serve in many prominent government positions; in fact, it was some 25 years ago that Atlanta became one of the first major Southern cities to elect a black mayor.

A Closer Look

GEOGRAPHY

Georgia, the largest state east of the Mississippi River, is geographically diverse. The jagged peaks (some approaching 5,000 feet in elevation in the northeast) of extreme **northern Georgia** rise above hardwood and pine forests, tumbling mountain streams, turbulent rivers, and waterfalls. Broad valleys separated by long, parallel ridges of sandstone characterize northwestern Georgia, while the **Blue Ridge Region** in the northeastern corner of the state has the steepest promontories. Atlanta, capital of the New South and site of the 1996 Summer Olympics, is the jewel city of this region.

    Central Georgia contains rolling hills, many lakes, and more gently flowing rivers. Descending from the mountains, the terrain drops to 1,500 feet in elevation through a broad region called the **Piedmont.** Macon, in the geographic center of the state, is this area's major city.

    Two coastal plains cover **southern Georgia.** The eastern Atlantic Coastal Plain is flat and identified by light, sandy terrain and slow moving rivers. Vegetation is dominated by scrub pine, live oaks draped with Spanish moss, palmettos, and underbrush of grasses and small shrubs. Georgia's coastline is over 2,300 miles long (approximately the distance between Atlanta and Boise, ID) if all the bays, offshore islands, and river mouths are included. Twelve barrier islands known as the **Golden Isles** protect the mainland and provide endless miles of pristine beaches. Rivers in the East Coast Coastal Plain in southwest Georgia empty into the Gulf of Mexico. Georgia's "West Coast" is formed by the mighty **Chattahoochee River,** which forms the border be-

---

DRIVING DISTANCES

Atlanta

114 mi S of Chattanooga, TN
139 mi W of Augusta
150 mi E of Birmingham, AL
197 mi S of Asheville, NC
215 mi SW of Columbia, SC
249 mi NE of Savannah

Columbus

83 mi E of Montgomery, AL
123 mi SW of Atlanta
139 mi SE of Birmingham, AL
159 mi NE of Mobile, AL
190 mi N of Tallahassee, FL
255 mi W of Savannah

Savannah

106 mi S of Charleston, SC
142 mi S of Columbia, SC
147 mi N of Jacksonville, FL
244 mi NE of Tallahassee, FL
249 mi SE of Atlanta
255 mi E of Columbus

---

tween the state and Alabama.

CLIMATE

Because of its latitude and proximity to the warm waters of the Gulf of Mexico, Georgia enjoys mild temperatures year-round and winters that are short and mild. Barring an occasional rogue gale, only the northern mountains experience snow and cold temperatures, and then only a few times a year. Cool summers characterize the mountainous regions, while the Piedmont has hot (but not overly humid) summers. The southern areas of the state are the hottest and the most humid. Fortunately, an ever-present sea breeze helps to moderate the high summer temperatures of the coast and barrier islands.

WHAT TO PACK

Georgia's mild temperatures make packing easy. Except during the winter in the mountainous regions, you almost never need a coat. Average winters require only a heavy jacket; hats, gloves, and boots are rarely needed. During summer in the mountains, you'll need a jacket or sweater in the evening. Cool, cotton clothing is appropriate throughout the state for nine months out of the year. Georgians, as a rule, tend to dress casually, although upscale resorts and some restaurants are dressier by night. Pack sturdy walking or hiking shoes and, if you're going to be spending a lot of time in the wilds, long pants are recommended to guard against ticks and mosquitoes.

TOURIST INFORMATION

For a free state map and a copy of *Georgia on My Mind,* a comprehensive guide to the state's many attractions, events, and accommodations, contact the **Georgia Department of Industry, Trade, and Tourism** at PO Box 1776, Atlanta, GA 30301 (tel 404/656-3590). Another organization that provides statewide information is the **Georgia Hospitality and Travel Association,** 600 W Peachtree St, Ste 1500, Atlanta, GA 30308 (tel 404/873-4482). The

Georgia Online Network maintains a Web page (http://www.state.ga.us) with general information about the state. To find out how to obtain tourist information for individual cities and parks in Georgia, look under specific cities in the listings section of this book.

DRIVING RULES AND REGULATIONS

The minimum age for drivers is 16. Unless otherwise noted, the speed limit on urban highways is 55 mph; 65 mph on rural interstates. Use of seat belts by the driver and any passenger under 18 is mandatory. Children under three years old must be secured in an approved child safety seat, and motorcyclists must wear a helmet. Auto insurance is mandatory and the registration and proof of insurance must be carried in the car. Right turns are allowed after stops at red lights. It is illegal to carry an open container of alcohol within arm's length of the driver.

AVG MONTHLY TEMPS (°F) & RAINFALL (IN)		
	Atlanta	Savannah
Jan	47/3.9	55/5.5
Feb	45/4.4	50/3.6
Mar	52/5.7	57/8.0
Apr	59/2.8	62/3.2
May	71/4.9	74/1.3
June	79/6.0	81/2.5
July	85/3.0	87/4.3
Aug	82/3.0	83/3.0
Sept	77/3.9	80/6.8
Oct	63/3.8	68/2.6
Nov	54/4.0	60/5.3
Dec	45/2.5	50/2.1

RENTING A CAR

All of the major car rental firms have offices statewide. Minimum age requirements vary and are set by the rental company. Collision Damage Waiver protection is sold separately, but check your credit card or auto insurance to see if you are already covered. To get the best rental rate, make your reservations as far in advance as possible.

- **Alamo** (tel toll free 800/327-9633)
- **Avis** (tel 800/831-2847)
- **Budget** (tel 800/527-0700)
- **Dollar** (tel 800/800-4000)
- **Hertz** (tel 800/654-3131)
- **National** (tel 800/227-7368)
- **Thrifty** (tel 800/367-2277)

ESSENTIALS

Area Code: The area code for the Atlanta metropolitan area (the area inside the I-285 perimeter) is **404**; the surrounding counties are now in **770**. Calls between the two zones are local but require dialing the area code. The rest of the northern part of the state, which includes Athens and Rome and extends down the western border of the state to Columbus, is **706**. The southern part of the state (including Macon, Savannah, Thomasville, and Valdosta) is in **912**.

Emergencies: To summon police, ambulance, or fire department, call 911.

Liquor Laws: You must be 21 years old and have proper identification to purchase or consume alcoholic beverages in Georgia. Local liquor laws vary widely: some counties are dry; others sell only beer and wine.

Road Info: To inquire about road conditions, call 404/656-5882 (weekdays 8:15am-4:45pm) or 404/656-5267 (nights and weekends).

Smoking: Smoking regulations are set at the local level. In some, but not all, local jurisdictions, restaurants are required to provide both nonsmoking and smoking sections. Many hotels offer nonsmoking guest rooms.

Taxes: The state sales tax is 4% and applies to most purchases (including food and beverages); local jurisdictions often add another percentage or two. Hotel taxes vary by county, but range from 5%-8%.

Time Zone: Georgia is in the Eastern time zone and the entire state observes daylight saving time.

Best of the State
WHAT TO SEE AND DO

Below is a general overview of some of the top sights and attractions in Georgia. To find out more detailed information, look under "Attractions" under individual cities in the listings portion of this book.

National Parks Several of the most enchanting parks in the national park system are found in Georgia. **Cumberland Island National Seashore** is an unspoiled and almost uninhabited barrier island with 20 miles of wide, flat, undeveloped beach and heavily wooded maritime forest. Wildlife includes a vast array of birds, alligators, deer, wild horses, sea turtles, and armadillos. Access is by ferry from St Marys; a mere 300 visitors are permitted on the island each day and no vehicles are allowed except those of park rangers and residents. Camping is available at one developed and several primitive campsites. Visitors may partake in fishing, hiking, shelling, wildlife observation, and wandering around several abandoned Carnegie mansions. A small museum chronicles the island's history.

Called by Native Americans the "land of the trembling earth," the untarnished wilderness of southeastern Georgia's intriguing 438,000-acre **Okefenokee Swamp National Wildlife Refuge** is the largest and most ecologically intact swamp in the country. The swamp is a mecca for canoeists, primitive campers, bird watchers, hikers, and fishing enthusiasts. Outdoor enthusiasts visiting Atlanta can find plenty of opportunities for rafting, canoeing, kayaking, rowing, fishing, hiking, mountain biking, and wildlife observation at the 14 units of the **Chattahoochee River National Recreation Area.** Georgia has two National Forests—the **Chattahoochee National Forest** (with 750,000 acres in the north Georgia mountains), and the **Oconee National Forest** (with 110,000 acres in the Piedmont region).

State Parks   Georgia is blessed with an extensive system of 58 state parks and historic sites that provide camping, hiking, fishing, boating, and biking. Some feature tennis courts, golf courses, and/or horseback riding. Many provide accommodations in lodges and cottages. Call the Department of Natural Resources at 404/656-3530 for more information.

Natural Wonders   Georgia is crammed with natural wonders. Among the most impressive are the "Seven Wonders of Georgia." **Amicalola Falls,** plummeting 729 feet in Amicalola State Park near Dawsonville, is the state's highest waterfall and one of the tallest in the eastern United States. **Tallulah Falls,** in the northeast mountains, courses through a spectacularly rugged gorge. Known as Georgia's Little Grand Canyon, breathtakingly beautiful **Providence Canyon,** near Lumpkin in the west-central part of the state, was formed by only 100 years of erosion. **Stone Mountain,** near Atlanta, is a gigantic granite outcropping. The restorative qualities of the mineral waters at **Warm Springs,** in west Georgia, attracted polio victims (including Franklin D Roosevelt) and are still being used for therapy. **Radium Springs,** near Albany in southwest Georgia, the state's largest natural spring, offers swimming in waters that remain at 68°F year round. **Okefenokee Swamp,** in southeastern Georgia, rounds out the list of seven (see "National Parks," above).

Manmade Wonders   Man's imprint is everywhere. The mysterious **Rock Eagle Effigy,** a 102-foot by 120-foot prone bird located near Eatonton, was created 6,000 years ago by Native Americans using thousands of stones. Other evidence of ancient peoples are the petroglyphs at the **Trackrock Archaeological Area,** south of Blairsville, and the Mississippian-era mounds at **Etowah Indian Mounds** near Cartersville, the **Kolomoki Indian Mounds** near Blakely, the mounds at the **Ocmulgee National Monument** near Macon, and the **Sautee-Nacoochee Indian Mound** just south of Helen. All the sites except the Sautee-Nacoochee Mound have interpretive museums.

Leaping ahead to this century, the world's largest bas-relief sculpture—on the granite outcropping at **Stone Mountain** near Atlanta—represents Confederate Civil War heroes Jefferson Davis, Robert E Lee, and Stonewall Jackson. Referred to as Georgia's Stonehenge, the **Georgia Guidestones** in Elberton are a set of gigantic granite monoliths inscribed in 12 different ancient languages. The **Walter F George Lock and Dam,** near Fort Gaines off GA 39, is the second-highest lock east of the Mississippi River. An interpretive center features displays and brochures.

Ruins   Remnants of the past are everywhere. The wealthy Carnegie family owned Cumberland Island at the turn of the century and built six vacation mansions there. **Dungeness,** the largest, burned down several years ago but visitors can still wander around the perimeter of the picturesque ruins. See where sugar cane was ground, boiled, and processed at the **McIntosh Sugar Mill Tabby Ruins** near St Marys.

Family Favorites   Always popular with families are amusement parks such as **Six Flags Over Georgia** in Marietta, Malibu Grand Prix (with two locations near Atlanta), or water parks such as **White Water/American Adventures** in Marietta. Stone Mountain Park, east of Atlanta, is a 3,200-acre park with an antebellum plantation, a train ride pulled by a steam-driven locomotive, a paddle wheel riverboat, museums filled with antique cars and Civil War memorabilia, and a nightly laser-light show in summer. **Rock City Gardens,** part of the Lookout Mountain complex near Chattanooga, TN, is actually located in Georgia. The famous park features unique rock formations, lush gardens, Fairyland Caverns, and a Mother Goose Village. See a century of memorabilia connected to the world's best-known soft drink at Atlanta's **World of Coca-Cola.** The Cabbage Patch Kids dolls are "born" at **Babyland General Hospital** in Cleveland. At the outdoor **Southeastern Railway Museum,** Duluth, you can explore restored and unrestored railway cars. The **Big Shanty Museum,** Kennesaw, houses a famous train that was kidnapped by Union soldiers during the Civil War. In Atlanta, **SciTrek** offers more than 100 hands-on exhibits, while the **Center for Puppetry Arts** is the largest center of its kind in the country.

Beaches Life breezes along at a languid pace on Georgia's Golden Isles. Each of the Peach State's barrier islands has a different personality. **Tybee Island,** off the coast of Savannah, retains a 1950s ambience with miles of uncrowded beaches and lots of mom-and-pop motels. The beach at **Skidaway Island State Park** is also uncrowded, but not as uncrowded as **Little St Simons,** a private island that accepts only 24 guests at a time. **St Simons Island** is the most-visited of the barrier islands, while **Sea Island,** an enclave of the wealthy, is the home of one of Georgia's most exclusive properties, The Cloister. Development has also been restricted on **Jekyll Island,** near Brunswick. Last, but certainly not least, 20 miles of pristine beaches are preserved forever at **Cumberland Island National Seashore** near the Florida state border.

Historic Buildings & Sites Georgia's past as a wealthy commercial center and playground for the rich have left it with a remarkable architectural legacy. Savannah's **National Historic Landmark District,** one of the largest in the country, covers 2 square miles and preserves more than 1,400 structures, most of them from the 18th century. Elaborate wrought-iron ornamentation is used in all styles of buildings—from Greek revival mansions to Romanesque civic offices to Gothic villas—to create the unique Savannah style. The **Jekyll Island Historic Landmark District** safeguards the palatial "cottages" of the millionaires who owned the island at the turn of the century.

Some other "don't miss" homes to visit in Georgia are **Roosevelt's Little White House Historic Site,** FDR's home in Warm Springs; the **Hofwyl-Broadfield Plantation** in Brunswick; **Hay House,** Macon, an elaborate Italianate Renaissance Revival mansion; **Pebble Hill Plantation,** Thomasville, a winter resort home; and **Heritage Corner,** Columbus, a collection of five houses including that of John Stith Pemberton—creator of Coca-Cola. The most visited spot in Atlanta is the **Martin Luther King Jr National Historic Site** encompassing Dr King's Birth Home, Ebenezer Baptist Church, and the Freedom Hall Complex which includes the civil rights leader's grave site.

A state that has always played a major role in defense, Georgia has preserved many of its forts including **Fort King George** near Darien, **Morris** near Midway, **McAllister** near Richmond Hill, **Frederica** on St Simons, **Jackson** and **Pulaski** near Savannah, **Screven** on Tybee Island, and **Benjamin Hawkins** near Macon. All are open for tours.

Museums The **High Museum of Art** in Atlanta and the **Columbus Museum of Art** in Columbus both feature exceptional collections of 18th- and 19th-century American art. Several museums chronicle Atlanta's history: the **Atlanta History Center** at Underground Atlanta; and the **Cyclorama** in Atlanta's Grant Park. Georgia's gold rush is illustrated at the **Dahlonega Courthouse Gold Museum.** The **Museum of Aviation,** Warner Robins, is the Southeast's fastest growing aviation museum. Two living history museums provide glimpses of life in 19th century Georgia: the **Georgia Agrirama,** Tifton, has 35 buildings that make up a restored town and several farms; buildings relocated to **Westville,** Lumpkin, recreate a rural Georgia town of 1850. Both sites feature costumed guides demonstrating pioneer skills.

Gardens The Peach State's balmy climate keeps nature's bounty blooming year-round. One of the most beloved spots in Georgia is **Callaway Gardens** in Pine Mountain, with 1,400 acres of formal and informal gardens, an indoor/outdoor conservatory, and an impressive free-flight butterfly center. Other "don't miss" gardens include **Barnsley Gardens** in Adairsville, which contains several old-fashioned gardens typical of an antebellum plantation; **Rock City Gardens** in Lookout Mountain, a series of informal gardens scattered among some of nature's most unusual rock formations; the **Atlanta Botanical Garden**, which features a formal Japanese tea garden; the **State Botanical Garden of Georgia** in Athens, which contains five miles of trails and gardens; and the **Rose Test Gardens** in Thomasville, where more than 250 varieties of roses are showcased.

Parks & Zoos Zoo Atlanta is particularly renowned for its primate collection and natural habitats. Several other wild animal parks provide an opportunity to see unusual wildlife: **Chehaw Wild Animal Park** in Albany; **Pine Mountain Wild Animal Park** in Pine Mountain; and **Yellow River Wildlife Game Ranch** in Lilburn. Each has a petting zoo that permits children to get up close and personal with wriggling critters.

EVENTS AND FESTIVALS

ATLANTA AND NORTH GEORGIA

* **Georgia Renaissance Festival,** Atlanta. Roving minstrels, rope walkers, jugglers, jousting, food. Six weekends in spring, four in fall. Call 770/964-8575.
* **Atlanta Dogwood Festival,** Atlanta. Art, hot-air balloons, food, hole-in-one golf contest, canine Frisbee championships, music. Second week in April. Call 770/952-9151.
* **Prater's Mill Country Fair,** Dalton. Crafts demonstrations, working gristmill, country store, arts and crafts festival. First weekend in May and October. Call 706/275-MILL.
* **Georgia Mountain Fair,** Hiawassee. Pioneer exhibits and demonstrations, national entertainers. August. Call 706/896-4191.
* **Helen's Oktoberfest,** Helen. German food, music, arts and crafts. September and October. Call 706/878-2181.

COLUMBUS AND SOUTHWEST GEORGIA

* **Andersonville Historic Fair and Civil War Re-enactment,** Andersonville. Civil War re-enactments, old-time artisans; dealers selling antiques, crafts, and Civil War items. Last weekend in May and first weekend in October. Call 912/924-2558.
* **Powers' Crossroads Country Fair and Art Festival,** Newnan. Arts and crafts, entertainment, food. Labor Day weekend. Call 770/253-2011.
* **Big Pig Jig Barbecue Cooking Championship,** Vienna. Barbecue competition, entertainment,

arts and crafts, midway. First week in October. Call 912/268-8275.
* **Fantasy in Lights,** Callaway Gardens Resort, Pine Mountain. Five-mile Christmas light extravaganza. Thanksgiving through New Years Day. Call 706/663-2281.

SAVANNAH AND SOUTHEAST GEORGIA

* **Augusta Futurity,** Augusta. Largest cutting-horse tournament east of the Mississippi. January. Call 706/724-0851.
* **Cherry Blossom Festival,** Macon. Mid-March. Call 912/751-7429.
* **St Patrick's Day Celebration,** Dublin. Parades, beauty contests, and the wearin' o' the green. Mid-March. Call 912/272-1822.
* **River Race Augusta,** Augusta. Premier event of the International Outboard Grand Prix Series. June. Call 706/860-6890.
* **Hardee's Augusta Southern Nationals Dragboat Races,** Augusta. July. Call 706/724-2452.
* **Savannah Maritime Festival,** Savannah. Activities related to the area's maritime heritage, with an emphasis on water sports and seafood. July through August. Call 912/236-3959.
* **Christmas in Savannah,** Savannah. A month of activities and tours of historic homes. Call toll free 800/444-CHARM.

SPECTATOR SPORTS

Auto Racing Two NASCAR Winston Cup races and the Busch Grand National, as well as IMSA and ARCA events, are run at the **Atlanta Motor Speedway** in Hampton just south of Atlanta (tel 770/946-4211). Gainesville's **Road Atlanta** (tel 770/967-6143) is the home of the Sports Car Club of America National Championship Race, while **Lanier Raceway** (tel 770/967-2131), also in Gainesville, sponsors a sanctioned NASCAR-Winston Racing Series. The quarter-mile track at **New Atlanta Dragway** in Commerce (tel 706/335-2301) hosts races every Saturday night.

Baseball America's team, the 1995 World Series champion **Atlanta Braves,** play at the new Olympic Stadium. For information about tickets, call Ticketmaster (tel 404/249-6400). There are five class-A teams in the state: the **Columbus Redstixx** (tel 706/571-8866) play at Golden Park; the **Macon Braves** (tel 912/745-8942) play at Luther Williams Stadium; the **Savannah Cardinals** (tel 912/351-

9150) play at Grayson Stadium; the **Augusta Green Jackets** (tel 706/736-7889) play at Lake Olmstead Stadium; and the **Albany Polecats** (tel 912/435-6444), a favorite of many minor-league fans because of their unique logo, play at Polecats Park.

Basketball The 17,000-seat Omni Coliseum is home to the NBA's **Atlanta Hawks** (tel 404/249-6400). College basketball fans can see the **Yellow Jackets** of Georgia Tech play at Alexander Memorial Coliseum/McDonald's Center (tel 404/894-5447) or watch the **University of Georgia Bulldogs** play at the UGA Coliseum in Athens (tel 706/542-1231).

College Football College football is akin to a religious cult in Georgia. Fans at the University of Georgia are taught to bark and everyone knows the meaning of "How 'Bout Them Dawgs?" You can watch the **UGA Bulldogs** (tel 706/542-1231) play "between the hedges" at Sanford Stadium in Athens. Fans of the Ramblin' Wreck from Georgia Tech can watch the **Yellow Jackets** (tel 404/894-5447) play at Bobby Dodd Stadium in Atlanta. The **Peach Bowl** (tel 404/586-8499) is played at the Georgia Dome in Atlanta every New Year.

Pro Football The NFL's **Atlanta Falcons** (tel 404/223-9200) play at the new ultramodern Georgia Dome, site of Super Bowl XXVIII and many 1996 Olympic events.

Hockey Hockey fans can catch an exciting game between the **Atlanta Knights** (tel 404/420-5000) and their competitors in the International Hockey League at the Omni Coliseum.

ACTIVITIES A TO Z

Bicycling Georgia's terrain offers a wide variety of biking experiences from rigorous mountain cycling to leisurely pedaling. Your best resource for information is the free *Georgia Bicycle Touring Guide*, which includes ten popular touring routes with terrain maps and lists of state parks along the way. Request a copy from the Tourism Division of the **Georgia Department of Industry, Trade and Tourism,** PO Box 1776, Atlanta, GA 30301 (tel 404/656-3590).

Camping Georgia's 39 state park campgrounds cater to tent, trailer, and RV campers; backpackers; and pioneer campers alike, and range from the ocean's edge to the highest mountain peak. For information, contact **Georgia State Parks and His-**toric Sites (tel toll free 800/5GA-PARK outside GA). Many of the state's lakes were created by the US Corps of Engineers, which supports several campsites as well. Contact the **US Corps of Engineers** (tel 404/688-7870 for Lake Allatoona; tel 770/945-9531 for Lake Lanier). **Georgia Power Company,** Georgia's electric utility, maintains several lakes for hydroelectric power generation and has developed recreation areas with campgrounds to give the public access to the lakes. For information about their facilities, contact them at 404/329-1455. Among the most-sought-after destinations for primitive camping are Cumberland Island and the Okefenokee Swamp. Due to their extreme popularity, reservations must be made months in advance. The **Georgia Department of Industry, Trade and Tourism** (tel 404/656-3590) can provide you with a list of private campgrounds.

Climbing The craggy mountains of north Georgia provide some of the best rock climbing in the Southeast. Exceptional Georgia sites include Mount Yonah and Tallulah Gorge (for experts), and Curahee Mountain, Pigeon Mountain, and Lookout Mountain. For advice, directions, instruction, and/or equipment contact **Call of the Wild,** Roswell (tel 770/992-5400). Other sources of instruction (all in Atlanta) are the **Atlanta Climbing Club** (tel 770/621-5070), the **Challenge Rock Climbing School** (tel 404/237-4021), and the **Sporting Club at Windy Hill** (tel 770/953-1100).

Fishing The Peach State offers a wide variety of fishing experiences, from deep-sea excursions or surf casting along the coastal beaches to angling in the tidal marshes, dipping your pole into the state's many lakes, and challenging your skills in tumbling mountain streams. Some premier spots include the Augusta Canal off the Savannah River in eastern Georgia, the Okefenokee Swamp in the southern part of the state, and the Waters Creek Trophy Trout Stream in the north Georgia mountains. For more information, contact the **Georgia Department of Natural Resources, Game and Fish Division** (tel 404/656-3524).

Golf Golf has a long tradition in Georgia, beginning in 1736 when a group of Scottish settlers laid out a course near the present coastal village of Darien. That legacy continued through the historic 1898 Oceanside course (used exclusively by a group of millionaires on Jekyll Island) and the hallowed

Augusta National (site of the Masters Tournament). Today, the state is home to over 300 courses, including the one at the **Château Elan Winery** in Braselton (tel toll free 800/233-9463). Five of Georgia's **state parks** sport golf courses: **Georgia Veterans Memorial** in Cordele (tel 912/276-2377); **Gordonia-Altamaha** in Reidsville (tel 912/557-6444); **Hard Labor Creek** in Rutledge (tel 706/557-2863); **Little Ocmulgee** in McRae (tel 912/868-7474); and **Victoria Bryant** in Royston (tel 706/245-6776).

Hang Gliding Lookout Mountain, on the Georgia/Tennessee border, provides excellent conditions for hang gliding. You can learn the sport at the **Lookout Mountain Flight Park and Training Center** (tel toll free 800/688-LMFP), where certified instructors provide daily lessons; rental equipment is also available, as are clinics, meets, and competitions. For more information about hang gliding, contact the **Georgia Hang Gliding Association,** c/o US Hang Gliding Association, Colorado Springs, CO 80933 (tel 719/632-8300).

Hiking Georgia is crisscrossed with a network of nationally renowned trails. The southern terminus of the Appalachian Trail, the most hiked footpath in the state, is located at Springer Mountain. The 50-mile Georgia segment of the 250-mile figure-eight-shaped Benton MacKaye Trail provides access and alternatives to the Appalachian Trail. The William Bartram Trail traces 37 miles of the route taken by the 18th-century explorer along the Georgia/North Carolina border. For information about these trails and others in the Chattahoochee National Forest, request the pamphlets *Directory to the Chattahoochee-Oconee National Forests Recreation Areas* and/or *Trail Guide to the Chattahoochee-Oconee National Forests* from the Forest Supervisor, US Forest Supervisor, 508 Oak St, NW, Gainesville, GA 30501 (tel 770/536-0541). To learn more about hiking in state parks and historic sites, contact **Georgia State Parks and Historic Sites** (tel 404/656-3590).

Horseback Riding The FDR Stables at **Franklin D Roosevelt State Park** in Pine Mountain (tel 706/628-4533) provide overnight horseback riding trips complete with chuck wagon cookouts, storytelling, and singing around the campfire. The stable also offers trail rides from one hour to five days in length. Rides on the beach originate at **Sea Island Stables** (tel 912/638-1032).

Pack Trips One of the newest fads in hiking is using a llama to carry your gear. **Hawksbell Farm** (tel 706/259-9310) offers llama treks in the Chattahoochee National Forest; lunch is included and they even bring hammocks so you can take an afternoon snooze. **Eagle Adventure Company** in McCaysville (tel toll free 800/288-3245) also offers llama treks.

Sailing Georgia offers sailing opportunities for every level of experience and in every setting from coastal inlets to tranquil lakes. Many coastal and inland marinas maintain rental fleets and offer instruction and/or skippered cruises. For coastal instruction or rentals, contact **Dunbar Sales, Inc** in St Simons (tel toll free 800/282-1411) or **Sail Harbor** in Savannah (tel 912/897-2135). Inland choices include **Lanier Sailing Academy Ltd** in Marietta (tel 770/945-8810) and **Windsong Sailing Academy** in Lithonia (tel 770/256-6700).

Skiing Yes, *snow* skiing. **Sky Valley Resort** (tel 706/746-5301), in the extreme northeastern corner of the state, is one of the southernmost ski resorts in the country. All that's required are temperatures cold enough to be able to use the snow-making equipment. A bunny hill and four slopes ranging in length from 400 to 2,000 feet are served by a double chairlift and rope tow. If conditions are right, you can be playing golf on the resort's course or playing tennis while other members of your party are skiing.

Tennis Georgia's moderate climate is so ideal for year-round tennis that residents and visitors alike take to the sport with a vengeance. In fact, the Atlanta Lawn Tennis Association (ALTA) is the largest and most active tennis association in the country. Most town parks feature tennis courts as do resort hotels and state parks. One of the most popular places to play is at the restored **J P Morgan Tennis Center** on Jekyll Island (tel 912/635-2600).

White-Water Rafting Georgia boasts three of the Top 10 white-water rivers in the country: the Chattooga, the Ocoee, and the Nantahala (although most of the Ocoee and Nantahala are in North Carolina). Five miles of action-packed Class III and IV rapids on the Ocoee were the site of the 1996 Summer Olympic white-water events. Best known as the setting for the movie *Deliverance*, the Chattooga was declared a National Wild and Scenic River in 1974, preserving it in its primitive state. Carving its way down a steep gorge as it tumbles through the Sumter and Chattahoochee National Forests between South

---

SELECTED PARKS & RECREATION AREAS

- **Fort Frederica National Monument,** Rte 9, Box 286-C, St Simons Island, GA 31522 (tel 912/638-3639)
- **Fort Pulaski National Monument,** PO Box 30757, Savannah, GA 31410 (tel 912/786-5787)
- **Ocmulgee National Monument,** 1207 Emery Hwy, Macon, GA 31201 (tel 912/752-8257)
- **Chattahoochee River National Recreation Area,** 1978 Island Ford Pkwy, Dunwoody, GA 30350 (tel 770/399-8070)
- **Okefenokee National Wildlife Refuge,** Rte 2, Box 338, Folkston, GA 31537 (tel 912/496-3331)
- **Cumberland Island National Seashore,** Box 806, St Marys, GA 31558 (tel 912/882-4337)
- **Chickamauga and Chattanooga National Military Park,** PO Box 2128, Fort Oglethorpe, GA 30742 (tel 615/752-5213)
- **Martin Luther King Jr National Historic Site,** c/o National Park Service, 522 Auburn Ave NE, Atlanta, GA 30312 (tel 404/331-5190)
- **A H Stephens State Historic Park,** 2 miles north of I-20, Crawfordville, GA 30631 (tel 706/456-2602)
- **Amicalola Falls State Park,** GA 183, Dawsonville, GA 30534 (tel 706/265-2885)
- **Crooked River State Park,** GA Spur 40, St Marys, GA 31558 (tel 912/882-5256)
- **F D Roosevelt State Park,** GA 190, Pine Mountain, GA 31822 (tel 706/663-4858)
- **Fort McAllister State Historic Park,** GA Spur 144, Richmond Hill, GA 31324 (tel 912/727-2339)
- **George T Bagby State Park,** off Cty Rd 39, Fort Gaines, GA 31751 (tel 912/768-2571)
- **Hard Labor Creek State Park,** US 278, Rutledge, GA 30663 (tel 706/557-2863)
- **Kolomoki Mounds State Historic Park,** off Cty Rd 27, Blakely, GA 31723 (tel 912/723-5296)
- **Little Ocmulgee State Park and Lodge,** US 441, McRae, GA 31055 (tel 912/868-2832)
- **Providence Canyon State Conservation Park,** GA 29C, Lumpkin, GA 31815 (tel 912/838-6202)
- **Red Top Mountain State Park and Lodge,** 1½ miles east of I-75 at exit 123, Cartersville, GA 30120 (tel 770/975-4203)
- **Unicoi State Park and Lodge,** GA 356, Helen, GA 30545 (tel 706/878-2824)

Carolina and Georgia, the Chattooga offers easy to moderate rapids in Section III and tight, technical drops in Section IV. The Chattahoochee, Etowah, and Chestatee Rivers also offer some white water. Outfitters include **Nantahala Outdoor Center** in Clayton (tel toll free 800/232-7238) and **Southeastern Expeditions** in Atlanta (tel toll free 800/868-RAFT). White-water activity isn't restricted to the northern part of the state, however. The Flint River in southwest Georgia provides Class I, II, and III rapids. The **Flint River Outdoor Center** in Thomaston (tel 706/647-2633) offers guided excursions, rentals, and shuttle service.

Driving the State

Start	Helen
Finish	West Point
Distance	Approximately 180 miles
Time	2 days
Highlights	Bavarian village, waterfalls, gold mine, gristmill, Indian mound, general store, covered bridge, nature centers, auto racing, Lake Lanier, football training camp, railway museum, historic homes, Civil War sites, West Point Lake

Emanating as a tiny trickle in the north Georgia mountains, the Chattahoochee River gains power and strength as it flows south—sometimes meandering, sometimes coursing—all the way to the Florida state border. This mighty river provides water and hydroelectric power to a major portion of the state, and endless recreational opportunities to everyone.

This driving tour will focus on the northern section of the river. The Upper Chattahoochee is characterized by the natural beauty of rugged mountains, gentle valleys, deep forests, rolling hills, and winding mountain roads that, coupled with the manmade marvels of Lake Sidney Lanier and West Point Lake, force you into a slower pace. Miles of totally uninhabited wilderness are punctuated by tiny hamlets and small towns, and in some areas you can easily believe that you've been propelled by time machine to the pioneer days of the early 19th century or to the luxury of the antebellum South. In other places—such as sophisticated, cosmopolitan Atlanta—you know that the 21st century is right around the corner.

For additional information on lodgings, dining, and attractions in the region covered by the tour, look under specific cities in the listings portion of this chapter.

The headwaters of the Chattahoochee River are about two hours north of Atlanta or two hours south of Asheville, NC. To reach the area from Atlanta, take I-85 north, then take I-985 north to Gainesville. From Gainesville take US 441 northeast about 16 miles and turn northwest on GA 384, which ends at GA 75. Take GA 75 north to Helen. From Asheville, take I-40/US 23 west to US 441, then south into Georgia and continue 25 miles. Turn west on GA 385 to Clarkesville, from which you will take GA 17 to GA 75, where you will turn north to the first stop:

1. **Helen.** You may wonder how this cutesy Bavarian alpine village ended up in the wilds of the north Georgia mountains. About 25 years ago, as the lumber business declined drastically, tiny Helen was gasping its last breath. When the town fathers got together to see if there was something they could do to save their hamlet, they decided to create a tourist attraction. Soon, Swiss/German facades were slapped onto Victorian building fronts; cobblestones covered narrow, winding alleys; German merchandise was brought into shops tended by costumed storekeepers; and German food made an appearance at the town's only restaurant. It was a huge gamble, but it paid off in a big way. Helen now boasts dozens and dozens of shops, restaurants, and hotels. Despite its completely manufactured appearance, Helen is blessed with the natural beauty of the headwaters of the Chattahoochee, as water burbles over a rock-strewn riverbed. Several of the most popular restaurants and lodgings overlook the river.

The **Welcome Center** in City Hall is a good source of advice and brochures. One of the town's most interesting attractions is the **Museum of the Hills,** Main St, a wax museum portraying the lifestyles of mountaineers at the turn of the century. A significant event in the history of the north Georgia mountains was the discovery of gold in 1836. Although the nation's first gold rush didn't last very long, you can still tour a mine and pan for gold at **Historic Gold Mines of Helen,** off GA 75.

Take GA 75 north of town and turn right onto GA 356 to **Unicoi State Park,** a popular spot for fishing and hiking. A half-mile north is **Anna Ruby Falls,** a 150-foot-high double waterfall.

Return to Helen and continue south on GA 75, making a stop at the **Nora Mill Granary** (a working gristmill where you can buy freshly ground grains of many kinds). Continue south on GA 75 to the **Sautee-Nacoochee Indian Mound,** a remnant of an ancient Native American culture. Turn left onto GA 17 and proceed 2 miles to:

2. **Sautee-Nacoochee,** twin mountain valley communities with rich histories. At the intersection of GA 17 and GA 255 is the **Old Sautee Store,** a 100-year-old museum depicting general stores of the turn of the century. Turn onto GA 255. Almost immediately on the left is the **Sautee-Nacoochee Community Cen-**

75

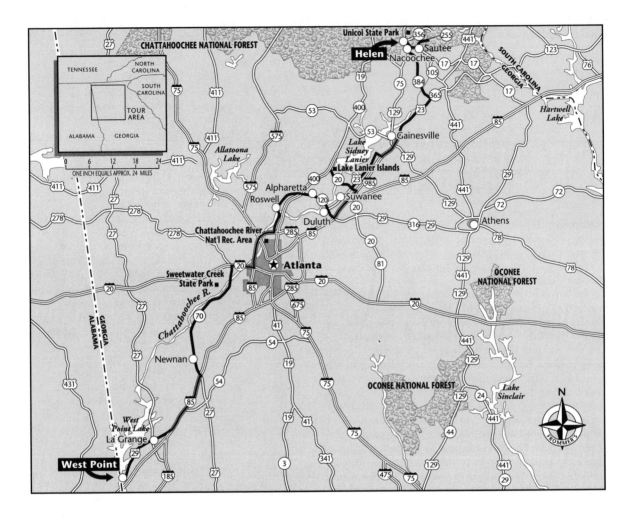

ter, which houses an art gallery and gift shop selling the work of north Georgia artists and a history museum that displays memorabilia from the two valleys. Continue 3 miles north on GA 255 to the **Stovall Covered Bridge.** The 33-foot, one-span Kingpost bridge, built in 1895, is Georgia's smallest covered bridge.

Take a Break

The **Stovall House Country Inn and Restaurant,** on GA 255 (tel 706/878-3355), is located in a historic 1837 farmhouse with wraparound porches and a 360° view of the surrounding valley and mountains. Dinner entrees (which range from $10 to $14) include chicken stuffed with cream cheese, citrus trout, and pork scaloppine—all served with choice of two vegetables.

Retrace GA 255 to GA 17, then back to GA 75. Turn south on GA 75, go 2 miles, and turn onto GA 384. Continue 15 miles south along the river to US 441, which you will take 16 miles southwest to the head of Lake Sidney Lanier and the next stop:

3. **Gainesville,** known as the Poultry Capital of the World. A garden and statuary in **Poultry Park,** Broad and Grove Sts, salute the local poultry industry. Nearby is the **Green Street Station and Georgia Mountains Museum,** 311 Green St SE, which houses eclectic displays of arts and crafts created by north Georgians, antique medical equipment, and the Ed Dodd/Mark Trail collection. (Gainesvillian Dodd was the creator of the first "environmentally correct" comic strip, Mark Trail.) While you're in the neighborhood, tour the **Green Street Historical District** to see the impressive Victorian and neoclassical homes.

Quinlan Arts Center, at the intersection of US 129 and GA 60, displays traveling exhibits of regional, state, and national artists. The natural history museum at the **Elachee Nature Center,** Old Atlanta Hwy, encompasses exhibits, botanical gardens, and nature trails.

If you're interested in motor racing, Gainesville offers two options. **Road Atlanta,** southeast of town on GA 53, is the home of the Sports Car Club of America National Championship Race and features sports-car, motorcycle, and go-cart racing. **Lanier Raceway,** GA 53, features a sanctioned NASCAR-Winston Racing Series.

Skirt Lake Lanier by taking either US 23 or I-985. Go approximately 18 miles south, then turn west on GA 20 about 5 miles and follow the signs to:

4. **Lake Lanier Islands,** a gigantic recreational resort with a beach, water park, boat rentals, horseback riding, and camping. The area is home to two resort hotels: the **Lake Lanier Islands Hilton Resort** (tel 770/945-8787), which offers golf, tennis, heated pool, health club, and boating; and the **Stouffer PineIsle Resort** (tel 770/945-8921), which also features golf, tennis, and water sports.

You might decide to spend the night at one of these upscale hotels. If not, return to GA 20 and I-985. Head south, and after 5 miles turn off the interstate at exit 44 to:

5. **Suwanee,** home of the Atlanta Falcons Training Camp at 2745 Burnette Rd. Some practice sessions of the NFL football team are open to the public in the summer. The remainder of the year you can browse through the NFL gift shop or make use of the fitness center.

Return to the interstate. (At Suwanee, I-985 merges with I-85.) Continue south 4 miles, then take GA 120 another 4 miles west to:

6. **Duluth,** a turn-of-the-century railroad town that is now home to the **Southeast Railway Museum,** 3966 Buford Hwy. An outdoor facility operated by the Atlanta Chapter of the National Railway Historical Society, the complex contains dozens of historic railway cars in various stages of restoration. You can explore the cars or watch work in progress at the machine shop. One Saturday per month, a train carries passengers around the perimeter of the property. (The museum is only open on Saturday.)

Continue 11 miles west on GA 120 to Alpharetta where the route turns south. Drive 6 miles to:

7. **Roswell,** which—although a suburb of Atlanta—has managed to retain its Southern history and character. A logical starting point for your tour is the **Welcome Center,** 617 Atlanta St in the historic downtown square, where you can pick up self-guided walking or driving tour brochures. Roswell features dozens of historic buildings dating back to 1839, and several of the structures are open to the public. One block west of the square is **Bulloch Hall,** 180 Bulloch Ave, the antebellum Greek Revival home of Mittie Bulloch (mother of Theodore Roosevelt). Several of Roswell's most impressive antebellum homes are along Mimosa Blvd, as is the historic Roswell Presbyterian Church and the **Teaching Museum-North,** 791 Mimosa Blvd, where displays of memorabilia relate to education as well as political, social, and historical interests.

A few blocks north of the square is the **Archibald Smith Plantation Home,** 935 Alpharetta St, Roswell's best preserved, unaltered landmark. Lived in by family members until only a few years ago, it is furnished with original pieces and retains authentic outbuildings. Just behind the Smith Plantation are the grounds of the Roswell City Complex. Along the nature trail behind City Hall is the beautiful **Vietnam Memorial,** dedicated in 1995.

Roswell was born and prospered as a textile mill town for more than 125 years. However, during the Civil War, several of the mills were destroyed by Union forces because they were producing gray fabric for Confederate uniforms. The surviving **Roswell Mill** has been transformed into a home for boutiques, restaurants, nightspots, and a summer outdoor music venue.

Less than a mile west on GA 120, turn south on Willeo Rd. On the right you'll come to the **Chattahoochee Nature Center,** 9135 Willeo Rd. Located on the Chattahoochee River, this science education center offers nature trails through the woods and along a pond, a scenic boardwalk across the river marshes, and a rehabilitation program for injured birds of prey.

Roswell has a charming bed-and-breakfast that would make an excellent place to spend the night. The cozy **Ten-Fifty Canton Street Bed and Breakfast,** 1050 Canton St, is located in a restored 1890s house within walking distance of the historic district. Its three guest rooms offer antique-filled decor and private baths.

Leave town via S Atlanta St. At the bottom of the hill, just before you cross the Chattahoochee River, turn left onto Dogwood Dr and make an immediate left into the:

8. **Chattahoochee River National Recreation Area/ Vickery Creek Unit.** As the river meanders its way 48 miles through the metropolitan Atlanta area, this unique urban refuge offers a wide variety of outdoor recreation. At the Vickery Creek Unit, you can fish, enjoy a picnic, or explore 11½ miles of

---

Take a Break

Located in a sprawling 1846 farmhouse on 5½ tree-shaded acres, the **Lickskillet Farm Restaurant,** 1380 Old Roswell Rd (tel 770/475-6484), serves up classic American/Continental cuisine. Light lunch entrees—such as the black-bean burger and the sautéed chicken with lemon and capers—range between $5 and $7. Choices such as Aussie rack of lamb with rosemary plum sauce and snapper Alicia are available at dinner, and cost $12 to $17. The generous Sunday brunch (which includes champagne, pastas, fresh fruit, Belgian waffles, garlic-cheese grits, and a carving station with lamb, pork, and beef) is $17.95.

---

mountainous hiking trails. Just south of the river, turn east onto Roberts Dr and follow it to the **Island Ford Unit,** park headquarters, which provides fishing, picnicking, and several miles of trails. Continue on Roberts Dr (which makes a big loop), turn south at Dunwoody Place, and then exit onto GA 400. Take this road south to I-285 and head west to Powers Ferry Rd. The **Powers Island Unit,** the most frequently used in the system, features raft rentals.

Return to I-285 and proceed approximately 15 miles south. Go west on I-20 one exit to GA 70 and turn south. Continue 7 miles to GA 154 and turn northwest to:

9. **Sweetwater Creek State Conservation Park,** Mount Vernon Rd. The park includes a lake, boat ramp, dock, fishing boats, canoes, lake and stream fishing, and hiking trails.

Retrace GA 154 and turn south on GA 70, which parallels the river as far as Roscoe, where it turns south to:

10. **Newnan,** the quintessential Old South city and county seat of Coweta County. First visit the **Male Academy Museum,** 30 Temple Ave. Among the exhibits are ones devoted to the Civil War, architecture, and *Gone with the Wind,* as well as an impressive collection of period clothing. While you're there, you can pick up a brochure for a driving tour of 23 historic homes, some of which date from the antebellum period. Make prior arrangements to visit **Windemere,** an 1850s Greek Revival plantation house with secret hideaways and an interesting Civil War history.

If you wish to spend the night, there's a bed-and-breakfast at the **Parrott-Camp-Soucy House,** probably the most outstanding example of Second Empire Victorian architecture in the state. The house has been featured in the book *Daughters of the Painted Ladies.*

From Newnan take I-85 south for 32 miles, back to the river and:

11. **LaGrange,** another town with Old South allure. Named for the French estate of the Marquis de Lafayette, the town honors the Revolutionary War hero with a statue and fountain in beautifully landscaped **Lafayette Square.** You can pick up a brochure for the National Register of Historic Places Driving Tour of Troup County from the Troup County Archives, 136 Main St, or the Troup County Chamber of Commerce, 224 Main St. Patterned after the Campanile of St Mark's Square in Venice, the **Callaway Memorial Tower,** Truitt and Fourth Ave, was built in 1929 to honor textile magnate Fuller E Callaway Sr. Visit the 1854 Greek Revival **Bellevue,** 204 Ben Hill St, former home of statesman Benjamin Harvey Hill.

Art lovers will want to check out LaGrange's impressive collections. The **Chattahoochee Valley Art Museum,** 112 Hines St, located in a 19th-century jail, houses a collection of 20th-century American art. Named in honor of LaGrange resident and nationally known artist Lamar Dodd, the **Lamar Dodd Art Center,** Forrest Ave on the grounds of LaGrange College, contains works by Dodd as well as Southwestern and Plains Indian art.

US 27, GA 219, GA 109, or US 29 are all choice routes to:

12. **West Point Lake,** and the end of this tour. The 25,900-acre artificial lake provides excellent fishing, and surrounding the lake are 27 day-use areas, 11 campgrounds, 2 marinas, and a wildlife management area. A visitor center and museum are located at the Resource Manager's office, 500 Resource Management Dr.

From West Point Lake, the Chattahoochee River flows south to the Georgia/Florida state border, where it empties into Lake Seminole. From West Point Lake, you can take I-85 south to Montgomery, AL, or return north on I-85 to Atlanta.

Georgia Listings

Albany

Located at head of the Flint River, this center of a pecan- and peanut-producing region was named for Albany, NY, by the Connecticut Yankee who founded the town in 1836. Kolomoki Indian Mounds from AD 800 are preserved here. **Information:** Albany Convention & Visitors Bureau, 225 W Broad Ave, Albany, 21701 (tel 912/434-8700).

HOTEL

≡≡≡ Comfort Suites Merry Acres
1400 Dawson Rd, 31707; or toll free 800/228-5150; fax 912/435-4431. A stylish property featuring a wooden staircase and a large, open lobby. Great for extended stays and for business travelers. **Rooms:** 60 stes. CI 2pm/CO noon. Nonsmoking rms avail. Rooms are comfortable and very well kept. **Amenities:** A/C, cable TV, refrig, dataport. Some units w/whirlpools. All the suites have microwaves; VCRs available on request. **Services:** Babysitting. **Facilities:** 1 restaurant, 1 bar, playground. Property shares pool, fitness center, lounge, restaurant, and meeting facilities with the adjacent Quality Inn. **Rates (CP):** $82–$95 ste. Extra person $5. Children under age 18 stay free. Parking: Outdoor, free. AE, CB, DC, DISC, MC, V.

MOTELS

≡≡ Hampton Inn Albany Mall
806 N Westover Blvd, 31707; tel 912/883-3300 or toll free 800/426-7866; fax 912/435-4092. Nice, new property located off the main bypass in Albany. **Rooms:** 82 rms. CI noon/CO noon. Nonsmoking rms avail. Sofa or recliner available in king rooms for an additional fee. **Amenities:** A/C, cable TV, dataport. Refrigerators can be requested in rooms at a charge per night. **Services:** Pets allowed only for the sight- or hearing-impaired. Coffee available 24 hours. **Facilities:** **Rates (CP):** $51–$55 D. Extra person $5. Children under age 18 stay free. Min stay special events. Parking: Outdoor, free. Weekend rates are lower. AE, CB, DC, DISC, MC, V.

≡≡ Jameson Inn
2720 Dawson Rd, 31707; tel 912/435-3737 or toll free 800/541-3268; fax 912/432-2308. Located right across from the Albany mall. A good place for business travelers and families. **Rooms:** 42 rms and stes. CI 1pm/CO 11am. Nonsmoking rms avail. **Amenities:** A/C, cable TV, dataport. Some units w/whirlpools. **Services:** **Facilities:** **Rates:** $50–$55 S or D; $95–$135 ste. Extra person $4. Children under age 12 stay free. Parking: Outdoor, free. AE, CB, DC, DISC, MC, V.

≡≡≡ Quality Inn Merry Acres
1500 Dawson Rd, PO Box 3349, 31708; tel 912/435-7721 or toll free 800/228-5151; fax 912/439-9386. A motel that does not look like one. The lobby is located in a 1934 manor house, the grounds are well kept, and the area has a "homey" atmosphere. Popular with business travelers. **Rooms:** 110 rms and effic. Executive level. CI 2pm/CO noon. **Amenities:** A/C, cable TV, dataport. All units w/terraces, some w/whirlpools. Quality Choice rooms have wet bars and refrigerators. VCRs available on request. Coffee in rooms. **Services:** Babysitting. **Facilities:** 1 restaurant, 1 bar, playground. Healthworks fitness center in adjacent mall. **Rates (CP):** $53–$64 S or D; $145 effic. Extra person $5. Children under age 18 stay free. Parking: Outdoor, free. AE, CB, DC, DISC, MC, V.

≡≡≡ Ramada Inn
2505 N Slappey Blvd, 31701; tel 912/883-3211 or toll free 800/525-6685; fax 912/883-3211 ext 113. Right off US 82 bypass. Recently renovated. **Rooms:** 158 rms and stes. CI 2pm/CO noon. Nonsmoking rms avail. **Amenities:** A/C, cable TV, dataport. Hair dryers in most rooms. **Services:** Car-rental desk, babysitting. **Facilities:** 1 restaurant, 1 bar, games rm. Adjacent restaurant/club, with entertainment. **Rates:** $54–$65 S or D; $65 ste. Extra person $7. Children under age 18 stay free. Parking: Outdoor, free. AE, CB, DC, DISC, EC, JCB, MC, V.

RESTAURANT

Villa Gargano
1604 N Slappey Blvd; tel 912/436-7265. Slappey Blvd exit off US 82. **Italian.** Very casual, family-owned eatery specializ-

ing in pizza, pasta, chicken, and veal entrees, as well as a variety of subs and hamburgers. The Gargano's shrimp pizza is a favorite. **FYI:** Reservations recommended. Children's menu. Beer and wine only. **Open:** Mon–Thurs 11am–10pm, Fri–Sat 11am–11pm. **Prices:** Main courses $6–$17. AE, MC, V. 🖼️ ⬧

ATTRACTIONS 📷

Thronateeska Heritage Center and Planetarium
100 W Roosevelt Ave; tel 912/432-6955. This multibuilding complex is anchored by the Museum of History and Science, which explores the history, geology, ecology, and culture of southwestern Georgia, and the Wetherbee Planetarium, with evening shows on the second and fourth Thursdays of each month. The site also includes a display consisting of several model trains, and a collection of railroad memorabilia housed in a set of historic railcars. **Open:** Mon–Fri 10am–4pm, Sat noon–4pm. Closed some hols. **$**

Chehaw Park
105 Chehaw Park Rd, Chehaw; tel 912/430-5275. Really two parks in one. The Front of the Park features a 3¼-mile scenic train ride, nature trails, camping facilities, two playgrounds, and a picnic pavilion. The Wild Animal Park (separate admission fee) houses native and exotic wildlife in natural habitats. **Open:** Daily 9am–sunset. Closed some hols. **$**

Americus

See also Plains

Founded in 1832, Americus soon became, and remains today, a prominent agricultural center and a county seat. Its historic district contains many Greek Revival, Victorian, and Gothic Revival homes. Former President Jimmy Carter put nearby Plains on the map. **Information:** Americus–Sumter County Chamber of Commerce, 400 W Lamar St, PO Box 724, Americus, 31709 (tel 912/924-2646).

HOTEL 🏨

≣≣≣≣ Windsor Hotel
125 W Lamar St, 31709; tel 912/924-1555; fax 912/924-1555. Unique Victorian hotel built in 1892, featuring castlelike towers on the outside and 12-foot ceilings on the inside. The beautiful three-story, open atrium lobby is accented with carved golden oak. **Rooms:** 53 rms and stes. CI 3pm/CO noon. Nonsmoking rms avail. Some rooms have beautiful views of downtown. **Amenities:** 🛁 ⚬ 📺 A/C, cable TV w/movies. **Services:** ✕ ⬥ 🖼️ ⬧ Social director. **Facilities:** 🚐 ⬧ 1 restaurant, 1 bar, beauty salon. **Rates:** $70 S or D; $80–$135 ste. Children under age 15 stay free. MAP rates avail. Parking: Outdoor, free. AE, DC, DISC, MC, V.

ATTRACTION 📷

Jimmy Carter National Historic Site
100 Main St; tel 912/824-3413. Tiny Plains, Georgia (population 716) is world-famous as the hometown of Jimmy Carter, the first person to be elected president from the Deep South since the Civil War. This 77-acre historic site includes a visitors center (housed in a converted 1888 railroad depot) offering self-guided walking tour brochures and auto-tour cassettes as well as a small museum of Carter family memorabilia. Other points of interest in town include the high school that the President and his wife Rosalynn attended, and his boyhood home. The Carters still maintain a residence here. **Open:** Daily 9am–5pm. Closed some hols. **Free**

Andersonville

This village in southwestern Georgia was the site of a notorious Confederate prison camp, where some 12,000 Union soldiers died. Andersonville National Cemetery is also here.

RESTAURANT 🍽️

Andersonville Restaurant
213 W Church; tel 912/928-2980. Off GA 228. **Soul/Southern.** One of the South's famous "meat and threes"—diners get their choice of meat plus three vegetables, homemade biscuits, beverage, and dessert, all for one low price. The house specialty is catfish, but shrimp, chicken, ham, and steak are also available at dinner. **FYI:** Reservations not accepted. Children's menu. No liquor license. **Open:** Lunch Tues–Fri 11:30am–2pm, Sun 11:30am–2pm; dinner Fri 5:30–9pm. **Prices:** Main courses $6–$11. No CC. ♜

Athens

Located on a high bluff above the Oconee River, Athens was spared the wrath of General William T Sherman's Union troops in their infamous "march to the sea." Today, preserved historic homes and buildings stand among stately oaks and elms. Home to the University of Georgia, the first chartered state university (1785) in the country. **Information:** Athens Convention & Visitors Bureau, 200 College Ave, PO Box 948, Athens, 30603 (tel 706/546-1805).

HOTEL 🏨

≣≣≣ Holiday Inn
197 E Broad St, PO Box 1666, 30603; tel 706/549-4433 or toll free 800/TO-ATHEN; fax 706/548-3031. Exceptionally nice property, located near historic district. **Rooms:** 308 rms and stes. CI 2pm/CO noon. Nonsmoking rms avail. **Amenities:** 🛁 ⚬ 📺 A/C, satel TV w/movies, voice mail. Some units w/terraces. **Services:** ✕ ⬥ 🚗 🖼️ ⬧ Car-rental desk, babysitting. Copy, fax, and transparency services. Shuttle service. **Facilities:** 🖼️ 🍴 🚐 💻 ⬧ 1 restaurant, 1 bar,

whirlpool, washer/dryer. **Rates:** $69–$89 S or D; $119–$149 ste. Extra person $10. Children under age 18 stay free. Min stay special events. Parking: Outdoor, free. AE, CB, DC, DISC, JCB, MC, V.

MOTELS

☰☰☰ Courtyard by Marriott

166 Finley St, 30601; tel 706/369-7000 or toll free 800/321-2211; fax 706/548-4224. Off Broad St. Popular with corporate guests and those seeking extended stays. Located near downtown and University of Georgia. **Rooms:** 105 rms and stes. CI 4pm/CO noon. Nonsmoking rms avail. **Amenities:** 🛁 🕹 📺 A/C, cable TV. Some units w/terraces. **Services:** ✗ 🚗 🛆 🛎 Car-rental desk. Shuttles available to Atlanta. Guest passes to local health club. **Facilities:** 🏊 🏐 🎱 & 1 restaurant (bkfst only), 1 bar, whirlpool, washer/dryer. **Rates:** Peak (Sept–Nov) $67 S; $77 D; $95 ste. Extra person $10. Children under age 18 stay free. Lower rates off-season. Parking: Outdoor, free. Higher rates on graduation and football weekends. AE, DC, DISC, MC, V.

☰ Days Inn History Village

295 E Dougherty St, 30601; tel 706/546-0410 or toll free 800/634-3862; fax 706/546-0410. Listed on the National Register of Historic Places. The complex was originally used as a munitions and foundry for the Confederate Army. It looks like a little village, with the pastel-colored buildings looking like separate townhouses. **Rooms:** 115 rms and stes. CI 4pm/CO 11am. Nonsmoking rms avail. Rooms contain only the bare necessities and are not well maintained. **Amenities:** 🛁 🕹 A/C, cable TV. **Services:** 🛎 🚗 Car-rental desk. $50 deposit for pets. **Facilities:** 🏊 🎱 Washer/dryer. **Rates (CP):** $45 S; $50 D; $125 ste. Extra person $10. Children under age 18 stay free. Min stay special events. Parking: Outdoor, free. AE, CB, DC, DISC, MC, V.

☰☰ Ramada Inn

513 W Broad St, 30601; tel 706/546-8122 or toll free 800/448-4245; fax 706/546-8122 ext 586. Basic accommodations, good for an overnight stay. Located three blocks from University of Georgia and downtown Athens. **Rooms:** 160 rms and stes. CI 2pm/CO noon. Nonsmoking rms avail. **Amenities:** 🛁 🕹 📺 A/C, cable TV, dataport. Business services and safe-deposit boxes available. **Services:** ✗ 🚗 🛆 🛎 Car-rental desk. Passes to local health club. **Facilities:** 🏊 🎱 & 1 restaurant, 1 bar (w/entertainment). **Rates:** $60 S; $57 D; $80 ste. Extra person $6. Children under age 18 stay free. Min stay special events. Parking: Outdoor, free. Higher rates on graduation and football weekends. AE, CB, DC, DISC, ER, JCB, MC, V.

☰☰ Travelodge

3791 Atlanta Hwy, Bogart, 30622; tel 706/548-3000 or toll free 800/578-7878; fax 706/353-8114. A typical chain motel offering standard-quality rooms. Located near campus and historic downtown. **Rooms:** 33 rms. CI noon/CO 11am. Nonsmoking rms avail. **Amenities:** 🛁 A/C, cable TV, refrig.

Some units w/whirlpools. **Services:** 🛆 🛎 🍽 **Facilities:** 🏊 & **Rates (CP):** $39–$65 S or D. Extra person $5. Children under age 17 stay free. Min stay special events. Parking: Outdoor, free. AE, DC, DISC, MC, V.

RESTAURANT 🍴

Harry Bissett's New Orleans Cafe

279 E Broad St; tel 706/548-0803. **Cajun/Creole.** Housed in an old, downtown building, with diners sitting in a brick-walled atrium. Menu selections include varied pasta, veal, chicken, and beef combinations, as well as seafood. **FYI:** Reservations not accepted. **Open:** Lunch Tues–Fri 11:30am–3pm; dinner Mon–Thurs 5:30–10pm, Fri–Sat 5:30–11pm, Sun 6–10pm; brunch Sat 11:30am–3:30pm, Sun noon–4pm. **Prices:** Main courses $7–$16. AE, DISC, MC, V.

ATTRACTIONS 🧳

Georgia Museum of Art

Jackson St, North Campus of University of Georgia; tel 706/542-3255. Permanent collection focusing on 19th- and 20th-century American paintings, along with European, American, and Oriental prints and drawings. **Open:** Mon–Sat 9am–5pm, Sun 1–5pm. Closed some hols. **Free**

The State Botanical Garden of Georgia

2450 S Milledge Ave; tel 706/542-1244. Set in a forest along the scenic Oconee River, this 313-acre preserve is made up of 11 botanical collections, including the Rose Garden, Dahlia Garden, Herb Garden, and Shade Garden. Five miles of nature trails enable the visitor to observe a multitude of native plants, wildlife, and birds. New features include the International Garden, which focuses on the role plants have played in global exploration, medicine, and cultures throughout the world. The Garden Room Cafe, located in the Conservatory, serves lunch daily. **Open:** Grounds, daily sunrise–sunset; visitor center, Mon–Sat 9am–4:30pm, Sun 11:30am–4:30pm. Closed some hols. **Free**

Atlanta

See also Buford, Duluth, Kennesaw, Lake Lanier Islands, Marietta, Norcross, Peachtree City, Roswell, Smyrna, Stone Mountain, Suwanee

Settled in 1837, prosperous Atlanta is Georgia's capital and largest city and is the most important commercial, industrial, and financial center in the Southeast. It is a major transportation hub and played host to the 1996 Summer Olympics. Captured and burned by General William T Sherman's army in 1864, the city was rebuilt and officially named the state capital in 1877. Among its many educational institutions are Emory University and the Georgia Institutes of Technology. Chamblee, in the metropolitan area north of Atlanta, features Antique Row, with more than 40 unique shops in historic old homes, churches, and stores, some dating back to the mid-1800s. **Information:** Atlanta Convention & Visitors Bureau, 233 Peachtree St #2000, Atlanta, 30303 (tel 404/ 521-6600).

PUBLIC TRANSPORTATION

The **Metropolitan Atlanta Rapid Transit Authority (MARTA)** runs two subway lines: the **Orange Line,** which runs south–north between the airport and Doraville; and the **Blue Line,** which runs east–west between Indian Creek and Hightower. Fare ($1.25) is payable in exact change, tokens, or TransCard (good for unlimited rail and bus travel for one week; available at the RideStore in the Five Points Station). MARTA **buses** travel on 150 routes; they require exact change ($1.25) or a token, transfer, or TransCard. Call 404/ 848-4711 for MARTA schedule and route information.

HOTELS 🏨

≡≡≡≡ Atlanta Hilton & Towers

255 Courtland St NE, 30303 (Downtown); tel 404/659-2000 or toll free 800/445-8667; fax 404/522-8926. 2 blocks E of Peachtree Center at Harris St. A glamorous, 30-story hotel. Its public areas are a mix of the traditional and the modern, with mahogany-paneled walls and sleek glass elevators. **Rooms:** 1,222 rms and stes. Executive level. CI 3pm/CO 11am. Nonsmoking rms avail. Every room is beautifully decorated with Quaker-style, cherry-finished furniture. **Amenities:** 🛁 🕭 A/C, cable TV w/movies, dataport, voice mail. Some units w/minibars, some w/whirlpools. Business-level rooms offer private registration, concierge service, and private lounge. **Services:** ✕ 🖰 VP 🖅 🕭 Car-rental desk, masseur, children's program, babysitting. **Facilities:** 🛋 🏋 🏊 🏑 🎯 ➁ 🖳 🕭 5 restaurants (*see* "Restaurants" below). Topped by Nikolai's Roof, one of the premier restaurants in town. **Rates:** $165–$185 S; $350–$450 ste. Extra person $20. Children under age 18 stay free. Parking: Indoor, $8/day. AE, CB, DC, DISC, JCB, MC, V.

≡≡≡ Atlanta Marriott Marquis

265 Peachtree Center Ave, 30303 (Downtown); tel 404/ 521-0000 or toll free 800/228-9290; fax 404/586-6299. A hotel designed by John Portman in his classic style, with beautiful glass elevators and a 50-story open atrium. Windows on every floor provide incredible views of downtown Atlanta. The city's largest (but not highest) hotel, the Marriott Marquis has everything—even direct access to Peachtree Center Mall and MARTA. **Rooms:** 1,672 rms and stes. Executive level. CI 4pm/CO noon. Nonsmoking rms avail. Rooms feature pale-peach color scheme, contemporary artwork, custom-designed bed linens, and walnut furnishings. **Amenities:** 🛁 🕭 🎐 A/C, cable TV w/movies, dataport, voice mail. Complimentary copies of *USA Today* delivered to room. **Services:** 🍽 🖰 VP 🖅 🕭 Car-rental desk, masseur, babysitting. Concierge-level rooms include complimentary snacks and beverages, as well as extra services such as nightly bed turndown. **Facilities:** 🛋 🏋 🎯 ➁ 🖳 🕭 4 restaurants, 1 bar, whirlpool, beauty salon. Florist, drugstore, Delta Air Lines

desk, travel agent, and various clothing stores are all on premises. **Rates:** $210 S or D; $350–$900 ste. Children under age 18 stay free. Parking: Indoor, $15/day. AE, CB, DC, DISC, EC, JCB, MC, V.

≡≡≡ Atlanta Marriott Perimeter Center

246 Perimeter Center Pkwy NE, 30346; tel 770/394-6500 or toll free 800/228-9290; fax 770/394-4338. Exit 21 off I-285. A solid, comfortable place to stay. Although it caters to business travelers, this Marriott is also popular with traveling shoppers due to its location next to Perimeter Mall and hundreds of little specialty shops. **Rooms:** 400 rms and stes. CI 4pm/CO 11am. Nonsmoking rms avail. **Amenities:** 🛁 🕭 A/C, cable TV w/movies, dataport, voice mail. **Services:** ✕ 🖰 🚗 🖅 🕭 Car-rental desk, masseur, babysitting. **Facilities:** 🛋 🏊➁ 🏋 🎯 🖳 🕭 1 restaurant, 1 bar, basketball, washer/dryer. **Rates:** $130–$140 S; $150–$160 D; $275 ste. Children under age 18 stay free. Parking: Outdoor, free. AE, DC, DISC, ER, JCB, MC, V.

≡≡≡ Atlanta Renaissance Hotel

590 W Peachtree St NW, 30309 (Midtown); tel 404/ 881-6000 or toll free 800/228-9898; fax 404/815-5012. European-style high-rise hotel, with ultramodern designs and art deco overtones. **Rooms:** 504 rms and stes. Executive level. CI 3pm/CO noon. Nonsmoking rms avail. Most rooms offer a great view of downtown area. **Amenities:** 🛁 🕭 🎐 🎐 A/C, cable TV w/movies, dataport. All units w/minibars, all w/terraces. **Services:** 🍽 🖰 VP 🚗 🖅 🕭 Twice-daily maid svce, car-rental desk, babysitting. **Facilities:** 🛋 🏋 🎯 🖳 🕭 2 restaurants, 2 bars, washer/dryer. German-style pub offers beer and snacks. **Rates:** $155–$220 S; $175–$250 D; $300– $750 ste. Extra person $20. Children under age 18 stay free. Parking: Indoor, $7/day. AE, CB, DC, DISC, EC, ER, JCB, MC, V.

≡≡ Best Western American Hotel

160 Spring St NW, 30303 (Downtown); tel 404/688-8600 or toll free 800/634-1234; fax 404/658-9458. At Williams St. Although the decor is decidedly retro, with late 1950s–early 1960s touches like mirrored columns and blond wood paneling, everything here is in tip-top shape thanks to a recent $2 million renovation. **Rooms:** 321 rms and stes. Executive level. CI 3pm/CO noon. Nonsmoking rms avail. Some rooms have sofas and love seats. **Amenities:** 🛁 🕭 A/C, cable TV w/movies, dataport. **Services:** ✕ 🚗 🖅 🕭 Babysitting. **Facilities:** 🛋 🏋 🎯 🕭 2 restaurants, 1 bar. **Rates:** $159– $179 S or D; $265–$1,200 ste. Extra person $20. Children under age 18 stay free. AP and MAP rates avail. Parking: Indoor, $8/day. AE, CB, JCB.

≡≡ Best Western Bradbury Suites

4500 Circle 75 Pkwy, 30339; tel 770/956-9919 or toll free 800/528-1234; fax 770/955-3270. Exit 110 off I-75. A quiet, pleasing, and beautifully landscaped hotel. A perfect respite for the interstate traveler. **Rooms:** 243 rms and stes. CI 2pm/ CO noon. Nonsmoking rms avail. **Amenities:** 🛁 🕭 🎐 A/C, cable TV. **Services:** 🖼 🍴 Babysitting. **Facilities:** 🏋 160 ♿ Whirlpool. **Rates (BB):** $40–$75 S or D; $65–$75 ste. Extra person $5. Children under age 6 stay free. Parking: Outdoor, free. AE, CB, DC, DISC, MC, V.

≣≣ Best Western Inn at the Peachtree

330 W Peachtree St NW, 30308 (Downtown); tel 404/577-6970 or toll free 800/242-4642; fax 404/659-3244. At Simpson St. A small-scale, charming establishment offering a comfortable alternative to the upscale high-rises of downtown. **Rooms:** 102 rms. CI 2pm/CO 11am. Nonsmoking rms avail. **Amenities:** 🛎 A/C, cable TV. **Services:** 🍽 🖼 🍴 **Facilities:** 50 **Rates (CP):** $59 S; $69 D. Extra person $10. Children under age 12 stay free. Parking: Indoor, free. AE, DC, DISC, JCB, MC, V.

≣≣ Biltmore Peachtree Hotel

330 Peachtree St NE, 30308 (Downtown); tel 404/577-1980 or toll free 800/241-4288; fax 404/688-3706. 2 blocks S of Peachtree Center. Nice, average hotel. A good place to stay for a no-frills visit to the city. **Rooms:** 94 rms. CI 3pm/CO noon. Nonsmoking rms avail. All rooms have spacious, walk-in closets. **Amenities:** 🛎 📺 A/C, cable TV, refrig. **Services:** 🖼 🍴 **Facilities:** 🏋 100 🖥 ♿ **Rates (CP):** Peak (fall/spring) $49–$250 S; $59–$260 D. Children under age 12 stay free. Lower rates off-season. Parking: Outdoor, $8/day. AE, CB, DC, DISC, MC, V.

≣≣ Budgetel Inn

2535 Chantilly Dr NE, 30324 (Buckhead); tel 404/321-0999 or toll free 800/428-3438; fax 404/634-3384. 2 mi S of Lenox Sq. A basic, but comfortable hotel with easy access to the interstate. **Rooms:** 102 rms. CI 2pm/CO noon. Nonsmoking rms avail. All rooms have oak furnishings and attractive prints on the walls, and windows can actually be opened. **Amenities:** 🛎 📺 A/C, cable TV w/movies, dataport. Leisure suites have refrigerators, microwaves, hair dryers, and sofa beds. **Services:** 🍴 Free local calls. **Facilities:** 10 ♿ Washer/dryer. **Rates:** $44–$54 S; $51–$61 D. Extra person $7. Children under age 18 stay free. Parking: Outdoor, free. AE, CB, DC, DISC, MC, V.

≣≣≣ Castlegate Hotel & Conference Center

Howell Mill Rd, 30318; tel 404/351-6100 or toll free 800/824-8657. Exit 104 off I-75. A hotel with a Tudor-style exterior and easy access to downtown. Perfect for corporate travel and conferences in Atlanta. **Rooms:** 365 rms and stes. CI 3pm/CO noon. Nonsmoking rms avail. **Amenities:** 🛎 A/C, cable TV. Some units w/whirlpools. **Services:** ✗ 🚗 🖼 🍴 Babysitting. **Facilities:** 🏋 ⛳ 3500 ♿ 1 restaurant, 1 bar. **Rates:** Peak (Jan–Mar/Sept–Nov) $85–$100 S; $95–$105 D; $150–$275 ste. Children under age 12 stay free. Lower rates off-season. Parking: Outdoor, free. AE, DC, DISC, ER, JCB, MC, V.

≣≣ Comfort Inn

101 International Blvd, 30303 (Downtown); tel 404/524-5555; fax 404/221-0702. 2 blocks E of W Peachtree. An appealingly modern 11-story property offering downtown convenience and comfortable rooms. **Rooms:** 260 rms and stes. CI 3pm/CO noon. Nonsmoking rms avail. Attractive oak furnishings, color-coordinated decor. **Amenities:** 🛎 ❄ A/C, cable TV, voice mail. **Services:** ✗ 🖼 🍴 **Facilities:** 🏋 50 ♿ 1 restaurant. **Rates:** $179 S; $189 D; $209–$299 ste. Extra person $10. Children under age 16 stay free. Parking: Outdoor, $8/day. AE, MC, V.

≣≣ Comfort Inn

4330 Fulton Industrial Blvd, 30336; tel 404/696-2274 or toll free 800/241-7343; fax 404/691-4466. Exit 14 off I-20. Popular with families and overnight guests. **Rooms:** 151 rms and stes. CI 2pm/CO 11am. Nonsmoking rms avail. **Amenities:** 🛎 A/C, cable TV. **Services:** 🍴 **Facilities:** 🏋 ⛳ 25 ♿ Games rm. **Rates:** $40–$55 S; $45–$65 D; $125 ste. Children under age 18 stay free. Parking: Outdoor, free. AE, CB, DC, DISC, MC, V.

≣≣≣ Courtyard by Marriott

1236 Executive Park Dr, 30329; tel 404/728-0708 or toll free 800/321-2211; fax 404/636-4019. Exit 31 off I-85. Located in a quiet neighborhood, not very far from downtown, this hotel is perfect for both business travelers and families. Housed in a four-story stucco building, with an attractively landscaped setting of trees, shrubbery, and well-tended flower beds. **Rooms:** 145 rms and stes. CI 4pm/CO noon. Nonsmoking rms avail. All rooms feature large desks and separate dressing-room areas. Suites have separate living area with sofa bed, and extra phones and TVs. **Amenities:** 🛎 ❄ A/C, cable TV w/movies, voice mail. All units w/terraces. **Services:** 🍽 🖼 🍴 Babysitting. Food-delivery service available. **Facilities:** 🏋 ⛳ 30 ♿ 1 restaurant (bkfst only), 1 bar, whirlpool, washer/dryer. Poolside gazebo. **Rates:** $92 S; $102 D; $106–$121 ste. Extra person $10. Children under age 16 stay free. Parking: Outdoor, free. AE, CB, DC, DISC, MC, V.

UNRATED Courtyard by Marriott

175 Piedmont Ave NE, 30303 (Downtown); tel 404/659-2727 or toll free 800/228-2828; fax 404/577-7805. 3 blocks W of W Peachtree. An aging but well-kept property, with a large and attractive lobby. Especially popular with convention-goers. **Rooms:** 173 rms. CI 3pm/CO noon. Nonsmoking rms avail. **Amenities:** 🛎 ❄ A/C, cable TV w/movies. **Services:** ✗ 🖼 🍴 Many of the staff people have been here for decades. **Facilities:** 🏋 132 ♿ 1 restaurant, 1 bar. **Rates:** $79–$109 S or D. Children under age 16 stay free. Parking: Outdoor, free. AE, CB, DC, DISC, EC, JCB, MC, V.

≣≣ Days Inn Downtown

300 Spring St, 30308 (Downtown); tel 404/523-1144 or toll free 800/329-7466; fax 404/577-8495. 3 blocks W of Peachtree Center at Spring St. A standard but comfortable hotel, offering comfortable no-frills accommodations in the heart of Atlanta's business district. **Rooms:** 263 rms and stes. Executive level. CI 3pm/CO 11am. Nonsmoking rms avail.

Amenities: 🛏 🛁 🖥 A/C, cable TV w/movies, dataport, voice mail, in-rm safe. Some units w/terraces. **Services:** 🚌 🖼 ↵ Babysitting. **Facilities:** 🏊 🍴100 ♿ 1 bar, games rm. **Rates:** $57–$150 S or D; $115–$269 ste. Extra person $10. Children under age 7 stay free. Min stay special events. Parking: Outdoor, $5/day. AE, CB, DC, DISC, ER, MC, V.

Days Inn Peachtree
683 Peachtree St, 30308 (Downtown); tel 404/874-9200 or toll free 800/DAYS-INN; fax 404/873-4245. A small, quaint hotel with a turn-of-the-century atmosphere. Impressive lobby features Persian rugs, a brass chandelier, and a grand piano. **Rooms:** 142 rms and stes. CI 1pm/CO noon. Nonsmoking rms avail. Rooms decorated with nautical- and equestrian-themed prints. Some rooms have sofas. **Amenities:** 🛏 A/C, cable TV w/movies, in-rm safe. 1 unit w/terrace, 1 w/whirlpool. **Services:** ↵ 🍴 Coffee served all day in lobby. Thurs evening cocktail party with complimentary wine, cheeses, and hot hors d'oeuvres. **Facilities:** 🍴25 ♿ Washer/dryer. **Rates (CP):** Peak (Mar–Sept) $69–$79 S or D; $150 ste. Extra person $10. Children under age 12 stay free. Lower rates off-season. Parking: Indoor, $5/day. AE, CB, DC, DISC, MC, V.

DoubleTree Hotel at Concourse
7 Concourse Pkwy, 30328; tel 770/395-3900; fax 770/395-3935. Exit 18 and 20 off I-285 W and E. Nestled among the trees at The Concourse, a 64-acre, wooded corporate convention center, the DoubleTree is perfect for the corporate traveler who likes to be pampered. Beautiful brass-and-wood elevators take guests to and from the elegant rooms. **Rooms:** 370 rms and stes. Executive level. CI 3pm/CO noon. Nonsmoking rms avail. **Amenities:** 🛏 🛁 A/C, cable TV w/movies, dataport, voice mail. 1 unit w/whirlpool. **Services:** 🍴 🔑 VP 🖼 ↵ 🍴 Babysitting. **Facilities:** 🏊 🏋 🍴600 🖥 ♿ 2 restaurants, 2 bars (1 w/entertainment), sauna, whirlpool. Access to nearby fitness center for nominal fee. **Rates:** $140–$160 S; $160–$180 D; $275–$900 ste. Extra person $10. Children under age 18 stay free. Parking: Indoor/outdoor, $8/day. AE, CB, DC, DISC, MC, V.

Embassy Suites
3285 Peachtree Rd, 30326 (Buckhead); tel 404/261-7733 or toll free 800/362-2779; fax 404/261-6857. ½ mi W of Lenox Sq. An all-suite hotel offering a home-away-from-home atmosphere. **Rooms:** 317 stes. CI 3pm/CO noon. Nonsmoking rms avail. **Amenities:** 🛏 🛁 🖥 🍴 A/C, cable TV w/movies, refrig, dataport, voice mail. **Services:** 🍴 VP 🖼 ↵ Free transportation to/from Lenox Mall, Phipps Plaza, Lenox MARTA station, and numerous bars and restaurants. **Facilities:** 🏊 🚲 🍴350 ♿ 1 restaurant (lunch and dinner only), 1 bar, whirlpool, washer/dryer. **Rates (BB):** $129–$169 ste. Children under age 18 stay free. Parking: Indoor, free. AE, CB, DC, DISC, JCB, MC, V.

Embassy Suites Galleria
2815 Akers Mill Road, 30339; tel 770/984-9300 or toll free 800/362-2779; fax 770/955-4183. S on Cobb Pkwy from exit 13 off I-285. Offers spacious, comfortable rooms, and beautiful fountains in its courtyard. **Rooms:** 261 stes. CI 3pm/CO noon. Nonsmoking rms avail. **Amenities:** 🛏 🛁 🖥 A/C, cable TV w/movies, refrig, dataport, voice mail. **Services:** 🍴 🖼 ↵ Babysitting. **Facilities:** 🏊 🍴75 ♿ 1 restaurant (lunch and dinner only), 1 bar, games rm, sauna, whirlpool. **Rates (BB):** $89–$250 ste. Extra person $10. Children under age 12 stay free. Parking: Outdoor, free. AE, CB, DC, DISC, MC, V.

Embassy Suites Hotel Perimeter Center
1030 Crown Pointe Pkwy, 30338; tel 770/394-5454 or toll free 800/362-2779; fax 770/955-4183. Exit 21 off I-285. Attractive and modern, offering spacious and comfortable accommodations. Popular with business travelers due to its location in a commercial park. **Rooms:** 241 stes. CI 3pm/CO noon. Nonsmoking rms avail. Rooms feature Early American–style furnishings and peach color scheme. Many rooms have views of the surrounding woods. **Amenities:** 🛏 🛁 🖥 A/C, cable TV w/movies, refrig, dataport, voice mail. Complimentary morning coffee. **Services:** ✗ 🖼 ↵ **Facilities:** 🏊 🍴35 ♿ 1 restaurant (lunch and dinner only). Guests may use Emory University fitness complex, with indoor pool, 12 night-lit tennis courts, weight machines, and more. **Rates (BB):** $144 ste. Parking: Outdoor, free. AE, MC, V.

The Grand Hotel Atlanta
75 14th St, 30309 (Midtown); tel 404/881-9898 or toll free 800/952-0702; fax 404/873-4692. For a "grand" visit to Atlanta, this is definitely the right hotel. Beautiful marble floors, stately columns, and a three-story lobby with a chandelier give this hotel an elegant air. **Rooms:** 244 rms and stes. CI 3pm/CO noon. Nonsmoking rms avail. Luxurious rooms offer sofa, armoire, marble desk, fine artwork. Lovely baths swathed in marble. **Amenities:** 🛏 🛁 🍴 A/C, cable TV w/movies, in-rm safe, bathrobes. All units w/minibars. **Services:** 🍴 🔑 VP 🖼 ↵ 🍴 Twice-daily maid svce, social director, masseur, children's program, babysitting. 24-hour concierge. Free town-car service. Currency exchange. Newspaper of choice delivered to room. Complimentary shoe shine. **Facilities:** 🏊 🚲 🍴400 🖥 ♿ 2 restaurants, 1 bar (w/entertainment), spa, sauna, steam rm, whirlpool, beauty salon. Well-equipped fitness center has adjoining sundeck and offers aerobics classes. Special children's program includes fun amenities package. Gift shop. **Rates:** $153–$275 S or D; $425–$1,500 ste. Parking: Indoor, $12/day. "Days of beauty" package avail. AE, CB, DC, DISC, MC, V.

Holiday Inn Atlanta Central
418 Armour Dr NE, 30324 (Buckhead); tel 404/873-4661 or toll free 800/282-8222; fax 404/872-1292. Exit 28 off I-85. Although located in an industrial area near the interstate, attractive landscaping and wonderful fountains make this a pleasant and relatively peaceful place to stay. **Rooms:** 322 rms and stes. CI 3pm/CO noon. Nonsmoking rms avail.

Amenities: 🔥 🛗 A/C, cable TV w/movies, dataport. Some units w/whirlpools. **Services:** ✗ 🖼 🛎 🏧 Car-rental desk. **Facilities:** 🏊 🖥 600 🛗 1 restaurant, 1 bar, games rm, beauty salon, washer/dryer. **Rates:** $68–$110 S; $78–$120 D; $150–$300 ste. Extra person $10. Children under age 17 stay free. Parking: Outdoor, free. AE, CB, DC, DISC, JCB, MC, V.

≣≣≣ Holiday Inn at Lenox

3377 Peachtree Rd NE, 30326 (Buckhead); tel 404/264-1111 or toll free 800/526-0247; fax 404/233-7061. An exceptionally attractive Holiday Inn, located near Lenox Square Mall and Phipps Plaza. A short walk to Lenox MARTA station puts all of Atlanta within minutes of the hotel's guests. **Rooms:** 297 rms and stes. CI 4pm/CO 11am. Nonsmoking rms avail. Rooms have coordinated color schemes and oak-trimmed furniture. **Amenities:** 🔥 🛗 A/C, cable TV w/movies, voice mail. Some rooms have refrigerators, and all have Nintendo. **Services:** ✗ 🖼 🛎 Car-rental desk, babysitting. **Facilities:** 🏊 150 🖥 🛗 1 restaurant, washer/dryer. **Rates:** $89–$109 S; $99–$119 D; $175–$225 ste. Extra person $15. Children under age 18 stay free. Parking: Outdoor, free. AE, CB, DC, DISC, EC, MC, V.

≣≣≣ Holiday Inn Crowne Plaza at Ravinia

4355 Ashford-Dunwoody Rd, 30346; tel 770/395-7700 or toll free 800/465-4329; fax 770/392-9503. 2 blocks N of I-285 exit 21, across from Perimeter Mall. A beautifully landscaped and attractive hotel, catering to the corporate traveler. **Rooms:** 500 rms and stes. Executive level. CI 3pm/CO noon. Nonsmoking rms avail. **Amenities:** 🔥 🛗 🍷 A/C, cable TV w/movies, dataport, voice mail. Some units w/minibars, 1 w/fireplace. **Services:** ✗ 🖼 VP 🖼 🛎 Twice-daily maid svce, social director, masseur. **Facilities:** 🏊 🖼 🖥 1500 🖥 🛗 2 restaurants, basketball, spa, sauna, steam rm, whirlpool. **Rates:** $89–$130 S or D; $175–$500 ste. Extra person $10. Children under age 12 stay free. Parking: Outdoor, free. AE, DC, DISC, MC, V.

≣≣≣ Holiday Inn Perimeter Dunwoody

4386 Chamblee Dunwoody Rd, 30341; tel 404/457-6363 or toll free 800/465-4329; fax 404/936-9592. ½ mi S of exit 22 off I-285. A beautiful, top-of-the-line Holiday Inn with art deco decor and comfortable accommodations. **Rooms:** 252 rms and stes. CI 3pm/CO noon. Nonsmoking rms avail. **Amenities:** 🔥 🛗 A/C, cable TV w/movies, voice mail. **Services:** 🖼 🛎 **Facilities:** 🏊 🖼 400 🛗 1 restaurant, 1 bar, washer/dryer. **Rates:** $119 S; $129 D; $325 ste. Extra person $10. MAP rates avail. Parking: Outdoor, free. AE, CB, DC, DISC, MC, V.

≣≣≣≣ Hotel Nikko Atlanta

3300 Peachtree Rd, 30305 (Buckhead); tel 404/365-8100 or toll free 800/645-5687; fax 404/233-5686. A 25-story fusion of Japanese restraint and American swank. Its postmodern architecture includes touches of classic Georgian; the striking marble-columned lobby and lounge features full-length Palladian windows facing a 9,000-sq-ft traditional Japanese garden. Well over a hundred works of original art from two continents adorn the walls. **Rooms:** 440 rms and stes. Executive level. CI 3pm/CO noon. Nonsmoking rms avail. Elegant and efficient but unremarkable furnishings (Lucite-topped desks, too-low desk chairs). Black and pink-marble bathrooms with TV extension speaker. **Amenities:** 🔥 🛗 🍷 A/C, cable TV, refrig, dataport, bathrobes. All units w/minibars, some w/terraces, some w/whirlpools. Exclusive Japanese soaps; Buddhist text alongside Gideon bible in desk drawers. **Services:** 🍽 🗝 VP 🚐 🖼 🛎 Twice-daily maid svce, car-rental desk, masseur, babysitting. 24-hour concierge. Courtesy limo for local transfers. Afternoon tea in lobby lounge. **Facilities:** 🏊 🖥 1000 🖥 🛗 2 restaurants, 3 bars (1 w/entertainment), sauna, steam rm. Health club has handsomely landscaped outdoor lap pool and sundeck (for hotel guests only). Permanently staffed business center (open weekdays only, until 4:30pm). Library Bay with fireplace and live music. **Rates:** $200–$220 S or D; $435–$1,500 ste. Extra person $10. Parking: Indoor/outdoor, $12/day. AE, CB, DC, DISC, JCB, MC, V.

≣≣≣ Hyatt Regency Atlanta

265 Peachtree St NE, 30303 (Downtown); tel 404/577-1234 or toll free 800/233-1234; fax 404/588-4137. 1 block N of Peachtree Center. Designed in 1967 by famed local architect John Portman, this high-rise hotel was the prototype for modern, urban hotel design. Its 23-story open-air atrium and central bank of glass elevators were revolutionary in the late 1960s, but are now seen in hotels all over the world. Two later towers have been added. **Rooms:** 1,279 rms and stes. Executive level. CI 3pm/CO noon. Nonsmoking rms avail. **Amenities:** 🔥 🛗 🍷 A/C, cable TV w/movies, dataport, voice mail. All units w/minibars, some w/terraces. **Services:** ✗ 🗝 VP 🖼 🛎 Car-rental desk, social director, children's program, babysitting. **Facilities:** 🏊 🖥 4000 🖥 🛗 4 restaurants, 2 bars, spa. The blue dome atop the Polaris (the Hyatt's revolving rooftop restaurant) is a landmark of the downtown Atlanta skyline. **Rates:** $170 S; $195 D; $405–$1,175 ste. Extra person $25. Children under age 18 stay free. Parking: Indoor, $15/day. Reduced rate on second room available for large families. AE, CB, DC, DISC, MC, V.

≣≣≣ The Marque of Atlanta

111 Perimeter Center W, 30346; tel 770/396-6800 or toll free 800/683-6100; fax 770/399-5514. Exit 21 off I-285. For a quiet, secluded stay in Atlanta, the Marque is perfect. **Rooms:** 254 rms and stes. Executive level. CI 4pm/CO noon. Nonsmoking rms avail. **Amenities:** 🔥 🛗 🍷 A/C, cable TV w/movies, dataport, voice mail. All units w/terraces. **Services:** ✗ VP 🚐 🖼 🛎 Masseur, babysitting. **Facilities:** 🏊 🖥 100 🖥 🛗 1 restaurant, 1 bar, basketball, whirlpool, washer/dryer. **Rates:** $64–$85 S or D; $74–$102 ste. Extra person $10. Children under age 18 stay free. Parking: Outdoor, free. AE, CB, DC, DISC, MC, V.

≣≣≣ Marriott Suites

35 14th St NE, 30309 (Midtown); tel 404/876-8888 or toll free 800/228-9290; fax 404/876-7727. A very hospitable property—it's clear that the customer's comfort comes first here. Spacious, comfortable suites draw lots of families, and would be great for an extended stay. **Rooms:** 254 stes. CI open/CO noon. Nonsmoking rms avail. All rooms have separate living area with a sofa bed and a desk with an extra phone. Lace-curtained french doors separate living room and bedroom. Most rooms have king-size beds. **Amenities:** 🚗 🐕 🖼 🍷 A/C, cable TV w/movies, refrig, dataport, voice mail. All units w/terraces. Complimentary copies of *USA Today* delivered to rooms. **Services:** 🍽 VP 🖼 ↩ Social director, babysitting. Turndown service (available on request) includes Godiva chocolates. **Facilities:** 🏋 ♨ 🖼150 💻 ⅁ 1 restaurant, 1 bar, spa, washer/dryer. **Rates:** $139 ste. Extra person $20. Children under age 18 stay free. Parking: Indoor, $9/day. AE, MC, V.

≣≣≣ Omni International

1 CNN Center, 30335 (Downtown); tel 404/659-0000 or toll free 800/THE-OMNI; fax 404/818-4322. ½ mi W of W Peachtree St. A self-contained conference center, convenient to Georgia Dome, Underground Atlanta, and other downtown attractions. Modern marble lobby features glass elevators and a 15-floor atrium. Perfect for corporate travel, but still provides plenty of entertainment options. **Rooms:** 457 rms and stes. CI 3pm/CO noon. Nonsmoking rms avail. **Amenities:** 🚗 🐕 🍷 A/C, cable TV w/movies, voice mail. All units w/minibars, some w/terraces. **Services:** ✗ 🗝 VP 🖼 ↩ Twice-daily maid svce, children's program, babysitting. Tennis and golf privileges. **Facilities:** ♨ 🖼2000 💻 ⅁ 2 restaurants, 1 bar (w/entertainment), sauna, steam rm, whirlpool. **Rates:** Peak (Feb–May/Sept–Dec) $180–$240 S; $200–$260 D; $500–$1,000 ste. Extra person $20. Children under age 17 stay free. Min stay special events. Lower rates off-season. Parking: Indoor, $9/day. AE, CB, DC, DISC, EC, ER, JCB, MC, V.

≣≣≣ Quality Hotel

89 Luckie St NW, 30303 (Downtown); tel 404/524-7991 or toll free 800/242-4551; fax 404/524-0672. Secluded in a quiet section of downtown, it's a nice alternative to upscale hotels and the hustle of downtown Atlanta. **Rooms:** 65 rms and stes. CI 3pm/CO noon. Nonsmoking rms avail. **Amenities:** 🚗 🐕 A/C, cable TV. **Services:** ✗ VP 🖼 **Facilities:** ♨ 🖼175 💻 ⅁ 1 restaurant (lunch and dinner only), washer/dryer. **Rates:** $75–$95 S; $85–$105 D; $150–$375 ste. Parking: Indoor, $7/day. AE, CB, DC, DISC, JCB, MC, V.

≣≣ The Ramada Hotel Downtown

70 John Wesley Dobbs Ave, 30303 (Downtown); tel 404/659-2660 or toll free 800/241-3828; fax 404/524-5390. Exit 97 and 98 off I-75/85 N and S. Housed in an eight-story cream-colored stucco building, this is a simple and convenient hotel with access to downtown areas. **Rooms:** 224 rms and stes. CI 3pm/CO noon. Nonsmoking rms avail. Some rooms are very small; all are furnished with traditional cherry-wood furniture. **Amenities:** 🚗 🐕 A/C, cable TV. **Services:** 🍽 VP 🚐 🖼 ↩ Twice-daily maid svce, social director, babysitting. **Facilities:** 🏋450 💻 ⅁ Games rm. Use of nearby health club for nominal fee. **Rates:** $69 S; $79 D; $125 ste. Extra person $10. Children under age 18 stay free. Parking: Indoor, AE, CB, DC, DISC, MC, V.

≣≣≣≣ Renaissance Waverly Hotel

2450 Galleria Pkwy, 30339; tel 770/953-4500 or toll free 800/468-3571; fax 770/953-0740. 1 block S of exit 13 off I-285. Built in a well-landscaped commercial district adjacent to Cumberland Mall and Cobb Galleria Centre convention facility, this luxurious hotel is perfect for corporate travelers. **Rooms:** 521 rms and stes. Executive level. CI 3pm/CO noon. Nonsmoking rms avail. **Amenities:** 🚗 🐕 🖼 A/C, cable TV w/movies. Some units w/minibars. Complimentary coffee and newspaper delivered with wake-up call. **Services:** 🍽 🗝 VP 🖼 ↩ Masseur, babysitting. Free transportation within five-mile radius. **Facilities:** 🏋2 🖼2000 ⅁ 3 restaurants, 3 bars, racquetball, spa, sauna, steam rm, whirlpool. **Rates:** $165–$235 S; $180–$215 D; $440–$1,200 ste. Extra person $20. Children under age 16 stay free. Parking: Outdoor, free. AE, CB, DC, DISC, EC, MC, V.

≣≣ Residence Inn by Marriott

1041 W Peachtree St, 30309 (Midtown); tel 404/872-8885 or toll free 800/331-3131; fax 404/872-8885. Exit 101 off I-85. Located in a former girls' Christian dormitory, this hotel has a cozy, homey atmosphere. **Rooms:** 66 stes and effic. CI 3pm/CO noon. Nonsmoking rms avail. **Amenities:** 🚗 🐕 🖼 A/C, cable TV, refrig, voice mail. **Services:** 🖼 ↩ 🏌 **Facilities:** 🏋 🖼12 ⅁ Washer/dryer. **Rates (CP):** $119–$149 ste; $119–$149 effic. Children under age 18 stay free. Parking: Outdoor, free. AE, CB, DC, DISC.

≣≣≣≣ The Ritz-Carlton Atlanta

181 Peachtree St NE, 30303 (Downtown); tel 404/659-0400 or toll free 800/241-3333; fax 404/659-7821. This 25-story hotel, though overshadowed by its Buckhead counterpart, is back in the limelight after a recent renovation. Features the usual Ritz-Carlton blend of spacious public areas and a generous array of art and antiques. **Rooms:** 447 rms and stes. Executive level. CI 2pm/CO noon. Nonsmoking rms avail. Rooms of generous proportions, with soothing color schemes, custom-designed cherry-wood furniture, sofas in bay windows. (But only one room has windows that open.) Executive suites have separate sitting rooms and two full bathrooms. **Amenities:** 🚗 🐕 🍷 A/C, cable TV w/movies, refrig, dataport, in-rm safe, bathrobes. All units w/minibars, some w/whirlpools. Two-line telephones; video games. Some rooms with fax machines. **Services:** 🍽 🗝 VP 🚐 🖼 ↩ Twice-daily maid svce, car-rental desk, masseur, babysitting. Afternoon tea in The Lobby Lounge. On-the-ball concierge staff. **Facilities:** 🖼 🖼1500 💻 ⅁ 2 restaurants (*see* "Restaurants" below), 2 bars (1 w/entertainment), sauna, steam rm. Business center has cellular phones and pagers for rent.

Rates: $165–$225 S or D; $450–$900 ste. Extra person $25. Children under age 12 stay free. Min stay peak. Parking: Indoor, $15/day. Rates vary with floor and view. AE, CB, DC, DISC, EC, ER, JCB, MC, V.

≡≡≡≡ The Ritz-Carlton Buckhead

3434 Peachtree Rd NE, 30326 (Buckhead); tel 404/237-2700 or toll free 800/241-3333; fax 404/239-0078. The 19-story flagship of the Ritz-Carlton fleet, all gleaming and glowing with polished woodwork and brass, original artwork, and 19th-century French marble fireplaces. Spacious driveway facilitates arrivals/departures from busy thoroughfare adjoining Phipps Plaza and Lenox Square shopping malls. **Rooms:** 582 rms and stes. Executive level. CI 3pm/CO noon. Nonsmoking rms avail. Functional but elegant rooms with refined decor and furniture, including sofas in sumptuously draped bay windows, desk with white marble top. **Amenities:** 🛎 🅰 🍽 A/C, cable TV w/movies, refrig, dataport, in-rm safe, bathrobes. All units w/minibars. Two-line phone (with hold and redial). Awkward outlets for laptops. Out-of-date *TV Guide* in some rooms. **Services:** 🍽 ☎ VP 🚗 🧺 🛎 Twice-daily maid svce, car-rental desk, masseur, children's program, babysitting. 24-hour concierge. Afternoon tea in The Lobby Lounge is an Atlanta institution (reservations recommended). **Facilities:** 🏋 🚣 800 🖥 ♿ 3 restaurants (*see* "Restaurants" below), 2 bars (1 w/entertainment), sauna, steam rm, whirlpool. Business center is well-equipped but open weekdays only (until 5pm). Fitness center with sixth-floor sundeck and high-ceilinged indoor pool (open until 10pm); complimentary workout clothes. **Rates:** $165–$255 S or D; $395–$1,200 ste. Children under age 18 stay free. Parking: Indoor/outdoor, $12/day. Minimum-rate rooms perfectly adequate for guests who don't need views. Special packages worth looking into. AE, CB, DC, DISC, EC, ER, JCB, MC, V.

≡≡≡ Sheraton Colony Square Hotel

188 14th St NE, 30361; tel 404/892-6000 or toll free 800/325-3535; fax 404/872-9192. 1 block E of Peachtree St. A theatrically themed property popular with entertainers playing at the nearby Woodruff Arts Center. A great choice for tennis and jogging enthusiasts, since Piedmont Park is just two blocks away. **Rooms:** 461 rms and stes. Executive level. CI 3pm/CO noon. Nonsmoking rms avail. Rooms are opulently decorated: plush armchairs and hassocks, beautiful marble desks, silk throw pillows, and handsome armoires. All have views of downtown. **Amenities:** 🛎 🅰 A/C, cable TV w/movies, dataport, voice mail. **Services:** ✕ ☎ VP 🚗 🧺 🛎 Masseur, babysitting. **Facilities:** 🏋 🚣 500 🖥 ♿ 1 restaurant, 1 bar. Colony Square complex includes a mall with 20 shops and restaurants. **Rates:** $139–$169 S or D; $169–$199 ste. Children under age 12 stay free. AP rates avail. Parking: Indoor, AE, CB, DC, MC, V.

≡≡≡ Sheraton Suites Cumberland

2844 Cobb Pkwy, 30339; tel 770/955-3900 or toll free 800/325-3535; fax 770/916-3165. Exit 13 off I-285. An all-suite hotel that is perfect for business travel. **Rooms:** 278 stes.

Executive level. CI 3pm/CO noon. Nonsmoking rms avail. **Amenities:** 🛎 🅰 📺 🍽 A/C, cable TV w/movies, VCR, voice mail. All units w/minibars, some w/whirlpools. **Services:** ✕ 🚗 🧺 🛎 Babysitting. Business center open 24 hours. Free transportation within a three-mile radius. **Facilities:** 🏋 🚣 175 🖥 ♿ 1 restaurant, 1 bar, sauna, whirlpool, washer/dryer. **Rates (BB):** $109–$214 ste. Extra person $15. Children under age 17 stay free. Parking: Outdoor, free. AE, DC, DISC, ER, JCB, MC, V.

≡≡≡ Suite Hotel Underground Atlanta

54 Peachtree St at Upper Alabama, 30303 (Downtown); tel 404/223-5555 or toll free 800/477-5549; fax 404/223-0467. With the popularity of Underground Atlanta, it seemed logical to build a hotel on top. This all-suite building, with a limestone-and-brick exterior and a plush, cozy interior, is in the midst of downtown yet has a relaxed, residential feel. Parking and noise can sometimes be troublesome. **Rooms:** 197 stes. CI 3pm/CO noon. Nonsmoking rms avail. **Amenities:** 🛎 🅰 A/C, cable TV w/movies, dataport. All units w/minibars, all w/terraces, some w/whirlpools. **Services:** ✕ ☎ VP 🧺 🛎 🐾 One pet under 10 lbs permitted. **Facilities:** 75 ♿ 1 restaurant (bkfst and dinner only), 1 bar. **Rates:** $135–$210 ste. Extra person $10. Children under age 12 stay free. AP and MAP rates avail. Parking: Indoor, $12/day. AE, CB, DC, DISC, ER, JCB, MC, V.

≡≡≡≡ Swissôtel Atlanta

3391 Peachtree Rd NE, 30326 (Buckhead); tel 404/365-0065 or toll free 800/253-1397; fax 404/365-8787. Drab office-block architecture and an undistinguished entrance give way to a soaring, three-story lobby/lounge at the top of a long flight of stairs. Contemporary and art deco–inspired furnishings are augmented by expressionist artworks. Across the street from Lenox Square and close to Phipps Plaza, two of the Southeast's major shopping centers. **Rooms:** 384 rms, stes, and effic. Executive level. CI 3pm/CO 1pm. Nonsmoking rms avail. Generally large rooms, with distinctive Biedermeier decor and handcrafted furniture in bird's-eye maple and Australian lacewood. Leather-topped desk with halogen lamp; custom-designed cabinet for minibar and TV. Black and pink-marble bathrooms offer lots of style but limited shelf space. Corner rooms are particularly bright and airy. (But note: Guest room windows cannot be opened.) **Amenities:** 🛎 🅰 🍽 A/C, cable TV w/movies, voice mail, bathrobes. All units w/minibars, some w/fireplaces, some w/whirlpools. Two-line phones. Some rooms with fax machines. TV extension speakers in bathrooms. **Services:** 🍽 ☎ VP 🚗 🧺 🛎 🐾 Twice-daily maid svce, car-rental desk, masseur, babysitting. "Coffee on the Run" from 6am in the lobby. Service in general lacks the "unrivaled Swiss commitment to precision" promised in the brochure. **Facilities:** 🏋 🚣 1500 🖥 ♿ 1 restaurant (*see* "Restaurants" below), 1 bar (w/entertainment), sauna, steam rm, beauty salon. Staffed business center adjoins extensive meeting rooms. Fitness center (with sundeck) open until 9pm. Restaurant is branch of New York's famed steak house, The Palm. **Rates:** $155 S; $180 D; $235–$260 ste; $1,050 effic. Children under age 11 stay free. Parking: Indoor, $7.50/day. AE, CB, DC, DISC, EC, ER, JCB, MC, V.

📰📰📰 Terrace Garden Inn

3405 Lenox Rd NE, 30326 (Buckhead); tel 404/261-9250 or toll free 800/241-8260; fax 404/848-7301. An elegant yet homey property, right across from Lenox Square Mall. Antiques, flowers, and greenery grace public areas, and spirited classical music replaces the usual din of Muzak. **Rooms:** 360 rms and stes. Executive level. CI 3pm/CO 11am. No smoking. Room decor features French country–style furniture and earth-tone color schemes. **Amenities:** 📺 🍸 A/C, cable TV w/movies, dataport, voice mail. Club-level rooms offer concierge, private lounge, complimentary cocktails, and shoeshine service. **Services:** ✕ 🛏 🕽 Car-rental desk, babysitting. **Facilities:** 🏋 💪 🔟 🖥 💪 1 restaurant, 1 bar, racquetball, spa, sauna, steam rm, whirlpool. **Rates:** $145 S; $155 D; $270–$405 ste. Children under age 12 stay free. Parking: Outdoor, $5/day. AE, CB, DC, DISC, MC, V.

📰📰📰 Wyndham Garden Hotel Buckhead

3340 Peachtree Rd NE, 30326 (Buckhead); tel 404/231-1234 or toll free 800/996-3426; fax 404/231-5236. 1 mi W of Lenox Square. This hotel, with its friendly and enthusiastic staff, offers a quiet alternative in the hub of busy Buckhead. Designed with the business traveler in mind, but it is also popular with tourists. **Rooms:** 221 rms and stes. CI 3pm/CO noon. Nonsmoking rms avail. Rooms have attractive color-coordinated decor, mahogany furnishings, and recliners. **Amenities:** 📺 🍸 🖥 A/C, cable TV w/movies, dataport. **Services:** ✕ 🛏 🕽 Babysitting. Free courtesy van to/from Lenox Square Mall, Phipps Plaza, and Lenox MARTA station. **Facilities:** 🏋 🔟 🖥 💪 1 restaurant, 1 bar. Guests may use Sports Life fitness center across the street. **Rates (CP):** $198 S; $208 D; $129–$199 ste. Extra person $10. Children under age 12 stay free. Parking: Outdoor, free. AE, CB, DC, DISC, MC, V.

📰📰📰 Wyndham Hotel Midtown

125 10th St NE, 30309 (Midtown); tel 404/873-4800 or toll free 800/996-3426; fax 404/870-1530. Offering spacious accommodations on the edge of Midtown's Victorian district, this hotel is a favorite of music stars touring in Atlanta. Near Fox Theater, Piedmont Park, and numerous bars and restaurants. **Rooms:** 191 rms. CI 3pm/CO noon. Nonsmoking rms avail. **Amenities:** 📺 🍸 🖥 A/C, cable TV w/movies, voice mail. **Services:** ✕ 🔑 🆅🅿 🚐 🛏 🕽 Babysitting. **Facilities:** 🏋 🔟 🔟 🖥 💪 1 restaurant, 1 bar, games rm, spa, sauna, steam rm, whirlpool. **Rates (BB):** $79–$115 S; $89–$125 D. Extra person $10. Parking: Outdoor, $7/day. AE, CB, DC, DISC, EC, ER, JCB, MC, V.

MOTELS

📰📰 Cheshire Motor Inn

1865 Cheshire Bridge Rd NE, 30324; tel 404/872-9628 or toll free 800/827-9628. Off I-85. Located near several local hangouts and restaurants and numerous antique dealers, this comfortable motel offers great entertainment and shopping options. **Rooms:** 50 rms. CI 1pm/CO noon. Nonsmoking rms avail. **Amenities:** 📺 A/C, cable TV. **Services:** 🛏 🕽 🕽 Babysitting. **Facilities:** 🔟 🖥 💪 Playground. **Rates:** $40–$50 S; $50–$60 D. Extra person $5. Children under age 16 stay free. Parking: Outdoor, free. AE, CB, DC, DISC, MC, V.

📰📰 Comfort Inn Buckhead

2115 Piedmont Rd NE, 30324 (Buckhead); tel 404/876-4365 or toll free 800/221-2222; fax 404/873-1007. A comfortable little chain motel with adequate accommodations. **Rooms:** 150 rms and stes. CI 3pm/CO noon. Nonsmoking rms avail. **Amenities:** 📺 🍸 A/C, cable TV, dataport. **Services:** 🕽 **Facilities:** 🏋 🔟 💪 1 restaurant (lunch and dinner only). **Rates (CP):** $49–$69 S; $85–$99 ste. Extra person $6. Children under age 13 stay free. Parking: Outdoor, free. AE, CB, DC, DISC, MC, V.

📰 Econo Lodge

2574 Candler Rd, 30032 (Decatur); tel 404/243-4422 or toll free 800/553-2666; fax 404/243-1162. Exit 33 off I-20. Built in a heavily commercial district, this hotel is adequate for interstate travelers looking for an overnight stop. **Rooms:** 59 rms. CI 11am/CO 11am. Nonsmoking rms avail. **Amenities:** 📺 A/C, cable TV. Some units w/whirlpools. **Services:** 🕽 **Facilities:** 💪 **Rates:** Peak (Mar–Labor Day) $40–$100 S; $45–$100 D. Extra person $4. Children under age 18 stay free. Lower rates off-season. Parking: Outdoor, free. AE, DC, DISC, JCB, MC, V.

📰📰 Emory Inn

1641 Clifton Rd, 30329; tel 404/712-6700 or toll free 800/933-6679; fax 404/712-6701. ½ mi from N Decatur Rd. Located right in the midst of Emory University and next to Emory Medical Complex, this motel is perfect for visitors to either. Charming, cozy lobby has a fireplace and piped-in classical music. **Rooms:** 107 rms. CI 3pm/CO noon. Nonsmoking rms avail. Rooms feature Early American–style furnishings and peach color scheme. Many rooms have views of the surrounding woods. **Amenities:** 📺 🍸 🖥 A/C, cable TV w/movies, voice mail. Complimentary morning coffee. **Services:** 🍽 🚐 🛏 🕽 🕽 Babysitting. **Facilities:** 🏋 🔟 🔟 💪 1 restaurant, 1 bar, washer/dryer. Guests may use Emory University fitness complex, with indoor pool, 12 night-lit tennis courts, weight machines, and more. **Rates:** $79–$130 S or D. Min stay special events. Parking: Outdoor, free. AE, CB, DC, DISC, ER, MC, V.

📰📰📰 Homewood Suites

3200 Cobb Pkwy, 30339; tel 770/988-9449 or toll free 800/225-5466; fax 770/933-9612. 1 mi S of exit 14 off I-285. A quaint hotel offering comfortable rooms and accessibility to shopping and dining. **Rooms:** 124 stes. CI 3pm/CO noon. Nonsmoking rms avail. **Amenities:** 🔐 ⚱ 📺 A/C, cable TV w/movies, refrig, dataport, VCR, voice mail. Some units w/fireplaces. Complimentary copy of *USA Today* delivered to room. **Services:** 🚐 📐 ⊂⊃ ⊲⊳ Babysitting. Nonrefundable $75 pet fee. Evening social hour with complimentary drinks. **Facilities:** 📷 🛁 📋25 🖥 ⚄ Basketball, spa, whirlpool, playground, washer/dryer. **Rates (CP):** $79–$102 ste. Children under age 18 stay free. Parking: Outdoor, free. AE, CB, DC, DISC, ER, JCB, MC, V.

≣≣ Lenox Inn
3387 Lenox Rd NE, 30326 (Buckhead); tel 404/261-5500 or toll free 800/241-0200; fax 404/261-6140. A comfortable, friendly property located near nightlife, Lenox Square Mall, and Lenox MARTA stop. Rooms are spread out over four brick buildings, only one of which has an elevator. **Rooms:** 180 rms and stes. CI 2pm/CO noon. No smoking. Pristine rooms feature antique-reproduction furniture and floral-print drapes. Some rooms have extra sink in dressing area. **Amenities:** 🔐 A/C, cable TV w/movies. **Services:** 📐 ⊂⊃ Babysitting. Free local calls. Room service consists of offerings from several local restaurants. **Facilities:** 📷 🛁 📋100 ⚄ 1 restaurant (bkfst only), spa. Guests may use fitness facilities at Terrace Garden Inn next door. **Rates (CP):** $66 S; $72 D; $140–$260 ste. Children under age 18 stay free. Parking: Outdoor, free. AE, CB, DC, DISC, MC, V.

≣ Motel 6
2565 Wesley Chapel Rd, 30035 (Decatur); tel 404/288-6911; fax 404/284-1068. Exit 36N off I-20. Clean, comfortable, no-frills property. **Rooms:** 99 rms. CI open/CO noon. Nonsmoking rms avail. **Amenities:** 🔐 A/C, cable TV. All units w/terraces. **Services:** ⊂⊃ ⊲⊳ **Facilities:** 📷 📋100 ⚄ 1 restaurant, washer/dryer. **Rates:** $36 S or D. Extra person $6. Children under age 18 stay free. Parking: Outdoor, free. AE, CB, DC, DISC, MC, V.

≣≣≣ Residence Inn Buckhead
2960 Piedmont Rd NE, 30305 (Buckhead); tel 404/239-0677 or toll free 800/331-3131; fax 404/262-9638. A nice, home-like property that encourages and caters to long-term guests. **Rooms:** 136 stes. CI 3pm/CO noon. Nonsmoking rms avail. Rooms are spacious and have large kitchens. **Amenities:** 🔐 ⚱ 📺 A/C, refrig, voice mail. **Services:** 📐 ⊂⊃ ⊲⊳ Babysitting. Grocery delivery available upon request. **Facilities:** 📷 📋36 ⚄ Basketball, whirlpool, washer/dryer. **Rates (CP):** Peak (June 15–Oct) $79–$160 ste. Children under age 18 stay free. Lower rates off-season. Parking: Outdoor, free. AE, CB, DC, DISC, MC, V.

≣ Travelodge Atlanta Downtown
311 Courtland St NE, 30303 (Downtown); tel 404/659-4545 or toll free 800/578-7878; fax 404/659-5934. Exit 99 and 100 off I-75/85 N and S. Provides clean, comfortable, but simple rooms near downtown Atlanta. **Rooms:** 71 rms. CI 3pm/CO noon. Nonsmoking rms avail. **Amenities:** 🔐 ⚱ 📺

A/C, cable TV w/movies, in-rm safe. Some units w/terraces. **Services:** 📐 ⊂⊃ Babysitting. **Facilities:** 📷 📋15 **Rates (CP):** $60–$105 S; $74–$119 D. Extra person $8. Children under age 18 stay free. Min stay special events. Parking: Indoor/outdoor, free. AE, CB, DC, DISC, JCB, MC, V.

≣ Travelodge Atlanta Midtown
1641 Peachtree St NE, 30309 (Midtown); tel 404/873-5731 or toll free 800/525-9055; fax 404/874-5599. Located in a small, commercial district, this standard motel provides easy access to downtown. **Rooms:** 56 rms. CI noon/CO 11am. Nonsmoking rms avail. **Amenities:** 🔐 A/C, cable TV. **Services:** ⊂⊃ **Facilities:** 📷 ⚄ **Rates:** $49 S; $59 D. Children under age 16 stay free. Parking: Outdoor, free. AE, MC, V.

INNS
≣≣≣ Beverly Hills Inn
65 Sheridan Dr NE, 30305 (Buckhead); tel 404/233-8520 or toll free 800/331-8520; fax 404/233-8520 ext 18. Originally built in 1929 as an apartment complex, it provides a simple, comfortable place to stay in a wonderfully quiet neighborhood. Beautiful furnishings, hardwood floors, and Oriental rugs set the homey tone. **Rooms:** 22 effic. CI 2pm CI open/CO open. Nonsmoking rms avail. Furnishings are an eclectic mix of period antiques, many of them English. Some rooms have canopied beds, and all are equipped with kitchenettes. **Amenities:** 🔐 ⚱ A/C, cable TV, refrig. Some units w/terraces. **Services:** ⊂⊃ ⊲⊳ Babysitting. Guests receive complimentary bottle of wine upon arrival. Free local calls. **Facilities:** Washer/dryer, guest lounge. Parlor, garden room, and two libraries. **Rates (CP):** $80–$140 effic. Extra person $5. Children under age 12 stay free. Parking: Outdoor, free. AE, CB, DC, DISC, MC, V.

≣≣≣ Shellmont Bed & Breakfast Lodge
821 Piedmont Ave NE, 30308 (Midtown); tel 404/872-9290. At 6th St. Situated in a century-old Victorian house, this inn offers relaxing, comfortable rooms and a beautiful wildflower garden. Located near Fox Theater and other Midtown attractions. Unsuitable for children under 12. **Rooms:** 5 rms; 1 cottage/villa. CI 3pm/CO 11am. No smoking. **Amenities:** 🔐 ⚱ 📺 🍴 A/C, cable TV, dataport, VCR. **Services:** ⊂⊃ Afternoon tea served. **Facilities:** Guest lounge. **Rates (BB):** $79 S; $109 D; $99–$109 cottage/villa. Extra person $20. Children under age 12 stay free. Min stay wknds. AE, DISC, MC, V.

RESTAURANTS 🍴

Atlanta Fish Market
265 Pharr Rd (Buckhead); tel 404/262-3165. ¼ mi E of Peachtree Rd. **Seafood.** Housed in a brick building inspired by a 1920s Savannah train station, and fronted by a covered veranda furnished with rocking chairs. The laid-back quality of the exterior is belied by a dramatic and elegant interior complete with vast globe lights, chandeliers, plush leather booths, and art-deco wall sconces. The ample daily menu features such appetizers as barbecued oysters topped with

applewood-smoked bacon; deep-fried calamari drizzled with aioli and served with a rich marinara sauce; and Dungeness crab cakes served with tartar and red-mustard sauces. A list of over a dozen fresh seafood entrees can be ordered charbroiled or steamed; steamed vegetables, mashed potatoes, and tartar sauce are served on the side. Also pasta dishes, salads. **FYI:** Reservations accepted. **Open:** Lunch Mon–Sat 11:30am–2:30pm; dinner Mon–Thurs 5:30–11pm, Fri–Sat 5pm–midnight, Sun 4:30–10pm. **Prices:** Main courses $15–$30. AE, CB, DC, DISC, MC. VP &

Bistango
1100 Peachtree St (Midtown); tel 404/724-0901. At 14th St. **Mediterranean.** Upscale bistro with large, stained-glass windows in the ceiling and art deco decor. The Mediterranean menu features grilled scampi, vegetarian lasagna, and thick grilled pork chops. One of the rich desserts is bread pudding in caramel sauce studded with golden raisins and topped with fresh whipped cream. First-rate wine list. **FYI:** Reservations recommended. Guitar/piano. Dress code. No smoking. **Open:** Lunch Mon–Fri 11:30am–2:30pm; dinner Mon–Sat 5:30–11pm. **Prices:** Main courses $16–$21. AE, CB, DC, DISC, ER, MC, V. &

★ **Bridgetown Grill**
1156 Euclid Ave NE (Little Five Points); tel 404/653-0110. At Moreland Ave. **Caribbean.** Eatery with a Caribbean flair. Lush tropical plantings and a beach bar set the tone for dishes like flaky-crusted Jamaican beef patties, bay scallops ceviche, and big baskets of jerk chicken wings. All main courses come with salad, black beans, and rice. Nonalcoholic ginger beer and other island coolers available. **FYI:** Reservations not accepted. Beer and wine only. No smoking. Additional locations: 691 Peachtree St (tel 873-5361); 7285 Roswell Rd, Sandy Springs (tel 770/394-1575). **Open:** Sun–Thurs 11:30am–10pm, Fri–Sat 11:30am–midnight. **Prices:** Main courses $6–$13. AE, MC, V.

★ **The Buckhead Diner**
3073 Piedmont Rd (Buckhead); tel 404/262-3336. **New American.** This art deco–style retro-chic diner recalls the 1920s and '30s. Inside its gleaming stainless-steel exterior is an Italian marble floor, a mahogany diner counter, and upholstered mahogany booths. Classic jazz plays in the background. The contemporary American menu features thick-cut grilled pork chops served with black-eyed-pea salsa; crispy fried oysters and scallops with fries and jalapeño coleslaw; and tamarind-glazed baby-back ribs with fried plaintains and black-bean and mango salsa. **FYI:** Reservations not accepted. Dress code. **Open:** Mon–Sat 11am–midnight, Sun 10am–10pm. **Prices:** Main courses $9–$18. AE, CB, DC, DISC, ER, MC, V. VP &

The Cafe
In The Ritz-Carlton Buckhead, 3434 Peachtree Rd NE (Buckhead); tel 404/237-2700. **New American/Continental.** A classy corner for informal dining, located down a few steps from The Lobby Lounge. Has the sort of relaxed ambience that allows the maitre d' to ask solo diners if they'd like to have copies of current newspapers. Sample dishes: roasted red pepper and celery root soup; Atlantic salmon wrapped in potato and braised leek; rack of Colorado lamb with herb pesto crust; peppered swordfish with key lime glacé. **FYI:** Reservations accepted. Piano. Children's menu. Dress code. **Open:** Daily 6am–11pm. **Prices:** Main courses $15–$28. AE, CB, DC, DISC, ER, MC, V. VP &

Ⓢ **The Cafe**
In The Ritz-Carlton Atlanta, 181 Peachtree St NE (Downtown); tel 404/659-0400. **Regional American/Continental.** Less formal than the adjoining Dining Room, but with its elegant setting, it's hardly a corner cafe in the everyday sense. Wood-paneled walls hung with candelabra sconces and 19th-century paintings set the scene for widely spaced tables, brocade banquettes, and armchairs in striped fabrics. The menu suits diners with time to spare as well as those dashing off to their next meeting, and dishes liven up classic flavors with Southern and Southwestern accents: Louisiana crab cake with lobster-orange beurre blanc; spinach basil gazpacho; vegetable strudel with cilantro–pistachio pesto; grilled veal chop with jalapeño corn cakes and apple-mango chutney; raspberry crème brûlée; peach cobbler. Also available is a selection of "Cuisine Vitale" dishes prepared according to American Heart Association guidelines. **FYI:** Reservations recommended. Children's menu. Dress code. **Open:** Daily 6:30am–11:30pm. **Prices:** Main courses $15–$28. AE, CB, DC, DISC, ER, MC, V. VP &

Cassis
In Hotel Nikko Atlanta, 3300 Peachtree Rd (Buckhead); tel 404/365-8100. **Mediterranean.** Relaxed but stylish informality coupled with the cuisine of southern France is presented against a backdrop of an authentic Japanese garden, all on the lower level of the Nikko's public areas. The emphasis here is on extra virgin olive oil and the herbs of Provence in intriguing combinations—duck confit strudel with shiitake mushrooms; escargot with Provençal herbs on a crispy potato nest; seared sea scallop salad with asparagus and radicchio; tagliatelle with julienne of smoked chicken and asparagus; seared fillet of grouper with langoustine and skordalia-flavored potatoes; toasted veal chop with grilled pancetta and balsamic jus. Dessert options include zabaglione and praline cheesecake. Cellar is noted for its selection of wines from southern France (among them, Bandols and Châteauneuf-du-Papes), available by the bottle and by the glass. **FYI:** Reservations accepted. Children's menu. Dress code. **Open:** Breakfast daily 6:30–11am; lunch Mon–Sat 11:30am–2:30pm; dinner Mon–Thurs 6–10:30pm, Fri–Sat 6–11pm, Sun 6–10pm; brunch Sun 11:30am–2:30pm. **Prices:** Main courses $20–$26. AE, CB, DC, DISC, MC, V. ❤ VP &

Chef's Cafe
2115 Piedmont Rd (Buckhead); tel 404/872-2284. 2 mi S of Peachtree Rd. **American.** Charming, unpretentious cafe.

Appetizers might include grilled pancetta-wrapped oysters on a bed of orange salsa cruda, while some of the favorite main course choices include superb spicy paella, grilled lamb loin, and steamed salmon. Homemade desserts. Extensive wine list, with mainly California selections. **FYI:** Reservations recommended. **Open:** Lunch Tues–Fri 11:30am–2pm; dinner Sun–Thurs 6–10pm, Fri–Sat 6–11pm; brunch Sun 11am–2:30pm. **Prices:** Main courses $9–$18. AE, CB, DC, DISC, MC, V. &

Chops

In Buckhead Plaza Bldg, 70 W Paces Ferry Rd (Buckhead); tel 404/262-2675. ¼ mi W of Peachtree Rd. **Seafood/Steak.** Elegant, clublike restaurant in an intimate setting, with dark decor, fine cuisine, and an impressive wine list. Steak tartare, swordfish served on a bed of mashed potatoes, and soft-shell crabs are among the highlights. **FYI:** Reservations recommended. Jacket required. **Open:** Lunch Mon–Fri 11:30am–2:30pm; dinner Mon–Thurs 5:30–11pm, Fri–Sat 5:30pm–midnight, Sun 5:30–10pm. **Prices:** Main courses $15–$32. AE, CB, DC, DISC, MC, V. VP &

Chow

1026B N Highland Ave (Virginia-Highlands); tel 404/872-0869. **New American/Seafood.** This bustling, hip eatery evokes the casual chic of New York's trendy SoHo district. Glossy cream walls function as gallery space for quality artworks, large lamps hang from a high pressed-tin ceiling, and bare oak floors further the minimalist ambience. Dinner might begin with rosemary- and thyme-marinated garlic cloves served with feta-cheese spread and toasted french bread croutons; a plate of hummus with pita bread; or lightly battered fried calamari. The lunch menu features salads, half-pound burgers, sandwiches, and pasta dishes, while the more extensive dinner menu focuses on fresh seafood and pasta entrees. Sunday brunch at Chow is an institution among Atlanta's in-crowd, who munch on omelettes, strawberry french toast, and Belgian waffles. **FYI:** Reservations not accepted. Additional location: 303 Peachtree Center Ave (tel 222-0210). **Open:** Lunch Mon–Fri 11:30am–3pm; dinner Mon–Thurs 6–10:30pm, Fri–Sat 6–11:30pm, Sun 6–10pm; brunch Sun 11am–3pm. **Prices:** Main courses $10–$18. AE, CB, DC, DISC, MC, V. &

Ciboulette

1529 Piedmont Ave NE (Buckhead); tel 404/874-7600. At Monroe. **French.** Foie gras, and any of the meats and seafood served in deep, rich sauces are good picks at this classic French restaurant. Cooking classes are offered every Sunday morning for the dedicated guest and amateur chef. **FYI:** Reservations accepted. Jacket required. No smoking. **Open:** Mon–Thurs 6–10pm, Fri–Sat 5:30–11pm. **Prices:** Main courses $16–$23. AE, CB, DC, DISC, MC, V.

★ The Colonnade

1879 Cheshire Bridge Rd (Buckhead); tel 404/874-5642. **American.** An Atlanta institution since 1927, offering up authentic regional specialties. The huge dining room is simply decorated with English prints and butcher-block tables. At lunch or dinner, you can feast on large helpings of turkey with dressing, sugar-cured ham in redeye gravy, or roast leg of lamb; all dishes come with corn bread, rolls, and choice of two vegetables. Homemade desserts. **FYI:** Reservations not accepted. No liquor license. **Open:** Lunch Mon–Sat 11am–2:30pm; dinner Mon–Thurs 5–9pm, Fri–Sat 5–10pm, Sun 11am–9pm. **Prices:** Main courses $7–$14. No CC. &

$ ★ Crescent Moon

254 W Ponce de Leon Ave (Decatur); tel 404/377-5623. **Eclectic.** This tiny, somewhat funky neighborhood hangout is most popular at breakfast, when locals and college students come in for the homemade multigrain biscuits, thick slabs of challah french toast, and scrambled eggs with fresh herbs and cream cheese. Lunch consists mainly of sandwiches and salads, while the dinner menu has a Mexican accent. **FYI:** Reservations not accepted. Beer and wine only. No smoking. **Open:** Lunch Mon–Fri 7:30am–3pm; dinner Tues–Sat 5:30–10pm; brunch Sat 8am–2pm, Sun 8am–2:30pm. **Prices:** Main courses $8–$17. DISC, MC, V.

Dailey's

17 International Blvd (Downtown); tel 404/681-3303. **Seafood.** Housed in a former warehouse with a 20-foot peaked ceiling crisscrossed with dark wooden beams, exposed-brick walls, and pine-plank floors is this cozy but often boisterous bistro. Creations include swordfish steak marinated in mustard sauce, grilled Gulf shrimp dredged in grated coconut, and fresh salmon fillet wrapped in edible rice paper and served in tangy sweet-and-sour sauce. Huge portions come with vegetable, salad, rolls. Dessert bar. **FYI:** Reservations not accepted. **Open:** Lunch Mon–Sat 11am–3:30pm; dinner Sun–Thurs 5:30–11pm, Fri–Sat 5:30pm–midnight. **Prices:** Main courses $13–$24. AE, DISC, MC, V. &

★ Dante's Down the Hatch

3380 Peachtree Rd (Buckhead); tel 404/266-1600. **Fondue.** Fun eatery filled with a mix of antiques and nautical kitsch. The specialty is cheese fondue, with dippers ranging from french bread croutons to fresh vegetables. Diners can also opt for a Mandarin fondue of beef, chicken, pork, and shrimp served with four Chinese dipping sauces. Award-winning wine list. Hot chocolate fudge cake for dessert. **FYI:** Reservations recommended. Folk/jazz. Dress code. Additional location: Underground Atlanta (tel 577-1800). **Open:** Mon–Sat 4–11:30pm, Sun 5–11pm. **Prices:** Main courses $11–$20. AE, DC, DISC, MC, V. &

♣ The Dining Room

In The Ritz-Carlton Buckhead, 3434 Peachtree Rd NE (Buckhead); tel 404/237-2700. **New American/Continental.** An outstanding dining experience in a gracious setting that's perfect for both whispered tête-à-têtes and exuberant celebrations of billion-dollar deals. The softly lighted sanctum is aglow with polished woods and massed flowers; muted colors match the hushed conversation. Chef Guenter Seeger is the city's top chef for serious, evening-long gourmandizing. Typical dishes: smoked salmon on crisp Oriental wafer with seaweed salad; roasted red peppers and celery root soup; peppered swordfish with key lime glacé; grilled squab with artichoke and vegetable risotto. **FYI:** Reservations recommended. Jacket required. **Open:** Mon–Sat 6–10pm. **Prices:** Prix fixe $58. AE, CB, DC, DISC, ER, MC, V. ♥ VP &

Fellini's Pizza

2809 Peachtree Rd (Buckhead); tel 404/266-0082. 2 mi S of Lenox Square. **Pizza.** You won't get fancy toppings on your New York–style pies here, but you will get the best-quality anchovies, Italian sausage, and meatballs, and other traditional items. The wacky decor includes statues of angels, gargoyles, and Egyptian pharaohs. **FYI:** Reservations not accepted. Beer and wine only. Additional location: 933 Ponce de Leon (tel 873-3088). **Open:** Mon–Sat 11:30am–2am, Sun 12:30pm–midnight. **Prices:** Main courses $5–$15. No CC.

★ French Quarter Food Shop

923 Peachtree St NE (Midtown); tel 404/875-2489. ⅕ mi S of 14th St. **Cajun/Creole.** The Cajun owners of this small, unpretentious eatery know what they're doing: The gumbo here is really special—dark, rich, and spicy, and loaded with savory chunks of andouille sausage. The crawfish étouffée and jambalaya are likewise fine choices, as are muffulettas and oyster po' boys. A small shop sells Louisiana food items. **FYI:** Reservations not accepted. Dress code. Beer and wine only. Additional location: 2144 Johnson Ferry Rd (tel 458-2148). **Open:** Mon–Thurs 11am–10pm, Fri–Sat 11am–11pm. **Prices:** Main courses $6–$14. AE, CB, DC, DISC, MC, V. &

Gorin's Diner

1170 Peachtree St (Midtown); tel 404/892-2500. At 14th St. **Diner.** Silver paneling and flashy neon signs greet the guests of this traditional diner. No frills, just good food. Sit at the multicolored bar stools and watch the cooks do their thing. **FYI:** Reservations not accepted. No liquor license. No smoking. **Open:** Sun 7:30am–midnight, Mon–Thurs 7am–midnight, Fri 7am–2am, Sat 7:30am–2am. **Prices:** Main courses $5–$9. AE, MC, V. &

Hard Rock Cafe

215 Peachtree St NE (Downtown); tel 404/688-7625. At International Blvd. **American.** A typical Hard Rock—loud, crowded, and decorated with authentic rock-and-roll memorabilia. It's just diner-style food, but then again, that's not why you're going. **FYI:** Reservations not accepted. Children's menu. **Open:** Mon–Sun 11am–2am. **Prices:** Main courses $6–$13. AE, CB, DC, MC, V. &

Harry & Sons

820 N Highland Ave (Virginia-Highlands); tel 404/873-2009. **Eclectic.** Under the same ownership as Surin of Thailand (see below), this comfortable neighborhood bistro offers great food in a friendly, casual setting. Diverse dining choices include Thai chicken panang, and grilled shrimp scampi served over angel-hair pasta. Sunday brunch menu offers eggs benedict, pecan waffles, and sourdough french toast. **FYI:** Reservations not accepted. **Open:** Lunch Mon–Sat 11am–2:30pm, Sun 11am–3pm; dinner Mon–Thurs 5:30–10:30pm, Fri–Sat 5:30–11:30pm. **Prices:** Main courses $8–$16. AE, DC, DISC, MC, V. &

♥ Hedgerose Heights Inn

490 Paces Ferry Rd NE (Buckhead); tel 404/233-7673. **American/Continental.** This warmly elegant restaurant, decorated with lovely flower arrangements, carved moldings, and crystal chandeliers, occupies a former townhouse. Classic dishes starring fish and wild game are often served with inventive sauces. The dessert soufflés are highly regarded. Over 300 wine selections, many available by the glass. **FYI:** Reservations accepted. Jacket required. No smoking. **Open:** Tues–Sat 6–10pm. **Prices:** Main courses $18–$25. AE, DC, MC, V. ♥ &

★ Honto Restaurant

3295 Chamblee-Dunwoody Rd, Chamblee; tel 770/458-8088. **Chinese.** It's a little out of the way, but the food can be well worth the trip. Specials change daily (and are not listed in English on the menu), but typically include tender sautéed beef with snow peas, carrots, and oyster mushrooms; clams steamed in garlic butter and served in cilantro-flavored broth; or sautéed Dungeness crab with ginger or black-bean sauce. Huge portions. Dim sum available. **FYI:** Reservations not accepted. **Open:** Sun–Thurs 11:30am–10pm, Fri–Sat 11:30am–11pm. **Prices:** Main courses $8–$13. AE, MC, V. &

Houston's

2166 Peachtree Rd (Buckhead); tel 404/351-2442. 3 mi S of Lenox Square. **American.** Inside this moderately lighted restaurant is a rough, wood interior designed like an old ship's cabin. Guests are encouraged to try the cheese soup. **FYI:** Reservations accepted. Additional location: Lenox Square, Buckhead (tel 237-7534). **Open:** Sun–Thurs 11am–11pm, Fri–Sat 6am–midnight. **Prices:** Main courses $9–$17. AE, MC, V. &

Indigo Coastal Grill

1397 N Highland Ave (Virginia-Highlands); tel 404/876-0676. **Seafood.** The energetic and whimsical atmosphere at this casual eatery make it the closest thing to taking a Caribbean cruise. Southern touches include country ham and jalapeño grits; pork dishes are excellent. Wine is available by the glass. **FYI:** Reservations accepted. Beer and wine only. No smoking. **Open:** Dinner daily 5:30–11pm; brunch Sat–Sun 9am–3pm. **Prices:** Main courses $13–$20. AE, MC, V.

Kudzu Cafe

3215 Peachtree Rd NE (Buckhead); tel 404/262-0661. **Regional American.** Named after the vine that proliferates throughout the South—and in the decor of the dining area. Highlights of the bold Southern cooking include fried green tomatoes battered with cornmeal and served with Creole tomato sauce, and hearty options like barbecued chicken and hickory-smoked pork shops. The vegetable side dishes—hickory-grilled corn on the cob, apple-cider slaw, sautéed spinach, and red skin mashed potatoes with horseradish—can make a meal in themselves. **FYI:** Reservations not accepted. **Open:** Sun–Thurs 11am–11pm, Fri–Sat 11am–midnight. **Prices:** Main courses $10–$22. AE, DISC, MC, V. VP &

La Fonda Latina

2813 Peachtree Rd NE (Buckhead); tel 404/816-8311. 2 mi S of Lenox Square. **Mexican.** Funky and festive, La Fonda is brightly painted in tropical colors and designs, and the food is both fresh and authentic. Sandwiches are stuffed with roast pork, ham, Swiss cheese, and "mojo" sauce and served on crusty Cuban bread; grilled quesadillas are served with yellow rice and black beans; and the paella—cooked with herbed baked chicken, calamari, shrimp, sausage, peppers, and onions—is heartily satisfying. **FYI:** Reservations not accepted. Beer and wine only. Additional location: 1150 B Euclid Ave (tel 557-8317). **Open:** Mon–Thurs 11:30am–11pm, Sat 11:30am–midnight, Sun 12:30–11pm. **Prices:** Main courses $4–$7. No CC.

★ Mary Mac's Tea Room

224 Ponce de Leon Ave NE (Midtown); tel 404/876-1800. Go ½ mi E of W Peachtree St. **Southern.** In business since 1945, this quaint and colorful Atlanta institution is a bastion of classic Southern cuisine. Cream-colored walls in the four dining rooms are covered with photos of famous customers and Atlanta landmarks. The menu changes daily, but some likely entree choices include fried chicken, fried rainbow trout, and chicken pot pie topped with thick giblet gravy. Loads of side dishes include corn bread, black-eyed peas, mashed potatoes, and macaroni and cheese. You can finish things off with Georgia peach cobbler, or pound cake topped with strawberries and whipped cream. **FYI:** Reservations not accepted. Piano. No smoking. **Open:** Lunch Mon–Fri 11am–3pm, Sun 11am–3pm; dinner Mon–Sat 5–9pm; brunch Sat–Sun 9–11am. **Prices:** Main courses $6–$12. No CC.

Mick's

557 Peachtree St (Downtown); tel 404/875-6425. **Diner.** A haven for young business types, this modern restaurant offers good burgers and sandwiches for lunch. Oreo cheesecake is available for sweet-tooths. **FYI:** Reservations not accepted. Children's menu. Beer and wine only. Additional locations: Peachtree St, Buckhead (tel 262-6425); Underground Atlanta (tel 525-2825). **Open:** Daily 11am–midnight. **Prices:** Main courses $6–$14. AE, CB, DC, DISC, MC, V. VP

Morton's of Chicago

3379 Peachtree Rd (Buckhead); tel 404/816-6535. **Steak.** One of the most elegant steak houses in Atlanta, with a classy, country club atmosphere. There's no printed menu. Servers roll up carts laden with several cuts of meat, a cooked chicken, and a frisky live lobster, and the diner picks one. Appetizers include lump crabmeat cocktail with remoulade

sauce, smoked Pacific salmon, and broiled scallops wrapped in bacon and covered with apricot chutney. Main course choices include prime midwestern steaks (porterhouse, sirloin, rib eye, or double filet mignon), lemon oregano chicken, whole baked Maine lobster, and prime rib. Complimentary onion loaf on every table. Extensive wine list. **FYI:** Reservations recommended. Dress code. Additional location: 215 Peachtree Center Ave (tel 577-4366). **Open:** Mon–Sat 5:30–11pm, Sun 5–10pm. **Prices:** Main courses $17–$30. AE, DC, MC, V. VP &

★ Murphy's

997 Virginia Ave NE (Virginia-Highlands); tel 404/872-0904. At N Highland Ave. **Regional American.** Murphy's cozy warren of dining rooms separated by french doors is a perfect setting for Sunday morning breakfast. Everything is fresh, from the Belgian waffles and french toast served at breakfast, to the quiches and haute-deli sandwiches offered for lunch (basil-flavored chicken salad tossed with mayonnaise and sour cream is a favorite), to the light entrees served for dinner. Try the hearty homemade soups, or Irish potatoes (sautéed with onion, peppers, and zucchini, and seasoned with Cajun spices). A small grocery/bakery is open in front of the brick-walled restaurant. **FYI:** Reservations not accepted. Beer and wine only. No smoking. **Open:** Mon–Thurs 7:30am–10pm, Fri 7:30am–midnight, Sat 8am–midnight, Sun 8am–10pm. **Prices:** Main courses $8–$13. AE, DISC, MC, V. &

Nikolai's Roof

In Atlanta Hilton & Towers, 255 Courtland St (Downtown); tel 404/659-2000. At Baker St. **Continental/Russian.** Offering a lovely view of Atlanta's skyline, this rooftop restaurant specializes in a five-course, prix-fixe dinner with two seatings per night (6:30 and 9:30pm). Tables are set with fine stemware and china. Solicitous, expert service. Menu changes monthly. **FYI:** Reservations recommended. Jacket required. **Open:** Daily 6:30–9:30pm. **Prices:** Main courses $30–$60; prix fixe $60. AE, CB, DC, DISC, ER, MC, V. ♥ ▲ VP

The OK Cafe

1284 W Paces Ferry Rd (Buckhead); tel 404/233-2888. Exit 107 off I-75. **Regional American/Diner.** Built in 1987 to resemble a 1950s rural Georgia roadhouse, with striped aluminum awnings and a neon sign. Inside are roomy leather booths, Formica tables, and a jukebox replete with oldies. The nostalgic food includes blue-plate specials: meat loaf, fried catfish, roast turkey with corn-bread stuffing. Homemade corn muffins come with meals. Sandwiches, burgers, and salads are also available. Country-style breakfast, too. **FYI:** Reservations not accepted. No liquor license. No smoking. **Open:** Daily 24 hrs. **Prices:** Main courses $4–$10. AE, MC, V. ▣ &

103 West

103 W Paces Ferry Rd (Buckhead); tel 404/233-5993. ¼ mi W of Peachtree Rd. **French.** From the valet parking to the elegant lounge, and from the marble-columned dining room

to the attentive wait staff, guests feel perfectly pampered in this fine, old world–style establishment. Specialties of the house include veal (prepared in any way), fresh Dover sole, venison, roasted duck, and soufflés. **FYI:** Reservations accepted. Jacket required. No smoking. **Open:** Mon–Sat 6–11pm. **Prices:** Main courses $16–$30. AE, CB, DC, DISC, MC, V. 🆅🅿 ♿

Palm Restaurant

In Swissôtel Atlanta, 3391 Peachtree Rd NE (Buckhead); tel 404/365-0065. **Continental/Steak.** A stylized version of its Manhattan namesake—with service that's less brusque and brassy. New York steak house styling (wood paneling, wooden booths), but brighter and more soothing. Menu offerings include clams blanco, casino, or oreganata; chopped tomato and onion salad; swordfish steak; three double-cut lamb chops; prime aged porterhouse; and the house specialty—a 36-oz New York strip for two. Key lime pie and New York cheesecake for dessert. **FYI:** Reservations accepted. Children's menu. **Open:** Breakfast daily 7–11am; lunch daily noon–3pm; dinner daily 6–10pm. **Prices:** Main courses $14–$51. AE, CB, DC, DISC, ER, MC, V. 🆅🅿 ♿

Pano & Paul's

1232 W Paces Ferry Rd (Buckhead); tel 404/261-3662. **American/Seafood.** Sophisticated and posh, featuring canopied booths, vases of fresh-cut flowers, and antique chandeliers and wall sconces. The innovative kitchen produces such delights as an appetizer of spinach- and ricotta-filled tortellini tossed in browned butter with fresh sage leaves and walnuts; and such entrees as lightly battered soft-shell crabs served with white lemon butter, Chinese-style roast duck, and lightly smoked salmon with Pommery honey cream served on a bed of sesame spinach. Distinguished wine list. **FYI:** Reservations recommended. Piano. Jacket required. No smoking. **Open:** Mon–Fri 6–11pm, Sat 5:30–11pm. **Prices:** Main courses $16–$32. AE, CB, DC, DISC, MC, V.

The Peasant Restaurant & Bar

3402 Piedmont Rd NE, Atlanta (Buckhead); tel 404/261-6341. **New American.** With its decor of black lacquer paneling, wicker furniture, and original oil paintings, this restaurant is perfect for a quiet dinner. Starters include grilled quesadilla stuffed with shrimp, black beans, cheese, and jalapeños; and sea scallops in soy-chili sauce. Entrees (all of which come with cheese toast and a huge green salad) include pan-sautéed boneless chicken breast topped with Jarlsberg cheese sauce and roasted tomatoes; grilled grouper with avocado, tomato, and couscous; and pork chops stuffed with black beans, rice, and melted cheddar. Lavish desserts include caramel-butter pecan pie. An extensive wine list highlights California labels. **FYI:** Reservations recommended. Children's menu. Dress code. **Open:** Lunch Mon–Fri 11:30am–2:30pm; dinner Sun–Thurs 5:30–10pm, Fri–Sat 5:30–11pm; brunch Sun 11:30am–2:30pm. **Prices:** Main courses $11–$21. AE, DC, DISC, MC, V. ♥ 🆅🅿

Pricci

500 Pharr Rd (Buckhead); tel 404/237-2941. ¼ mi from Peachtree Rd. **Italian.** A glamorous setting in which to enjoy hearty Italian cuisine. The art deco interior incorporates curved vaulted ceilings, terrazzo marble floors, and chrome dividers with crisp, white table linens and whimsical hand-blown light fixtures. The food is no less exciting: Gorgonzola- and walnut-filled risotto, thin-crusted, oak-fired pizzas, spicy Tuscan seafood stew. The pasta is homemade. Lunch menu offers lighter fare, including focaccia sandwiches, salads, and calzones. **FYI:** Reservations recommended. Jacket required. **Open:** Mon–Thurs 11am–11pm, Fri–Sat 11am–midnight, Sun 5–10pm. **Prices:** Main courses $11–$20. AE, CB, DC, DISC, MC, V. 🆅🅿

Restaurant Kamogawa

In Hotel Nikko Atlanta, 3300 Peachtree Rd (Buckhead); tel 404/365-8100. **Japanese.** A beguiling oasis of Japanese calm in bustling Atlanta. Traditional Japanese Sukiya interiors feature low lintels, shoji screens, and paper lanterns; a few tables overlook the Nikko's formal Japanese garden. Servers clad in kimonos. Tatami rooms and Sushi Counter. Standbys include shabu shabu, teriyaki, sukiyaki, and tempura, plus traditional Kaiseki dinners. The business lunch at $6.75 is hard to beat. **FYI:** Reservations recommended. **Open:** Breakfast Mon–Fri 7–10am; lunch Mon–Fri 11:30am–2pm; dinner Mon–Thurs 6–10pm, Fri–Sat 6–10:30pm, Sun 6–10pm. **Prices:** Main courses $17–$28; prix fixe $28–$50. AE, CB, DC, DISC, MC, V. 🆅🅿 ♿

The Rib Ranch

25 Irby Ave NW (Buckhead); tel 404/233-7644. **Barbecue.** There's no pretentious decor at this down-home joint—the walls are covered in pictures, license plates, posters, and dollar bills. People come here for the fork-tender Texas-style ribs, pork ribs, and barbecue chicken. There are all kinds of side dishes, the best being spicy Brunswick stew—a mix of tomato, shredded pork and beef, okra, onions, and lima beans. Beer is the beverage of choice, and you can have a brownie or some blackberry cobbler for dessert. **FYI:** Reservations not accepted. Beer and wine only. No smoking. **Open:** Mon–Sat 11am–11pm, Sun noon–10pm. **Prices:** Main courses $4–$15. MC, V.

★ R Thomas

1812 Peachtree St NW (Midtown); tel 404/881-0246. ½ mi N of jct with I-85. **Californian.** A laid-back yet zany atmosphere predominates here. Owner Richard Thomas occasionally offers a performance by his many exotic birds, and psychics and magicians are often found working the floor. As if all that weren't enough, there's also food: omelettes, veggie tacos, roasted chicken, caesar salad, and fresh-squeezed juices are popular choices. Very popular late at night. **FYI:** Reservations not accepted. Beer and wine only. **Open:** Mon–Thurs 11am–6am, Fri–Sat 24 hrs. **Prices:** Main courses $6–$16. AE, MC, V. 🍴 🈘

Ruth's Chris Steak House

950 E Paces Ferry Rd (Buckhead); tel 404/365-0660. Near Lenox Mall. **Seafood/Steak.** Aged prime strips, filets, and rib eyes are grilled to order at this upscale chain steak house that is a favorite with businesspeople. Also available are seafood (Maine lobster), several side dishes, a large wine list, and desserts like blueberry cheesecake and New Orleans–style praline freezes. **FYI:** Reservations accepted. Additional location: Roswell Rd, Sandy Springs (tel 255-0035). **Open:** Mon–Fri 11:30am–11pm, Sat–Sun 5–11pm. **Prices:** Main courses $16–$30. AE, CB, DC, DISC, MC, V. 🆅🅿 ♿

Shipfeifer on Peachtree

1814 Peachtree Rd (Buckhead); tel 404/875-1106. **Mediterranean/Vegetarian.** Typical Mediterranean-style fast food shop with minimal decor. Specializes in pita wraps. **FYI:** Reservations not accepted. Beer and wine only. **Open:** Mon–Fri 11am–11pm, Sat–Sun 11am–midnight. **Prices:** Main courses $4–$9. AE, DISC, MC, V. 🍴

South City Kitchen

1144 Crescent Ave (Midtown); tel 404/873-7358. Exit 102 off I-85/75. **Regional American/Southern.** Contemporary Southern-style eatery in a converted two-story house. There are two dining areas—upstairs and down—and both have fireplaces. The seasonally changing menu reflects a wide variety of influences. Some sample dishes are she-crab soup; arugula salad garnished with fresh Georgia peaches; jambalaya; and tangy barbecue swordfish served atop creamy cheese grits. Small but well-chosen wine list. **FYI:** Reservations recommended. **Open:** Sun–Thurs 11am–11pm, Fri–Sat 11am–midnight. **Prices:** Main courses $7–$24. AE, MC, V. 🍴 🖼

⭐ Sundown Cafe

2165 Cheshire Bridge Rd (Buckhead); tel 404/321-1118. ¼ mi S of jct with LaVista Rd. **Mexican.** A funky and relaxed eatery serving up handmade tortillas, inventive soups (shrimp soup, green chili stew), and entrees like ranchero steak and crab cakes. More than a dozen homemade salsas, plus fresh margaritas. An adventurous dessert is the chocolate chimichanga with tequila sauce. **FYI:** Reservations accepted. **Open:** Lunch Wed–Fri 11am–2pm; dinner Mon–Thurs 5:30–10pm, Fri–Sat 5:30–11pm. **Prices:** Main courses $9–$15. AE, DC, MC, V. ♿

Surin of Thailand

810 N Highland Ave (Virginia-Highlands); tel 404/892-7789. At Greenwood Ave NE. **Thai.** Surin has been garnering acclaim for its authentic fare since it opened in 1991. Chicken or beef satay, served with cucumber salad, is a popular starter, while the hearty chicken curry is a top entree. Seafood is very fresh. Beverages include mango daiquiris, sake, wine, and sweet Thai herbal iced tea. **FYI:** Reservations not accepted. **Open:** Mon–Thurs 11:30am–10:30pm, Fri 11:30am–11:30pm, Sat noon–11:30pm, Sun noon–10:30pm. **Prices:** Main courses $7–$15. AE, DISC, MC, V. ♿

⭐ The Swan Coach House

In Atlanta History Center, 3130 Slaton Dr NW (Buckhead); tel 404/261-0636. **American.** A fine choice when visiting the art museum. The elegant setting is marked by lovely flower arrangements, crystal chandeliers, and multipaned windows looking out to wooded grounds. Samples of the fare offered are salmon croquettes topped with white caper sauce; chicken salad in a pastry timbales served with cheese straws and creamy frozen fruit salad; and chicken à la king. Fresh muffins accompany all main courses. Elegant desserts. **FYI:** Reservations accepted. No smoking. **Open:** Mon–Sat 11:30am–2:30pm. **Prices:** Lunch main courses $7–$8. MC, V. 🍴 🆅🅿 ♿

Trader Vic's

In Atlanta Hilton & Towers, 255 Courtland St (Downtown); tel 404/659-2000. At Baker St. **Polynesian/Thai.** South Pacific cuisine and atmosphere. Seating is available with a view of the Hilton's beautiful gardens. Dim sum lunch is offered weekdays 11:30am–2pm. **FYI:** Reservations accepted. **Open:** Lunch Mon–Fri 11:30am–2pm; dinner daily 6–11pm. **Prices:** Main courses $14–$25. AE, CB, DC, DISC, ER, MC, V. 🅅 🆅🅿 ♿

⭐ The Varsity

61 North Ave (Downtown); tel 404/881-1706. At Spring St. **Diner/Fast food.** Adjacent to the Georgia Tech campus. Since 1928, generations of Atlantans have been flocking to this landmark drive-in restaurant. The spartan interior is dominated by a 150-foot stainless-steel counter, where red-shirted counterpeople rush out thousands of orders a day. Order up a chili dog or a couple of the small chili burgers, with fries, onion rings, and a frosted orange. Barbecued pork, homemade chicken salad, and deviled-egg sandwiches are other options. Curb service is still available, if you're in a hurry or you'd rather just stay in the car. **FYI:** Reservations not accepted. No liquor license. No smoking. **Open:** Sun–Thurs 9am–11:30pm, Fri–Sat 9am–1:30am. **Prices:** Main courses $1–$2. No CC. 🍴 ♿

Vickeny's Crescent Ave Bar and Grill

1106 Crescent Ave (Midtown); tel 404/881-1106. Exit 102 off I-85/75. **Eclectic.** A little rough around the edges and noisy, this restaurant with white-washed walls is worth the visit for the Cuban roast chicken and expertly grilled hamburgers. Salads are served with homemade dressing; black-bean cakes are offered for those preferring a meatless dish. **FYI:** Reservations not accepted. No smoking. **Open:** Lunch Mon–Fri 11am–5pm; dinner Mon–Sun 5pm–1am; brunch Sat–Sun 11am–3:30pm. **Prices:** Main courses $7–$15. AE, MC, V.

REFRESHMENT STOP 🍴

Gorin's

620 Peachtree St (Midtown); tel 404/874-0550. **Deli/Ice cream.** Over 200 flavors of rich homemade ice cream to choose from, plus quick, simple meals like the Reuben

sandwich, ham and cheese with honey mustard, and almond chicken salad platter. **Open:** Mon–Fri 9:30am–5pm, Sat–Sun 10am–5pm. No CC. &

ATTRACTIONS

MUSEUMS

Atlanta History Center
130 W Paces Ferry Rd NW (Buckhead); tel 404/814-4000. Covering 32 woodland acres, this complex maintains a vast collection of photographs, maps, books, newspaper accounts, furnishings, Civil War artifacts, and Margaret Mitchell memorabilia. The two-story Atlanta History Museum displays an entire 1890s shotgun house, a fire engine used in the great Atlanta fire of 1917, and a rare 1920 Hanson Six touring car. Historic houses on the grounds include an 1840s plantation farm (Tullie Smith House), the aristocratic Swan House, and a slave cabin. Self-guided walking trails connect the buildings, and there are five historical gardens. (Small additional admission charge for the historic houses.) **Open:** Mon–Sat 10am–5:30pm, Sun noon–5:30pm. Closed some hols. **$$$**

World of Coca-Cola
55 Martin Luther King Dr SW (Downtown); tel 404/676-5151. Adjacent to Underground Atlanta (see below). This three-story, multimedia extravaganza pays tribute to Atlanta's most famous export, with exhibits dedicated to the history and international appeal of this native drink. Contains more than 1,000 Coke-related artifacts and memorabilia, including a replica of a 1930s soda fountain and a 4,500-square-foot company store. **Open:** Mon–Sat 10am–8:30pm, Sun noon–5pm. Closed some hols. **$$**

High Museum of Art
1280 Peachtree St NE (Midtown); tel 404/892-3600 or 892-HIGH (24 hours). Housed in a $20 million, Richard Meier-designed, white porcelain building, this marvelous museum houses impressive collections of Western and African art. The permanent collection includes over 10,000 pieces, among them a significant group of 19th- and 20th-century American paintings by Hudson River School artists such as Thomas Cole and Frederic Church, as well as works by Thomas Sully, John Singer Sargent, and William Harnet. Other strong points include Italian art from the 14th to the 18th centuries and 19th-century French art. **Open:** Tues–Sat 10am–5pm, Fri 10am–9pm, Sun noon–5pm. Closed some hols. **$$**

SciTrek
395 Piedmont Ave; tel 404/522-5500. SciTrek houses more than 100 hands-on exhibits divided into nine categories such as "Electricity and Magnetism," "Light and Perception," "Mechanics," and "Mathematica." Kids can lift a race car with one hand, view the world from inside a bubble, control traffic for the city of Atlanta, and much more. Exhibits are supplemented by an ongoing series of lectures, demonstrations, and workshops, plus an IMAX theater. **Open:** Mon–Sat 10am–5pm, Sun noon–5pm. Closed some hols. **$$$**

Fernbank Museum of Natural History
767 Clifton Rd NE; tel 404/378-0127. The largest museum of natural sciences in the Southeast, this architecturally stunning facility adjoins 65 acres of pristine forest. The major permanent exhibit, "A Walk Through Time in Georgia," uses the state as a microcosm of the earth's development through time and the chronology of life upon it. Visitors travel back 15 billion years—to experience the Big Bang and the formation of galaxies and solar systems—and into the future to consider the planet's fate. Another permanent exhibit, "Spectrum of the Senses," features participatory displays in which visitors can step into a life-size kaleidoscope, see physical evidence of sound waves, or mix colors on a computer. Other museum attractions include a Caribbean coral-reef aquarium, the Star Gallery, and an IMAX theater (additional admission charge for IMAX films). **Open:** Mon–Thurs 10am–5pm, Fri 10am–9pm, Sat 10am–5pm, Sun noon–5pm. Closed some hols. **$$$**

Michael C Carlos Museum
571 S Kilgo St, Emory University; tel 404/727-4282. This intriguing museum was founded in 1919, in order to display art and artifacts collected by Emory faculty in Egypt, Cyprus, Greece, Sicily, the Sea of Galilee, and the sites of ancient Babylon and Palestine. Since then, the collection has expanded to include over 12,000 treasures from Rome, Central and South America, the Near East, and Mesoamerica, and aboriginal art from North America, Asia, Africa, and Oceania. Even the building itself is stunning. Listed on the National Register of Historic Places, it was built in 1916 with a beaux-arts exterior; its interior has since been redesigned by postmodernist architect Michael Graves, who also designed the new 35,000-square-foot annex. **Open:** Mon–Thurs, Sat 10am–5pm, Fri 10am–9pm, Sun noon–5pm. Closed some hols. **$**

Museum of the Jimmy Carter Library
441 Freedom Pkwy (Little Five Points); tel 404/331-0296. Located at the Carter Presidential Center. Visitors to this ultramodern building may view personal aspects of Carter's presidency, such as handmade gifts from the American people and elegant Gifts of State from foreign leaders. Several interactive video displays including a "Town Hall" and videotapes of state events. There's also a faithful replica of the White House's Oval Office, a Japanese garden, and a lovely view of the Atlanta skyline. **Open:** Mon–Sat 9am–4:45pm, Sun noon–4:45pm. Closed some hols. **$$**

Center for Puppetry Arts
1404 Spring St at 18th St (Midtown); tel 404/873-3391 or 874-0398 (recorded info). More than 200 puppets are on display, and there are shows and other activities regularly planned. Visitors are even given the opportunity to make their own puppets. There's a 300-seat theater, two galleries, a museum, lecture hall, education room, reference library, and gift shop. **Open:** Mon–Sat 9am–5pm. Closed some hols. **$$$**

MARTIN LUTHER KING JR HISTORIC DISTRICT

Martin Luther King Jr Center for Nonviolent Social Change

449 Auburn Ave (between Boulevard and Jackson St); tel 404/524-1956. As a nongovernmental member of the United Nations, the King Center works with government agencies and the private sector to reduce violence within the local community and among nations. Its library and archives house the world's largest collection of books and other materials documenting the civil rights movement, including Dr King's personal papers and a rare 87-volume edition of *The Collected Works of Mahatma Gandhi,* a gift from the government of India.

Visitors are given a self-guided tour brochure. The tour begins in the Exhibition Hall, where memorabilia of King and the civil rights movement are displayed in an exhibit called "King: Images of the Drum Major." Additional exhibits—including a room honoring Rosa Parks and another honoring Gandhi—are in Freedom Hall. Outside is Freedom Plaza, where Dr King's white-marble crypt rests on a beautiful five-tiered Reflecting Pool, a symbol of the life-giving nature of water. The tomb is inscribed with his words: "Free at last." Also on the premises is an information counter where visitors can find out about all Auburn Avenue attractions and obtain tickets to tour the King birth home (see below). **Open:** Daily 9:30am–5:30pm. Closed some hols. **Free**

Birth Home of Martin Luther King Jr

501 Auburn Ave (at Hogue St); tel 404/331-3920. Martin Luther King Jr, the oldest son of a Baptist minister and an elementary-school teacher, was born in this two-story Queen Anne–style house on January 15, 1929. King lived here through the age of 12, then moved with his family to a house a few blocks away. In 1971, King's mother deeded the home to the Martin Luther King Jr Center. It has since been restored to its appearance during the years of Martin's boyhood. The furnishings, wallpapers, linoleum, and paint colors are all originals or similar period reproductions, and many personal items belonging to the family are on display.

Tickets for a tour of the house must be obtained at the King Center (see above). Tours depart from the Center, taking in sights en route to the house. In summer months, especially, tickets often run out early. **Open:** Daily 10am–5pm. Closed some hols. **Free**

Ebenezer Baptist Church

407–413 Auburn Ave; tel 404/688-7263. Founded in 1886, Ebenezer was a spiritual center of the civil rights movement during the years 1960 to 1968, when Martin Luther King Jr served as a co-pastor. His grandfather, the Rev A D Williams, dedicated the church to "the advancement of black people and every righteous and social movement." Visitors can listen to a taped message on the history of the church and/or take a 10-minute guided tour. Sunday services at 7:45am and 10:45am. An ecumenical service takes place here every year during King week. Donations appreciated. **Open:** Mon–Fri 9:30am–noon and 1:30–4:30pm. **Free**

The African American Panoramic Experience Museum

135 Auburn Ave NE; tel 404/523-2739. African art, exhibits on local African American history, and rotating exhibits by local and national African American artists are the focus of this museum situated in Sweet Auburn, Atlanta's foremost black residential and business district. There's also a 12-minute multimedia presentation on the area's history narrated by Cicely Tyson and Julian Bond. **Open:** Tues–Sat 10am–5pm, Sun 1–5pm. Closed Sun Sept–Jan, Mar–May. Closed some hols. **$**

OTHER HISTORIC SITES

Georgia State Capitol

Capitol Hill at Washington St; tel 404/656-2844. Built in 1884, the capitol building is readily recognizable from its gold-topped dome standing 237 feet above the city. Besides a hall of fame (with busts of famous Georgians) and a hall of flags (with US, state, and Confederate battle flags), the building houses the **Georgia State Museum of Science and Industry,** which has collections of Georgia minerals and Indian artifacts, dioramas of famous places in the state, and fish and wildlife exhibits. Tours offered Monday–Friday at 10am, 11am, 1pm, and 2pm. **Open:** Mon–Fri 8am–5pm, Sat 10am–4pm, Sun noon–4pm. Closed some hols. **Free**

Wren's Nest

1050 Ralph David Abernathy Blvd, SW; tel 404/753-7735. Former home of Joel Chandler Harris, author, journalist, and creator of the Uncle Remus tales. Harris began his journalism career in 1861 at a plantation-based newspaper, where he befriended several of the older slaves. Harris absorbed the slaves' African folk tales and later adapted them for his stories, which he hoped would heal the racial wounds left by the Civil War. Harris's beautiful Victorian house is now a National Historic Landmark containing original family furnishings, photographs, and memorabilia. Special storytelling programs, picnic grounds, museum shop. Guided tours are given on the hour and half-hour. **Open:** Tues–Sat 10am–4pm, Sun 1–4pm. Closed some hols. **$$**

Hammonds House Galleries and Resource Center

503 Peeples St SW; tel 404/752-8730. Occupying the 1857 Eastlake Victorian-style former home of Dr Otis T Hammonds, a black anesthesiologist and art patron, Hammonds House is a national center for the exhibition, preservation, research, and documentation of African American art and artists. The house, now operated by the Fulton County Commission, houses Hammonds's extensive collection of works by African American and Haitian artists, as well as African masks and carvings. **Open:** Tues–Fri 10am–6pm, Sat–Sun 1–5pm. Closed some hols. **$**

Margaret Mitchell House
Peachtree and 10th Sts (Midtown); tel 404/249-7012. Mitchell wrote most of her epic novel *Gone With the Wind* in this turn-of-the-century Tudor Revival apartment house (circa 1899), where she lived with her husband from 1925 to 1932. The building, which Mitchell referred to as "the Dump," was engulfed by flames in 1994 and in 1996 but was subsequently restored. Mitchell's apartment has been renovated to its 1920s appearance, and the rest of the interior structure houses exhibits and special event facilities. **Open:** Call for schedule. **$$**

Alonzo F Herndon Home
587 University Place; tel 404/581-9813. Alonzo Herndon was one of the most remarkable financial success stories of African American history. Born into slavery in 1858, he later worked as a field hand and sharecropper before moving to Atlanta, where he worked as a barber. He eventually bought several barbershops, then went into real estate and insurance. By 1895 he was the richest black man in Atlanta.

In 1910, Herndon built this elegant 15-room beaux-arts house. Herndon and his wife, Adrienne, were the primary architects of the house and construction was accomplished almost entirely by black artisans. Guided tours begin in a receiving room, with a 10-minute introductory video, and continue through rooms full of Louis XV–style furnishings, rococo gilt-trim walls, and friezes depicting the accomplishments of Herndon's life. The family's impressive collection of ancient Greek and Roman vases and funerary objects is housed in the Collection Room. **Open:** Tues–Sat 10am–4pm. Closed some hols. **Free**

Oakland Cemetery
248 Oakland Ave SE (Downtown); tel 404/688-2107. This fascinating 88-acre Victorian cemetery, founded in 1850, survived the Civil War and remained the only cemetery in Atlanta for 34 years. The cemetery is remarkable not only for the people buried here—Confederate and Union soldiers (including five Southern generals), prominent families and paupers, governors and mayors, golf great Bobby Jones, and one of Atlanta's most famous natives, *Gone With the Wind* author Margaret Mitchell—but for its grandiose Gothic and classical-revival mausolea, urns, stained glass, and Victorian statuary. A self-guided walking tour brochure is available at the visitors center. **Open:** Cemetery, daily sunrise–7pm; visitors center, Mon–Fri 9am–5pm. **Free**

PARKS AND GARDENS

Atlanta Botanical Garden
Piedmont Ave between Monroe Dr and 14th St; tel 404/876-5859. An oasis of beauty and tranquillity in Piedmont Park, just minutes from downtown Atlanta. Includes 15 acres of landscaped gardens, a 15-acre woodland with walking trails, and the new Dorothy Chapman Fuqua Conservatory, a

16,000-square-foot, state-of-the-art facility housing tropical and desert plants from around the world. **Open:** Tues–Sun 9am–6pm, until 7pm during summer. Closed some hols. **$$$**

Centennial Olympic Park
Martin Luther King Jr Dr (Downtown); tel 404/744-1996. This 21-acre urban oasis is heralded by an Olympic ring–shaped fountain that spills into a reflecting pool flanked by a pair of century-old Georgia oak trees. The fountain is the central focus of a vast paved plaza bordered by the flags of the 23 countries that have hosted the modern Olympic Games. Other areas of the park include an 8,000-seat grassy outdoor amphitheater, lawns and gardens highlighting local greenery, pedestrian promenades, and pathways made from commemorative Olympic bricks. An Olympic Games museum is also planned for the site.

Chattahoochee River National Recreation Area
1978 Island Ford Pkwy; tel 770/399-8070. A very popular spot for Atlantans looking to commune with nature, this park consists of 13 different "units" along a 48-mile stretch of the Chattahoochee River from northwest Atlanta to Lake Lanier. Day hikes, fitness trails, nature trails, and picnic facilities are all available, all within easy access of the city. The river is also a popular spot for canoeing, kayaking, rafting, and fishing. The park concessioner, Chattahoochee Outdoor Center (tel 404/395-6851) rents watercraft from May through Labor Day at the Johnson Ferry and Powers Island units. **Open:** Daily sunrise–sunset. **$**

ENTERTAINMENT VENUES

The Fox Theatre
660 Peachtree St NE; tel 404/881-2100. This extravaganza of Moorish-Egyptian fantasy, with its minarets and onion domes, began life as a Shriners' temple back in 1916. Its exotic lobby was decorated with goldfish ponds and lush Oriental carpeting; in the auditorium itself, a skyscape was transformed to sunrise, sunset, or starry night skies as the occasion demanded, and a striped Bedouin canopy overhung the balcony. Recently restored to its former glory, it has positively thrived as a venue for live entertainment. Tours are available Monday and Thursday at 10am and Saturday at 10am and 11:30am.

Olympic Stadium
Capitol Ave SW; tel 404/589-5000. Built for the 1996 Olympics and donated to the city by Olympic organizers, this 45,000-seat facility is the new home of the Atlanta Braves. The Braves play 81 games here during the regular season. **$$$$**

Georgia Dome
1 Georgia Dome Rd (at International Blvd and Northside Dr) (Downtown); tel 404/223-9200 or 223-8427 (box office). Atlanta's 71,500-seat domed megastadium is the home of pro football's Atlanta Falcons. The facility combines with the adjacent two-million-square-foot **Georgia World Congress Center** to form the world's largest entertainment complex.

Its oval shape provides a close view of stadium action from every seat. It is also the site for college football's Peach Bowl, in addition to tennis matches, tractor pulls, college basketball, and track and field events. Tours of the Georgia Dome last 45 minutes and are offered on the hour Tues–Sat 10am–4pm, Sun noon–4pm. **$$$$**

Omni Coliseum

100 Techwood Dr NW (at Marietta St) (Downtown); tel 404/681-2100. The 17,000-seat oval-shaped Omni Coliseum is home to the Atlanta Hawks of the NBA, the Atlanta Knights hockey team (IHL), and WCW professional wrestling. The Omni is also used for varied sporting and entertainment events, including Harlem Globetrotters games, college basketball, and tennis exhibitions. **$$$$**

OTHER ATTRACTIONS

CNN Center

Marietta St at Techwood Dr (Downtown); tel 404/827-2400. Guided 45-minute tours take visitors through the entire process of news broadcasting, as they view the news team at work just beyond a glassed-in viewing room. Exhibits on Ted Turner's Cable News Network and WTBS Superstation include a scaled-down model of the Galaxy 5 satellite that carries the signal for the company's networks; an exhibit on TBS sports, and a duplicate of MGM's Oscar for *Gone With the Wind.* Also, one of the six theaters on the premises shows *Gone With the Wind* twice every day. **Open:** Daily 9am–5pm. Closed some hols. **$$$**

Underground Atlanta

50 Upper Alabama St (Downtown); tel 404/523-2311. Bounded by Wall St, Washington St, Martin Luther King Jr Dr, and S Peachtree St, and adjacent to the Five Points MARTA station. This "city under the city" was formed in 1920 when street viaducts were built over downtown Atlanta, essentially burying the neighborhood for several decades. (Despite its name and history, most of the current complex is actually aboveground.) Many significant architectural details still survive from these storefronts, including ornate marble, granite archways, cast-iron pilasters, decorative brickwork, and hard-carved wood posts and panels.

In 1989, a six-block stretch of Alabama St was reincarnated as Underground Atlanta. This $142-million project includes more than 200 retail and food shops. In **Kenny's Alley,** there are restaurants ranging from fast food to fine dining, and nightspots featuring every imaginable type of music. **Humbug Square Market,** with its restored turn-of-the-century wagons and pushcarts, offers unique merchandise in a typical street-market setting. The brand-new **Olympic Experience** commemorates Atlanta's role as host of the 1996 Summer Olympics. **Open:** Mon–Sat 10am–9:30pm, Sun 11am–7:30pm. Closed Dec 25. **Free**

Atlanta Heritage Row

55 Upper Alabama St (Downtown); tel 404/584-7879. Located in Underground Atlanta (see above). This 7,000-square-foot facility tells the story of Atlanta's history and spirit, from its inception as a railroad depot to its recent role as an international Olympic city and business center. Six interactive exhibition areas—with maps, models, and high-definition TV—include a re-created 1845 train depot, audio of Atlanta blues and country-music greats like Fiddlin' John Carson and Bessie Smith, a video presenting the movie premiere of *Gone With the Wind,* and a 1970 Conair 880 jet cockpit. **Open:** Tues–Sat 10am–5pm, Sun 1–5pm. Closed some hols. **$**

Zoo Atlanta

800 Cherokee Ave SE; tel 404/624-5600. A 40-acre zoo with habitats simulating the animals' native environments. There's an African rain forest with resident gorilla families and a walk-through aviary; and an East African savanna, with lions, giraffes, rhinos, ostriches, and other species. **Open:** Daily 10am–6:30pm. Closed some hols. **$$$**

Cyclorama

800 Cherokee Ave; tel 404/624-1071. For a breathtaking view of the Battle of Atlanta, go by the neoclassical building that houses this 42-foot-high, 356-foot-circumference, 100-year-old painting with a three-dimensional foreground and special lighting, music, and sound effects. This is only one of three cycloramas in the country, and it has recently been fully restored. There are 15 shows daily. **Open:** June–Aug, daily 9:20am–5:30pm; Sept–May, daily 9:20am–4:30pm. Closed some hols. **$$**

Chamblee's Antique Row

Peachtree Rd between Chamblee-Dunwoody and N Peachtree Rds, Chamblee; tel 770/458-1614. Quaint complex of more than 30 shops are housed in a row of 19th-century homes, churches, and storefronts. Dealers of antique American and European furniture; glassware and pottery; books; coins; dolls; jewelry; records; and political, Coca-Cola, and sports memorabilia are all represented. **Open:** Mon–Sat 10:30am–5pm, Sun 1–5pm. Closed some hols.

Atlanta Hartsfield Int'l Airport

HOTELS 🏨

≡≡≡ Courtyard by Marriott Atlanta Airport

2050 Sullivan Rd, College Park, 30337; tel 770/997-2220 or toll free 800/321-2211; fax 770/994-9743. Exit 16 off I-285. A winning, modern property with the trademark central courtyard. Clean, comfortable, and quiet, despite being near the airport. **Rooms:** 144 rms and stes. CI 3pm/CO noon. Nonsmoking rms avail. **Amenities:** 🛋 🕹 A/C, cable TV w/movies, voice mail. **Services:** ✕ 🚗 🛍 🛎 Car-rental desk. **Facilities:** 🔲 🅿 ⅙ 1 restaurant (bkfst only), whirlpool, washer/dryer. **Rates:** $89 S; $99 D; $109–$119 ste. Children under age 18 stay free. Parking: Outdoor, free. AE, CB, DC.

◼◼ Hampton Inn Airport

1888 Sullivan Rd, College Park, 30337; tel 770/996-2220 or toll free 800/426-7866; fax 770/996-2488. Exit 16 off I-285. A great place for families, and surprisingly quiet, considering its location. **Rooms:** 130 rms. CI 2pm/CO noon. Nonsmoking rms avail. **Amenities:** 🛏 💧 A/C, cable TV w/movies, dataport. **Services:** 🚐 ⚗ ↵ **Facilities:** 🛁 ⊡ 🛐 **Rates (CP):** $54–$60 S; $62–$68 D. Children under age 18 stay free. Parking: Outdoor, free. AE, CB, DC, DISC, MC, V.

◼◼ Holiday Inn Airport

1380 Virginia Ave, Atlanta, 30344; tel 404/762-8411 or toll free 800/465-4329; fax 404/767-4963. Exit 19 off I-85. A nice, basic property with a wonderful and expansive lobby and adequate rooms. **Rooms:** 492 rms and stes. CI 3pm/CO noon. Nonsmoking rms avail. **Amenities:** 🛏 💧 A/C, cable TV w/movies, dataport. **Services:** 🍴 🚐 ⚗ ↵ **Facilities:** 🛁 ⛆ ⊡ 🛐 1 restaurant, sauna, washer/dryer. **Rates:** $105–$175 S or D; $250 ste. Extra person $12. Children under age 19 stay free. Parking: Outdoor, free. AE, CB, DC, DISC, EC, ER, JCB, MC, V.

MOTELS

◼◼ Fairfield Inn by Marriott Airport

2451 Old National Hwy, College Park, 30349; tel 404/761-8371 or toll free 800/228-2800; fax 404/761-8371. Exit 16 off I-28. Standard chain motel, located in a commercial district near the airport. Oriented toward business travelers. **Rooms:** 132 rms. CI 3pm/CO noon. Nonsmoking rms avail. All rooms have well-lit work desks, separate vanity areas, and two double or one king-size bed. **Amenities:** 🛏 💧 A/C, cable TV w/movies. **Services:** 🚐 ⚗ ↵ **Facilities:** 🛁 🛐 **Rates (CP):** Peak (Feb–Sept) $40–$50 S; $46–$60 D. Extra person $7. Children under age 10 stay free. Lower rates off-season. Parking: Outdoor, free. AE, DC, DISC, MC, V.

◼◼ La Quinta Inn Airport

4874 Old National Hwy, College Park, 30337; tel 404/768-1241 or toll free 800/531-5900; fax 404/766-3642. Exit 16 off I-85. A simple, comfortable chain motel. **Rooms:** 120 rms. CI 3pm/CO noon. Nonsmoking rms avail. The suites are located in the old slave quarters and open into a private courtyard. **Amenities:** 🛏 💧 A/C, cable TV w/movies. **Services:** 🚐 ⚗ ↵ 🍴 Complimentary tea served every afternoon. **Facilities:** 🛁 ⊡ 🛐 **Rates (CP):** $50 S; $57 D. Extra person $7. Children under age 18 stay free. Parking: Outdoor, free. AE, CB, DC, DISC, MC, V.

RESTAURANTS 🍴

Flying Pig

856 Virginia Ave, College Park; tel 404/559-1000. 1 mi E of exit 19 off I-85. **Barbecue.** Although the decor here is nothing fancy—the restaurant is behind a liquor store and the seats are a little uncomfortable—the barbecue is 100% authentic. Chopped-pork sandwiches, huge portions of ribs and sliced pork, and homemade iced tea are popular with locals as well as with visitors rushing off to the airport. **FYI:** Reservations not accepted. No liquor license. **Open:** Tues–Fri 10:30am–8pm, Sat 11:30am–8pm. **Prices:** Main courses $3–$7. No CC.

Grecian Gyro Restaurant

855 Virginia Ave, College Park; tel 404/762-1627. 5 mi E of exit 19 off I-85. **Greek.** An utterly no-frills joint, with hard booths and a few padded stools at the counter. This is the place to go when you're stuck at the airport and have a craving for a big, greasy gyro. **FYI:** Reservations not accepted. No liquor license. **Open:** Mon–Fri 10am–10pm. **Prices:** Main courses $3–$6. No CC.

Zab-E-Lee

4837 Old National Hwy, College Park; tel 404/768-2705. **Thai.** Owned and operated by a local Thai family. Authentic dishes include papaya salad and tom yum soup with lemongrass and straw mushrooms. **FYI:** Reservations not accepted. BYO. **Open:** Lunch Mon–Fri 11am–3pm; dinner Mon–Fri 5–10pm, Sat 11am–10pm, Sun 4–9pm. **Prices:** Main courses $3–$9. AE, CB, DC, DISC, MC, V. ♿

Augusta

See also North Augusta, SC

The oldest and largest city in east-central Georgia, on the Savannah River. It was the state capital from 1783 to 1795. A trading port as early as 1717, it remains a trade center and features diversified industries. A popular resort known for its golf tournaments (especially the prestigious Masters), with Riverwalk the hub of tourism. **Information:** Augusta–Richmond County Convention & Visitors Bureau, 32 8th St, PO Box 1331, Augusta, 30903 (tel 706/823-6600).

HOTELS 🏨

◼◼ AmeriSuites

1062 Claussen Rd, 30907; tel 706/733-4656 or toll free 800/528-1234. Exit 66 off I-20. An attractive property offering comfortable and roomy suites. **Rooms:** 111 stes. CI 2pm/CO noon. Nonsmoking rms avail. Rooms are very well furnished. **Amenities:** 🛏 💧 🖬 A/C, cable TV, refrig. 1 unit w/whirlpool. **Services:** ↵ **Facilities:** 🛁 ⊡ 🛐 Washer/dryer. Guests may use tennis and swimming facilities at nearby Telfair Inn. **Rates (CP):** Peak (Apr) $90–$95 ste. Extra person $5. Children under age 18 stay free. Lower rates off-season. Parking: Outdoor, free. AE, DC, DISC, ER, JCB, MC, V.

UNRATED Augusta Landmark Hotel

640 Broad St, 30901; tel 706/722-5541; fax 706/724-0053. Exit 66 off I-20. A charming property housed in a sandstone building and surrounded by well-manicured grounds. **Rooms:** 200 rms and stes. Executive level. CI 2pm/CO noon. Nonsmoking rms avail. **Amenities:** 🛏 💧 🖬 A/C, cable TV. **Services:** ✗ ↵ 🍴 Babysitting. **Facilities:** 🛁 ⊡ 🛐 1

restaurant, 2 bars (w/entertainment). **Rates:** $52–$225 S; $57–$229 D; $125–$450 ste. Extra person $10. Lower rates off-season. Parking: Outdoor, free. AE, DC, DISC, MC, V.

≣≣≣ Courtyard by Marriott

1045 Stevens Creek Rd, 30907; tel 706/737-3737 or toll free 800/321-2211; fax 706/738-7851. Exit 65 off I-20. Everything you might expect from a Courtyard: modern decor, comfortable rooms, and well-landscaped grounds. A beautiful and appealing place for any traveler. **Rooms:** 130 rms and stes. CI 4pm/CO noon. Nonsmoking rms avail. **Amenities:** 📺 ⚴ A/C, cable TV w/movies. Some units w/terraces, 1 w/whirlpool. **Services:** ✗ ⤸ **Facilities:** 🎣 ⚑ 35 ⅁ 1 restaurant (bkfst only), 1 bar, whirlpool, washer/dryer. **Rates (BB):** Peak (Apr) $66–$76 S or D; $76–$104 ste. Children under age 18 stay free. Lower rates off-season. Parking: Outdoor, free. AE, DC, DISC, MC, V.

≣≣≣ The Partridge Inn

2110 Walton Way, 30904; tel 706/737-8888 or toll free 800/476-6888; fax 706/731-0826. Exit 65 off I-20. A relaxing inn housed in a century-old building with lots of homey Southern touches, like porches with rocking chairs. A comfortable place to spend a few days. **Rooms:** 155 rms and stes. Executive level. CI 2pm/CO noon. Nonsmoking rms avail. Rooms are very well decorated and comfortable. **Amenities:** 📺 ⚴ ⚑ ⚲ A/C, cable TV w/movies, refrig. Some units w/terraces. **Services:** ✗ VP ⚴ ⤸ Car-rental desk, social director, babysitting. **Facilities:** 🎣 200 ⌨ ⅁ 2 restaurants (see "Restaurants" below), 1 bar. **Rates (CP):** $65–$110 S; $75–$120 D; $90–$110 ste. Extra person $10. Children under age 18 stay free. Parking: Indoor/outdoor, free. AE, DC, DISC, MC, V.

≣≣≣ Radisson Hotel

Two 10th St, 30901; tel 706/722-8900 or toll free 800/333-3333; fax 706/823-6513. A modern, brick hotel located on the banks of the Savannah River. A wonderful choice for the traveler who wants extra comfort and a beautiful setting. **Rooms:** 234 rms and stes. CI 2pm/CO 11am. Nonsmoking rms avail. **Amenities:** 📺 ⚴ ⚑ A/C, cable TV w/movies. **Services:** ✗ ⤸ ⚴ Babysitting. **Facilities:** 🎣 ⚑ 700 ⅁ 1 restaurant, 1 bar, sauna. **Rates:** $69–$99 S or D; $125 ste. Children under age 18 stay free. Parking: Indoor, free. AE, CB, DC, DISC, MC, V.

UNRATED Sheraton Augusta Hotel

2651 Perimeter Pkwy, 30909; tel 706/855-8100 or toll free 800/325-3535. Exit 64A off I-20. A charming hotel offering comfortable rooms and surrounded by well-manicured grounds. **Rooms:** 240 rms and stes. CI 2pm/CO 11am. Nonsmoking rms avail. **Amenities:** 📺 ⚴ ⚑ A/C, cable TV w/movies, refrig. Some units w/whirlpools. **Services:** ✗ ⤸ **Facilities:** 🎣 100 ⅁ 1 restaurant, 1 bar, volleyball, games rm, spa, sauna, whirlpool. **Rates:** Peak (Apr) $82–$92 S; $139 ste.

Extra person $5. Children under age 12 stay free. Lower rates off-season. Parking: Outdoor, free. AE, CB, DC, DISC, MC, V.

MOTELS

≣≣≣ Days Inn

3026 Washington Rd, 30907; tel 706/738-0131 or toll free 800/DAYS-INN; fax 706/738-0131. Exit 65 off I-20. Standard chain accommodations housed in a pink, sandstone building. **Rooms:** 122 rms. CI 2pm/CO 11am. Nonsmoking rms avail. Rooms are large and comfortable, and have average-quality furnishings. **Amenities:** 📺 ⚑ A/C, cable TV w/movies, refrig, VCR, CD/tape player. All units w/terraces. **Services:** ✗ ⤸ **Facilities:** 🎣 ⅁ 1 restaurant. **Rates:** $35 S; $40–$50 D. Extra person $5. Children under age 17 stay free. Parking: Outdoor, free. AE, DC, DISC, MC, V.

≣≣ Shoney's Inn

3023 Washington Rd, 30907; tel 706/736-2595 or toll free 800/222-2222; fax 706/736-2595. Exit 65 off I-20. A comfortable, clean, dependable chain motel. Perfect for an overnight stay. **Rooms:** 120 rms. CI 2pm/CO noon. Nonsmoking rms avail. **Amenities:** 📺 A/C, cable TV. **Services:** 🚐 ⤸ ⚴ **Facilities:** 🎣 ⅁ **Rates:** Peak (Feb–June) $35 S; $37 D. Extra person $7. Children under age 12 stay free. Lower rates off-season. Parking: Outdoor, free. AE, DC, DISC, MC, V.

INNS

UNRATED Oglethorpe Inn

836-838 Greene St, 30901; tel 706/724-9774. Exit 66 off I-20. These green houses with red trim are adorned in Victorian style and are charming and inviting. Great service and a cozy atmosphere make this a great getaway. **Rooms:** 14 rms. CI 3pm/CO 11am. No smoking. Rooms are very well furnished. **Amenities:** 📺 ⚴ ⚲ A/C, cable TV. **Services:** ✗ ⤸ ⚴ Wine/sherry served. **Facilities:** Guest lounge w/TV. Guests may use tennis and swimming facilities at nearby Telfair Inn. **Rates (BB):** $85–$125 S or D. Extra person $10. Children under age 10 stay free. Higher rates for special events/hols. Parking: Outdoor, free. AE, CB, DC, DISC, MC, V.

≣≣≣ Telfair Inn

326 Greene St, 30901 (Downtown); tel 706/724-3315 or toll free 800/241-2407; fax 706/823-6623. Riverwatch Pkwy exit off I-20. This inn has two beautiful buildings—one is green with red trim, the other is white with green trim. Good service, friendly staff. **Rooms:** 61 rms and stes. CI 3pm/CO 11am. Nonsmoking rms avail. **Amenities:** 📺 ⚴ ⚲ A/C, cable TV. All units w/fireplaces, all w/whirlpools. **Services:** ✗ 🚐 ⤸ ⚴ Afternoon tea and wine/sherry served. **Facilities:** 🎣 350 ⅁ 1 restaurant (bkfst only), 1 bar, guest lounge. **Rates:** Peak (Apr) $67–$97 S; $77–$107 D; $97–$107 ste. Extra

person $10. Children under age 12 stay free. Lower rates off-season. Higher rates for special events/hols. Parking: Outdoor, free. AE, CB, DC, DISC, MC, V.

RESTAURANTS 🍴

Cotton Row Cafe
Six 8th St; tel 706/722-6901. **American.** An eatery offering a wide variety of sandwiches, burgers, and appetizers in a relaxing and gracious setting. **FYI:** Reservations not accepted. Dress code. **Open:** Daily 11am–11pm. **Prices:** Main courses $2–$7. AE, MC, V. 🛳 👥

Michael's
2860 Washington Rd; tel 706/733-2860. At Boy Scout Rd. **Continental.** Specializes in French and continental cuisine; the most popular entree is rack of lamb. **FYI:** Reservations accepted. Dress code. **Open:** Daily 6–10pm. **Prices:** Main courses $11–$25. AE, CB, DC, DISC, MC, V. ♥

⑤ ★ Restaurant
In the Partridge Inn, 2110 Walton Way; tel 706/737-8888. **American.** Diners here can enjoy fresh fish, beef, and fowl entrees in an elegant, high-ceilinged dining room with an antebellum atmosphere. **FYI:** Reservations recommended. Jazz. Children's menu. Dress code. **Open:** Peak (Apr) daily 11:30am–10pm. **Prices:** Main courses $12–$18. AE, DISC, MC, V. ♥ 🔊 📹 VP ♿

ATTRACTION 🧳

Morris Museum of Art
1 10th St; tel 706/724-7501. Located along the Riverwalk cultural corridor, the Morris is the only museum in the United States dedicated entirely to Southern art and artists. Galleries are devoted to topics such as Antebellum Portraiture, Civil War Art, the Black Presence in Southern Painting, Southern Impressionism, and Self-Taught Artists. **Open:** Tues–Sat 10am–5:30pm, Sun 12:30–5:30pm. Closed some hols. **$**

Bainbridge

The Flint River flows through the center of this town, once a Native American trading post. Victorian and neoclassical houses line several streets, and there is a freshwater beach. **Information:** Bainbridge–Decatur County Chamber of Commerce, PO Box 736, Bainbridge, 31717 (tel 912/246-4774).

MOTELS 🏨

🛏🛏 Charter House Inn
1401 Tallahassee Hwy, 31717; tel 912/246-8550 or toll free 800/768-8550; fax 912/246-0260. US 27 S and US 84 bypass. Good for overnight stays, this is the closest full-service facility to Lake Seminole. **Rooms:** 124 rms. CI 3pm/CO noon. Nonsmoking rms avail. **Amenities:** 🎬 A/C, cable TV. King rooms have coffeemakers. **Services:** 🛄 🍴 🐾 Car-

rental desk. **Facilities:** 🎬 🅿250 ♿ 1 restaurant, 1 bar (w/entertainment), volleyball. **Rates:** $38–$39 D. Extra person $5. Children under age 16 stay free. Parking: Outdoor, free. AE, CB, DC, DISC, MC, V.

🛏🛏 Holiday Inn Express
751 W Shotwell St, 31717; tel 912/246-0015 or toll free 800/HOLIDAY; fax 912/246-9972. Quiet hotel on the outskirts of the city, offering a convenient overnight stopover for visitors heading south to Florida. **Rooms:** 52 rms and stes. CI noon/CO 11am. Nonsmoking rms avail. **Amenities:** 🎬 ⚓ A/C, cable TV, dataport. 1 unit w/minibar, 1 w/whirlpool. Suites have refrigerators and wet bars. **Services:** ✗ 🛄 🍴 **Facilities:** 🎬 🅿50 ♿ Heated pool, whirlpool. **Rates (CP):** $50 S or D; $70 ste. Extra person $5. Children under age 12 stay free. Parking: Outdoor, free. AE, DC, DISC, MC, V.

🛏🛏 Jameson Inn
1403 Tallahassee Hwy, 31717; tel 912/243-7000 or toll free 800/541-3268. US 27 off US 84 bypass. Fine accommodations for business guests, though the surroundings—another lodging and a gas station—are not particularly appealing. **Rooms:** 42 rms and stes. CI 2pm/CO 11am. Nonsmoking rms avail. **Amenities:** 🎬 ⚓ A/C, cable TV, dataport, voice mail. Some units w/whirlpools. **Services:** 🍴 Car-rental desk. **Facilities:** 🎬 🏸 ♿ **Rates (CP):** $46 S or D; $85–$125 ste. Extra person $4. Children under age 16 stay free. Parking: Outdoor, free. AE, CB, DC, DISC, MC, V.

Braselton

North of Atlanta in rolling foothills. Georgia's premier winery tours are given here in a 16th-century-French-style château.

RESORT 🧳

🛏🛏🛏🛏 Château Elan Resort
7000 Old Winder Hwy, 30517; tel 404/932-0900 or toll free 800/233-WINE; fax 404/271-6005. Exit 48 off I-85. 2,400 acres. Wrought-iron detail, a pitch roof, and cornice moldings give this winery/resort the feel of a French country estate. The lobby area opens to an atrium washed in sunlight and housing restaurants. **Rooms:** 176 rms and stes; 18 cottages/villas. CI 3pm/CO noon. Nonsmoking rms avail. Each room is unique, with decor ranging from Country French to Victorian, high-tech modern to old-fashioned Western. **Amenities:** 🎬 ⚓ 📺 🍴 A/C, cable TV w/movies, refrig, dataport, voice mail, in-rm safe. Some units w/terraces, some w/fireplaces, some w/whirlpools. **Services:** ✗ 🔑 VP 🚗 🛄 🍴 Twice-daily maid svce, car-rental desk, masseur, children's program, babysitting. **Facilities:** 🎬 🏌45 🎾 🏌 🏸 🅿450 💻 ♿ 6 restaurants (see "Restaurants" below), 1 bar, volleyball, lawn games, spa, sauna, steam rm, whirlpool, beauty salon, playground. Award-winning winery. Olympic-size pool. European spa offers personalized treatments and

retreats. Legends golf course (home to Sarazen World Open) was designed by pros Gene Sarazen, Sam Snead, and Kathy Whitworth. Tennis courts include three clay, three hard, one stadium, and a pro shop. Horseback riding offered off premises, but resort provides transportation. **Rates:** Peak (Mar–June/Sept–mid-Nov) $109–$195 S or D; $225 ste; $210–$279 cottage/villa. Extra person $10. Children under age 18 stay free. Lower rates off-season. Parking: Outdoor, free. Spa has minimum stay on weekends. AE, DC, DISC, MC, V.

RESTAURANT 🍽️

♥ Cafe Elan
In Château Elan Resort and Conference Center, 7000 Old Winder Hwy; tel 404/932-0900. Exit 48 off I-85. **French Bistro.** Amidst the Château Elan Resort, this restaurant has an open and fresh decor and offers beautiful views of the surrounding landscape. The menu features sandwiches, salads, and continental entrees like chicken sautéed with pecans in red-wine cream sauce. **FYI:** Reservations recommended. Children's menu. Jacket required. Wine only. **Open:** Daily 11am–10pm. **Prices:** Main courses $13–$18. AE, DC, DISC, MC, V. VP &

ATTRACTION 🏛️

Château Elan Vineyards
Exit 48 off I-85; tel 404/867-8200. In the 10 years since wine has been produced here, this North Georgia winery has won 194 awards. Guided tours of the winery are given daily between 11am and 4pm; you can also take self-guided tours from 5pm to closing. On view are the grape-crushing and pressing machines, oak barrels used to age and flavor wines, the cask room, and the bottling area. (If you come during harvesting in August and September, you'll actually see the winemaking process.) All tours conclude with a wine tasting.

However, there's a lot more to Château Elan than just wine. The interior of the château, a stage-set version of a Parisian street, has a quarry-stone floor, wrought-iron fences, and streetlamps. Walls are adorned with large murals depicting the history of winemaking and two Parisian sites—the train station Gare du Nord and the Place des Vosges. The building also houses an art gallery with changing exhibits by regional and national artists, displays of antique European winemaking equipment, and a wine market. Outdoors, there are waterside nature trails, an 18-hole golf course, a full spa, and seven tennis courts. Outdoor concerts are fairly common in summer and entail an extra charge; call ahead to find out the current schedule. **Open:** Daily 10am–10pm. Closed Dec 25. **Free**

Brunswick

See also Jekyll Island, St Simons Island, Sea Island

Named for the ancestral German home of King George II, grantor of Georgia's original land charter, this quaint port city prides itself on its Old Towne section and waterfront. Claims to be the "shrimp capital of the world." Visitors can cross the famed Marshes of Glynn to the Golden Isles. **Information:** Brunswick–Golden Isles Visitors Bureau, 4 Glynn Ave, Brunswick, 31520 (tel 912/265-0620).

HOTEL 🏨

≣ ≣ ≣ Embassy Suites of the Golden Isles
500 Mall Blvd, 31525; tel 912/264-6100 or toll free 800/EMBASSY; fax 912/267-1615. 1 mi from exit 8 off I-95. Connected to the Brunswick Mall, this property features a lush courtyard lobby. Only a few miles from the beach. **Rooms:** 130 stes. CI 4pm/CO noon. Nonsmoking rms avail. **Amenities:** 🛁 ♨ 📶 ☕ A/C, cable TV, refrig. Some units w/whirlpools. **Services:** 🍽️ 🚗 🖼️ 🛎️ 🐕 Car-rental desk. **Facilities:** 🏋️ 🍴 500 ⚕️ 1 restaurant, 2 bars. **Rates (BB):** $99–$102 ste. Extra person $10. Children under age 16 stay free. Min stay special events. Parking: Outdoor, free. Honeymoon, golf, and *Emerald Prince* (a local gambling boat) packages avail. AE, DC, DISC, MC, V.

MOTELS

≣ ≣ ≣ Comfort Inn
5308 New Jesup Hwy, 31520; tel 912/264-6540 or toll free 800/551-7591; fax 912/264-9296. Exit 7 AB off I-95. A five-story property offering basic accommodations, right off I-95. Within 30 minutes of St Simons Island, Jekyll Island, and close to historic Brunswick. **Rooms:** 118 rms. Executive level. CI 2pm/CO noon. Nonsmoking rms avail. **Amenities:** 🛁 A/C, cable TV, dataport. **Services:** 🖼️ 🐕 🐕 Babysitting. **Facilities:** 🏋️ 200 ⚕️ 1 restaurant. **Rates (CP):** Peak (Feb–Apr; mid-June–Aug) $49–$54 S; $59–$69 D. Extra person $6. Children under age 18 stay free. Lower rates off-season. Parking: Outdoor, free. AE, CB, DC, DISC, JCB, MC, V.

≣ ≣ The Jameson Inn
661 Scranton Rd, 31520; tel 912/267-0800 or toll free 800/541-3268; fax 912/265-1922. Off Spur 25; close to Brunswick Mall. Located off a major highway, but quiet and secluded. **Rooms:** 42 rms and stes. CI 3pm/CO 11am. Nonsmoking rms avail. King rooms feature recliners. **Amenities:** 🛁 ♨ ☕ A/C, cable TV. Some units w/whirlpools. **Services:** 🖼️ 🐕 **Facilities:** 🏋️ 🍴 ⚕️ **Rates (CP):** $38–$50 S; $42–$54 D; $80–$135 ste. Extra person $4. Children under age 16 stay free. Parking: Outdoor, free. *Emerald Prince* (a local gambling boat) packages avail. AE, CB, DC, DISC, MC, V.

≣≣ Quality Inn

125 Benture Dr, 31525; tel 912/265-4600 or toll free 800/221-2222; fax 912/265-8268. Exit 8 off I-95. While this property is located on the interstate, the trees surrounding the property help cut the noise. **Rooms:** 83 rms. CI 1pm/CO 11am. Nonsmoking rms avail. **Amenities:** 🔒 ⚙ 🖥 A/C, cable TV. 1 unit w/whirlpool. **Services:** ✗ 🚐 🖼 ↵ 🔊 Car-rental desk. **Facilities:** 🔗 ⌷100⌷ ⚷ **Rates (CP):** $45–$59 S or D. Children under age 18 stay free. Parking: Outdoor, free. AE, DC, DISC, MC, V.

≣≣ Ramada Inn Downtown

3241 Glynn Ave, 31520; tel 912/264-8611 or toll free 800/272-6232; fax 912/264-8611 ext 302. Off US 17. Attractive property less than a mile from the toll road to St Simons and Sea Island, and within five miles of the Jekyll Island Causeway. **Rooms:** 100 rms. CI 4pm/CO noon. Nonsmoking rms avail. **Amenities:** 🔒 A/C, cable TV. **Services:** 🖼 ↵ 🔊 Car-rental desk. **Facilities:** 🔗 ⌷300⌷ ⚷ **Rates (CP):** $52 S; $57 D. Children under age 18 stay free. Parking: Outdoor, free. AE, CB, DC, DISC, JCB, MC, V.

≣≣ Sleep Inn

5272 New Jesup Hwy, 31525; tel 912/261-0670 or toll free 800/261-0670; fax 912/264-0441. Exit 7AB off I-95. Basic, no-frills motel, right off I-95 and within minutes of Jekyll Island and St Simons. **Rooms:** 93 rms. CI 2pm/CO noon. Nonsmoking rms avail. **Amenities:** A/C, cable TV, dataport. No phone. **Services:** 🖼 ↵ 🔊 Babysitting. Complimentary chocolate chip cookies available evenings. **Facilities:** 🔗 🖥 ⚷ **Rates (CP):** Peak (Feb–Apr/June–Aug) $42–$52 S; $55–$59 D. Extra person $6. Children under age 18 stay free. Lower rates off-season. Parking: Outdoor, free. AE, CB, DC, DISC, JCB, MC, V.

RESTAURANTS 🍴

★ The Royal Cafe

1618 Newcastle St (Old Towne); tel 912/262-1402. **Continental.** Gourmet cooking at reasonable prices. The elegant dining room—high ceilings, local art—attracts a trendy crowd who come for barbecue or grouper sandwiches at lunch and pasta specials in the evening. **FYI:** Reservations recommended. No smoking. **Open:** Lunch Mon–Fri 11am–2:30pm; dinner Fri–Sat 6:30–9pm; brunch Sun 11am–2pm. **Prices:** Main courses $12–$15. AE, MC, V. 🍴 ⚷

Spanky's

1200 Glynn Ave; tel 912/267-6100. Off US 17. **Eclectic.** This eatery, with a relaxed atmosphere and a central bar, offers fresh seafood (like grouper and scallops) as well as a large variety of popular items including fajitas, burgers, and the highly regarded chicken fingers. The dining patio overlooks a marsh. **FYI:** Reservations not accepted. Children's menu. **Open:** Sun 11am–8pm, Mon–Thurs 11am–10pm, Fri–Sat 11am–11pm. **Prices:** Main courses $5–$17. AE, DISC, MC, V. 🍴 ⚷

Buford

See also Lake Lanier Islands

Calhoun

This town founded in the 1850s suffered so severely during the Civil War that only a plain wood-frame plantation home survived—perhaps because it served briefly as General Sherman's headquarters. Nearby is the site of what was once the capital of the Cherokee nation, New Echota, now a national historic site. **Information:** Gordon County Convention & Visitors Bureau, 300 S Wall St, Calhoun, 30701 (tel toll free 800/887-3811).

MOTELS 🛏

≣≣≣ Holiday Inn

Redbud Rd, PO Box 252, 30703; tel 706/629-9191 or toll free 800/HOLIDAY. Off I-75. Located directly off the interstate, this comfortable Holiday Inn offers standard accommodations and amenities. **Rooms:** 98 rms. CI 2pm/CO 11am. Nonsmoking rms avail. **Amenities:** 🔒 ⚙ A/C, cable TV, voice mail. **Services:** 🍽 🚐 🖼 ↵ **Facilities:** 🔗 🏊 ⚷ 1 restaurant, 1 bar (w/entertainment). **Rates:** $45 S; $50 D. Extra person $5. Children under age 19 stay free. Parking: Outdoor, free. AE, CB, DC, DISC, JCB, MC, V.

≣≣ Quality Inn

915 GA 53E, 30701; tel 706/629-9501 or toll free 800/CALHOUN; fax 706/629-9501. Exit 129 off I-75. An average chain property with basic rooms. Fine for an overnight stay but not for an extended visit. **Rooms:** 100 rms. CI open/CO 11am. Nonsmoking rms avail. **Amenities:** 🔒 A/C, cable TV. **Services:** ✗ ↵ 🔊 Car-rental desk. Fax and copy services. **Facilities:** 🔗 ⌷300⌷ 1 restaurant, washer/dryer. **Rates (CP):** $36 S; $42 D. Extra person $4. Parking: Outdoor, free. AE, MC, V.

Carrollton

With rural roots and character, this town on the Chieftain's Trail offers evidence of the area's Creek heritage at McIntosh Reserve (on the Chattahoochee River), which features a river overlook. **Information:** Carrollton Area Convention & Visitors Bureau, PO Box 532, Carrollton, 30117 (tel 404/387-1357).

RESTAURANT 🍴

★ Maple Street Mansion

401 Maple St; tel 404/834-2657. Off US 27. **Eclectic.** Built in 1894 by industrial giant L C Mandeville, this old mansion has now been converted into a great dining complex. The original house features a cozy dining area, while there's an old converted boxcar for a more casual atmosphere. Drinks are

available in a separate bar area. The menu in all three dining areas is sandwiches, steak, pasta, and seafood. **FYI:** Reservations recommended. Big band. Children's menu. **Open:** Lunch Mon–Fri 11am–2pm; dinner Mon–Sat 5–10pm. **Prices:** Main courses $6–$23. AE, CB, DC, DISC, MC, V. ♥ 🍴 ⛁

Cartersville

The seat of Bartow County, in northwest Georgia. Native American temple mounds here, some dating as far back as AD 1000, abound at Etowah Indian Mounds State Historic Site. **Information:** Cartersville–Bartow County Chamber of Commerce, 3 Dixie Ave, PO Box 307, Cartersville, 30120 (tel 404/382-1466).

MOTELS 🏨

⊫⊫⊫ Holiday Inn
Exit 126 off I-75, PO Box 200306, 30120; tel 404/386-0830 or toll free 800/HOLIDAY; fax 404/386-0867. Suitable for all travelers. Located near Lake Allatoona and Red Top Mountain State Park. **Rooms:** 150 rms. CI 3pm/CO noon. Nonsmoking rms avail. **Amenities:** 🛁 ⊘ A/C, cable TV, dataport. **Services:** ✕ ⊠ ⊷ ⊛ Car-rental desk. Pets under 50 lbs only. **Facilities:** 🛋 🛎 177 ⛁ 1 restaurant, 1 bar, basketball, volleyball, sauna, whirlpool. Restaurant open 24 hours. **Rates:** $61 S or D. Extra person $6. Children under age 19 stay free. Parking: Outdoor, free. AE, CB, DC, DISC, JCB, MC, V.

⊫⊫⊫ Quality Inn
US 41 and Dixie Ave, PO Box 158, 30120; tel 770/386-0510 or toll free 800/598-5643; fax 770/386-1361. Suitable for all travelers; near downtown Cartersville, Red Top Mountain Park, and Lake Allatoona. **Rooms:** 82 rms. CI 1pm/CO 11am. Nonsmoking rms avail. **Amenities:** 🛁 A/C, cable TV, dataport. **Services:** ⊠ ⊷ Car-rental desk. **Facilities:** 🛋 85 ⛁ 1 restaurant, 1 bar. **Rates:** $33 S; $40 D. Extra person $5. Children under age 18 stay free. Parking: Outdoor, free. AE, CB, DC, DISC, JCB, MC, V.

LODGE

⊫⊫⊫ Red Top Mountain Lodge
653 Red Top Mountain Rd, 30120; tel 404/975-0055; fax 404/975-4211. Exit 123 off I-75. 1,950 acres. Conveniently located near Lake Allatoona and accessible to Etowah Indian Mounds, Kennesaw Mountain National Battlefield, White Water Park, and Chieftain's Indian Heritage Trail. **Rooms:** 33 rms and stes; 18 cottages/villas. CI 4pm/CO 11am. Nonsmoking rms avail. **Amenities:** 🛁 ⊘ 📺 A/C, cable TV. Some units w/terraces, some w/fireplaces. **Services:** ⊷ Linens changed in cottages every other day of multinight stay. Sat night storytelling and marshmallow roast for kids. **Facilities:** 🛋 ◩ ⊠ ⊠2 ⊱ 160 ⛁ 1 restaurant (*see* "Restau-

rants" below), 1 beach (lake shore), volleyball, playground. Hiking trails and boat rentals nearby. Picnic area, miniature golf, fishing. **Rates:** Peak (Apr–Oct) $60 S or D; $75 ste; $75 cottage/villa. Extra person $6. Children under age 12 stay free. Lower rates off-season. Parking: Outdoor, $2/day. Cabins require five-night minimum stay. AE, CB, DC, DISC, MC, V.

RESTAURANT 🍴

Mountain Cove Restaurant
In Red Top Mountain Lodge, 653 Red Top Mountain Rd; tel 404/975-0055. **Soul/Southern.** Large windows offer great views of the park and lodge while guests sit down to a family-style buffet. **FYI:** Reservations accepted. Children's menu. No liquor license. **Open:** Breakfast daily 7–10am; lunch daily 11:30am–2pm; dinner Mon–Sat 5–9pm. **Prices:** Prix fixe $5–$10. AE, CB, DC, DISC, MC, V. ⛰ ⛁

Chatsworth

This small town lies in an important talc-mining region in north Georgia; the talc-producing mountains also offer recreation. Host to the North Georgia International Horse Trials in November. **Information:** Chatsworth–Murray County Chamber of Commerce, 120 W Fort St #104, PO Box 327, Chatsworth, 30705 (tel 706/695-6060).

RESTAURANT 🍴

Little Rome, Inc
1201 N 3rd Ave; tel 706/695-7309. Off US 411-1201. **Italian.** A simple, no-frills decor predominates at this eatery. The menu offers an array of pizzas, pastas, and sandwiches, but Little Rome is probably best known for its Empire Pizza and lasagna. **FYI:** Reservations accepted. Children's menu. No liquor license. **Open:** Mon–Thurs 11am–11pm, Fri 11am–midnight, Sat 5pm–midnight, Sun 5–11pm. **Prices:** Main courses $3–$17. AE, DC, DISC, MC, V. 🅿 ⛁

Chickamauga and Chattanooga National Military Park

For lodgings and dining, see Chickamauga, GA and Chattanooga, TN

The country's most visited battlefield and its first military park, designated in 1890. Here, on Sept 19–20 and Nov 23–25, 1863, Confederates under Gen Braxton Bragg and Union troops under Gen George H Thomas fought two bloody battles, ending in a Northern victory that left 34,000 dead and wounded on both sides. Today, visitors can drive around the 8,000-acre site on a seven-mile signposted road; the visitors center provides maps and a 26-minute multimedia orientation (shown hourly; half-hourly during peak season). Various monuments and plaques mark the sites of important skirmishes, and some of the old artillery is still visible. For more information, contact PO Box 2128, Fort Oglethorpe, GA 30742 (tel 706/866-9241).

Clarkesville

County seat set in a mountain-ringed valley. Handicrafts are produced here at a 60-year-old grist mill on the Soque River.

INN 🏨

≣≣≣ Glen-Ella Springs Inn

Bear Gap Rd, PO Box 3304, 30523; tel 706/754-7295 or toll free 800/552-3479; fax 706/754-7295. 16 acres. Beautifully renovated 100-year-old inn set in the rolling hills of northern Georgia. All four floors feature wraparound porches with rocking chairs. Unsuitable for children under 6. **Rooms:** 16 rms and stes. CI 2pm/CO 11am. No smoking. Rooms are furnished with antiques that give an air of rustic luxury. **Amenities:** 🛁 ⌚ A/C. No TV. 1 unit w/terrace, some w/fireplaces, some w/whirlpools. **Facilities:** 🛱 🛏 25 🛏 ⚹ 1 restaurant (bkfst and dinner only), guest lounge w/TV. Pool surrounded by large, wood deck. Grounds offer both natural beauty and perfectly manicured gardens. **Rates (BB):** $80–$110 D; $125–$150 ste. Extra person $10. Min stay wknds. Parking: Outdoor, free. AE, MC, V.

Cleveland

Once prominent as a gold town, this county seat in the northeast mountains is now noted for zany Babyland General Hospital, housed in a circa-1900s clinic and the birthplace of the original Cabbage Patch Kids. **Information:** White County Chamber of Commerce, 122 N Main St, Cleveland, 30528 (tel 706/865-5356).

LODGE 🏨

≣≣≣ Villagio di Montagna

US 129 N, PO Box 174, 30528; tel 706/865-7000 or toll free 800/367-3922; fax 706/865-1422. 16 acres. European-style villa with beautiful gardens. **Rooms:** 8 rms; 21 cottages/villas. CI 4pm/CO noon. Nonsmoking rms avail. Rooms have an unappealing, 1980s decor. Some rooms have nice views overlooking river. **Amenities:** 🛁 ⌚ 🛏 🍴 A/C, cable TV, refrig, CD/tape player. All units w/terraces, some w/fireplaces, some w/whirlpools. Rooms have an ice maker. **Services:** 🛎 ⚬ Babysitting. Linens changed every other day. Pets allowed in certain rooms. **Facilities:** 🛱 🛏 🛏 75 ⚹ Spa, sauna, steam rm, whirlpool. Olympic-sized pool (closed in winter). Nearby activities include golf, horseback riding, hiking, and white-water rafting. **Rates (CP):** $80–$120 S or

D; $80–$450 cottage/villa. Min stay special events. Parking: Outdoor, free. Children stay free according to room choice. AE, DISC, MC, V.

Columbus

This bustling river city is the northernmost navigable point on the Chattahoochee River. Its Historic Riverfront Industrial District is a national historic landmark. **Information:** Columbus Convention & Visitors Bureau, 801 Front Ave, PO Box 2768, Columbus, 31902 (tel 706/322-1613).

HOTEL 🏨

≣≣≣ Courtyard by Marriott

3501 Courtyard Way, 31904; tel 706/323-2323 or toll free 800/321-2211; fax 706/327-6030. Off Manchester Expwy by Peachtree Mall. Comfortable accommodations good for corporate travelers and extended stays. Located near Callaway Gardens, Warm Springs, and Roosevelt National Park. **Rooms:** 139 rms and stes. CI 3pm/CO noon. Nonsmoking rms avail. Each apartmentlike room is unique in size and design. **Amenities:** 🛁 ⌚ 🛏 A/C, cable TV w/movies, dataport, voice mail. Some units w/terraces. Some rooms have refrigerators. **Services:** 🛎 ⚬ Masseur. **Facilities:** 🛱 🛏 50 🖥 ⚹ 1 restaurant (bkfst only), 1 bar, spa, whirlpool, washer/dryer. Access to local health club. **Rates:** $58–$68 S or D; $87 ste. Extra person $10. Children under age 12 stay free. Min stay special events. Parking: Outdoor, free. Rates vary widely, so be sure to specify your price range when you make a reservation. AE, CB, DC, DISC, MC, V.

MOTELS

≣≣ Comfort Inn

3443 B Macon Rd, 31907; tel 706/568-3300. Off I-185. Rooms at this attractive motel are nicely done up and very comfortable. Convenient to the interstate, Fort Benning, downtown Columbus, and several shopping malls. **Rooms:** 66 rms and stes. CI noon/CO noon. Nonsmoking rms avail. **Amenities:** 🛁 🛏 A/C, cable TV. Some units w/whirlpools. **Services:** 🛎 ⚬ 🚗 **Facilities:** 🛱 ⚹ Sauna, whirlpool. **Rates (CP):** $48 S; $54 D; $100 ste. Extra person $6. Children under age 18 stay free. Parking: Outdoor, free. AE, MC, V.

≣≣ Days Inn

3452 Macon Rd, 31907; tel 706/561-4400 or toll free 800/DAYS-INN; fax 706/568-3075. Exit 4 off I-185. No-frills chain motel. Located near dining, malls, and historic downtown Columbus. **Rooms:** 122 rms and stes. CI 2pm/CO noon. Nonsmoking rms avail. Basic, comfortable rooms. **Amenities:** 🛁 ⌚ A/C, cable TV, dataport. **Services:** 🛎 ⚬ 🚗 Car-rental desk. **Facilities:** 🛱 🛏 20 ⚹ Pool closed Oct–April. **Rates (CP):** $46–$55 S or D; $75 ste. Extra person $6. Children under age 18 stay free. Parking: Outdoor, free. AE, CB, DC, DISC, MC, V.

≣≣≣ **Holiday Inn North**
2800 Manchester Expwy, 31904; tel 706/324-0231 or toll free 800/605-8266; fax 706/596-0248. Exit 5 off I-185. Basic chain property, suitable for all travelers. Located near Peachtree Mall, restaurants, and airport. **Rooms:** 223 rms. CI 3pm/CO noon. Nonsmoking rms avail. **Amenities:** 🛏 🕯 A/C, satel TV w/movies, dataport, voice mail. All units w/terraces. **Services:** ✕ 🚐 🖵 🖵 Complimentary pass and transportation to nearby World Gym. **Facilities:** 🖼 🔲 150 🕭 1 restaurant (bkfst and dinner only), 1 bar, washer/dryer. **Rates:** $65 S or D. Children under age 18 stay free. Min stay special events. Parking: Outdoor, free. AE, CB, DC, DISC, JCB, MC, V.

≣≣ **La Quinta Motor Inn**
3201 Macon Rd, 31906; tel 706/568-1740 or toll free 800/531-5900; fax 706/569-7434. Exit 4 off I-185. Small property located in middle of a shopping center. Good for corporate and military guests (Fort Benning is just south of town). **Rooms:** 122 rms and stes. CI noon/CO noon. Nonsmoking rms avail. The size of each room varies from quite small to average. **Amenities:** 🛏 🕯 A/C, dataport. **Services:** 🖵 🖵 🖘 **Facilities:** 🖼 🔲 30 🕭 Washer/dryer. Discounts offered at nearby Denny's and Shoney's restaurants. **Rates (CP):** $56 S; $49 D. Extra person $6–$7. Children under age 18 stay free. Parking: Outdoor, free. AE, CB, DC, DISC, MC, V.

RESTAURANT 🍴

WD Crowley's
In Peachtree Mall, 3111 Manchester Expwy; tel 706/324-3463. Off I-185. **Eclectic.** Casual atmosphere reigns in this dining room. It's decorated in dark woods and tiles and has a sunken area in the floor with a big bar. Menu specialties include seafood, Australian lobster, and steak; soups, salads, sandwiches, and a variety of chicken dishes are also offered. Daily specials. Reservations required for parties of six or more. **FYI:** Reservations accepted. Guitar/piano. Children's menu. **Open:** Sun 11:30am–4:30pm, Mon–Thurs 11:30am–10pm, Fri–Sat 11:30am–11pm. **Prices:** Main courses $9–$50. AE, CB, DC, DISC, MC, V. 🖳

ATTRACTIONS 🏛

National Infantry Museum
Bldg 396 on Baltzell Ave, Fort Benning; tel 706/545-2958. Military museum reflecting the history of the foot soldier from the Revolutionary War to the present. Uniforms, weapons, and other military equipment (both foreign and domestic) are among the objects on display. **Open:** Mon–Fri 8am–4:30pm, Sat–Sun 12:30–4:30pm. **Free**

Columbus Museum
1251 Wynnton Rd; tel 706/649-0713. Exhibits prehistoric Native American relics along with artifacts of regional history, works of art from the late 1800s and the 1900s, decorative arts displays, and a restored log cabin. **Open:** Tues–Sat 10am–5pm, Sun 1–5pm. Closed some hols. **Free**

Commerce

The charm of the 19th- and 20th-century industrial structures in this northeast Georgia city's commercial historic district has been captured by Olive Ann Burns in her novel *Cold Sassy Tree.*

MOTEL 🏨

≣≣ **Holiday Inn Express**
30747 US 441 S, PO Box 247, 30529; tel 706/335-5183 or toll free 800/HOLIDAY; fax 706/335-6588. Exit 53 off I-85. Comfortable chain-motel accommodations. Located near outlet-mall shopping and the north Georgia mountains. **Rooms:** 96 rms. CI 2pm/CO noon. Nonsmoking rms avail. **Amenities:** 🛏 🕯 A/C, cable TV, dataport. **Services:** 🖵 🖵 🖘 Small pets only. **Facilities:** 🖼 🔲 🔲 20 🕭 Whirlpool. **Rates (CP):** $43–$46 S or D. Extra person $6. Children under age 18 stay free. Parking: Outdoor, free. AE, CB, DC, DISC, MC, V.

Conyers

Situated in north-central Georgia; once the train stop between Atlanta and Augusta. Visitors can tour the city's historic Olde Town District. **Information:** Conyers-Rockdale Chamber of Commerce, 1186 Scott St, PO Box 483, Conyers, 30207 (tel 404/483-7049).

MOTEL 🏨

≣≣≣ **Holiday Inn Conyers**
1351 Dogwood Dr, 30207; tel 404/483-3220 or toll free 800/HOLIDAY; fax 404/760-9413. Exit 41 off I-20. Decent rooms suitable for all travelers on an overnight stay. Located near Six Flags, Stone Mountain, and downtown Atlanta, so it's very popular with families. **Rooms:** 136 rms. CI noon/CO noon. Nonsmoking rms avail. Each room is individualized in terms of size and decor. All are comfortable and tastefully decorated. Rooms 3 and 4 face Toulouse St and have balcony access. **Amenities:** 🛏 🕯 A/C, cable TV, dataport. **Services:** ✕ 🖵 🖵 Car-rental desk. **Facilities:** 🖼 🔲 100 🕭 1 restaurant, 1 bar, washer/dryer. Golf and tennis nearby. **Rates:** $54 S or D. Extra person $10. Children under age 19 stay free. Min stay special events. Parking: Outdoor, free. AE, CB, DC, DISC, JCB, MC, V.

ATTRACTION 🏛

Monastery of the Holy Spirit
2625 GA 212; tel 404/483-8705. A blissfully peaceful haven open to all, regardless of religion. Visitors may stroll the grounds and watch ducks swim in the lake, or visit the greenhouse with its bonsai trees. The monks, who make all their own food, sell their delicious breads in the bookstore/

gift shop. Prayer services Mon–Sat 7am, 5:35 and 8:15pm, and Sunday mass 6:15 and 11am. **Open:** Mon–Sat 9:30am–4:30pm. **Free**

Cordele

Picturesque, rural community in the heart of Georgia's richest agricultural area. It claims to be the "watermelon capital of the world," producing 200 million pounds annually. Home to Georgia Veterans Memorial State Park. **Information:** Cordele-Crisp Chamber of Commerce, 302 E 16th Ave, PO Box 158, Cordele, 31015 (tel 912/273-3526).

MOTELS 🏨

≡≡ Econo Lodge

1618 E 16th Ave, 31015; tel 912/273-2456 or toll free 800/424-4777; fax 912/273-3251. Exit 33 off I-75. This two-building property is nothing fancy, but it is a suitable choice for the budget conscious. **Rooms:** 45 rms. CI noon/CO 11am. Nonsmoking rms avail. Decent, basic rooms. **Amenities:** 🗼 A/C, cable TV w/movies. Refrigerator and microwaves available on request. **Services:** 🔄 🍽 **Facilities:** ⅃ **Rates (CP):** Peak (Mem Day–Labor Day/Christmas) $38–$43 S or D. Extra person $5. Children under age 16 stay free. Lower rates off-season. Parking: Outdoor, free. AE, CB, DC, DISC, JCB, MC, V.

≡≡≡ Holiday Inn

1711 E 16th Ave, 31015; tel 912/273-4117 or toll free 800/HOLIDAY; fax 912/273-1344. Exit 33 off I-75. Above-average Holiday Inn, good for family overnight stays. **Rooms:** 187 rms. CI noon/CO noon. Nonsmoking rms avail. **Amenities:** 🗼 🔥 A/C, cable TV. **Services:** ✕ 🚗 🖼 🔄 🍽 24-hour security. **Facilities:** 🏊 300 ⅃ 1 restaurant, 1 bar, washer/dryer. Well-landscaped pool surrounded with flowers and trees. Driving range. **Rates:** Peak (Mem Day–Labor Day) $50 S or D. Extra person $6. Children under age 18 stay free. Lower rates off-season. Parking: Outdoor, free. Golf and ballroom-dancing packages avail. AE, CB, DC, DISC, JCB, MC, V.

RESTAURANT 🍽

♣ Daphne Lodge

US 280; tel 912/273-2596. 11 mi W of exit 33 off I-75. **Seafood.** In 1994, *Atlanta* magazine mentioned this restaurant as one of "the South's favorite restaurants." The interior is dark, with antique decorations and dark-paneled walls; outside, there's a full front porch with rocking chairs. House specialties are fresh catfish, aged Angus beef, quail dishes, and homemade biscuits. **FYI:** Reservations recommended. Dress code. Beer and wine only. No smoking. **Open:** Tues–Sat 6–10pm. **Prices:** Main courses $9–$19. AE, DISC, MC, V.

Cumberland Island National Seashore

For lodgings, see St Mary's

Of all the islands along the Atlantic coast, this is the one closest to an unspoiled, natural state. The 18-mile-long and 3-mile-wide island is covered in moss oaks and dwarf palmettos; marshes and empty beaches teem with ibis, duck, alligators, and wild ponies. Ranger-led walking tours let visitors get a close look at the wildlife, as well as structures built by the Carnegie family in the late 19th- and early 20th-centuries. Other recreational activities include swimming, hiking, camping, and picnicking. The island is reached by ferry from St Mary's, GA (tel 904/261-6408). Visitor access is limited to 300 people per day, so call to confirm ferry space. For more information, contact Superintendent, Cumberland Island National Seashore, PO Box 806, St Mary's, GA 31558 (tel 912/882-4337).

INN 🏨

≡≡≡ Greyfield Inn

Cumberland Island, ; tel 904/261-6408; fax 904/261-0946. 1,300 acres. Thomas Carnegie (brother and business partner of Andrew) built this three-story plantation mansion for his daughter in 1901. Family antiques and portraits are scattered throughout the house, wild ponies graze in the yard, and towering oak trees fill the surrounding forest. The only way to the island is by boat: A public ferry runs from St Mary's, and the Inn's private ferry, the *Lucy R Ferguson*, runs from Amelia Island, FL. Unsuitable for children under 6. **Rooms:** 9 rms and stes (8 w/shared bath); 1 cottage/villa. CI 12:30pm/CO 11:30am. No smoking. The rooms are spacious, and each has a delightful view. Some rooms share baths, and shower houses were built onto the back of the house. **Amenities:** Bathrobes. No A/C, phone, or TV. **Services:** Masseur, babysitting, afternoon tea served. Meals are served at the long Carnegie dining table, complete with heirloom silver candlesticks. (Semiformal attire is required at dinner—no shorts or jeans.) Coffee and tea are served after dinner, and lemonade is available all day. Staff naturalist will give guided tours. **Facilities:** 🚴 🏖 🏖 20 1 restaurant (bkfst and dinner only), 1 bar, 1 beach (ocean), guest lounge. Be forewarned that the house is antique, and so are the facilities. Very impressive library. **Rates (AP):** $245–$320 D w/shared bath, $315–$350 D w/private bath; $315–$350 ste; $315–$350 cottage/villa. Min stay wknds and special events. Parking: Outdoor, free. Closed Aug. MC, V.

Dahlonega

America's first major gold rush began here in 1828; mines are still open for panning. Its 19th-century square is surrounded by antique stores and Appalachian craft shops. **Information:** 101 S Park St, Dahlonega, 30533 (tel 706/864-3711).

INN 🏨

⊨⊨ Smith House Inn and Country Store
202 S Chestatee St, 30533; tel 706/867-7000 or toll free 800/852-9577. 1 block from Public Square on GA 60. 3 acres. Country inn built in 1884. Operated since 1946 by the same family, this unique property offers a spacious veranda and a homelike atmosphere. The building stands atop a vein of gold ore, and guests are invited to try their hand at gold panning on front lawn. **Rooms:** 16 rms. CI 2pm/CO 11am. No smoking. Rooms have modern decor. **Amenities:** 📺 🍸 📠 A/C, cable TV. Some units w/whirlpools. **Services:** Linens changed every other day of multinight stay. **Facilities:** 🛗 55 👍 1 restaurant (see "Restaurants" below), guest lounge w/TV. **Rates (CP):** Peak (Oct) $70–$150 S. Children under age 18 stay free. Min stay peak and special events. Lower rates off-season. Higher rates for special events/hols. Parking: Outdoor, free. AE, DISC, MC, V.

LODGE

⊨⊨ Mountain Top Lodge at Dahlonega
Old Ellijay Rd, PO Box 150, 30533; tel 706/864-5257. Off GA 52 to Siloam Rd. Situated on a remote mountainside road, this lodge offers beautiful scenery—especially when the leaves change. The lodge itself is a modern, wood structure with antique country decor. Perfect for a weekend getaway. **Rooms:** 13 rms and stes. CI 3pm/CO 11am. No smoking. Some rooms have balconies with spectacular mountain views. **Amenities:** A/C. No phone or TV. Some units w/terraces, some w/fireplaces, some w/whirlpools. Radio/alarm clocks available. Free access to kitchen microwave and refrigerator. **Services:** Complimentary cookies and soft drinks. Linens changed every other night during multinight stay. **Facilities:** 35 Games rm, whirlpool. Hiking on site. **Rates (BB):** $65–$85 S or D; $125 ste. Extra person $15. Min stay special events. Parking: Outdoor, free. In fall, additional person charge is 50% of room rate. AE, MC, V.

RESTAURANT 🍴

⑤ Restaurant
In Smith House Inn and Country Store, 202 S Chestatee St; tel 706/864-3566. **Soul/Southern.** A very simple, family-style eatery, located in the basement of the inn. Its monumental all-you-can-eat Southern buffets typically include fried chicken, ham, roast beef, barbecue, a dozen or more vegetables, and homemade biscuits and cinnamon rolls. **FYI:** Reservations not accepted. No liquor license. No smoking. **Open:** Lunch Tues–Sat 11am–3pm, Sun 11am–7:30pm; dinner Tues–Sat 4:30–8pm. **Prices:** Prix fixe $10–$15. AE, DISC, MC, V. 🍴 👍

ATTRACTIONS 🖼

Dahlonega Courthouse Gold Museum
Public Square; tel 706/864-3345. *Dahlonega* is a Cherokee word meaning "precious yellow." In 1828, according to legend, a trapper named Benjamin Parks stubbed his toe on a rock and uncovered a vein of gold that brought prospectors streaming into these hills for the next 20 years. Today, enough gold is still around to intrigue visitors who pan for it at various local mines. This museum chronicles the history of the Georgia gold rush and the many mines that once flourished here. A half-hour film entitled *Gold Fever* describes early mining techniques and chronicles the lifestyles of the prospectors. **Open:** Mon–Sat 9am–5pm, Sun 10am–5pm. Closed some hols. **$**

Consolidated Gold Mines
125 Gold Mine Rd; tel 706/864-8473. Visitors can tour an authentic underground mine and learn about the little-known "gold rush" that transformed this tiny North Georgia town in the early 19th century. Actual miners conduct 45-minute tours. If you get inspired after your tour, you can try your luck panning for gold; instructors are on the site and the mine claims that "gold is discovered daily." **Open:** Daily 10am–4pm. Closed Dec 25. **$$$**

Desoto Falls Scenic Area
US 129; tel 706/864-3711. A rugged, mountainous area, covering 650 acres, with an average elevation of 2,000–3,400 feet. Camping, fishing, and hiking are available amid exceptional views and several beautiful waterfalls. **Open:** Daily sunrise–sunset. **Free**

Dalton

A gateway city to the Chieftains Trail in the northwest mountains. Fully restored Prater's Mill, used as campsite by both Union and Confederate troops in 1864, is the site of a semiannual country fair. **Information:** Dalton Convention & Visitors Bureau, PO Box 2046, Dalton, 30720 (tel toll free 800/824-7469).

ATTRACTION 🖼

Prater's Mill
GA 2; tel 706/275-6455. Listed on the National Register of Historic Places, this beautifully restored, water-powered 1855 grist mill still grinds out corn and wheat twice a year. The Prater's Mill Country Fair, held every Mother's Day weekend and Columbus Day weekend (Sat–Sun 9am–6pm), raises money for the preservation of the mill and gives many local artisans, craftspeople, and antique dealers a chance to show and sell their wares. The mill itself is only open during the fair, but the grounds (including a country store, a restored cotton gin, and a barn with farm animals) are open year-round. **$$**

Douglas

Located in Georgia's rural "Magnolia Midlands," in Coffee County, with historic 18th- and 19th-century homes. **Information:** Douglas Tourism & Promotions, PO Box 470, Douglas, 31533 (tel 912/383-0277).

MOTEL

≡≡≡ Holiday Inn

1750 S Peterson Ave, PO Box 1170, 31533; tel 912/384-9100 or toll free 800/HOLIDAY; fax 912/384-9100. Located just off US 441 S and near many fast-food places. This is a good place to stay for traveling families. **Rooms:** 100 rms. CI 2pm/CO noon. Nonsmoking rms avail. Rooms were renovated in 1994. **Amenities:** A/C, cable TV, dataport. 1 unit w/minibar. **Services:** Car-rental desk, babysitting. **Facilities:** 1 restaurant, 1 bar, washer/dryer. **Rates:** $49 S or D. Extra person $5. Children under age 18 stay free. Min stay special events. Parking: Outdoor, free. AE, CB, DC, DISC, MC, V.

Dublin

On the banks of the Oconee River in Georgia's "Magnolia Midlands," with rural, pine-studded backroads. Dublin puts on an extravagant two-week salute to its Irish heritage in March. **Information:** Dublin–Laurens County Chamber of Commerce, 1200 Bellevue Ave, PO Box 818, Dublin, 31040 (tel 912/272-5546).

MOTEL

≡≡≡ Holiday Inn

I-16 at US 441, PO Box 768, 31021; tel 912/272-7862 or toll free 800/HOLIDAY; fax 912/272-1077. Exit 14 off I-16. Plain, two-story property with surprisingly nice accommodations. Near VA Hospital and Little Ocmulgee State Park. **Rooms:** 150 rms. CI 2pm/CO noon. Nonsmoking rms avail. Each room is individually decorated with antiques and oil paintings. The VIP suite has three bedrooms, a kitchen area, and a steam room. **Amenities:** A/C, satel TV w/movies, dataport. **Services:** X Facilities: 1 restaurant, 1 bar (w/entertainment). **Rates (BB):** $52 S or D. Extra person $4. Children under age 18 stay free. Parking: Outdoor, free. AE, CB, DC, DISC, JCB, MC, V.

Eatonton

A gateway to Lakes Oconee and Sinclair, this central Georgia city on the Antebellum Trail features a historic courthouse square. A statue of Brer Rabbit and the Uncle Remus Museum honor author Joel Chandler Harris, a one-time resident. Birthplace of Alice Walker, author of *The Color*

Purple. **Information:** Eatonton-Putnam Chamber of Commerce, 105 Sumter St, PO Box 4088, Eatonton, 31024 (tel 706/485-7701).

ATTRACTION

Uncle Remus Museum

US 441 S; tel 706/485-6856. Memorabilia about Brer Rabbit, Brer Fox, and Joel Chandler Harris's other storybook critters are housed in this log cabin (made from two former slave cabins similar to the one occupied by Uncle Remus). Colorful scenes in each of the windows capture the daily life of a Southern plantation during the antebellum days, and first editions of many of Harris's works are on display. **Open:** Mon–Sat 10am–5pm, Sun 2–5pm. Closed Tues Sept–May. **$**

Forsyth

Named for the secretary of state under presidents Jackson and Van Buren, the town received its first boost in 1834 when the railroad from Macon was completed. The historic courthouse square is the city's hub. Host to annual Forsythia Festival. Northeast of Forsyth is Juliette, a thriving mill town in the 1930s that was reborn in the early 1990s with the filming of *Fried Green Tomatoes*. **Information:** Forsyth–Monroe County Chamber of Commerce, 267 Tift College Dr, PO Box 811, Forsyth, 31029 (tel 912/994-9239).

MOTELS

≡≡ Best Western Hilltop Inn

Exit 63 off I-75 and GA 42, 31029; tel 912/994-9260 or toll free 800/447-3241; fax 912/781-0066. Standard chain accommodations suitable for an overnight stop. **Rooms:** 125 rms. CI open/CO noon. Nonsmoking rms avail. **Amenities:** A/C, cable TV. **Services:** X Car-rental desk. **Facilities:** 1 restaurant (bkfst and dinner only). **Rates:** Peak (May–Sept) $53–$57 S; $48–$52 D. Extra person $5. Children under age 12 stay free. Lower rates off-season. Parking: Outdoor, free. AE, CB, DC, DISC, MC, V.

≡≡≡ Hampton Inn

520 Holiday Circle, 31029; tel 912/994-9697 or toll free 800/HAMPTON; fax 912/994-3594. Exit 61 off I-75. Chain motel with four stories, located just off I-17. Popular with business travelers. Near Atlanta Raceway. **Rooms:** 124 rms and stes. CI 3pm/CO noon. Nonsmoking rms avail. All rooms are individually decorated, and some overlook the courtyard and gazebo. The management wishes to discourage children because of the rare and expensive antiques in every room. **Amenities:** A/C, cable TV, dataport. **Services:** Privileges at nearby health club. **Facilities:** **Rates (CP):** $49 S or D; $60 ste. Children under age 18 stay free. Parking: Outdoor, free. AE, CB, DC, DISC, JCB, MC, V.

≣≣≣ Holiday Inn

480 Holiday Circle, 31029; tel 912/994-5691 or toll free 800/HOLIDAY; fax 912/994-3254. I-75 at Tift College Dr. Standard-quality chain accommodations. Located near Atlanta Raceway. **Rooms:** 120 rms. CI noon/CO noon. Nonsmoking rms avail. **Amenities:** 🛏 ⚱ A/C, cable TV, dataport. **Services:** ✗ 🖼 ⊐ ⊲⊅ **Facilities:** ⬚ ⬚ 🌲 200 ⚹ 1 restaurant, 1 bar (w/entertainment), washer/dryer. **Rates:** $59 S or D. Extra person $5. Children under age 18 stay free. Parking: Outdoor, free. AE, CB, DC, DISC, JCB, MC, V.

RESTAURANT 🍴

★ Whistle Stop Cafe

Rte 1, Juliette; tel 912/994-3670. **Soul/Southern.** Site of the filming of the hit movie *Fried Green Tomatoes*. The building itself dates from 1927 and was used as a general store for 45 years. The decor features magnolias in window boxes, wooden booths, and photos of the stars of the movie, plus the store's original cash register. Menu specialties include barbecue ribs, fried chicken, and pork chops, as well as hamburgers and hot dogs for children—and of course, fried green tomatoes. Lines can be long, especially on the weekends. **FYI:** Reservations not accepted. Children's menu. No liquor license. **Open:** Mon–Sat 8am–2pm, Sun noon–7pm. **Prices:** Lunch main courses $3–$7. No CC. 🍽 👥 ⚹

Fort Frederica National Monument

See St Simon's Island

Gainesville

Founded in 1821, this town in the foothills of the Northeast Georgia Mountains is a gateway to the Blue Ridge region. **Information:** Gainesville–Hall County Convention & Visitors Bureau, 830 Green St, Gainesville, 30601 (tel 404/536-5209).

RESTAURANTS 🍴

★ Poor Richard's

1702 Park Hill Dr; tel 404/532-0499. **Seafood/Steak.** Good food and service in a dark, candlelit atmosphere. The specialty is prime rib; also available are other steaks, seafood, salads, and chicken. **FYI:** Reservations accepted. Children's menu. **Open:** Mon–Thurs 5–10pm, Fri–Sat 5–11pm. **Prices:** Main courses $7–$19. AE, MC, V. ♥ ⚹

Restaurant

In Ramada Inn Lanier Center, 400 E E Butler Pkwy; tel 404/531-0907. **Eclectic.** The decor is plain, as is the food during the week, when the menu offers only a few selections. What it's best for is the large Sunday brunch buffet. **FYI:** Reserva-

tions accepted. Piano/singer. Children's menu. **Open:** Breakfast daily 6:30–10:30am; lunch daily 11:30am–2pm; dinner daily 5–10pm. **Prices:** Main courses $9–$17. AE, CB, DC, DISC, MC, V. ☑ ⚹

Greensboro

Named for Revolutionary War general Nathaniel Greene and laid out in 1786, Greensboro sprung up around the mansions of plantation owners. Once Native American territory, the area is still a hunting ground for Creek and Cherokee artifacts. **Information:** Greene County Chamber of Commerce, 112 S Main St, PO Box 741, Greensboro, 30642 (tel 706/453-7592).

MOTEL 🏨

≣≣ Jameson Inn

2252 S Main St, 30642; tel 706/453-9135 or toll free 800/541-3268; fax 706/453-4004. Exit 53 off I-20. No-frills property. Attracts lots of golfers due to location near several courses. **Rooms:** 40 rms and stes. CI 2pm/CO 11am. Nonsmoking rms avail. **Amenities:** 🛏 A/C, cable TV, dataport. **Services:** ⊐ **Facilities:** ⬚ ⚹ **Rates (CP):** $46 S or D; $95–$135 ste. Extra person $4. Children under age 12 stay free. Parking: Outdoor, free. AE, CB, DC, DISC, MC, V.

RESORT

≣≣≣ Reynolds Plantation

100 Linger Longer Rd, 30642; tel 706/467-3151 or toll free 800/733-5253; fax 706/467-3152. Exit 53 off I-20. Located on Lake Oconee, 75 mi E of Atlanta. This quiet, peaceful resort, situated on 1,000 developed acres, is surrounded by an amazing variety of wildlife. Several homes on the property have been featured in *Southern Living* magazine, and Reynolds played host to the Andersen Consulting Championship of Golf in 1995 and 1996. **Rooms:** 60 cottages/villas. CI 4pm/CO 11am. Nonsmoking rms avail. Cottages have breathtaking views of the golf courses, Lake Oconee, and the forest area, and all feature two TVs and fully equipped kitchens. Decor is tasteful, comfortable, elegant. **Amenities:** 🛏 ⚱ 🖥 A/C, cable TV, refrig. All units w/terraces, all w/fireplaces, all w/whirlpools. **Services:** ⊐ Social director, babysitting. **Facilities:** ⬚ ⬚ ▶36 🏌 ⚓4 ⬚2 🌲 100 ⚹ 2 restaurants, 2 bars (1 w/entertainment), 1 beach (lake shore), basketball, volleyball, whirlpool, playground, washer/dryer. The Plantation Golf Course was designed by Bob Cupp (in association with champion golfers Fuzzy Zoeller and Hubert Green); the nine holes of the Jack Nicklaus–designed Great Waters Course stretch along the Lake Oconee shoreline. Junior Olympic–size pool, clay and hard courts for tennis. Beach area equipped with a building for parties and barbecues. Pro shop, boat/tackle shop, boat storage. Pontoon boats for rent. **Rates (BB):** Peak (mid-Mar–July 7; Sept–mid-Nov) $242–$358 cottage/villa. Children under age 18 stay

free. Min stay special events. Lower rates off-season. Parking: Outdoor, free. Children stay free (excluding special package rates). AE, DISC, JCB, MC, V.

Hamilton

See also Pine Mountain

Located in the central Georgia Piedmont region at Lake Harding, a recreational area. **Information:** Harris County Chamber of Commerce, PO Box 426, Hamilton, 31811 (tel 706/628-4381).

MOTEL

Valley Inn Resort

14420 GA 27, 31811; tel 706/628-4454 or toll free 800/944-9393. 3 mi S of Callaway Gardens. 67 acres. Comfortable cottages and motel-style rooms nestled on shore of a 22-acre lake. Callaway Gardens and Roosevelt State Park are only minutes away. **Rooms:** 20 rms and stes; 4 cottages/villas. CI 2pm/CO noon. The rooms are unusually spacious and each has its own distinctive features. Some rooms surround an enclosed French-style courtyard, although the rooms surrounding the rear courtyard are more popular. **Amenities:** A/C, cable TV. Coffee available in rooms. **Services:** Guest privileges at nearby health club. **Facilities:** Playground. Barbecue pits, picnic area. **Rates:** $65 S; $78 D; $80 ste; $95–$105 cottage/villa. Extra person $5–$12. Children under age 6 stay free. Min stay wknds. Parking: Outdoor, free. Rates are based on double occupancy and include free admission to Callaway Gardens. MC, V.

Helen

Incorporated in 1913, after a lumber company built a mill here in the Georgia hills (and named the site for an official's daughter). Tourism eventually won out over logging, and in 1969 Helen was transformed into a replica of a Bavarian village. The South's largest Oktoberfest is held here. Main Street buildings feature red roofs, flower boxes, balconies, and murals. Visitors can shop for sweaters, porcelains, and cuckoo clocks and enjoy wurst and beer to oompah music at an outdoor beer garden. **Information:** Helen Convention & Visitors Bureau, City Hall Building, Chattahoochee St, PO Box 730, Helen, 30545 (tel 706/878-2181).

MOTELS

The Castle Inn

8590 Main St, PO Box 258, 30545; tel 706/878-3140; fax 706/878-3130. Nice, well-furnished inn perched on the banks of the Chattahoochee River. **Rooms:** 11 rms. CI 3pm/CO 11am. Some rooms have balconies with views of river and downtown Helen. **Amenities:** A/C, cable TV. No phone.

Services: Complimentary morning coffee. **Facilities:** 1 restaurant (lunch and dinner only; see "Restaurants" below), 1 bar (w/entertainment), washer/dryer. Amusement park, golf, canoeing, horseback riding, and hiking nearby. **Rates:** Peak (Sept–Oct) $98 S or D. Extra person $10. Children under age 16 stay free. Min stay peak and special events. Lower rates off-season. Parking: Outdoor, free. AE, CB, DC, MC, V.

Helendorf River Inn & Towers

33 Munich Strasse, PO Box 305, 30545; tel 706/878-2271 or toll free 800/445-2271; fax 706/878-2271. Unimpressive facility situated along the Chattahoochee River. Decent and clean, but not well kept. Only for the very budget-minded. **Rooms:** 98 rms and effic. CI 3pm/CO 11am. Bare necessities. **Amenities:** A/C, cable TV. Some units w/terraces, some w/fireplaces, some w/whirlpools. Complimentary coffee. **Services:** Pets allowed only in designated rooms. **Facilities:** 1 restaurant. Hiking, horseback riding, golf, tennis, fishing, tubing, and swimming are nearby. **Rates:** Peak (Sept–Oct) $74–$84 S or D; $135–$150 effic. Extra person $5. Children under age 12 stay free. Min stay special events. Lower rates off-season. Parking: Outdoor, free. DC, MC, V.

LODGE

Unicoi State Park Lodge

GA 356, PO Box 849, 30545; tel 706/878-2201 or toll free 800/864-PARK; fax 706/878-1897. Remote, wood-beamed lodge offering single and double rooms as well as cottages. Good for families and getaways. **Rooms:** 100 rms; 30 cottages/villas. CI 4pm/CO 11am. Nonsmoking rms avail. Cottages have kitchens, but no TVs or telephones. **Amenities:** A/C, cable TV w/movies. Some units w/terraces, some w/fireplaces. Coffee brought to rooms. **Services:** Social director. Movies and VCRs available for rent. **Facilities:** 1 restaurant, games rm, playground, washer/dryer. Gift shop stocks local arts and crafts. Near hiking, white-water rafting, tubing, and golf. **Rates:** Peak (Oct) $69 D; $75–$95 cottage/villa. Extra person $6. Children under age 12 stay free. Min stay special events. Lower rates off-season. Parking: Indoor/outdoor, $2/day. AE, DC, DISC, MC, V.

RESTAURANTS

★ Hofbrauhaus Inn Restaurant

1 Main St; tel 706/878-2248. **International.** The menu is international, with a focus on German specialties. Highlights include steak au poivre, steak loupe, and seafood Wellington. **FYI:** Reservations recommended. Piano. Children's menu. **Open:** Mon–Thurs 5–10pm, Fri–Sat 5–10:30pm. **Prices:** Main courses $12–$20. AE, CB, DC, DISC, MC, V.

Troll Tavern and Restaurant

In Castle Inn, Main St; tel 706/878-3117. **Eclectic.** A typical Bavarian-style restaurant, especially noted for its German wurst and burgers. Outdoor diners can watch tubers float down the Chattahoochee River. **FYI:** Reservations not accepted. Guitar/singer. Children's menu. **Open:** Mon–Thurs 11am–10pm, Fri–Sat 11am–midnight, Sun 11am–6pm. **Prices:** Main courses $6–$8. AE, DISC, MC, V. ⬛ 🖼 ⅙

ATTRACTIONS 🖼

Unicoi State Park
GA 356; tel 706/878-2201. Nestled in the north Georgia mountains, Unicoi offers a wide variety of accommodations—cottages, campsites, and a beautiful 100-room lodge—and recreational opportunities. From Memorial Day through Labor Day, Unicoi's beach area (located on the shore of a 53-acre lake) offers swimming and fishing, and canoes and paddle boats are available for a small fee. Four hiking trails are located at Unicoi or nearby Anna Ruby Falls and there are four lighted tennis courts and picnic tables. **Open:** Daily 24 hours. **Free**

Fred's Famous Peanuts
GA 356 N; tel 706/878-3124. A unique country store specializing in Georgia's most famous agricultural product. Fred sells them roasted, boiled, and even fried, or made into peanut brittle or peanut butter. Also on sale are jams and jellies, honey, apple cider, pork rinds, and other mountain products and nonedible souvenirs. **Open:** Daily 10am–7pm. Closed some hols. **Free**

Hiawassee

On the shores of Lake Chatuge in the northeast mountains, Hiawassee offers the 10-day Fall Celebration, which includes the state Fiddlers Convention. **Information:** Towns County Chamber of Commerce, 1411 Fuller Circle, Young Harris, 30582 (tel 706/896-4966).

RESORT 🏨

📆📆📆 Fieldstone Inn
3499 US 76 W, PO Box 670, 30546; tel 706/896-2262 or toll free 800/896-2262; fax 706/896-4128. On Lake Chatuge. This lakeside property greets you with a beautiful stone-and-wood lobby containing a big, open fireplace. A wall of windows offers a peaceful view of Lake Chatuge. **Rooms:** 66 rms. CI 4pm/CO 11am. Nonsmoking rms avail. All rooms are well furnished. Luxury rooms feature whirlpool, wet bar, and sitting area. **Amenities:** 🛗 ⚬ A/C, cable TV w/movies. Some units w/terraces, some w/whirlpools. **Services:** ⌘ Social director, masseur, babysitting. Complimentary coffee in lobby. Tee times at nearby golf course can be arranged. **Facilities:** 🏕 ⛰ 🛶 🎣 🚣 📷 🚴 🎿 🏓 175 🖥 ⅙ 1 restaurant, 1 bar, volleyball, whirlpool, playground. Courtyard area with a walking path. Hiking nearby. **Rates:** Peak (Mem Day–Labor Day) $89–$99 S or D. Extra person $7. Children under age 14 stay free. Min stay special events. Lower rates off-season. Parking: Outdoor, free. AE, DISC, MC, V.

Jekyll Island

Southernmost of the Golden Isles, this 240-acre island was a retreat in the 19th century for some of America's richest families. There is a splendidly restored historic district. **Information:** Jekyll Island Convention & Visitors Bureau, 1 Beachview Dr, Jekyll Island, 31527 (tel 912/635-4080).

HOTELS 🏨

📆📆📆 Best Western Jekyll Inn
975 N Beachview Dr, 31527; tel 912/635-2531 or toll free 800/736-1046; fax 912/635-2332. Beachfront property located right off the highway. A good place for families due to its central location between the historical district of Jekyll and Summer Waves Park. **Rooms:** 188 rms; 76 cottages/villas. CI 4pm/CO 11am. Nonsmoking rms avail. Rooms have hardwood floors, area rugs, antique furnishings, and *frete livres* bed linens. **Amenities:** 🛗 ⚬ A/C, cable TV. Some units w/terraces. **Services:** ⌘ ⬦ Babysitting. $20 pet fee. **Facilities:** 🏕 🚴 500 ⅙ 1 restaurant, 2 bars (1 w/entertainment), 1 beach (ocean), volleyball, playground, washer/dryer. Putting green and driving range. Snack bar. Picnic area. **Rates:** Peak (Mar 21–Sept 7) $79–$104 S or D; $109–$150 cottage/villa. Extra person $5. Children under age 19 stay free. Min stay special events. Lower rates off-season. MAP rates avail. Parking: Outdoor, free. Golf, honeymoon packages avail. AE, CB, DC, DISC, MC, V.

📆📆📆 Clarion Resort Buccaneer
85 S Beachview Dr, 31520; tel 912/635-2261 or toll free 800/253-5955; fax 912/635-3230. Large oceanfront resort surrounded by lush tropical foliage. Quiet atmosphere, and a nice walkway to the beach. **Rooms:** 208 rms, stes, and effic. Executive level. CI 4pm/CO 11am. Nonsmoking rms avail. **Amenities:** 🛗 ⚬ A/C, cable TV w/movies, dataport, voice mail. All units w/terraces. **Services:** ✕ 🚗 🖼 ⌘ ⬦ Car-rental desk, social director, children's program, babysitting. **Facilities:** 🏕 🚴 🎾 🖼 600 ⅙ 1 restaurant, 1 bar (w/entertainment), 1 beach (ocean), lifeguard, games rm, whirlpool, playground, washer/dryer. **Rates:** Peak (June–Aug) $109–$139 S or D; $165–$175 ste; $139–$175 effic. Extra person $10. Children under age 18 stay free. Min stay special events. Lower rates off-season. Parking: Outdoor, free. AE, CB, DC, DISC, MC, V.

📆📆📆 Holiday Inn Beach Resort
200 S Beachview Dr, 31527; tel 912/635-3311 or toll free 800/753-5955; fax 912/635-2901. A family-style hotel with big oak trees and a good, wooden walkway to the beach. **Rooms:** 205 rms and stes. CI 4pm/CO 11am. Nonsmoking rms avail. **Amenities:** 🛗 ⚬ 🖥 A/C, cable TV. Some units w/terraces. Bidets in all rooms. **Services:** ✕ 🖼 ⌘ ⬦ Babysitting. **Facilities:** 🏕 🚴 🎾 800 ⅙ 1 restaurant, 1 bar (w/entertainment), 1 beach (ocean), playground, washer/dryer. The hotel shares a pool with the nearby St Ann, which is owned by the same company. **Rates:** Peak (May–Aug)

$110–$125 S or D; $157–$255 ste. Extra person $10. Children under age 19 stay free. Min stay special events. Lower rates off-season. Parking: Outdoor, free. AE, CB, DC, DISC, JCB, MC, V.

☰☰ Ramada Inn

150 S Beachview Dr, 31527; tel 912/635-2111 or toll free 800/835-2110; fax 912/635-2758. Located minutes away from Jekyll Island historic district and Summer Waves theme park. **Rooms:** 110 rms and stes. CI 4pm/CO noon. Non-smoking rms avail. **Amenities:** 🛎 A/C, cable TV. Some units w/terraces, some w/whirlpools. **Services:** ✗ 🛗 **Facilities:** 🛗 📶 1 restaurant, 1 bar (w/entertainment), 1 beach (ocean), volleyball, games rm, playground. **Rates:** Peak (May–Aug) $63–$80 S or D; $99–$129 ste. Extra person $8. Min stay special events. Lower rates off-season. Parking: Outdoor, free. AE, DC, DISC, MC, V.

MOTEL

☰☰☰ Comfort Inn Island Suites

711 N Beachview Dr, 31520; tel 912/635-2211 or toll free 800/204-0202. Beachfront hotel with beautifully landscaped grounds. Located near Jekyll Island historic district. **Rooms:** 180 rms, stes, and effic. CI 4pm/CO 11am. Nonsmoking rms avail. **Amenities:** 🛎 A/C, cable TV w/movies, refrig. All units w/terraces, some w/whirlpools. Some units have whirlpools overlooking the ocean. **Services:** 🚐 📶 🛗 🛎 Car-rental desk. **Facilities:** 🛗 📶 🛗 ☖ 2 restaurants, 1 beach (ocean), volleyball, whirlpool, playground, washer/dryer. Picnic area. Tennis complex nearby. **Rates (CP):** Peak (May–Aug) $95 S or D; $175 ste; $125–$145 effic. Extra person $10. Children under age 18 stay free. Min stay special events. Lower rates off-season. Parking: Outdoor, free. AE, CB, DC, DISC, MC, V.

RESORT

☰☰☰ Jekyll Island Club Hotel

371 Riverview Dr, 31527 (Historic District); tel 912/635-2600 or toll free 800/535-9547; fax 912/635-2818. 12 acres. This resort was built in 1888 by Astor, Gould, Rockefeller, Morgan, and Pulitzer. If that alone isn't impressive enough, the property is close to the personal homes of these famous families, which are open to the public. The hotel itself has a whimsical caramel-and-vanilla-colored exterior with lots of towers and turrets, and there are 10 miles of beaches for sunbathing, swimming, and wandering. **Rooms:** 134 rms and stes. CI 4pm/CO noon. Nonsmoking rms avail. All rooms are furnished with antique reproductions. Some have views of ocean or lawn. **Amenities:** 🛎 ☖ A/C, cable TV w/movies, VCR. Some units w/terraces, some w/fireplaces, some w/whirlpools. **Services:** ✗ 🛗 🆅🅿 🚐 🛗 🛎 Social director, masseur, children's program, babysitting. Horse-drawn carriage rides available. **Facilities:** 🛗 📶 ⛰ 🛗 📶 ▶63 ⛳ 🎿 🥎3 🛗6 🛟 📶 ☖ 2 restaurants (see "Restaurants" below), 1 bar, 1 beach (ocean), basketball, volleyball, lawn games. **Rates:** Peak

(Mar–Aug) $99–$139 S or D; $159–$230 ste. Extra person $20. Children under age 17 stay free. Min stay wknds and special events. Lower rates off-season. AP and MAP rates avail. Parking: Outdoor, free. AE, CB, DC, DISC, MC, V.

RESTAURANTS 🍴

Blackbeard's

200 N Beachview Dr; tel 912/635-3522. **Seafood.** Standard nautical decor in a relaxed, beachside setting with gorgeous ocean views. House specialties range from baked stuffed flounder to seafood fettuccine, and they all are made from the freshest local fish. Steak and chicken dishes also available. **FYI:** Reservations not accepted. Guitar. Children's menu. **Open:** Daily 11am–10pm. Closed Dec 14–Jan 5. **Prices:** Main courses $10–$19. AE, DISC, MC, V. 🛰 🛗 ☖

♛ Grand Dining Room

In Jekyll Island Club Hotel, 371 Riverview Dr; tel 912/635-2600. **Eclectic.** An elegant and roomy dining room, where guests can sample gourmet entrees—ranging from seafood platters to roast duck—along with regional favorites like fried green tomatoes and Georgia quail. Seafood is always the freshest available, the steaks are first rate, and all baking is done on the premises. **FYI:** Reservations recommended. Piano. Children's menu. Jacket required. No smoking. **Open:** Breakfast Mon–Sat 7–11am, Sun 7–10am; lunch Mon–Sat 11:30am–2pm; dinner daily 6–10pm; brunch Sun 10:45am–2pm. **Prices:** Main courses $19–$26; prix fixe $15. AE, CB, DC, DISC, MC, V. 🛰 🛗 🆅🅿 ☖

Zachry's

44 Beachview Dr; tel 912/635-3128. Opposite the convention center. **Seafood.** The decor is nothing fancy, but locals swear by the menu. The Seafood House Special contains every kind of seafood you can think of, prepared in a variety of ways. There are also steak and chicken entrees, and a huge salad bar. **FYI:** Reservations not accepted. Children's menu. Beer and wine only. **Open:** Peak (Apr–Oct) Sun–Thurs 11am–9pm, Fri–Sat 11am–10pm. Closed 2 weeks before Christmas. **Prices:** Main courses $8–$20. MC, V.

ATTRACTIONS 🏛

Faith Chapel

Historic District; tel 912/635-2762. A beautifully restored English Gothic–style chapel featuring stained glass windows by Louis Comfort Tiffany and D Maitland Armstrong. **Open:** Daily 2–4pm.

Summer Waves

210 S Riverview Dr; tel 912/635-2074 or toll free 800/841-6586. Water park featuring wave pool, water slides, children's area, and an endless river, as well as a snack bar and beach shop. **Open:** Mem Day–Labor Day, Sun–Fri 10am–6pm, Sat 10am–8pm. **$$$$**

Kennesaw

This Cobb County city 20 miles northwest of Atlanta is near Kennesaw Mountain National Battlefield Park, commemorating a decisive battle of the Civil War.

MOTEL

🏨 Holiday Inn Express Town Center Mall

2485 George Busbee Pkwy NW, 30144; tel 770/427-5210 or toll free 800/HOLIDAY; fax 770/425-4211. Exit 116 off I-75. Standard Holiday Inn–style accommodations. Perfectly adequate. **Rooms:** 147 rms and stes. CI 3pm/CO noon. Nonsmoking rms avail. King rooms feature microwave, refrigerator, and queen sofa bed. **Amenities:** 🛁 🕭 🖥 A/C, cable TV, dataport. Free copies of *USA Today.* **Services:** 🚗 🖼 🗘 Car-rental desk. Fax and copy services. **Facilities:** 🛗 182 🛗 Free use of Sportslife health club. Located near Cowboys, a country-music venue that can accommodate up to 4,000 people at its 19 bars. **Rates (CP):** $62 S or D; $125 ste. Extra person $6. Children under age 18 stay free. Min stay special events. Parking: Outdoor, free. AE, CB, DC, DISC, JCB, MC, V.

RESTAURANT

Skeeter's

2700 Town Center Dr; tel 770/499-0676. Exit 116 off I-75. **Seafood/Steak/Ribs.** The attractive Southwestern-style decor at this lively eatery includes original paintings and prints of Native American art. The kitchen is perhaps best known for its luscious baby-back ribs and salmon. **FYI:** Reservations not accepted. Children's menu. Additional location: 3505 Satellite Blvd, Duluth (tel 476-3131). **Open:** Mon–Thurs 11:15am–10:30pm, Fri 11:15am–11:30pm, Sat 4–11:30pm, Sun 4–10pm. **Prices:** Main courses $8–$18. AE, CB, DC, DISC, MC, V. 🛗

ATTRACTIONS

Kennesaw Mountain National Battlefield Park

900 Kennesaw Mountain Dr; tel 770/427-4686. This 2,882-acre park was established in 1917 on the site of a crucial 1864 Civil War battle. Gen Ulysses S Grant had ordered Sherman to break up the Confederate army in Georgia, and by summer Sherman's 100,000-strong army had pushed Rebel forces back to a well-prepared defensive position on Kennesaw Mountain. On June 27 of that year, following a few weeks of skirmishing, Sherman made a last-ditch effort to break through Confederate lines and annihilate them with a grand assault from two directions. Sherman's men, repelled by firepower and the huge rocks rolling down the mountain at them, suffered far more casualties than the Confederate side.

The park visitors center has maps, a 10-minute slide show about the battle, and exhibits of Civil War artifacts and memorabilia. On weekdays, visitors can drive or hike directly up the mountain to see the actual Confederate entrench-ments; a shuttle bus runs on weekends. Interpretive signs at key spots enhance the experience and on weekends (spring through fall), interpretive programs further elucidate the battle. There are 16 miles of hiking trails and picnicking is permitted in designated areas. **Open:** Daily 8:30am–5pm. Closed Dec 25. **Free**

Big Shanty Museum

2829 Cherokee St; tel 770/428-6039 or toll free 800/742-6897. Site of the Andrews Railroad Raid, one of the most unusual episodes of the Civil War. On April 12, 1862, Union spy James J Andrews and a group of 21 Northern soldiers disguised as civilians boarded a train in Marietta. When the locomotive, known as the *General,* made a breakfast stop at Big Shanty, they seized it and headed north toward Chattanooga, planning to destroy supply lines to the Confederate Army. But the *General*'s conductor, William Fuller, gave chase (commandeering several locomotives himself) and foiled the Yankees' plans. (The whole escapade was made into a Disney movie, *The Great Locomotive Chase.*)

The museum, occupying a former cotton gin, houses the *General,* exhibits of Civil War artifacts and memorabilia, and photographs relating to the raid. There's also a *Gone With the Wind* exhibit. **Open:** Mon–Sat 9:30am–5:30pm, Sun noon–5:30pm. **$**

La Grange

The prosperous textile industry of this city north of Columbus dates back to the turn of the century. Site of Bellevue, a mansion that was a home of statesman Benjamin Hill. Nearby to 25,900-acre West Point Lake. **Information:** La Grange–Troup County Chamber of Commerce, 234 Main St, PO Box 636, La Grange, 30241 (tel 706/884-8671).

MOTEL

🏨 Ramada Inn

1513 Lafayette Pkwy, 30240; tel 706/884-6175 or toll free 800/2-RAMADA; fax 706/884-1106. Exit 4 off I-85. Average accommodations with worn carpeting and rooms. Located near Callaway Gardens, FDR's Little White House, and Warm Springs. **Rooms:** 145 rms and stes. CI 2pm/CO noon. Nonsmoking rms avail. Rooms are slightly worn. **Amenities:** 🛁 🕭 🖥 A/C, cable TV w/movies, dataport, in-rm safe. **Services:** ✕ 🖼 🗘 VCRs and movies for rent. **Facilities:** 🛗 🍽 400 🛗 1 restaurant, 1 bar (w/entertainment). **Rates:** $56 S or D; $125–$145 ste. Extra person $6. Children under age 16 stay free. Parking: Outdoor, free. AE, CB, DC, DISC, JCB, MC, V.

Lake Lanier Islands

See also Buford

In the foothills of the Appalachians and home to golf resorts, hidden coves, and wooded inlets along beaches. "Magical Nights of Lights" festival is held throughout the late fall and winter.

RESORTS

≡≡≡ Lake Lanier Islands Hilton Resort

7000 Holiday Rd, 30518; tel 770/945-8787 or toll free 800/768-LAKE; fax 770/932-5471. Exit 2 off I-985. 1,250 acres. Situated on the banks of Lake Lanier, this resort welcomes you with a lobby dominated by a glass wall that allows for far-reaching views of lake and pool area. **Rooms:** 224 rms and stes. CI 3pm/CO noon. Nonsmoking rms avail. **Amenities:** A/C, cable TV w/movies, dataport. All units w/terraces. **Services:** Masseur, babysitting. Concierge. Shuttle service to Atlanta (for fee); free shuttle to nearby water park. Children's program in summer. **Facilities:** 18 3 restaurants (see "Restaurants" below), 1 bar, volleyball, sauna, steam rm, whirlpool, playground. Gift shop. Picnic area with grills. Pontoon boats for rent. **Rates:** Peak (Apr–Oct) $119 S or D; $190 ste. Extra person $10. Children under age 18 stay free. Min stay special events. Lower rates off-season. Parking: Outdoor, $4/day. AE, CB, DC, DISC, MC, V.

≡≡≡≡ Renaissance Pineisle Resort

9000 Holiday Rd, 30518; tel 770/945-8921 or toll free 800/HOTELS-1; fax 770/945-1024. Exit 2 off I-985. Located on the shore of Lake Lanier, minutes from downtown Atlanta but isolated from the hustle and bustle. Great for family vacations and conventions. **Rooms:** 250 rms and stes. CI 3pm/CO noon. Nonsmoking rms avail. **Amenities:** A/C, cable TV w/movies, dataport, in-rm safe, bathrobes. All units w/minibars, all w/terraces, some w/whirlpools. Coffee and newspaper delivered with morning wake-up call. **Services:** VP Car-rental desk, social director, masseur, children's program, babysitting. Small pets only. **Facilities:** 18 350 3 restaurants, 2 bars (1 w/entertainment), 1 beach (lake shore), basketball, volleyball, games rm, lawn games, sauna, whirlpool. Lake Lanier Islands Water Park is adjacent to property. **Rates:** Peak (mid-Mar–mid-Nov) $149–$169 S or D; $250–$960 ste. Extra person $20. Children under age 18 stay free. Min stay special events. Lower rates off-season. AE, CB, DC, DISC, JCB, MC, V.

RESTAURANT

Sylvan's on Lanier

In Lake Lanier Islands Hilton Resort, 7000 Holiday Rd; tel 770/945-8787. **American/Continental.** A tastefully decorated restaurant offering a very select menu of veal, salmon, steak, and various types of seafood. The views of Lake Lanier and the rest of the Hilton Resort are awe-inspiring. **FYI:** Reservations accepted. Children's menu. **Open:** Breakfast daily 6:30am–noon; lunch daily noon–2pm; dinner daily 5–10pm. **Prices:** Main courses $10–$20. AE, CB, DC, DISC, MC, V.

Lincolnton

This agricultural town in the eastern part of the state is the site of Chenault Plantation, where the entire Confederate treasury was last seen, but never located. There are beaches and outdoor activities on Clark's Hill Lake, the largest Army Corps of Engineers lake project east of the Mississippi River. **Information:** Lincolnton–Lincoln County Chamber of Commerce, 160 May Ave, PO Box 490, Lincolnton, 30817 (tel 706/359-7970).

RESTAURANT

★ Home Cafe of Lincolnton

120 Washington Hwy; tel 706/359-3815. **American.** Opened over 40 years ago and housed in an old building, this humble eatery specializes in traditional Southern foods like fried chicken and country ham. **FYI:** Reservations accepted. No liquor license. **Open:** Daily 10am–9pm. **Prices:** Main courses $6–$11. No CC.

Lookout Mountain

See also Chattanooga, TN

INN

≡≡ Chanticleer Inn

1300 Mockingbird Lane, 30750; tel 706/820-2015. Quaint and comfortable property consisting of separate stone buildings. Located near Chattanooga Aquarium, Rock City, and Ruby Falls. **Rooms:** 16 rms and stes. CI 4pm/CO 11am. Rooms are decorated in antiques. No frills, but really livable. All rooms have a stone patio. **Amenities:** A/C, cable TV. **Services:** Linens changed every other day. Kids get free passes to Ruby Falls. **Facilities:** Well-kept grounds offer picnic tables and grills. Pool with diving board. **Rates:** $40–$50 S; $56–$70 D; $86 ste.

ATTRACTION

Rock City Gardens

1400 Patten Rd; tel 706/820-2531 or toll free 800/854-0675. This 14-acre complex, six miles from Chattanooga, TN, offers something for everyone: the geologic marvel of gigantic rock formations, the serenity and beauty of its landscaped gardens, the famous view from Lover's Leap of seven different states, and a deer park and Fairyland Caverns theme park for the youngsters. **Open:** Daily 8:30am–sunset. Closed Dec 25. **$$$**

Macon

See also Ocmulgee National Monument

At Georgia's geographical center, in the rolling hills on the west side of the Ocmulgee River. Macon's wide streets and parks were first laid out in 1822. The city is a growing business center and a focus for education in central Georgia; Wesleyan College, chartered in 1836 as Georgia Female College, was the first college for women in the world. The 1855 Hay House, sometimes called the "Palace of the South," is one of the finest surviving antebellum houses. **Information:** Macon–Bibb County Convention & Visitors Bureau, 200 Cherry St, PO Box 6354, Macon, 31208 (tel 912/743-3401).

HOTEL 🏨

▤▤▤ Crowne Plaza Macon
108 1st St, PO Box 144, 31202 (Historic District); tel 912/746-1461 or toll free 800/333-3333; fax 912/738-2460. Modern, centrally located hotel, great for corporate guests and visitors to Cherry Blossom Festival. **Rooms:** 299 rms and stes. Executive level. CI 3pm/CO noon. Nonsmoking rms avail. Rooms are luxuriously furnished and offer nice views of downtown. **Amenities:** 🛏 🍷 📺 A/C, satel TV w/movies, dataport, voice mail. Some units w/minibars, some w/terraces. Executive-level accommodations feature complimentary hors d'oeuvres, continental breakfast, and fax machines in rooms. **Services:** ✕ ☛ 📹 🛎 🍴 🤵 Pets under 30 lbs only. **Facilities:** 🏋 🍴 🎰 ⅙ 2 restaurants, 2 bars. Guests may use local health club. Golf, tennis, fishing, guided tours, and water sports can be arranged. **Rates:** $89–$104 S; $85–$99 D; $165–$225 ste. Extra person $15. Children under age 18 stay free. Min stay special events. Parking: Indoor/outdoor, free. AE, CB, DC, DISC, MC, V.

MOTELS

▤▤ Best Western Riverside Inn
2400 Riverside Dr, 31204; tel 912/743-6311 or toll free 800/446-6835; fax 912/743-9420. A low-key, basic establishment. Located near downtown/historic Macon, Mercer University, and a variety of restaurants and shopping. **Rooms:** 122 rms. CI 4pm/CO noon. Nonsmoking rms avail. **Amenities:** 🛏 🍷 📺 A/C, cable TV, refrig. **Services:** ✕ 🛎 🍴 Car-rental desk. **Facilities:** 🏋 ⅛ 1 restaurant, 1 bar, washer/dryer. **Rates:** $44 S; $54 D. Extra person $7. Children under age 18 stay free. Parking: Outdoor, free. AE, CB, DC, DISC, JCB, MC, V.

▤▤ Comfort Inn North
2690 Riverside Dr, 31204; tel 912/746-8855 or toll free 800/221-2222; fax 912/746-8881. Exit 54 off I-75. Suitable for all travelers and near Lake Tobesofkee, the Macon Coliseum, the Confederate Museum, and the Grand Opera House. **Rooms:** 120 rms. CI 3pm/CO noon. Nonsmoking rms avail. **Amenities:** 🛏 🍷 A/C, cable TV, voice mail. Some units w/terraces. Some rooms have microwaves and refrigerators. Free copies of *USA Today*. **Services:** 🛎 🍴 🤵 Complimentary coffee in lobby. **Facilities:** 🏋 ⅛ Washer/dryer. **Rates (CP):** $54 S; $59 D. Parking: Outdoor, free. Higher rates during Cherry Blossom Festival. AE, CB, DC, DISC, MC, V.

▤▤ Hampton Inn I-75
3680 Riverside Dr, 31210; tel 912/471-0660 or toll free 800/HAMPTON; fax 912/471-2528. Exit 55A off I-75. A good property for overnight stops. Located near shopping and restaurants. **Rooms:** 151 rms. CI 3pm/CO 11am. Nonsmoking rms avail. **Amenities:** 🛏 🍷 A/C, cable TV w/movies. **Services:** 🛎 🍴 🤵 Car-rental desk. Pets under 40 lbs only. **Facilities:** 🏋 ⅛ Free access to Gold's Gym. **Rates (CP):** $55 S or D. Extra person $6. Children under age 12 stay free. Parking: Outdoor, free. AE, CB, DC, DISC, MC, V.

▤▤ Holiday Inn I-75
Arkwright Rd, PO Box 7006, 31298; tel 912/474-2610 or toll free 800/HOLIDAY; fax 912/471-0712. Exit 55 off I-75. Near all Macon's attractions, including historic downtown and Mercer University. A good choice for extended stays. **Rooms:** 200 rms. CI 3pm/CO 11am. Nonsmoking rms avail. **Amenities:** 🛏 🍷 📺 A/C, cable TV w/movies, dataport. **Services:** ✕ 🛎 🍴 🤵 Car-rental desk. Pets under 40 lbs only. **Facilities:** 🏋 🎰 🖥 ⅛ 1 restaurant, 1 bar (w/entertainment), washer/dryer. Access to nearby Gold's Gym. **Rates:** $65 S or D. Extra person $6. Children under age 12 stay free. Parking: Outdoor, free. AE, CB, DC, DISC, MC, V.

▤▤ Quality Inn
4630 Chambers Rd, 31206; tel 912/781-7000 or toll free 800/228-5151; fax 912/781-7000. Exit 1 off I-475. Average chain property located near area universities, the coliseum, and Macon Mall. **Rooms:** 108 rms. CI 1pm/CO 11am. Nonsmoking rms avail. **Amenities:** 🛏 A/C, cable TV, dataport. **Services:** 🛎 🍴 🤵 Car-rental desk. **Facilities:** 🏋 🎰 ⅛ Whirlpool. **Rates (CP):** $35–$55 S or D. Extra person $5. Children under age 16 stay free. Parking: Outdoor, free. AE, CB, DC, DISC, MC, V.

INN

▤▤▤ 1842 Inn
353 College St, 31201 (Historic District); tel 912/741-1842 or toll free 800/336-1842; fax 912/741-1842. Forsyth St exit off I-75; left onto College St. Restored Greek Revival inn set in the middle of historic downtown Macon. There's a beautiful courtyard between the main house (with its massive columns) and the cottage, as well as very nice landscaping.

Perfect for a romantic getaway or for the businessperson who wants to travel in style. Unsuitable for children under 11. **Rooms:** 21 rms. CI 3pm/CO 11am. Nonsmoking rms avail. Rooms are individually decorated and named. **Amenities:** 🛏 🕐 A/C, cable TV. Some units w/fireplaces, some w/whirlpools. **Services:** ✗ 🖛 🖾 Twice-daily maid svce, afternoon tea and wine/sherry served. Breakfast can be served in room, in courtyard, or on the porch. Complimentary coffee and tea all day. Complimentary hors d'oeuvres served 5:30–7pm; cash bar 3–11pm. **Facilities:** 🔲20 🖳 ₺ Guest lounge. Access to private gym and restaurant at the Macon City Club for a fee. **Rates (CP):** $95–$125 S; $105–$135 D. Extra person $10. Parking: Outdoor, free. AE, MC, V.

RESTAURANTS 🍽

The Green Jacket
325 5th St; tel 912/746-4680. At Mulberry St. **Seafood/ Steak/Chicken.** The motif here is golf. The primary color of the restaurant is green, and the walls are decorated with highlights of the Master's Tournament. House specialties are prime rib (available in 10-, 12-, or 16-ounce portions), seafood, and chicken. **FYI:** Reservations recommended. Children's menu. **Open:** Sun–Thurs 11am–10pm, Fri 11am–11pm, Sat 5–11pm. **Prices:** Main courses $9–$20. AE, DISC, MC, V. ₺

★ Len Berg's Restaurant
Old Post Office Alley; tel 912/742-9255. Off Walnut St behind the Federal Court building. **Soul/Southern.** A Macon institution for over 30 years, housed in a very plain cinder-block structure. The walls are decorated with old photos of Macon. Entrees include salmon croquettes, fried chicken, pork chops, and meat loaf; side dishes tend toward traditional Southern items: tomatoes and okra, beets in orange sauce, lima beans, fried fresh corn, black-eyed peas, and turnip greens. Desserts include macaroon pie and (during June and July) fresh peach ice cream. **FYI:** Reservations not accepted. No liquor license. Additional location: 2395 Ingleside Dr (tel 743-7011). **Open:** Mon–Sat 11am–2:30pm. **Prices:** Lunch main courses $4–$6. No CC. 👥

ATTRACTIONS 📷

Sidney Lanier Cottage
955 High St; tel 404/743-3851. This 1842 Gothic Revival cottage was home to Sidney Lanier, a poet best known for "Song of the Chattahoochee" and "The Marshes of Glynn." Behind the house is an ornamental garden. The house, outfitted in furnishings of the period, is home to the Middle Georgia Historical Society. **Open:** Mon–Fri 9am–1pm and 2–4pm, Sat 9:30am–12:30pm. Closed some hols. **$**

Harriet Tubman Historical and Cultural Museum
340 Walnut St; tel 912/743-8544. Celebrates the history, art, and achievements of all African Americans, with special attention paid to Underground Railroad "conductor" Tub-

man. A mural depicts her accomplishments in leading 300 slaves north to freedom, and there are African artifacts on display. **Open:** Mon–Sat 10am–5pm, Sun 2–5pm. Closed some hols. **$**

Cannonball House and Confederate Museum
856 Mulberry St; tel 404/745-5982. On July 30, 1864, Union forces led by Gen George Stoneman struck this building with a cannonball. The cannonball is on the floor in the entryway today. The building—an authentic example of Greek Revival design—is on the National Register of Historic Places. **Open:** Tues–Fri 10am–1pm and 2–4pm, Sat–Sun 1:30–4:30pm. Closed some hols. **$**

Hay House
934 Georgia Ave; tel 404/742-8155. Built between 1855 and 1860, this extravagant home of Italian Renaissance Revival design was the home of William Butler Johnston, the keeper of the Confederate treasury. The spectacular interiors are reminiscent of European palaces, complete with ornamental plasterwork, Victorian antiques, and stained-glass windows. More than 20 rooms in the house are not fully restored, but those that are complete are breathtaking. The house is listed on the National Register of Historic Places. **Open:** Mon–Sat 10am–5pm, Sun 1–5pm. Closed some hols. **$$$**

Ocmulgee National Monument
1207 Emery Hwy; tel 912/752-8257. This 683-acre complex celebrates 12,000 years of Southeastern history, from the first Native Americans to the present day. The visitors center features an archeological museum; a short film, *People of the Macon Plateau,* is shown every half-hour. Other highlights include a reconstructed Native American lodge, a burial mound, several temple mounds, prehistoric trenches, and the site of a colonial British trading post. **Open:** Daily 9am–5pm. Closed some hols. **Free**

Madison

On the Antebellum Trail, with a large historic district that encompasses most of the town. Much of the architecture remains unchanged from the 1830s. Referred to as "the town Sherman refused to burn." **Information:** Madison–Morgan County Convention & Visitors Bureau, 115 E Jefferson St, PO Box 826, Madison, 30650 (tel 706/342-4454).

MOTELS 🏨

🏨🏨 Days Inn
2001 Eatonton Rd, 30650; tel 706/342-1839 or toll free 800/325-2525; fax 706/342-1839. Exit 51 off I-20. Comfortable property, good for overnight stops. Popular with fishing enthusiasts (Lake Oconee is nearby) and U of GA visitors. **Rooms:** 77 rms. CI 2pm/CO noon. Nonsmoking rms avail. **Amenities:** 🛏 A/C, cable TV. **Services:** 🚗 🖾 🦮 🐾 $10 deposit for pets. **Facilities:** 🔲 🔲12 ₺ 1 restaurant, washer/dryer. Golf, boat rentals, horseback riding, and hiking at

nearby Hard Labor Creek State Park. **Rates:** $45 S or D. Extra person $5. Children under age 17 stay free. Parking: Outdoor, free. AE, CB, DC, DISC, MC, V.

🏯🏯 Holiday Inn Express

2080 Eatonton Rd, 30650; tel 706/342-3433 or toll free 800/HOLIDAY; fax 706/342-7060. Exit 51 off I-20. Standard chain accommodations. **Rooms:** 92 rms. CI 2pm/CO noon. Nonsmoking rms avail. **Amenities:** 🔐 A/C, cable TV w/movies, dataport. **Services:** 🛎 🍴 **Facilities:** 🛗 🏊 ⚐ **Rates (CP):** $45 S; $55 D. Extra person $10. Children under age 20 stay free. Min stay special events. Parking: Outdoor, free. AE, CB, DC, DISC, JCB, MC, V.

🏯🏯 Ramada Antebellum Inn

2020 Eatonton Rd, 30650; tel 706/342-2121 or toll free 800/2-RAMADA; fax 706/342-3738. Exit 51 off I-20 and US 441. Slightly dated, average property. Centrally located to Atlanta, Macon, and Athens, and near Lake Oconee and downtown Madison. **Rooms:** 120 rms. CI 2pm/CO noon. Nonsmoking rms avail. **Amenities:** 🔐 A/C, cable TV, dataport. **Services:** 🛎 🍴 🍽 **Facilities:** 🛗 🏊 ⚐ Washer/dryer. **Rates (BB):** Peak (Apr–Oct) $59–$65 S or D. Extra person $6. Children under age 18 stay free. Lower rates off-season. Parking: Outdoor, free. AE, DISC, MC, V.

RESTAURANT 🍴

Ye Old Colonial Restaurant

108 E Washington St (Historic District); tel 706/342-2211. At Main St on the Square. **Soul/Southern.** Housed in two beautiful old buildings: one was built in 1817 for use as a tavern, and the other is the former Morgan County Bank (circa 1900). The dining area features the original bank vault, patterned tile floors, and pressed tin ceiling. Breakfast is served à la carte, while lunch and dinner are served buffet-style with a selection of meats (fried chicken, ham, roast beef) and vegetables. **FYI:** Reservations not accepted. No liquor license. **Open:** Mon–Sat 5:30am–8:30pm. **Prices:** Main courses $5–$6. No CC. 🍴

ATTRACTIONS 🏛

Madison-Morgan Cultural Center

434 S Main St; tel 706/342-4743. Built circa 1895 as a schoolhouse, this red-brick Romanesque building now houses a history museum on the Piedmont region of Georgia, a classroom museum, art galleries with changing exhibits, and an auditorium featuring live performances ranging from Shakespeare and chamber music concerts to gospel singing and ballet. **Open:** Tues–Sat 10am–4:30pm, Sun 2–5pm. Closed some hols. $

Hard Labor Creek State Park

Off Knox Chapel Rd, Rutledge; tel 706/557-3001. *Golf* magazine rates this park's 18-hole course as one of the finest public courses in America. If golf is not your cup of tea, you can swim at a sand beach, fish for bass and catfish, or hike the

5,000 wooded acres. The park campground has 51 sites with electricity, water, rest rooms, and showers. **Open:** Daily 8am–10pm. Closed Dec 25. $

Marietta

Located in the northwest Atlanta metro area, Marietta—a major center of the aircraft industry–features a Victorian town square, Civil War sites, and antebellum mansions. **Information:** Cobb County Convention & Visitors Bureau, PO Box 672827, Marietta, 30067 (tel 770/933-7228).

HOTEL 🏨

🏯🏯🏯 Sheraton Inn Atlanta Northwest

1775 Parkway Place NW, 30067; tel 770/428-4400 or toll free 800/800-5756; fax 770/424-5756. Exit 112 off I-75. Everything travelers expect from a Sheraton: modern and attractive public areas, and spacious rooms with lots of comforts and amenities. **Rooms:** 221 rms and stes. CI 3pm/CO noon. Nonsmoking rms avail. **Amenities:** 🔐 🍴 📺 A/C, cable TV w/movies, dataport. **Services:** 🍽 🛎 🍴 Babysitting. **Facilities:** 🛗 🏊 🍽 ⚐ 1 restaurant, 1 bar. **Rates:** $109 S; $119 D; $129 ste. Extra person $10. Children under age 5 stay free. Parking: Outdoor, free. AE, CB, DC, DISC, MC, V.

MOTELS

🏯🏯 Best Western Bon Air Motel

859 Cobb Pkwy SE, 30062; tel 770/427-4676 or toll free 800/528-1234; fax 770/514-1327. Exit 112 off I-75. Though there are few modern amenities, this 1950s-style motel has its own unique charms. **Rooms:** 39 rms and stes. CI open/CO 11am. Nonsmoking rms avail. **Amenities:** 🔐 A/C, cable TV, refrig. **Services:** 🍴 **Facilities:** 🛗 ⚐ Playground. **Rates (CP):** Peak (Mem Day–Labor Day) $55–$70 S; $65–$72 D; $90–$110 ste. Extra person $3. Min stay special events. Lower rates off-season. Parking: Outdoor, free. AE, DC, DISC, MC, V.

🏯🏯 La Quinta Motor Inn

2170 Delk Rd, 30067; tel 770/951-0026 or toll free 800/531-5900; fax 770/952-5372. Exit 111 off I-75. A comfortable and convenient hotel for the interstate traveler. **Rooms:** 130 rms. CI 2pm/CO noon. Nonsmoking rms avail. **Amenities:** 🔐 🍴 A/C, cable TV. **Services:** 🔑 🛎 🍴 🍽 Babysitting. **Facilities:** 🛗 🏊 ⚐ **Rates (CP):** Peak (Mem Day–Labor Day) $85–$95 S; $92–$102 D. Extra person $8. Children under age 18 stay free. Lower rates off-season. Parking: Outdoor, free. AE, CB, DC, DISC, EC, ER, JCB, MC, V.

RESTAURANT 🍴

★ Jimmy's

164 Roswell St; tel 770/428-5627. Exit 112 off I-75. **Greek/Seafood/Steak.** This Greek steak house is reminiscent of old,

family-style dinner houses. An elegant dining experience with some superb steaks. **FYI:** Reservations recommended. Dress code. **Open:** Lunch Mon–Fri 11am–2:30pm; dinner Sun–Thurs 5–10pm, Fri–Sat 5–11pm. **Prices:** Main courses $10–$22. AE, MC, V.

ATTRACTIONS

Six Flags Over Georgia

7561 Six Flags Pkwy; tel 770/739-3400. With more than 100 rides, a multitude of shows, and several restaurants, Six Flags offers a full day's entertainment for families. The park's eight theme areas mirror the historical heritage of the region, both Southern (Cotton States, Confederate, Georgia, and Lickskillet) and European (France, Britain, Spain), plus of course "USA." Sylvester, Porky Pig, Daffy Duck, and other Looney Tunes cartoon characters roam the park greeting kids. Thrill rides include several wet ones such as Ragin' Rivers, Splashwater Falls, and Thunder River. White-knuckle roller coasters range from the corkscrew turns of the Ninja to the classic wooden-track Georgia Cyclone. Other highlights are the Great Gasp (a 20-story parachute jump) and Free Fall, which simulates a fall from a 10-story building.

Shows vary from year to year, but they usually include a musical revue, a country music show, a water show, an oldies rock show, a magic show, and an animated characters show. The 8,000-seat amphitheater hosts various pop and country stars. **Open:** Late May–Labor Day, Sun–Thurs 10am–10pm, Fri–Sat 10am–midnight; Labor Day–Oct and Apr–May, Sat–Sun 10am–10pm. **$$$$**

White Water

250 N Cobb Pkwy, exit 113 off I-75; tel 770/424-9283. A 40-acre theme park boasting over 40 water adventures, ranging from the Bahama Bob-Slide and White Water Rapids to the Atlanta Ocean wave pool and Little Squirt's Island for toddlers. The four-story Tree House Island features cargo netting, water jetting, and slides galore. (Visitors should bring bathing suits, since the park does not allow street clothes on the rides.) **Open:** Mem Day–Labor Day, daily 10am–8pm. **$$$$**

American Adventures

250 N Cobb Pkwy, exit 113 off I-75; tel 770/424-9283. Located next door to White Water (see above) and designed especially for families with kids age 12 and under, this amusement park features 15 rides, an 18-hole miniature-golf course, and an Indoor Park with a games arcade, carousel, and Imagination Station creative play area. **Open:** Labor Day–Mem Day, Sat–Sun 10am–8pm; Mem Day–Labor Day, daily 10am–8pm. Closed some hols. **$$$$**

Milledgeville

The "Antebellum Capital," it served as state capital from 1804 to 1868, and is the only other city besides Washington, DC that was designed to serve as a capital. Home to Southern novelist Flannery O'Connor for many years. **Information:** Milledgeville–Baldwin County Convention & Visitors Bureau, 200 W Hancock St, PO Box 219, Milledgeville, 31061 (tel 912/452-4687).

MOTELS

Holiday Inn

2627 N Columbia St, 31061; tel 912/452-3502 or toll free 800/HOLIDAY; fax 912/453-3591. A standard Holiday Inn near historic district and Georgia College. **Rooms:** 170 rms and stes. CI 3pm/CO noon. Nonsmoking rms avail. **Amenities:** A/C, cable TV w/movies. Some units w/whirlpools. Some suites have wet bar. **Services:** Car-rental desk. **Facilities:** 1 restaurant, 1 bar, washer/dryer. **Rates:** $64 S; $69 D; $125 ste. Extra person $5. Children under age 12 stay free. Parking: Outdoor, free. AE, CB, DC, DISC, JCB, MC, V.

Jameson Inn

2551 N Columbia St, 31061; tel 912/453-8471 or toll free 800/541-3268; fax 912/453-8482. Off US 441 N. Solid, two-story property, good for extended stays. Located near dining, shopping, and Lake Sinclair. **Rooms:** 100 rms, stes, and effic. CI 2pm/CO 11am. Nonsmoking rms avail. **Amenities:** A/C, cable TV. **Services:** A nearby vet will keep pets for a fee. **Facilities:** Sauna, whirlpool. Fitness center and spa are well kept. **Rates (CP):** $46–$51 S or D; $82–$125 ste; $105–$150 effic. Extra person $4. Children under age 12 stay free. Parking: Outdoor, free. AE, DC, DISC, MC, V.

ATTRACTION

The Old Governor's Mansion

120 S Clarke St; tel 912/453-4545. This pink-marble Palladian beauty has been restored and refurbished, and is now the home of the president of Georgia College. Listed on the Register of Historic Landmarks, the mansion features period antiques and displays on Georgia's history, especially during the years when Milledgeville served as its capital (1804–1868). Guided tours begin every hour on the hour. **Open:** Tues–Sat 10am–4pm, Sun 2–4pm. Closed some hols. **$**

Norcross

Northeast of Atlanta, with a quiet, picturesque downtown district. Its 123-year history can be found in its train depot, converted to a gathering spot.

HOTELS

Atlanta Marriott Norcross

475 Technology Pkwy, 30092; tel 770/263-8558 or toll free 800/228-9290; fax 770/263-0766. Exit 23 off I-285. Nestled in a quiet, commercial district. Friendly, efficient staff.

Rooms: 222 rms and stes. Executive level. CI 3pm/CO noon. Nonsmoking rms avail. **Amenities:** ☎ ⚖ ☕ A/C, cable TV w/movies, dataport, voice mail. **Services:** ✗ 🚐 ☒ ↩ ⤵ Babysitting. **Facilities:** 🎿 🏌 400 ⚿ 1 restaurant, 1 bar, whirlpool. **Rates:** $99 S; $109 D; $185–$250 ste. Extra person $10. Children under age 12 stay free. Parking: Outdoor, free. AE, DISC, ER, JCB, MC, V.

≣≣ Best Western Bradbury Inn
5985 Oakbrook Pkwy, 30093; tel 770/662-8175 or toll free 800/528-1234; fax 770/840-1183. Exit 37 off I-85. Mainly a corporate hotel during the week, traveling families will find this Tudor-style hotel very inviting and comfortable (and a good value) on weekends. **Rooms:** 123 rms and stes. CI 2pm/CO noon. Nonsmoking rms avail. **Amenities:** ☎ ⚖ ☕ A/C, cable TV, refrig. Some units w/whirlpools. **Services:** ☒ ↩ **Facilities:** 🎿 120 ⚿ 1 restaurant (bkfst only). **Rates (BB):** $59–$69 S; $69–$89 ste. Children under age 18 stay free. Parking: Outdoor, free. AE, CB, DC, DISC, JCB, MC, V.

≣≣ ClubHouse Inn
5945 Oakbrook Pkwy, 30093; tel 770/368-9400 or toll free 800/258-2460; fax 770/416-7370. Exit 37 off I-85. A basic, comfortable hotel for a pleasant stay in Norcross. **Rooms:** 172 rms and stes. CI 3pm/CO noon. Nonsmoking rms avail. **Amenities:** ☎ ⚖ A/C, cable TV. Some units w/terraces, 1 w/whirlpool. **Services:** ☒ ↩ **Facilities:** 🎿 50 ⚿ 1 restaurant (bkfst only), whirlpool, washer/dryer. **Rates (BB):** $56–$65 S; $56–$75 D; $85–$95 ste. Extra person $10. Children under age 10 stay free. Min stay special events. Parking: Outdoor, free. AE, DISC, MC, V.

≣≣≣ Courtyard by Marriott Peachtree Corners
3209 Holcomb Bridge Rd, 30092; tel 770/446-3777 or toll free 800/321-2211. Exit 23 off I-285. A wonderful hotel for corporate travelers; the grounds and pool area offer a relaxing haven for hardworking businesspeople. **Rooms:** 131 rms and stes. CI 4pm/CO noon. Nonsmoking rms avail. **Amenities:** ☎ ⚖ A/C, cable TV, voice mail. Some units w/terraces. **Services:** ☒ ↩ **Facilities:** 🎿 30 ⚿ 1 restaurant (bkfst only). **Rates:** $79 S; $89 D; $89–$99 ste. Children under age 18 stay free. Parking: Outdoor, free. AE, CB, DC, DISC, MC, V.

≣≣≣ Holiday Inn Select
6050 Peachtree Industrial Blvd, 30071; tel 770/448-4400 or toll free 800/HOLIDAY; fax 770/840-8008. 5½ mi N of exit 23 off I-285. Having just recently become a Holiday Select hotel, this Holiday Inn offers many of the amenities found at four-flag hotels. Although it is 10 miles from downtown, MARTA transportation makes this property very accessible. **Rooms:** 243 rms and stes. Executive level. CI 2pm/CO noon. Nonsmoking rms avail. **Amenities:** ☎ ⚖ ☕ 🍴 A/C, cable TV w/movies, refrig, voice mail. **Services:** ✗ ☒ ↩ ⤵ **Facilities:** 🎿 🏌 200 💻 ⚿ 1 restaurant, 1 bar (w/entertainment),

whirlpool, washer/dryer. **Rates:** $65–$114 S; $75–$124 D; $95–$135 ste. Children under age 12 stay free. Parking: Outdoor, free. AE, CB, DC, DISC, MC, V.

≣≣≣ Homewood Suites Peachtree Corners
450 Technology Pkwy, 30092; tel 770/448-4663 or toll free 800/225-5466; fax 770/242-6979. Exit 23 off I-285. Decorated in American/Country style, this hotel is suitable for both businesspeople and families. **Rooms:** 92 rms and stes. CI 3pm/CO noon. Nonsmoking rms avail. **Amenities:** ☎ ⚖ 🍴 A/C, cable TV w/movies, refrig, VCR, voice mail. Some units w/terraces. **Services:** ☒ ↩ ⤵ Babysitting. **Facilities:** 🎿 🏌 40 💻 ⚿ 1 restaurant (bkfst only), basketball, sauna, playground, washer/dryer. **Rates (BB):** $92 S; $102–$152 ste. Children under age 18 stay free. Parking: Outdoor, free. AE, CB, DC, DISC, MC, V.

MOTEL
≣≣ La Quinta Inn
5375 Peachtree Industrial Blvd, 30092; tel 770/449-5144 or toll free 800/531-5900; fax 770/840-8576. Exit 23 N off I-285. A surprisingly nice chain motel. Convenient to interstates and nearby Atlanta. **Rooms:** 130 rms and stes. CI 3pm/CO noon. Nonsmoking rms avail. **Amenities:** ☎ ⚖ A/C, cable TV w/movies. **Services:** ☒ ↩ ⤵ **Facilities:** 🎿 25 ⚿ **Rates (CP):** $69 S; $89 ste. Extra person $7. Children under age 18 stay free. Parking: Outdoor, free. AE, CB, DC, DISC, MC, V.

RESTAURANTS 🍴
Malasia House
5945 Jimmy Carter Blvd; tel 770/368-8368. ½ mi N of exit 37 off I-85. **Malaysian.** Decor includes a beautiful fish tank and Malaysian art, but the authentic cooking is all-important here. **FYI:** Reservations not accepted. No liquor license. No smoking. **Open:** Lunch Mon–Fri 11am–2:30pm, Sat 11am–3pm; dinner Mon–Thurs 4:30–9:30pm, Fri–Sat 4:30–10:30pm. **Prices:** Main courses $6–$14. AE, DISC, MC, V. ⚿

★ Slocums
6025 Peachtree Pkwy; tel 770/446-7725. **Seafood/Steak.** Noisy, publike atmosphere and nautical decor predominate at this home of great seafood. Big burgers, surf-and-turf platters, chicken wings, and nouvelle touches like marinated tuna steaks keep all members of the family happy. **FYI:** Reservations accepted. Additional locations: 8849 Roswell Rd, Atlanta (tel 404/587-3022); 1433 Terrell Mill Rd, Atlanta (tel 951-2090). **Open:** Mon–Sat 11am–11pm, Sun noon–10:30pm. **Prices:** Main courses $6–$17. AE, CB, DC, DISC, MC, V. ⚿

Okefenokee National Wildlife Refuge

Okefenokee is the largest wetlands park in the country after Florida's Everglades, with an area of 700 square miles. To get a closer look at the enormous variety of flora and fauna here—black bear, deer, lynx, alligators, water birds—visitors may wish to take a canoe trip (guided or unguided) through the swamp. Canoe trails must be reserved in advance by calling the number above; canoes and camping equipment are available for rent from the park concessioner (tel 912/ 496-7156). A 4½-mile wildlife observation drive, 4½ miles of walking trails, a pedestrian boardwalk into the swamp, and two observation towers are also available. The visitors center, near the refuge's east entrance in Folkston (on GA 121/23) provides information and maps. For more information, contact Refuge Manager, Rte 2, Box 338, Folkston, GA 31537 (tel 912/496-3331).

Peachtree City

Georgia's planned city has 70 miles of bike paths, two lakes, and some 30 restaurants.

RESORT 🏨

≣≣≣ Peachtree Executive Conference Center
2443 GA 54 W, 30269; tel 770/487-2000 or toll free 800/ PEACH-11. 19 acres. Great for conventions and business retreats. Located near antique shopping. **Rooms:** 250 rms and stes. CI 3pm/CO 11am. Nonsmoking rms avail. **Amenities:** 🛁 🅿 🖥 A/C, dataport. All units w/terraces. **Services:** ✕ 🗝 🚗 🖐 🤏 🐕 Masseur. Small pets only. **Facilities:** 🏋 🚴 ▶18 🏀 🎿 🏊3 🎱 550 🎮 ♿ 3 restaurants, 1 bar (w/entertainment), basketball, games rm, racquetball, sauna, steam rm, whirlpool. Ropes course and skeet shooting available. **Rates:** $135 S; $140 D; $280–$350 ste. Extra person $10. Parking: Outdoor, free. AE, DC, DISC, MC, V.

RESTAURANT 🍴

Partners II Pizza
In Aberdeen Village Center, 215 Northlake Dr; tel 770/ 487-9393. **Cafe/Pizza.** Plain, simple decor does not detract from the hearty fare served here. A variety of sandwiches, salads, and pasta dishes is available à la carte, and there's an all-you-can-eat lunch buffet (with pizza and salad) served every weekday. **FYI:** Reservations not accepted. Children's menu. Beer and wine only. **Open:** Daily 11am–10pm. **Prices:** Main courses $4–$16. AE, DC, DISC, MC, V. 👪 ♿

Perry

The antique center of Georgia, this charming, small central Georgia town is on the Antique and Peach Blossom Trails. Downtown includes a "living history" area. **Information:** Perry Area Convention & Visitors Bureau. 101 Gen Courtney Hodges Blvd, PO Box 1619, Perry, 31069 (tel 912/ 988-8000).

MOTELS 🏨

≣≣ Days Inn
800 Valley Dr, PO Box 615, 31069; tel 912/987-2142 or toll free 800/DAYS-INN; fax 912/987-0468. Off I-75. Basic two-story property, adequate for overnight stays. Near Aviation Museum, Agricultural Center, and Camelia Gardens. **Rooms:** 80 rms. CI 2pm/CO noon. Nonsmoking rms avail. **Amenities:** 🛁 🅿 A/C, cable TV, dataport. All units w/terraces. **Services:** 🚐 🗝 🖐 🐕 Car-rental desk. Complimentary coffee in lobby. **Facilities:** 🍴 1 restaurant. Guests have access to Perry Country Club for golf and other activities. **Rates:** $46 S or D. Children under age 18 stay free. Parking: Outdoor, free. AE, CB, DC, DISC, MC, V.

≣≣ Holiday Inn
700 Valley Dr, 31069; tel 912/987-3313 or toll free 800/ HOLIDAY; fax 912/988-8269. Exit 43 off I-75. A standard Holiday Inn with recently renovated rooms. **Rooms:** 203 rms. CI 3pm/CO noon. Nonsmoking rms avail. **Amenities:** 🛁 🅿 A/C, cable TV, dataport. **Services:** ✕ 🗝 🖐 **Facilities:** 🍴 250 ♿ 1 restaurant, 1 bar, washer/dryer. **Rates:** $44 S or D. Children under age 18 stay free. Parking: Outdoor, free. AE, CB, DC, DISC, JCB, MC, V.

Pine Mountain

See also Hamilton

This small town north of Columbus is named for the mountain on the slopes of which stands the house Franklin D Roosevelt built for himself in 1932, the "Little White House." Also a gateway to Callaway Gardens, a 2,500-acre resort for recreation and education. **Information:** Pine Mountain Tourism Association, 111 Broad St, Pine Mountain, 31822 (tel 706/663-4000).

MOTELS 🏨

≣≣ Davis Inn
State Park Rd, PO Box 830, 31822; tel 706/663-2522 or toll free 800/346-2668. At US 27. Southern hospitality reigns at this homey inn, where each guest is greeted with a loaf of homemade bread. **Rooms:** 22 rms and effic; 15 cottages/ villas. CI 1pm/CO noon. Nonsmoking rms avail. Rooms are well kept. **Amenities:** 🛁 🅿 🖥 A/C, cable TV. Some units w/terraces. Coffee brought to room. **Services:** 🚐 Babysitting. Linens changed every other day unless requested. Passes

to nearby health club and nearby Callaway Gardens. **Rates:** $85 S or D; $85 effic; $100–$195 cottage/villa. Extra person $5–$10. Children under age 6 stay free. Min stay wknds and special events. Parking: Outdoor, free. No CC.

〓〓 White Columns Motel

19727 US 27, PO Box 531, 31822; or toll free 800/722-5083. 1 mi N of Callaway Gardens. A small, homey property located near Callaway Gardens, Pine Mountain, and Roosevelt State Park. **Rooms:** 13 rms. CI 2pm/CO noon. Rooms are a little dated, but comfortable. **Amenities:** 📺 🍷 A/C, cable TV. **Services:** 🚐 🍽 🛎 Linens changed every other day during multinight stays. **Facilities:** ⅙ **Rates:** Peak (Mar–Oct/last of Nov–Dec) $45 S or D. Extra person $6. Min stay special events. Lower rates off-season. Parking: Outdoor, free. AE, DISC, MC, V.

LODGE

〓〓〓 Mountain Top Inn and Resort

GA 190 at Hines Gap Rd, PO Box 147, 31822; tel 706/663-4719 or toll free 800/NIGHT–NIGHT; fax 706/663-8380. Located in the middle of Roosevelt State Park, this rustic facility is a perfect place to get away. **Rooms:** 20 rms; 50 cottages/villas. CI 4pm/CO noon. Nonsmoking rms avail. Rooms are decorated in international themes, but not very tastefully done. Cabins, on the other hand, are very tasteful with full front porches, kitchens, whirlpool garden tubs, and nice views. **Amenities:** 🍷 A/C, TV w/movies. No phone. Some units w/terraces, some w/fireplaces, some w/whirlpools. **Services:** ✗ 🚐 Car-rental desk. Cottages receive daily linen delivery and complete clean-up on third day of multinight stays. Breakfast served in rooms. VCRs available for rent. **Facilities:** �ᵢ 🚲 📶 ⎡200⎤ ⌨ ⅙ 1 restaurant (bkfst and dinner only), playground. The Mountain Top Chapel (available for wedding parties) is tastefully decorated with dark and light woods and stained-glass windows. All park activities—including golf, swimming, and horseback riding—are just minutes from the lodge. **Rates (CP):** $62–$105 S or D; $94–$182 cottage/villa. Extra person $10. Children under age 12 stay free. Min stay wknds and special events. Parking: Outdoor, free. AE, DISC, MC, V.

RESORT

〓〓〓〓 Callaway Gardens Resort

US 27, 31822; tel 706/663-2281 or toll free 800/CALLAWAY; fax 706/663-5080. Although it is quiet and secluded, this resort surrounded by 12,000 of woodlands offers enough activities for anyone's taste. Popular with families as well as couples. Accommodations include rooms, two-bedroom cottages, and villas. **Rooms:** 350 rms and stes; 204 cottages/villas. CI 4pm/CO noon. Nonsmoking rms avail. Cottages and villas have fully equipped kitchens, grills, porches, and fireplaces. **Amenities:** 📺 🍷 A/C, cable TV, dataport. All units w/minibars, some w/terraces. Some rooms have refrigerators. **Services:** ✗ 🍷 🚐 🛎 🍽 Car-rental desk,

social director, children's program, babysitting. In summer, resort features Florida State University's "Flying High" Circus for children. **Facilities:** 🔳 🚲 △ 🚩63 🎿 💻20 ⛷ 🖥 ⎡800⎤ ⌨ ⅙ 9 restaurants (see "Restaurants" below), 2 bars (1 w/entertainment), 1 beach (lake shore), lifeguard, basketball, volleyball, games rm, lawn games, racquetball, sauna, steam rm, whirlpool, playground, washer/dryer. Grounds include 7½ miles of bicycle trails; fly fishing; tennis center; John A Sibley Horticultural Center; Cecil B Day Butterfly Center. Quail hunting and skeet shooting available in season. **Rates:** Peak (Mar–Dec) $89–$118 S or D; $200–$350 ste; $170–$485 cottage/villa. Extra person $15. Children under age 18 stay free. Min stay special events. Lower rates off-season. AP and MAP rates avail. Parking: Outdoor, free. Golf and tennis packages avail. AE, DISC, MC, V.

RESTAURANTS 🍴

The Country Kitchen

In Callaway Gardens Resort, US 27; tel 706/663-2281. **Southern.** The country-style, wooden-barn atmosphere is perfect for families, and the dining area has a great view of the valley. The menu includes many country favorites like "meat-and-two" (choice of ham, turkey, or chicken served with two vegetable side dishes). The food is nothing fancy, but the view alone makes it worth a trip. There's a small country store, near the entrance, where guests can browse while waiting to be seated. **FYI:** Reservations not accepted. Children's menu. No liquor license. **Open:** Daily 7am–8pm. **Prices:** Main courses $5–$7; prix fixe $7. AE, DISC, MC, V. ⛰ ⅙

The Gardens Restaurant

In Callaway Gardens Resort, US 27; tel 706/663-2281. **Seafood/Steak.** Relaxed yet elegant eatery, offering a great view of Mountain Creek Lake and the nearby golf course. The menu offers such Southern entrees as fried chicken, fried catfish, and barbecue, as well as steak and other seafood. Summertime diners are serenaded by a classical guitarist. **FYI:** Reservations recommended. Guitar. Children's menu. Beer and wine only. **Open:** Lunch daily 11am–3pm; dinner Mon–Sat 6–10pm. **Prices:** Main courses $10–$18. AE, DISC, MC, V. 🍽 ⛰ ⅙

The Georgia Room

In Callaway Gardens Resort, US 27; tel 706/663-2281. **Southern.** The dark and nicely furnished Georgia Room offers romantic dining for couples, or elegant dining for groups. The continental-style menu has a few select choices available at a time, including perhaps lamb, grouper, salmon, chicken, prime rib, and filet mignon. All baked goods are made on premises; extensive wine list. **FYI:** Reservations recommended. Dress code. No smoking. **Open:** Mon 6–10pm, Wed–Sat 6–10pm. **Prices:** Main courses $17–$23. AE, DISC, MC, V. ♥ ⅙

The Plantation Room

In Callaway Gardens Resort, US 27; tel 706/663-2281. **Southern.** A very casual and comfortable eatery that is great for hungry families. Offerings include a daily, all-you-can-eat Southern-style buffet; a Friday night seafood buffet; and a Sunday brunch. There's also an à la carte menu, with choices like baked country ham, fried chicken, and roast beef. **FYI:** Reservations not accepted. Children's menu. **Open:** Daily 6:30am–10pm. **Prices:** Main courses $6–$20; prix fixe $8–$20. AE, DISC, MC, V. 🖼️ &.

The Veranda

In Callaway Gardens Resort, US 27; tel 706/663-2281. **Southern Italian.** An upscale dining option for Callaway Gardens visitors. Choices include various pasta dishes, chicken, veal, and seafood. The atmosphere is light, airy, and comfortable. **FYI:** Reservations recommended. Guitar. Children's menu. Beer and wine only. No smoking. **Open:** Tues–Sun 6–10pm. Closed Jan–Feb. **Prices:** Main courses $9–$14. AE, DISC, MC, V. ❤️

ATTRACTIONS 🏛️

Callaway Gardens

US 27; tel 706/663-2281 or toll free 800/282-8181. Cason Callaway, head of one of Georgia's most prosperous textile mills, started rebuilding the soil here in the 1930s. He nurtured and imported plant life, built the largest manmade inland beach in the world, provided inn and cottage accommodations, and opened it all to the public. Highlights of the 2,500-acre park include the 5-acre John A Sibley Horticulture Center, the 7½-acre Mr Cason's Vegetable Garden, and the 160-year-old Pioneer Log Cabin. The nondenominational Ida Cason Callaway Memorial Chapel is a lovely native fieldstone structure by a waterfall on a small lake, with stained-glass windows depicting the seasons at the gardens. The information center, near the entrance, offers an eight-minute slide show on the fascinating history of this place. A country store, also near the entrance, sells country-cured bacon and ham, preserves, grits, water-ground cornmeal, and hundreds of other items. **Open:** Daily 7am–7pm. $$$

F D Roosevelt State Park

2970 GA 190; tel 706/663-4858. This wooded, 10,000-acre park has two connections to President Roosevelt: most of the facilities here were built as part of FDR's Civilian Conservation Corps program, and his rural Georgia retreat at Warm Springs is just 12 miles from the park. Today's visitors can stay at any of several campgrounds or cottages while they enjoy fishing and boating at Lake Delano; hiking, picnicking, horseback riding, guided trail rides, and swimming are also available. **Open:** Daily 7am–10pm. $

Plains

See Americus

Rome

Founded in the 1830s at the head of the Coosa Valley and built on seven hills, Rome is now the most important manufacturing town in northwestern Georgia. Home to the antebellum estate that is the ancestral home of Martha Berry (1866–1942), a legend of the area. Berry dedicated her life to educating mountain children and founded Berry Academy and College. **Information:** Greater Rome Convention & Visitors Bureau, 402 Civic Center Dr, PO Box 5823, Rome, 30162 (tel 706/295-5576).

MOTELS 🏨

≡≡≡ Days Inn

840 Turner McCall Blvd, 30161; tel 706/295-0400 or toll free 800/329-7466; fax 706/295-0400 ext 225. Basic, five-story motel located near downtown Rome and area colleges and malls. **Rooms:** 107 rms and stes. CI 2:30pm/CO 11am. Nonsmoking rms avail. Poolside rooms open onto pool decks. **Amenities:** 🛁 A/C, cable TV. **Services:** 🚐 🖼️ 🔧 **Facilities:** 🏋️ 🏊 & 1 restaurant (bkfst only). Free passes to nearby Gold's Gym. **Rates (BB):** $45 S or D; $90–$120 ste. Extra person $4. Children under age 12 stay free. Min stay special events. Parking: Outdoor, free. AE, CB, DC, DISC, MC, V.

≡≡≡ Holiday Inn Skytop Center

20 US 411 E, 30161; tel 706/295-1100 or toll free 800/HOLIDAY; fax 706/291-7128. Chateau Rd exit. Located right off a main highway on a hilltop, this place attracts all sorts of pleasure and business travelers. Holidome offers indoor recreational facilities. **Rooms:** 200 rms and stes. CI 1pm/CO noon. Nonsmoking rms avail. **Amenities:** 🛁 🔥 A/C, cable TV, dataport. **Services:** ✗ 🖼️ 🔧 🍴 Car-rental desk. **Facilities:** 🏋️ 🎱 🏊 & 1 restaurant, 1 bar (w/entertainment), sauna, whirlpool, washer/dryer. Indoor/outdoor pool. Near golf and tennis. **Rates:** $63 S; $59 D; $117 ste. Extra person $6. Children under age 18 stay free. Parking: Outdoor, free. AE, CB, DC, DISC, JCB, MC, V.

RESTAURANT 🍴

Country Gentleman East

26 Chateau Dr; tel 706/295-0205. Off US 411. **Italian/ Seafood.** Tastefully decorated, with dark-wood furnishings and light walls. Specializes in slow-roasted prime rib, but chicken, pasta, and seafood are also available. **FYI:** Reservations accepted. Children's menu. Dress code. **Open:** Lunch Mon–Fri 11:30am–2:30pm; dinner Mon–Sat 4–10:30pm. **Prices:** Main courses $10–$17. AE, CB, DC, DISC, MC, V. &

Roswell

Settled by Roswell King and his relatives and friends from Connecticut and modeled on a New England mill town. The palatial homes of the founders were spared by General

Sherman during the Civil War. **Information:** Historic Roswell Convention & Visitors Bureau, 617 Atlanta St, Roswell, 30075 (tel 770/640-3253).

HOTEL 📷

⊫⊫⊫ Holiday Inn

1075 Holcomb Bridge Rd, 30076; tel 770/992-9600 or toll free 800/HOLIDAY; fax 770/993-6539. Nestled on a small hill near downtown Roswell, and secluded from the hustle and bustle of Atlanta but still close enough for sightseeing. **Rooms:** 174 rms and stes. CI 3pm/CO noon. Nonsmoking rms avail. **Amenities:** 📺 ☎ A/C, cable TV, voice mail. **Services:** ✕ 🚐 ⊠ 🛎 Babysitting. **Facilities:** 🏋 400 ⅙ 1 restaurant, 2 bars (1 w/entertainment). **Rates:** $79–$139 S; $85–$149 ste. Extra person $10. Children under age 18 stay free. Parking: Outdoor, free. AE, CB, DC, DISC, JCB, MC, V.

RESTAURANT 🍴

★ The Public House on Roswell Square

In Roswell Square, 605 Atlanta St; tel 770/992-4646. **Regional American.** Originally a commissary, this restaurant dates back to the early 19th century. The house specialty is peach-pecan rack of lamb; chocolate-chip walnut pie is available for dessert. **FYI:** Reservations not accepted. Piano. **Open:** Lunch Mon–Fri 11:30am–2:30pm, Sat 11:30am–3pm; dinner Sun–Thurs 5:30–10pm, Fri–Sat 5:30–11pm; brunch Sun 11:30am–3pm. **Prices:** Main courses $12–$27. AE, CB, DC, DISC, MC, V. ♥ 🍷

ATTRACTIONS 📷

Museum–North Fulton County Schools

791 Mimosa Blvd; tel 770/552-6339. Although the Teaching Museum is designed to give Fulton County students hands-on experiences coordinated with classroom curricula, visitors of all ages are welcome and will certainly educate themselves. Permanent exhibits include the Toy Attic, the Decade Room (focusing on social, political, and cultural aspects of the 1930s), a replica of a post–Civil War Roswell log cabin, a courtroom where students can participate in or watch mock trials, and the Writer's Corner. **Open:** Mon–Fri 8am–4pm. Closed some hols. $

Chattahoochee Nature Center

9135 Willeo Rd; tel 770/992-2055. A nonprofit environmental education facility dedicated to informing the public about the importance of preserving nature. The Center is also a licensed rehabilitation center for birds of prey such as hawks and vultures. Birds who are too injured to be re-released into the wild are housed here, where visitors are invited to get a close look. **Open:** Mon–Sat 9am–5pm, Sun noon–5pm. Closed some hols. $

St Mary's

This sleepy little town with a waterfront pavilion serves as a departure point for trips to Cumberland Island. Elegance of days gone by is visible in the town's historic district, which includes some haunts of the family of industrialist Andrew Carnegie. **Information:** St Mary's Convention & Visitors Bureau, PO Box 1291, St Mary's, 31558 (tel 912/882-6200).

HOTEL 📷

⊫ Riverview Hotel

105 Osborne St, 31558 (Historic District); tel 912/882-3242. A 90-year-old brick building with stately columns. Situated on the banks of the St Mary's River, across from the Cumberland Island ferry. **Rooms:** 18 rms and stes. CI noon/CO 11:30am. **Amenities:** A/C, cable TV. No phone. 1 unit w/terrace. **Services:** ✕ 🚐 🛎 **Facilities:** 35 1 restaurant, 1 bar, washer/dryer. **Rates (CP):** $36 S; $45 D; $65 ste. Extra person $5. Children under age 3 stay free. Parking: Outdoor, free. AE, DC, DISC, MC, V.

INN

⊫⊫⊫ Spencer House Inn

101 E Bryant St, 31558 (Historic District); tel 912/882-1872; fax 912/882-9427. At Osborne St. This three-story inn was built in 1872 with a long, wide porch and a matching balcony on the second floor. Beautiful cypress rockers fill both spaces. The building is one block from the ferry to Cumberland Island. (This is not a place for toddlers or rambunctious young children.) **Rooms:** 14 rms and stes. CI 3pm/CO 11am. No smoking. The rooms are furnished with antiques. **Amenities:** 📺 ☎ A/C, cable TV. **Services:** 🛎 Babysitting, afternoon tea served. **Facilities:** 25 ⅙ Guest lounge. Discounts at Osprey Cove Golf Course. **Rates (CP):** $55 S; $65–$100 D; $100 ste. Extra person $15. Children under age 3 stay free. Min stay special events. Parking: Outdoor, free. AE, DISC, MC, V.

St Simons Island

The largest of the Golden Isles, featuring lush landscapes and historic remnants of an active colonial history, including several plantations. Little St Simons Island, reachable by boat from the main island, is secluded and privately owned, with 10,000 pristine acres for a limited number of guests. **Information:** St Simons Island Chamber of Commerce, 530B Beachwood Dr, St Simons Island, 31522 (tel 912/638-9014).

MOTELS 📷

⊫⊫ Days Inn

1701 Frederica Rd, 31522; tel 912/634-0660 or toll free 800/329-7466; fax 912/638-7115. Built in 1989, this standard property is slightly inland, just off the main road.

Rooms: 101 rms. CI 2pm/CO noon. Nonsmoking rms avail. **Amenities:** 🔲🐾🖥 A/C, cable TV, refrig. **Services:** 🚗🖼⤺ Complimentary wine and cheese party daily 5–7pm. **Facilities:** 🛗 🚲 125 ♿ **Rates (CP):** Peak (Mar–Aug) $65–$89 S; $75–$89 D. Extra person $10. Children under age 12 stay free. Lower rates off-season. Parking: Outdoor, free. AE, DC, DISC, MC, V.

≣≣ Queen's Court

437 Kings Way, 31522; tel 912/638-8459. This bare-bones property, marked by a large oak tree out front, has been run by the same family since 1948. Rooms are in great demand and many reservations for major weekends are booked a couple of years in advance. A great place to see the 4th of July fireworks. **Rooms:** 24 rms, stes, and effic. CI 2:30pm/CO 11am. Not much decor to speak of. **Amenities:** 🔲 A/C, cable TV. Some units w/terraces. Some rooms have refrigerators. **Services:** ⤺ **Facilities:** 🛗 **Rates:** Peak (Mar–Oct) $45–$50 S or D; $55–$62 ste; $64–$70 effic. Extra person $5. Min stay wknds and special events. Lower rates off-season. Parking: Outdoor, free. MC, V.

≣≣ Sea Gate Inn

1014 Ocean Blvd, 31522; tel 912/638-8661 or toll free 800/562-8812; fax 912/638-4932. This establishment may not be fancy, but it is very clean and neat. Some of the property is on the beach. **Rooms:** 48 rms, stes, and effic. CI 3pm/CO noon. Bright and colorful decor. About half the units are ocean-front; some have kitchens. **Amenities:** 🔲 A/C, cable TV. Some units w/terraces. **Services:** ⤺ **Facilities:** 🛗 ♿ 1 beach (ocean). **Rates (CP):** Peak (June–Aug) $69–$115 S or D; $115–$250 ste; $89–$115 effic. Extra person $7. Children under age 10 stay free. Min stay wknds and special events. Lower rates off-season. Parking: Outdoor, free. AE, MC, V.

RESORTS

≣≣≣ The King and Prince Beach Resort

201 Arnold Rd, PO Box 20798, 31522; tel 912/638-3631 or toll free 800/342-0212. 11 acres. A casual, yet elegant resort, featuring Spanish colonial architecture and a skylighted lobby. French doors and stained-glass windows in the dining room offer a lovely spot to dine amid spectacular ocean views. **Rooms:** 125 rms and stes; 50 cottages/villas. CI 4pm/CO 11am. Two- and three-room villas available. **Amenities:** 🔲🐾 A/C, cable TV, in-rm safe. Some units w/terraces, some w/fireplaces, some w/whirlpools. **Services:** ✕🗝🚗🖼⤺ Babysitting. Children's program offered Mem Day–Labor Day. **Facilities:** 🛗 ▶18 ♨4 🏓 325 ♿ 2 restaurants, 1 bar, 1 beach (ocean), whirlpool. **Rates:** Peak (May–Sept) $120–$145 S or D; $215–$255 ste; $235–$335 cottage/villa. Min stay special events. Lower rates off-season. Parking: Outdoor, free. AE, DC, DISC, MC, V.

≣≣≣ Little St Simons Island

PO Box 1078, 31522; tel 912/638-7472; fax 912/634-1811. 10,000 acres. Unique accommodations located on a privately owned, six-mile-long island. Each of the four comfortable lodges—some of them built before 1920—have screened-in porches and decks. The area surrounding the resort remains untouched and is home to deer, horses, raccoons, alligators, and over 200 species of birds. **Rooms:** 10 rms; 1 cottage/villa. CI open/CO open. No smoking. Each cottage has a view of the marsh or the forest. Ceiling fans keep guests cool. **Amenities:** 🖥 Refrig. No A/C, phone, or TV. All units w/terraces, all w/fireplaces. **Services:** ⤺ Social director, masseur, children's program. Tours, fly fishing instruction, and interpretive programs on the region and its wildlife are available. **Facilities:** 🛗 🚲 ⚠ 🏊 ♦ 🖼 24 ♿ 1 restaurant, 1 bar, 1 beach (ocean), washer/dryer. **Rates (AP):** Peak (Oct–May) $260–$400 S; $360–$500 D; $460–$500 cottage/villa. Extra person $100. Lower rates off-season. Parking: Outdoor, free. Two-night minimum stay. MC, V.

≣≣≣ Sea Palms Golf and Tennis Resort

5445 Frederica Rd, 31522; tel 912/638-3351 or toll free 800/841-6268; fax 912/634-8029. An 800-acre residential and vacation complex. Contemporary concrete-and-shell villas are scattered throughout this marshside property. **Rooms:** 122 rms, stes, and effic; 36 cottages/villas. CI 3pm/CO noon. Nonsmoking rms avail. Most suites have a foyer area that divides the bedrooms. **Amenities:** 🔲🐾 A/C, cable TV w/movies, refrig. Some units w/terraces. **Services:** 🖼⤺ Babysitting. **Facilities:** 🛗 🚲 ▶27 ♨9 ▣3 🏓 400 ♿ 1 restaurant, 1 bar, basketball, volleyball, sauna, playground, washer/dryer. There is a nearby golf course with pro shop and snack bars. The east course is the site of Georgia PGA tournaments and challenge matches. Tennis is also available on rubico (clay) courts. **Rates:** Peak (Mar–May) $119 S or D; $129–$248 ste; $119 effic. Extra person $15. Children under age 14 stay free. Lower rates off-season. Parking: Outdoor, free. AE, CB, DC, MC, V.

RESTAURANTS 🍴

★ Alfonza's Olde Plantation Supper Club

Harrington Lane; tel 912/638-9883. **Seafood.** Big portions and excellent quality in a welcoming atmosphere. Although seafood is the main star, the steaks and the Southern-style fried chicken are also outstanding. **FYI:** Reservations recommended. Guitar/singer/sax. Children's menu. **Open:** Mon–Sat 6–10pm. **Prices:** Main courses $13–$20. DC, DISC, MC, V. 🅿 VP

Blanche's Courtyard

440 Kings Way; tel 912/638-3030. **Seafood/Steak.** The atmosphere of Victorian New Orleans is re-created via old brickwork, antiques, a private patio, and a 300-year-old live oak tree growing in the courtyard. The menu highlights seafood and steak specialties; broiled catch of the day with Cajun spices is a popular option. **FYI:** Reservations recommended. Big band. Children's menu. Dress code. No smoking. **Open:** Peak (Mem Day–Labor Day) daily 5:30–10pm. Closed week after Thanksgiving. **Prices:** Main courses $12–$18. AE, CB, DC, MC, V. ❤♿

CJ's

405 Mallory St; tel 912/634-1022. **Italian.** Small, crowded, and family-oriented place specializing in pizza (both deep dish and crispy), pasta, and Italian-style subs. An open kitchen means that diners can watch their dinner being prepared. **FYI:** Reservations not accepted. Beer and wine only. No smoking. Additional location: 511 Ocean Blvd (tel 634-1022). **Open:** Sun–Thurs 5–9:30pm, Fri–Sat 5–10pm. **Prices:** Main courses $4–$16. No CC. 👥

★ The 4th of May

321 Mallory St; tel 912/638-5444. At King's Way. **Eclectic.** A fun-loving atmosphere reigns at this family-friendly eatery. The chef offers daily potluck specials. If you're *really* hungry, try Malcolm's Mile High Ultimate Sandwich—if you can finish it, it's free. **FYI:** Reservations not accepted. BYO. No smoking. **Open:** Peak (Apr–Oct) Sun 11am–8pm, Mon–Thurs 11am–9pm, Fri–Sat 11am–10pm. **Prices:** Main courses $4–$10; prix fixe $4–$6. MC, V. 👥 &

Frederica House

3611 Frederica Rd; tel 912/638-6789. **Seafood/Steak.** The interior walls of the unique dining rooms are made of intricately etched white cedar wood from a Florida swamp. Menu highlights include fresh local seafood and Iowa grain-fed beef. **FYI:** Reservations recommended. Children's menu. Dress code. **Open:** Sun–Thurs 5:30–9:30pm, Fri–Sat 5:30–10pm. Closed Christmas week. **Prices:** Main courses $10–$19. AE, CB, DC, DISC, MC, V. 👥 ♥ &

ATTRACTIONS 🏛

Fort Frederica National Monument

Frederica Rd; tel 912/638-3639. The English Gen Oglethorpe, founder of Savannah, built Fort Frederica in 1736. Burned down in 1758, the fort and the little town it protected were abandoned. About all that's left of the original construction is a small portion of the King's magazine and the barracks tower, but archeological excavations have unearthed many foundations of period homes and shops. The visitors center has a film on the history of the fort and the town. **Open:** Daily 8am–5pm. Closed Dec 25. $

Museum of Coastal History

101 12th St; tel 912/638-4666. Located in a restored lighthouse keeper's house. There is a gallery with information about the coastal region, and upstairs is a re-creation of what the lighthouse keeper's dwelling was like from the 1870s to the early 1900s. Hardy souls will want to climb the lighthouse's 129 steps for a spectacular view of the Golden Isles. **Open:** Tues–Sat 10am–5pm, Sun 1:30–5pm. Closed some hols. $

Savannah

See also Fort Pulaski National Monument, Tybee Island

This is Georgia's oldest city, founded in 1739 near the mouth of the Savannah River and called one of the most enchanting (and fastest growing) port cities in the world. Its 24 parklike squares are shaded by moss-draped oaks and magnolia trees, and its historic district contains many fine old homes and churches. Some of the oldest African American landmarks in the country are located here, and Gullah—a dialect of West African Krio combined with English—is still spoken by a few residents. **Information:** Savannah Area Convention & Visitors Bureau, 222 W Oglethorpe Ave, Savannah, 31401 (tel 912/944-0456).

HOTELS 🏨

🏨🏨 Best Western Savannah

412 W Bay St, 31401; tel 912/233-1011 or toll free 800/528-1234; fax 912/234-3963. Blooming flowers hang out of flower boxes in the exterior corridors of this unique property. Located on one of the city's major streets, adjacent to River St and its attractions. **Rooms:** 142 rms. CI 3pm/CO noon. Nonsmoking rms avail. **Amenities:** 🛏 & A/C, satel TV, dataport. **Services:** 🛎 Car-rental desk, babysitting. **Facilities:** 🏋 🛏 1 restaurant (bkfst only). **Rates:** Peak (Mar–Oct) $60–$76 D. Extra person $6. Children under age 12 stay free. Min stay special events. Lower rates off-season. Parking: Outdoor, free. AE, CB, DC, DISC, MC, V.

🏨🏨 Desoto Hilton

15 E Liberty St, 31412 (Historic District); tel 912/232-9000; fax 912/231-1633. Mid-rise property occupying a whole block in Savannah's historic district. Although it lacks a waterfront location, it does have fine—if a little dated and worn—interiors. **Rooms:** 250 rms and stes. CI 4pm/CO noon. Nonsmoking rms avail. Rooms are very dated and in need of renovation. **Amenities:** 🛏 & 🍽 A/C, cable TV. **Services:** ✕ ⌫ 🆅🅿 🛎 Twice-daily maid svce. The service is exceptional. **Facilities:** 🛏 & 2 restaurants, 1 bar (w/entertainment). **Rates:** Peak (Mar–Sept) $90 S; $155 D; $450 ste. Extra person $10. Children under age 18 stay free. Lower rates off-season. Parking: Indoor/outdoor, $5/day. AE, DC, DISC, MC, V.

🏨🏨🏨 Hyatt Regency Savannah

2 W Bay St, 31401 (Historic District); tel 912/238-1234 or toll free 800/233-1234; fax 912/944-3678. On the waterfront. Located in the heart of historic Savannah, with the front part of the property facing W Bay St and the back facing the Riverfront and River St. The lobby is located in an open air atrium with glass elevators. Great for families and anyone who prefers modern surroundings to the typical Savannah antebellum inns. **Rooms:** 346 rms and stes. CI 3pm/CO noon. Nonsmoking rms avail. Riverview rooms have a light to alert visitors when ships are coming by on the

Savannah River. **Amenities:** 🏨 🐾 ☂ A/C, cable TV w/movies, dataport, voice mail. Some units w/minibars, some w/terraces, some w/fireplaces. All rooms have irons and ironing boards; some have refrigerators. **Services:** ✗ 🛏 VP 🖨 🍴 🛎 Twice-daily maid svce, car-rental desk. $250 pet deposit. Multilingual staff. Tours can be arranged on the property. **Facilities:** 🍴 🚲 🍳 1000 💻 🔱 1 restaurant, 1 bar (w/entertainment). 17,000-sq-ft meeting space. Sun deck, docking space, shopping arcade. **Rates:** Peak (Mar–Oct) $99–$140 S; $124–$165 D; $210–$650 ste. Extra person $25. Children under age 18 stay free. Min stay special events. Lower rates off-season. Parking: Indoor, $7–$9/day. Romantic packages avail. AE, CB, DC, DISC, MC, V.

🏨🏨 Imperial Suites

7110 Hodgson Memorial Dr, 31406; tel 912/354-8560 or toll free 800/344-4378; fax 912/356-1438. Near Oglethorpe Mall. Quiet, airy motel. The lobby features an open atrium (complete with a pet bird) and plenty of chairs for relaxing. Perfect for businesspeople on long stays. **Rooms:** 52 stes. CI 1pm/CO 11am. Nonsmoking rms avail. Luxury suites have two phones. **Amenities:** 🏨 🎨 A/C, cable TV, refrig. Some units w/whirlpools. All suites have microwaves; luxury suites have two TVs, a wet bar, and a whirlpool tub. **Services:** 🖨 🍴 **Facilities:** 🍴 40 🔱 Steam rm, whirlpool, washer/dryer. Guest passes to Gold's Gym (one block away). **Rates:** $70–$90 ste. Extra person $8. Children under age 3 stay free. Min stay special events. Parking: Outdoor, free. Extra $4 charge for children 3–15 years old. AE, MC, V.

🏨🏨🏨 The Mulberry—A Holiday Inn Hotel

601 E Bay St, 31401 (Historic District); tel 912/238-1200 or toll free 800/HOLIDAY; fax 912/236-2184. Exquisite and unique Holiday Inn housed in a restored Victorian mansion. Lobby is set up in the large living room, with paintings and period antiques placed throughout. Beautiful courtyard contains a fountain, tables, and pool area surrounded by a privacy fence. St Patrick's Day parade (one of the biggest social events in Savannah) comes right by the hotel. **Rooms:** 122 rms and stes. CI 3pm/CO noon. Nonsmoking rms avail. Rooms are spacious and nicely decorated. **Amenities:** 🏨 🎨 A/C, dataport. Some units w/terraces. Suites feature coffeemakers, small refrigerators, and wet bars. **Services:** ✗ VP 🖨 🍴 Car-rental desk. Complimentary tea served 4–6pm in the lobby. **Facilities:** 🍴 120 🔱 2 restaurants, 1 bar, whirlpool. **Rates:** Peak (Mar–Oct) $102–$130 S or D; $170 ste. Extra person $10. Children under age 18 stay free. Min stay special events. Lower rates off-season. Parking: Indoor/outdoor, free. Honeymoon packages avail. AE, DISC, MC, V.

🏨🏨🏨 Savannah Marriott

100 Gen McIntosh Blvd, 31401; tel 912/233-7722 or toll free 800/228-9290; fax 912/233-3765. On the riverfront. Modern-looking property facing the Savannah River. Lobby has large open atrium and indoor pool. **Rooms:** 384 rms and stes. Executive level. CI 4pm/CO 11am. Nonsmoking rms avail. Some rooms have beautiful river views. **Amenities:** 🏨 🎨

A/C, satel TV w/movies, dataport. Some units w/terraces, some w/whirlpools. **Services:** ✗ 🛏 🖨 🍴 Car-rental desk, masseur. Historic tours leave from hotel every morning. **Facilities:** 🍴 🍳 2000 🔱 2 restaurants, 2 bars, games rm, whirlpool. **Rates:** Peak (spring and fall) $119–$169 S or D; $169–$399 ste. Extra person $20. Children under age 18 stay free. Min stay special events. Lower rates off-season. Parking: Indoor/outdoor, $7/day. AE, CB, DC, DISC, EC, JCB, MC, V.

MOTELS

🏨🏨 Club House Inn

6800 Abercorn St, 31405; tel 912/356-1234 or toll free 800/CLUB-INN; fax 912/352-2828. 12 mi E of I-95. Located near downtown and the historic area, this chain hotel may be a step down from the quaint historic inns of Savannah, but it's perfectly adequate for corporate guests and extended stays. **Rooms:** 138 rms and stes. CI 3pm/CO noon. Nonsmoking rms avail. Modern, color-coordinated decor. **Amenities:** 🏨 🎨 A/C, cable TV w/movies, dataport. Some units w/terraces, some w/whirlpools. **Services:** 🖨 🍴 Car-rental desk. Complimentary guest reception 5–7pm daily. **Facilities:** 🍴 35 🔱 Whirlpool. Access to Gold's Gym. **Rates (BB):** $60 S or D; $81 ste. Extra person $5. Children under age 16 stay free. Min stay special events. Parking: Outdoor, free. Senior discounts avail. AE, CB, DC, DISC, MC, V.

🏨🏨🏨 Days Inn Airport

2500 Dean Forest Rd, 31408 (Savannah Int'l Airport); tel 912/966-5000 or toll free 800/329-7466; fax 912/966-5000 ext 282. Property noted for its half-acre lake and "floating lounge." Standard chain-motel accommodations. **Rooms:** 121 rms. CI 3pm/CO 11am. Nonsmoking rms avail. **Amenities:** 🏨 🎨 A/C, satel TV w/movies, dataport, voice mail. Complimentary coffee served in room. **Services:** 🚐 🖨 🍴 Complimentary shuttle service to historic downtown Savannah. **Facilities:** 🍴 🍳 60 🔱 1 restaurant, 1 bar, whirlpool, washer/dryer. **Rates:** $58–$63 S or D. Extra person $5. Children under age 18 stay free. Min stay special events. Parking: Outdoor, free. AE, CB, DC, DISC, MC, V.

🏨🏨 Fairfield Inn

2 Lee Blvd, 31405; tel 912/353-7100 or toll free 800/228-2800; fax 912/353-7100. Off Abercorn St, 1 mi from Oglethorpe Mall. Plain-looking concrete motel with exterior corridors on the first and second floors, and an interior corridor on the third floor. The property is six miles from the historic district and a half-hour from the beach. Nice for people who want to be centrally located in Savannah, without staying in the historic district. **Rooms:** 135 rms. CI 3pm/CO noon. Nonsmoking rms avail. **Amenities:** 🏨 🎨 A/C, satel TV w/movies. Refrigerators available for a fee. Some rooms have dataports. **Services:** 🖨 🍴 Guest passes to Gold's Gym. **Facilities:** 🍴 🔱 **Rates (CP):** Peak (June–Aug) $51 S; $56 D.

Extra person $5. Children under age 18 stay free. Min stay special events. Lower rates off-season. Parking: Outdoor, free. AE, CB, DC, DISC, MC, V.

Howard Johnson Lodge Historic Downtown
224 W Boundary St, 31401; tel 912/232-4371 or toll free 800/673-6316; fax 912/232-4371 ext 250. Motel with only the bare necessities, located across from the Visitor's Center, where bus tours of the historic district and City Market depart daily. **Rooms:** 89 rms and stes. CI 3pm/CO noon. Nonsmoking rms avail. **Amenities:** A/C, cable TV. All units w/terraces. **Services:** Complimentary coffee in lobby. **Facilities:** 1 restaurant, 1 bar. **Rates:** $65 S or D; $68–$85 ste. Extra person $5. Children under age 18 stay free. Min stay special events. Parking: Outdoor, free. AE, CB, DC, DISC, MC, V.

La Quinta Motor Inn
6805 Abercorn St, 31405; tel 912/355-3004 or toll free 800/531-5900; fax 912/355-0143. Near Hunter Army Airbase. Modern-style property made up of two floors with exterior corridors. The gate to the Hunter Army Airbase is directly behind the motel. **Rooms:** 154 rms. CI 3pm/CO noon. Nonsmoking rms avail. **Amenities:** A/C, cable TV w/movies. **Services:** Car-rental desk. Pets must be under 30 lbs. **Facilities:** Rates (CP): $50–$67 D. Extra person $7–$10. Children under age 18 stay free. Min stay special events. Parking: Outdoor, free. AE, CB, DC, DISC, MC, V.

Sleep Inn
7206 GA 21, Port Wentworth, 31407; tel 912/966-9800 or toll free 800/62-SLEEP; fax 912/966-9800. Exit 19 off I-95. Located 10 miles from Savannah's Historic District. This no-frills property is a great way to visit Savannah on a budget—the drive won't matter. **Rooms:** 85 rms. CI 2pm/CO noon. Nonsmoking rms avail. Nice, basic rooms. **Amenities:** A/C, satel TV, dataport. **Services:** Car-rental desk. Fax and copy services. **Facilities:** Restaurant across parking lot. **Rates (CP):** $39–$45 S; $47–$64 D. Extra person $6. Children under age 18 stay free. Min stay special events. Parking: Outdoor, free. AE, CB, DC, DISC, MC, V.

INNS

Ballastone Inn & Townhouse
14 E Oglethorpe Ave, 31401 (Historic District); tel 912/236-1484 or toll free 800/822-4553; fax 912/236-4626. Four-story Regency-style mansion built in 1838 and named for the stones which were used as the foundation for most of Savannah. It is furnished with antiques and has a beautiful Queen Anne staircase and iron railings at the entrance. A beautiful courtyard with tables is the perfect setting for breakfast. **Rooms:** 22 rms and stes. CI 2pm/CO 11am. Rooms are uniquely decorated with specific themes. **Amenities:** A/C, cable TV w/movies, VCR, bathrobes. Some units w/fireplaces, some w/whirlpools. **Services:** Twice-daily maid svce, car-rental desk, babysitting,

afternoon tea and wine/sherry served. Breakfast can be served in room, courtyard, or parlor. Complimentary tea, sherry, and pastries served all day. Linens changed every second day during multinight stays. Movie library. Pets must be under 15 lbs. **Facilities:** 1 bar, guest lounge. Full bar in main house, honor bar in townhouse. **Rates (CP):** $100–$130 S; $140–$165 D; $195–$215 ste. Extra person $10. Min stay special events. Higher rates for special events/hols. Parking: Outdoor, free. AE, MC, V.

East Bay Inn
225 E Bay St, 31401 (Historic District); tel 912/238-1225 or toll free 800/500-1225; fax 912/232-2709. Former cotton warehouse, built in 1853. The brick exterior is not very attractive, but it is the closest property to River St without staying there. **Rooms:** 28 rms. CI 3pm/CO 11am. Nonsmoking rms avail. The rooms feature four-poster beds. **Amenities:** A/C, cable TV, dataport. Some units w/terraces. **Services:** Wine/sherry served. Turndown service includes chocolates. Pets allowed in selected rooms for $25 nonrefundable fee. **Facilities:** 1 restaurant, guest lounge. **Rates (CP):** $89–$119 S; $109–$129 D. Extra person $10. Children under age 12 stay free. Min stay special events. Higher rates for special events/hols. Parking: Outdoor, free. AE, CB, DC, DISC, MC, V.

Eliza Thompson House
5 W Jones St, 31401 (Historic District); tel 912/236-3620 or toll free 800/348-9378; fax 912/238-1920. Beautifully restored 1847 home located on one of Savannah's loveliest brick streets. The inn surrounds a small brick courtyard with quaint tables and chairs. **Rooms:** 23 rms. CI 2pm/CO 11am. **Amenities:** A/C, cable TV. Morning coffee, tea, and newspaper can be delivered to room. **Services:** Car-rental desk, babysitting. Wine, cheese, and desserts served 8–10pm. **Facilities:** Guest lounge. **Rates (CP):** $90–$110 S. Extra person $10. Children under age 12 stay free. Min stay special events. Higher rates for special events/hols. AE, MC, V.

Foley House Inn
14 W Hull St, 31401 (Historic District); tel 912/232-6622 or toll free 800/647-3708; fax 912/231-1218. Two nicely furnished parlors, with carved Griffin mantels, welcome guests to this restored brick inn built in 1896. The park across the street (Chippewa Square) is where Tom Hanks sat in *Forrest Gump*. **Rooms:** 19 rms and stes. CI 3pm/CO noon. Nonsmoking rms avail. All rooms are individually decorated. **Amenities:** A/C, cable TV w/movies, dataport. Some units w/terraces, some w/fireplaces, some w/whirlpools. Rooms in main house have VCRs. Suite equipped with refrigerator. Bathrobes available on request. **Services:** Afternoon tea and wine/sherry served. Complimentary iced tea and lemonade in summer, coffee in winter. Linen changed on second night of multinight stay. Shoe shine, turndown service on request. **Facilities:** 1 bar, guest lounge. **Rates (CP):** $85–$190 S; $125–$135 D. Extra person $10.

Children under age 12 stay free. Min stay special events. Higher rates for special events/hols. Parking: Outdoor, $5/day. AE, JCB, MC, V.

▤▤▤ Forsyth Park Inn

102 W Hull St, 31401 (Historic District); tel 912/233-6800. Across from Forsyth Park. Two-story woodframe Victorian mansion built in 1893, with wooden porches and ornately carved railings. The interior features beautiful parquet flooring and 16-ft ceilings. **Rooms:** 9 rms. CI 3pm/CO 11am. Nonsmoking rms avail. **Amenities:** 🕯 A/C, TV. No phone. Some units w/fireplaces, some w/whirlpools. Roll-away beds available for extra charge. **Services:** ⫣ Afternoon tea served. **Facilities:** Guest lounge. Tennis courts, basketball courts, and jogging path in adjacent Forsyth Park are all owned by the inn. **Rates (CP):** $80–$155 S; $165 D. Extra person $15. Min stay special events. Higher rates for special events/hols. Parking: Outdoor, free. AE, DISC, MC, V.

▤▤▤▤ The Gastonian

220 E Gaston St, 31401 (Historic District); tel 912/232-2869 or toll free 800/322-6603; fax 912/232-0710. At Lincoln St. The Gastonian was built in 1868, in Regency-Italianate style, from handmade brick that was then stuccoed white. A beautiful above-ground walkway leads from one house to the next. Balconies grace the side of the main house, and the parlor rooms are furnished with beautiful antiques. Unsuitable for children under 12. **Rooms:** 13 rms and stes. CI 3pm/CO noon. No smoking. All rooms have either canopied beds or Rice poster beds and are decorated with Georgian and Regency antiques. The Carriage House features an Oriental "Wedding Bed" and "Chinese-Red Birthday Bath" with its own balcony and kitchen facilities. **Amenities:** 🕯🗖 📺 🍴A/C, cable TV, bathrobes. Some units w/terraces, all w/fireplaces, some w/whirlpools. Rooms have private thermostats. **Services:** ⛝ 🖼 Afternoon tea served. Full, hot breakfast served in the parlor, or continental breakfast served in the room. Turndown service includes Savannah sweets and cordials. **Facilities:** 🕭 Whirlpool, guest lounge. **Rates (BB):** Peak (Mar–Apr/Oct) $135–$200 S; $150–$200 D; $175–$285 ste. Min stay special events. Lower rates off-season. Parking: Outdoor, free. AE, MC, V.

▤▤▤▤ The Kehoe House

123 Habersham St, 31401 (Historic District); tel 912/232-1020 or toll free 800/820-1020; fax 912/231-0208. On Columbia Square. Built in 1892, this beautiful brick structure features charming balconies, towerlike walls, and porches with wooden railings. The interior is enhanced by a dramatic wooden staircase. Unsuitable for children under 12. **Rooms:** 15 rms and stes; 1 cottage/villa. CI 3pm/CO 11am. No smoking. Rooms decorated with antiques. **Amenities:** 🕯🗖 🍴 A/C, cable TV, dataport, VCR, bathrobes. Some units w/terraces. **Services:** ⛝ 🖼 ⫣ Twice-daily maid svce, car-rental desk, masseur. English afternoon tea available by reservation (for a fee). Nightly hors d'oeuvres and cocktails. **Facilities:** 🍽 🔲 🕭 1 bar, guest lounge. Off-street parking. **Rates**

(BB): $150–$250 S; $250 ste. Extra person $35. Min stay special events. Higher rates for special events/hols. Parking: Outdoor, free. Theme packages—romantic, "ghostly," and others—avail. AE, CB, DC, DISC, MC, V.

▤▤▤ Magnolia Place

503 Whitaker St, 31401 (Historic District); tel 912/236-7674 or toll free 800/238-7674. Built in 1878, this Victorian mansion has large verandas and porches as well as typical Victorian woodwork. Don't miss the butterfly collection in the parlor. **Rooms:** 13 rms. CI 2:30pm/CO 11am. Rooms are nice and comfortable, but nothing special. All have four-poster beds. **Amenities:** 🕯🗖 A/C, cable TV w/movies, VCR. Some units w/terraces, some w/fireplaces, some w/whirlpools. **Services:** ⛝ 🖾 Twice-daily maid svce, car-rental desk, masseur, babysitting, afternoon tea and wine/sherry served. **Facilities:** Guest lounge. Film library. Located across from Forsyth Park, which has tennis courts and a bicycle/jogging path. **Rates (CP):** $100–$140 S; $175–$195 D. Extra person $15. Children under age 12 stay free. Min stay special events. Parking: Outdoor, free. AE, MC, V.

▤▤▤ Olde Harbour Inn

508 E Factors Walk, 31401 (Historic District); tel 912/234-4100 or toll free 800/553-6533; fax 912/233-5979. At River St. A late-Victorian brick building located right on the riverfront. Popular with families. **Rooms:** 24 effic. CI 3pm/CO 11am. Decor leans more toward modern than antique, and the rooms are laid out like condominiums. Riverfront suites have great views. **Amenities:** 🕯🗖 📺 A/C, cable TV, refrig, dataport. Some units w/terraces. **Services:** 🖾 ⫣ 🛎 Turndown service includes an ice cream treat. **Facilities:** Guest lounge. **Rates (CP):** $95–$155 effic. Extra person $10. Children under age 12 stay free. Min stay special events. Higher rates for special events/hols. Parking: Outdoor, free. AE, CB, DC, DISC, MC, V.

▤▤▤ Planters Inn

29 Abercorn St, 31401 (Historic District); tel 912/232-5678 or toll free 800/554-1187; fax 912/232-8893. Located on historic Reynolds Square, only four blocks from City Market. Good for corporate stays. **Rooms:** 56 rms, stes, and effic. CI 4pm/CO noon. Nonsmoking rms avail. Rooms feature period furnishings, four-poster beds, and pleasing color schemes. **Amenities:** 🕯🗖 A/C, satel TV, dataport. Some units w/terraces, some w/fireplaces. Honor bar. **Services:** ⛝ 🖼 VP 🖾 ⫣ Twice-daily maid svce, car-rental desk, babysitting, afternoon tea served. Guests have access to downtown athletic club for a fee. **Facilities:** 🔲 🕭 1 bar, guest lounge. **Rates (CP):** $109 S or D; $210 ste; $135 effic. Extra person $10. Children under age 12 stay free. Min stay special events. Higher rates for special events/hols. Parking: Indoor, $5/day. AE, DC, MC, V.

▤▤▤▤ Presidents' Quarters

225 E President St, 31401 (Historic District); tel 912/233-1600 or toll free 800/233-1776; fax 912/238-0849. Tall,

brick inn built in 1855, with guest rooms named after US presidents. Located across from Wright Square, the inn was used as the backdrop for the filming of Alex Haley's TV epic, *Roots.* **Rooms:** 16 rms and stes. CI 2pm/CO 11am. Nonsmoking rms avail. Rooms are decorated to reflect the presidents who have stayed here. Some rooms have gas log fireplaces, ceiling fans, and loft bedrooms. **Amenities:** 🛎 🕹 A/C, cable TV w/movies, refrig, VCR, bathrobes. Some units w/terraces, all w/fireplaces, some w/whirlpools. Complimentary fruit and wine upon arrival. **Services:** ✗ 🖾 🗘 Twice-daily maid svce, car-rental desk, babysitting, afternoon tea and wine/sherry served. Continental breakfast can be served either in room, lobby, or courtyard. Babysitting available with two hours' notice. Fax service. **Facilities:** 🕹 Whirlpool, guest lounge. Film library, whirlpool, walled-in parking. **Rates (CP):** Peak (Mar–June; Sept–Nov) $137–$147 S; $137 D; $137–$167 ste. Extra person $10. Children under age 10 stay free. Min stay special events. Lower rates off-season. Higher rates for special events/hols. Parking: Outdoor, free. Honeymoon packages avail. AE, CB, DC, DISC, MC, V.

▤▤▤ River Street Inn

115 E River St, 31401 (Historic District); tel 912/234-6400 or toll free 800/253-4229; fax 912/234-1478. Originally built in 1817 as an old cotton warehouse and characterized by its five-story atrium, beautiful hardwood floors, and Oriental rugs. **Rooms:** 44 rms. CI 4pm/CO noon. River and park views available. Some rooms have canopy beds. **Amenities:** 🛎 🕹 A/C, satel TV. Some units w/terraces. Weekday morning paper. **Services:** ✗ 🖾 🗘 🖘 Twice-daily maid svce, car-rental desk, babysitting, wine/sherry served. Concierge. Secretarial services available. Wine reception Mon–Sat. **Facilities:** ▭₃₅ 🕹 3 restaurants (*see* "Restaurants" below), 4 bars (3 w/entertainment), games rm, guest lounge. Access to a fitness center (with masseuse) two blocks away. **Rates (CP):** $69–$129 S or D. Extra person $10. Children under age 18 stay free. Min stay special events. Higher rates for special events/hols. Parking: Outdoor, free. AE, CB, DC, MC, V.

RESTAURANTS 🍴

Bistro Savannah

309 W Congress St; tel 912/333-6266. **Seafood.** The light, casual atmosphere at this authentic bistro is fostered by exposed-brick walls, cane chairs, and works of local artists. The menu changes daily, but is sure to include lots of local seafood, country game, and pastas. **FYI:** Reservations recommended. **Open:** Sun–Thurs 6–10:30pm, Fri–Sat 6pm–midnight. **Prices:** Main courses $8–$18. AE, MC, V. ●

♣ The Boar's Head

1 N Lincoln St; tel 912/232-3196. On River St. **Eclectic.** In a 250-year-old waterfront warehouse at River St, the Boar's Head offers English pub–style decor: dark colors, brick walls, huge wooden beams. Art adorns the walls, and there are hanging baskets of greenery everywhere. All tables have a

marvelous river view. Specializes in classic entrees like filet mignon, lobster tail, Boar's Head stuffed sirloin with shrimp, and baby-back ribs. **FYI:** Reservations recommended. Piano. **Open:** Lunch Tues–Thurs 11:30am–3pm, Fri–Sun 11:30am–4pm; dinner Tues–Thurs 5:30–10pm, Fri–Sat 5:30–11:30pm, Sun 5:30–10pm. **Prices:** Main courses $9–$25. AE, DISC, MC, V. ■ ▦

The Chart House

202 W Bay St; tel 912/233-6686. At River St. **Seafood/Steak.** From the outside deck, diners can enjoy hors d'oeuvres and cocktails within view of passing ships. Inside, the multilevel dining room is decorated in a nautical theme. Oysters, shrimp, and other local catches are excellent. Also on the menu are halibut steaks and beef steaks. **FYI:** Reservations recommended. Children's menu. **Open:** Sun–Thurs 5:30–10pm, Fri–Sat 5:30–11pm. **Prices:** Main courses $15–$24. AE, CB, DC, DISC, MC, V. ▱ ▦ ▼

♣ Elizabeth on 37th Restaurant & Dessert Cafe

105 E 37th St; tel 912/236-5547. At Drayton St. Housed in a grand turn-of-the-century mansion, and listed in *Food & Wine* magazine's "Top 25 Restaurants in America 1992." Chef Elizabeth Terry, who has researched 18th- and 19th-century Savannah cuisine, uses the freshest local ingredients (especially seafood) in her kitchen. The menu ranges from crisp, roasted grouper to Southern fried grits with country ham, and from Georgia goat-cheese salad to mustard barbecued quail with Savannah red rice. Desserts are not to be missed, especially the Savannah cream cake. Excellent wine list. **FYI:** Reservations recommended. Dress code. No smoking. **Open:** Mon–Sat 6–10:30pm. Closed 1 week in Aug. **Prices:** Main courses $20–$26. AE, DC, DISC, MC, V. ●

The Exchange Tavern

201 E River St; tel 912/232-7088. **Seafood.** There's a great selection of sandwiches and "Low Country Nibblers" here, amid an interesting collection of clocks. The extensive menu also features traditional seafood dishes, steaks, chicken, and shish kebob. A great "drop-in" place for beer, cocktails, and food on the riverfront. **FYI:** Reservations not accepted. **Open:** Sun–Thurs 11am–11pm, Fri–Sat 11am–1am. **Prices:** Main courses $6–$19. AE, DC, DISC, MC, V. 🕹

Garibaldi's

315 W Congress St; tel 912/232-7118. **Italian.** Located in the 1871 Germania Firehouse, the romantic decor features pressed-tin ceilings, 19th-century gilt mirrors, and lots of candles. Local seafood is prepared with an Italian accent. The seafood and veal combination plate, and the duck Garibaldi, are usually big hits. **FYI:** Reservations recommended. **Open:** Mon–Thurs 6–10:30pm, Fri–Sat 5:30pm–midnight, Sun 6–10:30pm. **Prices:** Main courses $6–$15. AE, MC, V. ● ■ ▼

Huey's

In River Street Inn, 115 River St; tel 912/234-7385. **Cajun/Creole.** This casual eatery on the riverfront offers some water views in a room with ceiling fans, red-and-gray decor, and exposed brick. Oyster po' boy, blackened chicken sandwich served with red beans and rice, other Louisiana specialties. **FYI:** Reservations not accepted. Children's menu. No smoking. **Open:** Mon–Thurs 7am–10pm, Fri 7am–11pm, Sat 8am–11pm, Sun 8am–10pm. **Prices:** Main courses $7–$16. AE, DISC, MC, V. 🖼️ 🔲 ▾

⭐ Kevin Barry's Irish Pub

117 W River St; tel 912/233-9626. By the Hyatt. **Irish.** Although the menu is rather limited, the woodsy atmosphere and live Irish folk music make this riverfront eatery worth checking out. In addition to the two-level dining area, there's also a large, beautiful bar. Menu options include prime rib, Maine lobster, Irish beef stew, and shepherd's pie. A separate bar menu is also available. **FYI:** Reservations not accepted. Guitar. **Open:** Mon–Fri 4pm–3am, Sat–Sun noon–3am. **Prices:** Main courses $6–$14. AE, CB, DC, DISC, MC, V. ▾

⑤ Mrs Wilkes's Dining Room

107 W Jones St; tel 912/232-5997. **Southern.** Mrs Sema Wilkes has been serving her classic Southern cooking to locals and Savannah visitors since the 1940s. Guests are seated at large tables in the basement dining room of Mrs Wilkes's 1870 gray brick house. The food, served out of big dishes placed in the middle of the table, reflects the cuisine Savannah residents have cherished for generations—collard greens, black-eyed peas, fried chicken, barbecued ribs, baked ham, pickled beets, candied yams, banana pudding, and a lot more. If you come for breakfast, you'll find the tables piled high with eggs, sausage, homemade biscuits, and grits. There's no sign outside, but you'll recognize the place from the long line outside. **FYI:** Reservations not accepted. No liquor license. No smoking. **Open:** Breakfast Mon–Fri 8–9am; lunch Mon–Fri 11:30am–3pm. Closed 1st 2 weeks in July. **Prices:** Prix fixe $5–$8. No CC. 🔲 ⅙

The Olde Pink House Restaurant & Planters' Tavern

23 Abercorn St; tel 912/232-4286. On Reynolds Square. **Regional American.** Built in 1771, this old brick mansion has been a private residence, a bank, headquarters for one of William T Sherman's generals, and a tea room. (It's now pink because its original red brick shows through the white plaster walls.) There are several dining areas, including the lovely colonial-style main room and the cozy Planters' Tavern. Riverfront gumbo, black turtle bean soup, baby flounder stuffed with crab, and Old Savannah trifle are all standouts. **FYI:** Reservations recommended. Piano. No smoking. **Open:** Daily 6–10:30pm. **Prices:** Main courses $13–$19. AE, MC, V. ♥ 🖥️

The Pirates' House

20 E Broad St; tel 912/233-5757. At Bay St. **Seafood.** Built in 1734, the Pirate's House is located next to the oldest building in Savannah. Tunnels leading from the Pirate's House to the dock still exist, and many sailors are said to have been shipped across the Atlantic from these tunnels by their cohorts after a night of heavy revelry. (The House was also used as a setting

in Robert Louis Stevenson's *Treasure Island*.) Today, diners can enjoy seafood specialties like oysters Savannah and sherry-flavored shrimp; other typical offerings include chicken cordon bleu and duck à l'orange. You'll also want to set aside time to explore all the 23 dining rooms and the colorful Treasure Island bar. **FYI:** Reservations recommended. Children's menu. **Open:** Lunch Sun 11am–3pm, Mon–Sat 11:30am–2:30pm; dinner daily 5–9:30pm; brunch Sun 11am–3pm. **Prices:** Main courses $15–$20. AE, CB, DC, DISC, MC, V. 🖥️ ⅙

River House

125 W River St (Historic District); tel 912/234-1900. **Seafood.** Housed in a converted cotton warehouse on the riverfront. The decor is dark wood and brick, and artworks line the walls. The kitchen excels in fresh seafood creations, steaks, sourdough bread, hickory-smoked chicken, and homemade pasta. The onsite bakery caters to guests who want to take home some bread, pecan pie, or cheesecake. **FYI:** Reservations recommended. Children's menu. **Open:** Mon–Thurs 11:30am–10pm, Fri–Sat 11:30am–11pm, Sun noon–10pm. **Prices:** Main courses $10–$23. AE, CB, DC, MC, V. ▾

The River's End

3122 River Dr, Thunderbolt; tel 912/354-2973. Next to Palmer Johnson Marina on the Intercoastal Waterway. **Seafood.** Diners here can watch the shrimp- and pleasure-boat traffic on the Waterway from the elegant, subdued dining room. Fresh fish and shellfish might include snapper, salmon, flounder, shrimp, and crab; other choices include steak, pasta, veal, lamb, and duck. Desserts are homemade. **FYI:** Reservations recommended. Piano. Children's menu. **Open:** Mon–Thurs 5–10pm, Fri–Sat 5–11pm. **Prices:** Main courses $10–$24. AE, CB, DC, DISC, MC, V. 🖼️ ▾ ⅙

Shrimp Factory

313 E River St; tel 912/236-4229. **Seafood.** Built with heart-pine beams and rafters, Savannah gray bricks, and dark woods, this eatery offers a great view of the River and River St. As you might expect, the menu is dominated by shrimp (prepared 50 different ways), but other seafood entrees and a few meat options are on hand as well. **FYI:** Reservations recommended. Children's menu. **Open:** Mon–Thurs 11am–10pm, Fri–Sat 11am–11pm, Sun noon–10pm. **Prices:** Main courses $15–$24. AE, CB, DC, DISC, MC, V. 🖼️ ▾

606 East Cafe

319 W Congress St; tel 912/233-2887. **Burgers/Deli.** Decorated with a cow motif, this cafe's motto is "To err . . . is human, to moo . . . bovine." From the dairy cow bar painted black and white to the outdoor dining area called the Cow Patio, this place is whimsical fun. The menu consists mainly of light dishes—salads, sandwiches, pitas, and pastas—and exceptionally rich desserts like peanut butter pie and Cha-Cha-Chocolate cake. **FYI:** Reservations accepted. Big band. **Open:** Sun noon–10pm, Mon–Wed 11am–10pm, Thurs–Sat 11am–11pm. **Prices:** Main courses $7–$13. AE, MC, V. 🔲 ⅙

ATTRACTIONS

Andrew Low House
329 Abercorn St; tel 912/233-6854. Girl Scouts founder Juliette Low lived in this 1848 house after her marriage, and it was here that she actually founded the group. She died here in 1927. The classic mid-19th-century house is made of stucco over brick, with elaborate ironwork, jalousied porches, carved woodwork, and crystal chandeliers. William Makepeace Thackeray visited here twice (the desk at which he worked is in one of the bedrooms), and Robert E Lee was entertained at a gala reception in 1870. **Open:** Mon–Wed and Fri–Sat 10:30am–4pm, Sun noon–4pm. Closed some hols. **$$**

Green-Meldrim Home
14 W Macon St; tel 912/233-3845. Gen Sherman headquartered here when his troops occupied Savannah in 1864. It was from this Gothic-style house that the general sent a telegram to President Lincoln offering him the city as a Christmas gift. The house now belongs to St John's Church, which uses the former kitchen, servants' quarters, and stable as its rectory. The rest of the premises are open to visitors. **Open:** Tues and Thurs 10am–4pm. **$**

Fort Pulaski National Monument
US 80 E; tel 912/786-5787. Located 15 mi E of Savannah. This fort is a remarkably well-preserved example of 19th-century military architecture. It took 18 years to complete the massive, pentagonally shaped structure, with its casemate galleries and drawbridges crossing the moat. When completed in 1847, Fort Pulaski was a state-of-the-art defensive structure, but the development of rifled artillery during the Civil War rendered the fort obsolete. Today, a visitors center at the monument offers an introductory video, historical exhibits, and a bookstore. The fort also provides spectacular views of surrounding salt marshes as well as the Atlantic Ocean. **Open:** Daily 8:30am–5:30pm; extended summer hours. Closed Dec 25. **$**

Savannah History Museum
303 Martin Luther King Jr Blvd; tel 912/238-1779. Housed in a restored train shed at the old Central of Georgia railway station, this museum offers a good introduction to the city. In the theater, the Siege of Savannah is replayed. In addition to the theatrics, there's an exhibition hall displaying memorabilia from every era of Savannah's history. **Open:** Daily 8:30am–5pm. Closed some hols. **$**

Savannah Science Museum
4405 Paulsen St; tel 912/355-6705. Features hands-on exhibits in natural history, astronomy, and science. Reptiles and amphibians of Georgia are also featured, and planetarium shows realistically re-create night skies. **Open:** Tues–Sat 10am–5pm, Sun 2–5pm. Closed some hols. **$**

Ships of the Sea Maritime Museum
503 E River St; tel 912/232-1511. Located in a renovated waterfront building, this museum features beautifully constructed models of seagoing vessels—from Viking warships right up to today's nuclear-powered ships. There's also a marvelous collection of ships-in-a-bottle. **Open:** Daily 10am–5pm. Closed some hols. **$**

The Isaiah Davenport House Museum and Shop
324 E State St; tel 912/236-8097. In 1955, hours before the dilapidated Davenport House was scheduled to be demolished, seven Savannah women managed to raise the funds to buy it. (These women went on to form the Historic Savannah Foundation, which has helped to "rescue" more than 800 of Savannah's 1,000 historic buildings.)

The Davenport House, built between 1815 and 1820 by master builder Isaiah Davenport, is one of the truly great Federal-style houses in America. Its delicate plasterwork, cantilevered staircase, dormer windows, and wrought-iron trim serve as lasting proof of Davenport's skill. Genuine Chippendale pieces are scattered throughout the house, and there's an exhibit of early 19th-century dolls in the attic. **Open:** Daily 10am–4pm. Closed some hols. **$$**

Juliette Gordon Low Girl Scout National Center
142 Bull St; tel 912/233-4501. The founder of the Girl Scouts lived in this Regency-style house that is now maintained both as a memorial to her and as a national program center for Girl Scouts of the USA. The Victorian additions to the 1818 house were made in 1886, just before Juliette Gordon married William Mackay Low. Low's art collection and personal artifacts are displayed throughout. **Open:** Mon–Tues and Thurs–Sat, 10am–4:30pm, Sun 12:30–4:30pm. Closed some hols. **$$**

Fort Jackson
Islands Expwy; tel 912/232-3945. Located 2½ mi E of downtown. Built at a strategic point on the Savannah River, this is the fort that Georgia troops occupied before the outbreak of the Civil War and held until Sherman arrived in 1864. Its arched rooms (designed to support the weight of heavy cannon mounted above, which commanded the harbor entrance) hold 13 exhibit areas. **Open:** Daily 9am–5pm. **$**

Flannery O'Connor Childhood Home
207 E Charlton St; tel 912/233-6014. Savannah-born Flannery O'Connor, best known for her powerful portraits of the South and its eccentric characters, lived in this house for the first 13 years of her life. Restoration of the house is ongoing, but already its heart-of-pine floors, heavy furniture, and lace curtains mark the house as reminiscent of 1930s Savannah. Between October and May, the association that maintains the house holds readings, films, lectures, and seminars about O'Connor and other Southern writers. **Open:** Fri–Sun 1–4pm and by appointment. Closed some hols. **Free**

Sea Island

Reached by a causeway from St Simons Island, Sea Island has been synonymous with luxurious living and has been luring the wealthy since the 1920s. The island is largely residential, and life centers around the Cloister, honored as one of the world's great hotels. The annual Sea Island Festival celebrates the area's African American culture and heritage.

RESORT 🏨

♨ The Cloister

Sea Island, 31561; tel 912/638-3611 or toll free 800/732-4752; fax 912/638-5159. On a barrier island, 10 mi from Brunswick. An American institution since 1946, this gracious, old-style resort sits on 10,000 acres of barrier island, with five miles of private shoreline and beautiful parklike grounds and flowering courtyards shaded by live oaks. One of the last bastions of decorum and jacket-and-tie evenings—no ifs, ands, or buts, even when half the guests are children. Nine of 10 guests are repeaters. **Rooms:** 261 rms and stes. CI open/CO noon. Tastefully decorated, luxurious accommodations are dispersed among the original low-rise, red-roofed, mission-style cloister wing, newer beachside wings, and various guest houses, but the most attractive are the originals (recently restyled with new fabrics, furniture, and louvered doors). For families planning to spend a lot of time on the beach, the rooms and suites beside the ocean—with their wonderful views and breezes—are ideal, since they eliminate the need for children to cross the county road that runs through the grounds. **Amenities:** 🛏 🔥 🗄 A/C, cable TV, dataport, in-rm safe, bathrobes. Some units w/minibars, some w/terraces. Large closets for guests settling in for a week or two. Two-line speakerphones for executives attending conferences. **Services:** ✕ ✦ 🆅🅿 🛎 ⬛ 🐾 Twice-daily maid svce, car-rental desk, social director, masseur, children's program, babysitting. Shuttle buses throughout the estate. Complimentary afternoon tea and refreshments in lobby. Outstanding children's program includes turtle nest patrols and nature walks. **Facilities:** 🛝 🚴 ⛰ 🎣 ▶54 ⛴ 🎿 🎱18 🐎 ⛳ 🏊900 🖥 🔧 2 restaurants, 3 bars (1 w/entertainment), 1 beach (ocean), lifeguard, volleyball, board surfing, games rm, lawn games, spa, sauna, steam rm, whirlpool, beauty salon, day-care ctr, playground. Enough facilities for a half-dozen resorts. Several spacious, elegant, antique-filled lounges and solariums; separate salon for dancing. Nearby golf courses shared with club members, but greens fees are only $50/day (courses of this caliber can cost twice as much). Equestrians have a choice of trail rides, evening cookouts, or bareback swim rides. Teenagers' games room is a large rotunda with 12-foot-high ceilings in a prime oceanside location; state-of-the-art fitness center has individual TVs and portable radio headsets; tennis center (all clay-composite courts) includes practice court. European-style spa. Dancing lessons. Boogie boarding, sea kayaking, boat tours through the marshes. **Rates (AP):** Peak (May 15–Nov 30; Christmas) $238–$452 S; $288–$502 D; $440–$552 ste. Extra person $70. Children under age 19 stay free. Min stay wknds. Lower rates off-season. Parking: Outdoor, free. Even with daily service charge of 15% and fees for most activities, this is exceptional value. No CC.

Smyrna

A residential suburb northwest of Atlanta, Smyrna was named for the ancient Greek seaport on the Aegean Sea. It boasts a circa-1848 bridge.

RESTAURANT 🍴

Haveli Indian Restaurant

2706 Cobb Pkwy NW; tel 770/955-4525. Exit 13 off I-285. **Indian.** Bas-relief plaster decorates most walls while some Indian carvings can be found on others. Come for the authentic decor and cuisine, including tandoor items, curries, stuffed breads, and mango ice cream. **FYI:** Reservations accepted. **Open:** Lunch Mon–Sat 11:30am–2:30pm; dinner daily 5:30–10:30pm. **Prices:** Main courses $7–$17. AE, MC, V.

Social Circle

This small town, spread between Newton and Walton Counties in north-central Georgia, probably derives its name for having been a rest station where people could socialize on an early westward migration route.

RESTAURANT 🍴

Ⓢ Blue Willow Inn Restaurant

294 N Cherokee; tel 770/464-2131. Exit 47 off I-20. **Soul/Southern.** Located in the historic district, this restaurant is housed in a Greek Revival mansion with hardwood floors, Oriental rugs, bright jade-and-maroon walls, and a beautiful central staircase. Each of the dining rooms is individually decorated and named (like the Lewis Grizzard Room, made famous in his writings). The authentically Southern cuisine includes fried chicken, fried green tomatoes, and other down-home favorites. **FYI:** Reservations recommended. Dress code. No liquor license. No smoking. **Open:** Lunch Mon–Fri 11am–2:30pm, Sat 11am–3:30pm, Sun 11am–9pm; dinner Mon–Fri 5:30–9pm, Sat 4:30–9pm. **Prices:** Prix fixe $11–$15. No CC. ♿

Statesboro

Statesboro combines the charm of a small Southern agricultural town with the cultural opportunities of a more urban area. Home of Georgia Southern University and magnolia and botanical gardens. **Information:** Statesboro Convention & Visitors Bureau, 204 S Main St, PO Box 1516, Statesboro, 30459 (tel 912/489-1869).

MOTELS 🏨

🏳🏳 Days Inn of Statesboro

461 S Main St, 30458; or toll free 800/DAYS-INN; fax 912/489-8193. Located near Georgia Southern College and within minutes of dining; fine for an overnight stay. **Rooms:** 44 rms. CI 1pm/CO 11am. Nonsmoking rms avail. **Amenities:** 🏨 A/C, cable TV. **Services:** 🛎️ 🍴 **Facilities:** 🍴 1 restaurant (lunch and dinner only). **Rates (CP):** $49 S or D. Extra person $5. Children under age 17 stay free. Lower rates off-season. Parking: Outdoor, free. AE, CB, DC, DISC, MC, V.

🏳🏳 Jameson Inn

1 Jameson Ave, 30458; tel 912/681-7900 or toll free 800/541-3268; fax 912/681-7905. Exit 25 off I-16; across from Georgia Southern College. A good, well-maintained place to stay, especially if you are attending a ball game. **Rooms:** 39 rms and stes. CI 2pm/CO 11am. Nonsmoking rms avail. **Amenities:** 🏨 A/C, cable TV. Some units w/whirlpools. Some rooms have refrigerators and microwaves. **Services:** 🍴 **Facilities:** 🍴 ♨️ 20 ♿ **Rates (CP):** $42–$46 S or D; $85 ste. Extra person $5. Children under age 18 stay free. Parking: Outdoor, free. AE, CB, DC, DISC, MC, V.

RESTAURANTS 🍴

Archibald's Restaurant & Tavern

470 S Main St; tel 912/764-6593. **Eclectic.** More sophisticated than most eateries in the area. Archibald's has a cozy, dark-wood interior and a large and varied menu that includes steak, pasta, chicken, seafood—even a few Mexican dishes. Large bar. **FYI:** Reservations accepted. Guitar/singer. Children's menu. Beer and wine only. **Open:** Mon–Sat 11am–midnight. **Prices:** Main courses $5–$13. AE, DC, DISC, MC, V. 🖼️

RJ's Steakery & Fishery

434 S Main St; tel 912/489-8658. **Seafood/Steak.** A very plain, casual eatery, with the menu painted on the wall, lots of booths and tables, and a cafeteria-style serving line for drinks and ordering. (Food is brought to the table by wait staff.) The simple menu offers a few chicken dishes, in addition to surf-and-turf. **FYI:** Reservations not accepted. Children's menu. No liquor license. **Open:** Sun–Thurs 11am–10pm, Fri–Sat 11am–11pm. **Prices:** Main courses $4–$14. AE, MC, V. 🖼️♿

Stone Mountain

This quaint 19th-century town just east of Atlanta lies just beyond the west entrance to Stone Mountain Park.

HOTEL 🏨

🏳🏳🏳 Hampton Inn Stone Mountain

1737 Mountain Industrial Blvd, 30083; tel 770/934-0004 or toll free 800/426-7866; fax 770/908-0940. S off US 78. A great hotel with an expansive front lawn. Located just three miles from Stone Mountain Park. **Rooms:** 129 rms and stes. CI 3pm/CO noon. Nonsmoking rms avail. **Amenities:** 🏨 ♨️ A/C, cable TV w/movies, dataport. **Services:** 🛎️ 🍴 **Facilities:** 🍴 ♨️ 50 ♿ **Rates (CP):** $49–$67 S; $54–$77 D; $80–$98 ste. Extra person $8. Children under age 18 stay free. Parking: Outdoor, free. AE, CB, DC, DISC, MC, V.

MOTELS

🏳🏳 Days Inn Stone Mountain

2006 Glen Club Dr, 30087; tel 770/879-0800 or toll free 800/325-2525; fax 770/879-0800. 1 mi E of Stone Mountain Park on US 78. Located in a quaint, secluded area away from the shopping strip, this hotel enjoys extraordinary peace and quiet. **Rooms:** 81 rms. CI 2pm/CO 11am. Nonsmoking rms avail. **Amenities:** 🏨 A/C, cable TV. **Services:** 🍴 **Facilities:** 🍴 ♿ **Rates (CP):** $45–$200 S or D. Extra person $5. Children under age 12 stay free. Parking: Outdoor, free. AE, CB, DC, DISC, MC, V.

🏳🏳 La Quinta Stone Mountain

1819 Mountain Industrial Blvd, Tucker, 30084; tel 770/496-1317 or toll free 800/531-5900; fax 770/493-4785. Off US 78. This comfortable chain motel is an oasis in the jungle of tacky commercial enterprises surrounding Stone Mountain Park. **Rooms:** 128 rms and stes. CI 4pm/CO 11am. Nonsmoking rms avail. **Amenities:** 🏨 ♨️ A/C, cable TV w/movies. **Services:** 🛎️ 🍴 **Facilities:** 🍴 150 💻 Washer/dryer. **Rates:** Peak (mid-May–mid-Sept) $54–$66 S; $61–$73 D; $150 ste. Extra person $7. Children under age 18 stay free. Lower rates off-season. Parking: Outdoor, free. AE, CB, DC, DISC, MC, V.

RESORT

🏳🏳🏳🏳 Evergreen Conference Center & Resort,

In Stone Mountain Park, One Lakeview Dr, 30086; tel 770/879-9900 or toll free 800/722-1000; fax 770/413-9052. 25 acres. A castlelike resort (complete with turrets) offering a remote, secluded atmosphere and wonderful views of Stone Mountain and Stone Mountain Lake. Popular with business travelers. **Rooms:** 249 rms and stes. Executive level. CI 4pm/CO noon. Nonsmoking rms avail. Large, luxuriously appointed rooms are decorated in neutral tones and furnished with floral-tapestried armchairs and mahogany furniture. **Amenities:** 🏨 ♨️ A/C, cable TV w/movies, refrig, dataport, voice mail. **Services:** 🍽️ 🗝️ 🚗 🍴 Car-rental desk, social director, masseur, babysitting. **Facilities:** 🍴 5 ⛰️ 🚣 ▶️ 36 ⛳ ♨️ 300 💻 ♿ 1 restaurant (see "Restaurants" below), 2 bars, 1 beach (lake shore), lifeguard, volleyball, whirlpool. **Rates:** $125–$145 S or D; $160–$329 ste. Children under age 18 stay free. Parking: Outdoor, $5/day. AE, CB, DC, DISC, ER, MC, V.

RESTAURANTS 🍴

Magnolia Tea Room

5459 E Mountain St; tel 770/498-6304. 1 block S of west entrance of Stone Mountain Park; ½ mile E of Main St.

American. Located in the historic 1854 Gormley House, this restaurant offers Southern cuisine in a truly Southern atmosphere. Lace curtains, hardwood floors, and antique furniture set the mood. Chicken salad is popular at lunch, while grilled fish and prime rib are typical dinner entrees. Homemade biscuits and jams. **FYI:** Reservations accepted. Beer and wine only. No smoking. **Open:** Lunch Tues–Sat 11am–2:30pm; dinner Fri–Sat 5:30–9:30pm; brunch Sun 11am–2:30pm. Closed Dec 25–31. **Prices:** Main courses $13–$20. No CC. ▧ ▨

Waterside Restaurant

In Evergreen Conference Center & Resort, One Lakeview Dr; tel 770/879-9900. **American.** Located on the fourth floor, this restaurant offers a great view of the woods and the surrounding Stone Mountain area. The menu changes regularly, and buffets are offered at all meals in addition to sophisticated à la carte regional fare. Even breakfast can get fancy, with selections like quail eggs and sautéed quail with grits. **FYI:** Reservations recommended. **Open:** Breakfast daily 6:30–11am; lunch daily 11am–5pm; dinner daily 5–10pm. **Prices:** Main courses $10–$22. AE, DC, DISC, MC, V. ▨ &

ATTRACTION 📷

Georgia's Stone Mountain Park

US 78; tel 770/498-5600. Millions flock to this 3,200-acre park each year to enjoy a wealth of attractions and recreation. Foremost, of course, is Stone Mountain itself. Carved on its sheer north flank is the world's largest sculpture, a 90-by-190-foot carving of Confederate heroes Robert E Lee, Thomas "Stonewall" Jackson, and President Jefferson Davis. You can take a skylift to the top, or hike up an easy trail on the other side. Elsewhere in the park you can play golf, swim from a sand beach, visit an authentic antebellum plantation, or ride around the mountain's base on a steam locomotive. There's also an ice skating rink, biking, fishing, and campgrounds. The six major attractions—skylift, auto/music museum, railroad, riverboat, plantation, and wildlife trails—charge an additional fee and close earlier than the rest of the park. **Open:** Daily 6am–midnight. **$**

Thomasville

The "City of Roses" and home to vast estates of earlier days when northerners arrived for winter sunshine and quail hunting. Pebble Hill mansion is at the center of a sprawling shooting plantation and is the site of the annual grand Plantation Ball. **Information:** Destination Thomasville Tourism, PO Box 1540, Thomasville, 31799 (tel 912/225-3919).

MOTEL 🛏

≣≣ Shoney's Inn

14866 US 19 S, 31792; tel 912/228-5555 or toll free 800/222-2222; fax 912/228-0663. Dated but well-kept property,

located about 10 miles from the Pebble Hill Plantation and 10 miles from the Florida state line. Good for overnight stays. **Rooms:** 96 rms. CI noon/CO noon. Nonsmoking rms avail. **Amenities:** ▧ A/C, cable TV. **Services:** ▨ ▨ ▨ **Facilities:** ▨ ▨ & **Rates (CP):** $41–$43 D. Extra person $4. Children under age 18 stay free. Parking: Outdoor, free. AE, CB, DC, DISC, MC, V.

INN

≣≣≣≣ 1884 Paxton House

445 Remington Ave, 31792; tel 912/226-5197 or toll free 800/278-0138. Beautiful Victorian Gothic home with neo-classical porches, a circular staircase, heart-pine floors, and claw-foot tubs. Unsuitable for children under 12. **Rooms:** 6 rms and stes. CI 3pm/CO 11am. No smoking. Each room is decorated with its own collection of antiques from all parts of the world. Refined and elegant, but comfortable. **Amenities:** ▧ ▨ ▨ A/C, cable TV. Some units w/fireplaces. Each room supplied with fresh flowers, bedside chocolates, and fresh fruit. Some rooms have VCRs. **Services:** ▨ Afternoon tea served. Fresh breads and pastries are baked daily for breakfast. **Facilities:** Guest lounge. **Rates (BB):** $65–$90 S; $80–$130 ste. Min stay special events. Parking: Outdoor, free. MC, V.

RESTAURANTS 🍴

♥ The Grand Old House

502 S Broad St (Historic District); tel 912/227-0108. **Continental/French.** Located in a turn-of-the-century home, with six tall white columns along its big front porch, and a half-circle open-air balcony on the second floor. Each room is individually decorated with period antiques. The menu changes daily in order to take advantage of the freshest available ingredients, but is sure to include seafood, steak, veal, lamb, and chicken entrees. The food is carefully prepared and perfectly seasoned. **FYI:** Reservations recommended. Dress code. **Open:** Lunch Tues–Sat 11:30am–2:30pm; dinner Mon–Fri 6–9:30pm. **Prices:** Main courses $12–$28. AE, DISC, MC, V. ♥

The Tavern

In The Grand Old House, 502 S Broad St (Historic District); tel 912/227-0108. **Bistro.** Located in the basement, this eatery uses the same chef but has a much more casual atmosphere. The bar-type menu offers steak, chicken, seafood, and various finger foods and sandwiches. **FYI:** Reservations not accepted. Blues. Children's menu. **Open:** Tues–Thurs 5–11pm, Fri 5pm–1:30am, Sat 5pm–midnight. **Prices:** Main courses $8–$16. AE, DISC, MC, V. ▨

ATTRACTION 📷

Pebble Hill Plantation

US 319 S; tel 912/226-2344. Rich in both art and history, Pebble Hill was established in the 1820s by Thomas Jefferson Johnson, the founder of Thomas County. In 1896, the house was sold to the Hanna family of Cleveland, who turned Pebble Hill into their winter home and hunting plantation. The house, almost totally consumed by fire in 1934 (although the furnishings were saved), was rebuilt in 1936.

Today, the mansion is filled with the collections of sportwoman Pansy Poe, its last Hanna family owner. Artwork by John James Audubon and other famous American and British artists, 19th-century antiques, silver, glassware, and a sizable collection of Native American memorabilia are a few of the highlights. (Note that children under age 6 are not allowed inside the Main House.) Outside, guests can peruse the stables (which house a large carriage collection), gardens, swimming pool and bathhouse, dog kennel, dog hospital, fire engine house, family schoolhouse, and cemetery. **Open:** Tues–Sat 10am–5pm, Sun 1–5pm. Closed some hols. **$$**

Tifton

The seat of Tift County in south-central Georgia, Tifton is a farming and manufacturing city and site of a state agricultural experiment station. Home to Jefferson Davis Memorial Park, which marks the site of Davis's capture by Union forces, as well as numerous theaters. **Information:** Tifton–Tift County Chamber of Commerce, 100 Central Ave, PO Box 165, Tifton, 31793 (tel 912/382-6200).

MOTELS 🏨

🏨🏨 Comfort Inn
1104 King Rd, 21794; tel 912/382-4410 or toll free 800/221-2222; fax 912/382-4410. Exit 19 off I-75. Popular with both families and business travelers. The only property in Tifton with an indoor pool. **Rooms:** 91 rms and stes. CI 2pm/CO 11am. Nonsmoking rms avail. **Amenities:** 🛏 A/C, cable TV. Some units w/whirlpools. Suites have refrigerators and wet bars. **Services:** 🛎 🖐 Car-rental desk, babysitting. **Facilities:** 🏋 🛢 ⅛ Whirlpool. **Rates (CP):** $49 S; $57 D; $90–$98 ste. Extra person $5. Children under age 16 stay free. Parking: Outdoor, free. AE, DC, DISC, MC, V.

🏨🏨 Hampton Inn
720 US 319S, 31794; tel 912/382-8800 or toll free 800/892-2753; fax 912/387-0563. Exit 18 off I-75. Popular with corporate guests as well as families, due to easy interstate access. **Rooms:** 82 rms. CI 2pm/CO 11am. Nonsmoking rms avail. King rooms are larger and have sofas. **Amenities:** 🛏 👁 A/C, cable TV, dataport. Refrigerators available for a fee. **Services:** 🛢 🖐 **Facilities:** 🏋 ⅛ **Rates (CP):** $50–$61 D. Children under age 18 stay free. Parking: Outdoor, free. AE, CB, DC, DISC, JCB, MC, V.

🏨🏨 Holiday Inn
At Jct I-75/US 82W, PO Box 1267, 31794; tel 912/382-6687 or toll free 800/HOLIDAY; fax 912/382-1533. Exit 18. Basic Holiday Inn, located right off I-75. **Rooms:** 189 rms. CI noon/CO noon. Nonsmoking rms avail. **Amenities:** 🛏 👁

A/C, satel TV w/movies. Microwaves and refrigerator available upon request. **Services:** ✕ 🚗 🖐 🖐 🖐 Car-rental desk. **Facilities:** 🏋 🛢 ⅛ 1 restaurant, 1 bar, playground, washer/dryer. Pool in courtyard. **Rates:** $47 S or D. Children under age 19 stay free. Parking: Outdoor, free. AE, CB, DC, DISC, JCB, MC, V.

RESTAURANT 🍴

Sonny's Real Pit Bar-B-Q
US 82W; tel 912/386-0606. **Barbecue.** Dark and rather plain decor, punctuated by simple wooden booths. The barbecue is the real star here: pork and beef ribs, slathered in thick sauce. Other selections include smoked turkey and charbroiled chicken, and daily specials are available. **FYI:** Reservations not accepted. Children's menu. No liquor license. **Open:** Daily 11am–9pm. **Prices:** Main courses $6–$9. AE, DC, DISC, MC, V. 🅿 ⅛

Tybee Island

Linked to Savannah by US 80, the island features large strands of hard-packed sand, surf, and fishing from beaches, tidal creeks, and deep-sea boats. The 1867 lighthouse is part of a museum. **Information:** Tybee Island Visitors Center, PO Box 491, Tybee Island, 31328 (tel 912/786-5444).

HOTEL 🏨

🏨🏨🏨 Ocean Plaza Beach Resort
15th St and Oceanfront, PO Box 158, 31328; tel 912/786-7664 or toll free 800/215-6750; fax 912/786-4531. Well-kept, beachfront property offering plain but comfortable accommodations. **Rooms:** 250 rms, stes, and effic. CI noon/CO 11am. Nonsmoking rms avail. **Amenities:** 🛏 👁 A/C, cable TV, dataport. All units w/terraces, some w/whirlpools. **Services:** ✕ 🚗 🖐 🖐 🖐 Car-rental desk, social director, babysitting. **Facilities:** 🏋 🛢 🖥 ⅛ 1 bar (w/entertainment), 1 beach (ocean), volleyball, washer/dryer. **Rates:** Peak (Mem Day–Labor Day) $75–$115 S or D; $85–$195 ste; $95 effic. Extra person $5. Children under age 2 stay free. Min stay special events. Lower rates off-season. Parking: Outdoor, free. Higher rates for oceanfront or poolside rooms. AE, CB, DC, DISC, MC, V.

RESTAURANT 🍴

The Oar House Restaurant
1311 Butler Ave; tel 912/786-5055. **Seafood/Steak.** Nautical-themed restaurant with a simple menu offering mostly seafood, with a few chicken and beef choices. Best for the bar's impressive selection of imported beers from Ireland, Italy, the Czech Republic, and Mexico. **FYI:** Reservations accepted. Children's menu. Dress code. **Open:** Daily 5–10pm. Closed Jan–Feb on Tues, Wed. **Prices:** Main courses $10–$18. AE, CB, DC, DISC, MC, V. 🅿 🖤

Valdosta

This south Georgia agricultural and manufacturing city showcases three different historic districts. Once called Troupville, the town picked up and moved in 1859 to be beside the railroad that had passed it by; the new settlement was named Valdosta. **Information:** Valdosta Lowndes Convention & Visitors Bureau, 1703 Norman Dr #F, PO Box 1964, Valdosta, 31603 (tel 912/245-0513).

MOTELS 🏨

≋≋ Best Western King of the Road

1403 N St Augustine Rd, 31601; tel 912/244-7600 or toll free 800/528-1234; fax 912/245-1734. Nice, clean, basic property. Nothing special, but fine for an overnight stay. **Rooms:** 137 rms, stes, and effic. CI 11am/CO 11am. Nonsmoking rms avail. **Amenities:** 🛏 A/C, cable TV w/movies. Some rooms have refrigerators. **Services:** ✕ 🚐 🖨 🗗 🕭 **Facilities:** 🏊 300 🕭 1 restaurant, 1 bar (w/entertainment), playground. **Rates:** $34 S; $39 D; $54 ste; $58 effic. Extra person $3. Children under age 12 stay free. Parking: Outdoor, free. AE, CB, DC, DISC, MC, V.

≋≋≋ Club House Inn

1800 Club House Dr, 31601; tel 912/247-7755 or toll free 800/CLUB-INN; fax 912/245-1359. Exit 5 off I-75. Comfortable property, good for extended stays and business travelers. Located within 10 miles of outlet shopping. **Rooms:** 121 rms and stes. CI 3pm/CO noon. Nonsmoking rms avail. **Amenities:** 🛏 ⚒ A/C, cable TV w/movies. Some units w/terraces, some w/whirlpools. Suites have kitchenettes with microwaves and refrigerators. **Services:** 🖨 🗗 Car-rental desk. Manager's reception with cocktails and snacks (5–7pm, Mon–Sat). **Facilities:** 🏊 50 🕭 1 bar, whirlpool, washer/dryer. Guests passes to YMCA. Courtyard area has barbecue grills and a gazebo by the pool. **Rates (BB):** $58 S or D; $80–$108 ste. Extra person $5. Children under age 16 stay free. Parking: Outdoor, free. Golf packages avail for Stone Creek Golf Course. AE, CB, DC, DISC, MC, V.

≋≋≋ Comfort Inn Conference Center

I-75 and US 84, PO Box 1191, 31603; tel 912/242-1212 or toll free 800/221-2222; fax 912/242-2639. Nice, basic accommodations, located minutes away from downtown Valdosta and the mall. **Rooms:** 138 rms and stes. CI 2pm/CO noon. Nonsmoking rms avail. **Amenities:** 🛏 📺 A/C, cable TV w/movies. Premium king bed rooms have refrigerators and microwaves. **Services:** ✕ 🚐 🖨 🗗 🕭 **Facilities:** 🏊 🍴 300 🖥 🕭 1 restaurant, 1 bar, volleyball, washer/dryer. Laundry facilities. Shuffleboard available. **Rates (CP):** $46–$54 D; $90 ste. Extra person $4. Children under age 18 stay free. Parking: Outdoor, free. AE, CB, DC, DISC, ER, MC, V.

≋≋ Hampton Inn

1705 Gornto Rd, 31601; tel 912/244-8800 or toll free 800/426-7866; fax 912/244-6602. Exit 5 off I-75. Chain motel on the same property as the Valdosta Mall. **Rooms:** 102 rms. CI 3pm/CO noon. Nonsmoking rms avail. **Amenities:** 🛏 ⚒ A/C, cable TV. **Services:** 🖨 🗗 **Facilities:** 🏊 🕭 Guests have access to Gold's Gym, on the other side of the mall. **Rates (CP):** $49–$64 S or D. Extra person $6. Children under age 18 stay free. Parking: Outdoor, free. AE, CB, DC, DISC, MC, V.

≋≋≋ Holiday Inn

1309 St Augustine Rd, PO Box 1047, 31602; tel 912/242-3881 or toll free 800/HOLIDAY; fax 912/242-3881. Exit 5 off I-75. Attractively landscaped property, with a nice courtyard and pool. The Valdosta Mall is only two blocks away, making this a popular choice with families as well as business travelers. **Rooms:** 281 rms and stes. CI 3pm/CO noon. Nonsmoking rms avail. **Amenities:** 🛏 ⚒ 📺 A/C, cable TV w/movies, VCR. **Services:** ✕ 🚐 🖨 🗗 🕭 Champagne reception in the lobby (Mon–Thurs). Copy and fax services available. **Facilities:** 🏊 250 🕭 1 restaurant (bkfst and dinner only), 1 bar (w/entertainment), games rm, washer/dryer. Guest passes to YMCA. **Rates:** $51–$53 S or D. Children under age 18 stay free. Parking: Outdoor, free. AE, CB, DC, DISC, MC, V.

≋≋ Jameson Inn

1725 Gornto Rd, 31601; tel 912/253-0009 or toll free 800/541-3268. Exit 5 off I-75. Basic, relatively new property adjacent to the Valdosta Mall. The surrounding square features restaurants, miniature golf, and grocery stores. **Rooms:** 40 rms and stes. CI 2pm/CO 11am. Nonsmoking rms avail. **Amenities:** 🛏 ⚒ A/C, cable TV, dataport. Some units w/whirlpools. **Services:** 🖨 🗗 **Facilities:** 🏊 🕭 **Rates (CP):** $46 S or D; $95–$135 ste. Extra person $4. Children under age 18 stay free. Parking: Outdoor, free. AE, CB, DC, DISC, MC, V.

≋≋ Quality Inn North

1209 St Augustine Rd, 31601; tel 912/244-8510 or toll free 800/228-5151; fax 912/249-8215. Exit 5 off I-75. Basic chain motel, located right off I-75. Fine for overnight stay. **Rooms:** 124 rms. CI noon/CO noon. Nonsmoking rms avail. **Amenities:** 🛏 A/C, cable TV. **Services:** 🖨 🗗 🕭 **Facilities:** 🏊 🍴 🎾 🖥 🕭 1 restaurant (lunch and dinner only), 1 bar, washer/dryer. **Rates (CP):** $40–$80 S; $45–$90 D. Extra person $5. Children under age 18 stay free. Parking: Outdoor, free. AE, DC, DISC, MC, V.

≋ Ramada Inn

2008 W Hill, 31601; tel 912/242-1225 or toll free 800/2-RAMADA; fax 912/247-2755. I-75 and US 84. Slightly worn but adequate property. OK for an overnight stay but nothing more. **Rooms:** 102 rms and effic. CI noon/CO noon. Nonsmoking rms avail. Decor and furniture are very dated. **Amenities:** 🛏 ⚒ A/C, cable TV. **Services:** ✕ 🚐 🖨 🗗 🕭 **Facilities:** 🏊 70 1 restaurant, 1 bar (w/entertainment), basketball. Putting green. Pool surrounded by unattractive green "carpet." Kids under 12 eat free in restaurant. **Rates:** $34 S or D; $34 effic. Children under age 18 stay free. Parking: Outdoor, free. AE, CB, DC, DISC, JCB, MC, V.

☰ Travelodge

1330 St Augustine Rd, 31601; tel 912/242-3464 or toll free 800/578-7878; fax 912/242-3464 ext 189. Exit 5 off I-75. Offers the bare necessities only. Fine for short stays. **Rooms:** 88 rms. CI open/CO noon. Nonsmoking rms avail. **Amenities:** ☎ ⊡ A/C, cable TV. Complimentary coffee in rooms. Refrigerators and sofas available by request in king rooms. **Services:** 🚗 ⊠ ↴ ⟨⟩ **Facilities:** ⓖ ⅁ 1 restaurant. **Rates:** Peak (Mem Day–Labor Day) $36 S; $41–$51 D. Extra person $5. Children under age 12 stay free. Lower rates off-season. Parking: Indoor, free. AE, CB, DC, DISC, MC, V.

RESTAURANTS ⑪

Covington's Dining & Catering

310 N Patterson (Historic district); tel 912/242-2261. **Deli.** A nice, quaint place for a quick lunch downtown, with a light and airy decor. Menu specialties include chicken salad and homemade cinnamon rolls plus a wide selection of sandwiches, salads, and pastas. **FYI:** Reservations recommended. No liquor license. **Open:** Daily 8am–2:30pm. **Prices:** Lunch main courses $4–$8. AE, CB, DC, DISC, MC, V. ⅁

Fiddlers Green

2575 N Valdosta Rd; tel 912/247-0366. Exit 6 off I-75. **Seafood/Steak.** Dark-wood decor and low lighting set the subdued mood. Specialty of the house is roast Black Angus prime rib au jus, available in 6- or 12-oz portions; larger cuts available on request. **FYI:** Reservations recommended. Piano. Children's menu. **Open:** Mon–Sat 6–10pm. **Prices:** Main courses $11–$16. AE, CB, DC, DISC, MC, V. ♥ ⅁

Guilio's Greek Italian Restaurant

105 E Ann; tel 912/333-0929. Across from Valdosta State University. **Greek/Italian.** Located in a renovated house dating from the 1920s. Each room has been individually and stylishly decorated and some of the dining rooms have artwork painted on the floor. The menu features salads, pastas, and meats prepared in Italian or Greek manner, as well as shrimp dishes and steak for the less adventuresome. **FYI:** Reservations recommended. Children's menu. Beer and wine only. **Open:** Tues–Sat 5–10pm. **Prices:** Main courses $7–$13. AE, MC, V. ⅁

Warm Springs

The village of Warm Springs, built between 1881 and 1907 and incorporated in 1924, has been revitalized in recent years and includes many shops and restaurants. It is most known, of course, for the nearby springs that produce its famously therapeutic waters. Franklin D Roosevelt first visited the springs in 1924 for treatment of his polio and later built the cottage known as the "Little White House," where he died in 1945. **Information:** Meriwether County Chamber of Commerce, Federal Building, PO Box 9, Warm Springs, 31830 (tel 706/655-2558).

RESTAURANT ⑪

★ The Bulloch House

47 Bulloch St; tel 706/655-9068. **Soul/Southern.** The Bulloch House, built atop a small knoll in 1892, is now the home of this restaurant that specializes in Southern buffet-style dinners. It is best-known for its fried green tomatoes, special tomato sauce, and homemade preserves. **FYI:** Reservations accepted. Children's menu. No liquor license. No smoking. **Open:** Lunch daily 11am–2:30pm; dinner Fri–Sat 5:30–8:30pm. **Prices:** Prix fixe $6–$8. MC, V. 🖳 ⅁

ATTRACTION 🖼

Little White House Historic Site

GA 85 W; tel 706/655-5870. Franklin Delano Roosevelt "discovered" Warm Springs in 1924, shortly after he contracted polio, when he went there for the beneficial effect of swimming in the warm spring water. In 1926 he bought the springs, a hotel, and some cottages, and began developing facilities to help paralytic patients from all over the country through the Georgia Warm Springs Foundation, which he founded. When he became president, this was the retreat he loved most, and the house today is much as he left it when he died here while sitting for a portrait in 1945. The unfinished portrait, his wheelchair, ship models, and gifts from citizens are preserved as he last saw them. Next door, the Little White House Museum holds more memorabilia and shows a 12-minute movie depicting FDR's life in Warm Springs. **Open:** Daily 9am–5pm. Closed some hols. **$$**

Warner Robins

Georgia's fastest-growing city, it was originally an agricultural village named Wellston before being renamed Warner Robins in 1943, after the neighboring army air depot. The town has evolved with Robins Air Force Base. Home to one of top aviation museums in the country. **Information:** Warner Robins Area Chamber of Commerce, 1420 Watson Blvd, Warner Robins, 31093 (tel 912/922-8585).

MOTEL 🖬

☰☰☰ Ramada Inn

2725 Watson Blvd, 31093; tel 912/953-3000 or toll free 800/2-RAMADA; fax 912/953-3000 ext 411. Exit 45 off I-75. This motel is good for corporate guests and extended stays and is located near Robins Air Base and Air Force Museum. **Rooms:** 164 rms and stes. CI 2pm/CO noon. Nonsmoking rms avail. **Amenities:** ☎ ⚬ A/C, satel TV w/movies. 1 unit w/whirlpool. **Services:** ✕ ⊠ ↴ ⟨⟩ Free newspapers in lobby. **Facilities:** ⓖ 🖾 🖳 ⬚ ⅁ 2 restaurants (bkfst and dinner only), 1 bar. **Rates:** $40–$77 S or D; $90–$150 ste. Extra person $8. Children under age 18 stay free. Parking: Outdoor, free. AE, DC, DISC, MC, V.

RESTAURANT

★ **Richard's**

604 Russell Pkwy; tel 912/922-1547. **Seafood/Steak.** Small dining room with wooden booths and a rather dark decor. The specialty is roast prime rib, and there's an extensive selection of seafood, steaks, poultry, and vegetarian plates. **FYI:** Reservations recommended. Children's menu. **Open:** Lunch Mon–Fri 11am–2:30pm; dinner Mon–Thurs 5:30–9:30pm, Fri–Sat 5–10pm. **Prices:** Main courses $7–$28. AE, CB, DC, MC, V. ♥ &

Washington

This small northeast Georgia town boasts an architectural legacy spanning three centuries. Within the city limits are 4 districts and 14 individual properties listed on the National Register. Kettle Creek Battlefield nearby was the site of a decisive 1779 Revolutionary War battle. **Information:** Washington-Wilkes Chamber of Commerce, 104 E Liberty St, PO Box 661, Washington, 30673 (tel 706/678-2013).

HOTEL

UNRATED **Jameson Inn**

115 Ann Denard Dr, 30673; tel 706/678-7925 or toll free 800/541-3268; fax 706/678-7925. Off US 78. Clean, comfortable accommodations with few frills and no surprises. **Rooms:** 41 rms and stes. CI 2pm/CO 11am. Nonsmoking rms avail. **Amenities:** 🔒 ＆ A/C, cable TV, refrig. Some units w/whirlpools. **Services:** ⊒ Babysitting. **Rates (CP):** $46 S; $50 D; $95–$135 ste. Extra person $4. Children under age 12 stay free. Parking: Outdoor, free. AE, DC, DISC, MC, V.

Waycross

The largest city in Ware County, located in the southeastern coastal area, is a bustling retail center and a gateway to mysterious Okefenokee Swamp Park. The largest bluegrass convention in southeast Georgia is held here. **Information:** Waycross–Ware County Convention & Visitors Bureau, PO Box 137, Waycross, 31502 (tel 912/283-3742).

MOTEL

▤▤▤ **Holiday Inn**

1725 Memorial Dr, PO Box 1357, 31501; tel 912/283-4490 or toll free 800/HOLIDAY. On US 82. Located in downtown Waycross, right off US 82 and within a few miles of the Okefenokee swamp. **Rooms:** 145 rms and stes. CI 1pm/CO 1pm. Nonsmoking rms avail. **Amenities:** 🔒 ☜ A/C, cable TV, dataport, voice mail. Some units w/terraces. **Services:** ✗ VP ⚌ ⊡ ⊒ ⇜ **Facilities:** 🚹 ⚇ 150 & 1 restaurant, 1 bar, games rm, playground, washer/dryer. Small putting green.

Rates (CP): $47 S; $52 D; $95 ste. Extra person $5. Children under age 19 stay free. Parking: Outdoor, free. AE, CB, DC, DISC, MC, V.

ATTRACTIONS

Okefenokee Heritage Center

N Augusta Ave; tel 912/285-4260. A 1,600-acre wildlife sanctuary located on Cowhouse Island, at the northern entrance to the Okefenokee Swamp. Guided boat trips let passengers see the unique habitat; a serpentarium offers reptile shows. A boardwalk into the swamp and a 90-foot observation tower allow for wildlife viewing. **Open:** Mon–Sat 9am–5pm, Sun 1–5pm. Closed some hols. **$**

Okefenokee Swamp Park

GA 177; tel 912/283-0583. Exhibits of fine arts and local history include a 1912 locomotive and restored depot, a late 1800s print shop, an 1840 farm house, antique vehicles; the Walt Kelly Room contains memorabilia of the creator of the "Pogo" comic strip. **Open:** June–Aug, daily 9am–6:30pm; Sept–May, daily 9am–5pm. **$$$**

KENTUCKY

Gateway to the South

In the spring, seemingly never-ending miles of white-railed fences stretch out to the horizon, enclosing countless acres of grass with a bluish-purple tint. Kentucky's famous bluegrass—nurtured by calcium-rich limestone soil—is ideal for raising thoroughbred horses, and the state's history has been profoundly influenced by the horse. The first thoroughbred was brought into the state in 1779 and by the next year, a race track had been designated along Lexington's Main Street and the state census counted more horses than people. A century later, the Kentucky Derby ("the greatest two minutes in sports") was born in Louisville, where it continues to capture the world's attention on the first Saturday in May.

If your first impression of Kentucky is horses, the second is probably bourbon whiskey. This type of "firewater" was named for Bourbon County, KY, where it was first produced in 1790. A mixture of corn, rye, and malt, bourbon must be aged in unused charred oak barrels for at least two years. As with horses, limestone plays a key role, in that the water used to make real Kentucky bourbon has been filtered through it. Visitors may observe the distilling process at several distilleries that are open to the public.

Kentucky is blessed with beautiful scenery—mountains, waterfalls, and gorges in the east; bluegrass pastures in the central region; giant lakes in the west; lush forests everywhere. The state boasts five nationally designated outdoor recreation areas (covering close to one million acres) as well as 47 state parks, 21 major lakes, 14 significant river systems, and 1,400 miles of hiking trails. Kentucky's historic sites deal with such illustrious former residents as Daniel Boone, Abraham Lincoln, and the industrious Shakers.

Kentucky is also a mecca for the arts. Kentucky's larger cities boast numerous museums and performing arts companies. (Actors Theater of Louisville, one of the most important regional theaters in the

STATE STATS

CAPITAL
Frankfort

AREA
40,395 square miles

BORDERS
Illinois, Indiana, Missouri, Ohio, Virginia, West Virginia, Tennessee

POPULATION
3,826,794 (1994 estimate)

ENTERED UNION
June 1, 1792 (15th state)

NICKNAME
Bluegrass State

STATE FLOWER
Goldenrod

STATE BIRD
Cardinal

FAMOUS NATIVES
Muhammad Ali, Abraham Lincoln, Diane Sawyer, Henry Clay

country, has hosted the likes of Kevin Bacon, Kathy Bates, Holly Hunter, and Mercedes Ruehl.) The quality of Kentucky's traditional, contemporary, and folk art handicrafts is recognized worldwide. More than 3,000 craftspeople sell their creations at co-ops, museums, galleries, shops, and studios throughout the state. And of course, bluegrass music—named after the state's famous turf—was born here and it continues to flourish.

Neither Southern nor Midwestern and neither urban nor rural, Kentucky offers a perfect blend of natural beauty, down-home hospitality, and sophisticated entertainment. No matter what you are looking for, you can probably find it in the Bluegrass State.

A Brief History

Gap to the West Before the arrival of white settlers, the Kentucky region was inhabited by the Shawnee and Cherokee and other Native Americans who hunted on the land and sometimes fought over it. Early in the 18th century, French and Spanish explorers pushed into the territory from the Mississippi River in the west, and a few intrepid explorers and traders made the trip through the Cumberland Gap in the east. The area was not seriously explored until Daniel Boone arrived in 1769. During a period of extensive settlement in the 1770s, the Cherokee chief Dragging Cloud predicted that whites would find Kentucky "a dark and bloody land." The British aided the Native Americans in fulfilling this prophecy during the American Revolution with sieges, scalpings, and skirmishes. After the war, however, settlers continued to pour in and the region separated from Virginia in the 1780s. By 1792—the year Kentucky was admitted to the Union as the 15th state—75,000 settlers were living there.

The ethnic makeup of these early settlers was exceptionally mixed. English and Scotch-Irish settlers arrived from Pennsylvania by way of Maryland and Virginia and the Cumberland Gap. French emigrés journeyed up the Mississippi and settled predominantly in the Louisville area; German settlers made their way down the Ohio from New England, western Pennsylvania, and other Middle Atlantic states.

Caught in the Middle Almost from the beginning, there were two societies with very different philosophies developing in Kentucky. Not only was the state a crossroads in east–west expansion, it was officially (but unsuccessfully) neutral in the Civil War. The plantation owners and businessmen of the Bluegrass and Pennyrile regions, who controlled the government, favored slavery, while the farmers who floated their grain, hides, and other products down the Mississippi allied themselves with antislavery forces. (An ironic historical footnote: US President Abraham Lincoln and Confederate President Jefferson Davis were both born in Kentucky—one year and 100 miles apart.)

In 1833 the legislature passed a bill forbidding the importation of slaves for resale, but slave owners continued to dominate the government. A Confederate capital was established at Bowling Green, yet Louisville was a major supply point for the Union Army and the Underground Railroad flourished throughout the state. Most men of fighting age actively supported one side or the other (with about twice as many fighting for the Union as siding with the Confederacy). Camp Nelson, near Nicholasville, was an important recruiting station for African Americans; the beginnings of the 5th and 6th US Cavalry and the 114th and 116th US Colored Heavy Artillery were formed there.

Only a few major battles were contested on Kentucky soil, but the Cumberland Gap seesawed back and forth between Confederate and Union control. Following the Confederate defeat at Perryville in 1862, action during the remainder of the conflict consisted primarily of guerrilla warfare. Many daring raids were carried out by Lexington native John Hunt Morgan, the so-called "Thunderbolt of the Confederacy."

Because Kentucky never officially left the Union, it survived the Reconstruction years better than did its neighbors in the Deep South. Ironically, after the

---

Fun Facts

• The first crude oil well was discovered in Kentucky in 1818, when a salt well unexpectedly filled with "black gold." But at that time there were no industrial uses for the stuff, and the well was abandoned.

• Col Harlan Sanders, the man who made Kentucky Fried Chicken famous, was actually born in neighboring Indiana. His first restaurant is still in operation in Corbin, KY.

• Basketball fever is so strong in Kentucky that the state legislature passed a bill in 1983 requiring the University of Louisville Cardinals and the University of Kentucky Wildcats to play each other every December.

• The door of the US Bullion Depository at Fort Knox weighs 28 tons.

war Kentucky aligned itself more with the South than it had previously.

Mountaineers & Moonshiners In years past, while the landed aristocracy raised and raced their stately horses, small farmers and coal miners in the mountainous eastern part of the state led a hardscrabble life, one that would give rise to a whole body of folklore. This is the home of the mountaineers and moonshiners, some of whom worked in the coal mines under unbelievably harsh conditions, supplementing the dinner pot with a little "coon huntin'" and taking the edge off desperate lives with a little backwoods whiskey. These fiercely independent mountain folk lived by a harsh law of "an eye for an eye," resulting in many a multigenerational family feud, most notoriously that between the Hatfields and the McCoys.

Moving On In the later years of the century, the opening of rail lines into the eastern coal fields and the introduction of tobacco stirred the economy. Lexington and the Ohio River cities of Louisville (once the nation's largest tobacco market), Owensboro, Paducah, and Covington grew rapidly. Continued economic diversification marked the 20th century, as industries from car manufacturing to hospital management moved into the state. The 1960s saw both laws requiring reforestation and restoration of the devastation caused by strip mining, and a relatively peaceful transition to racial integration.

A Closer Look

GEOGRAPHY

Rivers define most of Kentucky's borders. The **Tug** and **Big Sandy Rivers** separate it from West Virginia; the **Ohio River** creates the boundary between Kentucky and the states of Ohio, Indiana, and Illinois; and the **Mississippi River** divides Kentucky from Missouri. (The Ohio and Mississippi Rivers border Kentucky for 700 miles.) Together with their

---

DRIVING DISTANCES

Lexington

72 mi E of Louisville
76 mi S of Cincinnati, OH
175 mi N of Knoxville, TN
210 mi NE of Nashville, TN
261 mi NE of Paducah

Louisville

72 mi W of Lexington
101 mi SW of Cincinnati, OH
168 mi NE of Nashville, TN
219 mi NE of Paducah
247 mi NW of Knoxville, TN

Paducah

150 mi NW of Nashville, TN
177 mi N of Memphis, TN
178 mi SE of St Louis, MO
219 mi SW of Louisville
261 mi SW of Lexington

---

tributaries, these rivers provide Kentucky with more miles of navigable rivers and streams than any other state.

Within the state are several distinct geographic areas. More than 10,000 square miles of easternmost Kentucky lie in the **Mountain Region,** a sloping plateau of the Cumberland and Pine Mountain ranges. This area is distinguished by the state's highest summits, as well as by deep gorges, narrow valleys, rock arches, and transverse ridges. The district is drained by the Big Sandy and Cumberland Rivers, which created water passes such as the Cumberland Gap. Massive seams of coal are buried under the mountains.

The **Knobs,** a long narrow region shaped like an irregular horseshoe with both ends touching the Ohio River, is an area of cone-shaped or rounded hills and ancient escarpments. Its easily eroded shale soil makes it better for forest growth than cultivation. The major city in this region is Louisville, which was founded in 1778 at the Falls of the Ohio River and used as a base from which to harass British troops during the Revolutionary War. To the southeast of the Knobs is the **Bluegrass Region,** named for the long-stemmed, bluish grass that flourishes there. The underlying mineral-rich limestone makes for ideal pasture for thoroughbred horses; many world-class horse farms are located in these gently rolling hills. Frankfort, which was named the state capital in 1792, and Lexington, the state's second-largest city, are the principal cities of this region.

Caves dominate the **Pennyrile (or Pennyroyal) Region,** named for a plant of the mint family that grows in the area. Abundant water and limestone have combined to create such subterranean passages as Mammoth Cave—a 150-mile cavern that includes three rivers, two lakes, and an underground sea. Also in this region are rocky wooded hillsides, cliffs, and an area once known as the Barrens because the Native Americans burned it continuously to create grasslands for buffalo. Bowling Green, the state's fifth-largest city, is located here.

Bounded by the Tennessee, Mississippi, and Ohio Rivers in the western part of the state, **The Purchase** (also known as the Jackson Purchase) is the smallest —but most fertile—of the state's regions. Its wide flood plains are broken by low hills; bluffs, swamps, and lagoons dot the terrain. **Paducah,** located near the confluence of the Ohio and Tennessee Rivers, is the chief urban center.

CLIMATE

Kentucky has a temperate climate, with four distinct seasons moderated by prevailing winds from the south and southwest. Spring and summer can bring heavy thunderstorms and tornadoes. (Locals refer to the Ohio River Valley as "Tornado Alley.") Fall is often very warm, but nights can be chilly at almost any time of year. Although snowfall averages almost 14 inches per year statewide, its severity depends on location. In the southwestern section of the state, snow averages only 5 to 10 inches; that amount increases to 25 inches in the northeastern sections and as many as 40 inches can fall in the highest elevations each year.

AVG MONTHLY TEMPS (°F) & RAINFALL (IN)		
	Jackson	**Louisville**
Jan	31/3.9	33/3.4
Feb	33/3.7	36/3.2
Mar	41/4.6	45/4.7
Apr	53/4.0	57/4.1
May	62/3.5	66/4.2
June	69/3.8	74/3.6
July	73/4.9	78/4.1
Aug	72/3.6	77/3.3
Sept	66/3.1	70/3.4
Oct	55/2.1	58/2.6
Nov	43/3.2	47/3.5
Dec	34/3.5	37/3.5

WHAT TO PACK

The time of year and your destination govern what you should pack for a trip to Kentucky. Spring and fall usually require lightweight sweaters or jackets in the daytime and definitely in the evening. Summers can be very warm and humid, but cool evenings are not unusual. A heavy coat will be needed in winter, especially in the northern and mountainous regions.

For the most part, life in Kentucky is casual and you can pack accordingly. If you are planning to eat at a fancy restaurant or attend a cultural function in one of the cities, one nice dressy outfit should suffice.

TOURIST INFORMATION

For a copy of the *Official Kentucky Vacation Guide*, filled with information on attractions, resorts, campgrounds, marinas, golf courses, bed-and-breakfasts, and other accommodations, contact **Kentucky Travel**, Dept KVG, PO Box 2011, Frankfort, KY 40602 (tel toll free 800/225-TRIP). The **Commonwealth Data Center Web Server** maintains a Web page (http://www.state.ky.us) with general information about the state. To find out how to obtain tourist information for individual cities and parks in Kentucky, look under specific cities in the listings section of this book.

DRIVING RULES AND REGULATIONS

Drivers in Kentucky must be at least 16 years of age and have proof of automobile liability insurance. Kentucky has a mandatory seat belt law and all children 40 inches tall or less must be placed in a federally approved child restraint seat. Right turn on red is permitted unless otherwise posted. The speed limit is 65 mph on rural sections of interstates and most parkways; otherwise the speed on open highways is 55 mph.

RENTING A CAR

All the major car rental companies are represented in the larger cities. Visitors should make reservations as far in advance as possible, especially in the summer. The minimum age to rent a car varies by company. Always ask about special promotional deals offered by the company or by any credit card companies or clubs. Make sure whether your insurance or credit card coverage extends to rental cars. Major car rental firms in Kentucky include:

* **Alamo** (tel toll free 800/327-9633)
* **Avis** (tel 800/831-2847)
* **Budget** (tel 800/527-0700)
* **Dollar** (tel 800/800-4000)
* **Hertz** (tel 800/654-3131)
* **National** (tel 800/227-7368)
* **Thrifty** (tel 800/367-2277)

ESSENTIALS

Area Code: The eastern part of Kentucky (including Ashland and Lexington) uses the **606** area code, while the western portion (including Frankfort, Bowling Green, and Louisville) uses **502.**

Emergencies: 911 is used universally for summoning emergency help.

Liquor Laws: The legal age to drink in Kentucky is 21. Liquor laws are locally mandated and vary widely throughout the state. Liquor may be purchased at drug stores and retail liquor stores in 30 of the state's 120 counties and in 15 cities of the remaining 90 counties. It is sold in restaurants on Sunday according to local option.

Road Info: Call the Kentucky State Police (tel 606/x928-6421) for the latest information.

Smoking: There are no state-mandated smoking laws; any antismoking laws are on the local level. Many hotels, restaurants, and places of business voluntarily provide nonsmoking areas.

Taxes: The statewide sales tax is 6% and there are no additional local or county sales taxes.

Time Zones: Kentucky lies across two time zones. Most of north central and all of eastern Kentucky (including Lexington, Louisville, and Frankfort) are in the Eastern time zone; south central and all of western Kentucky (including Bowling Green and Paducah) are in the Central time zone. The entire state observes daylight saving time.

Best of the State

WHAT TO SEE AND DO

Below is a general overview of some of the top sights and attractions in Kentucky. To find out more detailed information, look under "Attractions" under individual cities in the listings portion of this book.

National Parks Kentucky's spectacular scenery makes the state a natural for national parks and recreation areas. The **Big South Fork National River and Recreation Area** straddles the Kentucky/Tennessee border for a total of more than 100,000 acres of fantastic natural geological formations bisected by the raging Big South Fork of the Cumberland River. With 20,305 acres of wilderness (80% of it without paved roads), **Cumberland Gap National Historical Park** is both the country's largest national historical park and a backcountry hiker's paradise. Within the park are overlooks, a Confederate fort, a pioneer settlement, hiking trails, and primitive campsites. (For information on **Mammoth Cave National Park,** see Natural Wonders.)

State Parks Kentucky has an outstanding system of 47 state parks. For a complete listing of parks, with a description of the facilities at each, request the brochure *Kentucky State Parks* by calling toll free 800/255-PARK. Among Kentucky's premier parks, **My Old Kentucky Home State Park,** US 31E/150 in Bardstown (tel 502/348-3502), is a rare jewel. Stephen Foster's famous song was inspired by his cousin's mansion, Federal Hill, which you can tour along with the formal gardens, carriage house, and smokehouse. *The Stephen Foster Story,* an outdoor musical with 50 Foster songs, is performed in the summer.

Natural Wonders Kentucky's diverse topography abounds with natural phenomena. **Mammoth Cave National Park** is the longest known cave system in the world. Named a World Heritage Site, the cave's 345 miles of explored passageways contain many types of unusual cave formations and several species of rare animal life. During the summer, 11 daily tours (lasting from 1¼ to 6½ hours) guide visitors past prehistoric artifacts and an 1812 saltpeter mining operation. South central Kentucky is riddled with caves. Among the others open to the public are **Hidden River Cave** and **Kentucky Caverns** in Horse Cave, **Crystal Onyx Cave** in Cave City, and **Diamond Caverns** in Park City.

Other wonders include huge **Reelfoot Lake,** a 13,000-acre depression created by the 1811 New Madrid earthquake. Visitors can step back 350 million years at the **Falls of the Ohio Fossil Beds** in Louisville. The world's largest exposed Devonian fossil bed was once at the bottom of an inland sea. Called the "Niagara of the South," **Cumberland Falls** (within Cumberland Falls State Resort Park, west of Corbin) is a 125-foot-wide curtain of roaring water that drops 68 feet into a gorge. **Yahoo Falls,** near Whitley City, drops 113 feet into a crystal-clear pool. A trail leads behind the falls under a massive rock roof. Natural Bridge State Resort Park is home to **Natural Bridge,** a 900-ton slab of ancient sandstone suspended across a mountainside. The craggy, untouched beauty of the largest canyon east of the

Mississippi is found in the **Breaks Interstate Park,** near Elkhorn City. The 5-mile-long and 1,600-foot-deep gorge, which sits astride the Kentucky/Virginia border, was formed by the Russell Fork River.

Manmade Wonders Man has never been content to rest on nature's laurels. A ceremonial site and trade center, the **Wickliffe Mounds,** northwest of Paducah at the confluence of the Mississippi and Ohio Rivers, were occupied from AD 800–1350. Several mounds are also preserved at **Central Park** in the Ashland/Greenup area. **Kentucky Lake** and **Lake Barkley,** connected by a canal, together form one of the largest manmade bodies of water in the country. Watch barges go through the huge 1,200-foot lock at the **Barkley Dam and Visitor Center,** near Cadiz.

Distilleries & Breweries Bourbon whiskey was first created in Kentucky and most of the world's supply is still produced in the state. At Bardstown's **Heaven Hill Distilleries,** the largest family-owned distillery in the country, guests can examine the bourbon-making process and watch the bottling operations of the Heaven Hill, Elijah Craig, and Evan Williams brands. In Frankfort, you can tour the **Leestown Company Ancient Age Distillery,** America's largest distillery. The famous Wild Turkey brand is made at the **Boulevard Distillery** in Lawrenceburg. The Samuels family has been making bourbon at the **Maker's Mark Distillery** in Loretto since 1953; it is the only operating distillery in the country that is a National Historic Landmark. Tours include the still house, warehouse, and bottling operation. At **Jim Beam's American Outpost** in Clermont, you can see the country's oldest moonshine still, an 1800s cooperage (barrel making) museum, 500 collector decanters, and a bourbon warehouse. Tour a microbrewery at Fort Mitchell's **Oldenberg Brewery** and see hundreds of items of beer memorabilia on display at the brewery's **American Museum of Brewing History and Arts.**

Family Favorites Families will enjoy most of the attractions listed under the other categories, but the following are special favorites. See baseball bats being made by taking the **Louisville Slugger Tour** at Hillerich and Bradsby in nearby Jeffersonville, IN. An on-site museum includes a bat used by Babe Ruth, among other treasures. **Kentucky Kingdom,** located at the Kentucky Fair and Exposition Center in Louisville, features "the world's most terrifying roller coaster" and a water theme park. The **Owensboro Area Museum of Science and History** displays exhibits on natural, cultural, and Native American history and features a discovery area and planetarium. The **Lexington Children's Museum** contains seven galleries and 90 hands-on exhibits.

Historic Sites Kentucky is home to two remaining villages founded in the early 1800s by a religious sect called the United Society of Believers in Christ's Second Appearing—better known as the Shakers because of the trembling they did during their devotional dancing. Innovative builders and farmers, the Shakers are credited with inventing such "modern" necessities as the clothespin, flat broom, circular saw, and water-repellent fabric. The most completely restored Shaker community in the country is **Shaker Village of Pleasant Hill.** The complex, which includes 30 original buildings surrounded by 20 miles of stone fences, features costumed interpreters who demonstrate traditional crafts and skills. The other village is **Shakertown at South Union,** 15 miles east of Russellville. Guests may tour its 1824 Centre House Museum, eat lunch at the **Shaker Tavern,** or stay in a bed-and-breakfast furnished with beautiful Shaker furniture.

Several sites in or near Hodgenville honor Abraham Lincoln, who was born here on February 12, 1809. The **Lincoln Museum,** on the downtown square, contains a dozen dioramas depicting scenes from his life, as well as an art collection and personal and Civil War memorabilia. Three miles south of town is the **Abraham Lincoln Birthplace National Historic Site,** where a traditional log cabin is enclosed in a granite memorial building. **Lincoln's Boyhood Home** at Knob Creek contains a reproduction of the log cabin where he lived. At the **Pate House,** Hawesville, 18-year-old Abraham Lincoln successfully defended himself for operating a ferry without a license. Judge Pate, who presided, was so impressed with Lincoln's defense, he suggested that the young man study law. In Lexington, you can visit the **Mary Todd Lincoln Home,** girlhood abode of Lincoln's wife, and the **Lincoln Homestead State Park** near Springfield features several sites significant to the lives of Lincoln's parents.

Relatively little attention is paid to Jefferson Davis, president of the Confederacy, who was also born in Kentucky. You can, however, ride to the top of the **Jefferson Davis Monument**—a 315-foot memorial obelisk honoring the Confederacy's only president, who was born near Hopkinsville. Among the homes of famous Kentuckians you can visit are: the **Hunt-Morgan House,** home of Confederate general John Hunt Morgan, in Lexington; **Ashland,** the home of Henry Clay, also in Lexington; and **Locust Grove,** the Louisville home of soldier-explorer George Rogers Clark.

Horse Attractions   Kentucky and thoroughbreds are synonymous. One of the most popular attractions in the state is the **Kentucky Horse Park** near Lexington. Two films—*Thou Shalt Fly Without Wings* and *All the King's Horses II*—provide a basic orientation to the history of horses in the state. Visitors can then take a walking tour of the working farm, see more than 40 breeds of horses performing in the show ring during the Parade of Breeds, or visit current and recent winners at the Hall of Champions. The collections at the fascinating International Museum of the Horse trace the history of the stately equine creature through the Horse in Sport gallery, the 500-piece Calumet Farm Trophy Collection, and an exhibit of horse-drawn vehicles. A variety of championship equestrian events, horse shows, and polo matches are held at the park.

Dioramas, life-size models, and multimedia presentations tell the story of Kentucky's own breed at the adjacent **American Saddle Horse Museum.** At the nearby **Kentucky Horse Center,** a working thoroughbred training operation, visitors can watch morning workouts and ask questions of trainers. Keeneland and The Red Mile, two race tracks in Lexington, offer tours at certain times of year, and a half-dozen companies around Lexington offer guided tours of surrounding horse farms.

In Louisville, the **Kentucky Derby Museum** features an exciting 360° multimedia show, hands-on displays, and racing-related memorabilia and art. Guests may visit resident thoroughbred Deputy Joe, then take a walking tour of Churchill Downs next door.

Museums   Examples of Cherokee culture are on display at the museum in the **Trail of Tears Commemorative Park,** on US 41S in western Kentucky on land used as a campground on the tribe's forced march to Oklahoma. The evolution of the 101st Airborne "Screaming Eagles" Division is showcased at the **Don F Pratt Museum** at Fort Campbell in Hopkinsville. Indoor exhibits trace the division's history while outdoor displays include World War II

cargo gliders, C-119 and C-47 aircraft, and helicopters. Personal effects that belonged to Gen George Patton as well as American and foreign armored combat vehicles, uniforms, and weapons are on display at Fort Knox's **Patton Museum of Cavalry and Armor.** The state's tobacco heritage is the focus of the **Western Kentucky Museum** in Mayfield, where you can inspect ledgers, stencils, sleds, a press, and other tobacco warehouse tools. Hands-on exhibits, electronic games, original Norman Rockwell artwork, scouting memorabilia, and a challenging obstacle course provide something for every age and interest at the **National Scouting Museum** in Murray. Changing exhibits of antique and contemporary quilts are displayed in three galleries at Paducah's **Museum of the American Quilter's Society.**

Spalding Hall, in Bardstown, houses two museums: the **Oscar Getz Museum of Whiskey History,** which contains a collection spanning 500 years from pre-colonial days to post-Prohibition including an authentic moonshine still; and the **Bardstown Historical Museum** where two hundred years of local history are exhibited. The incredible success story of the founder of Kentucky Fried Chicken is examined at the **Colonel Harlan Sanders Museum** in Louisville and the **Harlan Sanders Cafe and Museum** in Corbin. The avant-garde architecture of the **National Corvette Museum** in Bowling Green is as distinctive as the more than 50 unique, rare, and futuristic sports cars honored there.

Parks, Zoos & Gardens   Exotic animals from all over the world make Kentucky their home. Located on 73 acres of natural habitat, the **Louisville Zoo** is home to 1,600 animals representing 371 species. The zoo's arachnid exhibit is the only one of its kind in the country. Animals native to Kentucky are on display at the **Fish and Wildlife Game Farm,** near Frankfort. You'll think you've been transported to the Australian outback at **Kentucky Down Under** in Horse Cave, a wildlife refuge with kangaroos, emus, lorikeets, and other Australian animals, as well as aboriginal storytelling, demonstrations, and sheep-shearing.

The **Bernheim Arboretum and Research Forest** in Clermont is a parklike area with 18,000 plants. Fifteen of the 250 acres are devoted to ornamental gardens. Stroll through gardens, a conservatory, and wildflower meadows at **Broadmoor Gardens,** Irvington.

Train Excursions Fans of rail travel will think they've died and gone to heaven in Kentucky, the state offers such a variety of excursions from which to choose. New Haven's **Kentucky Railway Museum** conducts a 22-mile round trip through the valley between New Haven and Boston aboard a train pulled by a 1905 locomotive. Savor a gourmet meal as you travel on the **My Old Kentucky Home Dinner Train,** Bardstown. Relax and enjoy the 18-mile, two-hour roundtrip through the Clarks River Valley from Benton, aboard the **Hardin Southern Railroad's Nostalgia Train.** The historic **Kentucky Central Railway,** Paris, offers excursions to Carlisle in the summer and Maysville in October. A different way to enjoy the picturesque countryside of the Bluegrass is aboard the **Bluegrass Scenic Railroad** from Woodford County Park in Versailles. An exciting trip aboard the **Big South Fork Scenic Railway** follows an original coal-train route to the Blue Heron Mining Community.

EVENTS AND FESTIVALS

- **Hillbilly Days Spring Festival,** Pikeville. Antique cars, music, and re-creations of the feud between the Hatfields and the McCoys. Pikeville. Third weekend in April. Call 606/437-7331.
- **American Quilter's Society National Show,** Paducah. Hundreds of quilts and wall hangings, vendors, tours, cultural events. Late April. Call toll free 800/359-4775.
- **Kentucky Derby Festival,** Louisville. Kentucky Derby race, fireworks, basketball classic, balloon race, steamboat race. Late April through early May. Call toll free 800/928-FEST.
- **International Bar-B-Que Festival,** Owensboro. Chicken and burgoo, arts and crafts, bluegrass music. Mid-May. Call toll free 800/489-1131.
- **Summer Motion Festival,** Ashland. Tri-state fair and regatta featuring entertainment, arts and crafts, 10K race. July 4th weekend. Call 606/329-1007 or toll free 800/377-6249.
- **Great American Brass Band Festival,** Danville. Old-time brass band concert with national bands, hot-air balloon race, picnic. Mid-July. Call 606/236-7794 or toll free 800/755-0076.
- **Kentucky State Championship Old Time Fiddler's Contest,** Leitchfield. Also harmonicas, bluegrass banjo, flat top guitar, mandolin, jig dancing. Late July. Call 502/259-3578.
- **St Patrick's Irish Picnic and Homecoming,** McEwen. Homecoming of former residents and visitors, games, music, dancing, food. Late July. Call 615/582-3417.
- **Shelbyville Horse Show,** Shelbyville. Equine sporting competition, elegant lawn party, county fair. Early August. Call 502/633-7123.
- **Strassenfest,** Louisville. A celebration of the River City's German heritage, with lots of beer and brats and oompah music. Second weekend in August. Call 502/561-3440.
- **Kentucky Heartland Festival,** Elizabethtown. Parade, hot-air balloon race, fireworks, square dancing. Late August. Call 502/765-4334.
- **Historic Constitution Square Festival,** Danville. Arts and crafts, living history demonstrations. Mid-September. Call 606/236-5089.
- **World Chicken Festival,** London. Home of Colonel Sanders Original Restaurant and Museum celebrates with four days of entertainment, arts and crafts, parades, Chick-O-Lympics, Colonel Sanders Look-A-Like Contest, world's largest skillet. Late September. Call toll free 800/348-0095.
- **St James Court Art Fair,** Louisville. One of the largest craft fairs in the country, with over 700 booths and exhibitors from all over the world. First weekend in October. Call 502/635-1842.
- **Light Up Louisville/Dickens on Main St,** Louisville. Caroling, mulled cider, and Dickensian costumes, as the mayor turns on the city's Christmas lights in the Victorian cast-iron district downtown. Day after Thanksgiving. Call 502/568-7452.

SPECTATOR SPORTS

Auto & Motorcycle Racing Stock-car racing takes place at the **Louisville Motor Speedway** (tel 502/966-2277), **Central Park Raceway** in McHenry (tel 502/274-9455), and **Thunder Ridge Racing and Entertainment Complex** in Prestonsburg (tel toll free 800/941-7223). IHRA drag racing takes place at **Beech Bend Raceway Park** (tel 502/781-7634) in Bowling Green and at **River Cities Raceway Park** in Ashland (tel 606/928-3110). The AMA-sanctioned **Daniel Boone Motocross Park** in London (tel 606/877-1364) features racing May through November.

Baseball The **Louisville Redbirds** (tel 502/368-5120), the Triple-A farm team of the St Louis Cardinals, play at Cardinal Stadium at the state fairgrounds.

Basketball Kentucky's basketball fans are as enthusiastic as they come. You can see what the excitement is about at Rupp Arena in Lexington (tel 606/257-3838), which is home to the **University of Kentucky Wildcats;** intrastate rival **University of Louisville Cardinals** play at Freedom Hall at the state fairgrounds (tel 502/852-5151).

College Football Thought not as fiercely followed as basketball, the state's two major schools also have an active football rivalry. The U of K Wildcats play at Commonwealth Stadium in Lexington (tel 606/257-3838), while U of L plays at Freedom Hall (tel 502/852-5151).

Horse Racing The Kentucky Derby—the world's most famous horse race—has been run at **Churchill Downs** (tel 502/636-4400) on the first Saturday in May since 1875. The historic track hosts racing meets every spring and fall. Lexington boasts two tracks: **Keeneland** (tel toll free 800/456-3412), founded in 1936, is the scene of thoroughbred racing March through November; **The Red Mile** (tel 606/255-0752), established in 1875—the same year as the Kentucky Derby—has been the site of more world-record finish times than any other harness race course. There's a Grand Circuit meet in the fall and you can watch morning workouts all year. The pounding of horses' hoofs has replaced the crack of gunshots at **Dueling Grounds Race Course,** Franklin (tel 502/586-7778). Once the spot of many duels, the course offers live thoroughbred racing every September. Live thoroughbred racing takes place at **Ellis Park** in Henderson (tel 812/425-1456); **Players Bluegrass Downs** in Paducah (tel 502/444-7117); and at **Turfway Park** in Florence (tel toll free 800/733-0200). Harness racing is on tap July through mid-September at the **Thunder Ridge Racing and Entertainment Complex,** Prestonsburg (tel toll free 800/941-7223).

ACTIVITIES A TO Z

Bicycling Varied topography and a temperate climate team up to make Kentucky a great site for cycling adventures. More than 600 miles of the national **TransAmerica Trail** winds through the state. For more information on the trail, contact **Adventure Cycling Association,** PO Box 8308, Missoula, MT 59807 (tel 406/721-1776). For a free *Kentucky Bicycle Tours* pamphlet with six routes and other information, contact **Kentucky Travel** (tel toll free 800/255-TRIP).

Bird Watching The northwestern corner of Kentucky, where the Green River flows into the Ohio, is on one of the world's most significant migratory bird routes. More than 200 of the state's 300 species of birds frequent this area. The marshes of southwestern Kentucky provide excellent breeding places for waterfowl such as egrets, heron, and cormorants. For more information, contact the Louisville chapter of the Audubon Society (tel 502/339-9891).

Boating Kentucky's 10 major lakes and 1,100 miles of navigable rivers provide countless opportunities for every kind of boating. Boat rentals are available at marinas across the state. The 22-mile Little River Canoe Trail between Cadiz and Land Between the Lakes is an easy run. **Canoe Kentucky** (tel toll free 800/K-CANOE-1) offers guided canoe and raft trips at several locations throughout Kentucky.

Fishing The swift mountain streams, wide rivers, and natural and manmade lakes of Kentucky provide superb fishing opportunities for more than 100 species of fish. The muskellunge or muskie (the largest member of the pike family) is found in profusion, even though it is generally considered to be a Great Lakes fish. For a daily update on conditions on Kentucky Lake, considered the state's premier crappie lake, call 502/527-5952; for Lake Cumberland, call 606/679-5655. The **Kentucky Department of Fish and Wildlife Resources,** #1 Game Farm Rd, Frankfort, KY 40601 (tel 502/564-4336), can provide a list of licensed guides and a copy of the *Kentucky Fish* booklet.

Hiking With 1,500 miles of marked and maintained trails, Kentucky offers hikers experiences from casual strolls to strenuous wilderness backpacking adventures. Two major trails—the **Sheltowee Trace National Recreation Trail** and the **Jenny Wiley National Recreation Trail**—provide scenic routes through the forested highlands of eastern Kentucky. Sheltowee is marked for 257 miles through deep canyons, narrow ridge tops, and rimrock cliffs in the Daniel Boone National Forest and links up with the Jenny Wiley Trail and several other major trail systems. The Jenny Wiley Trail runs 185 miles from Kentucky's northeastern tip to the Jenny Wiley State Resort Park in Petersburg. There are two connector trails off the Jenny Wiley—the 25-mile Tygart Trail and the 9-mile Simon Kenton Trail. The peninsula between Kentucky Lake and Lake

Barkley, now known as the Land Between the Lakes, was developed by the Tennessee Valley Authority as a national recreation area. It contains 200 miles of heavily wooded trails including the 65-mile North-South Trail. The Little Shepherd Trail winds 38 miles through the Kentenia State Forest near Harlan; the Red River Gorge National Recreation Trail (also in eastern Kentucky) is a 36-mile system of loop trails leading to attractions within the gorge. For a complete list of trails in the state, request the *Kentucky Trails Guide* from **Kentucky State Parks** (tel toll free 800/255-PARK).

Horseback Riding   Kentucky is after all the Horse Capital of the World, so what better or more natural place could there be for horseback riding? The state offers a variety of options from pony rides to overnight trail rides. For a complete list of bridle trails in the state parks, request *Kentucky Trails Guide* from **Kentucky State Parks** (tel toll free 800/255-PARK). Wranglers Campground in the Land Between the Lakes has 23 miles of designated horseback riding trails. Visitors to Louisville can check out Iroquois Park, a magnificent 739-acre urban park with miles of riding trails.

Skiing   Although the mountainous areas of Kentucky experience frequent—though rarely heavy—snowfalls, the state has only one downhill ski area. **General Butler State Park** in Carrollton (tel toll free 800/456-3284 for the snow conditions; tel 502/732-4231 for other information) is the home of Ski Butler, which sports 23 acres of trails, three chair lifts, and a ski school. Cross-country ski trails are available at Daniel Boone National Forest.

White-Water Rafting   Nine of the state's most scenic and undeveloped river sections have been designated as Kentucky Wild Rivers. Among them are the Rockcastle, Red River, Bad Branch, Martins Fork, Big South Fork (considered to be among the Top 10 white-water rivers in the country), Rock Creek, Little South Fork, and the Green. To find out more about Kentucky's Wild Rivers, contact the **Kentucky Division of Water,** 14 Reilly Rd, Frankfort, KY 40601 (tel 502/564-3410). The Russell Fork River, near Elkhorn City, drops 350 feet as it smashes through the chasm in a succession of Class IV falls, rapids, pools, and twists.

SELECTED PARKS & RECREATION AREAS

- **Mammoth Cave National Park,** 8 mi W of I-65, Mammoth Cave, KY 42259 (tel 502/758-2251)
- **Cumberland Gap National Historical Park,** Box 1848, Middlesboro, KY 40965 (tel 606/248-2817)
- **Abraham Lincoln Birthplace National Historic Site,** 2995 Lincoln Farm Rd, Hodgenville, KY 42728 (tel 502/358-3874)
- **Ben Hawes State Park,** 400 Booth Field Rd, Owensboro, KY 42301 (tel 502/684-9808)
- **Big Bone Lick State Park,** 3380 Beaver Rd, Union, KY 41091-9627 (tel 606/384-3522)
- **Boone Station State Park,** off KY 418, Lexington, KY (tel 502/564-2172)
- **Buckhorn Lake State Resort Park,** KY 15/28W, Buckhorn, KY 41721-9602 (tel 606/398-7510)
- **Carter Caves State Resort Park,** KY 182N, Olive Hill, KY 41164-9032 (tel 606/286-4411)
- **Columbus-Belmont State Park,** KY 80, Columbus, KY 42032-0008 (tel 502/677-2327)
- **Dale Hollow Lake State Park,** KY 90/449, Burkesville, KY 42714-9728 (tel 502/433-7431)
- **E P "Tom" Sawyer State Park,** 3000 Freys Hill Rd, Louisville, KY 40241-2172 (tel 502/426-8950)
- **General Burnside State Park,** US 27, Burnside, KY 42519-0488 (tel 606/561-4104)
- **John James Audubon State Park,** US 41N, Henderson, KY 42420-0576 (tel 502/827-1893)
- **Kentucky Dam Village State Resort Park,** US 62E, Gilbertsville, KY 42044-0069 (tel 502/362-4271)
- **Lake Cumberland State Resort Park,** US 127S, Jamestown, KY 42629-7801 (tel 502/343-3111)
- **Levi Jackson Wilderness Road State Park,** 998 Levi Jackson Mill Rd, London, KY 40741-8944 (tel 606/878-8000)
- **Old Fort Harrod State Park,** US 68, Harrodsburg, KY 40330-0156 (tel 606/734-3314)
- **Pennyrile Forest State Resort Park,** KY 109S, Dawson Springs, KY 42408-9212 (tel 502/797-3421)
- **Rough River Dam State Resort Park,** KY 79N, Falls of Rough, KY 40119-9701 (tel 502/257-2311)

THE FRONTIER TRAIL

Start	Cumberland Gap National Historical Park
Finish	Lexington
Distance	170 miles
Time	2–3 days
Highlights	Wilderness, frontier trails, scenic overlooks, pioneer cabins, state parks, historic forts, museums, living history villages, Kentucky crafts, natural bridges, horse country

One of the most influential figures in Kentucky history and legend was Daniel Boone—woodsman, explorer, settler, tavern keeper, and statesman. Although Boone was born in Pennsylvania, married and began his family in North Carolina, and died in Missouri, he is forever associated with Kentucky because he opened the area to white settlers.

For the first 150 years that settlers had been in North America, the wilderness surrounding the forbidding Cumberland Mountains (part of the Allegheny mountain chain) had prevented colonists from venturing into the region that became Kentucky. Although a gap in the mountains was used by Native Americans, and a European explorer was known to have used it as early as in 1674, the exact location of the gap was not documented until 1750; many would-be explorers had to turn back in disappointment because they couldn't find the pass. Intrepid adventurer Daniel Boone, accompanied by John Finley, found the Cumberland Gap in 1769; six years later, Boone and a group of woodsmen marked two trails through the pass. In only eight short years, 12,000 settlers entered Kentucky through the Cumberland Gap. By the time Kentucky was admitted to the Union, 100,000 settlers had passed through the breach. Other, easier routes to the west caused traffic through the gap to decline after 1830.

Although Boone staked many claims in the Kentucky Territory, by 1788 all of them had been lost in legal battles. Like so many pioneers, Boone kept going west—this time to Missouri, where he died in 1820.

This scenic driving tour traces routes once traveled by Daniel Boone, beginning in the southeastern corner of the state at the all-important Cumberland Gap and continuing northward.

For additional information on lodgings, dining, and attractions in the region covered by the tour, look under specific cities in the listings portion of this chapter.

US 25E (Cumberland Gap Parkway), US 58, and US 63 give access to the first stop:

1. **Cumberland Gap National Historical Park,** where Kentucky, Tennessee, and Virginia meet. With more than 20,000 acres of rugged wilderness, Cumberland Gap National Historical Park is the largest national historical park in the country and actually straddles the three states, although most of it is in Tennessee. Predominantly rough back-country, the park contains relatively few paved roads. Begin at the **Visitor Center,** where you can watch an orientation program and explore both the museum and craft sales area. From **Pinnacle Overlook,** you can see into three states and perceive why the gap was so important to westward expansion. **Fort McCook** was built by Confederate troops to guard the vital passage through the mountains.

   Seventy miles of hiking trails provide every experience from a short stroll to a strenuous overnight backpacking trek. The rugged but scenic 21-mile **Ridge Trail** runs the length of the park and passes by the restored Appalachian community at **Hensley Settlement.** Characterized by log cabins enclosed by split-rail fences, the settlement was home to a dozen farms and over a hundred people. The park service has restored three of the farmsteads, where historical interpreters demonstrate many techniques used by the pioneers. Three-hour shuttle tours are available in the summer.

   Within the immediate area of the park are the **Falls Mountain Craft Center** (on KY 90) and **Cumberland Falls State Resort Park,** 7351 KY 90, which offers a lodge, cottages, camping, a museum, nature center, tennis, horseback riding, and more.

   Take US 25E for 4 miles to:

2. **Middlesboro,** established in 1889 and home of the country's oldest continuously operated nine-hole golf course. Middlesboro's historic district resembles that of its namesake: Middlesborough, England. At the **Middlesboro/Bell County Airport,** on Cumberland Ave, you can watch the restoration of the World War II P-38 fighter plane *Glacier Girl,* one of those recovered in 1992 from under 268 feet of ice in Greenland.

   If your timing is such that you can spend the

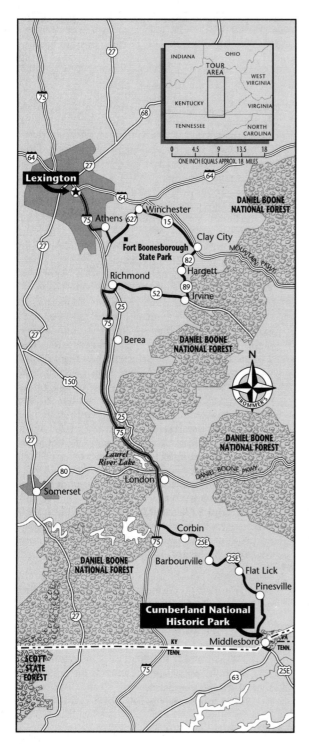

night, try the moderately priced **Ridge Runner,** 208 Arthur Heights (tel 606/248-4299), an 1894 Victorian inn nestled in the Cumberland Mountains.

Continue for 11 miles on US 25E to:

3. **Pineville,** first settled in 1781, and originally called Cumberland Ford because it was the best place for Daniel Boone and other frontiersmen to ford the Cumberland River. The state nature preserve in **Pine Mountain State Resort Park,** 1050 State Park Rd, is the site of the **Rock Hotel,** actually a large sandstone shelter used by prehistoric Native Americans. In addition, the park features a lodge, cottages, camping, a golf course, miniature golf, and hiking trails. Four miles from the resort is **Chained Rock,** two large jutting promontories connected by a "chain" of smaller rocks. From Chained Rock you can gaze on spectacular panoramas of the surrounding mountains.

Proceed 9 miles on US 25E to:

4. **Flat Lick,** where game animals used to congregate at the numerous salt licks. Located at the junction of a pioneer trail and the Warrior's Path, it was one of Kentucky's earliest settlements. Hike the nature trail in the **Daniel Boone Trail Memorial Park** on Evergreen Road. The **Daniel Boone Festival,** held in the park the first week in October each year, offers myriad activities; one of the most popular is the Husband Calling Contest.

Follow US 25E for 10 miles, to reach the next stop:

5. **Barbourville,** where you can see a replica of Kentucky's first pioneer house at the **Dr Thomas Walker State Historic Site,** KY 459. Although Boone gets almost all the credit, Dr Walker was actually the first frontiersman in Kentucky, leading a 1750 expedition through the Cumberland Gap. Exhibits at the **Knox Historical Museum,** Daniel Boone Dr, highlight area heritage.

Then, take US 25E for 18 miles to:

6. **Corbin,** former home of Colonel Harlan Sanders of Kentucky Fried Chicken fame. It was at the Colonel's cafe that he developed his "secret recipe" in the 1940s. You can dine in the restaurant at the **Harlan Sanders Cafe and Museum** on US 25, tour the kitchen, and peruse the memorabilia. Crafts demonstrations are given most days in the cabins at the **Kentucky Communities Crafts Village,** US 25E, where the finished products are for sale.

Stay on US 25E for 12 miles to the next stop:

7. **London.** Both of Daniel Boone's original roads pass near here: the Wilderness Road (which brought

more than 200,000 settlers into Kentucky) and Boone's Trace (which runs from Cumberland Gap to the Kentucky River). Both trails run through **Levi Jackson Wilderness Road State Park,** 998 Levi Jackson Mill Rd. This was the site of McNitt's Defeat, where 20 settlers were killed by Cherokee warriors in 1786. Discover colorful pioneer life in the park's **Mountain Life Museum.** Also in the park is **McHargue's Mill,** a working gristmill surrounded by the world's largest collection of millstones.

Nearby is **Mays Log Cabin Craft Village and Museum,** KY 229, a restored collection of 18th-century log cabins, a blacksmith shop, a loomhouse, and a woodworking shop where costumed interpreters give demonstrations of pioneer skills and crafts.

When you've soaked up your quota of history, you may want to look into the London area's recreational activities. Houseboating and fishing are renowned on the waters of 5,600-acre **Laurel River Lake**—one of Kentucky's finest recreational lakes—and **Wood Creek Lake.** The **Rockcastle River** offers challenges for canoeing, rafting, and kayaking enthusiasts; while hikers can get plenty of exercise on the Sheltowee Trace National Recreation Trail and the Jenny Wiley National Recreation Trail in nearby **Daniel Boone National Forest.** The 672,000-acre forest, which is home to more than 100 species of birds, 46 kinds of mammals, and 67 types of amphibians and reptiles, is also a popular site for camping, mountain biking, cross-country skiing, horseback riding, boating, fishing, and white-water rafting.

Continue on US 25 for 38 miles (or use I-75) to:

8. **Berea,** home of Berea College and considered a center for folk arts and crafts in Kentucky. Following a tradition that began in the late 1800s, many professional craftspeople and artists are still drawn to the town. Begin at the visitors center located in the **L&N Railroad Depot,** 201 N Broadway in Old Town Berea, for information and advice about touring the area.

Next you can tour the college, founded in 1855 as the South's first interracial institution of higher learning. Berea maintains its commitment to accessible education by making college affordable for all; students perform work on campus in exchange for their tuition. Students lead tours of the campus and their crafts are sold at the **Log House Sales Room.** The school's **Appalachian Museum,** Jackson St, features exhibits and audiovisuals focusing on Appalachian history and culture. On the loomhouse tour at **Churchill Weavers,** Lorraine Court,

Berea's first noncollege industry, visitors can watch every step in the process from warping to weaving.

Take a Break

The best Kentucky gourmet fare is served at the **Boone Tavern,** Main St in Berea (tel 606/986-9358). Among the more traditional menu items are plantation ham with raisin sauce and grits, prime rib with Yorkshire pudding, and roast Kentucky turkey with dressing and gravy. More unusual dishes include chicken flakes in a potato bird's nest or loin chop rolled in Parmesan cheese. A member of the National Trust for Historic Preservation's Historic Hotels of America. Entrees are $10 to $15.

Proceed north 18 miles on US 25 to:

9. **Richmond,** the birthplace of scout Kit Carson and home of abolitionist Cassius Marcellus Clay. At **White Hall State Historic Site,** 500 White Hall Shrine Rd, you'll learn more about the man who was Abraham Lincoln's friend, a newspaper publisher, and Minister to Russia. Clay's 44-room Italianate mansion was built in 1799; indoor plumbing and central heating were added in the 1860s. Richmond's other noteworthy sites include the **Richmond Area Arts Center** (located in an 1887 church on Lancaster); Eastern Kentucky University's **Hummel Planetarium** (the 11th-largest planetarium in the country); and **Bybee Pottery,** KY 52 (the oldest pottery studio west of the Alleghenies).

Travel east on KY 52 to Irvine, turn north on KY 89 to Harget, then east on KY 82. It is 21 miles to:

10. **Clay City,** another site on the ancient Warrior's Path. Pilot Knob, a 730-foot protuberance in the **Pilot Knob State Nature Preserve,** off KY 15 on Brush Creek Rd, is thought to be the spot from which Daniel Boone first saw the Bluegrass region. In the **Red River Historical Museum,** Main St, artifacts from the region's iron, logging, and railroad industries are exhibited. Nearby are the 80 natural arches in the **Red River Gorge Geological Area.**

Next, follow KY 15 west for 19 miles to:

11. **Winchester,** where the 1855 courthouse is the repository of many important Daniel Boone and Henry Clay papers. Begin by stopping at the **Visitor Center** at 2 S Maple. Winchester's Main Street is one of the few intact 19th-century commercial

streets in Kentucky. Among the significant buildings are the **Winchester Opera House,** built in 1887 and now an antique mall and tearoom, and the newly renovated 1925 **Leeds Theater,** now a performing arts center. **Holly Rood Clark Mansion,** on S Burns, was the home of the state's 12th governor, James Clark. Watch the bottling line in operation at the **Ale-8-One Bottling Company,** a manufacturer of ginger ale located on Carol Rd.

Take KY 627 to the Old Stone Church Rd to see the **Old Stone Meeting House,** possibly the oldest active church west of the Alleghenies. Established in 1784, the present building was erected in 1793; Daniel Boone's family attended services there.

Continue south for 10 miles on KY 627 to:

12. **Fort Boonesborough State Park,** 4375 Boonesborough Rd, the site Daniel Boone chose for Kentucky's first fortified settlement in 1755. By that summer the fort had grown to 26 cabins and four blockhouses, and in 1779 it became the first chartered town in Kentucky. Today, costumed artisans demonstrate pioneer crafts and skills at the replicated fort and an on-site museum offers a video presentation depicting the saga of Daniel Boone and the fort. In addition, the park offers camping, water activities, miniature golf, and hiking.

Take KY 418 north 5 miles to:

13. **Athens,** first called Cross Plains because of its location at the crossing of two buffalo trails. Daniel Boone established a settlement here in 1779 after Fort Boonesborough became too crowded for him. Several years later he, one of his sons, and a nephew helped defend Bryan's Station from attack by Native Americans. The son and nephew were killed and are buried at Boone's Station, as are two of Boone's brothers and a sister-in-law. The grave sites are commemorated at **Boone Station State Historic Site,** off KY 418.

Continue for a few miles more on KY 418 to US 25, then on into:

14. **Lexington,** the premier city in the Bluegrass region. Founded in 1775, by 1820 Lexington was so wealthy and cultured it was known as the Athens of the West. Centerpiece of **Waveland State Historic Site,** 225 Higbee Mill Rd, is the gracious Greek Revival mansion built in 1847 by Joseph Bryan, a grandnephew of Boone's. The property was surveyed by Boone himself for his nephew Daniel Boone Bryan in 1779 and the first dwelling on the grounds was a small stone house. Tours include the mansion, servants' quarters, smokehouse, and icehouse.

While in Lexington, you'll probably want to see some of the city's many horse-related sites. Brochures for self-guided walking or driving tours of the surrounding horse farms are available at the **Visitor Center,** 301 E Vine. The **Kentucky Horse Park,** on 1-75 at the northern edge of town, is one of the state's most popular attractions. The two orientation films—*Thou Shalt Fly Without Wings* and *All the King's Horses*—explain Kentucky's love affair with the horse. Guests can then take a walking tour of the on-site horse farm, see more than 40 breeds of horses during the Parade of Breeds, or visit current and recent race winners at the Hall of Champions. The collections at the fascinating **International Museum of the Horse** trace equine history through the Horse in Sport gallery, the 500-piece Calumet Farm Trophy Display, and a collection of horse-drawn vehicles. Dioramas, life-size models, and multimedia presentations tell the story of Kentucky's own breed at the adjacent **American Saddle Horse Museum.** During the year, a variety of championship equestrian events, horse shows, and polo matches are held at the park.

At the nearby **Kentucky Horse Center,** 3380 Paris Pike, you can watch the horses during their morning workout and ask trainers any questions you may have. You can also watch morning workouts, tour the facilities, or take in a thoroughbred flat race at **Keeneland,** US 60/Versailles Rd. **The Red Mile,** off S Broadway, a harness racing track, was founded in 1875—the same year as the Kentucky Derby. The Red Mile has seen more world-record harness racing times than any other course.

From Lexington, I-64 will take you west to Frankfort and Louisville or east to Ashland and into West Virginia, while I-75 heads south toward Knoxville and north to Cincinnati, OH.

Kentucky Listings

Ashland

This Ohio River city is home to the Ashland Oil Company, the largest corporation in the state. It was settled by Scotch-Irish in 1786 at Poage's Landing, the site of an ancient Native American village. **Information:** Chamber of Commerce of Boyd & Greenup Counties, 207 15th St, PO Box 830, Ashland, 41105 (tel 606/324-5111).

HOTEL 🏨

≡≡≡ Ashland Plaza Hotel

15th St and Winchester, 41101; tel 606/329-0055 or toll free 800/346-6133; fax 606/325-4513. Exit 185 off I-64. Downtown hotel popular with business travelers and people visiting the city's historic district. **Rooms:** 157 rms and stes. Executive level. CI 3pm/CO noon. Nonsmoking rms avail. Rooms offer excellent views of the surrounding area. **Amenities:** 🛎 ♨ A/C, cable TV w/movies, dataport, voice mail. Some units w/terraces. **Services:** ✕ ⬛ VP 🛺 ⬛ ↩ Babysitting. Friendly, attentive service. **Facilities:** 🏋 500 ⚹ 1 restaurant, 1 bar (w/entertainment), games rm. **Rates:** $76 S; $86 D; $145–$240 ste. Extra person $6. Children under age 12 stay free. Parking: Outdoor, free. AE, CB, DC, DISC, MC, V.

MOTEL

≡ Colonial Inn

1835 Winchester, 41101; tel 606/325-4747. Slightly run-down downtown motel. For overnights only. **Rooms:** 77 rms and effic. CI open/CO noon. Nonsmoking rms avail. No-frills rooms need some maintenance. **Amenities:** 🛎 A/C, cable TV. **Services:** ✕ ⬛ ↩ 🐾 **Facilities:** 1 restaurant (bkfst and lunch only), 1 bar. **Rates:** $26–$28 S; $32–$42 D; $90–$150 effic. Extra person $5. Children under age 12 stay free. Parking: Outdoor, free. AE, DC, DISC, MC, V.

Bardstown

Founded in 1775. Its historic downtown sites include Old Talbott Tavern (the oldest western stagecoach stop in America). Composer Stephen Foster spent summers here, and wrote "My Old Kentucky Home" (the state's anthem) about Federal Hill, a house just east of town. Today, Bardstown is the center of the state's distilling industry; Loretto (located 10 mi S of Bardstown) is the site of famous Maker's Mark Distillery, where sour-mash whiskey has been made since 1840. **Information:** Bardstown–Nelson County Visitors Bureau, 107 E Stephen Foster Ave, PO Box 867, Bardstown, 40004 (tel 502/348-4877).

MOTELS 🏨

≡≡≡ Best Western General Nelson Inn

411 W Stephen Foster Ave, 40004; tel 502/348-3977 or toll free 800/225-3977; fax 502/348-7596. Off US 62. Offers well-maintained rooms. Located in the historic district. **Rooms:** 52 rms and effic. CI 4pm/CO noon. Nonsmoking rms avail. **Amenities:** 🛎 A/C, cable TV, dataport. King rooms have refrigerators and microwaves. **Services:** 🛺 ⬛ ↩ **Facilities:** 🏋 ⚹ Washer/dryer. **Rates:** Peak (June–Sept 15) $45–$60 S or D; $55–$70 effic. Extra person $5. Children under age 12 stay free. Min stay special events. Lower rates off-season. Parking: Outdoor, free. AE, CB, DC, DISC, MC, V.

≡≡≡ Hampton Inn

985 Chambers Blvd, 40004; tel 502/349-1000 or toll free 800/HAMPTON; fax 502/349-1191. Off KY 245. Attractive, yet fairly standard, rooms. Close to shopping areas and restaurants. **Rooms:** 61 rms. CI 2pm/CO noon. Nonsmoking rms avail. Hospitality suite for meetings or celebrations. **Amenities:** 🛎 ♨ 📺 ☕ A/C, cable TV. **Services:** ⬛ ↩ 🐾 **Facilities:** 🏋 🍴 30 ⚹ Indoor pool. **Rates (CP):** Peak (June–Oct) $56 S; $62 D. Children under age 18 stay free. Lower rates off-season. Parking: Outdoor, free. AE, CB, DC, DISC, MC, V.

≡≡≡ Holiday Inn

1475 New Haven Rd, PO Box 520, 40004; tel 502/348-9253 or toll free 800/348-9253; fax 502/348-5478. Off Bluegrass Pkwy at exit 21. Standard motel with a very helpful staff. Located 1½ miles from historic downtown area. **Rooms:** 102 rms. CI 2pm/CO 11am. Nonsmoking rms avail. **Amenities:** 🛎 ♨ A/C, satel TV w/movies. Refrigerators and microwaves in some rooms. **Services:** ✕ 🛺 ⬛ ↩ 🐾 **Facilities:** 🏋 ▶9 🍴 390 ⚹ 1 restaurant, 1 bar (w/entertainment), playground,

155

washer/dryer. Golf driving range as well as putting course. **Rates:** Peak (June–Sept) $65 S or D. Extra person $5. Children under age 18 stay free. Min stay special events. Lower rates off-season. AP and MAP rates avail. Parking: Outdoor, free. AE, CB, DC, DISC, JCB, MC, V.

≣≣ Old Bardstown Inn
510 E Stephen Foster Ave, 40004; tel 502/349-0776 or toll free 800/894-1601. on US 150. Located across the street from "My Old Kentucky Home," the house that inspired Stephen Foster's ballad. **Rooms:** 34 rms. CI 2pm/CO 11am. Nonsmoking rms avail. **Amenities:** 🛏 A/C, cable TV. **Services:** 🛎 🐾 Helpful staff is knowledgeable about area attractions. **Facilities:** 🏋 ᕯ **Rates:** Peak (Apr–Oct) $36 S; $40 D. Extra person $5. Children under age 18 stay free. Lower rates off-season. Parking: Outdoor, free. AE, MC, V.

≣≣ Ramada Inn
523 N 3rd St, 40004; tel 502/349-0363 or toll free 800/2-RAMADA; fax 502/348-7109. Standard motel featuring very spacious rooms. **Rooms:** 40 rms. CI open/CO noon. Nonsmoking rms avail. **Amenities:** 🛏 ᕯ A/C, cable TV. **Services:** 🚗 🛎 🐾 Carriage rides can be arranged. Free local phone calls. **Facilities:** 🏋 ᕯ Whirlpool. **Rates (CP):** Peak (June 1–Sept 3) $40–$55 S; $50–$65 D. Extra person $5. Children under age 18 stay free. Lower rates off-season. Parking: Outdoor, free. AE, CB, DC, DISC, MC, V.

RESTAURANTS 🍴

Stephen Foster Restaurant
503 W Stephen Foster Ave; tel 502/348-5076. Off US 62. **Regional American.** A casual restaurant located in the historic district of the city with a menu featuring regional Kentucky fare. Buffets offer a large selection of choices. **FYI:** Reservations recommended. Children's menu. No liquor license. **Open:** Peak (Apr–Oct) Mon–Thurs 6:30am–9pm, Fri–Sun 6:30am–10pm. **Prices:** Prix fixe $7. No CC. 👪

★ Talbott Tavern
107 W Stephen Foster Ave; tel 502/348-3494. **Regional American.** Located downtown, on the square. Established in 1779, the tavern offers regional favorites such as country ham, steak, and chicken in a historical setting that makes for a unique dining experience. **FYI:** Reservations not accepted. Blues/country music/rock. Children's menu. **Open:** Peak (June–Aug) Sun–Fri 11am–9pm, Sat 11am–10pm. **Prices:** Main courses $10–$15. MC, V. 🍴 ᕯ

ATTRACTIONS 📷

My Old Kentucky Home State Park
501 E Stephen Foster Ave; tel 502/348-3502 or toll free 800/323-7803. Park honoring Federal Hill, the graceful 1818 mansion that inspired Stephen Foster to write "My Old Kentucky Home"(now Kentucky's official state song). Guides

in antebellum dress lead tours through the home, which is much as it was in the 1850s. Tours are given 8:30am–6:15pm June–Labor Day; 9am–4:45pm the rest of the year.

Besides the house, the 235-acre park also includes a 39-site campground, 18-hole golf course, and picnic area. One of the South's most famous outdoor dramas, **The Stephen Foster Story,** is performed here June to September. For ticket information, call toll free 800/626-1563. **Open:** June–Aug, daily 8:30am–6:15pm; Sept–May, daily 9am–4:45pm. Closed some hols. **$$**

St Joseph Proto-Cathedral
310 W Stephen Foster Ave; tel 502/348-3126. St Joseph's, built in 1816, was the first Roman Catholic cathedral west of the Alleghenies. It now contains an impressive art collection, including paintings presented to the church by King Louis-Phillipe of France and Pope Leo XII. Guides are available May–October; formal tours given by reservation only November–April. **Open:** May–Oct, Mon–Fri 9am–5pm, Sat 9am–3pm, Sun 1–5pm. **Free**

Oscar Getz Museum of Whiskey History
114 N 5th St; tel 502/348-2999. A unique museum housing a diverse collection of rare documents and artifacts concerning the American whiskey industry from precolonial days to the present. Exhibits include a copy of Abraham Lincoln's liquor license (he operated a tavern in Illinois in the 1830s), an authentic moonshine still, a room with over 200 antique whiskey bottles and jugs, and a display on temperance crusader Carry Nation (a Kentucky native). The building also houses the **Bardstown Historical Museum,** featuring Native American relics, Lincoln memorabilia, and Civil War artifacts. Free guided tours are offered at both museums. **Open:** May–Oct, Mon–Sat 9am–5pm, Sun 1–5pm; Nov–Apr, Tues–Sat 10am–4pm, Sun 1–4pm. Closed some hols. **Free**

Maker's Mark Distillery
Star Hill Farm, 3350 Burks Spring Rd, Loretto; tel 502/865-2099. Located 15 mi S of Bardstown. Maker's Mark is the only continuously operating distillery in the United States designated as a National Historical Landmark. Walking tours of the beautifully restored buildings allow visitors to see the bourbon being made and bottled, then sealed with red wax, Maker's Mark signature color. **Open:** Tours, Mon–Sat 10:30 and 11:30am, 12:30, 1:30, 2:30 and 3:30pm. Closed some hols. **Free**

Berea

Perched at the edge of the Appalachian foothills, Berea is the center of the state's folk arts and crafts movement and has had a national reputation as home and workplace for craftspeople and artists since the late 1800s. There are more than 50 shops and studios in town today. Site of Berea College, founded in 1855 as the first interracial college in the South. **Information:** Berea Chamber of Commerce, 105 Boone St, PO Box 318, Berea, 40403 (tel 606/986-9760).

HOTEL 🏨

≡≡≡ Boone Tavern Hotel of Berea College
CPO 2345 Main at Prospect, 40404; tel 606/986-9358 or toll free 800/366-9358; fax 606/986-7711. Jct US 25 and 21. Historic hotel, established in 1909 and now owned and operated by Berea College. Elegant lobby area allows guests to relax and enjoy Southern hospitality. **Rooms:** 59 rms. CI 2pm/CO noon. No smoking. Furnishings handcrafted by students at Berea College. **Amenities:** 🛎 A/C, cable TV. **Services:** ✕ 🍽 🐾 **Facilities:** 🛏 ⅙ 1 restaurant (*see* "Restaurants" below). **Rates:** $57–$76 S; $52–$97 D. Extra person $10. Children under age 12 stay free. Parking: Outdoor, free. AE, DC, DISC, MC, V.

RESTAURANT 🍴

♥★ Dining Room
In Boone Tavern Hotel, CPO 2345 Main St; tel 606/986-9358. Jct US 25 and 21. **Regional American.** Established in 1909 and staffed by students at nearby Berea College (even the furnishings were handmade by Berea students), this dining hall offers the perfect blend of elegance and down-home Southern hospitality. Menu selections change regularly, but usually focus on simple Kentucky-style meat and vegetables, and specialties such as spoonbread and cured country ham. **FYI:** Reservations recommended. Children's menu. Jacket required. No liquor license. No smoking. **Open:** Breakfast daily 7–9am; lunch Mon–Sat 11:30am–1:30pm, Sun noon–2pm; dinner daily 6–7:30pm. **Prices:** Main courses $10–$18. AE, DC, DISC, MC, V. ◼ ⅙

ATTRACTIONS 📷

Berea College Museum
103 Jackson St; tel 606/986-9341. Exhibits and multimedia presentations on the rich history and culture of Appalachia, including crafts, farm implements, baskets, clothing, and other household goods. Special attention is paid to the fascinating history of Berea College itself: its role as the first interracial college in the South, its innovative student labor program (work is part of every student's curriculum), and its efforts to preserve local crafts traditions. **Open:** Mon–Sat 9am–6pm, Sun 1–6pm. Closed Jan and some hols. **$**

Log House Craft Gallery
Berea College; tel 606/986-9341 or toll free 800/347-3892. This gallery serves as a showcase for the fine woodworking and craft skills of students at Berea College. This innovative school aims to integrate practical work experience, classic Kentucky crafts, and academic study as a way of empowering the local Appalachian community. Works by other local craftspeople are also available. The gallery also houses the Wallace Nutting Collection of Early American Furniture. **Open:** Mon–Sat 8am–5pm, also Apr–Dec 25, Sun 1–5pm. Closed some hols. **Free**

Bowling Green

Named for a type of lawn bowling the founding Moore brothers brought from the East in 1798. Though Kentucky never officially left the Union, the city was made a Confederate capital. Home to Western Kentucky University and the world's only Corvette manufacturing plant. **Information:** Bowling Green–Warren County Tourist & Convention Commission, 352 Three Springs Rd, Bowling Green, 42104 (tel 502/782-0800).

MOTELS 🏨

≡≡ Best Western Continental Inn
700 Interstate Dr, PO Box 96, 42102; tel 502/781-5200 or toll free 800/528-1234; fax 502/782-0314. Nice, clean accommodations located across the street from the Corvette Museum. **Rooms:** 100 rms. CI 2pm/CO noon. Nonsmoking rms avail. **Amenities:** 🛎 ⓐ A/C, cable TV. **Services:** ✕ 🖼 🐾 Friendly staff. **Facilities:** 🛏 🏊 1 restaurant. Well-maintained pool area. **Rates (CP):** Peak (Apr–Oct) $40–$45 S; $45–$60 D. Extra person $5. Lower rates off-season. Parking: Outdoor, free. AE, CB, DC, DISC, MC, V.

≡≡ Comfort Inn
4646 Scottsville Rd, 42101; tel 502/843-1163 or toll free 800/221-2222; fax 502/843-1166. Exit 22 off I-65. Pleasant, standard chain motel. **Rooms:** 82 rms. CI noon/CO 11am. Nonsmoking rms avail. Rooms are comfortable and well appointed. **Amenities:** 🛎 A/C, cable TV, dataport. Some rooms have coffeemakers, refrigerators, microwaves, and VCRs. **Services:** ✕ 🖼 🐾 Better-than-average security. **Facilities:** 🛏 1 restaurant (dinner only), 1 bar (w/entertainment). **Rates (CP):** Peak (Apr–Oct) $43–$63 S; $48–$68 D. Extra person $6. Children under age 13 stay free. Lower rates off-season. Parking: Outdoor, free. AE, DISC, MC, V.

≡≡≡ Greenwood Executive Inn
1000 Executive Way, 42102; tel 502/781-6610 or toll free 800/354-4394; fax 502/781-7985. Exit 22 off I-65. Exterior and entrance need some work, but the lobby is quite attractive. Near area attractions and shopping. **Rooms:** 152 rms and stes. CI noon/CO 2pm. Nonsmoking rms avail. **Amenities:** 🛎 📺 A/C, satel TV. **Services:** ✕ 🚐 🖼 🐾 **Facilities:** 🛏 🚌 ⅙ 1 restaurant, 1 bar (w/entertainment). Security 24 hours. Bar area regularly hosts live bands. Large parking lot can accommodate 18-wheel trucks. **Rates:** $50 S; $60 D; $90–$130 ste. Extra person $5. Children under age 16 stay free. Parking: Outdoor, free. AE, CB, DC, DISC, MC, V.

≋≋≋ Hampton Inn

233 Three Springs Rd, 42104; tel 502/842-4100 or toll free 800/HAMPTON; fax 502/782-3377. Exit 22 off I-65. Attractive motel, located close to the Corvette museum. **Rooms:** 131 rms. CI 2pm/CO noon. Nonsmoking rms avail. Attractive, well-furnished rooms. **Amenities:** 🛎 🕐 A/C, cable TV, dataport. Free local calls. **Services:** ⊠ 🍸 Friendly, helpful staff. **Facilities:** 🏋 ⌷15 🕭 **Rates (CP):** $54–$68 S; $64–$78 D. Children under age 18 stay free. Parking: Outdoor, free. AE, CB, DC, DISC, MC, V.

≋≋≋ Ramada Inn

4767 Scottsville Rd, 42104; tel 502/781-3000 or toll free 800/2-RAMADA; fax 502/782-0591. Exit 22 off I-65. Pleasant accommodations close to area attractions, restaurants, and shopping. **Rooms:** 122 rms and stes. CI 2pm/CO noon. Nonsmoking rms avail. The air conditioners in some rooms can be loud. **Amenities:** 🛎 🕐 🖳 A/C, cable TV w/movies, dataport. Some units w/terraces. **Services:** ✗ ⊠ 🍸 ⇢ **Facilities:** 🏋 ⌷225 🕭 1 restaurant, 1 bar (w/entertainment), spa. Health spa facilities available off-site at no cost. **Rates:** Peak (May–Oct) $42–$84 S; $45–$89 D; $60–$125 ste. Extra person $7. Children under age 18 stay free. Min stay special events. Lower rates off-season. Parking: Outdoor, free. AE, CB, DC, DISC, JCB, MC, V.

RESTAURANTS 🍽

Beijing

1951 Scottsville Rd; tel 502/842-2288. Exit 22 off I-65. **Chinese.** A lovely combination of Southern hospitality and authentic Chinese cuisine, Beijing offers a relaxed and comfortable atmosphere. The friendly staff will help diners choose an entree or explain how dishes are prepared. **FYI:** Reservations accepted. Children's menu. **Open:** Tues–Thurs 11am–10pm, Fri–Sat 11am–11pm, Sun 11am–9pm. **Prices:** Main courses $7–$18. AE, MC, V. 👪 🕭

♣ ✦ Mariah's

801 State St; tel 502/842-6878. **American/Eclectic/Steak.** Located in the 1818 Moriah Moore House, listed on the National Register of Historic Places. The antique bar dating from the 1880s has been refurbished, and many 19th-century pieces adorn the elegant dining room. Filet mignon, homemade salad dressings, and fresh hot rolls are among the menu's highlights. **FYI:** Reservations accepted. Children's menu. **Open:** Mon–Thurs 11am–10pm, Fri–Sat 11am–11pm, Sun 11am–9pm. **Prices:** Main courses $5–$15. AE, CB, DC, DISC, MC, V. 🍴 🚗 🕭

ATTRACTIONS 📷

Capitol Arts Center

416 E Main; tel 502/782-2787. This faithfully renovated 1939 art deco movie theater now hosts a wide variety of cultural activities, including theater, dance, and concerts. $$$$

Kentucky Museum

Kentucky Building on Western Kentucky University campus; tel 502/745-2592. Kentucky's cultural heritage comes alive through this fascinating collection of photographs, manuscripts, and other artifacts. Permanent exhibits include the Felts Log House (circa 1820); the original home of an early Logan County family, the cabin is now filled with reproduction 1830s furniture, fixtures, clothing, and tools. Guided tours, gift shop. **Open:** Tues–Sat 9:30am–4pm, Sun 1–4:30pm. Closed some hols. $

National Corvette Museum

350 Corvette Dr; tel 502/781-7973. A shrine to one of the world's most famous sports cars. This brand-new $15 million facility, owned and operated by a foundation representing Corvette owners and collectors, is located a quarter-mile south of the world's only GM Corvette assembly plant. Over 50 past, present, and future Corvettes are on permanent display, including rare models and one of a kind prototypes. Thousands of Corvette-related photos, movies, videos, advertisements, and scale models. An on-site gift shop sells Corvette memorabilia. **Open:** Daily 9am–7pm. Closed some hols. $$$

Brandenburg

Located 30 miles southwest of Louisville, on the banks of the Ohio River. Abraham Lincoln's father was a stonemason at nearby 1792 Doe Run Inn. **Information:** Meade County Area Chamber of Commerce, PO Box 483, Brandenburg, 40108 (tel 502/422-3626).

LODGE 🛏

≋≋ Otter Creek Park Lodge

850 Otter Creek Park Rd, 40108; tel 502/583-3577; fax 502/583-3577 ext 124. Off US 31 W. 3,000 acres. This rustic, secluded lodge offers rooms and cabins with scenic views. **Rooms:** 22 rms and effic; 12 cottages/villas. CI 2pm/CO 11am. **Amenities:** 🛎 A/C, TV. All units w/terraces. **Services:** 🍸 ⇢ **Facilities:** 🏋 △ 🎾 🏊2 ⌷100 🕭 1 restaurant, basketball. An animal reserve park and caves for touring and exploring are nearby. Picnic areas, hay rides, miniature golf, nature centers, and camping facilities are available. **Rates:** Peak (Apr–Nov) $58 S or D; $78 effic; $80–$240 cottage/villa. Extra person $8. Lower rates off-season. Parking: Outdoor, free. Closed Jan. MC, V.

ATTRACTION 📷

Otter Creek Park

850 Otter Creek Park Rd; tel 502/583-3577. Located approximately halfway between Fort Knox and Louisville, Otter Creek offers 3,600 acres of forest and rolling hills along the banks of the Ohio River. A nature center (open Mar–Nov) offers exhibits on the geology and wildlife of the area. Family picnic areas, nature trails, swimming, fishing, hiking, minia-

ture-golf course, tennis courts, and boat ramps are available. **Open:** Park, daily sunrise–sunset; office, Mon–Fri 8am–4:30pm. **Free**

Cadiz

Eastern gateway to Lake Barkley and site of Lake Barkley State Resort Park. The town's Main Street is home to an antique mall. **Information:** Cadiz–Trigg County Chamber of Commerce, PO Box 647, Cadiz, 42211 (tel 502/522-3892).

MOTEL

⊨⊨ Country Inn
5909 Hopkinsville Rd, 42211; tel 502/522-7007 or toll free 800/456-4000; fax 502/522-3893. At Jct US 68/I-24. Guests at this homey motel are greeted with a fireplace and television in the lobby and rocking chairs outside. **Rooms:** 48 rms. CI 3pm/CO noon. Nonsmoking rms avail. **Amenities:** A/C. **Services:** Movies available for rent. **Facilities:** **Rates (CP):** Peak (Mar 15–Oct) $44–$47 S; $49–$52 D. Extra person $4. Children under age 18 stay free. Lower rates off-season. Parking: Outdoor, free. AE, CB, DC, DISC, MC, V.

RESORT

⊨⊨⊨ Barkley Lodge
Blue Springs Rd, Lake Barkley State Resort Park, PO Box 790, 42211; tel 502/924-1131 or toll free 800/325-1708; fax 502/924-0013. Off US 68. 3,600 acres. A rustic complex consisting of a large main lodge and several individual cabins. The lodge lobby has a large fireplace and an observation porch with excellent views of the lake. **Rooms:** 124 rms and stes; 13 cottages/villas. CI 4pm/CO noon. Nonsmoking rms avail. All lodge rooms have view of the lake. **Amenities:** A/C, cable TV. All units w/terraces, some w/fireplaces. **Services:** Children's program, babysitting. **Facilities:** 1 restaurant, 1 beach (lake shore), lifeguard, basketball, volleyball, games rm, lawn games, racquetball, sauna, steam rm, whirlpool, playground, washer/dryer. Large fitness center with aerobic machines, tanning beds, and weight equipment. Pontoon boats available. **Rates:** Peak (May–Sept 5) $37–$58 S; $47–$68 D; $124–$144 ste; $104–$124 cottage/villa. Extra person $5. Children under age 16 stay free. Lower rates off-season. Parking: Outdoor, free. AE, DC, DISC, MC, V.

ATTRACTION

Lake Barkley State Resort Park
Off US 68; tel 502/924-1131 or toll free 800/325-1708. A heavily wooded park encompassing 3,700 acres on the eastern shores of 60,000-acre Lake Barkley (the second-largest in the state). Facilities include a marina, fishing and ski boats,

18-hole golf course, nine miles of hiking trails, four tennis courts, and picnic shelters. There's also a campground with 80 sites and two lodges. **Open:** Daily sunrise–sunset. **$**

Campbellsville

A central Kentucky town known for the handmade cherry furniture produced by area craftspeople. Nearby Green River attracts boaters and fishing enthusiasts. **Information:** Campbellsville–Taylor County Chamber of Commerce, Court St, PO Box 116, Campbellsville, 42719 (tel 502/465-8601).

MOTELS

⊨⊨ Best Western
1400 E Broadway, 42718; tel 502/465-7001 or toll free 800/528-1234; fax 502/465-7001. Close to Green River Reservoir and Campbellsville College. Popular with families. **Rooms:** 60 rms and stes. Executive level. CI open/CO 11am. Nonsmoking rms avail. Recliner in every room. **Amenities:** A/C, cable TV. 1 unit w/whirlpool. Free local calls. **Services:** Coffee available 24 hours, popcorn available in late afternoon. **Facilities:** Games rm, whirlpool, playground, washer/dryer. Wading pool. **Rates (CP):** $50–$58 S or D; $80–$85 ste. Extra person $5. Children under age 12 stay free. Parking: Outdoor, free. AE, CB, DC, DISC, MC, V.

⊨⊨ Lucky Vista Motel
1409 S Columbia, 42718; tel 502/465-8196 or toll free 800/649-4692; fax 502/465-3470. A real home-away-from-home located near Green River Lake State Park. A great value. **Rooms:** 18 rms; 3 cottages/villas. CI open/CO 11am. Nonsmoking rms avail. Rooms are individually decorated and feature handmade furniture. **Amenities:** A/C, cable TV w/movies. Some rooms have refrigerators. **Services:** Coffee available in office. Owners are very friendly and helpful. **Facilities:** Grills are provided so you can cook up the fish you catch in the lake. Fishing licenses sold in the office; electrical hook-ups available for boats. **Rates:** $35–$44 S or D; $42–$48 cottage/villa. Extra person $3. Children under age 16 stay free. Parking: Outdoor, free. AE, DISC, MC, V.

Carrollton

Founded in 1794 at confluence of the Kentucky and Ohio Rivers, with a historic district that covers 25 blocks. Site of one of the largest burley tobacco markets in the world. **Information:** Carroll County Chamber of Commerce, PO Box 535, Carrollton, 41008 (tel 502/732-7034).

HOTELS

Days Inn

61 Inn Rd, PO Box 108, Rte 3, 41008; tel 502/732-9301 or toll free 800/DAYS-INN; fax 502/732-5596. Exit 44 off I-71. A basic budget hotel geared to families. **Rooms:** 88 rms. CI 3pm/CO noon. Nonsmoking rms avail. King rooms have alarm clock and radio. **Amenities:** A/C, cable TV w/movies. **Services:** X ⌂ ⌂ **Facilities:** ⌂ ⌂ ⌂ 1 restaurant (dinner only). Children under 12 eat free in restaurant. **Rates (CP):** $52–$69 S or D. Extra person $6. Children under age 17 stay free. Parking: Outdoor, free. AE, CB, DC, DISC, JCB, MC, V.

Holiday Inn Express

141 Inn Rd, PO Box 108, Rte 3, 41008; tel 502/732-6661 or toll free 800/HOLIDAY; fax 502/732-6661 ext 410. Exit 44 off I-71. Comfortable chain hotel offering friendly, Southern-style service and a nice lobby. **Rooms:** 62 rms. CI 2pm/CO noon. Nonsmoking rms avail. Queen rooms have a desk. **Amenities:** A/C, cable TV w/movies, dataport. Hair dryers and VCRs available upon request. **Services:** ⌂ ⌂ **Facilities:** ⌂ ⌂ Guests may use pool at Days Inn next door. Skiing available at nearby General Butler State Park. **Rates (CP):** $55 S or D. Children under age 18 stay free. Parking: Outdoor, free. AE, CB, DC, DISC, MC, V.

RESORT

General Butler State Resort Park Lodge

US 227, PO Box 325, 41008; tel 502/732-4384 or toll free 800/325-0078; fax 502/732-4270. Exit 44 off I-71. 800 acres. Charming, rustic resort with cottages and motel-style rooms in a main lodge. Lodge lobby has a beautiful view of the woods. **Rooms:** 56 rms; 23 cottages/villas. CI 4pm/CO noon. Nonsmoking rms avail. Rooms are in need of some updating. Rustic decor, screen doors to patio. **Amenities:** ⌂ A/C, cable TV. All units w/terraces. **Services:** ⌂ Social director, children's program. **Facilities:** ⌂ ⌂ ⌂ 9 ⌂ ⌂ 2 ⌂ ⌂ ⌂ 1 restaurant (see "Restaurants" below), 1 beach (lake shore), lifeguard, basketball, volleyball, games rm, playground, washer/dryer. Nature trails, picnic/playground area, mini-golf, gift shop. **Rates:** $52–$62 S or D; $61–$144 cottage/villa. Extra person $6. Children under age 16 stay free. Parking: Outdoor, free. Closed Dec 25–31. AE, DC, DISC, MC, V.

RESTAURANT

Kentucky State Resort Park Restaurant

In General Butler State Resort Park, US 227; tel 502/732-4384. **Regional American.** This restaurant features a wonderful wooded view and comfortable seating. They have a buffet-style dinner, which includes your choice of entree, vegetables, soup and salad bar, and dessert. **FYI:** Reservations recommended. Children's menu. No liquor license. **Open:** Breakfast daily 7–10:30am; lunch Mon–Sat 11:30am–

4pm, Sun noon–4pm; dinner Mon–Sat 5–9pm, Sun 4:30–9pm. Closed Dec 22–29. **Prices:** Main courses $6–$13. AE, DISC, MC, V. ⌂ ⌂ ⌂

ATTRACTION

General Butler State Resort Park

I-71; tel 502/732-4384. Popular summer activities at this 791-acre park include swimming and fishing at the 30-acre lake, golfing at the park's nine-hole course, hiking, and miniature golf. There's also a year-round campground with 111 modern sites. In winter, Butler provides the state's only cross-country and downhill skiing, with 20 acres of trails and an on-site ski shop offering rental equipment. **Open:** Daily sunrise–sunset. $

Cave City

The center of south-central Kentucky's cave region and one of the state's richest agricultural sections. **Information:** Cave City Convention Center, 502 Mammoth Cave Rd, Cave City, 42127 (tel 502/773-3131).

MOTELS

Best Western Kentucky Inn

Exit 53 off I-65, PO Box 356, 42127; tel 502/773-3161 or toll free 800/528-1234; fax 502/773-5494. Jct KY 70/90. Located near Mammoth Cave and the Barren River, this establishment features ground-floor rooms only—all comfortable and very well kept. **Rooms:** 50 rms. CI 1pm/CO 11am. Nonsmoking rms avail. Some rooms have a nice view of the pool. **Amenities:** A/C, cable TV. **Services:** X ⌂ Friendly, personal service. **Facilities:** ⌂ Washer/dryer. **Rates:** Peak (mid-May–Sept) $54–$64 S; $59–$69 D. Extra person $5. Children under age 12 stay free. Lower rates off-season. Parking: Outdoor, free. AE, CB, DC, DISC, MC, V.

Days Inn

822 Mammoth Cave St, 42127; tel 502/773-2151 or toll free 800/DAYS-INN; fax 502/773-2151. Exit 53 off I-65. Basic, family-style accommodations. **Rooms:** 111 rms. CI 2pm/CO noon. Nonsmoking rms avail. **Amenities:** A/C, cable TV. Some units w/terraces. **Services:** ⌂ ⌂ Friendly staff. **Facilities:** ⌂ ⌂ 1 restaurant, games rm, washer/dryer. **Rates:** Peak (June–Aug) $42–$49 S; $52–$57 D. Extra person $5. Children under age 12 stay free. Lower rates off-season. Parking: Outdoor, free. AE, CB, DC, DISC, JCB, MC, V.

Holiday Inn Express

US 90, PO Box 675, 42127; tel 502/773-3101 or toll free 800/HOLIDAY; fax 502/773-6082. Exit 53 off I-65. Modern motel with updated rooms and facilities. **Rooms:** 104 rms. CI 2pm/CO 11am. Nonsmoking rms avail. **Amenities:** ⌂ ⌂ ⌂ A/C, cable TV w/movies, dataport, in-rm safe. **Services:** ⌂ ⌂ **Facilities:** ⌂ ⌂ ⌂ Games rm, washer/

dryer. **Rates (CP):** Peak (June–Sept) $65–$100 S or D. Extra person $5. Children under age 18 stay free. Lower rates off-season. Parking: Outdoor, free. AE, CB, DC, DISC, JCB, MC, V.

≣≣ Quality Inn

Mammoth Cave Rd, PO Box 547, 42127; tel 502/773-2181 or toll free 800/321-4245; fax 502/773-2181. Exit 53 off I-65. Comfortable two-story property near area attractions and outlet mall. **Rooms:** 100 rms. CI 11am/CO 11am. Nonsmoking rms avail. **Amenities:** ⊞ A/C, cable TV w/movies. **Services:** ✗ ⊅ ⊲⊅ **Facilities:** ⚑ ё 1 restaurant, playground. Attractive, relaxing pool area. **Rates:** Peak (Mem Day–Labor Day) $56 S; $62 D. Extra person $6. Children under age 18 stay free. Lower rates off-season. Parking: Outdoor, free. AE, CB, DC, DISC, ER, JCB, MC, V.

≣ Wigwam Village

601 N Dixie Hwy, 42127; tel 502/773-3381. On US 31 W. Listed on the National Register of Historic Places, this unique piece of Americana consists of separate concrete "wigwams." If you want something different, this is it. **Rooms:** 15 rms. CI 2pm/CO 11am. Rooms and baths are small and feature hickory furniture. Probably not comfortable for extended stays. **Amenities:** A/C, cable TV. No phone. **Services:** Friendly staff. Good morning coffee available. **Facilities:** Playground. Large play area for children. Outside grills and picnic tables. **Rates:** Peak (June–Labor Day) $35 S; $45 D. Extra person $2. Children under age 4 stay free. Lower rates off-season. Parking: Outdoor, free. Closed Dec–Feb. DISC, MC, V.

RESTAURANT ⍨

★ Hickory Villa

Sanders Lane; tel 502/773-3033. Exit 53 off I-65. **Regional American/Barbecue.** A well-known local favorite for barbecue. (Their famous sauce has been a secret handed down for over 100 years.) Although barbecue is their specialty, they also serve steak, ribs, chicken, and regional favorites. Buffet on Fri and Sat nights. **FYI:** Reservations not accepted. Children's menu. No liquor license. **Open:** Daily 10:30am–10pm. **Prices:** Main courses $6–$12. AE, DC, DISC, MC, V. 📷

ATTRACTIONS 🖼

Kentucky Action Park

KY 70; tel 502/773-2636. A family-oriented park offering an alpine slide, a chair lift, go carts, bumper boats, and horseback riding. **Open:** Mem Day–Labor Day, daily 9am–9pm; Easter–Mem Day and Labor Day–Oct, Sat–Sun 10am–7pm. $$

Guntown Mountain

KY 70; tel 502/773-3530. Accessible only by a 1,300-foot chair lift, Guntown Mountain is a reproduction of an 1880s Wild West Town, complete with live-action "gunfights" on the main street and dancing girls in the saloon. The park also offers tours of Onyx Cave, a water slide, and a haunted house. **Open:** Mem Day–Labor Day, daily 9am–10pm; May and Labor Day–mid-Oct, Sat–Sun 9am–9pm. $$

Corbin

Located on the Cumberland Plateau, with access to Kentucky's finest recreational lakes. Site of the Harlan Sanders Cafe and Museum, where the Colonel developed his secret recipe for Kentucky Fried Chicken in the 1940s. **Information:** Corbin Tourist & Convention Commission, 101 N Lynn Ave, Corbin, 40701 (tel 606/528-1583).

MOTEL 🏨

≣≣≣ Holiday Inn

I-75 & US 25W, 40701; tel 606/528-6301 or toll free 800/HOLIDAY; fax 606/523-0483. Exit 25. Right off I-75, but nestled among trees—a delightful retreat for the traveler. **Rooms:** 147 rms and stes. CI 3pm/CO noon. Nonsmoking rms avail. Some rooms have lovely view of the surrounding mountains. **Amenities:** ⊞ ё ▤ A/C, satel TV w/movies. Some rooms have dataports. Refrigerator available on request. **Services:** ✗ ⊠ ⊅ ⊲⊅ Copy service. Very friendly and helpful staff. **Facilities:** ⚑ ⊡ ё 1 restaurant, games rm. **Rates (BB):** Peak (Mem Day–Labor Day) $62 S or D; $65–$80 ste. Extra person $5. Children under age 19 stay free. Lower rates off-season. Parking: Outdoor, free. B&B package avail. AE, CB, DC, DISC, JCB, MC, V.

LODGE

≣≣≣ Dupont Lodge & Cottages

7351 KY 90, 40701; tel 606/528-4121 or toll free 800/325-0063. In Cumberland Falls State Resort Park. 1,800 acres. A quiet, rural hideaway, with scenic views and many opportunities for outdoor recreation. Romantic, lodge-type lobby. **Rooms:** 72 rms and stes; 27 cottages/villas. CI 4pm/CO noon. Nonsmoking rms avail. Some rooms have beautiful views. Cottages and woodland rooms available. **Amenities:** ⊞ A/C, satel TV. Some units w/fireplaces. **Services:** ⊅ Social director, children's program. Helpful, friendly staff. **Facilities:** ⚑ ⊡ ⚓ ⍟ ▣ ё 2 restaurants, basketball, volleyball, games rm, playground, washer/dryer. Scenic hiking trails and picnic area. **Rates:** Peak (Mem Day–Sept 3) $68 S or D; $78 ste; $70–$135 cottage/villa. Extra person $5. Children under age 16 stay free. Lower rates off-season. Parking: Outdoor, free. Closed Dec 24–31. AE, CB, DC, DISC, MC, V.

RESTAURANT ⍨

Harland Sanders Cafe & Museum

US 25; tel 606/528-2163. **American.** A restoration of Col Harlan Sanders' very first Kentucky Fried Chicken restaurant. The original dining room is still in use, and a museum area contains kitchen equipment and other artifacts. The menu is standard KFC fare. **FYI:** Reservations not accepted. Children's menu. No liquor license. **Open:** Daily 7am–11pm. **Prices:** Main courses $5–$7. No CC. 🍴♿

ATTRACTION 🏛

Cumberland Falls State Resort Park
7351 KY 90; tel 606/528-4121. Known as the "Niagara of the South," Cumberland Falls forms a 125-foot-wide curtain that plunges 60 feet into the gorge below. On clear nights during a full moon, you can sometimes see a "moonbow" form over the falls. Accommodations include a park lodge, cottages, and a 50-site campground; popular activities include fishing, white-water rafting, horseback riding, picnicking, swimming, and tennis. **Free**

Covington/ Cincinnati Airport

See also Cincinnati, OH; Erlanger, Florence, Fort Mitchell, and Walton, KY

Covington, one of the seats of Kenton County, was founded in 1815 at the confluence of the Ohio and Licking Rivers. Covington and the nearby towns of Fort Mitchell, Erlanger, and Florence are all part of the Cincinnati metropolitan area (see *America on Wheels: Midwest & Great Lakes*); Walton is surrounded by horse farms. Cincinnati/Northern Kentucky International Airport is eight miles west of Covington.

HOTELS 🏨

≣≣≣ Commonwealth Hilton
7373 Turfway Rd, Florence, 41042; tel 606/371-4400 or toll free 800/HILTONS; fax 606/371-3361. Exit 182 off I-75. Near Cincinnati airport and all area attractions. It is well equipped for the business traveler. **Rooms:** 206 rms and stes. Executive level. CI 3pm/CO noon. Nonsmoking rms avail. Rooms are well appointed and comfortable. **Amenities:** 🛁 🕹 🖥 A/C, cable TV w/movies. Some units w/whirlpools. Concierge-level rooms feature extra amenities, such as an honor bar. **Services:** ✗ 🔑 🚗 🖂 ⤴ Babysitting. Friendly and efficient staff. **Facilities:** 🏋 ⛳ 400 ♿ 1 restaurant, 1 bar (w/entertainment), steam rm. **Rates:** $109 S; $119 D; $130–$375 ste. Extra person $10. Children under age 18 stay free. Min stay special events. Parking: Outdoor, free. AE, CB, DC, DISC, MC, V.

≣≣≣ Embassy Suites at River Center
10 E River Center Blvd, Covington, 41011; tel 606/261-8400 or toll free 800/EMBASSY; fax 606/261-8486. Exit 192 off I-75. Downtown waterfront hotel, with a beautiful garden atrium. Located in the heart of the city's nightlife and within walking distance of Cincinnati's Riverfront Stadium. Popular

with business travelers. **Rooms:** 226 stes. CI 3pm/CO noon. Nonsmoking rms avail. All units are suites that separate into sleeping and living areas, to accommodate both the business traveler and families. **Amenities:** 🛁 🕹 🖥 🍴 A/C, cable TV w/movies, refrig, dataport, voice mail. Complimentary morning newspaper and coffee. **Services:** ✗ 🅿 🚗 🖂 ⤴ 🐾 Babysitting. Friendly staff. **Facilities:** 🏋 ⛳ 300 🖥 ♿ 1 restaurant, 1 bar (w/entertainment), sauna, whirlpool, washer/dryer. **Rates (BB):** Peak (Apr–Oct) $139–$159 ste. Extra person $10. Children under age 18 stay free. Min stay special events. Lower rates off-season. Parking: Indoor, free. Senior discounts avail. AE, CB, DC, DISC, JCB, MC, V.

≣≣≣ Quality Inn Riverview
666 W 5th St, Covington, 41011; tel 606/491-1200 or toll free 800/292-2079; fax 606/491-0326. Exit 192 off I-75. Located in downtown area; convenient to all area attractions. **Rooms:** 236 rms and stes. CI 3pm/CO 11am. Nonsmoking rms avail. Some rooms have great river views. **Amenities:** 🛁 🕹 🖥 A/C, satel TV w/movies, dataport, voice mail. All units w/terraces, some w/whirlpools. **Services:** ✗ 🚗 🖂 ⤴ 🐾 Car-rental desk, babysitting. **Facilities:** 🏋 ⛳ 600 ♿ 2 restaurants, 2 bars (1 w/entertainment), basketball, volleyball, games rm, whirlpool. Indoor pool has opening roof. The revolving restaurant atop the hotel allows for a unique dining experience and a fantastic view of the Cincinnati skyline. **Rates:** $85 S; $93 D; $140–$165 ste. Extra person $10. Children under age 18 stay free. Parking: Indoor/outdoor, free. AE, CB, DC, DISC, JCB, MC, V.

MOTELS

≣≣ Comfort Inn
630 Donaldson Rd, Erlanger, 41018; tel 606/727-3400 or toll free 800/221-2222; fax 606/727-1378. Exit 184B off I-75. Slightly run-down motel offering adequate facilities for an overnight stay. **Rooms:** 146 rms. CI noon/CO noon. Nonsmoking rms avail. **Amenities:** 🛁 A/C, cable TV w/movies. Some units w/terraces. **Services:** ✗ 🚗 🖂 ⤴ 🐾 **Facilities:** 🏋 62 ♿ 1 restaurant, 1 bar, washer/dryer. **Rates (CP):** Peak (May–Sept) $60 S; $67 D. Extra person $7. Children under age 18 stay free. Lower rates off-season. Parking: Outdoor, free. AE, CB, DC, DISC, JCB, MC, V.

≣≣ Days Inn
Jct I-75/KY 338, Walton, 41094; tel 606/485-4151 or toll free 800/DAYS-INN; fax 606/485-4151. Exit 175 off I-75. No-frills, budget-minded accommodations. There's nothing fancy here, but it's fine for an overnight stay. **Rooms:** 137 rms. CI 2pm/CO 11am. Nonsmoking rms avail. **Amenities:** 🛁 A/C, satel TV w/movies. **Services:** ⤴ 🐾 **Facilities:** 🏋 1 restaurant (bkfst and dinner only). **Rates:** $34–$36 S; $42–$48 D. Extra person $7. Children under age 12 stay free. Parking: Outdoor, free. AE, CB, DC, DISC, JCB, MC, V.

≣≣≣ Drawbridge Inn & Convention Center
Buttermilk Pike, Fort Mitchell, 41017; tel 606/341-2800 or toll free 800/354-9793, 800/352-9866 in KY; fax 606/

341-5644. Exit 186 off I-75. Tudor-style decor is the hallmark of this motel adjacent to the Oldenburg Brewery and entertainment complex. **Rooms:** 505 rms and stes. Executive level. CI 3pm/CO noon. Nonsmoking rms avail. **Amenities:** 📺 🛁 A/C, cable TV w/movies, dataport, voice mail. Some units w/minibars, 1 w/fireplace, 1 w/whirlpool. **Services:** ✗ 🔑 🚐 🛁 🍸 Car-rental desk, masseur, babysitting. **Facilities:** 🏊 ⛳ 🎾 1800 🚹 3 restaurants, 4 bars, basketball, volleyball, games rm, spa, sauna, whirlpool, beauty salon, playground, washer/dryer. Shopping arcade. Restaurant open 24 hours. **Rates:** $88–$118 S; $98–$128 D; $205–$270 ste. Extra person $10. Children under age 18 stay free. Parking: Outdoor, free. AE, CB, DC, DISC, MC, V.

🏨 Econo Lodge

633 Donaldson Rd, Erlanger, 41018; tel 606/342-5500 or toll free 800/424-4777; fax 606/342-5500. Exit 184 off I-75. No-frills motel, convenient to the interstate and airport. **Rooms:** 73 rms. CI 1pm/CO 11am. Nonsmoking rms avail. The rooms are clean but not fancy. **Amenities:** 📺 A/C. 1 unit w/whirlpool. Free local calls. **Services:** 🍸 🕭 Complimentary morning coffee. **Rates:** Peak (June–Aug) $30–$35 S or D. Extra person $5. Children under age 16 stay free. Lower rates off-season. Parking: Outdoor, free. AE, CB, DC, DISC, JCB, MC, V.

🏨🏨 Hampton Inn Cincinnati South

7393 Turfway Rd, Florence, 41042; tel 606/283-1600 or toll free 800/HAMPTON; fax 606/283-1600. Exit 182 off I-75. Basic chain motel, close to the airport and all area attractions. **Rooms:** 117 rms. CI 3pm/CO noon. Nonsmoking rms avail. **Amenities:** 📺 🛁 A/C, satel TV w/movies, dataport. Free local calls. **Services:** 🚐 🛁 🍸 Friendly staff. **Facilities:** 🏊 25 🚹 **Rates (CP):** Peak (Apr–Oct) $57 S; $62 D. Extra person $5. Children under age 18 stay free. Lower rates off-season. Parking: Outdoor, free. AE, CB, DC, DISC, MC, V.

🏨🏨 HoJo Airport Inn

648 Donaldson Rd, Erlanger, 41018; tel 606/342-6200 or toll free 800/446-4656; fax 606/342-6077. Exit 184B off I-75. No-frills chain motel, convenient to Cincinnati and area attractions. **Rooms:** 81 rms and stes. CI noon/CO noon. Nonsmoking rms avail. **Amenities:** 📺 A/C, cable TV. Some units w/terraces. **Services:** 🚐 🛁 🍸 Car-rental desk. Fax machine in lobby. **Facilities:** 🏊 75 🚹 Games rm, washer/dryer. **Rates (CP):** Peak (May–Aug) $39–$42 S; $50–$52 D; $95–$110 ste. Extra person $6. Children under age 18 stay free. Lower rates off-season. Parking: Outdoor, free. AE, CB, DC, DISC, JCB, MC, V.

🏨🏨 Holiday Inn

1717 Airport Exchange Blvd, Erlanger, 41018; tel 606/371-2233 or toll free 800/HOLIDAY; fax 606/371-5002. Exit 2 off I-275. Basic chain motel offers adequate accommodations and few surprises. **Rooms:** 306 rms and stes. CI 3pm/CO noon. Nonsmoking rms avail. Well-appointed, comfortable rooms. **Amenities:** 📺 🛁 🖥 A/C, satel TV w/movies, dataport. Some units w/whirlpools. Minibars in suites. **Services:** ✗ 🚐 🛁 🍸 Friendly staff. **Facilities:** 🏊 🎾 650 🖥 🚹 1 restaurant, 1 bar, sauna, whirlpool, washer/dryer. **Rates:** $79–$92 S or D; $149–$175 ste. Extra person $10. Children under age 18 stay free. Min stay special events. AP and MAP rates avail. Parking: Outdoor, free. AE, CB, DC, DISC, MC, V.

🏨🏨🏨 Holiday Inn Riverfront

600 W 3rd St, Covington, 41011; tel 606/291-4300 or toll free 800/HOLIDAY; fax 606/491-2331. Exit 192 off I-75. Motel located off I-75, convenient to Cincinnati and all area attractions. **Rooms:** 156 rms and stes. CI 3pm/CO noon. Nonsmoking rms avail. Average quality, recently renovated rooms. **Amenities:** 📺 🛁 A/C, satel TV w/movies. **Services:** ✗ 🛁 🍸 Hospitable, friendly staff. **Facilities:** 🏊 🎾 85 🚹 1 restaurant, 1 bar. Recently redone pool area. **Rates (CP):** $85 S or D; $99 ste. Extra person $5. Children under age 12 stay free. Parking: Outdoor, free. AE, CB, DC, DISC, MC, V.

RESTAURANTS 🍴

BB Riverboats

1 Madison Ave, Covington; tel 606/261-8500. **American.** Located at Covington Landing at the foot of Madison Avenue, BB Riverboats offers a unique dining experience. Buffet meals, a cash bar, and music for dancing are offered daily, and there are a wide variety of cruises and boats to choose from. **FYI:** Reservations recommended. Dancing. No smoking. **Open:** Peak (Apr–Nov) lunch daily noon–2pm; dinner Mon–Sun 7–9:30pm; brunch Sun noon–2pm. **Prices:** AE, CB, DC, DISC, MC, V. 🖼 VP 🚹

★ Coach and Four

214 Scott Blvd, Covington; tel 606/431-6700. Across from Embassy Suites. **Eclectic.** Pastoral Kentucky is reflected in the decor, which features hand-painted murals depicting the beauty of the state. The menu consists of a wide variety of pastas, steaks, and favorite regional dishes. There are also daily specials. **FYI:** Reservations recommended. **Open:** Lunch Mon–Fri 11am–3pm; dinner Mon–Thurs 5–10pm, Fri–Sat 5–11pm, Sun 5–9pm; brunch Sun 9am–3pm. **Prices:** Main courses $6–$20. AE, DC, MC, V.

★ Crockett's River Cafe

101 Riverboat Row, Newport; tel 606/581-2800. **Continental/Seafood.** Upscale bistro offering a mostly-seafood menu at both lunch and dinner. (Fresh seafood is flown in daily.) A selection of chicken, beef, and veal for those who don't want fish. They offer an award-winning crab cake appetizer and soups on their menus. **FYI:** Reservations accepted. Rock. Children's menu. **Open:** Mon–Thurs 11:30am–10pm, Fri–Sat 11:30am–11pm, Sun 1–11pm. **Prices:** Main courses $13–$25. AE, CB, DC, DISC, MC, V. ❤ 🖼 🚹

ATTRACTIONS ▣

Covington Landing
Madison Ave, Covington; tel 606/491-3100. This multimillion-dollar riverfront showcase is one of the largest complexes on the inland waterways. Located on the Ohio River next to the Roebling Suspension Bridge, the Landing offers spectacular views of the Cincinnati skyline, plus lots of venues for dancing, dining, shopping, entertainment, and special events. **Open:** Daily 10am–2am. **Free**

Behringer-Crawford Museum
1600 Montague Rd, Devou Park, Covington; tel 606/491-4003. Housed in the historic Devou family home (built circa 1848), this is the only museum focusing on the cultural and natural history of northern Kentucky. The museum's permanent collection spans 450 million years of paleontology, archeology, military history, home life, fine art, and crafts. The Cohen Special Exhibits Gallery features quarterly special exhibits highlighting a specific aspect of the area's heritage. **Open:** Tues–Fri 10am–5pm, Sat–Sun 1–5pm. Closed some hols. **$**

Daniel Boone National Forest

Established in 1937, the Daniel Boone National Forest covers 660,000 acres of both public and private land in 21 Kentucky counties. The lushly wooded area encompasses the fishing meccas of Cave Run and Laurel River Lakes, the spectacular rock formations of Red River Gorge and Natural Bridge, and the white-water rapids of Red and Big South Fork Rivers. The Sheltowee National Recreation Trail runs more than 250 miles north to south, beginning near Morehead and ending near Jamestown, TN.

Most of the developed recreation areas are clustered in the northern and southern ends of the forest, with campsites around Morehead (Zilpo, Clear Creek), Slade (Natural Bridge), and Whitley City (Cumberland Falls, General Burnside, Holly Bay, and others). There are picnic areas at Natural Bridge and Alpine; facilities for horseback riding, rafting, rock climbing, and cross-country skiing are scattered throughout the forest. Staff at the forest's two visitors centers (in the Morehead Ranger District off KY 801, and in the Gladie Ranger District in Red River Gorge on KY 715) can provide maps, brochures, and other information. For information on hunting, fishing, and backcountry camping permits, call 606/745-3100.

Danville

"Birthplace of the Bluegrass," Danville was the site of Kentucky's first seat of government. Ten constitutional conventions took place here between 1784 and 1792, and today the town features living history exhibits re-creating that era. Home of Centre College, founded in 1819. **Information:** Danville–Boyle County Chamber of Commerce, 304 S 4th St, Danville, 40422 (tel 606/236-2361).

MOTEL ▣

▤▤ Holiday Inn Express
96 Daniel Dr, 40422; tel 606/236-8600 or toll free 800/HOLIDAY; fax 606/236-4299. Convenient location off US 150 bypass. Popular with budget-minded travelers. **Rooms:** 63 rms. CI 3pm/CO noon. Nonsmoking rms avail. **Amenities:** ▣ ⚬ A/C, cable TV. Some units w/whirlpools. Free local phone calls. **Services:** ▨ ⌂ ⌂ **Facilities:** ▣ ⛱ ⚬ Sauna, whirlpool, washer/dryer. **Rates (CP):** $55–$69 S or D. Extra person $6. Children under age 19 stay free. Parking: Outdoor, free. AE, CB, DC, DISC, JCB, MC, V.

ATTRACTION ▣

Constitution Square State Historic Site
134 S 2nd St; tel 606/239-7089. In the years following the Revolutionary War, Danville evolved into a seat of local government due to its position on the much-traveled Wilderness Road. Soon, local citizens were contemplating statehood. Ten constitutional conventions were held in the Danville courthouse and in April 1792, a constitution was finally adopted. Soon after, Kentucky became the 15th state. Replicas of the original courthouse, jail, and meeting hall are here, along with the first post office west of the Alleghenies, a late 18th-century tavern, several historic homes converted into museums, and the gravesite of Isaac Shelby, the state's first governor. **Open:** June–Aug, Mon–Fri 9am–6pm, Sat 9am–5pm, Sun 1–4pm; Sept–Dec and Feb–May, Mon–Fri 10am–4pm. Closed some hols. **Free**

Dawson Springs

This western Kentucky town was one of the South's best-known health resorts at the turn of the century, offering curative spring waters. Today, nearby Pennyrile Forest State Park attracts the tourists. **Information:** Dawson Springs Chamber of Commerce, PO Box 107, Dawson Springs, 42408 (tel 502/797-2781).

RESORT ▣

▤▤ Pennyrile Lodge & Cottages
20781 Pennyrile Lodge Rd, 42408; tel 502/797-3421 or toll free 800/325-1711; fax 502/797-3413. 1,500 acres. A quiet, peaceful lodge surrounded by beautifully landscaped grounds featuring ferns and colorful flowers. The complex overlooks Pennyrile Lake. **Rooms:** 24 rms; 13 cottages/villas. CI 4pm/CO noon. Nonsmoking rms avail. **Amenities:** ▣ A/C, cable TV, dataport. All units w/terraces. **Services:** ⌂ Children's program. **Facilities:** ▣ ⛱ ⚬ ⚬2 ⌂ ⚬ 1 restau-

rant, 1 beach (lake shore), volleyball, games rm, lawn games, playground. Miniature-golf course. Rowboats and trolling motors available. **Rates:** Peak (May 3–Sept) $45–$55 S; $55–$65 D; $80–$90 cottage/villa. Extra person $5. Children under age 16 stay free. Lower rates off-season. Parking: Outdoor, free. AE, CB, DC, DISC, MC, V.

ATTRACTION 📷

Pennyrile Forest State Resort Park

20781 Pennyrile Lodge Rd; tel 502/797-3421. This wooded 15,000-acre park, surrounded by Pennyrile State Forest, provides almost every variety of outdoor recreation imaginable. Water lovers will love the boating, fishing, and swimming in 56-acre Pennyrile Lake; golfers can tackle the 9-hole regulation course or 18-hole miniature-golf course; and hikers can explore more than eight miles of marked trails. Facilities for camping, picnicking, and tennis are also available. **Open:** Daily sunrise–sunset. Closed week of Dec 25. **Free**

Elizabethtown

Located 35 miles south of Louisville, this 18th-century town is in the heart of Kentucky's Lincoln Trail area, with wealth of history, including ties to Abraham Lincoln's family and a past that includes Carrie Nation, Gen Custer, and Jenny Lind. **Information:** Elizabethtown–Hardin County Chamber of Commerce, 111 W Dixie Ave, Elizabethtown, 42701 (tel 502/765-4334).

MOTELS 🏨

🏨🏨 Comfort Inn

1043 Executive Dr, 42701; tel 502/769-3030 or toll free 800/682-5285; fax 502/765-7208. Exit 94 off I-65. Offers comfortable accommodations and one outstanding feature—an indoor pool set in lush, tropical surroundings. **Rooms:** 133 rms. CI 2:30pm/CO 11:30am. Nonsmoking rms avail. **Amenities:** 🛁 A/C, cable TV. Some units w/whirlpools. Some rooms have refrigerators and microwaves. **Services:** 🍽️ VCRs for rent. Fax and copy machines available. **Facilities:** 🛗 🏓 🏊 ⚍ Games rm, washer/dryer. Indoor putting green. **Rates (CP):** Peak (May–Dec) $49–$54 S; $54–$59 D. Extra person $5. Children under age 17 stay free. Min stay special events. Lower rates off-season. Parking: Outdoor, free. AE, CB, DC, DISC, JCB, MC, V.

🏨🏨 Holiday Inn

US 62 and I-65, PO Box G, 42702; tel 502/769-2344 or toll free 800/HOLIDAY; fax 502/737-2850. Exit 94 off I-65. Easily accessible from I-65, this motel is a good choice for overnight stays. **Rooms:** 150 rms. CI 3pm/CO noon. Nonsmoking rms avail. **Amenities:** 🛁 🏧 A/C, satel TV w/movies, dataport. **Services:** ✕ ⚍ 🍽️ 🐾 Very friendly staff. **Facilities:**

🛗 📺 ⚍ 1 restaurant. **Rates:** $59–$69 S or D. Extra person $10. Children under age 19 stay free. Parking: Outdoor, free. AE, CB, DC, DISC, JCB, MC, V.

🏨🏨 Howard Johnson Lodge

708 E Dixie Ave, 42701; tel 502/765-2185 or toll free 800/446-4656; fax 502/737-2065. Exit 91 off I-65. Basic, centrally located motel. **Rooms:** 81 rms and effic. CI 2pm/CO noon. Nonsmoking rms avail. **Amenities:** 🏧 A/C, cable TV. Some rooms have coffeemakers, hair dryers, dataports, and free local calls. **Services:** ✕ 🍽️ 🐾 Coffee available 24 hours, popcorn in evenings. **Facilities:** 🛗 📺 ⚍ 1 restaurant (dinner only), washer/dryer. **Rates (CP):** $36 S; $40 D; $95 effic. Extra person $5. Children under age 18 stay free. Min stay special events. Parking: Outdoor, free. AE, CB, DC, DISC, JCB, MC, V.

🏨🏨 Rodeway Inn

656 E Dixie Ave, 42701; tel 502/769-2331 or toll free 800/421-4777; fax 502/769-2331. Exit 91 off I-65. No-frills motel with the basic accommodations and amenities. **Rooms:** 80 rms. CI open/CO noon. Nonsmoking rms avail. **Amenities:** 🏧 A/C, cable TV w/movies, dataport. **Services:** ✕ 🍽️ **Facilities:** 🛗 1 restaurant. **Rates:** Peak (June–Labor Day) $35–$60 S; $39–$60 D. Extra person $5. Children under age 17 stay free. Min stay special events. Lower rates off-season. Parking: Outdoor, free. AE, DC, DISC, MC, V.

ATTRACTION 📷

Schmidt's Coca-Cola Museum

1201 N Dixie Ave; tel 502/737-4000. This unique museum is located within a Coca-Cola bottling plant that has been run by the Schmidt family for over 90 years. Visitors' first stopping point is the viewing gallery, where they can watch the bottling and canning process. The museum itself contains the largest privately owned collection of Coca-Cola memorabilia in the world, with jewelry, sheet music, knives, chewing gum, and the more familiar trays, signs, and glasses—all bearing the familiar Coke trademark. **Open:** Mon–Fri 9am–4pm. Closed some hols. **$**

Falls of Rough

Quaint Bluegrass Country town with many late-Victorian buildings. Nearby Rough River Dam State Resort Park attracts boating enthusiasts.

RESORT 🏨

🏨🏨🏨 Rough River Lodge & Cottages

450 Lodge Rd, 40119; tel 502/257-2311 or toll free 800/325-1713; fax 502/257-8682. 377 acres. Breathtaking views, peaceful surroundings, and great fishing make this lodge a great retreat. **Rooms:** 40 rms; 15 cottages/villas. CI open/CO noon. Nonsmoking rms avail. Rooms are comfortable and offer wonderful views of Rough River Lake. **Amenities:**

A/C, satel TV. Some units w/minibars, all w/terraces. **Services:** Children's program. **Facilities:** 1 restaurant, 1 beach (lake shore), lifeguard, basketball, volleyball, games rm, lawn games, playground, washer/dryer. Park has many recreational facilities: public beach, marina, nature trails, miniature golf. The property even has its own small airport. **Rates:** Peak (May 6–Sept 3) $52–$68 S or D; $79–$95 cottage/villa. Extra person $5. Children under age 16 stay free. Lower rates off-season. Parking: Outdoor, free. Closed Dec 22–29. AE, CB, DC, DISC, MC, V.

ATTRACTION

Rough River Dam State Resort Park
450 Lodge Rd; tel 502/257-2311 or toll free 800/325-1713. Very popular with locals, this park is located in the hilly, ruggedly beautiful Central Kentucky countryside overlooking a 4,860-acre lake. Rough River Lake, stocked with largemouth, white, and Kentucky bass, bluegill, channel catfish, crappie, and rough fish, offers some of the best fishing in the state. A 240-slip marina, boat launching ramp, and rental fishing boats are available. *Lady of the Lake* cruise boat offers daily trips during summer. On-site 9-hole golf course and 18-hole miniature-golf course, camping, hiking, tennis, volleyball, picnicking, and water sports of all varieties. Public beach with swimming and a sand volleyball court. **Open:** Daily 24 hours. Closed Dec 22–Dec 29. **Free**

Fort Knox

For lodgings, see Radcliff

Located 30 miles southwest of Louisville. Site of the nation's gold depository and the Patton Museum of Cavalry and Armor. Named for Maj Gen Henry Knox, the first Secretary of War.

ATTRACTIONS

US Army Armor Center and Fort Knox
Tel 502/624-3051. Site of the US Bullion Depository, the country's second-largest gold reserve. The treasure is kept in a two-level steel, granite, and concrete cave, sealed by an armored door weighing 28 tons. Unfortunately the depository is closed to visitors, but you may view its exterior (which may look familiar to you from the James Bond movie *Goldfinger*) from both KY 31W and Bullion Blvd. **Open:** Daily 7:30am–6pm. Closed some hols. **Free**

Patton Museum of Cavalry and Armor
4554 Fayette Ave; tel 502/624-3812. The Patton Museum is home to a variety of armored equipment and vehicles, weapons, art, and other memorabilia relating to cavalry and armor. Several displays commemorate the career of Gen George S Patton Jr, and there's a 14-foot section of the Berlin Wall. **Open:** May–Sept, Mon–Fri 9am–4:30pm, Sat–Sun 10am–6pm; Oct–Apr, Mon–Fri 9am–4:30pm, Sat–Sun 10am–4:30pm. Closed some hols. **Free**

Frankfort

Located in the Kentucky River Valley, in the rolling foothills of the Bluegrass Region. Frankfort was chosen the state capital in 1792, and its 1910 capitol building (with its famous floral clock) is considered one of the most beautiful in the country. The city's rich past includes Daniel and Rebecca Boone (now buried at the Frankfort Cemetery), Henry Clay, and Aaron Burr, and there are many well-preserved old homes. Nearby Lawrenceburg was established in 1820 and is home of the distillery that makes Wild Turkey bourbon. The area is also a major trade center for tobacco and livestock. **Information:** Frankfort Area Chamber of Commerce, 100 Capital Ave, Frankfort, 40601 (tel 502/223-8261).

HOTEL

Holiday Inn Capital Plaza
405 Wilkinson Blvd, 40601; tel 502/227-5100 or toll free 800/HOLIDAY; fax 502/875-7147. Location near Capitol Bldg draws mainly governmental and business travelers. **Rooms:** 189 rms and stes. Executive level. CI 3pm/CO noon. Nonsmoking rms avail. **Amenities:** A/C, cable TV w/movies, dataport. **Services:** Copying service available. **Facilities:** 1 restaurant (see "Restaurants" below), 2 bars (1 w/entertainment), games rm, sauna, whirlpool, beauty salon. **Rates:** $49–$100 S; $69–$100 D; $125 ste. Extra person $20. Children under age 12 stay free. Parking: Indoor, free. Rates may vary according to demand. AE, CB, DC, DISC, JCB, MC, V.

MOTELS

Bluegrass Inn
635 Versailles Rd, 40601; tel 502/695-1800 or toll free 800/322-1802; fax 502/695-6111. Jct US 60 and US 421. Motel situated in the heart of Bluegrass country. Convenient to nearby horse farms; easy access to I-75. **Rooms:** 61 rms. CI open/CO noon. Nonsmoking rms avail. **Amenities:** A/C, cable TV. Refrigerators in some rooms. **Services:** Very friendly staff. **Facilities:** **Rates:** $36–$52 S or D. Extra person $6. Children under age 17 stay free. Parking: Outdoor, free. AE, CB, DC, DISC, MC, V.

Knights Inn
855 Louisville Rd, 40601; tel 502/227-2282 or toll free 800/843-5644; fax 502/223-5159. On US 60. Slightly shabby chain motel. OK for an overnight stay. **Rooms:** 136 rms. CI 2pm/CO noon. Nonsmoking rms avail. Furnishings are in good shape but the walls, ceilings, and fixtures need attention. **Amenities:** A/C, cable TV. **Services:** **Facilities:** Exterior is a bit run down. **Rates:** $37 S;

$42 D. Extra person $5. Children under age 11 stay free. Parking: Outdoor, free. Group rates avail. AE, DC, DISC, MC, V.

RESTAURANTS

★ Columbia Steak House

In Franklin Square Shopping Center, US 127; tel 502/227-2380. **Regional American/Steak.** The Columbia chain has been in this area for 40 years, and is especially known for its tenderloin broiled in garlic butter. T-bone, prime rib, chicken, and seafood are also available. The decor is centered around the local love of horses and farm "silk" colors. **FYI:** Reservations accepted. Children's menu. **Open:** Mon–Thurs 11:30am–9:30pm, Fri 11:30am–10pm, Sat 5–10pm, Sun 12–9pm. **Prices:** Main courses $5–$15. AE, DC, DISC, MC, V.

Gabriel's

In Holiday Inn Capital Plaza, 405 Wilkinson Blvd; tel 502/227-5100. **Regional American.** Gabriel's offers a casually elegant setting with a relaxing view of a fountain area. The menu features regional dishes, as well as items from burgers and steaks to seafood and barbecue. Frequented by local political figures, as it's near the State Capitol and the Civic Center. **FYI:** Reservations accepted. Children's menu. **Open:** Daily 6:30am–10pm. **Prices:** Main courses $5–$20. AE, CB, DC, DISC, MC, V.

ATTRACTIONS

State Capitol

South end of Capitol Ave; tel 502/564-3000. The beaux-arts design of this 1910 building features 70 Ionic columns, decorative murals, and sculptures of Kentucky dignitaries. Also, the First Lady Doll Collection and changing history and culture exhibits. The capitol is perhaps best known for its outdoor Floral Clock, which is 34 feet in diameter and is supported by a 100-ton base. **Open:** Mon–Fri 8am–4:30pm, Sun 1–4:30pm. **Free**

Kentucky Historical Society

Broadway and Lewis Sts; tel 502/564-3016. The KHS operates three museums in historic downtown Frankfort. The **Old State Capitol** was the first prominent Greek Revival building west of the Alleghenies when it was completed in 1830. Today, it houses a fine collection of Kentucky paintings, sculptures, and prints, as well as temporary exhibits. In the annex of the Old Capitol is the **Kentucky History Museum,** which highlights the state's social and economic history with artifacts and interactive exhibits. A gift shop features traditional and contemporary Kentucky crafts. Four blocks from the Old Capitol, on E Main St in the Old State Arsenal, is the **Kentucky Military History Museum,** containing a diverse collection of weapons, uniforms, flags, and photographs from the Civil War to the Persian Gulf war. **Open:** Capitol and History Museum, Mon–Sat 9am–4pm, Sun noon–4pm. Closed some hols. **Free**

Governor's Mansion

East end of State Capitol St; tel 502/564-3000. The official governor's residence is situated on a high bluff overlooking the Kentucky River. The beaux-arts mansion, constructed in 1914 of native limestone, was modeled after the Petit Trianon, Marie Antoinette's summer villa. Free guided tours include the state dining room, ballroom, reception room, and formal salon. **Open:** Tues and Thurs 9am–11pm. **Free**

Frank Lloyd Wright's Zeigler House

509 Shelby St; tel 502/227-7164. Designed by Wright for the Rev Jesse R Zeigler, this 1910 house is a classic example of Wright's Prairie Style—low roof with overhanging eaves, glass walls, open floor plan. The house, which is now privately owned, features period antiques as well as original leaded windows, woodwork, stained glass, and brass. **Open:** Please phone ahead for private tour.

Wild Turkey Distillery

1525 Tyrone Rd, Lawrenceburg; tel 502/839-4544. Located 15 mi S of Frankfort. The rye used to make this whiskey comes from North Dakota, the barley from Montana, but it's the pure local water that makes this unmistakably Kentucky sour-mash whiskey. Free tours of the distillery offered Monday–Friday at 9am, 10:30am, 12:30pm, and 2:30pm. **Open:** Mon–Fri. Closed 1st week in Jan, last 2 weeks in July, and some hols. **Free**

Harrodsburg

Founded in 1774, this was the first permanent English settlement west of the Allegheny Mountains. Many visitors come today for the Shaker Village. **Information:** Harrodsburg/Mercer County Tour Commission, 103 S Main St, PO Box 283, Harrodsburg, 40330 (tel 606/734-2364).

HOTEL

≡≡≡ The Shaker Village at Pleasant Hill

3501 Lexington Rd, 40330; tel 606/734-5411; fax 606/734-5411. Off US 68. 2,700 acres. Spend the night in rooms where Shakers lived and worked over a century ago. The entire village is listed on the National Register of Historic Places. Reservations should be made well in advance. **Rooms:** 81 rms, stes, and effic; 2 cottages/villas. CI 3pm/CO 11am. Nonsmoking rms avail. Rooms, spread out over 15 restored buildings, are furnished with Shaker reproductions and hand-woven rugs and curtains. **Amenities:** A/C, TV. Some units w/fireplaces. **Services:** Friendly, informative staff. **Facilities:** 2 restaurants (*see* "Restaurants" below). **Rates:** $46–$90 S; $56–$100 D; $110–$150 ste; $150–$200 effic; $150–$200 cottage/villa. Extra person $8. Children under age 17 stay free. Parking: Outdoor, free. MC, V.

INN

≣≣≣ The Beaumont Inn

638 Beaumont Inn Dr, 40330; tel 606/734-3381 or toll free 800/352-3992; fax 606/734-6897. Off US 127. 30 acres. Listed on the National Register of Historic Places, this quaint inn is located in a quiet setting of trees and bushes. Operated by fourth-generation innkeepers. **Rooms:** 33 rms. CI 3pm/ CO noon. Nonsmoking rms avail. Rooms combine modern amenities with the elegant furnishings of the past. **Amenities:** ⚏ ♨ A/C, cable TV. Some units w/terraces. **Services:** ⊠ ⟲ Service-oriented staff. **Facilities:** ⚐ ⛨ 1 restaurant (*see* "Restaurants" below), guest lounge w/TV. **Rates:** $57–$75 S; $77–$95 D; $60–$80 cottage/villa. Extra person $20. MAP rates avail. Parking: Outdoor, free. Closed Jan–Feb. AE, CB, DC, DISC, MC, V.

RESORT

≣≣≣ Bright Leaf Golf Resort

1742 Danville Rd, 40330; tel 606/734-5481; fax 606/ 734-0530. Off US 127. 200 acres. Located in historic Harrodsburg. Convenient to many area historic sites. Operated by the same family for five generations. **Rooms:** 105 rms, stes, and effic. CI 2pm/CO noon. Nonsmoking rms avail. **Amenities:** ⚏ A/C, cable TV, refrig. All units w/terraces. **Services:** ✗ ⛐ ⊠ **Facilities:** ⚐ ▶₃₆ ⚑ ⛋ ⛁ & 2 restaurants, spa, sauna. Excellent golf facility. **Rates:** Peak (Apr–Oct) $50–$70 S; $60–$90 D; $100 ste; $150 effic. Extra person $10. Lower rates off-season. Parking: Outdoor, free. Golf packages avail. AE, DC, DISC, MC, V.

RESTAURANTS ⍢

♥★ Beaumont Inn

638 Beaumont Inn Dr; tel 606/734-3381. Off US 127. **Regional American.** The dining room of this venerable inn (listed on the National Register of Historic Places) offers Southern-style cooking in a comfortable setting featuring period antique furnishings. Regional favorites on the menu include fried chicken, country ham and biscuits, and corn pudding. The staff is most friendly and helpful. **FYI:** Reservations recommended. Children's menu. Dress code. No liquor license. No smoking. **Open:** Breakfast Mon–Fri 7–9:30am, Sat–Sun 8–9:30am; lunch Tues–Sat 11:30am–2pm, Sun 11am–2pm; dinner daily 5:30–8:30pm; brunch Sun 11am–2pm. Closed Jan–Feb. **Prices:** Main courses $15–$23. AE, CB, DC, DISC, MC, V. ♥ ⛟ &

♥★ Inn at Shaker Village

In Shaker Village at Pleasant Hill, 3501 Lexington Rd; tel 606/734-5411. **Regional American.** Visitors to this historic dining room, furnished with Shaker reproductions, dine on hearty Kentucky foods made from traditional Shaker recipes. At dinner, a selection of meats, salads, relishes, and vegetables is served family-style, with hot-from-the-oven bread and home-baked pies and cakes. **FYI:** Reservations recommend-ed. Children's menu. No liquor license. No smoking. **Open:** Breakfast daily 7:30–9:30am; lunch Mon–Sat 11:30am–2:30pm, Sun noon–7pm; dinner Mon–Sat 5:30–7:30pm, Sun noon–7pm. **Prices:** Main courses $12–$18. MC, V. ⛟ ⛲ &

ATTRACTIONS 🛍

Shaker Village at Pleasant Hill

3501 Lexington Rd; tel 606/734-5411. The United Society of Believers in Christ's Second Appearing, known to the world as Shakers because of their way of dancing during services, were America's largest and best-known communal society. Fifty years after the sect's founding in the late 18th century, nearly 6,000 Shakers were living in communities all over the eastern United States. One group of Shakers made their home here in central Kentucky. They lived simple, industrious lives, and their quest for simplicity and innovation is best exemplified by their famous furniture.

Although the Shaker faith has completely died out in Kentucky, the village at Pleasant Hill still contains 14 original buildings where 20th-century visitors can experience a bit of the lifestyle of the Shakers. Costumed historical interpreters perform demonstrations of broom-making, coopering, weaving, and furniture making. From April–October, Shaker music performances and special activities are scheduled each day. Also offered are riverboat cruises (additional fee) on the *Dixie Belle*, which makes its way up the Kentucky River. **Open:** Apr–Oct, daily 9am–6pm; Nov–Mar, daily 9am–5pm. Closed Dec 25. **$$$**

Old Fort Harrod State Park

S College St; tel 606/734-3314. Visitors can stroll through more than 10 cabins and blockhouses in this replica of the first permanent settlement west of the Allegheny Mountains. A museum, housed in a Greek Revival mansion dating from 1830, houses Civil War memorabilia, Native American artifacts, and a collection of pioneer firearms. From mid-April to mid-October, costumed craftspeople demonstrate the traditional arts of quilting, basketry, woodworking, broom-making, and blacksmithing. From mid-June to mid-August, the park is home to the popular outdoor drama *The Legend of Daniel Boone*, which chronicles the trials and tribulations of Kentucky's first settlers. Call 606/734-3346 for information or reservations. **Open:** Daily 8:30am–5pm. Closed some hols. **$$**

Hazard

Kentucky's oldest town, founded in 1790 by Elijah Combs and his seven brothers. Coal was discovered here some 39 years later, and transformed the area forever. A local museum illustrates the history of the area's coal and lumber industries and the coming of the railroad in the early 1900s. **Information:** Hazard–Perry County Chamber of Commerce, 601 Main St #3, Hazard, 41701 (tel 606/439-2659).

MOTELS

≣≣≣ Holiday Inn

200 Dawahare Dr, 41701; tel 606/436-4428 or toll free 800/ HOLIDAY; fax 606/436-4428 ext 317. Off Daniel Boone Pkwy. Motel located atop a hill in the heart of eastern Kentucky. A Victorian motif dominates in the lobby and dining room, which lends a romantic feel to the establishment. Large collection of antique dolls on display. **Rooms:** 80 rms and stes. CI 3pm/CO 11am. Nonsmoking rms avail. **Amenities:** ☎ ⚱ A/C, cable TV. **Services:** ✗ ⌖ ⌔ **Facilities:** ⌖ ⌖300⌖ ⅙ 1 restaurant, 1 bar, whirlpool. Indoor/outdoor pool is heated in winter. **Rates (BB):** $57–$70 S or D; $125 ste. Extra person $6. Children under age 18 stay free. Min stay special events. AP and MAP rates avail. Parking: Outdoor, free. AE, CB, DC, DISC, JCB, MC, V.

≣ Super 8 Motel

125 Village Lane, 41701; tel 606/436-8888 or toll free 800/ 800-8000; fax 606/439-0768. Off Daniel Boone Pkwy. No-frills chain motel offering only the bare minimum amenities. Adequate for overnight stay. **Rooms:** 86 rms and stes. CI open/CO 11am. Nonsmoking rms avail. Recliners available in some rooms. Waterbed and whirlpool suites available. **Amenities:** ☎ ⌖ A/C, cable TV w/movies. Some units w/whirlpools. **Services:** ⌔ ⌔ Fax service and free local calls. Complimentary coffee in lobby. **Facilities:** ⅙ **Rates (CP):** Peak (May, July, Sept) $43 S; $46 D; $50–$68 ste. Extra person $5. Children under age 12 stay free. Lower rates off-season. Parking: Outdoor, free. Extended-stay rates avail. AE, DC, DISC, MC, V.

Henderson

Since the city's founding in 1797, the Ohio River has been part of its history. The bustling river commerce of early years is still recalled in the downtown area. Naturalist-writer-artist John James Audubon did much of his pioneering work here. **Information:** Henderson Tourism Commission, 2961 US 41 N, Henderson, 42420 (tel 502/826-3128).

MOTELS

≣≣≣ Days Inn

2044 US 41 N, 42420; tel 502/826-6600 or toll free 800/ DAYS-INN; fax 502/826-3055. Engaging two-story establishment. **Rooms:** 117 rms and stes. CI 2pm/CO 11am. Nonsmoking rms avail. **Amenities:** ☎ ⌖ A/C, cable TV w/movies, in-rm safe. Some rooms have dataports. **Services:** ✗ ⌖ ⌔ ⌔ **Facilities:** ⌖ ⌖300⌖ ⅙ 1 restaurant, 1 bar (w/entertainment), washer/dryer. Guest privileges at local fitness center. **Rates:** Peak (June 26–Sept 4) $50–$60 S; $56–$66 D; $60– $85 ste. Extra person $6. Children under age 12 stay free. Lower rates off-season. Parking: Outdoor, free. AE, CB, DC, DISC, JCB, MC, V.

≣ Sugar Creek Inn

2077 US 41 N, 42420; tel 502/827-0127. Clean, simple accommodations. Fine for an overnight stay. **Rooms:** 65 rms. CI 2pm/CO noon. Nonsmoking rms avail. **Amenities:** ☎ ⌖ A/C, cable TV. Some units w/whirlpools. **Services:** ⌖ ⌔ ⌔ **Facilities:** ⌖30⌖ ⅙ **Rates (CP):** $33–$36 S; $38–$50 D. Extra person $5. Children under age 16 stay free. Parking: Outdoor, free. AE, CB, DC, DISC, MC, V.

≣≣ Super 8 Motel

2030 US 41 N, 42420; tel 502/827-5611 or toll free 800/ 800-8000; fax 502/827-5615. Basic, no-frills chain motel. More amenities than the average Super 8. **Rooms:** 100 rms and stes. CI 1pm/CO 11am. Nonsmoking rms avail. **Amenities:** ☎ ⌖ A/C, cable TV w/movies, dataport. Some units w/whirlpools. Some rooms come with coffeemakers, radios, hair dryers, and full-length mirrors. **Services:** ⌖ ⌔ **Facilities:** ⌖ ⌖100⌖ ⅙ 1 bar, washer/dryer. Large pool area. **Rates (CP):** Peak (June–Sept) $36–$57 S; $47–$62 D; $75 ste. Extra person $5. Children under age 12 stay free. Lower rates off-season. Parking: Outdoor, free. AE, CB, DC, DISC, JCB, MC, V.

ATTRACTION

John James Audubon State Park and Nature Center

3100 US 41 N; tel 502/826-2247. Famed naturalist John James Audubon came to Henderson in 1810 with his wife and infant son. While living here, along the bird migration route on the Mississippi flyway, Audubon had the idea of painting every bird in North America and selling the life-size paintings in books. Many of the paintings that eventually appeared in his 1838 masterpiece *Birds of America* were produced in Henderson. The state park aims to preserve the peaceful woods where Audubon walked as he observed the subjects of his paintings. Five and a half miles of trails wind through the nature preserve, which features over 150 varieties of wildflowers. The park also has facilities for fishing and tennis, as well as a nine-hole golf course, campground, and public beach.

The **Aububon Museum and Nature Center** contains Audubon memorabilia (letters, journals, paintings, prints, jewelry, and clothing) as well as one of the world's largest collections of Audubon's work, including watercolors, oils, and engravings. The Discovery Center has exhibits on bird locomotion, feeding, habitat, and behavior. **Open:** Daily 10am–5pm. Closed Dec 22–Dec 28. $$

Hodgenville

Birthplace of Abraham Lincoln. The small downtown square is dominated by the Lincoln Museum and an outdoor bronze statue of the Union's savior; the 116-acre Abraham Lincoln

Birthplace National Historic Site is just south of town. **Information:** LaRue County Chamber of Commerce, PO Box 176, Hodgenville, 42748 (tel 502/358-3411).

MOTEL ⬚

▤ Lincoln Memorial Motel

2765 Lincoln Farm Rd, 42748; tel 502/358-3197. Jct US 31E/61. No-frills property adjacent to Lincoln's birthplace. **Rooms:** 10 rms. CI 2pm/CO 11am. Nonsmoking rms avail. **Amenities:** ⬚ A/C, cable TV. **Services:** ⬚ ⬚ **Facilities:** ⬚ **Rates:** $34–$38 S or D. Extra person $5. Parking: Outdoor, free. AE, MC, V.

ATTRACTIONS ⬚

Abraham Lincoln Birthplace National Historic Site
2995 Lincoln Farm Rd; tel 502/358-3137. Located 3 mi S of Hodgenville on US 31E and KY 61. In 1808, Thomas and Nancy Lincoln moved to a $200 plot of land called Sinking Spring Farm, in central Kentucky. Three months later, on February 12, 1809, their second child, Abraham, was born. Somewhat incongruously, a stately marble and granite memorial now encloses the humble log cabin where the 16th president entered the world. Visitors may take a self-guided walking tour around the grounds. There are picnic facilities and hiking trails on site, as well as a visitors center. **Open:** Apr–May and Sept–Oct, daily 8am–5:45pm; June–Aug, daily 8am–6:45pm; Nov–Mar, daily 8am–4:45pm. Closed some hols. **Free**

The Lincoln Museum
66 Lincoln Square; tel 502/358-3163. Located in the Downtown Hodgenville Historic District, the Lincoln Museum offers an educational experience for all ages. A descriptive brochure leads the visitor through 12 dioramas illustrating scenes ranging from "The Cabin Years" to Lincoln's death at "Ford's Theater." The second level of the museum houses a collection of original art, a film about Lincoln's life in Kentucky, and special exhibits. Guided tours can be provided, with advance notice, for groups of 12 or more. **Open:** Mon–Sat 8:30am–5pm, Sun 12:30–5pm. Closed some hols. **$**

Hopkinsville

A stop on the Cherokee Trail of Tears and the site of the 1904 Tobacco War. The town is still a major tobacco market, though other industries have moved in as well. Country roadside stands sell crafts made by the area's Amish and Mennonite residents. **Information:** Hopkinsville–Christian County Chamber of Commerce, 1209 S Virginia St, PO Box 1382, Hopkinsville, 42241 (tel 502/885-9096).

HOTEL ⬚

▤▤▤ Holiday Inn

2910 Fort Campbell Blvd, 42240; tel 502/886-4413 or toll free 800/465-4329; fax 502/886-4413. Exit 7A off Pennyrile Pkwy. Nestled in the woods of eastern Kentucky, this hotel offers all the peace and quiet—and all the recreational activities—anyone could want. Fishing, boating, hiking, tennis, and camping are all available in the park or nearby. **Rooms:** 101 rms. CI noon/CO noon. Nonsmoking rms avail. Well-decorated, well-kept rooms have private balconies with fantastic views. **Amenities:** ⬚ ⬚ ⬚ A/C, cable TV w/movies, dataport. **Services:** ✗ ⬚ ⬚ ⬚ Planned activities for both adults and children. **Facilities:** ⬚ ⬚ ⬚ ⬚ 1 restaurant, 1 bar, sauna, whirlpool. Square dancing and "clogging" on nearby Hoedoun Island. Park has a nature center and a sky lift to Natural Bridge. **Rates:** $59–$69 S or D. Extra person $6. Children under age 19 stay free. Parking: Outdoor, free. AE, CB, DC, DISC, JCB, MC, V.

MOTEL

▤▤ Econo Lodge

2916 Fort Campbell Blvd, 42240; tel 502/886-5242 or toll free 800/553-2666; fax 502/886-5242. Exit 7A off Pennyrile Pkwy. An attractive chain motel offering comfortable accommodations. **Rooms:** 125 rms. CI 2pm/CO noon. Nonsmoking rms avail. **Amenities:** ⬚ A/C, satel TV w/movies. Dataports available. **Services:** ✗ ⬚ ⬚ ⬚ **Facilities:** ⬚ ⬚ ⬚ 1 bar, games rm, sauna, whirlpool, washer/dryer. Discount at local golf course. Sundeck. **Rates (CP):** Peak (May 26–Sept 5) $34–$39 S or D. Extra person $5. Children under age 18 stay free. Lower rates off-season. Parking: Outdoor, free. AE, CB, DC, DISC, EC, ER, JCB, MC, V.

Horse Cave

In the Mammoth Cave area, with spectacular caves and caverns. Site of the Mammoth Cave Wildlife Museum, and Kentucky Down Under (a 75-acre wildlife refuge re-creating the Australian outback).

ATTRACTIONS ⬚

American Cave Museum and Hidden River Cave
Main St; tel 502/786-1466. Operated by the American Cave Conservation Association, this facility aims to educate visitors about the formation and history of natural caverns. If you've ever wondered how nature sculpts huge subterranean chambers out of limestone rock, why our prehistoric ancestors were cave dwellers, or how stalactites are formed, this is the place for you. An elevator behind the museum gives access to **Hidden River,** the underground waterway that flows 150 feet below the town of Horse Cave. **Open:** Sept–May, daily 9am–5pm; June–Aug, daily 9am–7pm. Closed some hols. **$$$**

Kentucky Down Under

Exit 58 off I-65; tel 502/786-2634. A clever combination of Kentucky's underground caverns and animals from "down under." The Australian element of the park includes wool-shearing demonstrations, petting zoo, exotic bird garden, Australian Walkabout (where human visitors mingle with kangaroos and emus), and Outback Cafe featuring Australian and American cuisine. Then visitors can really head down under, to Kentucky Caverns (formerly known as Mammoth Onyx Cave). Easy 45-minute guided tours of the cave are available. **Open:** Apr–May and Sept–Oct, daily 9am–4pm; June–Aug, daily 8am–6pm. Closed some hols. $$$$

Jamestown

The seat of Russell County in southern Kentucky, this agricultural town is located near the north shore of Lake Cumberland, one of the largest manmade lakes in the world (63,000 acres).

LODGES

≣ ≣ ≣ Lure Lodge

5465 State Park Rd, 42629; tel 502/343-3111 or toll free 800/325-1709; fax 502/343-5510. In Lake Cumberland State Resort Park; 8 mi S of town. 2,791 acres. Quiet, rural lodge offering rooms and fully equipped cottages. **Rooms:** 63 rms; 30 cottages/villas. CI 4pm/CO noon. Nonsmoking rms avail. Comfortable rooms with excellent views. **Amenities:** A/C, cable TV. All units w/terraces. Cottages have fully equipped kitchens. **Services:** Social director, children's program. Friendly and helpful staff. **Facilities:** 1 restaurant, basketball, volleyball, games rm, lawn games, sauna, whirlpool, playground. Planned outdoor activities; miniature golf, and camping are also available. **Rates:** Peak (May 26–Sept 3) $57–$73 S or D; $84–$100 cottage/villa. Extra person $5. Children under age 16 stay free. Lower rates off-season. Parking: Outdoor, free. Closed Dec 24–31. AE, CB, DC, DISC, MC, V.

≣ ≣ Pumpkin Creek Lodge

5465 State Park Rd, 42629; tel 502/343-3111 or toll free 800/325-1709; fax 502/343-5510. In Lake Cumberland State Resort Park; 8 mi S of town. 2,791 acres. Pumpkin Creek—the original lodge at Lake Cumberland—is set in a very quiet and secluded area close to the newer Lure Lodge and all its facilities. **Rooms:** 13 rms and stes. CI 4pm/CO noon. Nonsmoking rms avail. Rooms are somewhat rustic, but that is to be expected at this type of lodge. Some rooms have excellent views. **Amenities:** A/C, cable TV. Some units w/terraces. Some rooms have wet bars. **Services:** Social director, children's program. **Facilities:** 1 restaurant, basketball, volleyball, games rm, lawn games, sauna, whirlpool, playground. All facilities—including registration and dining—are shared with nearby Lure Lodge. **Rates:** Peak (May 26–Sept 3) $57–$73 S or D;

$63–$78 ste. Extra person $5. Children under age 16 stay free. Lower rates off-season. Parking: Outdoor, free. Closed Dec 24–31. AE, CB, DC, DISC, MC, V.

ATTRACTION

Lake Cumberland State Resort Park

5465 State Park Rd; tel 502/343-3111. Located in the south-central part of the state, this 3,000-acre park includes several campgrounds and picnic areas, a boat marina, a nine-hole golf course, a miniature-golf course, and tennis courts. Serious anglers will want to try their luck on the lake, which has an abundance of smallmouth bass, bluegill, crappie, and rainbow trout. Naturalist-led interpretive programs are offered year-round, and there are daily recreational programs in the summer. **Open:** Daily dawn–dusk. **Free**

Lexington

See also Frankfort, Georgetown, Paris

Founded in 1775 (17 years before Kentucky became a state). By 1820, Lexington had become one of the largest and wealthiest towns west of the Alleghenies. The state's second-largest city, it is one of the international centers of the horse industry. Nearby Kentucky Horse Park, the "Showplace of the Bluegrass," covers over 1,000 acres. Historic houses abound in Lexington, including the Henry Clay Estate. Home of the University of Kentucky. Nearby Versailles, established in 1793 by the General Marquis Calmes, is popular with antiques shoppers. Old Frankfort Pike, one of state's Scenic Byways, stretches between Frankfort and Versailles, passing through six historic districts and four National Register properties. **Information:** Greater Lexington Convention & Visitors Bureau, 301 E Vine St, Lexington, 40507 (tel 606/233-1221).

PUBLIC TRANSPORTATION

LexTran operates 17 main bus routes, including 2 trolley routes downtown. Bus fare: adults 80¢, seniors and persons with disabilities 40¢, children (ages 6–18) 60¢; children under 6 ride free. Trolley fare is 25¢, 10¢ for seniors and persons with disabilities. For schedule and route information call 253-INFO, or visit the Transit Center at 220 Vine St.

HOTELS

≣ ≣ ≣ Campbell House Inn, Suites & Golf Club

1375 Harrodsburg Rd, 40504; tel 606/255-4281 or toll free 800/354-9235, 800/432-9254 in KY; fax 606/254-4368. Off I-75, exit 113. 110 acres. A gracious hotel, serving up Southern-style hospitality. Convenient location five minutes from downtown, University of Kentucky, Keeneland, and Red Mile Harness Track. Within walking distance of restaurants and shops. **Rooms:** 370 rms, stes, and effic. CI 2pm/CO noon. Nonsmoking rms avail. Variety of rooms and suites available. **Amenities:** A/C, cable TV, refrig, dataport.

Some units w/terraces, some w/whirlpools. **Services:** X 🆅🅿 🚐 🔳 ⤸ Babysitting. Friendly, helpful staff. **Facilities:** ⚸ ▶18 ☎2 🍴 📶600 ⚷ 3 restaurants (*see* "Restaurants" below), 2 bars (1 w/entertainment), volleyball, games rm, lawn games, beauty salon, washer/dryer. **Rates:** $50–$65 S; $60–$75 D; $70–$175 ste; $70–$175 effic. Extra person $8. Children under age 12 stay free. Parking: Outdoor, free. Golf packages avail. AE, CB, DC, DISC, JCB, MC, V.

☰☰☰☰ DoubleTree Guest Suites

2601 Richmond Rd, 40509; tel 606/268-0060 or toll free 800/262-3774; fax 606/268-6209. Off I-75. Located in the French Quarter Shops, close to restaurants and area attractions. An indoor courtyard is filled with greenery, fountains, and wrought-iron furniture. **Rooms:** 155 rms and stes. CI 3pm/CO noon. Nonsmoking rms avail. Large rooms with spacious living areas and elegant furnishings. **Amenities:** 🍸 🛁 🔳 🍴 A/C, cable TV w/movies, refrig, dataport. Some units w/terraces, all w/whirlpools. Complimentary newspaper. **Services:** X 🆅🅿 🚐 🔳 ⤸ Babysitting. Friendly, accommodating staff. **Facilities:** ⚸ 🍴 📶260 ⚷ 1 restaurant, 1 bar (w/entertainment). **Rates (BB):** $99–$139 S or D; $109–$139 ste. Extra person $10. Children under age 18 stay free. Parking: Outdoor, free. Honeymoon rates avail. AE, DC, DISC, JCB, MC, V.

☰☰☰ Gratz Park Inn

120 W 2nd St, 40507 (Downtown); tel 606/231-1777 or toll free 800/227-4362; fax 606/233-7593. Off I-75 exit 113. Located in a historical residential section of downtown, this luxurious hotel is within walking distance of shops and dining in the area. **Rooms:** 44 rms and stes. CI 3pm/CO noon. Nonsmoking rms avail. Each room is individually decorated in a tasteful style that is in keeping with the historic spirit of the location. **Amenities:** 🍸 🛁 A/C, cable TV, dataport. **Services:** X 🖛 🚐 🔳 ⤸ Twice-daily maid svce. Staff is very attentive to guests' needs. Free newspapers and fresh flowers provided to rooms every morning. Free limousine service in evenings for transportation to downtown restaurants. **Facilities:** 📶65 ⚷ 1 restaurant. Use of nearby sports club available for small fee. **Rates (CP):** $95 S or D; $109–$250 ste. Extra person $10. Children under age 18 stay free. Min stay special events. Parking: Outdoor, free. Some discounts and packages avail. AE, CB, DC, DISC, MC, V.

☰☰☰ Hilton Suites of Lexington Green

3195 Nicholasville Rd, 40503; tel 606/271-4000 or toll free 800/367-4754; fax 606/273-2975. Corner of New Circle Rd. Adjacent to restaurants and shopping at Lexington Green, as well as comedy club and movie theater. **Rooms:** 174 stes. Executive level. CI 3pm/CO noon. Nonsmoking rms avail. Well-equipped for travelers with disabilities. **Amenities:** 🍸 🛁 🔳 A/C, cable TV w/movies, refrig, dataport. All units w/minibars, 1 w/whirlpool. **Services:** X 🚐 🔳 ⤸ ⟳ Car-rental desk, babysitting. Business support services available. Very helpful staff. **Facilities:** ⚸ 🍴 📶100 ⚷ 1 restaurant, 1 bar, sauna, whirlpool. Privileges at local sports club are available for small fee. **Rates:** $89–$145 ste. Extra person $10. Children under age 18 stay free. Min stay special events. AP and MAP rates avail. Parking: Outdoor, free. AE, CB, DC, DISC, ER, JCB, MC, V.

☰☰☰ Hyatt Regency Lexington

400 W Vine St, 40507 (Downtown); tel 606/253-1234 or toll free 800/233-1234; fax 606/254-7430. Off I-75 at exit 113. This business hotel is part of the Lexington Center complex, which includes shops, the convention center, and Rupp Arena. Close to area attractions. **Rooms:** 365 rms and stes. Executive level. CI 3pm/CO noon. Nonsmoking rms avail. **Amenities:** 🍸 🛁 🔳 🍴 A/C, satel TV w/movies, dataport, voice mail. Some units w/whirlpools. **Services:** X 🖛 🆅🅿 🚐 🔳 ⤸ Car-rental desk, masseur, children's program, babysitting. Complete business services include faxing, copying, packaging, and shipping. **Facilities:** ⚸ 🍴 📶900 ⚷ 1 restaurant, 2 bars. Use of sports facilities within walking distance (small fee). **Rates:** $127–$152 S; $152–$177 D; $275–$875 ste. Extra person $10. Children under age 12 stay free. MAP rates avail. Parking: Outdoor, free. AE, CB, DC, DISC, JCB, MC, V.

☰☰☰ Radisson Plaza Hotel Lexington

369 W Vine St, 40507 (Downtown); tel 606/231-9000 or toll free 800/333-3333; fax 606/281-3737. From I-75 take exit 113. Within walking distance of many downtown restaurants and facilities. Convention center is across the street. **Rooms:** 367 rms and stes. Executive level. CI 3pm/CO noon. Nonsmoking rms avail. **Amenities:** 🍸 🛁 🔳 A/C, cable TV w/movies, dataport. Some units w/whirlpools. **Services:** X 🖛 🆅🅿 🚐 🔳 ⤸ ⟳ Car-rental desk, social director. **Facilities:** ⚸ 🍴 📶1000 ⚷ 1 restaurant, 2 bars (1 w/entertainment), sauna, whirlpool. For small fee, guests can use facilities of downtown sports club. **Rates:** $115–$135 S; $125–$145 D; $175–$365 ste. Extra person $10. Children under age 12 stay free. AP rates avail. Parking: Indoor, free. Some discounts and packages available, as well as extended-stay rates. AE, CB, DC, DISC, EC, ER, JCB, MC, V.

☰☰☰ Residence Inn by Marriott

1080 Newtown Pike, 40511; tel 606/231-6191 or toll free 800/331-3131; fax 606/231-6191. Off New Circle Rd (KY 4) 1 mi from I-75, I-64 at exit 115. Offers large, well-equipped rooms and kitchens for extended stays. Convenient to airport, Keeneland, Kentucky Horse Park, and other area attractions. **Rooms:** 80 stes and effic. CI 3pm/CO noon. Nonsmoking rms avail. **Amenities:** 🍸 🛁 🔳 A/C, cable TV, refrig, in-rm safe. Some units w/fireplaces. **Services:** 🔳 ⤸ ⟳ Babysitting. **Facilities:** ⚸ 🏀 ⚷ Basketball, whirlpool, washer/dryer. Access to fitness center; facilities of Courtyard by Marriott are within walking distance. **Rates (CP):** Peak (Apr–Oct) $125–$160 ste; $125–$160 effic. Extra person $10. Children under age 18 stay free. Lower rates off-season. Parking: Outdoor, free. Lower rates offered for longer stays. AE, CB, DC, DISC, JCB, MC, V.

MOTELS

≣≣≣ Best Western Regency—Lexington Inn
2241 Elkhorn Rd, 40505; tel 606/293-2202 or toll free 800/528-1234; fax 606/293-2202. Off I-75 at exit 110. A good choice for families with children, due to extra-large rooms. Pleasant and relaxing lobby area. **Rooms:** 112 rms and stes. CI 2pm/CO 11am. Nonsmoking rms avail. Rooms and baths are large and well appointed. **Amenities:** 🛏 🕭 A/C, cable TV. 1 unit w/whirlpool. **Services:** 🖢 **Facilities:** 🛴 🔲50 🕭 Sauna, whirlpool, washer/dryer. **Rates (CP):** Peak (Mar–Dec) $46–$50 S; $54–$58 D; $85 ste. Extra person $8. Children under age 12 stay free. Lower rates off-season. Parking: Outdoor, free. AE, CB, DC, DISC, MC, V.

≣≣≣ Comfort Inn
2381 Buena Vista Dr, 40505; tel 606/299-0302 or toll free 800/394-8403; fax 606/299-2306. Off I-75 at exit 110. Popular with business travelers due to central location. Elegant yet comfortable lobby. **Rooms:** 124 rms and stes. CI 2pm/CO noon. Nonsmoking rms avail. Many business-friendly amenities, including large desk areas. **Amenities:** 🛏 🕭 A/C, cable TV, dataport. 1 unit w/whirlpool. **Services:** 🖢 **Facilities:** 🛴 🔲100 🕭 **Rates (CP):** Peak (May–Oct) $60–$80 S or D; $115 ste. Extra person $5. Children under age 16 stay free. Lower rates off-season. Parking: Outdoor, free. AE, CB, DC, DISC, MC, V.

≣≣≣ Courtyard by Marriott
775 Newtown Court, 40511; tel 606/253-4646 or toll free 800/321-2211; fax 606/253-9118. Off New Circle Rd. Surrounded by trees, this very quiet facility offers nicely appointed rooms well suited for the business traveler. **Rooms:** 146 rms and stes. CI 4pm/CO noon. Nonsmoking rms avail. Most rooms offer nice views. **Amenities:** 🛏 🕭 🖬 A/C, cable TV w/movies, dataport. Some units w/terraces. **Services:** ✗ 🖢 🖢 **Facilities:** 🛴 🖢 🔲45 🕭 1 restaurant, 1 bar, whirlpool, washer/dryer. **Rates:** Peak (varies) $59–$89 S; $64–$94 D; $98–$108 ste. Extra person $5. Children under age 21 stay free. Lower rates off-season. Parking: Outdoor, free. AE, DC, DISC, MC, V.

≣≣ Days Inn
1987 N Broadway, 40505; tel 606/299-1202 or toll free 800/333-9843; fax 606/299-5760. Off I-75 at exit 113. Within convenient distance from area attractions as well as downtown, the University of Kentucky, and the airport. Exterior needs some maintenance work. OK for overnight stay. **Rooms:** 190 rms and stes. CI 2pm/CO noon. Nonsmoking rms avail. **Amenities:** 🛏 🖬 A/C, cable TV w/movies, dataport, in-rm safe. All units w/terraces. **Services:** ✗ 🚗 🖢 🖢 🖢 Twice-daily maid svce. **Facilities:** 🛴 🔲100 1 restaurant, 1 bar (w/entertainment), washer/dryer. **Rates:** Peak (April–Oct) $36–$39 S; $42–$48 D; $48–$52 ste. Extra person $5. Children under age 16 stay free. Lower rates off-season. Parking: Outdoor, free. AE, CB, DC, DISC, MC, V.

≣ Econo Lodge North
925 Newtown Pike, 40511; tel 606/231-6300 or toll free 800/394-8402; fax 606/231-6300. Off New Circle Rd (KY 4) 1 mile from I-75, and I-64 at exit 115. For budget travelers. Adequate, but nothing special; facilities could use better upkeep. **Rooms:** 110 rms. CI 1pm/CO noon. Nonsmoking rms avail. **Amenities:** 🛏 🕭 A/C, cable TV. **Services:** ✗ 🖢 🖢 🖢 **Facilities:** 🛴 🔲50 1 restaurant, 1 bar (w/entertainment), washer/dryer. **Rates:** Peak (Mar–Oct) $30–$35 S; $35–$40 D. Extra person $5. Children under age 18 stay free. Lower rates off-season. Parking: Outdoor, free. AE, DC, DISC, MC, V.

≣≣ Hampton Inn
3060 Lakecrest Circle, 40513; tel 606/223-0088 or toll free 800/HAMPTON; fax 606/223-0088. Off New Circle Rd. Basic chain motel situated near restaurants, shopping, area attractions. Airport is three miles away. **Rooms:** 68 rms. CI 2pm/CO 11am. Nonsmoking rms avail. **Amenities:** 🛏 🕭 A/C, cable TV w/movies. **Services:** 🖢 🖢 🖢 Fax machine available. **Facilities:** 🛴 🕭 Whirlpool. **Rates (CP):** Peak (Apr–Oct) $86–$96 S; $96–$106 D. Children under age 18 stay free. Min stay special events. Lower rates off-season. Parking: Outdoor, free. 13th-night-free program. AE, CB, DC, DISC, MC, V.

≣≣≣ Hampton Inn
2251 Elkhorn Rd, 40505; tel 606/299-2613 or toll free 800/HAMPTON; fax 606/299-9664. Off I-75 at exit 110. Popular with business travelers due to location near business and industrial center. Large, well-appointed lobby area. **Rooms:** 125 rms. CI 2pm/CO noon. Nonsmoking rms avail. Rooms are larger than average. **Amenities:** 🛏 🕭 A/C, cable TV, dataport. Microwave, refrigerator available. Some rooms have coffeemakers. **Services:** 🖢 Free copies of *USA Today* and *Wall Street Journal*. Friendly, helpful staff. **Facilities:** 🛴 🖢 🔲35 🕭 Large, indoor heated pool and spacious exercise facility. **Rates (CP):** Peak (May 26–Sept 24) $59–$67 S; $64–$75 D. Children under age 18 stay free. Lower rates off-season. Parking: Outdoor, free. AE, CB, DC, DISC, MC, V.

≣≣≣ Harley Hotel
2143 N Broadway, 40505; tel 606/299-1261 or toll free 800/321-2323; fax 606/293-0048. Off I-75 at exit 113. With a mini-resort atmosphere and superior service, this is just right for a comfortable stay. **Rooms:** 146 rms and stes. CI 3pm/CO 11am. Nonsmoking rms avail. Spacious, well-appointed rooms with many extras. Excellent views. **Amenities:** 🛏 🕭 A/C, cable TV w/movies, dataport. All units w/terraces. **Services:** ✗ 🚗 🖢 🖢 Car-rental desk, babysitting. **Facilities:** 🛴 🖢2 🖢 🚐 🕭 1 restaurant, 1 bar (w/entertainment), sauna, whirlpool. Beautiful indoor and outdoor pools, grounds area for relaxing. Patio and gazebo. **Rates:** Peak (Apr and Oct) $88 S; $98 D; $125–$200 ste. Extra person $10. Children under age 18 stay free. Min stay special events. Lower rates off-season. Parking: Outdoor, free. AE, CB, DC, DISC, MC, V.

▤▤▤ Holiday Inn South

5532 Athens-Boonesboro Rd, 40509; tel 606/263-5241 or toll free 800/HOLIDAY; fax 606/263-4333. Exit 104 off I-75. Family-style motel with a Holidome, featuring many recreational activities. Nice lobby area and poolside patio. **Rooms:** 149 rms, stes, and effic. CI 3pm/CO noon. Nonsmoking rms avail. **Amenities:** 🛎 ⚒ A/C, satel TV w/movies, dataport. Some units w/minibars, some w/whirlpools. **Services:** ✕ 🖨 ⌲ 🕭 Social director. **Facilities:** 🖼 🏐 📺 ⚒ 1 restaurant, 1 bar (w/entertainment), basketball, games rm, sauna, steam rm, whirlpool, washer/dryer. Holidome features miniature-golf course and pool tables. Guest passes to local gym. **Rates:** Peak (Apr–Oct) $72–$76 S or D; $115–$140 ste; $115–$140 effic. Extra person $6. Children under age 19 stay free. Lower rates off-season. Parking: Outdoor, free. AE, CB, DC, DISC, JCB, MC, V.

▤▤ Kentucky Inn

525 Waller Ave, 40504; tel 606/254-1177 or toll free 800/221-6652; fax 606/252-4913. Off New Circle Rd on US 68. Convenient location to university, airport, Keeneland, and downtown. **Rooms:** 105 rms and stes. CI 3pm/CO noon. Nonsmoking rms avail. Rooms have some maintenance problems. **Amenities:** 🛎 A/C, cable TV. Some rooms have hair dryers. **Services:** ✕ 🖨 ⌲ Pleasant, friendly staff. **Facilities:** 🖼 📺 ⚒ 1 restaurant, 1 bar, games rm. **Rates:** $48 S; $54 D; $75 ste. Extra person $4. Children under age 16 stay free. Parking: Outdoor, free. AE, CB, DC, DISC, MC, V.

▤▤ La Quinta Motor Inn

1919 Stanton Way, 40511; tel 606/231-7551 or toll free 800/531-5900; fax 606/281-6002. Off I-75 at exit 115. Five minutes from Kentucky Horse Park. Exterior and lobby were recently renovated. **Rooms:** 130 rms and stes. CI 1pm/CO noon. Nonsmoking rms avail. **Amenities:** 🛎 ⚒ A/C, cable TV w/movies, dataport. **Services:** 🖨 ⌲ 🕭 Free local phone calls. **Facilities:** 🖼 📺 ⚒ **Rates (CP):** $56–$72 S; $63–$79 D; $71–$87 ste. Extra person $7. Children under age 18 stay free. Parking: Outdoor, free. Special discounts for return guests and seniors. AE, CB, DC, DISC, MC, V.

▤▤ Microtel

2240 Buena Vista Dr, 40505; tel 606/299-9600 or toll free 800/844-8608; fax 606/299-8719. Off I-75 at exit 110. Easy access to I-75. Central location is convenient to many area attractions and restaurants. **Rooms:** 99 rms. CI 2pm/CO noon. Nonsmoking rms avail. All rooms have day bed. **Amenities:** 🛎 A/C, cable TV w/movies. **Services:** ⌲ 🕭 **Facilities:** 📺 ⚒ **Rates:** Peak (June–Oct) $27 S; $32 D. Children under age 18 stay free. Lower rates off-season. Parking: Outdoor, free. AE, CB, DC, DISC, MC, V.

▤▤ Quality Inn Northwest

1050 Newtown Pike, 40511; tel 606/233-0561 or toll free 800/228-5151; fax 606/231-6125. Off New Circle Rd (KY 4). Clean, standard rooms. Minutes from downtown and area attractions. **Rooms:** 109 rms and stes. CI noon/CO noon. Nonsmoking rms avail. **Amenities:** 🛎 A/C, cable TV,

dataport. **Services:** 🖨 ⌲ 🕭 Helpful staff can arrange tours of horse farms. **Facilities:** 🖼 📺 ⚒ **Rates (CP):** Peak (May–Oct) $46 S; $66 D; $130 ste. Extra person $5. Children under age 19 stay free. Lower rates off-season. Parking: Outdoor, free. AE, CB, DC, DISC, EC, ER, JCB, MC, V.

▤▤ Shoney's Inn Lexington

2753 Richmond Rd, 40509; tel 606/269-4999 or toll free 800/222-2222; fax 606/268-2346. Easy access from I-75. Popular with University of Kentucky visitors and families. **Rooms:** 100 rms. CI 2pm/CO noon. Nonsmoking rms avail. **Amenities:** 🛎 A/C, cable TV w/movies. Complimentary morning coffee and newspaper. **Services:** 🖨 ⌲ **Facilities:** 🖼 📺 ⚒ 1 restaurant. Discount at neighboring Shoney's restaurant. **Rates:** $48–$50 D. Extra person $5. Children under age 18 stay free. Parking: Outdoor, free. AE, DC, DISC, MC, V.

▤▤▤ The Springs Inn

2020 Harrodsburg Rd, 40503; tel 606/277-5751 or toll free 800/354-9503; fax 606/277-3142. Off New Circle Rd. Located five miles from airport, Keeneland, University of Kentucky, and downtown Lexington. **Rooms:** 196 rms, stes, and effic. CI 3pm/CO noon. Nonsmoking rms avail. **Amenities:** 🛎 A/C, cable TV. **Services:** ✕ 🚗 🖨 ⌲ **Facilities:** 🖼 📺 ⚒ 1 restaurant, 1 bar (w/entertainment). Large, attractive pool is a good spot for relaxing. **Rates:** $48–$53 S; $58–$63 D; $75–$120 ste; $53–$75 effic. Extra person $10. Children under age 12 stay free. Parking: Outdoor, free. AE, CB, DC, DISC, MC, V.

▤ Wilson Inn

2400 Buena Vista Dr, 40505; tel 606/293-6113 or toll free 800/WILSONS; fax 606/293-6113. Off I-75 at exit 110. Convenient to business and downtown, and popular with families because of the large rooms. **Rooms:** 109 rms and stes. CI 2pm/CO noon. Nonsmoking rms avail. At time of inspection, some rooms were in need of repair. **Amenities:** 🛎 A/C, cable TV, refrig. **Services:** 🚐 ⌲ 🕭 **Facilities:** 📺 ⚒ **Rates (CP):** $36–$46 S; $42–$52 D; $49–$56 ste. Extra person $6. Children under age 18 stay free. Parking: Outdoor, free. AE, DC, DISC, MC, V.

▤ Winner's Circle Motel

149 Edwards Ave, Georgetown, 40324; tel 502/863-6500 or toll free 800/999-6965. Off I-75 at exit 125 or 126. Very basic. Close to Kentucky Horse Park. **Rooms:** 73 rms. CI open/CO 11am. Nonsmoking rms avail. **Amenities:** 🛎 A/C, cable TV. **Services:** 🖨 ⌲ **Facilities:** 📺 ⚒ **Rates:** $24–$28 S; $28 D. Extra person $4. Parking: Outdoor, free. AE, CB, DC, MC, V.

RESORT

▤▤▤▤ Marriott's Griffin Gate Resort

1800 Newtown Pike, 40511; tel 606/231-5100 or toll free 800/228-9290; fax 606/231-5136. Off I-75. 250 acres. A posh property in the heart of the Bluegrass. Elegant lobby lends itself to business meetings. **Rooms:** 409 rms, stes, and effic. Executive level. CI 4pm/CO noon. Nonsmoking rms avail. Luxurious, elegantly appointed rooms. **Amenities:** 🎛️ 📶 🍷 A/C, satel TV w/movies, dataport, voice mail, bathrobes. Some units w/terraces, some w/fireplaces, some w/whirlpools. Bathroom scales, full-size ironing boards and irons in every room. Suites have refrigerators. **Services:** ✕ 🔑 📼 🚐 🗂️ 🛎️ 🙌 Car-rental desk, social director, masseur, children's program, babysitting. Knowledgeable and friendly staff. **Facilities:** 🏠 🏌️18 ⛷️ 🏊 🎾 🏓 💻 ⛳ & 4 restaurants (*see* "Restaurants" below), 3 bars (2 w/entertainment), basketball, volleyball, games rm, lawn games, spa, sauna, whirlpool, beauty salon, playground, washer/dryer. **Rates:** Peak (Apr–Oct) $99–$125 S; $99–$157 D; $175–$850 ste; $850 effic. Children under age 18 stay free. Min stay special events. Lower rates off-season. AP rates avail. MAP rates avail. Parking: Outdoor, free. AE, CB, DC, DISC, EC, ER, JCB, MC, V.

RESTAURANTS 🍴

★ Alfalfa

557 S Limestone St; tel 606/253-0014. Across from U of K campus. **International/Vegetarian.** An area landmark, where the locally famous mix with neighborhood regulars and students. Entrees feature high quality fresh ingredients, and breads and desserts are freshly made. **FYI:** Reservations not accepted. Folk/jazz. Children's menu. Beer and wine only. **Open:** Lunch Mon–Fri 11am–5:30pm; dinner Tues–Thurs 5:30–9pm, Fri–Sat 5:30–10pm; brunch Sat–Sun 10am–2pm. **Prices:** Main courses $6–$12. No CC.

★ AP Suggins Bar & Grill

345 Romany Rd (Chevy Chase); tel 606/268-0709. Between Tates Creek Rd and Chinoe Rd. **American.** A neighborhood favorite offering one of the most extensive menus in town: everything from burgers and fried chicken to salads and Mexican entrees. A whimsical wall painting contributes to the casual atmosphere. **FYI:** Reservations not accepted. Children's menu. **Open:** Mon–Sat 11am–1am. **Prices:** Main courses $4–$12. AE, MC, V.

★ Billy's Bar B-Q

101 Cochran Rd (Chevy Chase); tel 606/269-9593. Off Tates Creek Rd. **Regional American/Barbecue.** A friendly neighborhood restaurant known for its Western Kentucky–style barbecue. Pork, beef, mutton, chicken, and ribs are among the barbecue options, and they also serve the Kentucky specialty stew known as burgoo. Carryout available. **FYI:** Reservations accepted. Children's menu. Beer and wine only. **Open:** Peak (Apr–Nov) Mon–Sat 11am–10pm, Sun 11:30am–10pm. **Prices:** Main courses $3–$14. AE, CB, DC, MC, V. 🖼️ 🚐 &

♣ Bravo's of Lexington

In Victorian Square, 401 W Main St; tel 606/255-2222. **Italian.** Offers fine Italian cuisine in an elegant, relaxed atmosphere. The wait staff is attentive to every detail. **FYI:** Reservations accepted. Piano. Children's menu. **Open:** Peak (Nov–Mar) lunch Tues–Sat 11:30am–2:30pm; dinner Mon–Sat 5:30–10:30pm. Closed Aug 14–21. **Prices:** Main courses $11–$19. AE, CB, DC, DISC, MC, V. ♥ 🍴 &

Campbell House Inn

1375 Harrodsburg Rd; tel 606/255-4281. **American.** Elegant dining in a gracious atmosphere. Entrees include Southern specialties such as country ham and hot browns, as well as seafood and lamb chops. A nice selection of wines complement the menu. **FYI:** Reservations accepted. Dancing/jazz. Children's menu. **Open:** Daily 11:30am–10pm. **Prices:** Main courses $9–$30. AE, CB, DC, DISC, MC, V. ✅ 📼 &

♣ The Coach House

855 S Broadway; tel 606/252-7777. **Continental.** Many people say that this elegant, formal dining room—with its impeccable service and attention to detail—is the best restaurant in Lexington. Noted for quality and distinction, the menu here always boasts a wide selection; well-known specialties include Maryland crab cakes, rack of lamb, and veal Oscar. Award-winning wine list. **FYI:** Reservations recommended. Jazz/piano. **Open:** Lunch Mon–Fri 11am–2:30pm; dinner Mon–Sat 5–10:30pm. Closed Jan 1–7. **Prices:** Main courses $14–$30. AE, CB, DC, DISC, MC, V. ♥ ✅ &

★ Hall's on the River

1225 Athens-Boonesboro Rd, Boonesboro; tel 606/255-8105. Exit 104 or 95 off I-75 N and S. **Seafood/Steak.** The Kentucky River has flooded this restaurant many times; the "high water" marks and dates of each flood can be viewed. Hall's specializes in catfish, frog legs, and other regional dishes, and they are famous for their beer cheese. Tables on the outside deck have river views. **FYI:** Reservations accepted. Children's menu. **Open:** Peak (June–Aug) Mon–Thurs 11:30am–10pm, Fri–Sat 11:30am–11pm, Sun noon–8pm. **Prices:** Main courses $10–$15. AE, DC, MC, V. 🛳️ 🏞️ 🖼️ &

♣ The Mansion at Griffin Gate

In Marriott's Griffin Gate Resort & Golf Club, 1800 Newtown Pike; tel 606/231-5152. Off I-75. **Continental.** Located in a beautifully restored antebellum home. The menu features a wide selection of American and Continental entrees, and there's an extensive wine list. **FYI:** Reservations recommended. **Open:** Lunch Mon–Fri 11:30am–2pm; dinner Sun–Thurs 6–10pm, Fri–Sat 6–10:30pm. **Prices:** Main courses $20–$29. AE, CB, DC, DISC, ER, MC, V. ♥ 🍴 📼 &

Marikka's

411 Southland Dr; tel 606/275-1925. **American/German.** A unique, casual eatery offering authentic German dishes—sauerbraten, knockwurst, Wiener schnitzel, and more. And, of course, there's plenty of good beer—over 400 brands (not all of them German) are served. Red-and-white-check tablecloths, down-to-earth atmosphere. **FYI:** Reservations recom-

mended. Children's menu. **Open:** Mon–Thurs 4–10pm, Fri–Sat 4–11pm. **Prices:** Main courses $7–$12. AE, CB, DC, DISC, MC, V. ⑤

Nagasaki Inn
2013 Regency Rd; tel 606/278-8782. Off Nichollesville Rd at Southland Dr. **Japanese/Seafood.** Dinner is prepared by a teppanyaki chef at a tableside grill. Seafood, beef, and chicken are prepared with a variety of vegetables. Dining is made more enjoyable by the chef who prepares the food and entertains with his skillful use of knives. Sushi bar. **FYI:** Reservations accepted. Children's menu. **Open:** Mon–Thurs 4:30–10pm, Fri–Sat 4:30–11pm, Sun 4:30–9pm. **Prices:** Main courses $10–$24; prix fixe $10–$24. AE, CB, DC, DISC, MC, V. ▣

★ Rosebud Bar & Grill
121 N Mill St (Downtown); tel 606/254-1907. Between Main St and Short St. **Regional American/Caribbean.** A sky of clouds and Renaissance angels adorn the ceiling of this popular cafe. Standard offerings include Cuban black beans or Cajun red beans with rice, enchiladas, jerk chicken, and chili. More American-style dishes—meat loaf, stews, soups, salads, sandwiches, and pasta—are also available. **FYI:** Reservations not accepted. **Open:** Mon–Sat 11:30am–1am. **Prices:** Main courses $5–$8. MC, V. ■

Seoul Barbecue
In Gardenside Shopping Center, 1837 Alexandria Dr; tel 606/276-2328. Off Versailles Rd. **Chinese/Korean.** A casual, family-friendly eatery offering Korean- and Chinese-style barbecue. Food is prepared in front of you, and can be adjusted to suit your preferred degree of spiciness. **FYI:** Reservations accepted. Children's menu. **Open:** Mon–Thurs 11am–10pm, Fri 11am–10:30pm, Sat noon–10:30pm. **Prices:** Main courses $5–$19. AE, CB, DC, DISC, MC, V. ▣ ⑤

ATTRACTIONS 📷

Ashland, the Henry Clay Estate
120 Sycamore Rd; tel 606/266-8581. Henry Clay—Secretary of State under John Quincy Adams, Speaker of the House, three-time presidential candidate, and legendary orator—was the first national political figure that Kentucky produced and one of the most influential leaders in pre–Civil War America. He negotiated the Treaty of Ghent, which officially brought an end to the War of 1812, and won passage of the Missouri Compromise as well as the Compromise of 1850, but he is perhaps best known for his statement—after losing the presidency for the third time—"I'd rather be right than be President."

Clay built Ashland in 1806 and lived here with his wife Lucretia and their 11 children. The current house was built in 1856 by Clay's son, James, and contains personal furnishings of five generations of the Clay family. Guided tours start on the hour, with the last one at 4pm. Museum Store and gardens are open to the public, as are several original outbuildings still on the grounds. **Open:** Tues–Sat 10am–4:30pm, Sun 1–4:30pm. Closed Mon in Jan, some hols. **$$**

Mary Todd Lincoln House
578 W Main St; tel 606/233-9999. The first site restored to honor a First Lady, in this case the wife of 16th president Abraham Lincoln. Many fine 19th-century furnishings, some of them Todd family pieces, are part of the collection. Several of Mary Todd's personal possessions are also in the house, as well as pieces of her Meissen and Old Paris china. **Open:** Tues–Sat 10am–4pm. Closed Dec 15–Apr 1, some hols. **$$**

Lexington Children's Museum
401 W Main St; tel 606/258-3256. A 14,000-square-foot museum with hands-on exhibits including Natural Wonders, Around the World, and a physics and space section with a kid-size moonscape. **Open:** Memorial Day–Labor Day, 10am–6pm, Sat 10am–5pm, Sun 1–5pm. Closed Mon Labor Day–Mem Day, and some hols. **$**

Kentucky Horse Center
3380 Paris Pike; tel 606/293-1853. Educational 1½-hour guided tours of this 268-acre training facility give visitors a glimpse behind the scenes of thoroughbred racing. Visit a trainer and his horses, or watch a morning workout. **Open:** Tours Apr–Oct, Mon–Fri 9 and 10:30am, 1pm, Sat 9 and 10:30am. Closed some hols. **$$$$**

Kentucky Horse Park
Exit 20 off I-75, 4089 Iron Works Pike; tel 606/233-4303 or toll free 800-568-8813. Located in the heart of Kentucky bluegrass country, this unique facility attracts hundreds of thousands of visitors devoted to the cult of the thoroughbred. At the **International Museum of the Horse,** visitors can peruse 19th-century horse carriages, equine art, and nearly 600 racing trophies. A Breed's Display Barn housing 40 different breeds. Many world-class equestrian events are held at the ½-mile race track, steeplechase course, and show rings. Horseback and children's pony rides are available, and there are horse-drawn carriages are available for touring the 1,032-acre site.

The Visitors Information Center shows two films daily: *Thou Shalt Fly Without Wings* is dedicated to the relationship between humans and horses, and *All the King's Horses* tells the story of the Budweiser Clydesdales. There's also a Farrier's (blacksmith's) Shop and a Harness Maker's Shop. The American Saddle Horse Museum, located on the grounds, has a separate admission charge but discounted combination tickets are available. **Open:** Apr–Oct, daily 9am–5pm; Nov–Mar, Wed–Sun 9am–5pm. Closed some hols. **$$$**

Three Chimneys Farm
Rte 1, Old Frankfort Pike, Midway; tel 606/873-7053. Located 15 mi NW of downtown Lexington. Nestled in the heart of the Kentucky Bluegrass, this horse farm is home to several champion thoroughbreds, including 1977 Triple Crown winner Seattle Slew. Visitors are invited to tour the farm and the

stallion complex, where the grooms will explain the breeding operations and the daily running of the farm. **Open:** Office, daily 8:30am–4:30pm; tours, daily 10am and 1pm. Closed some hols. **Free**

Historic Horse Farm Tours

3429 Montavesta Rd; tel 606/268-2906. Lexington native Margaret Woods runs this series of passenger-van tours. Most itineraries last 2–3 hours, with stops at Keeneland Racecourse (see below) and the world-famous Calumet horse farm, birthplace of eight Kentucky Derby winners and two Triple Crown winners. Vans stop at all major Lexington hotels and motels, but call first to reserve a spot and check the current tour offerings. **Open:** Daily 7:30am–9:30pm. Closed some hols. **$$$$**

Keeneland Racecourse

4201 Versailles Rd; tel 606/254-3412, or toll free 800/ 456-3412. Keeneland, which has been designated a National Historic Landmark and is the only US racetrack ever visited by Queen Elizabeth II, runs two race meetings a year—three weeks each in April and October. The spring meet features a stakes race each day, highlighted by the Blue Grass Stakes, a popular prep race for the Kentucky Derby. The horses' morning workouts can be seen daily from mid-March to late November, and the prestigious July Selected Yearling Sale is open to visitors. **Open:** Daily 6am–6pm. **$$**

London

Surrounded by Daniel Boone National Forest, the seat of Laurel County is an outdoor recreation haven. **Information:** London/Laurel County Tourist Commission, 140 W Daniel Boone Pkwy, London, 40741 (tel 606/878-6900).

MOTELS

Comfort Suites

1918 KY 192 W, 40741; tel 606/877-7848 or toll free 800/ 221-2222; fax 606/877-7907. Off I-75 at exit 38. Modern, all-suites facility with a large lobby. **Rooms:** 62 rms and stes. CI 2pm/CO noon. Nonsmoking rms avail. Well-appointed rooms; all are equipped with a sofa sleeper. **Amenities:** A/C, cable TV, refrig, dataport. Some units w/whirlpools. **Services:** Facilities: Washer/dryer. **Rates (CP):** Peak (May–Oct) $56–$66 S or D; $56–$66 ste. Extra person $5. Children under age 18 stay free. Lower rates off-season. Parking: Outdoor, free. Winter packages avail. AE, CB, DC, DISC, JCB, MC, V.

Hampton Inn

2075 W KY 192, 40741; tel 606/877-1000 or toll free 800/ 394-8411; fax 606/864-8560. Off I-75 at exit 38. Attractive facility for vacationers and businesspeople alike. **Rooms:** 82 rms and stes. CI 2pm/CO noon. Nonsmoking rms avail. Spacious, attractive rooms. **Amenities:** A/C, satel TV w/movies, dataport. Some units w/whirlpools. Some rooms have coffeemakers, microwaves, refrigerators. **Services:** Security guard on duty 24 hours. **Facilities:** Rates (CP): Peak (June–Nov) $50 S; $60 D; $85–$95 ste. Children under age 18 stay free. Lower rates off-season. Parking: Outdoor, free. AE, CB, DC, DISC, MC, V.

Louisville

See also Shelbyville, Shepherdsville

The state's largest city, founded in 1778 at the Falls of the Ohio River in north-central Kentucky. It became a major trading city in the 19th century; today it is a mix of historic and modern, Southern and Midwestern. It remains one of the South's most important industrial, financial, marketing, and shipping centers. Home to the University of Louisville (one of the oldest municipal universities in the country, founded in 1798), the Tony Award–winning Actors Theater, and the annual Kentucky Derby, the most prestigious leg of horse racing's Triple Crown. **Information:** Louisville Convention & Visitors Bureau, 400 S 1st St, Louisville, 40202 (tel 502/ 584-2121).

PUBLIC TRANSPORTATION

Transit Authority of River City (TARC) bus stops are marked by red-and-white signs. Bus fare is 85¢ during peak hours, 50¢ at all other times; exact change required. Fare Saver tickets offer 10 trips for $4.50 ($3 for students, seniors, and persons with disabilities). Call 502/585-1234 for more information.

HOTELS

Best Western

1301 Kentucky Mills Rd, 40299; tel 502/267-8100 or toll free 800/528-1234; fax 502/267-8100. Blankenbaker Lane exit off I-64. A beautiful new property with a comforting color scheme and helpful staff. **Rooms:** 119 rms and stes. CI 2pm/CO 11am. Nonsmoking rms avail. Some rooms have vaulted ceilings and extra-large closets. **Amenities:** A/C, cable TV w/movies, dataport. Some units w/whirlpools. Refrigerators available in suites. **Services:** Babysitting. **Facilities:** Sauna, whirlpool, washer/dryer. Guests have free use of nearby World Gym. **Rates (CP):** $52–$85 S; $60–$85 D; $95 ste. Extra person $5. Children under age 18 stay free. Parking: Outdoor, free. AE, DC, DISC, MC, V.

Breckinridge Inn Hotel

2800 Breckinridge Lane, 40220; tel 502/456-5050; fax 502/ 451-1577. Off I-264. In Southern Colonial–style, with a comfortable lobby and modern decor. **Rooms:** 125 rms and stes. CI 2pm/CO noon. Nonsmoking rms avail. **Amenities:** A/C, cable TV. **Services:** Masseur. **Facilities:** 1 restaurant, 1 bar, spa, sauna, steam rm, whirlpool, beauty salon. Club Breckinridge fitness center contains a junior Olympic-size pool, locker facilities, sun decks, and aerobic and weight machines. **Rates:** $65–$75 S or D; $95 ste. Extra person $10. Children under age 16 stay free. Parking: Indoor, free. AE, DC, DISC, MC, V.

≣≣≣≣ The Brown Hotel

335 W Broadway, 40202 (Downtown); tel 502/583-1234 or toll free 800/555-8000; fax 502/587-7006. Originally built in 1922 by local millionaire J Graham Brown for the then-outrageous sum of $4 million, this elegant 15-story hotel housed movie stars, royalty, and foreign heads of state during its heyday. The venerable old hotel closed in 1971, but was resurrected in 1985 after a $25 million facelift. The breathtaking lobby is as stately as ever, with marble floors, cherry furniture, and hand-painted ceilings and archways. **Rooms:** 292 rms and stes. Executive level. CI 3pm/CO 11am. Nonsmoking rms avail. Rooms feature cherry furniture, polished brass, and fine artwork. **Amenities:** 🛋 🐾 A/C, cable TV w/movies, dataport. Club-level amenities include robes, turndown service, continental breakfast, honor bar, and evening hors d' oeuvres. **Services:** 🍴 🗝 📼 🚗 🛄 🧺 Babysitting. **Facilities:** 🖳 🖥 🖳 ⅄ 2 restaurants (*see* "Restaurants" below), 2 bars, beauty salon. Art gallery and men's clothing store located on first floor. Guests have free use of downtown YMCA. **Rates:** $145–$170 S or D; $350–$650 ste. Extra person $10. Children under age 18 stay free. Parking: Indoor, $7–$10/day. AE, CB, DC, DISC, MC, V.

≣≣≣ Courtyard by Marriott

9608 Blairwood Rd, 40222; tel 502/429-0006 or toll free 800/321-2211; fax 502/429-5926. Exit 15 off I-64. A small Courtyard featuring a beautiful lobby and spiffy, modern decor. **Rooms:** 151 rms and stes. CI 3pm/CO 1pm. Nonsmoking rms avail. **Amenities:** 🛋 🐾 A/C, satel TV w/movies, dataport. Some units w/terraces. **Services:** 🛄 🧺 **Facilities:** 🖳 🖳 🖳 ⅄ 1 restaurant (bkfst only), 1 bar, whirlpool, washer/dryer. **Rates:** $49–$99 S or D; $93–$108 ste. Extra person $10. Children under age 18 stay free. Parking: Outdoor, free. AE, DC, DISC, MC, V.

≣≣ Days Inn Hotel Downtown

101 E Jefferson St, 40202 (Downtown); tel 502/585-2200 or toll free 800/DAYS-INN; fax 502/584-5657. Brook St exit off I-65. Standard chain accommodations located near downtown medical centers. **Rooms:** 177 rms and stes. CI 3pm/CO noon. Nonsmoking rms avail. Rooms are clean but are in need of new carpeting. **Amenities:** 🛋 📺 A/C, cable TV w/movies, refrig, dataport, in-rm safe. **Services:** ✗ 🚗 🛄 🧺 **Facilities:** 🖳 ⅄ 1 restaurant, 1 bar. Guests may use local YMCA for a nominal fee. **Rates:** $49–$79 S or D; $250 ste. Extra person $8. Children under age 18 stay free. Min stay special events. Parking: Outdoor, free. AE, CB, DC, DISC, JCB, MC, V.

≣≣≣ Executive Inn

978 Phillips Lane, 40209-1399; tel 502/367-6161 or toll free 800/626-2706; fax 502/368-1880. A large facility, great for conferences. The decor is a bit out of date, but still very tasteful. **Rooms:** 465 rms and stes. CI 3pm/CO noon. Nonsmoking rms avail. **Amenities:** 🛋 🐾 A/C, cable TV w/movies, voice mail. Some units w/terraces. **Services:** ✗ 🚗 🛄 🧺 🛎 Masseur, babysitting. Swimming lessons available. **Facilities:** 🖳 🖳 🖳 ⅄ 2 restaurants, 1 bar (w/entertainment), games rm, spa, sauna, beauty salon. Guests receive free use of local health club. **Rates:** $85 S; $95 D; $95–$260 ste. Extra person $10. Children under age 17 stay free. Parking: Outdoor, free. AE, CB, DC, DISC, MC, V.

≣≣≣ Executive West

830 Phillips Lane, 40209; tel 502/367-2251 or toll free 800/626-2708, 800/633-8723 in KY; fax 502/363-2087. A business-oriented hotel that looks like an old-fashioned men's club, with its dark decor and heavy, maple furniture. Large meetings are its bread and butter. **Rooms:** 611 rms and stes. Executive level. CI 3pm/CO 1pm. Nonsmoking rms avail. Color scheme is out of date. **Amenities:** 🛋 🐾 A/C, cable TV w/movies, dataport, voice mail. Some units w/terraces. VCRs, CD/tape players, and refrigerators available upon request. **Services:** ✗ 🚗 🛄 🧺 🛎 Babysitting. Nonrefundable $100 pet fee. **Facilities:** 🖳 🖳 🖳 🖥 ⅄ 2 restaurants, 1 bar (w/entertainment), games rm. Indoor/outdoor pool (open 11 months a year) has a large patio. **Rates:** $65–$72 S; $65–$85 D; $105–$275 ste. Children under age 12 stay free. Parking: Outdoor, free. AE, CB, DC, DISC, MC, V.

≣≣ Fairfield Inn Louisville East

9400 Blairwood Rd, 40222; tel 502/339-1900 or toll free 800/228-2800; fax 502/339-1900. Off I-64. A fine example of Marriott's line of budget properties. Attractive and comfortable. **Rooms:** 105 rms. CI 3pm/CO noon. Nonsmoking rms avail. Excellent housekeeping standards. Rooms are equipped with well-lit work desks—perfect for the business traveler. **Amenities:** 🛋 🐾 A/C, satel TV w/movies, dataport. **Services:** ✗ 🛄 🧺 **Facilities:** 🖳 🖳 ⅄ Excellent security—a key card is required to enter almost any area of the hotel. **Rates (CP):** $50–$68 S; $59–$75 D. Extra person $4. Children under age 18 stay free. Parking: Outdoor, free. AE, DC, DISC, MC, V.

≣≣≣ The Galt House

4th St at the Ohio River, 40202 (Downtown); tel 502/589-5200 or toll free 800/626-1814; fax 502/589-3444. Located on Louisville's riverfront, the city's largest convention complex exudes a businesslike ambiance. The Galt House dates from 1972, while the all-suites Galt House East was added in 1986. **Rooms:** 1,300 rms and stes. CI 3pm/CO noon. Nonsmoking rms avail. The rooms are a bit out of date, with maple furniture from the late 1970s. Suites have at least three phones. **Amenities:** 🛋 🐾 A/C, cable TV, voice mail. Some units w/terraces. Each suite has a refrigerator and at least two TVs. Dataports available on request. **Services:** ✗ 🛄 🧺 Twice-daily maid svce, car-rental desk, babysitting. **Facilities:** 🖳 🖳 ⅄ 3 restaurants (*see* "Restaurants" below), 3 bars, beauty salon. Shopping mall on the premises. **Rates:**

Peak (Apr–Oct) $65–$95 S; $75–$115 D; $95–$475 ste. Extra person $10. Children under age 16 stay free. Lower rates off-season. Parking: Indoor, free. AE, CB, DC, DISC, MC, V.

⊫⊫ Hampton Inn

1902 Embassy Square Blvd, 40299; tel 502/491-2577 or toll free 800/426-7866; fax 502/491-1325. Off I-64. A small, charming hotel with nice decor and very high housekeeping standards. **Rooms:** 118 rms. CI 3pm/CO noon. Nonsmoking rms avail. **Amenities:** 📺 ⓒ ▣ A/C, satel TV w/movies, dataport. **Services:** ▨ ⌁ **Facilities:** ⌂ 25 ⑆ **Rates (CP):** $49–$68 S or D. Children under age 18 stay free. Parking: Outdoor, free. AE, DC, DISC, MC, V.

⊫⊫⊫ Holiday Inn Downtown

120 W Broadway, 40202; tel 502/582-2241 or toll free 800/626-1558; fax 502/584-8591. Older but well-kept; caters to all types of travelers. **Rooms:** 287 rms and stes. Executive level. CI 2pm/CO noon. Nonsmoking rms avail. Many of the rooms have great views of downtown. **Amenities:** 📺 ⓒ ▣ ⓦ A/C, cable TV. Visual alarms available for the deaf or hard-of-hearing. **Services:** ✕ 🚐 ▨ ⌁ ⍨ **Facilities:** ⌂ 500 ▢ ⑆ 1 restaurant, 1 bar (w/entertainment), beauty salon. **Rates:** $88–$108 S or D; $175–$275 ste. Extra person $10. Children under age 19 stay free. Parking: Outdoor, free. Senior discounts avail. AE, CB, DC, DISC, MC, V.

⊫⊫⊫ Holiday Inn South Holidome

3317 Fern Valley Rd, 40213; tel 502/904-3311 or toll free 800/HOLIDAY; fax 502/966-4874. Exit 128 off I-65. A typical Holiday Inn, with a large Holidome containing an indoor playground and other amenities. **Rooms:** 405 rms and stes. CI 3pm/CO noon. Nonsmoking rms avail. Rooms feature bleached oak furniture. **Amenities:** 📺 ⓒ A/C, cable TV w/movies, dataport. **Services:** ✕ 🚐 ▨ ⌁ ⍨ **Facilities:** ⌂ ⛽ 1000 ⑆ 1 restaurant, 2 bars, games rm, whirlpool, playground, washer/dryer. **Rates:** $74–$84 S or D; $125–$150 ste. Extra person $10. Children under age 16 stay free. Parking: Outdoor, free. AE, CB, DC, DISC, MC, V.

⊫⊫⊫ The Hurstbourne Hotel

9700 Bluegrass Pkwy, 40299; tel 502/491-4830 or toll free 800/289-1009; fax 502/499-2893. Exit 15 off I-64. A large conference center catering to the business traveler. **Rooms:** 399 rms and stes. CI 3pm/CO noon. Nonsmoking rms avail. **Amenities:** 📺 ⓒ ▣ A/C, cable TV w/movies. Some units w/whirlpools. **Services:** |◎| ☎ 🚐 ▨ ⌁ ⍨ **Facilities:** ⌂ ⛽ 600 ⑆ 1 restaurant, 2 bars (1 w/entertainment), games rm, sauna, whirlpool, beauty salon, playground. Tropidome houses swimming pools, sauna, and fitness facilities. **Rates:** $79–$99 S or D; $99–$180 ste. Extra person $10. Children under age 12 stay free. Parking: Outdoor, free. AE, CB, DISC, MC, V.

⊫⊫⊫ Hyatt Regency Louisville

320 W Jefferson St, 40202 (Downtown); tel 502/587-3444 or toll free 800/587-1234; fax 502/540-3128. 3rd St exit off I-64. Linked to the Commonwealth Convention Center and the Galleria shopping mall by a pedestrian walkway, this contemporary hotel is built around an 18-story glass atrium. **Rooms:**. Executive level. CI 4pm/CO noon. Nonsmoking rms avail. **Amenities:** 📺 ⓒ ▣ ⓦ A/C, satel TV w/movies, dataport, voice mail. Regency Club Level amenities include robes, continental breakfast, evening hors d' oeuvres, and honor bar. Business rooms have in-room fax machines. **Services:** ✕ ☎ ▨ ⌁ Passes to local YMCA available for a nominal fee. **Facilities:** ⌂ ▩ ⛽ 1000 ▢ ⑆ 3 restaurants, 1 bar, whirlpool. Commonwealth Art Gallery located in the lobby. Revolving rooftop restaurant. **Rates:** $89–$140 S or D; $250–$420 ste. Extra person $10. Children under age 16 stay free. Parking: Indoor, $7/day. AE, CB, DC, DISC, MC, V.

⊫⊫⊫ The Inn at Jewish Hospital—Marriott

100 E Jefferson St, 40202 (Downtown); tel 502/582-2481; fax 502/582-3511. Off I-65. Located in the heart of Louisville's medical community, this beautiful, contemporary hotel is owned in conjunction with nearby Jewish Hospital. **Rooms:** 97 rms and stes. Executive level. CI open/CO noon. Nonsmoking rms avail. Some rooms are set aside for hospital patients and their families. **Amenities:** 📺 ⓒ ⓦ A/C, satel TV w/movies, refrig, dataport. Some units w/whirlpools. **Services:** ✕ ▨ ⌁ ⍨ **Facilities:** ⌂ 350 ⑆ 1 restaurant. **Rates:** $70–$120 S; $70–$130 D; $100–$285 ste. Children under age 12 stay free. Parking: Outdoor, free. AE, CB, DC, DISC, MC, V.

⊫⊫⊫ Louisville Marriott Hotel

1903 Embassy Square Blvd, 40299; tel 502/499-6220 or toll free 800/228-9290; fax 502/499-2480. Hurstbourne Lane exit off I-65. A contemporary hotel built around a 10-story glass atrium. Glass elevators overlook the indoor pool area. **Rooms:** 255 rms and stes. Executive level. CI 3pm/CO noon. Nonsmoking rms avail. Some rooms have balconies with atrium views. **Amenities:** 📺 ⓒ A/C, satel TV w/movies, dataport. Some units w/terraces, 1 w/whirlpool. Shoeshine machine, intercom, voice mail, and e-mail available in all rooms. TV lists guest services in five languages. **Services:** ✕ ☎ 🚐 ▨ ⌁ ⍨ Babysitting. On-site travel agent. Nonrefundable $25 pet fee. **Facilities:** ⌂ ⛽ 600 ⑆ 1 restaurant, 1 bar (w/entertainment), games rm, whirlpool. **Rates:** $99–$119 S; $109–$120 D; $234–$468 ste. Extra person $10. Children under age 18 stay free. Parking: Outdoor, free. AE, DC, DISC, MC, V.

⊫⊫⊫ Ramada Hotel Airport East

1921 Bishop Lane, 40218; tel 502/456-4411 or toll free 800/2-RAMADA; fax 502/456-2592. Newburg Rd exit off I-264. Attractive, business-oriented hotel. Convenient to downtown and the malls. **Rooms:** 148 rms and stes. CI 3pm/CO noon. Nonsmoking rms avail. **Amenities:** 📺 ⓒ A/C, cable TV w/movies. **Services:** ✕ 🚐 ▨ ⌁ **Facilities:** ⌂ 300 ⑆ 1 restaurant, 1 bar (w/entertainment), washer/dryer. **Rates:**

Peak (Mar–Aug) $49–$90 S or D; $135 ste. Extra person $5. Children under age 18 stay free. Lower rates off-season. Parking: Outdoor, free. AE, CB, DC, DISC, JCB, MC, V.

☰ ☰ ☰ ☰ The Seelbach

500 4th St, 40202 (Downtown); tel 502/585-3200 or toll free 800/333-3399; fax 502/585-9239. 3rd St exit off I-64. The Seelbach, originally built in 1905, greets the visitor with exquisite Italian marble at its entrance and murals depicting the state's pioneer past in its lobby. Outstanding staff is the best in town. **Rooms:** 322 rms and stes. Executive level. CI 3pm/CO 1pm. Nonsmoking rms avail. The old-world elegance is also present in the rooms, which feature high post cherry beds, custom-made drapes, pedestal sinks, and marble tubs. **Amenities:** 🛁 🕹 🍽 A/C, cable TV w/movies, dataport, voice mail. Club-level rooms available, with honor bar, evening hors d'oeuvres, robes, and turndown service. **Services:** 🍽 🖨 VP 🚗 🖼 ⌨ ⚡ Twice-daily maid svce, social director, babysitting. Nonrefundable $125 pet fee. **Facilities:** 🏊 🖥 ♿ 3 restaurants (see "Restaurants" below), 1 bar (w/entertainment). The Oak Room is considered one of the city's finest restaurants. **Rates:** $79–$150 S; $89–$160 D; $135–$510 ste. Extra person $10. Children under age 16 stay free. Parking: Indoor, $8–$12/day. AE, CB, DC, DISC, MC, V.

MOTELS

☰ Days Inn Arthur St

1620 Arthur St, 40208 (Downtown); tel 502/636-3781 or toll free 800/937-3297; fax 502/634-9544. Off I-65. You'll find only the bare essentials at this basic interstate motel located near an industrial area. Very small lobby is dark with somewhat worn appointments. Suitable for the frugal traveler. **Rooms:** 144 rms and stes. CI 3pm/CO 11am. Nonsmoking rms avail. **Amenities:** 🛁 🕹 A/C, satel TV w/movies, in-rm safe. **Services:** ⌨ **Facilities:** 🖥 ♿ **Rates:** $42–$52 S; $52–$65 D; $120–$170 ste. Extra person $3. Children under age 14 stay free. Parking: Outdoor, free. AE, CB, DC, MC, V.

☰ ☰ ☰ Holiday Inn Express

1901 E Blue Lick Rd, Brooks, 40109; tel 502/955-1501 or toll free 800/HOLIDAY; fax 502/955-1574. Brooks exit off I-65. Opened in February 1995, this facility has excellent housekeeping standards. **Rooms:** 50 rms and stes. CI 2pm/CO 11am. Nonsmoking rms avail. **Amenities:** 🛁 🕹 A/C, cable TV w/movies, dataport. Some units w/whirlpools. **Services:** ⌨ **Facilities:** 🖥 ♿ Whirlpool. **Rates (CP):** Peak (Feb–Oct) $50–$65 S; $65–$75 D; $65–$100 ste. Extra person $5. Children under age 19 stay free. Lower rates off-season. Parking: Outdoor, free. AE, CB, DC, DISC, JCB, MC, V.

☰ Red Carpet Inn

1640 S Hurstbourne Pkwy, 40220; tel 502/491-7320 or toll free 800/251-1962; fax 502/499-7617. Off I-64. Basic budget motel; suitable for an overnight stay but nothing longer. **Rooms:** 174 rms and stes. CI 2pm/CO noon. Rooms have dated decor, and all the furnishings are bolted to the floor.

Amenities: 🛁 A/C, satel TV w/movies. **Services:** ⌨ **Rates:** $29 S; $36 D; $43 ste. Extra person $3. Children under age 12 stay free. Parking: Outdoor, free. AE, DISC, MC, V.

INN

☰ ☰ ☰ Old Louisville Inn

1359 S 3rd St, 40208; tel 502/635-1574; fax 502/637-5892. Off I-65. A charming 1901 mansion with ornate mahogany columns, high ceilings, chandeliers, and period antiques. Large murals on the first floor represent Norman Rockwell's four freedoms. **Rooms:** 11 rms and stes (3 w/shared bath). CI 3pm/CO noon. Each room differs greatly in size and function. Some have marble tubs with updated fixtures. **Amenities:** 🕹 A/C. No phone or TV. 1 unit w/whirlpool. E-mail and fax machines available. **Services:** Afternoon tea served. Full breakfasts with fruit, waffles, granola, muffins, and popovers. **Facilities:** Guest lounge w/TV. Parlor, game/TV room. **Rates (BB):** $65 w/shared bath, $95 w/private bath; $125–$195 ste. Extra person $10. Children under age 12 stay free. MAP rates avail. Parking: Outdoor, free. Different rates apply for each room. MC, V.

RESTAURANTS 🍴

Alameda

1381 Bardstown Rd (The Highlands); tel 502/459-6300. **Southwestern.** Alameda features festive dining in an interesting, eclectic area of the city. Excellent Texas jambalaya with andouille sausage and shrimp. **FYI:** Reservations accepted. Children's menu. **Open:** Lunch daily 11am–2pm; dinner Fri–Sat 5pm–midnight. **Prices:** Main courses $12–$15. AE, MC, V. 🍽 🖼 ⚡

Bristol Bar & Grille

1321 Bardstown Rd (The Highlands); tel 502/456-1702. **Eclectic.** The Bristol greets you with a warm, lively atmosphere, and offers excellent salads and fruits, as well as pasta and grilled chicken dishes. **FYI:** Reservations accepted. Children's menu. Additional location: 300 N Hurstbourne Pkwy (tel 426-0627). **Open:** Fri–Sat 11am–4am, Sun 11am–midnight, Mon–Thurs 11am–2am. **Prices:** Main courses $6–$18. AE, DISC, MC, V. ♿

Cafe Kilimanjaro

In Theater Square, 649 S 4th St (Downtown); tel 502/583-4332. **Caribbean/South American/African.** Lunch here is served cafe-style with a buffet. A casual atmosphere grows very lively in the evenings. Event calendars are published monthly. **FYI:** Reservations accepted. Latin dancing. Children's menu. **Open:** Lunch daily 11am–3pm; dinner Tues–Thurs 4–9:30pm, Fri–Sat 5–11pm. **Prices:** Main courses $6–$14. AE, MC, V.

Cafe Metro

1700 Bardstown Rd (The Highlands); tel 502/458-4830. **Continental.** A classy establishment with an elegant menu. The fresh grilled fish is wonderful, but leave the children at home. **FYI:** Reservations recommended. **Open:** Mon–Thurs 6–10pm, Fri–Sat 6–11pm. **Prices:** Prix fixe $18. AE, DC, DISC, MC, V. ❤ க

Captain's Quarters
In Captain's Quarters Marina, 5700 Captain's Quarter's Rd; tel 502/228-1629. Exit 2 off I-71. **American/Seafood.** This restaurant offers three dining options. The dining room serves seafood in a formal atmosphere, with the main room overlooking the Ohio River. Shrimp, king crab legs, and lobster are a few of the delicious selections you'll find on this menu. The lodge also features seafood, but in a more casual atmosphere, and the bar is open until 1am on Fri and Sat. The third option is the extra-casual (food is served in plastic baskets) Captain's Quarter's patio and deck, which features a limited menu of salads, fried seafood, and chowder and gumbo. All restaurants offer valet parking on weekends. **FYI:** Reservations recommended. Singer. **Open:** Peak (Spring–Fall) Mon–Thurs 5–10pm, Fri–Sun 5–11pm. **Prices:** Main courses $14–$22. AE, DC, MC, V. ⛴ 🖼 க

Empress of China
2249 Hikes Lane; tel 502/451-2500. Exit 16 off I-264E. **Chinese.** Large selection of pork, chicken and seafood dishes in a pleasant atmosphere. Dim sum and Peking duck are popular here. **FYI:** Reservations accepted. Additional location: Holiday Manor Shopping Center (tel 426-1717). **Open:** Lunch Mon–Fri 11:30am–2:30pm, Sat noon–2:30pm; dinner daily 4:30–10pm; brunch Sun 11:30am–4:30pm. **Prices:** Main courses $6–$15. AE, MC, V. 🖼 க

★ The English Grill
In Brown Hotel, 335 W Broadway (Downtown); tel 502/583-1234. At 4th St. **Continental.** Winner of the 1994 "Best of Louisville" award, this fine restaurant offers genteel English ambience and standbys like rack of lamb and steak, along with fresh seafood and pastas. Local and regional ingredients used. The soufflé du jour is the big winner for dessert. Definitely leave the kids at home. **FYI:** Reservations recommended. Piano. Jacket required. **Open:** Daily 5–10pm. **Prices:** Main courses $16–$23. AE, CB, DC, DISC, MC, V. ❤ 🍷 VP க

Flagship Room
In the Galt House, 4th St and River Rd (Downtown); tel 502/589-5200. **Continental/Seafood.** Located on the 25th floor of the hotel, this fine-dining restaurant features two revolving floors overlooking the Ohio River. Exceptional seafood and nightly dinner specials. **FYI:** Reservations recommended. Piano. Jacket required. **Open:** Mon–Sat 6–10pm, Sun 10am–3pm. **Prices:** Main courses $16–$20. AE, CB, DC, DISC, MC, V. 🖼 க

The Irish Rover
2319 Frankfort Ave (Crescent Hill); tel 502/899-3544. Off US 60. **Irish.** Louisville's only Irish restaurant. Owned and operated by Irishman Michael Reidy, the Rover serves a fine grilled salmon and cabbage with homemade mashed potatoes amidst a warm and friendly atmosphere. **FYI:** Reservations accepted. Irish music. Children's menu. **Open:** Mon–Thurs 11:30am–10pm, Fri 11:30am–11pm, Sat 11am–11pm. **Prices:** Main courses $4–$11. AE, DISC, MC, V. 📷

Jay's Cafeteria
1812 W Muhammad Ali Blvd (West End); tel 502/583-2534. **Southern.** Housed in a new building since 1994, this restaurant offers a good selection of soul food classics. Specialties change daily. **FYI:** Reservations not accepted. Children's menu. No liquor license. **Open:** Fri–Sat 11am–8pm, Sun noon–7pm, Mon–Thurs 11am–7pm. **Prices:** Main courses $6–$7. AE, DISC, MC, V. 📷 க

★ Kaelin's
1801 Newburg Rd; tel 502/451-1801. **American/Burgers.** This restaurant features burgers and chicken in a nice, comfortable dining room. Fried chicken, or Kentucky ham, is served with two vegetables and hot biscuits. The seniors menu (for diners over age 60) starts after 4:30 pm and is offered all day on Sunday. **FYI:** Reservations accepted. Children's menu. **Open:** Mon–Thurs 11:30am–10pm, Fri–Sat 11:30am–11pm, Sun 11am–10pm. **Prices:** Main courses $3–$13. DC, DISC, MC, V. 📷

★ Mamma Grisanti's
3938 Dupont Circle; tel 502/893-0141. Off I-264. **Italian.** This excellent, family-oriented Italian restaurant was the first of the Grisanti chain. Classics like lasagna and veal scaloppine are complemented by a large selection of vegetable side dishes. Salad and hot garlic bread are served with all meals. **FYI:** Reservations accepted. Children's menu. **Open:** Lunch Mon–Fri 11:30am–2pm, Sat–Sun 11:30am–3pm; dinner Mon–Thurs 5–10pm, Fri 5–11pm, Sat 3–11pm, Sun 3–9pm. **Prices:** Main courses $8–$13. AE, DC, DISC, MC, V. ❤ 📷

Mo Flav
3334 Frankfort Ave (Crescent Hill); tel 502/899-5555. Off US 60 at Shelbyville Rd. **Cajun/Caribbean/Southwestern.** This joint is hot and spicy, with a young, upbeat crowd to match. The walls are covered with fabulous frescoes, and the floors are of original, handmade tiles. Many grilled specialties. **FYI:** Reservations not accepted. Children's menu. Beer and wine only. **Open:** Mon–Thurs 4–10pm, Fri–Sat 4pm–midnight, Sun 4–10pm. **Prices:** Main courses $5–$16. AE, CB, DC, MC, V. 📷 க

New Orleans House
9424 Shelbyville Rd; tel 502/426-1577. **Seafood.** An almost unbelievable variety of seafood is available at this all-you-can-eat buffet: steamed shrimp, Alaskan king crab legs, smoked salmon, pickled herring, fried clams, oysters on the half shell, calamari with marinara sauce, shrimp Creole, clam chowder, and much more. If that's not enough, à la carte steaks and lobsters are available, as is a dessert bar piled high with cheesecake and ingredients for make-your-own sundaes. **FYI:** Reservations recommended. **Open:** Daily 6–9:30pm, Fri–Sat 5–10pm. **Prices:** Prix fixe $28. AE, CB, DC, MC, V. ❤ க

The Oak Room

In Seelbach Hotel, 500 4th St; tel 502/585-3200. **Regional American.** Fine dining in a dark, oak-paneled room on the mezzanine of the Seelbach. Selected entrees include roasted rack of lamb and roasted free-range Kentucky chicken breast. The wine list includes over 150 vintages and they offer beers from eight different countries. Chocolate-almond truffle mousse cake is one of the most popular desserts. **FYI:** Reservations recommended. Piano. Jacket required. **Open:** Lunch Mon–Fri 11:30am–2pm; dinner Sun–Thurs 5–10pm, Fri–Sat 5–10:30pm; brunch Sun 10am–2pm. **Prices:** Main courses $12–$25; prix fixe $20. AE, DC, DISC, MC, V. ▮ VP ⓖ

★ **Vince Staten's Old Time Barbecue**

9219 US 42; tel 502/228-7427. **Barbecue.** This casual, fun family barbecue restaurant specializes in pork barbecue sandwich platters and pork family picnics. Six different family picnics are offered for take out (call ahead). There's a choice of six homemade sauces, with Texas sweet sauce the most popular. **FYI:** Reservations not accepted. Children's menu. Beer and wine only. **Open:** Mon–Sat 11am–9pm, Sun noon–9pm. **Prices:** Main courses $7–$14. AE, MC, V. ▦ ⓖ

ATTRACTIONS 📷

HISTORIC HOMES AND SITES

Farmington Historic Home

3033 Bardstown Rd; tel 502/452-9920. This beautifully restored Federal-style house was built for John and Lucy Fry Speed in 1810, from a plan designed by Thomas Jefferson. Its many Jeffersonian touches include two central octagonal rooms and a "hidden" stairway. Many of the house's architectural details are original, even down to the woodwork, glass, and brass, and the house is filled with opulent 19th-century furniture, dinnerware, and silver. A visit to Farmington by Abraham Lincoln is memorialized in a small museum room. The 18-acre site includes an early 19th-century garden, stone springhouse and barn, cook's quarters and kitchen, blacksmith shop, apple orchard, and a museum store. **Open:** Mon–Fri 10am–4:30pm, Sat 10am–4:30pm, Sun 1–4:30pm. Closed some hols. **$**

Locust Grove Historic Home

561 Blankenbaker Lane; tel 502/897-9845. Beautifully restored home of explorer and general George Rogers Clark. Clark's younger brother, William, and Meriwether Lewis returned here after their adventure to the Pacific Northwest. In its heyday, Locust Grove was visited by Aaron Burr, John James Audubon, and presidents James Monroe, Andrew Jackson, and Zachary Taylor. The visitors' center presents a 15-minute film and guided tours are available. **Open:** Mon–Sat 10am–4:30pm, Sun 1:30–4:30pm. Closed some hols. **$$**

Old Louisville Information Center

1340 S 4th St, in Central Park; tel 502/635-5244. Old Louisville—the city's most desirable neighborhood in the 19th century—covers approximately 1,200 acres and contains three National Register districts. While many of the homes are not a pure example of any one architectural style, exemplary examples of Victorian Gothic, Italianate, Renaissance Revival, Romanesque, Queen Anne, Tudor, and beaux arts styles are represented. High turrets, leaded and stained-glass windows, gargoyles, cornices, sharply pointed gables, and English-style half timbering are all on display. The Information Center has information about guided house tours and copies of *Old Louisville: A Victorian Treasure,* a self-guided walking tour brochure. **Open:** Mon, Tues, Thurs 12:30–4:30pm, Wed 10:30am–4:40pm. Closed some hols. **Free**

MUSEUMS

Kentucky Derby Museum

704 Central Ave; tel 502/637-1111. The pageantry and color of the "Run for the Roses" come alive year-round at this $7.5 million museum. A 13-minute, 360° multimedia show, *The Greatest Race,* re-creates all the hair-raising excitement of the Kentucky Derby. (Screenings daily on the hour and half-hour from 9:30am to 4:30pm.) Other high-tech exhibits allow visitors to weigh in on an authentic jockey scale, climb on a horse in a real starting gate, and practice their handicapping skills. Displays of racing memorabilia (jockey's silks, trophies) commemorate the 120-year history of Churchill Downs, which is the oldest continuously operated racetrack in the country and has been designated a National Historic Landmark. Guided tours of the racetrack take approximately 30 minutes; tickets are available at the Museum. **Open:** Daily 9am–5pm. Closed some hols. **$$**

J B Speed Art Museum

2035 S 3rd St; tel 502/636-2893. On the University of Louisville Belknap Campus. More than 5,000 works ranging from 4000 BC to the present. The permanent collection includes works by great masters such as Rembrandt, Rubens, Monet, Rodin, and Picasso. Highlights include the medieval room, with its gorgeous wall tapestries, and the sculpture garden. **Open:** Tues–Sat 10am–4pm, Sun noon–5pm. Closed some hols. **Free**

Louisville Science Center

727 W Main St; tel 502/561-6100. A world of hands-on exhibits, ranging from ancient Egypt to outer space, invite participation and arouse curiosity. There's a four-story IMAX Theater, a replica of a Foucault pendulum, Science Center gift shop, and a Food for Thought snack shop on the premises. **Open:** Mon–Thurs 10am–5pm, Fri–Sat 10am–9pm, Sun noon–5pm. Closed some hols. **$$$**

OTHER ATTRACTIONS

Churchill Downs

700 Central Ave; tel 502/636-4400. Originally, the grandstand and clubhouse at this gracious racetrack were located where the present barns now stand. In 1895, the first unit of

today's stands was completed. These gleaming white twin spires are recognized instantly by racing fans all over the world. The Derby, "the greatest two minutes in sports" and the first jewel of horse racing's Triple Crown, is held here the first Saturday in May. Churchill Downs holds two racing meets each year, in spring and fall. Spring Meet (usually late April through late June) is particularly glorious, when the gardens at the track are filled with tulips, petunias, marigolds, and roses. Guided tours of the grounds start from the **Kentucky Derby Museum** next door (see above). **$$**

Louisville Zoological Garden
1100 Trevilian Way; tel 502/459-2181. This 75-acre zoo features a simulated rain forest, camel and elephant rides, a lakeside cafe, and miniature trains to take visitors from exhibit to exhibit. The complex houses over 1,600 animals representing 370 species, 30% of them endangered or threatened. For the kids, the Meta Zoo offers a hands-on opportunity to learn about the animal world. **Open:** Apr–Labor Day, daily 10am–5pm; Labor Day–March, daily 10am–4pm; June–Aug, Sat–Tues 10am–5pm, Wed–Fri 10am–8pm. Closed some hols. **$$$**

Rauch Memorial Planetarium
University of Louisville Belknap Campus; tel 502/852-6665. The highlight of this planetarium is its Spitz 512 telescope, which projects images from outer space onto the huge domed ceiling. State-of-the-art sound system complements the visuals. Public showings are given every Saturday and Sunday, and an on-site gift shop sells astronomy-related items. **Open:** Shows on Sat at 1pm and 2:30pm. Call ahead for additional show times. **$$**

Belle of Louisville
4th St and River Rd; tel 502/574-2355. Cruise the Ohio River and listen to the calliope on one of the last authentic sternwheelers in the country. Built in 1914, this National Historic Landmark is the oldest operating steamboat on the Mississippi River system. Saturday night dance cruise June–Sept. **Open:** Mem Day–Labor Day, Tues–Sun. **$$$**

Kentucky Art and Craft Foundation
609 W Main St; tel 502/589-0102 or toll free 800/446-0102. A nonprofit group, founded in 1981 by then–First Lady and former Miss America Phyllis George Brown, dedicated to the continuation of Kentucky's craft heritage. The group operates the **Kentucky Art and Craft Gallery,** located in the Main Street Historic District in downtown Louisville. Two exhibition galleries and one sales gallery feature everything from traditional wood carvings, baskets, and quilts to colorful hand-painted silk kimonos and blown glass. **Open:** Mon–Sat 10am–4pm. Closed some hols. **Free**

Kentucky Center for the Arts
5 Riverfront Plaza; tel 502/584-7777. From Broadway to Bach, from bluegrass to bagpipes, virtually any night of the year the three stages of this modern brick-and-glass center are alive with entertainment. Tours of the building and its

outdoor sculpture collection (including works by Alexander Calder and Jean Dubuffet) are available. **Open:** Buildings, daily 9am–9pm. **$$$$**

Kentucky Kingdom
At the Kentucky State Fairgrounds; tel 502/366-2231. Located on the grounds of the Kentucky Fair and Exposition Center, this amusement park offers more than 70 exciting rides, games, and attractions, including Thunder Run (a wooden roller coaster) and Hurricane Bay (a 750,000-gallon wave pool). Stage shows are presented several times daily. **Open:** Apr–May and Sept, Sat–Sun 11am–9pm; Mem Day–Labor Day, Sun–Thurs 11am–9pm, Fri–Sat 11am–11pm. **$$**

Lucas

Small community near Barren River Resort Lake Park, in the gentle rolling hills of south central Kentucky.

MOTEL 🏨

≡≡ The Glasgow Inn
1003 W Main, PO Box 353, Glasgow, 42141; tel 502/651-5191 or toll free 800/GLASGOW; fax 502/651-9233. Off US 31 E at Jct US 68. Located near Mammoth Cave (approximately 25 mi) and Barren River (10 mi), the Glasgow Inn invites its guests to relax at their unusually large and well-landscaped pool area. **Rooms:** 80 rms. CI 7am/CO 11am. Nonsmoking rms avail. **Amenities:** 🛁 A/C, cable TV w/movies, dataport. **Services:** ⚄ 🛏 🍽 Friendly staff. **Facilities:** 🏊 250 & **Rates (CP):** Peak (May–Oct) $45–$55 S; $50–$70 D. Extra person $4. Children under age 19 stay free. Lower rates off-season. Parking: Outdoor, free. AE, CB, DC, DISC, ER, MC, V.

LODGE

≡≡ Barren River Lake Lodge
1149 State Park Rd, 42156; tel 502/646-2151 or toll free 800/325-0057; fax 502/646-3645. Off US 31 E. 2,200 acres. Located in Barren River State Park, this is a water lover's paradise surrounded by forested, rolling hills. Only a short drive to Mammoth Cave and the Corvette Museum in Bowling Green. **Rooms:** 51 rms; 22 cottages/villas. CI 4pm/CO 11am. Nonsmoking rms avail. The newer cottages are exceptionally nice, and there are good views from the lodge rooms. **Amenities:** 🛁 A/C, satel TV w/movies. All units w/terraces. **Services:** 🛏 Social director, children's program. Friendly staff. **Facilities:** 🏊 ⛰ 🛶 ►18 ⛳ 🎿 🚣 ⛷ 🍴 400 & 1 restaurant, 1 beach (lake shore), lifeguard, basketball, volleyball, games rm, lawn games, playground, washer/dryer. Lake activities, boat rentals, nature trails. Camping, picnicking, planned recreation in the summer. **Rates:** Peak (Mem Day–Labor Day) $52 S; $62 D; $124–$154 cottage/villa. Extra person

$5. Children under age 16 stay free. Lower rates off-season. Parking: Outdoor, free. Closed Dec 25–31. AE, CB, DC, DISC, MC, V.

ATTRACTION 🖼

Barren River Lake State Resort Park
US 31 E; tel 502/646-2357 or toll free 800/325-0057. Covering 2,187 acres near Mammoth Cave National Park, the park features a marina, rental fishing boats, fishing, an 18-hole golf course, miniature golf, hiking trails, a heated pool, tennis courts, horseback and hiking trails, three nature trails, a beach, and picnic shelters. Camping sites and year-round lodge also available. **Open:** Daily sunrise–sunset. **$**

Madisonville

This western Kentucky city, named for the fourth US president, dates back to 1807. The historical society here offers some 4,000 items, including a large Civil War collection. **Information:** Madisonville–Hopkins County Chamber of Commerce, 140 S Main St, Madisonville, 42431 (tel 502/821-3435).

MOTELS 🏨

≣≣ Best Western Pennyrile Inn
Exit 37 off Pennyrile Pkwy, PO Box 612, 42440; tel 502/258-5201 or toll free 800/528-1234; fax 502/258-9072. Standard chain accommodations. **Rooms:** 60 rms. CI open/CO noon. Nonsmoking rms avail. **Amenities:** 🛅 ⚱ A/C, satel TV. Many rooms have refrigerators; some have dataports. **Services:** � 🛏 🛆 **Facilities:** 🛗 🖼 ⅊ Basketball, lawn games, washer/dryer. Guests receive coupon for full breakfast buffet at adjacent restaurant. Guest privileges at local fitness center. **Rates (BB):** $33–$43 S; $36–$46 D. Extra person $3. Children under age 12 stay free. Parking: Outdoor, free. AE, CB, DC, DISC, MC, V.

≣≣ Days Inn
1900 Lantaff Blvd, 42431; tel 502/821-8620 or toll free 800/DAYS-INN; fax 502/825-9282. Exit 44 off Pennyrile Pkwy. Standard two-story chain motel. **Rooms:** 143 rms and stes. CI 2pm/CO noon. Nonsmoking rms avail. **Amenities:** 🛅 ⚱ A/C, cable TV w/movies, in-rm safe. **Services:** ✗ 🛆 🛏 🛆 **Facilities:** 🛗 🖼 ⅊ 1 restaurant, 1 bar (w/entertainment), sauna, washer/dryer. Guest privileges at local fitness center. **Rates (CP):** $49–$75 S; $54–$80 D; $60–$100 ste. Extra person $5. Children under age 16 stay free. Parking: Outdoor, free. AE, CB, DC, DISC, MC, V.

Mammoth Cave National Park

For lodgings and dining, see Bowling Green, Cave City, Glasgow, Horse Cave, Park City

The Mammoth Caves make up the longest system of underground caves in the world. Only 300 miles have been explored so far, and some scientists believe there could be as many as 600 miles of as-yet-undiscovered passageways. Spectacular underground lakes and rivers are home to creatures who have evolved without any eyes; since they live in total darkness, they have no need of vision and use the rest of their bodies to sense their environment. Approximately 130 different forms of life can be found in Mammoth Cave. In fact, the ecosystem here is so diverse that it has been named an International Biosphere Reserve.

Many different types of guided cave tours are offered, including one especially for the mobility impaired and one for children 6–13. The longer tours can be quite grueling. Make sure you are rested and prepared, and wear sturdy shoes and warm clothes; cave temperature rarely rises above 60°F, even in summer.

The park itself offers 3 campgrounds, 60 miles of hiking trails, and 2 rivers (the Green and the Nolin) for fishing and boating. Horseback riding, rustic cottages, camp store, and on-site Mammoth Cave Hotel. For more information, contact the Superintendent, Mammoth Cave, KY 42259 (tel 502/758-2328).

HOTEL 🏨

≣≣ Mammoth Cave Hotel
Exit 53 off I-65, Mammoth Cave, 42259; tel 502/758-2225; fax 502/758-2301. Basic accommodations for park visitors. **Rooms:** 38 rms; 10 cottages/villas. CI 4pm/CO noon. Good views. Excellent rooms for guests with disabilities. **Amenities:** 🛅 A/C, cable TV. All units w/terraces. **Services:** ✗ 🛏 **Facilities:** 🍴2 🖼 ⅊ 3 restaurants, lawn games, washer/dryer. **Rates:** Peak (Mem Day–Labor Day) $59 S; $65 D. Extra person $6. Children under age 16 stay free. Lower rates off-season. Parking: Outdoor, free. AE, CB, DC, MC, V.

LODGES

≣ Sunset Point Lodge
Exit 53 off I-65, Mammoth Cave, 42259; tel 502/758-2225; fax 502/758-2301. No-frills property. **Rooms:** 20 rms. CI 4pm/CO noon. **Amenities:** A/C, cable TV. No phone. **Services:** ✗ 🛏 **Facilities:** 🍴2 🖼 ⅊ 3 restaurants, lawn games, washer/dryer. **Rates:** Peak (Mem Day–Labor Day) $62 S; $68 D. Extra person $6. Children under age 16 stay free. Lower rates off-season. Family rates avail. AE, CB, DC, MC, V.

≡ Woodland Cottages

Exit 53 off I-65, Mammoth Cave, 42259; tel 502/758-2225; fax 502/758-2301. Perfect for families who want to camp, but need more than a tent. **Rooms:** 50 cottages/villas. CI 4pm/CO noon. Woodland cottages are very primitive—no phones, heat, or air. Hotel cottages have more amenities. **Amenities:** A/C, cable TV. No phone. **Services:** ⌐ **Facilities:** ●2 ⌐160 3 restaurants, lawn games, washer/dryer. All Mammoth Cave Hotel facilities available to Woodland guests. **Rates:** $34–$49 cottage/villa. Extra person $6. Children under age 16 stay free. Parking: Outdoor, free. Closed Sept–mid-May. AE, CB, DC, MC, V.

Maysville

Settled in the late 1700s by pioneers, scouts, and foreign nobility who journeyed down Ohio River to the landing at Limestone. Maysville became a major port in the 19th century, and is still a bustling harbor town today. Contains 48 National Register buildings. **Information:** Maysville–Mason County Chamber of Commerce, 15 ½ W 2nd St, Maysville, 41056 (tel 606/564-5534).

MOTEL 🏨

≡≡≡ Ramada Inn

484 Moody Dr, 41056; tel 606/564-6793 or toll free 800/272-6232; fax 606/564-4486. Off US 68. A standard chain motel located near many historic sites in the area. A quiet location well equipped for large groups. **Rooms:** 119 rms, stes, and effic. CI 1pm/CO 1pm. Nonsmoking rms avail. **Amenities:** 🏨 A/C, cable TV w/movies. **Services:** ✗ ⊠ ⌐ ⌐ Pets under 25 lbs only. **Facilities:** ⌐ ●1 ⌐400 ⅙ 1 restaurant, 1 bar. **Rates:** $51 S; $57 D; $95–$130 ste; $56–$63 effic. Extra person $6. Children under age 18 stay free. Parking: Outdoor, free. Group rates avail. AE, CB, DC, DISC, JCB, MC, V.

Middlesboro

Located in the historic and beautiful Cumberland Gap area at the meeting point of Kentucky, Tennessee, and Virginia. The town is featured in guided tours of Cumberland Gap National Historical Park. **Information:** Bell County Chamber of Commerce, N 20th St, PO Box 788, Middlesboro, 40965 (tel 606/248-1075).

ATTRACTION 🖼

Cumberland Gap National Historical Park

US 25 E; tel 606/249-2817. For early American pioneers, the Cumberland Gap area of Kentucky, Tennessee, and Virginia served as a natural "door" through the otherwise impassable Appalachian Mountains. Native Americans, who had long known about the trail, used it to get to the rich hunting grounds of Kentucky. In 1775, Daniel Boone became the first white man to mark the trail; over the next 25 years, more than 300,000 settlers crossed the gap into the West. Today, the Kentucky portion of Cumberland Gap is home to a 20,000-acre park, which features camping, picnicking, hiking, and structured interpretive programs on the area's vital role in America's history. **Open:** Daily 8am–sunset. Closed Dec 25. **Free**

Monticello

Established in 1801 and named for Thomas Jefferson's famous home, this is the seat of Wayne County in southern Kentucky. **Information:** Monticello–Wayne County Chamber of Commerce, PO Box 566, Monticello, 42633 (tel 606/348-3064).

MOTEL 🏨

≡ Anchor Motel

1077 N Main, 42633; tel 606/348-8441; fax 606/348-5118. No-frills facility close to Lake Cumberland. OK for an overnight stay if budget is a priority. **Rooms:** 53 rms and effic. CI noon/CO noon. Some room furnishings need repair. **Amenities:** 🏨 A/C, cable TV. Some units w/terraces. **Services:** ⌐ ⌐ **Facilities:** ⌐ ⌐75 1 restaurant, washer/dryer. **Rates:** $32–$38 S or D; $45 effic. Extra person $4. Children under age 12 stay free. Parking: Outdoor, free. Some efficiencies available for monthly rentals. AE, DISC, MC, V.

Morehead

Seat of Rowan County, Morehead is the gateway to Cave Run Lake and is surrounded by Daniel Boone National Forest. Morehead State University is here. **Information:** Morehead–Rowan County Chamber of Commerce, 168 E Main St, Morehead, 40351 (tel 606/784-6221).

MOTELS 🏨

≡≡ Days Inn

I-64 and Old Flemingsburg Rd, 40351; tel 606/783-1484 or toll free 800/DAYS-INN; fax 606/783-1484. Exit 137. Two-story chain motel with very basic rooms; within walking distance of Morehead State University. Popular with university visitors. **Rooms:** 51 rms. CI 11am/CO 11am. Nonsmoking rms avail. **Amenities:** 🏨 A/C, cable TV. Some units w/whirlpools. Some rooms have refrigerators. **Services:** ⌐ Complimentary coffee. **Facilities:** ⅙ Washer/dryer. **Rates:** Peak (May–Oct) $50–$70 S; $50–$80 D. Extra person $5. Children under age 12 stay free. Lower rates off-season. Parking: Outdoor, free. Rates rise during graduation weekend. AE, CB, DC, DISC, MC, V.

⫸⫸⫸ Holiday Inn

1698 Flemingsburg Rd, 40351; tel 606/784-7591 or toll free 800/HOLIDAY; fax 606/783-1859. Exit 137 off I-64. Basic chain motel close to Morehead State University and Cave Run Lake. **Rooms:** 142 rms. CI 3pm/CO noon. Nonsmoking rms avail. **Amenities:** 🛏 ⚬ A/C, cable TV w/movies, dataport. Hair dryers available in some rooms. **Services:** ✗ 🖼 ⌂ Friendly staff. **Facilities:** 🖼 🄻50 & 1 restaurant, washer/dryer. Beautifully landscaped pool area with mature trees and a large terrace. **Rates:** Peak (May–Oct) $55–$60 S or D. Extra person $5. Children under age 18 stay free. Lower rates off-season. Parking: Outdoor, free. AE, CB, DC, DISC, JCB, MC, V.

Murray

This popular retirement town lies just north of 148,000-acre Kentucky Lake. Home of Murray State University. **Information:** Murray–Calloway County Chamber of Commerce, Hart County Courthouse, PO Box 719, Murray, 42071 (tel 502/753-5171).

MOTELS 🏨

⫸⫸⫸ Best Western Racer Inn

S 12th St (US 641S), PO Box 3, Rte 4, 42071; tel 502/753-5986 or toll free 800/808-0036; fax 502/753-5986 ext 147. An older yet well-maintained lodging located near shopping and restaurants. **Rooms:** 107 rms. CI 2pm/CO noon. Nonsmoking rms avail. **Amenities:** 🛏 ⚬ 🍽 A/C, satel TV w/movies. **Services:** ✗ 🖼 ⌂ Babysitting. **Facilities:** 🖼 🄻50 & 1 restaurant, washer/dryer. **Rates:** $40–$80 S or D. Extra person $5. Children under age 18 stay free. Min stay special events. Parking: Outdoor, free. AE, CB, DC, DISC, ER, JCB, MC, V.

⫸⫸ Days Inn

517 S 12th St, 42017; tel 502/753-6706 or toll free 800/DAYS-INN; fax 502/753-6708. Under new ownership, this motel features clean and comfortable accommodations and is close to shopping and restaurants. **Rooms:** 40 rms. CI open/CO noon. Nonsmoking rms avail. **Amenities:** 🛏 ⚬ A/C, cable TV, refrig, dataport. Some units w/whirlpools. Microwaves in some rooms. **Services:** ⌂ 🕭 **Facilities:** 🖼 🄻10 & **Rates (CP):** $40–$44 S; $44–$48 D. Extra person $4. Children under age 12 stay free. Parking: Outdoor, free. AE, CB, DC, DISC, EC, ER, JCB, MC, V.

⫸⫸ Shoney's Inn

1503 N 12th St, 42071; tel 502/753-5353 or toll free 800/222-2222; fax 502/753-5353. Off US 641 N. Relatively new; located near Murray State University. **Rooms:** 72 rms and stes. CI 3pm/CO noon. Nonsmoking rms avail. Rooms are clean and have modern decor. **Amenities:** 🛏 A/C, cable TV w/movies. Suites have microwaves and refrigerators. **Services:** 🖼 ⌂ 🕭 Babysitting. **Facilities:** 🖼 🄻75 & Pool

area enclosed by brick wall for privacy and security. **Rates:** $42 S; $42–$54 D; $64 ste. Extra person $4. Children under age 13 stay free. Min stay special events. Parking: Outdoor, free. AE, DC, DISC, JCB, MC, V.

RESORTS

⫸⫸ Kenlake Hotel & Cottages

542 Kenlake Rd, Hardin, 42048; tel 502/474-2211 or toll free 800/325-0143; fax 502/474-2018. 1,800 acres. This resort features a rustic lodge with an outdoor patio area overlooking Kentucky Lake. The front lawn has a small gazebo and colorful flowers. **Rooms:** 48 rms; 34 cottages/villas. CI 4pm/CO noon. Nonsmoking rms avail. Cottages have screened-in patios, refrigerators, stoves, coffeemakers, and cooking utensils and dishes. **Amenities:** 🛏 ⚬ A/C, cable TV. VCRs and movies for rent. **Services:** ⌂ Children's program. **Facilities:** 🖼 △ 🐎 ▶9 🏌 ⚓ 🄻450 & 1 restaurant, basketball, volleyball, games rm, lawn games, playground. Indoor tennis center and outdoor courts. Pontoons and rowboats available. Dataports available in meeting rooms. **Rates:** Peak (May 24–Sept 5) $40–$55 S; $55–$65 D; $80–$125 cottage/villa. Extra person $6. Children under age 16 stay free. Lower rates off-season. Parking: Outdoor, free. AE, CB, DC, DISC, MC, V.

⫸⫸⫸ Kentucky Dam Village Inn

KY 641, PO Box 69, Gilbertsville, 42044; tel 502/362-4271 or toll free 800/325-0146; fax 502/362-8747. E of Jct I-24/62 E. 1,200 acres. A rustic yet comfortable lodgelike resort. The lobby has a large, cozy fireplace and a stunning view of nearby Kentucky Lake. **Rooms:** 86 rms; 72 cottages/villas. CI 4pm/CO noon. Nonsmoking rms avail. Accommodations range from basic motel-type lodge rooms to upgraded three-bedroom executive cottages. Cottages have kitchen facilities. **Amenities:** 🛏 A/C, cable TV w/movies. **Services:** 🚐 ⌂ Children's program, babysitting. Courtesy car and driver available to shuttle guests to their cottages. **Facilities:** 🖼 🐎 ▶18 △ 🖼 🄻525 & 1 restaurant, 1 beach (lake shore), lifeguard, basketball, volleyball, games rm, playground. Large, handsomely landscaped pool area. Houseboats and pontoon boats available. **Rates:** Peak (Apr–Oct) $38–$63 S; $49–$74 D; $79–$168 cottage/villa. Extra person $5. Children under age 16 stay free. Lower rates off-season. Parking: Outdoor, free. Special event and golf packages avail. AE, DC, DISC, MC, V.

RESTAURANT 🍽

★ Seafood Express Restaurant & Market

In Olympic Plaza Shopping Center, 506 N 12th St (US 641 N); tel 502/753-6149. Near Murray State University. **Seafood/Steak.** This medium-size restaurant offers both tables and high-backed booths surrounded by nostalgic music and movie and US Navy posters. Broiled and fried seafood, and some Cajun and blackened dishes are offered—the blackened mahi-mahi is especially fine. Diners can start things off with a cup of spicy seafood gumbo. Limited steak menu. **FYI:**

Reservations accepted. Rock/bluegrass. Children's menu. No liquor license. **Open:** Sun–Fri 11am–9pm, Sat 4–9pm. **Prices:** Main courses $6–$17. DC, MC, V. 🏧

Olive Hill

Founded in the early 1800s, Olive Hill is nearby to Carter Caves State Resort Park and Tygarts State Forest in northeastern Kentucky. **Information:** Olive Hill Area Chamber of Commerce, PO Box 5584, Olive Hill, 41164 (tel 606/286-2927).

RESORT 🏨

≣≣≣ Carter Caves State Resort

Rte 5, PO Box 1120, 41164; tel 606/286-4411 or toll free 800/325-0059; fax 606/286-8165. Exit 161 off I-64. 1,600 acres. Rural resort offering beautiful views in a quiet forest setting. **Rooms:** 28 rms; 15 cottages/villas. CI 4pm/CO 11am. Nonsmoking rms avail. Well-appointed rooms offer great views of the area and have attractive, modern decor. **Amenities:** 🛋 ⚖ A/C, satel TV w/movies. All units w/terraces. Cottages have refrigerators. **Services:** 🛎 Social director, children's program. Friendly staff. **Facilities:** 🏊 ⚠ 🏕 ▶9 🔥 ◢2 🍴200 ⅃ 1 restaurant, basketball, volleyball, games rm, playground, washer/dryer. Resort sponsors planned recreational activities, festivals, and special events year-round. Picnic area with grills. **Rates:** Peak (Mem Day–Labor Day) $52 S; $62 D; $69–$87 cottage/villa. Extra person $5. Children under age 16 stay free. Lower rates off-season. Parking: Outdoor, free. Closed Dec 24–31. AE, DC, DISC, MC, V.

ATTRACTION 🏛

Carter Caves State Resort Park

KY 182; tel 606/286-4411. This state park is home to over 20 caverns. Visitors can explore the rolling, green hills of Eastern Kentucky or go underneath them on a cave tour. (There are even special tours for beginning and advanced spelunkers.) Other recreational activities include swimming, nine-hole golf, boating, fishing, hiking, tennis, and horseback riding. **Open:** Daily sunrise–sunset. Closed Dec 25. **Free**

Owensboro

The state's third-largest city was settled around 1800 on the Ohio River in western Kentucky and went on to become a transportation and manufacturing center for the region. Home to Kentucky Wesleyan and Brescia Colleges. Headquarters of the International Bluegrass Music Association, the town hosts several riverfront music festivals. The area is also known regionally for its barbecue. **Information:** Owensboro–Daviess County Tourist Commission, 326 St Elizabeth St, Owensboro, 42301 (tel 502/926-1100).

HOTEL 🏨

≣≣≣ Holiday Inn

3136 W 2nd St, PO Box 21401, 42802; tel 502/685-3941 or toll free 800/HOLIDAY; fax 502/926-2917. Off US 60. An exceptionally well-kept establishment located on the main street in town. Public areas are attractively decorated with contemporary furnishings and a subdued mauve color scheme. **Rooms:** 145 rms and stes. CI noon/CO noon. Nonsmoking rms avail. **Amenities:** 🛋 ⚖ 🖥 A/C, cable TV w/movies, dataport, voice mail. Some units w/whirlpools. **Services:** ✕ 🚗 🛄 ⅃ 🛎 **Facilities:** 🏊 🏋 ⅃ 1 restaurant, 1 bar, games rm, steam rm, whirlpool, playground. **Rates (CP):** $55 S or D; $95 ste. Extra person $5. Children under age 19 stay free. Parking: Outdoor, free. AE, CB, DC, DISC, JCB, MC, V.

MOTELS

≣≣ Days Inn

3720 New Hartford Rd, 42301; tel 502/684-9621 or toll free 800/DAYS-INN; fax 502/684-9626. Off US 60. No frills here—just clean and comfortable rooms. **Rooms:** 121 rms. CI noon/CO noon. Nonsmoking rms avail. **Amenities:** 🛋 🖥 A/C, satel TV w/movies. Nintendo available for a fee. VCRs available upon request. **Services:** ✕ 🛄 ⅃ 🛎 Pet deposit is $25. **Facilities:** 🏊 ⅃ 1 restaurant. **Rates (CP):** $38 S; $42 D. Extra person $4. Children under age 12 stay free. Parking: Outdoor, free. AE, DC, DISC, MC, V.

≣ Motel 6

4585 Frederica, 42301; tel 502/686-8606 or toll free 800/891-6161; fax 502/683-2689. Off US 60. No-frills; fine for overnight stays but nothing more. **Rooms:** 90 rms. CI 3pm/CO noon. Nonsmoking rms avail. **Amenities:** 🛋 A/C, cable TV w/movies. **Services:** ⅃ 🛎 **Facilities:** 🏊 **Rates:** $35–$41 S or D. Extra person $3. Children under age 17 stay free. Parking: Outdoor, free. AE, DC, DISC, MC, V.

RESTAURANTS 🍴

★ The Briarpatch

2760 Veach Rd; tel 502/685-3329. **American.** Charming restaurant offering a large choice of entrees, from lasagna and prime rib to fish, lobster, and shrimp dishes. **FYI:** Reservations not accepted. Children's menu. **Open:** Lunch Sun–Fri 11am–2pm; dinner Sun–Thurs 5–9:30pm, Fri–Sat 5–10:30pm. **Prices:** Main courses $8–$15. AE, DC, DISC, MC, V. 🏧 ⅃

★ Moonlite Bar-B-Q Inn

2840 W Parrish Ave; tel 502/684-8143. **Barbecue.** Famous for its barbecue. The large menu offers a choice of chicken, pork, beef, or country ham served with hot fresh vegetables and dinner rolls. Eat in or carry out. **FYI:** Reservations not accepted. Children's menu. Beer and wine only. **Open:** Mon–Thurs 9am–9pm, Fri–Sat 9am–10pm, Sun 10am–3pm. **Prices:** Main courses $4–$11. AE, DC, DISC, MC, V. 🏧 ⅃

ATTRACTION 🖼

Owensboro Area Museum of Science and History
220 Davies St; tel 502/683-0296. Brand-new facility with exhibits illustrating the cultural and natural history of the Ohio River valley. ScienceWorks demonstrations, reptile exhibits, DramaWorks performances cater to the entire family. **Open:** Mon–Sat 10am–5pm, Sun 1–4pm. Closed some hols. **$**

Paducah

Founded at the confluence of the Ohio and Tennessee Rivers in 1827 and named by Gen William Clark for his Chickasaw friend, Chief Paduke. Known today for its quilt manufacturing, the city is a tobacco market and a river port. **Information:** Paducah Area Chamber of Commerce, 417 S 4th St, PO Box 810, Paducah, 42002 (tel 502/443-1746).

HOTELS 🏨

≣≣ Drury Inn
3975 Hinkleville Rd, 42001; tel 502/443-3313 or toll free 800/325-8300; fax 502/443-3313. Near Jct I-24/US 60. An attractive facility geared toward the corporate traveler. The atrium-style lobby has a balcony and a large chandelier. **Rooms:** 118 rms and stes. CI 3pm/CO noon. Nonsmoking rms avail. **Amenities:** 🛏 ⚬ A/C, satel TV w/movies, dataport. Some rooms have microwaves, refrigerators, and two phones. **Services:** ⚏ ⟑ ⟐ **Facilities:** ⚏ ⚬ Whirlpool. **Rates (CP):** $58–$71 S; $68–$81 D; $71–$81 ste. Extra person $10. Children under age 18 stay free. Parking: Outdoor, free. AE, CB, DC, DISC, MC, V.

≣≣≣ JR's Executive Inn Riverfront
1 Executive Blvd, 42001; tel 502/443-8000 or toll free 800/866-3636; fax 502/444-5317. A riverfront hotel with an open courtyard filled with trees and vines. **Rooms:** 434 rms and stes. CI 2pm/CO noon. Nonsmoking rms avail. Rooms are tastefully decorated. **Amenities:** 🛏 A/C, cable TV w/movies, refrig. **Services:** ✗ 🚌 ⚏ ⟑ Babysitting. Business services. **Facilities:** ⚏ 2500 ⚬ 2 restaurants (*see* "Restaurants" below), 2 bars (w/entertainment), games rm, beauty salon, washer/dryer. Vegas-style showroom regularly hosts top-name entertainers. **Rates:** $52–$57 S; $64–$69 D; $115–$125 ste. Extra person $5. Children under age 12 stay free. Parking: Outdoor, free. AE, CB, DC, DISC, MC, V.

MOTEL

≣≣ Quality Inn
1380 S Irvin Cobb Dr, 42003; tel 502/443-8751 or toll free 800/221-2222; fax 502/442-0133. Located near downtown Paducah, this motel offers simple, clean accommodations. **Rooms:** 101 rms. CI 2pm/CO 11am. Nonsmoking rms avail. **Amenities:** 🛏 A/C, cable TV. **Services:** ⟑ ⟐ **Facilities:** ⚏ 100 ⚬ Pool is landscaped with colorful flowers. **Rates (CP):**

$36–$42 S; $45–$50 D. Extra person $7. Children under age 18 stay free. Parking: Outdoor, free. AE, CB, DC, DISC, JCB, MC, V.

RESTAURANTS 🍽

The Holman House
2714 Park Ave; tel 502/444-3903. Exit 4 off I-24. **Eclectic/Southern.** Diners at this charming eatery have a choice of several intimate dining rooms. One room features hanging wicker swing benches at the tables and a small fountain, while others are decorated with historic memorabilia and shadow-box tables. Menu specialties include Bob Holman's famous Italian roast beef (choice cuts of beef roasted in a special blend of spices and served hot on a French roll) and French pecan pie (covered with fluffy cream cheese topping, whipped cream, and nuts). Full buffet and à la carte items available. An adjacent gourmet shop sells cookbooks, spices, and gift items. **FYI:** Reservations not accepted. Children's menu. No liquor license. **Open:** Mon–Thurs 11am–9pm, Fri–Sat 11am–10pm. **Prices:** Main courses $7–$16. DC, DISC, MC, V. 📷 ⚬

Kincaid's Crossing
In JR's Executive Inn Riverfront, 1 Executive Blvd; tel 502/443-8000. Exit 4 off I-24. **American.** Located inside a gardenlike atrium, with a small fountain at the entrance and flower beds scattered throughout the dining areas. Offers buffet service for all meals, as well as an à la carte menu. **FYI:** Reservations accepted. Piano. Children's menu. **Open:** Mon–Thurs 6am–10pm, Fri–Sat 6am–11pm, Sun 6am–9pm. **Prices:** Main courses $8–$17. AE, CB, DC, DISC, MC, V. ⚬

The Pines Restaurant & Cafe Maurice
900 N 32nd St; tel 502/442-9304. Exit 4 off I-40. **Continental/Mediterranean.** Together, these two eateries offer a range of cuisines, atmosphere, and prices. The more formal Pines features steak and seafood items prepared on an open charcoal grill; there's also a salad bar. The more casual, bistro-like Cafe Maurice offers a cappuccino/espresso bar along with Mediterranean-style dishes. **FYI:** Reservations accepted. Children's menu. **Open:** Lunch Mon–Fri 11:30am–2pm; dinner Mon–Sat 5–10pm. **Prices:** Main courses $13–$35. AE, CB, DC, DISC, MC, V. ⚬

ATTRACTIONS 🖼

Market House
200 Broadway. Built in 1905, this building is now a local cultural center housing an art gallery, museum, and community theater. The **Yeiser Art Center** (tel 502/444-2453) features changing exhibits of traditional and contemporary art from the 19th and early 20th centuries. The complete interior of a local 1877 drugstore as well as local artifacts are housed in the **Market Museum** (tel 502/443-7759). And, the **Market House Theatre** (tel 502/444-6828) presents 12 theat-

rical productions a year. **Open:** Mar–Dec, Tues–Sat noon–4pm, Sun 1–5pm; Jan–Apr, Sat noon–4pm, Sun 1–5pm. Closed some hols. **$**

Paducah Jubilee
Broadway at the river; tel 502/443-8874 or toll free 800/788-1057. Visitors can explore the Ohio and Tennessee Rivers aboard this authentic paddlewheeler. A variety of sightseeing, dining, and theme cruises are available. **Open:** Apr–Oct, call for schedule. **$$**

Museum of the American Quilter's Society
215 Jefferson St; tel 502/442-8856. This colorful 30,000-square-foot museum dedicated to "honoring today's quilter" houses three climate-controlled galleries, spacious studio classrooms, a book and gift shop, a conference room, and a reference room. If you've never thought of quilts as artwork before, this museum might change your mind. **Open:** Nov–Mar, Tues–Sat 10am–5pm; Apr–Oct, Tues–Sat 10am–5pm, Sun 1–5pm. Closed some hols. **$$**

Park City

This is one of the satellite cities surrounding Mammoth Cave National Park.

RESORTS 🏨

≣≣ Best Western Park Mammoth Resort
Exit 48 off I-65, 42160; tel 502/749-4101 or toll free 800/528-1234. 1,600 acres. Located approximately 10 miles from Mammoth Cave National Park, this resort features train rides around the grounds on a replica of a Civil War–era train. Scheduled stops on the ride include a visit to the "Tilt" house, which is constructed on a gravity point. A unique sightseeing experience not to be missed. **Rooms:** 92 rms. CI 2pm/CO noon. **Amenities:** 🛁 A/C, cable TV w/movies. Some units w/terraces. **Services:** ✕ ⌂ **Facilities:** ⛳ ▶18 ⛵ 🏊 🏀 ⌂ 150 ⛳ 1 restaurant, basketball, games rm, lawn games, sauna, playground. Miniature golf. The dining room features a beautiful view. **Rates:** Peak (June–Oct) $44 S; $56 D. Extra person $5. Children under age 18 stay free. Lower rates off-season. Parking: Outdoor, free. AE, CB, DC, DISC, MC, V.

≣≣≣ Park Place Resort
Doyle Rd, 42160; tel 502/749-9466; fax 502/749-5805. Exit 48 off I-65. Apartment-style accommodations in a secluded area. A good value for a family vacation spot. **Rooms:** 82 cottages/villas. CI 4pm/CO 10am. Units are new-looking and well equipped. **Amenities:** 🛁 🌀 🖥 A/C, TV, refrig. All units w/terraces, some w/whirlpools. **Services:** ⌂ **Facilities:** 🛳 🎿 ▶18 ⛷ 🎿 🎱 30 1 restaurant, basketball, volleyball, games rm, lawn games, racquetball, spa, sauna, steam rm, whirlpool, playground, washer/dryer. Cave tours and camping available at nearby Diamond Cave. **Rates:** $25–$89 cottage/villa. Children under age 18 stay free. Parking: Outdoor, free. AE, CB, DISC, MC, V.

Perryville

Located 40 miles southwest of Lexington. The state's largest and bloodiest Civil War battle was fought here.

ATTRACTION 🏛

Perryville Battlefield State Historic Site
KY 1920 off US 150; tel 606/332-8631. One of the greatest Civil War battles in the state took place at this location on Oct 8, 1862. It was the South's last serious attempt to control Kentucky, but Confederate Gen Braxton Bragg was forced to withdraw his troops, and in the end Federal forces maintained control of the state. The park includes a cemetery and monuments to both armies. Annual re-enactment held weekend closest to battle anniversary date. **Open:** Apr–Oct, daily 9am–9pm; Nov–Mar, daily 8am–5pm. **$**

Pikeville

Located in Pike County, the world's largest producer of coal. Pikeville is most famous as site of the Hatfield–McCoy feud; clan leader Randolph McCoy is buried in Dils Cemetery. The Pikeville Cut Thru is one of the country's largest engineering and earth-moving achievements. **Information:** Pike County Chamber of Commerce, 225 College St #2, Pikeville, 41501 (tel 606/432-5504).

MOTEL 🏨

≣≣ Landmark Inn
146 S Mayo Trail, 41501; tel 606/432-2545 or toll free 800/831-1469; fax 606/432-2545. Off US 23. Basic motel accommodations located in downtown Pikeville. Popular with fishing enthusiasts who come to nearby Fishtrap Lake. **Rooms:** 103 rms, stes, and effic. CI noon/CO noon. Nonsmoking rms avail. **Amenities:** 🛁 A/C. No TV. Some units w/terraces. **Services:** ✕ 🚐 🖼 ⌂ ⌂ **Facilities:** ⛳ 425 ⛳ 1 restaurant, 2 bars (w/entertainment), washer/dryer. Rooftop restaurant. **Rates:** $55 S or D; $75 ste; $75 effic. Extra person $10. Children under age 12 stay free. Parking: Outdoor, free. AE, CB, DC, DISC, MC, V.

Prestonsburg

This eastern Kentucky town, located in an area of coal mines and truck farms, was the scene of the Civil War Battle of Middle Creek. The battlefield is now a National Historic Landmark. This was also the site of Daniel Boone's winter camp in 1767–68. **Information:** Floyd County Chamber of Commerce, 245 N Lake Dr, Prestonsburg, 41653 (tel 606/886-7827).

MOTEL 🏨

≣≣≣ Holiday Inn

575 S US 23, 41653; tel 606/886-0001 or toll free 800/ HOLIDAY; fax 606/886-9850. 1 mi S of KY 114. Standard chain motel. Popular with families, as it's three miles from Jenny Wiley State Resort Park. **Rooms:** 117 rms. CI 3pm/CO noon. Nonsmoking rms avail. **Amenities:** 🛢 🕭 A/C, cable TV, dataport. **Services:** ✕ 🖎 🛱 Many services available for the business traveler. **Facilities:** 🔏 🖢 🔟 & 1 restaurant, 1 bar (w/entertainment), sauna, whirlpool, washer/dryer. Heated pool. **Rates:** $60–$85 S or D. Extra person $6. Children under age 16 stay free. Parking: Outdoor, free. AE, CB, DC, DISC, JCB, MC, V.

LODGE

≣≣ May Lodge

Jenny Wiley State Resort Park, 39 Jenny Wiley Rd, 41653; tel 606/886-2711 or toll free 800/325-0142; fax 606/886-8052. 4 mi off US 23. 2,500 acres. Lakeside lodge offering quiet relaxation in the mountains of eastern Kentucky. **Rooms:** 49 rms and stes; 18 cottages/villas. CI 4pm/CO 11am. Nonsmoking rms avail. One- and two-bedroom cottages come with fully equipped kitchens. **Amenities:** 🛢 A/C, cable TV. Some units w/terraces. **Services:** 🛱 Social director, children's program. **Facilities:** 🔏 🖻 🏳₉ 🔟 & 1 restaurant, basketball, volleyball, games rm, lawn games. Hiking trails, picnic areas, sky lift, boat dock, marina, and campground are all available in the park. The Jenny Wiley Theater puts on Broadway musicals June–Aug. **Rates:** Peak (June–Oct) $54 S; $64 D; $64 ste; $72–$87 cottage/villa. Extra person $10. Children under age 16 stay free. Lower rates off-season. Parking: Outdoor, free. AE, CB, DC, DISC, MC, V.

Radcliff

Radcliff is in an area of hotels and restaurants near the nation's gold depository at Fort Knox. **Information:** Radcliff–Vine Grove Chamber of Commerce, 306 N Wilson Rd, Radcliff, 40160 (tel 502/351-4450).

MOTELS 🏨

≣≣ Best Western Gold Vault Inn

1225 N Dixie Blvd, 40160; tel 502/351-1141 or toll free 800/528-1234; fax 502/351-1157. Simple but friendly motel, close to Fort Knox and other area attractions. **Rooms:** 94 rms. CI noon/CO noon. Executive king rooms feature attractive extras like armoires. **Amenities:** 🛢 A/C, cable TV w/movies. Some units w/terraces. **Services:** 🖎 🛱 Fax service. Free local calls and complimentary coffee. **Facilities:** 🔏 🔟 & Sauna, whirlpool, washer/dryer. **Rates:** $49–$51 S; $55–$69 D. Extra person $5. Children under age 12 stay free. Parking: Outdoor, free. AE, CB, DC, DISC, MC, V.

≣ Econo Lodge

261 N Dixie Blvd, 40160; tel 502/351-4488 or toll free 800/ 553-2666; fax 502/352-4833. Basic, budget motel. Easily accessible from the Western Kentucky Parkway. **Rooms:** 49 rms. CI 11/CO noon. Nonsmoking rms avail. **Amenities:** 🛢 A/C, cable TV w/movies, refrig. Some rooms have microwaves. **Services:** 🖎 🛱 🛱 VCRs for rent. **Facilities:** 🔏 **Rates (CP):** Peak (Apr–Aug) $37–$40 S; $42–$45 D. Extra person $4. Children under age 18 stay free. Lower rates off-season. Parking: Outdoor, free. AE, CB, DC, DISC, JCB, MC, V.

Renfro Valley

Since 1939, this nationally known country-music center has been the site of stage shows and the country's second-oldest radio broadcast, "The Sunday Morning Gatherin'." Nearby Mount Vernon is the seat of Rockcastle County (named for the Rockcastle River and the castlelike rock formations along its banks).

MOTELS 🏨

≣≣ Best Western Kastle Inn

I-75, exit 59, PO Box 637, Mount Vernon, 40456; tel 606/ 256-5156 or toll free 800/528-1234; fax 606/256-5156. Cozy property perched on top of a large hill. Three miles from the country-music shows at Renfro Valley. **Rooms:** 50 rms. CI 2pm/CO 11am. Nonsmoking rms avail. Some rooms have scenic mountain views. **Amenities:** 🛢 A/C, satel TV w/movies. **Services:** ✕ 🛱 🛱 **Facilities:** 🔏 🔟 1 restaurant. Gazebo in pool area. **Rates:** Peak (Mar–Nov 15) $30–$36 S; $38–$44 D. Extra person $5. Children under age 12 stay free. Lower rates off-season. Parking: Outdoor, free. Group rates avail. AE, CB, DC, DISC, ER, JCB, MC, V.

≣≣ Days Inn

I-75, exit 62, 40456; tel 606/256-3300 or toll free 800/ DAYS INN; fax 606/256-3323. Off I-75 exit 62. Basic chain motel, located near Renfro Valley and within a 45-minute drive from Cumberland Falls. **Rooms:** 100 rms. CI 2pm/CO 11am. Nonsmoking rms avail. **Amenities:** 🛢 A/C, satel TV w/movies. **Services:** 🛱 🛱 **Facilities:** & Golf and canoeing nearby. **Rates:** Peak (Mar–Nov) $30–$65 S or D. Extra person $5. Children under age 16 stay free. Lower rates off-season. Parking: Outdoor, free. Group rates avail. AE, DC, DISC, MC, V.

ATTRACTION 🏛

Renfro Valley

Exit 62 off I-75; tel toll free 800/765-7464. Center of country music for over 50 years. Traditional country music is presented at the weekly Barn Dance (Saturday at 7pm), country-style gospel at the Mountain Gospel Jubilee, and contemporary country at the Jamboree. The Sunday Mornin'

Gathering is—after the Grand Ol' Opry—the country's second-oldest radio broadcast. **Open:** Mar–Nov. Call for schedules. **$$$$**

Richmond

Site of Daniel Boone's wilderness outpost, Kit Carson's birthplace, and a major Civil War battle. The city is best known today as the home of Eastern Kentucky University. **Information:** Richmond Chamber of Commerce, 201 E Main St, PO Box 876, Richmond, 40476 (tel 606/623-1720).

MOTELS 🛏

🏊🏊 Best Western Road Star Inn

1751 Lexington Rd, 40475; tel 606/623-9121 or toll free 800/528-1234; fax 606/623-3160. Off I-75 at exit 90. Nice chain motel, close to many area attractions and restaurants. **Rooms:** 96 rms and stes. CI 2pm/CO noon. Nonsmoking rms avail. **Amenities:** 🛏 🕐 A/C, cable TV. **Services:** 🖨 🍴 **Facilities:** 🏊 🏋 & Nice, well-landscaped pool. **Rates (CP):** Peak (July–Oct) $55 S or D; $75–$85 ste. Extra person $5. Children under age 12 stay free. Lower rates off-season. Parking: Outdoor, free. Corporate rates avail. AE, DC, DISC, MC, V.

🏊🏊 Days Inn

2109 Beemont Dr, 40475; tel 606/624-5769 or toll free 800/DAYS-INN; fax 606/624-1406. Off I-75 at exit 90. Standard chain motel. **Rooms:** 70 rms. CI 3pm/CO noon. Nonsmoking rms avail. **Amenities:** 🛏 A/C, cable TV. **Services:** 🍴 🖨 **Facilities:** 🏊 🏋 & Lovely pool area. **Rates:** $50 S; $60 D. Extra person $5. Children under age 17 stay free. Parking: Outdoor, free. AE, CB, DC, DISC, JCB, MC, V.

🏊🏊 Holiday Inn

100 Eastern Bypass, 40475; tel 606/623-9220 or toll free 800/HOLIDAY; fax 606/624-1458. Off I-75 at exit 87. Basic chain motel, located off I-75. Convenient to Eastern Kentucky University. **Rooms:** 141 rms. CI 2pm/CO noon. Nonsmoking rms avail. **Amenities:** 🛏 🕐 📺 A/C, dataport. Refrigerators in some rooms. **Services:** ✕ 🖨 🍴 **Facilities:** 🏊 🏋 & 1 restaurant, volleyball, playground. **Rates:** Peak (May–Oct) $65 S or D. Extra person $5. Children under age 12 stay free. Lower rates off-season. Parking: Outdoor, free. AE, CB, DC, DISC, MC, V.

RESTAURANT 🍴

Applebee's Neighborhood Grill & Bar

In Carriage Gate Shopping Center, 851 Eastern Bypass; tel 606/624-1224. **American/Mexican.** A fun, popular eatery with families and college students alike. Menu offerings include blackened-chicken sandwiches, and fajitas, as well as many varieties of pasta, steak, and seafood. The combined bar and restaurant area is open and spacious, and the friendly staff adds to the dining enjoyment. **FYI:** Reservations not

accepted. Children's menu. **Open:** Mon–Sat 11am–noon, Sun 11am–11pm. **Prices:** Main courses $5–$9. AE, DISC, MC, V. 🖼 &

ATTRACTION 🖼

Hummel Planetarium

Eastern Kentucky University; tel 606/622-1547. The second-largest university-based planetarium in the world. A state-of-the-art multimedia system allows visitors to see a recreation of the night sky complete with planets, nebulae, meteor showers, and exploding supernovas. The system can even be adjusted to any vantage point in our solar system. Once your curiosity is piqued, you can visit the gift shop, which offers items related to astronomy and the other physical sciences. **Open:** Shows Thurs–Fri 7:30pm, Sat–Sun 3:30 and 7:30pm. Closed some hols. **$$**

Shelbyville

Located 20 miles west of Frankfort, the city is notable for its late-Victorian downtown area and for its world-renowned galleries selling European antiques. **Information:** Shelby County Chamber of Commerce, 316 Main St, PO Box 335, Shelbyville, 40066 (tel 502/633-1636).

HOTEL 🛏

🏊🏊 Best Western

115 Isaac Shelby Dr, 40065; tel 502/633-4400 or toll free 800/528-1234; fax 502/633-6818. Off I-64. Comfortable, with huge rooms. **Rooms:** 79 rms and stes. CI 1pm/CO 11am. Nonsmoking rms avail. **Amenities:** 🛏 A/C, satel TV w/movies. **Services:** 🍴 🖨 **Facilities:** 🏊 🏋 & Whirlpool, washer/dryer. Use of the Shelby fitness center is free. **Rates (CP):** Peak (May–Sept) $47 S; $48 D; $64 ste. Extra person $6. Children under age 12 stay free. Lower rates off-season. Parking: Outdoor, free. AE, CB, DC, DISC, MC, V.

RESTAURANTS 🍴

Claudia Sanders Dinner House

US 60; tel 502/633-5600. Off US 60. **Regional American.** Located in a large white farmhouse on the outskirts of Shelbyville is this family-oriented, casual restaurant. Specialties include fried chicken and Kentucky country ham served with all the vegetables you can eat, family-style. **FYI:** Reservations accepted. Children's menu. No liquor license. **Open:** Tues–Sun 11am–9pm. **Prices:** Main courses $12–$17. AE, CB, DC, DISC, MC, V. 🖼

Old Stone Inn

6905 Shelbyville Rd, Simpsonville; tel 502/722-8882. Off US 60. **Regional American.** Listed on the National Register of Historic Places, the building was built in 1817 on the site of a frontier stage coach stop and is one of the oldest stone houses in Kentucky. The restaurant offers daily specials, soups, and desserts. Friendship tea served Tues and Thurs by reservation only. **FYI:** Reservations recommended. Children's menu. No liquor license. No smoking. **Open:** Tues–Sat 11am–8:30pm, Sun 11am–3:30pm. **Prices:** Main courses $12–$15. MC, V. ▨

★ Science Hill Inn

630 Main; tel 502/633-2825. Off US 60. **Regional American.** The Science Hill Inn has been serving meals continuously for 170 years. Listed on the National Register of Historic Places, the building was an esteemed all-girls school for 114 years and served as a stop on the Underground Railroad during the Civil War. Today's restaurant features a large, elegant dining room with high ceilings, chandeliers, and floor-to-ceiling windows that overlook a beautiful garden. Southern regional favorites include shrimp and grits and Kentucky rainbow trout. All desserts and breads are baked fresh daily. **FYI:** Reservations recommended. **Open:** Lunch Tues–Sun 11:30am–2:30pm; dinner Fri–Sat 5:30–8:30pm; brunch Sun 11:30am–2:30pm. **Prices:** Main courses $8–$9. AE, MC, V. ▨

ATTRACTION 📷

Science Hill Inn

525 Washington St; tel 502/633-4382. Science Hill began life in 1825 as a private school for girls; it graduated its last class in 1939. Today, Historic Science Hill houses the Science Hill Inn, Wakefield-Scearce Galleries, and a variety of other fine stores. The building contains one of the largest collections of English antique furniture, silver, and accessories in the United States. **Open:** Mon–Sat 9am–5pm. Closed some hols. **Free**

Shepherdsville

Seat of Bullitt County. Settled in the 1700s, Shepherdsville still features its old jail, one-room schoolhouse, and a bank thought to be the oldest west of the Alleghenies. **Information:** Bullitt County Tourist Commission, PO Box 808, Shepherdsville, 40165 (tel toll free 800/526-2068).

HOTEL 📷

🛏🛏 Best Western Louisville South

Lakeview Dr, PO Box 96, 40165; tel 502/543-7097 or toll free 800/528-1234. Exit 117 off I-65. A basic, no-frills interstate hotel. **Rooms:** 85 rms. CI 3pm/CO noon. Nonsmoking rms avail. **Amenities:** 🔋 A/C, cable TV w/movies. **Services:** ✗ ⤴ ⤴ Pets under 25 lbs only. **Facilities:** 🔳 ♿ 1 restaurant, 1 bar (w/entertainment). **Rates:** $48–$55 S or D. Extra person $6. Children under age 12 stay free. Parking: Outdoor, free. AE, DC, DISC, MC, V.

MOTEL

🛏 Days Inn

120 Lakeview Dr, 40065; tel 502/543-3011 or toll free 800/DAYS-INN; fax 502/543-3011 ext 272. Shepherdsville exit off I-65. Bare-bones motel. There's no real lobby—just a place to check in and pay. **Rooms:** 120 rms. CI noon/CO 11am. Nonsmoking rms avail. **Amenities:** 🔋 A/C, satel TV w/movies. Complimentary coffee available near check-in area. **Services:** ⤴ ⤴ **Facilities:** 🔳 **Rates:** Peak (Apr–Sept) $42–$52 S or D. Extra person $2. Children under age 12 stay free. Lower rates off-season. Parking: Outdoor, free. AE, DC, DISC, MC, V.

Slade

Situated off the Mountain Parkway, a red caboose here offers information for travelers heading for the 25,662-acre Red River Gorge, with its unique vegetation and 80 natural arches, in Daniel Boone National Forest.

LODGE 📷

🛏🛏🛏 Hemlock Lodge & Cottages

2135 Natural Bridge Rd, 40376; tel 606/663-2214 or toll free 800/325-1710; fax 606/663-5037. In Natural Bridge State Resort Park; exit 33 KY 11. 892 acres. Comfy lodge nestled in the woods of Natural Bridge State Park. **Rooms:** 35 rms; 10 cottages/villas. CI 4pm/CO noon. Nonsmoking rms avail. Rooms offer beautiful views and plenty of peace and quiet. **Amenities:** 🔋 ⚲ A/C, satel TV w/movies. All units w/terraces. Private balconies. **Services:** ⤴ Social director, children's program. **Facilities:** 🔳 ⛺ 🏊 🎱2 🚗200 ♿ 1 restaurant, volleyball, playground, washer/dryer. Sky lift to Natural Bridge, campgrounds, hiking trails, miniature golf, nature center, and picnic areas available. **Rates:** Peak (Apr–Oct) $64 S or D; $69–$87 cottage/villa. Extra person $5. Children under age 16 stay free. Lower rates off-season. Parking: Outdoor, free. AE, CB, DC, DISC, MC, V.

ATTRACTION 📷

Natural Bridge State Resort Park

Mountain Pkwy off KY 11; tel 606/663-2214. Located in the Daniel Boone National Forest, near the Red River Gorge Geological Area. The dramatic natural sandstone arch from which this park takes its name is 78 feet long and 65 feet high. Other highlights of the 1,900-acre park are 18 miles of hiking trails, a nature center, fishing, tennis courts, a pool, and picnic shelters. Camping and year-round lodge. **Open:** Daily sunrise–sunset. **$**

Somerset

Named for the Duke of Somerset, the town occupies a sloping ridge on the west side of the Cumberland Mountains.

Northeast entrance to Lake Cumberland. **Information:** Somerset–Pulaski County Chamber of Commerce, 209 E Mount Vernon St, PO Box 126, Somerset, 42501 (tel 606/679-7323).

MOTELS

≣≣≣ Landmark Inn

606 S US 27, 42501; tel 606/678-8115 or toll free 800/585-3503; fax 606/678-8115 ext 323. Two-story motel convenient to shopping and restaurants. Lake Cumberland and Lee's Ford Resort are also close by. **Rooms:** 159 rms and stes. CI 3pm/CO 11am. Nonsmoking rms avail. **Amenities:** A/C, cable TV, dataport. **Services:** Friendly staff. **Facilities:** 1 restaurant, playground, washer/dryer. Fitness center nearby. **Rates (CP):** Peak (May–Oct) $54–$72 S or D; $75 ste. Extra person $6. Children under age 18 stay free. Lower rates off-season. Parking: Outdoor, free. AE, CB, DC, DISC, JCB, MC, V.

≣ Super 8 Motel

601 S US 27, 42501; tel 606/679-9279 or toll free 800/800-8000; fax 606/679-9281. Nothing fancy here—just basic, clean accommodations close to Lake Cumberland. **Rooms:** 63 rms and stes. CI 1pm/CO 11am. Nonsmoking rms avail. **Amenities:** A/C, cable TV. **Services:** **Facilities:** **Rates (CP):** $35–$41 S; $43–$45 D; $51–$53 ste. Extra person $2. Children under age 12 stay free. Parking: Outdoor, free. Extended-stay rates avail. AE, CB, DC, DISC, MC, V.

Springfield

This central Kentucky town features the state's oldest courthouse in continuous use (housing the marriage certificate of Abraham Lincoln's parents, Nancy Hanks and Thomas Lincoln), and one of the oldest Catholic settlements in the eastern United States. Lincoln Homestead State Park includes site of the marriage of Lincoln's parents. **Information:** Springfield/Washington County Chamber of Commerce, 112 Cross Main St, Springfield, 40069 (tel 606/336-3810).

RESTAURANT

★ Linc's

1007 Lincoln Park Rd; tel 606/336-7493. **Seafood/Steak.** Although best known for its weekend seafood buffets, Linc's serves up an extensive menu all week long. Many regional favorites—catfish, frog legs—are on offer, along with classics like crab legs, fried shrimp, scallops, and oysters on the half shell. Non-seafood items include rib eye and filet mignon. **FYI:** Reservations accepted. Children's menu. Beer and wine only. **Open:** Mon–Thurs 11am–9pm, Fri–Sat 11am–10pm, Sun 11am–3pm. **Prices:** Main courses $7–$20. AE, DISC, MC, V.

Williamsburg

Just north of the Kentucky–Tennessee border lies this access point for the Cumberland Falls and Big South Fork areas. Has the largest welcome center between the Great Lakes and Gulf Coast. **Information:** Williamsburg Tourism and Convention Commission, PO Box 2, Williamsburg, 40769 (tel 606/549-0530).

MOTELS

≣ Best Western Convenient Motor Lodge

KY 92 & I-75, PO Box 204, 40769; tel 606/549-1500 or toll free 800/215-2995; fax 606/549-8312. At exit 11. Convenient location right off I-75, but traffic noise makes it difficult to sleep. Adequate for overnight stay. **Rooms:** 83 rms. CI 1pm/CO 11am. Nonsmoking rms avail. **Amenities:** A/C, cable TV. Free local calls. **Services:** Small pets allowed. **Facilities:** **Rates (CP):** Peak (Apr–Labor Day) $34 S; $38 D. Extra person $5. Children under age 12 stay free. Lower rates off-season. Parking: Outdoor, free. AE, CB, DC, DISC, MC, V.

≣ Holiday Inn

30 W KY 92, 40769; tel 606/549-3450 or toll free 800/HOLIDAY; fax 606/549-8161. Off I-75, exit 11. Convenient location, just off I-75. **Rooms:** 100 rms. CI 3pm/CO noon. Nonsmoking rms avail. Some stains on furnishings and worn carpet detract from room decor. **Amenities:** A/C, cable TV. **Services:** VCRs available. **Facilities:** 1 restaurant, washer/dryer. **Rates:** $36 S or D. Children under age 12 stay free. Parking: Outdoor, free. B&B and "home cooking" packages avail. AE, CB, DC, DISC, JCB, MC, V.

MISSISSIPPI

Something Old, Something New

STATE STATS

CAPITAL
Jackson

AREA
47,233 square miles

BORDERS
Alabama, Arkansas, Louisiana, Tennessee, Gulf of Mexico

POPULATION
2,669,111

ENTERED UNION
December 10, 1817
(20th state)

NICKNAMES
Magnolia State

STATE FLOWER
Magnolia

STATE BIRD
Mockingbird

FAMOUS NATIVES
William Faulkner, Jim Henson, Tennessee Williams, Richard Wright

Mississippi has a way of blending the past with the present. It's a vibrant New South state with deep Old South cultural roots, a place where antebellum mansions, Civil War battlefields, and Native American mounds exist alongside an exciting new gaming industry.

Southern culture and creativity have a rich foundation here. The legacies from early planters, small property owners, and former slaves have blended into the cultural and artistic heritage of today's Mississippians. The state has spawned an abundance of 20th-century literary giants. Consider the Nobel Prize winner William Faulkner, author of such probing novels of the South as *The Sound and the Fury* and *The Reivers* and considered one of the greatest American writers of this century. Pulitzer-winning playwright Thomas Lanier Williams—better known as Tennessee Williams—was born in Columbus and produced such remarkable dramas as *The Glass Menagerie* and *A Streetcar Named Desire*. Other well-known Mississippi authors and journalists include Richard Wright, Eudora Welty, Shelby Foote, Hodding Carter, and John Grisham.

The state's creativity seems to breed good music as well. The Mississippi Delta region is acknowleged as the birthplace of that unique American art form, the blues, a musical style that was an outgrowth of chants sung by slaves as they worked the fields. One of the most famous and influential blues singers and guitarists, BB King, was born in Itta Bena. Jimmie Rodgers—sometimes called the "father of country music"—and The King himself, Elvis Presley, were also born in Mississippi.

But a rich literary and musical legacy represent just one of the appealing aspects of this state. Bounded by the majestic Father of Waters on the west and the shimmering Gulf of Mexico on the south and blessed with a gentle climate, Mississippi abounds with enjoyable outdoor activities. It boasts 17 million acres of woodlands, and you're never far from a body of water. Visitors can choose from an incredible array of special events ranging from antebellum home tours to Civil War reenactments to literary festivals and art shows. Mississippi truly has something to offer everyone.

A Brief History

First Peoples Originally inhabited by the Choctaw, Chickasaw, and Natchez, what is now the state of Mississippi was named by them for the river that flows along the western boundary. (The name translates roughly to "Father of Waters.") The Choctaw, the largest of the Mississippi tribes, once numbered more than 25,000 members in 50 villages. *Choctaw* means "charming voices" and the tribe was so named because of its proficiency in singing.

The Trace A track that cuts from the northeast to the southwest was first traced out by buffalo as long as 8,000 years ago. Now known as the Natchez Trace, the route stretches from Nashville, TN to Natchez, MS. The Native Americans were the first to follow the buffalo's trail. Traders, trappers, and missionaries (who were often beset by bandits, hostile natives, and wild animals) trampled the path into a crude road. Andrew Jackson and his army used the road on their way to the Battle of New Orleans. From 1800 to 1820 the Natchez Trace was the busiest road in the Old Southwest, but the rise of steamboat transportation caused the road to be virtually abandoned by the late 1820s.

Although the Mississippi territory was explored by the Spanish in the 1500s, it was not colonized until 1699 when Pierre LeMoyne, Sieur d'Iberville, landed on the Gulf Coast (at what is now Ocean Springs) and claimed the region for France. The territory, originally considered to be part of the

Southwest, was for more than a century alternately claimed by the French, Spanish, and English. Natchez, settled by the French in 1716, is considered to be the oldest permanent settlement on the Mississippi River and later served as the first capital of the state. During the War of 1812, American gunboats fought against a British fleet in the Gulf of Mexico near Bay St Louis—the last battle between the US Navy and a foreign foe in US waters. Mississippi became the 20th state in 1817 and the capital was moved to Jackson in 1822. Early settlers—especially those who came overland into the northern part of the territory—were predominantly of Protestant British, Irish, and northern European ancestry. The coastal area was more Catholic and Mediterranean because it drew immigrants from France, Spain, and later Latin America. Slaves, who clung to their legends, music, and dance, were imported to work the plantations.

When Cotton Was King By the 1830s, when cotton was at its peak and land speculation earned tremendous profits, Mississippi was the wealthiest state in the country. Natchez once boasted 500 millionaires, more than any other city in the country—with the exception of New York City. It was during this period that all but a few Native Americans were rounded up and expelled to west of the Mississippi. Some Choctaws remained, however, and there is still a Choctaw reservation near Philadelphia. As in the other Southern states, tensions grew between the land- and slave-owning gentry who controlled the government and the small farmers who were in the majority but wielded no power.

After Mississippi seceded from the Union in 1861, Civil War battles raged in every corner of the state. Although Confederate President Jefferson Davis was born in Kentucky, he was raised in Mississippi and was serving as its senator when the state seceded. In 1862 the Confederates scored a coup when they sunk the USS *Cairo* with the first electrically detonated torpedo. Vicksburg suffered perhaps more than any other Southern city during the war;

Fun Facts

• One stretch of the Pascagoula River in southeastern Mississippi is known to buzz with sound. Legend has it that what is actually heard is a death chant of the Pascagoula Indians.

• Mississippi didn't repeal Prohibition until 1966—becoming the last state to do so.

• In 1870, during Reconstruction, Mississippi elected the first African American to the US Senate. Hiram Revels took the seat once held by Jefferson Davis.

• The first human heart transplant was performed in Mississippi in 1964, five years before Dr Christian Barnard's more famous operation.

• Tupelo is the birthplace of Elvis Presley. The tiny two-room shack where "The King" was born is now a national shrine.

its starving citizens driven to living in caves during the 47-day Union siege of the summer of 1863. When the city fell to Federal troops under Ulysses S Grant on July 4, 1863, the Mississippi River was open to the Union and the Confederacy was financially crippled.

Healing the Wounds By the war's end in 1865 the state was in economic ruin. The state was readmitted to the Union in 1870, but the state constitution of 1890 virtually disenfranchised African Americans. The state remained rural, agricultural, and poor until the buildup to World War II brought industry to the state for the first time.

The first break in racial segregation came in 1954 when the Supreme Court ordered that schools be integrated. During the 1950s and 1960s, Mississippi was a hotbed of protests, sit-ins, and marches by civil rights activists fighting for voting rights and an end to Jim Crow laws. Retaliatory actions by white racists included one of the most infamous episodes of the civil rights era—the murder of three northern "freedom riders" (two white, one African American), an incident depicted in the film *Mississippi Burning*.

Although such racial wounds are slow to heal, the state has come a long way from those dark days and has emerged as a key player in the New South. Today's Mississippi is the largest producer of upholstered furniture in the country, raises 80% of the world's farm-bred catfish, and has an active shipping and barging trade. Its burgeoning gaming industry and its beaches and historic districts attract thousands of tourists each year.

A Closer Look
GEOGRAPHY
The topography and underlying geologic foundation of Mississippi are remarkably similar throughout the state. In contrast to the numerous distinct geographic regions found in some other Southern states,

Mississippi has only two main regions. The **Mississippi Delta** is a region of fertile lowlands that covers a narrow band along the entire western portion of Mississippi from north to south. It is wider at the northwestern corner of the state—stretching from the Mississippi River to the Yazoo, Tallahatchie, and Coldwater Rivers—and becomes quite slim south of Vicksburg. Before modern levees, flood waters frequently invaded the Delta and blanketed it with rich deposits of black silt ideal for growing cotton and soybeans. Among the cities in this region are the antebellum Mississippi Rivers towns of Natchez, Vicksburg, and Greenville.

The **East Gulf Coastal Plain** covers most of the rest of Mississippi. This region is characterized by low, rolling, forested hills; prairies; and lowlands laced with rivers. (With the exception of a few northeastern rivers that drain into the Tennessee River, the remainder of the state's many rivers empty directly into the Gulf of Mexico or drain into the Mississippi.) In the Tennessee River Hills of the northeast is Mississippi's highest point—Woodall Mountain, all of 806 feet above sea level.

Mississippi has a short 44 miles of coastline, but with coves and bays the total mileage along the coast stretches to 359 miles. Several islands lie off the coast, among them **Deer, Cat, Horn, Ship,** and **Petit Bois Islands**. Ship Island was one island until Hurricane Camille's 240-mph winds literally cut it in two in 1969. Mississippi's coastal islands are intentionally undeveloped, and several are units of the Gulf Islands National Seashore.

CLIMATE
Mississippi has a moderate climate with mild winters and hot summers. Rainfall is abundant and temperature extremes are unusual. Snow is rare but falls occasionally in the extreme northern sections. Temperatures along the coastal area are cooled by sea breezes in the summer and warmed by proximity to the ocean in the winter, but the area is subject to hurricanes from June through October.

DRIVING DISTANCES
Jackson
93 mi W of Meridian
170 mi SW of Tupelo
178 mi NW of Gulfport
178 mi N of New Orleans, LA
212 mi S of Memphis, TN
Tupelo
93 mi S of Memphis, TN
123 mi W of Birmingham, AL
141 mi N of Meridian
170 mi NE of Jackson
298 mi N of Gulfport
Gulfport
56 mi E of New Orleans, LA
64 mi W of Mobile, AL
138 mi S of Meridian
178 mi SE of Jackson
298 mi S of Tupelo

WHAT TO PACK

Because Mississippi is blessed with such a mild climate and because its residents dress casually for all but the most formal occasions, it's easy to pack for a visit here. Layering with cottons in the spring and fall or lightweight wools in the winter is the most efficient use of a small amount of clothing. Bring a sweater or jacket for spring and fall evenings, perhaps a heavier coat for winter. You might want to bring one dressy outfit to wear to an expensive restaurant or cultural event. If you're camping or fishing from the docks, pack insect repellent and a rain poncho.

TOURIST INFORMATION

To get a *Mississippi Travel Planner* and other tourist information, contact the **Mississippi Division of Tourism Development,** PO Box 1705, Ocean Springs, MS 39566-1705 (tel toll free 800/WARMEST). The **Dept of Economic and Community Development** maintains a Web page (http://mississippi.org) with general information about the state. To find out how to obtain tourist information for individual cities and parks in Mississippi, look under specific cities in the listings section of this book.

DRIVING RULES AND REGULATIONS

The speed limit is 65 mph on rural interstates; 55 mph on most other highways. (The speed limit on the Natchez Trace Parkway is 50 mph.) Right turn on red is permitted. The operator and front seat passengers are required to wear seat belts. Children under four years old must be placed in an approved child restraint device. Motorcyclists must wear a helmet.

RENTING A CAR

All the major national car companies have outlets in Mississippi. The minimum age to rent a car varies from 21 to 25 depending on the company, so be sure to check ahead.

- **Alamo** (tel toll free 800/327-9633)
- **Avis** (tel 800/831-2847)
- **Budget** (tel 800/527-0700)
- **Dollar** (tel 800/800-4000)
- **Hertz** (tel 800/654-3131)
- **National** (tel 800/227-7368)
- **Thrifty** (tel 800/367-2277)

ESSENTIALS

Area Code: The entire state of Mississippi uses the **601** area code.

Emergencies: 911 is used statewide for summoning emergency help. On the Natchez Trace Parkway, dial 0 for a park ranger.

Liquor Laws: You must be 21 years of age to purchase liquor. Liquor laws are established by the county, so some jurisdictions are wet and some are dry. Even those that allow liquor sales may have different rules about sales on Sunday.

Road Info: Contact the Mississippi Highway Patrol at 601/987-1212.

Smoking: There is no state-mandated ban on smoking in Mississippi. Whatever laws exist are determined on the local level. Many restaurants voluntarily set aside a nonsmoking section and some hotels and chains provide nonsmoking rooms or nonsmoking floors.

Taxes: The state sales tax is 7%. Cities or counties may impose an additional tax. A hotel tax of 1–3% is added to overnight rates.

Time Zone: Mississippi is in the Central time zone and the entire state observes daylight saving time.

AVG MONTHLY TEMPS (°F) & RAINFALL (IN)		
	Jackson	Tupelo
Jan	46/5.0	41/5.6
Feb	49/4.5	45/4.6
Mar	56/5.9	53/6.7
Apr	65/5.8	63/5.7
May	73/4.8	71/5.2
June	79/2.9	78/3.7
July	82/4.4	81/4.6
Aug	81/3.7	80/2.8
Sept	77/3.6	74/3.6
Oct	65/2.6	62/3.0
Nov	55/4.2	51/4.6
Dec	49/5.4	44/5.6

Best of the State

WHAT TO SEE AND DO

Below is a general overview of some of the top sights and attractions in Mississippi. To find out more detailed information, see "Attractions" under individual cities in the listings portion of this book.

National Parks Mississippi is blessed with several national parks. Although the **Natchez Trace Nation-**

al Parkway, the historic 450-mile national highway that runs from Nashville, TN through the northeast corner of Mississippi to Natchez on the Mississippi River, was forsaken as a major thoroughfare in the 1820s, in 1909 the Daughters of the American Revolution made restoration of the trace a priority. The work they began resulted in the present parkway. To ensure that its natural beauty remains unsullied, the scenic route allows no commercial vehicles and no billboards. A speed limit of 50 mph is strictly enforced. Stop by the Natchez Trace Parkway Visitors Center in Tupelo to see a film about the history of the old trace and artifacts from the road. **Gulf Islands National Seashore** consists of several barrier islands in Florida and Mississippi. **West Ship Island,** which can be reached only by ferry from spring through fall, lies about 12 miles offshore from Biloxi where the Mississippi Sound meets the Gulf of Mexico. In addition to taking a tour of **Fort Massachusetts,,** visitors can swim and walk the beaches. The Visitor Center at **Davis Bayou** in Ocean Springs features exhibits, nature walks, and ranger programs. The other Mississippi sections—the wilderness areas on **East Ship, Horn,** and **Petit Bois Islands**—are reachable only by private or chartered boat. At Davis Bayou, a typical salt marsh, you can camp, fish, and boat, but there's no swimming allowed (because of alligators). Drive along the marked auto route at the 1,800-acre **Vicksburg National Military Park** to read about the progress of the Civil War battle and to see stirring monuments to both armies. The visitor center features a narrative film, artifacts, and dioramas. While at the park, explore the USS *Cairo,* a Union gunboat sunk during the Civil War and raised after 100 years under water. Artifacts found on board are displayed at the adjoining museum.

State Parks Mississippi's 27 state parks (including five historic sites) are all open year-round. In addition to hiking trails, picnicking, and fishing, some of the parks feature golf, tennis, and miniature golf. For more information, call toll free 800/GO-PARKS.

Natural Wonders Mississippi offers awe-inspiring natural marvels. The only petrified forest in the eastern United States, the **Mississippi Petrified Forest** near Flora, contains gigantic trees as ancient as 36 million years old. A 60-foot, 23-ton piece of an 11 million-year-old petrified hardwood tree rests in the **Danforth Chapel** on the University of Southern

Mississippi campus, Hattiesburg. **Devil's Punch Bowl,** Natchez, is a freak of nature—a gigantic, cone-shaped, semi-circular pit. Although it is of unknown origin, the pit is the subject of several legends. **Friendship Oak,** Long Beach, is a more than 500-year-old live oak with a trunk circumference of 17 feet and a foliage canopy that covers 16,000 square feet.

Manmade Wonders Man has left ample evidence of his creativity. One of the largest Native American mound groups remaining from the Mississippian Era (AD 1000 to 1200) can be seen at the **Winterville Mounds Museum State Park** in Greenville. Artifacts found in the area can be inspected at the museum there. **Emerald Mound,** Natchez, was built about AD 1300 by ancestors of the Choctaw and Natchez tribes. Covering eight acres, this ceremonial mound (the second-largest in the country) is 770 feet by 435 feet at its base and stands 35 feet high. The **Mississippi River levee** at Greenville is a feat of modern engineering. Along the **Million Dollar Mile** there you can see towboats and barges under construction as well as shipping, towing, and barging operations.

Beaches Until 1941 the state's natural coastal shoreline had few sand beaches. In a massive engineering effort, the nation's largest seawall and manmade beach was created, stretching from Biloxi to Pass Christian. Today, the coast is a study in contrasts. At one extreme is the pristine beauty of the Gulf Islands National Seashore; at the other is the explosion of Las Vegas–style casinos and hotels clustered around the Mississippi. In between are campgrounds and cozy family hotels and motels—and lots of white, sandy beach.

Boat Excursions There's no better way to explore the towns along the Mississippi than by paddlewheel steamboat. Several towns have replicas of old-time paddleboats that are used for sightseeing and dinner cruises or for casinos. For the ultimate adventure, however, you can take an overnight excursion aboard one of the authentic steamboats owned and operated by the Delta Steamboat Co—the only overnight accommodations on American rivers. The antiques-filled *Delta Queen* was built in 1927 and is a masterpiece of craftsmanship. The larger *Mississippi Queen* was built in 1976 to commemorate America's bicentennial, and the *American Queen* was launched in June 1995. All three boats travel at the leisurely pace of 6–12 mph, calling at Natchez, Vicksburg, and Greenville. Gulfport is the point of departure for daily excursions to Ship Island, part of the Gulf Islands National Seashore. Call 601/864-1014 for schedules and information. The *Riverboat Julie* in Columbus (tel 601/327-2268) offers cruises along the Tennessee-Tombigbee Waterway.

Casinos Since the Mississippi legislature legalized dockside gambling in 1990, casinos have been sprouting like weeds. These gaming emporiums (more than a dozen at last count, and more are under construction) usually offer hotels, restaurants, lounges, and Las Vegas–style shows. The casinos range in style—from ultra-contemporary buildings to paddlewheel river boats to a gigantic pirate ship attached to a castle—but all offer slot machines and a wide variety of wagering games, and they're all open 24 hours a day, 7 days a week. For the most up-to-date gaming information, call toll free 800/237-9493.

Civil War Sites Because the Mississippi River was one of the keys to cutting off the Confederacy, the state saw heavy fighting during the Civil War. **Corinth,** a railroad junction, was a highly sought-after prize. See battery sites, earthworks, and rifle pits at **Battery Robinette,** the site of fierce Civil War fighting. More than 6,000 soldiers are buried in the **Corinth National Cemetery** located on a portion of the **Corinth Civil War Battlefield.** Monuments commemorate both Union and Confederate armies at the **Tupelo Battlefield.** The Union gunboat *Star of the West* was sunk at **Fort Pemberton,** near Greenwood between the Yazoo and Tallahatchie Rivers, to block the Union from advancing in the Yazoo Pass during the early campaign against Vicksburg in 1863.

Gen William Tecumseh Sherman used the 1846 Greek Revival Boyd House called **The Oaks,** Jackson, as his headquarters during the siege of that city. Among the period furnishings is the sofa from Lincoln's Springfield law office. On **Ship Island,** off the coast from Biloxi, is **Fort Massachusetts,** which was used by Union Gen Benjamin "Beast" Butler as a Civil War POW camp. Civil War grave sites are located at the **Texas Hospital Cemetery,** Quitman, and the **Natchez National Cemetery.**

Civil War buffs can begin a tour of **Vicksburg** by seeing the half-hour film *The Vanishing Glory* (tel 601/634-1863) about the long siege and eventual fall of the city. The world's largest collection of Civil War gunboat models, as well as Civil War artifacts

and paintings, are displayed at the **Gray and Blue Naval Museum.** Located on the highest point in Vicksburg, the 1858 courthouse has been converted into the **Old Court House Museum** and now displays Civil War artifacts and documents. (Among the displays is an authentic "Sherman's necktie"—an iron railroad rail heated and bent around a tree.) One man's collection of 30,000 toy soldiers, Civil War shells and artifacts, and antique and new toys are displayed at the **Toys and Soldiers Museum.**

Family Favorites At the **John C Stennis Space Center,** Bay St Louis, guests of all ages can take a guided tour of NASA's space shuttle engine-testing complex; the adjacent museum and theater feature space-related presentations. The Mississippi Delta was the boyhood home of Muppets creator Jim Henson. Among the exhibits at the **Birthplace of the Frog** in Leland are original Muppets, Henson's Christmas card designs, early Henson TV videos, and other artifacts. Children will spend as much time admiring the workmanship in the 1890s Dentzel **Highland Park Carousel,** Meridian, as enjoying the ride. Designated a National Historic Landmark, the world's only two-row stationary Dentzel menagerie is meticulously hand-carved of basswood and poplar.

Gardens Mississippi's mild climate is conducive to lavish displays of lush vegetation. Among the flowers that bloom year-round at the **Mynelle Gardens** in Jackson are seven acres of perennials and annuals. Nestled among the 14 acres of scenic floral displays at **Wister Gardens** is a lake where domestic and exotic birds thrive. Hundreds of varieties of daylilies are among the star attractions at **No Mistake Plantation** in Satartia; tours are by appointment. During the late spring and summer, 740 hybrid tea and Grandiflora roses bloom at the **All-American Rose Garden,** Gulfport.

Historic Buildings Despite heavy destruction during the Civil War, Mississippi is a treasure chest of historic structures. **Natchez** alone has more than 500 pre–Civil War structures, one of the largest concentrations in the country. Vicksburg has many historic structures as well. Walking and driving tours of these towns allow you to admire the buildings on your own schedule. Some operate as bed-and-breakfasts, and many others are open for annual "pilgrimage" tours. Among the most significant and/or extravagant of the antebellum and Victorian mansions open to the public are: **Longwood,** Natchez, an unfinished Moorish-style octagonal showplace begun before the Civil War; **Isom Place,** Oxford, a classic example of planter-style architecture; **Waverly Mansion,** West Point, noted for its four circular staircases connecting unsupported balconies in a large dome over a 65-foot-high foyer; and **Redbud Inn,** Kosciusko, considered to be one of the finest examples of Queen Anne architecture in the South.

Several sites reveal the life of Confederate President Jefferson Davis. **Rosemont Plantation,** Woodville, was Davis's boyhood home. The property contains outbuildings and the family cemetery. He was married at **The Briers** in Natchez. Open to the public, the house also operates as a bed-and-breakfast. Davis spent his last years at **Beauvoir,** his Biloxi estate. Meaning "beautiful view," it overlooks the Biloxi Bay and the Gulf of Mexico. After the former president's death, Mrs Davis donated the house and grounds for use as a nursing home for former Confederate soldiers and their wives or widows. Contained within the complex in addition to the house are a Confederate Cemetery and a Civil War museum. President Andrew Jackson married Rachel Robards at **Springfield Plantation,** Fayette, in 1791. In addition to its historical interest, the house is important architecturally because of its hand-carved woodwork and full colonnade across the front facade. Mississippi has spawned several noted authors, but none are more typical of the state than William Faulkner. **Rowan Oak,** Faulkner's antebellum home in Oxford, remains as he left it—right down to the story outlines he scribbled on the wall of the study.

Two antebellum ruins survive as ghosts of that era. Twenty-three fluted columns known as the **Ruins of Windsor** stand as silent sentinels to what was once the most opulent antebellum plantation mansion along the Mississippi. In an ironic twist of fate, the home was spared during the Civil War, then destroyed in 1890 by a fire caused by a careless smoker. Ruins of an 1830s mansion are located on the grounds of the **Springdale Hills Arboretum,** Pocahontas.

Museums A variety of museums reflect the diversity of life in Mississippi. See original costumes from Hollywood movies, including a large collection of John Wayne outfits, at the **American Costume Museum,** Ruleville. Civil War artifacts, Chickasaw relics, and fossils are displayed at the **Northeast**

Mississippi Museum, Corinth. Artifacts at the **Cottonlandia Museum,** Greenwood, depict life in the Delta and include displays on Native Americans and pioneers. Personal memorabilia from famous St Louis Cardinals pitcher and sports commentator Dizzy Dean are displayed at the **Dizzy Dean Museum,** Jackson. New Orleans and Mobile aren't the only cities that celebrate Mardi Gras. The Biloxi/Gulfport area has an old and active Mardi Gras tradition. Costumes and other memorabilia from past Mardi Gras events are displayed at the **Mardi Gras Museum** in the Magnolia Hotel, an antebellum hostelry in Biloxi. The **Cobb Institute of Archaeology,** on the campus of the University of Southern Mississippi in Hattiesburg, is a repository of artifacts from the excavations of southeastern Native American mounds. More than 6,000 items of military artifacts from the Civil War to Desert Storm are displayed at the **Camp Shelby Armed Forces Museum,** also in Hattiesburg.

Commercial fishing has long been vital to the state's economy. A 70-foot commercial shrimping boat has been converted into Pascagoula's **Scranton Floating Museum.** In addition to depicting the life of a shrimper, the museum describes the local Gulf Coast environment. Exhibits at the **Maritime and Seafood Industry Museum,** Biloxi, trace the history and importance of the industry along the Gulf Coast through photographs, early boat engines, a lighthouse lens, nets, tongs, and other paraphernalia.

Music The blues and rock and roll owe much of their development to Mississippi. The **Elvis Presley Birthplace and Museum** in Tupelo includes the two-room shotgun house where he was born; a museum containing an extensive collection of never-published photographs; and a small chapel erected by fans. At the home of rock and roll legend Jerry Lee Lewis in Nesbit, visitors can tour the house and grounds and take a peek at the piano-shaped swimming pool. Clarkdale's **Delta Blues Museum** pays tribute to blues greats like Robert Johnson, B B King, and Muddy Waters with memorabilia and audiovisual displays. (The museum also hosts occasional live blues concerts.) Jimmie Rodgers, the Father of Country Music, is immortalized at the **Jimmie Rodgers Museum** in his hometown of Meridian. The equipment, instruments and amplifiers of the Peavey Electronics Corporation in Meridian are used by musicians around the world and in every musical form. You can peruse a display of current amplifiers, keyboards, and guitars at the **Peavey Visitors Center.** The **Templeton Music Museum and Archives** at Mississippi State University in Starkville houses an extensive collection of phonograph music boxes, recordings, and sheet music.

Native American Sites Mississippi, once populated by thousands of Native Americans, now is home to one tribe. Exhibits at the **Choctaw Museum of the Southern Indian,** on the Choctaw Reservation in Philadelphia, depict the history and culture of Native Americans within the region. Twenty miles north of the reservation is the **Nanih Waiya Historic Site,** site of Choctaw mounds that are several thousand years old. Once the center of activities for the now-extinct Natchez people in the late 1600s and early 1700s, the only thing you'll find now at the **Grand Village of the Natchez Indians** is a **Visitors Center Museum** containing artifacts excavated at the site.

Parks & Zoos Visitors can view the animal exhibits at the **Hattiesburg Zoo** at Kamper Park on foot or aboard a train pulled by a ⅓-scale 1950s locomotive. In addition to the 500 animals roaming over 100 acres of natural habitat at the **Jackson Zoological Park,** the facility features a children's petting zoo with hands-on exhibits. Exhibits at the **J L Scott Marine Education Center** in Biloxi focus on coastal-zone animals and fish. At the **Marine Life Oceanarium,** Gulfport, you can watch dolphin and sea-lion shows, a dive show, and a bird show, as well as examine the marine life in the giant reef tank.

Events and Festivals

JACKSON AND CENTRAL MISSISSIPPI

- **Jubilee Jam,** Jackson. Celebration of music, food, and arts. Late May. Call 601/960-1557.
- **Jimmy Rodgers Memorial Country Music Festival,** Meridian. Tribute to the Father of Country Music, including concerts, celebrity fishing rodeo, celebrity golf, and more. Late May. Call 601/483-5763.
- **Hog Wild in July,** Jackson. Teams from all over the Southeast compete in a barbecue cooking contest. Mid-July. Call 601/354-7098.
- **Neshoba County Fair,** Philadelphia. Mississippi's Giant Houseparty includes a triathlon, flea market, harness and running races, country music. Late July to early August. Call 601/656-1742.

- **Scottish Highland Games of Mississippi,** Jackson. Traditional Scottish music, dance, food, pipe and drum competitions, parade. Late August. Call 601/924-5270.
- **Sky Parade,** Jackson. US Jet Team, air races, hot-air balloons, air show, live bands, military aircraft display. Early September. Call 601/982-8088.
- **Delta Blues Festival,** Greenville. Well-known blues greats perform. Mid-September. Call 601/335-3523.

GULFPORT AND SOUTHERN MISSISSIPPI

- **Historic Home Tours,** Ocean Springs and Gulfport. Many of the antebellum homes open their doors to visitors. Early April. Call toll free 800/237-9493.
- **Shrimp Festival,** Biloxi. Thousands of pounds of boiled crustacean are served. Early May. Call 601/435-5578.
- **Deep-Sea Fishing Rodeo,** Gulfport. Fishing tournament. Early July. Call 601/388-2271.
- **Sand Sculpture Contest,** Gulfport. Teams sculpt objects relating to an assigned theme. Mid-September. Call 601/896-2434.

OXFORD AND NORTHERN MISSISSIPPI

- **Holly Springs Pilgrimage,** Holly Springs. Antebellum homes and churches are open for tours. Late April. Call 601/252-3315.
- **Southaven Spring Festival and Founder's Day,** Southaven. Barbecue contest, parade, street dance, arts and crafts, carnival. Late April. Call 601/342-0699.
- **Oleput Festival,** Tupelo. Mardi Gras theme, hot-air balloon rides, 5K run/walk, parade, food. Early June. Call toll free 800/267-3104.
- **Sunflower River Blues and Gospel Festival,** Clarksdale. Early August. Call 601/627-2209.

SPECTATOR SPORTS

Baseball Mississippi has no major league baseball teams, but the **Jackson Generals,** the Double-A farm team of the Houston Astros, play at Smith-Wills Stadium (tel 601/981-4669).

Basketball Basketball fans don't mind the absence of professional teams when they can cheer for the **University of Mississippi Rebels** (tel 601/232-7522), who play at the Basketball Arena in Oxford, or the **Mississippi State Bulldogs** (tel 601/325-2703), who play at Humphrey Coliseum in Starkville.

College Football As with the other Southern states, college football is as important as air, food, and water. The **University of Mississippi Rebels** football team (tel 601/232-7522) plays at Vaught-Hemingway Stadium in Oxford. The **Mississippi State Bulldogs** play at Scott Field (tel 601/325-2703) in Starkville.

ACTIVITIES A TO Z

Bicycling Cycling is smooth and easy along the coast, more strenuous elsewhere. The well-paved and gently graded **Natchez Trace Parkway** provides excellent conditions for cyclists. Commercial vehicles are not permitted on the parkway and the speed limit is 50 mph. At two locations, cyclists can ride along actual portions of the sunken Old Trace road. Contact the **Natchez Trace Parkway**, RR 1, NT-143, Tupelo, MS 38801 (tel 601/680-4025) for maps and information. Get a map for the Live Oak Bicycle Trail at the Davis Bayou unit of the Gulf Islands National Seashore in Ocean Springs at the **Colmer Visitor Center** (tel 601/875-9057).

Bird Watching The **Colmer Visitor Center,** at the Davis Bayou unit of the Gulf Islands National Seashore (tel 601/875-9057), distributes handouts identifying birds found in the Mississippi units of the park and the best times to spot them. The park's diverse habitats attract an eclectic avian population, including more than 280 species. In addition to the ever-present seagulls and terns, you may spot ducks, gallinules, coots, indigo buntings, warblers, and, if you're lucky, nesting ospreys.

Boating You can cruise to all four of the offshore barrier islands in the **Gulf Islands National Seashore** (tel 601/875-9057), anchoring near beaches on the leeward side. Contact the **Gulfport Small Craft Harbor** and **Biloxi Small Craft Harbor** (tel for both 601/436-4062) to get names and numbers of contacts for chartering and renting boats. **Ross Tours** (tel 601/432-8000) in Biloxi rents boats, as does **Shearwater** (tel 601/875-3511) in Ocean Springs. Charter prices on the coast range from about $200 for a half-day to $600 for 10 hours, depending on the craft. Only charters licensed by the Gulf Islands National Seashore are authorized to travel to East Ship, Horn, and Petit Bois islands; charters are not permitted to dock at West Ship Island. Contact the Mississippi District office for names and numbers of official charter services.

Camping The Gulf Islands National Seashore's **Davis Bayou Campground** (tel 601/875-9057) is relatively small, but its 51 sites, all with electricity and water hookups, are spacious and protected by live oaks. (Reservations are not accepted and there's no waiting list, so get there early.) With their dunes, gulf surf, slash pines, palmettos, occasional live oak trees, and wax-myrtle bushes, Horn, Petit Bois, and East Ship Islands are popular with primitive campers. Permits are not required, but it's wise to check in with the rangers who patrol the islands. Camping is also available at most of the state parks and at numerous private campgrounds.

SELECTED PARKS & RECREATION AREAS

- **Gulf Islands National Seashore,** 3500 Park Rd, Ocean Springs, MS 39564 (tel 904/934-2604)
- **Natchez National Historical Park,** Box 1208, Natchez, MS 39121 (tel 601/442-7047)
- **Vicksburg National Military Park,** 3201 Clay St, Vicksburg, MS 39180 (tel 601/636-0583)
- **Florewood River Plantation State Park,** PO Box 680, Greenwood, MS 38930 (tel 601/455-3821)
- **Great River Road State Park,** PO Box 292, Rosedale, MS 38769 (tel 601/759-6762)
- **Hugh White State Park,** PO Box 725, Grenada, MS 38902-0725 (tel 601/226-4934)
- **John W Kyle State Park,** Rte 1, Box 115, Sardis, MS 38666 (tel 601/487-1345)
- **Lake Lowndes State Park,** 3319 Lake Lowndes Rd, Columbus, MS 39702 (tel 601/328-2110)
- **LeFleur's Bluff State Park,** 2140 Riverside Dr, Jackson, MS 39202 (tel 601/987-3998)
- **Legion State Park,** 635 Legion Park Rd (Old MS 25), Louisville, MS 39339-8803 (tel 601/773-8323)
- **Leroy Percy State Park,** PO Box 176, Louisville, MS 39339-8803 (tel 601/827-5436)
- **Percy Quin State Park,** 1156 Camp Beaver Dr, McComb, MS 39648 (tel 601/684-3938)
- **Roosevelt State Park,** 2149 MS 13S, Morton, MS 39117 (tel 601/732-6316)
- **Tishomingo State Park,** PO Box 880 (MP 304, Natchez Trace Pkwy), Tishomingo, MS 38873 (tel 601/438-6914)
- **Tombigbee State Park,** Rte 2, Box 336-E, Tupelo, MS 38801 (tel 601/842-7669)
- **Wall Doxey State Park,** Rte 5, Box 245, Holly Springs, MS 38635 (tel 601/252-4231)
- **Winterville Mounds State Historic Site,** 2415 MS 1, Greenville, MS 38703 (tel 601/334-4684)

Fishing You're never far from a body of water in Mississippi. Saltwater anglers can cast a line from a pier, surf fish off the beaches, or take a charter for deep-sea fishing in the Gulf of Mexico. In addition to the Mississippi River, other rivers and streams as well as lakes, ponds, and reservoirs provide excellent fishing. The **Mississippi Department of Wildlife, Fisheries and Parks** manages 21 fishing lakes. Find out more about them by contacting the department at PO Box 451, Jackson, MS 39205-0451 (tel 601/364-2123). The Mississippi units of the Gulf Islands National Seashore are also popular fishing spots. Davis Bayou's pier is the hot spot for mullet and blue crabs; on West Ship Island you can catch sheepshead and redfish from the dock. Charters leaving from Biloxi and Gulfport take more serious aficionados into the Gulf in search of large red snappers, groupers, and amberjack. For information, contact the **Gulfport Small Craft Harbor** and **Biloxi Small Craft Harbor** (tel for both 601/436-4062) or **Point Cadet Marina** (tel 601/436-9312).

Hiking On the Gulf Islands National Seashore's West Ship Island, hikers can circumnavigate the entire island in one sandy, seven-mile trek. A short-er, more leisurely hike of two miles from the swimming area around the west tip of the island to Fort Massachusetts takes about two hours. Numerous hiking trails branch off the Natchez Trace Parkway. Call the Mississippi Division of Tourism (tel toll free 800/WARMEST) for maps and more info.

Sailing The waters off the Mississippi coast are ideal for sailing and windsurfing, but rentals are not common. Try **Mid South Sailing and Charter** (tel 601/863-6969) in Gulfport and **Coast Cat Sailboat Rentals** (tel 601/452-9564) in Long Beach. Sunfish rentals cost $5–$10 per hour, and two hours on a four-person catamaran can cost as much as $60 (a little more if you need instruction).

Scuba Diving For excursions to wrecks, marine ballast, and artificial reefs in Mississippi waters, call **SeaSpace Dive Center** (tel 601/497-1381) in Gautier and **Dive Five** (tel 601/385-7664) in Biloxi. One-week, accelerated certification courses are available, and scuba-equipment rental costs about $15–$35 per day; charters cost $40–$50 per half-day, $60–$70 per full day, and group dives $30–$60, depending on how far out you go and how many tanks you consume.

Driving the State

Start	Natchez
Finish	Corinth
Distance	335 miles
Time	2–3 days
Highlights	Historic homes, plantations, Civil War battlefields, state parks, museums, Indian mounds, ruins, gardens, zoo, Elvis sites

Trampled into a path by buffalo, followed by Native Americans, and worn into a real road by early settlers, the original Natchez Trace stretched 450 miles from Natchez, MS, through a corner of Alabama to Nashville, TN. In the late 1700s river men floated down the Mississippi River to Natchez or New Orleans, sold all their goods (including their flatboats and rafts), and used the road to walk back to wherever they had begun their journey. The Natchez Trace—the busiest road in the United States in the early part of the 19th century—was virtually abandoned when steamboats diverted traffic onto the Mississippi.

Early in this century, the Mississippi Chapter of the Daughters of the American Revolution set out on a campaign to preserve this picturesque and historic route; in the 1930s, President Franklin D Roosevelt authorized its reconstruction. Today's highway—where advertising, traffic lights, and commercial traffic are prohibited—is punctuated by historic markers, picnic areas, and nature trails. The landscape varies as it passes through six forest types, eight watersheds, elevations from 70 to 1,100 feet, flats, ridges, swamps, and meadows. For more information, contact the Natchez Trace Parkway, RR 1, NT-143, Tupelo, MS 38801 (tel 601/680-4025).

For additional information on lodgings, dining, and attractions in the region covered by the tour, look under specific cities in the listings portion of this chapter.

US 65 from the northwest and US 61 from the south and northeast give easy access to the first stop:

1. **Natchez,** founded by the French in 1716. Occupied early in the Civil War, Natchez escaped the destruction leveled against many parts of the South. More than 500 antebellum homes, churches, and public buildings survive to this day; that they endure is a testament to the tenacity of Natchez citizens. Particularly during the years of Reconstruction and later during the Great Depression, impoverished residents (who had no money to make needed repairs or even to keep up appearances) refused to let structures fall down or be torn down. Today, many of the palatial homes, now furnished with opulent original or period pieces, are open for tours; others operate as elegant bed-and-breakfasts.

Begin with a stop at the **Natchez Convention and Visitors Bureau,** 311 Liberty Rd, or **Natchez Pilgrimage Tours,** Canal and State Sts, from which you can purchase the *Natchez: Walking Guide to the Old Town* brochure or tickets for a carriage tour. A good starting point is **Longwood,** 140 Lower Woodville Rd, the largest and only unfinished octagonal house in the country. The extravagant home with Moorish embellishments was completed on the outside, but only the lowest level of the interior had been finished when the Civil War broke out. (Tools still lie where Yankee workmen dropped them to return north.) Bankrupted by the war, the owners of the house were never able to complete the mansion but they continued to live on the lower level until 1970, when they donated the estate to the Pilgrimage Garden Club.

The **Natchez National Historical Park,** #1 Melrose-Montebello Pkwy, contains the beautiful brick mansion **Melrose,** completed in 1845, and the **William Johnson House,** the restored 1841 home of a prominent "free man of color" which now houses a museum of African American history. **Rosalie,** Canal and Orleans Sts (built circa 1820), served as a Union headquarters throughout the occupation. The delicate, lacy wrought-iron railings on stately, palatial **Stanton Hall,** 401 High St, make it one of the most photographed homes in the country.

Approximately 3,000 graves of Union and Confederate soldiers and illustrious Natchez citizens lie in the **Natchez National Cemetery,** 41 Cemetery Rd. Native American history can be explored at the **Emerald Mound,** constructed in AD 1300, and located west of Natchez Trace Parkway MP 10.33. Built by ancestors of the Choctaw and Natchez Indians, it is the second-largest ceremonial mound in the country. Artifacts taken from the site of the **Grand Village of the Natchez Indians** are found at the **Visitor Center Museum,** 400 Jefferson Davis Blvd, while African Americans are the focus at the **Natchez Museum of African-American History and Culture,** 307-A Market St.

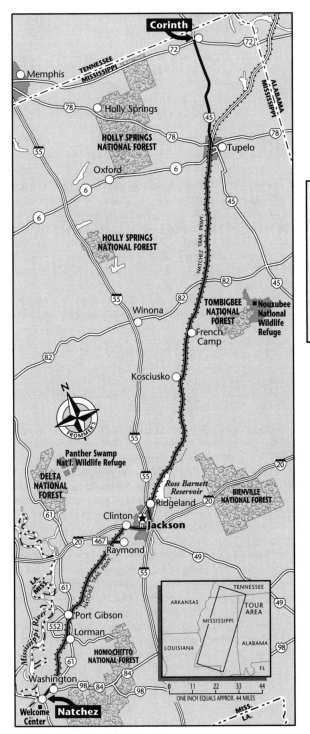

The tree-shaded streets of the historic downtown are filled with antique and specialty shops, housed in restored antebellum and Victorian storefronts. When you've had your fill of window shopping, you can walk or drive to the bottom of the riverfront bluff to **Natchez Under-the-Hill,** once a rough-and-tumble neighborhood of bars and bawdy houses known as the "Barbary Coast of Mississippi." Today it is the convivial site of several restaurants and taverns, the *Lady Luck* riverboat casino, and the Natchez riverboat landing.

Take a Break

Although you can eat inside, you'll probably want to choose a table on the rustic porch of **Natchez Landing,** 35 Silver St (tel 601/442-6639), overlooking the Mississippi River at Natchez-Under-the-Hill. Specialties include pork, chicken, and beef barbecue as well as fried or grilled catfish. All entrees are accompanied by hush puppies and country vegetables. A complete meal runs between $10 and $15.

Take US 61 northeast 10 miles to:

2. **Washington,** the old territorial capital and an early 19th-century seat of political, social, and cultural activity. Stop at **Historic Jefferson College,** US 61, the first educational institution chartered in Mississippi Territory. Aaron Burr was arraigned for treason here (under an oak tree that still stands) and Jefferson Davis was a student. The institution is no longer used as a school, but it does house a museum and archives and there are nature trails and picnicking on the grounds.

Not far north of Washington is the beginning of the Natchez Trace Parkway. Take the Parkway 26 miles north to:

3. **Lorman,** site of two plantations. The main house of **Canemount Plantation,** County Rd 552 W, is considered to be the finest example of Italianate Revival architecture in the country; it now operates as a bed-and-breakfast. White-tailed deer, Russian boar, and wild turkey roam the 6,000-acre grounds. The classic Greek Revival main house at **Rosswood Plantation,** County Rd 552, is also used as a B&B.

You can purchase souvenirs and snacks at the **Old Country Store** (tel 601/437-3661), US 61 in Lorman. This general store that has been in continuous operation for more than 100 years.

Return to the Natchez Trace Parkway and proceed 15 miles north to:

4. Port Gibson, MP 39.2, the oldest extant town on the Trace. It was the site of a bloody 1862 Civil War battle; the town fell but was spared destruction because Confederate Gen Ulysses S Grant declared it "too beautiful to burn." You may wish to stop by the **Claiborne County Visitor Center,** US 61S, to pick up a brochure for a self-guided tour of homes and battle sites.

Make your next stop the **Grand Gulf Military Monument Park,** Grand Gulf Rd, site of two forts and several other significant buildings. Just outside the park are the original earthworks of **Fort Coburn,** which never fell to Union troops. Inside are the original parapet, ammunition magazine earthworks, and fortifications of **Fort Wade.** The **Grand Gulf Cemetery** contains the remains of African Americans who fought in the Union Army. An on-site museum contains hundreds of Civil War artifacts and an outbuilding houses carriages and wagons including a Civil War ambulance and a one-of-a-kind Civil War submarine.

Twenty-three towering Corinthian columns at the **Ruins of Windsor,** County Rd 552 W, are all that remain of the largest mansion ever built in Mississippi. Its cupola served as a Confederate observation point because it commanded a panoramic view of the Mississippi River. After the Confederates were defeated at Port Gibson, Union troops commandeered the house for use as a hospital. The ardent pleas of Windsor's mistress saved the mansion from destruction three separate times; ironically, a careless smoker caused a fire that burned the house to the ground in 1890. Still picturesque, the ruins have been featured in several movies.

Back in town, the 1840 Greek Revival **City Hall,** 1005 College St, houses an intriguing collection of photographs chronicling life in the area between 1906 and 1915. At the 1859 **First Presbyterian Church,** Church St, note the 12-foot-tall gold hand pointing heavenward from the steeple and the ornate chandeliers from the steamboat *Robert E Lee.* If you want to spend the night in Port Gibson, consider **Oak Square,** 1207 Church St (tel 601/437-4350), a palatial 30-room Greek Revival mansion built in 1850 and now housing a moderately priced B&B.

One of the most beautiful and photographed spots on the parkway is the **Sunken Trace** at MP 41.5, where you can take a short hike on the only remaining section of the original road.

Return to the parkway and continue heading north for approximately 60 miles. At County Rd 467 take a detour east to:

5. Raymond, site of a Civil War skirmish between a small detachment of Confederate soldiers and Union forces fresh from their victory at Vicksburg. Among the highlights in town are the **Hinds County Courthouse** and **St Mark's Episcopal Church,** both of which served as hospitals and both of which are located on Main St. The **Marie Hull Gallery,** located in the Denton Art Building on the campus of Hinds Community College, exhibits works by Mississippi artists as well as changing displays of local, regional, and national works.

Retrace your route to the parkway and turn north for 8 miles to:

6. Clinton, once a popular health spa town. In the early 1800s, Clinton was known as Mount Salus ("mountain of health") due to its number of natural springs with reputed health-giving properties. Pick up a self-guided walking tour brochure at the **Clinton Chamber of Commerce,** 100 E Leake. Several significant sites are on the campus of **Mississippi College,** College St, founded in 1826 and one of the oldest institutions of higher learning in the country. **Provine Chapel** was spared by Sherman during the Civil War for use as a hospital and stables. Interior tours are available by appointment. **Robinson Spring,** Spring St, one of the town's healthful springs, is on the site of the home of the college's president.

The parkway is incomplete between MP 87 and 101.5. Take I-20 east for 9 miles to:

7. Jackson, capital of Mississippi, which alternated between Confederate and Union control during the Civil War. When Union troops first took the city in 1863, citizens fled with whatever they could carry. Scoundrels did some major looting and convicts released from the penitentiary set many buildings on fire. The second time Union troops captured the city, they burned so many buildings that Jackson earned the nickname "Chimneyville." Fortunately, several structures survived the war. The 1847 Greek Revival **City Hall,** 219 S President St, served as the center of government, a Masonic Hall, and during the Civil War as a hospital. The 1861 Ordinance of Secession was passed at the **Old Capitol,** 100 S State St; today, the building houses the **Mississippi State Historical Museum.** The **Governor's Mansion,** 300 E Capitol St, was the site of Sherman's victory dinner after the fall of Vicksburg. (When it was threatened with demolition in the early 1900s, concerned citizens saved the mansion by campaigning with the slogan "Will Mississippi destroy that which Sherman would not burn?") Open for tours, the governor's house is filled with 19th-century museum-quality decorative arts. **The Oaks,** 823 N Jefferson St, built in 1846 of hand-hewn timbers, is the oldest home in Jackson. Sherman occupied it during the 1863 siege. Its period furnishings include the sofa from Abraham Lincoln's Springfield law office. The **Manship House,** 420 E Fortification St, an 1857 Gothic Revival cottage, was the home of Jackson's Civil War mayor whose ornamental paintings hang throughout the house. The silver bell on the lawn rang when Mississippi seceded from the Union.

Jackson's attractions aren't limited to the Civil War era, however. Firmly planted in the 20th century, the **Russell C Davis Planetarium/Ronald McNair Space Theater,** 201 E Pascagoula St, presents high-tech programs ranging from astronomy to laser light shows to Cinema 360 films. More than 500 animals roam the 100-acre **Jackson Zoological Park,** 2918 W Capitol St. Educational exhibits, dioramas, and aquariums depict Mississippi's ecological history at the **Mississippi Museum of Natural Science,** 111 N Jefferson St. The **Mississippi Museum of Art,** 201 E Pascagoula St, features seven galleries of permanent and changing exhibits, as well as a children's hands-on Impressions Gallery.

The **Jim Buck Ross Mississippi Agriculture and Forestry/National Agricultural Aviation Museum,** 1150 Lakeland Dr, contains a little of everything: early crop-dusting airplanes; a miniature train; an impressive rose garden; and **Chimneyville Crafts Gallery,** which sells native, traditional, and contemporary pieces. If you want to spend the night in Jackson, the **Millsaps-Buie House,** 628 N State St (tel 601/352-0221), is a B&B located in a magnificently restored and exquisitely furnished 1888 Queen Anne–style home.

From Jackson, take I-55 north to Ridgeland and rejoin the parkway continuing northeast for 62 miles to the next stop:

8. **Kosciusko,** named for Polish freedom fighter Tadeusz Kosciusko. The **Kosciusko Museum and Welcome Center,** MS 35S, features an exhibit about the parkway as well as changing displays. Admire the beautiful stained-glass windows in the **Kosciusko–Attala County Cultural Center,** Washington and N Huntington Sts, located in an 1898 Gothic-style former Presbyterian church. A Greek Revival mansion, the **Hammond-Routt House,** 109 S Natchez, is filled with period antiques.

Continue northeast on the parkway for 15 more miles to:

8. **French Camp,** an early stopping point on the Old Natchez Trace. In 1812, Frenchman Louis LeFleur built a "stand" (inn) here and a small village grew up around it. Today you can explore the **French Camp Log Cabin,** an 1846 cabin furnished with

---

Take a Break

Lunch is served Monday through Friday in the tearoom at the **Redbud Inn,** 121 N Wells St (tel 601/289-5086). The inn, which also houses a B&B and an antiques shop, is located in an 1884 mansion considered to be the finest example of Queen Anne architecture in the South. Diners can choose from a chicken or seafood entree, accompanied by mountains of fresh vegetables and salads, for $8 to $10. Save room for the famous hot fudge cake. Dinner, which is by reservation only, might include filet mignon, the catch of the day, beef tenderloin, chicken, or catfish. Dinner ranges from $18 to $25 (including dessert).

Native American and early French artifacts; the grounds also house an operating sorghum mill, a workshop, and a gift shop. Adjacent to the cabin site is the **Colonel James Drane Plantation,** a restored two-story plantation house originally built in 1848. Both are at MP 180.8 on the parkway. The French Camp Academy operates the **Rainwater Observatory,** Mississippi's largest public access observatory. Tours of the observatory are by appointment only (tel 601/547-6113). The Academy also offers bed-and-breakfast accommodations.

From French Camp, it's a scenic 81-mile drive to the next stop:

9. **Tupelo,** best known as the birthplace of Elvis Presley. Seventy years before that momentous event, however, Tupelo—then called Harrisburg —was the site of several significant Civil War battles. First the Confederates routed the Union forces at **Brice's Cross Roads Battlefield,** County Rd 370, now a historic site. After that disastrous defeat, Gen Sherman is said to have proclaimed, "Go out and follow [Nathan Bedford] Forrest to the death, if it costs 10,000 lives and breaks the Treasury." When the opposing forces met at Tupelo, a wounded Forrest was forced to direct the battle from a carriage. A miscommunication cost the Confederates the battle, but the exhausted and poorly supplied Union troops withdrew, leaving their wounded behind. The **Tupelo National Battlefield,** W Main St, contains monuments and displays commemorating both armies. The **Tupelo Museum,** W Main St at James J Ballard Park, houses artifacts from the battle as well as a diorama of the battlefield. Other displays at the museum include an old-time country store, a working sorghum mill, and a turn-of-the-century Western Union office.

Outside, you can explore a train depot and a caboose.

Back in this century (1935 to be exact), Elvis Presley was born in a two-room shotgun house in Tupelo. The property, now designated as **Elvis Presley Park** (306 Elvis Presley Dr), contains the birthplace house (furnished as it would have been when the Presleys lived there), the Elvis Presley Museum, and the Elvis Presley Memorial Chapel.

From Tupelo, the parkway veers east into Alabama and on to Tennessee, so depart from it here and take US 45 north for 47 miles to our last stop:

10. **Corinth,** a strategic rail crossroads during the Civil War. In the spring of 1862, vastly outnumbered and inadequately supplied Confederate forces created one of the most ingenious hoaxes of the war. Fresh from defeat at the Battle of Shiloh in the spring of 1862, Confederate Gen Beauregard decided to retreat to Tupelo but left just enough of his troops in Corinth to fool the nearby Union encampment. Beauregard's subterfuge even involved dummy cannons and an empty train bringing nonexist-

ent Rebel reinforcements. The **Corinth Train Depot,** 213 Fillmore St, one of the keys of the whole plan, is open for tours.

Battery Robinette, W Linden St, is the best preserved of the fortifications, but the town is dotted with battery sites, earthworks, and rifle pits, as well as with historic homes and buildings. Pick up a brochure for a self-guided driving tour of Civil War sites from the **Northeast Mississippi Museum,** 4th and Washington Sts, a repository for artifacts related to the Chickasaw tribe, the Civil War, and other aspects of regional history, or from the **Corinth Chamber of Commerce,** 810 Tate St. More than 7,000 Union soldiers are interred at the **Corinth Battlefield and National Cemetery,** Horton St. At various times during the war, both Confederate and Union generals used the **Curlee House,** 301 Childs St, as their headquarters. Tours are available by appointment.

From Corinth you can take US 45 north into Tennessee or US 72 east into Alabama or west across Mississippi into Tennessee or Arkansas.

Mississippi Listings

Biloxi

See also Gulfport, Ocean Springs, Pascagoula

Largest and oldest of the Gulf coastal cities, Biloxi was settled by the French in 1699 and has since become one of the state's chief ports. It has been a popular resort since the mid-19th century. Crape myrtle, camellia, magnolias, and Spanish moss–draped oaks beautify the city's streets; innumerable boats ply the harbor. The Biloxi Shrimp Festival—the blessing of the shrimp fleet—is cited by many as the best state celebration. **Information:** Biloxi Chamber of Commerce, 1048 Beach Blvd, PO Box 1928, Biloxi, 39533 (tel 601/374-2717).

HOTELS

Edgewater Inn
1936 Beach Blvd, 39531; tel 601/388-1100 or toll free 800/323-9676; fax 601/385-2406. At Camelia St. Right across the street from the beach, the Edgewater is a popular homebase for family vacations. **Rooms:** 62 rms and stes; 1 cottage/villa. CI 3pm/CO noon. Nonsmoking rms avail. Whirlpool suites include a two-person whirlpool. Most have a separate living area with a dinette table and balcony. **Amenities:** A/C, cable TV w/movies, refrig, dataport, in-rm safe. Some units w/terraces, some w/whirlpools. All rooms have microwaves. **Services:** Babysitting. Shuttles can be arranged to the area casinos. **Facilities:** 1 restaurant, sauna, whirlpool. **Rates:** Peak (May–Labor Day) $69–$119 S; $59–$109 D; $129–$225 ste; $129–$225 cottage/villa. Extra person $6. Children under age 3 stay free. Min stay special events. Lower rates off-season. Parking: Outdoor, free. AE, CB, DC, DISC, EC, ER, JCB, MC, V.

Holiday Inn Coliseum
2400 Beach Blvd, 39531; tel 601/388-3551 or toll free 800/441-0882; fax 601/385-2032. On US 90. Next door to a casino and across the street from the beach, this large Holiday Inn draws many different kinds of guests and manages to cater to them all. **Rooms:** 268 rms and stes. CI 3pm/CO 11am. Nonsmoking rms avail. **Amenities:** A/C, cable TV w/movies, dataport. Some units w/minibars, some w/terraces, some w/whirlpools. **Services:** Babysit-ting. **Facilities:** 350 1 restaurant, 2 bars (1 w/entertainment), games rm, washer/dryer. **Rates:** Peak (May 5–Sept 5) $83–$93 S or D; $199–$209 ste. Extra person $10. Children under age 12 stay free. Min stay wknds. Lower rates off-season. Parking: Outdoor, free. AE, CB, DC, DISC, MC, V.

Treasure Bay Resort Hotel and Casino
1980 Beach Blvd, 39531; tel 601/385-6000 or toll free 800/747-2839; fax 601/385-6067. On US 90 E of I-110. A relatively new place, catering to couples and families. **Rooms:** 260 rms and stes. CI 4pm/CO 1pm. Nonsmoking rms avail. **Amenities:** A/C, cable TV w/movies. Some units w/terraces. **Services:** Social director, babysitting. Airport transportation may be arranged with prior notice. **Facilities:** 1500 2 restaurants, 4 bars (1 w/entertainment), games rm. **Rates:** Peak (June–Sept) $65–$85 S or D; $165–$185 ste. Extra person $10. Children under age 18 stay free. Lower rates off-season. Parking: Outdoor, free. AE, DC, DISC, MC, V.

RESORTS

Broadwater Beach Resort Hotel
2110 Beach Blvd, 39531; tel 601/388-2211 or toll free 800/647-3964; fax 601/385-4102. On US 90. 400 acres. Older but well-maintained. **Rooms:** 850 rms, stes, and effic; 13 cottages/villas. CI 3pm/CO noon. Nonsmoking rms avail. Rooms offer a nice view; many are near the pool. **Amenities:** A/C, cable TV w/movies, dataport. All units w/terraces. **Services:** Car-rental desk, social director, masseur, babysitting. Free shuttle service to area casinos. **Facilities:** 36 10 1000 5 restaurants, 4 bars (1 w/entertainment), basketball, volleyball, games rm, beauty salon, playground, washer/dryer. Claims to have the world's largest covered marina. **Rates:** Peak (May 27–Sept 5) $90–$150 S or D; $195–$350 ste; $90–$150 effic; $195–$350 cottage/villa. Extra person $10. Children under age 12 stay free. Min stay wknds and special events. Lower rates off-season. MAP rates avail. Parking: Outdoor, free. AE, CB, DC, DISC, MC, V.

Gulf Beach Resort
2428 Beach Blvd, 39531; tel 601/385-5555 or toll free 800/323-9164; fax 601/388-9015. On US 90. 10 acres. A seven-

story complex with lots of on-site recreational facilities. Located directly across from the beach and near local casinos. **Rooms:** 226 rms and stes. CI 3pm/CO 11am. Nonsmoking rms avail. **Amenities:** A/C, satel TV w/movies. All units w/terraces. **Services:** Social director. Casino shuttle service. **Facilities:** 1 restaurant (bkfst and lunch only), 3 bars (2 w/entertainment), games rm. **Rates:** Peak (May–Aug) $55–$85 S or D; $130–$150 ste. Extra person $10. Children under age 18 stay free. Min stay wknds. Lower rates off-season. Parking: Outdoor, free. AE, DC, DISC, MC, V.

RESTAURANTS

Alberti's
2028 Beach Blvd; tel 601/388-9507. On US 90 (Beach Blvd). **Italian.** Located across the street from the beach, this popular trattoria offers traditional fare: lasagna, chicken parmigiana, chicken piccata, and spaghetti. **FYI:** Reservations accepted. **Open:** Tues–Thurs 2–10:30pm, Fri–Sat 2–11:30pm, Sun 2–10:30pm. **Prices:** Main courses $11–$20. AE, CB, DC, MC, V.

The French Connection
1891 Pass Rd; tel 601/388-6367. 1 block W of VA Hospital. **Seafood/Steak.** Housed in a small, secluded building off Pass Rd, with limited parking. Some of their more popular hearth-cooked dishes include beloute of oysters, fillet of snapper, and seafood casserole. **FYI:** Reservations recommended. Children's menu. Dress code. **Open:** Mon–Sat 5:30–11pm. **Prices:** Main courses $12–$27. AE, DC, DISC, MC, V.

Mary Mahoney's Old French House and Cafe
138 Rue Magnolia; tel 601/374-0163. **Seafood/Steak.** Located across the street from the beach in a beautifully restored colonial house from 1737. The dining room is furnished with antiques and there's an Old South feel throughout. Popular among locals and tourists alike, Mary Mahoney's dining room is well known for fresh snapper, lobster, oyster stew, and other seafood specialties, as well as steaks. The cafe serves a more informal menu of po' boys and other sandwiches, and is open 24 hours. **FYI:** Reservations recommended. Children's menu. **Open:** Mon–Sat 11am–10pm. **Prices:** Main courses $16–$29. AE, CB, DC, DISC, MC, V.

McElroy's Harbor House Seafood Restaurant
695 Beach Blvd; tel 601/435-5001. 2 mi E of the Biloxi Belle Resort. **Seafood.** Although the decor is nothing special, the meals are hearty and the dining room offers views of the beach and harbor. Popular entrees include broiled stuffed flounder, Gulf shrimp, speckled trout fillet, red snapper, and Florida lobster. **FYI:** Reservations not accepted. Children's menu. **Open:** Mon–Sun 7am–10pm. Closed Dec 1–7. **Prices:** Main courses $4–$20. AE, CB, DC, DISC, MC, V.

Ole Biloxi Schooner
159 E Howard (Point Cadet); tel 601/374-8071. At Myrtle St. **Seafood.** Tiny family-owned establishment with a big reputation for good food. Thick, spicy gumbo and fresh seafood po' boys are joined on the menu by several seafood entrees. **FYI:** Reservations not accepted. Children's menu. Beer and wine only. **Open:** Daily 7am–9pm, Fri 7am–10pm. **Prices:** Main courses $7–$13. No CC.

ATTRACTIONS

Beauvoir, The Jefferson Davis Shrine
2244 Beach Blvd; tel 601/388-1313. The last home of the only President of the Confederate States of America, Beauvoir ("beautiful view") is perched on a 57-acre estate. Davis lived, worked, and entertained at the house, and hundreds of Confederate soldiers spent their last days here. A museum adjacent to the house contains Davis's library and family artifacts; also on the grounds is the Tomb of the Unknown Soldier of the Confederacy. **Open:** Daily 9am–5pm. Closed some hols. $$

Ship Island Excursion Ferry
MS 90 at Biloxi Point Cadet Marina; tel 601/432-2197. Ship Island, near the meeting point of the Mississippi River and the Gulf of Mexico, is popular for its beautiful beach and clear blue/green surf. Hour-long cruises leave from Biloxi. The island is also the site of Fort Massachusetts, a Civil War fortress (guided tours during summer). **Open:** Mem Day–Labor Day, daily, call for schedule. $$$$

J L Scott Marine Education Center
115 Beach Blvd; tel 601/374-5550. Live displays of coastal-zone marine life such as sharks, eels, and sea turtles are displayed in a 42,000-gallon aquarium (the largest in the state). Forty smaller tanks are home to snakes, fish, turtles, and alligators; there's also a sea shell collection and a partial whale skeleton. Touch Tank, gift shop, video presentation. **Open:** Mon–Sat 9am–4pm. Closed some hols. $

Magnolia Hotel/Mardi Gras Museum
119 Rue Magnolia; tel 601/432-8806. The Magnolia—the only remaining pre–Civil War hotel on the Mississippi Gulf coast—is now home to the Gulf Coast Carnival Association and their Mardi Gras Museum. Exhibits include costumes and memorabilia from local carnival celebrations. **Open:** Mon–Fri 11am–3pm. Closed some hols. $

Clarksdale

The Mississippi Delta region is the place of origin for America's unique musical form, the blues, and Clarksdale—located in the heart of the delta and home to pioneering blues master W C Handy—played a central role in the music's development. Nearby lakes provide recreational opportunities, while the surrounding farmland produces an abundance of cotton, soybeans, corn, and rice. **Information:** Clarksdale-Coahoma County Chamber of Commerce, PO Box 160, Clarksdale, 38614 (tel 601/627-7337).

RESTAURANT 🍴

★ Rest Haven

419 State St/US 61; tel 601/624-8601. **Diner/Mediterranean.** This unique eatery has been serving Mediterranean cuisine in the heart of the Mississippi Delta since 1947. Kibbie, cabbage rolls, and pita bread are popular favorites, along with baklava for dessert. The decor is simple yet very comfortable. **FYI:** Reservations accepted. Beer and wine only. **Open:** Mon–Thurs 5:30am–9pm, Fri–Sat 5:30am–10pm. **Prices:** Main courses $3–$14. No CC. 🏛

ATTRACTION 📷

Delta Blues Museum

114 Delta Ave; tel 601/624-4461 or toll free 800/626-3764. The uniquely American artform known as the blues was born in the Mississippi Delta, and so were many legendary bluesmen: W C Handy, Robert Johnson, Muddy Waters, Howlin' Wolf, and John Lee Hooker all lived and worked here. This museum, established at the Carnegie Public Library in 1979, acts as a repository for thousands of recordings, videos, books, and memorabilia. Exhibits include a copy of B B King's guitar "Lucille," and the "Muddywood" guitar built out of wood from Muddy Waters's childhood home. Live concerts are held here about once a month; call ahead for the schedule. **Open:** Mon–Fri 9am–5:30pm, Sat 10am–5pm. Closed some hols. **Free**

Cleveland

Located in the northwestern part of the state, in a cotton-growing area. Its Depot Library, in a 1915 train depot, has a special library dedicated to fostering literacy. Home to Delta State University. **Information:** Cleveland–Bolivar County Chamber of Commerce, Third St, PO Box 490, Cleveland, 38732 (tel 601/843-2712).

MOTEL 🛏

▤▤▤ Cleveland Inn

US 61 S, 38732; tel 601/846-1411 or toll free 800/533-8466; fax 601/843-1713. Formerly a Holiday Inn, this two-story motel boasts exquisite, well-maintained landscaping. **Rooms:** 119 rms. CI open/CO noon. Nonsmoking rms avail. Suites have sofabeds. **Amenities:** 🛁 A/C, cable TV w/movies. **Services:** ✗ 🖥 🍽 Babysitting. **Facilities:** 🏊 🛒12 🛎 1 restaurant, 1 bar. **Rates:** $35–$40 S or D. Extra person $5. Children under age 18 stay free. Parking: Outdoor, free. AE, CB, DC, DISC, MC, V.

ATTRACTION 📷

Fielding Wright Art Center

Delta State University Campus; tel 601/846-4720. Permanent collection includes work by Käthe Kollwitz and Salvador Dali. Changing exhibits of contemporary art by Southern artists. **Open:** Mon–Fri 7:30am–4:30pm. Closed some hols. **Free**

Columbus

Located 7 miles from the Alabama border and incorporated in 1821, Columbus was first called "Possum Town" because of the opossumlike features of an early trader. The city served as the temporary state capital during the time Jackson was occupied in the Civil War. Writer Tennessee Williams was born here and his home is open to the public. The first state college for women in the nation was established here in 1884. **Information:** Columbus Convention & Visitors Bureau, 321 7th St N, PO Box 789, Columbus, 39701 (tel 601/329-1191).

HOTELS 🏨

▤▤ Comfort Inn

1210 US 45 N, 39701; tel 601/329-2422 or toll free 800/221-2222; fax 601/327-0311. Standard, two-story hotel. Adequate for an overnight stay. **Rooms:** 106 rms. CI 3pm/CO 11am. Nonsmoking rms avail. Rooms are well maintained. **Amenities:** 🛁 🔌 A/C, cable TV w/movies, dataport. **Services:** 🖥 🍽 Babysitting. **Facilities:** 🛒40 🛎 **Rates (CP):** $48–$59 S or D. Extra person $4. Children under age 18 stay free. Parking: Outdoor, free. AE, CB, DC, DISC, EC, ER, JCB, MC, V.

▤▤ Hampton Inn

2015 Military Rd, 39701; tel 601/328-6720 or toll free 800/HAMPTON; fax 601/328-0843. At US 82. Relatively new hotel, highly recommended for businesspeople and families. **Rooms:** 60 rms. CI 1pm/CO noon. Nonsmoking rms avail. **Amenities:** 🛁 A/C, cable TV w/movies, refrig. **Services:** 🖥 🍽 **Facilities:** 🏊 🛒45 🛎 Washer/dryer. **Rates (CP):** $49–$55 S; $51–$60 D. Extra person $6. Children under age 18 stay free. Parking: Outdoor, free. AE, CB, DC, DISC, MC, V.

UNRATED Holiday Inn

506 US 45 N, 39701; tel 601/328-5202 or toll free 800/HOLIDAY; fax 601/328-5202. Two blocks from downtown Columbus. Landscaping is minimal but attractive. Popular with businesspeople. **Rooms:** 154 rms and stes. CI 3pm/CO noon. Nonsmoking rms avail. **Amenities:** 🛁 🔌 A/C, cable TV w/movies, dataport. 1 unit w/whirlpool. **Services:** ✗ 🖥 🍽 Babysitting. Very professional staff. Restaurant is a local favorite, well-known for its buffets. **Facilities:** 🏊 🛒300 🛎 1 restaurant, 1 bar (w/entertainment). **Rates:** $48–$54 S; $53–$59 D; $85–$125 ste. Extra person $5. Children under age 19 stay free. Min stay special events. Parking: Outdoor, free. AE, CB, DC, DISC, MC, V.

MOTELS

🚊 Gilmer Inn
321 Main St, 39701; tel 601/328-0070 or toll free 800/328-0722; fax 601/329-1700. At 3rd St. In good condition; fine for overnight stays. **Rooms:** 71 rms. CI 2pm/CO noon. Nonsmoking rms avail. **Amenities:** 🛅 A/C, cable TV w/movies. **Services:** ⬧ **Facilities:** 🔲 🔲 **Rates (CP):** $35–$38 S; $38–$44 D. Extra person $3. Children under age 12 stay free. Parking: Outdoor, free. AE, DISC, MC, V.

🚊🚊 Regency Park
2218 US 45 N, 39701; tel 601/327-2251 or toll free 800/346-7275; fax 601/329-1428. Well-maintained, locally owned motel. **Rooms:** 100 rms and stes. CI noon/CO noon. Nonsmoking rms avail. **Amenities:** 🛅 A/C, cable TV w/movies, dataport. **Services:** ⬧ ⬧ ⬧ 24-hour coffee. Fax service available at the front desk. **Facilities:** 🔲 🔲 🔲 Curbside electrical outlets for fishing boats. **Rates (CP):** $40–$45 S; $45–$50 D; $75–$80 ste. Extra person $5. Children under age 12 stay free. Parking: Outdoor, free. AE, CB, DC, DISC, MC, V.

RESTAURANTS 🍴

★ Browne's Downtown
509 Main St; tel 601/327-8880. At 5th St. **Eclectic.** A laid-back eatery, located in a historic downtown building. The dark green walls and ceilings are complemented by white table linens. Nouvelle cuisine predominates, with plenty of salads, pasta, and soups. **FYI:** Reservations accepted. **Open:** Lunch Mon–Sat 11am–2pm; dinner Mon–Sat 5–10pm. **Prices:** Main courses $6–$15. AE, DISC, MC, V. 🔲

★ Harvey's
200 Main St; tel 601/327-1639. At 2nd. **Cajun.** An attractive, family-oriented restaurant offering Cajun-style dishes and steak. There's also an array of salads, and all dressings are made in house. Semiprivate booths are surrounded by lots of plants, bricks, and exposed woodwork. **FYI:** Reservations accepted. Children's menu. **Open:** Mon–Thurs 11am–9:30pm, Fri–Sat 11am–10pm. **Prices:** Main courses $6–$16. AE, DISC, MC, V. 🔲

★ Proffitt's Porch
Officer's Lake Rd; tel 601/327-4485. **Cajun.** A small, out of the way place with a relaxing country atmosphere. (The owner recommends calling ahead for directions.) The clientele ranges from businesspeople to families and college students. Menu highlights include red beans and rice, po' boys, and homemade desserts. **FYI:** Reservations accepted. Beer and wine only. BYO. **Open:** Lunch Tues–Sun 11:30am–2pm; dinner Tues–Sun 5–9:30pm. Closed Dec 23–Jan 3. **Prices:** Main courses $3–$6. No CC. 🔲 🔲

Ruben's
171 Moores Creek Rd; tel 601/328-9880. ¼ mi S of jct US 45/US 82. **Seafood.** Located down a gravel road, ¼ mile from Main St. Guests arrive to find a very basic, country-style dining room filled with happy customers chowing down on the likes of fried catfish and grilled steak. All entrees come with salad bar, choice of potato, and hush puppies. **FYI:** Reservations accepted. **Open:** Daily 5–10pm. **Prices:** Main courses $6–$13. AE, DISC, MC, V. 🔲

ATTRACTION 🏛

Waverley Mansion
MS 50, West Point; tel 601/494-1399. Located 10 mi NW of Columbus, near West Point. Built in 1852 by Col George H Young, this architecturally unique plantation house features four circular staircases that connect unsupported balconies in a 65-foot cupola. The house has been beautifully restored, but it still contains its original ornamental plaster, gold-leaf mirrors, and Italian marble mantles. **Open:** Daily sunrise–sunset. $$

Corinth

This manufacturing and dairy town is located in the extreme northeast, near the Tennessee border and Shiloh National Military Park (see Tennessee). Corinth was a strategic railroad center during the Civil War and was one of the state's most sought-after prizes; countless battery sites and rifle pits can be seen throughout. **Information:** Corinth Area Tourism Promotion Council, PO Box 1988, Corinth, 38834 (tel 601/286-3759).

HOTEL 🏨

🚊🚊🚊 Comfort Inn
US 72W, PO Box 540, 38834; tel 601/287-4421 or toll free 800/228-5150; fax 601/286-9535. At US 45. A modern, relatively new hotel far enough from the highway to offer peace and quiet. Building and landscaping are very well kept. Small but attractive lobby. **Rooms:** 107 rms and stes. CI noon/CO 11am. Nonsmoking rms avail. **Amenities:** 🛅 A/C, cable TV w/movies. VCRs available upon request. **Services:** 🔲 🔲 🔲 🔲 Staff is very willing to help with guests' needs. **Facilities:** 🔲 🔲 🔲 1 restaurant, washer/dryer. **Rates (CP):** $37–$41 S; $39–$43 D; $55–$59 ste. Extra person $5. Children under age 18 stay free. Parking: Outdoor, free. AE, CB, DC, DISC, ER, JCB, MC, V.

Greenville

Gateway to the Mississippi Delta, this river port boasts a large fleet of boats and barges, and is sometimes referred to as the "towboat capital of the world." A crossroads for agribusiness as well as entertainment on the Mississippi River, Greenville is home of the famous Delta Blues Festival. **Information:** Greenwood–Leflore County Chamber of Commerce, 402 Sycamore St, PO Box 848, Greenwood, 38935 (tel 601/453-4152).

HOTELS

Best Western Regency Inn
2428 US 82 E, 38701; tel 601/334-6900 or toll free 800/528-1234; fax 601/332-5863. 1 mi E of US 1. Above-average chain hotel; a good choice for business travelers and families. **Rooms:** 119 rms, stes, and effic. CI noon/CO noon. Nonsmoking rms avail. **Amenities:** A/C, cable TV w/movies, refrig, dataport, voice mail. Some units w/terraces. **Services:** **Facilities:** 75 Racquetball, whirlpool, washer/dryer. **Rates (CP):** $48–$72 S or D; $62–$76 ste; $50–$65 effic. Extra person $6. Children under age 12 stay free. Parking: Outdoor, free. AE, CB, DC, DISC, MC, V.

Comfort Inn
3080 US 82 E, PO Box 1701, 38930; tel 601/378-4976 or toll free 800/221-2222; fax 601/378-4980. 2 mi E of US 1. One of the newest hotels in town. Suitable for anyone looking for above-average accommodations. **Rooms:** 77 rms and stes. Executive level. CI 1pm/CO 11am. Nonsmoking rms avail. Some suites have sofa sleepers with extra blankets and pillows. **Amenities:** A/C, cable TV w/movies, dataport. Some units w/terraces. **Services:** Babysitting. **Facilities:** 35 Washer/dryer. **Rates (CP):** Peak (May–Sept) $49–$58 S; $53–$58 D; $70–$75 ste. Extra person $4. Children under age 18 stay free. Lower rates off-season. Parking: Outdoor, free. AE, CB, DC, DISC, ER, JCB, MC, V.

Hampton Inn
2701 US 82 E, 38701; tel 601/334-1818 or toll free 800/426-7866; fax 601/334-1818. Two-story hotel with basic amenities. Attracts businesspeople and families. **Rooms:** 120 rms. CI 1pm/CO noon. Nonsmoking rms avail. **Amenities:** A/C, cable TV w/movies, refrig, dataport. **Services:** Babysitting. **Facilities:** 30 Basketball, whirlpool, washer/dryer. Basketball courts double as a tennis court. Health club with sauna and whirlpool. **Rates (CP):** $49–$55 S; $51–$57 D. Extra person $2. Children under age 21 stay free. Parking: Outdoor, free. AE, CB, DC, DISC, MC, V.

Ramada Inn
2700 US 82 E, 38701; tel 601/332-4411 or toll free 800/272-6232; fax 601/332-4411. 1½ mi E of US 1. Above-average accommodations make this Ramada a popular choice for families. **Rooms:** 121 rms and stes. CI 2pm/CO noon. Nonsmoking rms avail. **Amenities:** A/C, cable TV w/movies. Some rooms have refrigerators. **Services:** **Facilities:** 250 1 restaurant, 1 bar (w/entertainment), playground, washer/dryer. **Rates:** $45–$50 S; $48–$53 D; $150 ste. Extra person $5. Children under age 18 stay free. Min stay special events. Parking: Outdoor, free. AE, CB, DC, DISC, JCB, MC, V.

MOTEL

Days Inn
2500 US 82 E, PO Box 1139, MS; tel 601/335-1999 or toll free 800/329-7466; fax 601/332-1144. 1 mi E of US 1. This two-story motel is a little worn around the edges; recent renovations were expected to improve matters. OK for overnight family stays. **Rooms:** 154 rms. CI 2pm/CO noon. Nonsmoking rms avail. Rooms are comfortable, but decor is tacky. **Amenities:** A/C, cable TV w/movies. **Services:** **Facilities:** 25 Washer/dryer. **Rates (CP):** $32–$45 S or D. Extra person $3. Children under age 12 stay free. Parking: Outdoor, free. Rates based upon number of occupants. AE, CB, DC, DISC, MC, V.

INN

UNRATED **Miss Lois' Victorian Inn**
331 S Washington Ave, 38701; tel 601/335-6000. 1½ mi N of US 82. Graceful Victorian structure, built in 1898 and listed on the National Register of Historic Places. Unsuitable for children under 8. **Rooms:** 3 rms; 1 cottage/villa. CI 1pm/CO 11am. No smoking. Rooms are decorated with Victorian antiques. **Amenities:** A/C, cable TV w/movies. No phone. **Services:** Afternoon tea served. **Facilities:** 10 Guest lounge w/TV. **Rates (CP):** $65 S or D; $100 cottage/villa. Higher rates for special events/hols. Parking: Outdoor, free. MC, V.

RESTAURANTS

★ **Doe's Eat Place**
502 Nelson St; tel 601/334-3315. 1 block W of Broadway. **Eclectic/Southern.** Despite its humble and somewhat dilapidated appearance, this place is legendary. The specialties are huge, thick steaks (such as T-bone and porterhouse) and hot tamales. (Supposedly, Doe's tamales were a favorite of Elvis's.) There's also an extensive menu of simple items including spaghetti and meatballs, chili, fried and broiled shrimp, gumbo, and more. **FYI:** Reservations accepted. BYO. **Open:** Mon–Sat 5:30–11pm. **Prices:** Main courses $10–$35. No CC.

★ **How Joy**
3105 US 82 E; tel 601/335-1920. **Chinese.** How Joy, opened in 1968, claims to have been the first Chinese restaurant in Mississippi. Locals have been coming here regularly for years for the excellent butterfly shrimp and Cantonese specialties. The tables are set with high-quality stemware and silverware, and the walls are decorated with all kinds of Chinese bric-a-brac. **FYI:** Reservations recommended. Karaoke. **Open:** Lunch Sun–Fri 11:30am–2pm; dinner Sun–Fri 5–10pm, Sat 5–10:30pm. **Prices:** Main courses $7–$17. AE, MC, V.

($) **Shelton House**
217 S Washington Ave; tel 601/334-3083. **Eclectic.** The Shelton is known far and wide for delicious entrees, fresh coffee, and luscious homemade desserts. Converted in 1914 from a house to a restaurant, the interior is nicely decorated

with antiques and pictures. Chicken and artichoke casserole, quiche, and eight different varieties of cheesecake are available. A year-round Christmas shop (up in the attic) sells ornaments, trees, decorations, and gifts. **FYI:** Reservations accepted. BYO. **Open:** Peak (Oct–Jan) Mon–Fri 8am–5pm, Sat 10am–3pm. **Prices:** Lunch main courses $5–$8. MC, V. 🍴 ☕

★ Sherman's

1400 S Main St; tel 601/332-6924. At Reed Rd. **American/ Eclectic.** Located in a 60-year-old building in one of Greenville's oldest residential neighborhoods, this cozy eatery was once a corner grocery store. The interior is uniquely designed with stained glass, antique-style lamps, original photographs, and nice wooden furniture. The booths are semiprivate, and there's a private dining room located at the rear of the restaurant. Dishes include roasted prime rib, rib eye steak, filet mignon, seafood, and pasta. **FYI:** Reservations accepted. Children's menu. **Open:** Lunch Mon–Sat 11am–2pm; dinner Mon–Thurs 5–9:30pm, Fri–Sat 5–10pm. Closed July 4 week. **Prices:** Main courses $4–$20. AE, DISC, MC, V. 👥

ATTRACTION 🏛

Winterville Mounds Museum State Park

MS 1; tel 601/334-4684. One of the largest Indian mound groups in the Mississippi Valley, this site was once used as a ceremonial gathering place for thousands of native people. The central temple mound is over 55 feet high, and is surrounded by several smaller mounds. Today, a museum on site contains artifacts, such as jewelry, pottery, and utensils, recovered in the area. Picnic area, playground. **Open:** Wed–Sat 8am–5pm, Sun 1–5pm. Closed Dec 25. **$**

Greenwood

On the Yazoo River in the Mississippi Delta, Greenwood is a center of retail and trade in a productive farm region. Its Cotton Row district downtown is a historic landmark. The Mississippi International Balloon Classic is held here. **Information:** Greenwood Convention & Visitors Bureau, 1902 Leflore Ave, PO Box 739, Greenwood, 38930 (tel 601/ 453-9197).

HOTELS 🏨

☰☰ Comfort Inn

401 US 82 W, PO Box 1701, 38930; tel 601/453-5974 or toll free 800/221-2222; fax 601/455-6401. This well-kept property is suitable for families and businesspeople. **Rooms:** 60 rms and stes. Executive level. CI noon/CO 11am. Nonsmoking rms avail. Some rooms have pull-out sofas. **Amenities:** 🛁 📺 A/C, cable TV w/movies, refrig, dataport. Some units w/terraces. **Services:** 🚗 🧺 🧖 Babysitting. **Facilities:** 🏋 🏊 ⛏ **Rates (CP):** Peak (May–Sept 10) $45–$49 S; $49–$53 D;

$49–$59 ste. Extra person $4. Children under age 18 stay free. Lower rates off-season. Parking: Outdoor, free. AE, CB, DC, DISC, ER, JCB, MC, V.

☰☰☰ Hampton Inn

635 US 82 W, PO Box 8288, 38930; tel 601/455-5777 or toll free 800/HAMPTON. An unusually attractive Hampton catering to business travelers and discerning vacationers. Formerly a Best Western Regency Inn. **Rooms:** 100 rms and stes. CI 2pm/CO noon. Nonsmoking rms avail. Cherry-wood furniture. **Amenities:** 🛁 🧖 A/C, satel TV w/movies, refrig. All units w/terraces. Morning coffee delivered to room. **Services:** 🧺 🧖 **Facilities:** 🏋 📺 🛝 🏊 ⛏ Basketball, volleyball, racquetball, whirlpool, washer/dryer. **Rates (CP):** $50–$56 S; $50–$58 D; $75 ste. Children under age 18 stay free. Parking: Outdoor, free. AE, CB, DC, DISC, MC, V.

RESTAURANTS 🍽

★ The Crystal Grill

423 Carrollton Ave; tel 601/453-6530. 1 block E of Main St. **American/Eclectic/Greek.** Located in the historic part of downtown, this restaurant has been serving up basic Mississippi cooking for more than 80 years. The restaurant is spread out over five different dining rooms in three renovated buildings. Some of their more popular dishes include stuffed jumbo Gulf shrimp, deep-sea scallops, frog legs, rib eye steak, filet mignon, and homemade desserts. **FYI:** Reservations accepted. Children's menu. **Open:** Daily 11am–10pm. Closed July 4 week. **Prices:** Main courses $6–$20. AE, DC, DISC, MC, V. 🍴 👥

★ Yianni's

506 Yalobusha; tel 601/455-6789. **Eclectic.** Located in a quiet area near the business district. Yanni's is an airy, modern eatery offering fresh seafood, pastas, and other contemporary dishes. The chicken salad is especially popular. All of their homemade baked goods and desserts can be ordered through a unique drive-through window. A lounge area includes comfortable sofas for waiting and/or just relaxing. A good place for couples and families. **FYI:** Reservations accepted. Children's menu. **Open:** Lunch Mon–Fri 11am–2pm; dinner Mon–Sat 5–10pm. Closed varied summer weeks. **Prices:** Main courses $5–$22. AE, DISC, MC, V. ♥ 👥 ⛏

ATTRACTIONS 🏛

Cottonlandia Museum

1608 US 82 W; tel 601/453-0925. A local museum chronicling the heritage of the Mississippi Delta from 10,000 BC to the present. Displays include a Mastodon skeleton found in the Greenwood area, Native American pottery and beads, farming implements made and used by slaves, and contemporary local art and crafts. **Open:** Mon–Fri 9am–5pm, Sat–Sun 2–5pm. Closed some hols. **$**

Florewood River Plantation State Park

Jct US 82 and US 49E; tel 601/455-3821 or 455-3822. This unique state park consists of an exact reproduction of an 1850s antebellum cotton plantation, including the main house and outbuildings (school room, overseer's house, sorghum mill). Costumed historical interpreters conduct tours of the house and grounds. A cotton museum, illustrating the history of cotton in the region, is located near the park entrance. **Open:** Mar–Dec, Tues–Sat 9am–noon and 1–5pm, Sun 1–5pm. **$$**

Grenada

Historic Grenada is an important cotton market and trading hub in north-central Mississippi. Belle Flower Mount Baptist Church, which was bombed in 1960 and served as a focal point for marches and demonstrations during the civil rights era, is here. **Information:** Grenada County Chamber of Commerce, 701 Sunset Dr, PO Box 628, Grenada, 38902 (tel 601/226-2571).

HOTELS 🏨

☰☰ Hampton Inn

1622 Sunset Dr, 38901; tel 601/226-5555 or toll free 800/895-8555; fax 601/226-5581. ½ mi E of exit 206 off I-55. Located on a strip along with many other chain hotels. Inset farther than some, but still easy to find. Ideal for the business traveler. **Rooms:** 63 rms and stes. CI 2pm/CO noon. Nonsmoking rms avail. Very attractive room decor. **Amenities:** 🛁 A/C, cable TV w/movies, refrig, VCR. **Services:** 🖨 🛎 **Facilities:** 🏋 🏊 👤 Facilities are fairly new and very well maintained. **Rates (CP):** Peak (May–Sept) $59–$65 S or D; $75–$80 ste. Children under age 18 stay free. Lower rates off-season. Parking: Outdoor, free. AE, CB, DC, DISC, MC, V.

☰☰☰ Holiday Inn

1796 Sunset Dr, 38901; tel 601/226-2851 or toll free 800/HOLIDAY; fax 601/226-5058. At jct MS 8 and I-55. Attractive building features Holidome indoor recreational area. Popular with families. **Rooms:** 130 rms. CI 1pm/CO noon. Nonsmoking rms avail. **Amenities:** 🛁 🏋 🖥 A/C, cable TV w/movies, refrig, dataport. **Services:** ✕ 🆚 🐕 🖨 🛎 🕯 Babysitting. Nightly security patrol. **Facilities:** 🏋 🏊 👤 1 restaurant, 1 bar, washer/dryer. **Rates (BB):** $52–$56 S or D. Extra person $7. Children under age 12 stay free. Parking: Outdoor, free. AE, CB, DC, DISC, MC, V.

MOTEL

☰☰☰ Best Western Grenada

1750 Sunset Dr, 38901; tel 601/226-7816 or toll free 800/528-1234; fax 601/226-5623. Exit 206 off I-55. Ideal for families. **Rooms:** 61 rms and stes. CI 3pm/CO noon. Nonsmoking rms avail. **Amenities:** 🛁 🏋 A/C, cable TV w/movies, refrig, dataport. **Services:** ✕ 🐕 🖨 🛎 🕯 Turndown service

offered for groups and special events. **Facilities:** 🏋 🏊 1 restaurant (*see* "Restaurants" below), basketball, playground. **Rates (BB):** Peak (May 15–Sept 15) $40–$55 S; $51–$59 D; $61–$75 ste. Extra person $5. Children under age 12 stay free. Lower rates off-season. Parking: Outdoor, free. AE, CB, DC, DISC, MC, V.

RESTAURANT 🍽

Ⓢ Mr C's Best Western

In the Best Western Grenada, 1750 Sunset Dr; tel 601/226-7816. Exit 206 off I-55. **Regional American/Eclectic.** A cozy, friendly little place offering a wide variety of food but best known for its spaghetti, Southern fried chicken, and top sirloin. Very comfortable atmosphere. **FYI:** Reservations accepted. Children's menu. Beer and wine only. **Open:** Daily 6am–10pm. **Prices:** Main courses $3–$10. AE, CB, DC, DISC, MC, V. 👥

Gulfport

Gulfport, located where the Mississippi Sound meets the Gulf of Mexico, is a planned city with broad streets. A major rail and shipping center, it became a resort in the 1920s. The Deep Sea Fishing Rodeo is held here each summer. **Information:** Mississippi Beach Convention & Visitors Bureau, 135 Court House Rd, PO Box 6128, Gulfport, 39506 (tel 601/896-6699).

HOTELS 🏨

☰☰ Best Western Beach View Inn

2922 W Beach Blvd, 39501; tel 601/864-4650 or toll free 800/748-8969; fax 601/863-6867. ½ mi W of US 49 on US 90. In need of some exterior renovations but still an adequate place to stay. **Rooms:** 151 rms and stes. CI 3pm/CO noon. Nonsmoking rms avail. Basic, well-designed rooms. **Amenities:** 🛁 A/C, cable TV w/movies, dataport. **Services:** ✕ 🐕 🖨 🛎 Babysitting. **Facilities:** 🏋 🏊 👤 1 restaurant, 1 bar (w/entertainment), washer/dryer. **Rates:** Peak (May 15–Labor Day) $65–$89 S or D; $150–$170 ste. Extra person $10. Children under age 18 stay free. Min stay wknds. Lower rates off-season. Parking: Outdoor, free. AE, CB, DC, DISC, EC, MC, V.

☰☰ Hampton Inn

9445 US 49, 39503; tel 601/868-3300 or toll free 800/9-VISIT-9; fax 601/864-3347. Off I-10. Very nice chain hotel. Suitable for businesspeople and family vacationers. **Rooms:** 155 rms and stes. CI 3pm/CO noon. Nonsmoking rms avail. **Amenities:** 🛁 🏋 A/C, cable TV w/movies, refrig, dataport. Some units w/whirlpools. **Services:** 🐕 🖨 🛎 🕯 Babysitting. Twice-daily maid service upon request. Free casino shuttle service for hotel guests. **Facilities:** 🏋 🏊 👤 Washer/dryer.

Rates (CP): $59–$79 S or D; $100–$130 ste. Children under age 18 stay free. Min stay special events. Parking: Outdoor, free. AE, CB, DC, DISC, MC, V.

≣≣ Paradise Beach Resort

220 W Beach Blvd, 39560; tel 601/864-8811 or toll free 800/538-7752; fax 601/867-6392. On US 90 5 mi W of Biloxi. A winning, comfortable hideaway offering all sorts of travelers a place to relax. **Rooms:** 200 rms and stes. CI 3pm/CO 11am. Nonsmoking rms avail. **Amenities:** 🛏 🕯 A/C, cable TV w/movies. Some units w/terraces, some w/whirlpools. **Services:** ⤴ ⤴ Babysitting. **Facilities:** 🔧 200 🔧 **Rates:** Peak (Mar–July) $70–$89 S; $77–$95 D; $100–$150 ste. Extra person $6. Children under age 12 stay free. Lower rates off-season. Parking: Outdoor, free. AE, DC, DISC, MC, V.

MOTEL

≣≣ Shoney's Inn

9375 US 49, 39503; tel 601/868-8500 or toll free 800/222-2222; fax 601/865-0054. 3 mi S off I-10. Well-kept, family-friendly property. Shoney's restaurant next door. **Rooms:** 110 rms and stes. CI 2pm/CO noon. Nonsmoking rms avail. Rooms are nice and comfortable. **Amenities:** 🛏 A/C, cable TV w/movies. **Services:** ⤴ ⤴ ⤴ Babysitting. **Facilities:** 🔧 🔧 1 restaurant. **Rates:** Peak (June–Sept). Children under age 18 stay free. Lower rates off-season. Parking: Outdoor, free. AE, CB, DC, DISC, ER, JCB, MC, V.

RESTAURANTS 🍴

Chappy's Seafood Restaurant Inc

624 E Beach Blvd, Long Beach; tel 601/865-9755. 5 mi W of Gulfport. **Creole/Seafood.** A very popular establishment in a recently built area right across from the beach. Some of the more popular dishes include orange roughy, snapper, and various crab dishes. The extensive wine list includes domestic and imported labels. **FYI:** Reservations accepted. Piano. Children's menu. **Open:** Daily 11am–10pm. **Prices:** Main courses $13–$25. AE, CB, DC, DISC, MC, V. ● ■ ◗

♣ Vrazel's Fine Food Restaurant

3206 W Beach Blvd; tel 601/863-2229. On US 90 (Beach Blvd). **Eclectic.** Classy yet comfortable eatery known for good food and good service. The dining room decor is stylish and elegant, and the menu includes such items as stuffed snapper Bay St Louis, eggplant La Rosa, Gulf shrimp casserole, and rib eye steak. **FYI:** Reservations recommended. Children's menu. Dress code. **Open:** Lunch Mon–Fri 11am–2pm; dinner Mon–Sat 5–10pm. **Prices:** Main courses $13–$19. AE, CB, DC, DISC, MC, V. ●

ATTRACTIONS 🏛

NASA's John C Stennis Space Center

Building 1200, Stennis Space Center; tel 601/688-2370. Located 31 mi W of Gulfport. NASA's second-largest research center; this is where all space-vehicle engines are tested. The visitors center, with a 90-foot Space Tower, houses a Hall of Achievements tracing the history of space flight. Bus tours of the entire complex are available as well as films, lectures, and demonstrations. **Open:** Daily 9am–5pm. Closed some hols. **Free**

Marine Life Oceanarium

Jones Memorial Park; tel 601/864-2511. Highlights include an all-weather aquadome where dolphins and sea lions frolic; a re-creation of a South American rain forest complete with exotic birds; and a touch pool where visitors can get hands-on knowledge of starfish, horseshoe crabs, and other sea life. Also on site are the SS *Gravity* (which explores the effects of gravity) and the Harbor Tour Train. **Open:** Daily 9am–5pm. Closed some hols. **$$$**

Hattiesburg

Hattiesburg is a diversified industrial city located at the edge of De Soto National Forest. With the University of Southern Mississippi (which houses the largest collection of original manuscripts and illustrations of children's literature), it is a center for education in the southern part of the state. **Information:** Hattiesburg Convention & Visitors Bureau, PO Box 16122, Hattiesburg, 39404 (tel 601/264-0438).

HOTELS 🏨

≣≣ Hampton Inn

4301 Hardy St, 39402; tel 601/264-8080 or toll free 800/HAMPTON; fax 601/264-8080. Off I-55. Standard, two-story chain hotel, located in the heart of the business district. **Rooms:** 116 rms and stes. CI 1pm/CO noon. Nonsmoking rms avail. **Amenities:** 🛏 🕯 A/C, cable TV w/movies, dataport. **Services:** ⤴ ⤴ Babysitting. Coffee available all day. **Facilities:** 🔧 35 🔧 Guest privileges at local health club. **Rates (CP):** $52–$64 S; $61–$67 D; $63–$71 ste. Extra person $6. Children under age 12 stay free. Parking: Outdoor, free. AE, CB, DC, DISC, JCB, MC, V.

≣≣≣ Holiday Inn

6563 US 49 N, 39401; tel 601/268-2850 or toll free 800/HOLIDAY; fax 601/268-2823. ½ mi E off I-59. Modest, well-maintained property with nice landscaping. **Rooms:** 128 rms and stes. CI 3pm/CO noon. Nonsmoking rms avail. **Amenities:** 🛏 🕯 A/C, satel TV w/movies. Some units w/terraces. **Services:** ✗ ⤴ ⤴ **Facilities:** 🔧 220 🔧 1 restaurant, 1 bar, whirlpool. **Rates:** $57 S or D; $107 ste. Extra person $6. Children under age 12 stay free. Parking: Outdoor, free. AE, CB, DC, DISC, MC, V.

≣≣ Howard Johnson Hotel

6553 US 49 N, 39401; tel 601/268-2251 or toll free 800/327-0903; fax 601/264-7283. Nothing fancy here—just a clean, comfortable place to sleep. **Rooms:** 180 rms and stes. CI 3pm/CO noon. Nonsmoking rms avail. **Amenities:** 🛏 🕯 A/C, cable TV w/movies. **Services:** ⤴ ⤴ Babysitting. **Facilities:** 🔧 100 🔧 1 restaurant (bkfst only), washer/dryer.

Rates (CP): Peak (June–Aug) $40–$50 S or D; $46–$50 ste. Extra person $5. Children under age 12 stay free. Lower rates off-season. Parking: Outdoor, free. AE, CB, DC, DISC, MC, V.

MOTELS

≡≡ Best Western Northgate Inn
6757 US 49, 39402; tel 601/268-8816 or toll free 800/528-1234; fax 601/268-8816. 1 block W of I-59. This no-frills chain motel is a nice choice for families. Rooms: 87 rms and stes. CI 3pm/CO noon. Nonsmoking rms avail. Amenities: ☎ ⚱ A/C, cable TV w/movies, dataport. Services: ✗ ⬛ ⤴ Babysitting. Facilities: ⟨ ⟩ ♿ 1 restaurant, 1 bar (w/entertainment). Rates (BB): $45–$55 S; $47–$57 D; $89–$129 ste. Extra person $6. Children under age 12 stay free. Parking: Outdoor, free. AE, CB, DC, DISC, MC, V.

≡≡ Cabot Lodge
6541 US 49, 39401; tel 601/264-1881 or toll free 800/225-9429. 1 mi S off I-59. A very relaxing atmosphere reigns at this well-maintained property with a well-groomed yard. Suitable for all travelers. Rooms: 160 rms. CI noon/CO noon. Nonsmoking rms avail. Amenities: ☎ ⚱ A/C, cable TV w/movies, dataport. Services: ⬛ ⤴ Babysitting. Facilities: ⟨ ⟩ 20 ♿ Rates (CP): $55–$61 S; $52–$71 D. Extra person $6. Children under age 12 stay free. Parking: Outdoor, free. AE, CB, DC, DISC, MC, V.

RESTAURANTS ⍟

★ Chesterfield's
2507 Hardy St; tel 601/582-2778. At the corner of US 49 and US 98. American/Eclectic. Located in the center of town, this eatery has a very lively atmosphere and a casual, friendly ambience. The menu offers a nice variety of soups, sandwiches, and pastas, as well as chicken, beef, rib, and seafood entrees. FYI: Reservations not accepted. Children's menu. Open: Mon–Sat 11am–11pm, Sun 11am–10pm. Prices: Main courses $6–$15. AE, CB, DC, DISC, MC, V. ⬛ ♿

★ Crescent City Grill
3810 Hardy St; tel 601/264-0657. ½ mi E of I-59. Creole/Seafood. Adjacent to the Purple Parrot Cafe (see below), yet it offers a very different atmosphere. The very colorful, funky-looking dining room is decorated with all sorts of pictures and signs. The menu offers something for everyone, including sandwiches, steak, and seafood. The wine list offers 49 domestic and imported wines and there are 28 different types of beer available. FYI: Reservations not accepted. Children's menu. Open: Sun–Thurs 11am–10pm, Fri–Sat 11am–11pm. Prices: Main courses $5–$17. AE, DISC, MC, V. ⬛ ♿

★ The Front Porch Bar-B-Q & Seafood
205 Thornhill Dr; tel 601/264-3536. Off I-55 at US 98. Cajun. A quiet place offering lunch and dinner buffets plus a small sandwich menu. Buffet choices focus primarily on Cajun-style seafood and barbecue items. The building is new and the interior is very basic. FYI: Reservations accepted. No liquor license. Open: Daily 11am–9pm. Prices: Main courses $4–$10. AE, MC, V. ⬛ ♿

♣ Purple Parrot Cafe
3810 Hardy St; tel 601/264-0656. ½ mi E of I-59. Eclectic/Seafood. Low, soft lighting adds to the ambience of this cozy dining room. The menu offers a variety of sandwiches, seafood, and appetizers; some of the top sellers are chicken picatta, chicken pesto rotini, and eggplant bayou teche. FYI: Reservations accepted. Children's menu. Open: Lunch Mon–Fri 11am–2pm; dinner Mon–Thurs 5–10pm, Fri–Sat 5–11pm; brunch Sat 11am–2pm. Prices: Main courses $10–$20. AE, DISC, MC, V. ♥ ♿

Rocket City Diner
In Arbor Shopping Mall, 4700 Hardy St; tel 601/264-7893. 1 block W of I-59. American. Colorful 1960s-style diner, complete with radios on the tables and very friendly service. Burgers, steak, and down-home specialties dominate the menu. FYI: Reservations not accepted. Comedy. Beer and wine only. Open: Sun–Thurs 6am–10pm, Fri–Sat 6am–11pm. Prices: Main courses $6–$17. AE, CB, DC, DISC, MC, V. ⬛ ♿

♣ Wild Magnolia
1311 Hardy St; tel 601/543-0908. 1 mi E of US 49 N, on US 98. Italian/Seafood/Steak. Semi-elegant yet cozy dining room is decorated with art and artifacts. The menu offers a variety of pasta, poultry, steak, and seafood, such as filet mignon, lobster tail, and chicken Rossini. Full service bar and lounge on the second floor is available for private parties. FYI: Reservations accepted. Blues/guitar/rock. Children's menu. Open: Mon–Fri 11am–10pm, Sat 5–10pm. Prices: Main courses $10–$20. AE, DC, DISC, MC, V. ♥ ♿

ATTRACTIONS ⌸

Turner House Collection
500 Bay St; tel 601/582-1771. Classical revival house built 1908–1910. Some original furnishings are scattered among French and English antiques and a small collection of art. Open: Daily, by appointment. Closed last 2 weeks of July and some hols. Free

Mvuli Gallery
340 N 25th Ave; tel 601/582-9118 or toll free 800/99MVULI. African American art gallery displaying authentic African carvings, masks, sculptures, fabric, prints, and artifacts. Open: Tues–Sat 10am–6pm. Closed some hols. Free

Hattiesburg Zoo
107 S 17th Ave; tel 601/545-4576. One of only two zoos in the state of Mississippi. A passenger train called the Southern Railroad runs a half-mile loop around the various animal exhibits, which include wild cats, monkeys, and other popular favorites. Open: Mar–Oct, call for schedule. $

Holly Springs

This Old South city boasts more than 60 intact houses erected before the Civil War. Situated in the path of Union invasions of the state, the town changed hands so many times that citizens made a daily practice of checking to see which flag was flying. **Information:** Holly Springs Chamber of Commerce, 154 S Memphis St, Holly Springs, 38635 (tel 601/252-2943).

INN 🛏

☰ Holly Inn

US 78 W, 38635; tel 601/252-4105. 7 acres. Standard, comfortable accommodations; suitable for families. **Rooms:** 36 rms. CI noon/CO 11am. **Amenities:** 🕾 A/C, cable TV. **Services:** 🛎 🍽 **Facilities:** 1 restaurant, guest lounge. **Rates:** $30 S; $35 D. Children under age 18 stay free. Parking: Outdoor, free. No charge for additional guests in rooms. MC, V.

ATTRACTION 📷

Kate Freeman Clark Art Gallery

292 E College Ave; tel 601/252-4211 or 252-2511. Houses more than 1,200 paintings of Kate Freeman Clark, late 19th-century painter and student of noted artist William M Chase. Upon her death, Clark willed her entire collection to her hometown of Holly Springs. The gallery also features paintings by Chase, Rockwell Kent, and Alice Johns. **Open:** By appointment. **Free**

Indianola

The seat of Sunflower County in western Mississippi, this cotton-processing town is the original home of blues artist B B King. The first weekend in June marks his homecoming concert. **Information:** Indianola Chamber of Commerce, 104 E Percy St, PO Box 151, Indianola, 38751 (tel 601/887-4454).

HOTEL 🛏

UNRATED Comfort Inn

910 US 82 E, 38751; tel 601/887-6611 or toll free 800/228-5150; fax 601/887-1317. Recently updated property, recommended for businesspeople and families. **Rooms:** 50 rms and stes. Executive level. CI noon/CO noon. Nonsmoking rms avail. **Amenities:** 🕾 🛁 A/C, cable TV. Some units w/whirlpools. **Services:** 🍴 🛄 🍽 **Facilities:** 🏋 🏊50 🛗 **Rates (CP):** $44–$49 S; $41–$46 D; $52–$65 ste. Extra person $5. Children under age 18 stay free. Parking: Outdoor, free. AE, CB, DC, DISC, ER, JCB, MC, V.

RESTAURANT 🍴

$ ✹ The Crown Restaurant

In Antique Mall, 316 Sunflower Rd; tel 601/887-2522. Off MS 448 and US 82. **Seafood.** The Crown, which shares space with an antique shop, is furnished with an ever-changing array of antiques. (The antiques are all for sale, so if you like your dining table, you can take it home with you!) The menu is very basic, offering only two entrees per day. One of the choices is usually catfish of some sort (the Crown's famous catfish pâté is even exported overseas). Salad, vegetable, and dessert are available to round out your meal. **FYI:** Reservations recommended. BYO. No smoking. **Open:** Lunch Tues–Sat noon–2pm. Closed Dec 24–Jan 2. **Prices:** Lunch main courses $7. AE, DISC, MC, V. 🍷 📷

Jackson

Originally a trading station known as Le Fleur's Bluff and later renamed for Andrew Jackson, the state capital and largest city sits on the bluffs of the Pearl River in southwest-central Mississippi. The city center is laid out in a checkerboard pattern suggested by Thomas Jefferson. Mississippi's heart and hub—the center of government, commerce, and manufacturing—is sometimes referred to as "the crossroads of the South." Jackson was burned on three separate occasions during the Civil War, earning it the sardonic sobriquet "Chimneyville." The city boasts more colleges and universities—including Jackson State University, over 100 years old—than any other area of the state. **Information:** Metro Jackson Convention & Visitors Bureau, 921 N President St, PO Box 1450, Jackson, 39215 (tel toll free 800/354-7695).

HOTELS 🛏

☰☰☰ Cabot Lodge

2375 N State St, 39157; tel 601/948-8650 or toll free 800/874-4737; fax 601/948-8650. 1 mi W of Woodrow Wilson exit off I-55. Offers a very classy, quiet atmosphere. The lobby is decorated with color-coordinated furniture and pictures, and there are plenty of cozy sitting areas. **Rooms:** 205 rms and stes. Executive level. CI 3pm/CO noon. Nonsmoking rms avail. **Amenities:** 🕾 🛁 🍴 A/C, cable TV w/movies, dataport, voice mail. Robes are available in business, executive, and deluxe suites. **Services:** ✗ 🛄 🍽 Complimentary beverage service (including 24-hour coffee). Cocktail reception every evening. **Facilities:** 🏋 🍽150 🖥 🛗 Washer/dryer. **Rates (CP):** $56–$74 S; $64–$82 D; $135 ste. Extra person $8. Children under age 12 stay free. Parking: Outdoor, free. AE, CB, DC, DISC, MC, V.

☰☰ Cabot Lodge Jackson North

120 Dyess Rd, 39157; tel 601/957-0757 or toll free 800/342-2268; fax 601/957-0757. 1 block E of I-55 at County Line Rd. Well maintained and tastefully decorated. **Rooms:** 208 rms. Executive level. CI 3pm/CO noon. Nonsmoking

rms avail. **Amenities:** 📶 🕯 A/C, satel TV w/movies, dataport. Some units w/terraces. Coffeemakers in some rooms. Safe-deposit boxes are available. **Services:** 📇 🛎 Car-rental desk, babysitting. Cocktails and snacks are available every morning and evening. **Facilities:** 🏊 🛏35 🛁 **Rates (CP):** $67 S; $63 D. Extra person $8. Children under age 12 stay free. Min stay special events. Parking: Outdoor, free. AE, DC, DISC, MC, V.

≡≡≡ Edison Walthall Hotel

225 E Capitol St, 39201; tel 601/948-6161. At State St. This very elegant hotel has chandeliers in the lobby and throughout the public areas. **Rooms:** 200 rms and stes. Executive level. CI 3pm/CO noon. Nonsmoking rms avail. Each room is nicely decorated with color-coordinated wallpaper and furniture. **Amenities:** 📶 🕯 📺 🍷 A/C, cable TV w/movies, dataport, voice mail. Some units w/minibars, some w/whirlpools. **Services:** ✕ 🍽 🚗 📇 🛎 Twice-daily maid svce, social director, babysitting. Airline ticket office located on ground floor of lobby. **Facilities:** 🍴 🛏30 💻 🛁 1 restaurant, 1 bar (w/entertainment), games rm, beauty salon. Parking garage connected to building. **Rates:** Peak (Aug–Oct) $65–$85 S; $80–$100 D; $135–$195 ste. Extra person $10. Children under age 12 stay free. Lower rates off-season. Parking: Indoor, $5/day. AE, CB, DC, DISC, MC, V.

≡≡ Hampton Inn

465 Briarwood Dr, 39206; tel 601/956-3611 or toll free 800/HAMPTON; fax 601/956-4999. Off I-55. A very basic, but well-maintained hotel. The well-designed lobby offers comfortable seating for guests. **Rooms:** 117 rms. CI noon/CO noon. Nonsmoking rms avail. **Amenities:** 📶 🕯 A/C, cable TV w/movies, dataport. **Services:** 📇 🛎 **Facilities:** 🏊 🛁 **Rates (CP):** $59 S; $65 D. Children under age 18 stay free. Min stay special events. Parking: Outdoor, free. AE, CB, DC, DISC, MC, V.

≡≡≡ Marriott Residence Inn

881 E River Place, 39202; tel 601/355-3599 or toll free 800/331-3131; fax 601/355-5127. ½ mi E of I-55. A very well-maintained hotel located in a rather remote area. The apartment-style rooms and quiet setting make this a good choice for an extended stay. **Rooms:** 120 stes. CI 3pm/CO noon. Nonsmoking rms avail. Six apartment-style room/suites are accessible for guests with disabilities. **Amenities:** 📶 🕯 📺 A/C, satel TV w/movies, refrig, voice mail. Some units w/terraces, all w/fireplaces, some w/whirlpools. **Services:** 📇 🛎 🍹 Car-rental desk, babysitting. **Facilities:** 🏊 🎾 🛏25 🛁 Basketball, volleyball, spa, whirlpool, washer/dryer. Guest privileges at local YMCA. **Rates:** Peak (Jan–Nov) $99–$149 ste. Children under age 21 stay free. Lower rates off-season. Parking: Outdoor, free. AE, CB, DC, DISC, EC, JCB, MC, V.

≡≡≡ Ramada Coliseum

400 Greymont Ave, PO Box 893, 39205; tel 601/969-2141 or toll free 800/272-6232; fax 601/355-1704. I-55, exit 96B. Attractive property offering a wide variety of accommodations—everything from "standard" rooms to suites to honeymoon suites—for a wide variety of travelers. **Rooms:** 396 rms and stes. CI 3pm/CO noon. Nonsmoking rms avail. Suites have whirlpool, patio, bathrobes, and two phones. **Amenities:** 📶 🕯 📺 🍷 A/C, satel TV w/movies, refrig. Some units w/terraces, some w/whirlpools. VCR available upon request. **Services:** ✕ 🚗 📇 🛎 🍹 Babysitting. **Facilities:** 🏊 🛏2000 🛁 1 restaurant, 1 bar (w/entertainment), washer/dryer. **Rates:** $55–$68 S; $62–$75 D; $215–$365 ste. Extra person $7. Children under age 18 stay free. AP and MAP rates avail. Parking: Outdoor, free. AE, CB, DC, DISC, MC, V.

≡≡ Wilson Inn

310 Greymont Ave, 39202; tel 601/948-4466 or toll free 800/WILSONS; fax 601/948-4466 ext 157. Exit 96B off I-55. Well-maintained hotel. **Rooms:** 110 rms and stes. CI 2pm/CO noon. Nonsmoking rms avail. All rooms have king-size beds. **Amenities:** 📶 A/C, satel TV w/movies, refrig. Hair dryers available upon request. **Services:** 📇 🛎 🍹 Complimentary coffee and refreshments (including popcorn) available 24 hours. **Facilities:** 🛏25 Playground. **Rates (CP):** Peak (Oct and Feb) $42–$54 S; $48–$60 D; $53–$65 ste. Extra person $6. Children under age 18 stay free. Lower rates off-season. Parking: Outdoor, free. AE, CB, DC, DISC, MC, V.

MOTEL

≡ Quality Inn North

4641 I-55 N, 39206; tel 601/982-1044 or toll free 800/221-2222; fax 601/366-3381. Exit 100 off I-55. Wear your sunglasses on arrival—the room doors and trim here are painted bright pink. Most suitable for overnight stays. **Rooms:** 162 rms and stes. CI 3pm/CO noon. Nonsmoking rms avail. Several minor problems were noticed on inspection: buckled-up wallpaper, unpolished woodwork, and cracked grouting in the sink area. **Amenities:** 📶 🕯 A/C, cable TV w/movies. Some units w/terraces. Some rooms have hair dryers; refrigerators available upon request. **Services:** 🍽 🚗 🛎 🍹 Safe-deposit boxes available for use at front desk. **Facilities:** 🏊 🛏150 🛁 1 restaurant. **Rates:** $49 S; $59 D; $85 ste. Extra person $6. Children under age 6 stay free. Parking: Outdoor, free. AE, DC, DISC, JCB, MC, V.

INN

≡≡≡ Millsaps-Buie House

628 N State St, 39202; tel 601/352-0221 or toll free 800/784-0221; fax 601/352-0221. N of downtown. 5 acres. Located in the heart of Jackson's historic district, this popular establishment is well maintained and adorned with superb antiques and beautiful paintings. Unsuitable for children under 12. **Rooms:** 11 rms and stes. CI 2pm/CO 11am. No smoking. Each room is furnished with antiques and has fresh fruit and flowers. **Amenities:** 📶 🕯 🍷 A/C, cable TV w/movies, dataport. Some units w/terraces. Three rooms have refrigerators. **Services:** ✕ 🔑 📇 Alcoholic beverages available upon request. **Facilities:** 🛏10 🛁 Guest lounge. **Rates**

(BB): $85–$155 S; $100–$170 D; $150–$165 ste. Extra person $15. Children under age 12 stay free. Parking: Outdoor, free. AE, DC, DISC, MC, V.

RESTAURANTS 🍴

★ Dennery's

330 Greymont Ave; tel 601/354-2527. Exit 95 off I-55. **Greek.** The lovely decor is dominated by an interior fountain with a statue of Aphrodite (the Greek goddess of love) in its center; there are also photos of past guests and lots of plants. In addition to Greek specialties, steak and seafood are also popular. **FYI:** Reservations recommended. Children's menu. **Open:** Mon–Fri 11am–10pm, Sat 5–10pm. **Prices:** Main courses $5–$27. AE, DC, DISC, MC, V. ♥ 👥

★ The Elite

141 E Capitol; tel 601/352-5606. At Congress St. **Regional American.** Nice, friendly spot known for its simple yet tasty meals. The very simple decor is reminiscent of an old-time diner, with lots of mirrors and pictures, and the meals are similarly humble. Southern-style vegetables and fresh dinner rolls accompany entrees like veal cutlet and fried chicken. **FYI:** Reservations not accepted. Beer and wine only. **Open:** Mon–Fri 7am–9:30pm, Sat 5–9:30pm. **Prices:** Main courses $4–$13. No CC. 👥

Gridley's Fine Barbecue

1428 Old Square Rd; tel 601/362-8600. 1 block E of E Frontage Rd, exit 100 off I-55. **Barbecue.** The decor here is very casual—just a few pictures, and plain wooden booths and tables. Guests come here for the wide variety of barbecue dishes: ribs, pork, chicken, beef, and shrimp. Coleslaw and baked beans are available on the side. **FYI:** Reservations accepted. Additional location: Winchester Rd, Memphis (tel 901/794-5997). **Open:** Sun–Thurs 11am–9pm, Fri–Sat 11am–10pm. **Prices:** Main courses $3–$14. AE, DISC, MC, V. 👥 ♿

The Iron Horse Bar & Grill

320 W Pearl; tel 601/355-8419. **Southwestern/Steak.** Located in an old smokehouse constructed in 1906–1907; the building has undergone some minor restoration but it still retains its basic character. There are three floors, and the building has 42-inch walls. The third floor houses the main part of the restaurant. Featured dishes include certified Angus beef, fajitas, pollo relleno, and different types of pastas. **FYI:** Reservations accepted. Children's menu. **Open:** Mon–Thurs 11am–10pm, Fri–Sat 11am–11pm. **Prices:** Main courses $13–$20. AE, CB, DC, MC, V. 👥

New Orleans Cafe

1536 E County Line Rd; tel 601/957-2459. 1½ mi E of I-55. **Cajun/Creole.** Designed like a New Orleans–style enclosed courtyard, complete with wrought-iron fences. The menu matches the decor, with many Cajun-style dishes like jambalaya, crawfish étoufée, and crawfish enchiladas. **FYI:** Reservations accepted. Children's menu. **Open:** Mon–Thurs 11am–10pm, Fri–Sat 11am–11pm, Sun 11am–3pm. **Prices:** Main courses $5–$15. AE, DISC, MC, V. 👥

★ Old Tyme Delicatessen & Bakery

1305 E Northside Dr; tel 601/362-2565. At I-55. **Deli.** The only "kosher" deli in Jackson has a clientele that spans the state (although the only authentically kosher items offered are knockwurst and frankfurters). Some of their more popular items include sandwiches like the Rebel (imported ham, Genoa salami, cheddar cheese, lettuce, tomato and Russian dressing). A small shop offers an assortment of gourmet items. **FYI:** Reservations accepted. Beer and wine only. **Open:** Tues–Sat 6am–9pm. **Prices:** Main courses $3–$7. MC, V. 👥

ATTRACTIONS 📷

Governor's Mansion

300 E Capitol St; tel 601/359-3175. This restored Greek Revival mansion has been home to Mississippi's governors since 1842; the beautifully restored building houses an impressive collection of 19th-century decorative arts and museum-quality antiques. It is one of only two executive residences designated a National Historic Landmark and is one of the few historic buildings in Jackson to survive the Civil War. Grounds include landscaped gardens and a gazebo. Guided tours given on the half-hour. **Open:** Tues–Fri 9:30–11am. **Free**

Old Capitol Museum

100 S State St; tel 601/359-6920. Mississippians are justly proud of this beautifully restored Greek Revival–style building, which served as the new state's capitol from 1839 to 1903 and which has survived several attempts to have it demolished. Exhibits and historic rooms include approximately 30,000 artifacts chronicling the story of Mississippi from prehistory through the civil rights movement of the 1960s, and portraits of 84 distinguished Mississippians are hung throughout the building. **Open:** Mon–Fri 8am–5pm, Sat 9:30am–4:30pm, Sun 12:30–4:30pm. Closed some hols. **Free**

Mississippi Museum of Art

201 E Pascagoula St; tel 601/960-1515. The largest art museum in Mississippi, the MMA owns over 5,000 works. Besides concentrating in the work of Mississippi and Southern natives, the permanent collection is strong in 19th- and 20th-century landscape painting, 18th-century British paintings and furniture, Japanese prints, and pre-Columbian ceramics. The Art Cafe serves light, gourmet lunches. **Open:** Tues–Sat 10am–5pm. Closed some hols. **$**

Dizzy Dean Museum

1204 Lakeland Dr; tel 601/960-2404. A small, local museum housing artifacts and personal effects of Mississippi native, famous St Louis Cardinals pitcher, and radio announcer Jay Hanna "Dizzy" Dean. **Open:** Apr–Sept, Tues–Sat 11am–6pm, Sun 1–5pm. **$**

Smith Robertson Museum and Cultural Center
528 Bloom St; tel 601/960-1457. Housed in the city's first public school open to black children, this facility portrays the experiences and contributions of Mississippi's African Americans in the fields of history, education, business, politics, and the arts. Historical exhibits, folk art demonstrations, workshops, and public forums are offered, as is a gift shop selling an array of local African American crafts. **Open:** Mon–Fri 9am–5pm, Sat 9am–noon, Sun 2–5pm. Closed some hols. **$**

Laurel

Laurel, in southeastern Mississippi, maintains a country homestead and village. An industrial and manufacturing city, it is home to Masonite Corporation, which has the world's largest hardboard manufacturing plant. Birthplace of opera star Leontyne Price. **Information:** Jones County Chamber of Commerce, 153 Base Dr #3, PO Box 527, Laurel, 39440 (tel 601/428-2047).

MOTELS 🏨

≣≣ Days Inn
At jct US 11 N/I-59, PO Box 4116, 39441; tel 601/428-8421 or toll free 800/329-7466; fax 601/649-0938. Dependable accommodations are the attraction at this typical chain motel. **Rooms:** 85 rms. CI 3pm/CO 11am. Nonsmoking rms avail. **Amenities:** 🛁 A/C, cable TV w/movies. **Services:** ✗ 🖼 🛏 🐾 **Facilities:** 🔧 🍴 ⅙ 1 restaurant, 1 bar (w/entertainment), washer/dryer. **Rates:** $29–$33 S; $34–$40 D. Extra person $5. Children under age 12 stay free. **Parking:** Outdoor, free. AE, CB, DC, DISC, JCB, MC, V.

≣≣ Ramada Inn
1105 Sawmill Rd, PO Box 688, 39441; tel 601/649-9100 or toll free 800/272-6232; fax 601/649-6045. At jct US 1/US 84 off I-59. Well-kept and attractive Ramada offering lots of family-friendly amenities. **Rooms:** 207 rms, stes, and effic. CI 3pm/CO 11am. Nonsmoking rms avail. **Amenities:** 🛁 A/C, cable TV w/movies. Some units w/whirlpools. **Services:** 🛏 🐾 Babysitting. **Facilities:** 🔧 🍴 ⅙ **Rates:** $42–$51 S; $47–$56 D; $100–$120 ste. Extra person $5. Children under age 12 stay free. **Parking:** Outdoor, free. AE, DC, DISC, MC, V.

ATTRACTION 🏛

Lauren Rogers Museum of Art
5th Ave at 7th St; tel 601/649-6374. The permanent collection includes European paintings, drawings, and prints of the 19th century, as well as American works of the 19th and 20th centuries. The museum is particularly noted for its collections of English Georgian silver, Japanese wood block prints, and Native American baskets. **Open:** Tues–Sat 10am–4:45pm, Sun 1–4pm. Closed some hols. **Free**

Louisville

Located in the Redhills 45 miles southwest of Columbus, Louisville is host to the Redhills Festival in May. Lake Tiak O'Khata is here, and nearby is Tombigbee National Forest. **Information:** Louisville–Winston County Chamber of Commerce, 311 W Park St, PO Box 551, Louisville, 39339 (tel 601/773-3921).

RESTAURANT 🍽

★ Lake Tiak O'Khata Restaurant
Smyth Lake Rd; tel 601/773-7853. ¼ mi W of US 15. **Regional American.** This eatery offers relaxing resort atmosphere and good country cooking. Fried chicken, chicken and dumplings, and pork chops with gravy (with side dishes like collard greens and lima beans) star on the dinner menu and at the daily buffet. Seafood buffet offered Sat 5:30–9pm. **FYI:** Reservations recommended. Piano. Children's menu. Beer and wine only. **Open:** Daily 6am–10pm. **Prices:** Main courses $6–$15. AE, DC, DISC, MC, V. 🍽 🏞 👥 ⅙

McComb

Located in the southern part of the state, an hour's drive east of Natchez. Famous native son Will Price was the script consultant for *Gone With the Wind* (and later married one of the film's stars, Maureen O'Hara). **Information:** Pike County Chamber of Commerce, 617 Delaware Ave, PO Box 83, McComb, 39648 (tel 601/684-2291)

HOTEL 🏨

≣≣≣ Holiday Inn
1900 Delaware Ave, 39648; tel 601/684-6211 or toll free 800/HOLIDAY; fax 601/684-0408. Off I-55. Quiet, laid-back hotel with a leisure courtyard. **Rooms:** 148 rms and stes. CI 3pm/CO noon. Nonsmoking rms avail. Comfortable, well-decorated rooms. **Amenities:** 🛁 ⚙ A/C, satel TV w/movies. **Services:** ✗ 🖼 🛏 🐾 **Facilities:** 🔧 🍴 ⅙ 1 restaurant, 1 bar (w/entertainment). Enclosed, Olympic-size swimming pool. **Rates (BB):** $46 S; $52 D; $75 ste. Extra person $7. Children under age 18 stay free. **Parking:** Outdoor, free. AE, DC, DISC, JCB, MC, V.

MOTEL 🏨

≣≣≣ Ramada Inn
I-55 at Delaware Ave, PO Box 1460, 39648; tel 601/684-5566 or toll free 800/2-RAMADA; fax 601/684-0641. Designed for businesspeople who require a lot of meeting space, this motel is suitable for families as well. **Rooms:** 150 rms and stes. Executive level. CI open/CO 1pm. Nonsmoking rms avail. Comfortable, basic rooms. **Amenities:** 🛁 ⚙ A/C, cable TV w/movies. 1 unit w/whirlpool. **Services:** ✗ 🖼 🛏 🐾 Room service available depending on how busy the

restaurant is. **Facilities:** 🖼 📷 ⛱ 1 restaurant, 1 bar (w/entertainment). **Rates (BB):** Peak (May–Aug) $43–$49 S; $49–$55 D; $145–$155 ste. Extra person $6. Children under age 18 stay free. Lower rates off-season. Parking: Outdoor, free. AE, CB, DC, DISC, JCB, MC, V.

Meridian

Located 10 miles west of the Alabama state border, this rural town was founded in the early 18th century at the intersection of two major rail lines; today, its grand Opera House hints at former glories. **Information:** Meridian–Lauderdale County Partnership, PO Box 790, Meridian, 39302 (tel 601/ 693-1306).

HOTELS 🏨

📋 Best Western Meridian
2219 S Frontage Rd, 39301; tel 601/693-3210 or toll free 800/528-1234; fax 601/693-3210. Exit 153 off I-20 at I-59. Average hotel with few frills; adequate for an overnight stay. **Rooms:** 120 rms. CI 2pm/CO noon. Nonsmoking rms avail. Larger-than-average rooms. **Amenities:** 🛁 A/C, cable TV w/movies. **Services:** ✗ 🖼 ⛱ Babysitting. **Facilities:** 🖼 📷 ⛱ 1 restaurant, 1 bar (w/entertainment), playground, washer/dryer. **Rates (CP):** $33–$39 S; $43–$53 D. Extra person $5. Children under age 12 stay free. Parking: Outdoor, free. AE, CB, DC, DISC, EC, MC, V.

📋 Hampton Inn
103 US 11/80, 39301; tel 601/483-3000 or toll free 800/426-7866; fax 601/483-3000. A business-oriented hotel. **Rooms:** 116 rms and stes. CI 3pm/CO noon. Nonsmoking rms avail. Rooms are large and have relatively new beds and bedding. **Amenities:** 🛁 A/C, cable TV w/movies. **Services:** ✗ 🖼 ⛱ Whirlpool. **Rates (CP):** $49–$54 S or D; $92 ste. Extra person $5. Children under age 18 stay free. Parking: Outdoor, free. AE, DC, DISC, MC, V.

📋 Holiday Inn Northeast
111 US 11/80, 39302; tel 601/485-5101 or toll free 800/HOLIDAY; fax 601/485-5101. ½ mi from I-20. Gorgeous landscaping sets this property apart from the competition. **Rooms:** 191 rms and stes. CI 2pm/CO noon. Nonsmoking rms avail. **Amenities:** 🛁 A/C, cable TV w/movies. **Services:** 🍽 🖼 ⛱ Babysitting. **Facilities:** 🖼 🎱 📷 ⛱ 1 restaurant, 1 bar, playground, washer/dryer. **Rates (CP):** $54 S; $59 D; $95–$100 ste. Extra person $5. Children under age 12 stay free. Parking: Outdoor, free. Rates are based on occupancy. AE, CB, DC, DISC, JCB, MC, V.

📋 Holiday Inn South
1401 Roebuck Dr, 39301; tel 601/693-4521 or toll free 800/HOLIDAY; fax 601/693-4521. S of US 45. Well-maintained low-rise property; more than adequate for interstate travelers. **Rooms:** 172 rms and stes. CI open/CO noon. Nonsmok-

ing rms avail. **Amenities:** 🛁 🎱 📷 A/C, cable TV w/movies, dataport. **Services:** ✗ 🖼 ⛱ Facilities: 🖼 📷 ⛱ 1 restaurant, 1 bar, playground, washer/dryer. **Rates:** $47–$57 S; $52–$62 D; $144–$149 ste. Extra person $5. Children under age 18 stay free. Min stay special events. Parking: Outdoor, free. AE, CB, DC, DISC, JCB, MC, V.

📋 Ramada Limited
2915 St Paul St, 39301; tel 601/485-2722 or toll free 800/2-RAMADA; fax 601/485-3960. Exit 152 off I-20/I-59. Secluded hotel, good for those wanting to get away and relax. **Rooms:** 50 rms and stes. CI noon/CO noon. Nonsmoking rms avail. Rooms are well decorated. **Amenities:** 🛁 🎱 A/C, cable TV w/movies. **Services:** ⛱ Facilities: 🖼 📷 ⛱ Sauna, steam rm, whirlpool. **Rates (CP):** Peak (June 15–Aug) $36–$56 S; $40–$70 D; $55–$65 ste. Extra person $5. Children under age 18 stay free. Lower rates off-season. Parking: Outdoor, free. AE, CB, DC, DISC, EC, JCB, MC, V.

MOTELS

📋 Days Inn
145 US 80 E, 39301; tel 601/483-3812 or toll free 800/DAYS-INN; fax 601/483-3812. At US 11. Basic, bare-bones accommodations suitable for an overnight stay. **Rooms:** 115 rms and stes. CI 1pm/CO 11am. Nonsmoking rms avail. **Amenities:** 🛁 A/C, cable TV w/movies. **Services:** ✗ 🖼 ⛱ Facilities: 🖼 ⛱ 1 restaurant, washer/dryer. **Rates:** Peak (May 25–Aug) $36–$45 S; $44–$65 D; $65–$85 ste. Extra person $5. Children under age 12 stay free. Lower rates off-season. Parking: Outdoor, free. AE, DC, DISC, JCB, MC, V.

📋 Howard Johnson's
110 US 80 E, PO Box 588, 39301; tel 601/483-8281 or toll free 800/446-4656; fax 601/483-8281. A nice place for a short stay. Good value. **Rooms:** 136 rms and stes. Executive level. CI noon/CO noon. Nonsmoking rms avail. **Amenities:** 🛁 A/C, cable TV w/movies. All units w/terraces. **Services:** ⛱ Babysitting. **Facilities:** 🖼 📷 ⛱ 1 bar (w/entertainment), games rm, whirlpool, washer/dryer. **Rates:** $48–$80 S; $50–$85 D; $95–$175 ste. Extra person $4. Children under age 18 stay free. Parking: Outdoor, free. AE, CB, DC, DISC, JCB, MC, V.

RESTAURANTS 🍴

🌿 Hollybrook Fine Dining
1200 22nd Ave (Downtown); tel 601/693-7584. Near Front St. **Seafood/Steak.** Housed in an old two-story building with well-decorated rooms and a menu focusing on steaks and seafood. All desserts are homemade. **FYI:** Reservations accepted. Guitar/piano. Children's menu. **Open:** Lunch Mon–Sat 11am–2pm; dinner Mon–Sat 5–9pm. Closed Jan 1–7. **Prices:** Main courses $11–$22. AE, DISC, MC, V. ♥ 🍴 👪

★ Threefoot Deli
In Threefoot Building, 601 22nd Ave, Suite 100 (Downtown); tel 601/693-9952. At 6th St. **Deli.** The decor here is nothing

fancy—they use paper plates and plastic silverware—but the food is wonderful. Hearty, Southern-style breakfasts and hot and cold deli sandwiches keep loyal customers coming back. **FYI:** Reservations accepted. BYO. No smoking. **Open:** Mon–Fri 7am–3pm. **Prices:** Lunch main courses $4–$6. MC, V.

★ Weidman's

210 22nd Ave (Downtown); tel 601/693-1751. at 5th St. **Seafood/Steak.** Opened in 1870, this has become a landmark in the Meridian area. The building still sports its original sign and has decorations dating back to the 19th century. Some of their more popular dishes include prime rib, crab Belvedere, trout amandine, crab Norfolk, stuffed shrimp, stuffed flounder, and garlic-broiled shrimp. **FYI:** Reservations accepted. Children's menu. Jacket required. **Open:** Daily 7am–9:30pm. **Prices:** Main courses $8–$18. AE, CB, DC, DISC, MC, V. 🍴 🖼

ATTRACTIONS 🖼

Jimmie Rodgers Museum

1725 Jimmie Rodgers Rd; tel 601/485-1808 or toll free 800/748-9970. The "Father of Country Music" is immortalized in this collection of memorabilia, including guitars and costumes, located in a reconstructed train depot. **Open:** Mon–Sat 10am–4pm, Sun 1–5pm. Closed some hols. **$**

Highland Park Dentzel Carousel

Highland Park Dr; tel 601/485-1801. This gorgeous two-row antique carousel features 28 handcarved-wood animals including deer with real antlers, goats, giraffes, lions, tigers, and 20 horses with real horsehair tails, as well as two chariots. Originally part of the 1905 St Louis Exposition, the carousel moved to Meridian in 1909 and was designated a National Historic Landmark in 1986. **Open:** June–Aug, Mon–Fri 1–6pm, Sat–Sun 1–5pm; Sept–May, Sat–Sun 1–5pm. Closed some hols. **Free**

Natchez

The oldest settlement along the Mississippi River. Situated on 200-foot bluffs overlooking the river, it was claimed "the most desirable site on the river" by 17th-century French explorer LaSalle. Prior to the Civil War, over half of America's millionaires lived here; many of their elegant antebellum houses are still extant. Its historic district, once a steamboat landing and notorious hangout for rowdy travelers, now features popular nightlife, including casino gambling.

Romantic legend has it that the 1791 marriage of Andrew Jackson to Rachel Robards took place at the Springfield Plantation in nearby Fayette (20 miles northeast of Natchez). In 1969, political history was made in Fayette with the election of Charles Evers, the first black mayor of a racially mixed city. **Information:** Natchez–Adams County Convention & Visitors Bureau, 422 Main St, PO Box 1485, Natchez, 39121 (tel 601/446-6345).

HOTELS 🏨

≡≡≡ Best Western River Park Hotel

645 S Canal St, 39120; tel 601/446-6688 or toll free 800/274-5532; fax 601/442-9823. At US 84. Mid-rise hotel with comfortable rooms and a recently renovated lobby. **Rooms:** 147 rms and stes. CI 1pm/CO noon. Nonsmoking rms avail. **Amenities:** 🛁 👗 A/C, cable TV w/movies. **Services:** ✕ 🛄 👐 **Facilities:** 🛗 [160] 👟 1 restaurant, 1 bar (w/entertainment), whirlpool. **Rates:** Peak (Mar, Apr, Oct) $59–$69 S; $69–$79 D; $118–$177 ste. Extra person $5. Children under age 12 stay free. Lower rates off-season. Parking: Outdoor, free. AE, CB, DC, DISC, MC, V.

≡≡ Holiday Inn

271 D'Evereux Dr, 39120; tel 601/442-3686 or toll free 800/HOLIDAY; fax 601/446-9998. At US 84. 7 acres. Well-kept two-story hotel. Popular with vacationing families. **Rooms:** 139 rms and stes. CI 3pm/CO 1pm. Nonsmoking rms avail. **Amenities:** 🛁 👗 A/C, cable TV w/movies, dataport. **Services:** ✕ 🛄 👐 👐 Free continental breakfast or $2 off any breakfast menu order. **Facilities:** 🛗 [130] 👟 1 restaurant, washer/dryer. **Rates (CP):** Peak (Mar–Apr) $53–$59 S or D; $125–$175 ste. Extra person $6. Children under age 18 stay free. Lower rates off-season. Parking: Outdoor, free. AE, CB, DC, DISC, JCB, MC, V.

≡≡≡ Natchez Eola Hotel

110 N Pearl St, 39120; tel 601/445-6000 or toll free 800/888-9140; fax 601/446-5310. At Main St. A gracious hotel, originally built in the 1920s, offering Southern ambience and lovely views of the Mississippi. **Rooms:** 125 rms and stes. Executive level. CI 2pm/CO noon. Nonsmoking rms avail. Some rooms have full-length mirrors. Suites have two baths and two phones. **Amenities:** 🛁 👗 A/C, cable TV. Some units w/terraces. **Services:** ✕ 🆅🅿 🛄 👐 👐 Car-rental desk, social director, children's program, babysitting. **Facilities:** [400] 2 restaurants, 2 bars. **Rates:** $60 S; $70 D; $125 ste. Children under age 12 stay free. Parking: Outdoor, free. AE, CB, DC, MC, V.

≡≡≡ Ramada Inn Hilltop

130 John R Junkin Dr, 39120; tel 601/446-6311 or toll free 800/256-6311; fax 601/446-6321. Guests at this hotel will appreciate the spectacular views of the Mississippi and the "customer comes first" attitude of the staff. Located five minutes from downtown. **Rooms:** 162 rms and stes. CI 2pm/CO 1pm. Nonsmoking rms avail. Some suites have wet bars. Suites can accommodate small meetings or conferences (up to about 16 people). **Amenities:** 🛁 👗 A/C, cable TV w/movies. Some units w/terraces. **Services:** ✕ 🍴 🛄 👐 👐 Staff is very service-oriented. **Facilities:** 🛗 [300] 👟 1 restaurant, 1 bar (w/entertainment), washer/dryer. **Rates:** Peak (Mar, Oct) $42–$60 S; $45–$70 D; $85–$140 ste. Extra person $5. Children under age 12 stay free. Lower rates off-season. Parking: Outdoor, free. AE, CB, DC, DISC, JCB, MC, V.

MOTELS

▬▬ Days Inn

109 US 61 S, 39120; tel 601/445-8291 or toll free 800/ DAYS-INN; fax 601/442-4861. Well-maintained motel with the basic amenities, attractive views, and well-kept grounds. **Rooms:**. CI 3pm/CO 11am. Nonsmoking rms avail. **Amenities:** 🛏 🅰 A/C, cable TV w/movies. **Services:** 🖼 🍽 🍴 **Facilities:** 🛗 🏊 **Rates (CP):** Peak (Mar and Oct) $42–$47 S; $47–$62 D; $57–$72 ste. Extra person $5. Children under age 12 stay free. Lower rates off-season. Parking: Outdoor, free. AE, DC, DISC, MC, V.

▬▬ Howard Johnson Lodge

45 Sargeant Prentiss, 39120; tel 601/442-1691 or toll free 800/446-4656; fax 601/445-5895. A winning two-story chain motel. Popular with business travelers. **Rooms:** 120 rms and stes. CI 3pm/CO noon. Nonsmoking rms avail. **Amenities:** 🛏 🅰 A/C, cable TV w/movies. **Services:** 🍽 🍴 Babysitting. **Facilities:** 🛗 🏊 🅰 **Rates (CP):** Peak (Oct, Nov) $46–$51 S; $51–$56 D; $70–$90 ste. Extra person $5. Children under age 12 stay free. Lower rates off-season. Parking: Outdoor, free. AE, CB, DC, DISC, MC, V.

INNS

▬▬▬ The Burn

712 N Union St, 39120; tel 601/442-1344 or toll free 800/ 654-8859; fax 601/445-0606. 4½ acres. Romantic three-story inn (built in 1834) featuring formal gardens, antiques, and plantationlike white columns. Good choice for couples. Unsuitable for children under 12. **Rooms:** 7 rms and stes. CI 2pm/CO 11am. No smoking. Rather large rooms, some with garden views. **Amenities:** 🛏 🅰 A/C, cable TV w/movies, bathrobes. Some units w/fireplaces. Morning coffee can be delivered to room, with prior arrangement. **Services:** Wine/ sherry served. **Facilities:** 🛗 🏊 Washer/dryer, guest lounge. Well-maintained pool is open all day and all evening. **Rates (BB):** $80–$90 S; $90–$100 D; $115–$125 ste. Extra person $20. Parking: Outdoor, free. AE, DISC, MC, V.

▬▬▬ Monmouth Plantation

36 Melrose Ave, 39120; tel 601/442-5852 or toll free 800/ 828-4531; fax 601/446-7762. At John Quitman Pkwy. 26 acres. Built in 1818, this handsome two-story mansion has been completely renovated to provide excellent comfort and relaxation for its guests. Wonderful antique furniture makes the atmosphere very romantic. Unsuitable for children under 14. **Rooms:** 25 rms and stes. CI 3pm/CO 11am. No smoking. All rooms are individually decorated. **Amenities:** 🛏 🅰 🍽 A/C, cable TV w/movies, dataport, bathrobes. Some units w/terraces, some w/fireplaces, some w/whirlpools. **Services:** 🖼 Afternoon tea and wine/sherry served. Tours may be prearranged. **Facilities:** 🍴 🏊 🅰 1 restaurant (bkfst and dinner only), 1 bar, guest lounge w/TV. **Rates (BB):** $105–$145 S or

D; $150–$185 ste. Extra person $35. MAP rates avail. Parking: Outdoor, free. Rates are fixed according to suite. AE, DC, DISC, MC, V.

RESTAURANTS 🍽

★ Cock-of-the-Walk

In On the Bluff, 200 N Broadway (Downtown); tel 601/ 446-8920. At Franklin. **Regional American.** The dining area has the feel of an old-time railroad station, with antique-looking chairs and tables and old decorations such as tobacco trays. Entrees include fried catfish fillets, blackened catfish, and Downriver Chicken; unique side dishes include fried dill pickles, hush puppies, and coleslaw. **FYI:** Reservations not accepted. Piano. Children's menu. Additional locations: Cock of the Walk, Jackson (tel 856-5500); Cock of the Walk, Nashville (tel 615/889-1930). **Open:** Mon–Thurs 5–9pm, Fri–Sat 5–10pm, Sun 11:30am–1:30pm 5–8pm. **Prices:** Main courses $9–$11. AE, CB, DC, DISC, ER, MC, V. 🖼

⑤ The Fare Cafe

109 N Pearl St; tel 601/442-5299. Across from the Natchez Eola Hotel. **American.** Small diner-type establishment with mostly burgers and sandwiches, plus a few other items. Great selection of homemade desserts. Will prepare box lunches to go. **FYI:** Reservations accepted. BYO. **Open:** Peak (Mar, Apr, Oct) breakfast Mon–Sat 7:30–10am; lunch Mon–Sat 11am– 3pm. **Prices:** Main courses $4–$6. MC, V. 🛥

★ Liza's Contemporary Cuisine

657 S Canal St; tel 601/446-6368. 1 block N of US 84. **Regional American.** Housed in a 1852 house with glorious views of the Mississippi, this establishment is known throughout Natchez for its inventive cuisine made from fresh local ingredients. The menu changes regularly, but always includes a variety of steaks, pasta, seafood, veal, and pork. Vegetarian selections and luscious desserts are also available. **FYI:** Reservations recommended. **Open:** Peak (Oct, Mar) Tues–Thurs 6–9pm, Fri–Sat 6–10pm. **Prices:** Main courses $13–$17. AE, DISC, MC, V. 💗 🍴

Pearl Street Pasta

105 S Pearl St (Downtown); tel 601/442-9284. At Main Street. **Italian.** A small, cozy place built in the early 1960s. Pasta options include the classic favorites: lasagna, fettuccine Alfredo, pasta primavera, and spaghetti. All entrees come with house salad and garlic bread. **FYI:** Reservations not accepted. No liquor license. **Open:** Lunch Mon–Fri 11am– 2pm; dinner Mon–Sat 6–9pm. **Prices:** Main courses $8–$14. AE, DISC, MC, V.

ATTRACTIONS 🏛

Natchez National Historical Park

Tel 601/442-7047 or 446-5790. The main draw here is 80-acre Melrose Estate, the former home of John and Mary McMurran. The antebellum Greek Revival mansion was completed in 1845; the house, its outbuildings, a formal garden, and a re-created slave cabin are included as part of a self-guided tour. **Open:** Daily 8:30am–5pm. Closed some hols. **Free**

Historic Springfield Plantation

Jct MS 553 and Natchez Trace Pkwy, Fayette; tel 601/786-3802. Located 20 mi NE of Natchez, just off the Natchez Trace Parkway. Built in 1784 by wealthy Virginia planter Thomas Marston Green Jr, Springfield was one of the first mansions in Mississippi, and the first to be built with a full colonnade across its facade. The house itself remains almost entirely original, with hand-carved 18th-century woodwork and mantels. Displays of Civil War and railroad memorabilia. **Open:** Daily 10am–sunset. Closed Dec 25. **$$$**

Dunleith

84 Homochitto St; tel 601/446-8500 or toll free 800/433-2445. The lower floor of this 1856 Greek Revival mansion is open for tours by the public, while the second floor serves as a B&B. Built in 1856, the graceful white columns of Dunleith's exterior, and the opulent, French-inspired furnishings of its exterior, provide a fine example of antebellum elegance. The 40-acre grounds encompass bayous, pastures, and formal gardens. Tours begin every 20 minutes between the hours of 9am and 4:25pm. **Open:** Daily 9am–5pm. Closed some hols. **$$**

The Grand Village of the Natchez Indians

400 Jefferson Davis Blvd; tel 601/446-6502. The center of Natchez Indian culture during the 1500s. The Natchez, an agriculture-based and matrilineal society, were driven out of their "Grand Village" by the French in 1730. Today's visitors can see a reconstructed Natchez house and corn granary, a prehistoric ceremonial plaza, and several earthen mounds that were used as foundations for culturally important buildings such as temples. **Open:** Mon–Sat 9am–5pm, Sun 1:30–5pm. Closed some hols. **Free**

Old South Winery

64 S Concord Ave; tel 601/445-9924. Muscadine grapes have been grown in the Mississippi delta for centuries, and for most of that time people have been turning the local grapes into wine. But as a result of Prohibition, it was illegal to produce wine in Mississippi until 1978. That same year the Galbreath family opened Old South, one of very few wineries in the Deep South. Winery visitors are invited to sample 12 varieties of wine on the winery tour, or take a few bottles home as souvenirs. (Each label depicts a different Natchez scene.) **Open:** Mon–Sat 10am–5pm, Sun 11am–5pm. Closed some hols. **Free**

Ocean Springs

Site of the first permanent European settlement in the lower Mississippi Valley, established in 1699 by Pierre Le Moyne, sieur d'Iberville. The annual D'Iberville Festival commemorates the event. **Information:** Ocean Springs Chamber of Commerce, PO Box 187, Ocean Springs, 39564 (tel 601/875-4424).

RESORT

≡≡ Seven Oaks Gulf Hills Resort

13701 Paso Rd, 39564; tel 601/875-4211 or toll free 800/638-4902; fax 601/872-3504. 80 acres. A well-maintained resort offering a private oceanside getaway. Suitable for families or couples. **Rooms:** 65 rms and stes. Executive level. CI 4pm/CO 1pm. Nonsmoking rms avail. Many rooms are very large and offer extra closet space. **Amenities:** A/C, cable TV w/movies, dataport. 1 unit w/minibar. **Services:** X Social director, children's program, babysitting. **Facilities:** 18 8 200 1 restaurant, 1 bar (w/entertainment), volleyball, sauna, playground. Huge outdoor pool with nice tables and chairs, and a partially covered deck area. **Rates:** Peak (June–Aug) $65–$75 S or D; $110–$125 ste. Extra person $8. Children under age 21 stay free. Lower rates off-season. Parking: Outdoor, free. AE, CB, DC, DISC, MC, V.

RESTAURANTS

★ Germaine's

1203 Bienville Blvd/US 90 E; tel 601/875-4426. **Seafood.** Ensconced in a beautifully remodeled old house, with contemporary art on the walls and antique clocks scattered throughout. Some of the more popular entrees include crabmeat au gratin (lump crabmeat baked in a rich cheese sauce) and mushroom Le Marin. **FYI:** Reservations accepted. Children's menu. **Open:** Lunch Tues–Sun 11:30am–2pm; dinner Tues–Sat 6–10pm. Closed Jan 1–Jan 14. **Prices:** Main courses $4–$22. AE, CB, DC, DISC, MC, V.

★ Jocelyn's Restaurant

US 90 E; tel 601/875-1925. On US 90 E. **Creole.** A well-known, cozy place located in a remodeled, four-bedroom house. Some of the more popular Creole/Cajun dishes include the 10-oz rib eye and the trout and seafood casserole. **FYI:** Reservations not accepted. Children's menu. **Open:** Mon–Sat 5–10pm. **Prices:** Main courses $9–$16. No CC.

ATTRACTION

Gulf Islands National Seashore

3500 Park Rd; tel 601/875-9057. These barrier islands off the northeastern shore of the Gulf of Mexico stretch all the way into western Florida. Their sandy white beaches, clear blue waters, lush greenery, and abundant wildlife make them an ideal spot for a long vacation or a day at the beach, but these islands perform a much more important function. The barrier formed by this 150-mile stretch of islands and sandbars protects the coastline from violent storms and provides a safe haven for valuable marine life. The nutrient-rich waters between the islands and the mainland are ideal for shrimp, crab, and oyster.

The park itself is located partly on the mainland and partly on the islands. The section in Ocean Springs offers a fishing pier, boating ramp, campground, and picnic area. The islands themselves are less developed and can be reached only by boat. **West Ship Island,** the most accessible of the Mississippi islands, has picnicking facilities and a beach for swimming. Ranger stations are located on West Ship Island and Horn Island in Mississippi and Johnson Beach and Fort Barrancas in Florida. **Open:** Visitor center, daily 8am–5pm; park, sunrise–sunset. Closed Dec 25. **Free**

Oxford

Oxford is home of the University of Mississippi, founded in 1848. General Grant and his troops occupied the campus in 1862 and a handful of the original buildings survived the 1864 burning of the city. Oxford was home to writer William Faulkner, who modeled fictional Yoknapatawpha County after it; his antebellum home is now open to visitors. The university's library displays Faulkner's 1950 Nobel Prize, first edition prints of his books, and other memorabilia; while its Blues Archive contains the world's largest collection of blues music. **Information:** Oxford Tourism Council, 299 W Jackson Ave, PO Box 965, Oxford, 38655 (tel 601/234-4651).

HOTELS 🏨

🛏🛏 Best Western Oxford Inn
1101 Frontage Rd, 38655; tel 601/234-9500 or toll free 800/528-1234; fax 601/234-9500. Just off US 6. An engaging place with a family-friendly atmosphere. **Rooms:** 100 rms. CI 2pm/CO noon. Nonsmoking rms avail. **Amenities:** 🛎 📺 🍴 A/C, cable TV w/movies. VCRs available upon request. **Services:** ✗ 🛗 🚸 ⟳ **Facilities:** 🔥 🏊120 1 restaurant (bkfst and dinner only), 1 bar. **Rates:** Peak (Sept–Oct) $49–$54 S; $44–$59 D. Extra person $4. Children under age 12 stay free. Lower rates off-season. Parking: Outdoor, free. AE, DC, DISC, MC, V.

🛏🛏 Comfort Inn
290 Power Dr, Batesville, 38606; tel 601/563-1188 or toll free 800/228-5150; fax 601/563-1188. Exit 243B off I-55. A fine choice for businesspeople. The well-decorated lobby has plenty of seating for conducting meetings or just relaxing. **Rooms:** 51 rms. Executive level. CI 2pm/CO 11am. Nonsmoking rms avail. **Amenities:** 🛎 🔥 A/C, cable TV w/movies, refrig, dataport, voice mail. **Services:** 🍴 🚐 🚸 **Facilities:** 🔥 🔥 Washer/dryer. **Rates (CP):** Peak (Mar–Nov) $42–$65 S; $48–$80 D. Extra person $5. Children under age 17 stay free. Lower rates off-season. Parking: Outdoor, free. AE, CB, DC, DISC, JCB, MC, V.

🛏🛏🛏 Days Inn
280 Power Dr, Batesville, 38606; tel 601/563-4999 or toll free 800/329-7466; fax 601/563-4999. Exit 243 B off I-55. The management here is very conscious of their guests'

needs. Ideal for any type of traveler. **Rooms:** 49 rms and stes. Executive level. CI 2pm/CO 11am. Nonsmoking rms avail. Very attractive decor. **Amenities:** 🛎 A/C, cable TV w/movies, refrig, dataport, voice mail. **Services:** 🍴 🚐 🚸 ⟳ **Facilities:** 🔥 🏊50 🔥 Washer/dryer. **Rates (CP):** Peak (Mar–Nov) $36–$60 S; $42–$70 D; $50–$95 ste. Extra person $5. Children under age 17 stay free. Lower rates off-season. Parking: Outdoor, free. AE, CB, DC, DISC, JCB, MC, V.

🛏🛏🛏 Holiday Inn
400 N Lamar, PO Box 647, 38655; tel 601/234-3031 or toll free 800/HOLIDAY; fax 601/234-2834. Recently renovated hotel located one block north of town square. Most suitable for businesspeople. **Rooms:** 123 rms and stes. Executive level. CI 2pm/CO 1pm. Nonsmoking rms avail. **Amenities:** 🛎 🔥 📺 🍴 A/C, cable TV w/movies, dataport. Some rooms have microwaves and refrigerators. **Services:** ✗ 🚐 🛗 🚸 ⟳ Babysitting. **Facilities:** 🔥 🏊175 1 restaurant, 1 bar, washer/dryer. Free passes to Gold's Gym. **Rates:** $57–$75 S; $65–$80 D; $80–$175 ste. Extra person $6. Children under age 12 stay free. Min stay special events. Parking: Outdoor, free. AE, CB, DC, DISC, JCB, MC, V.

🛏🛏 Ramada Inn University
2201 Jackson Ave, 38655; tel 601/234-7013 or toll free 800/2-RAMADA; fax 601/236-4378. 1½ mi W of the university. Very new, modern-looking facility, best suited for businesspeople, families, students, and long-term stays. **Rooms:** 116 rms and stes. CI 2pm/CO noon. Nonsmoking rms avail. Suites feature sofa sectionals with recliners, desks. **Amenities:** 🛎 🔥 📺 A/C, cable TV w/movies, refrig. Some units w/whirlpools. All suites have hair dryers and three telephones (one in bathroom), some have tape players. **Services:** 🛗 🚸 ⟳ Manager's reception (Mon–Thurs, 5:30–7pm) includes a complimentary drink. **Facilities:** 🔥 🏊100 No elevators. Room keys act as guest passes at gym (a minimal charge may apply). **Rates:** $44–$75 S; $46–$75 D; $115–$150 ste. Extra person $6. Children under age 12 stay free. Min stay special events. Parking: Outdoor, free. AE, DC, DISC, ER, JCB, MC, V.

RESTAURANTS 🍽

Downtown Grill
1115 Jackson Ave; tel 601/234-2659. **Regional American.** Some of the more popular dishes at this simple yet elegant restaurant include filet mignon, coated with cracked black pepper and sautéed with vegetables and a butter cream sauce; tournedos Nantua—filet mignon topped with crawfish tails in a lobster sauce, and garnished with petite lobster tails; and seasoned catfish filet. All desserts (except the cheesecake) are homemade. Two floors, with several separate dining areas, offer more privacy. **FYI:** Reservations accepted. Jazz/piano. **Open:** Mon–Wed 11am–10pm, Thurs–Sat 11am–11pm. **Prices:** Main courses $12–$23. AE, DISC, MC, V. ❤ 🎪 🔥

★ **El Charro**
1417 W Jackson Ave; tel 601/236-0058. ½ mile from US 6. **Mexican.** Popular establishment known for hearty burritos, quesadillas, and other specialties. The two small dining areas are decorated with a colorful collection of authentic decorative ponchos and piñatas. **FYI:** Reservations accepted. Children's menu. Additional location: MS 6 E 569, Batesville (tel 563-8299). **Open:** Daily 11am–10pm. **Prices:** Main courses $6–$11. AE, MC, V. 👥

⑤ **Smitty's**
208 S Lamar; tel 601/234-9111. ½ block from town square behind Square Books Store. **Southern.** Housed in a 75-year-old building just off the town square, Smitty's menu is as basic as the decor. The chairs and tables here are often filled by regular, everyday customers (it was once frequented by William Faulkner) who come back for Smitty's breakfast, catfish, homemade bread, and homemade desserts. A buffet-style meal is available at all times. **FYI:** Reservations not accepted. BYO. **Open:** Mon–Sat 6am–9pm, Sun 8am–9pm. **Prices:** Main courses $2–$10. MC, V. 👥

ATTRACTIONS 📷

Rowan Oak
Old Taylor Rd; tel 601/234-4651. Built in 1844, this two-story white-frame house was the home of Nobel Prize-winning author William Faulkner for the last 30 years of his life. The author wrote most of his works here; the outline of his novel, *A Fable,* is scribbled on the study wall and his Underwood typewriter still sits on the desk where he worked. The house is now owned by the University of Mississippi. **Open:** Tues–Sat 10am–noon and 2–4pm, Sun 2–4pm. Closed some hols. **Free**

Center for the Study of Southern Culture
University of Mississippi, Barnard Observatory, University; tel 601/232-5993. Founded at the University of Mississippi in 1977, the Center promotes public understanding of the South through publications, media productions, lectures, performances, and exhibitions on Southern folklore, music, art, and literature. **Open:** Mon–Fri 8am–5pm. Closed some hols. **Free**

Pascagoula

An important shipbuilding center since World War II, the town is part of an important commercial fishing area. The oldest building in the Mississippi Valley is here (a Spanish fort built circa 1718). **Information:** Jackson County Area Chamber of Commerce, 825 Denny Ave, PO Box 480, Pascagoula, 39567 (tel 601/234-3391).

HOTEL 🏨

≣≣ Hampton Inn
6800 MS 63 N, PO Box 8660, 39567; tel 601/475-2477 or toll free 800/HAMPTON; fax 601/475-2477. Exit 69 off I-10. Well-maintained hotel, suitable for businesspeople, tourists, and families. **Rooms:** 115 rms and stes. CI 3pm/CO 11am. Nonsmoking rms avail. **Amenities:** 🛁 ⚲ A/C, cable TV w/movies, dataport. **Services:** 🛄 🛎 Facilities: 🛗 🏊 ⚅ Washer/dryer. **Rates (CP):** $44 S; $50–$55 D; $49–$59 ste. Extra person $5. Children under age 18 stay free. Parking: Outdoor, free. AE, CB, DC, DISC, MC, V.

MOTEL

≣≣ La Font Inn
2703 Denny Ave, PO Box 1028, 39567; tel 601/762-7111. Locally owned motel offering all the services and amenities guests need for a comfortable stay. **Rooms:** 192 rms, stes, and effic. Executive level. CI 2pm/CO 1pm. Nonsmoking rms avail. **Amenities:** 🛁 ⚲ 📺 A/C, cable TV w/movies, refrig, voice mail. **Services:** ✕ 🍴 🛄 🛎 Car-rental desk, babysitting. **Facilities:** 🛗 🏊 🎱 ⚅ ⚅ 1 restaurant, 1 bar (w/entertainment), basketball, sauna, whirlpool, playground, washer/dryer. Shuffleboard. **Rates:** $61–$63 S; $68–$73 D; $78–$132 ste; $78–$132 effic. Extra person $5. Children under age 14 stay free. Parking: Outdoor, free. AE, CB, DC, DISC, EC, MC, V.

RESTAURANT 🍴

★ **Marguerite's Italian Village**
2318 Ingalls Ave; tel 601/762-7464. 1½ mi S of US 98. **Italian.** The small but comfortable dining room with a small service bar is supplemented by a back dining room that can accommodate approximately 20 people. The menu offers a number of Italian dishes including veal and chicken entrees. The wine list, although not extensive, does offer good variety. **FYI:** Reservations not accepted. Children's menu. **Open:** Mon–Sat 5–10pm. **Prices:** Main courses $5–$14. AE, MC, V. 👥

ATTRACTION 📷

Old Spanish Fort and Museum
4602 Fort Ave; tel 601/769-1505. This modest, cottagelike structure was actually built by a French-Canadian, Joseph Simon de la Pointe, in 1718. The fort is open for tours and an adjacent museum houses historical artifacts, including Native American relics, a slave poster, and an original Civil War muster roll. **Open:** Mon–Sat 9:30am–4:30pm, Sun noon–4:30pm. Closed some hols. **$**

Philadelphia

Located in central Mississippi, Philadelphia occupies the site of sacred Indian mounds dating back thousands of years.

Nearby Choctaw Indian Reservation features casino gambling and hosts the Annual Choctaw Indian Fair. **Information:** Philadelphia–Neshoba County Chamber of Commerce, 410 Poplar Ave #101, PO Box 51, Philadelphia, 39350 (tel 601/656-1742).

HOTEL 🏨

⊫ ⊫ ⊫ Silver Star Resort & Casino

US 16 W, PO Box 6048, 39350; tel 601/650-1234 or toll free 800/557-0711; fax 601/650-1282. 3 mi W of US 15. This 150,000-square-foot complex is owned by the Mississippi Band of the Choctaw, and is built on their reservation. **Rooms:** 500 rms and stes. CI 3pm/CO noon. Wide variety of rooms offer differing decor and amenities. **Amenities:** 🛁 A/C, cable TV w/movies. Some units w/whirlpools. **Services:** 🆅🅿 ⬛ **Facilities:** 🎣 2500 ⬛ 4 restaurants (see "Restaurants" below), 3 bars (1 w/entertainment), whirlpool. 40,000-square-foot casino (the only land-based one in the state) offers slot machines, gaming tables, bingo. **Rates:** $64–$79 S or D; $150–$300 ste. Extra person $5. Children under age 12 stay free. Parking: Outdoor, free. AE, CB, DC, DISC, MC, V.

RESTAURANT 🍴

★ Phillip M's

In Silver Star Hotel & Casino, US 16 W; tel 601/650-1234. **Seafood/Steak.** Elegant food, large portions, and attentive service—at a good price. Dining room decor includes plants and pictures and each table is decorated with a fresh-cut rose. Some of the more popular items on the menu are Maine lobster, orange roughy, Alaskan king crablegs, filet mignon, and shrimp fettuccini with pecan pesto. Extensive wine list. **FYI:** Reservations recommended. **Open:** Sun–Thurs 5–11pm, Fri–Sat 5pm–midnight. **Prices:** Main courses $4–$19. AE, CB, DC, DISC, MC, V. 🌑 ⬛ 🆅🅿 ⬛

Port Gibson

The picturesque Mississippi Delta town that General Grant called "too beautiful to burn." Its stately homes and lovely gardens draw thousands of visitors each year. Nearby Lorman (10 mi S of Port Gibson) is home to Alcorn State University, established in 1830 and now the oldest land-grant college for African Americans. Lorman plantation owner Capt Isaac Ross freed his slaves in 1834 and sent them to Africa, where they founded the country of Liberia. His gravesite has been visited by representatives of Liberia and a stone placed there in honor of his kindness. **Information:** Port Gibson–Claiborne County Chamber of Commerce, US 61 S, PO Box 491, Port Gibson, 39150 (tel 601/437-4351).

INN 🏠

⊫ ⊫ ⊫ Oak Square Country Inn

1207 Church St, 39150; tel 601/437-4350 or toll free 800/729-0240; fax 601/437-5768. Housed in a restored 1850 mansion, this inn offers a quiet getaway (good for couples), even though it's located in the middle of town. Unsuitable for children under 10. **Rooms:** 12 rms and stes. CI noon/CO 11am. No smoking. Rooms are individually decorated. **Amenities:** 🛁 ⓐ A/C, cable TV w/movies. Some units w/terraces. **Services:** Afternoon tea and wine/sherry served. **Facilities:** 🔟 Guest lounge w/TV. Large grounds give visitors room to take walks, cook out, or just sit and relax. **Rates (BB):** $85–$105 S or D; $125 ste. Extra person $20. Parking: Outdoor, free. MC, V.

ATTRACTIONS 🏛

Samuel Gibson House

US 61 S; tel 601/437-4351. The oldest remaining house in Port Gibson, built around 1805, this was once the home of town founder Samuel Gibson. The guest room is open to the public, where a pencil sketch of Samuel Gibson and his wife can be found. **Open:** Mon–Fri 8am–4pm, Sat 9am–4pm, Sun noon–4pm. Closed weekends Dec and Jan, some hols. **Free**

The Old Country Store

US 61, Lorman; tel 601/437-3661. Located 10 mi S of Port Gibson. This old-time general store, perched just off the Natchez Trace, was constructed in 1890 and most store fixtures are original. Even the cheese cutter is 70 years old, and the walls are lined with over 30,000 calling cards left by previous visitors. The store still sells souvenirs, snacks, toys, and local crafts. **Open:** Mon–Sat 8am–6pm, Sun noon–6pm. Closed some hols. **Free**

Robinsonville

In the Northwest Delta, this tiny town is home to several major riverboat gambling facilities.

HOTEL 🏨

⊫ ⊫ ⊫ Sam's Town Hotel & Gambling Hall

Robinsonville Rd at Commerce Landing, 38664; tel 601/363-0711 or toll free 800/456-0711; fax 601/363-0760. On US 304 W. Designed to look like an Old West town, incorporating colorful designs reminiscent of a livery stable, a general store, and a blacksmith shop. The decor is carried through in the courtyard. **Rooms:** 508 rms and stes. CI 3pm/CO 11am. Nonsmoking rms avail. Rooms have well-maintained furniture and are decorated with Western-style art. **Amenities:** 🛁 ⓐ A/C, cable TV w/movies. Some units w/whirlpools. Some rooms have refrigerators, microwaves, and hair dryers. **Services:** ✕ 🆅🅿 ⬛ 🎧 Car-rental desk. **Facilities:** 🎣 100 ⬛ 1 restaurant, 5 bars (1 w/entertainment), games rm, whirlpool. Full-service casino connected to the hotel. Pool area has a gazebo. **Rates:** $59–$89 S or D; $89–$109 ste. Extra person $7. Children under age 12 stay free. Parking: Outdoor, free. AE, DISC, MC, V.

Sardis

In the northwestern portion of the state, the town is home to Sardis Reservoir and Dam. Named for a city mentioned in the biblical Book of Revelations. **Information:** 114 W Lee St, PO Box 377, Sardis, 38666 (tel 601/487-3451).

MOTEL 🎞

≣ Super 8 Motel

601 E Lee St, PO Box 28, 38666; tel 601/487-2311 or toll free 800/800-8000; fax 601/487-1905. Exit 252 off I-55. Budget motel suitable for a casual, short stay. **Rooms:** 41 rms. CI open/CO 11am. Nonsmoking rms avail. **Amenities:** 🛗 A/C, cable TV w/movies. **Services:** 🍽 **Facilities:** 🛗 **Rates (CP):** Peak (Apr–Oct) $38–$43 S; $46–$49 D. Extra person $5. Children under age 12 stay free. Lower rates off-season. Parking: Outdoor, free. AE, DISC, EC, MC, V.

Starkville

Site of Mississippi State University and its rich archives of blues and ragtime sheet music and original recordings. Home of the Oktibbeha County Western Singing Convention, a consortium of eight rural churches whose members practice a variety of "shape note singing." **Information:** Starkville Convention & Visitors Bureau, 322 University Dr, Starkville, 39759 (tel 601/323-3322).

HOTELS 🎞

≣≣≣ Holiday Inn

403 MS 12, PO Box 751, 39760-0751; tel 601/323-6161 or toll free 800/HOLIDAY; fax 601/323-8073. 1 mi W of MSU campus. Popular with businesspeople and visiting families. **Rooms:** 173 rms and stes. CI 1pm/CO noon. Nonsmoking rms avail. **Amenities:** 🛗 🐾 A/C, cable TV w/movies. Some units w/whirlpools. **Services:** ✕ 🖼 🍽 🐾 Babysitting. **Facilities:** 🛗 🖼250 🕏 2 restaurants, 2 bars, washer/dryer. Restaurant is well regarded for its buffets. Meeting facilities include teleconferencing capabilities. **Rates:** $40–$48 S; $48–$52 D; $100 ste. Children under age 18 stay free. Parking: Outdoor, free. Higher rates on football weekends. AE, CB, DC, DISC, JCB, MC, V.

≣≣ Starkville Best Western

119 MS 12 W, 39759; tel 601/324-5555 or toll free 800/528-1234; fax 601/323-4615. Basic chain hotel, with well-kept landscaping. **Rooms:** 60 rms and stes. CI 2pm/CO noon. Nonsmoking rms avail. All rooms have queen- or king-size bed. **Amenities:** 🛗 A/C, cable TV w/movies. 1 unit w/whirlpool. **Services:** 🖼 🍽 🐾 Fax and copy service

available. Small pets allowed. **Facilities:** 🛗 🖼20 🕏 **Rates:** $44–$49 S; $49–$54 D; $49–$54 ste. Extra person $5. Children under age 12 stay free. Min stay special events. Parking: Outdoor, free. AE, CB, DC, DISC, MC, V.

≣≣≣ The Statehouse Hotel

At Jackson and Main Sts, PO Box 2002, 39759; tel 601/323-2000 or toll free 800/722-1903; fax 601/323-4948. Well-maintained hotel offering an elegant lobby with dark-wood appointments and antique furnishings. Originally built in 1925, the property was totally renovated in 1985. **Rooms:** 43 rms and stes. CI 3pm/CO noon. Nonsmoking rms avail. Rooms are furnished with antique reproductions. **Amenities:** 🛗 🐾 🖼 A/C, cable TV w/movies, dataport. **Services:** ✕ 🖼 🍽 Complimentary restaurant discount card issued upon check-in. **Facilities:** 🖼30 🕏 1 restaurant, 1 bar (w/entertainment). **Rates:** $48–$68 S; $62–$72 D; $78–$108 ste. Extra person $8. Children under age 12 stay free. Min stay special events. Parking: Outdoor, free. AE, DC, DISC, MC, V.

MOTEL

≣ The Regal Inn

410 Lee St/US 82 E, 39759; tel 601/323-8251; fax 601/324-2469. Standard motor inn, suitable for overnight stays. **Rooms:** 60 rms. CI 2pm/CO noon. Nonsmoking rms avail. **Amenities:** 🛗 A/C, cable TV w/movies. **Services:** 🍽 VCRs available for rent. **Facilities:** 🛗 **Rates:** $33–$35 S; $40–$45 D. Children under age 21 stay free. Parking: Outdoor, free. AE, DC, DISC, MC, V.

RESTAURANTS 🍴

The District Cafe

In University Inn, 705 Spring; tel 601/323-9696. Off MS 12. **Regional American.** A cozy cafe, with semiprivate booths and a bar area with sofas and a TV. Menu offerings range from basic soups and sandwiches to Cajun-style entrees. **FYI:** Reservations accepted. Children's menu. **Open:** Mon–Thurs 11am–10pm, Fri–Sat 11am–11pm. **Prices:** Main courses $5–$15. AE, DISC, MC, V. 🎦

♣ Richey's Restaurant

513 Academy Rd; tel 601/324-2737. 1 block W of Main St (US 25). **Seafood/Steak.** Well-known for its hand-cut steaks, Richey's also boasts some of the area's best barbecue shrimp, chateaubriand, broiled orange roughy, and broiled chicken. All entrees come with vegetable and house salad. **FYI:** Reservations accepted. Children's menu. **Open:** Peak (Sept–Nov) Mon–Sat 4–10pm. **Prices:** Main courses $9–$33. AE, CB, DC, DISC, MC, V. ♥

Tupelo

Elvis Presley put this town on the map, and the legendary rock-and-roller's birthplace still attracts visitors from around the world. Natchez Trace Parkway Headquarters is here, as is a nature trail that passes near the Old Trace, a scenic path over 8,000 years old winding from Natchez to Nashville, Tennessee. **Information:** Tupelo Convention & Visitors Bureau, 399 E Main St, PO Drawer 47, Tupelo, 38802 (tel 601/841-6521).

HOTELS 🏨

🛏🛏 Comfort Inn

1190 N Gloster St, 38801; tel 601/842-5100 or toll free 800/221-2222; fax 601/844-0554. Off Business 45 N ½ block E of McCollough Blvd. Modern hotel, suitable for businesspeople or families. Located near several popular restaurants. **Rooms:** 83 rms. CI 3pm/CO 11am. Nonsmoking rms avail. **Amenities:** 🔒 A/C, cable TV w/movies. **Services:** 🚐 ⊠ 🛎 Fax and copier service. **Facilities:** 📠 40 **Rates (CP):** Peak (June–Aug) $46–$52 S; $43–$50 D. Extra person $4. Children under age 18 stay free. Lower rates off-season. Parking: Outdoor, free. AE, DC, DISC, MC, V.

🛏🛏 Days Inn

1015 N Gloster St, 38801; tel 601/842-0088 or toll free 800/329-7466; fax 601/842-3659. Spiffy-looking property. Ideal for the businessperson. **Rooms:** 40 rms and stes. CI 1pm/CO noon. Nonsmoking rms avail. New furniture in rooms. **Amenities:** 🔒 🖥 A/C, cable TV w/movies. **Services:** 🚐 ⊠ 🛎 **Facilities:** 📠 10 🏊 Washer/dryer. Pool is shared with inn next door (under same ownership). **Rates (CP):** $44–$59 D; $49–$59 ste. Extra person $5. Children under age 18 stay free. Parking: Outdoor, free. AE, CB, DC, DISC, JCB, MC, V.

🛏🛏🛏 Executive Inn

1011 N Gloster St, PO Box 1603, 38802; tel 601/841-2222 or toll free 800/533-3220; fax 601/844-7836. Off McCollough Blvd. Older yet well-maintained five-story hotel, perched at end of long driveway that serves to seclude it from the highway. **Rooms:** 115 rms and stes. CI 2pm/CO noon. Nonsmoking rms avail. **Amenities:** 🔒 🖥 A/C, satel TV w/movies. **Services:** ✕ ⊠ 🛎 ⬦ **Facilities:** 📠 200 🏊 1 restaurant (see "Restaurants" below), 1 bar, sauna, steam rm, whirlpool. **Rates:** $55–$63 S; $64–$72 D; $220 ste. Extra person $8. Children under age 18 stay free. Parking: Outdoor, free. AE, CB, DC, DISC, JCB, MC, V.

🛏🛏 Holiday Inn Express

923 N Gloster St, 38802; tel 601/842-8811 or toll free 800/800-6891; fax 601/844-6884. At McCollough. Suitable for all travelers. **Rooms:** 125 rms. CI 2pm/CO noon. Nonsmoking rms avail. **Amenities:** 🔒 A/C, satel TV w/movies, voice mail. **Services:** ⊠ 🛎 **Facilities:** 📠 50 Washer/dryer. **Rates (CP):** $42–$44 S; $46–$48 D. Extra person $7. Children under age 12 stay free. Parking: Outdoor, free. AE, CB, DC, DISC, JCB, MC, V.

🛏🛏🛏 Ramada Inn

854 N Gloster St, 38801; tel 601/844-4111 or toll free 800/228-2828; fax 601/844-4111. W of McCollough. Typical Ramada. **Rooms:** 232 rms and stes. CI open/CO 1pm. Nonsmoking rms avail. **Amenities:** 🔒 🖥 A/C, cable TV, refrig. 1 unit w/whirlpool. **Services:** ✕ 🚐 ⊠ 🛎 **Facilities:** 📠 1000 1 restaurant, washer/dryer. **Rates:** $47–$57 S or D; $100–$175 ste. Extra person $5. Children under age 18 stay free. Parking: Outdoor, free. AE, DC, DISC, MC, V.

🛏🛏🛏 Rex Plaza

619 N Gloster St, 38801; tel 601/840-8000 or toll free 800/203-5917; fax 601/840-1116. ½ mi S of US 78. A spacious, well-maintained hotel. Perfect for families. **Rooms:** 64 rms, stes, and effic. CI noon/CO noon. Nonsmoking rms avail. A 3-bedroom, 2½-bath house is available. **Amenities:** 🔒 🖥 🖥 A/C, cable TV w/movies, refrig. 1 unit w/terrace. Dataports and VCRs in one-bedroom suites. Some rooms have whirlpool tubs. **Services:** ✕ 🚐 ⊠ 🛎 **Facilities:** 📠 100 1 restaurant (dinner only; see "Restaurants" below), 1 bar (w/entertainment), washer/dryer. **Rates (CP):** $57–$65 S; $65–$70 D; $94–$189 ste. Children under age 18 stay free. Parking: Outdoor, free. Long-term rentals avail. No extra charge for extra guests. AE, DC, DISC, MC, V.

🛏🛏🛏 Trace Inn

3400 W Main, 38801; tel 601/842-5555; fax 601/844-3105. A 21-year-old hotel located near historic Natchez Trace and several Civil War sites. Suitable for businesspeople and families. No alcohol allowed on grounds. **Rooms:** 155 rms and stes. Executive level. CI 2pm/CO 11am. Nonsmoking rms avail. **Amenities:** 🔒 🖥 A/C, satel TV w/movies, refrig, dataport. 1 unit w/minibar, some w/terraces. **Services:** 🚐 ⊠ 🛎 ⬦ Children's program, babysitting. **Facilities:** 📠 2000 🏊 1 restaurant (lunch and dinner only), playground, washer/dryer. Kennel on the premises. RV hook-ups available for additional fee. **Rates:** $30–$34 S; $35–$39 D; $50–$60 ste. Extra person $5. Children under age 12 stay free. Parking: Outdoor, free. Rates cover up to four people per unit. Efficiencies rented monthly with no lease ($200 refundable deposit). AE, CB, DC, DISC, JCB, MC, V.

RESTAURANTS 🍴

Garden Terrace

In Executive Inn, 1011 N Gloster St; tel 601/841-2222. **American.** A relaxing eatery specializing in steak and seafood. Elevated above the main lobby floor, to offer private atmosphere and great views. Moderately priced California and other domestic wines. Lunch buffet daily. **FYI:** Reservations recommended. **Open:** Breakfast Mon–Fri 6–11am, Sat–Sun 7–11am; lunch Mon–Fri 11am–2pm, Sat–Sun 11am–2pm; dinner Mon–Sat 5–10pm. **Prices:** Main courses $5–$15. AE, CB, DC, DISC, MC, V. 🍴 🏊

♦ Gloster 205 Restaurant

205 N Gloster St; tel 601/842-7205. 1½ mi S of US 78. **Seafood/Steak.** A quite elegant establishment with an excellent interior design. Several different dining rooms each offer a different atmosphere. The solid menu focuses on steak (especially prime rib), seafood, and pasta dishes. Attractive

bar/lounge area. **FYI:** Reservations accepted. **Open:** Daily 5–10pm. **Prices:** Main courses $11–$23. AE, CB, DC, DISC, ER, MC, V. ♥

Harvey's
424 S Gloster St; tel 601/842-6763. 2–3 mi S of Old US 78. **Seafood/Steak.** This branch of the popular local restaurant chain is housed in a former Coca-Cola bottling plant. The exterior landscaping features lots of flowers, but the interior decorations are quite simple. Booths and tables are separate by tall sections, making all the tables semiprivate. The menu leans toward Cajun; and Harvey's is well known for its salads, seafood, and pasta. **FYI:** Reservations accepted. Children's menu. Additional location: 406 MS 12 E, Starkville (tel 323-1639). **Open:** Mon–Thurs 11am–9pm, Fri–Sat 11am–10pm. **Prices:** Main courses $5–$16. AE, DISC, MC, V. 👥 &

★ Jefferson Place
823 Jefferson; tel 601/844-8696. 1 block W of Gloster St. **American.** Housed in a beautifully restored 19th-century home, Jefferson Place is supposedly "haunted" by a resident ghost called Dr Nash, but don't let him scare you away. The restaurant is known for its steaks, which are top-choice, trimmed, and hand-cut. Several dishes are offered for the health-conscious, including grilled chicken salad. Desserts are homemade. Small wine list. **FYI:** Reservations accepted. Blues/jazz/rock. **Open:** Mon–Sat 11am–midnight. **Prices:** Main courses $7–$16. AE, DC, MC, V. ♥ ♟

★ Vanelli's
1302 N Gloster St; tel 601/844-4410. Located off Alt US 45. **Greek/Italian.** Very relaxed and friendly, and owned by the same Greek family for over 20 years. The offbeat (at least for Mississippi) decor features Greek statues, sculpted lion's heads, photos of celebrity visitors, newspaper clippings, and original artwork. The food is a Greek-Italian mix, with the emphasis on pizza and pasta entrees. Typical options include manicotti, Grecian spaghetti, and baked-cheese spaghetti. Wines are mostly California varieties, with some French selections as well. **FYI:** Reservations not accepted. **Open:** Mon–Sat 11am–10pm, Sun 11am–9pm. **Prices:** Main courses $9–$18. AE, CB, DC, DISC, MC, V. 👥 &

♣ Woody's Restaurant & Captain's Den
In Rex Plaza, 619 N Gloster St; tel 601/840-0460. ½ mi S of US 78. **Seafood/Steak.** Although the exterior of this building is quite modern, the interior design of the restaurant has an elegant, romantic mood, with lantern-type candles on each table. The menu choices are basic steak and seafood dishes. **FYI:** Reservations accepted. Blues/karaoke/rock. Children's menu. Dress code. Additional location: 2420 Military Rd, Columbus (tel 327-7869). **Open:** Daily 5–10pm. **Prices:** Main courses $9–$34. AE, DC, DISC, MC, V. ♥ ▼ &

ATTRACTIONS 🏛

Elvis Presley Birthplace and Museum
306 Elvis Presley Dr; tel 601/841-1245. The Man Who Would Be King was born January 8, 1935, in this two-room shotgun house built by his father. The tiny frame house was repossessed when Elvis was three, and the family moved in and out of several other houses in Tupelo before heading north to Memphis in 1948. The adjacent **Elvis Presley Museum** houses an extensive collection of Elvis memorabilia, including rare photographs and articles of clothing. Also on the grounds of the four-acre Elvis Presley Center are the Elvis Presley Memorial Chapel, a gift shop, and picnic grounds. **Open:** Daily 9am–5pm. Closed some hols. **$$**

Natchez Trace Parkway Visitors Center
Tel 601/680-4025 or toll free 800/305-7417. The Natchez Trace began as a trail carved out of the wilderness by the Choctaw and Chickasaw peoples, who used it as a hunting path. By the late 18th century, American settlers used it for hunting and as a trade route. By the beginning of the 19th century, farmers and merchants had begun traveling down the Mississippi River in search of new markets. Since the flatboats used for transporting goods were typically sold for their lumber in Natchez or New Orleans, the boatmen either walked or rode back home along the trace, which eventually became trampled into a clearly marked path.

Today, this route is commemorated by a two-lane, 450-mile scenic highway running from Nashville, TN in the north to Natchez, MS in the south. Tupelo, approximately the halfway point along the route, is home to the Parkway **visitors center,** at milepost 266. The visitors center has a nature trail, exhibits, and an orientation program. Ask at the visitors center for a copy of their brochure detailing historic and scenic sites along the Parkway. **Open:** Visitors center, daily 8am–5pm. Closed Dec 25. **Free**

Brices Cross Roads National Battlefield Site
MS 370; tel 601/680-4025. Located 15 mi N of Tupelo. Interpretive maps and markers tell the story of a crucial Confederate victory over Union forces that took place here in June 1864. Adjacent cemetery contains the graves of 100 Confederate soldiers. **Open:** Daily sunrise–sunset. **Free**

Vicksburg

Located on a bluff overlooking the Mississippi River in the western part of the state, Vicksburg was one of the key strategic points of the Civil War. The town is surrounded by Vicksburg National Military Park, which commemorates the site of some of the bloodiest battles of the War, and the Old Courthouse Museum has one of the largest collections of Civil War relics in the world. Once a main drag for paddleboats, gambling aristocrats, and scoundrels, now dockside casinos afford nightly entertainment. **Information:** Vicksburg–Warren County Convention & Visitors Bureau, PO Box 110, Vicksburg, 39181 (tel 601/636-9421).

HOTELS 🏨

⬛⬛ Hampton Inn of Vicksburg

3330 Clay St, 39180; tel 601/636-6100 or toll free 800/HAMPTON; fax 601/634-1962. At jct US 80/I-20. Well-maintained property close to the interstate, but surrounded with trees that provide some seclusion. **Rooms:** 148 rms and stes. CI 3pm/CO noon. Nonsmoking rms avail. Suites have pull-out sofas, king-size rooms have desks and recliners. **Amenities:** 🔒 ⚙ A/C, cable TV w/movies. **Services:** ✗ ⬛ ⤴ ⟲ **Facilities:** 🏋 30 ⛾ Washer/dryer. **Rates (CP):** $51–$56 S; $56–$61 D; $51–$61 ste. Extra person $5. Children under age 18 stay free. Parking: Outdoor, free. AE, DC, DISC, MC, V.

⬛⬛⬛ Harrah's Casino & Hotel

1310 S Mulberry St, 39180; tel 601/636-3423 or toll free 800/843-2343; fax 601/630-2194. Lively, seven-story hotel is the on-shore component of this entertainment complex. Attracts casino visitors (of course), but a surprising number of families stay here as well. Huge lobby with plenty of seating. **Rooms:** 117 rms and stes. CI 3pm/CO noon. Nonsmoking rms avail. **Amenities:** 🔒 ⚙ 🖥 A/C, cable TV w/movies. **Services:** VP ⬛ ⤴ Twice-daily maid service available upon request. **Facilities:** 250 ⛾ 2 restaurants, 2 bars (1 w/entertainment), games rm, day-care ctr. Adjacent 295-foot riverboat casino features three decks of gambling, bars, and stores. **Rates (BB):** $69–$89 S; $79–$99 D; $99–$149 ste. Extra person $10. Children under age 18 stay free. Min stay special events. Parking: Indoor/outdoor, free. Separate weekend and weekday rates. AE, CB, DC, DISC, EC, JCB, MC, V.

⬛⬛ Holiday Inn

3330 Clay St, 39180; tel 601/636-4551 or toll free 800/847-0372; fax 601/636-4552. At jct US 80/I-20. Older (built 35 years ago) but nicely maintained Holiday Inn located adjacent to the National Military Park. Holidome offers indoor recreational activities. **Rooms:** 172 rms and stes. CI 3pm/CO noon. Nonsmoking rms avail. Room decor is nice, but nothing fancy. **Amenities:** 🔒 ⚙ A/C, cable TV w/movies. **Services:** ✗ 🚐 ⬛ ⤴ ⟲ **Facilities:** 🏋 250 ⛾ 1 restaurant, 1 bar, games rm, whirlpool, washer/dryer. **Rates (BB):** Peak (May 15–Aug 15) $60–$65 S; $70–$77 D; $77–$82 ste. Extra person $5. Children under age 18 stay free. Lower rates off-season. AP and MAP rates avail. Parking: Outdoor, free. AE, CB, DC, DISC, MC, V.

⬛⬛⬛ Park Inn International Hotel

4137 Frontage Rd, 39180; tel 601/638-5811 or toll free 800/359-9363; fax 601/638-9249. Exit 4B off I-20. A well-maintained hotel with nice landscaping. For businesspeople and families. **Rooms:** 117 rms and stes. Executive level. CI 3pm/CO 12:30pm. Nonsmoking rms avail. All rooms have ceiling fans and better-than-average furniture. **Amenities:** 🔒 A/C, cable TV w/movies, dataport. Some units w/whirlpools. **Services:** ✗ 🚐 ⬛ ⤴ ⟲ 24-hour coffee service in lobby. Free complimentary cocktail service (Mon–Fri, 5:30–7:30pm). **Facilities:** 🏋 450 1 restaurant (bkfst and dinner only; see "Restaurants" below), 1 bar (w/entertainment), basketball, playground, washer/dryer. Poolside barbecue grills and four live parrots add character to the grounds. Free use of miniature-golf course. **Rates (BB):** $35–$67 S or D; $120–$127 ste. Extra person $7. Children under age 17 stay free. Parking: Outdoor, free. AE, CB, DC, DISC, MC, V.

MOTELS

⬛ Delta Point Inn

4155 Washington St, 39180; tel 601/636-5145 or toll free 800/700-7770; fax 601/636-5314. Primarily for casino visitors. (The Ameristar is across the street.) This property could use a little work, but it's adequate for an overnight stay. **Rooms:** 54 rms. Executive level. CI 1pm/CO noon. Nonsmoking rms avail. **Amenities:** 🔒 A/C, cable TV w/movies. Some units w/terraces. **Services:** 🚐 Linens changed every other night for multinight stays. **Facilities:** 🏋 **Rates:** $55–$75 S or D; $75–$90 ste. Extra person $5. Children under age 21 stay free. Parking: Outdoor, free. Casino packages avail. Higher rates on weekends. AE, DC, DISC, MC, V.

⬛ Super 8 Motel

4127 Frontage Rd, 39180; tel 601/638-5077 or toll free 800/800-8000; fax 601/638-5077. Exit 4B off I-20. Quiet, basic accommodations. **Rooms:** 62 rms. CI 1pm/CO 11am. Nonsmoking rms avail. **Amenities:** 🔒 A/C, cable TV w/movies. **Services:** ⤴ ⟲ Nightly patrols by local police department. **Facilities:** 🏋 ⛾ Whirlpool. **Rates:** Peak (Apr–Sept) $46–$51 S; $57–$62 D. Extra person $5. Children under age 12 stay free. Lower rates off-season. Parking: Outdoor, free. AE, CB, DC, DISC, MC, V.

INNS

⬛⬛⬛ Anchuca

1010 1st East St, 39180; tel 601/631-6800; fax 601/631-6800. At Cherry St. 8 acres. Well-maintained, Greek Revival–style inn (built in 1830) located in the historic district. Recommended for couples as well as families. **Rooms:** 10 rms and stes. CI 2pm/CO noon. Nonsmoking rms avail. Large, individually decorated rooms feature antiques and gas burning chandeliers. **Amenities:** 🔒 ⚙ 🖥 A/C, cable TV w/movies, refrig. **Services:** ✗ ⬛ ⤴ ⟲ Afternoon tea and wine/sherry served. **Facilities:** 🏋 12 Whirlpool, washer/dryer, guest lounge. Pool area with indoor-outdoor cabana. **Rates (BB):** $135–$175 S or D; $135–$175 ste; $100–$175 cottage/villa. Children under age 21 stay free. Parking: Outdoor, free. AE, CB, DC, DISC, ER, JCB, MC, V.

⬛⬛⬛ Cedar Grove Mansion Inn

2200 Oak St, 39180; tel 601/636-1000 or toll free 800/862-1300; fax 601/634-6126. 40 acres. Historic inn with a nice quiet atmosphere. Perfect for honeymooners, couples, and history buffs. Unsuitable for children under 6. **Rooms:** 27 rms and stes; 5 cottages/villas. CI 2pm/CO noon. No smoking. Individually decorated rooms feature antiques and photos; many rooms have canopy beds. **Amenities:** 📞 ⚬ 🍽 A/C, cable TV w/movies. Some units w/minibars, some w/terraces, some w/fireplaces, some w/whirlpools. Ice buckets brought to rooms twice daily. **Services:** ✗ ⌧ Afternoon tea and wine/sherry served. Guests are entitled to a free guided tour of the mansion and its grounds (reservations required). **Facilities:** 🔐 ⟦25⟧ 1 restaurant (bkfst and dinner only), 1 bar (w/entertainment), guest lounge w/TV. Rooftop sundeck with small bar area. **Rates (BB):** $90–$165 S or D; $90–$165 ste; $90–$150 cottage/villa. Extra person $20. Parking: Outdoor, free. AE, DISC, MC, V.

▤▤▤ The Corners

601 Klein St, 39180; tel 601/636-7421 or toll free 800/444-7421. ½ block W of Washington St. Spectacular two-story inn, built in 1872, with elements of Italianate and Greek Revival–style architecture. Property is surrounded by a cast-iron fence; the front porch offers views of the Yazoo and Mississippi Rivers. Original gardens, 14-foot ceilings, and floor-to-ceiling windows are all breathtaking. **Rooms:** 15 rms and stes; 1 cottage/villa. CI noon/CO 11am. No smoking. All accommodations, with the exception of one two-bedroom suite, are located in the main house. Rooms and suites are all well kept and enjoy above-average housekeeping. **Amenities:** ⚬ A/C, cable TV w/movies. No phone. Some units w/terraces, some w/fireplaces, some w/whirlpools. Only some rooms have phones. **Services:** ✗ ⌫ ⌬ Babysitting, afternoon tea and wine/sherry served. **Facilities:** ⟦35⟧ ⚬ Washer/dryer, guest lounge. **Rates (BB):** $75–$95 S; $85–$105 D; $95–$150 ste; $105–$150 cottage/villa. Extra person $20. Children under age 3 stay free. Parking: Outdoor, free. AE, CB, DC, DISC, EC, MC, V.

RESTAURANTS 🍴

♣ Delta Point River Restaurant

4144 Washington St; tel 601/636-5317. Next to Ameristar Casino. **Continental.** Owned and operated by Ameristar Casino, this elegant waterfront eatery offers a spectacular view of the Mississippi. The menu features veal, steaks, and seafood; some dishes are prepared and cooked tableside. Expert wait staff. **FYI:** Reservations recommended. Piano. **Open:** Tues–Thurs 5–10pm, Fri–Sat 5–11pm. **Prices:** Main courses $13–$40. AE, CB, DC, DISC, MC, V. ❤ 🏞 ⚬

Jacques Cafe

In Park Inn International Hotel, 4137 Frontage Rd; tel 601/638-5811. **Italian/Seafood/Steak.** A comfortable hotel cafe, with a touch of casual elegance. Highlights of the eclectic menu include steaks, redfish, and orange roughy. If you're in a competitive mood, the adjacent bar area has more than a dozen dart boards. **FYI:** Reservations recommended.

Karaoke. Dress code. **Open:** Mon–Fri 6am–9:30pm, Sat–Sun 6am–10:30pm. **Prices:** Main courses $6–$15. AE, DC, DISC, MC, V. ▦ ⚬

Walnut Hills

1214 Adams St; tel 601/638-4910. N of Clay St. **Regional American/Eclectic.** Down-home dining in an 1880s house. The dining areas include "round table" rooms and private dining rooms. At the round tables, guests may help themselves to any of the several entrees, vegetables, and other side dishes (cornbread, fruit cobbler) heaped onto platters on the central table. Some of the more popular à la carte selections served in the main dining room include Mississippi pond-raised catfish, beef kabobs, country-fried steak, and Walnut Hills's famous fried chicken. **FYI:** Reservations recommended. Children's menu. **Open:** Mon–Fri 11am–9pm, Sun 11am–2pm. **Prices:** Main courses $4–$16. AE, CB, DC, DISC, MC, V. ❤ 🍴 ▦

ATTRACTIONS 📷

Vicksburg National Military Park

3201 Clay St; tel 601/636-0583. Vicksburg's location on a cliff overlooking the Mississippi River gave it strategic importance to both the Confederate and Union sides during the Civil War, since whoever controlled the city could also control traffic along the river. General Ulysses S Grant and his men spent the winter of 1862–1863 trying to take the city, but they did not succeed. The following spring, Grant began formal siege operations. Union artillery and gunboats attacked Confederate fortifications for over a month before the Confederate leader John C Pemberton agreed to surrender on July 4, 1863. For the first time since the war began, Union forces held total control of the mighty Mississippi.

The national park, located in the northeastern portion of Vicksburg, contains remnants of fortifications, artillery batteries, and stockades used in the siege. Nearly 17,000 Union soldiers are buried in **Vicksburg National Cemetery.** The **USS Cairo,** one of the Union gunboats used to carry out the siege, is now on display in the northwest corner of the park. The visitors center, near the Clay St entrance, offers exhibits and a film entitled *Vanishing Glory.* A self-guided, 16-mile driving tour (map available at visitors center) covers major battle sites. **Open:** Daily 8am–5pm. Closed Dec 25. **Free**

Biederharn Coca-Cola Museum

1107 Washington St; tel 601/638-6514. In 1894, a Vicksburg candy merchant named Joseph Biedenharn had an idea that would soon change the way America (and the world) drinks. He took the popular soda fountain beverage Coca-Cola, put it in bottles, and shipped it to rural areas. This museum, housed in the restored Biedenharn Candy Company, contains original Coca-Cola advertising and memorabilia, as well as early bottling equipment. Ice cream, homemade candies, and Coca-Cola souvenirs are available for sale. **Open:** Mon–Sat 9am–5pm, Sun 1:30–4:30pm. **$**

Toys and Soldiers Museum
1100 Cherry St; tel 601/638-1986. This museum, a labor of love for Ann and Jim Morris of A&J Miniatures, houses the largest privately owned toy soldier collection open to the public in the world. In addition to the soldiers, there are Civil War artifacts; toy trains, planes, and automobiles; antique dolls; and a miniature circus. **Open:** Tues–Sat 9am–5pm. Closed some hols. **$**

Gray and Blue Naval Museum
1823 Clay St; tel 601/638-6500. Houses the world's largest collection of Civil War gunboat models. The museum is also home to unique paintings, reference files, and artifacts which offer a chance for visitors to see the many different designs of warships. **Open:** Mon–Sat 9am–5pm, Sun 1–5pm. Closed some hols. **$**

Cedar Grove Mansion
2200 Oak St; tel 601/636-1000 or toll free 800/862-1300. This Greek Revival mansion, built as a wedding gift for Gen Sherman's cousin, still has a cannonball lodged in its parlor wall from the Siege of Vicksburg. The entire house, which also serves as a B&B, is filled with period antiques and the grounds are studded with gazebos. **Open:** Daily 8am–10pm. Closed Dec 25. **$$**

Mississippi River Adventures
City Waterfront at foot of Clay St; tel 601/638-5443 or toll free 800/521-4363. Hydrojet boat takes visitors on a 40-mile, 2-hour narrated sightseeing adventure of historical landmarks, such as Grant's Canal and Fort Nogales, and river wildlife. Dinner cruises on Fridays. **Open:** Mar–Nov, daily. **$$$$**

Ameristar Casino Vicksburg
4146 Washington St; tel 601/638-1000. The style and grace of the old South in a facility modeled after the riverboats of the 1870s, where you can enjoy magnificent views of the mighty Mississippi. Slot machines and table games, a showroom featuring top music and comedy acts, and two restaurants. **Open:** Daily 24 hours. **Free**

Waveland

Located on the Mississippi Sound just southwest of Gulfport, this village is filled with marinas and old-time fishing fleets, with Bayou Caddy the quaint home of the Waveland shrimping fleet.

RESTAURANT

★ **Lil Ray's**
613 US 90; tel 601/467-4566. **Seafood.** Established nearly two decades ago, this down-home diner has a large and loyal following. Some of their more popular dishes include fried oysters and fried shrimp, but don't miss the boiled entrees or the po' boys. Thanks to their Coast location, all the seafood here is fresh. **FYI:** Reservations accepted. Children's menu.

Beer and wine only. Additional location: 500-A Courthouse Rd, Gulfport (tel 896-9601). **Open:** Sun–Thurs 10am–9pm, Fri–Sat 10am–10pm. **Prices:** Main courses $4–$11. DISC, MC, V.

Yazoo City

This city 42 miles north of Jackson is in an area of catfish farms and cotton gins. Its historic district includes the Bethel African Methodist Church (erected in 1890). **Information:** Yazoo County Convention & Visitors Bureau, 332 N Main, PO Box 186, Yazoo City, 39194 (tel 601/746-1815).

RESTAURANT

★ **The Main Event**
310 S Main St; tel 601/746-4171. 1½ blocks S of US 49 E. **Regional American.** This very casual lounge-type restaurant in downtown Yazoo City serves up a wide variety of dishes—from fajitas to Mississippi-style ribs. Many dishes that kids will enjoy (though no separate children's menu). **FYI:** Reservations not accepted. **Open:** Lunch Mon–Sat 11am–2pm; dinner Mon–Sat 5–10pm. **Prices:** Main courses $5–$16. AE, MC, V.

NORTH CAROLINA

The Small-Town State

A sizable and diverse state, North Carolina runs 540 miles east to west and its elevations vary from sea level to 6,600 feet. It's not surprising, therefore, that the state satisfies the cravings of so many visitors, whether they come seeking history and culture or exciting outdoor recreational pursuits. Located in a strategic position midway between New York and Florida, North Carolina has long been a center for commerce and a magnet for tourists.

In addition to three distinct physical regions, the state is also divided into thirds by history, tradition, and economic pursuits. The economy of the coastal region is highly geared toward tourism. The Piedmont region in the central part of the state is the industrial, technological, and political hub. A lively folk culture, tourism, and the largest group of Native Americans in the East characterize the Appalachian Mountains region. Although North Carolina is the 10th most populous state in the country, it does not have any megacities. It is essentially a state noted for its small-town character and hospitable, friendly people.

North Carolina's mild climate and diverse topography combine to offer something for everyone. The state's natural vegetation is complex, varying from subtropical plants found along the coast to dwarf tundra foliage discovered in the mountains. Forests cover nearly two-thirds of the state. A water wonderland, North Carolina not only fronts on the ocean but is crisscrossed by 16 major river basins. Just about every outdoor activity from archery to white-water rafting can be enjoyed in North Carolina.

Cultural activities are unsurpassed. The state is the home of several first-rate fine arts festivals (such as the North Carolina Shakespeare Festival) and a large selection of outdoor dramas, as well as cloggers, ballet troupes, jazz ensembles, symphony orchestras, museums, and arts and crafts shows. Historic preservation is an ongoing enterprise, and the Historic Preservation Foundation of North Carolina is one of the nation's largest and most successful state

ommer's
#1

preservation groups. North Carolina has been called ". . . an oasis between Northern realities and Southern dreams," an apt description for a state with so many roots in the past but such vision toward the future.

A Brief History

Lost & Found When the first European explorers arrived, there were between 35,000 and 50,000 Native Americans living in the territory. Although the coast was explored by the Spanish and French early in the 16th century, the state's origins are most closely tied to the earliest English attempts at colonization. In 1584, English explorers returned to England with reports of "the goodliest land under the cope of heaven." In 1587, a group led by Sir Walter Raleigh established a colony at Roanoke Island. The colony soon failed and the settlers disappeared without a trace, resulting in one of this country's greatest unsolved mysteries.

No permanent settlement was made until the 1650s, when farmers from Virginia moved into the Albemarle Sound area of the northeastern part of the colony. North Carolina's growth was hampered by restrictions on shipping imposed by Virginia, economic and religious quarrels with the absentee proprietors, war with the Native Americans, and coastal piracy. The colony had no town until Bath was settled by French Huguenots from Virginia in 1700, and between 1712 and 1729 North Carolina was considered a separate province of Carolina, which was governed out of Charleston. A boundary to divide the province into two independent states was agreed on in 1735 but not actually surveyed until 1815.

During the period of royal rule beginning in 1729, the population rose rapidly and spread westward. Settlers came down the wagon road from Pennsylvania through the Great Appalachian Valley into the Piedmont, while still others immigrated from Europe. Unlike the homogeneous population of some of the other Southern states, North Carolinians were a heterogeneous lot representing a variety of religions, economic and social classes, and nationalities. A large slave population was imported to maintain the state's core crops of tobacco, rice, indigo, and cotton.

Colonial Conflict As in several neighboring Southern states, class hostility divided the rich, educated landowners in the eastern part of the colony whose livelihood was based on the plantation and the hardscrabble individualists of the western regions who were primarily small farmers. Residents were also divided over loyalty to Britain and desire for independence. After the outbreak of the American Revolution and the collapse of royal authority in the colony, a provisional government was set up. Most loyalists, including Highland Scots, fled North Carolina following their defeat in 1776 at the battle of Moores Creek Bridge near Wilmington. The bloody Carolina Campaign (1780–81), which pitted American Gen Nathanael Greene against Lord Cornwallis, was the beginning of the end for the British. The American Revolution had the side effect of suppressing the Cherokee uprisings in the western part of the state.

North Carolina opposed a strong central government and did not ratify the Constitution until November 1789, several months after the US government had already begun operation. Social and economic progress was slow in the state until a new, more democratic constitution was adopted in 1835, when the interests of the more populous but less powerful western region at last won out over the politically dominant tidewater planter aristocracy. Also in that year, the Cherokee began their final forced exodus from North Carolina.

Reluctant Rebel Unlike South Carolina, which

Fun Facts

- The designation of North Carolinians as "Tar Heels" has been traced back to the Revolutionary War, when patriotic residents poured tar into a stream across which British troops led by Lord Cornwallis retreated. The Redcoats emerged from the stream with the stuff sticking to their heels.

- P T Barnum made the first stop of his circus in Rocky Mount, North Carolina, on November 12, 1836.

- Biltmore Estate, in Asheville, is the largest private residence ever built in America. The 255-room mansion, built by George W Vanderbilt, was modeled after the châteaux in France's Loire Valley.

- North Carolina refused to ratify the US Constitution until the Bill of Rights was added.

- Natives of North Carolina's Outer Banks, a string of small islands, sandbars, and reefs along the coast, are said to be the descendants of pirates. In fact, the notorious pirate Blackbeard (Edward Teach) was killed on Ocracoke Island in the Outer Banks in 1718.

led the South into secession from the Union, North Carolina at first sought compromise in an effort to remain in the Union. Few North Carolinians held slaves, and there was in fact considerable antislavery sentiment. But the firing on Fort Sumter finally prompted the state to follow its neighbor states into the Confederacy in May 1861 (the next-to-last state to do so). Once it seceded, however, the state sent more troops to the Confederate forces than any other state. Although many small engagements were fought on North Carolina soil, the state was not seriously invaded until late in the Civil War, when Sherman's rampaging army advanced north from Georgia. Confederate Gen J E Johnston surrendered his huge army to Sherman near Durham on April 26, 1865.

Economic Revival Although the state suffered the political corruption and social instability of the Reconstruction years, there did begin a sharp rise in industry in the Piedmont region during this time. Tobacco manufacturing, first centered in Durham, received a tremendous boost from the sharp increase in tobacco consumption during the war and later from the introduction of cigarette-making machines. Tobacco barons like R J Reynolds and James B Duke flourished as a result. The textile and furniture industries also brought jobs to the state in the late 19th century.

The New Century A new progressive era marked the turn of the century, reaching its zenith in the successful airplane flight of the Wright Brothers near Kitty Hawk. An ambitious effort to expand public education for both whites and blacks achieved notable success, and a renewed focus was placed on developing agricultural and industrial resources. Unfortunately, this progressivism did not extend to the area of black voting rights, which were virtually stripped away by the adoption of a "grandfather" clause to the state constitution in 1900, thus assuring white supremacy for decades to come. Still, North Carolina underwent relatively peaceful integration of its public schools following the 1954 de-

segregation ruling.

After World War II, North Carolina's industry blossomed, and during the 1950s the state was the industrial leader of the South. Tremendous growth continued into the early 1970s. The shift toward high-technology industries has led to the prominence of the Research Triangle area, a region anchored by three of the state's leading universities: the University of North Carolina at Chapel Hill, Duke University at Durham, and North Carolina State University at Raleigh. Though North Carolina ranks near the top in the nation in industry and technology, the state also mines a significant amount of minerals and is highly regarded for the fine craftsmanship of its furniture.

DRIVING DISTANCES
Cape Hatteras
142 miles SE of Norfolk, VA
232 miles SE of Richmond, VA
250 miles E of Raleigh
449 miles NE of Charleston, SC
487 miles E of Asheville
Raleigh
143 miles NE of Charlotte
151 miles S of Richmond, VA
248 miles E of Asheville
250 miles W of Cape Hatteras
289 miles NW of Charleston, SC
Asheville
111 miles E of Knoxville, TN
112 miles NW of Charlotte
197 miles NE of Atlanta, GA
248 miles W of Raleigh
487 miles W of Cape Hatteras

A Closer Look
GEOGRAPHY

North Carolina contains three distinct geographical regions. Comprising nearly half of the state, the **Coastal Plain** region is further divided into a swampy tidewater portion right on the coast and a gently rolling, well-drained interior. The tidewater region contains a long chain of barrier islands known as the **Outer Banks.** These islands, which extend from Virginia to South Carolina, are covered with sand dunes that range from a few feet to 100 feet high. The remainder of the tidewater averages about 20 feet above sea level. Three capes (Hatteras, Lookout, and Fear) jut out into the dangerous offshore waters (known as the "Graveyard of the Atlantic" because of the tremendous number of shipwrecks that have occurred there). Although there are several ports and the **Intracoastal Waterway** wends its way between the Outer Banks and the mainland, the remainder of the Coastal Plain is navigable only by small craft because of silting and shallow sounds and estuaries. Among the cities in the Coastal Plain are New Bern (the state's first capital and second-oldest town), the deep-sea port of Morehead City, and the historic waterfront towns of Beaufort and Wilmington.

The **Coastal Plain** region extends from 120

120 to 140 miles westward rising gradually to the **Fall Line**—a 30-mile-wide zone where upland rivers drop to the flatter lowlands. Above the Fall Line is the third region, the **Piedmont,** a region of rolling forested hills making up about 40% of the state's area. The prominent ridges and hills of the eastern Piedmont are the remnants of an ancient mountain chain that paralleled the Appalachians. Cities in the Piedmont include the Research Triangle cities (Raleigh, Chapel Hill, and Durham); the Triad area of High Point, Greensboro, and Winston-Salem; and Charlotte, the state's largest city.

The **Appalachian Mountain** region in the far west is bordered by the **Blue Ridge Mountains** on the east and the **Great Smoky Mountains** on the west. Summits in the Blue Ridge chain generally rise to between 3,000 and 4,000 feet, but a few peak at over 6,000 feet. In contrast, more than 80 peaks in the Great Smoky Mountains rise to above 5,000 feet and more than 43 rise above 6,000 feet. The Smokies are also characterized by cross ridges, plateaus, and basins. In this region the Blue Ridge Parkway snakes along the spines of the Blue Ridge and Great Smoky Mountains. The world's second-oldest river (the only older river is the Nile), ironically named the New River, flows through the high country and dozens of waterfalls along its course plunge over steep slopes and ledges. The cultural centers of this region are Asheville and Hickory.

AVG MONTHLY TEMPS (°F) & RAINFALL (IN)		
	Cape Hatteras	Raleigh
Jan	46/4.7	40/3.6
Feb	46/4.1	42/3.4
Mar	51/4.0	50/3.7
Apr	67/3.2	59/2.9
May	67/4.1	69/3.7
June	74/4.2	74/3.7
July	78/5.4	78/4.4
Aug	78/6.1	77/4.4
Sept	74/5.8	71/3.3
Oct	65/4.8	60/2.7
Nov	56/4.8	50/2.9
Dec	49/4.5	42/3.1

CLIMATE

Because of its size, location, exposure to the ocean, and regions of high elevations, North Carolina has the most varied climate of any eastern state. The coastal area enjoys subtropical conditions with some severe storms and hurricanes, while the mountainous west experiences a medium continental climate characterized by cool summers and heavier rainfall than the rest of the state. Although the mountains experience enough snow (four to six inches per year) for an active ski industry, winter weather rarely interferes with travel opportunities. Some lodgings and attractions in the mountains, however, are closed for several of the winter months. Be sure to check ahead before traveling in the mountains between December and March.

WHAT TO PACK

Packing decisions should be based on the season of the year and the region you are visiting. Winter in the mountains may require heavy coats, gloves, and boots, while cool weather in the remainder of the state may require little more than layered cottons or lightweight woolens with sweaters or jackets. Mountain nights can be chilly at any time of year.

TOURIST INFORMATION

For a North Carolina vacation guide, contact the **North Carolina Travel and Tourism Division,** Department of Commerce, 430 North Salisbury St, Raleigh, NC 27611 (tel toll free 800/VISIT-NC). The **NC Dept of Public Information** maintains a Web page (http://www.state.nc.us) with general information about the state. To find out how to obtain tourist information for individual cities and parks in North Carolina, look under specific cities in the listings section of this book.

DRIVING RULES AND REGULATIONS

The speed limit is 65 mph on rural interstates, 55 mph elsewhere. Right turns on red are permitted (after a complete stop) unless otherwise indicated. All front seat passengers must wear a seat belt. The state's child restraint law requires that children three years of age and younger must be secured in a child safety seat, while children ages three to six may ride in a child safety seat or be secured by a seat belt. Motorcyclists are required to wear a helmet. Insurance is mandatory.

RENTING A CAR

All the major car rental companies maintain outlets in the mid- to large-size cities of North Carolina. The minimum age to rent a car varies by company, so be sure to check ahead if age might create a problem.

Don't forget to check with your insurance company or credit card to see if your insurance coverage extends to rental vehicles.

- **Alamo** (tel toll free 800/327-9633)
- **Avis** (tel 800/831-2847)
- **Budget** (tel 800/527-0700)
- **Dollar** (tel 800/800-4000)
- **Hertz** (tel 800/654-3131)
- **National** (tel 800/227-7368)
- **Thrifty** (tel 800/367-2277)

ESSENTIALS

Area Code: The western part of the state (including Asheville and Charlotte) uses the **704** area code. In the central part of the state (including Greensboro and Winston-Salem), the **910** area code is used. Raleigh and the eastern portion of the state use **919.**

Emergencies: In approximately 75% of North Carolina (including all the major metropolitan areas), use 911 to summon emergency help.

Liquor Laws: Alcoholic beverages are sold only through government-operated stores and by qualified restaurants and clubs. Liquor may be sold between the hours of 7am and 2am except on Sunday, when it may not be sold until noon. (Local jurisdictions may prohibit *any* sales on Sunday, however.) You must be 21 years of age to purchase alcoholic beverages.

Road Info: To find out about road conditions, call the State Department of Transportation at 919/549-5100.

Smoking: North Carolina has no statewide smoking laws, although many hotels, restaurants, and places of business voluntarily designate nonsmoking sections.

Taxes: The statewide sales tax is 4%, although some local jurisdictions levy an additional 2%. Hotel taxes, which are imposed in certain counties and municipalities, average 3%.

Time Zone: North Carolina is in the Eastern time zone and the entire state observes daylight saving time.

Best of the State

WHAT TO SEE AND DO

Below is a general overview of some of the top sights and attractions in North Carolina. To find out more detailed information, look under "Attractions" under individual cities in the listings portion of this book.

National Parks More than half of the 515,000 acres of the **Great Smoky Mountains National Park,** America's most popular and most visited national park, are in North Carolina. Within the park is a **Pioneer Homestead;** miles of hiking trails; and **Clingman's Dome**—highest mountain in the park, second-highest in the eastern United States, and the highest point on the Appalachian Trail. Located near Kitty Hawk and Kill Devil Hill on the Outer Banks, the **Wright Brothers National Memorial** commemorates the first powered flight in 1903 with a visitors center/museum, an airport, a reconstructed hangar and shop, a monument, and several historical markers. Learn about the Lost Colony at **Fort Raleigh National Historic Site,** Manteo. The first patriot victory in the American Revolution was at the **Moores Creek National Battlefield,** northwest of Wilmington. A pivotal Revolutionary War battle is commemorated at the **Guilford Courthouse National Military Park,** Greensboro. Pulitzer Prize–winning author Carl Sandburg spent the last 22 years of his life at Connemara, his farm near Flat Rock. Now at the **Carl Sandburg Home National Historic Site,** the complex includes the house furnished as if the author just went out for a walk, as well as the outbuildings where his wife and daughters operated a goat farm. Twenty-six miles of the New River have been designated as a National Wild and Scenic River.

State Parks Among the most visited state parks is **Merchants Millpond State Park** (tel 919/357-1191), located in a swamp forest where you can canoe to a stand of 1,000-year-old virgin cypress. The remains of one of two Confederate ironclad gunboats completed in North Carolina, and the grave site of the state's first constitutionally elected governor, are among the attractions at the **CSS *Neuse* State Historic Site** in Kinston (tel 919/522-2091). Hang gliders and kite flyers head for **Jockey's Ridge State Park** in Nags Head (tel 919/441-7132), site of the largest sand dune on the East Coast.

Natural Wonders Wind, water, and time have created many spectacular natural formations in North Carolina. At 6,684 feet, **Mount Mitchell** is the highest peak in the eastern United States. **Chimney Rock** is a giant 500 million-year-old "chimney" with a spectacular 75-mile view of the surrounding area, including Lake Lure. If you follow the trail to 404-foot **Hickory Nut Falls,** you'll recognize much of the magnificent scenery from the movie *Last of the Mohicans.* Nearby, the **Bottomless Pools** are deep holes caused by stream erosion. Reportedly, air currents from the Johns River Gorge return objects tossed from the rock formation called **Blowing Rock,** in the Boone/Blowing Rock area. In addition to Hickory Nut Falls, a concentration of falls connects the mountain towns of Brevard, Cashiers, and Highlands earning the area the title **Land of Water-falls.** Among the cascades in this series are **Kalakaleskies Falls,** 18 small falls in a ¼-mile stretch of river; 250-foot **Cullasaja Falls;** and **Bridal Veil Falls,** which you can drive under. Other falls in North Carolina include **Linville Falls,** which plunges hundreds of feet into a gorge near the Blue Ridge Parkway, and **Whitewater Falls** near Sapphire, which at 441 feet is among the tallest in the East.

You don't need to go to a water theme park when nature provides one of its own. Fast-moving currents gliding over its mirror-slick surface at **Sliding Rock,** located north of Brevard, allow you to ride 150 feet down its slope. Explore the well-marked passages that follow an underground stream at **Linville Caverns,** near the Blue Ridge Parkway. Modern whirlpool baths are fed by hot natural mineral water at **Hot Springs Spa Mineral Baths** in Hot Springs.

Manmade Wonders What nature hasn't created, man attempts. One section of the Blue Ridge Parkway southwest of Blowing Rock, the **Linn Cove Viaduct,** appears to be a floating highway. This feat of modern engineering winds around Grandfather Mountain without appearing to be connected to anything but thin air. The 480-foot-high **Fontana Dam,** near Bryson City, is the highest dam in the Tennessee Valley Authority (TVA) system. Visitors ride an incline railway to the powerhouse, visitors center, and observation point. Atop Grandfather Mountain, the view from the **Mile-High Swinging Bridge** will take your breath away. Manmade marvels aren't confined to this century, however. Centuries ago, the **Town Creek Indian Mound,** Mount

Gilead, served as a ceremonial center with temples and a mortuary.

Family Favorites Families and children of all ages will want to visit many of the attractions listed in the other categories as well as these perennial favorites. **Paramount Carowinds** is located astride the North Carolina/South Carolina border near Charlotte. The park's historical ambience is home to over 30 rides, a wave pool, and live entertainment. Ride a chairlift or incline railway to **Ghost Town in the Sky,** a Maggie Valley amusement park with an Old West theme. On summer nights a sound and light show is presented onboard the **USS *North Carolina* Battleship Memorial.** Those city slickers who want to live the cowpoke lifestyle can have an overnight trail ride adventure at **Cataloochee Ranch** in Maggie Valley (the ranch also offers skiing in the winter). Visitors can tour a re-creation of a mid-18th-century Cherokee village at the **Oconaluftee Indian Village,** Cherokee. *Elizabeth II,* a replica of the 16th-century ship that brought English settlers to the Outer Banks, is berthed along the waterfront as part of the visitor center at the **Elizabeth II State Historic Site** in Manteo.

Beaches The sound of the surf is both your lullaby and your alarm clock along North Carolina's 300 miles of shore. The **Cape Hatteras National Seashore,** the country's first national seashore, runs 75 miles through the Outer Banks islands of Bodie, Hatteras, and Ocracoke, covering more than 30,000 acres. **Cape Lookout National Seashore** is known for its isolated beauty, outstanding fishing, exceptional shelling, the Cape Lookout Lighthouse, and the ghost village of Portsmouth. Other popular beaches include **Wrightsville Beach** (east of Wilmington) and **Hammocks Beach** (south of Swansboro).

Historic Buildings North Carolina is blessed with a legacy of structures that reveal its rich past. In colonial times, New Bern's **Tryon Palace** was called the most beautiful public building in America. Today the reconstruction of the grand brick government house is the focal point among 150 landmarks in the historic town that once served as North Carolina's capital. Wilmington's **Cotton Exchange,** a 19th-century structure from which more cotton was once shipped than from any other place in the world, and **Chandler's Wharf,** another historic complex, both now contain shops and boutiques. Chandler's Wharf is also home to a nautical museum. Asheville's 255-room French Renaissance–style **Biltmore House** was built as a summer home in 1898 by George Vanderbilt, grandson of tycoon Cornelius Vanderbilt. The grand château is furnished with exquisite antiques and art and surrounded by formal gardens, vineyards, and a winery. See the glorious stained-glass windows and listen to a pipe organ recital at Duke University's Gothic **Duke Chapel,** Durham, which was patterned after England's Canterbury Cathedral. Reminiscent of the great lodges of the western national parks, the **Grove Park Inn** was built in 1913—without a blueprint. Although well-heeled tourists in Asheville may have been able to stay at the Grove Park Inn, the less affluent may have rented rooms at the boardinghouse operated by the mother of author Thomas Wolfe. He later used his life there as the setting of his novel *Look Homeward, Angel.* Today the site is operated as the **Thomas Wolfe Memorial State Historic Site.**

Museums The $29 million **North Carolina Museum of History and Natural Sciences** in Raleigh features a Folklife Gallery that presents a chronological history of the area from prehistory to the present; a Women's History exhibit; and the North Carolina Sports Hall of Fame. **Discovery Place,** in Charlotte, is the state's largest museum of science and technology. In the same complex are an aviary, aquariums, the Charlotte Observer Omnimax Theater, and the Kelly Space Voyager Planetarium. You can see (and smell) bread being baked, watch cloth being woven, and listen to hymns being sung at **Old Salem,** a living history museum in a restored and reconstructed Moravian village in Winston-Salem. The small **Mint Museum** in Charlotte, housed in the first US Mint branch outside Washington, showcases fine collections of American, European, and pre-Columbian art. Relive the golden age of the railroads at the **North Carolina Transportation Museum** at the **Spencer Shops State Historic Site** in Spencer, a one-time railroad hub. Shouts of "All aboard!" call you to weekend rides around the site of the Southern Railway's former central repair shops. At the **Duke Homestead State Historic Site** in Durham, you can learn how the city became the brightleaf tobacco hub of the state after the Civil War. In addition to the homestead itself, the complex contains a museum, farm buildings, and exhibits. Not far away you can visit **Bennett Place,** the isolated log cabin where Confederate Gen Joseph E Johnston surrendered to Union Gen William T Sherman—the largest troop surrender of the Civil War. Cherokee history and culture are chronicled at the **Museum of the Cherokee Indian,** Cherokee.

Gardens **Craggy Gardens,** northeast of Asheville, is famous for its profusion of crimson-purple rhododendrons. A 16th-century English pleasure garden is re-created at the **Elizabethan Gardens,** on Roanoke Island. The Southeast's largest collection of native plants and herbs is displayed at the **North Carolina Botanical Gardens,** Chapel Hill. Gardens surround the **Reynolda House Museum of American Art,** Winston-Salem, the former home of tobacco magnate R J Reynolds. Stroll along the lily ponds and through the rose arbors at the **Sarah P Duke Gardens** on the campus of Duke University, Durham. In the Boone area, six gardens of native plants are found at the **Daniel Boone Native Gardens.**

Outdoor Dramas Dramatic things happen in North Carolina during the summer, as numerous outdoor theatrical productions are performed against backdrops of natural scenic beauty. *The Lost Colony,* by Pulitzer Prize–winning author Paul Green, portrays the hardships of the state's original band of English colonists on Roanoke Island. The oldest of the nation's outdoor dramas, *Unto These Hills* is performed at the Cherokee Reservation and tells the tragic story of the Cherokee exodus over the Trail of Tears. The life of Daniel Boone is recounted in *Horn in the West,* performed each summer in Boone.

Zoos & Aquariums You can see both native and exotic animals at several zoos and game preserves around the state. The **North Carolina Zoological Park** in Asheboro is the world's largest natural habitat zoo. Its African region features eight outdoor exhibits. As part of a $32 million expansion, the zoo has opened a 200-acre version of North America with four major new habitats: Rocky Coast, Cypress Swamp, Marsh, and Touch and Learn Center. North Carolina is home to three **aquariums** that display marine life. They are in **Manteo** on Roanoke Island, and in **Kure Beach** and **Pine Knoll Shores.** Ride a stagecoach through herds of buffalo and other animals at the **Buffalo Ranch** near Concord.

Train Excursions At one time railroads were instrumental in opening up almost inaccessible areas of the state to commerce. Although the Iron Horses are almost gone, you can still do some of your sightseeing by rail. The **Great Smoky Mountains Railway,** headquartered in Dillsboro, chugs through the steep mountains, skirts tumultuous rivers and placid lakes, crosses fearfully high trestles, and disappears into dark tunnels between Bryson City, Andrews, Murphy, and Dillsboro. Passengers can enjoy the experience in club cars, coaches, or open cars. Blowing Rock is the home of the **Tweetsie Railroad,** a narrow-gauge railroad where steam locomotives puff through mountain passes and around a frontier village and an amusement park.

EVENTS AND FESTIVALS

ASHEVILLE AND WESTERN NORTH CAROLINA

- **Spring Festival,** Hawksnest Golf and Ski Resort, Seven Devils. Ski racing, snow-related festivities. First weekend in March. Call 704/963-6561.
- **Festival of Flowers,** Biltmore Estate, Asheville. Profusion of flowers inside mansion and outside in gardens. Early April through early May. Call 704/255-1700 or toll free 800/543-2961.
- **Grandfather Mountain Highland Games and Gathering of the Scottish Clans,** Linville. Scottish dance, music, and athletic events. Early July. Call 704/733-1333.
- **North Carolina International Folk Festival— Folkmoot USA,** Waynesville and Maggie Valley. International music and dance. Late July. Call 704/648-2730.
- **North Carolina Apple Festival,** Hendersonville. Orchard tours, cooking contests, crafts, food, parade. Early September. Call 704/697-4669.

CAPE HATTERAS AND EASTERN NORTH CAROLINA

- **North Carolina Azalea Festival,** Wilmington. Parade, entertainment, garden tours. Early April. Call 910/763-0905.
- **Spring Historic Homes and Gardens Tour,** New Bern. Tour Tryon Palace and other area homes, gardens, and historic sites. Early April. Call 919/633-6448.
- **RiverSpree,** Elizabeth City. Dancing, parades, food, crafts, live entertainment. Mem Day weekend. Call 919/335-4365.
- **Hillsborough Hog Day,** Hillsborough. Barbecue, potbellied pig contest, entertainment, crafts, vintage car show. Mid-June. Call 919/968-2060.
- **Virginia Dare Day Celebration,** Fort Raleigh National Historic Site, Manteo. Commemoration of the birth of Virginia Dare, with interpretive programs and tours. Mid-August. Call 919/473-2127 or toll free 800/488-5012.

RALEIGH AND CENTRAL NORTH CAROLINA

- **Annual Star Fiddlers Convention,** Biscoe. Bluegrass fiddlers from all over the South. First weekend in March. Call 919/428-2972.
- **Stoneybrook Steeplechase,** Southern Pines. Five-card race, tailgate parties, hat competition. Mid-April. Call 910/692-8000.
- **National Hollerin' Contest,** Spivey's Corner. Hollerin' as a traditional form of communication. Mid-June. Call 910/567-2156.
- **Eastern Music Festival,** Greensboro. Concert series including orchestras, chamber ensembles, recitals. Late June through early August. Call 910/333-7450.
- **Mayberry Days,** Mount Airy. Celebration of *The Andy Griffith Show,* with entertainment, golf tournament, walking tours, pig pickin'. Late September. Call toll free 800/286-6193.

SPECTATOR SPORTS

Auto Racing North Carolinians are enthusiastic race fans. The one-mile oval at the **North Carolina Motor Speedway** in Rockingham (tel 910/582-2861) is one of NASCAR's oldest racetracks. Both the Pro-Am Nationals and the US Nationals roar into the **Rockingham International Dragway** on US 1 (tel 910/582-3400) in the spring and fall. Some of NASCAR's fastest action occurs at ultramodern **Concord Motor Speedway,** 5707 Shoreview Dr (tel 704/782-5863), and **Charlotte Motor Speedway** (tel 704/455-3200), which seats the second-largest audience in racing. On nonracing days, you can take a behind-the-scenes tour of the facility. The **North Wilkesboro Speedway** (tel 910/667-6663) is the home of the First Union 400 and the Tyson–Holly Farms 400 and the **Hickory Motor Speedway** (tel 704/464-3655) is the site of several Grand National races. **Bahari Racing,** 208 Rolling Hills Rd near Mooresville (tel 704/664-6670), is where Michael Waltrip's Winston Cup and Grand National cars are built.

Baseball Although North Carolina has no major league teams, you can take your pick from a number of minor league teams. The two most popular are the **Durham Bulls,** who play at Durham Athletic Park (tel 919/688-8211), and the **Charlotte**

Knights, who play at Knights Castle (tel 704/332-3746).

Basketball The NBA's **Charlotte Hornets** continue to set attendance records by packing the Charlotte Coliseum (tel 704/357-0489) with close to 24,000 screaming fans. North Carolina—home to three perennial powerhouse teams—also has a serious love affair with college basketball. The **University of North Carolina Tar Heels** play at the Dean E Smith Center in Chapel Hill (tel 919/962-2296); the **Duke Blue Devils** play at Cameron Indoor Stadium in Durham (tel 919/681-2583); the **North Carolina State University Wolfpack** play at Reynolds Coliseum in Raleigh (tel 919/515-2106).

College Football The **University of North Carolina Tar Heels** play at Kenan Memorial Stadium in Chapel Hill (tel 919/962-2296); the **Duke University Blue Devils** play at Wallace Wade Stadium in Durham (tel 919/681-2583); and the **North Carolina State University Wolfpack** play at Carter-Finley Stadium in Raleigh (tel 919/515-2106).

Pro Football North Carolina is home to one of the newest NFL expansion teams: the Charlotte-based **Carolina Panthers** (tel 704/358-1644).

Hockey Being located in the South doesn't prevent North Carolinians from enjoying three hockey teams: the **Charlotte Checkers** (tel 704/372-3600); **Greensboro Monarchs** (tel 910/852-6170); and the **Raleigh Ice Caps,** who play at Dorton Arena at the North Carolina State Fairgrounds (tel 919/755-0022).

Soccer The **Charlotte Eagles** (tel 704/841-8644) play at The Latin School and the **Raleigh Flyers** (tel 919/890-6026) play at Broaden High School.

ACTIVITIES A TO Z

Bicycling Pedalers can find a type of terrain appropriate to their level of expertise. Leisurely riding is the norm along the coast, while those interested in mud, sweat, and gears gravitate to rugged trails in the western forests. Trails and roads good for sturdy bikes are found around Fontana Lake, Nantahala Gorge, Brevard, and Highlands. A 27-mile loop snakes through gorgeous scenery in the Great Smoky Mountains National Park, while several trails in the Pisgah National Forest wind past spectacular streams and waterfalls. There are ten state-designated bike routes all around the state, ranging

from the 300-mile Ports of Call route (connecting historic coastal towns) to the 700-mile Mountains to the Sea route. For more information, contact the **North Carolina Office of Bicycle and Pedestrian Transportation,** PO Box 25201, Raleigh, NC 27611 (tel 919/733-2804).

Boating More than two dozen large lakes and reservoirs are scattered through the Piedmont and several TVA reservoirs are found in the mountains. With 40,000 acres, coastal Lake Mattamuskeet is North Carolina's largest natural lake. Charlotte's 34-mile-long Lake Norman, the state's largest man-made lake, boasts 32,500 acres of water activities and 10 public access areas. There's plenty of access to water in North Carolina's state parks, some of which have rental boats. Elizabeth City, on the Intracoastal Waterway, welcomes visiting yachts with zeal—dock slips are free for the first 48 hours, a rose is proffered to each female passenger, and when there are enough boats in port there's a wine and cheese party.

Camping Whether you want to pitch your tent on a wind-swept beach or in a cool mountain glen, North Carolina's 60 public and 300 private campgrounds will offer an appropriate site. Your two best sources of information are the brochures *North Carolina State Parks,* published by **North Carolina Parks and Recreation** (tel toll free 800/VISIT-NC), and *North Carolina Camping Guide,* a publication of the **North Carolina Campground Owners Association** (tel 919/779-5709).

Climbing & Rapelling With 43 peaks that tower above 6,000 feet, it's no surprise that North Carolina is so popular with climbers. With the highest cliffs in the East, Whiteside Mountain (between Highlands and Cashiers) is a big attraction for experienced climbers. Other exciting challenges await climbers at Table Rock, Looking Glass Rock, and Linville Gorge —all in the Pisgah National Forest; Crowders Mountain, near Gastonia; and Hanging Rock, near Winston-Salem. For more information on destinations as well as suggestions for guides and outfitters, contact the **North Carolina High Country Host** (tel toll free 800/438-7500).

Diving Curious divers can plumb the depths at many of the 2,000 shipwrecks off North Carolina's coast. Although the Civil War iron clad *Monitor* is off-limits, the USS *Huron* Historic Shipwreck Preserve is a popular spot. Both beginning and expert divers can explore sunken submarines, ocean liners, armed trawlers, and freighters in the Graveyard of the Atlantic. To find out more about what's available as well as to obtain suggestions for guides and dive shops, contact the **North Carolina Coast Host** (tel 910/754-2505).

Fishing The state offers anglers an impressive set of options: from deep-sea fishing to pier and surf casting along the beaches to trolling in natural lakes and countless mountain streams. You can get all kinds of fishing information from the **North Carolina Wildlife Resources Commission** (tel 919/733-3391) or request the guide *Fishing in North Carolina* from North Carolina Travel and Tourism.

Golf Tee off at more than 450 courses throughout North Carolina. For more than a century since famed Scotsman Donald Ross designed the area's first nine holes, **Pinehurst** in Southern Pines (tel toll free 800/346-5362) has been considered the golf capital of the state. Today it sports seven (soon to be eight) signature courses. Thirty courses are clustered around Moore County alone. Elsewhere in the state, the golf course at **Tanglewood Park,** US 158 in Clemmons (tel 910/766-5082), is rated among the Top 10 public courses in the country. The Greater Greensboro Open, a popular event on the PGA Tour, is played in Greensboro each spring.

Hang Gliding It's appropriate that those intent on trying their own wings should congregate at Kitty Hawk—the spot where the Wright brothers launched the first powered flight—to propel themselves off the tall sand dunes. National champions gather at **Jockey's Ridge State Park** (tel 919/441-7132) every May for the Hang Gliding Spectacular.

Hiking More than 285 miles of the Appalachian Trail thread through the high ridges of the Pisgah and Nantahala National Forests and the Great Smoky Mountains National Park. For more information about the trail, contact the **Appalachian Trail Conference,** 100 Otis St, Asheville, NC 28802 (tel 704/254-3708). The 75.8-mile Cape Hatteras Beach Trail (part of which requires you to take the Hatteras Ferry) begins at Whalebone Junction in Nags Head and follows NC 12 to Ocracoke. The Neusiok Trail, located in the Croatan National Forest, runs 21.7 miles through areas of dense vegetation and swampland before ending along the shore of Newport River in Carteret County.

Horseback Riding Several stables offer extensive trail systems in North Carolina's mountains, heartland, or along its coast: **Blowing Rock Stables** (tel 704/295-7851); **Cataloochee Ranch** in Maggie Valley (tel toll free 800/868-1401); **Earthshine Mountain Lodge** at Lake Toxaway (tel 704/862-4207); and **Tanglewood Park,** off US 158 in Clemmons (tel 910/766-5082). **Foothills Equestrian Nature Center** in Tryon (tel toll free 800/440-7848) offers a steeplechase course, show rings, and carriage trails.

Pack Trips North Carolina was the first state east of the Rockies with a llama outfitter guide service. The most comprehensive outfitters include **Noah Llama Treks, Inc** in Valle Crucis (tel 704/297-2171), **Windsong Llama Treks** in Clyde (tel 704/627-6111), and **Avalon Llama Treks** in Swannanoa (tel 704/299-7155).

Sailing & Windsurfing On weekends, North Carolina's hundreds of lakes are bright with colorful sailboats skimming over the waters. Lake Norman, in particular, hosts many sailing regattas and its gusts are favored by windsurfers as well. Both sailing and windsurfing are extremely popular along the coast and the Intracoastal Waterway. Canadian Hole, on the sound side from Cape Hatteras, is the most popular coastal windsurfing spot. Whether you're a novice or looking for bareboat certification, Wrightsville Beach is the place to go for nationally recognized sailing courses.

Skiing For most of the winter, temperatures are low enough for snowmaking equipment to blanket the more than 50 slopes in the western mountains. Among the top resorts are **Appalachian Ski Mountain** in Blowing Rock (tel 704/295-7828), **Cataloochee Ski Area** in Maggie Valley (tel 704/926-0285), **Hawksnest Golf and Ski Resort** in Seven Devils (tel 704/963-6561), and **Sugar Mountain Resort** in Banner Elk (tel 704/898-4521). For ski information, contact the **North Carolina Ski Areas Association,** PO Box 106, Blowing Rock, NC 28605 (tel 704/295-3277).

White-Water Rafting North Carolina's rivers offer an abundance of white-water adventures for rafters of all skill levels. The turbulent Nantahala River offers eight miles of Class I–Class III rapids, while the wide, uncrowded nine miles of the French Broad River provide lively Class II–Class IV rapids and calm pools. Class III–Class IV rapids on the narrow, rocky nine miles of the Nolichucky River

SELECTED PARKS & RECREATION AREAS

• **Great Smoky Mountains National Park,** Oconaluftee Center, US 441, Cherokee, NC 28719 (tel 704/497-9146)

• **Cape Hatteras National Seashore,** Rte 1, Box 675, Manteo, NC 27954 (tel 919/473-5772)

• **Cape Lookout National Seashore,** 3601 Bridges St, Ste F, Morehead City, NC 28557 (tel 919/240-1409)

• **Croatan National Forest,** off US 17, New Bern, NC 28560 (tel 919/638-5628)

• **Nantahala National Forest,** Franklin, NC 28734 (tel 704/524-6441)

• **Pisgah National Forest,** NW of town on US 276, Brevard, NC 28712 (tel 704/257-4200)

• **Pee Dee National Wildlife Refuge,** Box 780, Wadesboro, NC 28170 (tel 704/694-4424)

• **Wright Brothers National Memorial,** Rte 1, Box 675, Manteo, NC 27954 (tel 919/441-7430)

• **Fort Raleigh National Historic Site,** Rte 1, Box 675, Manteo, NC 27954 (tel 919/473-5772)

• **Guilford Courthouse National Military Park,** Box 9806, Greensboro, NC 27429-0806 (tel 919/288-1776)

• **Carolina Beach State Park,** off US 421, Carolina Beach, NC 28428 (tel 910/458-7770)

• **Cliffs of the Neuse State Park,** 345-A Park Entrance Rd, Seven Springs, NC 28578 (tel 919/778-6234)

• **Fort Macon State Park,** E Fort Macon Rd, PO Box 127, Atlantic Beach, NC 28512 (tel 919/726-3775)

• **Hanging Rock State Park,** off NC 1101, Danbury, NC 27016 (tel 910/593-8480)

• **Jockey's Ridge State Park,** off US 158, PO Box 592, Nags Head, NC 27959 (tel 919/441-7132)

• **Lake Waccamaw State Park,** US 74/76, Lake Waccamaw, NC 28450 (tel 910/646-4748)

• **Merchant's Millpond State Park,** Rte 1, Box 141-A, Gatesville, NC 27938 (tel 919/357-1191)

• **Morrow Mountain State Park,** 49104 Morrow Mountain Rd, Albemarle, NC 28001 (tel 704/982-4402)

• **Mount Mitchell State Park,** NC 128, Burnsville, NC 28714 (tel 704/675-4611)

• **New River State Park,** NC 1588, Jefferson, NC 28640 (tel 910/982-2587)

• **Pilot Mountain State Park,** US 52, Pilot Mountain, NC 27041 (tel 910/325-2355)

• **Raven Rock State Park,** NC 1314, Lillington, NC 27546 (tel 910/893-4888)

boasts roaring rapids and big drops. The five-mile upper section of Wilson Creek is an easy Class II–Class III float trip, while the three-mile lower section offers Class III–Class IV plunges over steep waterfalls. Beginners might want to start on the 4½-mile Class I–Class II Tuckasegee River. Numerous commercial outfitters lead guided and semi-guided half-day, all-day, and overnight float trips on all these rivers. For more information or a list of outfitters, contact **North Carolina High Country Host** (tel toll free 800/438-7500), or **Smoky Mountain Host** (tel toll free 800/432-4678).

Driving the State

Start	Asheville
Finish	Asheville
Distance	Approximately 155 miles
Time	2 days
Highlights	Mountains, overlooks, waterfalls, rock formations, museums, crafts, largest private home in America, Carl Sandburg's home, cultural and outdoors activities, scenic railroad

The high elevations and moderate temperatures of North Carolina's rugged mountains have been luring lowlanders for more than 150 summers. Flat Rock is the oldest of the resort towns, but there are many other rustic hamlets. Vacationers—then and now—have been attracted by the delightful coolness, the pollution-free air, the dramatic scenery, the glorious isolation, and the endless variety of outdoor recreational activities. The spectacular Blue Ridge Mountains, part of the Appalachian chain, run in elongated crests overlaid by one of the most botanically abundant forests in the world. Icy, crystal-clear rivers tumble down the steep slopes providing exhilarating white-water adventures, while lakes provide unlimited opportunities for swimming, boating, and fishing. Long, inviting trails draw hikers, mountain bikers, and equestrians throughout the year; plentiful snowfall and ideal conditions for manmade snow attract winter skiers.

Fabulously wealthy George Vanderbilt constructed a summer home near Asheville, and authors Thomas Wolfe, Carl Sandburg, O Henry, and F Scott Fitzgerald spent time in the region. Today, thousands of artisans draw inspiration for their work from the peace, solitude, and natural beauty surrounding them. Along this route you'll meet colorful hill characters, sophisticated urban dwellers, and transplants from all over the country who have become zealous converts to the mountain way of life.

For additional information on lodgings, dining, and attractions in the region covered by the tour, look under specific cities in the listings portion of this chapter. (Note: Many mountain accommodations and attractions are closed between December and March, so be sure to check ahead before you set out on a winter trip to this area.)

Located at the intersection of I-40 and I-26, just off the Blue Ridge Parkway, is the first stop:

1. Asheville, consistently rated as one of the "most livable" cities in the country. Visitors and residents alike may enjoy its stunning mountain scenery, sporting activities, arts and crafts, and architectural treasures. An extravagant testimonial to turn-of-the-century affluence, the **Biltmore Estate,** Biltmore Ave off US 25, is the largest private home ever constructed in America. Built for a grandson of Cornelius Vanderbilt, the 250-room French châteauesque mansion was designed by Richard Hunt Morris and landscaped by Frederick Law Olmstead (who planned New York's Central Park). The house is furnished with exquisite antiques, Flemish tapestries, and works of art by Renoir, Sargent, Whistler, and others; the formal upstairs rooms include the Winter Garden conservatory, the 90-foot-long Gallery, the library (with over 10,000 volumes), and the baronial Banquet Hall. Informal play rooms include a bowling alley, a gymnasium, and an indoor pool with 17 dressing rooms. The guided tour also includes the working area of the house: the kitchens, pantries, laundries, and servants' quarters. In the adjoining Carriage House are harness, saddle, blanket, and tack rooms, as well as two restaurants. Formal gardens—the Library Terrace Garden, the Italian Gardens, the Rose Garden, and the Victorian Conservatory—surround the mansion.

Also on the estate is the **Biltmore Winery,** winner of more than 100 medals for excellence. Visitors can follow the wine-making process through production rooms, state-of-the-art chemical and biological laboratories, and the cavelike tunnels where the wine is stored during the fermentation stage. Outside the gates of the estate is **Biltmore Village,** a town created by Vanderbilt for the workers and artisans who constructed his castle. Today the English Tudor buildings house a variety of cafes and boutiques.

Guided walking tours of downtown are offered by **Tour Services of Historic Asheville,** 14 Battery Park Ave, or you can pick up self-guided tour brochures from **Asheville City Development** (29 Haywood St) or the **Asheville Visitors Center** (151 Haywood St). You'll be surprised to learn that Asheville has more art deco architecture than any Southeastern city other than Miami. Noteworthy structures include **City Hall** (70 Court Plaza), the **First Baptist Church of Asheville** (5 Oak St), the **Basilica of St Lawrence** (97 Haywood St), and the **Grove Arcade** in Battery Park (the country's first enclosed mall).

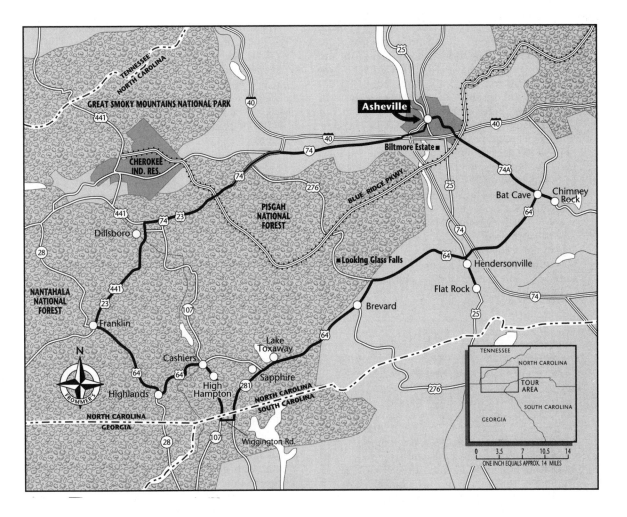

Take a Break

One of the most renowned resorts in the Southeast is the **Grove Park Inn and Country Club,** 290 Macon Ave in Asheville (tel 704/252-2711). Built in 1913 from boulders blasted from the mountain on which it sits, the inn is reminiscent of the national park lodges at Yosemite and Yellowstone. The most popular of the inn's several restaurants is the **Sunset Terrace,** open April–October. Light lunches range from $7 to $14, and include choices such as pasta or chicken. A five-course dinner—built around elegant entrees like steak and lobster, prime rib, New York strip, or grilled Alaska salmon— is $32–$46.

Because this scenic driving tour makes a circle and returns to Asheville, save the remaining sights

until you return. Take US 74 southeast for 20 miles to:

2. **Bat Cave/Chimney Rock,** a spectacularly scenic area of rugged outcroppings. At **Chimney Rock Park,** US 74, ride an elevator up 26 stories through the mountain, then take a short path and some steep stairs to Chimney Rock—a 500-million-year-old granite monolith. From the top of the rock you can see for 75 miles through **Hickory Nut Gorge** to beautiful **Lake Lure** and beyond. Several hiking trails wend through the park (past scenery you may recognize from the movie *Last of the Mohicans*) to **Hickory Nut Falls.** At 404 feet, Hickory Nut is twice the height of Niagara Falls.

   Take US 64 southwest, then turn south on US 25 and continue 22 miles to:

3. **Flat Rock,** whose most famous visitor decided to stay. Pulitzer Prize–winning author Carl Sandburg

came to Flat Rock in 1945, and he liked it so much he bought the local farm where he lived until his death in 1967. While Sandburg wrote, his wife and daughters ran a goat farm. Now the **Carl Sandburg National Historic Site,** Little River Rd off US 25, the farmstead includes the 1838 house and 24 outbuildings. Filled with personal belongings (including books, documents, and an extensive collection of phonograph records), the interior of the house looks as if the family had just gone out for a walk. During the summer, performances of several of Sandburg's works take place on the grounds. Built in 1832, nearby **St John's in the Wilderness Church,** US 25, is one of the oldest churches in western North Carolina. Many prominent Southerners are buried in the peaceful cemetery. The **Vagabond Players** perform each summer at the **Flat Rock Playhouse,** Thomas Wolfe Dr, North Carolina's state theater and the oldest professional summer theater in the state.

Take a Break

The **Woodfield Inn,** US 25 (tel 704/693-6016), has been a preferred stopover for travelers for more than 135 years. Perched at the top of a hill, the hotel boasts rocker-filled porches, a wine room, and three dining rooms. Luncheon entrees such as chicken salad, quiche, and teriyaki chicken salad run between $5 and $8; dinners of honey-baked ham, prime rib, and leg of lamb range from $10 to $14. Folks drive from miles around for the Sunday brunch: quiche, eggs, french toast, ham, potatoes, salads, vegetables, and pastries, all for $7.95.

Retrace US 25 north for 7 miles to:

4. **Hendersonville,** an archetypal turn-of-the-century resort town noted for its shops and cultural activities. As you wander along Main Street, stop in at **Days Gone By,** 303 N Main St. This old-fashioned pharmacy was established in 1882 and still serves up soda fountain treats, as well as collectibles and antiques. The **Apple Valley HO-Scale Model Railroad** is housed in the 1879 **Hendersonville Depot,** Seventh Ave E. Restored and replica antique airplanes are displayed at the **Western North Carolina Air Museum,** 1340 Gilbert St. The **Hendersonville Little Theater** and the **Belfry Players** present several plays annually.

Next, take US 64 west for 22 miles to:

5. **Brevard,** best known for the **Brevard Music Center,** 1000 Provart St, and its summer series of orchestral, choral, opera, and chamber-music concerts. Nature creates a musical melody of its own as it spills over the 250 waterfalls in the area, earning Brevard the nickname "Land of Waterfalls." Gaze in awe at the twin cataracts at **Connestee Falls,** off US 276 south of town, or **Looking Glass Falls,** off US 276 north of town. You can even slide down 150-foot **Sliding Rock**—nature's original water chute.

The surrounding **Pisgah National Forest** offers endless opportunities for hiking, mountain biking, fishing, camping, and other outdoor pursuits. Within the forest, the **Cradle of Forestry in America National Historic Site,** US 276, encompasses a visitor center/museum, a logging locomotive, and two trails that interpret the history of forestry and logging. At the **Holmes Educational State Forest,** Crab Creek Rd, a Talking Tree Trail features listening stations with information on the names and origins of the trees and the ecology of a managed forest. Before leaving the Brevard area, drive along the **North Carolina Forest Heritage National Scenic Byway,** a 79-mile loop through the Pisgah National Forest. From Brevard, go north on US 64 to US 276, then to the **Blue Ridge Parkway,** which you will take to NC 215, then back to US 64 and Brevard. Along the way, you'll see old settlement roads, logging towns, mountain communities, and turn-of-the-century railroads.

Continue west on US 64 to:

6. **Lake Toxaway,** a controlled-access vacation getaway with golf, tennis, and water sports. On the shores of the lake is the luxurious **Greystone Inn,** as good a place as any to spend the night if your schedule allows. Amenities include a high-country breakfast, six-course dinner, and most recreational activities. In the immediately surrounding area, climb the **Toxaway Fire Tower** on Hogback Mountain for a panoramic mountain view, or explore 123-foot **Toxaway Falls.**

Then, follow US 64 west for 20 miles to:

7. **Sapphire,** a mountain town at 3,120 feet in elevation. South of town on NC 281 are several colorfully named waterfalls on the Horsepasture River: Drift, Rainbow, Turtle, Bust-Your-Butt, and the 441-foot-tall Whitewater (one of the tallest falls in the East). Take NC 281 south (you will briefly cross into South Carolina) and take Wiggington Road west to NC 107 and **Silver Run Falls,** a 40-foot cascade reached by a short footpath.

Continue north on NC 107 for 4 miles to:

8. **High Hampton,** home of the **High Hampton Inn and Country Club,** NC 107. Accommodations at this 1,400-acre estate (once owned by Confederate

hero Wade Hampton) include hotel-type rooms in a rustic main lodge or in several cottages. The resort offers golf, sailing, hiking, swimming, and tennis.

Return to US 64 and travel 3 miles west to:

9. **Cashiers,** which sits on an isolated plateau surrounded by the **Nantahala National Forest.** Just as it has been for more than 100 years, Cashiers is a resort town specializing in outdoor activities such as fishing, boating, white-water rafting, and horseback riding. The tiny town has only one traffic light and claims to have the smallest post office in America. Small, attractive shops offer antiques, local crafts, and homemade goodies.

From Cashiers, stay on US 64 west and go 5 miles to the appropriately named:

10. **Highlands.** At an elevation of 4,118 feet, this is one of the highest incorporated municipalities east of the Mississippi. Founded as a resort in 1875, the town is still so popular that the year-round population of 2,000 increases to 20,000 in the summer. The **Chamber of Commerce,** Fifth and Oak Sts, offers free maps and modestly priced audiotapes for 12 different walking and driving tours. Unique shops offer one-of-a-kind creations that range from jewelry to bat houses. The works of outstanding local artists are displayed at the **Bascom-Louise Gallery in the Hudson Library,** E Main St.

But most visitors come to Highlands to enjoy the outdoors. Special programs are scheduled weekly at the Botanical Gardens at the **Highlands Nature Center,** Horse Cove Road. The town's scenic overlooks include **Blue Valley Overlook** on NC 106 and **Whiteside Overlook** on US 64E. The area is also graced with many waterfalls; along US 64 north of town, you'll come to 120-foot **Bridal Veil Falls** (which you can drive under), 75-foot **Dry Falls,** 250-foot **Lower Cullasaja Falls,** and the **Kalakaleskies** (a series of 18 small falls in a quarter-square-mile area).

Take a Break

The **Frog and Owl Cafe,** located in an old mill on Buck Creek Rd in Highlands (tel 704/526-5500), serves exquisite Continental and American cuisine. Entrees such as Roquefort duck or rack of lamb with pistachio-nut sauce are followed by delicious desserts. Dinner is served Tuesday through Saturday and costs $19–$28.

Follow US 64 northwest to Franklin, where you will turn north on US 441 and continue 38 miles to:

11. **Dillsboro,** home of the **Great Smoky Mountain Railroad** on Front St. Four different ½-day excursions (with both open and closed rail cars) are offered. The highlight of the Tuskasegee River Excursion is passing the train wreck site used in the movie *The Fugitive.* On weekends, passengers can enjoy a gourmet dinner excursion, while in December, the train becomes the Santa Express, with onboard festivities including a visit from Santa himself. Before or after your excursion, visit the **Floyd McEachern Historic Railway Museum** at the depot, then browse through Dillsboro's 40 shops; take a break at one of several restaurants; or spend the night at one of the bed-and-breakfasts such as the **Squire Watkins Inn,** located in a charming turn-of-the-century house on W Haywood Rd.

Take US 74 for 14 miles and you will be back at our starting point:

12. **Asheville.** Author Thomas Wolfe grew up here, and he used events from his life at his mother's boardinghouse for his semi-autobiographical novel *Look Homeward, Angel.* The boardinghouse, now the **Thomas Wolfe Memorial,** 48 Spruce St, is open for tours. During a festival in May, costumed actors give readings from Wolfe's works.

Asheville is known for its high concentration of artisans. The **Southern Highland Handicraft Guild** has represented Southern Appalachian artisans since 1930. You'll find members of the guild demonstrating their crafts at the **Folk Art Center** at MP 382 on the Blue Ridge Parkway, where the works are displayed and offered for sale. **Pack Place,** a downtown cultural center at 2 Pack Square, houses the **Asheville Art Museum,** the **Colburn Gem and Mineral Museum,** the **Health Adventure** (a hands-on health-oriented museum for kids), the **Diana Wortham Theatre,** and the **YMI Cultural Center** (highlighting African-American heritage).

Asheville sits at the crossroads of I-40, I-26, and the Blue Ridge Parkway. From here, you may choose to go west to the Great Smoky Mountains National Park and beyond to Knoxville, TN; south to Columbia, SC; or northeast along the parkway into Virginia.

Driving the State

Start	Kitty Hawk
Finish	Beaufort
Distance	Approximately 115 miles by highway, 19 miles by ferry
Time	1–2 days
Highlights	Sea, sand, and surf; the Wright Brothers National Memorial; national seashores; outdoor drama; 16th-century sailing vessel; English gardens; lighthouses; ghost town; historic homes and cemeteries

Most visitors come to the Outer Banks for the endless beaches and the fishing and water sports they offer, but other attractions await those who are willing to look for them. In addition to sun and fun, the Outer Banks (a chain of barrier islands stretching for 120 miles along North Carolina's coastline) are steeped in history and mystery. The sands here cover many secrets. The first mystery is the fate of the lost Roanoke Colony, the first English settlement in the New World. Then came 18th-century pirates (including the infamous Blackbeard) who supposedly buried much of their booty on or near these islands. Until the 1940s, ships regularly foundered in the rough waters of this area, earning it the grim nickname "Graveyard of the Atlantic." You never know when you may be walking along an expanse of beach and suddenly stumble on the remains of a 17th-century schooner.

All along the north/south route of NC 12, there are plenty of places to pull off the highway, so you can park, hike through breaks in the dunes, and find your own secluded stretch of beach. Although this entire route can be driven in a day, such a rush wouldn't allow you to sample from the many distractions along the way. You also need to factor in waiting time for the ferries, which depart every half hour in the summer and every hour in the winter and are loaded on a first-come, first-served basis. (Some businesses are closed during the winter months, so check before you plan a winter trip to the area.)

For additional information on lodgings, dining, and attractions in the region covered by the tour, look under specific cities in the listings portion of this chapter.

A tradition in the Outer Banks is to give directions in terms of the mile markers. Instead of describing places by street names or giving directions in relation to major intersections, natives and newcomers refer to the mile markers ("turn left two streets after MM 14" or "it's between MM 20 and MM 21 on your right"). These directions work well because there is only one major north/south road.

To reach the Outer Banks take US 158 or US 64/264 from the mainland to your first stop:

1. **Kitty Hawk/Kill Devil Hills,** where Orville and Wilbur Wright set humanity soaring with the first powered aircraft flight—even though it lasted only 12 seconds and covered only 120 feet. Although the brothers had been working on their invention in Ohio, they came to the Outer Banks for more tests because of the area's windy conditions, high sand dunes, and clear weather. The site of their historic flight has been designated as the **Wright Brothers National Memorial,** where a granite monument (resembling the tail of an airplane) marks the spot from which the momentous event was launched. There's also a visitor center/museum, an airport, and a reconstructed hangar and shop. The museum contains a wind tunnel used by the Wright brothers, their 1902 gliders, and a replica of the 1903 *Wright Flyer.* You can watch present-day flight enthusiasts launch their hang gliders from the tops of the 140-foot sand dunes at **Jockey's Ridge State Park,** four miles south of the memorial.

   From the state park, take NC 12 south for 11 miles to the next stop:

2. **Nags Head.** According to legend, local pirates used to tie a lantern to a horse's head (hence the town's name) and walk it back and forth on the beach so that ships coming toward shore thought they were seeing the lazy swing of a lantern on a ship anchored in a safe harbor. Once sailors headed for the light, their ship broke up on the rocks and the pirates could salvage whatever portions of the cargo washed ashore. Today Nags Head is a popular vacation community with hotels, condominiums, and rental cottages.

   Make a brief 7-mile detour west on US 64/264 to:

3. **Manteo** on Roanoke Island, the site of the mysterious Lost Colony. This island, sheltered between the Outer Banks and the mainland, was the site of the first permanent English colony in the New World. A

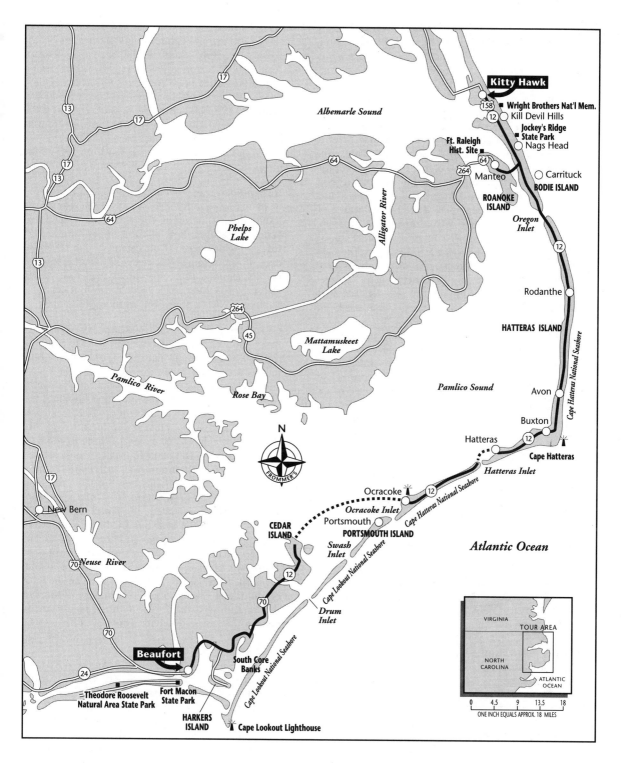

total of 112 men, women, and children arrived in 1585 and a fort was erected. Leader Sir Walter Raleigh then returned to England for supplies, but when he returned the following spring, all the settlers had disappeared. Over the years legends about their fate have grown, but no one has ever found out what really happened. The fort has been excavated and reconstructed on its original foundation. At **Fort Raleigh National Historic Site,** a restored earthworks and a visitor center/museum four miles north of Manteo, learn about Sir Walter Raleigh's attempt to establish the colony; Virginia Dare, the first colonist born in the Americas; and the baffling disappearance of all the colonists. If you travel to Roanoke Island during the summer months, take the opportunity to learn more about the lives and hardships of the colonists at *The Lost Colony,* an outdoor drama performed at the Waterside Amphitheatre. Written by Pulitzer Prize–winning author Paul Green, the play was the first outdoor historic drama in the nation and has been running continuously since 1937.

Although their first colony failed, the English did settle Roanoke Island later. So pervasive is the Anglo influence that some of today's inhabitants still speak with a discernible British accent. The island's English roots are remembered at two other attractions: the **Elizabethan Gardens,** a re-creation of a 16th-century formal pleasure garden; and, berthed at the waterfront, the *Elizabeth II,* a 69-foot, square-rigged ship modeled on the 16th-century sailing vessel that brought the colonists to these shores. The boat serves as the visitor center for the *Elizabeth II* **State Historic Site.** While you are on Roanoke Island, visit the **North Carolina Aquarium** to see displays of marine life.

Take a Break

Although you'd expect a 16th-century Elizabethan motif, the **Elizabethan Inn,** US 64 (tel 919/473-2101), actually specializes in Italian and seafood entrees. Luncheon choices range from $4 to $6 and change daily. Dinner entrees might include baked stuffed eggplant Parmesan, sausage cacciatore, baked salmon with peppercorns and Parmesan cheese, or grilled tuna. Dinner entrees are $10 to $15.

Retrace US 64/264 back onto the Outer Banks and turn north on NC 12 for 32 miles to:

4. **Currituck Beach Lighthouse and Bodie Island Lighthouses.** First lit in 1875, the Currituck Light-house is now open for tours. Visitors can climb to the top to see the rotating light fixture and enjoy panoramic, 360° views of the beach and ocean. Although the horizontally striped Bodie Island Lighthouse isn't open for tours, displays detailing its history are available in the old keeper's cottage. Built in 1872, the lighthouse at Bodie Island is the only one remaining in North Carolina to retain its original Fresnel glass lens.

From Currituck, backtrack south on NC 12 for 40 miles to:

5. **Rodanthe,** where you can watch the many varieties of waterfowl that live at least part of the year on the 5,000 marshy acres of the **Pea Island National Wildlife Refuge.** Parts of the **Chicamacomico US Lifesaving Service Station,** established in 1875, are open in the summer. Its museum tells the story of the 24 stations that once lined the coast; living history reenactments are held in the summer.

Follow NC 12 south for 15 miles to:

6. **Cape Hatteras National Seashore,** the country's first national seashore. Created in 1953 to preserve the beaches in their natural state, the national seashore runs 80 miles through Bodie, Hatteras, and Ocracoke Islands and covers 30,000 acres. Along with swimming, sunning, and shelling, the beaches are famous for surf fishing. Deep-sea charters are available from marinas in the towns, as are charters for inland/intracoastal fishing in the bays and estuaries. The 208-foot-tall, candy-striped **Cape Hatteras Lighthouse** was built in 1870 and is the tallest of all America's lighthouses—the light keeper had 268 steps to climb to reach the top! When it was constructed, the tower stood 1,500 feet back from the sea, but by 1935 waves were lapping around the base and the Coast Guard abandoned it. The light was restored to the tower in 1950, but plans are underway to move it inland. From the iron balcony at the top, you can see most of the island. Memorabilia relating the history of the lighthouse is the focus of the **Museum of the Sea,** in the restored keeper's cottage. Offshore lie the remains of the *Monitor,* the famous ironclad Confederate ship that sank in 1862.

The cold Labrador Current from the north and the warm waters of the Gulf Stream from the south converge offshore at **Diamond Shoals,** just off the southern tip of Cape Hatteras. The mixture of these waters causes turbulent seas that have wreaked havoc with sailors; the currents are so strong that they've actually moved the islands. These barrier islands consist of tall dunes covered with sea oats, small shrubs, maritime forest, and salt marshes. Among the rare and/or endangered species that inhabit the islands are the piping plover and the giant loggerhead turtle. Whistling swans, snow geese, Canada geese, and 25 species of ducks winter here.

Canadian Hole, on the sound side of Hatteras Island opposite the lighthouse, has evolved into the windsurfing capital of the Outer Banks. Strong, consistent winds make the area ideal for both the neophyte and the master windsurfer. Almost any day you drop by, you'll see surfers gathered to hone their skills.

From Hatteras, take the free auto ferry to:

7. **Ocracoke Island,** once a sanctuary for pirates. The infamous Blackbeard was captured in nearby waters and, according to local legend, part of the treasures he stole are buried somewhere in the vicinity. Many a vacationer has amused himself searching for the mysterious treasure. On the way to **Ocracoke Village,** watch for the ponies that used to roam wild in such profusion; these are descendants of the beasts brought to this country by Spanish and English sailors. In the village is the **British Cemetery,** where four British sailors—killed when a German U-boat sunk the HMS *Bedfordshire* 40 miles off the US coast during World War II—are buried. A British flag flies over the plot of ground, which was deeded to Britain forever. **Ocracoke Lighthouse,** built in 1823, is the oldest operating lighthouse in North Carolina. Standing a mere 75 feet tall, its sides are bare of any design. Overnight accommodations are available at the **Island Inn,** a turn-of-the-century hotel with a front porch filled with rocking chairs.

Take a Break

Best known for its oyster omelettes, Island Inn crab cakes, and hush puppies, the dining room at the **Island Inn** (tel 919/928-7821) is filled with Outer Banks character. For lunch, ask for a soft-shell crab sandwich; dinner often includes crab cakes, other seafood, beef, chicken, and pasta. Entrees are $5–$12; reservations advised for dinner.

Next, take the toll ferry from Ocracoke to Cedar Island, then follow NC 12 to US 70S. Depending on which of the three national seashore islands you want to visit, passenger ferry service is available from Harkers Island to Shackleford Banks or the southern tip of South Core Banks; Davis to the midpoint of South Core Banks; and Atlantic to the southern end of North Core Banks—all components of the:

8. **Cape Lookout National Seashore,** a protected 55-mile span of three unconnected barrier islands of deserted beaches and superb fishing. The seashore has few roads; if you have a four-wheel drive vehicle, motoring on the beach is the best method of transportation. You can camp anywhere, but there are no facilities.

It's a 40-minute drive from the ferry landing to **Portsmouth Village,** a modern-day ghost town. Established in 1753, this was at one time North Carolina's busiest seaport. When Wilmington and Morehead City drew maritime business away, the town declined drastically. (The last family finally left in 1971.) Of the 21 remaining structures, 2 are open to the public: the church and the Dixon/Salter House, which is used as a visitor center. On display are a town genealogy, old photos, and other memorabilia. Portsmouth is also accessible by ferry from Ocracoke and then a short walk from the dock.

At the southern end of South Core Banks is the **Cape Lookout Lighthouse.** Constructed in 1859, it is still operational. The old keeper's house serves as a visitor center (staffed March–November). Continue around the point to see massive, partially submerged gun mounts that served as submarine defenses during World War II.

Return on the ferry and continue south on US 70 for 25 miles to:

9. **Beaufort,** a popular stop on the Intracoastal Waterway. The historic village, settled in 1710 and once North Carolina's third-largest port, was attacked by pirates in 1747. Several structures from the 1700s and 1800s are part of an extensive preservation and restoration project in the historic district. Learn more about the role the sea has played in North Carolina's history at the **North Carolina Maritime Museum,** Front St, where exhibits include boats, boat models, and natural-history displays. Among the historic sites, homes, and businesses you can visit are: the **Old Burying Grounds** (built in 1731), the **Joseph Bell House** (1767), the **Carteret County Courthouse** (1796), the **Josiah Bell House** (1825), the **Carteret County Jail** (1829), the **J Pigott House** (1830), and the **Apothecary Shop and Doctor's Office** (1859). At the **Harvey W Smith Watercraft Center,** Front St, visitors can watch boats being constructed or restored.

From Beaufort, you can go to New Bern via US 70, or continue south along North Carolina's coast via US 17 to Wilmington.

North Carolina Listings

Asheboro

Incorporated in 1796 and located in the heart of the Uwharrie Mountains. The area is known for its handcrafted pottery. **Information:** Asheboro/Randolph Chamber of Commerce & Tourism Bureau, 317 E Dixie Dr, Asheboro, 27203 (tel 910/626-2626).

ATTRACTIONS 🏛

North Carolina Zoo
4401 Zoo Pkwy; tel 910/879-7000 or toll free 800/488-0444. Located 6 mi SE of Asheboro. In this still-developing, world-class zoo, gorillas and 200 rare animals (like meerkats) inhabit the African Pavilion, while lions, elephants, and chimpanzees dwell in spacious outdoor habitats. A 37-acre African Plains exhibit is home to a dozen species of antelope, gazelles, and oryx. The R J Reynolds Forest Aviary holds 150 exotic birds flying free amid lush tropical trees and plants. There's also a tram ride, a picnic area, restaurants, and gift shops. **Open:** Daily 9am–5pm. **$$$**

Seagrove Area Potteries
124 E Main St, Seagrove; tel 910/873-7887. Located 14 mi S of Asheboro. The red and gray clays of this region were first used by settlers from Staffordshire, England, to make jugs for transporting whiskey. The art of pottery is practiced today just as it was then: Clays are ground and mixed by machines turned by mules, simple designs are fashioned on kick wheels, and glazing is done in wood-burning kilns. Currently, there are approximately 75 pottery shops in this area; each of them is individually owned and sells its own unique style of pottery. A pottery museum is in the works and may be open by press time; call ahead. **Open:** Mon–Sat 9am–5pm. Closed some hols. **Free**

Asheville

See also Candler

Set amid the Blue Ridge Mountains. Site of George Vanderbilt's French Renaissance château (Biltmore Estates) and birthplace of author Thomas Wolfe. Today, Asheville is a mecca for galleries, craft shops, and the arts. **Information:** Asheville Area Convention & Visitors Bureau, 151 Haywood St, Asheville, 28801 (tel 704/258-6111).

HOTELS 🏨

≣≣ Comfort Suites Hotel
890 Brevard Rd, 28806; tel 704/665-4000 or toll free 800/622-4005; fax 704/665-4082. Exit 2 off I-26. Basic hotel, with comfortable accommodations, located directly across from the Biltmore Square Mall. **Rooms:** 125 rms. CI 3pm/CO noon. Nonsmoking rms avail. "Suites" are actually just large rooms with sofas, but they are attractive. **Amenities:** 🛗 🛁 A/C, cable TV w/movies, refrig. **Services:** 🚗 🖨 🛎 **Facilities:** 🏊 🎱 ♿ Whirlpool. **Rates (CP):** Peak (May–Oct) $80–$125 S; $87–$125 D. Extra person $7. Children under age 18 stay free. Lower rates off-season. Parking: Outdoor, free. AE, DISC, MC, V.

≣≣≣ Haywood Park Hotel
1 Battery Park Ave, 28801; tel 704/252-2522 or toll free 800/228-2522; fax 704/253-0481. A spacious, relaxed property with modern-looking mauve and gray decor in its lobby. Suitable for business or pleasure travelers. **Rooms:** 33 stes. CI 2pm/CO noon. Nonsmoking rms avail. Huge rooms have handsome brass and oak furnishings, and modern prints and patterns. Handmade porcelain in each room adds a classy touch. **Amenities:** 🛗 🛁 A/C, cable TV w/movies, refrig, dataport, voice mail. Some units w/whirlpools. Safes, bathrobes, and hair dryers available upon request. **Services:** ✕ 🖨 VP 🛎 Twice-daily maid svce, masseur. **Facilities:** 🍽 ♿ 4 restaurants, 2 bars. Excellent restaurant. **Rates (CP):** $108–$280 ste. Extra person $15. Children under age 18 stay free. Parking: Indoor/outdoor, free. Corporate rates avail Sun–Thurs. AE, DC, DISC, MC, V.

≣≣ Quality Inn Biltmore
115 Hendersonville Rd, 28803; tel 704/274-1800 or toll free 800/228-5151; fax 704/274-5960. Exit 50 off I-40. A beautiful little courtyard in the middle of the hotel with a flower garden and fountain adds a nice touch. Lobby is spacious and beautiful. **Rooms:** 160 rms and stes. CI 3pm/CO noon. Nonsmoking rms avail. Several rooms have nice views of the garden. **Amenities:** 🛗 🛁 🖥 A/C, cable TV, dataport. Some

units w/terraces, some w/whirlpools. Refrigerators available on request. **Services:** ✕ 🖼 🛎 Twice-daily maid svce, babysitting. **Facilities:** 🔲 🔲120 🔲 2 restaurants, 1 bar (w/entertainment). Free use of Gold's Gym (one block away). **Rates:** Peak (June–Dec) $75–$95 S or D; $95–$130 ste. Extra person $8. Children under age 18 stay free. Lower rates off-season. Parking: Outdoor, free. Special fall foliage packages avail. AE, DC, DISC, MC, V.

🏨🏨🏨 Radisson Hotel Asheville

1 Thomas Wolfe Plaza, 28801; tel 704/252-8211 or toll free 800/333-3333; fax 704/254-1374. Exit 5A off I-240. Located near the downtown area, this property is popular with business travelers. **Rooms:** 281 rms and stes. Executive level. CI 3pm/CO noon. Nonsmoking rms avail. Standard rooms are comfortable and attractive with few frills. Most rooms have good mountain views. **Amenities:** 🔲 🛁 🔲 A/C, cable TV w/movies, dataport, voice mail. All units w/minibars. Some rooms have refrigerators. **Services:** ✕ 🔑 🖼 🛎 Masseur. Staff is professional and friendly. **Facilities:** 🔲 🔲 🔲1000 🔲 2 restaurants, 2 bars, games rm. Gift shop. Golf courses and tennis courts are located minutes away. **Rates:** Peak (Apr 15–Nov 15) $89–$109 S; $89–$119 D; $195–$350 ste. Extra person $10. Children under age 18 stay free. Lower rates off-season. Parking: Outdoor, free. AE, CB, DC, DISC, JCB, MC, V.

🏨🏨🏨 Ramada Inn West

435 Smoky Park Hwy, 28806; tel 704/665-2161 or toll free 800/678-2161; fax 704/667-9744. Exit 44 off I-40. A spacious and airy property, with terrific views of the surrounding Smoky Mountains. **Rooms:** 156 rms. CI open/CO noon. Nicer-than-average rooms, with very nice furnishings. **Amenities:** 🔲 A/C, cable TV, dataport. Some units w/terraces. **Services:** ✕ 🖼 🛎 Babysitting. **Facilities:** 🔲 🔲300 🔲 1 restaurant, 1 bar, sauna, whirlpool. Very large swimming pool. **Rates:** Peak (May–Oct) $39 S; $39–$109 S or D. Extra person $10. Children under age 18 stay free. Lower rates off-season. Parking: Outdoor, free. AE, CB, DC, DISC, EC, ER, JCB, MC, V.

MOTELS

🏨🏨 Comfort Inn

800 Fairview Rd, 28803; tel 704/298-9141 or toll free 800/228-5150; fax 704/298-6629. Exit 53B off I-40. Average motel, sufficient for travelers just passing through. **Rooms:** 178 rms, stes, and effic. Executive level. CI 3pm/CO 11am. Nonsmoking rms avail. **Amenities:** 🔲 🛁 A/C, cable TV. Some units w/terraces, some w/whirlpools. Suites have refrigerators. **Services:** 🖼 🛎 🧺 Complimentary refreshments (nuts and cookies) in lobby. **Facilities:** 🔲 🔲40 🔲 Whirlpool, playground, washer/dryer. **Rates (CP):** Peak (June–Nov) $89 S; $149 ste; $149 effic. Extra person $6. Children under age 18 stay free. Lower rates off-season. Parking: Outdoor, free. AE, CB, DC, DISC, EC, ER, JCB, MC, V.

🏨 Days Inn Downtown

120 Patton Ave, 28801; tel 704/254-9661 or toll free 800/DAYS-INN; fax 704/254-9661. Located on a busy main street, so lower floors are a bad choice for light sleepers. The building itself is slightly run down. Popular with business travelers because of its convenient downtown location. **Rooms:** 92 rms. CI 3pm/CO 11am. Nonsmoking rms avail. Rooms are fairly attractive, though bathrooms are old and slightly grimy. **Amenities:** 🔲 🛁 A/C, cable TV. **Services:** 🛎 **Facilities:** 🔲 🔲 🔲20 🔲 🔲 Games rm, spa, beauty salon, daycare ctr, playground, washer/dryer. **Rates (CP):** Peak (May–Nov) $55–$70 S or D. Extra person $5. Children under age 15 stay free. Lower rates off-season. Parking: Outdoor, free. AE, CB, DC, DISC, JCB, MC, V.

🏨 Econo Lodge Biltmore East

1430 Tunnel Rd, PO Box 9676, 28815; tel 704/298-5519 or toll free 800/424-4777; fax 704/298-4739. Exit 55 off I-40. A slightly run-down chain motel with cheap-looking grounds. But it's livable, and it offers a decent room for a good price. **Rooms:** 141 rms. CI open/CO 11am. Nonsmoking rms avail. Nice color TVs. **Amenities:** 🔲 A/C, cable TV w/movies. **Services:** 🛎 Phones and fire alarm geared for guests who are deaf or hard-of-hearing. **Facilities:** 🔲 🔲12 🔲 **Rates (CP):** Peak (June–Nov) $46 S; $51 D. Extra person $5. Children under age 18 stay free. Lower rates off-season. Parking: Outdoor, free. AE, CB, DC, DISC, MC, V.

🏨🏨 Forest Manor Motor Lodge

866 Hendersonville Rd, 28803; tel 704/274-3531 or toll free 800/866-3531; fax 704/274-3036. 1 mi S of I-40 and 1 mi N of the Blue Ridge Pkwy. 5 acres. Rustic inn situated on five acres of pretty, well-manicured grounds with tall pines and informal flower gardens. Perfect for newlyweds and retired couples looking for a charming, homelike atmosphere. **Rooms:** 21 rms. CI 2pm/CO 11am. Nonsmoking rms avail. Rooms are surprisingly nice compared to the exterior, and feature dark hardwood furniture and ruffled white eyelet bedspreads. Walls are of beveled wood and are hung with old Audubon prints; headboards are carved. Bathrooms are old but meticulously clean. **Amenities:** 🔲 🛁 🔲 A/C, cable TV, VCR. All units w/terraces. Refrigerators available upon request. **Services:** 🛎 Babysitting. **Facilities:** 🔲 🔲 Lawn games. Good deals on golf and tennis nearby. **Rates (CP):** Peak (July–Oct) $79–$119 S or D. Extra person $10. Lower rates off-season. Parking: Indoor/outdoor, free. AE, DISC, EC, JCB, MC, V.

🏨🏨 The Mountaineer Inn

155 Tunnel Rd, 28805; tel 704/254-5331 or toll free 800/255-4080; fax 704/254-5331. Exit 6 off I-240. The outside is slightly run down and the lower levels are noisy, but the back sections are large and newly furnished. **Rooms:** 77 rms. CI open/CO 11am. Nonsmoking rms avail. Lower rooms are old but well kept, while rooms in the back are impressively nice, with dark-wood furniture and bedspreads. **Amenities:** 🔲 🛁 🔲 A/C, cable TV, refrig, dataport. **Services:** 🛎 Babysitting.

Extremely friendly and helpful staff. **Facilities:** 🛗 📷 80 ⅃ ⅄ Outdoor pool. **Rates:** Peak (June–Oct) $50–$85 S or D. Children under age 18 stay free. Lower rates off-season. Parking: Outdoor, free. AE, CB, DC, DISC, MC, V.

≣ Red Roof Inn West

16 Crowell Rd, 28806; tel 704/667-9803 or toll free 800/843-7663; fax 704/667-9810. Exit 44 off I-40. Located right off of the freeway, so it can be noisy. Sufficient for overnight stays. **Rooms:** 109 rms. CI 2pm/CO noon. Nonsmoking rms avail. Comfort and decoration are minimal. **Amenities:** 🛗 A/C, satel TV w/movies. **Services:** ⅃ ⅄ Complimentary coffee in lobby. **Facilities:** ⅄ **Rates:** Peak (May–Oct) $44–$50 S; $50–$62 D. Extra person $5. Children under age 18 stay free. Lower rates off-season. Parking: Outdoor, free. AE, CB, DC, DISC, MC, V.

INNS

≣≣≣ Cedar Crest Victorian Inn

674 Biltmore Ave, 28803; tel 704/252-1389. Exit 50B off 240 and I-40. 4 acres. Beautiful Victorian mansion, with intricate interior woodwork and winding staircases. Antiques abound, giving the inn a wonderful air of dignity and history. Unsuitable for children under 10. **Rooms:** 11 rms and stes. CI 3pm/CO 11am. No smoking. Every room is unique in its decor. Some have a floral/rose motif, hung with heavy dark draperies, and others offer light pastels and canopied beds. **Amenities:** 🛗 🜕 A/C. No TV. Some units w/fireplaces, 1 w/whirlpool. **Services:** Afternoon tea served. Breakfast in bed served upon request. **Facilities:** Lawn games, guest lounge w/TV. Pretty Victorian gardens with croquet and swings. **Rates (CP):** $109–$143 S; $115–$195 ste. Extra person $10. Children under age 10 stay free. Min stay wknds. Parking: Outdoor, free. AE, DISC, MC, V.

≣≣≣ Richmond Hill Inn

87 Richmond Hill Dr, 28806; tel 704/252-7313 or toll free 800/545-9238; fax 704/252-8726. Exit 251 off I-240. 40 acres. Tasteful and elegant, this Queen Anne–style inn with an impressive grand entrance hall is a perfect mountain getaway. Richly furnished guest parlors and sitting rooms abound, offering lovely views of the grounds and mountains. **Rooms:** 21 rms and stes; 9 cottages/villas. CI 3pm/CO 11am. No smoking. Each of the large, lovely rooms has a character of its own. Typical furnishings include plush couches, antique clawfoot chairs, heavy silk canopy beds, feather bedspreads, heavily embroidered sheets, and dark cherry-wood armoires and dressers. **Amenities:** 🛗 🜕 🍶 A/C, cable TV, voice mail, bathrobes. Some units w/minibars, some w/terraces, some w/fireplaces, 1 w/whirlpool. **Services:** ✕ ☞ ⅃ ⅃ Twice-daily maid svce, afternoon tea and wine/sherry served. Upon check-in, the friendly concierge gives you a personal tour of the historic property. **Facilities:** 📷 60 ⅄ 1 restaurant (bkfst and dinner only), lawn games, guest lounge w/TV. Only a quarter of the inn's acreage is developed; peaceful walking paths and gardens are abundant. Restaurant boasts an im-

pressive wine list. **Rates (BB):** $150–$325 D; $325 ste; $175–$230 cottage/villa. Extra person $20. Children under age 5 stay free. Min stay wknds. Parking: Outdoor, free. AE, MC, V.

≣≣≣ The Wright Inn

235 Pearson Dr, 28801 (Montford District); tel 704/251-0789 or toll free 800/552-5724; fax 704/351-0929. Lovely Victorian house filled with bright, cheery fabrics and period antiques. Unsuitable for children under 12. **Rooms:** 9 rms. CI 3–7pm/CO 11am. No smoking. Period furnishings and attention to detail distinguish this property from others in area. **Amenities:** 🛗 🜕 A/C, cable TV. 1 unit w/terrace, some w/fireplaces. **Services:** ☞ Afternoon tea served. **Facilities:** 🚲 Lawn games, guest lounge. Gazebo. A large carriage house is available for parties of up to eight people. **Rates (BB):** $85–$190 S. Extra person $20. Min stay wknds. Parking: Outdoor, free. Weekday discounts during off-season. MC, V.

RESORTS

≣≣≣≣ Grove Park Inn Resort

290 Macon Ave, 28804; tel 704/252-2711 or toll free 800/438-0050; fax 704/253-7053. Exit 5B (Charlotte Street) off I-240. 40 acres. Early in this century, the rich and powerful—including F Scott Fitzgerald, Thomas Edison, Henry Ford, and Woodrow Wilson—flocked to this massive stone inn dating back to 1913. Everything here is on a grand scale—even the fireplaces in the lobby burn 12-foot logs. Antique furnishings and lighting fixtures are employed throughout, and outdoor terraces provide awe-inspiring views of the surrounding Blue Ridge Mountains (the lodge itself is at an elevation of over 3,000 feet). Two outer wings were added in the 1980s. **Rooms:** 510 rms and stes. Executive level. CI 3pm/CO noon. Nonsmoking rms avail. Rooms in the old section are smaller than those in the new sections, but they have a unique feeling, with arched doors and large bathrooms. **Amenities:** 🛗 🍶 A/C, satel TV w/movies, dataport, voice mail, in-rm safe. Some units w/terraces, some w/whirlpools. **Services:** ✕ ☞ VP 🚐 🖾 ⅃ Social director, masseur, children's program, babysitting. Extremely pleasant staff is eager to assist guests. **Facilities:** 📷 🚲 ▶18 🖾 🖾 9 🛶 1500 ⅄ 5 restaurants (see "Restaurants" below), 3 bars (1 w/entertainment), basketball, volleyball, games rm, lawn games, racquetball, squash, spa, sauna, steam rm, whirlpool, playground. Shopping arcade. Sports club; hunting club nearby. Championship golf course designed by Donald Ross. **Rates:** Peak (Apr–Jan) $105–$205 D; $425 ste. Extra person $25. Children under age 16 stay free. Lower rates off-season. AP and MAP rates avail. Parking: Indoor/outdoor, free. Golf, tennis, and romance packages avail. AE, CB, DISC, MC, V.

≣≣ Pisgah View Ranch

Rte 1, Candler, 28715; tel 704/667-9100. 2,000 acres. The beautiful grounds, forests, and streams at this quaint property are a great way to break away from the daily grind.

Frequented by families with small children and retired couples. **Rooms:** 48 cottages/villas. CI 2pm/CO 11am. Rooms have the basic necessities, and are clean and comfortable. **Amenities:** A/C, TV. No phone. All units w/terraces, some w/fireplaces, 1 w/whirlpool. **Services:** ⬜ 🍽 **Facilities:** 🎣 ⚓ 🏊 🚲 🏊₁ 🚤 ⛷ 1 restaurant, basketball, volleyball, lawn games, squash. **Rates (AP):** $50–$125 cottage/villa. Extra person $30–45. Min stay. Parking: Outdoor, free. Closed Nov–May. No CC.

RESTAURANTS 🍴

⭐ Blue Moon Bakery
60 Biltmore Ave; tel 704/252-6063. **Eclectic/French/Mediterranean.** European-style cafe offering light lunch options (sandwiches and salads) in addition to home-baked breads and pastries. **FYI:** Reservations not accepted. No liquor license. No smoking. **Open:** Mon–Fri 7:30am–6pm, Sat 9am–5pm. **Prices:** Lunch main courses $3–$6. MC, V. &

Blue Ridge Dining Room
In Grove Park Inn Resort, 290 Macon Ave; tel 704/252-2711. Charlotte St exit off I-240. **International.** The dining room, located in the new wing of the inn, features large picture windows with gorgeous views of the forest and mountains. Two or three nights a week they offer specialty buffets—usually with prime rib or seafood. The Sunday brunch buffet is a local tradition, and offers omelettes, waffles, and other hearty fare. The staff will cater to unusual requests. **FYI:** Reservations accepted. Children's menu. **Open:** Peak (Apr 12–Dec) daily 6:30am–10pm. **Prices:** Main courses $13–$27; prix fixe $35. AE, DC, DISC, MC, V. 💟 🏔 ✅&

Carolina Cafe
In Grove Park Inn Resort, 290 Macon Ave; tel 704/252-2711. Charlotte St exit off I-240. **International.** Indoor cafe serving up mountain views along with specialties such as roast rack of New Zealand lamb with Zinfandel sauce, and grilled Alaskan salmon fillet with lemon-saffron sauce. The wine list includes some local brands, such as Biltmore wines. **FYI:** Reservations recommended. Children's menu. **Open:** Peak (June–Sept) breakfast daily 8–10:30am; lunch daily 11:30am–2:30pm; dinner daily 6–9pm. **Prices:** Main courses $32–$48; prix fixe $32–$48. AE, DC, DISC, MC, V. 🛎 🏔&

⭐ Depot Restaurant
30 Lodge St; tel 704/277-7651. Off Biltmore Ave. **American.** Housed in a restored 1896 railway station, this relaxing place offers a large menu that includes chicken, seafood, pork, veal, and beef dishes. Prime rib is very popular, and a very good deal. A scale-model train runs overhead in the bar area. **FYI:** Reservations not accepted. Children's menu. No smoking. **Open:** Daily 11am–9pm. **Prices:** Main courses $6–$13. AE, MC, V. 🍲&

♥ Horizons Restaurant
In Grove Park Inn Resort, 290 Macon Ave; tel 704/252-2711. Charlotte St exit off I-240. **International.** Upscale, opulent dining room specializing in unusual game dishes, such as medallion of South Texas antelope and roasted boar chop with stuffed quail. Dramatic soufflés also available. The staff is extraordinarily professional. **FYI:** Reservations recommended. Piano. Jacket required. **Open:** Tues–Sat 6–10pm. **Prices:** Main courses $19–$29; prix fixe $44. AE, CB, DC, DISC, ER, MC, V. ♥&

The Market Place
20 Wall St; tel 704/252-4162. **American/Continental.** Actually two different eateries: a casual cafe in the front features caesar salads, rack of lamb with rosemary, and cedar-roasted salmon with almond crust; while the back section is more upscale in decor (white tablecloths, fresh flowers, fine tableware) and menu (filet mignon, pan-seared scallops). **FYI:** Reservations recommended. No smoking. **Open:** Peak (June–Oct) daily 6–9:30pm. **Prices:** Main courses $7–$23. AE, DC, MC, V. ♥&

⭐ Mountain Smokehouse Barbecue and Bluegrass
20 S Spruce St; tel 704/253-4871. Exit 5 off 240W. **Barbecue/Soul/Southern.** Good ol' country cooking offered in a welcoming, rustic atmosphere. Friday nights feature a whole roasted pig. **FYI:** Reservations accepted. Dancing/bluegrass. Children's menu. **Open:** Mon–Thurs 5:30–9pm, Fri–Sat 5:30–10pm. Closed Jan–Feb. **Prices:** Main courses $8–$14. AE, CB, DC, DISC, ER, MC, V. ✅&

Steven's Restaurant and Pub
159 Charlotte St; tel 704/253-5348. **Eclectic.** Marvelous Victorian decor in the second-floor dining area adds informal elegance to any meal. Heading the list of specialties here is the rack of lamb. Freshly baked bread and homemade desserts also star, and there's a very good and extensive wine list. The lower-level room is less formal, with a big screen TV, booths, and an extensive selection of beer. **FYI:** Reservations recommended. **Open:** Lunch Mon–Fri 11am–2:30pm; dinner Sun–Thurs 5–9pm, Fri–Sat 5–10pm. **Prices:** Main courses $9–$21. AE, DISC, MC, V. ♥✅&

Top of the Plaza
In Radisson Hotel Asheville, 1 Thomas Wolfe Plaza; tel 704/252-8211. Exit 5A off I-240. **New American.** The versatile menu at this upscale eatery ranges from sandwiches and salads to prime rib. A particularly popular entree is the seafood symphony—a blend of seafood served in pastry shell with Newburg sauce and angel-hair pasta. **FYI:** Reservations recommended. Jazz/piano. Children's menu. **Open:** Breakfast daily 6–11am; dinner daily 5–10pm; brunch Sun 11am–3pm. **Prices:** Main courses $6–$18. AE, DC, DISC, MC, V. 🏔 🍴&

Windmill European Grill/Il Pescatore
85 Tunnel Rd; tel 704/253-5285. **Continental.** Located in a cool, grottolike cellar, this eatery offers fine dining in a

relaxed atmosphere. The extensive menu offers delicacies from all over Europe, including baked Norwegian salmon and tricolor tortellini carbonara. **FYI:** Reservations recommended. **Open:** Tues–Thurs 5:30–9:30pm, Fri–Sat 5:30–10pm. **Prices:** Main courses $9–$19. AE, MC, V.

ATTRACTIONS

Biltmore Estate

1 N Pack Sq; tel 704/255-1700 or toll free 800/543-2961. A sumptuous French Renaissance château that is a reminder of the era when North Carolina was considered the ultimate getaway for the nation's rich and powerful. Built by George W Vanderbilt in 1895, the house has 250 rooms. Vanderbilt personally oversaw its construction and decoration, gathering furnishings and art treasures from all over the world; for instance, Napoleon's chess set and table from St Helena are here and masterpieces by Dürer, Sargent, and Renoir hang on the walls. Today's visitors can see the Billiard Room, Bowling Alley, gymnasium, tapestry gallery, and other rooms where Vanderbilt entertained his guests. The 8,000 acres of grounds were designed by Frederick Law Olmsted, the designer of New York's Central Park. Lavish formal gardens contain more than 200 varieties of azaleas, plus thousands of other plants and shrubs.

Visitors should allow a minimum of two hours for the self-guided house tour, and plan to stay at least twice as long if they want to see everything. There's a charming restaurant in a renovated barn, as well as an interesting winery. **Open:** Daily 9am–5pm. Closed some hols. **$$$$**

Pack Place Education, Arts, and Science Center

2 S Pack Sq; tel 704/257-4500 or toll free 800/935-0204. Home of the Asheville Art Museum, Colburn Gem and Mineral Museum, Health Adventure (interactive health/science exhibits), YMI Cultural Center (African American art, culture, and history), and the Diana Wortham Theatre, this 92,000-square-foot downtown complex combines the arts, science, culture, and entertainment in one package. There are also art exhibitions in the common area. Combination tickets include admission to all individual attractions. Courtyard Cafe serves lunch and pretheater drinks and snacks. **Open:** Tues–Sat 10am–5pm, also June–Oct, Sun 1–5pm. Closed some hols. **$$**

Folk Art Center

MP 382, Blue Ridge Pkwy; tel 704/298-7928. Operated by the Southern Highland Handicraft Guild, a nonprofit organization of craftspeople. The contemporary wood-and-stone structure houses the finest in both traditional and contemporary handcrafts of the region, the Allanstand Craft Shop (one of the oldest craft shops in the country, established in 1895), and exhibition and museum areas. **Open:** Daily 9am–6pm. Closed some hols. **Free**

Grove Wood Gallery

Macon St via Charlotte St; tel 704/253-7651. Located 2 mi N of Asheville, on the grounds of the Grove Park Inn. This complex was a pet project of Mrs George Vanderbilt, who wanted to preserve the traditional wool-manufacturing skills of the mountain people and help the weavers turn those skills into a paying industry. Shops occupying the charming, ivy-covered buildings display a wide range of goods, from crafts to books to antiques. In addition to the retail shops, there is an Automobile Museum and a craft gallery. **Open:** Mon–Sat 9am–5pm, Sun 1–5pm. **Free**

Blue Ridge Parkway Visitors Center

1 Pack Place; tel 704/271-4779. Stretching 469 miles from Waynesboro, VA to the Great Smoky Mountains, the Parkway—one of America's most scenic drives— is a worthwhile destination in itself, or it can serve as an ideal base for side trips to many of the area's other attractions. Elevations along the route range from 649 to 6,053 feet above sea level. Marked walking trails are denoted by signs with a rifle-and-powderhorn symbol and the word "Trail"; some take only 10 or 20 minutes and are the best way to experience the natural beauty of the area.

There is no toll on the parkway, and frequent exits allow access to towns along the route. There are 11 visitor contact stations (the main one is in Asheville), 9 campgrounds (open May–October only; no reservations), restaurants and gas stations, and 3 lodges. For maps and detailed information, contact the Superintendent, Blue Ridge Parkway, 200 BB&T Building, One Pack Square, Asheville, NC 28801 (tel 704/259-0779). **Open:** Parkway, daily 24 hours; headquarters, daily 8am–4:45pm. **Free**

The Thomas Wolfe Memorial

48 Spruce St; tel 704/253-8304. Thomas Wolfe grew up in Asheville and immortalized the town and its citizens (much to their dismay) in his *Look Homeward, Angel*. The Dixieland boarding house, which was run by his mother and which figures so prominently in the book, is now maintained as a literary shrine. Many of the Wolfe family's furnishings and personal effects are on display. Guided tours available. **Open:** Apr–Oct, daily 9am–5pm; Nov–Mar, daily 10am–4pm. Closed some hols. **$**

Atlantic Beach

See also Beaufort, Morehead City

Located on the southern end of the Outer Banks, this resort town features white sands and an unhurried, uncrowded pace.

HOTELS

≡≡≡ Days Inn

602 W Fort Macon Rd, 28512; tel 919/247-6400 or toll free 800/325-2525; fax 919/247-2264. ¼ mi W of Atlantic Beach Bridge. A well-designed, shingle-style motel on the Sound and located two blocks from the ocean. **Rooms:** 90 rms. CI 4pm/CO noon. Nonsmoking rms avail. Some rooms have

view of the Sound. Oversized family rooms available. **Amenities:** 🏠 🛁 A/C, cable TV w/movies, refrig, dataport. All units w/terraces. **Services:** 🏊 🍽 **Facilities:** 🎣 ♿ Winding dock crosses the marsh to sundeck and gazebo overlooking the hotel marina. Motel also has a picnic area. **Rates (CP):** Peak (Mem Day–Labor Day) $70–$120 S; $77–$125 D. Extra person $5. Children under age 18 stay free. Lower rates off-season. Parking: Outdoor, free. AE, CB, DC, DISC, MC, V.

▤▤ Holiday Inn
Salter Path Rd, PO Box 280, 28512; tel 919/726-2544 or toll free 800/HOLIDAY; fax 919/726-6570. 2½ mi W of Atlantic Beach Bridge. A comfortable, oceanfront hotel. **Rooms:** 114 rms. CI 3pm/CO 11am. Nonsmoking rms avail. **Amenities:** 🏠 A/C, cable TV w/movies, dataport. Some units w/terraces. **Services:** 🍽 **Facilities:** 🎣 🏊 1 restaurant, 1 bar, 1 beach (ocean). **Rates:** Peak (Mem Day–Labor Day) $100–$140 S or D. Extra person $10. Children under age 18 stay free. Min stay special events. Lower rates off-season. Parking: Outdoor, free. AE, CB, DC, DISC, MC, V.

▤▤▤ Ramada Inn
Salter Path Rd, PO Box 846, 28512; tel 919/247-4155 or toll free 800/228-2828. Comfortable hotel on a quiet stretch of beach. **Rooms:** 100 rms. CI 4pm/CO noon. Nonsmoking rms avail. All rooms have an ocean view. **Amenities:** 🏠 A/C, cable TV, refrig, in-rm safe. All units w/terraces. **Services:** ✗ 🏊 🍽 **Facilities:** 🎣 🏊 ♿ 1 restaurant, 1 bar (w/entertainment), 1 beach (ocean). Golf and tennis privileges available at nearby facilities. **Rates:** Peak (Mem Day–Aug) $79 S or D. Extra person $6. Children under age 18 stay free. Lower rates off-season. Parking: Outdoor, free. AE, CB, DC, DISC, MC, V.

▤▤▤ Sands Villa Resort
E Fort Macon Rd, PO Box 1090, 28512; tel 919/247-2636 or toll free 800/334-2667; fax 919/247-1067. Luxurious, oceanfront villas placed along an especially quiet section of beach. **Rooms:** 28 cottages/villas. CI 4pm/CO 10am. Nonsmoking rms avail. Each villa has full kitchen, washer/dryer, two baths, two bedrooms, and ocean view from a private balcony. **Amenities:** 🏠 🛁 🖭 A/C, cable TV w/movies, refrig. All units w/terraces, all w/whirlpools. **Services:** 🏊 🍽 Babysitting. **Facilities:** 🎣 🏐 🍽 🛁 ♿ 1 restaurant (dinner only), 1 bar, 1 beach (ocean), games rm, sauna, whirlpool, washer/dryer. **Rates:** Peak (Mem Day–Labor Day) $173–$218 ste. Min stay peak. Lower rates off-season. Parking: Outdoor, free. AE, DISC, MC, V.

▤▤▤ Sheraton Atlantic Beach Resort
Salter Path Rd, PO Box 3040, 28512; tel 919/240-1155 or toll free 800/624-8875; fax 919/240-1452. Beautiful oceanfront hotel with its own 800-foot pier. Lobby decorated with wicker and bamboo furniture. **Rooms:** 200 rms and stes. CI 4pm/CO noon. Nonsmoking rms avail. All rooms have a breathtaking ocean view. **Amenities:** 🏠 🛁 🖭 A/C, cable TV w/movies, refrig, dataport. All units w/terraces, some w/whirlpools. All rooms have microwaves. **Services:** ✗ 🏊 🍽

Babysitting. Arts and crafts children's program daily. **Facilities:** 🏠 △ 🏊 🍽 600 ♿ 2 restaurants, 2 bars (1 w/entertainment), 1 beach (ocean), volleyball, games rm, whirlpool, playground. **Rates:** Peak (Mem Day–Labor Day) $129–$159 S or D; $199 ste. Extra person $15. Lower rates off-season. Parking: Outdoor, free. Golf and Seasonal Getaway packages avail. AE, CB, DC, DISC, MC, V.

MOTELS

▤▤ Atlantis Lodge
MP 5 Salter Path Rd, PO Box 310, 28512; tel 919/726-5168 or toll free 800/682-7057; fax 919/726-8103. A peaceful, older lodging that has aged well. Much of the grounds are covered by shady coastal woodland, and there is beach access. **Rooms:** 42 rms and stes. CI 4pm/CO noon. Ocean view from some rooms. **Amenities:** 🏠 🖭 A/C, cable TV w/movies, refrig. Some units w/terraces. **Services:** 🍽 **Facilities:** 🎣 🏊 40 ♿ 1 beach (ocean), lifeguard, games rm. Large game room with a pool table. **Rates:** Peak (June 15–Labor Day) $79 S or D; $98–$117 ste. Extra person $6. Min stay special events. Lower rates off-season. Parking: Outdoor, free. AE, MC, V.

▤ Oceana Resort Motel
600 Fort Macon Rd, PO Box 250, 28512; tel 919/726-4111. ¼ mi E on Fort Macon Rd. A relaxing family place, this comfortable motel offers plenty to do. **Rooms:** 109 rms and stes. CI 4pm/CO 1:30pm. **Amenities:** 🏠 A/C, cable TV. **Services:** 🍽 Babysitting. Twice-weekly watermelon parties are held for the guests. **Facilities:** 🎣 🚲 🏊 1 restaurant, 1 beach (ocean), games rm, playground. Large, colorful playground; 1,200-ft pier; private beach. **Rates (CP):** Peak (May 19–Labor Day) $70–$82 S or D; $98 ste. Extra person $8. Lower rates off-season. Parking: Outdoor, free. Closed Nov 12–Mar. MC, V.

▤▤ Windjammer Inn
Salter Path Rd, PO Box 2906, 28512; tel 919/247-7123 or toll free 800/233-6466. 2½ mi W of Atlantic Beach Bridge. A modern, five-story, oceanfront motel. **Rooms:** 50 rms. CI 1pm/CO 11am. All rooms have a view of the ocean. **Amenities:** 🏠 🛁 A/C, cable TV w/movies, refrig. All units w/terraces. **Services:** 🍽 **Facilities:** 🎣 1 beach (ocean). **Rates:** Peak (Mem Day–Labor Day) $82–$107 S or D. Extra person $6. Children under age 12 stay free. Min stay special events. Lower rates off-season. Parking: Outdoor, free. AE, MC, V.

RESTAURANT 🍽

★ DJ Shooters
Salter Path Rd; tel 919/240-1188. **Seafood/Steak.** A family place by day and a lounge at night, DJ's is sure to please all. They are most famous for their hearty country breakfasts. Later in the day, they offer a variety of seafood and steak entrees and a selection of sandwiches. **FYI:** Reservations

accepted. Dancing/rock. Children's menu. **Open:** Closed Dec 15–Feb 1. **Prices:** Main courses $9–$17. AE, DISC, MC, V. 👨‍👧 ♿

Balsam

Just off the Blue Ridge Parkway in the Great Smoky Mountains, this quaint town features many small inns.

INN 🏨

▤▤▤ Balsam Mountain Inn

NC 1974, PO Box 40, 28707; tel 704/456-9498 or toll free 800/224-9498; fax 704/456-9298. Off US 23. 26 acres. A comfortable, airy inn in relaxed surroundings. A grand two-tier porch welcomes visitors into a beautiful lobby with white wicker furniture and Oriental rugs. Local art is displayed throughout. **Rooms:** 34 rms and stes. CI 3pm/CO 11am. Nonsmoking rms avail. **Amenities:** ♨ No A/C, phone, or TV. **Services:** ⌂ Babysitting, afternoon tea served. **Facilities:** 🏊 ♿ 1 restaurant (*see* "Restaurants" below), games rm, guest lounge. Library with 2,000 volumes. Hiking and biking trails nearby. **Rates (BB):** Peak (June–Oct) $85–$100 D; $130 ste. Extra person $15. Children under age 2 stay free. Min stay wknds. Lower rates off-season. Parking: Outdoor, free. DISC, MC, V.

RESTAURANT 🍴

Balsam Mountain Inn

Balsam Mountain Inn Rd; tel 704/456-9498. Off NC 23/74. **American.** Beautifully restored hardwood floors and early American antiques set the decor at this elegant yet casual dining room. Menu selections change daily, but are likely to include fresh mountain trout and various grilled, sautéed, and broiled seafood and poultry dishes. All entrees are accompanied by fresh fruits, vegetables, and fresh-baked breads. **FYI:** Reservations recommended. Beer and wine only. **Open:** Breakfast Tues–Sun 8–9:30am; lunch Tues–Sun noon–1:30pm; dinner Tues–Thurs 6–7:30pm, Fri–Sat 6–8:30pm, Sun 6–7:30pm. **Prices:** Main courses $10–$18. DISC, MC, V. ♿

Banner Elk

Northeast of Asheville, the town was incorporated in 1912 and named for the Banner family, who settled on the Elk River in the early 1800s. Nearby Seven Devils, established in the 1960s, is a commercially developed recreation area.

MOTELS 🏨

▤▤ Beech Alpen Inn

700 Beech Mountain Pkwy, 28604; tel 704/387-2252; fax 704/387-2229. An establishment that lacks the modern amenities, but makes up for it with a rustic atmosphere,

panoramic views, and friendly service. The exposed beams and stone fireplaces of the Swiss-style construction are different and interesting. **Rooms:** 24 rms. CI 2pm/CO 11am. Nonsmoking rms avail. **Amenities:** Cable TV. No A/C or phone. Some units w/terraces, some w/fireplaces. **Services:** ✗ ⌂ **Facilities:** 🏊 🏓 60 1 restaurant (dinner only), lawn games, racquetball. **Rates (CP):** Peak (Dec–Mar/July–Aug) $69–$135 S or D. Extra person $9. Children under age 18 stay free. Min stay peak. Lower rates off-season. Parking: Outdoor, free. AE, DISC, MC, V.

▤▤ Holiday Inn Beech Mountain

NC 184, PO Box 1478, 28604; tel 704/898-4571 or toll free 800/HOLIDAY; fax 704/898-8437. A small property with decent, comfortable accommodations. Pleasant lobby with large birch fireplace and antiques. Suitable for all travelers. **Rooms:** 101 rms. CI 2pm/CO noon. Nonsmoking rms avail. **Amenities:** 🛁 ♨ 🍴 A/C, cable TV. **Services:** ✗ 🛏 ⌂ **Facilities:** 🏊 🏊 🏓 150 ♿ 1 restaurant, 1 bar (w/entertainment). **Rates:** Peak (Dec–Mar) $99 S or D. Extra person $5. Children under age 18 stay free. Min stay special events. Lower rates off-season. Parking: Outdoor, free. AE, CB, DC, DISC, MC, V.

RESTAURANTS 🍴

Heidi's Swiss Inn

PO Box 621; tel 704/898-5020. **German/Swiss.** Located in a 90-year-old farmhouse, the Swiss theme is carried throughout this cozy restaurant, from the knickknacks on the walls to the schnitzel and sauerbraten on the menu. The chocolate fondue is a great finish to any meal. **FYI:** Reservations recommended. Children's menu. **Open:** Tues–Sat 5:30–10pm. Closed mid-Oct–mid-Nov/mid-Feb–mid-Apr. **Prices:** Main courses $13–$21. DISC, MC, V. ♥ 🍽 🍷

Mike's Inland Seafood

In Sugarfoot Shops Plaza, 2941 Pine Castle Hwy; tel 704/264-4967. **American/Seafood.** Flounder and calabash are the best sellers at this branch of the local minichain. Decor is whimsical, colorful, and nautical. **FYI:** Reservations accepted. Children's menu. Beer and wine only. **Open:** Lunch Tues–Fri 11am–2pm; dinner Tues–Thurs 5–9pm, Fri–Sat 4–10pm, Sun noon–8pm. Closed Apr. **Prices:** Main courses $6–$25. AE, CB, DC, MC, V. ♿

Stonewalls

NC 194; tel 704/898-5550. **American/Seafood/Steak.** As the name implies, this eatery is housed in a stone building. The dark, quiet interior has carved wooden chairs and wood tables, a wood grill ceiling, and a blue color scheme. The menu features steak, prime rib, chicken, and seafood, in addition to a delicious salad bar. Frequented by a more mature crowd. **FYI:** Reservations not accepted. Jazz. Children's menu. **Open:** Sun–Thurs 5–10pm, Fri–Sat 5–11pm. **Prices:** Main courses $11–$19. AE, DISC, MC, V. ♿

ATTRACTIONS 📷

Ski Beech Ski Resort
Beech Mountain Pkwy/NC 184N; tel 704/387-2011. Some say this resort offers the best skiing in the South, especially for beginners. (Half of its 13 trails are rated for the beginning skier.) The 5,500-foot peak (with 830-foot vertical lift) allows for excellent views of the surrounding Blue Ridge Mountains, and nine lifts make for few lines. Skis can be rented, and a professional ski school offers classes as well as private lessons. There's a children's ski program, or nonskiing tykes can stay and play in the Land of Oz nursery. **Open:** Mid-Nov–mid-Mar, daily dawn–dusk. **$$$$**

Sugar Mountain Ski Resort
NC 184; tel 704/898-4521 or toll free 800/SUGAR-MT. Eighteen slopes and trails spread over 115 acres provide terrain for all skiing abilities. A total of eight lifts (one triple, four doubles, and three surface) shuttle skiers up the 5,300-foot mountain, where the vertical lift is 1,200 feet—by far the highest lift in the state and the second-highest in the South. Ski school; base lodge offers equipment rentals, cafeteria, lounge, and game room. **Open:** Dec–Mar, daily 9am–4:30pm, 6–10pm. Closed Dec 25 am. **$$$$**

Beaufort

In the southern Outer Banks, it was settled around 1710 and became a watering hole for the wealthy and a target of pirates. Much of its historic past is preserved in homes and museums. Site of Rachel Carson Reserve.

HOTELS 🏨

≣≣≣ Beaufort Inn
101 Ann St, 28516; tel 919/728-2600 or toll free 800/726-0321. Off US 70. Charming, with handsomely decorated rooms; located only a few blocks from the historic district. **Rooms:** 44 rms. CI 3pm/CO 11am. Nonsmoking rms avail. Some rooms have view of the marina and Beaufort Channel. **Amenities:** 🎱 🛁 A/C, cable TV w/movies. All units w/terraces. **Services:** Babysitting. **Facilities:** 🚲 🛶 🎱 Whirlpool. Boat slips provided for guests who arrive by water. **Rates (BB):** Peak (May–Sept) $99–$119 S or D. Extra person $10. Children under age 6 stay free. Min stay wknds. Lower rates off-season. Parking: Outdoor, free. AE, CB, DC, DISC, MC, V.

≣≣≣ Inlet Inn
601 Front St, 28516; tel 919/728-3600; fax 919/728-5833. At Queen St. An attractive, clapboard motel across the street from the inlet in the heart of the historic district. **Rooms:** 35 rms. CI 3pm/CO noon. Nonsmoking rms avail. Balconies in each room have rocking chairs, and many have view of the inlet. **Amenities:** 🎱 🛁 A/C, cable TV w/movies, refrig, dataport. All units w/terraces, some w/fireplaces. **Services:** 🛁 🐕 Babysitting. Complimentary evening beverages.

Facilities: 🚲 🛶 The fourth floor houses the Widow's Walk Lounge. **Rates (CP):** Peak (Mem Day–Labor Day) $99–$114 S or D. Extra person $15. Children under age 18 stay free. Min stay wknds. Lower rates off-season. Parking: Outdoor, free. AE, MC, V.

INN

≣≣≣ The Cedars Inn
305 Front St, 28516; tel 919/728-7036 or toll free 800/732-7036. Two houses built in 1768 and 1851 provide gracious bed and breakfast accommodations. **Rooms:** 15 rms and stes. CI 2pm/CO 11am. No smoking. Rooms are individually decorated with period furnishings, and the bathrooms have claw-foot tubs. **Amenities:** 🛁 A/C, cable TV. No phone. Some units w/fireplaces, 1 w/whirlpool. Complimentary beverages are provided for guests. **Services:** 🛎 🛁 🐕 Babysitting. Full breakfast is served in dining room and is cooked to order. This inn provides very personalized hospitality. **Facilities:** 🛶 Guest lounge. **Rates (BB):** Peak (May–Dec) $95–$140 D; $140–$185 ste. Extra person $10. Lower rates off-season. Higher rates for special events/hols. Parking: Outdoor, free. AE, DISC, MC, V.

RESTAURANTS 🍴

Beaufort House
502 Front St; tel 919/728-7541. On the waterfront. **Seafood.** On the boardwalk overlooking the harbor, this is a relaxed sort of place, specializing in fresh seafood from local waters. The large menu also includes prime steaks, Southern-fried chicken, and home-baked breads. Most entrees come with choice of two vegetables. **FYI:** Reservations not accepted. Rock. Children's menu. **Open:** Lunch Mon–Sat 11am–2pm; dinner Sun–Thurs 5–9pm, Fri–Sat 5–10pm; brunch Sun 11am–3pm. **Prices:** Main courses $12–$14. DISC, MC, V. 🍷 🌊

★ Clawson's 1905 Restaurant
429 Front St; tel 919/728-2133. **Eclectic/Seafood.** Housed in the former Clawson's General Store; today's dining room reflects the building's turn-of-the-century heritage. Dinner entrees include grilled, fried, and sautéed seafood; steaks and ribs; chicken; and pasta. **FYI:** Reservations recommended. Children's menu. **Open:** Peak (Mem Day–Labor Day) lunch daily 11:30am–5pm; dinner Sun–Thurs 5–9:30pm, Fri–Sat 5–10pm. **Prices:** Main courses $10–$15. DISC, MC, V. 🍷 ♿

The Spouter Inn
218 Front St; tel 919/728-5190. Off US 70. **Seafood/Steak.** A small waterfront place offering an excellent view of the Beaufort Inlet. Dinner entrees include grilled dolphin, prime rib, and a combination seafood platter with an array of the day's catch. Sunday champagne brunch offered. **FYI:** Reservations recommended. Children's menu. **Open:** Peak (Apr–Oct) lunch daily 11:30am–2:30pm; dinner daily 6–9:30pm; brunch Sun 11:30am–2pm. **Prices:** Main courses $11–$20. MC, V. 🍷 🌊 ♿

ATTRACTION

North Carolina Maritime Museum

315 Front St; tel 919/728-7317. Ship models, shell collections, and exhibits on the natural and maritime history of the state are complemented by field trips, lectures, and programs for visitors of all ages. **Open:** Mon–Fri 9am–5pm, Sat 10am–5pm, Sun 1–5pm. Closed some hols. **Free**

Blowing Rock

Named after the Blowing Rock, a rock formation that uses air currents from the Johns River Gorge to return objects tossed from a high cliff. **Information:** Blowing Rock Chamber of Commerce, PO Box 406, Blowing Rock, 28605 (tel 704/295-7851).

MOTELS

Cliff Dwellers Inn

116 Lakeview Terrace, PO Box 366, 28605; tel 704/295-3121 or toll free 800/322-7380. Off US 321. Outside there are beautiful wildflower gardens, and the interior is very nice and well decorated. **Rooms:** 19 rms and stes. CI noon/CO 11am. Nonsmoking rms avail. Country-style decor, with lots of flowers. Patios offer beautiful views of the lake and mountains. **Amenities:** A/C, cable TV w/movies. All units w/terraces, some w/fireplaces, some w/whirlpools. Some rooms have refrigerators. Complimentary coffee in rooms. **Services:** **Facilities:** Whirlpool. **Rates:** Peak (May 12–Nov) $50–$98 S or D; $135–$205 ste. Extra person $5. Children under age 12 stay free. Min stay wknds. Lower rates off-season. Parking: Outdoor, free. AE, CB, DC, MC, V.

Green Park Inn

US 321, PO Box 7, 28605; tel 704/295-3141 or toll free 800/852-2462; fax 704/295-3141 ext 116. 14 acres. This century-old inn is slightly run down and has an unimpressive interior, but the gardens are nice. A popular stopover with retired travelers. **Rooms:** 85 rms and stes. CI 3pm/CO 11am. Nonsmoking rms avail. Rooms show their age but are interestingly decorated and offer good views. **Amenities:** Cable TV. No A/C. Some units w/terraces. VCRs available upon request. **Services:** Babysitting. **Facilities:** 3 restaurants (see "Restaurants" below), 1 bar, lawn games. Use of country club behind the inn for additional fee. **Rates:** Peak (May–Nov) $94–$104 S or D; $135–$160 ste. Children under age 18 stay free. Lower rates off-season. AP and MAP rates avail. Parking: Outdoor, free. No charge for extra persons in room. AE, DISC, MC, V.

Meadowbrook Inn

N Main St, PO Box 2005, 28605; tel 704/295-4300 or toll free 800/456-5456; fax 704/295-4300. Off US 321. A European-style property nestled in the heart of Blowing Rock village. The Meadowbrook greets its guests with manicured grounds featuring a large pond in the gardens behind the property. The lobby is warm and inviting, with a fireplace and rose-colored walls. **Rooms:** 46 rms and stes. Executive level. CI 3pm/CO 11am. Nonsmoking rms avail. Standard rooms are unusually large, but not exceptionally appointed; deluxe rooms offer much higher quality, with fireplaces, whirlpool tubs, reproduction antiques, and a muted, classic decor. **Amenities:** A/C, cable TV, VCR. Some units w/terraces, some w/fireplaces, some w/whirlpools. **Services:** Masseur, babysitting. **Facilities:** 1 restaurant (lunch and dinner only), 1 bar (w/entertainment), whirlpool, washer/dryer. **Rates (CP):** Peak (May–Oct) $99–$159 S or D; $99–$159 ste. Extra person $10. Children under age 12 stay free. Min stay wknds. Lower rates off-season. Parking: Outdoor, free. AE, CB, DC, DISC, MC, V.

RESORTS

Chetola Resort

N Main St, PO Box 17, 28605; tel 704/295-5500 or toll free 800/243-8652; fax 704/295-5529. Just off Hwy 321 one mi south of the Pkwy junction. 75 acres. A lakefront resort with extensive, well-manicured grounds, convenient to Blue Ridge Parkway, Moses Cove National Park, and other attractions. Popular with families because of its many recreational opportunities. **Rooms:** 42 rms and stes. CI 3pm/CO 11am. Nonsmoking rms avail. Attractive, spacious rooms furnished with handsome dark-wood furniture; windows overlook forest and lake. **Amenities:** A/C, cable TV, refrig, VCR. Some units w/terraces, some w/whirlpools. **Services:** Social director, masseur, children's program, babysitting. Guard at main gate for added security. **Facilities:** 1 restaurant (see "Restaurants" below), 1 bar, games rm, racquetball, sauna, whirlpool, playground, washer/dryer. Extensive hiking trails. **Rates (CP):** Peak (May–Oct) $109–$149 S or D; $159–$198 ste. Extra person $10. Children under age 12 stay free. Lower rates off-season. Parking: Outdoor, free. AE, DISC, MC, V.

Hound Ears Lodge

NC 105, PO Box 188, 28605; tel 704/963-4321; fax 704/963-8030. 900 acres. Situated in a beautiful mountain valley, with breathtaking views on all sides. The lodge captures the charm of an exclusive resort club, with an air of old elegance. It is a favorite of retired couples who enjoy golf, but it offers many more options to visitors of every age. Beautiful lobby with live potted orchids and ivy, a stately grandfather clock, and a large sitting room overlooking the golf course. **Rooms:** 28 rms. CI 1:30pm/CO noon. Rooms have huge closets, and prints (floral and Audubon) on the walls. **Amenities:** A/C, cable TV w/movies, refrig. All units w/terraces. Complimentary newspapers. **Services:** Twice-daily maid svce, social director, masseur, babysitting. Exceptionally thorough 24-hour security at the main gate and throughout the lodge. Many extra services available, such as having your clubs cleaned at the end of each golf excursion. Children's camp program available. **Facilities:** 🏌️ 🏊 ▶18 ⛳ 🎿 🚴 🎾 🎱3 🎳3 🍸 [60] 🦽 2 restaurants, 2 bars (1 w/entertainment), lawn games, steam rm, beauty salon, playground, washer/dryer. Sleigh rides in winter. **Rates (MAP):** Peak (June–Aug) $122–$244 S or D. Extra person $65. Children under age 3 stay free. Min stay. Lower rates off-season. AP and MAP rates avail. Parking: Outdoor, free. Closed Mar. AE, MC, V.

RESTAURANTS 🍽️

The Garden Restaurant

In Meadowbrook Inn, N Main St; tel 704/295-4300. **American.** The main view from this airy, open restaurant is of the beautiful plaza and fountain, with lots of mountains beyond. Best known for its desserts: raspberry pies, fresh cobblers, and light-as-air soufflés. **FYI:** Reservations recommended. Dancing/piano/singer. Children's menu. Dress code. **Open:** Lunch daily 11am–2pm; dinner daily 6–9pm. **Prices:** Main courses $10–$24. AE, DC, DISC, MC, V. 🏔️ 🦽

Hearthside Cafe

In Chetola Resort, N Main St; tel 704/295-5505. **International.** Upscale interior, with mirrored walls and orchids and lilies on the tables, with an upscale menu to match. The kitchen's trademarks include sautéed quail Frangelico, breast of Long Island duck, and New Zealand rack of lamb. **FYI:** Reservations recommended. Piano. Children's menu. No smoking. **Open:** Peak (May–Oct) breakfast daily 8–10am; lunch daily 11:30am–2pm; dinner Tues–Thurs 5:30–8:30pm, Fri–Sat 5:30–9pm, Sun 5:30–8:30pm. **Prices:** Main courses $15–$24. AE, DISC, MC, V. 🦽

ATTRACTIONS 🏛️

The Blowing Rock

Rock Rd/US 321; tel 704/295-7111. "The Rock," as it is affectionately called, is a 4,000-foot-high cliff perched in the midst of a strong updraft so that a handkerchief or some other light object thrown off the edge will come right back up again. In addition, the observation tower, gazebos, and gardens offer splendid views of the John's River Gorge and nearby Blue Ridge peaks. **Open:** May–Oct, daily 8am–8pm; Nov–Apr, daily 9am–5pm. Closed Dec 25. **$$**

Tweetsie Railroad Theme Park

US 321; tel 704/264-9061 or toll free 800/526-5740. An old narrow-gauge train winds along a three-mile route, suffering mock attacks by "Indians" and "outlaws." There's also a petting zoo, amusement park rides, and live shows in the Old West saloon. **Open:** May–Oct, daily 9am–6pm. **$$$$**

Mystery Hill Entertainment Complex

Rte 1; tel 704/264-2792. Another natural phenomenon near The Blowing Rock (see above). Here, balls roll and water runs uphill, rocks glow in the dark, and shadows seem to disappear. The adjacent pioneer museum is also worth a visit.

Admission is on an all-day basis, so visitors can come and go as they like. (Ticket sales stop one hour before closing time.) **Open:** June–Aug, Mon–Sat 8am–8pm, Sun 1–8pm; Sept–May, Mon–Sat 9am–5pm, Sun 1–5pm. **$$$**

Boone

Mountain town in northwest North Carolina. Named for Daniel Boone, the town stages a summer outdoor drama by playwright Kermit Hunter that tells the frontiersman's story. Home of Appalachian State University. **Information:** Boone Convention & Visitors Bureau, 208 Howard St, Boone, 28607 (tel 704/262-3516).

HOTEL 🏨

≣≣≣ Broyhill Inn

96 Bodenheimer Dr, 28607; tel 704/262-2204 or toll free 800/489-6049; fax 704/262-2946. Spectacular views of the valley and nearby mountains are available from this hilltop hotel. Convenient to the Appalachian State University, this hotel is a good choice for retired couples and businesspeople. **Rooms:** 83 rms and stes. CI 3pm/CO noon. Nonsmoking rms avail. The rooms offer wonderful views and are pleasant and comfortable. **Amenities:** 📺 🅰️ 🔲 A/C, cable TV w/movies. Some units w/minibars. Complimentary coffee in rooms. **Services:** 🛎️ Social director, babysitting. **Facilities:** 🚴 🎿 [600] 🦽 1 restaurant, 1 bar. **Rates:** Peak (May–Oct/Dec–Jan) $60 S or D; $85–$150 ste. Extra person $4. Children under age 12 stay free. Lower rates off-season. AP and MAP rates avail. Parking: Outdoor, free. AE, MC, V.

MOTELS

≣≣ High Country Inn

NC 105 S, PO Box 1339, 28607; tel 704/264-1000 or toll free 800/334-5605; fax 704/264-1000. A nice little place with a pleasant, comfortable atmosphere and rooms suitable to families or groups. **Rooms:** 120 rms and stes. CI 4pm/CO 11am. Nonsmoking rms avail. The rooms are attractive, with relatively new carpet and accessories. **Amenities:** 📺 🅰️ A/C, cable TV w/movies, dataport. Some units w/fireplaces, some w/whirlpools. **Services:** ✕ 🛋️ 🛎️ Personable employees are eager to help with guests' needs. **Facilities:** 🏊 🚴 🎿 🍸 [75] 🦽 1 restaurant, 2 bars, sauna, whirlpool, playground, washer/dryer. The grounds are not extensive, but are in good condition. Walkways lead to the trout pond, rabbit compound, and waterwheel. **Rates:** Peak (Dec–Jan/May–Oct) $35–$64 S; $40–$69 D; $95–$175 ste. Extra person $5. Children under age 16 stay free. Lower rates off-season. Parking: Outdoor, free. AE, DISC, MC, V.

≣≣ Quality Inn Appalachian Conference Center

344 Blowing Rock Rd, 28607; tel 704/262-0020 or toll free 800/362-2777; fax 704/262-0020. An attractive, well-maintained seven-story property with a spacious lobby and recent-

ly refurbished rooms. A comfortable choice for extended stays. **Rooms:** 134 rms and stes. CI 3pm/CO 11am. Nonsmoking rms avail. Pleasant, comfortable rooms. **Amenities:** 🛏 ⚲ A/C, cable TV w/movies, dataport. 1 unit w/whirlpool. Suites have refrigerators. **Services:** ✗ ⌷ ⌷ Babysitting. **Facilities:** ⌷ ⌷ ⌷ ⌷ ⌷ 1 restaurant, 1 bar, washer/dryer. **Rates:** Peak (June 16–Oct/Dec 26–Mar) $66–$110 S; $74–$110 D; $82–$110 ste. Extra person $6. Children under age 18 stay free. Min stay special events. Lower rates off-season. Parking: Outdoor, free. Ski, golf packages avail. AE, CB, DC, DISC, EC, ER, JCB, MC, V.

RESTAURANTS 🍴

★ Dan'l Boone Inn

105 Hardin St; tel 704/264-8657. Jct US 321/US 421. **American.** Located in an old white boardinghouse surrounded by hedges and rambling roses, the country-style dining room is furnished with wooden trestle tables and wicker chairs. The food is good, plain, country fare: choice of three entrees—such as fried chicken, country-fried steak, or country ham—served with any of five homecooked vegetables, fresh biscuits, dessert, and beverage. Handmade strawberry shortcake is by far the most popular dessert. **FYI:** Reservations accepted. Children's menu. No liquor license. **Open:** Mon–Fri 11am–9pm, Sat–Sun 8am–9pm. **Prices:** Prix fixe $11. No CC. ⌷

Mike's Inland Seafood

US 321; tel 704/262-5605. **Seafood/Steak.** Nautical decor features fish—painted, stuffed, and in aquariums—while the menu serves up fresh seafood, baked, broiled, or fried. **FYI:** Reservations accepted. Children's menu. Beer and wine only. **Open:** Lunch Tues 11am–2pm; dinner Tues–Thurs 5–9pm, Fri–Sat 4–10pm, Sun noon–8pm. **Prices:** Main courses $6–$25. AE, MC, V. ⌷

Shadrack's

US 321; tel 704/264-1737. **Barbecue/Seafood.** Food is served buffet-style at long wooden tables, and is likely to include down-home favorites like fried chicken and country ham, barbecue ribs and fried fish fillets. **FYI:** Reservations recommended. Country music/dancing. Children's menu. No liquor license. **Open:** Fri 6–10pm, Sat 6–11pm. **Prices:** Prix fixe $13. DISC, MC, V. ⌷ ⌷

ATTRACTIONS 📷

Hickory Ridge Homestead Museum

US 421; tel 704/264-2120. An 18th-century living-history museum housed in a re-created log cabin, where traditional craftspeople demonstrate their skills. Some of the crafts are on sale at the adjacent homestead store. **Open:** June–Aug, Tues–Sun 1–8:30pm; May and Sept–Oct, Sat–Sun 1–8:30pm. **$**

"Horn in the West," at the Daniel Boone Theater

Horn in the West Dr; tel 704/264-2120. A vivid story of efforts by the rugged mountain pioneers of the area to win freedom from the British Redcoats during the American Revolution. Performances begin at 8:30pm. The theater is surrounded by the Daniel Boone Native Gardens, which aims to re-create the environment of Daniel Boone's day, with native plants, a log cabin, and a wishing well. **Open:** Mid-June–mid-August, Tues–Sun 9am–9pm. **$$$**

Brevard

In the central mountains of the state, the Brevard summer resort area is sometimes called the "land of waterfalls." The Brevard Music Center and Brevard College are here. **Information:** Brevard-Transylvania Chamber of Commerce, 35 W Main St, PO Box 589, Brevard, 28712 (tel 704/883-3700).

MOTEL 🏨

📧📧 Imperial Motor Lodge

Jct US 64/US 276, PO Box 586, 28712; tel 704/884-2887 or toll free 800/869-3335; fax 704/883-9811. A small, dated property, but one that has been well cared for over the years. **Rooms:** 95 rms. CI noon/CO 11:30am. Nonsmoking rms avail. Rooms are small and adequately clean. **Amenities:** 🛏 A/C, cable TV, refrig. **Services:** ⌷ **Facilities:** ⌷ ⌷ ⌷ Picnic area. **Rates (CP):** Peak (May–Oct) $60–$70 S or D. Extra person $5. Children under age 15 stay free. Lower rates off-season. Parking: Outdoor, free. AE, DC, MC, V.

INN

📧📧 The Inn at Brevard

410 E Main St, 28712; tel 704/884-2105. Less well-kept than would be expected, this inn still has a surprising old-world charm that makes it a nice place to stay. Unsuitable for children under 12. **Rooms:** 14 rms and stes (2 w/shared bath). CI 2pm/CO 11am. No smoking. Room quality varies widely. While some rooms are slightly run down (with peeling wall paper and tile), others are well kept and gorgeously decorated with throw pillows, crocheted bedspreads, and Oriental throw rugs. **Amenities:** A/C. No phone or TV. **Facilities:** ⌷ 1 restaurant (bkfst and dinner only), guest lounge w/TV. **Rates (BB):** $78–$89 S or D w/shared bath; $78–$89 S or D w/private bath; $125 ste. Extra person $10. Min stay wknds. Parking: Outdoor, free. Closed Thanksgiving–Easter. MC, V.

Brunswick Islands/Cape Fear Coast

See Calabash, Bald Head Island, Kure Beach, Ocean Isle Beach, Southport, Sunset Beach

Bryson City

This resort town is located west of Asheville on the edge of Great Smoky Mountains National Park. Incorporated in 1889, it was named for Capt Thaddeus Bryson, one of the founders of Charleston, SC. **Information:** Swain County Chamber of Commerce, 16 Everett St, PO Box 509, Bryson City, 28713 (tel 704/488-3681).

HOTELS

Hemlock Inn

911 Galbrith Creek Rd, PO Box EE, 28713; tel 704/488-2885. Across from Dairy Farm. 65 acres. A delightful mountain retreat with an informal atmosphere, beautiful vistas, and peaceful rooms. **Rooms:** 26 rms; 3 cottages/villas. CI 1pm/CO 11am. Handmade quilts and other country crafts give each room a cozy quality. **Amenities:** No A/C, phone, or TV. Some units w/terraces. **Services:** **Facilities:** 1 restaurant (bkfst and dinner only), games rm. **Rates (MAP):** $95–$115 S; $120–$140 D; $151–$162 cottage/villa. Extra person $20–$39. Children under age 4 stay free. Parking: Outdoor, free. Extended-stay discounts avail in June and Sept. Closed Nov–Apr 15. DISC, MC, V.

Randolph House Country Inn

223 Fryemont Rd, PO Box 816, 28713; tel 704/488-3472 or toll free 800/480-3472. Off US 74. This 1895 mansion, listed in the National Register of Historic Places, contains many original furnishings and antiques. Very hospitable staff. **Rooms:** 7 rms; 1 cottage/villa. CI 2pm/CO 11am. No smoking. **Amenities:** A/C. No phone or TV. **Services:** **Facilities:** 1 restaurant (bkfst and dinner only), washer/dryer. **Rates (MAP):** Peak (July, Aug, Oct) $60–$65 S; $120–$130 D; $550 cottage/villa. Extra person $18. Min stay wknds and special events. Lower rates off-season. Parking: Outdoor, free. Extended-stay discounts avail. Closed Nov–Mar. AE, DISC, MC, V.

MOTEL

Lloyds on the River

1 US 19, PO Box 429, 28713; tel 704/488-3767. On US 19 between Cherokee and Bryson City. Care and effort are put into every individually decorated room at this riverside property. The peaceful, quiet atmosphere make it a good choice for a long, relaxing vacation. **Rooms:** 21 rms and effic. CI 1pm/CO 10am. Nonsmoking rms avail. All rooms have rocking chairs; those on the river also have porches and picnic tables. **Amenities:** A/C, cable TV w/movies. No phone. Some units w/terraces. **Services:** **Facilities:** **Rates:** Peak (June–Aug, Oct) $55–$60 S; $58–$70 D; $55–$90 effic. Extra person $7. Children under age 16 stay free. Lower rates off-season. Parking: Outdoor, free. Closed Nov–Mar. DISC, MC, V.

RESORT

Nantahala Village Resort

9400 US 19W, 28713; tel 704/488-2826 or toll free 800/438-1507; fax 704/488-9634. This native stone lodge, built in 1948, is still a wonderful place to spend a weekend. **Rooms:** 14 rms; 44 cottages/villas. CI 2pm/CO 10am. Every cabin has a separate living room, invitingly furnished with couches around the fireplace. **Amenities:** A/C, satel TV. No phone. **Services:** **Facilities:** 1 restaurant, basketball, volleyball, games rm, lawn games, playground, washer/dryer. **Rates:** Peak (May–Oct) $70 S or D; $80–$225 cottage/villa. Extra person $5. Children under age 6 stay free. Min stay wknds. Lower rates off-season. Parking: Outdoor, free. Closed Jan–Mar. DISC, MC, V.

RESTAURANT

Restaurant in the Fryemont Inn

In Fryemont Inn, 1 Fryemont Rd; tel 704/488-2159. Off US 74. **American.** Specialty entrees at this family-style Southern eatery include fresh rainbow trout sautéed with mushrooms and white wine, and prime rib served au jus or blackened with Cajun spices. All entrees come with appetizer, salad, vegetables, dessert, and beverage. **FYI:** Reservations recommended. Children's menu. **Open:** Breakfast daily 8–10am; dinner Sun–Thurs 6–8pm, Fri–Sat 6–9pm. Closed Nov–Mar. **Prices:** Prix fixe $14–$17. DISC, MC, V.

Burlington

The birthplace of textile pioneer Edwin M Holt, this rural town between Greensboro and Durham is still a center of the textile industry, with over 150 factory and discount stores. **Information:** Burlington/Alamance County Convention & Visitors Bureau, 610 S Lexington Ave, PO Box 519, Burlington, 27216 (tel 910/570-1444).

HOTELS

Best Western Burlington Inn

770 Huffman Mill Rd, 27215; tel 910/584-0151 or toll free 800/528-1234. Exit 141 off I-85/I-40. An exquisite, comfortable hotel with covered, multitiered courtyard. **Rooms:** 140 rms and stes. CI 2pm/CO noon. Nonsmoking rms avail. Better-than-average housekeeping. **Amenities:** A/C, cable TV. **Services:** **Facilities:** 1 restaurant (bkfst and lunch only), 1 bar (w/entertainment).

Rates: $44 S or D; $123–$125 ste. Extra person $6. Children under age 6 stay free. Parking: Outdoor, free. AE, CB, DC, DISC, MC, V.

≡≡≡ Hampton Inn

2701 Kirkpatrick Rd, 27215; tel 910/584-4447 or toll free 800/HAMPTON; fax 910/721-1325. Exit 141 off I-40. Above-average chain hotel, with a sunroom lobby. Suitable for all travelers. **Rooms:** 118 rms. CI 3pm/CO noon. Nonsmoking rms avail. **Amenities:** 🛋 ⚙ A/C, cable TV, dataport. **Services:** 🖨 🛎 Complimentary coffee in lobby. **Facilities:** 🏊 ⚽ 25 ⚙ Sauna, whirlpool. **Rates (CP):** $51–$55 S; $58–$61 D. Min stay special events. Parking: Outdoor, free. AE, DISC, MC, V.

≡≡≡ Holiday Inn

2444 Maple Ave, 27216; tel 910/229-5203 or toll free 800/HOLIDAY; fax 910/570-0529. Exit 145 off I-85/I-40. This pleasant hotel with an attractive courtyard caters to the business traveler. **Rooms:** 132 rms and stes. Executive level. CI 3pm/CO noon. Nonsmoking rms avail. **Amenities:** 🛋 ⚙ 🗔 A/C, cable TV. Some units w/whirlpools. **Services:** ✕ 🖨 🛎 🖤 Babysitting. **Facilities:** 🏊 300 ⚙ 1 restaurant, 1 bar. Complimentary use of local fitness center. **Rates:** $69 S; $75 D; $125 ste. Extra person $6. Children under age 18 stay free. Parking: Outdoor, free. AE, CB, DC, DISC, MC, V.

MOTELS

≡≡ Comfort Inn

978 Plantation Dr, 27215; tel 910/227-3681 or toll free 800/334-6838; fax 910/570-0900. Exit 145 off I-85/I-40. Standard chain property offering adequate accommodations within walking distance of outlet shopping. **Rooms:** 127 rms. CI 2pm/CO noon. Nonsmoking rms avail. **Amenities:** 🛋 ⚙ 🗔 A/C, cable TV w/movies, dataport. **Services:** 🖨 🛎 🖤 Small pets only. **Facilities:** 🏊 ⚽ 250 **Rates (CP):** $51 S; $55 D. Extra person $4. Children under age 18 stay free. Parking: Outdoor, free. Rates increase during Furniture Mart. AE, CB, DC, DISC, JCB, MC, V.

≡≡≡ Ramada Inn

2703 Ramada Rd, 27215; tel 910/227-5541 or toll free 800/272-6232; fax 910/570-9158. Exit 143 off I-85/I-40. Located near the interstate, this Ramada is modern and convenient. **Rooms:** 138 rms and stes. CI 2pm/CO noon. Nonsmoking rms avail. **Amenities:** 🛋 ⚙ 🗔 A/C, cable TV, dataport. **Services:** ✕ 🖨 🛎 **Facilities:** 🏊 ⚽ 700 ⚙ 1 restaurant (bkfst and lunch only), 1 bar. Use of local health club for nominal fee. **Rates:** $43 S; $48 D; $50–$75 ste. Extra person $5. Children under age 18 stay free. AP rates avail. Parking: Outdoor, free. AE, CB, DC, DISC, MC, V.

ATTRACTION 📷

Alamance Battleground State Historic Site

Exit 143 off I-85 to NC 62; tel 910/227-4785. The site where upstart farmers marched against Royal Governor Tyron in 1771 to protest corrupt government practices. Ill-trained and poorly equipped, the farmers were soundly defeated—the battle lasted only two hours—but the stout-hearted "Regulators" were among the first Southern colonists to demonstrate their objection to royal rule. The visitor center has an audiovisual presentation on the battle. Guests may also tour the John Allen House, a restored log dwelling typical of North Carolina backwoods homes at the time of the battle. **Open:** Apr–Oct, Mon–Sat 9am–5pm, Sun 1–5pm; Nov–Mar, Tues–Sat 10am–4pm, Sun 1–4pm. **Free**

Burnsville

This small town in Yancey County on the state's northwestern border was incorporated in 1833 and named for Otway Burns, a privateer during the War of 1812. **Information:** Yancey County Chamber of Commerce, 2 Town Sq, Rm #3, Burnsville, 28714 (tel 704/682-7413).

ATTRACTION 📷

Mount Mitchell State Park

NC 128, off Blue Ridge Pkwy; tel 704/675-4611. Stately Mount Mitchell, highest mountain east of the Mississippi River at an elevation of 6,300 feet, towers over the state park that bears its name. The Black Mountain range, of which Mount Mitchell is a part, doesn't get as much attention (or as many tourists) as the Smokies or the Blue Ridge Mountains, even though it is at least as beautiful.

The park boasts a museum exploring the area's geological and natural history, an observation tower and lodge, five hiking trails ranging from easy to strenuous, and a mile-high picnicking area. There's a nine-site tent campground, or pack-in camping at two designated shelters is available for backpackers. **Open:** Nov–Feb, daily 8am–6pm; March and Oct, daily 8am–7pm; Apr–May and Sept, daily 8am–8pm; June–Aug, daily 8am–9pm. **Free**

Buxton

Imposing Hatteras Lighthouse stands watch near this Outer Banks beach town.

MOTELS 🏨

≡≡ Cape Pines Motel

NC 12, PO Box 279, 27920; tel 919/995-5666 or toll free 800/864-2707. ½ mi S of Cape Hatteras Lighthouse. Basic, oceanfront motel. **Rooms:** 28 rms and effic. CI 3pm/CO 10am. Nonsmoking rms avail. **Amenities:** 🛋 A/C, cable TV. Refrigerators and microwaves available. **Services:** 🖨 🛎 **Facilities:** 🏊 Picnic tables and grills on grounds. **Rates:** Peak (Mem Day–Labor Day) $54–$65 S or D; $70 effic. Extra person $3. Lower rates off-season. Parking: Outdoor, free. Weekly rates available for all efficiencies. Weekly rates range from $444–$534. AE, DISC, MC, V.

≣≣ The Falcon Motel

NC 12, PO Box 633, 27920; tel 919/995-5968 or toll free 800/635-6911. Basic motel in a quiet setting; a short walk from the beach and several restaurants and shops. **Rooms:** 35 rms and effic. CI 3pm/CO 11am. Nonsmoking rms avail. Larger-than-average rooms are clean and airy. **Amenities:** A/C, cable TV. No phone. Refrigerators and microwaves available. **Facilities:** ⛱ Shaded picnic area with picnic tables and grills. **Rates:** Peak (July–Aug) $68–$72 S or D; $50–$65 effic. Extra person $5. Children under age 5 stay free. Min stay special events. Lower rates off-season. Parking: Outdoor, free. Cottages require one-week minimum stay during peak season. Closed mid-Dec–Apr. MC, V.

≣≣ Lighthouse View Motel

NC 12, PO Box 39, 27920; tel 919/995-5680 or toll free 800/225-7651. An attractive oceanfront motel. **Rooms:** 51 rms and effic; 21 cottages/villas. CI 3pm/CO 10am. Nonsmoking rms avail. Most rooms have ocean views. **Amenities:** 📺 🕹 A/C, cable TV. Some units w/terraces. **Services:** 📠 Cottages do not have daily maid service. **Facilities:** ⛱ ♿ 1 beach (ocean), whirlpool. **Rates:** Peak (June–Aug) $79–$98 S or D; $85–$105 effic; $93–$158 cottage/villa. Extra person $7. Lower rates off-season. Parking: Outdoor, free. DISC, MC, V.

RESTAURANT 🍴

The Great Salt Marsh

In Osprey Shopping Center, NC 12; tel 919/995-6200. **Seafood.** A contemporary art deco motif dominates the interior, while the wraparound porch lends a more traditionally Southern flavor to the exterior. The menu is similarly eclectic, with options like fried oysters parmesan and sautéed crab cakes. **FYI:** Reservations accepted. Children's menu. Beer and wine only. **Open:** Peak (Mem Day–Labor Day) lunch Mon–Sat 11am–2:30pm; dinner Mon–Sat 5:30–10pm. Closed Dec–Jan. **Prices:** Main courses $13–$18. AE, MC, V. 🍷 🍴 ♿

ATTRACTION 📷

Cape Hatteras Lighthouse

NC 12; tel 919/995-4474. This 208-foot-tall lighthouse, the tallest on the Atlantic coast, has stood since 1870 as a beacon for ships passing through these treacherous waters, which have earned the title "Graveyard of the Atlantic." The lighthouse's rotating duplex beacon has a 1,000-watt, 250,000-candlepower lamp in each side, and is visible for 20 miles. It underwent a $1 million renovation in 1993. **Open:** Lighthouse, Mem Day–Labor Day, daily 9:30am–3:30pm; visitors center, daily 9am–5pm. Closed Dec 25. **Free**

Calabash

Proclaimed by some as the seafood capital of the world, this small fishing village in the southernmost coastal area is known for "Calabash-style" cooking, a lightly fried seafood featured in local restaurants.

RESTAURANTS 🍴

★ Calabash Seafood Hut

1125 River Rd; tel 910/579-6723. Off NC 17. **Seafood.** Typical example of Calabash's many seafood offerings: a small, unpretentious dining room and a menu serving a variety of well-prepared seafood. **FYI:** Reservations not accepted. Children's menu. No liquor license. **Open:** Tues–Sun 11am–9pm. **Prices:** Main courses $7–$11. No CC. 👥

Haley's Restaurant

10068 Beach Dr; tel 910/579-6032. **Italian/Seafood.** Diners sit in an attractive semiformal dining area while they enjoy various seafood and Italian specialties: lobster, Alaskan king-crab legs, chicken parmesan, veal parmesan, and several types of steak. **FYI:** Reservations accepted. Blues. Children's menu. **Open:** Daily 5–9pm. Closed Jan. **Prices:** Main courses $10–$20. MC, V. ♿

Larry's Calabash Seafood Barn

Rte 7; tel 910/579-6976. On Beach Dr in Calabash. **Seafood.** A bright place with a lot of windows in the dining room, and outdoor seating on a wraparound front porch with rocking chairs. Seafood specialties include tuna, flounder, mahimahi, and lobster tail. Salad bar included with all entrees. **FYI:** Reservations recommended. Children's menu. **Open:** Daily 4–9pm. **Prices:** Main courses $10–$19; prix fixe $14–$17. DISC, MC, V. 🍴 👥

Cape Hatteras National Seashore

From Whalebone Junction in South Nags Head, America's first National Seashore (established in 1953) stretches 70 miles southward, encompassing the Outer Banks barrier islands. The drive along NC 12 (about 4½ hrs) takes tourists through a wildlife refuge and pleasant villages, past gorgeous sand beaches. The hardy local people ("Bankers") can recount tales of heroism at sea, the ghostly light that bobs over Teach's Hole, and the wild ponies that have roamed Ocracoke Island for over 400 years—all in a soft accent that some say harks back to Devon, England.

At the little village of Hatteras, a free auto ferry makes the 40-minute crossing to **Ocracoke Island,** where more than 5,000 acres, including 16 miles of beach, are preserved by the National Park Service. According to legend, this is where the pirate Edward Teach—more commonly known as Blackbeard—met his end. From the southern end of the island, a toll auto ferry makes the 2¼-hour voyage across Pamlico Sound to Cedar Island.

The area is best explored in an all-day trip, or several half-day trips, from a Nags Head base. Swimming, fishing (channel bass, cobia, and mackerel are especially common), surfing, or just walking along the sand are the most popular pastimes here. There are also five campgrounds located on park grounds. For further information, contact the Superintendent, Rte 1, Box 675, Manteo, NC 27954 (tel 919/473-2111).

Cashiers

This Great Smokies mountain town is noted for its famous golf courses.

INN

▤▤▤ The Millstone Inn

US 64W, 28717; tel 704/743-2737; fax 704/743-0208. 7 acres. The rustic elegance of this inn is apparent in its exposed-beam ceilings and polished pine walls. A marvelous getaway, with breathtaking views of the Nantahala National Forest from the veranda. Unsuitable for children under 12. **Rooms:** 11 rms and stes. CI 3pm/CO 11am. No smoking. Rooms are tastefully yet comfortably decorated, with huge stuffed sofas and quilt bedspreads. **Amenities:** TV, refrig. No A/C or phone. Some units w/terraces. **Services:** Afternoon tea and wine/sherry served. **Facilities:** Guest lounge w/TV. **Rates (BB):** $101–$139 S or D; $109–$139 ste. Extra person $25. Parking: Outdoor, free. Closed Jan–Feb. AE, DISC, MC, V.

RESORTS

▤▤ Fairfield Sapphire Valley Resort

4000 US 64W, 28774; tel 704/743-5022 or toll free 800/533-8268; fax 704/743-2641. 6,000 acres. Particularly extensive grounds with easy access to lake activities, hiking, and many other wilderness sports. **Rooms:** 185 rms, stes, and effic; 25 cottages/villas. CI 4pm/CO 10am. Nonsmoking rms avail. Rooms offer a nice view of the grounds. **Amenities:** A/C, cable TV, voice mail. Some units w/terraces, some w/fireplaces. **Services:** Children's program, babysitting. **Facilities:** 2 restaurants, 1 bar (w/entertainment), 2 beaches (lake shore), basketball, volleyball, games rm, racquetball, sauna, whirlpool. **Rates:** Peak (Mar–Nov) $85–$225 S or D; $165 ste; $85–$105 effic; $175–$225 cottage/villa. Children under age 18 stay free. Lower rates off-season. Parking: Outdoor, free. Ski, golf, tennis packages avail. AE, DISC, MC, V.

▤▤▤ High Hampton Inn & Country Club

NC 107S, PO Box 338, 28717; tel 704/743-2411 or toll free 800/334-2551; fax 704/743-5991. 1,400 acres. A property

barely changed since its founding in the 1920s, with an interesting, old-world feel. While it doesn't offer luxury, it does have lovely scenery and a peaceful, noncommercial atmosphere. **Rooms:** 130 rms; 32 cottages/villas. CI open/CO 1pm. Modern, up-to-date cottages have many amenities and sleek appointments: cathedral ceilings, fireplaces, TVs, full kitchens. Rooms are more rustic. **Amenities:** No A/C, phone, or TV. Some units w/terraces, some w/fireplaces. **Services:** Social director, masseur, children's program, babysitting. Complimentary afternoon tea. **Facilities:** 2 restaurants (see "Restaurants" below), 1 bar (w/entertainment), 1 beach (lake shore), volleyball, lawn games, day-care ctr, playground, washer/dryer. The 1,400-acre grounds include two lakes, boat launch, docking facilities. Pet kennels. TV room in inn. **Rates (AP):** $72–$93 S; $144–$186 D; $190–$356 cottage/villa. Extra person $50–$57. Children under age 2 stay free. AP and MAP rates avail. Parking: Outdoor, free. Golf and tennis packages avail. Closed Nov–Apr. AE, MC, V.

RESTAURANT

Dining Room

In High Hampton Inn, NC 107S; tel 704/743-2411. **American/Southern.** An unimposing dining room with carved wooden chairs, snow-white tablecloths, and spectacular views of Lake Thorpe and the surrounding 1,400-acre estate. The buffet typically includes such specialties as London broil, Cornish game hens, and fresh mountain trout. All guests of the Inn are assigned their own table and waiter for the duration of their stay. **FYI:** Reservations recommended. Jacket required. Beer and wine only. No smoking. **Open:** Breakfast daily 7–9:30am; lunch daily noon–2:15pm; dinner daily 6:30–8:15pm. Closed Dec–Apr. **Prices:** Main courses $13–$16; prix fixe $13–$16. AE, MC, V.

Chapel Hill

See also Durham, Raleigh, Morrisville

Life in this picturesque, largely residential town at the edge of the Piedmont region centers around the main campus of the University of North Carolina, the oldest state-supported institution in the country. Along with Raleigh and Durham, Chapel Hill is part of the Research Triangle area. **Information:** Chapel Hill–Carrboro Chamber of Commerce, 104 S Estes Dr, PO Box 2897, Chapel Hill, 27515 (tel 919/967-7075).

HOTELS

▤▤▤ Carolina Inn

105 W Cameron Ave, 27514; tel 919/933-2001 or toll free 800/962-8519; fax 919/962-3400. Across from UNC Campus. The Carolina Inn opened in 1924 and was donated to

the University 11 years ago. Today it's a beacon of Carolina tradition, shining brightly after a recent $13.5 million renovation and expansion project. **Rooms:** 185 rms and stes. CI 3pm/CO noon. Nonsmoking rms avail. Rooms have Southern elegance and charm. Rhododendron bedspreads are a nice, regional touch. **Amenities:** 🗝 🕯 A/C, cable TV w/movies, dataport, voice mail. **Services:** ✕ VP 🖨 ↵ Fax and copy services available. **Facilities:** 🍽 450 🕭 1 restaurant, 1 bar. For its guests, the Hotel provides a sun room with courtyard view and complimentary periodicals. **Rates:** $99–$135 S; $109–$145 D; $155–$525 ste. Extra person $10. Children under age 17 stay free. Min stay special events. Parking: Outdoor, free. AE, CB, DC, DISC, MC, V.

UNRATED Omni Europa
1 Europa Dr, 27514; tel 919/968-4900 or toll free 800/THE-OMNI; fax 919/968-3520. ½ mi W of exit 270 off I-40. An elegant, modern hotel with an open lobby decorated in contemporary marble and exquisite Oriental pieces. **Rooms:** 168 rms and stes. Executive level. CI 5pm/CO noon. Nonsmoking rms avail. **Amenities:** 🗝 🕯 A/C, cable TV w/movies, dataport. Some units w/terraces. **Services:** ✕ 🔑 VP 🚌 🖨 ↵ Babysitting. Fax and copy services. **Facilities:** 🍽 🍴 900 🕭 2 restaurants, 1 bar. Health club privileges. **Rates:** $95–$135 S or D; $200–$310 ste. Extra person $10. Children under age 12 stay free. Min stay special events. Parking: Outdoor, free. AE, CB, DC, DISC, MC, V.

☰☰☰ Siena Hotel
1505 E Franklin St, 27514; tel 919/929-4000 or toll free 800/223-7379. Old-world Italian charm and elegance, with exceptional service. **Rooms:** 80 rms and stes. CI 4pm/CO noon. Nonsmoking rms avail. Most rooms are independently decorated. **Amenities:** 🗝 🕯 🍷 A/C, refrig, dataport, bathrobes. **Services:** ✕ 🔑 VP 🚌 🖨 ↵ Twice-daily maid svce, social director, masseur, babysitting. Free shoeshine. Free local limousine service (by appointment). Complimentary use of local health spa. **Facilities:** 175 🖥 🕭 1 restaurant, 1 bar (w/entertainment). **Rates (CP):** $175–$250 S or D; $220–$250 ste. Children under age 12 stay free. Min stay special events. Parking: Outdoor, free. AE, CB, DC, MC, V.

MOTELS

☰☰ Best Western University Inn
NC 54 E, PO Box 2118, 27515; tel 919/932-3000 or toll free 800/528-1234. NC 54; W off I-40; E off US 15/501 bypass. Motor inn with a classic look and feel. **Rooms:** 84 rms. CI 1pm/CO noon. Nonsmoking rms avail. **Amenities:** 🗝 🕯 📺 A/C, cable TV. **Services:** 🖨 ↵ **Facilities:** 🍽 🕭 **Rates (CP):** $54–$76 S; $59–$90 D. Children under age 18 stay free. Min stay special events. Parking: Outdoor, free. AE, DC, DISC, MC, V.

☰☰ Hampton Inn
1740 US 15/501, 27514; tel 919/968-3000 or toll free 800/HAMPTON; fax 919/929-0322. Exit 270 off I-40. Comfortable, pleasant property aimed at the business or leisure traveler. **Rooms:** 122 rms. CI 2pm/CO noon. Nonsmoking rms avail. Property is undergoing continual renovation. **Amenities:** 🗝 🕯 A/C, satel TV w/movies, refrig. Dataports available. **Services:** 🖨 ↵ **Facilities:** 🍽 🕭 **Rates (BB):** $53–$70 S or D. Extra person $8. Children under age 18 stay free. Min stay special events. Parking: Outdoor, free. AE, CB, DC, DISC, MC, V.

☰☰☰ Holiday Inn
1301 N Fordham Blvd, 27514; tel 919/929-2171 or toll free 800/HOLIDAY. Exit 270 off I-40. Comfortable hotel. Close to local shopping and the University of North Carolina at Chapel Hill campus. **Rooms:** 135 rms and stes. CI 3pm/CO noon. Nonsmoking rms avail. All rooms for guests with disabilities are on the first floor, and they are superior: visual alarms, closed captioning, etc. Executive rooms/minisuites (with king-size beds) available. **Amenities:** 🗝 🕯 📺 A/C, cable TV w/movies. **Services:** ✕ 🖨 ↵ Twice-daily maid svce. Turndown service available upon request. **Facilities:** 🍽 🍴 250 🕭 1 restaurant (bkfst and dinner only), 1 bar. No elevators. Complimentary use of local health spa. **Rates (BB):** $65 S or D; $85 ste. Extra person $5. Children under age 19 stay free. Min stay special events. Parking: Outdoor, free. Higher rates on graduation and football weekends, and minimum stay of two nights (football) or three nights (graduation). AE, CB, DC, JCB, MC, V.

RESTAURANTS 🍽

Armadillo Grill
120 E Main St, Carrboro; tel 919/929-4669. **Mexican.** A laid-back, mostly-self-service eatery. Diners design their own tacos, fajitas, and chalupas from the items on display, pay at the register, then wait for their name to be called. **FYI:** Reservations not accepted. No smoking. **Open:** Sun–Thurs 11am–11pm, Fri–Sat 11am–midnight. **Prices:** Main courses $2–$5. MC, V. 🍴 🎦 🕭

Aurora
In Carr Mill Mall, 200 N Greensboro St, Carrboro; tel 919/942-2400. Off Franklin St. **Italian.** An upscale trattoria housed in a restored 19th-century cotton mill. The dinner menu changes daily, but is likely to include elegant creations like scallops sautéed with shiitake mushrooms, rosemary, and white wine. A light menu is also available. **FYI:** Reservations recommended. No smoking. **Open:** Lunch Mon–Fri 11:30am–2pm; dinner Mon–Fri 6–10pm, Sat–Sun 6–10:30pm. **Prices:** Main courses $11–$20. MC, V. ❤ 🍴 🕭

★ Breadman's
224 W Rosemary St; tel 919/967-7110. **American.** A family establishment with a laid-back, casual atmosphere. Dinner entrees (which include Southern favorites like baked ham and steaks) come with vegetables; burgers and sandwiches are also available. **FYI:** Reservations not accepted. Children's menu. No smoking. **Open:** Daily 7am–10pm. **Prices:** Main courses $6–$8. No CC. 🎦 🕭

♥ Crook's Corner

610 W Franklin St; tel 919/929-7643. **Regional American.** The unique decor at this contemporary diner consists of original artwork by local painters, a bamboo-enclosed patio dominated by a pig sculpture, and mood lighting. The food, representing the various cuisines of the South, is similarly creative: El Paso chicken, grilled mahimahi, filet mignon with bourbon brown sauce, and Crook's trademark shrimp and grits. Pit-cooked barbecue is also available. Popular side dishes include cheese grits, hoppin' John (black-eyed peas and rice), and collard greens. **FYI:** Reservations accepted. No smoking. **Open:** Mon–Sat 6–10:30pm, Sun 10:30am–2pm. **Prices:** Main courses $12–$19. AE, MC, V. ♥ ♨ &

★ 411 West Italian Cafe

411 W Franklin St; tel 919/967-2782. **Italian.** A very popular trattoria with high vaulted ceilings and cosmopolitan decor. The menu includes gourmet pizza and a variety of chicken dishes. Everything is homemade and baked in a wood-burning oven. **FYI:** Reservations recommended. Children's menu. No smoking. **Open:** Lunch Mon–Fri 11:30am–2:30pm, Sat 11:30am–4pm; dinner Mon–Thurs 5–10pm, Fri–Sat 5–10:30pm, Sun 5:30–10pm. **Prices:** Main courses $6–$15. AE, DISC, MC, V. ♥ &

Il Palio

In Sienna Hotel, 1505 E Franklin St; tel 919/929-4000. **Italian/Mediterranean.** A plush dining room serving refined Northern Italian cuisine. The menu focuses on pasta, chicken, beef, fish, and veal entrees. **FYI:** Reservations recommended. Guitar/piano. Children's menu. No smoking. **Open:** Breakfast daily 6–10:30am; lunch daily 11:30am–2:30pm; dinner daily 6–10:30pm. **Prices:** Main courses $21–$30. AE, CB, DC, DISC, MC, V. ♥ &

India Palace

508 W Franklin St; tel 919/942-8201. **Indian.** A simple restaurant with an Indian-accented decor. The large menu includes a wide variety of traditional Indian entrees (including chicken, lamb, and vegetarian plates), breads like nan and poori, and South Asian sweets. **FYI:** Reservations accepted. Beer and wine only. No smoking. **Open:** Lunch daily 11:30am–2:30pm; dinner daily 5–10:30pm. **Prices:** Main courses $8–$12. AE, MC, V. 👥 &

♥ La Residence

220 W Rosemary St; tel 919/967-2506. Off Franklin St. **French.** Housed in a half-century-old residence surrounded by a patio and gardens, this charming bistro has several small dining rooms, each with its own decor. The dinner menu changes frequently to accommodate seasonal availability of ingredients. Desserts include homemade ice creams or sorbets, and chocolate soufflé cake. **FYI:** Reservations recommended. No smoking. **Open:** Tues–Sat 6–9:30pm, Sun 6–8:30pm. **Prices:** Main courses $12–$30. AE, CB, DC, MC, V. ♥ ♨ ♥ &

★ Mariakakis Restaurant & Bakery

1 Mariakakis Plaza; tel 919/942-1453. Across from Holiday Inn. **Greek/Italian.** Since 1969, Mariakakis has been offering fresh baked Greek pastries and breads to grateful locals. Over the years, the menu has diversified to include a number of Italian dishes; the specialty now is gourmet pizza (which goes well with a Greek salad). More than 20 sandwiches are available, and the desserts are heavenly. **FYI:** Reservations not accepted. Beer and wine only. No smoking. **Open:** Mon–Sat 11am–9pm. **Prices:** Main courses $3–$6. MC, V.

The Pines

1350 Raleigh Rd; tel 919/929-0428. **American.** A fashionable but friendly place that is a favorite among UNC alums returning to town for football weekends. Famous for its prime rib, but other cuts of beef as well as chicken, seafood, and veal entrees are also available. **FYI:** Reservations recommended. Children's menu. No smoking. **Open:** Mon–Thurs 5:30–10pm, Fri–Sat 5:30–10:30pm, Sun 5:30–9:30pm. **Prices:** Main courses $14–$29. AE, MC, V. &

Pyewacket Restaurant

In The Courtyard, 431 W Franklin St; tel 919/929-0297. Off US 15/501. **Eclectic.** A cosmopolitan eatery with stylish, contemporary decor consisting of a cozy lounge with comfortable couches, two high-ceilinged rooms done in soft reddish browns, and a "greenhouse" dining room with windows all around. Lunch choices include a selection of pasta, soups, sandwiches, omelettes, salads, and desserts; at dinner, seafood, vegetarian, and chicken specialties are featured. Low-calorie dishes are available for the health conscious. **FYI:** Reservations recommended. Folk/jazz/rock. No smoking. **Open:** Lunch Mon–Fri 11:30am–2:30pm; dinner Mon–Thurs 6–10pm, Fri–Sat 6–10:30pm, Sun 5:30–9:30pm. **Prices:** Main courses $11–$20. AE, MC, V. ♥ ♨ &

Red Hot & Blue

115 S Elliott Rd; tel 919/942-7427. **Barbecue.** A casual place, with low lighting and photos of famous blues musicians lining the walls. The menu features Memphis-style barbecue, prepared in a variety of ways; there's also an excellent dessert menu. **FYI:** Reservations not accepted. Children's menu. **Open:** Mon–Thurs 11am–10pm, Fri–Sat 11am–11pm, Sun 11am–9pm. **Prices:** Main courses $5–$15. AE, MC, V. &

Squid's Restaurant, Market & Oyster Bar

1201 N Fordham Blvd; tel 919/942-8757. Elliot Rd. **Seafood.** A large aquarium, filled with exotic fish and sea creatures, is the centerpiece of the pastel-and-gray interior. Diners can visit the oyster bar before heading to the dining room, where the waitstaff serves up a variety of grilled, broiled, and blackened seafood. Specialties include honey-grilled scallops, blackened-tuna burritos, and barbecue shrimp kebob. **FYI:** Reservations accepted. Children's menu. No smoking. **Open:** Mon–Thurs 5–9:30pm, Fri–Sat 5–10pm, Sun 5–9pm. **Prices:** Main courses $8–$16. AE, DC, MC, V. 👥 &

★ Ye Olde Waffle Shop

173 E Franklin St; tel 919/929-9192. Across from University of North Carolina. **Burgers/Breakfast.** The plain front room is reminiscent of a diner, but the back dining room (decorated in a Swiss motif) offers a more intimate environment. Breakfast selections include 12 omelette choices, pecan and blueberry pancakes, and, of course, waffles. Burgers and sandwiches also available. **FYI:** Reservations not accepted. No liquor license. No smoking. **Open:** Mon–Fri 7am–2pm, Sat–Sun 8am–2pm. **Prices:** Lunch main courses $3–$6. No CC. 🖼️ ♿

ATTRACTIONS 🖼️

Ackland Art Museum

S Columbia St, UNC Campus; tel 919/966-5736. Features a permanent collection of European and American paintings, sculpture from the Renaissance to the present, Asian art, North Carolina pottery and folk art, and ancient Greek and Roman art. Artists represented include Rubens, Delacroix, Degas, and Pissarro. **Open:** Wed–Sat 10am–5pm, Sun 1–5pm. Closed some hols. **Free**

Morehead Planetarium

E Franklin St; tel 919/549-6863. The "star" of the permanent scientific exhibits here is a large orrery showing the simultaneous action of planets revolving around the sun, moons revolving around the planets, and planets rotating on their axes. There's also a stargazing theater with a 68-foot dome. Show times vary considerably; call for the current schedule. **Open:** Sun–Fri 12:30–5pm and 7–9:45pm, Sat 10am–5pm and 7–9:45 pm. Closed Dec 25. **$**

North Carolina Botanical Garden

University of North Carolina, Old Mason Farm Rd; tel 919/962-0522. Boasts 330 acres of nature trails, as well as one of the South's largest herb gardens, a collection of carnivorous plants, and native plants in habitat settings. **Open:** Mar–Nov, daily 8am–5pm; Dec–Apr, Mon–Fri 8am–5pm. Closed some hols. **Free**

Dean E Smith Center

Skipper Bowles Dr, UNC Campus; tel 919/942-7818. Home of the UNC Tarheels men's basketball games, concerts, and special events. The Carolina Athletic Memorabilia Room features artifacts, highlight tapes, and other mementos from the University's rich athletic history. Call for schedule.

Charlotte

The state's largest city, Charlotte is rich in commerce and industry and is a distribution hub for the Carolina textile manufacturing belt. Located in the Piedmont region near the South Carolina border, it was established in 1748 and named for the wife of King George III; ironically, Charlotte was an early center of rebellion against the British crown (the Mecklenburg Declaration of Independence was signed here).

The first branch of the US Mint outside Washington, DC, was established here in the early 1800s to handle gold discovered at nearby Reed Gold Mine. Among the colleges and universities is the University of North Carolina at Charlotte. **Information:** Charlotte Convention & Visitors Bureau, 122 E Stonewall St, Charlotte, 28202 (tel 704/331-2700).

PUBLIC TRANSPORTATION

The **Transit Mall** has bus shelters on Trade and Tryon Sts in Uptown. Local fares are 80¢, express fares $1.15; seniors pay 35¢ during off-peak hours. Free bus service is provided Mon–Fri 9am–3pm between Mint and Kings Dr on Trade and between Stonewall and 11th Sts on Tryon. Call 704/336-3366 for information.

HOTELS 🏨

≡≡≡ Adam's Mark

555 S McDowell St, 28204 (Downtown); tel 704/372-4100 or toll free 800/444-ADAM; fax 704/348-4646. Corner of McDowell and Stonewall. A stately, elegant hostelry overlooking Marshall Park. This is Charlotte's largest hotel, and it offers incredible views of the city. **Rooms:** 598 rms and stes. Executive level. CI 3pm/CO noon. Nonsmoking rms avail. Rooms are stylishly decorated in deep jewel tones and dark-wood furnishings. **Amenities:** 🛆 A/C, cable TV w/movies, dataport, voice mail, bathrobes. **Services:** Twice-daily maid svce, babysitting. Staff is warm and friendly. **Facilities:** 2 restaurants (see "Restaurants" below), 1 bar (w/entertainment), racquetball, spa. **Rates:** $89–$109 S or D; $175–$225 ste. Parking: Indoor, free. AE, CB, DC, DISC, EC, MC, V.

≡≡ Best Western Luxury Inn—Sugar Creek

4904 N I-85 Service Rd, 28206; tel 704/596-9229 or toll free 800/252-7748; fax 704/598-6725. Exit 41 off I-85. Clean, well-maintained rooms are the main attraction of this chain property. **Rooms:** 98 rms and stes. CI 2pm/CO 11am. Nonsmoking rms avail. **Amenities:** 🛆 A/C, cable TV, dataport. Some units w/minibars. **Services:** Very friendly staff. **Facilities:** **Rates (CP):** $52 S; $49 D; $69–$101 ste. Extra person $6. Children under age 18 stay free. Lower rates off-season. Parking: Outdoor, free. AE, DC, DISC, MC, V.

UNRATED Charlotte Marriott Executive Park

5700 Westpark Dr, 28217; tel 704/527-9650 or toll free 800/541-4089; fax 704/527-7458. Exit 5 off I-77. An attractive property with lots of family-friendly amenities. Caters to business travelers during the week, families on weekends. **Rooms:** 297 rms and stes. Executive level. CI 3pm/CO noon. Nonsmoking rms avail. **Amenities:** 🛆 A/C, satel TV w/movies, refrig, dataport, voice mail. Some units w/terraces. **Services:** **Facilities:** 1 restaurant, 1 bar, basketball, volleyball, sauna, steam rm, whirlpool. **Rates:** $139 S; $149 D; $225–$400 ste. Children under age 18 stay free. Parking: Outdoor, free. AE, CB, DC, DISC, JCB, MC, V.

≡≡ Comfort Inn

5111 I-85 N Service Rd, 28269; tel 704/598-0007 or toll free 800/221-2222; fax 704/598-0007 ext 303. Off I-85. Standard chain property offering accommodations suitable for both overnight travelers and extended guests. **Rooms:** 87 rms. CI 2pm/CO 11am. Nonsmoking rms avail. **Amenities:** 🛅 ⚋ A/C, cable TV, dataport. Some units w/whirlpools. **Services:** 🖎 ⏌ **Facilities:** 🔗 🖳 🎱 🖫 Whirlpool. **Rates (CP):** $40–$70 S; $58 D. Extra person $6. Children under age 18 stay free. Parking: Outdoor, free. AE, DC, DISC, JCB, MC, V.

≡≡≡ Hilton at University Place

8629 JM Keynes Blvd, 28262; tel 704/547-7444 or toll free 800/HILTONS; fax 704/548-1081. Exit 45A off I-85. This very modern structure with a sleek, three-story atrium is the home of one of Charlotte's nicest luxury hotels. **Rooms:** 243 rms and stes. Executive level. CI 3pm/CO noon. Nonsmoking rms avail. **Amenities:** 🛅 ⚋ 🖭 🖢 A/C, cable TV w/movies, dataport, voice mail. Some units w/minibars. Every guest receives complimentary juice, coffee, and newspaper within a half-hour of their morning wake-up call. **Services:** ✕ 🖎 ⏌ 🖐 **Facilities:** 🔗 🖳 🎱 🖫 1 restaurant, 1 bar (w/entertainment), games rm. **Rates:** $105 S or D; $150–$275 ste. Parking: Outdoor, free. AE, CB, DC, DISC, JCB, MC, V.

≡≡≡ Holiday Inn University

8520 University Executive Park Dr, 28262; tel 704/547-0999 or toll free 800/SMILE-2-U; fax 704/549-4018. Exit 45A off I-85. A very nice chain property offering lots of amenities for the person traveling on business. **Rooms:** 177 rms and stes. Executive level. CI 3pm/CO noon. Nonsmoking rms avail. **Amenities:** 🛅 ⚋ A/C, cable TV, dataport. Coffeemakers and hair dryers available in executive-level rooms. **Services:** ✕ 🖐 🖎 ⏌ 🖐 **Facilities:** 🔗 🖳 🎱 🖫 1 restaurant, 1 bar, sauna, steam rm, whirlpool. **Rates:** $79 S or D; $179 ste. Extra person $10. Children under age 12 stay free. Parking: Outdoor, free. AE, CB, DC, DISC, MC, V.

≡≡≡ Homewood Suites North

8340 N Tryon St, 28262; tel 704/549-8800 or toll free 800/CALL-HOME; fax 704/549-8800 ext 520. Exit 45A off I-85. Homey, roomy suites make this property a great choice for those planning an extended stay. **Rooms:** 112 stes. CI 3pm/CO noon. Nonsmoking rms avail. Nice, comfortable units with separate living and sleeping areas and full kitchens. **Amenities:** 🛅 ⚋ 🖭 🖢 A/C, cable TV, refrig, dataport, VCR, voice mail. Some units w/fireplaces. **Services:** 🖎 ⏌ Babysitting. **Facilities:** 🔗 🖳 🎱 🖳 🖫 Sauna, whirlpool, washer/dryer. Private lake is stocked with catfish, bream, and bass. **Rates (CP):** $92–$142 ste. Parking: Outdoor, free. AE, CB, DC, DISC, MC, V.

≡≡≡≡ The Park—A Bissell Hotel

2200 Rexford Rd, 28211 (South Park); tel 704/364-8220 or toll free 800/334-0331; fax 704/365-4712. Exit 6A off I-77. Situated in the heart of one of Charlotte's premier neighborhoods, this small gem offers a warm, residential atmosphere. Guests are greeted by a beautiful four-tier fountain standing amidst manicured shrubbery and cheerful flowers. The cozy yet elegant lobby features black marble floors, deep wood accents, and recessed lighting. Excellent shopping and restaurant options are nearby. **Rooms:** 194 rms and stes. CI 4pm/CO noon. Nonsmoking rms avail. Individually decorated rooms ensure that guests will never experience that "institutional" feel. **Amenities:** 🛅 ⚋ 🖢 A/C, cable TV w/movies, dataport, voice mail, in-rm safe, bathrobes. Some units w/terraces. **Services:** 🖊 🖙 🖾 🖦 🖎 ⏌ Twice-daily maid svce, car-rental desk, masseur, babysitting. **Facilities:** 🔗 🖳 🎱 🖵 🖫 1 restaurant, 1 bar (w/entertainment), spa, sauna, steam rm, whirlpool, beauty salon. **Rates:** $150 S; $165 D; $275–$600 ste. Children under age 18 stay free. Parking: Outdoor, free. Weekend rates start at $89. AE, CB, DC, DISC, EC, JCB, MC, V.

MOTELS

≡≡ Comfort Inn

3100 Cloverleaf Pkwy, Kannapolis, 28081; tel 704/786-3100 or toll free 800/221-2222; fax 704/784-3114. Good for business travelers, offering the necessities for a short visit. **Rooms:** 71 rms, stes, and effic. CI 3pm/CO 11am. Nonsmoking rms avail. **Amenities:** 🛅 ⚋ 🖭 A/C, cable TV, refrig, dataport, in-rm safe. **Services:** 🖎 ⏌ **Facilities:** 🔗 🖫 🖫 Washer/dryer. **Rates (CP):** $56 D; $61 ste; $64 effic. Children under age 18 stay free. Parking: Outdoor, free. AE, CB, DC, DISC, MC, V.

≡≡≡ Comfort Inn Lake Norman

20740 Torrence Chapel Rd, Davidson, 28036; tel 704/892-3500 or toll free 800/848-9751; fax 704/892-6473. Exit 28 off I-77. Next door to shopping center. **Rooms:** 90 rms and stes. CI 3pm/CO 11am. Nonsmoking rms avail. **Amenities:** 🛅 ⚋ 🖭 A/C, cable TV w/movies, refrig, in-rm safe. Some units w/whirlpools. Suites have whirlpool baths. VCRs available upon request. **Services:** 🖎 ⏌ **Facilities:** 🔗 🖫 🖫 Washer/dryer. **Rates (CP):** $64 S or D; $82 ste. Children under age 18 stay free. Parking: Outdoor, free. AE, CB, DC, DISC, JCB, MC, V.

≡≡≡ Courtyard by Marriott

333 West WT Harris Blvd, 28262; tel 704/549-4888 or toll free 800/321-2211; fax 704/549-4946. off I-85. Next to UNC-Charlotte, this standard Courtyard boasts attractive, well-appointed rooms and a relaxing courtyard area surrounding the pool. **Rooms:** 152 rms and stes. CI 3pm/CO noon. Nonsmoking rms avail. **Amenities:** 🛅 ⚋ A/C, satel TV w/movies, dataport. Some units w/terraces. **Services:** 🖎 ⏌ **Facilities:** 🔗 🖳 🖫 🖫 1 restaurant (bkfst only), 1 bar, whirlpool, washer/dryer. **Rates:** $70 S; $80 S or D; $86 ste. Extra person $10. Parking: Outdoor, free. AE, CB, DC, DISC, MC, V.

≡≡ Cricket Inn

1200 W Sugar Creek Rd, 28213; tel 704/597-8500; fax 704/598-1815. Exit 41 off I-85. A recently renovated, clean, and comfortable motel offering great value for all travelers. **Rooms:** 132 rms and stes. CI 3pm/CO 11am. Nonsmoking rms avail. **Amenities:** 🏧 A/C, cable TV w/movies. **Services:** ⟿ **Facilities:** 🗗 🕭 Washer/dryer. **Rates (CP):** $36–$42 S or D; $54–$60 ste. Extra person $5. Parking: Outdoor, free. AE, CB, DC, DISC, MC, V.

🗏🗏 Days Inn
1408 W Sugar Creek Rd, 29713; tel 704/597-8110 or toll free 800/DAYS-INN; fax 704/597-9717. Exit 41 off I-85. These basic chain accommodations are a good choice for vacationing families or frugal business travelers. **Rooms:** 151 rms. CI 3pm/CO noon. Nonsmoking rms avail. **Amenities:** 🏧 A/C, satel TV, dataport. **Services:** ⟿ ⟿ **Facilities:** 🗗 🕭 1 restaurant (lunch and dinner only). **Rates (CP):** $28–$43 S. Extra person $5. Children under age 12 stay free. Parking: Outdoor, free. AE, CB, DC, DISC, JCB, MC, V.

🗏🗏 Fairfield Inn Charlotte Airport
3400 S I-85 Service Rd, 28208; tel 704/392-0600 or toll free 800/228-2800; fax 704/392-0600. Exit 41 off I-85. A chain property offering basic amenities. Very popular with families. **Rooms:** 135 rms. CI 3pm/CO noon. Nonsmoking rms avail. **Amenities:** 🏧 🕭 A/C, cable TV w/movies, dataport. **Services:** 🚐 ⟿ ⟿ **Facilities:** 🗗 🕭 **Rates (CP):** $46 S; $55 D. Extra person $3. Children under age 18 stay free. Parking: Outdoor, free. AE, CB, DC, DISC, MC, V.

🗏🗏🗏 Hampton Inn University Place
8419 N Tryon St, 28262; tel 704/548-0905 or toll free 800/HAMPTON; fax 704/548-0971. A very nice motel catering to the frugal businessperson. Near UNC-Charlotte and convenient to most everything. **Rooms:** 125 rms. CI 3pm/CO noon. Nonsmoking rms avail. **Amenities:** 🏧 🕭 A/C, cable TV, dataport. **Services:** ⟿ ⟿ **Facilities:** 🗗 🏊 🏊25 🕭 1 bar. Cash bar Mon–Thurs, 5–8pm. **Rates (CP):** $64 S; $72 D. Children under age 18 stay free. Parking: Outdoor, free. AE, CB, DC, DISC, MC, V.

🗏🗏 Holiday Inn Express
14135 Statesville Rd, PO Box 1349, Huntersville, 28078; tel 704/875-1165 or toll free 800/HOLIDAY; fax 704/875-1894. Exit 18 off I-77. Visitors will not be surprised—favorably or unfavorably—at this basic, dependable property. **Rooms:** 60 rms and stes. CI 2pm/CO 11am. Nonsmoking rms avail. **Amenities:** 🏧 🕭 A/C, cable TV, dataport, voice mail. **Services:** ⟿ **Facilities:** 🗗 🏊25 🕭 **Rates (CP):** $59–$64 S or D; $85 ste. Extra person $5. Children under age 16 stay free. Parking: Outdoor, free. AE, CB, DC, DISC, JCB, MC, V.

🗏🗏 Red Roof Inn
3300 I-85 S, 28208; tel 704/392-2316 or toll free 800/843-9999; fax 704/392-7149. Exit 33 off I-85. A great value for overnight guests, this standard property offers a nice, affordable place to stay near the interstate. **Rooms:** 84 rms. CI 1pm/CO noon. Nonsmoking rms avail. **Amenities:** 🏧

A/C, satel TV, dataport. **Services:** 🚐 ⟿ ⟿ **Facilities:** 🕭 **Rates:** $37 D. Extra person $5. Children under age 18 stay free. Parking: Outdoor, free. AE, CB, DC, DISC, MC, V.

🗏🗏 Red Roof Inn
5116 N I-85, 28206; tel 704/596-8222 or toll free 800/843-7663; fax 704/596-8298. Exit 41 off I-85. Basic chain accommodations, adequate for an overnight stay. **Rooms:** 108 rms. CI open/CO noon. Nonsmoking rms avail. **Amenities:** 🏧 A/C, satel TV, dataport. **Services:** ⟿ ⟿ **Facilities:** 🕭 **Rates:** $30 S; $37 D. Extra person $5. Children under age 18 stay free. Parking: Outdoor, free. AE, CB, DC, DISC, MC, V.

🗏🗏 Rodeway Inn
1416 W Sugar Creek Rd, 28213; tel 704/597-5074 or toll free 800/228-2000; fax 704/597-5074. Exit 41 off I-85. A bare-bones motel with simple but clean rooms and dependable service. **Rooms:** 56 rms. CI open/CO 11am. Nonsmoking rms avail. **Amenities:** 🏧 🕭 🖵 A/C, cable TV. **Services:** ⟿ **Facilities:** 🗗 🕭 **Rates (CP):** $38 S; $46 D. Extra person $3. Children under age 18 stay free. Parking: Outdoor, free. AE, CB, DC, DISC, MC, V.

RESTAURANTS 🍽

Anntony's Caribbean Cafe
In Pecan Point Shopping Center, 2001 E 7th St; tel 704/342-0749. **Caribbean.** A fun, casual restaurant decorated in bright Caribbean colors. The kitchen specializes in rotisserie chicken, chops, and ribs. **FYI:** Reservations not accepted. Blues/jazz/reggae. Children's menu. Beer and wine only. **Open:** Lunch Mon–Fri 11:30am–2:30pm; dinner Mon–Sat 5:30–10pm. **Prices:** Main courses $4–$9. MC, V. 🍴

★ Arthur's on Trade
In Euro-American Cultural Center, 129 W Trade St; tel 704/333-4867. **Cafe.** Offers hot and cold sandwiches, hoagies, quiches, burgers, and steak subs in a comfortable cafe atmosphere. Wine shop on premises. **FYI:** Reservations not accepted. No liquor license. **Open:** Mon–Fri 11:30am–2pm. **Prices:** Lunch main courses $3–$5. MC, V. 🕭

Bravo!
In Adam's Mark Hotel, 555 S McDowell St; tel 704/372-5440. **Italian/Mediterranean.** Since all the waitstaff here are trained singers, diners can expect show tunes or arias along with their meal. The Mediterranean decor complements the menu, which includes specialties such as fillet alla Rossini (charbroiled tenderloin of beef) and vitello alla Parmigiana (breaded veal chop). Prix fixe dinner includes appetizer, salad, entree, dessert, and coffee. **FYI:** Reservations recommended. Piano/singer. Dress code. **Open:** Sun–Thurs 6–10pm, Fri–Sat 6–11pm. **Prices:** Main courses $12–$30. AE, CB, DC, MC, V. ♥ 🆅🅿 🕭

Cajun Queen
1800 E 7th St; tel 704/377-9017. **Cajun.** Located in a renovated house, with each room uniquely decorated in

festive New Orleans colors. Steak, chicken, shrimp, and fish entrees are served with Cajun spice and flair. Specialties include blackened fish filet and pork tenderloin. **FYI:** Reservations recommended. Jazz. **Open:** Mon–Fri 5:30–10pm, Sat 5:30–10:30pm, Sun 5:30–9:30pm. **Prices:** Main courses $11–$20. AE, DC, DISC, MC, V.

5th St Cafe

118 W 5th St; tel 704/358-8334. **Cafe.** An artsy cafe (the dining area doubles as a gallery) known for its low-key ambience and well-prepared cuisine. Menu specialties include pork tenderloin, chicken Ballentine, and several pasta dishes. **FYI:** Reservations recommended. **Open:** Mon–Thurs 11am–5pm, Fri 11:30am–10:30pm, Sat 5–9:30pm. **Prices:** Main courses $12–$15. AE, DISC, MC, V. �

The Ginger Root

In International Trade Center, 201 E 5th St; tel 704/377-9429. **Chinese.** An elegant, contemporary restaurant decorated in muted colors accented with modern and traditional Chinese elements. Menu specialties include the Double Twist (jumbo shrimp and sea scallops sautéed in a hot sauce) and Hunan Dual (shredded chicken served with asparagus and shrimp). **FYI:** Reservations recommended. No smoking. **Open:** Lunch daily 11:30am–2:30pm; dinner daily 5–10pm. **Prices:** Main courses $8–$15. AE, CB, DC, MC, V. 🚗 &

Grady's American Grill

In Reddman Square, 5546 Albemarle Rd; tel 704/537-4663. 1¼ mi E of Independence Ave. **New American.** The classy yet casual dining room features brick walls adorned with original oil paintings, and brick archways dividing each section. The menu is mostly American, with Grady's New York strip, slow roasted prime rib, Southern-style quail, and several pasta dishes. **FYI:** Reservations not accepted. Children's menu. **Open:** Lunch daily 11am–4pm; dinner Sun–Thurs 4–11pm, Fri–Sat 4pm–midnight. **Prices:** Main courses $10–$15. AE, DC, MC, V. 🌑 &

India Palace

6140 E Independence; tel 704/568-7176. **Indian.** The simple decor consists mainly of Indian artwork and beads. The North Indian menu lists chicken, lamb, seafood, and vegetable entrees, as well as kabobs. **FYI:** Reservations not accepted. Beer and wine only. **Open:** Sun–Thurs 11:30am–11:30pm, Fri–Sat 11:30am–11pm. **Prices:** Main courses $7–$13. AE, DISC, MC, V. &

The Lamplighter

1065 E Morehead St (Dilworth); tel 704/372-5343. Off I-277. **Continental.** This restaurant is located in a restored 1920s-era Mediterranean-style house, with tables in many of the rooms. Private rooms are also available for small groups or for intimate dining. Elegant leather furnishings make it a nice place for couples. Entrees include lamb loin stroganoff, cold-water lobster tail, and mahimahi. **FYI:** Reservations

recommended. Dress code. **Open:** Mon–Thurs 5:30–10pm, Fri–Sat 5:30–10:30pm, Sun 5:30–9pm. **Prices:** Main courses $15–$25. AE, DC, MC, V. 🌑 &

★ Landmark Diner

4429 Central Ave; tel 704/532-1153. **Eclectic.** A spacious and colorful dining room with a pleasant, family-friendly atmosphere. The large menu covers seafood, steaks, roasts, chicken, and Italian dishes. Breakfast is served all day, and the cheesecake is as good as anything found in New York. **FYI:** Reservations not accepted. Children's menu. **Open:** Mon–Thurs 6am–3am, Fri–Sat 24 hrs, Sun noon–midnight. **Prices:** Main courses $5–$13. AE, MC, V. &

Longhorn's Steak Restaurant & Saloon

700 E Morehead; tel 704/332-2300. Off I-277. **Steak.** Low lighting, stuffed game and deer heads, neon beer signs, and rodeo posters add to the festive, carefree Western atmosphere. Eight steak choices (including the 22-oz Porterhouse, New York strip, and rib eye) are supplemented by chicken and seafood entrees. All meals come with salad, rolls, and "Texas taters" or rice. **FYI:** Reservations not accepted. Children's menu. **Open:** Lunch Mon–Fri 11am–4pm; dinner Mon–Thurs 4–10:30pm, Fri–Sat 4–11pm, Sun 5–10pm. **Prices:** Main courses $8–$19. DISC, MC, V. &

Morrocrofts

In The Park Hotel, 2200 Rexford Rd; tel 704/364-8220. **American.** A charming place decorated with American style. The rotating menu features such updated classics as grilled appleberry-smoked pork chops and smoked chicken ravioli with goat-cheese sauce. **FYI:** Reservations recommended. Children's menu. Dress code. **Open:** Breakfast daily 6:30–10:30am; lunch daily 10:30am–2pm; dinner daily 5–10:30pm; brunch Sun 10:30am–2pm. **Prices:** Main courses $10–$24. AE, DC, DISC, MC, V. 🌑 ⬇ VP &

♣ Pewter Rose Bistro

In Dilworth Court Shopping Complex, 1820 South Blvd; tel 704/332-8149. **Eclectic.** The decor is delightfully varied—handmade quilts, Broadway posters, dried roses. A second-story patio has garden furniture and flower pots along with painted canvas canopies overhead. Menu items include Chesapeake crab cakes and black tea–smoked suckling. A wide array of appetizers and a tremendous wine list are also available. **FYI:** Reservations not accepted. **Open:** Lunch Mon–Sat 11am–2pm; dinner Mon–Thurs 5–10pm, Fri–Sat 5–11pm, Sun 5–9pm; brunch Sun 11am–3pm. **Prices:** Main courses $12–$17. AE, DC, DISC, MC, V.

Providence Cafe

110 Perrin Place; tel 704/376-2008. Off Providence Rd. **Cafe.** An airy, light, and contemporary dining room with high windows and exposed painted rafters. Lunch offerings revolve around sandwiches on homemade focaccia bread, while dinner specialties include yellowfin tuna with shrimp jambalaya, and hickory-grilled tenderloin medallions. **FYI:**

Reservations not accepted. Jazz. **Open:** Mon–Thurs 11am–11pm, Fri–Sat 11am–midnight, Sun 10am–10pm. **Prices:** Main courses $7–$16. AE, DC, DISC, MC, V. ♨ ⅙

Thai Orchid

In Strawberry Hill Shopping Center, 4223 Providence Rd; tel 704/364-1134. **Thai.** This delightfully bright eatery is decorated in an orchid motif with traditional Thai accents. Menu options include dishes such as curry duck and *ka ta ron* (a sizzling plate of beef served with pineapples and vegetables covered in a brown sauce). **FYI:** Reservations not accepted. Beer and wine only. No smoking. **Open:** Lunch Wed–Mon 11:30am–2:30pm; dinner Mon–Thurs 5–9:45pm, Fri–Sat 5–10:45pm. **Prices:** Main courses $8–$14. DISC, MC, V. ♨ ⅙

ATTRACTIONS 🏛

Mint Museum of Art

2730 Randolph Rd; tel 704/337-2000 or (recorded info) 704/333-MINT. Stately museum containing a fine survey of European and American art, as well as the internationally recognized Delhom Collection of porcelain and pottery. Also featured are pre-Columbian art, contemporary American prints, North Carolina crafts, African objects, vast collections of costumes and antique maps. There's an especially impressive collection of gold coins originally minted at the facility, which was built in 1837 as the first branch of the US Mint. **Open:** Tues 10am–10pm, Wed–Sat 10am–5pm, Sun noon–5pm. Closed some hols. **$$**

Charlotte Nature Museum

1658 Sterling Rd; tel 704/372-6261. Exhibits and displays designed to develop an awareness and appreciation of nature, especially for young children. There's a room with live animals, a nature trail, and a gallery explaining the geological history of the area. **Open:** Mon–Fri 9am–5pm, Sat 9am–6pm, Sun 1–6pm. Closed some hols. **$**

Discovery Place

301 N Tryon St; tel 704/372-6261 or toll free 800/935-0553. Joining with the Nature Museum to form the combined Science Museums of Charlotte, Inc, this award-winning uptown center features such permanent exhibits as a tropical rain forest and an aquarium. Combination tickets are available, which include admission to the center's Omnimax theater and/or the Kelly Space Voyager Planetarium. **Open:** Daily, call for schedule. Closed some hols. **$$$**

James K Polk Memorial

US 521, Pineville; tel 704/889-9191. Located 10 mi S of Charlotte. The 11th president of the United States was born in Mecklenburg County in 1795, and today his birthplace is one of North Carolina's historic sites. Guided tours take visitors through reconstructed log buildings typical of the early 19th century, and exhibits in the modern visitors center illustrate Polk's life and times. **Open:** Apr–Oct, Mon–Sat 9am–5pm, Sun 1–5pm; Nov–Mar, Tues–Sat 10am–4pm, Sun 1–4pm. Closed some hols. **Free**

Wing Haven Gardens and Bird Sanctuary

248 Ridgewood Ave; tel 704/331-0664. These gardens were the inspiration and longtime labor of love of Mrs Elizabeth Clarkson, known as Charlotte's "bird lady"; 142 winged species have been sighted in the three-acre walled garden she created from a once-bare clay field. Birdwatchers and garden-lovers will have a field day, as they browse through the Upper, Lower, Main, Wild, and Herb gardens. The gardens are perhaps at their most splendid in the spring, when birds are returning from their winter sojourn in warmer climes. A bulletin board tells visitors which birds are around at the moment. **Open:** Sun, Tues–Wed 3–5pm. Hours may vary. **Free**

Paramount's Carowinds

14523 Carowinds Blvd; tel 704/588-2606 or toll free 800/888-4FUN. If you're taking children along on your Charlotte trip, you undoubtedly already know about this $40-million, 92-acre park straddling the North and South Carolina state line. Even without the kids, it's definitely worth a visit. The rides are entertaining and inventive, especially the flume and mine train rides. The Thunder Road and Carolina Cyclone rollercoasters may beckon the more adventurous. For sightseers, there's Pirate Island and a re-creation of the Old Charleston waterfront. Fast-paced revues are on view at Paramount and Troubador's Roost Theater. In Blue Ridge Junction, you'll enjoy the shops and crafts at Queen's Colony; and you can tap your toes to bluegrass music in Harmony Hall. The *Paramount on Ice* show features professional skaters and Paramount Pictures' most memorable movie themes. **Open:** Apr–May, Sept–Oct, Sat–Sun; June–Aug, daily; call for hours. **$$$$**

Cherokee

Located in the Great Smoky Mountains. Oconaluftee Indian Village re-creates the Cherokee community of 200 years ago. The Qualla Reservation is still home to the Eastern band of the Cherokee, whose members are descended from those who avoided forced exile on the Trail of Tears. **Information:** Cherokee Travel & Promotion, Main St, PO Box 460, Cherokee, 28719 (tel 704/497-9195).

MOTELS 🏨

≋≋≋ Best Western Great Smokies Inn

Acquoni Rd, PO Box 1809, 28719; tel 704/497-2020 or toll free 800/528-1234; fax 704/497-3903. A standard motel with spacious rooms, nice decor, and comfortable furnishings. Located near a Native American–run casino, and many crafts shops, restaurants, and other attractions. **Rooms:** 152 rms. CI 2pm/CO 11am. Nonsmoking rms avail. **Amenities:** 🛏 A/C, cable TV w/movies. Some units w/whirlpools. **Services:** ✗ ⌑ **Facilities:** 🛗 ⅙ 1 restaurant (*see* "Restaurants" below), games rm, washer/dryer. **Rates:** $75–$95 S or D. Extra person $6. Children under age 12 stay free. Parking: Outdoor, free. AE, CB, DC, DISC, JCB, MC, V.

≡≡ Carriage Inn Resort

US 19, PO Box 1506, 28719; tel 704/488-2398 or toll free 800/480-2398. Very comfortable motel conveniently located near area attractions. **Rooms:** 25 rms. CI noon/CO 11am. Nonsmoking rms avail. Very spacious rooms. **Amenities:** A/C, cable TV. No phone. **Services:** ⟲ **Facilities:** ⚅ ⚆ Playground. **Rates:** Peak (June–Aug, Oct) $32–$68 S or D. Extra person $4–$6. Children under age 12 stay free. Lower rates off-season. Parking: Outdoor, free. Closed Dec–Mar. AE, DISC, MC, V.

≡≡≡ Holiday Inn

US 19, PO Box 1929, 28719; tel 704/497-9181 or toll free 800/HOLIDAY; fax 704/497-5973. A pleasant chain motel located near many shops and restaurants. **Rooms:** 154 rms. CI 2pm/CO 11am. Nonsmoking rms avail. **Amenities:** ⚆ ⚆ A/C, cable TV w/movies, dataport. **Services:** ✗ ⟲ Babysitting. **Facilities:** ⚅ ⚏ ⚆ 1 restaurant (bkfst and dinner only; see "Restaurants" below), games rm, sauna, whirlpool, playground, washer/dryer. **Rates:** Peak (June–Aug, Oct) $69–$100 S or D. Extra person $6. Children under age 18 stay free. Min stay special events. Lower rates off-season. Parking: Outdoor, free. AE, CB, DC, DISC, JCB, MC, V.

≡≡ Pioneer Motel and Cottages

US 19, PO Box 397, 28719; tel 704/497-2435. Comfortable and convenient, offering standard accommodations. **Rooms:** 21 rms; 4 cottages/villas. CI 1pm/CO 11am. Nonsmoking rms avail. **Amenities:** ⚆ ⚆ A/C, cable TV w/movies. **Services:** ⟲ **Facilities:** ⚅ Basketball, lawn games. **Rates:** Peak (June–Oct) $48–$60 S or D; $65–$150 cottage/villa. Extra person $5. Children under age 12 stay free. Lower rates off-season. Parking: Outdoor, free. Cabins have a two-night minimum, and the seventh night is free. Closed Nov–Mar. AE, DISC, MC, V.

RESTAURANTS 🍴

Chestnut Tree Restaurant

In Holiday Inn, US 19; tel 704/497-9181. **Regional American/American.** Pleasant dining room serving up specialties such as trout amandine and Southern-fried chicken. **FYI:** Reservations accepted. Children's menu. BYO. **Open:** Breakfast daily 6:30–11am; dinner daily 5–10pm. **Prices:** Main courses $6–$13; prix fixe $10–$13. AE, CB, DC, DISC, MC, V. 📷 ⚆

Myrtle's Table

In Best Western Great Smokies Inn, 441 Acquoni Rd; tel 704/497-2020. Off US 441 N. **Regional American.** A family-friendly place offering a wide variety of food—from burgers, soups, salads, and sandwiches to steaks and chicken dishes. The Smoky Mountain trout is especially popular. **FYI:** Reser-

vations not accepted. Children's menu. BYO. **Open:** Daily 7am–9pm. Closed Dec–Feb. **Prices:** Main courses $8–$11. AE, CB, DC, DISC, MC, V. 📷

ATTRACTIONS 📷

Oconaluftee Indian Village

US 441; tel 704/497-2111 or 497-2315. An authentic Cherokee community whose residents wear the tribal dress and practice the same crafts as their ancestors. Guests can see dart guns being made or a log canoe being shaped by fire, and beautiful beadwork taking shape under skilled fingers. The seven-sided Council House conjures up images of the leaders of seven tribes gathered to thrash out problems or to worship their gods together. **Open:** May–Oct, daily 9am–5:30pm. $$$

Museum of the Cherokee Indian

Jct US 441 and Drama Rd; tel 704/497-3481. Tells the story of the Cherokee through exhibits of such items as spear points several centuries old and multimedia theater shows. Contemporary Cherokee arts and crafts are also on display. **Open:** June–Aug, Mon–Sat 9am–8pm, Sun 9am–5:30pm; Sept–May, daily 9am–5pm. Closed some hols. $$

Santa's Land Fun Park and Zoo

Rte 1, Box 134-A; tel 704/497-9191. Santa and his helpers are busy getting ready for December 25 in a charming Christmas village complete with amusement rides, paddleboat rides, picnic facilities, gift shops, and heritage exhibits. A small zoo houses reindeer and other domestic and exotic animals. **Open:** May–Sept, daily 9am–5pm. $$$$

Chimney Rock

Nestled in the state's central mountains and named for a spectacular granite edifice, carved by wind, water, and time. Trails in Chimney Rock Park lead to Hickory Nut Falls, one of the highest waterfalls in the eastern United States. **Information:** Hickory Nut Gorge Chamber of Commerce, US 64/74A, PO Box 32, Chimney Rock, 28720 (tel 704/625-2725).

INN 📷

≡≡ Esmerelda Inn

US 74, PO Box 57, 28720; tel 704/625-9105. A relaxed, rustic little place, not big on modern luxuries and conveniences but located right next to a lovely mountain stream and miles of hiking trails. A good place for people hoping to find some peace and quiet. **Rooms:** 13 rms and stes (2 w/shared bath). CI 2pm/CO 11am. No smoking. Comfortable rooms. **Amenities:** ⚆ A/C. No phone or TV. 1 unit w/terrace. **Services:** ✗ **Facilities:** ⚏ 1 restaurant, guest lounge. Restaurant is a local favorite. **Rates (CP):** $45–$51 S or D w/shared bath; $70 ste. Children under age 21 stay free. Parking: Outdoor, free. Closed Dec–Mar. AE, DISC, MC, V.

ATTRACTION 📷

Chimney Rock Park
US 64/74-A; tel 704/625-9611 or toll free 800/277-9611. A privately owned, 1,000-acre park offering the best of the mountains all in one place. The top of the 315-foot granite monolith known as Chimney Rock can be reached by stairway, trail, or elevator; on a clear day there's a 75-mile view. Several scenic nature trails make their way to Hickory Nut Falls, twice the height of Niagara and one of the locations for the 1992 movie *The Last of the Mohicans*. The park offers a year-round array of special events, including guided bird and wildflower walks, rock-climbing demonstrations, musical performances, craft demonstrations, and sports-car races. **Open:** Ticket office, daily 8:30am–4:30pm, park closes at 6pm. Closed some hols. $$$

Concord

Graced by tree-lined streets and a 105-year-old courthouse, this lovely town is also home to the Charlotte Motor Speedway and the NASCAR speedway (called one of the finest racetracks in the world). **Information:** Concord–Carbarrus County Chamber of Commerce, 23 Union St N, PO Box 1029, Concord, 28026 (tel 704/782-4111).

MOTEL 🛏

≣≣≣ Holiday Inn Express
1601 US 29 N, 28025; tel 704/786-5181 or toll free 800/HOLIDAY; fax 704/788-5181 ext 189. Exit 58 off I-85. Pleasant-looking property with nice, clean rooms. Good for an overnight stop, or maybe even an extended stay. **Rooms:** 95 rms. CI 2pm/CO noon. Nonsmoking rms avail. Rooms are very clean and new-looking. **Amenities:** 🛁 ⚲ A/C, cable TV, refrig, dataport. **Services:** ⟁ ⟲ ⟳ Babysitting. **Facilities:** ⟦⟧ ⟦⟧ ⟦250⟧ ⟐ **Rates (CP):** $48 S or D. Extra person $5. Children under age 18 stay free. Parking: Outdoor, free. AE, CB, DC, DISC, MC, V.

ATTRACTION 📷

Charlotte Motor Speedway
US 29; tel 704/455-3200. Located 12 mi N of downtown Charlotte. The speedway is host in late May (Memorial Day Sunday) of each year to the Coca-Cola 600 NASCAR Winston Cup Stock Car Race, the longest and richest such race in the US, which draws upward of 160,000 enthusiastic fans. In early October, the Mello Yello 500 Winston Cup Stock Car Race is run here.

Cornelius

Located 15 miles north of Charlotte in the Piedmont region. Founded as Liverpool in 1893, but renamed in 1905 in honor of Joe Cornelius, a principal stockholder in a local textiles

mill. **Information:** North Mecklenburg Chamber of Commerce & Visitors Center, PO Box 760, Cornelius, 28031 (tel 704/892-1922).

HOTELS 🏨

≣≣≣ Best Western Lake Norman
19608 Liverpool Pkwy, PO Box 2037, 28031; tel 704/896-0660 or toll free 800/528-1234; fax 704/896-8633. Exit 28 off I-77. A very attractive property, perfect for a short visit. Popular with fishing enthusiasts and families. **Rooms:** 80 rms and stes. CI 2pm/CO 11am. Nonsmoking rms avail. **Amenities:** 🛁 A/C, cable TV w/movies, refrig, dataport, VCR. Some units w/whirlpools. **Services:** ⟁ ⟲ Babysitting. **Facilities:** ⟦⟧ ⟦⟧ ⟦125⟧ ⟐ Whirlpool. **Rates (CP):** $55–$65 S; $76–$86 ste. Extra person $7. Children under age 13 stay free. Parking: Outdoor, free. AE, CB, DC, DISC, MC, V.

≣≣ Hampton Inn Lake Norman
19501 Old Statesville Rd, PO Box 1349, 28031; tel 704/892-9900 or toll free 800/HAMPTON; fax 704/892-9900. Exit 28 off I-77. Five-story motel with clean, dependable accommodations. Southern hospitality is dished out by a very friendly staff. **Rooms:** 117 rms. CI 2pm/CO 11am. Nonsmoking rms avail. **Amenities:** 🛁 ⚲ A/C, cable TV w/movies, dataport. **Services:** ⟁ ⟲ **Facilities:** ⟦⟧ ⟦⟧ ⟦25⟧ ⟐ **Rates (CP):** $44–$49 S; $49–$54 D. Extra person $8. Children under age 18 stay free. Parking: Outdoor, free. AE, CB, DC, DISC, MC, V.

Dillsboro

This quaint village in the Great Smoky Mountains offers mountain vistas and a colorful maze of crafts shops and artists' studios.

ATTRACTION 📷

Great Smoky Mountains Railway
1 Front St, Dillsboro; tel 704/586-8811 or toll free 800/872-4681. Round-trip scenic excursions through western North Carolina, with views of the Smoky Mountains, several national forests, lakes, and much more. Holiday theme excursions at Halloween, Christmas, and New Year's Eve; dinner excursions; raft 'n' rail packages. The depot at Dillsboro also houses a railway museum with over 3,000 articles of historic railway memorabilia. **Open:** Office hours, Apr–Oct, daily 8am–9pm; call for train schedule. $$$$

Duck

North of Oregon Inlet on the Outer Banks. Once known for the good duck hunting available here, the town is now an exclusive residential area and retirement resort.

RESORT

≡≡≡ Sanderling Inn Resort

1461 Duck Rd, 27949; tel 919/261-4111 or toll free 800/701-4111; fax 919/261-1638. 12 acres. A quiet, oceanfront resort with accommodations in three separate structures. The spacious, two-story lobby in the main inn has hardwood floors and wood-panel walls. Accents include Audubon prints and impressive bird carvings. **Rooms:** 87 rms and stes. Executive level. CI 4pm/CO 11am. Nonsmoking rms avail. Rooms and suites are beautifully furnished with wicker and wood appointments. Many have ocean view. **Amenities:** A/C, cable TV w/movies, refrig, dataport, bathrobes. All units w/terraces, some w/whirlpools. Luxury suites have VCR and stereo systems. Some rooms have wet bars and kitchenettes. **Services:** Masseur, babysitting. Afternoon tea is served in the Audubon Room. **Facilities:** 1 restaurant (see "Restaurants" below), 1 bar, 1 beach (ocean), spa, sauna, whirlpool. Spacious porches and decks offer relaxation in rocking chairs and a view of the sea oats and gazebos. Golf course nearby. **Rates (CP):** Peak (May 20–Oct) $175–$215 S or D; $210–$800 ste. Extra person $30. Children under age 4 stay free. Lower rates off-season. Parking: Outdoor, free. AE, CB, DC, DISC, MC, V.

RESTAURANT

♥ Restaurant

In Sanderling Inn Resort, 1461 Duck Rd; tel 919/261-4111. **Regional American.** Located in a restored lifesaving station in a National Historic Site, this dining room offers true Outer Banks elegance. Multiple dining rooms with wood floors and walls are decorated tastefully with nautical elements. Chef Connell's progressive Southern cuisine focuses on local seafood: pan-fried crab, scallop cake, and hickory-grilled seafood. Pasta dishes also available. **FYI:** Reservations accepted. Children's menu. **Open:** Breakfast daily 8–10am; lunch daily noon–2pm; dinner daily 5–9:30pm; brunch Sun 9am–2pm. **Prices:** Main courses $15–$19. AE, DISC, MC, V.

Dunn

Located in central North Carolina, 24 miles northeast of Fayetteville. **Information:** Dunn Area Chamber of Commerce, 209 W Divine St, PO Box 548, Dunn, 28335 (tel 910/892-4113).

MOTELS

≡≡ Best Western of Dunn

Exit 72 off I-95, PO Box 1000, 28334; tel 910/892-2162 or toll free 800/528-1234; fax 910/892-2162. A comfortable, clean economy motel with few frills. **Rooms:** 142 rms. CI noon/CO noon. Nonsmoking rms avail. **Amenities:** A/C, cable TV w/movies. **Services:** **Facilities:** **Rates:** $29–$49 S; $35–$59 D. Extra person $6. Children under age 12 stay free. Parking: Outdoor, free. AE, CB, DC, DISC, MC, V.

≡ Econo Lodge

Pope Rd, 28334; tel 919/892-6181 or toll free 800/446-6900. Exit 72 off I-95. Very basic economy accommodations with good housekeeping standards. A good choice for the frugal traveler. **Rooms:** 60 rms. CI 2pm/CO 11am. Nonsmoking rms avail. **Amenities:** A/C, cable TV. **Services:** **Facilities:** Basketball, playground. **Rates:** $35–$50 S or D. Extra person $5. Children under age 18 stay free. Parking: Outdoor, free. AE, DISC, MC, V.

≡≡ Ramada Inn

1011 E Cumberland St, PO Box 729, 28334; tel 910/892-8101 or toll free 800/2-RAMADA; fax 910/892-2836. Exit 73 off I-95. Pleasant motel with attractive public areas. Convenient to the interstate. **Rooms:** 100 rms. CI 1pm/CO noon. Nonsmoking rms avail. **Amenities:** A/C, cable TV w/movies. Refrigerators available. **Services:** Small pets only. **Facilities:** 1 restaurant. **Rates:** $47–$60 S; $57–$70 D. Extra person $6. Children under age 18 stay free. Parking: Outdoor, free. AE, CB, DC, DISC, JCB, MC, V.

Durham

See also Chapel Hill, Durham, Morrisville

Known as "The City of Medicine," and home of historic Duke University and its famous chapel and gardens. Some of the nation's finest African American art can be found at the NC Central University Museum. **Information:** Durham Convention & Visitors Bureau, 101 E Morgan St, Durham, 27701 (tel 919/687-0288).

HOTELS

≡≡≡ Best Western Hotel Crown Park

4620 S Miami Blvd, 27703; tel 919/941-6066 or toll free 800/972-0264. Exit 281 off I-40. Comfortable hotel in peaceful, convenient setting. **Rooms:** 175 rms and stes. Executive level. CI 3pm/CO noon. Nonsmoking rms avail. **Amenities:** A/C, cable TV w/movies, dataport. Some rooms have refrigerators. Complimentary coffee in rooms. **Services:** **Facilities:** 1 restaurant, 1 bar. **Rates:** $104 S; $124 D; $175 ste. Extra person $20. Children under age 12 stay free. Parking: Outdoor, free. Golf packages avail. AE, DC, DISC, MC, V.

≡≡ Brownstone Medcenter Inn

2424 Erwin Rd, 27705; tel 919/286-7761 or toll free 800/367-0293, 800/872-9009 in NC. Fulton St exit off I-40. Some parts of the facility show their age, although the lobby is stylish. Indoor pool makes property a year-round family favorite. **Rooms:** 140 rms and stes. Executive level. CI 3pm/

CO noon. Nonsmoking rms avail. No drapes in rooms. **Amenities:** ⏰ ⚲ A/C, cable TV w/movies, voice mail. Very minimal toiletries. **Services:** ✗ 🚐 ⛱ 🛏 🕭 Babysitting. Pets under 15 lbs allowed under special circumstances. **Facilities:** 🏋 💱 ⛷ 1 restaurant, 1 bar, sauna, whirlpool. Special rates at local fitness center. **Rates (CP):** $59 S; $65 D; $85–$95 ste. Children under age 18 stay free. Min stay special events. Parking: Outdoor, free. Dinner and weekend packages avail. AE, DC, DISC, MC, V.

≣≣ Comfort Inn University
3508 New Mount Moriah Rd, 27707; tel 919/490-4949 or toll free 800/221-2222. I-40 at US 15/US 501, exit 270. A comfortable hotel near I-40. Close to Durham and Chapel Hill. **Rooms:** 138 rms and stes. CI 3pm/CO noon. Nonsmoking rms avail. Room decor doesn't always match. **Amenities:** ⏰ ⚲ A/C, cable TV. **Services:** ⓋⓅ ⛱ 🛏 **Facilities:** 🏋 💱 ⛷ ⚲ Sauna, whirlpool. **Rates (CP):** $61–$63 S or D; $99–$125 ste. Extra person $6. Children under age 12 stay free. Min stay special events. Parking: Outdoor, free. AE, CB, DC, DISC, MC, V.

≣ Cricket Inn University
2306 Elba St, 27705; tel 919/286-3111; fax 919/286-5115. Cameron Blvd exit off US 15/US 501. A basic hotel, located one block from entrance to Duke University Medical Center. **Rooms:** 150 rms and stes. CI 3pm/CO noon. Nonsmoking rms avail. **Amenities:** ⏰ ⚲ A/C, satel TV. **Services:** 🛏 **Facilities:** ⚲ 1 restaurant, washer/dryer. **Rates:** $47–$61 S or D; $75 ste. Extra person $5. Children under age 18 stay free. Min stay special events. Parking: Outdoor, free. AE, CB, DC, DISC, MC, V.

≣≣≣ DoubleTree Guest Suites
2515 Meridian Pkwy, 27713; tel 919/361-4660 or toll free 800/424-2900; fax 919/361-2256. Exit 278 off I-40. A modern property located next to a small manmade lake. Paddleboats and waterside dining are available. **Rooms:** 203 stes. Executive level. CI 3pm/CO noon. Nonsmoking rms avail. **Amenities:** ⏰ ⚲ 📺 🍴 A/C, cable TV w/movies, dataport. All units w/minibars, some w/terraces, some w/whirlpools. Small TV in bathroom. Microwaves available upon request. **Services:** ✗ 🚐 ⛱ 🛏 Twice-daily maid svce, babysitting. **Facilities:** 🏋 🔺 2 💱 🚪 🖥 ⚲ 1 restaurant, 1 bar, basketball, steam rm, whirlpool, playground. **Rates (CP):** $150 ste. Extra person $10. Children under age 18 stay free. Min stay special events. Parking: Outdoor, free. Minimum stay according to availability. AE, CB, DC, DISC, MC, V.

≣≣≣ Durham Hilton
3800 Hillsborough Rd, 27705; tel 919/383-8033 or toll free 800/HILTONS; fax 919/383-4287. From exit I-85 S, take exit 173; from I-85 N, exit 174B. Modern, elegant hotel. Exceptional choice for business travel. **Rooms:** 154 rms and stes. Executive level. CI 3pm/CO noon. Nonsmoking rms avail. **Amenities:** ⏰ 2 ⚲ A/C, satel TV w/movies, dataport. Telephones feature push-button guide to local dining and

entertainment. **Services:** ✗ 🔑 ⓋⓅ 🚐 ⛱ 🛏 Car-rental desk, masseur, babysitting. **Facilities:** 🏋 💱 350 🖥 ⚲ 1 restaurant, 2 bars (1 w/entertainment). **Rates:** $75–$119 S or D; $145–$205 ste. Extra person $10. Children under age 18 stay free. Min stay special events. Parking: Outdoor, free. AE, DC, DISC, MC, V.

≣≣ The Forest Inn
3460 Hillsborough Rd, 27705; tel 919/383-1551. Off I-85. A good-looking property featuring a grassy courtyard and a unique pool with a children's area. **Rooms:** 94 rms and stes. CI 3pm/CO noon. Nonsmoking rms avail. **Amenities:** ⏰ ⚲ A/C, cable TV w/movies. **Services:** ✗ ⛱ 🛏 **Facilities:** 🏋 220 🖥 ⚲ 1 restaurant, 1 bar, washer/dryer. **Rates (CP):** $50 S; $51 D; $91 ste. Extra person $5. Children under age 18 stay free. Min stay special events. Parking: Outdoor, free. AE, CB, DC, JCB, MC, V.

≣≣ Hampton Inn
1816 Hillandale Rd, 27705; tel 919/471-6100 or toll free 800/HAMPTON. Off I-85. A comfortable hotel for business travelers or the whole family. Convenient to I-85. **Rooms:** 131 rms. Executive level. CI 2pm/CO noon. Nonsmoking rms avail. **Amenities:** ⏰ ⚲ A/C, cable TV. **Services:** 🔑 🚐 🛏 **Facilities:** 🏋 💱 30 ⚲ Steam rm. **Rates (CP):** $58 S; $124 D. Children under age 18 stay free. Min stay special events. Parking: Outdoor, free. AE, DC, DISC, MC, V.

≣≣≣ Hawthorn Suites
300 Meredith Dr, 27713; tel 919/361-1234 or toll free 800/866-4787. Exit 278 off I-40. Attractive hotel decorated with an unusual mix of traditional and modern elements. **Rooms:** 96 stes. Executive level. CI 3pm/CO 11am. Nonsmoking rms avail. **Amenities:** ⏰ ⚲ 📺 A/C, cable TV w/movies, refrig, dataport. Rooms have microwaves and full-size ranges. **Services:** 🚐 ⛱ 🛏 Babysitting. Full breakfast offered Mon–Fri; continental breakfast on weekends. **Facilities:** 🏋 🎾 125 🖥 ⚲ 1 restaurant, 1 bar, basketball, racquetball. Quiet courtyard and pool area. Free use of a local fitness center. **Rates (BB):** $99–$130 ste. Children under age 18 stay free. Min stay special events. Parking: Outdoor, free. AE, DC, MC, V.

≣≣≣ Holiday Inn Raleigh-Durham Airport
4810 New Page Rd, 27703; tel 919/941-6000 or toll free 800/HOLIDAY. Exit 282 off I-40. This property has the look and feel of a country inn: a white exterior, shutters, and rocking chairs on the porch. **Rooms:** 249 rms and stes. Executive level. CI 2pm/CO noon. Nonsmoking rms avail. **Amenities:** ⏰ ⚲ A/C, cable TV w/movies, dataport, VCR, voice mail. Some units w/terraces, some w/whirlpools. **Services:** ✗ 🔑 ⓋⓅ 🚐 ⛱ 🛏 🕭 Twice-daily maid svce, babysitting. **Facilities:** 🏋 💱 400 ⚲ 2 restaurants, 2 bars (1 w/entertainment), sauna, whirlpool. **Rates:** $109 S or D; $135 ste. Extra person $10. Children under age 12 stay free. Min stay special events. Parking: Outdoor, free. AE, DC, DISC, MC, V.

Marriott at Research Triangle Park

4700 Guardian Dr, 27703; tel 919/941-6200 or toll free 800/228-9290; fax 919/941-6229. Off I-40. The business-oriented location of this beautiful hotel is its biggest draw. Close to the interstate, office parks, and shopping. Lobby with skylights and courtyard. **Rooms:** 224 rms and stes. Executive level. CI 4pm/CO noon. Nonsmoking rms avail. **Amenities:** A/C, cable TV w/movies, dataport. **Services:** Twice-daily maid svce, babysitting. **Facilities:** 1 restaurant, 1 bar, sauna, whirlpool, washer/dryer. **Rates:** $112 S; $124 D; $175–$225 ste. Children under age 12 stay free. Min stay special events. Parking: Outdoor, free. AE, CB, DC, DISC, JCB, MC, V.

Omni Durham Hotel

201 Foster St, 27701; tel 919/683-6664 or toll free 800/THE-OMNI. Gregson St exit off I-85 and Roxboro/Mangum Sts off Durham Expressway. A downtown Durham landmark, this hotel is adjacent to the Durham Civic Center and the historic Carolina Theater. **Rooms:** 191 rms and stes. CI 3pm/CO noon. Nonsmoking rms avail. Some rooms offer views of Duke University Chapel. **Amenities:** A/C, cable TV w/movies, dataport. **Services:** Babysitting. **Facilities:** 1 restaurant (see "Restaurants" below), 1 bar. Guests may use nearby Gold's Gym and swimming pool off-site. **Rates:** $105–$135 S or D; $180–$275 ste. Extra person $10. Children under age 16 stay free. Min stay special events. Parking: Outdoor, free. AE, CB, DC, DISC, MC, V.

Radisson Governors Inn

Davis Dr, 27703; tel 919/549-8631 or toll free 800/333-3333. Exit 280 off I-40. Caters to guests doing business in the Research Triangle area. **Rooms:** 193 rms and stes. Executive level. CI 3pm/CO noon. Nonsmoking rms avail. **Amenities:** A/C, cable TV w/movies, refrig, dataport, VCR, voice mail. **Services:** **Facilities:** 1 restaurant, 1 bar, basketball. Free use of local health club. **Rates:** $109 S; $119 D; $185–$250 ste. Extra person $10. Children under age 12 stay free. Min stay special events. Parking: Outdoor, free. AE, DC, DISC, MC, V.

Regal University Hotel

2800 Middleton Ave, 27705; tel 919/383-8575 or toll free 800/633-5379. Morreen St exit off US 15/US 501 bypass. A stylish hotel with much to offer. The lounge features a baby grand piano and a billiards table. **Rooms:** 312 rms and stes. Executive level. CI 3pm/CO noon. Nonsmoking rms avail. **Amenities:** A/C, cable TV w/movies, voice mail. **Services:** Masseur. **Facilities:** 1 restaurant, 1 bar, whirlpool, beauty salon, washer/dryer. **Rates:** $95 S; $105 D; $140–$190 ste. Extra person $10. Children under age 18 stay free. Min stay special events. Parking: Outdoor, free. AE, CB, DC, DISC, MC, V.

Residence Inn by Marriott

1919 NC 54E, 27713; tel 919/361-1266 or toll free 800/331-3131; fax 919/361-1200. Exit 278 off I-40. Apartment-style property tucked away in a quiet, suburban area. A community feeling is fostered by the central athletic facility and weekly cookouts. **Rooms:** 122 stes. CI 3pm/CO noon. Nonsmoking rms avail. Furnished apartmentlike units, all with kitchens. **Amenities:** A/C, cable TV w/movies, refrig, dataport, voice mail, in-rm safe. All units w/fireplaces. **Services:** Children's program. **Facilities:** Basketball, volleyball, racquetball, whirlpool, washer/dryer. Multipurpose athletic court on property. Complimentary use of local health spa. **Rates (CP):** $109–$139 ste. Children under age 18 stay free. Min stay special events. Parking: Outdoor, free. Discounts for extended stays. AE, CB, DC, DISC, JCB, MC, V.

Sheraton Imperial Hotel

4700 Emperor Blvd, 27703; tel 919/941-5050 or toll free 800/325-3535; fax 919/941-5156. Exit 282 off I-40. A sleek, modern property, with marble floors and unique lighting. Modern art adorns the walls. **Rooms:** 331 rms and stes. Executive level. CI 3pm/CO noon. Nonsmoking rms avail. **Amenities:** A/C, cable TV w/movies, dataport, voice mail. **Services:** Car-rental desk, masseur, babysitting. **Facilities:** 2 restaurants, 2 bars (1 w/entertainment), whirlpool. Use of adjacent health spa for nominal fee. **Rates:** $114–$128 S or D; $140–$406 ste. Extra person $10. Children under age 16 stay free. Min stay special events. Parking: Outdoor, free. AE, CB, DC, DISC, MC, V.

MOTELS

Days Inn

Redwood Rd, 27704; tel 919/688-4338 or toll free 800/DAYS-INN. At exit 183 off I-85. A good place for an overnight stop off the interstate. **Rooms:** 119 rms and effic. CI 3pm/CO noon. Nonsmoking rms avail. **Amenities:** A/C, cable TV, refrig. **Services:** Pets allowed in onsite kennel only. **Facilities:** 1 restaurant, washer/dryer. **Rates:** Peak (Apr–Sept) $40–$60 S; $35–$44 D; $35–$50 effic. Extra person $5. Children under age 18 stay free. Lower rates off-season. Parking: Outdoor, free. AE, DISC, MC, V.

Fairfield Inn

4507 NC 55E, 27713; tel 919/361-2656 or toll free 800/228-2800; fax 919/544-0288. Exit 278 off I-40. A clean, pleasant place to stay. **Rooms:** 96 rms. Executive level. CI 2pm/CO noon. Nonsmoking rms avail. **Amenities:** A/C, cable TV w/movies, dataport. Some units w/whirlpools. Nintendo in all rooms. **Services:** **Facilities:** Whirlpool. **Rates (CP):** $49–$54 S or D. Extra person $5. Children under age 18 stay free. Parking: Outdoor, free. AE, DC, DISC, MC, V.

Fairfield Inn by Marriott

3710 Hillsborough Rd, 27705; tel 919/382-3388 or toll free 800/228-2800. From I-85 S take exit 173; from I-85 N, exit 174B. Very pleasant motel. Rooms have many high-tech conveniences. **Rooms:** 135 rms. CI 3pm/CO noon. Nonsmoking rms avail. **Amenities:** A/C, cable TV, dataport.

Telephones equipped with push-button directory of local dining and entertainment. Credit-card slide for pizza orders, car rentals, etc. **Services:** 🖼 ⌐ **Facilities:** 📶 💻 ⅙ **Rates (CP):** $46 S; $54 D. Children under age 18 stay free. Min stay special events. Parking: Outdoor, free. AE, DC, DISC, MC, V.

☰ Howard Johnson Lodge Durham

1800 Hillandale Rd, PO Box 2992, 27705; tel 919/477-7381 or toll free 800/1-GOHOJO; fax 919/477-3857. Off I-85. Basic, no-frills motel. **Rooms:** 80 rms. CI 2pm/CO noon. Nonsmoking rms avail. **Amenities:** 🛋 ⅙ A/C, cable TV w/movies. **Services:** 🖥 **Facilities:** 📶 ⅙ 1 restaurant. Restaurant open 24 hours. **Rates:** Peak (May–Oct) $36–$70 S; $40–$80 D. Extra person $5. Children under age 18 stay free. Lower rates off-season. Parking: Outdoor, free. Special hospital/clinic rates avail. AE, DC, DISC, MC, V.

☰ Red Roof Inn

4405 NC 55E, 27713; tel 919/361-1950 or toll free 800/THE-ROOF; fax 919/361-1950. Exit 278 off I-40. Basic chain motel, popular with university visitors and parents. **Rooms:** 120 rms. CI 2pm/CO noon. Nonsmoking rms avail. **Amenities:** 🛋 ⅙ A/C, cable TV w/movies. **Services:** ⌐ **Facilities:** ⅙ **Rates:** $38 S; $43–$48 D. Extra person $6. Children under age 18 stay free. Parking: Outdoor, free. AE, DC, MC, V.

RESORT

☰☰☰☰ Washington Duke Inn & Golf Club

3001 Cameron Blvd, 27706; tel 919/490-0999 or toll free 800/443-3853; fax 919/688-0105. US 15/501 Bypass to NC 751, ⅓ mile on right. Massive mahogany and glass doors open into beautiful lobby with view of the golf course. Adjoining corridors and sitting areas display artifacts and memorabilia from Duke University's history. **Rooms:** 171 rms and stes. CI 3pm/CO noon. Nonsmoking rms avail. **Amenities:** 🛋 ⅙ 🍴 A/C, cable TV, dataport. 1 unit w/whirlpool. **Services:** 🍽 🔑 📼 🖼 ⌐ Twice-daily maid svce, babysitting. Complimentary use of area health spa. **Facilities:** 📶 ▶18 🎿 🐟4 450 💻 ⅙ 1 restaurant, 1 bar, playground. **Rates:** $130–$160 S or D; $285–$485 ste. Extra person $10. Children under age 17 stay free. Min stay special events. Parking: Outdoor, free. AE, DC, MC, V.

RESTAURANTS 🍴

AnotherThyme

109 N Gregson St; tel 919/682-5225. 1 block off Main St. **Seafood/Vegetarian.** A rustic, contemporary motif lends this place a casual ambience, and the food is health conscious. The menu crosses ethnic culinary borders with innovative dishes that emphasize vegetables, seafood, and pasta. Chargoal-grilled swordfish steaks and seafood kabobs are popular with locals. For those with a sweet tooth, the dessert menu is excellent. **FYI:** Reservations recommended. **Open:** Lunch Mon–Fri 11:30am–2:30pm; dinner Mon–Thurs 6–10pm, Fri–Sat 6–11pm, Sun 6–9:30pm. **Prices:** Main courses $11–$20. AE, MC, V. 🌑⅙

Darryl's 1890 Restaurant and Bar

4603 Chapel Hill Blvd; tel 919/489-1890. **Eclectic.** A fun restaurant with a Southern theme. The exterior and interior are decorated with a variety of "Southern" elements and symbols; idiosyncratic features include row boats in the rafters and fishing lures in the chandeliers. The menu is classic Southern fare, with some variation (like beef and chicken fajitas), and the desserts are huge and very rich. **FYI:** Reservations accepted. Children's menu. **Open:** Lunch daily 11am–4pm; dinner Sun–Thurs 4–11pm, Fri–Sat 4pm–1am. **Prices:** Main courses $9–$14. AE, CB, DC, DISC, MC, V. ⅙

El Rodeo Mexican Restaurant

In Brightleaf Square, 905 W Main St; tel 919/683-2417. **Mexican.** A festive atmosphere is created via colorful decor and Hispanic music. The extensive menu (with more than 60 dinner options) includes beef steaks à la Tampiqueña (steak with rice, beans, and salad) and mole ranchero (chicken breast topped with mole sauce). Vegetarian dishes also available. **FYI:** Reservations not accepted. Children's menu. Beer and wine only. Additional location: 140 E Franklin St, Chapel Hill (tel 929-6566). **Open:** Lunch Mon–Fri 11am–2:30pm, Sat–Sun noon–5pm; dinner Mon–Thurs 5–10pm, Fri 5–11pm, Sat 5–10pm, Sun 5–9pm. **Prices:** Main courses $6–$9. DISC, MC, V. 🖼⅙

♥ Magnolia Grill

1002 9th St; tel 919/286-3609. **Seafood/Vegetarian.** Chef Ben Barker scouts local farmers' markets for fresh ingredients to be used in his seasonal recipes. The menu is always full of surprises, but will include the likes of grilled Norwegian salmon on green lentils with mustard-rosemary sauce. There's mouth-watering homemade ice cream for dessert. **FYI:** Reservations recommended. No smoking. **Open:** Mon–Thurs 6–9:30pm, Fri 6–10pm, Sat 5:30–10pm. Closed Jan 1–10. **Prices:** Main courses $12–$20. MC, V. ⅙

★ Ninth Street Bakery

776 9th St; tel 919/286-0303. Near Duke University. **Cafe.** A laid-back hangout frequented by local artists, writers, and students. Baked goods (all made with organic flour) include an assortment of breads, pastries, cookies, and cakes; they also serve sandwiches such as egg salad with organic sprouts and "Tofuna," and salads. **FYI:** Reservations not accepted. Blues/folk. Beer and wine only. No smoking. **Open:** Mon–Thurs 7am–6pm, Fri 7am–11pm, Sat 8am–11pm, Sun 8am–4pm. **Prices:** Main courses $6–$9. DISC, MC, V. ⅙

Outback Steak House

3500 Mount Moriah Rd; tel 919/493-2202. ¼ mi W of jct I-40/US 15/US 501. **Steak.** A laid-back place, with rough wood floors and walls. The Australian theme of the decor (stuffed koala bears hang from the light fixtures) makes for a fun and friendly atmosphere. Delicious appetizers such as the "bloomin' onion" and coconut-battered fried shrimp make a fine introduction for the thick and juicy steaks. **FYI:** Reservations not accepted. Children's menu. **Open:** Mon–Thurs 4:30–10:30pm, Fri 4:30–11:30pm, Sat 3–11:30pm, Sun 3–10pm. **Prices:** Main courses $8–$18. AE, DC, DISC, MC, V. &

Ravena's Restaurant, Cafe & Bookstore
716 9th St; tel 919/286-3170. Near Duke University. **Cafe/Vegetarian.** Diners are invited to sip cappuccino while they linger over the selection of 25,000 used books, or play the board games that are provided. On the menu are eggplant ravena, spinach and mushroom marinara over pasta, honey-mustard chicken dinner, and many sandwiches and vegetarian items. **FYI:** Reservations not accepted. Children's menu. Beer and wine only. No smoking. **Open:** Sun–Thurs 10am–10pm, Fri–Sat 10am–11pm. **Prices:** Main courses $6–$8. DISC, MC, V. &

Regulator Cafe
In Daniel Boone Plaza, 107 Freeland Memorial Dr, Hillsborough; tel 919/732-5600. **New American.** A unique and charming place located in a two-story historic house where George Washington once slept. The ambience may be old, but the food is entirely modern. The menu includes pasta, grilled seafood, and fajitas, and other dishes employing a variety of unusual ingredients. **FYI:** Reservations recommended. No smoking. **Open:** Dinner Tues–Sun 5:30–9:30pm. **Prices:** Main courses $7–$18. AE, MC, V. ▇

Restaurant
In The Colonial Inn, 153 W King St, Hillsborough; tel 919/732-2461. Off Main St. **American.** The Inn was opened in 1759 and was host to Revolutionary War–era dignitaries, including Lord Cornwallis. The prix fixe dinner includes unlimited portions of fried chicken, barbecue pork, baked ham, and choice of several vegetables and desserts. **FYI:** Reservations recommended. Children's menu. Beer and wine only. **Open:** Lunch Tues–Sun 11:30am–2pm; dinner Tues–Sat 5–8:30pm, Sun 5–8pm. **Prices:** Main courses $8–$15; prix fixe $13. MC, V. ▇

Romano's Macaroni Grill
4020 Chapel Hill Blvd; tel 919/489-0313. **Italian.** A fashionable establishment with high ceilings and rock walls; the tables are covered with paper and crayons for guests' enjoyment. The menu includes pasta, beef, chicken, and fish along with several pizzas and some luscious desserts. House wines are brought to the table and dispensed on the honor system. **FYI:** Reservations not accepted. Singer. Children's menu. **Open:** Sun–Thurs 11am–10pm, Fri–Sat 11am–11pm. **Prices:** Main courses $7–$14. AE, DISC, MC, V. ● ▦ &

Satisfaction Restaurant and Bar
19-J Brightleaf Sq; tel 919/682-7397. **Deli/Pizza.** A casual eatery popular with students. The brick walls of the dining room are decorated with neon signs and automobile posters; there's even a half of a VW Beetle hanging on the wall. The extensive menu features subs, burgers, and gyros. Create-your-own pizzas are available, with more than 20 toppings to choose from. **FYI:** Reservations not accepted. **Open:** Mon–Fri 11am–1am. **Prices:** Main courses $4–$13. AE, DISC, MC, V. &

REFRESHMENT STOP ▽

Francesca's Dessert Caffe
706 9th St; tel 919/286-4177. Near Duke University. **Desserts.** This cafe offers something for everyone's sweet tooth. Desserts (all of which are made fresh daily) include pound cakes, pies, tarts, cheesecakes, Black Forest cherry cake, banana Frangelico torte, and coconut-apricot torte. There's also ice cream by the scoop and an assortment of flavored coffees. **Open:** DISC, MC, V. &

ATTRACTIONS 🗂

Duke Homestead and Tobacco Museum
2828 Duke Homestead Rd; tel 919/477-5498. Duke Homestead is a national historical landmark consisting of the Duke family's ancestral home (built in 1852), the original American Tobacco Company factory building, and the Duke tobacco farm. The Tobacco Museum traces the history of tobacco from colonial days (when it was used as currency) to the present. A 22-minute film, *Carolina Bright,* provides introductory information on the Duke family and the state's tobacco industry. **Open:** Apr–Oct, Mon–Sat 9am–5pm, Sun 1–5pm; Nov–Mar, Tues–Sat 10am–4pm, Sun 1–4pm. Closed some hols. **Free**

Duke University Chapel
West Campus, Duke University; tel 919/684-2572. In 1925, James B Duke directed that a "great towering church" be built at the center of the new university that would bear his name. This magnificent Gothic chapel, reminiscent of England's Canterbury Cathedral, is the result. Its bell tower rises 210 feet and houses a 50-bell carillon that rings out at the end of each workday and on Sunday. There's a half-million-dollar organ with more than 5,000 pipes, and 77 stained-glass windows depicting Biblical scenes. The chapel is sometimes closed on weekends for private functions (it's a very popular site for weddings), so be sure to call ahead. Group tours available by appointment, as the chapel schedule permits. **Open:** Sept–May, daily 8am–10pm; June–Aug, daily 8am–8pm. Closed some hols. **Free**

Sarah P Duke Gardens
Tel 919/684-3698. Fifty-five acres of gardens on the West Campus of Duke that draw more than 200,000 visitors each year. In a valley bordered by a pine forest, the garden features a lily pond, stone terraces, a rose garden, a native-plant garden, an Asiatic arboretum, a wisteria-draped pergola, and colorful seasonal plantings. **Open:** Daily 8am–sunset. **Free**

North Carolina Museum of Life and Science
433 Murray Ave; tel 919/220-5429. Although it is especially geared toward children, visitors of all ages can enjoy this museum's exhibits on the human body, weather, geology, and physics. There's a large diorama of the *Apollo 15* lunar landing (complete with a sample of moon rock) and many hands-on exhibits in the Science Arcade and in the Nature Center's Discovery Room. The 78 acres also hold the Farmyard Loblolly Park and a mile-long narrow-gauge railroad. **Open:** Daily 10am–5pm. Closed some hols. **$$$**

Edenton

On Albemarle Sound near the mouth of the Chowan River. The colonial capital from 1722 to 1743, it was a prosperous port until the War of 1812. Former prosperity is still in evidence at several historic sites, including the home of James Iredell, a member of the first US Supreme Court. **Information:** Chowan County Tourism Division Authority, 116 E King St, PO Box 245, Edenton, 27932 (tel 919/ 482-3400).

MOTELS 🏨

≣ Coach House Inn
919 N Broad St, 27932; tel 919/482-2107. A basic, no-frills motel. **Rooms:** 38 rms. CI 2pm/CO 11am. **Amenities:** 🛎 A/C, cable TV. **Services:** 🆅🅿 **Rates:** $32 S; $42 D. Extra person $4. Children under age 12 stay free. Parking: Outdoor, free. AE, DISC, MC, V.

≣≣ Travel Host Inn
501 Virginia Rd, 27932; tel 919/482-2017. At jct US 17/US 32. A very pleasant and attractive motel, it has a brick exterior with white trim and is less than two miles from the historic district. **Rooms:** 65 rms. CI 2pm/CO 11am. Nonsmoking rms avail. **Amenities:** 🛎 🅰 A/C, cable TV, dataport. **Services:** 🖂 🍴 Babysitting. **Facilities:** 🔓 🛏25 🚹 **Rates (CP):** $47–$54 S or D. Extra person $5. Children under age 12 stay free. Parking: Outdoor, free. AE, DC, DISC, MC, V.

INN

≣≣≣ The Lords Proprietors' Inn
300 N Broad St, 27932; tel 919/482-3641 or toll free 800/ 348-8933; fax 919/482-2432. On US 17. 5 acres. Located in the heart of the historic district, this inn comprises three restored 18th- and 19th-century homes—a large brick Victorian with a wraparound porch, a smaller frame house, and a converted tobacco pack house. Sitting areas are beautifully decorated. **Rooms:** 20 rms. CI 1pm/CO 11am. No smoking. Every room has a charm of its own, with antiques and designer fabrics chosen with care and taste. **Amenities:** 🛎 🅰 A/C, cable TV, dataport, VCR. Some units w/terraces. **Services:** 🖂 🍴 Babysitting. **Facilities:** 🛏35 🚹 Guest lounge. Shaded garden courtyard and two large porches with rocking chairs. Guests may use pool at innkeeper's private home (10

min away). Library, gift shop. **Rates (MAP):** $120–$180 S; $165–$215 D. Extra person $20. Parking: Outdoor, free. No CC.

RESTAURANT 🍴

Dram Tree Inn
112 W Water St; tel 919/482-2711. On the waterfront. **American.** A surreal mural on the interior wall depicts coastal scenes ranging from the Caribbean to the Edenton Waterfront. Meats are cut on the premises for beef dishes such as beef Wellington, and fresh seafood is brought in daily for dishes such as crab Imperial. **FYI:** Reservations recommended. Dress code. **Open:** Lunch Mon–Sat 11:30am–3pm; dinner Mon–Sun 5–9pm. **Prices:** Main courses $11–$22. AE, DISC, MC, V. ♥

ATTRACTION 📷

Historic Edenton Visitor Center
108 N Broad St; tel 919/482-3663. A lovely old town whose streets are lined with homes built by the planters and merchants who settled along the Albemarle Sound. The visitors center features a free 14-minute slide show and sells maps of the historic district for a nominal fee. Guided tours of four historic buildings—the 1767 Chowan County Courthouse, the 1725 Cupola House, the 1773 James Iredell House State Historic Site, and restored St Paul's Episcopal Church—are conducted daily. (Tickets can be purchased, individually or as a package, at the visitors center.) **Open:** Mon–Sat 9am–5pm, Sun 1–5pm. Closed some hols. **Free**

Elizabeth City

Located on the state's scenic northern coast, the town's historic district has the largest number of pre–Civil War commercial buildings in the state. **Information:** Elizabeth City Chamber of Commerce, PO Box 426, Elizabeth City, 27907 (tel 919/335-4365).

HOTEL 🏨

≣≣ Comfort Inn
306 S Hughes Blvd, 27909; tel 919/338-8900 or toll free 800/228-5150; fax 919/338-6420. An attractive hotel. **Rooms:** 80 rms. CI 2:30pm/CO 11am. Nonsmoking rms avail. **Amenities:** 🛎 A/C, cable TV w/movies, dataport. Refrigerators available. **Services:** 🍴 **Facilities:** 🔓 🚹 **Rates (CP):** $49–$95 S; $57–$95 D. Extra person $6. Children under age 18 stay free. Parking: Outdoor, free. AE, CB, DC, DISC, MC, V.

MOTEL

≣≣ Holiday Inn
522 S Hughes Blvd, 27909; tel 919/338-3951 or toll free 800/HOLIDAY; fax 919/338-6225. On US 17. A comfort-

able motel with well-kept grounds. **Rooms:** 158 rms. CI 2pm/ CO noon. Nonsmoking rms avail. **Amenities:** 🛅 🐧 🎮 A/C, cable TV w/movies. **Services:** 🛥 🖢 **Facilities:** 🈳 🛖 🔢 🛆 1 restaurant, 1 bar, washer/dryer. **Rates:** $60–$65 S; $65–$70 D. Extra person $5. Children under age 18 stay free. Parking: Outdoor, free. AE, CB, DC, DISC, MC, V.

INN

≡≡≡ The Culpepper Inn

609 W Main St, 27909; tel 919/335-1993. An old and historic house as well, this lovely bed-and-breakfast inn is located in the heart of the historic district. Unsuitable for children under 12. **Rooms:** 11 rms. CI 3pm/CO 11am. No smoking. Rooms are individually decorated with handsome, traditional furnishings. **Amenities:** 🐧 A/C. No phone or TV. **Services:** 🛥 Babysitting, wine/sherry served. **Facilities:** 🈳 🔢 **Rates (BB):** $85–$105 D. Extra person $10. Higher rates for special events/hols. Parking: Outdoor, free. AE, MC, V.

ATTRACTION 📷

Museum of the Albemarle

1116 US 17S; tel 919/335-1453. Exhibits tell the stories of all the various peoples who have lived in this region of North Carolina, from the Native Americans to the Elizabethan-era English colonists. Programs include guided tours of the town and "Hands On History" presentations. **Open:** Tue–Sat 9am–5pm, Sun 2–5pm. Closed some hols. **Free**

Fayetteville

General Sherman spared the market building here (built in the 1830s on the site of the old statehouse) because of its unusual architecture. Home to Fort Bragg and the 82nd Airborne Division War Memorial Museum. **Information:** Fayetteville Area Convention & Visitors Bureau, 245 Person St, Fayetteville, 28301 (tel 910/483-5311).

HOTELS 🛏

≡≡≡ Courtyard by Marriott

4192 Sycamore Dairy Rd, 28303; tel 910/487-5557 or toll free 800/321-2211; fax 910/323-3946. Morganton Rd exit off All American Fwy. Very attractive hotel, convenient to dining and shopping options, and a good choice for business travel. **Rooms:** 108 rms and stes. CI 3pm/CO noon. Nonsmoking rms avail. **Amenities:** 🛅 🐧 🎮 A/C, cable TV, dataport. Some units w/terraces. **Services:** 🛥 **Facilities:** 🈳 🛖 🔢 🛆 1 restaurant (bkfst only), 1 bar, whirlpool, washer/dryer. **Rates:** $50–$65 S or D; $95 ste. Extra person $10. Children under age 18 stay free. Min stay special events. Parking: Outdoor, free. AE, CB, DC, DISC, JCB, MC, V.

≡≡ Days Inn

2065 Cedar Creek Rd, PO Box 2086, 28301; tel 910/483-6191 or toll free 800/DAYS-INN; fax 910/483-4113.

Exit 49 off I-95. A standard hotel decorated in soft colors and featuring a relaxing courtyard area. **Rooms:** 122 rms. CI 3pm/CO noon. Nonsmoking rms avail. **Amenities:** 🛅 🐧 A/C, cable TV, dataport. Devices for the deaf or hard-of-hearing available upon request. **Services:** 🛥 🖢 **Facilities:** 🈳 🔢 🛆 1 restaurant, 1 bar, games rm. **Rates:** $39 S; $42 D. Extra person $6. Children under age 18 stay free. Parking: Outdoor, free. AE, DC, DISC, JCB, MC, V.

≡≡ Holiday Inn

1944 Cedar Creek Rd, PO Box 2245, 28301; tel 910/323-1600 or toll free 800/HOLIDAY; fax 910/323-0691. Exit 49 off I-95. Decorated in pastels throughout, this pleasant hotel has a beautifully landscaped courtyard for lounging on sunny days. **Rooms:** 201 rms and stes. CI 2pm/ CO noon. Nonsmoking rms avail. **Amenities:** 🛅 🐧 🎮 A/C, cable TV w/movies. **Services:** ✗ 🚗 🛥 🖢 **Facilities:** 🈳 🛖 🔢 🛆 1 restaurant, 1 bar, whirlpool, washer/dryer. Indoor pool ensures year-round fun. **Rates:** $74–$95 S or D; $89–$120 ste. Extra person $10. Children under age 12 stay free. Min stay special events. AP and MAP rates avail. Parking: Outdoor, free. Golf packages avail. AE, CB, DC, DISC, JCB, MC, V.

≡≡≡ Howard Johnson Plaza Hotel

1965 Cedar Creek Rd, PO Box 2086, 28302; tel 910/323-8282 or toll free 800/253-7808. Exit 49 off I-95. Modern-looking hotel with an atrium lobby and nicely designed indoor and outdoor pools. **Rooms:** 168 rms and stes. Executive level. CI 2pm/CO noon. Nonsmoking rms avail. **Amenities:** 🛅 A/C, cable TV, dataport. **Services:** ✗ 🚗 🛥 🖢 **Facilities:** 🈳 🛖 🔢 💻 🛆 1 restaurant, 1 bar, sauna, whirlpool. **Rates:** $55–$65 S or D; $65–$76 ste. Extra person $6. Children under age 12 stay free. Min stay special events. Parking: Outdoor, free. AE, CB, DC, DISC, ER, JCB, MC, V.

≡≡ Quality Inn Ambassador

2205 Gillespie St, PO Box 64166, 28306; tel 910/485-8135 or toll free 800/228-5151; fax 910/485-8682. I-95 business and US 301 S at Owen Dr. A well-kept, quaint hotel with benches in exterior corridors and shutters on the windows. Located near airport and civic center. **Rooms:** 62 rms. CI 1pm/CO noon. Nonsmoking rms avail. **Amenities:** 🛅 🐧 A/C, cable TV w/movies. **Services:** 🖢 **Facilities:** 🈳 🛆 1 restaurant, playground. Courtyard with a gazebo and swings for kids. Picnic area. **Rates:** $36–$42 S; $42–$52 D. Extra person $6. Children under age 18 stay free. Min stay special events. Parking: Outdoor, free. Golf packages avail. AE, CB, DC, DISC, JCB, MC, V.

≡≡ Quality Inn East

2111 Cedar Creek Rd, 28301; tel 910/323-9850 or toll free 800/228-5151. Exit 49 off I-95. A basic, comfortable, but no-frills property. Convenient to the interstate. **Rooms:** 100 rms. CI 11am/CO 11am. Nonsmoking rms avail. **Amenities:** 🛅 🐧 A/C, cable TV. **Services:** 🛥 🖢 Babysitting. **Facilities:**

1 restaurant (bkfst and dinner only), 1 bar. **Rates:** $41–$47 S or D. Extra person $6. Children under age 16 stay free. Parking: Outdoor, free. AE, CB, DC, DISC, MC, V.

≣≣≣ Radisson Prince Charles Hotel

450 Hay St, 28301; tel 910/433-4444 or toll free 800/333-3333; fax 910/485-8269. A fine historic hotel dating to the early 1920s. Elegant lobby has marble floors and staircases. While the abandoned buildings surrounding the hotel make for an unattractive view, the Radisson is still among the best in town. **Rooms:** 83 rms and stes. Executive level. CI 3pm/CO noon. Nonsmoking rms avail. Rooms and suites are handsomely decorated. Housekeeping standards are better than average. **Amenities:** A/C, cable TV. **Services:** Babysitting. **Facilities:** 1 restaurant, 1 bar (w/entertainment). **Rates:** $65 S or D; $75 ste. Extra person $10. Children under age 12 stay free. Parking: Outdoor, free. AE, CB, DC, DISC, MC, V.

≣≣ Ramada Inn

511 Eastern Blvd, 28302; tel 910/484-8101 or toll free 800/2-RAMADA; fax 910/484-2516. A comfortable, homey Ramada with attractive public areas decorated in soft colors. **Rooms:** 138 rms and stes. CI 3pm/CO noon. Nonsmoking rms avail. **Amenities:** A/C, satel TV. **Services:** **Facilities:** 1 restaurant (bkfst and dinner only), 1 bar (w/entertainment). **Rates:** $52 S; $54 D; $75 ste. Extra person $7. Children under age 18 stay free. Parking: Outdoor, free. AE, CB, DC, MC, V.

MOTELS

≣≣ Fairfield Inn

562 Cross Creek Mall, 28303; tel 910/487-1400 or toll free 800/228-2800; fax 910/487-1400. Off US 401. A pleasant motel with a newly renovated appearance. **Rooms:** 135 rms. CI noon/CO noon. Nonsmoking rms avail. **Amenities:** A/C, cable TV, dataport. **Services:** **Facilities:** **Rates (CP):** $41–$48 S; $46–$51 D. Extra person $3. Children under age 18 stay free. Parking: Outdoor, free. AE, CB, DC, DISC, MC, V.

≣≣ Hampton Inn

1922 Cedar Creek Rd, 28301; tel 910/323-0011 or toll free 800/HAMPTON; fax 910/323-8764. Exit 49 off I-95. A clean, comfortable motel with a small, unassuming lobby and the trademark Hampton stucco exterior. **Rooms:** 122 rms. CI 2pm/CO noon. Nonsmoking rms avail. **Amenities:** A/C, cable TV w/movies. **Services:** **Facilities:** **Rates (CP):** $48–$53 S; $53–$58 D. Parking: Outdoor, free. AE, CB, DC, DISC, MC, V.

RESTAURANTS

Canton Station

301 N McPherson Church Rd; tel 910/864-5555. **Chinese.** Traditional Chinese fare—with beef, chicken, and several vegetarian specialties—served amidst a stylish Chinese decor, with low lighting and high-backed booths. **FYI:** Reservations accepted. Children's menu. **Open:** Lunch Mon–Fri 11am–2:30pm, Sat–Sun noon–5pm; dinner Mon–Sat 5–10pm, Sun 5–9pm. **Prices:** Main courses $7. AE, MC, V.

De Lafayette

6112 Cliffdale Rd; tel 910/868-4600. ½ mi W of Skipbo Rd. **Creole.** Soft blue decor and wicker-backed chairs with a view from the sunroom windows provides a beautiful setting for continental, Creole, and Cajun recipes such as shrimp étouffée and rack of lamb. **FYI:** Reservations recommended. Dress code. **Open:** Tues–Sat 5:30–10pm. **Prices:** Main courses $14–$29. AE, CB, DC, DISC, MC, V.

Fontana Dam

An incline railway takes visitors to this 480-foot dam—the highest in the Tennessee Valley Authority system.

RESORT

≣≣≣ Fontana Village Resort

NC 28, PO Box 68, 28733; tel 704/498-2211 or toll free 800/849-2258; fax 704/498-2209. on NC 28. Offering the ultimate in peacefulness and beautiful mountain scenery, this resort provides recreational activities for all seasons. **Rooms:** 94 rms and stes; 165 cottages/villas. CI 4pm/CO 10am. Nonsmoking rms avail. Small TV in bathrooms. **Amenities:** A/C, satel TV. Some units w/terraces, some w/fireplaces. **Services:** Children's program, babysitting. Instruction is available for many of the recreational activities offered here. **Facilities:** 3 restaurants (see "Restaurants" below), volleyball, games rm, lawn games, sauna, day-care ctr, playground, washer/dryer. **Rates:** Peak (Apr–Oct) $79 S or D; $99–$149 ste; $69–$189 cottage/villa. Children under age 12 stay free. Lower rates off-season. Parking: Outdoor, free. AE, DISC, MC, V.

RESTAURANTS

The Peppercorn Dining Room

In Fontana Village Resort, NC 28; tel 704/498-2211. **American.** The upscale option at Fontana Village, serving specialties such as scallops with herb, white wine, and cream sauce. Broiled trout mendillo is especially popular. **FYI:** Reservations accepted. Children's menu. No liquor license. **Open:** Daily 5–10pm. **Prices:** Main courses $13–$17. AE, DISC, MC, V.

The Peppermill Cafeteria

In Fontana Village Resort, NC 28; tel 704/498-2211. **American.** Menu specialties include veal parmesan, spaghetti, and many Southern dishes. Very casual atmosphere. **FYI:** Reservations not accepted. No liquor license. **Open:** Breakfast daily 7–10:30am; lunch daily 11:30am–2pm; dinner daily 5–8:30pm. Closed Nov–Mar. **Prices:** Main courses $7–$10. AE, DISC, MC, V.

Franklin

Called the "Gem Capital of the South" and location of the Cowee Valley Mines. The area was once mined by the Tiffany jewelry firm. **Information:** Franklin Area Chamber of Commerce, 180 Porter St, Franklin, 28734 (tel 704/524-3161).

MOTEL 🏨

🏳 Country Inn Town
277 E Main St, 28734; tel 704/524-4451 or toll free 800/233-7555. Off US 28. Peeling wallpaper and cracked tile make this unsuitable for extended stays, but it makes a sufficient overnight resting place. **Rooms:** 46 rms. CI 3pm/CO 11am. Nonsmoking rms avail. Rooms are surprisingly large. **Amenities:** 🛏 A/C, cable TV. **Services:** ⌐ **Facilities:** ⏢ 🛁 **Rates:** Peak (May–Oct) $45–$75 S or D. Extra person $3. Children under age 12 stay free. Min stay wknds. Lower rates off-season. Parking: Outdoor, free. AE, DISC, MC, V.

INN

🏳 Summit Inn
125 E Rogers St, 28734; tel 704/524-2006. Spartan accommodations. **Rooms:** 13 rms (10 w/shared bath). CI 4pm/CO noon. No smoking. Rooms are clean but not exceptional. **Amenities:** No A/C, phone, or TV. Some units w/fireplaces. **Services:** ⌐ **Facilities:** 🛐 1 restaurant (bkfst and dinner only), 1 bar, guest lounge w/TV. **Rates (BB):** $50 S or D w/shared bath, $60 S or D w/private bath. Extra person $10. Children under age 12 stay free. Parking: Outdoor, free. No CC.

ATTRACTION 🏛

Sheffield Mine
160 Leatherman Gap Rd; tel 704/369-8383. Visitors at this mountain-side gemstone mine receive a screening tray and bucket; the very helpful staff will help identify any finds. Picnic area and snack bar on-site. **Open:** Apr–Oct, daily 8am–5pm. Closed Dec 25. $$$

Gastonia

Gaston County seat. Its natural history museum has the Southeast's largest collection of North American mammals mounted in natural habitat settings. **Information:** Gaston County Chamber of Commerce, 601 W Franklin Blvd, PO Box 2168, Gastonia, 28053 (tel 704/864-2621).

HOTEL 🏨

🏳🏳🏳 Holiday Inn Express
1400 E Franklin Blvd, 28054; tel 704/864-8744 or toll free 800/HOLIDAY; fax 704/864-8744. Off I-85 at New Hope Rd. Exactly what is expected from a Holiday Inn Express, this hotel offers dependable, clean rooms. Great for overnight visits or a weekend getaway. **Rooms:** 60 rms. CI 2pm/CO noon. Nonsmoking rms avail. **Amenities:** 🛏 🛁 🖥 A/C, cable TV w/movies, dataport. **Services:** 🖂 ⌐ **Facilities:** 🍴 🛢 🛁 **Rates (CP):** $49–$59 D. Extra person $5. Children under age 16 stay free. Parking: Outdoor, free. AE, CB, DC, DISC, MC, V.

MOTELS

🏳🏳🏳 Hampton Inn
1859 Remault Rd, 28054; tel 704/866-9090 or toll free 800/HAMPTON; fax 704/866-7070. Off I-85 at New Hope Rd. A great place for a short visit, this Hampton Inn offers clean, comfortable rooms and dependable service. **Rooms:** 109 rms. CI 2pm/CO noon. Nonsmoking rms avail. **Amenities:** 🛏 Cable TV. No A/C. **Services:** 🖂 Car-rental desk. **Facilities:** ⏢ 🛢 🛁 **Rates (CP):** $54–$61 S or D. Children under age 18 stay free. Parking: Outdoor, free. AE, CB, DC, DISC, EC, ER, MC, V.

🏳🏳 Innkeeper
360 McNeil St, 28054; tel 704/868-2000 or toll free 800/822-9889; fax 704/868-2000. Off I-85 at New Hope Rd. Common, average motel that offers a good, clean place to sleep but not much else. **Rooms:** 64 rms. CI open/CO 11am. Nonsmoking rms avail. **Amenities:** 🛏 🛁 A/C, cable TV. **Facilities:** ⏢ 🛁 **Rates (CP):** $46 S; $53 D. Parking: Outdoor, free. AE, CB, DC, DISC, MC, V.

Glenville

Incorporated in 1891. Located in a mountainous region on the Thorpe River, between Thorpe Reservoir and Glassy Rock Ridge.

INN 🏨

🏳🏳🏳🏳 Innisfree Inn—A Victorian B&B
#7 Lakeside Knoll, PO Box 469, 28736; tel 704/743-2946. S of Sylva. 12 acres. A romantic retreat catering to couples. The lovely grounds include a beautiful water garden with a gazebo and award-winning flower gardens. Unsuitable for children under 18. **Rooms:** 10 rms and stes. CI 2:30pm/CO 11am. No smoking. Rooms show exceptional attention to detail, and the bathrooms are especially lovely. The garden house has modern amenities, but rooms at the inn are more secluded. **Amenities:** 🛁 Bathrobes. No A/C, phone, or TV. Some units w/terraces, some w/fireplaces, some w/whirlpools. Each room has a journal where visitors can record their thoughts, and read those of earlier visitors. Piped-in classical music. **Services:** ✕ 🖂 Twice-daily maid svce, afternoon tea and wine/sherry served. Full breakfast includes homemade bread. Complimentary Irish coffee and schnapps served nightly on the veranda. Extensive library. **Facilities:** 🏖 🛢 1 beach (lake shore), guest lounge w/TV. The highest lake east of the Rockies is on site, with waterfalls and islands—perfect for

exploring. **Rates (BB):** Peak (June–Nov) $140–$300 D; $140–$300 ste. Min stay wknds. Lower rates off-season. Parking: Outdoor, free. AE, DISC, MC, V.

Goldsboro

Located on the Neuse River, southeast of Raleigh. Incorporated in 1847 and named for Maj Matthew Goldsborough, a railroad engineer. **Information:** Chamber of Commerce of Wayne County, 308 N William St, PO Box 1107, Goldsboro, 27533 (tel 919/734-2241).

HOTELS 🏨

▤▤ Comfort Inn
909 N Spence Ave, 27534; tel 919/751-1999 or toll free 800/221-2222; fax 919/751-1506. Off US 70. A comfortable hotel. **Rooms:** 122 rms and stes. CI 3pm/CO Open. Nonsmoking rms avail. **Amenities:** 🛏 ⚘ A/C, cable TV w/movies. Some units w/whirlpools. **Services:** ⚞ ⚲ Fax and copy services. **Facilities:** ⛱ ⛴ ⚹ 1 bar. Restaurant located adjacent to hotel. **Rates (CP):** $52–$56 S or D; $110 ste. Extra person $6. Children under age 18 stay free. Parking: Outdoor, free. AE, CB, DC, DISC, MC, V.

▤▤▤ Hampton Inn
905 N Spence Ave, 27534; tel 919/778-1800 or toll free 800/HAMPTON; fax 919/778-5891. A beautiful, contemporary hotel opened in the summer of 1995. **Rooms:** 111 rms. CI 3pm/CO noon. Nonsmoking rms avail. **Amenities:** 🛏 ⚘ A/C, cable TV w/movies, dataport. Some units w/whirlpools. **Services:** ⚞ ⚲ Babysitting. **Facilities:** ⛱ ⛴ ⛳ 💻 ⚹ Washer/dryer. **Rates (CP):** $57–$59 S; $63–$65 D. Extra person $6. Children under age 18 stay free. Parking: Outdoor, free. AE, DC, DISC, MC, V.

▤▤ Ramada Inn
808 W Grantham St, 27530; tel 919/736-4590 or toll free 800/2-RAMADA; fax 919/735-3218. Off US 70. An attractive hotel with tastefully decorated public areas and rooms. **Rooms:** 128 rms and stes. CI 4pm/CO noon. Nonsmoking rms avail. **Amenities:** 🛏 A/C, cable TV. **Services:** ⚞ ⚲ **Facilities:** ⛱ ⛴ ⚹ 1 restaurant, 1 bar. **Rates:** $36–$57 S; $41–$62 D; $85–$95 ste. Extra person $6. Children under age 18 stay free. Parking: Outdoor, free. AE, CB, DC, DISC, JCB, MC, V.

MOTELS

▤▤ Days Inn
2000 Wayne Memorial Dr, 27534; tel 919/734-9471 or toll free 800/DAYS-INN; fax 919/736-2623. Off US 70. Basic, well-maintained motel with attractive grounds. Suitable for the traveler on a tight budget. **Rooms:** 120 rms. CI 2pm/CO noon. Nonsmoking rms avail. **Amenities:** 🛏 A/C, cable TV w/movies, dataport. **Services:** ⚲ **Facilities:** ⛱ ⛴ **Rates:** $36–$46 S; $40–$53 D. Extra person $4. Children under age 18 stay free. Parking: Outdoor, free. AE, CB, DC, DISC, MC, V.

▤▤ Holiday Inn
Williams St exit off US 70E, PO Box 1973, 27530; tel 919/735-7901 or toll free 800/HOLIDAY; fax 919/734-2946. At US 13N. A well-maintained, comfortable establishment with attractive public areas and tastefully furnished rooms. **Rooms:** 120 rms. CI 2pm/CO 11am. Nonsmoking rms avail. **Amenities:** 🛏 A/C, cable TV w/movies, dataport. **Services:** ⚞ ⚲ ⚔ **Facilities:** ⛱ ⛴ ⚹ 1 restaurant, 1 bar. **Rates:** $45–$50 S or D. Extra person $5. Children under age 17 stay free. Parking: Outdoor, free. AE, CB, DC, DISC, MC, V.

UNRATED Squires Vintage Inn
748 NC 24-50, PO Box 130R, Warsaw, 28398; tel 910/296-1831. Exit 364 off I-40. A rustic but beautiful motel. **Rooms:** 12 rms. CI 1pm/CO 11am. Nonsmoking rms avail. All rooms are individually decorated. **Amenities:** 🛏 A/C, TV. **Services:** Continental breakfast can be brought to room. **Facilities:** ⛴ ⚹ 1 restaurant, 1 bar. A spacious English garden has a gazebo and a sunken patio with fountain. **Rates (CP):** $49–$56 S or D. Extra person $15. Children under age 12 stay free. Parking: Outdoor, free. AE, DC, MC, V.

Great Smoky Mountains National Park

See Tennessee; For NC lodgings and dining, see Asheville, Bryson City, Cashiers, Maggie Valley, Robbinsville, Waynesville

Greensboro

See also High Point

First settled in 1749, now a bustling Piedmont city and seat of Guilford County. Important producer of textiles, tobacco, and machinery. The city's Old Greensborough section is listed on the National Register of Historic Places. Birthplace of author O Henry and first lady Dolley Madison; site of a number of colleges. **Information:** Greensboro Area Convention & Visitors Bureau, 317 S Greene St, Greensboro, 27401 (tel 910/274-2282).

HOTELS 🏨

▤▤ Best Western Windsor Suites
2006 Veasley St, 27407; tel 910/294-9100 or toll free 800/528-1234. Exit 217A off I-40. A stylish hotel with a variety of offerings. Lounge features a baby grand piano and a billiards table. **Rooms:** 76 stes. CI 3pm/CO 11am. Nonsmoking rms avail. **Amenities:** 🛏 ⚘ ⚐ A/C, cable TV w/movies, refrig, dataport. Some units w/whirlpools. **Services:** ⚞ ⚲ Babysitting. **Facilities:** ⛱ ⛴ ⛳ ⚹ Sauna, washer/dryer. **Rates**

(CP): $72–$82 ste. Extra person $6. Children under age 12 stay free. Min stay special events. Parking: Outdoor, free. AE, CB, DC, DISC, JCB, MC, V.

Biltmore Greensboro Hotel
111 W Washington St, 27401; tel 910/272-3474 or toll free 800/868-5064; fax 910/275-2523. Between Green and Elm Sts. A historic, downtown hotel. **Rooms:** 25 rms and stes. CI 3pm/CO noon. Nonsmoking rms avail. Rooms are individually decorated with early American reproductions. **Amenities:** A/C, cable TV w/movies, refrig, dataport. **Services:** Limousine service within five-mile radius. **Facilities:** Rates (BB): $75–$110 S or D; $99–$110 ste. Min stay special events. Parking: Outdoor, free. AE, CB, DC, DISC, MC, V.

Courtyard by Marriott
4400 W Wendover Ave, 27407; tel 910/294-3800 or toll free 800/321-2211; fax 910/294-9982. Off I-40. A stylish hotel with a bright, pleasant lobby. Courtyard area has gazebo. Great for business travel. **Rooms:** 149 rms and stes. CI 3pm/CO noon. Nonsmoking rms avail. Rooms are clean and comfortable. **Amenities:** A/C, cable TV w/movies, dataport. Some units w/terraces. **Services:** Babysitting. **Facilities:** 1 restaurant (bkfst only), 1 bar, whirlpool, washer/dryer. **Rates:** $77–$87 S or D; $92 ste. Children under age 18 stay free. Parking: Outdoor, free. AE, DC, DISC, MC, V.

Embassy Suites
204 Centre Port Dr, 27409; tel 910/668-4535 or toll free 800/EMBASSY. Exit 210 off I-40. Gorgeously designed hotel with an elaborate indoor courtyard, palm trees, terra-cotta tile floors, glass elevators, and fountains. Convenient to airport and interstate. **Rooms:** 221 stes. CI 2pm/CO noon. Nonsmoking rms avail. Housekeeping far exceeds average. **Amenities:** A/C, cable TV w/movies, dataport, voice mail. Some rooms have refrigerators and wet bars. **Services:** Babysitting. **Facilities:** 1 restaurant (lunch and dinner only), 1 bar (w/entertainment), sauna, steam rm, whirlpool. **Rates (BB):** $139–$250 ste. Extra person $10. Children under age 12 stay free. Min stay special events. Lower rates off-season. Parking: Outdoor, free. AE, CB, DC, DISC, MC, V.

Greensboro–High Point Marriott
1 Marriott Dr, 27409; tel 910/852-6450 or toll free 800/228-9290; fax 910/665-6522. At Piedmont Triad International Airport. This hotel has luxurious accommodations, a beautiful lobby decorated with fine marble furniture, and is conveniently located near the airport. **Rooms:** 232 rms and stes. Executive level. CI 3pm/CO noon. Nonsmoking rms avail. **Amenities:** A/C, cable TV w/movies, dataport, voice mail. Some units w/terraces. **Services:** Babysitting. **Facilities:** 2 restaurants, 1

bar (w/entertainment), volleyball, whirlpool. **Rates:** $99–$109 S or D; $169–$200 ste. Min stay special events. Parking: Outdoor, free. AE, CB, DC, DISC, MC, V.

Hilton Greensboro
304 N Green St, 27401; tel 910/379-8000 or toll free 800/325-3535; fax 910/275-2810. Off I-40/I-85. A mid-rise hotel, featuring a two-story lobby with a grand staircase, tapestries, and Oriental rugs. **Rooms:** 283 rms and stes. Executive level. CI 3pm/CO 11am. Nonsmoking rms avail. **Amenities:** A/C, cable TV w/movies, dataport. 1 unit w/whirlpool. **Services:** **Facilities:** 2 restaurants, 2 bars, spa, sauna, whirlpool. Exceptional health facility includes tanning beds and fitness staff. **Rates:** $110 S; $117 D; $150–$495 ste. Children under age 18 stay free. Min stay special events. Parking: Indoor, free. AE, CB, DC, DISC, MC, V.

Holiday Inn Four Seasons
3121 High Point Rd, 27407; tel 910/292-9161 or toll free 800/242-6556; fax 910/292-9161. Exit 217-A off I-40. An excellent choice for business travel, this Holiday Inn is next to the Koury Convention Center and a large shopping mall. **Rooms:** 530 rms and stes. CI 3pm/CO noon. Nonsmoking rms avail. **Amenities:** A/C, cable TV w/movies, dataport. Some units w/terraces. **Services:** Carrental desk. **Facilities:** 3 restaurants, 4 bars (1 w/entertainment), sauna, whirlpool, washer/dryer. **Rates:** $115 S; $125 D; $155–$425 ste. Extra person $10. Children under age 18 stay free. Min stay special events. Parking: Outdoor, free. AE, CB, DC, DISC, MC, V.

Howard Johnson Greensboro Coliseum
3630 High Point Rd, 27403; tel 910/294-4920 or toll free 800/446-4656; fax 910/299-0503. Exit 217B off I-40. A comfortable hotel conveniently located near the Greensboro Coliseum and local shopping and dining. **Rooms:** 176 rms and stes. Executive level. CI 3pm/CO 11am. Nonsmoking rms avail. **Amenities:** A/C, cable TV w/movies, dataport, voice mail. Some units w/terraces. **Services:** **Facilities:** Rates (CP): $49 S; $59 D; $65–$75 ste. Extra person $5. Children under age 18 stay free. Parking: Outdoor, free. AE, CB, DC, DISC, MC, V.

Park Lane Hotel—Four Seasons
3005 High Point Rd, 27403; tel 919/294-4565 or toll free 800/294-4565; fax 910/294-0572. Exit 217B off I-40. Formal, upscale property with white marble and many plants. **Rooms:** 161 rms and stes. CI 3pm/CO noon. Nonsmoking rms avail. **Amenities:** A/C, cable TV w/movies, dataport. Some units w/whirlpools. **Services:** Babysitting. Free transportation to Holiday Inn Four Seasons Convention Center (with indoor pool) and Four Seasons Towne Center (for shopping). **Facilities:** Sauna, washer/dryer. Exceptional workout area. **Rates (CP):** $97–$102 S or D; $125–$200 ste. Extra person $10. Children under age 18 stay free. Min stay special events. Lower rates

off-season. Parking: Outdoor, free. Seven-night minimum stay during the Furniture Mart. AE, CB, DC, DISC, JCB, MC, V.

Residence Inn by Marriott
2000 Veasley St, 27407; tel 910/294-8600 or toll free 800/331-3131; fax 910/294-2201. Exit 217A off I-40. A hotel with apartment-style accommodations. **Rooms:** 128 stes. CI 3pm/CO noon. Nonsmoking rms avail. All suites have kitchens. **Amenities:** A/C, cable TV w/movies, dataport. Some units w/fireplaces. Complimentary evening beverages. **Services:** Babysitting. **Facilities:** Basketball, volleyball, whirlpool, washer/dryer. Health club privileges Mon–Thurs. **Rates (CP):** $69–$122 ste. Min stay special events. Parking: Outdoor, free. Extended-stay discounts avail. AE, CB, DC, DISC, JCB, MC, V.

Shoney's Inn Greensboro
1103 Lanada Dr, 27407; tel 910/297-1055 or toll free 800/222-2222; fax 910/297-1904. Wendover exit (214) off I-40. Handsome stucco exterior. Convenient to local shopping/dining and interstate. **Rooms:** 115 rms and stes. CI 3pm/CO noon. Nonsmoking rms avail. Housekeeping is above average. **Amenities:** A/C, dataport. **Services:** Facilities: Washer/dryer. Small pets only. Nice view from pool area. **Rates:** $69–$73 S or D; $75–$105 ste. Extra person $6. Children under age 18 stay free. Parking: Outdoor, free. AE, CB, DC, DISC, MC, V.

MOTELS

Days Inn
120 Seneca Rd, 27406; tel 910/275-9571 or toll free 800/DAYS-INN. S Elm St exit off I-40. Convenient to I-40 and only three miles from downtown, the lobby and exterior of this hotel are accented with pleasant pastels. **Rooms:** 122 rms. CI 2pm/CO 11am. Nonsmoking rms avail. **Amenities:** A/C, cable TV, in-rm safe. **Facilities:** Playground. **Rates (CP):** $33 S; $39 D. Extra person $6. Children under age 12 stay free. Min stay special events. Parking: Outdoor, free. AE, CB, DC, DISC, MC, V.

Fairfield Inn Greensboro–High Point
2003 Athena Ct, 27407; tel 910/294-9922 or toll free 800/228-2800. Exit 217A off I-40. A pleasant property with no surprises; good for the business traveler. **Rooms:** 135 rms. Executive level. CI 3pm/CO noon. Nonsmoking rms avail. **Amenities:** A/C, cable TV. **Services:** Facilities: **Rates (CP):** $50 S or D. Extra person $6. Children under age 18 stay free. Parking: Outdoor, free. AE, CB, DC, DISC, MC, V.

Ramada Limited
2838 S Elm St, 27406; tel 910/275-0741 or toll free 800/2-RAMADA; fax 910/379-1267. Exit 125 off I-85 and I-40. No-frills accommodations, adequate for an overnight stay. Near I-40 and downtown. **Rooms:** 126 rms. CI 2pm/CO noon. Nonsmoking rms avail. **Amenities:** A/C, cable TV

w/movies. **Facilities:** 1 restaurant, 1 bar (w/entertainment). **Rates (CP):** $36–$40 S; $36–$44 D. Extra person $6. Children under age 12 stay free. Parking: Outdoor, free. AE, CB, DC, DISC, MC, V.

Travelodge
2112 W Meadowview Rd, 27403; tel 910/292-2020 or toll free 800/578-7878; fax 910/852-3476. Exit 217B off I-40. Pleasant, stylish motel. **Rooms:** 108 rms. Executive level. CI 3pm/CO noon. Nonsmoking rms avail. **Amenities:** A/C, cable TV. Complimentary coffee in rooms. **Services:** Babysitting. **Facilities:** Free use of local health spa. **Rates (CP):** $40 S; $50 D. Extra person $5. Children under age 18 stay free. Min stay special events. Parking: Outdoor, free. Five-night minimum stay (and higher rates) during Furniture Mart. AE, DC, DISC, MC, V.

University Inn
1000 W Market St, 27401; tel 910/273-5503. A basic, independently owned motel with very few extras. Located near University of North Carolina at Greensboro. **Rooms:** 70 rms. CI 2pm/CO noon. Nonsmoking rms avail. **Amenities:** A/C, cable TV. **Services:** Facilities: 1 restaurant (dinner only), 1 bar. **Rates:** $34 S; $38 D. Extra person $4. Children under age 16 stay free. Min stay special events. Parking: Outdoor, free. AE, DC, DISC, MC, V.

RESTAURANTS

★ Anton's
1628 Battleground Ave; tel 919/273-1386. N of Wendover. **Italian.** The upscale, casual atmosphere of this cellar eatery is set by stucco walls, hanging baskets, checkered tablecloths, and candlelight. The menu includes mostly traditional Italian food with some seafood options such as seafood Anton's (jumbo shrimp in wine sauce over angel-hair pasta) and stuffed flounder. All pastas are homemade. **FYI:** Reservations accepted. Children's menu. **Open:** Mon–Thurs 11am–10pm, Fri 11am–10:30pm, Sat 4:30–10:30pm. **Prices:** Main courses $10–$14. AE, MC, V.

★ Bert's Seafood Grill
2419 Spring Garden St; tel 910/854-2314. **Seafood.** A casual place with pink walls sporting colorful hand-painted fish. Bert's creative entrees include sesame flounder, crab-stuffed sea bass with leeks, and grilled trout amandine. **FYI:** Reservations not accepted. Children's menu. No smoking. **Open:** Daily 5–10pm. **Prices:** Main courses $9–$16. AE, DISC, MC, V.

Gate City Chop House
106 S Holden Rd; tel 910/294-9977. At Market St. **Seafood.** An elegant place with deep green walls accented with burgundy and oak tables. Dinner specialties include sautéed veal loin chops, grilled Norwegian salmon, and "Tide and Tundra" (filet mignon and Maine lobster tail). Creative desserts like Seventh Heaven (vanilla Pierre ice cream in sweet biscuit nestled in a warm raspberry/blueberry compote) provide a

perfect ending. **FYI:** Reservations accepted. **Open:** Mon–Fri 11:30am–11pm, Sat 4:30–11pm. **Prices:** Main courses $13–$26. AE, DISC, MC, V. 🌑 ⚹

♣ Kabuto Japanese Steak House

In Friendly Forum VI, Friendly Ave; tel 910/855-3400. **Japanese.** The decor features a mix of traditional and contemporary Japanese elements with low lighting. Talented chefs prepare the food at Japanese-style cooking tables with seating for up to eight. Entrees feature chicken, shrimp, and steak, with lobster combinations available. **FYI:** Reservations recommended. **Open:** Lunch daily 11:30am–2pm; dinner Sun–Thurs 5:30–9:30pm, Fri–Sat 5:30–10:30pm. **Prices:** Main courses $10–$24. AE, DISC, MC, V. ⚹

Lucky 32

1421 Westover Terrace; tel 910/370-0707. At Battleground Ave. **Regional American.** The avant-garde setting consists of a red-and-black color scheme, with murals and modern accent pieces. Diverse culinary offerings include hickory-grilled lamb loin chops and citrus-marinated chicken. A variety of gourmet pizzas, pasta, and seafood are also available. **FYI:** Reservations accepted. Additional location: 109 S Stratford Rd, Winston-Salem (tel 724-3232). **Open:** Mon–Thurs 11:15am–10:30pm, Fri–Sat 11:15am–11pm, Sun 10:45am–10pm. **Prices:** Main courses $7–$15. AE, DC, MC, V. 🌑 ⚹

Madison Park

616 Madison Park Rd; tel 910/294-6505. Across from Quaker Village Shopping Center. **New American.** Located in a restored home, with atmosphere and service as first-rate as the food. (Each course is brought to the table by a brigade of servers.) Entrees include black Angus beef tenderloin, lamb chops, Gulf shrimp, and grilled salmon. The dessert tray is magnificent, and their wine list is among the best in the region. **FYI:** Reservations accepted. Jacket required. **Open:** Mon–Sat 6–10pm. **Prices:** Main courses $15–$24. AE, MC, V. 🌑 ⚹

Sunset Cafe

4608 W Market St; tel 910/855-0349. **Cafe.** Lunch focuses on soups and sandwiches, while dinner entrees include Louisiana crab cakes (served with red beans and rice) and eggplant moussaka. **FYI:** Reservations not accepted. Children's menu. **Open:** Lunch Mon–Fri 11:30am–2pm; dinner Tues–Sat 5:30–9:30pm, Sun 5:30–9pm. **Prices:** Main courses $5–$15. MC, V. 📷 ⚹

REFRESHMENT STOP 🗗

The Bakery

1932 Spring Garden St; tel 910/272-8199. **Desserts.** A no-frills dining room filled with the aroma of fresh baked pastries, cookies, and muffins. **Open:** Mon–Fri 7:30am–6pm, Sat 9am–4pm. No CC. ⚹

ATTRACTIONS 📷

Guilford Courthouse National Military Park

2332 New Garden Rd; tel 910/288-1776. A 220-acre park marking one of the closing battles of the Revolution, the Battle of Guilford Courthouse on March 15, 1781. Gen Nathanael Greene (Greensboro's namesake) led a group of inexperienced troops against Lord Cornwallis; although they were defeated, his troops inflicted severe losses on the British. Following the battle, Cornwallis abandoned this part of the country and headed for Yorktown, VA, where he would surrender his depleted forces just seven months later.

The park visitors center has films, brochures, and displays about the historic battle, along with Revolutionary War weaponry. There are also many wayside exhibits along the two-mile road that connects some of the many monuments (self-guided auto tour maps available). For additional information, contact the Superintendent, PO Box 9806, Greensboro, NC 27429 (tel 910/288-1776). **Open:** Daily 8:30am–5pm. Closed some hols. **Free**

Greensboro Historical Museum

130 Summit Ave; tel 910/373-2043. Exhibits here illustrate the lives and works of North Carolina natives, including short-story author O Henry (born in Greensboro) and First Lady Dolley Madison. Other exhibits include early modes of transportation, furnishings, pottery, textiles, and military artifacts. One of the most moving displays re-creates a civil rights lunch counter sit-in at Woolworth's. The museum itself is housed in a restored 19th-century church. **Open:** Tues–Sat 10am–5pm, Sun 2–5pm. Closed some hols. **Free**

Charlotte Hawkins Brown Memorial State Historic Site

Exit 135 off I-85, Sedalia; tel 919/449-4846. North Carolina's first official historic site to honor an African American woman. The site is the former location of the Palmer Institute, a black preparatory school established by Charlotte Brown in 1902. Guided tours of the original campus include visits to several restored classrooms; an audiovisual history program tells Brown's story. **Open:** Sept–May, Tues–Fri 10am–4pm, Sun 1–4pm; June–Aug, Mon–Sat 9am–5pm, Sun 1–5pm. **Free**

Weatherspoon Art Gallery

Spring Garden and Tate Sts, UNCG Campus; tel 919/334-5770. Extensive permanent collection contains over 4,000 works, with special emphasis on 20th century American art. There's also an impressive collection of lithographs and bronzes by Matisse. **Open:** Tues, Thurs, Fri 10am–5pm, Wed 10am–8pm, Sat–Sun 1–5pm. Closed some hols. **Free**

Greenville

Pitt County seat and home of East Carolina University. The Greenville Museum of Art, founded in 1939 as a Works

Progress Administration Gallery, now houses works by local artists. **Information:** Pitt-Greenville Chamber of Commerce, 302 S Greene St, Greenville, 27834 (tel 919/752-4101).

HOTELS ⌂

⊟⊟⊟ Hilton Inn

207 SW Greenville Blvd, 27834; tel 919/355-5000 or toll free 800/HILTONS; fax 919/355-5099. on US 264 Alt. A thoroughly modern six-story luxury hotel, with impressive woodwork in public areas. Caters mainly to corporate travelers. **Rooms:** 121 rms and stes. Executive level. CI 2pm/CO noon. Nonsmoking rms avail. Contemporary decor; large windows offer plenty of natural lighting. **Amenities:** 🛆 🕭 🖵 A/C, cable TV w/movies, dataport. Refrigerators in suites. **Services:** ✗ 🚐 🖼 🖵 Babysitting. Secretarial services available. **Facilities:** 🛆 🕹 560 🕭 1 restaurant (*see* "Restaurants" below), 1 bar (w/entertainment), whirlpool. **Rates:** $85–$95 S; $95–$105 D; $165–$250 ste. Extra person $10. Children under age 18 stay free. Min stay special events. Parking: Outdoor, free. AE, CB, DC, DISC, JCB, MC, V.

⊟⊟⊟ Ramada Plaza Hotel

203 W Greenville Blvd, 27834; tel 919/355-8300 or toll free 800/2-RAMADA; fax 919/756-3553. Recently renovated property, suitable for all travelers. **Rooms:** 192 rms and stes. CI 2pm/CO noon. Nonsmoking rms avail. Stylish, modern furnishings. **Amenities:** 🛆 🕭 A/C, cable TV w/movies, dataport. **Services:** ✗ 🖼 🖵 Babysitting. Fax and copy services. **Facilities:** 🛆 🕹 525 🕭 1 restaurant, 1 bar (w/entertainment). **Rates:** $70–$80 S or D; $80–$100 ste. Extra person $6. Children under age 18 stay free. Min stay special events. Parking: Outdoor, free. AE, DC, DISC, MC, V.

MOTELS

⊟ Fairfield Inn

821 S Memorial Dr, 27834; tel 919/758-5544 or toll free 800/228-2800; fax 919/758-1416. A pleasant and new motel. **Rooms:** 115 rms. CI 2pm/CO noon. Nonsmoking rms avail. **Amenities:** 🛆 🕭 A/C, cable TV w/movies, dataport. **Services:** 🚐 🖼 🖵 **Facilities:** 🛆 🕭 **Rates (CP):** $43 S; $49 D. Children under age 17 stay free. Parking: Outdoor, free. AE, CB, DC, DISC, MC, V.

⊟⊟ Hampton Inn

3439 S Memorial Dr, 27834; tel 919/355-2521 or toll free 800/HAMPTON; fax 919/355-2521. On US 264. Comfortable, standard chain motel. Located across highway from a shopping mall. **Rooms:** 121 rms. CI 2pm/CO noon. Nonsmoking rms avail. **Amenities:** 🛆 🕭 A/C, cable TV w/movies, dataport. **Services:** 🖼 🖵 **Facilities:** 🛆 25 🕭 **Rates (CP):** $47–$49 S; $52–$55 D. Children under age 18 stay free. Min stay special events. Parking: Outdoor, free. AE, DC, DISC, MC, V.

⊟⊟ Howard Johnson's

702 S Memorial Dr, 27834; tel 919/758-3401. A spacious indoor courtyard with pool and game room, decorated with plants, rock walls, and patios, give these basic accommodations a special twist. **Rooms:** 137 rms. CI 2pm/CO noon. Nonsmoking rms avail. Some rooms face indoor courtyard. **Amenities:** 🛆 A/C, cable TV. **Services:** ✗ 🚐 🖼 🖵 **Facilities:** 🛆 300 🕭 1 restaurant (bkfst and dinner only), 1 bar (w/entertainment), whirlpool. **Rates:** Peak (May–Oct) $42 S; $48–$52 D. Extra person $5. Children under age 12 stay free. Min stay special events. Lower rates off-season. Parking: Outdoor, free. AE, DC, DISC, MC, V.

RESTAURANTS ♨

★ Chico's Mexican Restaurant

521 Cotanche St; tel 919/757-1666. Across from ECU campus. **Mexican.** Chico's casual dining room features hand-painted wall murals depicting Mexican scenery. The menu offers a variety of authentic south-of-the-border specialties, including a special children's menu. **FYI:** Reservations recommended. Children's menu. Additional location: 1701 Sunset Ave, Rocky Mount (tel 446-8600). **Open:** Sun–Thurs 11am–10pm, Fri–Sat 11am–11pm. **Prices:** Main courses $5–$10. AE, DISC, MC, V. 🍴 🕭

♣ Christinne's

In Hilton Inn, 207 SW Greenville Blvd; tel 919/355-9500. **Continental.** An attractive setting featuring vaulted ceilings, Victorian accents, and dividers between tables for added privacy. The menu offers mainly Italian and Greek selections, including veal cacciatore and Athenian chicken. They also have an impressive wine list and a delicious dessert tray. **FYI:** Reservations recommended. Children's menu. **Open:** Breakfast Mon–Fri 6:30–10:30am, Sat–Sun 7–10:30am; lunch Mon–Fri 11:30am–2pm; dinner Mon–Sat 5–10pm; brunch Sun 11:30am–2pm. **Prices:** Main courses $11–$29. AE, DISC, MC, V. ♥ 🕭

Mandarin Restaurant

2217 S Memorial Dr; tel 919/756-9687. **Chinese.** The Chinese-style decor consists of a pagodalike exterior and a simple, modern interior. Menu offerings include a large buffet for lunch, a variety of Hunan-style entrees for dinner, and a weekend seafood buffet. **FYI:** Reservations accepted. **Open:** Sun–Thurs 11am–10pm, Fri–Sat 11:30am–10:30pm. **Prices:** Main courses $6–$10. MC, V. 🚐 🕭

Ⓢ Sonic Drive-In

618 Greenville Blvd; tel 919/355-9815. **Diner.** Just like an old-fashioned drive-in, the Sonic has no indoor dining area. Visitors just drive up and order, and the food is whisked out to the parking lot on a tray. The menu includes hamburgers, hot dogs, milkshakes, and malts. There's a creatively designed playground for restless children. **FYI:** Reservations not accepted. Children's menu. No liquor license. **Open:** Sun–Thurs 9am–11pm, Fri–Sat 9am–midnight. **Prices:** Main courses $1–$3; prix fixe $3–$6. No CC. 🍴

Hatteras

Site of the Cape Hatteras lighthouse, built in 1870. The tallest lighthouse in America, its beacon projected a light over treacherous Diamond Shoals for more than a century.

MOTEL 🏨

▤▤ Sea Gull Motel

NC 12, PO Box 280, 27943; tel 919/986-2550. Well-kept basic motel, only 125 yards from the ocean. **Rooms:** 41 rms and effic; 4 cottages/villas. CI 2pm/CO 11am. High dunes prevent ocean views from rooms. **Amenities:** A/C, cable TV. No phone. **Services:** ⊂⊃ **Facilities:** 🏋 ⅙ 1 beach (ocean). Picnic tables, grills, and fish-cleaning tables on site. **Rates:** Peak (May 16–Sept 15) $55–$70 S or D; $70–$75 effic; $80–$90 cottage/villa. Extra person $5. Children under age 5 stay free. Lower rates off-season. Parking: Outdoor, free. Three-night minimum stay for efficiencies and villas. Closed Dec–Apr. DC, MC, V.

RESTAURANT 🍴

★ The Channel Bass

NC 12; tel 919/986-2250. **Seafood.** The large menu at this peaceful waterfront eatery includes a steamed sampler appetizer (with oysters, clams, and shrimp); homemade clam chowder; and platters of broiled, fried, and steamed seafood. Charbroiled steaks are also available, and delicious homemade desserts make an excellent finish to any meal. **FYI:** Reservations recommended. Children's menu. Beer and wine only. **Open:** Sun 5–10pm, Mon–Sat 5:30–10pm. Closed Thanksgiving–Easter. **Prices:** Main courses $10–$19. MC, V. 🏔 👪 ▽

Henderson

Incorporated in 1841 and located along the Virginia state border. Named for Leonard Henderson, former chief justice of the State Supreme Court. **Information:** Henderson–Vance County Chamber of Commerce, 414 S Garnett St, PO Box 1302, Henderson, 27536 (tel 919/438-8414).

HOTEL 🏨

▤▤ Howard Johnson Lodge

Exit 215 off I-85 at Parham Rd, PO Box Drawer F, 27536; tel 919/492-7001 or toll free 800/654-2000; fax 919/438-2389. A standard motor inn with few frills. **Rooms:** 98 rms. CI 2pm/CO 11am. Nonsmoking rms avail. **Amenities:** 🏋 A/C, cable TV w/movies. All units w/terraces. Refrigerators and microwaves available. **Services:** ⊂⊃ **Facilities:** 🏋 🏊 ⅙ 1 restaurant. **Rates:** $45–$55 S; $48–$57 D. Extra person $6. Children under age 17 stay free. Parking: Outdoor, free. AE, CB, DC, DISC, MC, V.

MOTEL

▤▤ Quality Inn

Exit 215 off I-85, PO Box 845, 27536; tel 919/492-1126; fax 919/492-2575. A clean, well-kept motel just off the interstate. Fine for an overnight stay. **Rooms:** 156 rms. CI 2pm/CO noon. Nonsmoking rms avail. **Amenities:** 🏋 A/C, cable TV w/movies, dataport. **Services:** ⊂⊃ **Facilities:** 🏋 1 restaurant, 1 bar. **Rates:** $46 S; $52–$55 D. Extra person $6. Children under age 18 stay free. Parking: Outdoor, free. AE, CB, DC, DISC, MC, V.

Hendersonville

Nestled in the Blue Ridge Mountains of western North Carolina, this small historic town calls itself "the Apple Capital" of the state and features vista views and the Flat Rock Playhouse. **Information:** Henderson County Travel & Tourism, 201 S Main St, PO Box 721, Hendersonville, 28793 (tel 704/693-9708).

HOTEL 🏨

▤▤ Hampton Inn

155 Sugarloaf Rd, 28739; tel 704/697-2333 or toll free 800/HAMPTON; fax 704/693-5280. Exit 18A off I-26. Attractive, well-maintained hotel. **Rooms:** 119 rms and stes. CI 2pm/CO noon. Nonsmoking rms avail. The bathrooms are looking dated, but are clean and large. **Amenities:** 🏋 ⅙ A/C, cable TV. **Services:** ▧ ⊂⊃ **Facilities:** 🏋 🏊 ⅙ **Rates (CP):** Peak (May–Oct) $60 S; $70 D; $100 ste. Children under age 18 stay free. Lower rates off-season. Parking: Outdoor, free. AE, CB, DC, DISC, MC, V.

MOTEL

▤▤▤ Quality Inn

201 Sugarloaf Rd, 28739; tel 704/692-7231 or toll free 800/424-6423; fax 704/693-9905. Exit 18A off I-26. Housed in a pretty brick and stucco building, this above-average chain motel features an indoor fountain and new interior. **Rooms:** 150 rms. CI 3pm/CO 11am. Nonsmoking rms avail. Recently remodeled rooms feature gaily colored bedspreads and plush chairs. **Amenities:** 🏋 ⅙ A/C, cable TV, voice mail. **Services:** ✕ 🚐 ▧ ⊂⊃ **Facilities:** 🏋 🏊 ⅙ 1 restaurant (bkfst and dinner only), 1 bar, games rm, sauna, whirlpool. Putting green. **Rates (CP):** $38–$85 S; $45–$85 D. Extra person $5. Children under age 12 stay free. Parking: Outdoor, free. Corporate packages avail. AE, CB, DC, DISC, JCB, MC, V.

INN

▤▤▤ Claddagh Inn

755 N Main St, 28792; tel 704/697-7778 or toll free 800/225-4700; fax 704/697-8664. Exit 18 off I-26. Country-style inn housed in a pretty, old yellow building. Accommodations are beautifully decorated. Families with children are the usual

guests. **Rooms:** 14 rms and stes. CI 3pm/CO 11am. No smoking. Quaint decorating theme, with lots of ruffles and embroidery and sometimes floral arrangements. **Amenities:** 🔒 ⚗ A/C, cable TV, dataport. **Services:** 🛏 Babysitting, afternoon tea and wine/sherry served. **Facilities:** 🍽30 ⚓ ᕒ 1 restaurant (bkfst only), guest lounge w/TV. **Rates (BB):** Peak (May–Dec) $69–$89 S; $79–$99 D; $99 ste. Extra person $10. Children under age 6 stay free. Lower rates off-season. Parking: Outdoor, free. AE, DISC, MC, V.

RESTAURANTS 🍴

Expressions

114 N Main St; tel 704/693-8516. Off US 25. **New American.** Award-winning chef Tom Young creates an ever-changing menu using only the freshest ingredients. His trademarks include pork tenderloin with sesame fried spinach, shiitake mushrooms, and apple-garlic sauce; or grilled duck breast with pickled blackberries and sour raspberry sauce. Young makes his own fresh bread, churns fresh ice cream, and makes pastries by hand. **FYI:** Reservations recommended. Dress code. **Open:** Peak (June–Aug) Mon–Sat 6–9:30pm. **Prices:** Main courses $14–$19. DISC, MC, V. ᕒ

Heritage House

1201 Asheville Hwy; tel 704/693-5449. Exit 18 off I-26. **American.** Heritage House caters to a busy breakfast crowd. They are famous for their Polish-style potato pancakes. **FYI:** Reservations accepted. Children's menu. No smoking. **Open:** Breakfast daily 7:30am–2:30pm; lunch daily noon–2:30pm; dinner Fri–Sun 5–8pm. **Prices:** Main courses $6–$13. AE, V. 🖼️ᕒ

ATTRACTION 🖼️

Carl Sandburg Home National Historic Site

1428 Little River Rd, Flat Rock; tel 704/693-4178. Located 2 mi S of Hendersonville. Last home of the two-time Pulitzer Prize–winning writer-poet-historian, who lived here for some 22 years, longer than he'd ever lived in any other place. His white, colonial-style home (built in 1838) and farm are preserved just as they were in his lifetime—his typewriter sitting on an orange crate in his top-floor hideaway and his guitar propped against a chair in the living room. (Guided tours of the house are available.) The 264-acre site also includes the pastures and mountain trails where Sandburg roamed. **Open:** Daily 9am–5pm. Closed Dec 25. **$**

Hickory

Located in the center of a major furniture-manufacturing area, this town was named for a hickory log tavern built at the site in the 1850s. Home to Lenoir Ryan College. **Information:** Greater Hickory Convention & Visitors Bureau, 470 US 70 SW, PO Box 1828, Hickory, 28603 (tel 704/328-6111).

HOTEL 🏨

⬛ Howard Johnson Lodge

483 US 70, PO Box 129, 28603; tel 704/322-1600 or toll free 800/446-4656; fax 704/327-2041. Off I-40. A comfortable, albeit unimpressive, hotel. Fine for all types of travelers. **Rooms:** 64 rms. CI 1pm/CO noon. Nonsmoking rms avail. Rooms are a bit larger than most in this price range. **Amenities:** 🔒 ⚗ A/C, cable TV. All units w/terraces. **Services:** ✕ 🚗 ⚓ 🛏 ⚓ **Facilities:** ⚓ 🍽 🍽125 ᕒ 1 restaurant, 1 bar, sauna, washer/dryer. **Rates:** $38–$52 S or D. Extra person $6. Children under age 16 stay free. Parking: Outdoor, free. AE, CB, DC, DISC, MC, V.

MOTELS

⬛⬛ Comfort Suites

1125 13th Ave SE, PO Box 3062, 28603; tel 704/323-1211 or toll free 800/228-5150; fax 704/322-4395. Exit 125 off I-40. Comfortable and pleasant lodgings suitable for families or business travelers. **Rooms:** 116 stes and effic. CI 3pm/CO 11am. Nonsmoking rms avail. Rooms have eye-popping aqua carpet, but furnishings are in good shape. **Amenities:** 🔒 ⚗ 🖥 A/C, cable TV, refrig. Some units w/whirlpools. Microwave in every unit. **Services:** ⚓ 🛏 **Facilities:** ⚓ 🍽 🍽65 ᕒ Washer/dryer. **Rates (BB):** $60–$100 ste; $100 effic. Extra person $7. Children under age 18 stay free. Parking: Outdoor, free. AE, CB, DC, DISC, ER, JCB, MC, V.

⬛⬛⬛ Holiday Inn

1385 Lenoir-Rhyne Blvd SE, 28602; tel 704/323-1000 or toll free 800/HOLIDAY; fax 704/322-3510. Exit 125 off I-40. A beautiful, elegant hotel with good facilities and friendly staff. The outside is not impressive, but the inside is surprisingly large and well decorated. **Rooms:** 201 rms and stes. Executive level. CI 3pm/CO noon. Nonsmoking rms avail. **Amenities:** 🔒 ⚗ 🖥 ☕ A/C, cable TV w/movies, dataport. Some units w/terraces. Some rooms have refrigerators. **Services:** ✕ 🚗 ⚓ 🛏 Social director, babysitting. **Facilities:** ⚓ 🍽 🍽350 ᕒ 1 restaurant, 1 bar, sauna, whirlpool, beauty salon, washer/dryer. **Rates (BB):** $75–$85 S or D; $125 ste. Extra person $6. Children under age 18 stay free. Parking: Outdoor, free. AE, CB, DC, DISC, JCB, MC, V.

Highlands

In the state's southern mountains, Highlands features a 120-foot waterfall you can drive beneath. **Information:** Highlands Area Chamber of Commerce, 396 Oak St, PO Box 404, Highlands, 28741 (tel 704/526-2112).

MOTELS 🏨

⬛⬛⬛ The Highlands Inn

E Main St, PO Box 1030, 28741; tel 704/526-9380; fax 704/526-5036. A unique 1880 property, with lots of character. The lobby has interesting touches such as gnarled driftwood benches that look like works of art, and twining ivy painted along the wall. **Rooms:** 32 rms and stes. CI 3pm/CO 11am. No smoking. Small canopies hung above each bed add a quaint touch. Rooms on the inside of the courtyard lead out into a garden with stone pathways and a tiny stream. **Amenities:** 🔥 A/C, cable TV. No phone. Some units w/terraces. Toiletries are displayed in wicker baskets with ceramic bluebirds. **Services:** 🔔 Coffee and cookies served nightly in the lobby. **Facilities:** 🍽 🛁 👌 1 restaurant (dinner only), games rm. **Rates (CP):** $74–$94 S or D; $74–$95 ste. Extra person $5. Children under age 18 stay free. Parking: Outdoor, free. Closed Dec–Mar. AE, MC, V.

≣≣≣ Highlands Suite Hotel
E Main St, PO Box 459, 28741; tel 704/526-4502 or toll free 800/221-5078; fax 704/526-4840. A small motel located conveniently in the downtown area, this is a pretty place with spacious attractive rooms and a wonderful open-air atmosphere with a terrific view of the mountains. **Rooms:** 28 stes. CI 3:30pm/CO noon. Nonsmoking rms avail. Rooms are small and adequately clean. **Amenities:** 🔥 🔥 🔲 A/C, cable TV, refrig, VCR. All units w/terraces, some w/fireplaces, all w/whirlpools. Each room has 2 TVs. Kitchen area with microwave, wet bar, and dishes. **Services:** 🔔 **Facilities:** 🍽 🛁 👌 **Rates (CP):** Peak (June–Oct) $69–$169 ste. Extra person $10. Children under age 15 stay free. Min stay wknds. Lower rates off-season. Parking: Indoor/outdoor, free. AE, MC, V.

RESTAURANT 🍴

On the Verandah
US 64W; tel 704/526-2338. **American/International.** The real attraction of this place is its lovely, peaceful open-air dining. The decor is simple but it has an interesting personality. Specials range from fresh trout to an excellent stuffed filet mignon. The restaurant is famous for its crème brûlée. **FYI:** Reservations recommended. Jazz. Wine only. No smoking. **Open:** Dinner daily 5–10pm; brunch Sun noon–2:30pm. Closed Nov–Mar. **Prices:** Main courses $14–$25. MC, V. 🏔 👌

High Point

One of the world's largest furniture markets; its Furniture Discovery Center is the nation's only museum dealing with furniture manufacturing. **Information:** High Point Convention & Visitors Bureau, 300 S Main, PO Box 2273, High Point, 27261 (tel 910/884-5255).

HOTEL 🏨

≣≣≣ Radisson Hotel
135 S Main St, 27260; tel 910/889-8888 or toll free 800/333-3333; fax 910/889-8888. On US 311. An attractive, eight-story hotel with fine furnishings throughout. **Rooms:**

249 rms and stes. Executive level. CI 3pm/CO noon. Nonsmoking rms avail. Suites are individually decorated. **Amenities:** 🔥 🔥 A/C, cable TV w/movies, dataport. **Services:** ✕ 🚐 🛁 🔔 Babysitting. **Facilities:** 🏋 🏊 👌 1 restaurant, 1 bar, sauna, whirlpool. **Rates:** $65–$90 S or D; $312–$449 ste. Min stay special events. Parking: Outdoor, free. AE, CB, DC, DISC, JCB, MC, V.

MOTEL

≣≣ Holiday Inn Market Square
236 S Main St, 27260; tel 910/886-7011 or toll free 800/HOLIDAY; fax 910/886-5595. A very comfortable motel. **Rooms:** 165 rms and stes. CI 3pm/CO noon. Nonsmoking rms avail. **Amenities:** 🔥 A/C, cable TV w/movies, dataport. **Services:** 🛁 🔔 **Facilities:** 🏋 👌 1 restaurant, 1 bar, washer/dryer. **Rates:** $50–$53 S; $60–$63 D; $95–$110 ste. Extra person $10. Children under age 18 stay free. Min stay special events. Parking: Outdoor, free. AE, CB, DC, DISC, MC, V.

Jacksonville

Home to the huge amphibious training complex of Camp Lejeune Marine Corps Base. Nearby Beirut Memorial dedicated to the marines and sailors who lost their lives in Lebanon in 1983. **Information:** Greater Jacksonville/Onslow Chamber of Commerce, 1 Marine Blvd N, PO Box 765, Jacksonville, 28541 (tel 910/347-3141).

MOTELS 📷

≣ Best Rest Inn
258 S Marine Blvd, 28540; tel 910/455-2063. Basic, no-frills motel. **Rooms:** 36 rms. CI 3pm/CO 11am. **Amenities:** 🔥 A/C, cable TV. **Rates:** $32.50 S; $35 D. Parking: Outdoor, free. AE, MC, V.

≣≣ Hampton Inn
474 Western Blvd, 28546; tel 910/347-6500 or toll free 800/888-5785; fax 910/347-6858. Attractive and comfortable accommodations near Camp Lejeune. **Rooms:** 80 rms. CI 2pm/CO noon. Nonsmoking rms avail. **Amenities:** 🔥 🔥 A/C, cable TV, dataport. **Services:** 🛁 **Facilities:** 🏋 🏊 👌 **Rates (CP):** $50 S; $55 D. Min stay special events. Parking: Outdoor, free. AE, CB, DC, DISC, MC, V.

≣ Onslow Inn
201 Marine Blvd, 28540; tel 910/347-2147 or toll free 800/763-3151; fax 910/346-4000. On US 17. Basic motel, with a pier and boat dock. **Rooms:** 92 rms. CI noon/CO 11am. Nonsmoking rms avail. **Amenities:** 🔥 🔥 A/C, cable TV w/movies, refrig. **Services:** 🛁 🔔 Complimentary coffee in lobby. **Facilities:** 🏋 🔲 👌 1 restaurant, 1 bar, playground. Picnic area. **Rates:** $38–$42 S or D. Extra person $4. Children under age 16 stay free. Parking: Outdoor, free. AE, CB, DC, DISC, MC, V.

Jefferson

Quaint mountain town near New River and 1,229-acre New River State Park.

MOTEL 🏨

🏨🏨🏨 Best Western Eldreth Inn

US 221 and NC 88, PO Box 12, 28640; tel 910/246-8845 or toll free 800/221-8802; fax 910/246-5620. By far the nicest motel in the area, with wooden rocking chairs set out on the terraces in front of the rooms. Flower boxes along the rail make for a quaint view. **Rooms:** 47 rms. CI 2pm/CO 11am. Nonsmoking rms avail. Rooms are clean and large, and have attractive touches like white, louvered doors on the closets. **Amenities:** 🏨 ⓩ A/C, cable TV. Some units have microwaves, refrigerators, and hair dryers. **Services:** ✗ ⌂ VCRs and movies for rent. **Facilities:** 🍴 ⅄ 1 restaurant, sauna. **Rates (BB):** $46–$58 S; $52–$66 D. Extra person $6. Children under age 12 stay free. Min stay wknds. Parking: Outdoor, free. AE, DC, DISC, MC, V.

ATTRACTION 🏛

New River State Park

1477 Wagoner Access Rd; tel 910/982-2587. Actually the *oldest* river in North America, its waters have followed the same course for millions of years and humans have lived in this area for at least 10,000 years. (The river was named the New River by Peter Jefferson, father of Thomas Jefferson, in 1749.) The river's shallow, slow moving waters are ideal for fishing (mostly bass and trout) and canoeing. Three access areas provide primitive camping and a picnic area; the access at Wagoner Road (at the south end of the park, just off NC 1590) also has a nature trail and a park office. Commercial campgrounds are available off NC 1308 and NC 1549, near the north fork of the river. **Open:** Nov–Feb, daily 8am–6pm; Mar, Oct, daily 8am–7pm; Apr–May, Sept, daily 8am–8pm; June–Aug, daily 8am–9pm. **Free**

Kill Devil Hills

Site of the Wright Brothers' earliest experiments with powered flight, and now the home of the Wright Brothers National Memorial. **Information:** Outer Banks Chamber of Commerce, Ocean Bay Blvd and Mustian St, PO Box 1757, Kill Devil Hills, 27948 (tel 919/441-8144).

HOTELS 🏨

🏨🏨🏨 Best Western Ocean Reef

107 Virginia Dare Trail, PO Box 1440, 27948; tel 919/441-1611 or toll free 800/528-1234. At MP 8½. An all-suites, oceanfront hotel. **Rooms:** 70 stes. CI 4pm/CO 11am. Nonsmoking rms avail. All suites have a full kitchen. Private balconies have view of the ocean or the Wright Brothers Memorial. **Amenities:** 🏨 ⓩ A/C, cable TV w/movies, refrig. All units w/terraces, 1 w/whirlpool. **Services:** ⌂ ⅄ **Facilities:** 🍴 ⅄ 1 restaurant, 1 bar, 1 beach (ocean), lifeguard, spa, sauna, whirlpool, washer/dryer. **Rates:** Peak (Mem Day–Labor Day) $147–$175 ste. Extra person $10. Children under age 18 stay free. Min stay special events. Lower rates off-season. Parking: Outdoor, free. Weekly rates avail. AE, DC, DISC, MC, V.

UNRATED Quality Inn Sea Ranch

Beach Rd, PO Box 325, 27959; tel 919/441-7126 or toll free 800/228-5151; fax 919/441-3795. At MP 7. A relaxing, oceanfront hotel. **Rooms:** 50 rms and effic. CI 4pm/CO 11am. Nonsmoking rms avail. Many rooms have ocean view. All suites have glass-enclosed balconies with view of the ocean. Two bedrooms available. **Amenities:** 🏨 A/C, cable TV w/movies, refrig. All units w/terraces. Rooms have microwaves. **Services:** ✗ ⌂ ⅄ **Facilities:** 🍴 ⅄ 🥗 1 restaurant, 1 bar (w/entertainment), 1 beach (ocean), lifeguard, spa, sauna, whirlpool, beauty salon. **Rates:** Peak (June 23–Aug) $85–$120 S or D; $100–$200 effic. Extra person $10. Children under age 18 stay free. Lower rates off-season. Parking: Outdoor, free. Sports packages avail. AE, CB, DC, DISC, MC, V.

🏨🏨🏨 Ramada Inn

1701 S Virginia Dare Trail, PO Box 2716, 27948; tel 919/441-2151 or toll free 800/2-RAMADA; fax 919/441-1830. Winning, modern hotel located on the oceanfront. **Rooms:** 172 rms. CI 1pm/CO 11am. Nonsmoking rms avail. **Amenities:** 🏨 ⓩ A/C, cable TV w/movies, refrig, dataport. All units w/terraces. **Services:** ✗ ⌂ ⅄ 🍽 **Facilities:** 🍴 🅿300 ⅄ 1 restaurant (see "Restaurants" below), 2 bars (1 w/entertainment), 1 beach (ocean), lifeguard, whirlpool. **Rates:** Peak (Mem Day–Aug) $84–$159 S or D. Extra person $10. Children under age 18 stay free. Min stay special events. Lower rates off-season. Parking: Outdoor, free. AE, CB, DC, DISC, EC, JCB, MC, V.

MOTELS

🏨🏨 Colony IV Motel

405 Virginia Dare Trail, PO Box 287, 27948; tel 919/441-5581 or toll free 800/848-3728. A family-oriented, oceanfront motel. **Rooms:** 87 rms and effic. CI 4pm/CO 11am. Nonsmoking rms avail. Comfortable rooms. Some have direct access to beach. **Amenities:** 🏨 A/C, cable TV, refrig. Some units w/terraces, 1 w/whirlpool. **Facilities:** 🍴 ⅄ 1 beach (ocean), games rm, whirlpool, playground, washer/dryer. Nine-hole miniature-golf course, horseshoes, and picnic area with grills. **Rates (CP):** Peak (June–Labor Day) $75–$95 S or D; $85–$115 effic. Extra person $5. Children under age 12 stay free. Lower rates off-season. Parking: Outdoor, free. Closed Dec, Jan. MC, V.

🏨🏨🏨 Comfort Inn North Oceanfront

401 N Virginia Dare Trail, PO Box 3427, 27948; tel 919/480-2600 or toll free 800/228-5150. An attractive, ocean-

front motel. Especially good for corporate travel. **Rooms:** 121 rms. CI 4pm/CO 11am. Nonsmoking rms avail. Rooms are attractively decorated; some have ocean view and some have a view of the Wright Brothers Memorial. **Amenities:** 🛢 🐦 A/C, cable TV w/movies, dataport. **Services:** 🖼 🍽 **Facilities:** 🖼 ⚒ ⚹ 1 beach (ocean), lifeguard, games rm. **Rates:** Peak (June 16–Aug 20) $100–$145 S or D. Extra person $5. Children under age 16 stay free. Min stay special events. Lower rates off-season. Parking: Outdoor, free. AE, DISC, MC, V.

≣≣ Days Inn Mariner
NC 12, PO Box 407, 27948; tel 919/441-2021 or toll free 800/DAYS-INN. At MP 7. Basic, homey accommodations on the oceanfront. **Rooms:** 70 rms and effic. CI 4pm/CO 11am. Nonsmoking rms avail. **Amenities:** 🛢 A/C, cable TV, refrig. Some units w/terraces. **Services:** 🍽 **Facilities:** 🖼 ⚹ 1 beach (ocean), lifeguard. **Rates (CP):** Peak (June–Labor Day) $90–$100 S or D; $100–$155 effic. Extra person $5. Children under age 12 stay free. Min stay peak. Lower rates off-season. Parking: Outdoor, free. AE, DC, DISC, MC, V.

≣≣≣ Days Inn Oceanfront
101 N Virginia Dare Trail, PO Box 3189, Kitty Hawk, 27948; tel 919/441-7211 or toll free 800/DAYS-INN. A unique mountain lodge–style motel on the Carolina shore. The lobby has hardwood floors with Oriental rugs, a fireplace, and leather furnishings. **Rooms:** 52 rms and effic. CI 4pm/CO 11am. Nonsmoking rms avail. Some rooms have interior corridors. One- and two-room efficiencies available. **Amenities:** 🛢 A/C, cable TV. **Services:** 🖼 🍽 **Facilities:** 🖼 ⚹ 1 beach (ocean), lifeguard, volleyball. Grills available. **Rates (CP):** Peak (June–Labor Day) $75–$140 S or D; $130–$140 effic. Extra person $5. Children under age 12 stay free. Lower rates off-season. Parking: Outdoor, free. AE, DC, DISC, MC, V.

UNRATED Hampton Inn
804 N Virginia Dare Trail, 27948; tel 919/441-0411 or toll free 800/338-7761; fax 919/441-7811. Off NC 12. Comfortable hotel located across the street from the beach. **Rooms:** 97 rms. CI 4pm/CO 11am. Nonsmoking rms avail. Some rooms have an ocean view. **Amenities:** 🛢 A/C, cable TV, refrig, dataport. All units w/terraces. Microwaves available. **Services:** 🖼 🍽 🛎 **Facilities:** 🖼 ⚹ Games rm. **Rates (CP):** Peak (June 18–Sept 2) $68–$78 S; $78–$98 D. Children under age 18 stay free. Lower rates off-season. Parking: Outdoor, free. Extended-stay packages avail. AE, DC, DISC, MC, V.

UNRATED Holiday Inn
MP 9½ US 158, Nags Head, PO Box 308, Kill Devil Hills, 27941; tel 919/441-6333 or toll free 800/HOLIDAY. Attractive oceanfront chain accommodations. **Rooms:** 105 rms. CI 4pm/CO 11am. Nonsmoking rms avail. **Amenities:** 🛢 A/C, cable TV. Some units w/terraces. **Services:** ✗ 🖼 🍽 **Facilities:** 🖼 🏊300 ⚹ 1 restaurant, 1 bar, 1 beach (ocean),

lifeguard, whirlpool. Small gazebo with hot tub. Children under 12 eat free in hotel restaurant. **Rates:** Peak (Mem Day–Labor Day) $115–$155 S or D. Extra person $10. Children under age 18 stay free. Lower rates off-season. Parking: Outdoor, free. AE, DC, DISC, MC, V.

≣≣≣ Quality Inn John Yancey
MP 10 NC 12, PO Box 422, 27948; tel 919/441-7141 or toll free 800/367-5941. Family-oriented oceanfront motel. **Rooms:** 107 rms and effic. CI 4pm/CO 11am. Nonsmoking rms avail. Rooms are decorated in soft beach colors. Oceanfront rooms are literally steps away from the surf. **Amenities:** 🛢 A/C, cable TV w/movies, refrig. Some units w/terraces, some w/whirlpools. **Services:** 🖼 🍽 **Facilities:** 🖼 1 beach (ocean), lifeguard, lawn games, playground. **Rates:** Peak (July–Aug 19) $99–$145 S or D; $109–$119 effic. Extra person $10. Children under age 12 stay free. Lower rates off-season. Parking: Outdoor, free. AE, DISC, MC, V.

≣≣ Tanya's Ocean House Motel
MP 9½ NC 12, PO Box 747, 27948; tel 919/441-2900. A basic oceanfront motel consisting of an unusual collection of theme rooms. **Rooms:** 43 rms. CI 4pm/CO 11am. Theme rooms include the Dixieland room, the Waterloo room, the Broadway room, and the Tobacco Belt room. Regular rooms are available for those who prefer more traditional decor. **Amenities:** 🛢 A/C, cable TV w/movies, refrig. **Facilities:** 🖼 1 beach (ocean), lifeguard. **Rates:** Peak (June 23–Labor Day) $62–$100 S or D. Extra person $8. Children under age 18 stay free. Min stay special events. Lower rates off-season. Parking: Outdoor, free. Closed Oct 15–Mar. AE, DISC, MC, V.

RESTAURANTS 🍴

Goombay's Grille & Raw Bar
MP 7½ on Beach Rd; tel 919/441-6001. Off US 158. **Seafood.** The lively and colorful decor consists of Caribbean colors, fish paintings, knotty-pine walls, and ceiling fans. The menu is similarly flavored by the islands, with pecan-fried flounder and shrimp with mandarin oranges among the seafood standouts. Some chicken and pasta dishes available, and they also serve Mexican dishes and a number of burgers for lunch. **FYI:** Reservations not accepted. Children's menu. **Open:** Mon–Fri 11:30am–10pm, Sun noon–10pm. **Prices:** Main courses $10–$17. DISC, MC, V. 👥 ⚹

Peppercorns Restaurant
In Ramada Inn, MP 9.5 US 158; tel 919/441-2151. **Eclectic.** Diners can enjoy oceanfront views while feasting on specialties such as steamed shrimp, grilled chicken Milano, and sautéed pork St James served with scallops. Chef's specials available daily. **FYI:** Reservations accepted. Blues/jazz/rock. Children's menu. **Open:** Breakfast daily 7–11:30am; lunch daily noon–2pm; dinner Sun–Thurs 5–9pm, Fri–Sat 5–9:30pm. **Prices:** Main courses $12–$15. AE, DC, DISC, MC, V. 🏔 ⚹

ATTRACTION

Wright Brothers National Memorial

Tel 919/441-7430. Both the hangar and Orville and Wilbur's living quarters have been restored, and the visitors center holds a replica of that first airplane, as well as exhibits that tell the story of the two brothers who came here on vacations from their Dayton, Ohio, bicycle business to turn their dream of flying into a reality. The site of the brothers' first December 1903 flight is marked off, with plaques showing where the plane took off and landed. Administered out of the same Manteo office that manages Fort Raleigh National Historic Site and Cape Hatteras National Seashore.

Kure Beach

Located on the Cape Fear Coast, this is one of the state's tropical, southernmost communities. Pristine beaches and state aquarium draw visitors.

MOTEL

UNRATED Docksider Inn

202 N US 421, PO Box 373, 28449; tel 910/458-4200; fax 910/458-6468. A comfortable, oceanfront motel. **Rooms:** 34 rms and effic. CI 3pm/CO noon. Nonsmoking rms avail. **Amenities:** A/C, cable TV. Some units w/terraces. **Facilities:** 1 beach (ocean). **Rates:** Peak (Mem Day–Labor Day) $102–$112 S or D; $115–$129 effic. Extra person $5. Children under age 10 stay free. Min stay special events. Lower rates off-season. Parking: Outdoor, free. Weekly rates avail. DC, DISC, MC, V.

ATTRACTION

Fort Fisher State Historic Site

1610 Fort Fisher Blvd S; tel 910/458-5538. One of the Confederacy's largest, most technically advanced forts, Fort Fisher protected blockade runners bringing in vital goods to the port of Wilmington. After withstanding two of the heaviest naval bombardments of the Civil War, the fort finally fell to Union forces in the conflict's largest land-sea battle. The visitors center exhibits artifacts of that era, and there's an audiovisual program as well. Costumed tour guides welcome visitors, and living-history events take place seasonally. **Open:** Apr–Oct, Mon–Sat 9am–5pm; Nov–Mar, Tues–Sat 10am–4pm, Sun 1–4pm. Closed some hols. **Free**

Lake Toxaway

Resort nearby to Pisgah National Forest in the northwestern part of the state.

LODGE

Earthshine Mountain Lodge

Rte 1, PO Box 216-C, 28747; tel 704/862-4207. Off NC 216. 70 acres. Though the gravel road leading to the lodge is rough, once you arrive, it is a nature lover's dream come true. A hewn-pine building houses the charming rooms and the grounds are stunningly beautiful. **Rooms:** 10 rms and stes; 1 cottage/villa. CI 3pm/CO 11am. No smoking. Rough-wood paneled rooms with log-frame beds and colorful patchwork quilts give a log cabin feel, although the beds are new and the bathrooms are modern. Some rooms also have lofts. **Amenities:** No A/C, phone, or TV. 1 unit w/terrace, 1 w/fireplace. **Services:** Social director, children's program, babysitting. **Facilities:** 1 restaurant, lawn games. Cherokee-style lawn games and amusements. Evening programs such as folk dances, campfire stories, and night hikes. Adventure programs for biking, hiking, and canoeing. **Rates (AP):** $100 S; $150 D; $100–$150 cottage/villa. Extra person $50. Min stay. Parking: Outdoor, free. MC, V.

RESORT

The Greystone Inn

Greystone Lane, PO Box 6, 28747; tel 704/966-4700 or toll free 800/824-5766; fax 704/862-5689. On US 64 between Brevard and Cashiers. 9,000 acres. Located on beautiful Lake Toxaway, this quiet property (housed in a restored 1915 mansion) provides beautiful views of the surrounding mountains. **Rooms:** 33 rms and stes. Executive level. CI 3pm/CO noon. Nonsmoking rms avail. Antique and period reproduction rooms are individually decorated with beautiful old furniture and architecture. Six cottages come equipped with full kitchens. **Amenities:** A/C, cable TV, refrig, VCR, bathrobes. Some units w/terraces, some w/fireplaces, all w/whirlpools. **Services:** Twice-daily maid svce, social director, masseur, children's program, babysitting. Guests are treated with care and individually shown around the grounds. Complimentary afternoon tea; daily champagne cruise on Lake Toxaway. **Facilities:** 1 restaurant, 1 bar (w/entertainment), 1 beach (lake shore), volleyball, lawn games, spa, sauna, whirlpool, beauty salon. Full spa for men and women. Bass boat and fishing gear provided. Complimentary country club memberships include free golf (except July–August). **Rates (MAP):** Peak (May–Oct) $220–$400 S; $295–$475 D; $345–$380 ste. Extra person $80. Children under age 1 stay free. Min stay wknds. Lower rates off-season. Parking: Outdoor, free. AE, MC, V.

Laurinburg

Founded by Scottish settlers in the early 18th century. This small, tree-lined town boomed with the addition of St Andrews Presbyterian College in the mid-1960s. **Information:**

Laurinburg/Scotland County Area Chamber of Commerce, 606 Atkinson St, PO Box 1025, Laurinburg, 28353 (tel 910/276-7420).

HOTEL

≣≣≣ Comfort Inn

1705 US 401 Bypass, 28352; tel 910/277-7788 or toll free 800/221-2222; fax 910/277-7229. A welcoming three-story property with a handsome lobby, old English furnishings, and a fireplace. **Rooms:** 80 rms. CI 3pm/CO noon. Nonsmoking rms avail. **Amenities:** 🛅 🐧 📺 A/C, cable TV. Some units w/whirlpools. **Services:** 🖼 🕬 **Facilities:** 🛗 🛁 📶 🔁 & **Rates (CP):** $51–$57 S; $54–$61 D. Extra person $6. Children under age 18 stay free. Parking: Outdoor, free. AE, CB, DC, DISC, JCB, MC, V.

MOTELS

≣≣ Holiday Inn

Jct US 15/US 401, PO Box 1688, 28352; tel 910/276-6555 or toll free 800/HOLIDAY. Extremely attractive, two-story motel. **Rooms:.** CI noon/CO noon. Nonsmoking rms avail. Rooms are comfortable and well kept. **Amenities:** 🛅 🐧 A/C, cable TV, dataport. **Services:** ✗ 🖼 🕬 🍴 **Facilities:** 🛗 📶 & 1 restaurant, 1 bar (w/entertainment). **Rates:** $48–$58 S or D. Extra person $6. Children under age 19 stay free. Min stay special events. Parking: Outdoor, free. AE, DC, DISC, MC, V.

≣ Pine Acres Lodge

401 S Lauringburg, PO Box 135A, Rt 5, 28352; tel 910/276-1531 or toll free 800/348-8242. This roadside motel sits among the pine trees. Beautiful, relaxing grounds. **Rooms:** 72 rms. CI 11am/CO 11am. **Amenities:** 🛅 🐧 🍴 A/C, cable TV, refrig. **Services:** 🍴 **Facilities:** 🛗 & 1 restaurant (lunch only). **Rates (CP):** $30–$60 S or D. Extra person $6. Children under age 4 stay free. Parking: Outdoor, free. AE, CB, DC, DISC, MC, V.

Lenoir

Caldwell County seat, located in the foothills of the Blue Ridge Mountains. One of the major furniture manufacturing areas of the state. **Information:** Caldwell County Chamber of Commerce, 1 Commerce Center Dr, PO Box 510, Lenoir, 28645 (tel 704/726-0616).

MOTEL

≣≣ Holiday Inn Express

142 Wilkesboro Blvd SE, 28645; tel 704/758-4403 or toll free 800/HOLIDAY; fax 704/758-4403. Off US 321. A small property with spotless rooms and friendly service. **Rooms:** 100 rms. CI 2pm/CO 11am. Nonsmoking rms avail. Nicely decorated rooms with new furniture, carpeting, and linens. Charming and functional. **Amenities:** 🛅 🐧 A/C, cable

TV. **Services:** 🖼 🕬 **Facilities:** 🛗 📶 & Volleyball, lawn games, washer/dryer. **Rates (CP):** Peak (June–Oct) $55–$60 S; $65–$70 D. Extra person $10. Children under age 18 stay free. Lower rates off-season. Parking: Outdoor, free. AE, CB, DC, DISC, JCB, MC, V.

Linville

Resort town located on the Blue Ridge Parkway. Linville Falls and Linville Caverns attract many tourists. Host to annual Grandfather Mountain Highland Games and Gathering of the Scottish Clans each summer.

RESORT

≣≣≣≣ Eseeola Lodge

175 Linville Ave, PO Box 99, 28646; tel 704/733-4311 or toll free 800/742-6717; fax 704/733-3227. Off NC 105. 1,600 acres. A quiet, rural hotel with country appeal and open, manicured grounds. The entrance is unusual, with log pillars entwined with ivy and flowers. A favorite getaway for retired couples. **Rooms:** 30 rms; 1 cottage/villa. CI 3pm/CO noon. Charming, country-decorated rooms have wildflower wallpaper, white quilted bedspreads, and large porches with views. **Amenities:** 🛅 🐧 📺 🍴 Cable TV, bathrobes. No A/C. All units w/terraces. **Services:** ✗ 🆅🅿 🖼 🕬 Twice-daily maid svce, social director, children's program, babysitting. Security patrol. **Facilities:** 🛗 🛁 ▶18 🎿 ⛳8 📶 2 restaurants (see "Restaurants" below), 1 bar, lawn games, playground. Lots of quiet walking paths through the extensive grounds. **Rates (MAP):** $150–$190 S; $200–$240 D; $350–$550 cottage/villa. Extra person $50. Children under age 5 stay free. Min stay peak. Parking: Outdoor, free. Closed Nov–Apr. MC, V.

RESTAURANT

♣ Eseeola Lodge Restaurant

US 221; tel 704/733-4311. **New American/French.** Quiet, formal atmosphere with lovely views of the hotel grounds and careful attention to extras like handmade wildflower arrangements and carved glass oil lamps on every table. Menus change often, but offer a wide variety of gourmet dishes such as sautéed North Carolina rainbow trout with jumbo crab, tossed macadamia nuts, and grapes with lemon-butter sauce. Frequented by an older (and very loyal) clientele. **FYI:** Reservations recommended. Piano. Children's menu. **Open:** Breakfast daily 7:30–9:30am; lunch daily 11:30am–2:30pm; dinner daily 7–9pm. Closed Nov–Apr. **Prices:** Prix fixe $28–$29. MC, V. 🏔

ATTRACTIONS

Grandfather Mountain

US 221 N; tel 704/733-4337 or toll free 800/468-7325. The highest peak in the Blue Ridge Mountains. Views of up to 100 miles can be had from the famous **Mile High Swinging**

Bridge, the highest suspension footbridge in the United States. An Environmental Habitat houses black bears and other animals native to the area. Spacious separate sections contain native deer, cougars, and bald and golden eagles which have been injured and cannot live in the wild on their own. The entrance to Grandfather Mountain is one mile from the Linville exit on the Blue Ridge Parkway at MP 305. **Open:** Apr–Oct, daily 8am–7pm; Nov–Mar, daily 8am–5pm. Closed some hols. **$$$**

Linville Caverns

US 221, Marion; tel 704/756-4171. Located within Humpback Mountain. The caverns, which served as a hiding place for deserters from both armies during the Civil War, contain a system of underground streams with schools of eyeless, sightless trout. Today's visitors can follow paths to see stalactite and stalagmite formations with descriptive names: Frozen Waterfall, Natural Bridge, the Franciscan Monk. Guided tours available. **Open:** June–Aug, daily 9am–6pm; Apr–May and Sept–Oct, daily 9am–5pm; Nov and Mar, daily 9am–4:30pm; Dec–Feb, Sat–Sun 9am–4:30pm. Closed some hols. **$$**

Little Switzerland

Summer resort town in the mountains of western North Carolina, at the head of Three-Mile Creek. Named for its mountainous location.

MOTEL

Big Lynn Lodge

US 226A, PO Box 459, 28749; tel 704/765-6771 or toll free 800/654-5232. 22 acres. A charming place with a wonderfully airy atmosphere and an unequaled view. **Rooms:** 42 rms and stes; 4 cottages/villas. CI 3pm/CO 11am. Nonsmoking rms avail. Rooms range from rustic cottage rooms, to standard motel rooms, to beautiful condominium-style suites. **Amenities:** No A/C or TV. All units w/terraces. Only some rooms have TV and air conditioning. Suites have coffeemaker, washer/dryer, dishwasher, and full-size kitchen appliances. **Services:** **Facilities:** 1 restaurant (bkfst and dinner only), lawn games. Hiking trails. **Rates (MAP):** $69–$78 S; $78–$95 D; $110 ste; $85 cottage/villa. Extra person $23. Children under age 5 stay free. Min stay wknds. Parking: Outdoor, free. Closed Nov–Apr. MC, V.

Lumberton

In the southern heartland of eastern North Carolina, this small town offers a restored one-room schoolhouse, a planetarium, and a state park. Named for its location on the Lumber River. **Information:** Lumberton Area Chamber of Commerce & Visitors Bureau, 800 N Chestnut St, PO Box 1008, Lumberton, 28359 (tel 910/739-4750).

HOTEL

Comfort Suites

215 Wintergreen Dr, 28358; tel 910/739-8800 or toll free 800/964-7700. Exit 22 off I-95. Beautiful, modern hotel with high ceilings in lobby and rooms. An excellent choice for business travelers. **Rooms:** 93 stes. CI 2pm/CO 11am. Nonsmoking rms avail. Suites consist of one room with a sitting area. **Amenities:** A/C, cable TV, refrig, dataport. Some units w/whirlpools. **Services:** Guest membership at local health club. **Facilities:** Sauna, whirlpool. **Rates (CP):** Peak (May–Aug) $55–$85 ste. Extra person $5. Children under age 18 stay free. Lower rates off-season. Parking: Outdoor, free. AE, CB, DC, DISC, MC, V.

MOTELS

Best Western of Lumberton

201 Jackson Court, 28358; tel 910/618-9799 or toll free 800/528-1234; fax 910/618-9057. Exit 22 off I-95. A very attractive motel opened in spring 1995. **Rooms:** 74 rms. CI 11am/CO 11am. Nonsmoking rms avail. **Amenities:** A/C, cable TV, refrig, dataport. **Services:** **Facilities:** **Rates (CP):** $45–$55 S; $49–$59 D. Extra person $5. Children under age 18 stay free. Parking: Outdoor, free. AE, CB, DC, DISC, MC, V.

Fairfield Inn

3361 Lackey St, 28358; tel 910/739-8444 or toll free 800/228-2800; fax 910/739-8466. Exit 20 off I-95. A pleasant new motel with excellent housekeeping. **Rooms:** 105 rms. CI 3pm/CO noon. Nonsmoking rms avail. **Amenities:** A/C, cable TV w/movies, dataport. **Services:** **Facilities:** **Rates (CP):** $42–$46 S; $46–$53 D. Extra person $7. Children under age 18 stay free. Parking: Outdoor, free. AE, CB, DC, DISC, MC, V.

Howard Johnson Lodge

3540 Capuano Dr, 28358; tel 910/738-4281 or toll free 800/IGO-HOJO. Off I-95. A standard, national chain motel. **Rooms:** 64 rms. CI 2pm/CO noon. Nonsmoking rms avail. Has nicely decorated rooms. **Amenities:** A/C, cable TV. Some units w/terraces. **Facilities:** 1 restaurant. **Rates:** $38–$42 S or D. Extra person $6. Children under age 17 stay free. Parking: Outdoor, free. AE, DISC, MC, V.

Quality Inn & Suites

3608 Kahn Dr, 28358; tel 910/738-8261. Off I-95 and NC 211, on Service Rd. An attractive motel that is convenient to the interstate. **Rooms:** 120 rms and stes. CI 2pm/CO noon. Nonsmoking rms avail. Some rooms have interior corridors. **Amenities:** A/C, cable TV w/movies, dataport. **Services:** **Facilities:** 1 restaurant, 1 bar (w/entertainment), sauna. Health club privileges. **Rates:** $54–$77 S; $60–$83 D; $65–$85 ste. Extra person $6. Children under age 11 stay free. Parking: Outdoor, free. AE, CB, DC, DISC, JCB, MC, V.

RESTAURANT

Fuller's Old Fashioned Bar-B-Q

NC 211; tel 910/738-8694. ¼ mi W of jct I-95/NC 211. **Barbecue/Seafood/Steak.** Old-fashioned is the operative word at this eatery, both in the decor and the food. The dining room is decorated with country crafts and old fashioned scenes, while the menu offers seafood plates, steaks, barbecue, and sandwiches as well as a buffet at dinner time. **FYI:** Reservations not accepted. Children's menu. No liquor license. **Open:** Daily 11am–9pm. **Prices:** Main courses $4–$9; prix fixe $5–$8. MC, V.

Maggie Valley

One of the state's gateways to Great Smoky Mountains National Park, this tourist mecca is a center for clogging (a dance that evolved from old Scotch and Irish reels and jigs) and other mountains arts. **Information:** Maggie Valley Area Chamber of Commerce, 623 Soco Rd, PO Box 87, Maggie Valley, 28751 (tel 704/926-1686).

MOTELS

Best Western Mountainbrook Inn

Soco Rd, 28751; tel 704/926-3962 or toll free 800/752-6230; fax 704/926-2947. On US 19, ½ mi from Ghost Town. A comfortable and dependable place to relax after a day of enjoying area attractions and activities. **Rooms:** 48 rms. CI 3pm/CO 11am. Nonsmoking rms avail. **Amenities:** A/C, cable TV w/movies, refrig. Microwaves. **Services:** Babysitting. **Facilities:** Whirlpool. Rocking chairs located outside every room. **Rates (CP):** Peak (May–Oct) $65–$89 S or D. Extra person $8. Children under age 12 stay free. Min stay special events. Lower rates off-season. Parking: Outdoor, free. Ski packages avail. AE, CB, DC, DISC, MC, V.

Comfort Inn

848 Soco Rd, 28751; tel 704/926-9106 or toll free 800/624-8259; fax 704/926-9106. On US 19. Well-maintained rooms and a convenient location are the strong points of this chain property. **Rooms:** 68 rms and stes. CI 4pm/CO 11am. Nonsmoking rms avail. **Amenities:** A/C, cable TV w/movies. Some units w/terraces. **Services:** **Facilities:** Playground, washer/dryer. **Rates (CP):** Peak (June–Oct) $55–$75 S; $65–$89 D; $125 ste. Extra person $10. Children under age 18 stay free. Min stay special events. Lower rates off-season. Parking: Outdoor, free. AE, CB, DC, DISC, ER, JCB, MC, V.

Opry House Motel

1005 Soco Rd, 28751; tel 704/926-3385. On US 19, 1 mi E of Ghost Town. Basic, no-frills accommodations convenient to Smokies and nearby attractions. **Rooms:** 20 rms and effic. CI 2pm/CO 10am. Nonsmoking rms avail. Rooms in the back building offer two double beds and a shower, while rooms in the front have two queen beds and tub/shower combos. **Amenities:** A/C, cable TV w/movies, refrig. **Services:** **Facilities:** Washer/dryer. **Rates:** Peak (July, Aug, Oct) $45–$65 S or D; $60–$70 effic. Extra person $5. Children under age 12 stay free. Min stay special events. Lower rates off-season. Parking: Outdoor, free. Seventh day is free. Closed Dec–Mar. MC, V.

RESORTS

Cataloochee Ranch

Fie Top Rd, PO Box 500, Rte 1, 28751; tel 704/926-1401 or toll free 800/868-1401; fax 704/926-9249. 3 mi off US 19. 1,000 acres. These great, little split-log cabins have been managed by the same family for over 60 years. The vistas at this mountain resort near Smoky Mountain National Park are unbelievable. **Rooms:** 12 rms and stes; 6 cottages/villas. CI 3pm/CO 11am. **Amenities:** TV w/movies. No A/C or phone. Some units w/fireplaces. **Services:** Three private gateways into the park. **Facilities:** 1 restaurant (see "Restaurants" below), lawn games, whirlpool. **Rates (MAP):** Peak (June 16–Aug 19, Oct) $100–$115 S; $120–$225 D; $210–$225 ste; $180–$340 cottage/villa. Extra person $50–60. Min stay. Lower rates off-season. Parking: Outdoor, free. AE, MC, V.

Maggie Valley Resort & Country Club

340 Country Club Rd, 28751; tel 704/926-1616 or toll free 800/438-3861; fax 704/926-2906. ½ mi off US 19. A comfortable resort near the picturesque Smoky Mountains. **Rooms:** 75 rms; 11 cottages/villas. CI 3pm/CO noon. Rooms offer stunning views of the resort grounds and distant mountains through a full wall of windows. **Amenities:** A/C, cable TV w/movies. All units w/terraces. **Services:** **Facilities:** 1 restaurant (see "Restaurants" below), 1 bar. Golf available year round, as are golf lessons. **Rates:** Peak (Apr–Oct) $89–$99 S; $99–$109 D; $119–$129 cottage/villa. Extra person $10. Children under age 14 stay free. Lower rates off-season. Parking: Outdoor, free. Golf packages avail. AE, DISC, MC, V.

Twinbrook Resort Cottages

Twinbrook Lane, PO Box 683, 28751; tel 704/926-1388 or toll free 800/305-8946; fax 704/926-2943. Off US 19. 20 acres. Secluded private cottages, each with its own front porch. A perfect place for a peaceful, family vacation. **Rooms:** 14 cottages/villas. CI 2pm/CO 11am. Cabin porches offer a great view of nearby mountains and streams. **Amenities:** Cable TV w/movies, refrig. No A/C. All units w/terraces, all w/fireplaces, some w/whirlpools. **Services:** **Facilities:** Basketball, volleyball, lawn games, whirlpool. **Rates:** $85–$250 cottage/villa. Extra person $5–$10. Parking: Outdoor, free. AE, DISC, MC, V.

RESTAURANTS 🍴

Cataloochee Ranch
Fie Top Rd; tel 704/926-1401. 3 mi off US 19. **Regional American.** Down-home, Appalachian-style cuisine, including pan-fried Smoky Mountain trout, prime rib, and sweet potatoes served with brown sugar, cinnamon, and butter. **FYI:** Reservations recommended. Beer and wine only. **Open:** Breakfast daily 8–9am; lunch daily 12:30–1:30pm; dinner daily 7pm. Closed Dec–Mar. **Prices:** Prix fixe $18. AE, MC, V. &

J Arthur's Restaurant
US 19; tel 704/926-1817. **American.** Specialties include prime rib, lamb, and trout. Gourmet coffee is available to finish off the meal. **FYI:** Reservations not accepted. Children's menu. **Open:** Peak (Apr–Oct) dinner daily 5–9:30pm. **Prices:** Main courses $9–$23. AE, CB, DC, DISC, MC, V. &

The Valley Room
In Maggie Valley Resort and Country Club, 340 Country Club Rd; tel 704/926-1616. ½ mi off US 19. **American.** Diners at this fine restaurant enjoy splendid views of the surrounding country club along with their filet mignon, prime rib, and trout amandine. **FYI:** Reservations recommended. Country music/dancing. Dress code. **Open:** Breakfast daily 6:30–9:30am; lunch daily 11am–5pm; dinner Sun–Thurs 6–9pm, Fri–Sat 6–10pm. **Prices:** Main courses $15–$18; prix fixe $15–$18. AE, MC, V. 🖤 &

ATTRACTIONS 🖼

Ghost Town in the Sky
US 19; tel 704/926-1140. Separate Western, mining, and mountaineer towns have been re-created on different levels of the mountaintop. Shows are staged in the saloons, there are street gunfights, and all sorts of Western and mountaineer types wander about. Kids will love the amusement park rides, including a roller coaster built into the side of a mountain. The park (which is 3,364 feet up) is accessible by means of twin inclined railways, shuttle bus, or chairlift. **Open:** Sept–Oct and May, daily 9:30am–6pm; June–Aug, daily 9am–7pm. $$$$

Cataloochee Ski Area
Exit 20 off I-40W or exit 27 off I-40E; tel 704/926-0285 or toll free 800/768-0285. The nine trails at this family-oriented resort (with a vertical drop of 740 feet) offer skiing for everyone from novices to expert schussboomers. The PSIA-registered Cataloochee Ski School offers classes and private instruction, and a base lodge serves three hearty meals daily in ski season. Many discount programs available; call ahead to check current rates. **Open:** Dec–Mar, daily 9am–4:30pm, Tues–Sat 6–10pm. $$$$

Manteo
See also Cape Hatteras National Seashore, Nags Head

The major town on Roanoke Island. Waterfront *Elizabeth II* State Historic Site re-creates the 16th-century ship that brought the first English colonists to America. One of the state's three aquariums is located three miles north of town.

MOTEL 🏨

≣ Elizabethan Inn
814 US 64, PO Box 549, 27954; tel 919/473-2101 or toll free 800/346-2466; fax 919/473-6688. English Tudor–style motel, convenient to historic waterfront and business district. **Rooms:** 105 rms and effic. CI 3:30pm/CO noon. Nonsmoking rms avail. **Amenities:** 🛏 A/C, cable TV w/movies, refrig. **Services:** 🛎 Babysitting. **Facilities:** 🗂 🍽 🚐 1 restaurant (*see* "Restaurants" below), spa, sauna. **Rates:** Peak (Mem Day–Labor Day) $70–$85 S or D; $60 effic. Extra person $10. Children under age 18 stay free. Lower rates off-season. Parking: Outdoor, free. AE, DISC, MC, V.

INNS

≣≣ Scarborough Inn
524 US 64/264, PO Box 1310, 27954; tel 919/473-3979. A charming, shingle-style inn in the center of town. **Rooms:** 10 rms and stes. CI 2pm/CO 11am. Rooms are furnished with antiques. **Amenities:** 🛏 A/C, cable TV, refrig. **Services:** ⬜ **Rates (CP):** Peak (Mem Day–Labor Day) $50 S or D; $55 ste. Extra person $5. Children under age 2 stay free. Lower rates off-season. Higher rates for special events/hols. Parking: Outdoor, free. DISC, MC, V.

≣≣≣ Tranquil House Inn
Queen Elizabeth St, PO Box 2045, 27954; tel 919/473-1404 or toll free 800/458-7069. 5 acres. Located on the waterfront, the Tranquil House Inn offers serene accommodations year-round. The original inn was built in 1885 but burned to the ground in the 1950s. The current structure was built in 1988. **Rooms:** 27 rms, stes, and effic. CI 3pm/CO 11am. Nonsmoking rms avail. Designer wallpaper, stencil work, and stained glass make each room uniquely beautiful, and Oriental carpets adorn the hardwood floors. Some rooms have poster or canopy beds, and some suites have small sitting rooms. **Amenities:** 🛏 A/C, cable TV, dataport. **Services:** ⬜ Babysitting, wine/sherry served. Wine and cheese reception each evening. Secretarial services. **Facilities:** 🚲 🛶 🍽 & 1 restaurant (dinner only; *see* "Restaurants" below), 1 bar, guest lounge. The fourth-story observatory has been converted into a library and game room. A second-story veranda provides a relaxing view of the bay and marina, and health club privileges are provided for guests. **Rates (CP):** Peak (Mem Day–Labor Day) $119–$159 D; $159 ste; $159

effic. Extra person $10. Children under age 16 stay free. Lower rates off-season. Higher rates for special events/hols. Parking: Outdoor, free. AE, DISC, MC, V.

RESTAURANTS

Anna Livia's Restaurant

In The Elizabethan Inn, US 64; tel 919/473-3753. **Italian/ Seafood.** A family restaurant with an English Tudor decor. Menu offerings include baked stuffed eggplant parmigiana, and grilled fresh tuna putanesca. **FYI:** Reservations accepted. Children's menu. Beer and wine only. **Open:** Breakfast daily 6:30–11:30am; lunch Sun–Fri 11:30am–2pm; dinner daily 4–9pm. Closed Christmas week. **Prices:** Main courses $9–$15. AE, DC, MC, V.

Clara's Steam Bar & Seafood Grill

In Waterfront Shops, Queen Elizabeth Ave; tel 919/473-1727. **Seafood/Steak.** A casual eatery with one of the best views in Manteo—a stunning panorama of the bay, marsh, and marina. The menu offers creative seafood options like tuna kabob, scallops Florentine, and Manteo fish-in-a-bag (fresh local fish, vegetables, rice pilaf, and spices—all baked in a bag). **FYI:** Reservations recommended. Children's menu. Beer and wine only. **Open:** Daily 11:30am–9:30pm. Closed Jan–Feb. **Prices:** Main courses $8–$18. AE, DISC, MC, V.

✿ 1587

In Tranquil House Inn, Queen Elizabeth Ave; tel 919/473-1404. On the waterfront. **Regional American.** The walls here are painted with a marble effect and are accented with blond-wood trim. This unique flair continues with the cuisine. Many of Chef Jason Melton's creations are unique twists on Southern fare, and some have tropical touches. The duck, steak, lamb, and seafood entrees are bold and very filling; all desserts are homemade. **FYI:** Reservations recommended. Children's menu. Beer and wine only. **Open:** Daily 5–10pm. Closed Jan–Mar. **Prices:** Main courses $15–$27. AE, DISC, MC, V.

★ Fisherman's Wharf

NC 345S, Wanchese; tel 919/473-5205. **Seafood.** Nestled on the waterfront at the south end of Roanoke Island, so that diners can see the fishing boats that bring in the fresh seafood served here. Dinners focus on fresh shellfish and fish, while steaks, chicken, and pasta are also available. Wanchese crab cakes are a favorite. **FYI:** Reservations not accepted. Children's menu. No liquor license. No smoking. **Open:** Mon–Sat noon–9pm. Closed Mid-Dec–mid-Apr. **Prices:** Main courses $10–$20. AE, DC, DISC, MC, V.

★ Poor Richard's Sandwich Shop

Queen Elizabeth Ave; tel 919/473-3333. On the waterfront. **Deli.** Serves a variety of cold and grilled sandwiches, all with pickles and chips on the side. Breakfast sandwiches and soft-serve ice cream are also available. The deli has a cozy dining room and a patio with table tops that rest on wooden barrels.

FYI: Reservations not accepted. Children's menu. No liquor license. **Open:** Peak (June–Aug) Mon–Fri 8am–8pm, Sat 8am–3pm. **Prices:** Main courses $3–$5. No CC.

ATTRACTIONS

Fort Raleigh National Historic Site

US 64/264; tel 919/473-5772. Sir Walter Raleigh's colony of more than 100 men, women, and children settled here in 1585, in what was to be England's first permanent foothold in the New World. Colony governor John White sailed back to England that same year; when he returned in 1590, all he found was a sign at the entrance of the settlement that spelled out the word "CROATAN." Since their prearranged distress signal—a cross—was not there, and no evidence of violence was found, White concluded that the colonists must have joined the friendly Croatan tribe, but he had to return to England before a search could be made. No clue has ever been unearthed to reveal exactly what did happen to the "lost" colonists.

The old fort has been excavated and reconstructed just as it stood in 1585. The visitors center is a fascinating first stop, with a museum and audiovisual program. A nature trail looks out over Roanoke Sound, and during the summer costumed interpreters play 16th-century music. **Open:** Daily 9am–5pm. Closed Dec 25. **Free**

Elizabeth II State Historic Site

Hwy 400; tel 919/473-1144. This 69-foot-long three-master bark was built in 1984 for the 400th anniversary commemoration of the Roanoke landing. The visitors center contains exhibits describing the tense political climate between Protestant England and Catholic Spain, as well as Native American life on the island. A 20-minute multimedia presentation realistically depicts life aboard such a ship from the perspective of the voyagers. During the summer months, living-history interpreters portray roles of colonists and mariners. **Open:** Apr–Oct, daily 10am–6pm; Nov–Mar, Tues–Sun 10am–4pm. Closed some hols. **$**

Elizabethan Gardens

US 64; tel 919/473-3234. Located at the site of the first English colony in the New World. The Tudor-style Gate House is filled with period furniture and portraits of many of the English settlers. Grounds are dotted with ancient garden statuary, a Shakespearean herb garden, a Sunken Garden with parterres and fountain, and a terrace overlooking Roanoke Sound. **Open:** March and Nov, daily 9am–5pm; Apr and Oct, daily 9am–6pm; May and Sept, daily 9am–7pm; June–Aug, daily 9am–8pm. Closed some hols. **$**

North Carolina Aquarium on Roanoke Island

Airport Rd; tel 919/473-3494. One of three state aquariums along the coast of North Carolina; the others are in Morehead City and Wilmington. Displays of sharks, eels, sea turtles, and other marine life, interspersed with educational exhibits and films. Touch tanks are available for visitors who want a more hands-on experience. **Open:** Mon–Sat 9am–5pm, Sun 1–5pm. Closed some hols. **$**

Morehead City

See also Atlantic Beach, Beaufort

Located across the Intracoastal Waterway from Beaufort, this resort town is noted for charter boat fishing. (The nearby Gulf Stream brings in a bountiful catch.) There is a 1,000-foot pier. **Information:** Carteret County Chamber of Commerce, 3615 Arendell St, PO Box 1198, Morehead City, 28557 (tel 919/726-6350).

HOTEL

≡≡≡ Hampton Inn
4035 Arendell St, 28557; tel 919/240-2300 or toll free 800/HAMPTON; fax 919/240-2311. Relaxing grounds and a pastel stucco exterior are highlights at this attractive hotel. **Rooms:** 120 rms and stes. CI 4pm/CO 11am. Nonsmoking rms avail. Some rooms have a view of Bogue Sound. **Amenities:** A/C, cable TV w/movies, dataport. **Services:** **Facilities:** 100 Rates (CP): Peak (Apr–Labor Day) $53–$56 S; $59–$62 D. Lower rates off-season. Parking: Outdoor, free. AE, CB, DC, DISC, MC, V.

MOTELS

≡≡ Best Western Buccaneer Motor Inn
2806 Arendell St, 28557; tel 919/726-3115 or toll free 800/682-4982; fax 919/726-3864. On US 70. A standard motel located only two miles from the beach. **Rooms:** 91 rms. CI 3pm/CO noon. Nonsmoking rms avail. Rooms have modern decor; some have whirlpools. **Amenities:** A/C, cable TV w/movies, dataport. Free coffee and local phone calls. **Services:** **Facilities:** 1 restaurant, 1 bar. **Rates (BB):** Peak (Mem Day–Labor Day) $59–$78 S; $62–$75 D. Extra person $5. Children under age 18 stay free. Lower rates off-season. Parking: Outdoor, free. Golf packages avail. AE, CB, DC, DISC, MC, V.

≡≡ Comfort Inn
3100 Arendell St, 28557; tel 919/247-3434 or toll free 800/422-5404; fax 919/247-4411. Standard motel, with an attractive color scheme. Located two miles from local beach. **Rooms:** 100 rms. CI 3pm/CO 11am. Nonsmoking rms avail. **Amenities:** A/C, cable TV w/movies. **Services:** **Facilities:** 20 Golf privileges at nearby courses can be arranged for a nominal fee. **Rates (CP):** Peak (May–Labor Day) $52–$74 S; $62–$77 D. Extra person $5. Children under age 18 stay free. Lower rates off-season. Parking: Outdoor, free. AE, DC, DISC, MC, V.

RESTAURANTS

Captain Bill's Waterfront Restaurant
701 Evans St; tel 919/726-2166. On the waterfront. **Seafood.** Overlooking colorful fishing boats on Bogue Sound, this family-style eatery has wraparound walkways where visitors often feed hungry seagulls. The menu includes broiled and fried seafood entrees, combination platters, and seafood casseroles such as shrimp au gratin and shrimp Creole with rice. Desserts, sauces, and salad dressings are all homemade. **FYI:** Reservations not accepted. Children's menu. No liquor license. **Open:** Peak (Mem Day–Labor Day) daily 11am–9pm. Closed Feb. **Prices:** Main courses $7–$19. DISC, MC, V.

★ Mrs Willis Restaurant
3002 Bridges St; tel 919/726-3741. **American/Seafood.** Mrs Willis (and now her family) has been serving the public since 1952. Entrees include hearty portions of seafood, prime rib, choice chargrilled steak, barbecue pork, and baked ham; everything is made from family recipes and it all comes with choice of vegetable. Sandwiches, burgers, and homemade desserts also available. **FYI:** Reservations not accepted. Children's menu. **Open:** Peak (May–Oct) daily 11:30am–9pm. Closed Dec 24–Dec 31. **Prices:** Main courses $5–$17. DISC, MC, V.

★ Sanitary Fish Market and Restaurant
501 Evans St; tel 919/247-3111. On the waterfront. **Seafood.** Morehead City's first waterfront restaurant, the Sanitary has been a local landmark since 1938. The current building extends over the water, offering guests a wonderful view of the Beaufort Inlet from all directions. The large menu (with over 50 items) emphasizes seafood, with broiled and fried fish, homemade clam chowder, and she-crab soup among the favorite choices. **FYI:** Reservations not accepted. Children's menu. No liquor license. **Open:** Daily 11am–9pm. Closed Nov 27–Jan. **Prices:** Main courses $6–$22. DISC, MC, V.

Morganton

Founded in 1784 on the Catawba River in the foothills of the Blue Ridge Mountains, the seat of Burke County is a lake resort and a furniture and clothing manufacturer. Home to Western Piedmont Community College. **Information:** Burke County Chamber of Commerce, 110 E Meeting St, PO Box 751, Morganton, 28680 (tel 704/437-3021).

MOTELS

≡ Days Inn
2402 S Sterling St, 28655; tel 704/433-0011 or toll free 800/DAYS-INN; fax 704/437-0985. Exit 105 off I-40. Decent, well-kept property. **Rooms:** 115 rms. CI 2pm/CO 11am. Nonsmoking rms avail. **Amenities:** A/C, cable TV, dataport. **Services:** **Facilities:** 1 restaurant (lunch

and dinner only). **Rates (CP):** $30–$40 S; $40–$50 D. Extra person $5. Children under age 12 stay free. Parking: Outdoor, free. AE, DC, DISC, MC, V.

≋≋≋ Holiday Inn

2400 S Sterling St, 28655; tel 704/437-0171 or toll free 800/HOLIDAY; fax 704/437-0171 ext 297. Exit 105 off I-40. Although the exterior is not impressive, the interior is wonderfully decorated and extremely livable. **Rooms:** 267 rms. CI 3pm/CO noon. Nonsmoking rms avail. **Amenities:** 🅣 🅐 A/C, cable TV, dataport. **Services:** ✕ 🖼 ⇨ ⬦ Babysitting. **Facilities:** 🔃 🔟 ⅙ 1 restaurant, 1 bar. **Rates:** Peak (June–Aug) $45–$54 S; $50–$59 D. Extra person $5. Children under age 19 stay free. Lower rates off-season. Parking: Outdoor, free. AE, CB, DC, DISC, MC, V.

Morrisville

See also Chapel Hill, Durham, Raleigh

Nags Head

See also Manteo

This small resort town on the Outer Banks is a popular center for hang gliders. The largest natural sand dune on the East Coast, about 140 feet high, is here.

HOTELS 🏨

≋≋ The Carolinian Hotel

MP 10½ NC 12, PO Box 370, 27959; tel 919/441-7171 or toll free 800/852-0756. This older hotel has a lobby with knotted-pine floors and walls and reminds its guests of a time when life kept a slower pace. **Rooms:** 88 rms, stes, and effic; 2 cottages/villas. CI 3pm/CO 11am. Rooms are small. **Amenities:** 🅣 A/C, cable TV. Some rooms available with refrigerators. **Services:** ⇨ ⬦ **Facilities:** 🔃 🌅 1 restaurant (dinner only), 2 bars (1 w/entertainment), 1 beach (ocean), games rm. Large platform deck (with gazebo) overlooks the beach. **Rates:** Peak (Mem Day–Labor Day) $65–$95 S or D; $65–$95 ste; $95–$175 cottage/villa. Extra person $5. Children under age 12 stay free. Lower rates off-season. MAP rates avail. Parking: Outdoor, free. Weekly rates avail. Closed Thanksgiving–Easter. AE, MC, V.

≋≋ Comfort Inn

8031 Old Oregon Inlet Rd, 27959; tel 919/441-6315 or toll free 800/334-3302. A comfortable, modern-looking oceanfront hotel. **Rooms:** 105 rms and stes. CI 4pm/CO 11am. Nonsmoking rms avail. Most rooms have ocean or bay view. **Amenities:** 🅣 A/C, cable TV w/movies. Some units w/terraces. Microwaves and refrigerators available. **Services:** ⇨ Fax and copy services available. **Facilities:** 🔃 🌅 ⅙ 1 beach (ocean), games rm. **Rates (CP):** Peak (Mem Day–Labor Day)

$115–$155 S or D; $250 ste. Extra person $10. Children under age 18 stay free. Min stay special events. Lower rates off-season. Parking: Outdoor, free. AE, DISC, MC, V.

≋≋≋ Nags Head Inn

4701 S Virginia Dare Trail, PO Box 1599, 27959; tel 919/441-0454 or toll free 800/327-0454. MP 14. Comfortable, five-story oceanfront hotel. **Rooms:** 100 rms and stes. CI 4pm/CO 11am. Nonsmoking rms avail. Some rooms have oceanfront balconies. **Amenities:** 🅣 A/C, cable TV w/movies, refrig, dataport. Some units w/terraces. **Services:** ⇨ Complimentary coffee in lobby. **Facilities:** 🔃 🌅 ⅙ 1 beach (ocean), lifeguard, whirlpool. Indoor pool has large glass doors that open onto a sun deck. Whirlpool. **Rates:** Peak (June 23–Sept 4) $99–$139 S or D; $199 ste. Extra person $5. Lower rates off-season. Parking: Outdoor, free. AE, CB, DC, DISC, MC, V.

MOTELS

≋≋ Beacon Motor Lodge

2617 S Virginia Dare Trail, PO Box 729, 27959; tel 919/441-5501; fax 919/441-2178. MP 11. Clean, basic oceanfront accommodations. **Rooms:** 48 rms and effic; 2 cottages/villas. CI 4pm/CO 11am. Nonsmoking rms avail. **Amenities:** 🅣 A/C, cable TV w/movies, refrig. **Services:** ⇨ **Facilities:** 🔃 1 beach (ocean), lifeguard, playground. Picnic area with grills. **Rates:** Peak (June 9–Labor Day) $75–$92 S or D; $80–$105 effic; $95–$115 cottage/villa. Extra person $5. Lower rates off-season. Parking: Outdoor, free. Two-bedroom efficiency apartments and cottages require one-week minimum stay during peak season. Closed Nov–Feb. AE, DISC, MC, V.

≋≋ Cabana East Motel

MP 11 NC 12, PO Box 395, 27959; tel 919/441-7106. A comfortable, oceanfront motel. **Rooms:** 40 rms and effic; 1 cottage/villa. CI 4pm/CO 11am. Nonsmoking rms avail. **Amenities:** 🅣 A/C, cable TV w/movies. All units w/terraces. **Services:** ⇨ **Facilities:** 🔃 ⅙ **Rates:** Peak (June 16–Labor Day) $73 S or D; $79–$88 effic; $110 cottage/villa. Extra person $8. Children under age 18 stay free. Min stay special events. Lower rates off-season. Parking: Outdoor, free. Cottages require a three-night minimum stay during peak season. AE, MC, V.

≋≋ Quality Inn Sea Oatel

7123 S Virginia Dare Trail, 27959; tel 919/441-7191 or toll free 800/440-4-FUN; fax 919/441-1961. A comfortable, attractive, seaside motel. **Rooms:** 111 rms. CI 4pm/CO 11am. Nonsmoking rms avail. Rooms are decorated in soft colors and most have an ocean view. **Amenities:** 🅣 🅐 A/C, cable TV w/movies. All units w/terraces. **Services:** 🖼 ⇨ **Facilities:** ⅙ 1 beach (ocean), volleyball. **Rates:** Peak (Mem Day–Labor Day) $50–$125 S or D. Extra person $8. Children under age 18 stay free. Lower rates off-season. Parking: Outdoor, free. AE, CB, DC, DISC, MC, V.

⊨⊨ Surf Side Motel

Beach Rd, PO Box 400, 27959; tel 919/441-2105 or toll free 800/552-SURF; fax 919/441-2456. MP 16. A comfortable, five-story, oceanfront motel. **Rooms:** 76 rms and stes. CI 3pm/CO 11am. Nonsmoking rms avail. All rooms have ocean view. **Amenities:** 📺 🔥 A/C, cable TV. All units w/terraces, 1 w/whirlpool. **Services:** 🛎 🍴 **Facilities:** 🏋 🔥 1 beach (ocean), lifeguard, whirlpool. **Rates (CP):** Peak (June 16–Sept 23) $99–$139 D; $139–$149 ste. Extra person $5. Children under age 13 stay free. Lower rates off-season. Parking: Outdoor, free. Weekly rates avail. AE, DC, DISC, MC, V.

INN

⊨⊨⊨ First Colony Inn

6720 S Virginia Dare Trail, 27959; tel 919/441-2343 or toll free 800/368-9390; fax 919/441-9234. MP 16. The first Inn opened in 1932 but was moved and remodeled in 1988 to avoid the encroaching surf. Still a charming, shingle-style inn with wraparound porches, this island of Southern hospitality has retained its old fashioned elegance and added modern conveniences. **Rooms:** 27 rms and effic. CI 3pm/CO 11am. No smoking. Rooms are individually decorated with English antiques, and some have private, screened porches. **Amenities:** 📺 🔥 A/C, cable TV, refrig, dataport. Some units w/terraces, 1 w/whirlpool. Luxury rooms have wet bars. **Services:** 🚐 🛎 🍴 Babysitting, afternoon tea served. Secretarial services. **Facilities:** 🏋 🛏 Second story houses a cozy reading and game room, and the inn has a private beach access. **Rates (CP):** Peak (June 9–Sept 3) $125–$200 D; $125 effic. Extra person $30. Lower rates off-season. Higher rates for special events/hols. Parking: Outdoor, free. Extended-stay discounts avail. $10 charge for infants under 2. AE, DISC, MC, V.

RESTAURANTS 🍴

Lance's Seafood Bar & Market

MP 14 US 158 Bypass; tel 919/441-7501. **Seafood.** A pink exterior leads to a dining room with antelope and deer heads, beer signs, fish, and nautical items adorning the walls. Dinner entrees include grilled, fried, and broiled seafood items. Prime rib is also available. **FYI:** Reservations not accepted. **Open:** Peak (Mem Day–Labor Day) daily noon–11pm. **Prices:** Main courses $10–$19. AE, MC, V.

Owens' Restaurant

MP 16½ US 158; tel 919/441-7309. **Seafood.** The Owens family has owned and operated this comfortable eatery for over 40 years. An aura of times past still prevails, with nautical antiques and friendly service throughout. Hearty menu options include coconut shrimp (for starters) and innovative entrees such as spicy pecan pork tenderloin, Low Country shrimp and grits, and salmon glazed with honey and apple butter. **FYI:** Reservations not accepted. Children's

menu. **Open:** Peak (June–Aug) daily 5–10pm. Closed Jan–Mar 15. **Prices:** Main courses $14–$24. AE, DISC, MC, V. 🍴 👪 🔥

★ The Thai Room

MP 8.5 US 158; tel 919/441-1180. **Thai.** A pleasant switch from the standard seafood fare of the Outer Banks, the Thai Room features decor representative of the owner's Thailand roots. The staff are also Thai and will be glad to help the diner sort out the options. Specialties include beef curry and spicy Thai noodles. All menu items are "rated" for the level of spiciness. **FYI:** Reservations accepted. **Open:** Lunch daily 11:30am–2:30pm; dinner daily 5pm–close. Closed Jan–Feb. **Prices:** Main courses $6–$13. DISC, MC, V.

ATTRACTION 🏛

Jockey's Ridge State Park

West Carolista Dr off US 158; tel 919/441-7132. The tallest natural sand dune system on the eastern seaboard. According to legend, "Jockey's Ridge" refers to the early inhabitants' practice of racing wild ponies along the base of the dunes. Although the environment here often seems more like the Sahara than North Carolina, the area is far from desolate. Rabbits, foxes, lizards, and many varieties of birds populate the area, especially at night, and salt marshes and shrub forests dot the miles of shifting sand.

The park is popular with hang gliders, who use the tall dunes and sharp winds to their advantage in much the same way that the Wright brothers did. A hike to the top of the tallest dune gives a spectacular view of the coast. Picnicking facilities and a museum are also available. **Open:** Nov–Feb, daily 8am–6pm; Mar and Oct, daily 8am–7pm; Apr–May, and Sept, daily 8am–8pm; June–Aug, daily 8am–9pm. Closed Dec 25. **Free**

New Bern

The state's first capital and its second-oldest town, New Bern was settled around 1710 by Palatine Germans and Swiss. Home to 18th-century restored Tryon Palace and surrounding buildings. **Information:** New Bern Area Chamber of Commerce, 233 Middle St, PO Drawer C, New Bern, 28563 (tel 919/637-3111).

HOTELS 🏨

⊨⊨⊨ Comfort Suites and Marina

218 E Front St, 28560; tel 919/636-0022 or toll free 800/638-7322; fax 919/636-0051. New hotel with traditional-looking exterior and decor that fits in with the surrounding historic district. Spacious and finely furnished lobby features a fireplace. **Rooms:** 100 stes. CI 2pm/CO noon. Nonsmoking rms avail. Some suites have balconies overlooking milewide Neuse River. **Amenities:** 📺 🔥 🖥 A/C, cable TV w/movies, refrig, dataport. Some units w/terraces, some w/whirlpools.

Services: ✕ ⊠ ⊐ Complimentary evening beverages. **Facilities:** ⌂ ⊟ 50 ⅙ Beautifully landscaped waterfront courtyard. Golf privileges available. **Rates (CP):** $62–$125 ste. Extra person $7. Children under age 17 stay free. Parking: Outdoor, free. AE, CB, DC, DISC, MC, V.

≣≣ Days Inn

925 Broad St, 28560; tel 919/636-0150 or toll free 800/ 329-7466. Standard chain motel located on outskirts of the historic district. **Rooms:** 110 rms. CI 3pm/CO noon. Nonsmoking rms avail. **Amenities:** ⊟ ⊡ A/C, cable TV. Some units w/terraces. **Services:** ⊠ ⊐ **Facilities:** ⌂ 300 ⅙ 1 restaurant, 1 bar. **Rates (CP):** Peak (June–Sept) $39–$56 S; $42–$61 D. Extra person $5. Lower rates off-season. Parking: Outdoor, free. AE, DC, DISC, MC, V.

≣≣≣ Hampton Inn

200 Hotel Dr, 28562; tel 919/637-2111 or toll free 800/ 448-8288; fax 919/637-2000. Relatively new property, located near shopping, dining, and the historic district. Good choice for business travelers. **Rooms:** 101 rms. Executive level. CI 3pm/CO noon. Nonsmoking rms avail. **Amenities:** ⊟ ⊡ A/C, cable TV w/movies, dataport. **Services:** ⊠ ⊐ **Facilities:** ⌂ ⊟ 60 ⅙ Whirlpool. **Rates (CP):** $51–$56 S; $58–$63 D. Parking: Outdoor, free. AE, CB, DC, DISC, MC, V.

≣≣≣ Ramada Inn Waterfront & Marina

101 Howell Rd, 28562; tel 919/636-3637 or toll free 800/2-RAMADA; fax 919/637-5028. Well-kept, four-story property features a sun deck and many amenities. **Rooms:** 116 rms and stes. CI 2pm/CO noon. Nonsmoking rms avail. Modern rooms feature pine furnishings and views of either the Neuse or Trent Rivers. **Amenities:** ⊟ ⊡ A/C, cable TV w/movies, dataport. Some units w/whirlpools. Suites have refrigerator and whirlpool. **Services:** ✕ ⊠ **Facilities:** ⌂ ⊰ 150 ⅙ 1 restaurant, 1 bar. Health club privileges. **Rates:** $60–$80 S or D; $100 ste. Extra person $5. Children under age 18 stay free. Parking: Outdoor, free. AE, CB, DC, DISC, MC, V.

≣≣≣ Sheraton Hotel & Marina

1 Bicentennial Park, PO Box 130, 28560; tel 919/638-3585 or toll free 800/326-3745. This Sheraton advertises New Bern's best view with one side of the hotel facing the Trent River and the other offering a stunning panorama of the town's historic storefronts and steeples. The newer of the two buildings was designed with a country-inn theme. It has gracious patios and sitting areas. The other has a much more modern theme. **Rooms:** 172 rms and stes. Executive level. CI 2pm/CO noon. Nonsmoking rms avail. **Amenities:** ⊟ ⊡ A/C, cable TV, dataport. Some units w/terraces, some w/whirlpools. **Services:** ✕ ⊠ ⊐ Babysitting. **Facilities:** ⌂ ⊰ ⊟ 200 ⅙ 2 restaurants, 2 bars (1 w/entertainment). **Rates:** Peak (Apr–Oct) $90–$110 S or D; $125–$250 ste. Extra person $10. Children under age 18 stay free. Lower rates off-season. MAP rates avail. Parking: Outdoor, free. Golf packages avail. AE, CB, DC, DISC, MC, V.

INN

≣≣≣ Harmony House Inn

215 Pollock St, 28560; tel 919/636-3810 or toll free 800/ 636-3110. A beautiful, Southern house, this bed-and-breakfast inn has an elegant parlor and a relaxing front porch with rocking chairs. **Rooms:** 10 rms and stes. CI 3pm/CO 11am. No smoking. Rooms are individually decorated with antiques and reproductions. **Amenities:** ⊟ ⊡ A/C, cable TV. Complimentary evening beverages provided. **Services:** ⊠ Babysitting, wine/sherry served. **Facilities:** Guest lounge. **Rates (BB):** $85–$95 D. Extra person $20. Children under age 10 stay free. Higher rates for special events/hols. Parking: Outdoor, free. AE, MC, V.

RESTAURANTS 🍴

✹ The Chelsea

335 Middle St; tel 919/637-5469. At Broad St. **Eclectic.** The building that now houses the Chelsea was built in 1920 to be used as a drug store by Caleb Bradham, whose concoction (originally known as "Brad's drink") became popular worldwide as Pepsi-Cola. The Chelsea serves sandwiches all day, while its dinner menu adds seafood, poultry, beef, pasta, and vegetarian entrees. **FYI:** Reservations not accepted. **Open:** Mon–Thurs 11am–9pm, Fri–Sat 11am–10pm, Sun 9am–2pm. **Prices:** Main courses $10–$14. DISC, MC, V. ▆ ⅙

The Harvey Mansion

221 Tryon Palace Dr; tel 919/638-3205. **Continental.** Located in a three-story building constructed in the 1790s by John Harvey. The structure served many different purposes over the years—private home, boarding house, military academy and college—before falling into severe disrepair prior to its renovation and opening as a restaurant in 1979. Chef Beat Zuttle creates classic entrees (scallops à la menthe, shrimp Provençal) as well as unique dishes with a Southern twist such as entrecôte de boeuf Dixie (New York strip grilled in barbecue sauce and garnished with baked beans). Food is either poached, grilled, or sautéed for maximum flavor and minimum fat. **FYI:** Reservations recommended. Dress code. **Open:** Lunch Mon–Sat 11:45am–2:30pm; dinner daily 5:30–10pm; brunch Sun 10am–2pm. **Prices:** Main courses $12–$25. AE, DC, DISC, MC, V. ♥ ▆ ▣

♣ Henderson House

216 Pollock St; tel 919/637-4784. **Continental.** Elegant dining in a restored historic home, with candlelight atmosphere and original artwork on display for guests to enjoy. Specialties include pheasant sesame, lobster au whiskey, and veal chop chanterelles. There's also a large dessert menu for those with a sweet tooth. **FYI:** Reservations recommended. Dress code. No smoking. **Open:** Lunch Wed–Sat 11:30am–2pm; dinner Wed–Sat 6–9pm. **Prices:** Main courses $16–$27. AE, MC, V. ♥ ▆

Scalzo's

415 Broad St; tel 919/633-9898. **Italian.** A traditional trattoria, with checked tablecloths and a large wall mural. Diners can choose from 8 pastas and 19 sauces including Alfredo, shrimp, meat sauce, and carbonara. Specialties include veal parmigiana, veal marsala, and chicken cacciatore. **FYI:** Reservations recommended. Children's menu. **Open:** Mon–Sat 5–10pm. **Prices:** Main courses $10–$18. AE, MC, V. ● &

ATTRACTION 🏛

Tyron Palace Historic Sites and Gardens

610 Pollock St; tel 919/514-4900. Built in 1767–1770 as residence for the royal governor, the palace became North Carolina's first state capitol in 1777. In recent years, Tryon Palace has been authentically restored and turned into a 48-room museum. The handsome grounds and gardens surrounding Tryon Palace are also designed in grand 18th-century style. Two highlights of the 13-acre complex are the **John Wright Stanly House** (1780), a sophisticated late-Georgian-style mansion with town-house gardens, and the **Stevenson House** (1805), built by a merchant and noted for its rare Federal antiques. On the grounds, craftspeople demonstrate 18th-century home arts such as cooking, weaving, and blacksmithing. Historical dramas supplement the regular guided tours during the summer months. Special events, including candlelight tours of the complex, are held at Christmas and other seasons. **Open:** Mon–Sat 9am–4pm, Sun 1–4pm. Closed some hols. $$$$

Ocean Isle Beach

One of the state's tropical, quiet, southernmost islands, located between Cape Fear River and the Atlantic.

HOTEL 🏨

🟰🟰🟰 Winds Clarion Carriage House Inn

310 E 1st St, 28469; tel 910/579-6275 or toll free 800/334-3581; fax 910/579-2884. Relaxing oceanfront miniresort hidden among private homes that dot the quiet shoreline. Beautiful tropical plants and palm trees surround the hotel. **Rooms:** 73 rms and stes; 5 cottages/villas. CI 4pm/CO 11am. Nonsmoking rms avail. One-, two-, and three-bedroom suites have kitchen facilities. **Amenities:** 🟥 ⚬ 🗓 A/C, cable TV, refrig. All units w/terraces, 1 w/whirlpool. **Services:** 🔺 🍽 Babysitting. **Facilities:** 🔥 🚴 ⛰ 🏐 🏊 & 1 beach (ocean), volleyball, lawn games, sauna, whirlpool, washer/dryer. Pool covered in winter. **Rates (CP):** Peak (June–Sept 20) $119–$135 S or D; $138–$337 ste; $389–$439 cottage/villa. Extra person $15. Children under age 18 stay free. Lower rates off-season. Parking: Outdoor, free. Golf packages avail. AE, CB, DC, DISC, MC, V.

MOTELS

🟰 Cooke's Inn Motel

12 Causeway, 28469; tel 910/579-9001. Comfortable accommodations one block from the beach and close to water slides, miniature golf, and boutique shopping. **Rooms:** 37 rms. CI 1pm/CO 11am. Nonsmoking rms avail. **Amenities:** 🟥 A/C, cable TV, refrig. **Facilities:** 🔥 & Small swimming pool. **Rates:** Peak (June–Aug) $75 S or D. Children under age 18 stay free. Lower rates off-season. Parking: Outdoor, free. DISC, MC, V.

🟰🟰 Ocean Isle Motel

35 W 1st St, 28469; tel 910/579-0750 or toll free 800/352-5988. Simple yet attractive oceanfront motel. **Rooms:** 50 rms. CI 3pm/CO 11am. Nonsmoking rms avail. **Amenities:** 🟥 ⚬ A/C, cable TV, refrig. Some units w/terraces,. **Services:** 🍽 **Facilities:** 🔥 🏊 & 1 beach (ocean), whirlpool. Heated indoor pool. **Rates (CP):** Peak (May 12–Sept 10) $94–$114 S or D. Lower rates off-season. Parking: Outdoor, free. Max of five people allowed per room. Seventh night free during high season. MC, V.

Ocracoke

This island has shown up on maps as far back as the late 16th century, when Sir Walter Raleigh's Roanoke Island party landed here. It is rumored to have been the last headquarters of Edward Teach—the infamous Blackbeard—and tales persist that the famous pirate's treasure is stashed nearby (though none has ever been found). At one time as many as a thousand wild ponies roamed the dunes here; small remnants of the herd (whose origin is a mystery) now live on a range seven miles north of Ocracoke Village. The village is the site of the oldest lighthouse (built circa 1823) still operating in North Carolina.

MOTELS 🏨

🟰🟰🟰 Anchorage Inn

NC 12, PO Box 130, 27960; tel 919/928-1581. Modest and relaxing, with breathtaking views of the entire harbor encompassing the lighthouses, the marina, and the Coast Guard Station. **Rooms:** 41 rms and effic. CI 2pm/CO 11am. Nonsmoking rms avail. Rooms are attractive and simply furnished. Six waterfront efficiencies available. **Amenities:** 🟥 ⚬ 🍴 A/C, cable TV w/movies. **Services:** 🔺 🍽 **Facilities:** 🔥 & **Rates (CP):** Peak (Mem Day–Labor Day) $79–$99 S or D; $99 effic. Extra person $10. Children under age 18 stay free. Min stay special events. Lower rates off-season. Parking: Outdoor, free. Closed 3 weeks in Jan. AE, DISC, MC, V.

🟰🟰 The Boyette House

NC 12, PO Box 39, 27960; tel 919/928-4261. Resembling a quiet country inn, this motel is mesmerizing and relaxing. Hammocks are stretched between aged cedar trees and a multilevel deck. **Rooms:** 24 rms and stes. CI 2pm/CO 11am.

Nonsmoking rms avail. Attractively furnished rooms with simple decor. Two suites have wicker rockers and beautiful views on the third floor. **Amenities:** 🛍 🍸 A/C, cable TV w/movies. Some units w/terraces, some w/whirlpools. Some rooms have refrigerator, microwave, and coffeemaker. **Services:** ⬜ 🛏 Babysitting. **Facilities:** ⅙ **Rates:** Peak (Mem Day–Labor Day) $55–$90 S or D; $140 ste. Extra person $5. Children under age 2 stay free. Lower rates off-season. Parking: Outdoor, free. Closed Jan, Feb. AE, DISC, MC, V.

UNRATED **Harborside Motel**

NC 12, PO Box 116, 27960; tel 919/928-3111. Simple, seaside motel with blue clapboard siding and white trim. Located across the street from marina and boardwalk in heart of the village. **Rooms:** 18 rms and effic. CI 2pm/CO 11am. Nonsmoking rms avail. **Amenities:** 🛍 A/C, cable TV, refrig. **Services:** 🛏 **Facilities:** 🚲 **Rates (CP):** Peak (May 19–Aug) $70 S or D; $80 effic. Extra person $7. Children under age 5 stay free. Lower rates off-season. Parking: Outdoor, free. Efficiencies require a six-night minimum stay. DISC, MC, V.

INN

🏨 **Island Inn**

NC 12, PO Box 9, Rte 12, 27960; tel 919/928-4351. A historic inn built in 1901. Some rooms are in a modern wing. **Rooms:** 35 rms; 4 cottages/villas. CI 1pm/CO 11am. Nonsmoking rms avail. Rooms in inn are mostly furnished with antiques, but rooms in new addition have a more modern decor. Some rooms have harbor views. **Amenities:** A/C, cable TV. No phone. Some units w/terraces. Rooms in modern wing have telephones. **Services:** ⬜ 🛏 🍽 **Facilities:** 🚲 🔟 1 restaurant (*see* "Restaurants" below), guest lounge. No elevator. **Rates:** Peak (Mem Day–Labor Day) $35–$95 S or D; $85 cottage/villa. Extra person $5. Children under age 7 stay free. Min stay peak. Lower rates off-season. Higher rates for special events/hols. Parking: Outdoor, free. One-week minimum stay for cottages during peak season ($525–$650 per week). Two-night minimum for rooms and suites on weekends, holidays, and during peak season. DISC, MC, V.

LODGE

🏨 **Black Beard's Lodge**

NC 12, PO Box 298, 27960; tel 919/928-3421 or toll free 800/892-5314. From NC 12, turn right at Medical Clinic sign, then 2 blocks. A rustic lodge built in 1936 and set in a quiet, residential area, it is just a short walk to the village shops and boardwalks. **Rooms:** 37 rms and effic. CI 2pm/CO 11am. Nonsmoking rms avail. Some rooms have been renovated, but most are rustic, yet comfortable and clean. **Amenities:** 🛍 🍸 A/C, cable TV. **Services:** 🛏 **Facilities:** 🚲 Games rm. The Back Porch Restaurant is across the street. **Rates:** Peak (June 15–Labor Day) $40–$90 S or D; $65–$100 effic. Extra person $5. Children under age 2 stay

free. Lower rates off-season. Parking: Outdoor, free. Efficiency apartments avail (three-day minimum stay). Closed Nov–Mar. DISC, MC, V.

RESTAURANTS 🍽

Back Porch Restaurant

NC 12; tel 919/928-6401. **Seafood.** Located in a peaceful residential setting, this eatery offers a relaxing atmosphere and fine Southern dining. The menu includes a variety of creatively prepared seafood entrees (filet of fish Nipon, for example); non-seafood dishes include Cuban-style casserole made with black beans and Monterey Jack cheese. **FYI:** Reservations not accepted. Beer and wine only. **Open:** Daily 5–9:30pm. Closed Oct 15–Apr 15. **Prices:** Main courses $13–$18. MC, V. 🍴 🖼 📷 ⅙

Cafe Atlantic

NC 12; tel 919/928-4861. **Cafe/Seafood.** A bright and airy place with unique geometric ceilings, walls, and windows. The menu is as fresh as the decor, offering seafood (grilled, baked, and fried) as well as pasta and salad. **FYI:** Reservations accepted. Children's menu. Beer and wine only. **Open:** Lunch daily 11am–3:30pm; dinner daily 5:30–9:30pm. Closed Dec–Apr. **Prices:** Main courses $9–$15. AE, DISC, MC, V. ❤ 🖼 ⅙

Dining Room

In Island Inn, 100 Lighthouse Rd; tel 919/928-7821. **Eclectic.** The laid-back dining area—with white washed walls and an enclosed porch—lends this eatery a bright and airy feel. The lunch menu features salads, sandwiches, and a couple of hot seafood platters; dinner brings sautéed crabmeat, clam chowder, and an enormous seafood platter as well as beef, chicken, and pasta. **FYI:** Reservations not accepted. Children's menu. Beer and wine only. **Open:** Peak (Mem Day–Labor Day) breakfast daily 7–11am; lunch daily 11am–2pm; dinner daily 5–9pm. Closed Thanksgiving–Feb 15. **Prices:** Main courses $8–$14. DISC, MC, V. 🍷 📷

⭐ **Howard's Pub and Raw Bar**

NC 12; tel 919/928-4441. **Pub.** A laid-back place decorated with athletic pennants, nautical paraphernalia, and beer signs. Diners may eat inside or on the screened-in porch. The regular menu offers burgers, subs, pizzas, and sandwiches, while the raw bar serves steamed shrimp, oysters, clams, and mussels. **FYI:** Reservations not accepted. Children's menu. Beer and wine only. **Open:** Daily 11am–2am. **Prices:** Main courses $6–$9. DISC, MC, V. ⅙

Outer Banks Islands

See Duck, Elizabeth City, Hatteras, Kill Devil Hills, Kitty Hawk, Manteo, Nags Head, Ocracoke

Pilot Mountain

Named for a 1,400-foot quartzite formation rising out of the landscape.

MOTEL 🏨

≣≣ Holiday Inn Express

US 52 and NC 268, PO Box 668, 27041; tel 910/368-2237 or toll free 800/HOLIDAY; fax 910/368-1212. With a well-kept but spartan exterior, this motel is surprisingly nice from the inside. New carpeting, linens, and furniture make it a popular place for vacationers and overnight travelers alike. **Rooms:** 68 rms. CI noon/CO 11am. Nonsmoking rms avail. Rooms are basic, and offer mountain views. **Amenities:** 🛢 🧖 A/C, cable TV. **Services:** 🛎 🍷 **Facilities:** 🏋 💺 ₤ **Rates (CP):** Peak (Apr; Sept) $47–$55 S; $52–$57 D. Extra person $5. Children under age 12 stay free. Lower rates off-season. Parking: Outdoor, free. AE, DC, DISC, MC, V.

Pinehurst

Known to many as one of the golfing capitals of the world, Pinehurst features more than three dozen courses in the immediate area. The winter resort's prestigious country club will host the 1999 US Open golf championships.

HOTEL 🏨

≣≣≣ Holly Inn

Cherokee Rd, Box 2300, 28374; tel 910/295-2300 or toll free 800/682-6901; fax 910/295-0988. First opened in 1895, this picture-perfect inn is adjacent to Frederick Law Olmsted's carefully designed, charming village. **Rooms:** 76 rms and stes. CI 3pm/CO noon. **Amenities:** 🛢 🧖 A/C, cable TV. **Services:** 🗝 🛎 🍷 Babysitting. **Facilities:** 🏋 🚲 1 restaurant (bkfst and dinner only; see "Restaurants" below), 1 bar (w/entertainment). **Rates (BB):** Peak (Mar–mid-June/Sept–mid-Nov) $119–$144 S; $119–$139 D; $169 ste. Extra person $10. Children under age 10 stay free. Lower rates off-season. Parking: Outdoor, free. Golf packages avail. AE, CB, DC, MC, V.

INNS

≣≣≣ Magnolia Inn

65 Magnolia Rd, 28374; tel 910/295-6900 or toll free 800/526-5562; fax 910/215-0858. Lovely, restored Victorian inn, originally built in 1896, offers terrific views of the village shopping district. **Rooms:** 12 rms; 2 cottages/villas. CI 3pm/CO noon. No smoking. Spacious and extremely comfortable rooms are decorated with period antiques. Housekeeping is above average. **Amenities:** 🧖 A/C, cable TV. No phone. Some units w/fireplaces. **Services:** 🛎 🍷 Babysitting. **Facilities:** 🏋 💺 1 restaurant (see "Restaurants" below), 1 bar, guest lounge w/TV. **Rates (MAP):** $80 S; $160 D. Children under age 12 stay free. Min stay wknds and special events. AP and MAP rates avail. Parking: Outdoor, free. Rates increase during major golf tournaments. Golf packages avail. AE, MC, V.

≣≣≣ Manor Inn

Community Rd, 28374; tel 910/295-8472 or toll free 800/ITS-GOLF; fax 910/295-6546. 5,000 acres. Open since the 1920s, this inn welcomes its guests to a beautiful lobby decorated with wicker furniture and floral accents. Guests may relax in an adjoining sunroom. **Rooms:** 46 rms and stes. CI 4pm/CO noon. Nonsmoking rms avail. **Amenities:** 🛢 🧖 A/C, cable TV w/movies, dataport. Some units w/terraces. Refrigerators available. **Services:** 🚐 🛎 Masseur, children's program, afternoon tea served. **Facilities:** 1 restaurant (dinner only), 1 bar, guest lounge w/TV. Guests have privileges at resort hotel. **Rates (MAP):** Peak (Mar–May) $344 D; $344 ste. Extra person $38. Children under age 6 stay free. Min stay peak. Lower rates off-season. Higher rates for special events/hols. Parking: Outdoor, free. Golf and tennis packages avail. AE, DC, DISC, MC, V.

≣≣≣ Pine Crest Inn

200 Pine Crest Lane, 28374; tel 910/295-6121. This Inn has a rock exterior with a cozy front porch and garden terrace and is walking distance from a New England–style shopping village. **Rooms:** 40 rms. CI 2pm/CO noon. Rooms are handsomely furnished. **Amenities:** 🛢 🧖 A/C, cable TV. **Services:** 🛎 **Facilities:** 1 restaurant (bkfst and dinner only; see "Restaurants" below), 1 bar, guest lounge w/TV. **Rates (MAP):** Peak (Mar 23–May 11/Sept 28–Nov 11) $76–$106 S; $112–$150 D. Extra person $51. Children under age 12 stay free. Min stay peak. Lower rates off-season. Higher rates for special events/hols. Parking: Outdoor, free. AE, DC, DISC, MC, V.

RESORT

≣≣≣≣ Pinehurst Resort and Country Club

Carolina Vista, PO Box 4000, 28374; tel 910/295-6811 or toll free 800/487-4653; fax 910/295-8503. On NC 2. The meticulously polished, copper roofs accentuate the bright spacious lobby, and its peaceful, wraparound porch, amply supplied with rocking chairs, provides a wonderful view of the beautiful grounds. **Rooms:** 299 rms and stes; 40 cottages/villas. CI 4pm/CO noon. Nonsmoking rms avail. **Amenities:** 🛢 🧖 A/C, cable TV w/movies, dataport, in-rm safe. Some units w/minibars, some w/terraces. **Services:** ✗ 🆅🅿 🚐 🛎 🍷 Social director, masseur, children's program, babysitting. Secretarial services. **Facilities:** 🏋 ⛳ 📶 ₁₂₆ 🎾₂₀ 🏊₈ 🏌 🎳 💺 ₤ 2 restaurants (see "Restaurants" below), 2 bars (1 w/entertainment), 1 beach (lake shore), lifeguard, lawn games. Renowned golf course. **Rates (MAP):** Peak (Mar–May/Sept–mid-Nov) $157 S or D; $172 ste; $157 cottage/villa. Extra person $100. Children under age 18 stay free. Min stay peak. Lower rates off-season. Parking: Outdoor, free. AE, CB, DC, DISC, MC, V.

RESTAURANTS 🍽

♥ Carolina Dining Room

In Pinehurst Resort and Country Club, Carolina Vista; tel 910/295-6811. **American.** A formal, elegant dining room with crystal chandeliers and lit candles at every table. Professional waitstaff serve classic American specialties like double Smithfield pork chop, tangy chicken roulade, and pan-fried Dover sole. **FYI:** Reservations recommended. Piano. Jacket required. **Open:** Breakfast daily 6:30–10am; lunch daily noon–2pm; dinner daily 6:30–9pm. **Prices:** Main courses $21–$30. AE, DC, MC, V. ♥ VP �

Greenhouse Restaurant

905 Linden Rd; tel 910/295-1761. **Cafe.** A light and airy place with blond bentwood chairs and lots of hanging plants. The menu has a garden theme with each entree named after a plant or flower, such as the Morning Glory (omelette and crepes) and the Snap Dragon (roast beef sandwich with melted Swiss cheese). The soups are memorable, as are the desserts, such as the Greenhouse mud pie and strawberry shortcake. **FYI:** Reservations not accepted. **Open:** Daily 11:30am–3pm. **Prices:** Lunch main courses $6–$7. MC, V. �

✹ Magnolia Inn Restaurant

65 Magnolia Rd; tel 910/295-6900. **Neo-European.** Located in a beautifully restored Victorian house that is now used as a B&B. The pink-and-white dining room is decorated with period antiques and original artwork. "Neo-European" menu specialties include tenderloin of pork, veal medallion, and roast quail. **FYI:** Reservations recommended. **Open:** Peak (Sept–Nov/Mar–May) breakfast Mon–Sat 7–9am; lunch Mon–Sat 11:30am–2pm; dinner daily 6–9:30pm; brunch Sun 7–11am. **Prices:** Main courses $16–$28. AE, MC, V. ♥ ▮ ⊜

Pinehurst Playhouse Restaurant & Yogurt

100 West Village Green; tel 910/295-8873. **Cafe.** A casual place located within a renovated theater building. Sandwiches have "stage" names such as the Hamlet (sliced ham and Swiss) or the Camelot (Italian marinated chicken breast). Yogurt is offered throughout the day. **FYI:** Reservations not accepted. Beer and wine only. No smoking. **Open:** Mon–Fri 9am–3pm. **Prices:** Lunch main courses $5–$6. No CC. ⊜ �

Restaurant

In Pine Crest Inn, Dogwood Rd; tel 910/295-6121. **American.** Elegant dining in a cozy, Colonial American setting. Traditional specialties include prime rib au jus, ham steak with pineapple sauce, and stuffed pork chops. All pastries are homemade. **FYI:** Reservations recommended. Dress code. **Open:** Peak (Mar 23–May 11/Sept 28–Nov 11) daily 7–9pm. **Prices:** Main courses $12–$22. AE, CB, DC, DISC, MC, V. ▮

♥ Restaurant

In Holly Inn, Cherokee Rd; tel 910/295-2300. **American.** Elegant dining in a historic inn decorated with ornate oak paneling and handcrafted accents. The menu focuses on hearty yet creative dishes: roast duck, cornbread-crusted Carolina mountain trout, and meat loaf terrine made of ground beef, pork, and veal served with a port-wine sauce. **FYI:** Reservations recommended. Piano. Children's menu. Dress code. **Open:** Breakfast Mon–Fri 6–10am, Sat–Sun 6–11am; dinner daily 6:30–10pm. **Prices:** Main courses $13–$22. AE, CB, DC, MC, V. ♥ ▮

ATTRACTION 🏛

World Golf Hall of Fame

PGA Blvd; tel 919/295-6651. Even nongolfers will be impressed by the white-columned porticoes and sparkling fountains of the Entrance Pavilion, which overlooks Pinehurst Country Club's Number Two course. The north and south wings tell the story of the development of golf and people associated with it. Hundreds of golf items are displayed, including early golf balls made of tanned animal hides stuffed with leather. The Ryder Cup Room, Old Clubmakers Shop, and new Walter Hagen exhibit offer insights into the game. There's also a theater (the only one in the world devoted exclusively to golf) featuring films of major tournaments as well as instructional films. The actual Hall of Fame, with bronzes of the inductees, is in the rear of the building. **Open:** Mar–Nov, daily 9am–5pm. Closed some hols. $

Pittsboro

Established in 1778, it is the Chatham County seat. Named for William Pitt, Earl of Chatham, a defender of American rights in the British Parliament.

INN 🏨

⯆⯆⯆⯆ Fearrington House Inn

2000 Fearrington Village Center, 27312; tel 919/542-2121; fax 919/542-4202. 12 acres. An entire village has been built around this 200-year-old farm. The original homestead has been turned into a restaurant; adjacent inn rooms are clustered around courtyards and parks. The pastoral ambience has been preserved by serene country gardens, winding paths, and hedge sculptures. **Rooms:** 24 rms and stes. CI 3pm/CO noon. No smoking. Rooms and suites are individually decorated with English pine antiques and original artwork. **Amenities:** 🛁 🅰 ♥ A/C, cable TV w/movies, dataport. Some units w/fireplaces. Rooms have marble vanities, heated towel racks, and individual stereo systems. **Services:** ◐ ◪ ⌂ Masseur, babysitting, afternoon tea served. Secretarial services available. **Facilities:** ◻ ⬜ � 2 restaurants (see "Restaurants" below), 1 bar, lawn games, whirlpool, playground, guest lounge. Fearrington Village offers several shops, including a bookstore, a gallery and gift shops. **Rates (BB):** $150 D w/shared bath; $200–$250 ste. Extra person $10. Min stay special events. Higher rates for special events/hols. Parking: Outdoor, free. MC, V.

RESTAURANTS

The Market Cafe at Fearrington
2000 Fearrington Village Center; tel 919/542-5505. **Cafe.** Positioned on the second floor of Fearrington Village Market with a serene view of the rolling farmland and picturesque gardens and shops, the Cafe is bright and airy and the food is fresh and healthy. Salads with unique twists are a favorite, and entrees include burgers, shrimp kabobs, and vegetarian chili. **FYI:** Reservations accepted. Children's menu. Beer and wine only. No smoking. **Open:** Lunch Mon–Fri 11am–3pm; dinner Wed–Fri 5:30–8:30pm; brunch Sat–Sun 9am–3pm. **Prices:** Main courses $10–$17. AE, MC, V. ♥ ⛰

♥ Restaurant
In Fearrington House Inn, 2000 Fearrington Village Center; tel 919/542-2121. **New American.** Housed in a structure built in 1927 and fully restored in 1980, this spot offers the ultimate in fine dining. Not only is the exterior exceptionally beautiful; the country furnishings make the interior a sight to behold. The menu changes monthly. Pecan-crusted pork tenderloin, yellowfin tuna wrapped in rice paper, and grilled beef tenderloin on a parmesan disk are a sample of some of the wonderful dishes. Full vegetarian menu also available. **FYI:** Reservations recommended. Jacket required. Beer and wine only. No smoking. **Open:** Dinner Tues–Sat 6–9pm, Sun 6–8pm; brunch Sun noon–2pm. **Prices:** Prix fixe $48. AE, MC, V. ♥ ▮ ⛱

Raleigh

See also Chapel Hill, Durham

Raleigh is a governmental, cultural, and industrial center and, along with Chapel Hill and Durham, it is part of North Carolina's Research Triangle complex. Selected as the state capital in 1788 and incorporated in 1792, the city is the birthplace (in 1808) of President Andrew Johnson. Home of the nation's first state symphony and museum of art, and site of a number of colleges, including North Carolina State University. **Information:** Greater Raleigh Convention & Visitors Bureau, 225 Hillsborough St, #400, PO Box 1879, Raleigh, 27602 (tel 919/834-5900).

PUBLIC TRANSPORTATION
Raleigh's **Capital Area Transit (CAT)** (tel 919/828-7228) provides bus service. Fares are 50¢ (25¢ for seniors); children under age 4 ride free. The **Trolley Through Raleigh** (tel 833-5701) makes six stops around the city, including the Capital Area Visitor Center and City Market, Mon–Fri 10am–2pm. Fare is 10¢.

HOTELS

The Brownestone Hotel
1707 Hillsborough St, 27605; tel 919/828-0811 or toll free 800/331-7919 in NC; fax 919/834-0904. An example of simple elegance, this property is convenient to NC State University and downtown. **Rooms:** 210 rms. Executive level. CI 3pm/CO 1pm. Nonsmoking rms avail. **Amenities:** 📺 ⌚ A/C, cable TV w/movies. Some units w/minibars, all w/terraces. **Services:** ✕ 🚐 📠 🛎 Twice-daily maid svce, babysitting. **Facilities:** 🏊 🛎 1000 🖥 🔌 1 restaurant (bkfst and lunch only), 1 bar (w/entertainment). Complimentary use of YMCA next door. **Rates:** $73 S; $80 D. Extra person $4. Children under age 10 stay free. Min stay special events. Parking: Outdoor, free. AE, CB, DC, DISC, MC, V.

Courtyard by Marriott
1041 Wake Towne Dr, 27609; tel 919/821-3400 or toll free 800/321-2211. Wake Forest Rd exit off I-440. Very quaint, quiet, and peaceful four-story property. **Rooms:** 153 rms and stes. CI 3pm/CO noon. Nonsmoking rms avail. **Amenities:** 📺 ⌚ 🔌 A/C, cable TV w/movies, dataport, voice mail. Some units w/terraces. Complimentary coffee in rooms. Suites have refrigerators. **Services:** 📠 🛎 Babysitting. **Facilities:** 🏊 🛎 49 🖥 🔌 1 restaurant (bkfst only), 1 bar, whirlpool, washer/dryer. Gazebo. **Rates:** $74 S; $84 D; $84–$94 ste. Extra person $10. Children under age 18 stay free. Parking: Outdoor, free. AE, CB, DC, DISC, JCB, MC, V.

Courtyard by Marriott Airport
2001 Hospitality Court, 27560; tel 919/467-9444 or toll free 800/321-2211; fax 919/467-9322. Exit 284 off I-40. This standard Courtyard is conveniently located near Raleigh-Durham Airport. **Rooms:** 152 rms and stes. CI 3pm/CO 11am. Nonsmoking rms avail. **Amenities:** 📺 ⌚ 🔌 A/C, cable TV w/movies, dataport, voice mail. Some units w/terraces. **Services:** ✕ 🚐 📠 🛎 Babysitting. **Facilities:** 🏊 🛎 30 🔌 1 restaurant, 1 bar, whirlpool, washer/dryer. **Rates:** $84 S; $94 D; $98–$108 ste. Children under age 16 stay free. Parking: Outdoor, free. AE, DC, DISC, MC, V.

Crabtree Summit Hotel
3908 Arrow Dr, 27609; tel 919/782-6868 or toll free 800/521-7521. Off US 70. Ornate and stately mid-rise property. **Rooms:** 88 rms and stes. CI 1pm/CO 11am. Nonsmoking rms avail. **Amenities:** 📺 ⌚ 🔌 A/C, cable TV w/movies, refrig. 1 unit w/fireplace, some w/whirlpools. All units have microwaves. **Services:** VP 🚐 📠 🛎 Babysitting. Free transportation to points around Raleigh. **Facilities:** 🏊 20 🔌 Use of nearby health club for nominal fee. **Rates (BB):** $91–$96 S or D; $108–$135 ste. Extra person $10. Children under age 12 stay free. Min stay special events. Parking: Outdoor, free. AE, CB, DC, DISC, JCB, MC, V.

Embassy Suites Hotel Raleigh
4700 Creedmoor Rd, 27612; tel 919/881-0000 or toll free 800/EMBASSY; fax 919/782-7225. Near Crabtree Valley Mall. Beautiful nine-story hotel. Elegant, sunlit courtyard houses indoor pool and multitiered restaurant/lounge. **Rooms:** 225 stes. Executive level. CI 3pm/CO noon. Nonsmoking rms avail. Suites overlook courtyard. **Amenities:** 📺 ⌚ 🔌 🍴 A/C, cable TV w/movies, refrig, dataport, voice mail.

Some units w/minibars, some w/whirlpools. Microwaves available upon request. **Services:** ✕ VP 🚐 🛌 🛎 Babysitting. Complimentary evening beverage. **Facilities:** 🛗 🎱 200 ⚂ 1 restaurant, 1 bar (w/entertainment), spa, sauna, whirlpool. Above-average security. Whirlpool, sauna. **Rates (BB):** $124–$289 ste. Extra person $15. Children under age 12 stay free. Min stay special events. Parking: Indoor/outdoor, free. AE, CB, DC, DISC, JCB, MC, V.

Hampton Inn Crabtree

6209 Glenwood Ave, 27612; tel 919/782-1112 or toll free 800/HAMPTON. 2½ mi W of I-440 on US 70W. Standard Hampton Inn offering pleasant accommodations. **Rooms:** 141 rms and stes. CI 3pm/CO noon. Nonsmoking rms avail. **Amenities:** 🛗 🎱 A/C, cable TV. Some units w/whirlpools. **Services:** ✕ 🚐 🛌 🛎 Complimentary evening cocktails. **Facilities:** 🛗 🎱 125 ⚂ Sauna, whirlpool. **Rates (CP):** $59 S; $64 D; $89–$125 ste. Extra person $5. Children under age 18 stay free. Min stay special events. Parking: Indoor/outdoor, free. AE, DC, DISC, MC, V.

Hampton Inn North Raleigh

1001 Wake Towne Dr, 27609; tel 919/828-1813 or toll free 800/HAMPTON. Wake Forest Rd exit off I-440. A standard but stylish hotel. Perfect for the business traveler. **Rooms:** 130 rms. CI 2pm/CO noon. Nonsmoking rms avail. Excellent housekeeping. **Amenities:** 🛗 🎱 A/C, cable TV w/movies, dataport. **Services:** 🛌 🛎 🐾 Small pets only. **Facilities:** 🛗 10 ⚂ Use of local health club for nominal fee. **Rates (CP):** $52 S; $55–$62 D. Extra person $6. Children under age 18 stay free. Parking: Outdoor, free. AE, DC, DISC, MC, V.

Holiday Inn Downtown

320 Hillsborough St, 27603; tel 919/832-0501 or toll free 800/HOLIDAY. Saunders St exit off I-40; 2 mi N to Hillsborough St, then left. Round, high-rise property with exceptional views of historic downtown Raleigh. **Rooms:** 202 rms and stes. CI 3pm/CO noon. Nonsmoking rms avail. **Amenities:** 🛗 🎱 📺 A/C, cable TV w/movies, dataport. All units w/terraces. **Services:** ✕ 🚐 🛌 🛎 **Facilities:** 🛗 🎱 200 ⚂ 1 restaurant, 1 bar. **Rates:** $72 S or D; $129–$159 ste. Extra person $10. Children under age 12 stay free. Parking: Indoor, free. AE, CB, DC, DISC, MC, V.

Holiday Inn North

2815 Capitol Blvd, 27604; tel 919/872-7666 or toll free 800/HOLIDAY. Off I-40. A wonderful design of colorful geometric shapes and indoor gardens greet visitors at this enchanting hotel. The lobby is spacious and well lighted. **Rooms:** 272 rms and stes. Executive level. CI 2pm/CO noon. Nonsmoking rms avail. **Amenities:** 🛗 🎱 A/C, cable TV. Some units w/terraces. **Services:** ✕ VP 🛌 🛎 **Facilities:** 🛗 🎱 300 ⚂ 1 restaurant, 1 bar, games rm, whirlpool. Putting green. **Rates:** $59 S or D; $125 ste. Extra person $8. Children under age 12 stay free. Parking: Outdoor, free. AE, CB, DC, DISC, MC, V.

Meredith Guest House

2603 Village Court, 27607; tel 919/787-2800 or toll free 800/237-9363. Lake Boone exit off I-440. Spacious, apartment-style accommodations nestled in quiet suburb. **Rooms:** 60 stes. CI 2pm/CO 11am. All suites feature a full kitchen. Some suites face a beautiful pond with gazebo and weeping willows. **Amenities:** 🛗 📺 A/C, cable TV, refrig. All units w/terraces. **Services:** 🚐 🛌 🛎 🐾 Babysitting. Maid service washes dishes. **Facilities:** 🛗 🎱 50 Volleyball. Free use of local health spa. **Rates (CP):** $70–$125 ste. Parking: Outdoor, free. AE, CB, DC, DISC, MC, V.

North Raleigh Hilton

3415 Wake Forest Rd, 27609; tel 919/872-2323 or toll free 800/HILTONS; fax 919/876-6890. Exit off I-440. Beautiful hotel, featuring Oriental accents and marble floors. **Rooms:** 340 rms and stes. Executive level. CI 3pm/CO noon. Nonsmoking rms avail. **Amenities:** 🛗 🎱 📺 A/C, cable TV w/movies, dataport. **Services:** ✕ VP 🚐 🛌 🛎 **Facilities:** 🛗 🎱 1500 ⚂ 🖥 ⚂ 1 restaurant, 2 bars (w/entertainment), sauna, whirlpool. **Rates:** $105–$130 S; $115–$140 D; $350–$450 ste. Extra person $10. Children under age 18 stay free. Min stay special events. Parking: Outdoor, free. AE, CB, DC, DISC, MC, V.

Quality Suites Hotel

4400 Capital Blvd, 27604; tel 919/876-2211 or toll free 800/543-5497; fax 919/876-2211. 3 mi N of I-440. A stylish, comfortable hotel with brick courtyard, beautiful landscaping, and tables for outdoor dining and cocktails. Convenient to many shopping and dining options. **Rooms:** 114 stes. CI 3pm/CO noon. Nonsmoking rms avail. **Amenities:** 🛗 🎱 📺 A/C, cable TV, refrig, dataport, VCR, CD/tape player. Some units w/terraces. Microwaves available. **Services:** 🚐 🛌 🛎 Computerized concierge, videotape rentals, and local transportation within 15 mi of hotel. Complimentary evening beverages. **Facilities:** 🛗 🎱 80 ⚂ 1 bar. **Rates (BB):** $65–$114 ste. Extra person $10. Children under age 16 stay free. Min stay special events. Parking: Outdoor, free. AE, CB, DC, DISC, JCB, MC, V.

Radisson Plaza Hotel Raleigh

421 S Salisbury St, 27601; tel 919/834-9900 or toll free 800/333-3333. At corner of Davie and Salisbury Sts. Downtown high-rise hotel adjacent to office buildings and shops. The property has a contemporary feel, and features indoor gardens and an atrium restaurant. **Rooms:** 360 rms and stes. Executive level. CI 3pm/CO noon. Nonsmoking rms avail. **Amenities:** 🛗 🎱 📺 A/C, cable TV w/movies, dataport, voice mail. **Services:** ✕ 🚐 🛌 🛎 **Facilities:** 🛗 🎱 500 ⚂ 1 restaurant, 1 bar (w/entertainment), sauna, whirlpool. **Rates (CP):** $110 S; $120 D; $200–$400 ste. Extra person $10. Children under age 18 stay free. Min stay special events. Parking: Indoor, $5/day. AE, CB, DC, DISC, MC, V.

Raleigh Marriott Crabtree Valley

4500 Marriott Dr, 27612; tel 919/781-7000 or toll free 800/228-9290; fax 919/781-3059. Across from Crabtree Valley

Mall on US 70. A sunlit, contemporary hotel, nestled away in a wooded area but close to shopping and restaurants. **Rooms:** 379 rms and stes. Executive level. CI 3pm/CO noon. Non-smoking rms avail. **Amenities:** 🛁 🛎 A/C, cable TV w/movies, voice mail. **Services:** ✕ 🗝 VP 🚐 ⬛ 🛎 Car-rental desk. Complimentary morning coffee. **Facilities:** 🛗 🏋 🛠 400 🛗 1 restaurant, 1 bar, games rm, whirlpool. **Rates:** $104 S or D; $150–$225 ste. Children under age 18 stay free. Min stay special events. Parking: Outdoor, free. AE, CB, DC, DISC, MC, V.

≡≡≡ Residence Inn by Marriott
1000 Navaho Dr, 27609; tel 919/878-6100 or toll free 800/331-3131; fax 919/876-4117. Wake Forest Rd exit off I-440. This hotel features comfortable suites and a friendly environment. Stone fireplace in lobby. **Rooms:** 144 effic. CI 3pm/CO noon. Nonsmoking rms avail. All rooms have fully equipped kitchens. **Amenities:** 🛁 🛎 🖥 A/C, cable TV, refrig, dataport. Some units w/fireplaces. Some rooms have microwaves. **Services:** ⬛ 🛎 🚲 Children's program, babysitting. Hospitality service Mon–Thurs with cookouts and other dining options. Complimentary wine-and-cheese reception every evening. **Facilities:** 🛗 🛎 🛠 25 🛗 Basketball, whirlpool, washer/dryer. Health club privileges. Barbecue and picnic facilities. **Rates (CP):** $69–$125 effic. Parking: Outdoor, free. Weekly and monthly rates avail. AE, CB, DC, DISC, JCB, MC, V.

≡≡ Sundown Inn North
3801 Capital Blvd, 27604; tel 919/790-8480 or toll free 800/553-7749; fax 919/954-9025. 1½ mi N of I-440. Basic, no-frills hotel. A good value. **Rooms:** 123 rms. CI 3pm/CO noon. Nonsmoking rms avail. Sparse but adequate furnishings. **Amenities:** 🛁 🛎 A/C, cable TV w/movies, dataport. **Services:** ⬛ 🚲 Small pets only. **Facilities:** 🛗 25 🛗 **Rates (CP):** $42–$46 S or D. Extra person $4. Children under age 18 stay free. Parking: Outdoor, free. AE, CB, DC, DISC, MC, V.

≡≡≡ Velvet Cloak Inn
1505 Hillsborough St, 27605; tel 919/828-0333 or toll free 800/662-8829, 800/334-4372 in NC. A New Orleans–style property, with lots of exposed brick and wrought–iron touches. **Rooms:** 172 rms and stes. Executive level. CI 3pm/CO noon. Nonsmoking rms avail. **Amenities:** 🛁 🛎 A/C, cable TV w/movies, dataport. All units w/terraces, some w/whirlpools. **Services:** ✕ VP 🚐 ⬛ 🛎 🚲 Babysitting. Complimentary coffee and morning newspapers in lobby. **Facilities:** 🛗 200 🛗 1 restaurant, 1 bar. Indoor pool set amid tropical garden. Guests may use YMCA next door for nominal fee. **Rates (CP):** $75–$93 S; $85–$103 D; $125–$285 ste. Extra person $10. Children under age 17 stay free. Lower rates off-season. Parking: Outdoor, free. AE, CB, DC, DISC, MC, V.

MOTELS

≡≡ Days Inn South
3901 S Wilmington St, 27603; tel 919/772-8900 or toll free 800/DAYS-INN; fax 919/772-1536. Exit 298A off I-40. A very basic property, close to downtown. **Rooms:** 103 rms. CI 2pm/CO 11am. Nonsmoking rms avail. **Amenities:** 🛁 🛎 A/C, cable TV w/movies. **Services:** 🚲 **Facilities:** 🛗 🛗 Adjacent restaurant open 24 hours. **Rates (CP):** $44–$49 S; $49–$54 D. Extra person $5. Children under age 12 stay free. Parking: Outdoor, free. AE, DC, DISC, MC, V.

≡≡ Fairfield Inn by Marriott
2641 Appliance Court, 27604; tel 919/856-9800 or toll free 800/228-2800. Exit 11B off I-440. A bright and comfortable—yet budget-minded—property. **Rooms:** 132 rms. CI 3pm/CO noon. Nonsmoking rms avail. All rooms have seating area and work area with desk. **Amenities:** 🛁 🛎 A/C, cable TV w/movies, dataport. **Services:** ⬛ 🚲 Complimentary coffee in lobby. **Facilities:** 🛗 🛗 **Rates (CP):** $48 S; $53 D. Extra person $3. Children under age 18 stay free. Parking: Outdoor, free. AE, CB, DC, DISC, MC, V.

≡≡≡ The Plantation Inn Resort
6401 Capital Blvd, PO Box 11333, 27604; tel 919/876-1411; fax 919/790-7093. 5 mi N on US 1 off I-440. Surrounded by tall pines and azaleas, the main building of this motel looks like an old Southern plantation house with large, white columns and a weather vane. Good for the whole family. **Rooms:** 101 rms and stes. CI 2pm/CO noon. Nonsmoking rms avail. Rooms are decorated with traditional furnishings. **Amenities:** 🛁 🛎 A/C, cable TV w/movies, dataport. Coffee-makers and refrigerators available. **Services:** 🚐 ⬛ 🛎 🚲 Babysitting. **Facilities:** 🛗 🛎 125 🛗 2 restaurants, 1 bar, playground. This motel provides health club privileges to guests, as well as nature trails and a putting green. **Rates:** $46–$51 S or D; $55–$75 ste. Extra person $5. Children under age 18 stay free. Min stay special events. Parking: Outdoor, free. AE, CB, DISC, MC, V.

≡≡≡ Ramada Inn Crabtree
3920 Arrow Dr, 27612; tel 919/782-7525 or toll free 800/2-RAMADA. Off US 70. Colonial-style motor inn. **Rooms:** 174 rms and stes. CI 1pm/CO 1pm. Nonsmoking rms avail. **Amenities:** 🛁 🛎 A/C, cable TV. Portable dataports available. **Services:** ✕ VP 🚐 ⬛ 🚲 Babysitting. Each day of their stay, guests receive vouchers for two free dinners and two movie passes. **Facilities:** 🛗 🛠 200 🖥 🛗 1 restaurant, 1 bar. **Rates (CP):** $64 S; $70 D; $64–$85 ste. Extra person $6. Children under age 18 stay free. Parking: Outdoor, free. AE, CB, DC, DISC, JCB, MC, V.

≡≡ Ramada Inn South Apex
Exit 145 off I-95 at NC 55, PO Box 1090, 27502; tel 919/362-8621 or toll free 800/2-RAMADA; fax 919/362-9383. I-95 exit 145. A standard motel. **Rooms:** 109 rms. CI 3pm/CO noon. Nonsmoking rms avail. Some rooms available with waterbeds. **Amenities:** 🛁 🛎 A/C, cable TV w/movies,

dataport. **Services:** 🖨 ⏻ **Facilities:** 🛗 🅿 ♿ 1 restaurant, 1 bar (w/entertainment). Health club privileges. **Rates:** $52–$75 S; $75 D. Extra person $10. Children under age 18 stay free. Min stay special events. Parking: Outdoor, free. AE, CB, DC, DISC, MC, V.

RESTAURANTS 🍴

Big Ed's Restaurant
In City Market, 220 Wolfe St; tel 919/836-9909. **Cafe.** A simple, casual place with a country decor and menu. Big Ed's is known for its great breakfasts, which include ham, hotcakes, and omelettes. The lunch menu includes fresh vegetables from the farmer's market, roast pork with dressing, and hot barbecued chicken. **FYI:** Reservations not accepted. No liquor license. No smoking. **Open:** Mon–Fri 6am–2pm, Sat 7am–noon. **Prices:** Lunch main courses $7. No CC.

Black Dog Cafe
In City Market, 208 E Martin St; tel 919/828-1994. **Eclectic.** A fun place for dog lovers, with doggie decor (a fire hydrant indicates the rest room), a gift shop selling canine toys, and sandwiches named after dogs. Entrees include pork tenderloin and grilled shrimp and vegetables. **FYI:** Reservations not accepted. Children's menu. **Open:** Lunch Tues–Sun 11am–2:30pm; dinner Wed–Sat 5–10pm. **Prices:** Main courses $12–$17. DC, MC, V. 👥 ♿

Carver's Creek
2711 Capital Blvd; tel 919/872-2300. **Seafood/Steak.** Catering to a younger crowd, Mountain Jack's has a rustic, fun decor. Hearty entrees focus on steak and seafood, with soup, salad, potatoes, and rice as side dishes. The restaurant is most famous for its prime rib (cooked in an herb crust) and whisky peppercorn steak. **FYI:** Reservations accepted. **Open:** Lunch Mon–Fri 11:30am–2pm; dinner Mon–Thurs 5–10pm, Sat 4:30–11pm, Sun 4–9pm. **Prices:** Main courses $12–$20. AE, DC, DISC, MC, V.

Casa Carbone Ristorante
In Oak Park Shopping Center, 6019-A Glenwood Ave; tel 919/781-8750. **Italian.** An upscale Italian eatery with elegant decor that lends itself to casual or semicasual dining. The menu offers a host of well-prepared Italian entrees, including pasta, veal, and chicken dishes. Homemade breads and desserts furnish the finishing touches. **FYI:** Reservations not accepted. **Open:** Tues–Sat 5–10pm, Sun 4–9pm. **Prices:** Main courses $6–$14. AE, CB, DC, DISC, MC, V. ♥ ♿

Ⓢ Cooper's Barbecue
109 E Davie St; tel 919/832-7614. 1 block W of Artspace. **Barbecue.** Cooper's is a Raleigh tradition, with an authentic diner interior and walls decorated with old photos of town. The house specialty is slow-cooked pork barbecue, served chopped or sliced, with hush puppies and coleslaw on the side. Ribs, chicken, and seafood also available. **FYI:** Reserva-tions not accepted. Children's menu. No liquor license. **Open:** Mon–Sat 10am–6pm. **Prices:** Main courses $5–$6. No CC. 👥

★ 42nd Street Oyster Bar and Seafood Grill
508 W Jones St; tel 919/831-2811. At West St. **Seafood.** Housed in a restored seafood warehouse that dates from the 1930s, this place has made its name by serving the freshest Carolina seafood. Oysters on the half shell share menu honors with platters of fried or steamed fish and lobster, shrimp Creole, seafood fettuccine, prime rib, and fried chicken. Servings are plentiful, and there's also a children's menu. **FYI:** Reservations recommended. Children's menu. Beer and wine only. **Open:** Mon–Fri 11am–11pm, Sat 5–11pm, Sun 5–10pm. **Prices:** Main courses $10–$27. DC, MC, V. ♿

Greenshields Brewery & Pub
In City Market, 214 E Martin St; tel 919/829-0214. **American/Pub.** This upscale yet casual place has a plush interior with high-backed upholstered chairs and oak paneling. Grilled pork tenderloin, chicken pot pie, and chargrilled caesar salad are a few of the menu's highlights. A pub menu is available in the afternoons and late at night; the brewery makes four different microbrews. **FYI:** Reservations accept-ed. Singer. Children's menu. **Open:** Lunch daily 11:30am–2pm; dinner daily 5:30–10:30pm. **Prices:** Main courses $6–$16. AE, DC, MC, V. ♥ ♿

India Mahal
3212 Hillsborough St; tel 919/836-9742. Across from NC State University. **Indian.** The rather plain decor belies the spiciness of the menu at this humble eatery. The North Indian specialties include vegetable, chicken, lamb, and sea-food entrees, with Indian breads and condiments on the side. There's a lot to choose from—all of it entirely authentic. **FYI:** Reservations accepted. Beer and wine only. No smoking. **Open:** Lunch daily 11:30am–3pm; dinner daily 5–10pm. **Prices:** Main courses $7–$12. MC, V. ♿

Irregardless Cafe
901 W Morgan St; tel 919/833-8898. 1 block from Hillsbor-ough St. **Cafe.** Pastel colors and works by local artists brighten up the dining room. All entrees are health con-scious, and no pork or red meat is served. Sample specialties include a sweet vidalia tart (filled with sautéed onions and blue-cheese custard); scarecrow chicken (baked half-chicken served with raspberry sauce); and grouper moutarde. **FYI:** Reservations not accepted. Blues/jazz. No smoking. **Open:** Lunch Mon–Sat 11:30am–2:30pm; dinner Mon–Thurs 5:30–10pm, Fri–Sat 5:30–11pm; brunch Sun 10am–2:30pm. **Prices:** Main courses $10–$15. AE, MC, V. ♿

Lucky 32
832 Spring Forest Rd; tel 919/876-9932. Exit 10 off I-440. **Regional American.** A contemporary bistro decorated in red and black with art deco accents and bold mahogany trim, Lucky 32 features a menu that is mostly Northwestern fare.

Specialties include hickory-grilled lamb chops, citrus-marinated grilled chicken, and several gourmet pizzas. **FYI:** Reservations recommended. **Open:** Mon–Thurs 11:15am–10:30pm, Fri–Sat 11:15am–11pm, Sun 10:45am–10pm. **Prices:** Main courses $7–$15. AE, DC, MC, V. ♥ ᕕ

Pizza Amore
In Artspace, 329 S Blount St; tel 919/832-2255. Near City Market. **Italian/Pizza.** A classic trattoria serving up a variety of gourmet pizzas (with Tunisian, Hawaiian, and Mediterranean toppings) along with calzones, stromboli, spaghetti, and lasagna. **FYI:** Reservations accepted. **Open:** Mon–Thurs 11am–9pm, Fri–Sat 11am–10pm. **Prices:** Main courses $4–$6. AE, MC, V. 🚗 ᕕ

ATTRACTIONS 🏛

The State Capitol
Capitol Sq; tel 919/733-4994. This stately Greek Revival structure (constructed 1833–1840) has been named a National Historic Landmark. All state business was conducted here until 1888. The building now contains the offices of the governor and lieutenant governor as well as restored legislative chambers. Beneath the awe-inspiring 97½-foot copper dome there's a duplicate of Antonio Canova's marble statue of George Washington dressed as a Roman general. Guided tours last about 45 minutes. **Open:** Mon–Fri 8am–5pm, Sat 9am–5pm, Sun 1–5pm. Closed some hols. **Free**

North Carolina Museum of History
109 E Jones St; tel 919/733-3894. The state's history is pictured in exhibits that tell the story of the Roanoke Island colonists and display relics of colonial, Revolutionary, and Civil War eras (costumes, shops, and period rooms). There's also a North Carolina Sports Hall of Fame, a display tracing the development of firearms, and a collection of local folk art. **Open:** Tues–Sat 9am–5pm, Sun 1–6pm. Closed some hols. **Free**

North Carolina State Museum of Natural Sciences
Bicentennial Plaza; tel 919/733-7450. Outstanding features include a fossil lab, where volunteers work on dinosaur bones; an exhibit of the state's most common gems; Bioscanner, an interactive exhibit of living animals shown enlarged on color video monitors; and the hands-on Discovery Room. There's even a bird hall, a dinosaur hall, a live snake collection, and four whale skeletons. **Open:** Mon–Sat 9am–5pm, Sun 1–5pm. Closed some hols. **Free**

North Carolina Museum of Art
2110 Blue Ridge Rd; tel 919/833-1935. This museum houses an important collection of European paintings, plus American, African, Oceanic, and Judaica collections. Masters like Botticetti, Giotto, Rubens, and Monet are represented in the permanent collection, and a variety of special exhibitions and programs are offered. **Open:** Tues–Sat 9am–5pm, Fri 9am–9pm, Sun 11am–6pm. Closed some hols. **Free**

Andrew Johnson's Birthplace (Mordecai Historic Park and Mordecai House)
1 Mimosa St; tel 919/834-4844. One of three North Carolina natives who became president, Andrew Johnson was born in a small cabin about a block from the capitol building. The 17th president's birthplace has been moved to Mordecai Historic Park and is open to visitors. The restored Mordecai House, with the original furnishings, was the plantation home of five generations of one of North Carolina's oldest families. Other historic buildings have also been relocated to the park to re-create an entire 19th-century village, including a kitchen, a law office, and a post office. **Open:** Mar–Nov, Tues–Fri 10am–3pm, Sat–Sun 1:30–3:30pm. **$**

Research Triangle Park

See also Durham, Raleigh

Site of a 6,800-acre industrial park that is home to corporate and government institutions like IBM, Du Pont, and the Environmental Protection Agency. Raleigh-Durham Airport is another big draw. **Information:** Morrisville Chamber of Commerce, 222 N Church St, PO Box 548, Morrisville, 27560 (tel 919/380-9026).

MOTEL 🏨

≡≡ Triangle Inn Airport
RDU Airport, PO Box 80084, Raleigh, 27623; tel 919/840-9000 or toll free 800/662-8850. Across from Terminal A. Proximity to the airport is this property's biggest draw, but be aware that the noise and bustle of the surrounding area is not conducive for extended stays. **Rooms:** 150 rms. CI 9:30am/CO noon. Nonsmoking rms avail. **Amenities:** 🛏 ☕ A/C, cable TV. **Services:** 🅥🅟 ⬜ ᐧ **Facilities:** ⬜ ⬜ ⬜ ᕕ Washer/dryer. **Rates (CP):** $53 S; $59 D. Extra person $6. Children under age 12 stay free. Parking: Outdoor, free. AE, CB, DC, DISC, JCB, MC, V.

RESTAURANT 🍴

Angus Barn
US 70W at Airport Rd, Raleigh; tel 919/787-3505. **Steak.** A landmark in area dining, this eatery is housed in an enormous barn with a country decor—quilts, antiques, and farm equipment decorate the establishment. Charcoal-broiled steak is the main attraction, with cuts to satisfy any appetite. There is also a lobster-and-steak combo, and other seafood dishes are available. Portions are large, and the wine list is extensive. **FYI:** Reservations recommended. Country music/jazz. Children's menu. **Open:** Mon–Sat 5–11pm, Sun 5–10pm. **Prices:** Main courses $17–$33. AE, CB, DC, MC, V.

Roanoke Rapids

On the Roanoke River, near the Virginia state line. Founded in 1893 by John Armstrong Chaloner as a cotton mill site, it is today a lumber and paper product manufacturer. **Information:** Roanoke Valley Chamber of Commerce, 1640 Weldon Rd, PO Box 519, Roanoke Rapids, 27870 (tel 919/537-3519).

MOTELS 🏨

≣≣ Comfort Inn North

NC 46, PO Box 716, 27870; tel 919/537-1011 or toll free 800/228-5150; fax 919/537-9258. Exit 176 off I-95. A pleasant and new motel. **Rooms:** 100 rms. CI 3pm/CO 11am. Nonsmoking rms avail. **Amenities:** 🛏 A/C, cable TV w/movies. Some units w/whirlpools. **Services:** 🛎 **Facilities:** 🛗 🖳 ⅋ 1 restaurant, whirlpool. **Rates (CP):** $38–$40 S; $40–$50 D. Extra person $5. Children under age 18 stay free. Parking: Outdoor, free. AE, CB, DC, DISC, MC, V.

≣≣ Hampton Inn

1914 Weldon Rd, 27870; tel 919/537-7555 or toll free 800/HAMPTON; fax 919/537-9852. Exit 173 off I-95. An attractive, standard motel. **Rooms:** 124 rms. CI 3pm/CO noon. Nonsmoking rms avail. **Amenities:** 🛏 A/C, cable TV w/movies, dataport. **Services:** 🖼 🛎 **Facilities:** 🛗 🖳25 ⅋ Health-club privileges provided to guests. **Rates (CP):** $48–$55 S; $51–$60 D. Children under age 18 stay free. Parking: Outdoor, free. AE, CB, DC, DISC, MC, V.

≣≣ Holiday Inn

100 Holiday Dr, 27870; tel 919/537-1031 or toll free 800/HOLIDAY; fax 919/537-7848. Exit 173 at US 158 and I-95. A comfortable, garden motel. **Rooms:** 140 rms and stes. CI 3pm/CO noon. Nonsmoking rms avail. **Amenities:** 🛏 ⚖ A/C, cable TV w/movies, dataport. **Services:** 🖼 🛎 Babysitting. **Facilities:** 🛗 🖳300 ⅋ 1 restaurant, 1 bar. The pool area is nicely landscaped with rock walls and a waterfall. **Rates:** $60–$65 S or D; $76 ste. Extra person $6. Children under age 19 stay free. Parking: Outdoor, free. AE, CB, DC, DISC, JCB, MC, V.

Robbinsville

Located near the southwest corner of Great Smoky Mountains National Park. Nearby lakes—Nantahala, Santeetlah, Fontana—draw many boaters and fishing enthusiasts. **Information:** Graham County Chamber of Commerce, Main St, PO Box 1206, Robbinsville, 28771 (tel 704/479-3790).

LODGE 🏨

≣≣ Snowbird Mountain Lodge

275 Santeetlah Rd, 28771; tel 704/479-3433. Off US 129. A peaceful, secluded lodge, with a flagstone terrace, rustic lobby, and magnificent views of the surrounding mountains and Nantahala National Forest. **Rooms:** 22 rms and stes; 7 cottages/villas. CI noon/CO 10am. Nonsmoking rms avail. **Amenities:** No A/C, phone, or TV. Some units w/terraces. **Facilities:** 🖳20 ⅋ 1 restaurant, games rm, lawn games. The only phone is in the lobby. **Rates (AP):** $89 S; $118 S or D; $124 ste; $118–$124 cottage/villa. Extra person $20–$42. Min stay wknds. Parking: Outdoor, free. Closed Dec–Mar. MC, V.

Rocky Mount

This growing city on the Tar River is a large tobacco market and the commercial center of a rich farming region. North Carolina Wesleyan College is here. Home to an arts center housed in a late Federalist building representing the pre–Civil War lifestyle of planters. **Information:** Rocky Mount Area Chamber of Commerce, 437 Falls Rd, PO Box 392, Rocky Mount, 27802 (tel 919/442-5111).

HOTEL 🏨

UNRATED Comfort Inn

200 Gateway Blvd, 27804; tel 919/937-7765 or toll free 800/221-2222; fax 919/937-7765. Across from Nash General Hospital. A nice hotel with tastefully decorated public areas. **Rooms:** 125 rms. CI 3pm/CO 11am. Nonsmoking rms avail. **Amenities:** 🛏 A/C, cable TV w/movies, dataport. Refrigerators and microwaves available. **Services:** 🖼 🛎 **Facilities:** 🛗 🖳40 ⅋ Walking distance from a full-service restaurant. **Rates (CP):** $50–$55 S; $56–$62 D. Extra person $5. Parking: Outdoor, free. AE, CB, DC, DISC, MC, V.

MOTELS

≣≣ Best Western Inn Rocky Mount

NC 4, PO Box 121, Rte 1, 27809; tel 919/985-1450 or toll free 800/528-1234; fax 919/985-2236. Exit 145 off I-95. A very attractive motel that is conveniently located near the interstate and shopping and dining options. **Rooms:** 81 rms. CI 3pm/CO 11am. Nonsmoking rms avail. **Amenities:** 🛏 A/C, cable TV w/movies. **Services:** 🛎 **Facilities:** 🛗 ⅋ **Rates:** $39–$49 S; $44–$54 D. Extra person $5. Children under age 12 stay free. Parking: Outdoor, free. AE, CB, DC, DISC, MC, V.

≣≣ Best Western Rocky Mount Inn

1921 N Wesleyan Blvd, 27804; tel 919/442-8101 or toll free 800/528-1234; fax 919/442-1048. Basic, older motel with excellent housekeeping standards. **Rooms:** 72 rms. CI 2pm/CO 11am. Nonsmoking rms avail. **Amenities:** 🛏 A/C, cable TV w/movies. **Facilities:** 🛗 🖳60 1 restaurant. **Rates (CP):** Peak (May–Sept) $37–$42 S; $42–$47 D. Extra person $5. Children under age 12 stay free. Lower rates off-season. Parking: Outdoor, free. AE, CB, DC, DISC, MC, V.

⊨⊨⊨ Carleton House

215 N Church St, 27804; tel 919/977-0410. 4½ mi E of I-95 on US 64. An attractive, traditional motel with a brick exterior. **Rooms:** 42 rms. CI 3pm/CO noon. Nonsmoking rms avail. Some "theme rooms" are available. **Amenities:** 📶 🅰 ⬛ A/C, cable TV w/movies. Some units w/whirlpools. Coffee delivered to rooms. **Services:** ⛱ 🔄 Guest privileges at local health club. **Facilities:** 🔒 250 ⚓ 1 restaurant, 1 bar. **Rates (BB):** $38–$40 S; $45 D. Children under age 16 stay free. Parking: Outdoor, free. AE, CB, DC, MC, V.

⊨ Mosley's Shady Lake Motel

1621 Wesleyan Blvd, 27804; tel 919/446-7195. One mi E of I-95 on US 64. A motel from the 1950s era, it has been well kept and still retains its kitschy decor. Visitors are welcomed by a 15-foot statue of a bathing beauty holding a beach ball and clad in a red bikini. **Rooms:** 30 rms. CI noon/CO 11am. **Amenities:** 📶 A/C, cable TV, refrig. **Rates:** $28 S or D. Extra person $5. Children under age 4 stay free. Parking: Outdoor, free. AE, DISC, MC, V.

RESTAURANTS 🍴

Atlantis Restaurant & Oyster Bar

US 301 Business N; tel 919/977-2239. **Seafood.** The very attractive nautical decor features large aquariums. They serve a variety of broiled and fried seafood, and the oyster bar offers steamed shrimp and oysters. **FYI:** Reservations accepted. Children's menu. Beer and wine only. **Open:** Tues–Sun 5–10pm. Closed Aug. **Prices:** Main courses $8–$12. AE, DISC, MC, V. ♥⚓

Bob Melton's Barbecue

631 E Ridge St; tel 919/977-2239. ¼ mi off US 301 N Business. **Barbecue/Seafood.** A family restaurant serving pit-cooked barbecue since 1924, Bob Melton's sits on the banks of the Tar River and has a peaceful view of the small river and the weeping trees along the opposite shore. Menu specialties include barbecued chicken and ribs, Brunswick stew, and several seafood dinners (mostly fried). **FYI:** Reservations not accepted. Children's menu. No liquor license. **Open:** Mon–Thurs 10am–8pm, Fri–Sat 10am–9pm, Sun 10am–3pm. **Prices:** Main courses $5–$9. No CC. 🖼 🎰

Salisbury

A quiet Piedmont town, with graceful homes and old-fashioned shops with original turn-of-the-century architecture. Once a jumping off point for the West, this is where Daniel Boone's trail began in 1765; Andrew Jackson studied law here. **Information:** Rowan County Chamber of Commerce, 620 W Innes St, PO Box 559, Salisbury, 28145 (tel 704/633-4221).

HOTEL 🏨

⊨⊨ Hampton Inn

1001 Klumac Rd, 28144; tel 704/637-8000 or toll free 800/HAMPTON. Exit 75 off I-85. Attractively decorated hotel with contemporary decor and tastefully appointed public areas. **Rooms:** 121 rms. CI 2pm/CO noon. Nonsmoking rms avail. **Amenities:** 📶 🅰 A/C, cable TV w/movies, dataport. **Services:** ⛱ 🔄 **Facilities:** 🔒 🏋 20 💻 ⚓ **Rates (CP):** $47–$55 S or D. Children under age 18 stay free. Parking: Outdoor, free. AE, CB, DC, DISC, MC, V.

MOTEL 🏨

⊨⊨⊨ Holiday Inn

530 Jake Alexander Blvd, 28144; tel 704/637-3100 or toll free 800/HOLIDAY; fax 704/637-9152. Exit 75 off I-85. A modern motor inn with Southern comfort and style. **Rooms:** 124 rms. CI 2pm/CO noon. Nonsmoking rms avail. **Amenities:** 📶 🅰 ⬛ 🍽 A/C, cable TV w/movies, dataport. Some units w/whirlpools. **Services:** ✗ ⛱ 🔄 🍸 **Facilities:** 🔒 🏋 500 ⚓ 1 restaurant, 1 bar, games rm, whirlpool. **Rates:** $59–$65 S or D. Extra person $6. Children under age 12 stay free. Parking: Outdoor, free. AE, CB, DC, DISC, MC, V.

ATTRACTION 🖼

North Carolina Transportation Museum

411 S Salisbury Ave, Spencer; tel 704/636-2889. Located 4 mi NE of Salisbury, on the site of Historic Spencer Shops (once a major repair facility for the Southern Railway). Visitors are free to wander and inspect the 57-acre site and its growing collection of transportation memorabilia, engines, freight cars, and trolleys. It's a friendly, informal place, and staff members are likely to jump in with anecdotes about the shops' history. Guests may take a 50-minute tour on board a restored steam locomotive, and a large museum shop offers unusual railroad items ranging from 15¢ maps to *Orient Express* crystal. **Open:** Apr–Oct, Mon–Sat 9am–5pm, Sun 1–5pm; Nov–Mar, Tues–Sat, 10am–4pm, Sun 1–4pm. Closed some hols.

Sanford

Lee County seat, established in the Piedmont region in 1872. Named for Col C O Sanford, locating engineer for the Chatam Railroad. **Information:** Sanford Area Chamber of Commerce, 229 Carthage St, PO Box 519, Sanford, 27331 (tel 919/775-7341).

MOTELS 🏨

⊨⊨ Best Western Executive Inn

Horner Blvd N, PO Box 186, 27330; tel 919/776-5121 or toll free 800/528-1234; fax 919/774-3533. At US 1. A basic, comfortable motel. **Rooms:** 100 rms. CI noon/CO noon. Nonsmoking rms avail. **Amenities:** 📶 🅰 🍽 A/C, cable TV, dataport. **Services:** 🛎 **Facilities:** 🖨 📠 ⅄ 1 restaurant, 1 bar. **Rates (CP):** $38–$42 S; $40–$48 D. Extra person $5. Children under age 12 stay free. Parking: Outdoor, free. AE, CB, DC, DISC, MC, V.

⊨ Palomino Motor Inn

1508 Westover Dr, PO Box 777, 27331; tel 919/776-7531 or toll free 800/641-6060; fax 919/776-9670. Fifties-style motel best suited for golfers or families on a budget. **Rooms:** 92 rms and stes. CI noon/CO noon. Nonsmoking rms avail. **Amenities:** 🖥 🅑 A/C, satel TV, refrig, dataport. **Services:** 🛎 ⇗ **Facilities:** 🖨 📦 🍴 📠 ⅄ 1 restaurant, sauna, whirlpool, playground. Indoor golf simulator. Picnic area. **Rates:** $30–$36 S or D; $48–$50 ste; $108 cottage/villa. Extra person $4. Parking: Outdoor, free. Golf packages avail. AE, DC, DISC, MC, V.

ATTRACTION 🏛

House in the Horseshoe

324 Alston House Rd; tel 910/947-2051. Located 10 mi W of Sanford on NC 42. More properly known as Alston House (the house's nickname refers to its location in a bend of the Deep River), this two-story frame structure, built in the late 1770s, is typical of plantation houses of that era. Several bullet holes were made in 1781 when Whigs and Tories battled it out on the grounds. "Miss Ruby" Newton, who takes visitors through the house, will fill you in with other anecdotes about the house and its owners down through the years. **Open:** Apr–Oct, Mon–Sat 9am–5pm, Sun 1–5pm; Nov–Mar, Tues–Sat 10am–4pm, Sun 1–4pm. Closed some hols. **Free**

Smithfield

The seat of Johnston County, this is one of North Carolina's oldest towns, incorporated in 1777. Hometown of Ava Gardner and the site of a museum filled with the world's largest collection of memorabilia from her life. **Information:** Greater Smithfield–Selma Area Chamber of Commerce, Industrial Park Dr, PO Box 467, Smithfield, 27577 (tel 919/934-9166).

MOTELS 🏨

⊫⊨ Comfort Inn

1705 Industrial Park Dr, 27576; tel 919/965-5200 or toll free 800/228-5150. Exit 97 off I-95. A standard motel with easy access to the interstate. **Rooms:** 80 rms and stes. CI 2pm/CO 11am. Nonsmoking rms avail. **Amenities:** 🖥 A/C, cable TV w/movies. Some units w/whirlpools. **Services:** 🛎 **Facilities:** 🖨 📦 ⅄ Sauna, whirlpool. **Rates (CP):** $42–$85 S; $44–$85 D; $85 ste. Extra person $7. Children under age 18 stay free. Parking: Outdoor, free. AE, CB, DC, DISC, MC, V.

⊫⊨ Masters Economy Inn

Exit 97 off I-40 at US 70A, PO Box 529, 27577; tel 919/965-3771 or toll free 800/633-3434. A well-maintained motel that is convenient to the interstate and several restaurants. **Rooms:** 116 rms. CI 3pm/CO noon. Nonsmoking rms avail. **Amenities:** 🖥 A/C, cable TV w/movies. **Services:** 🛎 Fax and copy services. **Facilities:** 🖨 📦 ⅄ Washer/dryer. **Rates:** $27 S or D. Children under age 18 stay free. Parking: Outdoor, free. AE, CB, DC, DISC, MC, V.

Sneads Ferry

RESORT 🏨

⊫⊫⊨ Villa Capriani Resort

1 N Topsail Shores, 28460; tel 910/328-1900 or toll free 800/934-2400. A beautiful, Spanish-style resort on a secluded section of beach, this horseshoe-shaped hotel has a stucco exterior and terra-cotta roofing. The multilevel courtyard has gazebos and waterfalls. **Rooms:** 116 cottages/villas. CI 4pm/CO 11am. Nonsmoking rms avail. One-, two-, and three-bedroom villas are available. All are tastefully decorated and have full kitchens and washers/dryers. **Amenities:** 🖥 🅑 📺 A/C, cable TV w/movies, refrig. All units w/terraces. **Services:** 🏊 🛎 Children's program. **Facilities:** 🖨 📦 ⚓ 1 restaurant (lunch and dinner only), 1 bar, 1 beach (ocean), whirlpool, washer/dryer. **Rates:** Peak (June 3–Sept 10) $110–$765 cottage/villa. Min stay peak. Lower rates off-season. Parking: Outdoor, free. AE, CB, DC, DISC, MC, V.

Southern Pines

Part of the Sandhills golf mecca in central North Carolina. Site of Weymouth Center, the former estate of writer and publisher James Boyd. **Information:** Pinehurst Convention & Visitors Bureau, PO Box 2270, Southern Pines, 28388 (tel 910/692-3330).

MOTELS 🏨

⊫⊨ Best Western Pinehurst Motor Inn

1500 Sandhills Blvd, 28387; tel 910/944-2367 or toll free 800/528-1234; fax 910/944-2730. Recently renovated motel, with the look and feel of a lodge. Located five miles from Pinehurst Country Club. **Rooms:** 50 rms. CI noon/CO noon. Nonsmoking rms avail. Good-quality housekeeping. **Amenities:** 🖥 🅑 A/C, cable TV w/movies, dataport. **Services:** 🏊 🛎 🐕 Babysitting. **Facilities:** 🖨 📦 ⅄ Washer/dryer. **Rates (CP):** $50–$60 S or D. Extra person $5. Children under age 12 stay free. Parking: Outdoor, free. Golfing packages avail. AE, CB, DC, DISC, MC, V.

⊫⊨ Days Inn

1420 US 1, 28387; tel 910/692-7581 or toll free 800/972-3096; fax 910/692-7581. An average motel with better-than-average offerings for its guests. **Rooms:** 120 rms. CI 2pm/CO 11am. Nonsmoking rms avail. Adequately furnished and exceptionally clean. **Amenities:** 🛎 ⚲ A/C, cable TV w/movies, dataport. Refrigerators and microwaves available upon request. **Services:** ⌷ ⇄ ⌣ Small pets only. **Facilities:** 🖼 650 ⌷ ⚱ Volleyball. Business center. **Rates:** Peak (Mar–May/Sept–Dec) $40–$45 S or D. Extra person $6. Children under age 12 stay free. Min stay special events. Lower rates off-season. Parking: Outdoor, free. Golf packages avail. AE, CB, DC, DISC, JCB, MC, V.

📧📧📧 Holiday Inn

US 1 at Morganton Rd, PO Box 1467, 28387; tel 910/692-8585 or toll free 800/465-4329. Delightfully pleasant, modern hotel. Popular with golfers. **Rooms:** 160 rms and stes. Executive level. CI 3pm/CO noon. Nonsmoking rms avail. Brightly decorated rooms. **Amenities:** 🛎 ⚲ A/C, cable TV w/movies, dataport. Some units w/whirlpools. **Services:** ✗ 🚐 ⌷ ⌣ Babysitting. **Facilities:** 🖼 ⚐ 350 ⚱ 1 restaurant, 1 bar, games rm. Game room. **Rates (CP):** $65 S; $75 D; $110–$130 ste. Extra person $10. Children under age 10 stay free. Min stay special events. Parking: Outdoor, free. AE, CB, DC, DISC, MC, V.

📧📧 Innkeeper

US 1, Aberdeen, PO Box 150, Southern Pines, 28387; tel 910/944-2324 or toll free 800/344-2324. At jct US 1/US 15/501. Basic hotel within five miles of a golf course. Perfect for a business trip stay. **Rooms:** 77 rms. CI 1pm/CO 11am. Nonsmoking rms avail. Adequate furnishings and better-than-average housekeeping. **Amenities:** 🛎 ⚲ A/C, cable TV. Some units w/terraces, some w/whirlpools. **Services:** ⌣ **Facilities:** 🖼 25 ⌷ ⚱ Indoor/outdoor pool. **Rates (CP):** $80 S or D. Extra person $5. Children under age 16 stay free. Min stay special events. Parking: Outdoor, free. Golf package avail. AE, CB, DC, DISC, MC, V.

RESORTS

📧 Hyland Hills Resort

41110 US 1, 28387; tel 910/692-7615 or toll free 800/841-0638. 200 acres. This resort provides affordable golfing accommodations. **Rooms:** 60 rms and stes. CI 7am/CO noon. Out-of-date decor. **Amenities:** 🛎 ⚲ A/C, cable TV. All units w/terraces. **Facilities:** 🖼 ▶18 ⚱ 1 restaurant (bkfst and lunch only). **Rates (CP):** Peak (Mar 16–May) $98–$108 S or D; $108 ste. Extra person $10. Lower rates off-season. Parking: Outdoor, free. AE, DISC, MC, V.

📧📧 Mid Pines

1010 Midland Rd, 28387; tel 910/692-2114 or toll free 800/323-2114. 250 acres. A midlevel luxury golf resort, it has beautiful, quiet grounds studded with magnolia and pine trees and is a great choice for family vacations. **Rooms:** 118 rms and stes; 9 cottages/villas. CI 2pm/CO 11am. Nonsmoking rms avail. Some rooms need slight renovation. Some have showers only. Two- to ten-room villas available. **Amenities:** 🛎 📺 A/C, cable TV. Some units w/terraces. **Services:** ✗ 📼 🚐

⌷ ⌣ Children's program, babysitting. **Facilities:** 🖼 🚲 ▶18 🟦4 250 ⚱ 1 restaurant, 1 bar, playground. **Rates:** Peak (mid-Mar–June/mid-Sept–mid-Nov) $46–$86 S or D; $56–$96 ste; $61–$102 cottage/villa. Extra person $10. Children under age 12 stay free. Lower rates off-season. MAP rates avail. Parking: Outdoor, free. Golf packages avail. AE, DISC, MC, V.

📧📧📧 Pine Needles Resort

Ridge Rd, PO Box 88, 28387; tel 910/692-7111 or toll free 800/747-7272. 250 acres. This charming lodge in a natural setting houses a golf course designed by Donald Ross in 1927, and a charming, rustic clubhouse. **Rooms:** 75 rms. CI 2pm/CO 11am. The rooms have a simple elegance with their pine paneling. **Amenities:** 🛎 ⚲ 🍽 A/C, cable TV, refrig. **Services:** 📼 ⌷ ⌣ **Facilities:** 🖼 ▶18 🟦2 🏓 250 ⚱ 1 restaurant, 1 bar, games rm, sauna, whirlpool. **Rates (AP):** Peak (Sept 13–Nov 18/Mar 14–June 8) $115–$135 S or D. Children under age 4 stay free. Min stay peak. Lower rates off-season. Parking: Outdoor, free. Golf and holiday packages avail. AE, DC, DISC, MC, V.

RESTAURANTS 🍴

★ La Terrace

270 SW Broad St; tel 910/692-5622. **French.** The airy dining room, with its peach-painted, mirrored walls, makes a wonderful setting. The menu is primarily French with some traditional American dishes. Specialties include roasted rack of lamb and sautéed frog legs in garlic butter (served as an appetizer or an entree). **FYI:** Reservations recommended. **Open:** Lunch Tues–Sat 11:30am–2pm; dinner Tues–Sat 6–10pm. **Prices:** Main courses $13–$23. MC, V. 🍽 ⚱

★ Lob Steer Inn

Morganton Rd; tel 910/692-3503. Off US 1 N. **Seafood/Steak.** One of the best and most popular places in the area for prime steaks, lobster, and fresh seafood. The menu includes steak-and-lobster combination plates, king-crab legs, stuffed shrimp, and filet mignon. The classy dining room features low lighting and a dark-green color scheme; golf scenes adorn the walls. **FYI:** Reservations recommended. Children's menu. **Open:** Daily 5–10:30pm. **Prices:** Main courses $11–$26. AE, DC, MC, V. 👪 ⚱

Whiskey McNeill's Restaurant

Northeast Blvd; tel 910/692-5440. At Broad St. **Cafe.** The automobile motif still remains in this former service station featuring automobile pictures and gas pumps. Dinner sandwiches include French dip and chicken sandwich. Spaghetti is also available. **FYI:** Reservations accepted. Children's menu. Beer and wine only. **Open:** Lunch Mon–Fri 11:30am–5pm, Sun noon–5pm; dinner Sun–Thurs 5–9pm, Fri–Sat 5–10pm. **Prices:** Main courses $6–$16. MC, V. 👪

ATTRACTION

Weymouth Woods—Sandhills Nature Preserve

1024 Fort Bragg Rd; tel 910/692-2167. This beautiful 676-acre natural preserve is home to rare and endangered species such as the red-cockaded woodpecker and the pine barrens tree frog. Carolina longleaf pines, with needles up to 18 inches long, are the dominant plant species here. The survival of these delicate trees depends on "prescribed burning," controlled fires which serve to remove competing hardwoods and replenish the soil with nutrients. A natural history museum contains displays on the area's delicate ecology, and foot and bridle paths wind through the sandhills. **Open:** Mon–Sat 9am–6pm, Sun noon–5pm. Closed Dec 25. **Free**

Southport

Founded in 1792 and located at the mouth of the Cape Fear River, south of Wilmington. Fishermen still meet at the "whittler's bench" on the waterfront to swap stories. **Information:** Southport–Oak Island Chamber of Commerce, 4841 Long Beach Rd SE, Southport, 28461 (tel 910/457-6964).

MOTEL

Sea Captain Motor Lodge

608 W West St, 28461; tel 910/457-5263. Basic accommodation located within walking distance of a charming historic district. **Rooms:** 294 rms and effic. CI 1pm/CO 11am. Nonsmoking rms avail. **Amenities:** A/C, cable TV, refrig. **Services:** **Facilities:** 1 restaurant, 1 bar. **Rates:** $52 S or D; $62 effic. Children under age 12 stay free. Parking: Outdoor, free. AE, CB, DC, DISC, MC, V.

RESTAURANT

Lucky Fisherman Seafood Buffet

Long Beach Rd; tel 910/457-9499. **Seafood/Steak.** A quaint seafood diner with nautical decor and aquariums. In addition to the nightly seafood buffet, there are four steak entrees and a surf-and-turf combo with steak and lobster. Salad bar included with all entrees. **FYI:** Reservations not accepted. Children's menu. No liquor license. **Open:** Tues–Sun 5–10pm. **Prices:** Main courses $8–$24; prix fixe $10. MC, V.

Statesville

Four historic districts are featured in this Piedmont area city, home to fiddlers' conventions and festivals. **Information:** Greater Statesville Chamber of Commerce, 115 E Front St, PO Box 1064, Statesville, 28687 (tel 704/873-2892).

MOTELS

Best Western

1121 Morland Dr, 28677; tel 704/881-0111 or toll free 800/528-1234; fax 704/872-5056. Exit 49A off I-77. Dependable service and basic but nice rooms. **Rooms:** 70 rms and stes. Executive level. CI 1pm/CO 11am. Nonsmoking rms avail. **Amenities:** A/C, cable TV, dataport. Some units w/whirlpools. **Services:** **Facilities:** **Rates (CP):** $50 S; $54 D; $190 ste. Parking: Outdoor, free. AE, CB, DC, DISC, MC, V.

Days Inn

703 Gaither Rd, 28677; tel 704/872-9891 or toll free 800/DAYS-INN; fax 704/872-0480. Exit 151 off I-40. A standard chain property, perfect for I-40 travelers in need of an overnight stay. **Rooms:** 104 rms. CI 3pm/CO 11am. Nonsmoking rms avail. Rooms are clean and comfortable. **Amenities:** A/C, satel TV. **Services:** **Facilities:** **Rates (CP):** $38 S; $43 D. Children under age 13 stay free. Parking: Outdoor, free. AE, CB, DC, DISC, MC, V.

Econo Lodge South

1023 Salisbury Rd, 28677; tel 704/872-5215 or toll free 800/424-4777; fax 704/872-4936. Exit 49B off I-77. A standard and dependable property, adequate for a short stay. **Rooms:** 120 rms. CI open/CO noon. Nonsmoking rms avail. Rooms are in need of renovation. **Amenities:** A/C, cable TV. **Services:** **Facilities:** **Rates (CP):** $42–$49 S or D. Extra person $3. Children under age 18 stay free. Parking: Outdoor, free. AE, CB, DC, DISC, JCB, MC, V.

Fairfield Inn by Marriott

1505 E Broad, 28677; tel 704/878-2091 or toll free 800/228-2800; fax 704/873-1368. Exit 50 off I-77. Clean, well-maintained motel near the interstate and a local shopping center. **Rooms:** 118 rms. CI noon/CO noon. Nonsmoking rms avail. **Amenities:** A/C, satel TV w/movies, dataport. **Services:** Twice-daily maid svce. **Facilities:** **Rates (CP):** $54 S or D. Extra person $5. Children under age 18 stay free. Parking: Outdoor, free. AE, CB, DC, DISC, MC, V.

Hampton Inn

715 Sullivan Rd, 28677; tel 704/878-2721 or toll free 800/HAMPTON; fax 704/873-6694. Exit 151 off I-40. Standard, dependable chain accommodations with amenities catering to business travelers. **Rooms:** 122 rms. CI 3pm/CO 11am. Nonsmoking rms avail. **Amenities:** A/C, cable TV, dataport. **Services:** **Facilities:** **Rates (CP):** $47–$53 S or D. Extra person $6. Children under age 18 stay free. Parking: Outdoor, free. AE, CB, DC, DISC, JCB, MC, V.

Holiday Inn

1209 Bagnal Blvd, 28677; tel 704/878-9691 or toll free 800/446-4656. Exit 49A off I-77. A comfortable two-story motel offering dependable, no-frills accommodations. **Rooms:** 135 rms. CI 3pm/CO noon. Nonsmoking rms avail. **Amenities:**

🔌🖥 A/C, satel TV. **Services:** ✗ 🚗 🖼 🔔 **Facilities:** 🔗 🛏️500️ 🔗 1 restaurant, 1 bar. **Rates:** $74 S or D. Children under age 14 stay free. Parking: Outdoor, free. AE, CB, DC, DISC, JCB, MC, V.

Sunset Beach

One of the state's southernmost coastal island communities, it is a popular beach resort.

RESORT 🏨

UNRATED **Sea Trail Plantation**
211 Clubhouse Rd, 28468; tel 910/287-1100 or toll free 800/624-6601; fax 910/287-1104. Off Old Georgetown Rd. 2,000 acres. Peaceful resort with attractive stucco and wood exterior, screened porches, and well-spaced villas. **Rooms:** 100 effic; 300 cottages/villas. CI 4pm/CO 11am. Nonsmoking rms avail. Minisuites (efficiencies) available. **Amenities:** 📺 🔌 A/C, cable TV, refrig. All units w/terraces. **Services:** 🚗 🖼 🔔 Golf school. **Facilities:** 🔗 ▶54 🏊2 🎾 🛏️750️ 🔗 2 restaurants, 1 bar, basketball, volleyball, lawn games, sauna, whirlpool. Resort has two driving ranges. **Rates:** Peak (mid-Mar–July/Oct–Nov) $89–$99 effic; $130–$310 cottage/villa. Lower rates off-season. MAP rates avail. Parking: Outdoor, free. Golf packages avail. AE, CB, DC, DISC, MC, V.

RESTAURANT 🍴

🍴 **Twin Lakes Seafood Restaurant**
3852 Holden Rd, South Brunswick; tel 910/579-6373. At the entrance to Sunset Beach. **Seafood.** A comfortable family place, with pastel colors to set you at ease. (The artwork on the walls is for sale.) A changing menu of grilled and broiled seafood entrees is likely to include popular favorites like "Grouper in a Garden" and broiled shrimp with crabmeat dressing. **FYI:** Reservations not accepted. Children's menu. Beer and wine only. **Open:** Daily 5–9:30pm. Closed Thanksgiving–Feb. **Prices:** Main courses $8–$18. MC, V. 🏞️ 🎴

Swansboro

See also Atlantic Beach, Beaufort, Morehead City

Home of shifting sand dunes, a maritime forest, marshlands, and miles of unspoiled beach.

RESTAURANT 🍴

★ **T&W Oyster Bar and Restaurant**
3231 NC 58 N; tel 919/393-8838. **Seafood.** This place looks like a country roadhouse on the outside; on the inside, the beamed ceilings and two large dining rooms have a simplicity bordering on sophistication. Menu specialties include homemade clam chowder and an array of seafood entrees. Combination plates are available, and the oyster bar offers a variety of steamed seafood items, sold by the peck (eight quarts) or half-peck. Steak and chicken available for landlubbers. **FYI:** Reservations not accepted. Children's menu. Beer and wine only. **Open:** Peak (June–Sept) Mon–Sat 5–9pm, Sun noon–9pm. **Prices:** Main courses $8–$12. AE, MC, V. 🎴

Troy

ATTRACTION 🏛️

Town Creek Indian Mound State Historic Site
NC 1542, Mount Gilead; tel 910/439-6802. Native Americans established this religious, ceremonial, and burial center some 300 years ago on a bluff overlooking the junction of Little River and Town Creek. The remnants have now been excavated and/or reconstructed: a major temple, the dwelling place of priests, ceremonial grounds, and many, many artifacts are on view. **Open:** Apr–Oct, Mon–Sat 9am–5pm, Sun 1–5pm; Nov–Mar, Tues–Sat 10am–4pm, Sun 1–4pm. Closed some hols. **Free**

Tryon

This mountain community, settled in 1885, lies just north of the South Carolina border. Nearby to 90-foot falls and Tryon Mountain, for which the town is named. **Information:** Polk County Travel & Tourism, 401 N Trade St, Tryon, 28782 (tel 704/859-8300).

INN 🏨

☰ ☰ ☰ **Pine Crest Inn**
200 Pine Crest Lane, 28782; tel 704/859-9135 or toll free 800/633-3001; fax 704/859-9135. Off I-26. A quaint inn nestled in the foothills of the Blue Ridge Mountains. The extensive grounds are a wonderland of shade trees, climbing ivy, and wildflowers, and the beautiful lobby features wildflower arrangements, chandeliers, and antiques. **Rooms:** 24 rms and effic; 3 cottages/villas. CI 3pm/CO 11am. Nonsmoking rms avail. Private and semiprivate cottages are furnished in country-style with leather armchairs, Oriental rugs, and dark paneling. **Amenities:** 📺 🔌 🍷 A/C, cable TV w/movies, VCR, bathrobes. Some units w/terraces, some w/fireplaces, some w/whirlpools. About half the rooms have refrigerators. **Services:** ✗ 🆅🅿 🖼 🔔 Twice-daily maid svce, children's program, babysitting. **Facilities:** 🛏️75️ 🖥 1 restaurant (bkfst and dinner only), 1 bar, lawn games. **Rates (CP):** Peak (Mar–May/Sept–Dec) $120–$165 S or D; $120–$185 effic; $165–$450 cottage/villa. Children under age 12 stay free. Min stay peak and wknds. Lower rates off-season. Higher rates for special events/hols. AP and MAP rates avail. Parking: Outdoor, free. Closed Jan. AE, DISC, MC, V.

Washington

The first town named after George Washington, who visited here in 1791. The restored waterfront includes "Fowles Dock," former mooring site of the boat that inspired Edna Ferber's *Showboat*. **Information:** Washington–Beaufort County Chamber of Commerce, 102 W Stewart Pkwy, PO Box 665, Washington, 27889 (tel 919/946-9168).

HOTEL 🏨

≣≣ Comfort Inn

1636 Carolina Ave, 27889; tel 919/946-4444 or toll free 800/221-2222. Small, relatively new hotel. Located 1½ miles from historic downtown and waterfront, and within walking distance of fast-food restaurants. **Rooms:** 55 rms. CI 2pm/CO noon. Nonsmoking rms avail. **Amenities:** 🔧 🗄 A/C, cable TV, dataport. **Services:** 🛆 🖅 Fax and copy services. **Facilities:** 🏋 🛟 🐟 👗 **Rates:** Peak (May–Aug) $49–$61 S; $54–$66 D. Extra person $5. Children under age 18 stay free. Lower rates off-season. Parking: Outdoor, free. AE, DISC, MC, V.

MOTEL

≣ Econo Lodge

1220 W 15th St, 27889; tel 919/946-7781 or toll free 800/55-ECONO; fax 919/946-7050. At jct US 17/US 264. Very basic motel, with no surprises. **Rooms:** 48 rms. CI 11am/CO 11am. Nonsmoking rms avail. **Amenities:** 🔧 A/C, cable TV w/movies. **Facilities:** 👗 Chinese restaurant next door. **Rates:** $35 S; $38–$41 D. Extra person $4. Children under age 11 stay free. Parking: Outdoor, free. AE, DISC, MC, V.

Waynesville

Quaint mountain town in the Great Smoky Mountains, incorporated in 1810. Host to Folk Moot, an international festival of folk dancing. **Information:** Haywood County Chamber of Commerce, 107 Woodland Dr, PO Box 600, Waynesville, 28786 (tel 704/456-3021).

MOTELS 🏨

≣≣ Best Western Smoky Mountain Inn

200 Westream Dr, 28786; tel 704/456-4402 or toll free 800/528-1234; fax 704/456-4885. Exit 98 off US 23/74. A comfortable and reliable chain motel with great mountain views and large, pleasant rooms. **Rooms:** 58 rms and effic. CI 2pm/CO 11am. Nonsmoking rms avail. Rooms between 201 and 221 have the best mountain views. **Amenities:** 🔧 A/C, cable TV w/movies. **Services:** 🖅 **Facilities:** 🏋 🛟 👗 **Rates (CP):** Peak (June–Oct) $59–$75 S; $69–$95 D; $70–$125 effic. Extra person $7. Children under age 15 stay free. Lower rates off-season. Parking: Outdoor, free. AE, CB, DC, DISC, MC, V.

≣≣ Days Inn

3325 Dellwood Rd, 28786; tel 704/926-0201 or toll free 800/325-2525; fax 704/926-1461. Exit 20 off I-40. A comfortable chain hotel popular with vacationing families. **Rooms:** 102 rms and stes. CI 3pm/CO 11am. Nonsmoking rms avail. **Amenities:** 🔧 A/C, cable TV w/movies. **Services:** 🖅 **Facilities:** 🏋 🛟 👗 1 restaurant (bkfst only), games rm, whirlpool, playground, washer/dryer. **Rates:** Peak (June–Oct) $55–$75 S or D; $85 ste. Children under age 18 stay free. Lower rates off-season. Parking: Outdoor, free. AE, CB, DC, DISC, JCB, MC, V.

≣≣ Econo Lodge

1202 Russ Ave, 28786; tel 704/452-0353 or toll free 800/424-4777; fax 704/452-3329. Exit 102 off US 23/74. No-frills motel, located in the mountains and near many restaurants. **Rooms:** 40 rms. CI 2pm/CO 11am. Nonsmoking rms avail. Very comfortable rooms. **Amenities:** 🔧 A/C, cable TV w/movies. All units w/terraces. Pool-view rooms have balconies with rocking chairs. **Services:** 🖅 **Facilities:** 🏋 🛟 👗 **Rates (CP):** Peak (June–Oct) $40 S; $59 S or D. Extra person $5. Children under age 18 stay free. Lower rates off-season. Parking: Outdoor, free. AE, CB, DC, DISC, MC, V.

UNRATED Pisgah Inn

Blue Ridge Pkwy, PO Box 749, 28786; tel 704/235-8228; fax 704/648-9719. On Blue Ridge Pkwy N of US 276. A wonderfully picturesque place to stay in the mountains, with vistas of forested mountains, rhododendrons, and mountain laurel and azaleas. **Rooms:** 51 rms and stes. CI 2pm/CO 11am. Nonsmoking rms avail. Rooms have incredible views of the surrounding landscape. **Amenities:** TV w/movies. No A/C or phone. All units w/terraces, 1 w/fireplace. **Services:** 🖅 **Facilities:** 🏋 🛟 👗 2 restaurants, washer/dryer. **Rates:** $60–$65 S; $65–$70 D; $105 ste. Extra person $6. Children under age 12 stay free. Parking: Outdoor, free. Closed Dec–Mar. MC, V.

INN

≣≣≣ The Old Stone Inn

900 Dolan Rd, 28786; tel 704/456-3333 or toll free 800/432-8499. Off US 23. A rustic, restful retreat surrounded by giant oak trees and beautiful landscapes. Rocking chairs on the front porch provide a great place to relax. **Rooms:** 20 rms and stes; 2 cottages/villas. CI 3pm/CO 10am. Nonsmoking rms avail. **Amenities:** Cable TV. No A/C or phone. **Services:** ✗ 🛒 🖅 Babysitting. A feast of freshly baked specialties is served at breakfast. **Facilities:** 🛟 1 restaurant (bkfst and dinner only), games rm, lawn games. **Rates (BB):** Peak (June–Aug, Oct) $59–$79 S; $74–$94 D; $89–$104 ste; $89–$104 cottage/villa. Extra person $18. Children under age 5 stay free. Min stay special events. Lower rates off-season. MAP rates avail. Parking: Outdoor, free. DISC, MC, V.

RESORT

≣≣≣ Waynesville Country Club Inn

Country Club Dr, PO Box 390, 28786; tel 704/452-2258 or toll free 800/627-6250; fax 704/456-3555. Exit 27 off I-40. A pleasant and relaxing resort offering beautiful grounds and spectacular mountain vistas. **Rooms:** 92 rms and stes; 3 cottages/villas. CI 2pm/CO noon. **Amenities:** 🛕 A/C, cable TV. Some units w/terraces. **Services:** 🚗 🖼 🔧 **Facilities:** 🖼 ▶27 🏊2 🏏200 🔥 1 restaurant, 1 bar. **Rates (MAP):** Peak (May–Oct) $106–$150 S; $140–$208 D; $174 ste; $174–$208 cottage/villa. Extra person $50. Lower rates off-season. Parking: Outdoor, free. Golf and holiday packages avail. MC, V.

Wilkesboro

Seat of Wilkes County. Its historic jail (built in 1770) housed legendary Tom Dula (of "The Ballad of Tom Dooley" fame) before he was sent to the gallows in 1868.

MOTEL 🏨

≣≣≣ Holiday Inn Express

US 421 at Wilkes Mall, 28697; tel 910/838-1800 or toll free 800/HOLIDAY; fax 910/838-1800. An exceptionally well-maintained property, with a spacious, pleasant lobby including palm leaf–patterned carpeting and a spectacular indoor garden. **Rooms:** 101 rms and stes. CI 2pm/CO noon. Nonsmoking rms avail. Spacious, comfortable rooms, with relatively new furnishings and carpeting. **Amenities:** 🛕 🔌 A/C, cable TV. VCRs available upon request. **Services:** ✗ 🖼 🔧 **Facilities:** 🖼 🏏400 🔥 **Rates (CP):** Peak (June–Sept) $70 S or D; $82 ste. Extra person $6. Children under age 19 stay free. Min stay special events. Lower rates off-season. Parking: Outdoor, free. AE, DC, DISC, MC, V.

Williamston

Situated on the Roanoke River in a farming area, the town was incorporated in 1779 as William's Town, in honor of William Williams, a colonel in the Revolutionary War. **Information:** Martin County Chamber of Commerce, 620 E Blvd, PO Box 311, Williamston, 27892 (tel 919/792-4131).

HOTEL 🏨

≣≣ Comfort Inn

US 17 and US 64 Bypass, PO Box 663, 27892; tel 919/792-8400 or toll free 800/228-5150. Recently renovated hotel featuring a brick exterior and a columned portico entrance. **Rooms:** 59 rms and stes. CI 1pm/CO noon. Nonsmoking rms avail. **Amenities:** 🛕 🔌 A/C, cable TV w/movies, dataport. **Services:** 🖼 🔧 **Facilities:** 🔥 **Rates (CP):**

$47–$52 S; $51–$56 D; $50–$60 ste. Extra person $5. Children under age 18 stay free. Parking: Outdoor, free. AE, CB, DC, DISC, MC, V.

MOTEL

≣≣ Holiday Inn

At jct US 13/17/64, PO Box 711, 27892; tel 919/792-3184 or toll free 800/792-3101; fax 919/792-9003. Standard motel, with contemporary furnishings and coordinated color schemes throughout. Don't expect any extras, though. **Rooms:** 100 rms. CI 3pm/CO noon. Nonsmoking rms avail. **Amenities:** 🛕 🔌 A/C, satel TV w/movies, dataport. **Services:** 🖼 🔧 **Facilities:** 🖼 🏏175 🖥 🔥 1 restaurant, 1 bar. **Rates:** $46 S; $50 D. Extra person $4. Children under age 18 stay free. Parking: Outdoor, free. AE, CB, DC, DISC, MC, V.

Wilmington

See also Brunswick Islands/Cape Fear Coast

The state's largest coastal city, this historic seaport once exported more cotton than any other port in the world. Restored Cotton Exchange houses shops and boutiques, and Chandler's Wharf surrounds a nautical museum. **Information:** Greater Wilmington Chamber of Commerce, 1 Estell Lee Place, Wilmington, 28401 (tel 910/762-2611).

HOTELS 🏨

≣≣≣ Coast Line Inn

503 Nutt St, 28401; tel 910/763-2800. On the waterfront. Classy property featuring warm decor with lots of mahogany, brass, and dark leather, as well as a dock and boardwalk with benches. Located next to Coast Line Convention Center, a restored railroad depot. **Rooms:** 50 rms and stes. CI 3pm/CO noon. All rooms offer serene views of Cape Fear River. **Amenities:** 🛕 🔌 📺 A/C, cable TV w/movies. **Services:** ✗ 🚗 🔧 **Facilities:** 🏏700 🔥 1 bar (w/entertainment). **Rates (CP):** $72 S or D; $92 ste. Extra person $10. Children under age 12 stay free. Min stay special events. Parking: Outdoor, free. AE, CB, DC, DISC, MC, V.

≣≣ Comfort Inn Executive Center

151 S College Rd, 28403; tel 910/791-4841 or toll free 800/444-4841. ¼ mi S of US 17. A bright, coastal decor dominates this comfortable hotel convenient to UNC Wilmington. **Rooms:** 146 rms and stes. CI 3pm/CO noon. Nonsmoking rms avail. **Amenities:** 🛕 🔌 A/C, cable TV w/movies. **Services:** 🚗 🖼 🔧 Babysitting. **Facilities:** 🖼 🏊 🏏50 🔥 Washer/dryer. **Rates (CP):** Peak (Mar 25–Oct 10) $75–$110 S or D; $85–$110 ste. Extra person $5. Children under age 18 stay free. Min stay peak. Lower rates off-season. Parking: Outdoor, free. AE, DC, DISC, MC, V.

≣≣≣ Howard Johnson Plaza Hotel

5032 Market St, 28405; tel 910/392-1101 or toll free 800/I-GO-HOJO. ½ mi W of I-40/NC 132. A contemporary and stylish hotel. **Rooms:** 124 rms and stes. Executive level. CI 3pm/CO noon. Nonsmoking rms avail. **Amenities:** 🛏 ⓐ 🔲 A/C, cable TV w/movies, dataport. Refrigerators and microwaves available. **Services:** ✗ 🚗 🖼 ⌁ **Facilities:** 🔧 🏊300 ⓖ 1 restaurant, 1 bar, sauna, whirlpool, washer/dryer. **Rates:** Peak (Apr–Labor Day) $76–$84 S or D; $125–$150 ste. Extra person $10. Children under age 18 stay free. Min stay special events. Lower rates off-season. Parking: Outdoor, free. AE, CB, DC, DISC, MC, V.

≣≣≣ The Inn at St Thomas Court
101 S 2nd St, 28401; tel 910/343-1800 or toll free 800/525-0909; fax 910/251-1149. Off Market St. Located in the heart of the historic district, this quaint inn boasts beautiful courtyard gardens with fountains, patios, and shade trees. **Rooms:** 34 stes. CI 3pm/CO 11am. No smoking. Individually decorated units have shared balconies with rocking chairs. One- and two-bedroom suites (with kitchen facilities) available. **Amenities:** 🛏 ⓐ 🔲 A/C, cable TV w/movies, refrig, dataport. All units w/terraces, 1 w/fireplace, some w/whirlpools. **Services:** 🚗 🖼 ⌁ Babysitting. Fax and copy services. **Facilities:** 🍴 🏊300 ⓖ **Rates (CP):** Peak (Apr–Oct) $115–$185 ste. Extra person $5. Children under age 12 stay free. Min stay special events. Lower rates off-season. Parking: Outdoor, free. AE, CB, DC, DISC, MC, V.

≣≣ Ramada Inn Conference Center
5001 Market St, 28405; tel 910/799-1730 or toll free 800/433-7144. ½ mi W of jct I-40/NC 132. Standard hotel accommodations. **Rooms:** 100 rms and stes. CI 3pm/CO noon. Nonsmoking rms avail. **Amenities:** 🛏 ⓐ A/C, cable TV. **Services:** 🚗 🖼 ⌁ Breakfast available weekdays only. **Facilities:** 🔧 🏊150 ⓖ 1 restaurant, 1 bar, playground. **Rates (BB):** Peak (Apr–Sept) $59–$69 S or D; $85–$95 ste. Extra person $8. Children under age 18 stay free. Min stay special events. Lower rates off-season. MAP rates avail. Parking: Outdoor, free. Golf packages avail. AE, CB, DC, DISC, MC, V.

≣≣≣ Wilmington Hilton Inn
301 N Water St, 28401; tel 910/763-5900 or toll free 800/HILTONS; fax 910/763-0038. Beautiful luxury hotel located on the water. **Rooms:** 178 rms and stes. Executive level. CI 4pm/CO noon. Nonsmoking rms avail. Some rooms have view of Cape Fear River and the USS *North Carolina*. **Amenities:** 🛏 ⓐ 🔲 A/C, cable TV w/movies, dataport. **Services:** ✗ VP 🚗 🖼 ⌁ Babysitting. **Facilities:** 🔧 🍴 🏊700 ⓖ 1 restaurant, 1 bar, whirlpool. **Rates:** $99–$119 S; $109–$129 D; $225–$300 ste. Extra person $10. Children under age 18 stay free. Min stay special events. Parking: Outdoor, free. AE, CB, DC, DISC, MC, V.

MOTELS

≣ The Azalea Inn
311 N 3rd St, 28401; tel 910/763-0121; fax 910/343-8102. Motel is located at the outer limits of the historic district. **Rooms:** 70 rms. CI 2pm/CO 11am. Nonsmoking rms avail.

Amenities: 🛏 A/C, cable TV. **Services:** ⌁ **Facilities:** 🔧 🏊200 1 restaurant, 1 bar. **Rates:** Peak (May–Sept) $58–$78 S or D. Extra person $7.50. Children under age 12 stay free. Min stay special events. Lower rates off-season. Parking: Outdoor, free. AE, DISC, MC, V.

≣≣≣ Beau Rivage Plantation
6230 Carolina Beach Rd, 28412; tel 910/392-9021 or toll free 800/628-7080. 7 mi S of Wilmington. A peaceful coastal resort only minutes from the beach. The main building looks like an antebellum plantation house with its white columns. **Rooms:** 30 stes. CI 3pm/CO noon. Nonsmoking rms avail. Decorated with traditional furnishings. **Amenities:** 🛏 A/C, cable TV. **Services:** 🖼 Babysitting. **Facilities:** 🔧 ⛳18 🏌2 🏊250 1 restaurant (bkfst and lunch only). Breakfast and lunch served daily at the snack bar; the full-service restaurant is open Fri night only. **Rates:** Peak (Mar–May/Sept–Nov) $85 ste. Extra person $5. Children under age 12 stay free. Min stay peak. Lower rates off-season. Parking: Outdoor, free. Golf package avail. AE, DC, DISC, EC, MC, V.

≣≣ Best Western Carolinian
2916 Market St, 28403; tel 910/763-4653 or toll free 800/528-1234; fax 910/763-0486. 1½ mi W of Jct I-40/NC 132. Beautifully landscaped grounds and gardens brighten up this otherwise standard property. **Rooms:** 61 rms. CI 2pm/CO 11am. Nonsmoking rms avail. **Amenities:** 🛏 ⓐ A/C, cable TV. **Facilities:** 🔧 🏊25 **Rates (CP):** Peak (Mem Day–Labor Day) $49 S; $63–$73 D. Extra person $8. Children under age 12 stay free. Min stay special events. Lower rates off-season. Parking: Outdoor, free. AE, DISC, MC, V.

≣≣ Days Inn
5040 Market St, 28405; tel 910/799-6300 or toll free 800/DAYS-INN. Property stands out for its pastel exterior and bright, islandlike interior. **Rooms:** 122 rms. CI 3pm/CO 11am. Nonsmoking rms avail. **Amenities:** 🛏 ⓐ A/C, cable TV w/movies. **Facilities:** 🔧 ⓖ 1 restaurant. **Rates:** Peak (Apr–Sept) $32–$70 S; $38–$70 D. Extra person $6. Lower rates off-season. Parking: Outdoor, free. AE, DC, DISC, MC, V.

≣≣ Fairfield Inn Market St
4926 Market St, 28403; tel 910/791-8850 or toll free 800/228-2800. A comfortable motel with a clean, fresh look. **Rooms:**. CI 2pm/CO noon. Nonsmoking rms avail. **Amenities:** 🛏 ⓐ A/C, cable TV w/movies. Nintendo in rooms. **Services:** 🖼 ⌁ **Facilities:** 🔧 🏊10 🖥 ⓖ Health club privileges. **Rates (CP):** Peak (Apr–Sept 15) $59–$79 S; $64–$84 D. Extra person $5. Children under age 17 stay free. Lower rates off-season. Parking: Outdoor, free. AE, CB, DC, DISC, MC, V.

≣≣ Fairfield Inn Wilmington
306 S College Rd, 28403; tel 910/392-6767 or toll free 800/228-2800. Off I-40. Basic yet pleasant three-story motel, not far from University of North Carolina–Wilmington. **Rooms:** 134 rms. CI 3pm/CO noon. Nonsmoking rms avail. **Amenities:** 🛏 ⓐ A/C, cable TV w/movies, dataport. **Services:**

⊠ ⊐ Coffee in lobby. **Facilities:** 🔲 🔲 ⅃ **Rates (CP):** Peak (Apr–Sept) $49–$69 S; $58–$69 D. Extra person $5. Children under age 18 stay free. Lower rates off-season. Parking: Outdoor, free. AE, CB, DC, DISC, MC, V.

☰ Greentree Inn
5025 Market St, 28405; tel 910/799-6001 or toll free 800/ 225-ROOM in the US. ½ mi W of jct I-40/NC 132S. A basic, well-kept place with few frills. Suitable for the frugal traveler. **Rooms:** 123 rms and stes. CI 3pm/CO noon. Nonsmoking rms avail. **Amenities:** 🔲 A/C, cable TV w/movies. **Services:** ⊠ ⊐ Breakfast served on weekdays only. **Facilities:** 🔲 ⅃ **Rates (BB):** Peak (Mem Day–Labor Day) $38–$45 S; $43– $50 D; $100 ste. Extra person $4. Children under age 16 stay free. Min stay special events. Lower rates off-season. Parking: Outdoor, free. Golf packages avail. AE, DISC, MC, V.

☰☰ Hampton Inn
5107 Market St, 28403; tel 910/395-5045 or toll free 800/ HAMPTON; fax 910/799-1974. ¼ mi W of Jct I-40/NC 132. No-frills, two-story motel. **Rooms:.** CI 2pm/CO noon. Nonsmoking rms avail. **Amenities:** 🔲 ⚱ A/C, cable TV, dataport. **Services:** ⊠ ⊐ Babysitting. **Facilities:** 🔲 🔲 ⅃ Guest privileges at local health club. **Rates (CP):** Peak (Apr–Labor Day) $60 S; $67–$75 D. Children under age 18 stay free. Lower rates off-season. Parking: Outdoor, free. AE, CB, DC, DISC, MC, V.

☰☰☰ Holiday Inn
4903 Market St, 28405; tel 910/799-1440 or toll free 800/ HOLIDAY; fax 910/799-2683. Attractive complex with a beautiful courtyard and a large bean-shaped pool landscaped with trees and crape myrtles. **Rooms:** 233 rms. CI 3pm/CO noon. Nonsmoking rms avail. **Amenities:** 🔲 ⚱ A/C, cable TV w/movies. Some units w/whirlpools. **Services:** ✗ ⊠ ⊐ **Facilities:** 🔲 🔲 ⅃ 1 restaurant, 1 bar. Health club privileges. **Rates:** Peak (Apr–Sept) $68 S; $70 D. Extra person $5. Children under age 12 stay free. Lower rates off-season. Parking: Outdoor, free. AE, CB, DC, DISC, MC, V.

☰☰ Rodeway Inn Intown
2929 Market St, 28403; tel 910/763-3318 or toll free 800/ 424-4777. 1½ mi W of I-40/NC 132 on US 17. A classic 1950s-era motel, which has been recently refurbished. Guests will enjoy swaying trees and flower gardens, which lend property a secluded atmosphere. **Rooms:** 48 rms. CI 2pm/ CO 11am. Nonsmoking rms avail. **Amenities:** 🔲 A/C, cable TV. **Services:** ⊠ ⊐ **Facilities:** 🔲 ⅃ **Rates (CP):** Peak (May– Aug) $36–$49 S; $45–$65 D. Extra person $5. Children under age 17 stay free. Lower rates off-season. Parking: Outdoor, free. AE, DISC, MC, V.

RESORT

UNRATED St Regis Resort
2000 New River Inlet Rd, PO Box 4000, 28460; tel 910/ 328-0778 or toll free 800/682-4882. At N Topsail Beach. This is a very modern, secluded, oceanfront resort. **Rooms:**

224 cottages/villas. CI 4pm/CO 11am. Nonsmoking rms avail. **Amenities:** 🔲 ⚱ 🔲 A/C, cable TV w/movies, refrig. All units w/terraces, some w/whirlpools. **Services:** ⊠ ⊐ Babysitting. **Facilities:** 🔲 🔺 🔲 🔲 🔲 1 restaurant (dinner only), 1 bar, 1 beach (ocean), volleyball, sauna, steam rm, whirlpool. **Rates:** Peak (June 10–Aug 18) $150–$235 cottage/villa. Lower rates off-season. Parking: Outdoor, free. Extended-stay rates avail. AE, CB, DC, DISC, MC, V.

RESTAURANTS 🍴

Bridge Tender
Airlie Rd at Wrightsville Beach Bridge; tel 910/256-4519. **Seafood/Steak.** Most tables have a view of the waterway, Wrightsville Beach, and the many boats and yachts parked at the marina next door. Certified Angus beef and 14 seafood entrees—including sautéed scallops, baked red snapper, and grouper Florentine—are available. Desserts are made fresh daily. **FYI:** Reservations recommended. **Open:** Peak (Mem Day–Labor Day) lunch Mon–Fri 11:30am–2pm; dinner daily 5:30–11pm. **Prices:** Main courses $17–$23. AE, DC, DISC, MC, V. 🔲 ⅃

♦ Crook's on the River
138 S Front St; tel 919/762-8898. **Southern.** Crook's innovative kitchen, which has drawn praise from national critics, specializes in dishes like shrimp and grits, Cajun rib eye, alligator and okra, red beans and rice, and crab cakes. The outside patio boasts fantastic views of Cape Fear River, while the indoor dining area offers diner-style tables and chairs along with original local artwork. **FYI:** Reservations accepted. Blues/jazz. **Open:** Dinner Sun–Wed 6–10pm, Thurs–Sat 6– 10:30pm; brunch Sun 11am–2pm. **Prices:** Main courses $9– $17. AE, MC, V. 🔲 🔲 ⅃

Elijah's
In Chandler's Wharf, 2 Ann St; tel 910/343-1448. **Seafood.** A stylish and elegant waterfront eatery with beautiful views from the window tables and the outside covered patio. The menu focuses on classic renditions of fresh local seafood. **FYI:** Reservations recommended. Children's menu. **Open:** Lunch daily 11:30am–3pm; dinner Sun–Thurs 5–10pm, Fri– Sat 5–11pm. **Prices:** Main courses $13–$17. AE, DISC, MC, V. ♥ 🔲 🔲 ⅃

Front Street Brewery
9 N Front St; tel 910/251-1935. **Pub.** A new brewery housed in a historic 1883 structure; the original tin ceiling and pine floors are still in place, and the great copper vats used in the brewing process are on display in the front window. Culinary specialties include fish-and-chips, black pepper–crusted New York strip, and grilled boneless pork chops. Seasonal beers feature fruit flavors in the spring and summer, and spiced ales in the cooler months. **FYI:** Reservations not accepted. Children's menu. **Open:** Mon–Thurs 11:30am–midnight, Fri–Sat 11:30am–1am, Sun noon–10pm. **Prices:** Main courses $6–$13. AE, MC, V. ♥ ▮ 🔲 ⅃

The Paleo Sun Cafe

35 N Front St; tel 910/762-7700. **Eclectic.** An Aztec sun sculpture, wooden sun carvings, and loads of fresh-cut sunflowers give this cafe a "sunny" feel. Innovative dinner specialties include seared pork tenderloin with wild mushrooms and Jamaican paella (chicken, sausage, and seafood mixed with rice). **FYI:** Reservations accepted. Blues/jazz. **Open:** Daily 11:30am–11pm. **Prices:** Main courses $12–$15. AE, DISC, MC, V. ● &

♥ The Pilot House

In Chandler's Wharf, 2 Ann St; tel 910/343-0200. **Seafood/ Southern.** Casual dining in an elegant atmosphere with a stunning view of Cape Fear River. Diners can enjoy seafood dishes like crab cakes, grilled salmon with grits, and crab quiche. Other dishes include smoked barbecue pork chops served with potato cakes, and veal medallions served with fried green tomatoes. **FYI:** Reservations recommended. Children's menu. **Open:** Peak (Mem Day–Labor Day) lunch Mon–Sat 11:30am–3pm; dinner Mon–Thurs 5–10pm, Fri–Sat 5–11pm; brunch Sun 11:30am–3pm. **Prices:** Main courses $13–$19. AE, DISC, MC, V. ⛴ 🏞 &

⑤ Skinner & Daniels Barbecue and Seafood

5214 Market St; tel 910/799-1790. ¼ mi W of jct I-40/NC 132. **Southern.** Good country cooking served in a simple dining room with minimal decor. The kitchen serves up hearty portions of barbecue pork, chicken, and ribs along with several seafood plates. Southern vegetables (blackeyed peas, greens, grits) round out the meal. **FYI:** Reservations not accepted. Children's menu. No liquor license. **Open:** Mon–Sat 11am–9pm. **Prices:** Main courses $4–$10. No CC. 📷

Szechuan 130

130 N Front St; tel 910/762-5782. Between Princess and Chestnut Sts. **Chinese.** Widely regarded as having the best Chinese food in Wilmington. The large menu includes the usual Chinese offerings along with surprises like Genghis Khan beef (a heavy slab of beef marinated with ginger, garlic, and wine) and Neptune Delight (a sampler platter of sautéed seafood). Most seafood options are a good bet. **FYI:** Reservations accepted. **Open:** Lunch Sun–Fri 11:30am–2:30pm, Sat noon–2:30pm; dinner Sun–Fri 4:30–9pm, Sat 2:30–10pm. **Prices:** Main courses $6–$12. MC, V. &

REFRESHMENT STOP 🗗

Port City Java

7 N Front St; tel 910/762-JAVA. **Coffeehouse.** This small coffee bar serves up fresh-baked muffins, cakes, and pies; ice cream shakes such as the Colossal Coffee Shake and Java Super Shake; and, of course, gourmet coffees. **Open:** Sun–Thurs 6:30am–11pm, Fri–Sat 6:30am–midnight. No CC. &

ATTRACTIONS 🏛

Burgwin-Wright House and Gardens

224 Market St; tel 910/762-0570. This beautifully restored example of a colonial gentleman's town house was built in 1771 over an abandoned city jail. Later, Lord Cornwallis used the house as his headquarters in the weeks before his final defeat at Yorktown. (Cornwallis kept war prisoners in the house's dungeon.) Today, the Georgian house has been restored and displays an array of fine 18th-century antiques; the parterre garden is also of typical 18th-century design. **Open:** Tues–Sat 10am–4pm. Closed Jan and some hols. $

Poplar Grove Plantation

10200 US 17 N; tel 910/686-9989. A restored Greek Revival manor house and estate dating from 1850 and inhabited for several generations by the Foy family. Outbuildings include a smokehouse, tenant house, and restored old kitchen, with demonstrations by a basket weaver, a fabric weaver, and a blacksmith. The Plantation Tea Room serves country-style meals and a country store sells souvenirs. **Open:** Mon–Sat 9am–5pm, Sun noon–5pm. Closed mid-Dec–Jan, some hols. $$$

Battleship USS *North Carolina*

Eagle Island; tel 910/251-5797. Commissioned in 1941, this warship was involved in almost every major naval offensive in the Pacific during World War II. Today, it is permanently berthed here as a memorial to the state's 10,000 World War II dead. Visitors can choose from two self-guided tours, both of them beginning with a 10-minute orientation film; the full tour takes approximately two hours and the shorter tour takes one hour. A museum presents a pictorial history of the *North Carolina*'s Pacific campaigns. From early June through Labor Day, there's a 70-minute sound and light show, *The Immortal Showboat*. **Open:** Daily 8am–sunset. $$$

Capt J N Maffitt Riverboat

Foot of Market St; tel 919/343-1611. The 45-minute narrated cruise departs from the foot of Market St for a five-mile loop of the Cape Fear River. The route skirts the busy harbor, passes the Cotton Exchange renovation and the new Waterfront Park, and stops at the dock for passengers who wish to disembark to tour the battleship USS *North Carolina* (see above). $$

Wilson

This eastern North Carolina city is the South's leading antique market, with a number of shops in the area. **Information:** Wilson Chamber of Commerce, 220 Broad St, PO Box 1146, Wilson, 27894 (tel 919/237-0165).

MOTELS 🏨

≡≡≡ Best Western La Sammana

400 Ward Blvd SW, 27893; tel 919/237-8700 or toll free 800/528-1234; fax 919/237-8092. Attractive pink-stucco exterior and copper roof make this newish motel a stand-out. **Rooms:** 83 rms and stes. CI noon/CO 11am. Nonsmoking rms avail. Nicely furnished. **Amenities:** 🛁 Ⓐ A/C, cable TV w/movies, dataport. Some units w/whirlpools. **Services:** 🛎

Facilities: 🔲 [20] ♿ Whirlpool. **Rates (CP):** $54 S or D; $75–$95 ste. Extra person $5. Children under age 12 stay free. Parking: Outdoor, free. AE, DC, DISC, MC, V.

🔳🔳 Quality Inn South
US 301 S, 27893; tel 919/243-5165 or toll free 800/243-6540; fax 919/243-5109. Standard motel offering comfortable accommodations and a location convenient to restaurants and antique shopping. **Rooms:** 101 rms. CI 2pm/CO 11am. Nonsmoking rms avail. **Amenities:** 🔳 A/C, cable TV w/movies. King suites equipped with microwaves. **Services:** 🔲🔲🔲 Fax and copy services. **Facilities:** 🔲 ♿ 2 restaurants, 1 bar, whirlpool. **Rates (CP):** $52–$70 S or D. Extra person $5. Children under age 18 stay free. Min stay wknds. Parking: Outdoor, free. AE, CB, DC, DISC, MC, V.

•

INN

🔳🔳🔳 Miss Betty's Bed & Breakfast Inn
600 W Nash St, 27893; tel 919/243-4447 or toll free 800/243-4447. This inn is well suited for both corporate or leisure travel. Guests here are in for a hearty dose of Southern hospitality in an elegant Victorian setting. The main house, built in 1858, has been beautifully restored, and breakfast is served there at a large dining room table. Unsuitable for children under 12. **Rooms:** 10 rms and stes. CI 3pm/CO 11am. Each room is individually decorated with antiques, most of which are for sale. **Amenities:** 🔳 A/C, cable TV. **Services:** 🔲 Provides very unique, personal service. **Facilities:** ♿ Guest lounge. One house has a conference room with audio/visual equipment. **Rates (BB):** $50–$60 S; $65–$75 D; $75 ste. Higher rates for special events/hols. Parking: Outdoor, free. AE, MC, V.

RESTAURANTS 🍴

★ Beef Master Inn
2066 US 301S; tel 919/237-7343. 1 mi S of downtown. **Steak.** A simple "hole in the wall" place that locals can't get enough of. The typical dinner includes an eight-ounce steak, baked potato, salad, and a drink. **FYI:** Reservations not accepted. **Open:** Daily 6–10:30pm. **Prices:** Prix fixe $12. AE, MC, V.

Griff's Steak Barn
US 301S; tel 919/237-5935. 1½ mi S of downtown. **Steak.** A full-service steak house with a decor that is reminiscent of the Old West saloons of the movies. The menu includes a wide range of steaks, chicken, and seafood, and the dessert menu includes three "flaming" desserts—cherries jubilee, peach flambé, and bananas Foster. **FYI:** Reservations accepted. **Open:** Lunch Mon–Fri 11:30am–5pm, Sun 11:30am–2:30pm; dinner Mon–Sat 5–11pm, Sun 5–10pm. **Prices:** Main courses $9–$15. AE, DISC, MC, V. ■ 🔲 ♿

$ ★ Parker's Barbecue
US 301S; tel 919/237-0972. 1½ mi S of downtown. **Barbecue.** Since 1946, Parker's has been serving up pit-cooked North Carolina barbecue in sandwiches or piled high on plates. Order à la carte, or try the family-style dinner (barbecue, chicken, Brunswick stew, boiled potatoes, cole slaw, and corn sticks). **FYI:** Reservations not accepted. Children's menu. No liquor license. **Open:** Daily 9am–9pm. Closed 1 week after Father's Day. **Prices:** Main courses $4–$8; prix fixe $6. No CC. 🔲

ATTRACTION 🖼

Imagination Station Hands On Science Museum
224 E Nash St; tel 919/291-5113. Visitors to this interactive museum can take in more than 100 experiential science exhibits (including the Wright Brothers Flying Machine Gallery, a Mini-Planetarium, and more), daily live science shows, and even a state-of-the-art computer lab. **Open:** Mon–Sat 9am–5pm, Sun 1–5pm. Closed some hols. $$

Winston-Salem

Located in the agriculturally rich Piedmont area, this industrial city (the result of the consolidation of the cities of Winston and Salem in 1913) is perhaps best known as a major tobacco market and cigarette producer. The village of Old Salem recalls the city's origins as a mid-1700s Moravian settlement. Wake Forest University is here. **Information:** Winston-Salem Convention & Visitors Bureau, 601 W 4th St, PO Box 1408, Winston-Salem, 27102 (tel 910/725-2361).

HOTELS 🏨

🔳🔳🔳 Adam's Mark Winston Plaza
425 N Cherry St, 27101; tel 910/725-3500 or toll free 800/444-ADAM; fax 910/721-2240. Off I-40. Classy, modern hotel with fine, contemporary furnishings and high ceilings throughout. The spacious lobby is decorated in muted colors. **Rooms:** 315 rms and stes. Executive level. CI 3pm/CO noon. Nonsmoking rms avail. Luxury accommodations with exceptional decor. **Amenities:** 🔳 A/C, cable TV w/movies, dataport, voice mail. **Services:** 🔲🔲 VP 🔲🔲 Complimentary shoe shine available. **Facilities:** 🔲 🔲 [600] 🔲 ♿ 2 restaurants, 2 bars (1 w/entertainment), games rm, sauna. **Rates:** $135 S; $145 D; $250–$900 ste. Min stay special events. Parking: Outdoor, $5/day. AE, DC, DISC, MC, V.

🔳🔳🔳 Comfort Inn Cloverdale Place
110 Miller St, 27103; tel 910/721-0220 or toll free 800/228-5150. Cloverdale exit off I-40. One of the most comfortable places to stay in the area. Conveniently located to the interstate. **Rooms:** 122 rms. CI 4pm/CO noon. Nonsmoking rms avail. Well-kept rooms. **Amenities:** 🔳 A/C, cable TV, dataport. **Services:** 🔲🔲 **Facilities:** 🔲 🔲 [30] 🔲 ♿ Sauna, whirlpool. **Rates (CP):** $53–$67 S or D. Children under age 18 stay free. Min stay special events. Parking: Outdoor, free. AE, CB, DISC, MC, V.

≣≣≣ Courtyard by Marriott

3111 University Pkwy, 27105; tel 910/727-1277 or toll free 800/321-2211; fax 910/722-8219. 2 blocks from Wake Forest University. Excellent for business guests or college parents. **Rooms:** 123 rms. CI 3pm/CO 11am. Nonsmoking rms avail. Adequately furnished, with plenty of drawer and closet space for a lengthy stay. Up to three phones per room. **Amenities:** 🛏 ⚬ 🖬 A/C, cable TV w/movies, dataport. Some units w/whirlpools. **Services:** ✕ 🚗 ⌂ ⌐ Babysitting. **Facilities:** 🖻 ⌂ 🔲25 ⌐ 🖳 ⌂ 1 restaurant (bkfst only), 1 bar, whirlpool, washer/dryer. On-site exercise facility, plus guest passes to Gold's Gym. Complimentary greens fees at the local golf course. **Rates:** $57 S or D. Extra person $10. Parking: Outdoor, free. Accommodations for up to four people per room with no additional charge. Holiday package avail Nov–Dec. AE, CB, DC, DISC, MC, V.

≣≣≣ Hampton Inn

1990 Hampton Inn Court, 27103; tel 910/760-1660 or toll free 800/HAMPTON; fax 910/768-9168. Stratford Rd exit (189) off I-40. Attractive property convenient to I-40, shopping malls, and hospital. Multiroom lobby has built-in oak shelving and spectacular view of the garden patio. **Rooms:** 131 rms and stes. CI 2pm/CO noon. Nonsmoking rms avail. **Amenities:** 🛏 ⚬ A/C, cable TV, dataport. Some units w/whirlpools. **Services:** ⌂ ⌐ **Facilities:** 🖻 ⌂ 🔲60 🖳 ⌂ **Rates (CP):** $51–$53 S; $57–$59 D; $75–$96 ste. Extra person $6. Children under age 18 stay free. Min stay special events. Parking: Outdoor, free. AE, CB, DC, DISC, MC, V.

≣≣≣ Hawthorne Inn & Conference Center

420 High St, 27101; tel 910/777-3000 or toll free 800/972-3774; fax 910/777-3282. Cherry St exit off I-40. This contemporary hotel has a lobby with black-marble floors, light wood paneling, and modern furnishings. **Rooms:** 160 rms and stes. CI 3pm/CO noon. Nonsmoking rms avail. Comfortable rooms with up-to-date furnishings. **Amenities:** 🛏 ⚬ 🖬 A/C, cable TV, dataport. Some units w/terraces. TDD cases available. **Services:** 🍴 🚗 ⌂ ⌐ ⌐ Babysitting. Small pets only. **Facilities:** 🖻 ⌂ 🔲500 🖳 ⌂ 1 restaurant, 1 bar. **Rates (CP):** $75 S; $85 D; $99–$109 ste. Extra person $10. Children under age 18 stay free. Parking: Outdoor, free. AE, DC, DISC, MC, V.

≣≣ Holiday Inn North

3050 University Pkwy, 27105; tel 910/723-2911 or toll free 800/HOLIDAY. 2 blocks from Wake Forest University. This modern hotel greets its guests with a cozy, attractively appointed lobby and a neatly landscaped courtyard/pool area. **Rooms:** 191 rms. CI 3pm/CO 3pm. Nonsmoking rms avail. **Amenities:** 🛏 ⚬ A/C, cable TV. Some units w/terraces. **Services:** ✕ 🚗 ⌂ ⌐ **Facilities:** 🖻 ⌂ 🔲500 ⌂ 1 restaurant, 1 bar. **Rates:** $80 S or D. Parking: Outdoor, free. AE, CB, DC, DISC, MC, V.

≣≣≣ Radisson Marque Hotel

460 N Cherry St, 27101; tel 910/725-1234 or toll free 800/333-3333; fax 910/722-9182. Off I-40 across from Civic Center. Spectacular, modern hotel with an indoor glass elevator and nine-story atrium. The interior is lavishly furnished in leather. **Rooms:** 293 rms and stes. Executive level. CI 4pm/CO noon. Nonsmoking rms avail. Comfortable rooms. **Amenities:** 🛏 ⚬ 🖬 A/C, cable TV w/movies, voice mail. Some units w/terraces, some w/whirlpools. **Services:** ✕ 🅥🅟 ⌂ ⌐ Babysitting. **Facilities:** 🖻 ⌂ 🔲500 ⌂ 1 restaurant, 1 bar (w/entertainment), sauna. Heated pool, whirlpool. **Rates:** $125 S or D; $225 ste. Extra person $10. Children under age 12 stay free. Min stay special events. Parking: Indoor, $5/day. Higher rates during basketball season and Furniture Market. AE, CB, DC, DISC, MC, V.

≣≣ Regency Inn

128 N Cherry St, 27101; tel 910/723-8861 or toll free 800/528-1234; fax 910/723-2997. Cherry St exit off I-40. Comfortable, basic accommodations. Convenient to I-40 business district and downtown. **Rooms:** 147 rms and stes. CI 3pm/CO noon. Nonsmoking rms avail. Many rooms have a great view of the city. **Amenities:** 🛏 ⚬ A/C, cable TV w/movies, dataport. Microwaves and refrigerators available. **Services:** ⌂ ⌐ **Facilities:** 🖻 🔲250 🖳 ⌂ 1 restaurant, 1 bar. **Rates (CP):** $55–$88 S or D; $75 ste. Extra person $10. Children under age 16 stay free. Parking: Outdoor, free. AE, CB, DC, DISC, MC, V.

≣≣ Residence Inn by Marriott

7835 North Point Blvd, 27106; tel 910/759-0777 or toll free 800/331-3131; fax 910/759-9671. A hotel with apartment-like accommodations, it is an excellent choice for extended business travel. **Rooms:** 88 effic. CI 3pm/CO noon. Nonsmoking rms avail. One- and two-bedroom efficiencies. Some have lofts. **Amenities:** 🛏 ⚬ A/C, cable TV w/movies, refrig, dataport. Some units w/fireplaces. **Services:** ⌂ ⌐ ⌐ Babysitting. **Facilities:** 🖻 🖿 ⌂ Basketball, volleyball, washer/dryer. **Rates (CP):** $86–$106 effic. Min stay special events. Parking: Outdoor, free. Weekly and monthly rates avail. AE, CB, DC, DISC, MC, V.

≣≣≣ Tanglewood Manor House

NC 158 off I-40, PO Box 1040, 27012; tel 910/766-0591. At Tanglewood Park. In a quiet corner of 1200-acre Tanglewood Park, this mansion was once the home of the brother of tobacco magnate R J Reynolds. **Rooms:** 28 rms; 6 cottages/villas. CI 3pm/CO 11am. Nonsmoking rms avail. Rooms are tastefully decorated with antique reproductions. **Amenities:** 🛏 A/C, cable TV. **Facilities:** 🖻 ⚲ △ 🔲 ▶36 ♠ 🏃 ●3 🔲6 🔲500 Playground. Miniature-golf course. **Rates (BB):** $66–$107 S or D; $75–$125 cottage/villa. Extra person $10. Children under age 3 stay free. Parking: Outdoor, free. AE, DISC, MC, V.

MOTEL

≣ Stratford Inn

160 S Stratford Rd, 27104; tel 910/725-7501. Exit 191 off I-40 Business. Located near I-40, this basic motel offers a surprisingly secluded atmosphere since it is set apart from the

interstate by a wooded area. **Rooms:** 62 rms. CI noon/CO noon. Nonsmoking rms avail. Rooms feature slightly outdated decor, but they are scrupulously clean and well kept. **Amenities:** 🚪 A/C, cable TV. **Services:** ⇦ **Facilities:** ⬧ **Rates:** $37–$43 S or D. Extra person $5. Children under age 11 stay free. Min stay special events. Parking: Outdoor, free. AE, CB, DC, DISC, MC, V.

INN

☷☷☷ Brookstown Inn

200 Brookstown Ave, 27101; tel 910/725-1120 or toll free 800/845-4262; fax 910/773-0147. Set in a restored 1837 cotton mill that once supplied material for Confederate Army uniforms, this inn offers modern amenities and conveniences amid old-world charm. Silk flowers, quilts, baskets, and wooden decoys adorn the parlor areas, which are decorated in lovely Wedgwood blue, burgundy, gold, and olive. Listed on the National Register of Historic Places. **Rooms:** 71 rms and stes. CI 2pm/CO noon. Nonsmoking rms avail. Rooms and suites have high ceilings with bare wooden beams, hardwood floors, and period furnishings. **Amenities:** 🚪 ⬧ A/C, cable TV, dataport. Some units w/fireplaces, some w/whirlpools. **Services:** 🖾 ⇦ Babysitting, wine/sherry served. **Facilities:** 🔲 ⬜ ⬧ Guest lounge. Adjacent restaurant. **Rates (CP):** $95 S; $115 D; $105–$135 ste. Extra person $20. Children under age 12 stay free. Min stay special events. Higher rates for special events/hols. Parking: Outdoor, free. AE, CB, DC, DISC, MC, V.

RESTAURANTS ▥

Cactus Jack's Steakhouse and Saloon

3001 University Pkwy; tel 910/721-0055. **Steak.** Beer signs and antlers cover the rough-wood walls at this laid-back eatery. The menu consists mainly of cooked-to-order steaks, as well as a few chicken and ribs platters. **FYI:** Reservations not accepted. Children's menu. **Open:** Mon–Fri 11am–11pm, Sat noon–11pm, Sun noon–10pm. **Prices:** Main courses $10–$14. DISC, MC, V. ⬧

⑤ K&W Cafeteria

3300 Healey Dr; tel 410/768-1066. **Cafeteria.** A traditional cafeteria with a surprisingly cosmopolitan decor, K&W serves a wide variety of foods. Regular items include roast beef, country-fried steak, fried chicken, and veal parmesan. A selection of vegetables and breads is always available, and all cakes and pies are baked on the premises. **FYI:** Reservations not accepted. No liquor license. **Open:** Breakfast Mon–Fri 6:30–10:30am; lunch Mon–Fri 11am–2pm, Sat–Sun 11am–4pm; dinner daily 4–8pm. **Prices:** Main courses $5–$8. No CC. ⬧

Leon's Cafe

924 S Marshall St; tel 910/725-9593. At Walnut St. **Cafe.** A low-key local cafe with a surprisingly nouvelle menu. Main courses vary from week to week; typical listings might include grilled twin duck breasts topped with crabmeat or grilled grouper with Japanese barbecue sauce and Chinese spinach. **FYI:** Reservations recommended. **Open:** Lunch Mon–Fri 11am–2pm; dinner Tues–Sat 6–10pm. **Prices:** Main courses $11–$19. DISC, MC, V. ⬧

Old Salem Tavern Dining Room

736 S Main St; tel 910/748-8585. **American.** Housed in an early-19th-century tavern; the area's Moravian heritage is reflected in the dining room's period furnishings and costumed waiters. Favorite dishes include Tavern chicken pie, rack of lamb, roast duck, baked salmon, and sautéed veal medallions. Moravian gingerbread topped with homemade lemon ice cream is available for dessert. Outdoor dining is available in the arbor during the summer months. **FYI:** Reservations recommended. Children's menu. **Open:** Lunch Sun–Fri 11:30am–2pm, Sat 11:30am–2:30pm; dinner Mon–Thurs 5–9pm, Sat–Sun 5–9:30pm. **Prices:** Main courses $11–$19. AE, MC, V. ▮ ⬃ ◪

Rainbow News & Cafe

712 Brookstown Ave; tel 919/723-0858. At Broad St. **Cafe.** Located in an old house, this funky cafe features new and used books and magazines amidst a comfortable, homey atmosphere. The menu changes daily, but there will be vegetarian entrees, sandwiches, and salads for lunch; daily dinner specials range from red beans and rice to chile rellenos and blackened swordfish. Fresh-baked breads and muffins are always available, as are rich brownies made with Belgian chocolate and cream cheese. **FYI:** Reservations not accepted. Folk/jazz. Beer and wine only. **Open:** Mon–Fri 9am–9pm, Sat 10am–9pm, Sun 10am–6pm. **Prices:** Main courses $6–$13. DISC, MC, V. ⬃

Village Tavern

In Reynolda Village, 221 Reynolda Village; tel 910/748-0221. **New American/Pub.** An extensive lunch menu includes hearty sandwiches and lighter fare such as salads. (The hot chicken Mexican salad is especially popular.) Dinner includes seafood, pasta, and steaks. The Southwestern Grill platter (marinated chicken breast topped with black-bean salsa) is a favorite, as are the Maryland crab cakes. **FYI:** Reservations not accepted. Children's menu. **Open:** Mon–Thurs 11am–midnight, Fri–Sat 11am–1am, Sun 11am–10pm. **Prices:** Main courses $5–$9. AE, MC, V. ♥ ⬃ ⬧

ATTRACTIONS ▥

Reynolda House Museum of American Art

2250 Reynolda Rd; tel 910/725-5325. Tobacco tycoon R J Reynolds built this mansion, which now holds an excellent collection of furnishings, American paintings, and textiles. The lake porch has been enclosed to provide an additional 2,000 square feet of space for programs and exhibits. **Open:** Tues–Sat 9:30–4:30pm, Sun 1:30–4:30pm. $$$

Historic Bethabara Park

2147 Bethabara Rd; tel 919/924-8191. Located 3 mi NW of downtown. A reconstruction of the 1753 site of the first

Moravian settlement in North Carolina, with two 18th-century homes, a 200-year-old Moravian church, the excavated foundations of the town of Bethabara, and a rebuilt French and Indian War fort, nature trails, and picnic tables. The visitors center provides a slide presentation about Bethabara and the beginnings of Winston-Salem; and there are nature trails and picnic tables spread throughout the grounds. **Open:** Apr–Nov, Mon–Fri 9:30am–4:30pm, Sat–Sun 1:30–4:30pm. **Free**

Old Salem

600 S Main St; tel 910/721-7300 or toll free 800/441-5305. The Moravians—devout people who fled persecution in Europe and brought to the New World their artisans' skills, a deep love of music and education, and an absolute rejection of violence in any form—first came to this area from Pennsylvania in 1766. Today, this village of 80 restored buildings aims to re-create the Moravian lifestyle. The visitors center, on Old Salem Rd, has exhibits that trace the history of the settlers. Costumed hosts and hostesses give guided tours of the complex, and craftspeople in Moravian dress practice the trades of the original settlement. In 1791, George Washington spent two nights in the village's tavern, and sleeping rooms, barns, and grounds are not much different now from when he stopped by. **Open:** Mon–Sat 9:30am–4:30pm, Sun 1–4:30pm. Closed some hols. **$$$$**

Southeastern Center for Contemporary Art

750 Marguerite Dr; tel 910/725-1904. Housed in an English-style cottage surrounded by 32 wooded acres, this cultural resource center showcases artwork by nationally recognized artists as well as local favorites. Educational programs are emphasized, and guided tours are offered for groups of all ages. The Center shop sells gifts, artwork, and children's books. **Open:** Tues–Sat 10am–5pm, Sun 2–5pm. Closed some hols. **$**

R J Reynolds Tobacco Company Tour

Reynolds Blvd (Whitaker Park Cigarette Plant); tel 919/741-5718. Visitors are given a tour of the plant, which produces 300 million cigarettes every day. Colorful murals illustrate the various stages of tobacco production. **Open:** Mon–Fri 8:15am–6pm. **Free**

Stroh Brewery

S Main St exit off US 52; tel 919/788-6710. Visitors here are treated to a 30-minute guided tour of the plant and a first-rate explanation of the brewing process. Guided tours begin on the hour. **Open:** Mon–Fri 11am–4pm. Closed some hols. **Free**

Wrightsville Beach

Located just east of Wilmington, on the Cape Fear Coast. Its white-sand beaches draw many sun worshippers.

HOTELS 🏨

≝≝≝ Blockade Runner Resort Hotel

275 Waynick Blvd, 28480; tel 910/256-2251 or toll free 800/805-2252; fax 910/256-5502. Nice, seven-story, oceanfront hotel. **Rooms:** 150 rms. CI 3pm/CO 11:30 am. Nonsmoking rms avail. **Amenities:** 🛏 ⚡ A/C, cable TV w/movies. Some units w/terraces, some w/whirlpools. **Services:** ✕ VP 🚗 ⊠ ⏰ Babysitting. **Facilities:** 🔧 ♿ ⚠ 🔲 🍴 250 👤 1 restaurant (see "Restaurants" below), 2 bars (1 w/entertainment), 1 beach (ocean), spa, sauna, whirlpool. Outdoor, heated pool is open year-round. **Rates:** Peak (mid-May–mid-Aug) $82–$225 S or D. Extra person $15. Children under age 12 stay free. Lower rates off-season. Parking: Outdoor, free. AE, CB, DC, DISC, MC, V.

≝≝≝ Shell Island Resort Hotel

2700 N Lumina Ave, 28480; tel 910/256-8696 or toll free 800/689-6765; fax 910/256-8337. 1½ mi N on US 74. A beautiful, comfortable, suite resort. **Rooms:** 43 stes. CI 3pm/CO 11am. Nonsmoking rms avail. Each suite has separate bedroom and living area, full kitchen, 1½ baths, and ocean view. **Amenities:** 🛏 ⚡ 📺 A/C, cable TV w/movies, refrig, dataport. All units w/terraces. **Services:** VP 🚗 ⊠ ⏰ Children's program, babysitting. **Facilities:** 🔧 👤 1 restaurant, 1 bar, 1 beach (ocean), lifeguard, sauna, whirlpool. **Rates:** Peak (mid-May–Labor Day) $185–$195 ste. Extra person $10. Children under age 18 stay free. Lower rates off-season. Parking: Indoor/outdoor, free. AE, CB, DC, DISC, MC, V.

≝≝≝ Surf Motel Suites

711 S Lumina Ave, PO Box 489, 28480; tel 910/256-2275. Oceanfront property with a spacious sun deck and a gazebo by the pool area. **Rooms:** 45 effic. CI 2:30pm/CO 11:30am. All suites have ocean views, separate bedroom and living area, and a fully equipped kitchen. **Amenities:** 🛏 ⚡ A/C, cable TV, refrig. All units w/terraces. **Services:** ⊠ ⏰ **Facilities:** 🔧 👤 1 beach (ocean), lifeguard, washer/dryer. **Rates:** Peak (Mem Day–Labor Day) $130–$150 effic. Lower rates off-season. Parking: Outdoor, free. AE, CB, DC, DISC, MC, V.

MOTELS

≝≝ Ocean View Motel

17 E Salisbury St, PO Box 795, 28480; tel 910/256-3785. A basic motel less than one block from the beach. **Rooms:** 40 rms and effic. CI 2pm/CO 11am. **Amenities:** 🛏 A/C, cable TV. **Services:** ⏰ **Rates:** Peak (Mar–Labor Day) $75–$85 S or D; $135 effic. Extra person $5. Children under age 18 stay free. Min stay wknds. Lower rates off-season. Parking: Outdoor, free. AE, CB, DC, MC, V.

≝≝ Waterway Lodge

7246 Wrightsville Ave, PO Box 857, 28480; tel 910/256-3771 or toll free 800/677-3771. At Arlie Rd and Wrightsville Beach Bridge. This motel is conveniently located near local seafood restaurants and within ½ mi of the beach. **Rooms:** 35 rms and stes. CI 3pm/CO 11:30am. Nonsmoking rms avail. Rooms and suites are custom decorated, and all suites are equipped with kitchens. **Amenities:** 🛏 A/C, cable TV w/movies, refrig. **Services:** ⟨◊⟩ **Facilities:** 🛗 **Rates:** Peak (May–Sept) $80 S or D; $90–$115 ste. Extra person $5. Children under age 12 stay free. Min stay special events. Lower rates off-season. Parking: Outdoor, free. Golf packages avail. AE, DISC, MC, V.

RESTAURANTS 🍴

The King Neptune

11 N Lumina Ave; tel 910/256-2525. **Seafood.** A very informal, very nautical place with two large dining rooms and a lounge to one side. Pictures of Wrightsville Beach in the 1920s and 1930s adorn the walls. The atmosphere is lively, and the food is superb. In addition to seafood entrees such as Creole shrimp over grits and Atlantic grouper, there is also a good selection of beef and pizza. **FYI:** Reservations not accepted. Children's menu. **Open:** Daily 5–10pm. **Prices:** Main courses $9–$16. AE, MC, V.

Oceanic Restaurant and Grill

703 S Lumina Ave; tel 910/256-5551. Off US 76. **Seafood.** Indoor or outdoor dining provides breathtaking views of the ocean. Menu specialties include Carolina crab cakes and "Super-Duper Grouper" (served on a bed of cashews over celery mashed potatoes). **FYI:** Reservations not accepted. Children's menu. **Open:** Mon–Sat 11:30am–11pm, Sun 10am–11pm. **Prices:** Main courses $14–$25. AE, MC, V. ⛴ ▟ ⅋

Ocean Terrace Restaurant

In Blockade Runner Resort Hotel, 275 Waynick Blvd; tel 910/256-2251. **Eclectic.** Large windows allow ample views of the surrounding dunes and breakers and the delightful nautical decor sets a casual mood. The kitchen serves up innovative fare: New York strip with bourbon sauce and sautéed chicken breast with toasted pecans and apples are among the offerings. **FYI:** Reservations accepted. Guitar/jazz/piano. Children's menu. **Open:** Sun–Wed 6:30am–10pm, Thurs–Sat 6:30am–11pm. **Prices:** Main courses $14–$21. AE, CB, DC, DISC, MC, V. ▟ ⅋

The Raw Bar

13 E Salisbury St; tel 910/256-2974. By the pier. **Seafood.** A laid-back place with rough pine paneling and high-backed wooden booths. The extensive menu includes shrimp scampi, seafood Alfredo, shrimp and scallop linguini with Alfredo sauce, and oysters on the half shell. Combination platters available. **FYI:** Reservations accepted. Children's menu. **Open:** Mon–Fri 5–10:30pm, Sat–Sun 5–11pm. Closed Dec 6. **Prices:** Main courses $8–$15. AE, MC, V.

SOUTH CAROLINA
The South's Gracious Beauty

Stretching from the Atlantic Ocean in the east to the foothills of the Blue Ridge Mountains in the northwest, compact South Carolina—only 40th in geographic size among the 50 states but 25th in population—is a principal playground for tourists from all over the world. Throughout the year in every area of the state, there's a ceaseless whirl of activities. Beautifully restored antebellum homes, miles of sandy beaches, Civil War sites, and many more attractions await the visitor.

South Carolina's antebellum aristocracy produced a culture that was unique even for the Deep South. Their interest in education and the arts, as well as love of entertainment and gracious living, are still very much in evidence today. It is believed that the first play produced in America was performed at the Dock Street Theater in Charleston in 1736. Columbia's Town Theater claims to be the oldest continuously performing theater company in the country. Prolific novelist William Gilmore Simms, South Carolina's greatest antebellum literary figure, was instrumental in founding the prestigious *Southern Review* in 1828. Today, symphony orchestras, opera and ballet companies, and other cultural institutions and events thrive in metropolitan areas. The state's premier event is Charleston's performing arts festival, Spoleto USA; however, myriad other festivals range from the frivolous to the sublime.

From early on in South Carolina's history, the landed gentry migrated to the barrier islands or the Upcountry during the heat of summer, but in the last century wealthy Northerners discovered that the areas around Aiken and Camden were ideal wintering spots for their thoroughbred and standardbred horses. These winter colonies—with facilities for raising, training, and racing horses, and winter "cottages" of up to 90 rooms—are still frequented by the jet set today.

Descendants of slaves maintain several proud communities where natives speak the musical Gullah dialect (a curious combination of King's English, American English, and several African languages). One of the most-prized mementos you can bring home from a trip to South Carolina is a sweet-grass basket woven by the artisans from these close-knit communities. Basket weavers can be found at the Old City Market in Charleston and along US 17 near Mount Pleasant.

South Carolina is not as geographically diverse as some of its neighbors, but that doesn't mean there aren't plenty of natural attractions and outdoor recreational activities. The Atlantic coast and the surrounding bays, inlets, and estuaries provide all types of water sports—from boating to scuba diving. The gentle, rolling hills of the midlands are perfect for biking, golf, and hiking, while inland lakes offer acres of water on which to fish or boat. The rugged Upcountry provides the challenges of wilderness backpacking and white-water rafting. Whether you come to explore the great outdoors or relax in Southern gentility, South Carolina will show you a good time.

A Brief History

Colonial Days South Carolina's recorded history begins less than 30 years after Columbus discovered the Americas. Spanish explorers sailed along the coast as early as 1514. A 1526 attempt to establish a settlement on Winyah Bay (near present-day Georgetown) was doomed to failure because of a severe winter, Native American attacks, and disease, but Hernando De Soto explored the central part of the state and made peaceful contact with native residents in 1540.

It was the British, however, who were to establish the first permanent European settlement in South Carolina. The colony founded by eight English

---

Fun Facts

• Many of the classic 18th- and 19th-century buildings in Charleston still stand today because the city's residents—impoverished in the years following the Civil War—lacked the funds to build new structures. In fact, patches made in those days can still be seen on some buildings.

• Route I-26, which runs from northwestern South Carolina diagonally southeast to Charleston, follows the famous Cherokee Path blazed by Native Americans centuries ago.

• Palmetto trees, indigenous to South Carolina, grow throughout much of the state. They even played a role during the Revolutionary War, when forts made from the sturdy trunks helped defend against British attack.

• One of the first public libraries in the United States was founded at Charleston in 1698. The selection of titles was a bit limited, though—just Bibles and other religious books.

---

noblemen at Albemarle Point in the Ashley River in 1670 set the tone for settlement in South Carolina for the next two hundred years. Indigo and rice plantations were set up, and black slaves were imported from Barbados to work them. By 1680 the English had expanded across the Ashley to the present site of Charleston. South Carolina came to resemble the West Indian plantation economy more closely than any of the other North American colonies. By 1708 the majority of the nonnative inhabitants were African slaves. (Native Americans—ravaged by the old-world diseases introduced by Europeans—could no longer significantly threaten the colony after 1715.)

The success of their rice and indigo crops made the plantation owners the wealthiest men in North America. At the same time, white Protestants from Europe or from Pennsylvania, North Carolina, and Virginia were encouraged to settle the interior central and Upcountry regions. These German, Scotch-Irish, and Welsh settlers were different in both inclination and background from the tidewater planters. The majority of the new settlers farmed small pieces of property and weren't able to wrest control of the government from the landed aristocracy of the Low Country.

Pushing for Independence

Most South Carolinians, both rich and poor, were staunch supporters of local rights. As such they were in the forefront of resistance to the Stamp Act in 1765 and took an active role when difficulties with England escalated into the war for American independence. The initial overt act of the war involved the seizing of British property by Colonial forces at Fort Charlotte in 1775; the next year, the rebels won their first significant naval victory when the British fleet was turned back at Fort Moultrie (on Sullivans Island, near Charleston). During the course of the Revolutionary War, more than 200 battles and skirmishes took place on South Carolina soil—more than in any other state. In 1788, South Carolina became the eighth state to ratify the US Constitution. Two years later, the midlands city of Columbia—designed specifically to serve as a capital—became the seat of the new state government.

Civil War South Carolina—preeminent among the states in resisting the abolition of slavery and in supporting states' rights—was the first to leave the Union. The Ordinance of Secession was passed on December 20, 1860, and the first shots of the Civil War were fired at Fort Sumter five months later. Although Union troops occupied the sea islands near Beaufort throughout the war and successfully barricaded the Charleston harbor, few military engagements occurred within South Carolina until the spring of 1865, when Gen William Sherman marched north fresh from his occupation of Savannah. Columbia suffered the most devastating effects of his notorious scorched-earth policy.

Recovery South Carolina lay in ruins in the years following the Civil War, and poverty marked the state for generations. The constitution of 1868, which granted universal male suffrage and ended property qualifications for holding office, gained the state readmittance to the Union. Although African Americans played a prominent role in state government during Reconstruction, the transition from a slave state to a free society was difficult and the corruptness of some carpetbaggers and scalawags left bad feelings that exist to this day. Return to a white-dominated government and disenfranchisement of African Americans occurred barely 10 years after the end of the war. (It was not until a 1947 state court decision that blacks were allowed to vote again in Democratic primaries.)

Rapid expansion of the textile industry in the 1880s and 1890s began the state's economic recovery. That industry, however, was still heavily dependent on the production of cotton, and the devastation wreaked by the notorious boll weevil gave the Great Depression a head start in South Carolina. The state's economy did not really recover until

World War II. The war brought an expansion of military bases and in the half-century since then, domestic and foreign investment in manufacturing has revitalized this Sunbelt state and hastened the migration of residents from rural to urban areas.

South Carolina has likewise undergone a full recovery from the devastating effects of Hurricane Hugo, which struck the state in 1989. That powerful storm caused 26 deaths and some $5 billion in property damage.

DRIVING DISTANCES

Charleston

94 mi S of Myrtle Beach
104 mi N of Savannah, GA
113 mi SE of Columbia
139 mi E of Augusta, GA
210 mi SE of Greenville

Columbia

72 mi E of Augusta, GA
94 mi S of Charlotte, NC
101 mi SE of Greenville
113 mi NE of Charleston
143 mi SW of Myrtle Beach

Greenville

62 mi S of Asheville, NC
101 mi NW of Columbia
112 mi NE of Atlanta, GA
210 mi NW of Charleston
235 mi NW of Savannah, GA

A Closer Look

GEOGRAPHY

Two-thirds of South Carolina is covered by the Atlantic Coastal Plain, a lowland that rises gradually from southeast to northwest. This area, locally known as the **Low Country,** includes a coastline of 187 miles. (If the wide bays and inlets were also measured, the coastline would actually amount to 2,876 miles.) The northern coast—an almost unbroken stretch of beach, which includes the town of Myrtle Beach—is called the **Grand Strand.** The southern area is marshy, with tidal rivers cutting well inland. Barrier islands lying off the coast include Pawleys, Bull, Isle of Palms, Sullivan's, Kiawah, Edisto, Hunting, Fripp, Parris, Hilton Head, and Daufuskie. The **Sand Hills** mark the western edge of the coastal plain and indicate that the Atlantic Ocean once reached this far inland. Most of South Carolina's major cities are located in the Low Country, including Aiken, Camden, Charleston, Columbia, Florence, and Sumter.

Much of the rest of South Carolina is in the **Piedmont Plateau**—an area marked on its eastern edge by the **Fall Line,** where rivers tumble from the highlands to the lowlands. The Piedmont is distinguished by land that varies in elevation from 400 to 1,400 feet. Swift-flowing rivers are a major source of hydroelectric power and have helped to make this an important manufacturing region. Key cities here include Anderson, Greenville, and Spartanburg.

Occupying a very narrow band in the extreme

northwestern corner of the state is the **Blue Ridge,** part of the Appalachian Mountain chain. Known as the **Upcountry,** this forested area is characterized by peaks of up to 3,500 feet. The Upcountry has no large cities, just small towns such as Clemson, Walhalla, Pickens, and Westminster.

CLIMATE

South Carolina is blessed with a moderate climate. Temperatures—in both winter and summer—are markedly higher in the Low Country and especially on the coast. More than 100 years ago planters began the tradition of summering on one of the barrier islands (where they were cooled by the sea breezes) or in the Upcountry (where higher elevations provided some relief from the heat). The Upcountry, especially in the mountainous areas, may experience a dusting of snow in the winter.

WHAT TO PACK

Packing for a trip to South Carolina is a cinch. Winter weather is almost nonexistent and although summers are hot, temperatures are moderated by sea breezes along the coast and by high elevations in the Upcountry. Nights may be cool in the higher reaches of the Upcountry, so you may need a sweater or jacket for evenings in those areas. South Carolinians dress casually and layers of cool cotton are both appropriate and comfortable most of the year. You will probably want to pack one dressier outfit for upscale restaurants and resorts or for a cultural performance in one of the larger cities.

TOURIST INFORMATION

For the *South Carolina Travel Guide,* an excellent and comprehensive handbook to the state's attractions, contact the **South Carolina Division of Tourism,** PO Box 71, Columbia, SC 29202 (tel 803/734-0122). The **SC Office of Information Resources** maintains a Web page (http://www.state.sc.us) with general information about the state. To find out how to obtain tourist information for individual cities and parks in South Carolina, look under specific cities in the listings section of this book.

AVG MONTHLY TEMPS (°F) & RAINFALL (IN)		
	Charleston	Greenville
Jan	48/3.3	41/4.2
Feb	50/3.4	44/4.4
Mar	56/4.4	51/5.9
Apr	64/2.6	61/4.4
May	72/4.4	69/4.2
June	78/6.5	75/4.8
July	81/7.3	78/4.1
Aug	80/6.5	79/3.7
Sept	76/4.9	72/4.4
Oct	66/2.9	61/3.5
Nov	57/2.2	54/3.9
Dec	50/3.1	44/3.9

DRIVING RULES AND REGULATIONS

Minimum age for drivers is 16. Unless otherwise posted, the speed limit is 65 mph on rural interstates and 55 mph on other highways. The driver and front seat passengers must wear seat belts. Child restraints are required for any child under one year of age. (In the front seat, children between 1 and 4 must use a child seat while children 4 to 6 may use a seat belt. In the back seat, children 1 to 5 years old must use seat belts.) It is illegal to possess an open container of alcohol in a moving vehicle.

RENTING A CAR

All of the major car rental firms have outlets throughout the state. Minimum age requirements for renting a car vary between 21 and 25, depending on the company, so be sure to check. Collision Damage Waiver (CDW) protection is sold separately. Check with your insurance company or the credit card company you will use to rent the car to see if you are already covered.

- **Alamo** (tel toll free 800/327-9633)
- **Avis** (tel 800/831-2847)
- **Budget** (tel 800/527-0700)
- **Dollar** (tel 800/800-4000)
- **Hertz** (tel 800/654-3131)
- **National** (tel 800/227-7368)
- **Thrifty** (tel 800/367-2277)

ESSENTIALS

Area Code: Northern and central South Carolina use the **864** area code; the rest of the state uses the **803** area code.

Emergencies: Call 911 from anywhere in the state to summon emergency police, fire, or ambulance assistance.

Liquor Laws: Alcoholic beverages may be purchased by anyone 21 years of age or older, with proof of age. Beer and wine are sold in supermarkets, while hard liquor is sold only in liquor stores. Alcoholic beverages cannot be served after midnight on Saturday and all day Sunday except in establishments with special permits in Charleston, Columbia, Edisto Beach, Hilton Head, Myrtle Beach, and Santee.

Road Info: For information about road conditions, call toll free 800/768-1501.

Smoking: There is no state law pertaining to smoking; rules vary by municipality. The city of Greenville mandates that restaurants seating 50 or more must provide a nonsmoking area. Otherwise, most restaurants around the state voluntarily maintain nonsmoking sections and many large hotels offer nonsmoking rooms or floors.

Taxes: South Carolina's base statewide sales tax is 5%. Many cities and counties impose an additional tax. The statewide hotel room tax is 2%.

Time Zone: South Carolina is in the Eastern time tone and the entire state observes daylight saving time.

Best of the State
WHAT TO SEE AND DO

Below is a general overview of some of the top sights and attractions in South Carolina. To find out more detailed information, look under "Attractions" under individual cities in the listings portion of this book.

National Parks Several decisive Revolutionary War battles were fought on South Carolina soil. A 1780 battle where an army of Tennessee irregulars defeated a superior Tory force is commemorated at the **Kings Mountain National Military Park** in York. Authentically dressed reenactors periodically demonstrate black-powder shooting on the craggy promontory. A 1781 battle at a drover's shelter called "The Cowpens" is remembered at the **Cowpens National Battlefield,** in the northwest corner of the state. A park features walking trails, road tours, and a visitor center with exhibits, memorabilia, and a multimedia presentation. Another Revolutionary War battle site, the **Ninety Six National Historic Site** (south of the town of Ninety Six), began as a star fort. The site features restorations, an archaeological dig, a visitors center, and an interpretive trail. A dark-water wonderland renowned for its biological diversity and record-size trees, the **Congaree Swamp National Monument,** near Columbia, features self-guided canoe trips, a ¾-mile boardwalk, and 18 miles of hiking trails.

State Parks South Carolina maintains a system of 48 parks, many with cabin rentals and/or campsites. The most popular state parks are those on the Grand Strand: **Myrtle Beach State Park** offers swimming, surfing, hiking, and camping; **Huntington Beach State Park** offers swimming, fishing, and camping.

Natural Wonders South Carolina boasts some impressive natural phenomena. The Upcountry's best-known landmark is the rounded dome called **Table Rock,** now part of a state park. The **Flat Creek Heritage Preserve** in Kershaw is a 1,436-acre National Natural Landmark where many rare plants thrive. At 3,548 feet in elevation, **Sassafras Mountain,** at Rocky Bottom, is the highest point in South Carolina. A bumpy 6-mile road leads to the summit of 3,208-foot **Caesar's Head**—the state's second-highest spot—located on the North Carolina/South Carolina border. Dropping an astounding 49.3 feet per mile as it tears 40 tumultuous miles through densely wooded Sumter National Forest, the **Chattooga Wild and Scenic River** forms the border between Georgia and South Carolina.

For a state without an abundance of mountainous areas, South Carolina nonetheless has several impressive waterfalls. **Raven Cliff Falls,** in Greenville County above Caesar's Head, drops 400 feet. **Issaqueena Falls,** located near Walhalla, is a lovely 200-foot cataract. At **Whitewater Falls,** two cascades plunge more than 400 feet into Lake Jocassee. Since the beginning of recorded history the artesian wells of the **Healing Springs,** found in Barnwell State Park, have supplied legendary mineral waters to pilgrims seeking relief from a variety of ailments.

Manmade Wonders The **Peachoid,** Gaffney's peach-shaped water tower, is one of the most-photographed water tanks in the country. **Patriot's Point Naval and Maritime Museum,** across the harbor from Charleston, contains several ships open for tours: the aircraft carrier USS *Yorktown*; the submarine *Clagmore*; the Coast Guard cutter *Ingham*; and the destroyer *Laffey*. In addition, the park features a re-created Vietnam naval support base, the Medal of Honor Museum, and an 18-hole golf course.

Ruins   Ghostly remnants of the past lurk in quiet corners of the state. The graceful remains known as the **Sheldon Church Ruins,** located between Gardens Corner and Yemassee, are a haunting reminder of the tragedy of war. Built in 1753, the church was burned not once, but twice—first by the British in 1779, again by Sherman's troops in 1865. Ruins of the **Old Stone Church,** near Clemson, stand watch over a cemetery where several prominent South Carolinians are buried. Tours of the ruins of famous Confederate Gen Wade Hampton's plantation **Millwood,** near Columbia, are conducted by reservation the last Sunday of each month from March through November. Only one wing survived Civil War destruction at **Middleton Plantation,** SC Scenic Hwy 61.

Family Favorites   The biggest amusement park in the state is **Paramount's Carowinds,** near Rock Hill on the South Carolina/North Carolina border. The park features exciting rides such as the Vortex (the only stand-up roller coaster east of the Mississippi), a water theme park, and top-notch entertainment. Not far away in Fort Hill is **New Heritage USA,** a Christian resort and theme park with a water park and facilities for horseback riding, boating, tennis, and roller skating. The Myrtle Beach area is a favorite of families who frequent the amusement parks and other diverting attractions in the evenings and on rainy days. (See the South Carolina scenic driving tour for more details). Next door to the **Darlington Raceway** is the **NMPA Stock Car Hall of Fame,** repository of the largest collection of stock racing cars in the world.

Beaches   South Carolina's 187 miles of coastline are lined with wide, hard-packed beaches backed by high, sea oat–covered dunes. These popular destinations provide ample opportunities for swimming, sunbathing, strolling, shelling, surfing, and fishing. Miles of unspoiled beaches and golden marshlands in the southern part of the state include the coastal resort islands of Hilton Head, Kiawah, Edisto, and Daufuskie. Some of these world-renowned vacation retreats have controlled access, others have unlimited entry, and several sport state parks.

Historic Buildings   Contrary to popular opinion, Gen William Tecumseh Sherman's Federal troops didn't destroy all of South Carolina's magnificent plantations and antebellum homes. Many towns, districts, and individual structures survived, so state-wide you can find numerous examples of antebellum architecture. Charleston organized the first Preservation Society in the country in the 1920s and many other cities and towns quickly followed. The results of their Herculean efforts are on display in Charleston, Aiken, Abbeville, Beaufort, Camden, and elsewhere around the state. Several plantations are open for you to tour. Near Charleston you can visit **Boone Hall Plantation, Magnolia Plantation and Gardens, Drayton Hall,** and **Middleton Place.** (For more information about Charleston's historic district and the surrounding plantations, see the driving tour for South Carolina). Original family pieces and personal effects of the Hammond-Billings family furnish **Redcliffe,** a huge 1850s plantation home overlooking the Savannah River in northwest South Carolina. **Ashtabula** and **Woodburn,** two plantations near Pendleton, portray the period of the early 1800s when Low Country planters built Upcountry mansions and moved their families to the more healthful foothills. **Fort Hill** was the antebellum home of statesman, US senator, and two-time vice president John C Calhoun; it was later occupied by his daughter Anna and her husband Thomas Green Clemson. (Thomas Clemson willed the plantation to the state for the creation of an agricultural college, known today as Clemson University.)

Museums   Most of South Carolina's many museums chronicle the history of the state. The absolutely amazing array of collections belonging to the **Aiken County Historical Museum** is housed at Banksia, a former winter colony mansion. Also on the grounds are the 1808 Erle log cabin (believed to be the oldest edifice in Aiken County), and an 1890 one-room schoolhouse. Horse racing memorabilia pertaining to Aiken-raised and/or -trained championship horses is displayed at the **Thoroughbred Hall of Fame,** housed in the former stables at Hopeland Gardens estate in Aiken. Adjacent to Hopeland is the **Carriage Museum** at Rye Patch estate, a collection of restored vintage carriages, coaches, surreys, and buggies. The **World of Energy,** Duke Power Company's energy-education center/museum at the Oconee Nuclear Plant on Lake Keowee north of Seneca, tells the story of energy through animated displays, computer games, and a control-room simulator.

Gardens   South Carolina's climate is ideal for growing flowers year-round. **Brookgreen Gardens** near Murrells Inlet is a showplace of art and nature.

Created in the 1930s on the site of a former rice plantation, the gardens showcase more than 500 sculptures from the 19th and 20th centuries among 2,000 species of plants. It is considered to be the world's largest outdoor collection of American statuary. Also on the grounds are an aviary and a wildlife park featuring native birds and animals. Several of the state's surviving plantations boast outstanding gardens. **Magnolia Plantation and Gardens,** north of Charleston, features this country's oldest colonial estate garden. The grounds include an 18th-century herb garden, Biblical garden, topiary garden, and a horticultural maze. You can tour the plantation house, enjoy the petting zoo and miniature-horse ranch, explore the 125-acre waterfowl refuge, and rent bicycles or canoes. Adjacent to Magnolia Plantation is the **Audubon Swamp Garden**—60 acres of primeval blackwater cypress and tupelo trees punctuated by flowers and ferns, traversed by bridges, boardwalks, and dikes. Nearby **Middleton Place** boasts America's oldest formal landscaped gardens. Rising from the river's edge in butterfly lakes and sweeping terraces, the French- and English-style gardens feature intricate walks, and exquisite plantings of roses, camellias, azaleas, and magnolias—some of which are original from the construction of the gardens in the mid-1700s. The one wing of the plantation house that wasn't destroyed during the Civil War is open for tours, as is the stableyard and a rice museum.

The 250 acres of public floral displays at the **South Carolina Botanical Garden** at Clemson University is considered to be the state's most diverse garden. In addition to areas devoted to wildflowers and ferns, the facility boasts bog and turf gardens, a pioneer village, a Braille Trail for the visually impaired, and a special garden for the mobility impaired. At **Cypress Gardens,** between Charleston and Moncks Corner, paths and water trails lead through a blackwater swamp highlighted by cypress forest, and in season azaleas, camellias, and spring bulbs. A testing ground for the All America Rose selection process, **Edisto Memorial Gardens** in Orangeburg also blankets the river banks with masses of azaleas, wisteria, and other Southern favorites; a wetlands park permits visitors to glimpse plants and animals found in the wetlands via a 2,600-foot boardwalk. In the spring, the dark, swampy lake at Sumter's **Swan Lake Iris Gardens** is wreathed in splashes of color provided by Dutch and Japanese irises. In addition to formal boxwood gardens,

Hopeland Gardens, a former estate in Aiken, blossoms with azaleas, wisteria, dogwood, crepe myrtle, magnolias, lilies, and roses, and features a Braille trail for the visually impaired. **Glencairn Gardens,** Rock Hill, contains six acres of sculpted terraces, flower beds, and a reflecting pool.

Parks & Zoos Visitors can journey through a microcosmic rain forest, desert, undersea kingdom, and a typical Southern farm at Columbia's **Riverbanks Zoo.** Ranked among the Top 10 zoos in the country, Riverbanks uses water and light to create wild, unlimited space for 2,000 animals. Visit the hundreds of exotic animals that reside at the **Greenville Zoo** or the **Hollywild Animal Park,** Inman.

EVENTS AND FESTIVALS

NORTHERN AND CENTRAL SOUTH CAROLINA

- **Battle of Cowpens Reenactment,** Cowpens National Battlefield, Cowpens. Living history encampments and tactical demonstrations mark the popular Revolutionary War reenactment. Mid-January. Call 864/461-2828.
- **Aiken Triple Crown,** Aiken. Three successive weekends of horse racing include flat racing, harness racing, and steeplechasing. Mid- to late March. Call 803/641-1111.
- **Carolina Cup,** Camden. Steeplechasing and flat racing. Early April. Call 803/432-6513.
- **Historic Pendleton Spring Jubilee,** Pendleton. Arts and crafts, entertainment, antiques shows, museum exhibits. Spring opening of the Agricultural Museum and Ashtabula and Woodburn plantations. Early April. Call 864/646-3782.
- **Sunsets at Sidney,** Columbia. A 13-week concert series in magnificent Sidney Park. June through August. Call 803/343-8750.
- **Freedom Weekend Aloft,** Greenville. Nation's second-largest hot-air balloon event. July 4 weekend. Call 864/232-3700.
- **The Lights Before Christmas,** Columbia. Riverbanks Zoo becomes a winter wonderland of 200,000 holiday lights. December. Call 803/779-8717.

CHARLESTON AND BEAUFORT

- **Oyster Festival,** Boone Hall Plantation, Charleston. Crafts, exhibits, food, oyster-eating contests. Late January or early February. Call 803/577-4030.

- **Charleston Blues Festival,** Charleston. Ten-day festival celebrating the blues. Mid-March. Call 803/723-1075.
- **Festival of Houses and Gardens,** Charleston. Legendary tour of treasured historic homes and courtyard gardens. Late March through early April. Call 803/723-1623.
- **Spoleto Festival USA,** Charleston. International festival with world-renowned performers in drama, dance, music, and art. Late May through early June. Call 803/722-2764.
- **Piccolo Spoleto,** Charleston. Companion festival to Spoleto USA features local and regional artists. Late May through early June. Call 803/724-7309.
- **Gullah Festival,** Beaufort. Sea island cultural festival based on African-influenced heritage features storytelling, fine arts, dance, and special events. Late May. Call 803/525-0628.

THE GRAND STRAND

- **Georgetown Plantation Tours,** Georgetown. See antebellum rice plantations, colonial townhouses, and magnificent gardens. Mid-April. Call 803/527-3653.
- **Seafood Festival,** Murrells Inlet. Seafood samples from popular local restaurants. Mid-April. Call 803/651-3232.
- **Georgetown County Expo and Fair,** Georgetown. Community and commercial exhibits, crafts, and rides. Mid-October. Call 803/546-9705.
- **Brookgreenfest,** Murrells Inlet. Music, visual and performing arts, and food in the sculpture garden. Late October. Call 803/237-4218.
- **Ghost Hunt,** Georgetown. Self-guided tour of the Ghost Capital of the World as well as other festival activities. Late October. Call 803/546-8437.
- **Treasures by the Sea,** Myrtle Beach. A festival of lights covering the area with images of mermaids, seashells, seahorses, and other nautical likenesses. November through February. Call 803/626-7444.

SPECTATOR SPORTS

Auto Racing   Home of the NASCAR TranSouth 500 stock car race in April and the Mountain Dew 500 on Labor Day weekend, the **Darlington Raceway** on SC 34 (tel 803/393-4041) attracts champion drivers and a massive tide of fans.

Baseball   Although South Carolina has no major league baseball team, it does field several minor league teams. The **Columbia Bombers** (tel 803/256-4110), a Class A farm team of the New York Mets, play at Capital City Stadium; the **Greenville Braves** (tel 864/299-3456) play at Greenville Municipal Stadium; and the **Charleston Riverdogs** (tel 803/723-7241) play at College Park.

College Athletics   Despite the state's lack of professional basketball and football teams, there's no lack of enthusiasm on the part of fans. Most sports fans in the state side with one of the major university teams. The **University of South Carolina Gamecocks** (tel 803/777-5204) play basketball at Frank McGuire Arena and football at Williams-Brice Stadium, both in Columbia. The **Clemson University Tigers** (tel 864/656-2114) play basketball at Littlejohn Coliseum, while football games are at Clemson Memorial Stadium.

Horse Racing   The **Carolina Cup** in late March or early April and the **Colonial Cup** in November are run in Camden (tel 803/432-6513). Steeplechasing is one of the three events in Aiken's annual **Triple Crown,** which also includes flat racing and harness racing (tel 803/641-1111).

Polo   There are polo matches at **Rose Hill Plantation** in Bluffton (tel 803/757-4945) every other Sunday in the spring and fall. In Aiken, matches are played at **Whitney Field** (tel 803/648-7874) on Sunday afternoons between September and November and between March and July.

ACTIVITIES A TO Z

Boating   South Carolina offers every boating experience from ocean cruising to black-water paddling. Lakes Murray, Norman, Hartwell, and Richard B Russell, among others, provide thousands of acres of boating opportunities. The Edisto River Canoe and Kayak Trail is a 56-mile black-water river course at **Colleton State Park** (tel 803/538-8206), where five boat landings make public access easy. Guided trips are available. You can canoe the black waters of Biggin Creek and the Old Santee Canal at **Old Santee Canal State Park** off of US 52 (tel 803/899-5200). Built in 1800, the canal was the first channel dug in America. Rental fishing boats, pedal boats, and/or canoes are available at most of the state parks. South Carolina offers a Basic Boating Education Course, which includes instruction in navigation, legal requirements, safety, and trailering. The course is recognized by all states requiring operators to take courses. Contact Boating Safety, PO Box 12559, Charleston, SC 29412 (tel 803/762-5041).

Camping From sandy campgrounds lapped by Atlantic Ocean waves to the rugged hills of the Upcountry, South Carolina offers a tremendous variety of camping experiences at state parks and private campgrounds. Contact the **South Carolina Campground Owner's Association** (tel 803/726-5733) and request a copy of their *Camping Guide to South Carolina,* a compendium of private and state park campgrounds. In addition to listing and describing member campgrounds, the guide also divulges plenty of information on various tourist attractions.

Fishing Pier, surf, inlet, river, and deep-sea fishing opportunities abound along the coast. The longest fishing pier on the East Coast is the 1,200-foot Apache Pier in Myrtle Beach. Unless you fish from a private boat, no license is required for fishing in salt water. The state's river systems and inland lakes offer many other challenges. Many of the best fishing experiences can be found in the South Carolina State Parks. Contact the **South Carolina Department of Natural Resources** (tel 803/734-3888) for a copy of the *South Carolina Rules and Regulations* booklet, which also contains descriptions of all the wildlife management areas in the state.

Golf Although not as spectacularly diverse in terrain as some of its neighboring states, South Carolina offers enough changes in a relatively short area to provide varied challenges for the avid golfer. Designed by such great course architects as George and Tom Fazio, Robert Trent and Rees Jones, Pete and P B Dye, and Arthur Hills, salty seaside links vie with the dogwood-lined fairways in the rolling hills of Thoroughbred Country, the wooded terrain of the midlands, and the scenic elevations of the Blue Ridge Mountains. More than 200 public, semiprivate, and resort courses dot South Carolina with 70 courses in the Grand Strand alone. Hickory Knob and Goodale State Parks offer golf links and a course is under construction at Cheraw. Your best source of golfing information is the *South Carolina Golf Guide* published by the **South Carolina Department of Parks, Recreation, and Tourism** (tel toll free 800/346-3634).

Hiking Hiking in South Carolina can be as easy as a stroll along a hard-packed beach or as arduous as a five-mile trek up Caesar's Head Mountain. Although the name of the Foothills Trail seems to indicate a nonstrenuous hiking track, this 85-mile footpath is actually a wilderness adventure with a steep, rugged trail that winds over the mountain ridges along the North Carolina/South Carolina line from Table

---

SELECTED PARKS & RECREATION AREAS

- **Congaree Swamp National Monument,** 20 mi SE of town on SC 48, Columbia, SC (tel 803/776-4396)
- **Fort Sumter National Monument,** 1214 Middle St, Sullivans Island, SC 29482 (tel 803/883-3123)
- **Francis Marion National Forest,** NE of town on SC 41, Charleston, SC (tel 803/765-5222)
- **Santee National Wildlife Refuge,** Rte 2, Box 66, Summerton, SC 29148 (tel 803/478-2217)
- **Ninety Six National Historic Site,** Box 496, Ninety Six, SC 29666 (tel 864/543-4068)
- **Kings Mountain National Military Park,** 20 miles NE of town off I-85, Gaffney, SC (tel 803/936-7921)
- **Aiken State Park,** 1145 State Park Rd, Aiken, SC 29856 (tel 803/649-2857)
- **Colleton State Park,** US 15, Canadys, SC 29433 (tel 803/538-8206)
- **Edisto Beach State Park,** 8377 State Cabin Rd, Edisto Island, SC 29438 (tel 803/869-2156)
- **Hampton Plantation State Park,** 1950 Rutledge Rd, McClellanville, SC 29458 (tel 803/546-9361)
- **Hickory Knob State Resort Park,** Rte 1, Box 199-B, McCormick, SC 29835 (tel 864/391-2450)
- **Hunting Island State Park,** 1775 Sea Island Pkwy, St Helena Island, SC 29920 (tel 803/838-2011)
- **Huntington Beach State Park,** US 17S, Murrells Inlet, SC 29576 (tel 803/237-4440)
- **Lake Warren State Park,** Rte 1-A, Box 208-D, Hampton, SC 29924 (tel 803/943-5051)
- **Little Pee Dee State Park,** Rte 2, Box 250, Dillon, SC 29536 (tel 803/774-8872)
- **Myrtle Beach State Park,** 4401 S Kings Hwy, Myrtle Beach, SC 29575 (tel 803/238-5325)
- **Old Dorchester State Park,** 300 State Park Rd, Summerville, SC 29485 (tel 803/873-1740)
- **Rose Hill Plantation State Park,** 2677 Sardis Rd, Union, SC 29379 (tel 864/427-5966)
- **Santee State Park,** 251 State Park Rd, Santee, SC 29142 (tel 803/854-2408)

Rock to Oconee State Park. Eighteen miles of hiking trails give access to the biological diversity of Congaree Swamp National Monument, near Columbia.

White-Water Rafting Rafting, canoeing, and kayaking are major adventures in the Upcountry, where the tumultuous Chattooga National Wild and Scenic River forms the border between South Carolina and Georgia. The Chattooga, familiar to many as the setting for the movie *Deliverance,* offers some of the finest wilderness white-water experiences in the country. Colorfully named rapids—Screaming Left Turn, Rock Jumble, Corkscrew, and Soc'em Dog—provide extraordinary challenges. For information about guided tours, contact **Wildwater Ltd** (tel toll free 800/451-9972), **Southeastern Expeditions** (tel toll free 800/868-7238), or the **Nantahala Outdoor Center** (tel toll free 800/232-7238).

Driving the State

THE SOUTH CAROLINA COAST

Start	Little River
Finish	Daufuskie Island
Distance	300 miles
Time	2–4 days
Highlights	Beaches, resorts, historic homes and churches, plantations, gardens, museums

The Gulf Stream—an undersea river originating in the tropics—flows 40 miles off the coast of South Carolina, moderating the climate for humans and nurturing an ideally balanced ecological environment for a vast population of marine life. Along this wide ribbon of sea-washed sand, temperatures average in the low 90s in summer and rarely dip below the 50s in winter. This scenic driving tour will allow you the opportunity to surf along the beaches of the Grand Strand, Sullivan's Island, and Folly; play golf and tennis at every resort island from Litchfield to Kiawah to Hilton Head; or take a stroll in the narrow streets and esplanades of Georgetown, Charleston, and Beaufort. Seafood from the ocean and estuaries abounds—and you may even catch some of it yourself.

For additional information on lodgings, dining, and attractions in the region covered by the tour, look under specific cities in the listings portion of this chapter.

US 17 traces a pre-colonial Native American trail that came south from Massachusetts. To begin this great escape, start at:

1. **Little River,** a quaint oceanside village near the North Carolina border. This is the departure point of many fishing boats heading out to sea to angle for grouper and red snapper or troll for amberjack and sailfish.

   Follow US 17 south for 24 miles, stopping as the mood strikes you at any of the beaches—Cherry Grove, Ocean Drive, Crescent, Atlantic, or Windy Hill—on the way to the next stop:

2. **Myrtle Beach,** the sun-and-fun capital of the Grand Strand. Of all South Carolina's beach resorts, Myrtle Beach is the one with the most to offer those

who can't sit still. Fishing piers and deep-sea charters lure the fishing enthusiast. Golfers can tee off on more than 70 courses while tennis buffs can ace on more than 200 courts. Charted shipwrecks call from the ocean depths to the adventurous diver. Shopping ranges from handcrafted treasures to outlet bargains. If all that's not enough, there's also dinner cruises, helicopter rides, amusement parks, water parks, wax museums, dinner theater, several country music venues, and dancing. Kids can ride the antique carousel horses on the Herschel-Spillman Merry-Go-Round at the **Myrtle Beach Pavilion Amusement Park,** Ninth Ave N at Ocean Blvd, or try out the legendary wooden roller coaster at **Family Kingdom Amusement Park,** Third Ave S. Wax museums are represented by **Ripley's Believe It or Not Museum,** 901 N Ocean Blvd, and the animated figures at the **Myrtle Beach National Wax Museum,** 1000 N Ocean Blvd. There are even two water theme parks: **Myrtle Waves Water Park,** US 17 Bypass and 10th Ave N, and **Wild Water and Wheels,** US 17 Business. The **All Children's Park,** S Hollywood and 10th Ave S, is a barrier-free playground designed for children with disabilities.

   If you're not too exhausted from all this frenetic activity, continue south on US 17 (through Surfside Beach and Garden City) for 13 miles to:

3. **Murrells Inlet,** known as the Seafood Capital of the South. This picturesque fishing village is famous for its Restaurant Row, with more than 20 seafood eateries. Fishing charters depart daily from several docks and the inlets provide outstanding opportunities for fishing and crabbing. While in Murrells Inlet, make time to visit **Brookgreen Gardens/ Huntington Beach State Park,** US 17. The gardens, located on the site of a colonial rice plantation, were the 1930s creation of Archer and Anna Huntington. Herself an artist, Mrs Huntington gathered exquisite pieces of 19th- and 20th-century American sculpture and developed an outdoor setting for them amidst 2,000 species of plants. Across US 17 in what is now Huntington Beach State Park is the Huntington's home, **Atalaya**—a fortresslike 30-room Moorish castle, now open for tours.

   Keep going south on US 17 for 9½ miles (passing through upscale Litchfield Beach) to:

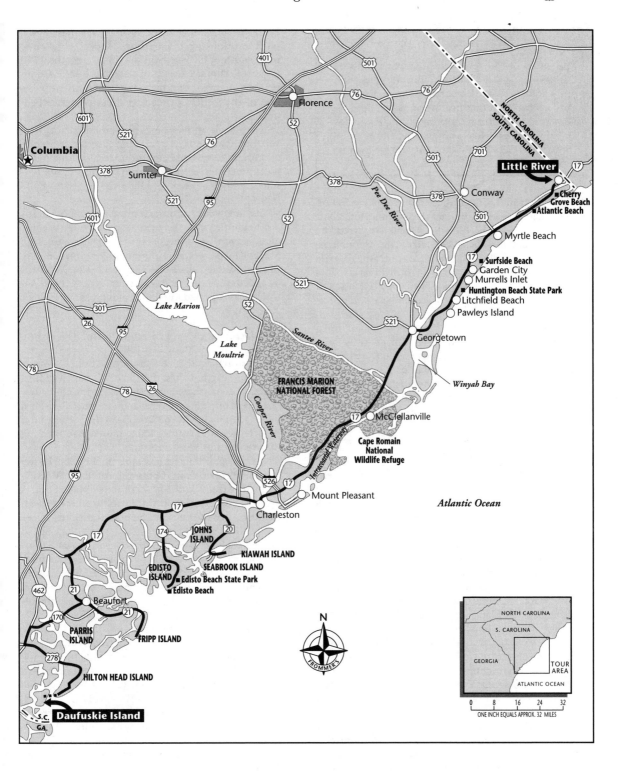

Take a Break

The oldest of Murrells Inlet's many restaurants, **Oliver's Lodge,** 4204 US 17 Business (tel 803/651-2963), is located in a rustic summer cottage with wraparound porches overlooking the inlet. Dinner entrees focus on prime rib, steaks, ribs, and chicken, as well as seafood, and prices range from $10 to $23. The Light Fare menu features smaller portions for $7 to $12.

4. **Pawleys Island,** one of the oldest beach resorts on the Atlantic Coast. Colonial rice planters and their families escaped here in the summer to avoid the malaria that they believed stalked the woodlands, rivers, and marshes. In complete contrast to Myrtle Beach, Pawleys Island comprises individual cottages and almost nothing else except broad expanses of beach. Still, this island retreat does have two claims to fame. The Pawleys Island hammock—a woven-cotton creation in which to enfold yourself for a lazy summer nap—has been handmade in the area for as long as anyone can remember and is available at several shops. The island is also home to the mysterious Gray Man of Pawleys Island; according to legend, he is the ghost of a colonist who appears whenever danger (such as an impending hurricane) is imminent.

From Pawleys Island, it's another 12½ miles south on US 17 to the next stop:

5. **Georgetown,** which claims to be the first settlement in North America. Although that early Spanish colony, attempted in 1526, ultimately failed as a result of hostile encounters with a hurricane and with Native Americans, a permanent English settlement was established here in 1726. For many years Georgetown was an important seaport serving the area's once-thriving rice plantations. The town's old docks have been converted into the charming **Harbor Walk,** where a boardwalk stretches along the waterfront and old commercial buildings have been converted into shops and restaurants.

The story of rice and indigo, and how they once made Georgetown County the wealthiest county in the nation, is told through artifacts and dioramas at the **Rice Museum,** Front and Screven Sts. There's also a fine historic district, with dozens of structures dating from the 18th and 19th centuries. The **Prince George Winyah Episcopal Church,** 301 Broad St, was established in 1721. The church's graveyard is filled with old tombstones, some of which lean drunkenly or rest in the clutches of massive tree roots. An exquisite collection of antiques is displayed at the **Kaminski House,** 1003 Front St, an 18th-century townhouse situated on a bluff overlooking the harbor. **Hopsewee Plantation,** south of Georgetown on US 17, was the 1740 home of Thomas Lynch, a delegate to the Continental Congress, and his son Thomas Jr, who was one of the signers of the Declaration of Independence.

With such an extensive historic district, it's no surprise that Georgetown offers overnight accommodations in several bed-and-breakfasts; one of the most amenable is the moderately priced, antiques-filled **1790 House,** 630 Highmarket St (tel 803/546-4821).

Resume your southward progress on US 17. It's a 60-mile drive to the next stop. If your schedule allows, you can make brief detours through McClellanville—an authentic Spanish moss-draped fishing village on the Intracoastal Waterway—and the historic Old Village in Mount Pleasant, which was founded in 1680. Then cross the Cooper River to:

6. **Charleston,** the jewel in South Carolina's crown. Founded in 1670 by British and Irish emigrés, Charleston has survived many catastrophes—hurricanes and earthquakes, the Revolutionary and Civil Wars, the encroachments of modern architecture—to remain the proud and aristocratic Southern belle. The city has been vigorous in the preservation of its legacy, and is now a living museum showcasing 300 years of architecture styles.

Begin your visit with a stop at the **Charleston Visitor Information Center,** located at Meeting and Ann Streets in a 19th-century railway depot. A film, *Forever Charleston,* will introduce you to both the history of the city and the important sites in and around it. From the visitor center, you can take a guided walking tour, a horse-drawn carriage tour, or hop aboard the trolley to explore on your own. Right across Meeting Street are the **Charleston Museum,** founded in 1773 and filled with local memorabilia, and the 1803 **Joseph Manigault House.**

Charleston's house museums number in the dozens, but some of the most attractive include the 1817 **Aiken-Rhett House** (48 Elizabeth St), the 1876 **Calhoun Mansion** (16 Meeting St), the 1828 **Edmondston-Alston House** (21 E Battery), the 1772 **Heyward-Washington House** (87 Church St), and the circa-1800 **Nathaniel Russell House** (51 Meeting St). There are so many examples of historic religious architecture in Charleston, the city has earned the nickname The Holy City. **Congregation Beth Elohim,** 90 Hassel St, is the oldest synagogue in continuous use in the country; the oldest Roman Catholic church in the South—**St Mary's Roman**

Catholic Church, built in 1839—is right across the street.

Plantation life in the Low Country was once described as "quiet as Sunday." To absorb a sense of that tranquillity, make a point to see some of these gracious old homes. Three of the best are on SC 61 along the banks of the Ashley River. **Middleton Place** was built circa 1740 by Henry Middleton, a signer of the Declaration of Independence; today the grounds include the ruins of the original house, a restored house wing, a stable yard, and several magnificent gardens. **Drayton Hall,** built circa 1738, is considered to be the finest example of Georgian Palladian architecture in the country and is the only Ashley River plantation not vandalized by Union troops in 1865. **Magnolia Plantation** offers a 19th-century house, formal and cypress gardens, and a petting zoo. North of Charleston on the banks of the Cooper River is **Boone Hall Plantation,** dating from 1681. You may recognize its breathtakingly beautiful ¾-mile, oak tree–lined entrance from the TV miniseries *North and South.* Near Summerville is the garden and chapel of **Mepkin Abbey,** formerly Mepkin Plantation, on River Rd off SC 402. Originally the home of patriot Henry Laurens, Mepkin was the last home of Henry and Clare Boothe Luce, who donated it to the Catholic Church for use as a monastery.

Charleston has one of the largest collections of historic bed-and-breakfasts in the country. Premier hostelries include: the **John Rutledge House Inn,** 116 Broad St (tel 803/723-7999); the **Planters Inn,** Market and Meeting Sts (tel 803/722-2345); and the **Lodge Alley Inn,** 195 E Bay St (tel 803/722-1611).

After leaving Charleston, continue west on US 17. After about 23 miles, take Main Rd on Johns Island south to:

7. **Kiawah and Seabrook Islands,** both controlled-access resort islands. Kiawah is a 10,000-acre retreat with two resort villages, an inn, restaurants, shopping arcades, tennis, four championship golf courses, miles of bike trails, and 10 miles of pristine beach. Seabrook features tennis courts, two golf courses, restaurants, an equestrian center and bridle trails, and bike trails.

Return to US 17 and proceed west to SC 174, which you will take south for 61 miles to:

8. **Edisto Island,** settled in 1690 and once famous for growing Sea Island cotton. Archeological excavations show that the Edisto tribe inhabited the island thousands of years ago. Bought by the British in 1674 in exchange for a few trinkets, the island went on to produce indigo and, later, cotton. Campsites and cabins, as well as many recreational facilities, are available at **Edisto Beach State Park,** SC 174.

Return to US 17 and go west to US 21, taking it south for 51 miles to:

9. **Beaufort,** which you may recognize from such films as *The Big Chill* and *The Great Santini.* This romantic Southern town is graced with many antebellum homes, and ancient oak trees dripping with Spanish moss. Carriage tours of the **Old Point Historic District** leave from the visitor center at **Henry C Chambers Waterfront Park** on the Intracoastal Waterway, or you can explore on your own. To learn more about Beaufort and the Low Country coastal area, visit the **Beaufort Museum,** 713 Craven St. The exterior of the building itself is interesting: Once an arsenal, it was constructed of tabby—a material of burned oyster shells, sand, and whole shells unique to the South Carolina and Georgia coasts. The **George Parsons Elliott House Museum,** Bay and Charles Sts, is an antebellum Greek Revival home filled with period antiques. The federal-style **John Mark Verdier House,** 801 Bay St, was built in 1790 by a prosperous merchant, visited by the Marquis de Lafayette in 1825, and commandeered for use as a Union headquarters during the Civil War. The flat tombstones of **St Helena's Episcopal Church,** 505 Church St, were used as operating tables during the Civil War.

In 1863 Abraham Lincoln created a **National Cemetery,** US 21, at Beaufort to bury victims of the battles in the South. Eventually the cemetery was used for the remains of 9,000 Union soldiers and 122 Confederates. Near Beaufort on SC 280 are the ruins of **Fort Frederick,** a tabby fortress built by the English in 1732 to protect themselves from the Spanish, French, and Native Americans.

If your schedule allows, you could spend a romantic night in Beaufort at the moderately priced **Rhett House Inn,** 1705 Bay St (tel 803/524-9030). Shaded by Spanish moss–draped live oaks and

Take a Break

Diners enjoy spectacular views of the seawall promenade, crafts market, gardens, and marina from the dining room at the **Gadsby Tavern,** 822 Bay St (tel 803/525-1800). Menu highlights include fresh seafood and Low Country specialties. Lunch choices (which might include crab cakes, an oyster or vegetarian sandwich, or gourmet pizza) range from $4 to $8, while dinner entrees (grouper Daufuskie stuffed with crabmeat, shrimp Gadsby) cost $6 to $19.

magnolias, the inn is filled with priceless art and antiques.

From Beaufort, explore the rest of:

10. **Parris and Fripp Islands.** Parris Island, best known for the US Marine Corps Recruit Depot, was settled by the Spanish in 1566. Archeological digs reveal remnants of **Fort San Felipe, Santa Elena,** and **Fort San Marcos.** First the Spanish built Fort San Felipe and formed the village of Santa Elena. When the Native Americans destroyed the village in 1576, the Spanish rebuilt the village and constructed a larger fort they called San Marcos. Displays detailing the history of the island as well as marine uniforms and weapons can be seen at the **Parris Island Museum** at the Marine Corps Recruit Depot.

    An ancient hunting ground of the Yemassee tribe, the land of Fripp Island was acquired in colonial times by Capt Johannes Fripp, a hero in battles against the Spanish. Because the resort island has controlled access, walking or getting around by bicycle or golf-cart are the most popular method of transportation. Its most famous resident today is novelist Pat Conroy, author of the best-sellers *The Great Santini* and *The Prince of Tides.*

It's a scenic 35-mile drive to the next stop. Return to US 17, go west to I-95, then southwest to US 278, and turn south to:

11. **Hilton Head,** one of the most popular resort islands on the East Coast. (Ironically, in the 18th century, discoverer William Hilton had to advertise for settlers in the London newspapers.) Today, the peak tourist season brings 55,000 visitors to the 42-square-mile island, which wasn't even connected to the mainland until 1956. In addition to its 12 miles of sandy beaches, the planned resort offers the limited-access communities of **Palmetto Dunes, Port Royal Resort, Sea Pines,** and **Shipyard Plantation,** 20 public or semi-private championship golf courses, 300 tennis courts, marinas, nature preserves, upscale and outlet shopping, restaurants, and nightspots. Learn more about Native American life on 15th-century Hilton Head and see changing exhibits at the **Museum of Hilton Head Island,** 100 William Hilton Hwy. Visitors can tour 24 ponds and the research building to see methods of raising seafood commercially at the **James M Waddell Jr Mariculture Research and Development Center,** Sawmill Creek Rd.

    From several Hilton Head marinas, you can gain boat access to:

12. **Daufuskie Island,** the setting for Pat Conroy's novel *The Water is Wide,* which was later made into the movie *Conrack.* A rural, remote, self-sufficient island inhabited by the descendants of former slaves, the community is characterized by small farms interspersed with the remains of antebellum structures.

    Return to Hilton Head, where you can pick up I-26 W and I-95 S toward Savannah, GA, or head north on I-36 toward Columbia.

South Carolina Listings

Abbeville

The Confederacy was born here with the first reading of the secession papers in 1860, and the rebel cause died when the War Council formally disbanded here. Abbeville's grand 18th-century Opera House—still in use—has seen the likes of Fanny Brice and Jimmy Durante on its stage. **Information:** Abbeville Chamber of Commerce, 104 Pickens St, Abbeville, 29620 (tel 864/459-4600).

HOTEL

≣≣≣ Belmont Inn

106 Court Sq, 29620; tel 864/459-9625; fax 864/459-9625. Next to Opry House. An innlike hotel housed in a building listed on the National Register of Historic Places. Fireplace in the lobby adds a cozy feel. **Rooms:** 25 rms and stes. CI 3pm/CO noon. Nonsmoking rms avail. J C Calhoun Suite can sleep up to 10 people in three connecting rooms. Regular rooms have two twin beds or one queen. Furniture is simple and somewhat antique (wardrobes instead of closets). **Amenities:** A/C, cable TV. 1 unit w/terrace. **Facilities:** 1 restaurant (lunch and dinner only; see "Restaurants" below), 1 bar. Huge, Southern-style front porch. **Rates (CP):** $67–$77 S or D; $261 ste. Extra person $10. Children under age 12 stay free. Parking: Outdoor, free. Higher rates on weekends. Weekend theater package includes wine/cheese, dinner, coffee/dessert, and two theater tickets. AE, CB, DC, DISC, EC, ER, JCB, MC, V.

RESTAURANT

★ Belmont Inn Restaurant

106 Court Sq; tel 864/459-9625. **Continental/Southern.** A cozy eatery located just off the lobby of this quaint, historic inn. The building is on the National Register of Historic Places, and interesting renovation pictures can be found downstairs, just outside the bar. The lunch buffet features Southern country cooking, while the dinner menu is continental. Menu choices are few: stuffed flounder, rib eye steak, and two chicken entrees. Fresh soups daily. **FYI:** Reservations recommended. Children's menu. Dress code. **Open:** Lunch Mon–Fri 11:30am–2pm, Sun 11:30am–2pm; dinner Mon–Sat 6–9pm. **Prices:** Main courses $13–$17. AE, CB, DC, DISC, ER, MC, V.

Aiken

A watering place and winter resort for the wealthy for over a century. Year-round green pastures produce one of the state's most celebrated "crops": fine thoroughbred horses. Aiken was the scene of a Civil War battle in early 1865.

HOTEL

UNRATED Holly Inn

235 Richland Ave, PO Box 588, SC; tel 803/648-4265; fax 803/648-4265. Comfortable accommodations in a cream building with green trim. Older, but very well-maintained. **Rooms:** 56 rms and stes. CI 7am/CO noon. **Amenities:** A/C, cable TV. **Services:** Children's program. **Facilities:** 1 restaurant (bkfst and lunch only), 1 bar. **Rates:** Peak (Apr) $32–$40 S; $34–$45 D; $34–$45 ste. Extra person $3. Children under age 12 stay free. Lower rates off-season. Parking: Outdoor, free. AE, DC, DISC, MC, V.

MOTEL

≣≣ Days Inn Downtown

1204 Richland Ave W, 29801; tel 803/649-5524 or toll free 800/329-7466; fax 803/649-5524 ext 101. Housed in an attractive sandstone building, this chain motel offers clean and comfortable accommodations and neat, well-maintained grounds. **Rooms:** 42 rms and stes. CI 2pm/CO 11am. Nonsmoking rms avail. **Amenities:** A/C, refrig. **Services:** **Facilities:** **Rates:** Peak (Apr) $28 S; $34–$38 D; $45 ste. Extra person $4. Children under age 12 stay free. Lower rates off-season. Parking: Outdoor, free. AE, DC, DISC, JCB, MC, V.

INN

≣≣≣ Wilcox Inn

100 Colleton Ave, 29801; tel 803/649-1377; fax 803/643-0971. At Wiskey Rd. A quaint, Old South atmosphere reigns at this inn, housed in an old white building with large

347

columns. Lobby is beautifully appointed with polished wood paneling and plush furniture. **Rooms:** 30 rms and stes. CI 3pm/CO noon. Nonsmoking rms avail. **Amenities:** 🛁 🅰 A/C, cable TV w/movies. Some units w/terraces, all w/fireplaces. Suites have two telephones. **Services:** ✕ ⌫ Babysitting. **Facilities:** 🏊 ‚ 1 restaurant (bkfst and dinner only), 1 bar (w/entertainment), guest lounge w/TV. Complimentary pass to Aiken Health Club. **Rates:** Peak (Sept–May) $105 S or D; $140 ste. Extra person $15. Children under age 18 stay free. Lower rates off-season. Higher rates for special events/hols. Parking: Outdoor, free. AE, DISC, JCB, MC, V.

RESTAURANT 🍽️

★ No 10 Downing Street

241 Laurens St; tel 803/642-9062. **Eclectic.** Listed on the National Register of Historic Homes, this 1837 Colonial has been converted into a lovely and unique eatery. The menu changes regularly to focus on a different ethnic or regional American cuisine. Past favorites have included pollo al proscuitto, grilled swordfish, salmon, and rack of lamb. Baking is done on premises. **FYI:** Reservations accepted. No smoking. **Open:** Lunch Tues–Sat 11:30am–2:30pm; dinner Tues–Sat 6–9:30pm. **Prices:** Main courses $3–$10. AE, DISC, MC. 🍸 🖼️ ‚

ATTRACTIONS 🏛️

Aiken County Historical Museum

433 Newberry St SW; tel 803/642-2015. This museum occupies part of a former "Winter Colony" millionaire's estate. Of special interest are Native American artifacts, an old-time drugstore from a little South Carolina town that no longer exists, a 19th-century schoolhouse, and early firefighting equipment. **Open:** Tues–Fri 9:30am–4:30pm, Sat 9:30am–12:30pm, Sun 2–5pm. Closed some hols. **Free**

Hopeland Gardens

149 Dupree Place; tel 803/648-5461. The grounds hold the Thoroughbred Racing Hall of Fame in a restored carriage house. The gardens have a trail, dubbed the "touch and scent" trail, which has plaques in standard type and Braille to identify the plants, and to lead visitors to a performing arts stage. There, open-air concerts are performed Monday evenings in summer, and theatrical productions are offered periodically. **Open:** Gardens, daily 10am–sunset; Hall of Fame, Tues–Sun 2–5pm. **Free**

Anderson

See also Starr

A busy cotton-spinning and -weaving center from the late 18th century, this industrial city is a commercial and shipping center for an agricultural region of northwest South Caroli-na. **Information:** Anderson Area Chamber of Commerce, 706 E Greenville St, PO Box 1568, Anderson, 29622 (tel 864/226-3454).

MOTELS 🏨

UNRATED Holiday Inn

3025 N Main St, 29621; tel 864/226-6051 or toll free 800/HOLIDAY; fax 864/226-6051. 2½ mi off I-85. A basic Holiday Inn on the town's main drag. Attractive water fountains at entrance. **Rooms:** 130 rms. CI 2pm/CO noon. Nonsmoking rms avail. All units have either two double beds or one king-size bed. Suites have kitchenettes. **Amenities:** 🛁 🅰 🔲 A/C, satel TV w/movies, dataport. **Services:** ✕ 🖼️ ⌫ **Facilities:** 🏋️ 🏊 ‚ 1 restaurant, 1 bar. **Rates:** $59–$64 S; $55–$70 D. Extra person $6. Children under age 19 stay free. Parking: Outdoor, free. Higher rates on football weekends. AE, DC, DISC, MC, V.

≣≣ La Quinta Inn

3430 N Main St, 29621; tel 864/225-3721 or toll free 800/531-5900. 2 mi off I-85. Bright white-stucco exterior, Southwestern decor, and a subtle, updated look are the highlights here. **Rooms:** 100 rms. CI 3pm/CO noon. Nonsmoking rms avail. Spotless rooms have well-coordinated decor. **Amenities:** 🛁 🅰 A/C, cable TV. Bigger-than-average TVs. **Services:** 🖼️ ⌫ Twice-daily maid svce. Pets must be under 15 lbs. **Facilities:** 🏋️ 🏊 ‚ Grounds are larger than those of average motel in area. **Rates (CP):** $50–$57 S; $56–$63 D. Extra person $5. Children under age 18 stay free. Parking: Outdoor, free. AE, DC, DISC, MC, V.

RESTAURANT 🍽️

★ The Gray House

111 Stones Throw Ave, Starr; tel 864/352-6778. **Southern.** Located on the first floor of a Victorian bed-and-breakfast, which is itself part of a working farm well known for its prize cattle and fresh produce. The charming decor consists of pine floors, beaded-wood walls, and period antiques. Each of the dining rooms has a slightly different color scheme and decor. Although there is no fixed menu, entrees usually include beef, lamb, pork, and seafood selections. **FYI:** Reservations recommended. Piano. **Open:** Lunch daily 11:30am–2pm; dinner Thurs–Sun 6:30–10pm. **Prices:** Main courses $12–$16. AE, DISC. ❤️

Beaufort

On Port Royal along the southern coast. Spaniards first came ashore here in 1520, and a city was established in 1710. The area achieved prosperity when Sea Island cotton was introduced toward the close of the 18th century; today the economy is based on commercial fisheries, truck farms, and tourism. Hunting Island, a state park off the coast of Beaufort, was once a hunting reserve for the wealthy. The beach here, considered one of the most beautiful of the Barrier Islands, is preserved in its natural state. Parris Island, another component of the Sea Islands, is the site of 16th-century forts and a village built by the Spaniards. **Information:** Greater Beaufort Chamber of Commerce, 1006 Bay St, PO Box 910, Beaufort, 29901 (tel 803/524-3163).

MOTEL

Holiday Inn
2001 Boundary St, 29902; tel 803/524-2144 or toll free 800/465-4329; fax 803/524-2144. Off US 170 and I-95. This four-story brick building looks like a classic Southern mansion, complete with stately white columns. Lobby is exquisitely decorated. **Rooms:** 152 rms. CI 2pm/CO noon. Nonsmoking rms avail. Rooms are nice and comfortable. **Amenities:** A/C, cable TV. **Services:** Pet fee is $20. Horse-and-buggy tour of the historic district can be arranged for fee. **Facilities:** 1 restaurant, 1 bar (w/entertainment). **Rates:** $51–$59 S or D. Extra person $8. Children under age 18 stay free. Min stay special events. Parking: Outdoor, free. AE, DC, DISC, MC, V.

INN

Rhett House Inn
1009 Craven St, 29902; tel 803/524-9030; fax 803/524-1310. Off Charles St. Restored in 1986, Rhett House is a stately 1820 home with grand Doric columns and verandas on both floors. Outside, guests may relax on the "piazza" and sip tea while enjoying the evening breeze among the moss-draped oaks. The interior is warm and inviting, with paintings by one of the original owner's descendants scattered throughout the house. Unsuitable for children under 16. **Rooms:** 10 rms. CI 3pm/CO 11am. No smoking. Every room is uniquely decorated with family antiques and handmade comforters. **Amenities:** A/C, cable TV, bathrobes. Some units w/terraces. Fresh flowers in every room. **Services:** Twice-daily maid svce, afternoon tea served. Complimentary bicycles and beach chairs; picnic baskets for lunch and dinner available for small fee. **Facilities:** Guest lounge. **Rates (BB):** Peak (Sept–Dec/Mar–May) $125–$175 S or D. Extra person $25. Min stay special events. Lower rates off-season. Parking: Outdoor, free. AE, MC, V.

RESTAURANT

The New Gadsby Tavern
822 Bay St; tel 803/525-1800. Off US 21. **Eclectic.** A very formal dining room, serving everything from seafood and steak to vegetarian plates. **FYI:** Reservations recommended. Children's menu. **Open:** Lunch daily 11:30am–3pm; dinner daily 5:30–10pm; brunch Sun 11am–3pm. **Prices:** Main courses $5–$9. AE, DISC, MC, V.

ATTRACTIONS

Parris Island Museum
Building III, Parris Island; tel 803/525-2951. Located 10 mi S of Beaufort. Through its displays, this museum depicts the history of Parris Island, as a Spanish and then an English colony, up to its present day role as the site of a Marine base. The archeology, military history, and social history of the area are explored.

Today, Parris Island is responsible for training all new female Marine recruits, and roughly half of the male recruits, in the United States. One room even includes a display following the experience of "boots," or new recruits going through boot camp. On the grounds, a replica of the Iwo Jima Memorial stands near the parade ground. **Open:** Daily 10am–4:30pm. Closed some hols. **Free**

Hunting Island State Park
1775 Sea Island Pkwy, Hunting Island; tel 803/838-2011. Located 15 mi SE of Beaufort. This state park encompasses over 5,000 acres of sandy beach, maritime forest, and saltwater marsh. The unique ecosystem of this barrier island includes deer, raccoon, amphibians, and over 125 species of birds. A visitors center features displays about the cultural and natural history of the area; inquire here about park ranger tours. Park facilities include a 200-site camping area, 15 cabins, 2 beaches, 2 nature trails, and a fishing pier. **Open:** Daily 6am–10pm. **Free**

Camden

One of the state's oldest inland towns and a major center for the training and breeding of thoroughbreds. Many roads remain unpaved for the sake of horses' hooves. **Information:** Kershaw County Chamber of Commerce, 724 S Broad St, PO Box 605, Camden, 29020 (tel 803/432-2525).

MOTELS

Hampton Park Motel
322 DeKalb St, 29020; tel 803/432-2453. A basic budget motel located just off the main street. Fine for an overnight stay. **Rooms:** 34 rms. CI open/CO 11am. Nonsmoking rms avail. **Amenities:** A/C, cable TV. **Services:** **Facilities:** Pool is located in parking lot. **Rates:** $25–$32 S or D. Children under age 18 stay free. Parking: Outdoor, free. AE, DISC, MC, V.

Holiday Inn
US 1 S, PO Box 96, 29078; tel 803/438-9441 or toll free 800/HOLIDAY; fax 803/438-9441 ext 518. Exit 92 off I-20. A nicer-than-average Holiday Inn located several miles from downtown. Beautiful lobby was recently renovated. Popular with business travelers. **Rooms:** 117 rms. Executive level. CI noon/CO noon. Nonsmoking rms avail. **Amenities:** A/C, satel TV w/movies. Some units w/whirlpools. Many rooms have dataports and two telephone lines. **Services:** X

🖼️🛏️🔊 Babysitting. **Facilities:** 🏋️📷 ♿ 1 restaurant, 1 bar (w/entertainment), washer/dryer. Guests receive free passes to a local health club. Nightclub offers karaoke, a DJ, and a bar and lounge area. Exceptionally roomy and secluded pool area. **Rates (BB):** $49–$54 S; $54–$59 D. Extra person $5. Children under age 19 stay free. Parking: Outdoor, free. Golf packages avail. AE, CB, DC, DISC, ER, MC, V.

INN

▦▦▦ Greenleaf Inn

1308/10 Broad St, 29020; tel 803/425-1806 or toll free 800/437-5874; fax 803/425-5853. Quaint and comfortable inn located in a century-old building listed on National Register of Historic Places. **Rooms:** 13 rms; 1 cottage/villa. CI 1pm/CO 11am. Nonsmoking rms avail. Spacious rooms feature beautiful hardwood floors and white embroidered spreads but there are some maintenance problems, such as peeling paint and wallpaper. **Amenities:** 📺 ♨ 🍴 A/C, cable TV. Some units w/fireplaces. **Services:** ✗ 🖼️🛏️🔊 Wine/sherry served. Occasionally, there's a piano player. **Facilities:** 📷 1 restaurant, 1 bar (w/entertainment). Community balcony with comfortable lawn seating. **Rates (CP):** $55–$65 S; $65–$75 D; $135 cottage/villa. Extra person $10. Children under age 12 stay free. Parking: Outdoor, free. AE, MC, V.

RESTAURANT 🍽️

The Paddock Restaurant and Pub

514 Rutledge St; tel 803/432-3222. **Continental.** With dark decor and clubby atmosphere, this spot is popular with horse trainers and owners, and fans of the annual Colonial Cup Steeplechase. The menu serves up the usual steaks, ribs, sandwiches, salads, and pastas, and there's a good selection of beer. **FYI:** Reservations recommended. Piano. No smoking. **Open:** Tues–Fri 11am–2am, Sat 11am–midnight. **Prices:** Main courses $10–$28. AE, DISC, MC, V. ♨

ATTRACTION 🏛️

Historic Camden, Revolutionary War Site

S Broad St, Hwy 521; tel 803/432-9841. A Revolutionary War park affiliated with the National Park Service. There are restored log houses with museum exhibits, fortifications, the Cornwallis House, powder magazine, a model of the original town, and miniature dioramas. The guided tour includes a narrated slide presentation and access to all museums. **Open:** Tues–Sat 10am–5pm, Sun 1–5pm. Closed some hols. $$

Charleston

See also Edisto Island, Kiawah Island

The state's oldest city (founded 1680) and one of the chief ports of entry in the Southeast, Charleston lies on a narrow peninsula in the bay formed by the confluence of the Ashley and Cooper Rivers. Reminders of its early importance as a prosperous and cosmopolitan seaport are everywhere, and it is famous for its picturesque streets, houses, and other 18th-century monuments. The incident that ignited the Civil War occurred at nearby Fort Sumter. Across the river from Charleston lies the port town of Mount Pleasant, with its 1860 Old Village boasting several antebellum homes. Quiet little Edisto Island, once famous for its Sea Island cotton, is cut off from the mainland by the Edisto River. Settlers bought the island from its native inhabitants in 1674; in recent years, archeologists have unearthed many Native American artifacts. **Information:** Charleston Trident Convention & Visitors Bureau, PO Box 975, Charleston, 29402 (tel 803/853-8000).

PUBLIC TRANSPORTATION

Regular bus service is provided. Fare is 75¢ (25¢ for seniors and persons with disabilities during off-peak hours); exact change required. **Downtown Area Shuttle (DASH)** trolley-style buses service main downtown areas. Fare is 75¢, $1 for all-day pass. For bus schedules and DASH information, call 803/747-0922

HOTELS 🏨

▦▦▦ Best Western King Charles Inn

237 Meeting St, 29401; tel 803/723-7451 or toll free 800/528-1234; fax 803/723-2041. Off I-26. Recently remodeled and tastefully decorated, this hotel is a five-minute walk from historic district sights. Popular with families because of the pool. **Rooms:** 91 rms. CI 2pm/CO noon. Nonsmoking rms avail. Relatively new furnishings, drapes, carpets, and bedding make for a comfortable stay. **Amenities:** 📺 ♨ A/C, cable TV. Some units w/terraces. **Services:** ✗ 🚗 🖼️🛏️ **Facilities:** 🏋️📷 ♿ 1 restaurant (bkfst only). One of very few downtown hotels with a pool. **Rates:** $79–$159 S or D. Extra person $10. Children under age 17 stay free. Min stay wknds. Parking: Outdoor, free. AE, CB, DC, DISC, MC, V.

▦▦▦ Charleston Hilton

4770 Goer Dr, 29418; tel 803/747-1900 or toll free 800/228-9290; fax 803/747-2530. Exit 213B off I-26E and exit 213 off I-26W. Although it lacks the individuality of the historic Charleston inns, this upscale, modern hotel is a good choice for businesspeople or anyone else who wants or needs all the amenities and services offered by Hilton. The attractive lobby has parquet floors, fluted columns, and knotty-pine furnishings. **Rooms:** 297 rms and stes. Executive level. CI 4pm/CO noon. Nonsmoking rms avail. Spacious, handsome rooms. **Amenities:** 📺 ♨ A/C, cable TV. **Services:** ✗ 🚗 🖼️🛏️ Babysitting. **Facilities:** 📷 🏋️ 📷 ♿ 1 restaurant, 1 bar, spa, whirlpool, washer/dryer. During winter, kids under eight eat free in hotel restaurant. **Rates:** Peak (Mar–June/Sept–Nov) $109 S or D; $149 ste. Extra person $18. Children under age 18 stay free. Lower rates off-season. Parking: Outdoor, free. Weekend packages avail. AE, DISC, MC, V.

≣≣≣ Hampton Inn

345 Meeting St, 29401; tel 803/723-4000 or toll free 800/ HAMPTON; fax 803/722-3725. Exit 221 at I-26. A unique chain hotel housed in a converted 19th-century baggage factory. The colonial-style lobby is filled with natural woods and Oriental rugs, and there's a cozy fireplace. **Rooms:** 171 rms and stes. CI 4pm/CO noon. Nonsmoking rms avail. **Amenities:** 🛏 ⚙ A/C, cable TV. Some units w/terraces, 1 w/whirlpool. **Services:** 🖙 VP 🖭 ⌁ Babysitting. **Facilities:** 🖼 🚗 ⅙ **Rates (CP):** Peak (Mar–Oct) $89–$109 S; $89–$119 D; $115–$160 ste. Extra person $10. Children under age 18 stay free. Min stay special events. Lower rates off-season. Parking: Outdoor, $9/day. AE, CB, DC, DISC, MC, V.

≣≣ Hampton Inn Mount Pleasant

255 US 17 N Bypass, 29464; tel 803/881-3300 or toll free 800/HAMPTON; fax 803/881-6288. Off US 17 N. A spiffy new place located 10 minutes from the island beaches. **Rooms:** 121 rms and stes. CI 3pm/CO noon. Nonsmoking rms avail. Well-designed rooms with fairly new furnishings. **Amenities:** 🛏 ⚙ A/C, cable TV. **Services:** 🖭 ⌁ Babysitting. Expanded continental breakfast includes muffins, waffles, juice, rolls, cereals, and coffee. **Facilities:** 🖼 ⅙ **Rates (CP):** Peak (Mar–Sept) $65 S; $78 D; $95 ste. Extra person $10. Children under age 18 stay free. Min stay peak and wknds. Lower rates off-season. Parking: Outdoor, free. AE, CB, DC, DISC, MC, V.

≣≣≣ Hawthorne Suites Hotel

181 Church St, 29401 (Old Market); tel 803/577-2644 or toll free 800/527-1133; fax 803/577-2697. Off Hayne St. In the center of downtown, this relatively new hotel has been well maintained. Perfect for families or business travelers. **Rooms:** 182 rms and stes. Executive level. CI 3pm/CO noon. Nonsmoking rms avail. **Amenities:** 🛏 ⚙ 🖥 A/C, cable TV, refrig, voice mail. **Services:** X VP 🖭 ⌁ Babysitting. **Facilities:** 🖼 🖳 ⅙ Games rm, spa, whirlpool, washer/dryer. Limited parking available. **Rates (BB):** Peak (Mar–June/Sept–Nov) $100–$145 S or D; $115–$155 ste. Children under age 18 stay free. Lower rates off-season. Parking: Outdoor, free. Honeymoon and golf packages avail. MC, V.

≣≣≣ Heart of Charleston Quality Inn

125 Calhoun St, 29401; tel 803/722-3391 or toll free 800/845-2504; fax 803/577-0361. At Meeting St. Located a half-block from the city visitor's center, this hotel is nicer inside than outside. **Rooms:** 126 rms and stes. Executive level. CI 4pm/CO 11am. Nonsmoking rms avail. Rooms are clean and spacious. **Amenities:** 🛏 ⚙ 🖥 A/C, cable TV, dataport. Some units w/terraces. **Services:** X 🚗 🖭 ⌁ Car-rental desk. A free shuttle to downtown is available. **Facilities:** 🖼 🚗 ⅙ 1 restaurant, 1 bar, washer/dryer. **Rates:** Peak (Mar–Oct) $72–$88 S or D; $150 ste. Extra person $5. Children under age 18 stay free. Lower rates off-season. Parking: Indoor/outdoor, free. AE, DISC, MC, V.

≣≣≣ Holiday Inn Riverview

301 Savannah Hwy, 29407; tel 803/556-7100 or toll free 800/HOLIDAY; fax 803/556-6176. Exit 221A off I-26 to US 17S. A unique, cylindrical 13-story hotel overlooking the Ashley River. **Rooms:** 181 rms and stes. CI 3pm/CO noon. Nonsmoking rms avail. Some rooms have river views. **Amenities:** 🛏 ⚙ A/C, satel TV w/movies, dataport. All units w/terraces. Some rooms have Nintendo for a fee. **Services:** X 🖭 ⌁ 🚐 Free shuttle to historic downtown. **Facilities:** 🖼 🍴 🚗 ⅙ 1 restaurant, 1 bar (w/entertainment), washer/dryer. Guests have free access to local health club. **Rates:** Peak (Mar–Oct) $79–$129 S; $85–$135 D; $125–$175 ste. Extra person $6. Children under age 19 stay free. Lower rates off-season. Parking: Outdoor, free. AE, CB, DC, DISC, JCB, MC, V.

≣≣≣≣ Mills House Hotel

115 Meeting St, 29401; tel 803/577-2400 or toll free 800/874-9600; fax 803/722-2112. Off US 17 at Calhoun St. This large, pink hotel with wrought-iron balconies is a completely rebuilt reproduction of an 1853 hotel which hosted Stephen Douglas, Robert E Lee, and Theodore Roosevelt. Filled with period antiques, it is an elegant antebellum hotel for both families and business travelers. **Rooms:** 214 rms and stes. CI 3pm/CO 11am. Nonsmoking rms avail. **Amenities:** 🛏 ⚙ A/C, cable TV. **Services:** X 🖙 VP 🚐 🖭 ⌁ Masseur, babysitting. Very hospitable staff. **Facilities:** 🖼 🍴 ⅙ 1 restaurant (see "Restaurants" below), 2 bars (w/entertainment). **Rates:** Peak (Mar–June/Sept–Nov) $210 S or D; $220–$600 ste. Min stay special events. Lower rates off-season. Parking: Indoor, $11/day. MC, V.

≣≣≣≣ Orient Express Hotel at Charleston Place

130 Market St, 29401; tel 803/722-4900 or toll free 800/843-6664; fax 803/724-7215. Off Meeting St. A big-city hotel in the heart of old-town Charleston. Although this property looks modern on the outside, the interior has an old-fashioned and elegant feel. **Rooms:** 440 rms and stes. Executive level. CI 4pm/CO noon. Nonsmoking rms avail. Rooms facing hectic Market St can be noisy. **Amenities:** 🛏 ⚙ 🍴 A/C, cable TV w/movies, voice mail. Some units w/terraces, 1 w/whirlpool. **Services:** 🍽 🖙 VP 🖭 ⌁ Car-rental desk, masseur, children's program, babysitting. Service is brusque and hurried. Don't expect old-fashioned charm. **Facilities:** 🖼 🍴 🍴 🖳 ⅙ 2 restaurants, 2 bars (w/entertainment), spa, sauna, steam rm, whirlpool, day-care ctr. **Rates:** Peak (Mar–May/Sept–Nov) $139–$239 S or D; $290 ste. Extra person $20. Min stay wknds. Lower rates off-season. Parking: Indoor, $11/day. AE, DC, DISC, MC, V.

≣≣≣ Residence Inn by Marriott

7645 Northwoods Blvd, North Charleston, 29418; tel 803/572-5757 or toll free 800/331-3131; fax 803/797-8529. Exit 209 off I-265. A recently remodeled all-suite hotel, specializing in extended stays. **Rooms:** 96 rms and stes. CI 3pm/CO noon. Nonsmoking rms avail. Units are comfortable and scrupulously clean. **Amenities:** 🚗 ⚱ 🔲 A/C, refrig, dataport. Some units w/terraces, some w/fireplaces. **Services:** 🛏 🍴 ⟳ Social hour (from 5–7pm, Mon–Thurs) with hors d'oeuvres. **Facilities:** 🍴 ⚲¹ [30] ♿ Basketball, volleyball, whirlpool, washer/dryer. Guests have free use of local fitness center. **Rates (CP):** Peak (June–Sept) $90 S; $100 D; $130 ste. Children under age 18 stay free. Lower rates off-season. Parking: Outdoor, free. Honeymoon packages avail. AE, DC, DISC, MC, V.

≣≣≣ Sheraton Charleston Hotel

170 Lockwood Blvd, 29403; tel 803/723-3000 or toll free 800/968-3569; fax 803/720-0844. Off US 17. Tall and pink, this luxury hotel overlooks the Ashley River. It is particularly good for business travelers who need extensive facilities and proximity to downtown. **Rooms:** 333 rms and stes. Executive level. CI 3pm/CO noon. Nonsmoking rms avail. Some rooms have nice views of the river. **Amenities:** 🚗 ⚱ 🔲 🍴 A/C, cable TV, voice mail. Some units w/terraces. **Services:** ✗ 🚗 🛏 🍴 Free shuttle to downtown. **Facilities:** 🍴 🏋 [800] ♿ 1 restaurant, 1 bar. **Rates:** Peak (Mar–June/Sept–Nov) $120–$135 S or D; $175–$350 ste. Extra person $10. Children under age 18 stay free. Min stay peak. Lower rates off-season. Parking: Outdoor, free. Rates vary according to view. AE, CB, DC, DISC, MC, V.

MOTELS

≣≣ Days Inn Historic District

155 Meeting St, 29401; tel 803/722-8411 or toll free 800/DAYS-INN; fax 803/723-5361. Off Calhoun St. A simple two-story motel with ironwork fences. **Rooms:** 124 rms. CI 2pm/CO noon. Nonsmoking rms avail. The rooms are nice and clean. **Amenities:** 🚗 A/C, cable TV w/movies, in-rm safe. **Services:** 🚗 🛏 🍴 **Facilities:** 🍴 [40] ♿ 1 restaurant (bkfst and lunch only). **Rates:** Peak (Feb–Sept) $99–$110 S or D. Extra person $6. Children under age 12 stay free. Lower rates off-season. Parking: Outdoor, free. AE, DC, DISC, MC, V.

UNRATED Dorchester Motor Lodge

3668 Dorchester Ave, 29405; tel 803/747-0961; fax 803/747-3230. Exit 215 off I-26. Basic accommodations, suitable for a one-night stay. **Rooms:** 199 rms and stes. Executive level. CI open/CO 11:30am. Nonsmoking rms avail. Suites are spacious and well maintained. **Amenities:** 🚗 ⚱ A/C, cable TV w/movies, refrig. **Services:** ✗ 🍴 **Facilities:** 🍴 [100] ♿ 1 restaurant, 1 bar. **Rates:** Peak (Mar–Sept) $41–$56 S or D; $56–$66 ste. Extra person $5. Children under age 12 stay free. Lower rates off-season. Parking: Outdoor, free. AE, MC, V.

≣ Econo Lodge

2237 Savannah Hwy, 29407; tel 803/571-1880 or toll free 800/424-4777. A basic property located 10 miles outside the city on a busy commercial strip. Fine for a night or two. **Rooms:** 48 rms. CI 11am/CO 11am. Nonsmoking rms avail. Clean, decent rooms. **Amenities:** 🚗 A/C, cable TV. **Services:**

🍴 **Facilities:** Several golf courses nearby. **Rates (CP):** Peak (Mar–Oct) $32–$49 S; $41–$59 D. Extra person $5. Children under age 18 stay free. Lower rates off-season. Parking: Outdoor, free. AE, DISC, MC, V.

≣≣ La Quinta Motor Inn

2499 La Quinta Lane, North Charleston, 29405; tel 803/797-8181 or toll free 800/531-5900; fax 803/569-1608. Exit 209 off I-26. Located right off the highway on a busy corner, this is a relatively nice stay for a night. **Rooms:** 122 rms. CI 1pm/CO noon. Nonsmoking rms avail. **Amenities:** 🚗 ⚱ A/C, satel TV w/movies. **Services:** 🛏 🍴 ⟳ Coffee available 24 hours. **Facilities:** 🍴 [35] ♿ **Rates (CP):** Peak (Apr–Sept) $48 S; $54 D. Extra person $6. Children under age 18 stay free. Lower rates off-season. Parking: Outdoor, free. AARP and military discounts avail. AE, CB, DC, DISC, MC, V.

≣≣ Motel 6 South

2058 Savannah Hwy, 29407; tel 803/556-5144 or toll free 800/440-6000; fax 803/556-2241. On US 17S. Located on the very busy and noisy commercial strip leading to Charleston; adequate if you just need a quick overnight stay. **Rooms:** 111 rms. CI noon/CO noon. Nonsmoking rms avail. **Amenities:** 🚗 A/C, cable TV. **Services:** 🍴 **Facilities:** 🍴 ♿ **Rates:** $33 S; $37 D. Extra person $4. Children under age 16 stay free. Parking: Outdoor, free. AARP discount avail. AE, DC, DISC, MC, V.

INNS

≣≣≣ Anchorage Inn

26 Vendue Range, 29401; tel 803/723-8300 or toll free 800/421-2952. Off Bay St. A relatively new inn in the historic district and near the waterfront. European atmosphere. Unsuitable for children under 16. **Rooms:** 19 rms and stes. CI 2pm/CO noon. No smoking. Quiet and elegantly cozy, each room is designed with beautiful antiques. **Amenities:** 🚗 ⚱ 🍴 A/C, satel TV, dataport. Some units w/whirlpools. Complimentary newspaper. **Services:** 🔑 🛏 Babysitting, afternoon tea and wine/sherry served. Turndown service with chocolates. **Facilities:** ♿ Guest lounge. **Rates (CP):** Peak (Mar–June/Sept–Nov) $134–$184 S or D; $229 ste. Min stay wknds. Lower rates off-season. Parking: Indoor, $6/day. Maximum of two people per room. AE, MC, V.

≣≣≣ Ansonborough Inn

21 Hasell St, 29401; tel 803/723-1655 or toll free 800/522-2073; fax 803/577-6888. At E Bay St. Located in a paper warehouse built in 1901, this building has been transformed into a cozy inn. The striking atrium lobby combines original heart-pine beams and red brick with modern-looking decor. An inviting place to stay. **Rooms:** 38 rms and stes. CI 3pm/CO noon. Nonsmoking rms avail. Antique reproduction furniture with colorful chintz upholstery and prints depicting local scenes. **Amenities:** 🚗 ⚱ A/C, cable TV, refrig, bathrobes. Some units w/terraces. Complimentary morning newspaper. **Services:** ✗ 🔑 🛏 🍴 Babysitting, afternoon tea and wine/sherry served. Wine and cheese served in the

afternoon, coffee served all day. **Facilities:** [16] Whirlpool, guest lounge. **Rates (CP):** Peak (Mar–June/Sept–Nov) $139–$229 D; $139–$159 ste. Extra person $10. Children under age 12 stay free. Lower rates off-season. Higher rates for special events/hols. Parking: Outdoor, free. AE, DISC, MC, V.

Barksdale House Inn

27 George St, 29401; tel 803/577-4800; fax 803/853-0482. A comfortable 1778 home, now completely restored and charmingly decorated. There are two verandas, and a backyard patio with a fountain. This is a quiet, peaceful place downtown—outside the bustle. Friendly staff and personal attention make for an even more enjoyable stay. Unsuitable for children under 10. **Rooms:** 14 rms. CI 3pm/CO 11am. Nonsmoking rms avail. Dramatically decorated rooms with period antiques. All rooms have queen-size four-poster beds (with brass headboards) and ceiling fans. Four of the rooms are in the carriage house. **Amenities:** 🛏 ⚱ A/C, cable TV. Some units w/fireplaces, some w/whirlpools. **Services:** ✕ ☛ ☒ Babysitting, wine/sherry served. Nightly turndown service with chocolates on pillow. Sherry and tea are served in the parlor (or on the back porch, weather permitting). **Facilities:** Guest lounge. Guests may use swimming pool, weight room, and tennis and racquetball courts across the street for a nominal fee. **Rates (CP):** Peak (Feb–June/Sept–Nov) $80–$160 S or D. Lower rates off-season. Parking: Outdoor, free. MC, V.

Battery Carriage House Inn

20 S Battery, 29401; tel 803/727-3100 or toll free 800/775-5575; fax 803/727-3130. Off Meeting St. This 1843 carriage house overlooking the Battery and Charleston Harbor has survived war, natural disasters, and even (according to legend) has a few ghosts. There's a faux-stone floor and walls in the reception area, and wrought-iron tables in the bricked garden. A very peaceful place to stay along Charleston's most popular walking area. Unsuitable for children under 12. **Rooms:** 11 rms and stes. CI 3pm/CO noon. No smoking. Rooms are not large, but they are well appointed. Four-poster beds, quilts, and armoires add to the romantic atmosphere. **Amenities:** 🛏 ⚱ A/C, cable TV, dataport, bathrobes. Some units w/terraces, some w/whirlpools. Some rooms have steam bath showers; all have answering machines. **Services:** ✕ ☛ ☒ Babysitting, wine/sherry served. **Facilities:** Guest lounge. The beautiful garden is a great place for breakfast or relaxation. **Rates (CP):** Peak (Mar–June/Sept–Nov) $149–$169 S; $179 D; $179 ste. Extra person $25. Min stay wknds. Lower rates off-season. Higher rates for special events/hols. Parking: Outdoor, free. MC, V.

Elliott House Inn

78 Queen St, 29401; tel 803/723-1855 or toll free 800/729-1855; fax 803/722-1567. Off Meeting St. Built in 1861 in the heart of the historic district, this inn has two levels that open into a shady courtyard with tables, umbrellas, trees, beautiful flowers, and a whirlpool. The smallish lobby is much more humble than the luxurious guest rooms. Unsuitable for children under 16. **Rooms:** 26 rms and stes. CI 3pm/CO noon. Nonsmoking rms avail. Each room is furnished in antiques, dark wood appointments, and canopied beds. **Amenities:** 🛏 ⚱ A/C, cable TV. Some units w/terraces. Chocolates at turndown and freshly cut flowers in each room. **Services:** ✕ ☛ ☒ ☐ Wine/sherry served. Picnic baskets can be arranged. **Facilities:** ☉ Whirlpool. **Rates (CP):** Peak (Apr–June/Sept–Nov) $120 S or D; $140 ste. Extra person $10. Min stay special events. Lower rates off-season. AE, DISC, MC, V.

Indigo Inn

1 Maiden Lane, 29401; tel 803/577-5900 or toll free 800/845-7639; fax 803/577-0378. At Meeting and Pickney Sts. Once an 1850 indigo warehouse, the rooms of this large building surround an inner courtyard with a fountain. The wood-paneled lobby has a flagstone floor, Oriental rugs, and a slightly nautical feel. **Rooms:** 40 rms. CI 3pm/CO noon. Nonsmoking rms avail. Rooms come in bright colors (green, red, mustard), but are somewhat dark with small windows facing the courtyard. They are nicely appointed with 18th-century antique reproductions; some rooms have four-poster beds. **Amenities:** 🛏 ⚱ A/C, cable TV. All units w/terraces. **Services:** ✕ ☛ 🚗 ☒ ☐ ☐ Twice-daily maid svce, masseur, babysitting. Very congenial staff. Afternoon tea and wine served. Expanded continental breakfast includes ham, biscuits, fruit, and homemade breads. $10 per night per pet. **Facilities:** ⚹ Guest lounge. **Rates (CP):** Peak (Mar–June/Sept–Nov) $140 S; $155 D. Extra person $10. Children under age 12 stay free. Min stay wknds. Lower rates off-season. Higher rates for special events/hols. Parking: Outdoor, free. AE, DISC, MC, V.

Jasmine House

64 Hasell St, 29401; tel 803/577-5900 or toll free 800/845-7639; fax 803/577-0378. Off Calhoun St. A sunny yellow 1843 Greek Revival mansion with 14-foot ceilings, Italian marble baths, and hardwood floors. Two white-columned piazzas are great for catching the evening breeze, and a courtyard with tables is also available. **Rooms:** 10 rms and stes. CI 3pm/CO noon. Spacious, elegant rooms. Some have four-poster beds. **Amenities:** 🛏 ⚱ A/C, cable TV. All units w/terraces. Complimentary newspapers. **Services:** ✕ 🚗 ☒ ☐ Twice-daily maid svce, masseur, babysitting. Clothes pressed upon request. **Facilities:** Whirlpool. **Rates (CP):** Peak (Mar–June/Sept–Nov) $140 S; $155 D; $180 ste. Extra person $10. Children under age 12 stay free. Min stay wknds. Lower rates off-season. Higher rates for special events/hols. Parking: Outdoor, free. AE, DISC, MC, V.

John Rutledge House Inn

116 Broad St, 29401; tel 803/723-7999. Off King St. Built in 1763 by one of the signers of the US Constitution; it is one of only 15 surviving homes of these men, and the only one with guest lodging. The elaborate ironwork, inlaid floors, carved marble mantles and original plasterwork exude beauty and

charm. George Washington supposedly ate here in 1791. **Rooms:** 19 rms and stes. CI 3pm/CO noon. Nonsmoking rms avail. Rooms are furnished mostly in reproductions, although a minimum of one piece in each room is a genuine period antique. **Amenities:** 📶 🔥 A/C, cable TV, refrig, bathrobes. Some units w/terraces, some w/fireplaces, some w/whirlpools. Turndown service, with Godiva chocolate and brandy. **Services:** 🔑 🖼 ⊙ Babysitting, afternoon tea and wine/sherry served. **Facilities:** 🔲50 👌 Guest lounge. **Rates (CP):** Peak (Mar–June/Sept–Nov) $165 S; $180 D; $285 ste. Extra person $15. Children under age 12 stay free. Min stay special events. Lower rates off-season. Parking: Outdoor, free. "Discover Charleston" package avail. AE, MC, V.

≡≡≡ Kings Courtyard Inn

198 King St, 29401 (Historic Downtown); tel 803/723-7000 or toll free 800/845-6119; fax 803/720-2608. In the heart of the antique shopping area, this 1853 Greek Revival building used to be an inn for plantation owners. The charming lobby is accented by a fireplace and a brass chandelier, and there are a total of three courtyards (one with fountain). A charter member of Historic Hotels of America. **Rooms:** 43 rms and stes. CI 3pm/CO noon. Nonsmoking rms avail. Rooms overlook the courtyard or garden and are furnished with canopied beds, 18th-century reproduction furnishings, and Oriental rugs. **Amenities:** 📶 🔥 A/C, cable TV, refrig, voice mail, bathrobes. Some units w/terraces, some w/fireplaces, some w/whirlpools. **Services:** 🔑 🖼 ⊙ Babysitting, wine/sherry served. Continental breakfast can be served in guest's room or on the patio. Complimentary brandy and chocolates at turndown. **Facilities:** 🔲70 👌 1 restaurant (bkfst only), guest lounge. **Rates (CP):** Peak (Mar–June/Sept–Nov) $125 S; $140–$180 D; $210 ste. Extra person $15. Children under age 12 stay free. Min stay special events. Lower rates off-season. Parking: Outdoor, free. AE, MC, V.

≡≡≡ Lodge Alley Inn

195 E Bay St, 29401; tel 803/722-1611 or toll free 800/845-1004, 800/821-2791 in SC. Off Cumberland St. This former beer warehouse—now miraculously transformed into an elegant and hospitable inn—was one of the first E Bay St properties to undergo restoration. **Rooms:** 95 rms and stes. CI 4pm/CO noon. Rooms are sometimes noisy because of all the activity on E Bay St, but they are large and luxuriously appointed. All are decorated with period reproduction furnishings, pine floors, Windsor desks, butler's tables, and Oriental carpets. **Amenities:** 📶 🔥 🖥 A/C, cable TV. All units w/minibars, some w/terraces, some w/fireplaces, some w/whirlpools. **Services:** ✗ 🆅🅿 🖼 ⊙ Babysitting, wine/sherry served. **Facilities:** 🔲200 👌 1 restaurant, 1 bar (w/entertainment), guest lounge. **Rates (CP):** Peak (Mar–June/Sept–Nov) $125–$145 S or D; $145–$285 ste. Extra person $15. Children under age 12 stay free. Lower rates off-season. Parking: Indoor, free. Honeymoon and third-night-free packages avail. AE, MC, V.

≡≡≡ Maison Dupre

317 E Bay St, 29401; tel 803/723-8691 or toll free 800/844-4667; fax 803/723-3722. At George St. A photogenic French Country–style inn made up of three restored "single houses" and two carriage houses. (The original house was built in 1803, while the two other buildings were later moved to the property.) Reception is in the former kitchen, where two fireplaces burn. Tall garden walls and wrought-iron gates give a feeling of privacy. **Rooms:** 15 rms and stes. CI 2pm/CO noon. No smoking. All rooms have tile and marble baths with brass fittings, antique armoires, and Oriental rugs; some have canopied beds. Owner Lucille Mulholland has filled the rooms with her impressionist paintings. **Amenities:** 📶 🔥 A/C, cable TV. All units w/terraces. Complimentary morning newspaper. Turndown service with chocolates. **Services:** ✗ 🔑 🚗 ⊙ Afternoon tea served. Afternoon "Low Country" tea with sandwiches and cake; beer and wine served for an additional fee. **Facilities:** 🔲15 Guest lounge. **Rates (CP):** Peak (Feb–June/Sept–Nov) $160–$200 ste. Children under age 18 stay free. Lower rates off-season. Parking: Outdoor, free. Corporate rates avail; romantic, beach, and golf packages avail. Closed Thanksgiving, Dec 25. MC, V.

≡≡≡ Meeting Street Inn

173 Meeting St, 29401 (Historic Downtown); tel 803/723-1882 or toll free 800/842-8022; fax 803/577-0851. Off I-26. A pink-stucco house, originally built as a hotel in 1874 and now beautifully restored and furnished with period antiques and reproductions. Central to all downtown attractions. **Rooms:** 56 rms. CI 3pm/CO noon. Nonsmoking rms avail. All rooms have four-poster rice beds, Oriental rugs, shuttered windows, and tiny balconies opening onto a central piazza. **Amenities:** 📶 A/C, cable TV. All units w/terraces. Complimentary newspapers. **Services:** ✗ 🆅🅿 🖼 ⊙ Afternoon tea and wine/sherry served. **Facilities:** 🔲25 👌 Whirlpool, guest lounge. Guests can use swimming pool at the hotel next door. **Rates (CP):** Peak (Mar–June/Sept–Dec) $93–$146 S; $103–$156 D. Extra person $10. Children under age 12 stay free. Min stay wknds. Lower rates off-season. Parking: Indoor, $6/day. AE, DISC, MC, V.

≡≡≡ Middleton Inn at Middleton Place

Ashley River Rd, 29414; tel 803/556-0500 or toll free 800/543-4774; fax 803/556-0500. Off US 17 and 61 N. 6,000 acres. Visitors expecting to see a colonial mansion will be shocked by Middleton's postmodern concrete block structures. Some have praised it as a striking example of 20th-century architecture in comparison with Charleston's typical 18th- and 19th-century inns, while others are disappointed in its concrete sterility. But whatever you think of the exterior, the interior is exquisite. **Rooms:** 55 rms and stes. CI 3pm/CO noon. Nonsmoking rms avail. The calm, Zenlike rooms are spotless, with minimalist blond-wood floors and ceiling-to-floor shutters which open onto a sprawling view of the peaceful Ashley River. A welcome alternative to the many lavishly decorated Charleston homes. **Amenities:** 📶 🔥 A/C,

TV, refrig. All units w/fireplaces. **Services:** 🛎 🐕 Cypress swamp tours available in the fall. $15 pet fee; $20 to board horses. **Facilities:** ⛳ 🚴 ⛰ 🏕 🎣 🏊³⁵ 🔥 1 restaurant (*see* "Restaurants" below), guest lounge. Six miles of nature trails. **Rates (CP):** Peak (Mar–June) $100–$110 D; $119–$140 ste. Extra person $10. Lower rates off-season. Higher rates for special events/hols. Parking: Outdoor, free. Rates include free admission to Middleton Gardens. MC, V.

▤▤▤ Planters Inn

112 N Market St, 29401 (Old Market); tel 803/722-2345 or toll free 800/845-8072. At Meeting St. Housed in a beautifully restored 1840 building in the heart of Old City Market, this inn succeeds in providing the ambience and amenities of a fine hotel with the personal care and charisma of an old-fashioned hostelry. **Rooms:** 41 rms and stes. CI 3pm/CO noon. Nonsmoking rms avail. Rooms are large and individually decorated with antiques. **Amenities:** 🔥 A/C, cable TV w/movies, bathrobes. All units w/minibars, some w/fireplaces. **Services:** ✕ 🔑 |VP| 🚗 🧺 🐕 Car-rental desk, babysitting, afternoon tea and wine/sherry served. Turndown service, with chocolates on every pillow. Deluxe continental breakfast is delivered to room. **Facilities:** ⬛³⁰ 🔥 1 restaurant (*see* "Restaurants" below), 1 bar, guest lounge. **Rates (CP):** Peak (Apr–May/Oct–Nov) $120–$150 S; $140–$165 D; $165–$200 ste. Extra person $15. Children under age 16 stay free. Min stay special events. Lower rates off-season. Higher rates for special events/hols. Parking: Outdoor, free. AE, CB, DC, DISC, MC, V.

▤▤▤▤ Vendue Inn

19 Vendue Range, 29401; tel 803/577-7970 or toll free 800/845-7900, 800/922-7900 in SC; fax 803/577-2913. At E Bay St. An ideal location near the center of downtown but without the noise. The inn is decorated in 18th-century period furnishings, and there are comfortable sitting parlors tucked unexpectedly in the corners of the hallway. **Rooms:** 45 rms and stes. CI 3pm/CO noon. Nonsmoking rms avail. **Amenities:** 🔥 A/C, satel TV. Some units w/minibars, some w/fireplaces, some w/whirlpools. Some rooms have separate sitting areas with wet bars and sofa beds. **Services:** ✕ 🔑 |VP| 🧺 🐕 Babysitting, wine/sherry served. Wine and cheese served every afternoon. Aperitifs and chocolates available at turndown. **Facilities:** ⬛³⁰ 🔥 1 restaurant, 1 bar (w/entertainment), guest lounge. Library; roof-top bar with views of the waterfront and the city. **Rates (CP):** Peak (Mar–June/Sept–Nov) $120–$130 S; $135–$145 D; $210 ste. Extra person $15. Min stay wknds and special events. Lower rates off-season. Parking: Outdoor, free. AE, DISC, MC, V.

▤▤▤ Victoria House Inn

208 King St, 29401; tel 803/720-2944 or toll free 800/933-5464. At Calhoun St off US 17 N. A 1889 Victorian structure built in the Romanesque style. Rooms are upstairs and the ground level is occupied by antique shops. **Rooms:** 18 rms and stes. CI 3pm/CO noon. Nonsmoking rms avail. Victorian-style furniture is found in every room. **Amenities:**

🔥 A/C, cable TV, refrig, bathrobes. Some units w/fireplaces, some w/whirlpools. Breakfast is served in the guest's room, along with a complimentary morning paper. **Services:** 🔑 🧺 🐕 Babysitting, wine/sherry served. Turndown with chocolates. **Facilities:** ⬛⁷⁰ 🔥 **Rates (CP):** Peak (Mar–June/Sept–Nov) $145 S; $160 D; $200 ste. Extra person $15. Children under age 12 stay free. Min stay special events. Lower rates off-season. Parking: Outdoor, free. MC, V.

RESORT

UNRATED Seabrook Island Resort

1002 Landfall Way, Seabrook Island, 29455; tel 803/768-1000 or toll free 800/845-2475; fax 803/768-3096. Off US 17. 22,000 acres. Located in an upscale community off the Charleston coast, this resort is popular with golfers and boaters. **Rooms:** 165 cottages/villas. CI 4pm/CO 11am. Nonsmoking rms avail. **Amenities:** 🔥 🏠 📺 A/C, cable TV, refrig, voice mail. All units w/terraces, some w/fireplaces, some w/whirlpools. **Services:** 🚗 🧺 🐕 Car-rental desk, social director, masseur, children's program, babysitting. **Facilities:** ⛳ 🚴 🚤 🏕 🎣 🐎¹³ ⬛⁴⁰⁰ 🖥 🔥 4 restaurants, 2 bars, 2 beaches (ocean, cove/inlet), basketball, volleyball, games rm, playground, washer/dryer. **Rates:** Peak (Apr–Aug) $150–$195 cottage/villa. Children under age 18 stay free. Min stay peak. Lower rates off-season. Parking: Outdoor, free. Golf, tennis, equestrian, and honeymoon packages avail. AE, DISC, MC, V.

RESTAURANTS 🍴

♣ Anson

12 Anson St; tel 803/577-0551. Off Market St. **Regional American/Seafood.** Renowned for its crispy flounder and cashew-crusted grouper with champagne sauce, this elegant spot boasts a white, neoclassical upstairs dining room with white leather chairs and a billowy ceiling; the downstairs rooms have soft, elegant lighting and plush seating. **FYI:** Reservations accepted. **Open:** Sun–Thurs 5:30–11pm, Fri–Sat 5:30–11:30pm. **Prices:** Main courses $10–$20. AE, CB, DC, DISC, MC, V. 💟 🍽 🔥

A W Shucks

70 State St (Old Market); tel 803/723-1151. **Seafood.** Housed in an old, cracker factory-turned-speakeasy with beach views. In addition to its delectable Low Country seafood dishes (like sautéed baby shrimp and scallops over deviled crab with lobster-cheese sauce), A W Shucks specializes in steamed and raw oysters, steamed mussels, and clams. They also have a good selection of salads. **FYI:** Reservations accepted. Caribbean music. Children's menu. **Open:** Daily 11:30am–10:30pm. **Prices:** Main courses $9–$14. AE, DC, DISC, MC, V. 🍽 🔥

The Baker's Cafe

214 King St; tel 803/577-2694. Off Calhoun St. **American French.** Elegant little eatery offering French-style dishes like poached eggs, smoked salmon, and caviar and capers with

hollandaise sauce. Homemade desserts. **FYI:** Reservations not accepted. Dress code. Beer and wine only. **Open:** Mon–Fri 8am–3pm, Sat–Sun 9am–3pm. **Prices:** Lunch main courses $7–$10. DC, MC, V. &

Barbadoes Room

In Mills House Hotel, 115 Meeting St; tel 803/577-2400. At Calhoun St. **Regional American.** Italianate archways, plush chairs, and paddle fans set the mood at this very classy restaurant, best known for its extensive Sunday brunch. Menu specialties include filet mignon and shrimp andouille; for dessert, you can try famous Mills House mud pie (mocha ice cream in chocolate-cookie crust, topped with fudge, whipped cream, and pecans). **FYI:** Reservations recommended. Piano/singer. Children's menu. **Open:** Breakfast daily 6:30–10am; lunch daily 11am–2pm; dinner daily 5:30–10pm; brunch Sun 11am–2pm. **Prices:** Main courses $15–$20. AE, CB, DC, DISC, MC, V. ◉ &

♥ ✖ Blossom Cafe

17 E Bay St; tel 803/722-9200. **Eclectic.** A very "in" place, with stylish, art deco design, a high-beamed ceiling, curvy lamps, and weathered mirrors. The menu is heavy on nouvelle Mediterranean dishes like lobster pizza and linguine with roasted chicken. **FYI:** Reservations accepted. Children's menu. **Open:** Lunch Mon–Sat 11:30am–2:30pm; dinner Mon–Thurs 2:30–11pm, Fri–Sat 2:30pm–1am, Sun 5–11pm; brunch Sun 11am–2:30pm. **Prices:** Main courses $7–$19. AE, MC, V. ⛴ &

Bookstore Cafe

412 King St; tel 803/720-8843. Off Calhoun St. **Cafe.** The walls are covered with wallpaper that looks like bookshelves, in honor of the history of this quaint, little cafe housed in a former bookstore. Menu highlights Low Country favorites like jerk chicken, Kiawah sausage and gravy, and fried green tomatoes. All pastries and desserts are fresh and homemade. **FYI:** Reservations accepted. Beer and wine only. **Open:** Breakfast Mon–Fri 8–11:30am, Sat–Sun 9am–2pm; lunch Mon–Fri 11:30am–2:30pm, Sat–Sun 11:30am–2pm; dinner daily 5:30–9pm. **Prices:** Main courses $7–$13. MC, V. &

♥ ✖ Carolina's

10 Exchange St; tel 803/724-3800. Off Broad St. **Eclectic.** The walls of this secluded but popular bistro display local artwork, and the bar room is decorated with black and white tables, chairs, columns, and arches. The varied and creative menu features items like crawfish tails in a spicy cream sauce over fettuccine, and hazelnut-wasabi tempura shrimp with soy-lime-ginger sauce. **FYI:** Reservations recommended. Children's menu. Dress code. **Open:** Daily 5pm–2am. **Prices:** Main courses $6–$20. AE, DISC, MC, V. ◉ ▮ ▦ &

East Bay Trading Company

161 E Bay St; tel 803/722-0722. Off Calhoun St. **Eclectic.** Housed in an 1880 trading company warehouse, the three-level dining room surrounds an atrium with a San Francisco trolley car and many antique treasures. The 100 year-old dumbwaiter is still used daily, and much of the original floor, beams, windows, and facade have been preserved. The most favored dish on the menu is the East Bay bouillabaisse (a stew made with saffron, Pernod, vegetables, fish broth, and fresh local seafood); great desserts include chocolate-bourbon pecan pie and peanut butter pie with Oreo cookie crust. **FYI:** Reservations accepted. Piano. Children's menu. **Open:** Sun–Fri 5:30–10pm, Sat 5–10pm. Closed Jan 1–7. **Prices:** Main courses $9–$15. AE, CB, DC, DISC, MC, V. ▮ ▦ &

82 Queen

82 Queen St; tel 803/723-7591. Off Meeting St. **Regional American.** Located in a handsomely restored 19th-century town house that was built around a giant magnolia tree. Specialties include Carolina crab cakes, Daufuskie crab, sautéed veal and mushrooms, and she-crab soup. The tourists' favorite is fried alligator with black-bean sauce. **FYI:** Reservations accepted. Children's menu. **Open:** Lunch daily 11:30am–4pm; dinner Sun–Thurs 5:30–10pm, Fri–Sat 5:30–10:30pm. **Prices:** Main courses $9–$18. AE, CB, DC, MC, V. ▮ ⛴ &

Fannie's Diner

137 Market St (Old Market); tel 803/723-7121. Off King St. **Diner.** The decor is right out of the glory days of the diner, the 1950s. Chrome-trimmed red booths, pink and blue neon, 1950s photos, and a Wurlitzer jukebox stocked with classic oldies create a fun mood. On the menu is french toast, blueberry pancakes, chicken-breast sandwiches, and ice cream specialties. **FYI:** Reservations not accepted. Children's menu. Beer and wine only. **Open:** Daily 24 hrs. **Prices:** Main courses $4–$8. DISC, MC, V. ⫴⯀⫴ &

Garibaldi's

49 S Market St; tel 803/723-7153. At Meeting St. **Italian/ Seafood.** Specializes in creative seafood dishes (such as dolphin, stuffed grouper, and blackened tuna) and pasta. The tables in the lower dining room are a little too close together, but the upstairs is spacious and serene. **FYI:** Reservations recommended. **Open:** Dinner Sun–Thurs 6–10:30pm, Fri–Sat 6–11pm. **Prices:** Main courses $8–$19. AE, MC, V. ▮ ⛴ &

Magnolia's

185 E Bay St; tel 803/577-7771. **Southern.** Fine Southern food prepared with local ingredients, served in a refined and sophisticated atmosphere. Although the decor is anything but down-home, the service is warm and friendly. You might want to try the seafood succotash (with shrimp, scallops, lobster, cornbread, veggies, and herbs); the spicy seared soft-shell crabs with Creole sauce; or the crab-stuffed pasilla pepper with yellow corn, tomato, and scallion salsa. Hushpuppies, red rice, and other classic side dishes to choose from. Many "Heart Healthy" dishes available. **FYI:** Reservations recommended. Children's menu. Dress code. **Open:** Sun–Thurs 11:30am–11pm, Fri–Sat 11:30am–midnight. **Prices:** Main courses $8–$20. AE, MC, V. ◉ ▮

Marina Variety Store Restaurant
In City Marina, 17 Lockwood Blvd; tel 803/723-6325. Off US 17 N. **Seafood.** This humble establishment, housed in one side of a store that sells fishing supplies and souvenirs, has been serving up simple, hearty food for over 25 years and is now in its third generation of family ownership. Picture windows in the dining area look out onto the yacht basin. Okra soup, chili, sandwiches, and fried fish dinners are the mainstays. **FYI:** Reservations recommended. Karaoke. **Open:** Sun–Thurs 6:30am–9pm, Fri–Sat 6:30am–9:30pm. **Prices:** Main courses $9–$21. AE, MC, V. 🏔 ⅙

Market Street Food Court
In Charleston Market, S Market and Church Sts; tel 803/722-4455. Calhoun St exit off US 17. **Eclectic/Fast food.** A diverse food court serving up international cuisines (Greek, Japanese, Chinese) as well as American specialty items (seafood, bagels, sandwiches, hot dogs, burgers, barbecue, and cookies). Good for a quick, inexpensive meal. **FYI:** Reservations not accepted. No liquor license. **Open:** Daily 8:30am–5pm. **Prices:** Main courses $2–$8. MC, V. 📷

Ⓢ McCrady's Deli/Bakery
159 E Bay St; tel 803/937-4131. Off Calhoun St. **Cafe/Deli.** One of the few places open early for breakfast, McCrady's dishes up omelettes and pancakes (and mainly sandwiches for lunch) to an eager crowd of regulars. This hip little place was once the site of one of America's oldest taverns. George Washington did not have cappuccino here (as the rumor goes), but he did have a dinner party here in 1791. **FYI:** Reservations not accepted. **Open:** Daily 7am–midnight. **Prices:** Main courses $4–$6. AE, MC, V. ▮ 📷 ⅙

Mesa Grill & Cantina
32½ N Market St; tel 803/723-3770. Off US 17 N at Bay St. **Southwestern.** Housed in an old church and decorated in a Southwestern motif with Indian blankets, tile, and other various pieces of art. Fajitas and margaritas are the house specialties; vegetarian alternatives available. **FYI:** Reservations accepted. Guitar/singer. Children's menu. **Open:** Daily 11am–11pm. **Prices:** Main courses $6–$14. AE, CB, DC, DISC, MC, V.

Middleton Place
Ashley River Rd; tel 803/556-6020. Off US 17. **American.** Built in the 1930s as a guest house on the Middleton plantation, this charming restaurant now offers lunch (to visitors with paid admission to the gardens) and dinner (to the general public). The house, situated in the oldest landscaped gardens in America, overlooks an old rice mill pond. Typical menu offerings include panned quail with julienned ham and spoon bread; sea scallops with butter on a bed of spinach; and beef tenderloin laced with fresh chervil sauce, tarragon, and shallots. **FYI:** Reservations recommended. **Open:** Lunch daily 11am–3pm; dinner Fri–Sat 6–9pm. **Prices:** Main courses $13–$18; prix fixe $12–$18. DISC, MC, V. ▮ 📷

Mistral
99 S Market St; tel 803/722-5708. At Meeting St. **French.** The jazzy, sophisticated decor at this popular eatery features dark-wood fixtures and mauve walls. Specialty dishes include braised rabbit with shallot, mushrooms, and tomato sauce with wild rice; coq au vin; and duck ravioli. **FYI:** Reservations recommended. Jazz. Children's menu. Dress code. **Open:** Mon–Sat 11am–10pm. **Prices:** Main courses $11–$19. AE, DC, DISC, MC, V. ♥ ⅙

Old Towne Restaurant
229 King St; tel 803/723-8170. Off Calhoun St. **Greek.** This long, narrow restaurant with booths against the wall is a popular place for lunch near the antique shopping area. Pork and beef kebobs, Greek-style hamburgers, gyros, spanakopita, baklava, and other homemade Greek specialties. **FYI:** Reservations accepted. Children's menu. **Open:** Sun–Thurs 11am–10pm, Fri–Sat 11am–10:30pm. **Prices:** Main courses $5–$13. AE, DC, DISC, MC, V. ◧ ⅙

★ Pinckney Cafe and Espresso
18 Pinckney St; tel 803/577-0961. Off E Bay St. **Cafe.** Although it looks like a quiet, quaint home from the outside, this joint really jumps, especially at lunchtime. The menu (written on a blackboard brought to your table) features light specialties such as curried chicken salad, seafood salad croissant, spinach quesadilla, and turkey marsala. Full complement of coffee drinks, including Café Market Street (espresso with cocoa, sugar, cinnamon, nutmeg, and whipped cream). **FYI:** Reservations accepted. Beer and wine only. **Open:** Lunch Tues–Thurs 11:30am–3pm, Fri–Sat 11:30am–2:30pm; dinner Tues–Sat 6–10pm. Closed Mid-June–June 30. **Prices:** Main courses $6–$15. No CC. ▮ ⚓

♣ Planters Cafe
In Planters Inn, 112 N Market St (Old Market); tel 803/723-0700. Calhoun exit off US 17 at Meeting St. **New American.** Diners here may choose between sitting under crape-myrtle trees on the patio or in the cool mauve-colored dining room (which features a jazz brunch on Sundays). Creative nightly specials and menu mainstays include grilled medallions of lobster basted with Tahitian vanilla bean oil and tossed with black pepper, fettuccine, and fresh tarragon cream; and grilled ostrich steak with tawny port demiglacé with sautéed spinach, portobello mushrooms, and new potato-and-leek gratin. **FYI:** Reservations accepted. Jazz. Dress code. **Open:** Lunch Mon–Sat 11:30am–4pm; dinner Sun 4–9pm, Mon–Fri 4–10pm, Sat 4–10:30pm; brunch Sun 10am–3pm. **Prices:** Main courses $12–$23. AE, CB, DC, DISC, MC, V. ♥ ▮ ⚓ ⅙

Slightly North of Broad
192 E Bay St; tel 803/723-3424. Off S Market St. **Regional American.** Offbeat decor features ethereal-looking walls and columns, funky chairs, and antique chandeliers and rugs. The self-proclaimed "maverick Southern kitchen" serves up food with a flair. Specialties include grilled barbecued tuna glazed with mustard and topped with fried oysters, corn and crab

soup, and smoked sausage and ham. **FYI:** Reservations not accepted. Dress code. **Open:** Lunch Mon–Fri 11:30am–3pm; dinner daily 5:30–11pm. **Prices:** Main courses $9–$17. AE, DC, DISC, MC, V. ⅚

Swensen's Cafe
57 S Market St; tel 803/722-1411. Off Meeting St. **Cafe.** A good place to bring the kids, or just to have a quick but filling lunch. The decor is reminiscent of an old-time ice cream parlor—with Tiffany lamps, marble tables, and brick walls—while the menu offers up everything from grilled turkey, bacon, and cheddar sandwiches on sourdough bread, to Greek salads, to eight-scoop ice cream sundaes. **FYI:** Reservations not accepted. Children's menu. Beer and wine only. **Open:** Peak (Mar–Sept) Mon–Thurs 11am–6pm, Fri–Sat 11am–11pm, Sun 11am–10pm. **Prices:** Main courses $4–$7. No CC. ⛴ 🖼

Taste of India
273 King St; tel 803/723-8132. Off Calhoun St. **Indian.** Dishes at this traditional Indian restaurant range from mild to extremely hot. One of the best bets is tandoori chicken, marinated for 24 hours in yogurt and spices before it's cooked on a skewer, and then served on a bed of greens or fresh minced vegetables simmered in a light cream sauce spiced with saffron, garlic, and cashews. **FYI:** Reservations accepted. Beer and wine only. **Open:** Lunch Mon–Sat 11:30am–3pm; dinner daily 5–10:30pm; brunch Sun noon–3pm. **Prices:** Main courses $7–$11. AE, DISC, MC, V. ⅚

★ Vickery's
15 Beaufain St; tel 803/577-5300. Off King St. **Cuban.** Housed in a former Goodyear tire store, this hip eatery sports a funky '70s-style decor complete with a rust, mustard, and chartreuse color scheme and tacky ashtrays adorning the walls. Traces of Spain, Cuba, and Asia are evident in the cooking, producing such specialties as black-bean cakes, jerk chicken, "Cuban Reuben," and paella. **FYI:** Reservations accepted. Children's menu. **Open:** Daily 11:30am–1am. **Prices:** Main courses $5–$14. AE, DISC, MC, V. ⅚

Wild Wing Cafe
36 N Market St (Old Market); tel 803/722-WING. **Chicken.** Casual atmosphere and great food. In addition to hot wings (offered in various flavors and degrees of heat) and cold beer, they also offer chicken quesadillas and salads. **FYI:** Reservations not accepted. Local bands. Children's menu. **Open:** Daily 11am–2am. **Prices:** Main courses $5–$7. AE, DISC, MC, V. 🖼 ⅚

REFRESHMENT STOPS ☕

★ Cafe Rainbow
282 King St; tel 803/853-9777. Off Calhoun St. **Coffeehouse.** A bohemian ambience reigns here, as people play chess on the large board in the front window and others sit on big sacks of coffee beans and watch. It's the only coffee roaster in Charleston, and many people stop by just for

coffee, caffè mocha, or iced cappuccino. The menu also offers soups, salads, sandwiches, quiche, and desserts. Great, homemade Belgian waffles are available for breakfast. **Open:** Peak (Sept–May) daily 8am–10pm. AE, DISC, MC, V. ⅚

Fulford-Egan Coffees & Teas
231 Meeting St; tel 803/577-4553. Off Calhoun St. **Coffeehouse.** The aroma wafting from open coffee bags entices customers off busy Meeting Street; once inside, they can choose from 30 coffee blends and almost as many teas. Bagels, pastries, scones, cakes, pies, and milkshakes are also available, and Fulford-Egan sells teapots, mugs, and gift items. **Open:** Sun–Thurs 8am–11pm, Fri–Sat 8am–midnight. AE, MC, V. ⅚

Kaminsky's Most Excellent Cafe
78 N Market St (Old Market); tel 803/853-8270. **Coffeehouse.** The perfect place for a respite from shopping in the Old Market area, this coffeehouse has a full bar and freshly baked desserts. Famed specialties include the 6-foot-high "Mountain of Chocolate" cake. Additional location: Johnny Dodds Blvd, Mount Pleasant (tel 971-7437). **Open:** Daily noon–2am. AE, DISC, MC, V. 🍴

ATTRACTIONS 🏛

HISTORIC BUILDINGS

Edmondston-Alston House
21 E Battery (Historic District); tel 803/722-7171. Built in 1828 as the home of wealthy Scottish merchant Charles Edmondston, the house was later bought by a Colonel Alston, whose son redid it in the Greek Revival style. The house, which has a breathtaking view of Charleston Harbor, contains some notable woodwork and holds family furnishings, paintings, and documents. **Open:** Tues–Sat 10am–4:40pm, Sun–Mon 1:30–4:40pm. Closed Dec 25. **$$$**

Calhoun Mansion
16 Meeting St (Historic District); tel 803/722-8205. This 1876 Victorian showplace boasts fine period furnishings (including a few original pieces), porcelain and etched-glass gas chandeliers, ornate plastering, and woodwork of cherry, oak, and walnut. The ballroom's 45-foot-high ceiling has a skylight. **Open:** Wed–Sun 10am–4pm. Closed some hols. **$$$$**

Congregation Beth Elohim
90 Hassel St (Downtown); tel 803/723-1090. Dating from 1840, this is the oldest synagogue in continuous use in the United States. The original building, built in 1794, burned in 1838; its Greek Revival replacement is considered one of America's finest examples of that style. **Open:** Mon–Fri 10am–noon. **Free**

Old Exchange Building and Provost Dungeon
122 E Bay St (Historic District); tel 803/727-2165. The **Exchange Building**, originally used as a customhouse, was a small British fort where American patriots were imprisoned during the Revolutionary War (**Provost Dungeon**). Exhibits

dedicated to the British colonial period, plus films about Charleston's artistic heritage. **Open:** Daily 9am–5pm. Closed some hols. **$$**

Powder Magazine

79 Cumberland St; tel 803/722-1623. This former Revolutionary War gunpowder factory was part of the original city fortifications and is Charleston's oldest public building (1713). Artifacts from Charleston's early history, including furniture, textiles, and Revolutionary War weaponry, are on display. **$**

MUSEUMS

American Military Museum

40 Pinckney St; tel 803/723-9620. Dedicated to the men and women who have served in the US armed forces, this museum displays uniforms and artifacts from all branches of the military and relics of virtually every armed conflict in which this country has been involved. **Open:** Mon–Sat 10am–6pm, Sun 1–6pm. Closed some hols. **$**

Charleston Museum

360 Meeting St; tel 803/722-2996. Founded in 1773, the oldest museum in America houses collections that preserve and interpret the social and natural history of Charleston and the South Carolina coastal region. The full-scale replica of the famed Confederate submarine *Hunley* standing outside the museum is one of the most photographed subjects in the city. The museum also exhibits the largest Charleston silver collection, early crafts, historic relics, and a children's "Discover Me" room with hands-on exhibits for youngsters.

The **Joseph Manigault House,** at 350 Meeting St (diagonally across from the visitors center on the corner of John St), is also under the auspices of the Museum. This 1803 Adams-style residence, a National Historic Landmark, was the home of a wealthy rice planter. Outstanding features include a curved central staircase and a collection of Charleston, American, English, and French period furnishing. The **Heyward-Washington House** (1772), at 87 Church St (several blocks south of the main museum grounds), was the home of Thomas Heyward Jr, a signer of the Declaration of Independence. Behind the main house are a garden, a kitchen, and servants' quarters. **Open:** Mon–Sat 9am–5pm, Sun 1–5pm. Closed some hols. **$$**

Gibbes Museum of Art

135 Meeting St; tel 803/722-2706. One of the country's finest collections of American art from the 18th century to the present—paintings, prints, drawings, and a fine collection of portraits—is on exhibit here. Don't miss the Elizabeth Wallace Miniature Rooms: 10 rooms representing different traditions in American and French architecture, decorative, arts, and design, all done on a miniature scale. There's also a very good museum shop. **Open:** Tues–Sat 10am–5pm, Sun–Mon 1–5pm. Closed some hols. **$$**

PLANTATIONS

Boone Hall Plantation

1235 Long Point Rd, Mount Pleasant; tel 803/884-4371. Located 12 mi NE of downtown Charleston. "America's most photographed plantation." This 738-acre estate is justly famous for its half-mile approach—an avenue of dramatically moss-draped oaks planted in 1743 by Capt Thomas Boone. (The Boones were one of the state's most influential families; members included a signer of the Declaration of Independence and the first governor of South Carolina.) At one time, handmade bricks and tiles were produced here, many of which can still be seen in Charleston's most beautiful old buildings. The first floor of the elegantly furnished plantation house is open to the public. The grounds contain a cotton-gin house, a smokehouse, and an entire "slave street" of nine original brick cabins. The Plantation Kitchen Restaurant, on the second floor of the gin house, serves Southern-style breakfast and lunch. **Open:** Apr–Labor Day, Mon–Sat 8:30am–6:30pm, Sun 1–5pm; Labor Day–Apr, Mon–Sat 9am–5pm, Sun 1–4pm. Closed some hols. **$$$**

Middleton Place

Ashley River Rd; tel 803/556-6020 or toll free 800/782-3608. Home of Henry Middleton, president of the First Continental Congress, whose son, Arthur, was a signer of the Declaration of Independence. Today, this National Historic Landmark includes America's oldest landscaped gardens, the Middleton Place House, and the Plantation Stableyards. The gardens, begun in 1741, reflect the elegant symmetry of European gardens of the period. Ornamental lakes, terraces, and plantings of camellias, azaleas, magnolias, and crape myrtle accent the grand design.

Most of **Middleton Place House** (1755) was ransacked and burned by Union troops in the Civil War. Restored in the 1870s as a family residence, it houses collections of fine silver, furniture, rare first editions by Catesby and Audubon, and portraits by Benjamin West and Thomas Sully. In the stableyards, where horses, mules, hogs, milk cows, sheep, and goats roam about, busy craftspeople provide a glimpse of working life on a plantation of yesteryear. **Open:** Daily 9am–5pm. **$$$$**

Magnolia Plantation and Gardens

SC 61; tel 803/571-1266. Ten generations of the Drayton family have lived here continuously since the 1670s. The first mansion at this site burned just after the Revolution, while the second was burned by Sherman's troops. The third house, a simple, pre-Revolutionary structure, was barged down from Summerville and set on the basement foundations of its predecessors. Visitors can tour the house, the gardens (which include an herb garden, horticultural maze, topiary garden, and biblical garden), and a petting zoo; climb the observation tower; ride canoes through a 125-acre waterfowl refuge; or walk or cycle through wildlife trails. Newer features on the grounds are a restored antebellum cabin, a rice barge that sits beside the Ashley River, and the **Nature Train,** which takes guests on a 45-minute ride around the perimeter of the plantation. Low Country wildlife is visible in marsh, woodland, and swamp settings.

The **Audubon Swamp Garden,** also on the grounds, is an independently operated 60-acre cypress swamp offering a close look at other Low Country wildlife, including egrets, alligators, wood ducks, anhingas, otters, turtles, and herons. **Open:** Daily 8am–5pm. **$$$$**

PARKS AND GARDENS

Cypress Gardens

US 52, Moncks Corner; tel 803/552-0515. Located 23 mi N of Charleston. This swamp garden was used as a freshwater reserve for Dean Hall, a huge Cooper River rice plantation, and was given to the city in 1963. Today, its giant cypress trees draped with Spanish moss provide an unforgettable setting for boats that glide among their knobby roots. Footpaths in the garden wind through a profusion of azaleas, camellias, daffodils, and other colorful blooms. The gardens are worth a visit at any time of year, but they're at their most colorful from March through April. **Open:** Daily 9am–5pm. **$$$**

Edisto Beach State Park

Edisto Island; tel 803/869-2756. Located 21 mi W of Charleston on US 17, then 29 mi S on SC 174. Its 1,255 acres are ideal for a day away from organized sightseeing. Swimming and fishing are good along two miles of beach, and there's a well-marked nature trail and a sheltered picnic area. **Open:** Daily sunrise–sunset. **$**

OTHER ATTRACTIONS

Avery Research Center for African-American History and Culture

College of Charleston, 125 Bull St; tel 803/727-2009. This research center, housed in a 19th-century African American school, aims to collect, preserve, and document the history and culture of African Americans in Charleston and in the Low Country of South Carolina. One gallery recreates a classroom in the Avery School, another contains archival materials such as manuscripts, personal papers, family records, photographs, and rare books. A site-specific art piece called "The New Charleston" is in the upstairs gallery, and a fourth gallery is reserved for special installations. **Open:** Mon–Sat noon–5pm. Closed some hols. **Free**

Charles Town Landing–1670

SC 171; tel 803/852-4200. This 663-acre park is located on the site of South Carolina's first permanent English settlement. Underground exhibits show the colony's history, and there's a re-creation of a small village, a full-scale replica of a 17th-century trading ship, and a tram tour. There's no flashy "theme park" atmosphere here: What you see as you walk under huge old oaks, past freshwater lagoons, and through the Animal Forest (which has animals of the same species that lived here in 1670) is what those early settlers saw. **Open:** Daily 9am–5pm. Closed Dec 25. **$$**

Fort Sumter Tours

City Marina, Lockwood Dr; tel 803/722-1691. Board specially built sightseeing yachts for a comfortable ride out to Fort Sumter, the site where the Civil War began in April 1861. In addition to a visit to Fort Sumter National Monument (see), you'll enjoy a harbor tour with brief commentary as you view Charleston's beautiful waterfront. Tours leave from both Patriots Point and City Marina. **Open:** Daily, call for schedule. Closed Dec 25. **$$$**

Harbor and Naval Base Tour

Patriots Point; tel 803/722-1691. Provides a waterside view of the many historic and engaging sights of the city and Charleston Harbor. On the cruise, you'll see gigantic cargo ships leaving the busy state port terminals. You cruise by beautiful Revolutionary War–era mansions and historic Fort Sumter, as your tour guide informs you of the importance of each site. **Open:** Daily, call for schedule. Closed Dec 25. **$$$**

The Citadel, The Military College of South Carolina

171 Moultrie St; tel 803/953-5006. Known as "the West Point of the South," this military academy occupies the site of an early 19th-century fort built to quell slave revolts. The campus, with its buildings of Moorish design, including crenellated battlements and sentry towers, is architecturally striking.

For more information on the school's history, stop by the Citadel Memorial Archives Museum (open during the school year only, Sunday–Friday 2–5pm and Saturday noon–5pm). When the college is in session, the public is invited to a precision drill parade on the quadrangle at 3:45pm almost every Friday. **Open:** Daily 8am–6pm. **Free**

The Market

188 Meeting St (Downtown); tel 803/723-9819. Charleston's most unique place to shop and dine offers dozens of fascinating specialty and crafts shops, open-air vendors, and fine restaurants. The Market's history goes back to 1788, when Charles Cotesworth Pinckney (a signer of the US Constitution) ceded the land on which the Market is built to the city of Charleston—on the condition that a public market be built on the site. There's been a market here ever since. Also located within the market is the Confederate Museum, which houses an extensive collection of Confederate relics including uniforms, guns, swords, flags, quilts, pictures, and documents. **Open:** Daily 9:30am–5:30pm. Closed some hols. **Free**

Patriots Point

US 17; tel 803/884-2727. Located here is the aircraft carrier the USS *Yorktown.* Visitors can wander through the bridge, wheelhouse, flight and hangar decks, chapel, sick bay, and several other areas, and view the film "The Fighting Lady," depicting life aboard the carrier. Other ships welcoming visitors aboard are the *Savannah,* the world's first nuclear-powered merchant ship; the World War II destroyer *Laffey;*

the World War II submarine *Clamagore;* and the cutter *Ingham.* **Open:** Apr–Oct, daily 9am–6pm; Nov–Mar, daily 9am–5pm. **$$$**

Clemson

Located in northwest South Carolina, the town is home to the state's botanical gardens and to Clemson University. **Information:** Clemson Area Chamber of Commerce, 103 Clemson St, PO Box 202, Clemson, 29633 (tel 864/654-1200).

HOTEL 📠

🏛🏛🏛 Ramada Inn

US 76 and SC 123, PO Box 1706, 29631; tel 864/654-7501 or toll free 800/2-RAMADA; fax 864/654-7301. 1 mi from Clemson University. Popular site for conventions because of the particularly nice indoor pool area and gazebo. **Rooms:** 149 rms and stes. CI 3pm/CO 11am. Nonsmoking rms avail. Rooms are simple and institutional-looking. All rooms facing pool area have balconies and sliding doors. **Amenities:** 🛏 🐾 A/C, cable TV. Some units w/terraces. **Services:** ✕ 🚗 🖃 🕬 🕬 Car-rental desk, babysitting. **Facilities:** 🚃 600 🚾 1 restaurant, 1 bar, sauna, steam rm, whirlpool. **Rates (CP):** $42–$49 S or D; $65–$125 ste. Extra person $7. Children under age 12 stay free. AP and MAP rates avail. Parking: Outdoor, free. AE, CB, DC, DISC, EC, ER, JCB, MC, V.

MOTEL

🏛🏛 Holiday Inn

894 Tiger Blvd, PO Box 512, 29633; tel 864/654-4450 or toll free 800/HOLIDAY; fax 864/654-8451. 2 mi from Clemson University. Basic Holiday Inn. Gets lots of use from students' families and visiting football fans. **Rooms:** 219 rms and stes. CI 2pm/CO noon. Nonsmoking rms avail. Average, slightly dated rooms. Views from one section overlook scenic lake. **Amenities:** 🛏 🐾 🖭 A/C, cable TV w/movies. Skimpy toiletries. **Services:** ✕ 🚗 🖃 🕬 🕬 Golf tee times can be arranged. Same-day dry cleaning available Mon–Fri. **Facilities:** 🚃 🔲 500 🖳 🚾 1 restaurant, 1 bar, washer/dryer. Boat dock but no launch. No elevators. **Rates:** $50–$55 S or D; $75 ste. Children under age 19 stay free. Parking: Outdoor, free. Rates increase during special Clemson University events. AE, CB, DC, DISC, EC, JCB, MC, V.

Clinton

This northwest South Carolina town was founded in 1850 and named for attorney Col Henry Clinton Young. Presbyterian College is here.

MOTEL 📠

🏛🏛🏛 Holiday Inn

SC 56, 29325; tel 864/833-4900 or toll free 800/HOLIDAY; fax 864/833-4916. Exit 52 off I-26. Standard chain motel with pleasant, yet simple rooms. **Rooms:** 102 rms and stes. CI noon/CO noon. Nonsmoking rms avail. **Amenities:** 🛏 🐾 A/C, cable TV. **Services:** ✕ 🖃 🕬 🕬 Babysitting. **Facilities:** 🚃 🕬 150 🚾 1 restaurant, 1 bar, washer/dryer. The bar features karaoke. **Rates (CP):** Peak (Apr–Sept) $59–$64 S or D; $100 ste. Extra person $5. Children under age 18 stay free. Min stay special events. Lower rates off-season. Parking: Outdoor, free. AE, CB, DISC, MC, V.

Columbia

Incorporated in 1805, this is South Carolina's capital and its largest city. One of the nation's first planned cities, its streets are among the widest in America. Two-thirds of the city was burned by Sherman's troops during the Civil War, but today Columbia is the state's center of agricultural trade, manufacturing, and higher education. Seat of the University of South Carolina. **Information:** Greater Columbia Convention & Visitors Bureau, 1200 Main St, PO Box 15, Columbia, 29202 (tel 803/254-0479).

HOTELS 📠

🏛🏛🏛 Adam's Mark

1200 Hampton St, 29201; tel 803/771-7000 or toll free 800/444-ADAM; fax 803/254-2911. Considered one of the nicest lodgings in the downtown area—and certainly the tallest, at 13 stories—this basic, concrete hotel features extremely large meeting facilities and caters to corporate travelers. **Rooms:** 298 rms, stes, and effic. Executive level. CI 3pm/CO noon. Nonsmoking rms avail. Rooms are fairly standard, though some have views of the city. **Amenities:** 🛏 🐾 🍽 A/C, cable TV w/movies, voice mail. Some units w/terraces. Iron and ironing board in each room. **Services:** ✕ 🍴 🚗 🖃 🕬 🕬 Babysitting. Concierge available on club level only. **Facilities:** 🚃 🕬 800 🖳 🚾 1 restaurant, 1 bar (w/entertainment), spa, sauna, steam rm, whirlpool. **Rates:** $109 S; $119 D; $368–$488 ste. Parking: Indoor, free. AE, DC, DISC, MC, V.

🏛🏛 Best Western Bradbury Suites

7525 Two Notch Rd, 29223; tel 803/736-6666 or toll free 800/699-1301; fax 803/788-6011. Exit 74 off I-20. Although the rooms here are downright plush, the public areas are very basic. **Rooms:** 103 stes. CI 2pm/CO noon. Nonsmoking rms avail. A partial wall separates the living area and bedroom. **Amenities:** 🛏 🐾 🖭 A/C, refrig. Some units w/minibars. All rooms have a microwave and a TV in the bathroom. **Services:** 🖃 🕬 Complimentary newspaper. **Facilities:** 🚃 🕬 100 🚾 Whirlpool. Pool area with gazebo and sundeck. **Rates (BB):** $65–$90 ste. Extra person $5. Children under age 18 stay free. Parking: Outdoor, free. AE, DC, DISC, MC, V.

Claussen's Inn
2003 Green St, 29205 (Five Points); tel 803/765-0440 or toll free 800/622-3382; fax 803/799-7924. Well-preserved hotel with the comfortable, homey ambiance of an inn. Open, airy lobby features terra-cotta tile, lush greenery, a vaulted ceiling with skylights, and overstuffed seating. **Rooms:** 29 rms. CI 3pm/CO noon. Nonsmoking rms avail. Each room has individual character; some have white, embroidered bedspreads and four-poster beds. **Amenities:** A/C, cable TV, refrig. **Services:** Twice-daily maid svce. Sherry is offered in lobby, and brandy and chocolates are offered at bedtime. **Facilities:** Whirlpool. **Rates (CP):** $95–$120 S or D. Extra person $10. Children under age 12 stay free. Parking: Outdoor, free. AE, MC, V.

Courtyard by Marriott
347 Zimalcrest Dr, 29210; tel 803/731-2300 or toll free 800/321-2211; fax 803/772-6965. Off I-26 at Bush River Rd. A standard Courtyard, with an attractive cafe and fireplace in the lobby. Located in a busy commercial area but set back from the road. **Rooms:** 149 rms and stes. CI 4pm/CO noon. Nonsmoking rms avail. Comfortable rooms feature an armchair with an ottoman. **Amenities:** A/C, cable TV, voice mail. Some units w/terraces. Each room has an iron and ironing board, plus a hot water tap for instant coffee or tea. **Services:** Babysitting. Very good security—all outside doors require a key card to enter. **Facilities:** 1 restaurant (bkfst and dinner only), 1 bar, whirlpool, washer/dryer. **Rates:** $45–$69 S or D; $69–$86 ste. Parking: Outdoor, free. AE, DC, DISC, MC, V.

Embassy Suites Hotel Columbia
200 Stoneridge Dr, 29210; tel 803/252-8700 or toll free 800/362-2779; fax 803/256-8749. A comfortable, family-friendly spot, located in a quiet neighborhood across from Riverbanks Zoo. Exceptionally helpful and pleasant staff. **Rooms:** 214 stes. Executive level. CI 3pm/CO noon. Nonsmoking rms avail. **Amenities:** A/C, cable TV w/movies, refrig, voice mail. Each room has a hideaway bed. **Services:** VP Facilities: 1 restaurant, 1 bar (w/entertainment), games rm, sauna, whirlpool, washer/dryer. **Rates (BB):** $94–$99 ste. Extra person $10. Children under age 18 stay free. Parking: Outdoor, free. AE, DC, DISC, MC, V.

Holiday Inn Coliseum at USC
630 Assembly St, 29201; tel 803/799-7800 or toll free 800/HOLIDAY; fax 803/252-5909. A standard Holiday Inn, with easy access to downtown and the University. **Rooms:** 174 rms and stes. CI 3pm/CO noon. Nonsmoking rms avail. Some rooms have good views of the city. **Amenities:** A/C, satel TV w/movies. 1 unit w/whirlpool. **Services:** Facilities: 1 restaurant, 1 bar. Large parking

garage—a luxury for a downtown hotel. **Rates:** $89 S or D; $135 ste. Extra person $7. Children under age 18 stay free. Parking: Indoor, free. AE, DC, DISC, JCB, MC, V.

Quality Inn
1539 Horseshoe Dr, 29223; tel 803/736-1600 or toll free 800/228-5151; fax 803/736-1600 ext 515. Exit 74 off I-20. An unusually shaped building with slanting ceilings and skylights in the lobby. Perfect location for large groups. **Rooms:** 192 rms and stes. Executive level. CI 2pm/CO noon. Nonsmoking rms avail. **Amenities:** A/C, cable TV, voice mail. Some units w/whirlpools. **Services:** Twice-daily maid svce. **Facilities:** 1 restaurant, 1 bar, games rm, whirlpool. Bar in lobby offers three TVs and lots of seating. Secluded pool area. **Rates (BB):** Peak (Sept–Nov) $54 S or D; $64 ste. Extra person $5. Children under age 18 stay free. Lower rates off-season. Parking: Outdoor, free. AE, DC, DISC, JCB, MC, V.

Ramada Townhouse
1615 Gervais St, 29201; tel 803/771-8711 or toll free 800/2-RAMADA; fax 803/252-5347. This historically significant location was once headquarters of Gen Sherman during one of his marches through the South. Today, it welcomes its guests with an impressive chandelier in the lobby. **Rooms:** 142 rms and stes. CI 3pm/CO noon. Nonsmoking rms avail. Rooms look old and worn. **Amenities:** A/C, satel TV w/movies. **Services:** $10 deposit for small pets. Iced tea offered every afternoon in lobby. **Facilities:** 1 restaurant, 1 bar, washer/dryer. Guests receive special rate at a local health club. **Rates:** $72 S or D; $99–$149 ste. Extra person $6. Children under age 12 stay free. Parking: Outdoor, free. AE, DC, DISC, MC, V.

Residence Inn by Marriott
150 Stoneridge Dr, 29210; tel 803/779-7000 or toll free 800/331-3131. At Grey Stone Blvd. Individual cottage-style buildings located on a quiet residential street. **Rooms:** 128 stes. CI 3pm/CO noon. Nonsmoking rms avail. **Amenities:** A/C, cable TV w/movies, refrig, voice mail. Some units w/terraces, all w/fireplaces. **Services:** Masseur. Social hour every evening includes complimentary beer, wine, and snacks. Grocery service available. **Facilities:** Basketball, volleyball, whirlpool, playground, washer/dryer. Outdoor grill located near pool. **Rates (CP):** $94–$131 ste. Parking: Outdoor, free. AE, DC, DISC, MC, V.

Sheraton Hotel & Conference Center
2100 Bush River Rd, 29210; tel 803/731-0300 or toll free 800/325-3535; fax 803/731-2839. Jct I-20. This fine hotel is located in a busy commercial area and offers the largest meeting facilities in the area. A beautiful lobby features glass elevators and a pond. **Rooms:** 237 rms and stes. Executive level. CI 3pm/CO noon. Nonsmoking rms avail. **Amenities:** A/C, cable TV w/movies, voice mail. Some units w/terraces, some w/whirlpools. Business suites offer fax

machines and office supplies. **Services:** ✗ ☞ VP 🚗 🖨 ⤴
🔊 **Facilities:** 🎰 🎿 ⛳ 1200 ⚓ 1 restaurant, 1 bar, volleyball, sauna, whirlpool. On-site nightclub with DJ. **Rates:** $55–$85 S or D; $119–$350 ste. Extra person $10. Children under age 18 stay free. Parking: Outdoor, free. AE, DC, DISC, MC, V.

▤▤▤▤ Whitney Hotel

700 Woodrow St, 29205; tel 803/252-0845 or toll free 800/637-4008; fax 803/771-0495. A beautiful, all-suite hotel located in a quiet, commercial neighborhood. Guests are greeted by a wrought-iron arch entrance and an impressive foyer with marble floors. Several miles from town, but well worth the drive. **Rooms:** 74 stes. Executive level. CI 3pm/CO noon. Nonsmoking rms avail. Each one- or two-bedroom suite is furnished with American and English antiques (including comfortable wing-back chairs in the living room) plus full kitchens, two closets, and washer/dryer sets. **Amenities:** 🛏 🅰 🖵 A/C, cable TV, refrig. All units w/terraces, some w/whirlpools. Complimentary morning newspaper and coffee. Cookies and milk in refrigerator when you arrive. **Services:** ☞ 🚗 🖨 ⤴ **Facilities:** 🎰 ⛳ 50 ⚓ Washer/dryer. Fitness room offers free weights only—no machines. **Rates (CP):** $119–$159 ste. Parking: Outdoor, free. AE, DC, DISC, MC, V.

MOTELS

▤▤ Comfort Inn

499 Piney Grove Rd, 29210; tel 803/798-0500 or toll free 800/228-5150. Exit 104 off I-26. A busy, nicer-than-average chain property. Reservations are advisable. **Rooms:** 102 rms. CI 2pm/CO 11am. Nonsmoking rms avail. Pleasant rooms sport a Southwestern theme, with arched doors. **Amenities:** 🛏 🅰 A/C, cable TV. Some units w/whirlpools. **Services:** ⤴ **Facilities:** 🎰 30 ⚓ **Rates (CP):** Peak (Apr–Aug) $54 S or D. Extra person $5. Children under age 12 stay free. Lower rates off-season. Parking: Outdoor, free. AE, CB, DC, DISC, MC, V.

▤▤ La Quinta Motor Inn

1335 Garner Lane, 29210; tel 803/798-9590 or toll free 800/531-5900; fax 803/731-5574. Exit 65 off I-20. A standard motel just off the interstate, with the Southwestern decor typical of the La Quinta chain. Bright white stucco exterior. **Rooms:** 120 rms. Executive level. CI 3pm/CO noon. Nonsmoking rms avail. **Amenities:** 🛏 🅰 A/C, cable TV. King-plus rooms have two phones. **Services:** 🖨 ⤴ 🔊 **Facilities:** 🎰 25 ⚓ Free passes to Gold's Gym. **Rates (CP):** $45–$52 S or D. Extra person $7. Children under age 18 stay free. Parking: Outdoor, free. Golf packages avail. AE, CB, DC, DISC, MC, V.

RESTAURANTS 🍴

Adriana's

721 Saluda Ave (Five Points); tel 803/799-7595. **Cafe/Italian.** A very casual place; food is served from a central counter and tables are available inside and outside. Longtime favorites include hero sandwiches, Bulgarian red pepper stew, and pizza with tomato, basil, and onion. Daily Italian specials include all the old standbys, such as ravioli, tortellini, and manicotti. Their popular gelato and black-and-white-swirl cheesecake make great finishers. **FYI:** Reservations recommended. No liquor license. **Open:** Mon–Thurs 10am–midnight, Fri–Sat 10am–12:30am, Sun 10am–11pm. **Prices:** Main courses $6. MC, V.

California Dreaming

401 S Main St; tel 803/254-6767. **Continental.** Historic pictures hang on the walls, and the high ceilings and wood floors give a crisp, clean feel. The menu features a variety of fare from steaks to sandwiches, but they are most famous for their salads. Good variety of beer served in chilled mugs. **FYI:** Reservations not accepted. Children's menu. **Open:** Sun–Thurs 11am–10pm, Fri–Sat 11am–11pm. **Prices:** Main courses $8–$20. AE, MC, V. ⚓

Garibaldi's

2013 Greene St (Five Points); tel 803/771-8888. **Italian/Seafood.** The strong point at this innovative trattoria is the wide selection of pizzas (with toppings like eggplant, sweet peppers, andouille sausage, and goat cheese). There's also a nightly fresh seafood special, and pasta dishes such penne palla and fettuccine with seafood. Appetizers include crab cakes, black-bean soup, and wild mushroom ravioli. **FYI:** Reservations recommended. **Open:** Sun–Thurs 5:30–10:30pm, Fri–Sat 5:30–11pm. **Prices:** Main courses $10–$20. AE, MC, V. ⚓

Gourmet Shop Cafe

724 Saluda Ave (Five Points); tel 803/799-3705. **Cafe/International.** A great stop for a healthy breakfast of granola and a croissant, or a salad lunch. A delicious cup of gourmet coffee (like Guatemala Antigua) is only $1, and refills are free. The gourmet kitchen and wine shop connected to the restaurant carries an enormous selection of breads, cheeses, coffees, and more. **FYI:** Reservations not accepted. Beer and wine only. **Open:** Mon–Sat 9am–3:45pm, Sun 10am–5pm. **Prices:** Lunch main courses $5–$8. AE, MC, V.

Hennessey's

1649 Main St; tel 803/799-8280. **Continental.** Occupying a converted old hardware store, this atmospheric restaurant is one of Columbia's most interesting. The emphasis is on seafood and steak, and cakes here deserve top billing. Extensive salad bar at lunch. All desserts are homemade. **FYI:** Reservations recommended. **Open:** Lunch Mon–Fri 11:30am–2:30pm; dinner Mon–Sat 6–10pm. **Prices:** Main courses $10–$24. AE, DC, MC, V. ⚓

★ Maurice Piggie Park

1600 Charleston Hwy; tel 803/796-0220. 1½ mi from exit 113 off I-26. **Barbecue.** A "must" for barbecue lovers; this is the home of Maurice's BBQ sauce, sold in grocery stores across the country. The restaurant is easily spotted—there's a

100-foot, flashing "Little Joe's Pig" sign out front. Inside, eye-catching red-and-white decor distracts one from the cleanliness problems. Dinner baskets with slaw, hush puppies, fries, and rice or beans are available with each entree; the fresh lemonade is perfect for washing it all down. Homemade ice cream. **FYI:** Reservations not accepted. Children's menu. No liquor license. **Open:** Sun–Thurs 10am–11pm, Fri–Sat 10am–midnight. **Prices:** Main courses $5–$12. DISC, MC, V.

Zorba's

In Seven Oaks Shopping Center, 6169 St Andrews; tel 803/772-4617. At Bush River Rd. **Greek/Pizza.** Casual dining with primarily booth seating; a few pictures of Greece line the walls. Menu highlights include gyros, moussaka, and spanakopita, as well as pizzas, subs, salads, steak, and chicken. Greek beers available. **FYI:** Reservations not accepted. Children's menu. Beer and wine only. Additional location: 2628 Decker Blvd (tel 736-5200). **Open:** Mon–Thurs 10:30am–10pm, Fri–Sat 10:30am–11pm. **Prices:** Main courses $6–$14. AE, MC, V.

ATTRACTIONS

South Carolina State Museum

301 Gervais St; tel 803/737-4921. Housed in what was once the world's first all-electric textile mill. There are four floors, each dedicated to one of four areas: art, history, natural history, and science and technology. Hands-on exhibits, realistic dioramas, and laser displays make for exciting browsing through South Carolina's past, from prehistory through the present and even into the future. **Open:** Mon–Sat 10am–5pm, Sun 1–5pm. Closed some hols. **$$**

Columbia Museum of Art and Gibbes Planetarium

1112 Bull St; tel 803/799-2810. Eight galleries house a permanent collection featuring paintings, furniture, and sculpture (totaling more than 5,000 items) of the baroque and Renaissance periods. A focus of the collection is the work of native South Carolinians, including turn-of-the-century photographs. The museum also hosts various musical presentations. The Gibbes Planetarium, an extravaganza of sight and sound, is located within the museum. Museum is free; planetarium admission varies from show to show. **Open:** Tues–Fri 10am–5pm, Sat–Sun 12:30–5pm. Closed some hols. **Free**

Hampton-Preston Mansion

1616 Blanding St; tel 803/252-1770. The home of Gen Wade Hampton, a Confederate leader who later became one of the state's most popular governors. The restored 1818 mansion features furnishings that belonged to the owners. Lavish dining room, brightly colored mantelpieces, rococo-style furniture. 45-minute guided tours. **Open:** Tues–Sat 10:15am–3:15pm, Sun 1:15–4:15pm. Closed some hols. **$**

Woodrow Wilson Boyhood Home

1705 Hampton St; tel 803/252-1770. Victorian-style setting with arched doorways, gas lighting, antimacassars, and a clutter of ornaments. President Wilson spent three years as a teenager here while his father taught at Columbia Theological Seminary. Among the furniture in the 1872 house is the desk Wilson used while governor of New Jersey. 45-minute guided tours. **Open:** Tues–Sat 10:15am–3:15pm, Sun 1:15–3:15pm. Closed some hols. **$**

Riverbanks Zoo and Botanical Garden

500 Wildlife Pkwy; tel 803/779-8717 or 779-8730. A refuge for many endangered species, including the rare American bald eagle. The animals and birds here are among the healthiest and liveliest you'll ever see in a zoo. Penguins are kept happy in an environment that duplicates the bacteria-free Antarctic ice shelf. All kinds of domestic animals can be seen at the Farm, which also has an automated milking parlor in action for the education of city-bred folk. The Aquarium Reptile Complex is a spectacular facility that introduces the aquatic and reptilian creatures of South Carolina. The new 70-acre botanical park boasts woodlands, gardens, historic ruins, and plant collections from around the world. **Open:** Daily 9am–4pm. Closed some hols. **$$$**

Congaree Swamp National Monument

200 Caroline Sims Rd, Hopkins; tel 803/776-4396. Located 20 mi SE of Columbia. This 22,000-acre nature preserve is home to more than 320 plant, 41 mammal, 24 reptile, 52 fish, and 200 bird species. Its designation as a national monument assures the protection of perhaps the last significant old-growth riverbottom forest in the country. It is not rare to see ancient trees whose trunks measure more than 20 feet in circumference and are over 150 feet tall; the forest canopy is so thick that rain seldom falls unimpeded to the ground below. Facilities include 20 miles of walking trails, 20 miles of self-guided canoe trails, and a 3,000-foot boardwalk (accessible to visitors with disabilities) through a spectacular cypress-tupelo forest. **Open:** Daily 8:30am–5pm. Closed Dec 25. **Free**

Darlington

In Pee Dee country (named for the Pee Dee tribe), the town is a trade center in an agricultural region. Home of Darlington Raceway, site of the NASCAR TranSouth Financial 400 and the Mountain Dew Southern 500 auto races. **Information:** Darlington County Chamber of Commerce, 102 Orange St, PO Box 274, Darlington, 29532 (tel 803/393-2641).

ATTRACTION

NMPA Stock Car Hall of Fame/Joe Weatherly Museum

SC 34; tel 803/393-2103. At the Darlington Raceway, home of the TransSouth 500 and Southern 500 NASCAR races. The museum holds the world's largest collection of stock-racing cars, including those of such racing greats as Richard Petty, Fireball Roberts, and Bill Elliott. **Open:** Daily 8:30am–5pm. Closed some hols. **$**

Florence

Born in the 1880s with the coming of the railroad, this manufacturing city in a farm and timber region served as a transportation and supply point during the Civil War and was the site of a prison camp. Florence is a mecca for the performing arts in the northeastern part of the state. **Information:** Greater Florence Chamber of Commerce, 610 W Palmetto St, PO Box 948, Florence, 29503 (tel 803/665-0515).

ATTRACTION 🏛

Florence Museum of Art, Science, and History

558 Spruce St; tel 803/662-3351. Artifacts and artwork from Asia, Africa, and ancient Greece and Rome housed in an art deco–style building. Highlights include a collection of Native American ceramics, a History Room detailing the story of Florence, and the propellers from the *Pee Dee Cruiser* (the only ship built by the Confederate States). Wildflower Garden in back of the museum features native South Carolina plants and trees. **Open:** Tues–Sat 10am–5pm, Sun 2–5pm. Closed some hols. **Free**

Fort Mill

A producer of corn and wheat, the town is also headquarters for one of the world's largest textile manufacturers. **Information:** Fort Mill Area Chamber of Commerce, 101 S White St, PO Box 1357, Fort Mill, 29715 (tel 803/547-5900).

HOTELS 🏨

🎗🎗🎗 Comfort Inn at Carowinds

3725 Ave of the Carolinas, 29715; tel 803/548-5200 or toll free 800/221-2222; fax 803/548-6692. Housed in a concrete high-rise just off the interstate, this Comfort Inn is an obvious choice for families visiting Carowinds. **Rooms:** 153 rms, stes, and effic. CI 2pm/CO 11am. Nonsmoking rms avail. Rooms are very clean and nicely appointed. **Amenities:** 🛁 🦴 A/C, cable TV. Some units w/whirlpools. **Services:** 🚐 🖨 🐾 **Facilities:** 🏋 ⛳ 🏊50 👤 **Rates (CP):** Peak (Mar–Nov) $59–$79 S; $69–$89 D; $139–$159 ste. Extra person $10. Children under age 18 stay free. Lower rates off-season. Parking: Outdoor, free. AE, CB, DC, DISC, EC, ER, JCB, MC, V.

🎗🎗 Holiday Inn Express

3560 Lakemont Blvd, 29715; tel 803/548-0100 or toll free 800/HOLIDAY; fax 803/548-5305. Across from Carowinds. Very inviting decor and all the basic amenities. **Rooms:** 68 rms. CI 2pm/CO 11am. Nonsmoking rms avail. **Amenities:** 🛁 🦴 A/C, cable TV. **Services:** 🚐 🖨 🐾 **Facilities:** 🏋 ⛳ 🏊35 👤 **Rates (CP):** $69–$79 S or D. Extra person $6. Children under age 12 stay free. Parking: Outdoor, free. AE, CB, DC, DISC, MC, V.

Fort Sumter National Monument

Considered to be one of the most important military sites in the history of the nation, the first shot of the War Between the States was fired at Fort Sumter from Fort Johnson in 1861. The restored fort is located on a small man-made island at the entrance to Charleston's harbor and is accessible only by boat. Located at the fort is a museum with exhibits on military uniforms and local artifacts. Ranger-led tours. For information on tours and ferry service contact Fort Sumter Tours, 205 King St, Suite 204, Charleston SC 29401 (tel 803/722-1691).

Georgetown

Spaniards first established a settlement here in 1526, although it was eventually abandoned due to disease and attacks by Native Americans. The city was founded in 1726, after surrounding rice and indigo plantations brought economic prosperity to the region. Today, Georgetown is a magnet for tourism. **Information:** Georgetown County Chamber of Commerce, 102 Broad St, PO Box 1776, Georgetown, 29442 (tel 803/546-8436).

MOTEL 🏩

🎗🎗🎗 Clarion Carriage House Carolinian Inn

706 Church St, 29440; tel 803/546-5191 or toll free 800/722-4667; fax 803/546-1514. Off US 17. Situated on the grounds of a former rice plantation. The lobby is a replica of a 1734 rice planter's house. **Rooms:** 89 rms. CI 2pm/CO 11am. Nonsmoking rms avail. Very nice rooms feature solid, nicely designed furniture; some have large desks. **Amenities:** 🛁 🦴 A/C. **Services:** 🖨 🐾 **Facilities:** 🏋 🏊35 👤 1 restaurant (dinner only), 1 bar. **Rates (CP):** Peak (Mar–Sept) $63 S or D. Extra person $10. Children under age 17 stay free. Min stay special events. Lower rates off-season. Parking: Outdoor, free. AE, CB, DC, DISC, JCB, MC, V.

RESTAURANTS 🍴

Pink Magnolia

719 Front St (Historic Waterfront); tel 803/527-6506. Off US 17. **Southern.** A casual and comfortable atmosphere prevails; diners can sit on an outdoor terrace overlooking the water or in the indoor dining room. The best-seller is fried chicken salad: slices of lightly battered fried chicken breast served on a bed of mixed greens and vegetables with potato

wedges and sweet-and-sour dressing. **FYI:** Reservations accepted. Children's menu. Beer and wine only. **Open:** Breakfast daily 8–10am; lunch daily 11:30am–2pm. **Prices:** Lunch main courses $4–$7. AE, DISC, MC, V.

Rice Paddy

408 Duke St; tel 803/546-2021. Off US 17 N. **New American.** The space is as imaginative as the menu—each table is individually hand-painted and local art hangs throughout. Paddle fans spin overhead and a stone fountain splashes outside the window. Creative daily specials are offered in addition to the regular fare—baked snapper stuffed with spinach and shrimp; lump crab cakes; and fillet of beef with shiitake mushrooms, brandy, and cream. **FYI:** Reservations recommended. **Open:** Lunch Tues–Fri 11:30am–2:30pm; dinner Tues–Sat 6–10pm. **Prices:** Main courses $15–$20. AE, DISC, MC, V.

River Room

801 Front St (Historic Waterfront); tel 803/527-4110. Off US 17 at Broad St. **Seafood.** An upscale, riverfront restaurant with an extraordinarily dark, nautical decor. Fresh local seafood dishes, soup, poultry, and beef are served. There's a view of the river at the rear, and a tiny bar area. **FYI:** Reservations not accepted. **Open:** Lunch daily 11am–2:30pm; dinner daily 5–10pm. **Prices:** Main courses $12–$20. AE, MC, V.

Ⓢ ★ Thomas Cafe

703 Front St (Historic Waterfront); tel 803/546-7776. Off US 17. **Cafe.** A morning meeting place (especially for judges and lawyers) for the last 75 years, the Thomas Cafe is the prototypical small-town luncheonette. You might feel as if you've stepped back in time when you look at the prices—pancakes are $2.50 and a peanut butter and jelly sandwich will set you back $1.25. Homemade biscuits with sausage and ham are tops with locals. Lots of big booths. **FYI:** Reservations not accepted. No liquor license. **Open:** Daily 6am–2pm. **Prices:** Lunch main courses $1–$5. No CC.

REFRESHMENT STOP 🗗

★ Kudzu Bakery

714 Front St; tel 803/546-1847. Off US 17. **Bakery.** Small-town bakery offering a huge variety of goods made from scratch daily. There are usually 10 cakes and 5 pies on offer, besides cookies, muffins, and bread. Deep-dish apple-blackberry pie, praline cheesecake topped with fresh peaches, red velvet cake, and carrot cake are often available; bread specialties include black pepper brioche, sour white bread, and cornmeal yeast loaf. Jellies and jams for sale. **Open:** Mon–Fri 8am–4pm, Sat 9am–2pm. No CC.

ATTRACTIONS 🏛

The Kaminski House Museum

1003 Front St; tel 803/546-7706. A pre-Revolutionary home (ca 1760) furnished with antiques, mostly from the 18th and mid-19th centuries. Outstanding pieces include a 15th-century Spanish wedding chest and an authentic Chippendale dining room table. House tours are offered on the hour. In the summer, "Made in the Shade" concerts are held on the outside of the house and visitors may picnic on the lawn; call ahead for schedule. **Open:** Mon–Sat 10am–4pm, Sun 1–4pm. Closed some hols. **$$**

Prince George Episcopal Church

301 Broad St; tel 803/546-4358. Services in this church, which dates to about 1750, have been interrupted only by the Revolution and the Civil War. The stained-glass window behind the altar was once part of the slaves' chapel on a nearby plantation. **Open:** Mar–Oct, daily 11:30am–4:30pm. Closed some hols. **Free**

Greenville

Established in 1776 as a trading post on the Falls of Reedy River, this small town on the Piedmont plateau was one of the first inland settlements in the state. It has been a textile center in recent years. **Information:** Greater Greenville Convention & Visitors Bureau, PO Box 10527, Greenville, 29603 (tel 864/233-0461).

HOTELS 🏨

⬗⬗⬗ Courtyard by Marriott

70 Orchard Park Dr, 29615; tel 864/234-0300 or toll free 800/321-2211; fax 864/234-0296. Haywood exit off I-385. A standard hotel in a commercial district near downtown. It caters mainly to business travelers. **Rooms:** 146 rms and stes. Executive level. CI 4pm/CO noon. Nonsmoking rms avail. Rooms are comfortable and well-decorated. **Amenities:** 🛜 🖥 🧊 A/C, cable TV. Some units w/terraces. Hot water tap for making coffee and tea. **Services:** 📠 🚗 **Facilities:** 🏋 📺 500 ♿ 1 restaurant (bkfst only), 1 bar, whirlpool, washer/dryer. Fitness room has a TV. Secluded courtyard with gazebo. **Rates:** $53–$60 S or D; $69–$84 ste. Extra person $10. Children under age 18 stay free. Parking: Outdoor, free. AE, DC, DISC, MC, V.

⬗⬗⬗ Greenville Hilton and Towers

45 W Orchard Park Dr, 29615; tel 864/232-4747 or toll free 800/HILTON; fax 864/235-6248. Haywood exit off I-385. Three miles out of the center of town, this Hilton is a rather impressive choice. The beautiful glass motor entry leads to an equally striking lobby faced with marble and appointed with rich detail, custom fixtures, and expensive furniture. **Rooms:** 206 rms and stes. CI 3pm/CO noon. Nonsmoking rms avail. Rooms are fairly drab compared to grand lobby, though there are great views from the fourth floor up. **Amenities:** 🛜 🧊 A/C, cable TV w/movies. 1 unit w/whirlpool. **Services:** ✕ 🅥🅟 🚗 📠 🚗 **Facilities:** 🏋 📺 500 ♿ 1 restaurant, sauna, whirlpool. Indoor pool is completely surrounded by glass. **Rates:** $134 S; $149 D; $200–$350 ste. Extra person $10.

Children under age 12 stay free. Parking: Outdoor, free. Romance package (including flowers, champagne, and breakfast) avail. AE, CB, DC, DISC, EC, ER, JCB, MC, V.

☰☰☰ Greenville-Spartanburg Airport Marriott

One Parkway East, 29615; tel 864/297-0300 or toll free 800/441-1737; fax 864/281-0801. Exit 54 off I-85. A luxurious, full-service hotel offering smart accommodations with modern decor and lots of amenities. Elegant lobby boasts marble floors, high ceilings, towering potted plants, and heavy drapery on windows. **Rooms:** 204 rms and stes. Executive level. CI 3pm/CO noon. Nonsmoking rms avail. Recently renovated rooms are very plush and well appointed. **Amenities:** 🛁 ⚱ 🖭 🗑 A/C, cable TV, voice mail. **Services:** ✗ 🛏 VP 🚗 🖎 🗘 🕮 Only small pets allowed. **Facilities:** 🖼 ᜆ 1 restaurant (*see* "Restaurants" below), 1 bar, sauna, whirlpool. Extra large pool area with lots of seating, umbrellas, and even a few shade trees. **Rates:** $125 S; $135 D; $200–$350 ste. Extra person $10. Children under age 18 stay free. Min stay special events. Parking: Outdoor, free. Honeymoon packages (including champagne and breakfast) avail. AE, CB, DC, DISC, EC, ER, JCB, MC, V.

☰☰☰ Hyatt Regency Greenville

220 N Main St, 29601; tel 864/235-1234 or toll free 800/233-1234; fax 864/370-9204. The only lodging in downtown Greenville. Spacious lobby (open to the eighth floor) features sleek glass elevators and a waterfall. **Rooms:** 327 rms and stes. Executive level. CI noon/CO noon. Nonsmoking rms avail. Rooms feature particularly nice paintings and expansive windows overlooking the city. Many inner rooms open into lobby atrium. **Amenities:** 🛁 ⚱ 🗑 A/C, cable TV, voice mail. Some units w/minibars. **Services:** ✗ 🚗 🖎 🗘 Children's program, babysitting. **Facilities:** 🖼 🚲 🖪 1500 🖵 ᜆ 1 restaurant (*see* "Restaurants" below), 1 bar (w/entertainment), whirlpool. Free parking lot nearby. **Rates:** Peak (Labor Day–Dec) $109 S or D; $150–$475 ste. Extra person $25. Lower rates off-season. Honeymoon and family packages avail. AE, CB, DC, DISC, EC, ER, JCB, MC, V.

☰☰ Residence Inn

48 McPrice Court, 29615; tel 864/297-0099 or toll free 800/331-3131; fax 864/288-8203. Haywood exit off I-385. Corporate-type hotel offering apartmentlike accommodations in a commercial area. Inviting lobby features fireplace and lots of flowers. **Rooms:** 96 stes. CI 3pm/CO noon. Nonsmoking rms avail. **Amenities:** 🛁 ⚱ 🗑 A/C, cable TV, refrig. All units w/terraces, some w/fireplaces. **Services:** 🖎 🗘 🕮 Babysitting. Complimentary coffee, popcorn, and snacks offered in main room. Board games available. Complimentary grocery service. Pets can stay for a $50 deposit, and $5 per day. **Facilities:** 🖼 📷 🖪 15 ᜆ Basketball, whirlpool, washer/dryer. All-in-one basketball, tennis, and volleyball area. **Rates (CP):** $94–$114 ste. Children under age 19 stay free. Parking: Outdoor, free. AE, CB, DC, DISC, EC, ER, JCB, MC, V.

MOTELS

☰☰ Holiday Inn Express

5009 Pelham Rd, 29615; tel 864/297-5353 or toll free 800/HOLIDAY; fax 864/297-5353. Exit 54 off I-85. Well-kept property with a particularly well-coordinated pale-green color scheme. **Rooms:** 178 rms. CI 3pm/CO 1pm. Nonsmoking rms avail. Standard rooms are pleasant and clean. **Amenities:** 🛁 ⚱ A/C, satel TV w/movies. **Services:** 🚗 🖎 🗘 🕮 $25 pet deposit. **Facilities:** 🖼 ᜆ **Rates (CP):** $55 S or D. Extra person $5. Children under age 18 stay free. Parking: Outdoor, free. AE, DC, DISC, MC, V.

☰☰☰ The Phoenix

246 N Pleasantburg Dr, 29607; tel 864/233-4651 or toll free 800/257-3529; fax 864/233-4651. Off I-385. A well-managed, locally owned establishment with the air of a country home. A white picket fence, and fruit trees lining the long drive, lend a quaint atmosphere. The lovely courtyard area by the pool has water fountains, an enclosed gazebo, and gardens with walking paths and statues. **Rooms:** 186 rms. CI 2pm/CO noon. Nonsmoking rms avail. White, embroidered bedspreads and beautiful prints on the walls give these rooms character. **Amenities:** 🛁 ⚱ 🗑 A/C, cable TV. **Services:** ✗ 🚗 🖎 🗘 🕮 Car-rental desk, babysitting. Turndown service for some rooms. Van service transports guests to shopping and gym. **Facilities:** 🖼 300 ᜆ 1 restaurant, 1 bar (w/entertainment). Complimentary guest passes to Gold's Gym. **Rates:** $56–$110 S or D. Extra person $7. Children under age 18 stay free. Parking: Outdoor, free. Room rates are based on location and appointments of rooms. AE, CB, DC, DISC, MC, V.

☰☰ Quality Inn Haywood

50 Orchard Park Dr, 29615; tel 864/297-9000 or toll free 800/525-8250; fax 864/297-8292. Haywood exit off I-385. Located in a commercial district close to downtown and interstates, this comfortable Quality Inn features a lobby with a big screen TV. **Rooms:** 145 rms and stes. CI 2pm/CO noon. Nonsmoking rms avail. **Amenities:** 🛁 ⚱ 🗑 A/C, cable TV w/movies, voice mail. Two suites equipped with refrigerators and microwaves. **Services:** 🖎 🗘 🕮 Free cocktails on Mon and Wed evenings. Extra charge for pets. **Facilities:** 🖼 40 ᜆ Guests may use nearby fitness center for nominal fee. Parking for large trucks available. **Rates (CP):** $50–$56 S; $56–$62 D; $75–$79 ste. Extra person $6. Children under age 18 stay free. Parking: Outdoor, free. AE, DC, DISC, MC, V.

☰☰ Ramada Inn South

1314 S Pleasantburg Dr, 29605; tel 864/277-3734 or toll free 800/272-6232; fax 864/277-3734 ext 167. At Mauldin St. An older motel located at a busy intersection in a commercial area. **Rooms:** 118 rms and effic. CI 3pm/CO noon. Nonsmoking rms avail. **Amenities:** 🛁 ⚱ A/C, cable TV. **Services:** 🖎 🗘 🕮 **Facilities:** 🖼 200 ᜆ 1 restaurant, 1 bar. **Rates (CP):** Peak (June–Oct) $44 S; $49 D; $44–$49 effic.

Extra person $5. Children under age 18 stay free. Lower rates off-season. Parking: Outdoor, free. Pool-side efficiency is same rate as standard rooms. AE, CB, DC, EC, JCB, MC, V.

RESORT

≣≣≣ Embassy Suites Hotel

670 Verdae Blvd, 29607; tel 864/676-9090 or toll free 800/EMBASSY; fax 864/676-0669. Exit 48B off I-85. This lovely all-suites resort property features a championship golf course. Particularly impressive lobby, with an atrium open to all floors, fountains, a grand piano, ponds complete with fish, and glass elevators. **Rooms:** 268 stes. CI 3pm/CO noon. Nonsmoking rms avail. All units offer separate eating area with wet bar and microwave, living area with pullout sofa, and a separate sink in bedroom. **Amenities:** ☎ ▲ ▣ A/C, refrig, VCR, voice mail. TVs in bathrooms. **Services:** ✕ VP 🚗 ⊿ ↵ Children's program, babysitting. Complimentary newspapers. Free cocktails served nightly (5–7pm) in lobby. **Facilities:** ⚑ ▶₁₈ ⚑ 🔲 ₁₀₀₀ ⅙ 1 restaurant (lunch and dinner only; *see* "Restaurants" below), 1 bar, sauna, steam rm, whirlpool, washer/dryer. Party deck holds up to 500 guests. Golf club has its own pro. **Rates (BB):** $119–$129 ste. Extra person $10. Children under age 12 stay free. Parking: Outdoor, free. AE, DISC, MC, V.

RESTAURANTS 🍴

Addy's Dutch Cafe & Restaurant

17 E Coffee St; tel 864/232-2339. **International.** Located in an older building with funky interior wall decor (old hats, signs). The menu reflects the cuisines of a former colonial power and its one-time colony—the Netherlands and Indonesia. Other ethnic influences can be seen in dishes like Hungarian goulash and vegetable bahmi. Roasted duck is especially popular. An extensive beer selection includes mostly European imports and microbrews. **FYI:** Reservations recommended. Jazz. Dress code. **Open:** Mon–Sat 6–11:30pm. **Prices:** Main courses $15–$30. AE, DC, DISC, MC, V.

Austin's

In Greenville-Spartanburg Airport Marriott, 1 Parkway East; tel 864/297-0300. Exit 54 off I-85. **Continental.** This pleasant, airy dining room fortunately lacks the institutional atmosphere found in so many hotel restaurants. Solid, if unspectacular, food includes New York strip, grilled pork chops, osso buco, and various chicken dishes—though spinach salad with mandarin oranges and walnuts is a real treat. Dessert tray. **FYI:** Reservations accepted. Children's menu. **Open:** Daily 6:30am–10pm. **Prices:** Main courses $6–$15. AE, CB, DC, DISC, ER, MC, V. ⅙

Cafe Verdae

In Embassy Suites Hotel, Golf, and Conference Center, 670 Verdae Blvd; tel 864/676-9090. Exit 48B off I-85. **Regional American.** Tables are scattered throughout the lush, indoor garden, with a goldfish pond and a player piano to help keep

waiting customers amused. Entrees include pork medallions, linguine with smoked salmon and dill, and snowy grouper with grapefruit beurre blanc. The specialty dessert is cheesecake. **FYI:** Reservations accepted. Piano. Children's menu. **Open:** Lunch Mon–Sat 11am–2pm; dinner Mon–Sat 5–10pm; brunch Sun 11am–2pm. **Prices:** Main courses $13–$18. AE, DISC, MC, V. ⅙

McGuffy's

711 Congaree Rd; tel 864/288-3116. Off I-385. **Eclectic.** The decor, based on the McGuffy's reader, is carried out through historic pictures, a "reader" menu, and a chalkboard for specials. Many items are homemade, such as the fresh-squeezed lemonade and hamburger that is ground daily. About 35 types of beer are available. On Sundays, it's classical music, fancy tablecloths, and a more sophisticated menu. **FYI:** Reservations not accepted. Children's menu. **Open:** Mon–Fri 11am–2am, Sat 11am–midnight, Sun 11am–10pm. **Prices:** Main courses $13. AE, DISC, MC, V. ⅙

Omega Diner/Stax's Bakery

72 Orchard Park Dr; tel 864/297-6639. Haywood exit off I-385. **Continental.** Sort of an upscale Denny's, without all the charmless chain trimmings. Diners can choose from waffles, biscuits, french toast, pancakes, sandwiches, burgers, and chicken. There are over 30 varieties of pies, pastries, and cakes. The bakery, next door, offers gourmet coffee and fancier desserts. **FYI:** Reservations accepted. Children's menu. Beer and wine only. **Open:** Sun–Tues 6:30am–midnight, Wed–Thurs 6:30am–2am, Fri–Sat 6:30am–4am. **Prices:** Main courses $5–$13. AE, DC, MC, V. 🖵 ⅙

Provencia

In Hyatt Regency Greenville, 220 N Main St; tel 864/235-1234. **Eclectic/Italian.** Open and airy hotel restaurant, with a ceiling that soars eight floors and a waterfall that drowns out the hustle and bustle of the lobby. Diners can choose from among linguine primavera, salmon and vegetables, gamberoni portofino, and a wide variety of pasta dishes. **FYI:** Reservations accepted. Children's menu. **Open:** Breakfast Mon–Fri 6:30–11am, Sat 6:30am–noon, Sun 6:30–10:30am; lunch Mon–Sat 11:30am–2pm, Sun 11am–2pm; dinner daily 5–10:30pm. **Prices:** Main courses $9–$17. AE, CB, DC, DISC, ER, MC, V. ⅙

Seven Oaks

104 Broadus Ave; tel 864/232-1895. Near Auditorium. **Continental.** Fine dining located in a beautiful 1895 home with original fireplace, stained-glass windows, and rare 14-foot curved ceilings. Servers dressed in black and white bring out specialties like rack of lamb, chicken Wellington, and beef medallions. Wonderful appetizers include crab cakes, baked Brie, and a seafood sampler. Homemade desserts include maple gingerbread soufflé. **FYI:** Reservations accepted. Dress code. **Open:** Mon–Sat 6–10pm. **Prices:** Main courses $18. AE, CB, DC, DISC, MC, V. ● ▮ 🔲 ⅙

ATTRACTION 🖼

The Greenville County Museum of Art
420 College St; tel 864/271-7570. Home of one of the best collections of Southern art in the country, with works by native-born or transplanted Southerners ranging from the early 18th century to the present day. Other highlights include pieces by such artists as Romare Bearden, Jasper Johns, Georgia O'Keeffe, and Andy Warhol. **Open:** Tues–Sat 10am–5pm, Sun 1–5pm. Closed some hols. **Free**

Greenwood

This manufacturing city in the western part of the state was founded in 1802 by Irish settlers; the town was named in 1830 in honor of a local plantation. **Information:** Greenwood Chamber of Commerce, 24 Cleveland St, PO Box 10048, Greenwood, 29648 (tel 864/242-1050).

HOTEL 🏨

▤▤▤ The Inn on the Square
104 Court St, 29648 (Downtown); tel 864/223-4488 or toll free 800/231-9109; fax 864/223-7067. This former warehouse was beautifully renovated in the 1980s and now houses a luxurious hotel. The strikingly large lobby boasts cozy seating nooks and lots of fresh flowers. Caters to business travelers. **Rooms:** 48 rms. CI 2pm/CO 11am. Nonsmoking rms avail. Rooms are beautifully furnished with genuine antiques. **Amenities:** 🔽 🜂 A/C, cable TV. Rooms are stocked with bottled water, wine, and crackers. Complimentary copy of *USA Today*, coffee, and juice in morning. Nordic Track available upon request. **Services:** ✕ 🔼 🔁 Twice-daily maid svce. **Facilities:** 🔼 🔲 🔼 1 restaurant (*see* "Restaurants" below), 1 bar (w/entertainment). **Rates (CP):** $66–$76 S or D. Extra person $15. Children under age 18 stay free. Parking: Outdoor, free. AE, DC, DISC, MC, V.

MOTELS

▤▤ Days Inn
919 Montague Ave, 29649; tel 864/223-3979 or toll free 800/329-7466; fax 864/223-3297. This standard Days Inn is located in a quiet commercial district near Lander University. It is popular with visiting parents and alumni. **Rooms:** 100 rms. CI 2pm/CO noon. Nonsmoking rms avail. Simple, clean rooms. **Amenities:** 🔽 A/C, cable TV. **Services:** 🔼 🔁 **Facilities:** 🔼 🔼 1 restaurant (lunch and dinner only), 1 bar. Large, grassy area surrounding pool offers a great place for kids to play. **Rates (CP):** $35–$49 S or D. Extra person $5. Children under age 12 stay free. Parking: Outdoor, free. AE, CB, DC, DISC, MC, V.

▤▤ Holiday Inn
1014 Montague Ave, 29649; tel 864/223-4231 or toll free 800/HOLIDAY. ½ mile from Lander University; across from Crosscreek Mall. Two-story motel housed in two buildings.

Typical 1960s design has been updated with an above-average pool/deck area. **Rooms:** 100 rms. CI 2pm/CO noon. Nonsmoking rms avail. All rooms overlook parking area or inner courtyard/pool. **Amenities:** 🔽 🜂 A/C, cable TV. Some units w/terraces. Complimentary midday snack basket. **Services:** ✕ 🔼 🔁 🔁 Babysitting. Passes to local fitness center. Wed night cocktail party for guests. **Facilities:** 🔼 🔲 🔲 🔼 1 restaurant (bkfst and dinner only), 1 bar. Business center. Inner courtyard/pool is a bit nicer than average. **Rates (BB):** $58 S or D. Extra person $6. Children under age 19 stay free. Parking: Outdoor, free. AARP discounts avail. AE, CB, DC, DISC, EC, JCB, MC, V.

RESTAURANT 🍴

Restaurant
In The Inn on the Square, 104 Court St; tel 864/223-4488. **Continental.** A friendly hangout with an English pub atmosphere (leather furnishings, plaid accents, and a dart board). One of their most popular dishes is grilled salmon, but pasta, chicken, beef, and other kinds of seafood are served also. Appetizers include escargot and smoked salmon. Desserts such as strawberry Romanoff and bananas Foster (prepared at table) are a nice finish. **FYI:** Reservations recommended. **Open:** Breakfast Mon–Fri 7–10am; lunch Mon–Fri 11:30am–2pm; dinner Mon–Sat 5:30–10pm; brunch Sun 11:30am–2pm. **Prices:** Main courses $15–$18. AE, DC, DISC, MC, V. 🔽 🔼

ATTRACTION 🖼

Ninety Six National Historic Site
US 248, Ninety Six; tel 864/543-4068. Located 8 mi SE of Greenwood. This was a frontier trading post, and served as a fort during the French and Indian War. South Carolina's first Revolutionary War battle also erupted here. The visitors' center, operated by the National Park Service, has loads of information on the archeological digs and the restoration work now being done. Along the one-mile foot trail, you'll see the old earthworks, traces of the old village, a reconstructed stockade, and an early log cabin. **Open:** Visitors center, daily 8am–5pm. Closed some hols. **Free**

Hardeeville

Headquarters of the Hardee's fast-food restaurant chain, the small town has a Main Street, a town hall, and a 1910 steam locomotive that for many years hauled logs for a local lumber company. **Information:** Greater Hardeeville Chamber of Commerce, 301 Main St, PO Box 307, Hardeeville, 29927 (tel 803/784-3606).

MOTELS

≣≣ Holiday Inn Express

I-95 & US 17, PO Box 613, 29927; tel 803/784-2221 or toll free 800/465-4329. Exit 5 off I-95 at US 17. Completely renovated in July 1995. This property is perfect for anyone looking to visit Hilton Head (28 miles away) but looking to stay away from the crowds. **Rooms:** 112 rms and stes. CI 2pm/CO 11am. Nonsmoking rms avail. Comfortable, well-furnished rooms. **Amenities:** 📺 🍸 🖳 A/C, cable TV. Some units w/whirlpools. **Services:** 🍴 **Facilities:** 🛝 🔲 👤 **Rates (CP):** Peak (Mar–Sept) $59 S or D; $79 ste. Extra person $5. Children under age 19 stay free. Min stay special events. Lower rates off-season. Parking: Outdoor, free. AE, CB, DC, DISC, JCB, MC, V.

≣≣ Howard Johnson Lodge

Exit 5 off I-95 at US 17, PO Box 1107, 29927; tel 803/784-2271 or toll free 800/654-2000; fax 803/784-2217. Pleasant exterior and well-decorated lobby, but rooms are only so-so. **Rooms:** 127 rms. CI 1pm/CO noon. Nonsmoking rms avail. Rooms are not particularly well lit; bathrooms are small. **Amenities:** 📺 A/C, cable TV. All units w/terraces. **Services:** ✕ 🍴 🍽 Free coffee in lobby. **Facilities:** 🛝 👤 1 restaurant. **Rates:** $33–$50 S; $37–$55 D. Extra person $7. Children under age 18 stay free. Parking: Outdoor, free. AE, CB, DC, DISC, MC, V.

Hilton Head Island

The largest resort island between New Jersey and Florida, with four main resort communities featuring 12 miles of broad beaches. Noted for its golf courses, fine restaurants, and specialty shops and boutiques. **Information:** Hilton Head Island Convention & Visitors Bureau, PO Box 5647, Hilton Head Island, 29938 (tel 803/785-7110).

MOTELS

≣≣ Fairfield Inn by Marriott

9 Marina Side Dr, 29928; tel 803/842-4800 or toll free 800/228-2800; fax 803/842-4800. Attractive three-story motel near the center of Hilton Head action. Located across the street from an elaborate and popular miniature-golf course, this motel is a sure win with families. **Rooms:** 119 rms and stes. CI 3pm/CO 11am. Nonsmoking rms avail. Modern decor in rooms. **Amenities:** 📺 🍸 A/C, cable TV. **Services:** 🆅🅿 🖳 🍴 Staff is extremely accommodating. **Facilities:** 🛝 👤 **Rates (CP):** Peak (Apr–Sept) $80 S or D; $79–$114 ste. Children under age 18 stay free. Min stay special events. Lower rates off-season. Parking: Outdoor, free. AE, DC, DISC, MC, V.

≣ Motel 6

830 William Hilton Pkwy, 29938; tel 803/785-2700. A humble, one-story establishment offering dependable accommodations to budget-minded Hilton Head vacationers. **Rooms:** 116 rms. CI open/CO noon. Nonsmoking rms avail. **Amenities:** 📺 A/C, cable TV. **Services:** 🍴 🍽 **Facilities:** 🛝 **Rates:** Peak (May–Dec) $37–$41 S; $43–$48 D. Extra person $3. Children under age 17 stay free. Min stay special events. Lower rates off-season. Parking: Outdoor, free. AE, CB, DC, DISC, MC, V.

≣ Red Roof Inn

5 Regency Pkwy, 29928; tel 803/686-6808 or toll free 800/843-7663; fax 803/842-3352. Standard two-floor motel located close to the center of Hilton Head Island. **Rooms:** 112 rms. CI 3pm/CO noon. Nonsmoking rms avail. **Amenities:** 📺 A/C, cable TV w/movies. **Services:** 🍴 **Facilities:** 🛝 👤 **Rates:** Peak (Mar–Sept) $39 S; $60 D. Extra person $9. Children under age 18 stay free. Lower rates off-season. Parking: Outdoor, free. AE, CB, DC, DISC, MC, V.

≣ Sea Crest Motel

Avocet St, PO Box 5818, 29938; tel 803/785-2121 or toll free 800/845-7014; fax 803/842-6945. Basic, two-story oceanfront motel. **Rooms:** 87 rms. CI 4pm/CO 11am. Nonsmoking rms avail. Upper-floor rooms have patio and chairs and nice ocean view. **Amenities:** 📺 A/C, cable TV. Some units w/terraces. **Services:** 🍴 **Facilities:** 🛝 1 beach (ocean). **Rates:** Peak (Mar–Nov) $79–$110 S or D. Extra person $9. Children under age 12 stay free. Min stay special events. Lower rates off-season. Parking: Outdoor, free. AE, DC, MC, V.

RESORTS

≣≣≣≣ Crystal Sands Crowne Plaza Resort

130 Shipyard Dr, 29928; tel 803/842-2400 or toll free 800/334-1881; fax 803/842-9975. 13 acres. A true resort in every sense of the word, boasting beautifully landscaped tropical grounds, an elegant yacht club–like lobby, and a friendly staff that makes visitors feel more like house guests than customers. Wooden walkways lead you to the pool and ocean beaches. A great place for families. **Rooms:** 340 rms and stes. CI 4pm/CO noon. Nonsmoking rms avail. Nicely furnished. Many rooms open out onto square above lobby. **Amenities:** 📺 🍸 🖳 🍷 A/C, satel TV w/movies, dataport, voice mail, in-rm safe. All units w/terraces. **Services:** ✕ 🗝 🆅🅿 🚗 🛥 🍴 Twice-daily maid svce, car-rental desk, social director, masseur, children's program, babysitting. Complimentary valet parking. **Facilities:** 🛝 🚴 ⛳ 27 🎾 🎱 6 🎳 5 🏊 🛶 1000 🖳 👤 2 restaurants (*see* "Restaurants" below), 2 bars (1 w/entertainment), 1 beach (ocean), lifeguard, volleyball, board surfing, lawn games, spa, sauna, whirlpool, playground, washer/dryer. **Rates:** Peak (Apr–Oct) $199–$249 S or D; $350–$550 ste. Extra person $15. Children under age 19 stay free. Min stay special events. Lower rates off-season. Parking: Outdoor, free. AE, CB, DC, DISC, JCB, MC, V.

≣≣≣ Hilton Resort

23 Ocean Lane, PO Box 6165, 29938; tel 803/842-8000 or toll free 800/842-8001; fax 803/842-4988. 20 acres. This resort features guest rooms that open to hallways that are not

air conditioned—much like a motor inn. The landscaping is attractive, with many flowers, palms, and ponds surrounding the pool area, but guests may be disappointed by the lack of luxury at this supposedly upscale property. **Rooms:** 323 rms and stes. CI 4pm/CO noon. Nonsmoking rms avail. Rooms feature a dark decor with a burgundy color scheme; and all have kitchenettes with microwaves. **Amenities:** A/C, satel TV w/movies, refrig, in-rm safe. All units w/terraces. **Services:** Twice-daily maid svce, social director, children's program, babysitting. **Facilities:** [350] 3 restaurants, 2 bars (w/entertainment), 1 beach (ocean), lifeguard, basketball, volleyball, spa, sauna, whirlpool, playground. **Rates:** Peak (Mar–Sept) $185–$289 S or D; $350–$450 ste. Extra person $15. Children under age 18 stay free. Lower rates off-season. Parking: Outdoor, free. AE, CB, DC, DISC, MC, V.

Holiday Inn Oceanfront Resort

1 S Forest Beach Dr, PO Box 5728, 29938; tel 803/785-5126 or toll free 800/405-4329; fax 803/785-6678. Colorful resort, ideal for families. The three murals that adorn the walls were painted by the concierge. **Rooms:** 202 rms. CI 3pm/CO 11am. Nonsmoking rms avail. Well-decorated rooms have either partial or full ocean view. **Amenities:** A/C, cable TV w/movies. All units w/terraces. **Services:** Social director, children's program, babysitting. Concierge can secure all types of sports activity reservations. Full recreational program for children. **Facilities:** [200] 2 restaurants, 3 bars (2 w/entertainment), 1 beach (ocean), volleyball, day-care ctr, playground. Sand court volleyball. Poolside tiki bar with live music in evening. **Rates:** Peak (Mar–Oct) $139–$179 S or D. Children under age 12 stay free. Lower rates off-season. Parking: Outdoor, free. AE, CB, DC, DISC, MC, V.

Hyatt Regency Hilton Head

1 Hyatt Circle, PO Box 6167, 29938; tel 803/785-1234 or toll free 800/233-1234; fax 803/842-4369. 16 acres. The largest resort on the island, surrounded by wooden walkways and beautifully landscaped grounds. Elegant, dark-wood lobby and extensive meeting facilities are attractive to businesspeople, but this property is perfect for all. **Rooms:** 505 rms and stes. Executive level. CI 4pm/CO noon. Nonsmoking rms avail. Spacious and tastefully decorated rooms; most of them have full or partial ocean views. Bathrooms stocked with full-size toiletries. **Amenities:** A/C, cable TV w/movies, dataport, in-rm safe. All units w/terraces. **Services:** Social director, masseur, children's program, babysitting. Delta Airlines Reservations Counter located at front desk. **Facilities:** [2000] 3 restaurants (see "Restaurants" below), 2 bars (w/entertainment), 1 beach (ocean), lifeguard, games rm, spa, sauna, steam rm, whirlpool, beauty salon. **Rates:** Peak (Mar–June) $205–$280 S or D; $400–$975 ste. Extra person $20.

Children under age 21 stay free. Min stay special events. Lower rates off-season. Parking: Indoor/outdoor, free. Rates vary according to floor and view. AE, CB, DC, DISC, MC, V.

Palmetto Dunes Resort

4 Queens Folly Rd, PO Box 5606, 29938; tel 803/785-1161 or toll free 800/845-6130; fax 803/842-4482. 2,000 acres. Accommodations—from ocean-view villas to golf course units in a shady, tree-lined "plantation" house—are spread out over the 2,000-acre grounds. **Rooms:** 75 rms; 544 cottages/villas. CI 4pm/CO 10am. Nonsmoking rms avail. All rooms/villas are remarkable in decor and location. **Amenities:** A/C, cable TV, refrig, VCR, CD/tape player, in-rm safe. Some units w/terraces, some w/fireplaces, some w/whirlpools. **Services:** Maid service by request (additional charge). **Facilities:** [175] 7 restaurants (see "Restaurants" below), 4 bars (w/entertainment), 1 beach (ocean), lifeguard, volleyball, board surfing, washer/dryer. Each villa has its own pool. **Rates:** Peak (Apr–Sept) $100–$155 S; $161–$221 D; $131–$446 cottage/villa. Min stay. Lower rates off-season. Parking: Outdoor, free. Minimum stay of five to seven nights required during high season, two-night minimum rest of the year. AE, CB, DC, DISC, MC, V.

Sea Pines Resort

32 Greenwood, PO Box 7000, 29938; tel 803/785-3333 or toll free 800/732-7463; fax 803/842-1475. 5,000 acres. The perfect choice for golf or tennis buffs, offering many properties from which to choose. **Rooms:** 300 cottages/villas. Executive level. CI 4pm/CO 10am. Nonsmoking rms avail. No "hotel-style" rooms—only condos and villas. Rooms are tastefully furnished and decorated; some have harbor views. **Amenities:** A/C, cable TV, refrig, voice mail. All units w/terraces, some w/fireplaces, some w/whirlpools. **Services:** Car-rental desk, social director, masseur, children's program, babysitting. Maid service by request (additional fee). **Facilities:** [200] 15 restaurants (see "Restaurants" below), 15 bars (10 w/entertainment), 1 beach (ocean), spa, beauty salon, day-care ctr, playground. Sea Pines Racquet Club is the site of the Family Circle Cup Tennis Championships and the MCI Classic Golf Tournament, both held in March. **Rates:** Peak (June–Aug) $153 cottage/villa. Children under age 21 stay free. Min stay. Lower rates off-season. Parking: Outdoor, free. AE, DC, DISC, MC, V.

The Westin Resort

2 Grasslawn Ave, 29928; tel 803/681-4000 or toll free 800/933-3102; fax 803/681-1087. 24 acres. World-class resort, with an incredibly elegant lobby, comfortable furnishings, and a lovely balustraded art gallery on the second floor. **Rooms:** 492 rms and stes; 80 cottages/villas. Executive level. CI 4pm/CO noon. Nonsmoking rms avail. Rooms are cozy; nice ocean views. **Amenities:** A/C, cable TV w/movies, voice mail, in-rm safe. Some units w/minibars, all w/terraces, some w/whirlpools. **Services:**

Twice-daily maid svce, social director, masseur, children's program, babysitting. **Facilities:** 🏌 🚴 🅿54 🎿 ☎12 🏊 🛥 ⛵ 🔒960 💻 ♿ 3 restaurants (*see* "Restaurants" below), 2 bars (w/entertainment), 1 beach (ocean), lifeguard, volleyball, lawn games, spa, sauna, steam rm, whirlpool, playground. Indoor pool in glass atrium, children's pool, and three whirlpools. **Rates (AP):** Peak (Mar–Nov) $230–$350 S or D; $380–$2,000 ste; $255–$320 cottage/villa. Children under age 18 stay free. Lower rates off-season. Parking: Indoor/outdoor, free. AE, CB, DC, DISC, MC, V.

RESTAURANTS 🍽

⭐ Alexander's

In Palmetto Dunes Plantation, 76 Queen's Folly Rd; tel 803/785-4999. **Seafood.** The airy atmosphere at Alexander's features lots of windows overlooking a picturesque lagoon. Two classic motorcycles hang from the high ceiling of the main dining room. Menu specialties include shrimp, crab, and fresh fish dishes, with salmon Oscar a standout. **FYI:** Reservations recommended. Children's menu. Dress code. **Open:** Daily 5–10pm. Closed Dec 4–26. **Prices:** Main courses $16–$46. AE, DISC, MC, V. 🖼 💟 🆅🅿 ♿

The Barony Grill

In Westin Resort, 2 Grasslawn Ave; tel 803/681-4000. **American.** A hunt-club atmosphere prevails at this elegant resort eatery—the chandelier was imported from Europe, and fine oil paintings hang on the brick walls. Pine armoires and fine china add to the elegant ambience. Fresh local seafood, lamb, prime rib, and veal are among the menu highlights. **FYI:** Reservations recommended. Dress code. No smoking. **Open:** Daily 6–10pm. **Prices:** Main courses $21–$30. AE, CB, DC, DISC, MC, V. 💟 🆅🅿 ♿

Brellas Cafe

In Crystal Sands Crowne Plaza Resort, 130 Shipyard Dr; tel 803/842-2400. **Eclectic.** A nice airy cafe, with pastel decor, tiled floors, and tables overlooking the resort patio. Lunch options range from salad to ravioli. For dinner, the restaurant changes to "Portz," and decorations are changed accordingly (tablecloths and candles are added, etc). Nightly themed buffets feature Italian food, seafood, or barbecue. Kids eat free when accompanied by an adult. **FYI:** Reservations accepted. Children's menu. **Open:** Daily 7am–midnight. **Prices:** Main courses $7–$13. CB, DC, DISC, MC, V. 🖼 🆅🅿 ♿

The Cafe

In Hyatt Regency Hilton Head, 1 Hyatt Circle; tel 803/785-1234. **Regional American.** An elegant cafe with low lighting and windows facing the tree-lined patio of the resort. The widely varied dinner menu includes everything from simple chicken and beef dishes to fajitas. The Cafe also offers "Cuisine Naturelle," a specially prepared menu of health-conscious entrees made from wholesome ingredients. Large breakfast and dinner buffets available. **FYI:** Reservations

recommended. Children's menu. **Open:** Daily 6:30am–11pm. **Prices:** Main courses $5–$19. AE, CB, DC, DISC, MC, V. 🖼 🖼 ♿

Carmine's

1 Hudson Rd; tel 803/681-2771. **Seafood/Steak.** The rustic decor at this dark, cozy eatery includes a hodgepodge of horse saddles, guns, and old photographs. The menu focuses on high-quality prime rib and local seafood. Owned by the same proprietor as Hudson's on the Docks. **FYI:** Reservations not accepted. Children's menu. **Open:** Peak (Apr/June–Aug) daily 6–9:30pm. Closed Dec 1–27. **Prices:** Main courses $10–$27. AE, DC, MC, V. 🖼 🖼 💟 ♿

Carolina Cafe

In Westin Resort, 2 Grasslawn Ave; tel 803/681-4000. **Regional American.** Southern-style decor with high ceilings and ceiling fans cover two large rooms; pink-cushioned bamboo chairs and candlelit tables with single roses add to the atmosphere. The lower dining room overlooks the patio, pool, and ocean beyond. Menu specialties include tri-color tortellini with shrimp and scallops in basil cream sauce. **FYI:** Reservations not accepted. Children's menu. Beer and wine only. **Open:** Mon–Sat 6:30am–10pm, Sun 10:30am–2pm. **Prices:** Main courses $17–$19. AE, CB, DC, DISC, ER, MC, V. 🖼 🆅🅿 ♿

♣ CQ's

In Sea Pines Plantation, 140 Lighthouse Rd (Harbour Town); tel 803/671-2779. **Regional American.** The architecture of CQ's is reminiscent of the 19th century–style rice barns common in the Carolina low country, complete with wooden staircases and pine floors. One of the dining rooms—appropriately known as the Cotton Room—even contains cotton-harvesting tools from the 1800s. Nestled under the oaks inside Harbour Town, CQ's has served the island's "primest rib," seafood, and other specialties for over 20 years. (Harbour Town is accessible via Sea Pines Plantation, which charges $3 per car to enter.) **FYI:** Reservations recommended. Singer. Children's menu. Dress code. **Open:** Lunch daily 11:30am–2pm; dinner daily 5:30–10pm; brunch Sat–Sun 11:30am–2pm. Closed Jan 1–10. **Prices:** Main courses $14–$25. AE, CB, DC, DISC, MC, V. 🍴 ⛴ 💟

Crazy Crab

114 Executive Center; tel 803/363-2722. **Seafood.** Located in the heart of Harbour Town Marina, Crazy Crab serves only the freshest local seafood. The nautical decor includes old fishermen's gear, buoys, lifesaving rings, nets, and lanterns, and most tables afford a view of the million-dollar yachts in the marina. (Harbour Town is accessible via Sea Pines Plantation, which charges $3 per car to enter.) **FYI:** Reservations not accepted. Children's menu. Additional location: US 278E (tel 681-5021). **Open:** Lunch daily 11:30am–3pm; dinner daily 5–10pm. **Prices:** Main courses $12–$14. AE, DISC, MC, V. 🖼 🖼 💟

Damon's

In Village at Wexford, US 278E; tel 803/785-6677. **Barbecue/Steak.** In stark contrast to Hilton Head's array of seafood restaurants, Damon's specializes in prime rib and ribs. This casual, dark place, with Formica tables and booths, turns out a terrific onion loaf as well. A magician performs Tues–Sat evenings. **FYI:** Reservations not accepted. Magician. Children's menu. **Open:** Daily 11am–10pm. **Prices:** Main courses $8–$17. AE, DISC, MC, V. 🎦

Fuddrucker's

32 Shelter Cove Lane; tel 803/686-5161. **Burgers.** A typical hamburger joint with self-serve drinks and fast food–type order counter. Other menu offerings include hot dogs, steaks, chicken, and salad. Bakery goods (the brownies are a local favorite) and ice cream are also available. Decor is made up of school pennants and neon signs. **FYI:** Reservations not accepted. Children's menu. Beer and wine only. **Open:** Daily 11am–10pm. **Prices:** Main courses $4–$6. AE, DISC, MC, V. 🎦&

★ **Gaslight Restaurant**

303 Market Place; tel 803/785-5814. Off US 278E. **French.** Located in a quiet, elegant setting near the Sea Pines Plantation, this is a local favorite for formal dining in a leafy garden setting. Highlights include snapper, Dover sole, rack of lamb, and beef Wellington. There's a fine wine list, and all breads and rolls are freshly baked on site. **FYI:** Reservations recommended. Dress code. **Open:** Lunch Mon–Fri 11:30am–2pm; dinner Mon–Sat 6–10pm. **Prices:** Main courses $17–$24. AE, DC, MC, V. ♥&

♦ **Harbourmaster's**

1 Shelter Cove Lane; tel 803/785-3030. **Continental.** The three glassed-in floors and many outdoor tables at this waterfront restaurant provide spectacular views of the ocean and the setting sun, making this a lovely spot for a romantic dinner. Their specialty is rack of lamb, but the varied menu can suit any taste—from fresh local seafood to steak. Delicious desserts. **FYI:** Reservations recommended. Children's menu. Dress code. **Open:** Daily 6–10pm. **Prices:** Main courses $16–$24. AE, CB, DC, DISC, MC, V. ♥ 🎦&

Hemingway's

In Hyatt Regency Hilton Head, 1 Hyatt Circle; tel 803/785-1234. **Seafood.** Turquoise tiles, ceiling fans, and palm trees add to the laid-back but elegant atmosphere. Seafood is predictably popular—especially the lobster ravioli wrapped in thin "mu shu" skin served with spicy Thai sauce—and fruit cobbler is a hit at dessert. Piano bar features a singer nightly. **FYI:** Reservations recommended. Piano/singer. Dress code. **Open:** Dinner daily 5–11pm; brunch Sun 10am–2pm. **Prices:** Main courses $20–$30; prix fixe $13. AE, DC, DISC, MC, V. 🎦 💟 VP &

★ **Hudson's on the Docks**

In The Landing, 1 Hudson Rd; tel 803/681-2772. **Seafood.** Hudson's has been serving the freshest seafood in town for over 25 years. The historic building—located right on the docks where shrimp boats dock daily—was originally used as a seafood processing plant. Naturally the menu changes with the catch of the day, but entrees such as stuffed prawns and deep-fried local oysters regularly show up on the menu. Guests can sit on the dock, where a guitar player will serenade them while they wait for their orders. **FYI:** Reservations not accepted. Singer/Magician. Children's menu. **Open:** Lunch daily 11am–2pm; dinner daily 5:30–10pm. **Prices:** Main courses $10–$16. AE, DC, DISC, MC, V. 🔲 🍔 🎦

The Little Venice Ristorante

Harbourside II and Shelter Cove Rds; tel 803/785-3300. **Italian.** A charming trattoria overlooking Shelter Cove Harbour, with an outdoor pavilion that provides musical entertainment and outdoor dining (in season). The pasta is homemade (like linguine with clams), and veal comes in several incarnations. Local seafood is prepared Italian style—shrimp fra diavolo is especially fine. Hazelnut gelato is a popular dessert. **FYI:** Reservations accepted. **Open:** Lunch daily noon–2:30pm; dinner daily 5–10pm. **Prices:** Main courses $13–$20. AE, CB, DC, DISC, MC, V. 🎦 🎦 💟 &

♦ **Old Fort Pub**

In Hilton Head Plantation, 65 Skawl Creek Dr; tel 803/681-2386. **Regional American.** Inspired by Civil War structures built by Union forces, this 20-year-old restaurant has heart-pine floors, a covered veranda, clapboard trim, a tin roof, and shuttered windows. A third-floor observation deck provides panoramic views of the remains of old Fort Mitchel. The menu offerings lean toward Low Country specialties such as she-crab soup, oyster pie, and baked fish Daufuskie. **FYI:** Reservations recommended. Piano. Children's menu. Dress code. **Open:** Lunch daily noon–2:30pm; dinner daily 5:30–10pm; brunch Sun noon–2:30pm. Closed Jan 1–11. **Prices:** Main courses $16–$21. AE, DC, DISC, MC, V. ♥ 🔲 🍔 🎦

REFRESHMENT STOP ☕

The Playful Pelican

In Westin Resort, 2 Grasslawn Ave; tel 803/681-4000. **Eclectic.** The pastel decor at this beautiful, airy beachside bar/restaurant is accented by ceiling fans and glass walls. Only serves light fare, but location and ambience make it the perfect spot to relax with an after-dinner drink or watch the dramatic Hilton Head sunset. **Open:** Peak (Mar–Oct) daily 4pm–2am. Closed Nov–Feb. AE, CB, DC, DISC, MC, V. 🎦 VP &

Kiawah Island

Located south of Charleston, this privately owned 10,000-acre island is home to 10 miles of continuous beach.

RESORT 🏨

▤▤▤ Kiawah Island Resort
12 Kiawah Beach Dr, 29455; tel 803/768-2121 or toll free 800/654-2924; fax 803/768-6099. Off US 17. 10,000 acres. A good choice for a private and secluded getaway. Villas are cozily tucked away among the vast wooded grounds. **Rooms:** 150 rms; 350 cottages/villas. CI 4pm/CO 11am. Nonsmoking rms avail. Light oak–furnished rooms provide either an ocean, dunes, or nature view. **Amenities:** 🏨 ⚬ ▤ ⚬ A/C, cable TV w/movies, refrig, dataport, voice mail, bathrobes. Some units w/minibars, all w/terraces, some w/whirlpools. **Services:** ✕ ⚮ ⚬ ⚬ Car-rental desk, social director, masseur, children's program, babysitting. **Facilities:** ⚬ ⚲ ⚬ ▶72 ⚬ ⚬24 ⚬ ⚬ 650 ⚬ ⚬ 7 restaurants, 2 bars (1 w/entertainment), 1 beach (ocean), basketball, volleyball, games rm, lawn games, spa, sauna, beauty salon, playground, washer/dryer. **Rates:** Peak (June–Aug) $170–$230 S or D; $826–$1,365 cottage/villa. Lower rates off-season. Parking: Outdoor, free. During high season, large villas and ocean-view villas are rented by the week. AE, DC, DISC, MC, V.

Kings Mountain

ATTRACTION 📷

Kings Mountain National Military Park
SC 216; tel 803/936-7921. Marks the site of a crucial Revolutionary War battle. The southern Appalachians had been virtually undisturbed by the war until 1780, when British Maj Patrick Ferguson, who had threatened to "lay the country waste with fire and sword," set up camp here with a large loyalist force. The local backwoodsmen recruited Whigs from Virginia and North Carolina to form a largely un-trained, but very determined, army to throw the invaders out. The ill-trained and outnumbered colonists converged on Kings Mountain and kept advancing on Ferguson's men—in spite of wave after wave of bayonet charges—until they took the summit. Ferguson was killed in the battle, and the Appalachians were once more under colonial control. You can see relics and a diorama of the battle at the visitors' center. **Open:** Daily 9am–5pm. Closed some hols. **Free**

Litchfield Beach

At the southern end of the South Carolina's famous Grand Strand coastline, this oceanside community, noted for its quiet elegance, blooms along a highway that follows a pre-colonial Native American trail.

HOTEL 🏨

▤▤ Litchfield Inn
1 Norris Dr, Litchfield, 29585; tel 803/237-4211 or toll free 800/637-4211; fax 803/237-8921. Beachfront hotel rooms and private villas rented on an individual basis. The hotel is in a weathered, shingled building on a quiet residential beach. A good place for families. **Rooms:** 118 rms, stes, and effic; 8 cottages/villas. CI 3pm/CO 11am. Nonsmoking rms avail. Hotel rooms and 1-, 2- and 3-bedroom villas available. Hotel rooms are decent, if a bit on the plain and small side. **Amenities:** 🏨 A/C, cable TV. Some units w/terraces. **Services:** ⚬ Babysitting. **Facilities:** ⚬ 150 ⚬ 1 restaurant, 1 bar, 1 beach (ocean), lifeguard. **Rates:** Peak (May–Aug) $70–$115 S or D; $150–$214 ste; $130 effic; $175–$214 cottage/villa. Extra person $10. Children under age 12 stay free. Lower rates off-season. Parking: Outdoor, free. Weekday discounts avail. Room rates vary with view. AE, MC, V.

RESTAURANT 🍴

★ Pastaria 811 Italian Restaurant
In 111 Litchfield Exchange Mall, Litchfield; tel 803/237-0388. **Italian/Pizza.** The decor is nothing fancy, but the excellent, hearty fare keeps people coming back. Classics include lasagna, fettuccine Alfredo, veal, and pastas galore. **FYI:** Reservations accepted. Beer and wine only. **Open:** Peak (June–Aug) daily 11am–7pm. Closed 1 week at Christmas. **Prices:** Main courses $5–$13. MC, V. ⚬

Murrells Inlet

This small, picturesque fishing village lies along the 60-mile stretch of coast known as the Grand Strand. An abundance of excellent seafood is available at local markets and restaurants.

RESTAURANT 🍴

Prosser's Bar-B-Que at the Back Porch
US 17 S and Wachesaw Rd; tel 803/651-5263. **Regional American.** Housed for over 20 years in a late-19th-century farmhouse, the Back Porch offers hearty fare in a gracious garden setting. Guests may dine on enclosed porches that run along each side, or in the main dining room, with its cathedral ceiling. Low Country specialties include Carolina cured ham, Southern fried chicken, and homemade biscuits. A buffet is offered for lunch and dinner. **FYI:** Reservations not accept-ed. **Open:** Sun–Fri 11am–9pm, Sat 5–9pm. **Prices:** Main courses $5–$17. AE, DISC, MC, V. ⚬ ⚬

ATTRACTIONS 📷

Brookgreen Gardens
US 17 S; tel 803/237-4218 or toll free 800/849-1931. A unique sculpture garden and wildlife park on the grounds of four colonial rice plantations. The garden was laid out in 1931 as a setting for American garden sculpture from the mid-19th century to the present. Archer Milton and Anna Hyatt Huntington planned the garden walks in the shape of a butterfly with outspread wings, all leading back to the central space, which was the site of a plantation house. On opposite

sides of this space are the Small Sculpture Gallery and an original plantation kitchen. In the wildlife park, an outstanding feature is the Cypress Bird Sanctuary, a 90-foot-tall aviary housing species of wading birds within half an acre of cypress swamp. **Open:** Daily 9:30am–5:30pm. Closed Dec 25. **$$$**

Huntington Beach State Park

US 17 S; tel 803/237-4440. The park was once the estate of philanthropist Archer Huntington and his wife, the sculptor Anna Hyatt Huntington. They built a Moorish-style castle called Atalaya to serve as a home and studio. Today the structure is the main attraction of the beachfront park. A boardwalk nature trail provides a unique opportunity for observing marshlife, including alligators. Nature trails, beach area, camping, picnicking. **Open:** Apr–Sept, daily 6am–9pm; Oct–Mar, daily 6am–6pm. **$**

Myrtle Beach

See also Georgetown, Murrell's Inlet, Pawleys Island

The "capital" of the Grand Strand stretch of coastline offers lovely beaches, semitropical temperatures, warm waters, and plentiful golf. The population of this popular vacation spot rises from 24,000 in winter to over 350,000 during the peak summer season. North Myrtle Beach comprises the merged communities of Cherry Grove, Ocean Drive, Crescent Beach, and Windy Hill. **Information:** Myrtle Beach Area Convention & Visitors Bureau, PO Box 2115, Myrtle Beach, 29577 (tel 803/448-1629).

HOTELS 🏨

≣≣≣ Captain's Quarters Resort

901 S Ocean Blvd, PO Box 2486, 29578; tel 803/448-1404 or toll free 800/843-3561 in the US, 800/874-1923 in Canada. At 9th Ave S. Although this establishment has been in Myrtle Beach longer than most, it also looks better than most. A well-maintained, comfortable, and clean place to stay. **Rooms:** 328 rms and stes. CI 2pm/CO 11am. Nonsmoking rms avail. **Amenities:** 🛢 👌 🔳 A/C, cable TV w/movies, refrig. **Services:** ✕ ⱽᴾ 🛌 ⟿ **Facilities:** 🔏 🏊 ₅₀ 👌 1 restaurant, 1 bar, 1 beach (ocean). Extremely large game arcade. **Rates:** Peak (June–Sept) $105–$120 S; $120–$130 D; $150–$195 ste. Extra person $10. Children under age 18 stay free. Lower rates off-season. Parking: Indoor, free. Golf privileges offered at over 70 area courses. AE, CB, DC, DISC, MC, V.

≣≣≣ Coral Beach Hotel

1105 S Ocean Blvd, 29577; tel 803/448-8421 or toll free 800/843-2684; fax 803/626-0156. A large, pink-sandstone hotel that calls to mind Miami Beach instead of Myrtle Beach. One of the trendiest places in town, it has more to offer than the average Myrtle Beach resort. **Rooms:** 301 rms and stes. CI 3pm/CO 11am. Nonsmoking rms avail. **Amenities:** 🛢 👌 🔳 A/C, cable TV w/movies, refrig, in-rm safe. All units w/terraces, some w/whirlpools. **Services:** ✕ ⟿ Social direc-

tor, children's program. **Facilities:** 🔏 🛌 👌 1 restaurant, 2 bars (w/entertainment), 1 beach (ocean), games rm, sauna, steam rm, whirlpool, playground, washer/dryer. On-site bowling alley. **Rates:** Peak (June–Sept) $100 S; $108 D; $143 ste. Extra person $5. Children under age 18 stay free. Lower rates off-season. Parking: Indoor, free. AE, CB, DC, DISC, MC, V.

≣≣≣ Holiday Inn Oceanfront

6th Ave S at S Ocean Blvd, 29577; tel 803/448-4481 or toll free 800/845-0313; fax 803/448-0086. A large, comfortable, chain hotel located on a beautiful stretch of South Carolina beach. This attractive, pink-and-tan sandstone property is right in the middle of everything. **Rooms:** 311 rms and stes. CI 3pm/CO 11am. Nonsmoking rms avail. **Amenities:** 🛢 👌 A/C, cable TV w/movies, in-rm safe. Some units w/terraces. **Services:** ✕ 🖎 Children's program, babysitting. **Facilities:** 🔏 🛌 ₅₀₀ 👌 1 restaurant, 3 bars (1 w/entertainment), 1 beach (ocean), games rm, spa, sauna, steam rm, whirlpool, washer/dryer. **Rates:** Peak (June–Sept) $129 S; $149 D; $169–$189 ste. Children under age 12 stay free. Lower rates off-season. Parking: Outdoor, free. AE, DISC, MC, V.

≣≣≣ Landmark Resort

1501 S Ocean Blvd, 29577; tel 803/448-9441 or toll free 800/845-0658; fax 803/448-6701. At 15th Ave S. This light, sandstone building with orange trim is famous for its poolside parties on the Yellowbird deck and entertainment in the English-style pub. Friendly staff specializes in group tours and conventions. **Rooms:** 237 rms and stes. CI 3pm/CO 11am. Nonsmoking rms avail. Some rooms have ocean views. **Amenities:** 🛢 A/C, satel TV w/movies, refrig. **Services:** 🍽 🚗 🖎 Babysitting. **Facilities:** 🔏 ₂₅₀ 👌 1 restaurant, 1 bar (w/entertainment), 1 beach (ocean). **Rates:** Peak (June–Aug) $114 S; $142–$250 ste. Extra person $10. Children under age 18 stay free. Min stay wknds. Lower rates off-season. Parking: Indoor/outdoor, free. AE, DC, DISC.

UNRATED Ramada Ocean Forest Hotel

5523 N Ocean Blvd, 29577; tel 803/497-0044 or toll free 800/522-0818. This large oceanfront hotel is clean, comfortable, and conveniently located near North Myrtle Beach. **Rooms:** 175 rms. CI 2pm/CO 11am. Nonsmoking rms avail. Carpet and furniture are average, but rooms are well kept. **Amenities:** 🛢 👌 🔳 A/C, cable TV w/movies. All units w/terraces. **Services:** ✕ 🖎 Children's program, babysitting. **Facilities:** 🔏 ₇₅ 👌 1 restaurant, 1 bar, 1 beach (ocean), sauna, steam rm, whirlpool. **Rates:** Peak (June–Labor Day) $85–$95 S; $95–$105 D. Children under age 12 stay free. Lower rates off-season. Parking: Outdoor, free. AE, DISC, MC, V.

≣≣≣ St John's Inn

6801 N Ocean Blvd, 29577; tel 803/449-5251 or toll free 800/845-0624. At 68th St. Very well landscaped with a pleasing combination of shrubbery and palms, St John's is a beautiful little establishment with clean, comfortable rooms.

Rooms: 90 rms, stes, and effic. CI 2pm/CO 11am. Nonsmoking rms avail. **Amenities:** ⊟ A/C, cable TV w/movies, refrig. No phone. **Services:** ✕ 🚐 ⌂ Babysitting. **Facilities:** 🄵 ▣ ⅃ 1 restaurant, 1 bar, 1 beach (ocean). **Rates:** Peak (June–Sept) $93 S; $123 ste; $123 effic. Extra person $5. Children under age 12 stay free. Lower rates off-season. Parking: Indoor/outdoor, free. AE, DISC, MC, V.

▤▤▤ Sand Dunes Resort Hotel
201 74th Ave N, 29572; or toll free 800/845-1011; fax 803/449-5036. A large, sandstone hotel with a new 200-room tower and well-maintained grounds. A Myrtle Beach "hot spot." **Rooms:** 245 rms and stes. Executive level. CI 3pm/CO 11am. Nonsmoking rms avail. **Amenities:** 🔂 ⌀ ▣ A/C, cable TV w/movies. **Services:** ✕ ⌂ **Facilities:** 🄵 ▣ ⅃ 1 restaurant, 2 bars, 1 beach (ocean). Peak (June–Sept) $115–$119 S; $109–$315 ste. Extra person $10. Children under age 18 stay free. Min stay wknds. Lower rates off-season. Parking: Indoor/outdoor, free. AE, DISC, MC, V.

▤▤▤ Sea Mist Resort
1200 S Ocean Blvd, PO Box 2548, 29577; tel 803/448-1551 or toll free 800/SEA-MIST; fax 803/448-5858. Everything a guest could need is found at this self-contained community. With an on-site water park, miniature golf, game rooms, and more, the Sea Mist is designed to entertain both kids and adults. **Rooms:** 825 rms and stes. CI 2pm/CO 11am. **Amenities:** 🔂 ⌀ A/C, satel TV w/movies, dataport. Some units w/terraces. **Services:** ◎ 🚐 ⌂ Social director, children's program, babysitting. **Facilities:** 🄵 ▣ ▣ 🖳 ⅃ 3 restaurants, 1 bar, 1 beach (ocean), racquetball, sauna, steam rm, whirlpool, day-care ctr, washer/dryer. Water park features an inner-tube slide, an activity pool, and a floating river ride. Ice cream parlor and doughnut shop on site. **Rates:** Peak (June–Sept) $75 S; $84 D; $137 ste. Extra person $6. Children under age 15 stay free. Lower rates off-season. Parking: Indoor/outdoor, free. AE, DISC, MC, V.

UNRATED Sheraton Myrtle Beach Resort
2701 S Ocean Blvd, 29577; tel 803/448-2518 or toll free 800/669-9772; fax 803/448-1506. An excellent vacation choice for adults, the Sheraton is located right in the middle of the action. Nautical colors and modern appointments make this one of the classiest-looking places on the beach. **Rooms:** 219 rms and stes. Executive level. CI 3pm/CO 11am. Nonsmoking rms avail. **Amenities:** 🔂 ⌀ ▣ A/C, satel TV w/movies, refrig, in-rm safe. Some units w/terraces. **Services:** ✕ ⌂ Social director, children's program, babysitting. **Facilities:** 🄵 ▣ ▣ 🖳 ⅃ 1 restaurant, 2 bars (w/entertainment), 1 beach (ocean), games rm, spa, sauna, whirlpool, day-care ctr, playground, washer/dryer. **Rates:** Peak (June–Sept) $95–$179 S; $105–$189 D; $189–$229 ste. Extra person $10. Children under age 12 stay free. Lower rates off-season. Parking: Indoor/outdoor, free. Honeymoon and golf packages avail. AE, DISC, MC, V.

MOTELS

▤▤▤ The Beachcomber
1705 S Ocean Blvd, 29577; tel 803/448-4345 or toll free 800/262-2113; fax 803/626-8155. Housed in a sandstone building that is painted white with red and blue trim. Although there is very little landscaping, this motel provides a convenient and comfortable place to stay in Myrtle Beach. **Rooms:** 45 rms and effic. CI 2pm/CO 11am. Nonsmoking rms avail. Oceanfront rooms are available. **Amenities:** 🔂 ▣ A/C, refrig, in-rm safe. All units w/terraces. **Services:** ◎ ⌂ **Facilities:** 🄵 ⅃ 1 beach (ocean). Kiddie pool. **Rates:** Peak (June) $64 S; $88 D; $114 effic. Extra person $5. Children under age 18 stay free. Lower rates off-season. Parking: Outdoor, free. AE, DC, DISC, V.

▤▤ Chesterfield Inn
700 N Ocean Blvd, 29578; tel 803/448-3177 or toll free 800/392-3869; fax 803/626-4736. Owned by the same family for over 60 years, and one of the oldest establishments on the beach. The colonial-style brick property maintains its reputation by combining the best aspects of a beachfront vacation with bed-and-breakfast charm. **Rooms:** 57 rms. CI 1pm/CO 11am. Nonsmoking rms avail. Relatively new carpet and drapes. **Amenities:** 🔂 ▣ A/C, cable TV, refrig. **Services:** ✕ ⌂ **Facilities:** 🄵 ⅃ 1 restaurant (bkfst and dinner only), 1 beach (ocean). Quaint dining room features an incredible, panoramic view of the ocean. **Rates:** Peak (June–Sept) $91 S; $99 D. Extra person $8. Lower rates off-season. MAP rates avail. Parking: Outdoor, free. Golf and entertainment packages avail. Closed Dec–Jan. AE, DISC, MC, V.

▤▤▤ Driftwood on the Oceanfront
1600 N Ocean Blvd, PO Box 275, 29578; tel 803/448-1544 or toll free 800/942-3456; fax 803/448-2917. Housed in a large, white sandstone building, it provides a comfortable and clean place to stay. Six blocks from downtown Pavilion area. **Rooms:** 90 rms. CI 2pm/CO 11am. **Amenities:** 🔂 ⌀ ▣ ⌐ A/C, cable TV, refrig. **Services:** ⌂ Babysitting. **Facilities:** 🄵 ▣ ▣ ⅃ 1 beach (ocean), games rm, washer/dryer. **Rates:** Peak (June–Sept) $110 S or D. Extra person $5. Children under age 12 stay free. Lower rates off-season. Parking: Outdoor, free. AE, DC, DISC, MC, V.

▤▤ Jamaican
3006 N Ocean Blvd, 29577; tel 803/448-4321 or toll free 800/258-1164. Housed in a small, white, clapboard building with nice, well-manicured grounds, offering bright, airy accommodations on a (relatively) sparsely crowded strip of beach. **Rooms:** 48 rms and stes. CI 2pm/CO 11am. Rooms are well appointed and have attractive wall coverings. **Amenities:** 🔂 ▣ A/C, cable TV, refrig, in-rm safe. All units w/terraces. **Services:** ⌂ Babysitting. **Facilities:** 🄵 ⅃ 1 beach (ocean). **Rates:** Peak (June–Oct) $92 S or D; $105 ste. Extra person $5. Min stay peak and special events. Lower rates off-season. Parking: Outdoor, free. AE, DISC, MC, V.

☰☰☰ Red Roof Inn

2801 S Kings Hwy, 29577; tel 803/626-4444 or toll free 800/868-1990; fax 803/626-0753. At 28th Ave S. A dependable, clean place to stay while visiting Myrtle Beach. **Rooms:** 151 rms and stes. CI 3pm/CO 11am. Nonsmoking rms avail. **Amenities:** 🛏 ⚬ 🍽 A/C, satel TV w/movies, refrig. Some units w/terraces, some w/whirlpools. **Services:** ✗ 🕽 🖐 Babysitting. **Facilities:** 🏊 ☂ **Rates (CP):** Peak (June–Sept) $96 S or D; $149 ste. Children under age 18 stay free. Min stay wknds. Lower rates off-season. Parking: Outdoor, free. AE, DISC, MC, V.

☰☰ Teakwood Motel

7201 N Ocean Blvd, 29577; tel 803/449-5653. A family-oriented motel located five miles north of the town center. Clean, comfortable. **Rooms:** 25 rms and effic. CI 2pm/CO 11am. Nonsmoking rms avail. Rooms and efficiencies are attractively furnished, some in Polynesian decor. **Amenities:** A/C, cable TV w/movies, refrig. No phone. **Services:** 🚐 🕽 Twice-daily maid svce. **Facilities:** 🏊 ☂ 1 beach (ocean). **Rates:** Peak (Apr–Sept) $65 S; $70 D; $48 effic. Extra person $5. Lower rates off-season. Parking: Outdoor, free. Closed mid-Nov–mid-Feb. No CC.

RESORTS

☰☰☰ Myrtle Beach Martinique Resort

71st Ave N, 29578; tel 803/449-4441 or toll free 800/542-0048; fax 803/497-3041. At N Ocean Blvd. 3 acres. Located on the northern end of the beaches near a residential community, this resort has a secluded and austere quality. **Rooms:** 203 rms and stes. Executive level. CI 3pm/CO 11am. Nonsmoking rms avail. **Amenities:** 🛏 ⚬ 🖥 A/C, cable TV w/movies, refrig, in-rm safe. All units w/terraces, some w/whirlpools. **Services:** ✗ 🕽 Children's program, babysitting. **Facilities:** 🏊 🍴 🏊 ☂ 1 restaurant, 2 bars (1 w/entertainment), 1 beach (ocean), games rm, spa, sauna, steam rm, whirlpool, day-care ctr, washer/dryer. **Rates:** Peak (May–Sept) $119 S or D; $300 ste. Extra person $10. Children under age 17 stay free. Min stay wknds. Lower rates off-season. Parking: Outdoor, free. Golf packages avail. AE, DC, MC, V.

☰☰☰ Ocean Creek Plantation

10600 N Kings Hwy, PO Box 1557, North Myrtle Beach, 29572; tel 803/272-7724 or toll free 800/845-0353; fax 803/272-9606. 57 acres. A large, sandstone complex with well-maintained grounds. **Rooms:** 800 cottages/villas. CI 4pm/CO 11am. **Amenities:** 🛏 ⚬ 🖥 A/C, cable TV w/movies, refrig. Some units w/terraces. **Services:** 🕽 Social director, children's program, babysitting. **Facilities:** 🏊 ▶18 🎾4 🗾300 ☂ 1 restaurant, 1 bar, 1 beach (ocean), sauna, steam rm, whirlpool, playground. **Rates:** Peak (June–Sept) $78–$135 cottage/villa. Children under age 18 stay free. Min stay peak. Lower rates off-season. Parking: Indoor, free. Parking: Outdoor, free. AE, DISC, MC, V.

☰☰☰ Ocean Dunes/Ocean Sands Resort

201 74th Ave N, 29572; tel 803/449-7441 or toll free 800/845-0635; fax 803/449-0558. With organized children's entertainment and safety programs during summer months, this resort keeps children entertained so adults can relax. A good choice for families. **Rooms:** 400 rms and stes. Executive level. CI 3pm/CO 11am. Nonsmoking rms avail. Besides standard rooms and suites, guests may choose from apartments and town houses. **Amenities:** 🛏 ⚬ A/C, cable TV w/movies, refrig. All units w/terraces. **Services:** ✗ 🚐 🗾 🕽 Social director, masseur, children's program, babysitting. **Facilities:** 🏊 🍴 🗾175 ☂ 1 restaurant (bkfst and dinner only), 2 bars, 1 beach (ocean), games rm, spa, sauna, steam rm, whirlpool, beauty salon, day-care ctr, playground, washer/dryer. Convenience store and pizza parlor on site. **Rates:** Peak (June–mid-Aug) $105 S; $115 D; $115–$315 ste. Extra person $10. Children under age 18 stay free. Lower rates off-season. Parking: Indoor/outdoor, free. AE, DC, DISC, MC, V.

☰☰☰ Ocean Forest Villa Resort

5601 N Ocean Blvd, 29577; tel 803/449-9661 or toll free 800/845-0347; fax 803/449-9207. A beautifully appointed sandstone complex, right on the beach. The very accommodating staff help to make this a top choice for discerning travelers. **Rooms:** 160 cottages/villas. CI 3pm/CO 11am. **Amenities:** 🛏 ⚬ 🖥 🍽 A/C, cable TV w/movies, refrig, dataport, VCR, in-rm safe. All units w/terraces. **Services:** 🚐 🗾 🕽 Social director, children's program, babysitting. **Facilities:** 🏊 🎿 ☂ 1 beach (ocean), whirlpool, washer/dryer. **Rates:** Peak (June–mid-May) $135–$175 cottage/villa. Extra person $10. Children under age 18 stay free. Lower rates off-season. Parking: Outdoor, free. AE, CB, DC, DISC, MC, V.

☰☰☰ Sands Ocean Club Resort

9550 Shore Dr, 29572; tel 803/449-6461 or toll free 800/845-2202; fax 803/449-1837. This upscale property is perfect for the vacationing golf addict, since the Sands Ocean Club offers golf privileges at more than 70 local courses. **Rooms:** 175 rms, stes, and effic. CI 3pm/CO 11am. **Amenities:** 🛏 ⚬ 🖥 🍽 A/C, cable TV w/movies, refrig, dataport, in-rm safe. **Services:** ✗ 🚐 🗾 🕽 Social director, children's program, babysitting. **Facilities:** 🏊 🚴 🎾2 🗾120 ☂ 2 restaurants, 2 bars (w/entertainment), 1 beach (ocean), basketball, volleyball, games rm, spa, sauna, steam rm, whirlpool, washer/dryer. **Rates:** Peak (June–Sept) $90–$110 S or D; $150–$280 ste; $90–$110 effic. Extra person $10. Children under age 18 stay free. Lower rates off-season. Parking: Indoor/outdoor, free. AE, CB, DC, DISC, MC, V.

UNRATED Tidewater Golf Club and Plantation

4901 Little River Neck Rd, 29582; tel 803/249-1403 or toll free 800/843-3234; fax 803/249-6675. With the largest, most famous, and most luxurious course in the area, the Tidewater should not be missed by any golfer. Even nongolfers flock here for secluded atmosphere and beautiful views of the Intracoastal Waterway. A great vacation getaway. **Rooms:** 120 cottages/villas. CI 4pm/CO 11am. Nonsmoking rms avail. **Amenities:** ⬛ ⬛ ⬛ ⬛ A/C, cable TV w/movies, refrig, VCR, CD/tape player. All units w/terraces, some w/whirlpools. **Services:** ✗ ⬛ Children's program, babysitting. **Facilities:** ⬛ ⬛ ▶18 ⬛1 ⬛ 🔲75 & 1 beach (ocean). **Rates:** Peak (June–Sept) $100 cottage/villa. Min stay peak. Lower rates off-season. Parking: Outdoor, free. AE, CB, DISC, MC, V.

RESTAURANTS 🍴

Horst Gersthaus

802 37th Ave S; tel 803/272-3351. **German.** German offerings—sauerbraten, knockwurst, schnitzel—provide an interesting alternative to typical seafood-focused Myrtle Beach dining. Decor is reminiscent of a German beer hall; traditional German music most nights. **FYI:** Reservations accepted. **Open:** Mon–Sat 5–10pm. **Prices:** Main courses $5–$16. DISC, MC, V. ⬛ &

★ Marina Raw Bar

1203 US 17 N; tel 803/249-3972. **Seafood.** As the name suggests, this seaside eatery specializes in oysters, but there is also a variety of other seafood (served fried, grilled, or broiled) to go along with the seafaring decor. **FYI:** Reservations accepted. **Open:** Peak (June–Aug/Mar–Apr) daily 11:30am–10pm. **Prices:** Main courses $5–$16. AE, MC, V. ⬛

Sea Captain's House

3000 N Ocean Blvd; tel 803/448-8082. **Seafood.** Oceanfront eatery run by the same family for over 30 years. The paneled inner dining room has a warm, informal feel, and the glassed-in patio offers superb ocean views. Menu highlights include grilled salmon fillets with roasted garlic sauce, baked breast of chicken topped with Cajun-spiced shrimp, Southern fried chicken, and she-crab soup. Typical side dishes are cole slaw, potatoes, and hush puppies. **FYI:** Reservations accepted. Children's menu. **Open:** Breakfast daily 7–10:30am; lunch daily 11:30am–2pm; dinner daily 5–10pm. **Prices:** Main courses $10–$18. AE, DISC, MC, V. ⬛ ⬛ &

Tony's Italian Restaurant

1407 US 17, North Myrtle Beach; tel 803/249-1314. **Italian.** Attractive and contemporary-looking dining room with wine and teal decor. The menu focuses on classics like veal scaloppine, flounder primavera, and homemade pastas. Fresh clams are usually available, too. **FYI:** Reservations recommended. **Open:** Daily 11am–10pm. **Prices:** Main courses $5–$14. MC, V. ⬛ &

ATTRACTIONS 🏛️

Ripley's Believe It or Not! Museum

901 N Ocean Blvd; tel 803/448-2331. Unusual hobbies, habits, traditions, and people from all over the world. See a boat made entirely out of sugar, a wax figure of the world's tallest man (who reached nearly nine feet), a six-legged pig, and a cherry pit with the entire Lord's Prayer inscribed on it. **Open:** Daily 9am–10pm. **$$$**

Myrtle Beach Pavilion Amusement Park

Ocean Blvd between 8th and 9th Aves; tel 803/448-6456. The pavilion features more than 35 rides, restaurants, gift shops, a boardwalk, and dance hall. Two special features are the handcrafted 1900 German pipe organ, originally built for the World Exposition in Paris at the turn of the century, and the antique Herschell-Spillman merry-go-round. **Open:** June–Aug, daily 1pm–midnight; May and Sept, Mon–Fri 6–11pm, Sat–Sun 1pm–midnight.

Myrtle Waves Water Park

3000 10th Ave N; tel 803/448-1026 or toll free 800/524-9283. This 20-acre park boasts a variety of water slides and inner-tube rides, as well as a wave pool, children's playpool, video arcade, and tanning deck. **Open:** May and Sept, daily 10am–5pm; June–Aug, daily 10am–7pm. **$$$$**

North Augusta

See also Augusta, GA

Orangeburg

Swiss, German, and Dutch immigrants settled this city on the North Fork of the Edisto River in the 18th century; it was named for William, Prince of Orange. Home to South Carolina State University; the Festival of Roses is held in Edisto Memorial Gardens each spring. **Information:** Orangeburg County Chamber of Commerce, 570 J C Calhoun Dr SW, PO Box 328, Orangeburg, 29116 (tel 803/534-6821).

MOTEL 🏨

≡≡ Holiday Inn

1415 John C Calhoun Dr SE, 29115; tel 803/531-4600 or toll free 800/HOLIDAY; fax 803/531-4600. Exit 154A off US 60. A standard but pleasant motel, offering the basic amenities. Fine for a one night stay. **Rooms:** 160 rms and stes. CI 3pm/CO noon. Nonsmoking rms avail. **Amenities:** ⬛ ⬛ A/C, cable TV w/movies, dataport. **Services:** ⬛ ⬛ ⬛ **Facilities:** ⬛ 🔲300 & 1 restaurant, 1 bar (w/entertainment). **Rates:** $58 S; $66 D; $61 ste. Children under age 19 stay free. Parking: Outdoor, free. AE, CB, DC, DISC, MC, V.

Paramount's Carowinds

See Charlotte, NC. For SC lodgings, see Fort Mill, Rock Hill.

Pawleys Island

One of the oldest resorts on the Atlantic coast, this island was a refuge for rice planters' families fleeing from outbreaks of malaria. Famous for its woven cord hammocks, which are still made by local craftspeople.

MOTEL 🏨

🔲 Ramada Inn Seagull

US 17 S, PO Box 2212, 29585; tel 803/237-4261 or toll free 800/553-7008; fax 803/237-9703. An older, low-rise brick motel, located on Sea Gull Golf Course. Clean, comfortable rooms with no surprises. **Rooms:** 99 rms. CI 3pm/CO noon. Nonsmoking rms avail. Plain, worn rooms. **Amenities:** 🔲 A/C, cable TV w/movies. **Services:** ✗ ↩ **Facilities:** 🔲 🔲 🔲 1 restaurant, 1 bar (w/entertainment). **Rates:** Peak (May–Sept) $85 S; $90 D. Extra person $5. Children under age 18 stay free. Min stay wknds. Lower rates off-season. Parking: Outdoor, free. Rates are set per person, not per room. Golf packages avail. AE, CB, DC, DISC, MC, V.

INN

🔲🔲 Sea View Inn

414 Myrtle Ave, PO Box 210, 29585; tel 803/237-4253. Located in a wood-frame house with a commanding view of the dunes and the ocean, this inn has a comfortable, relaxed attitude reminiscent of summer camp—but without the counselors. "A whole lot of nothin' to do" is the motto here. The oceanfront veranda is equipped with rocking chairs so that guests can catch the constant sea breeze. Unsuitable for children under 3. **Rooms:** 20 rms (all w/shared bath). CI noon/CO 11am. Rooms have pickled wood walls, ceiling, and floors. Privacy is a bit lacking; rooms have swinging shutter doors. **Amenities:** No A/C, phone, or TV. House phone located in lounge. Six cottage rooms have air conditioning and screened porches. **Facilities:** 1 beach (ocean), guest lounge. Meals are served in the communal dining room with pre-set menu and dining times. Guests are summoned by chimes. **Rates (AP):** $95–$120 S w/shared bath; $140–$196 D w/shared bath. Extra person $50. Min stay. Parking: Outdoor, free. Closed Nov–Mar. No CC.

RESORT

🔲🔲🔲 Litchfield Beach & Golf Resort

US 17, 29577; tel 803/237-3000 or toll free 800/845-1897; fax 803/237-4282. Off US 17N. 4,500 acres. A sprawling combination of privately owned villas and a stucco hotel. Although the facility is posh in some areas, the main building is a bit worn and decor needs an update. **Rooms:** 96 stes; 230 cottages/villas. CI 4pm/CO 11am. A variety of accommodations are offered—an all-suite hotel, oceanfront condos, marsh view villas, and golf cottages. **Amenities:** 🔲 🔲 🔲 🔲 A/C, cable TV w/movies, refrig. Some units w/terraces, some w/whirlpools. **Services:** ✗ 🔲 🔲 🔲 ↩ Social director, masseur, children's program, babysitting. Summer Adventure program (for kids 5–15) teaches about nature and environment while improving sports skills. Yoga and aerobics also available. Shuttle runs from hotel to beach. **Facilities:** 🔲 🔲 🔲 🔲 🔲 🔲 🔲 3 restaurants (bkfst and dinner only), 2 bars (1 w/entertainment), 1 beach (ocean), basketball, volleyball, games rm, racquetball, spa, sauna, whirlpool, beauty salon, washer/dryer. Guests can only use the pool at their villa or the main pool. Tennis school. **Rates:** Peak (Apr–Oct) $99–$129 ste; $125–$345 cottage/villa. Min stay wknds. Lower rates off-season. Parking: Outdoor, free. Golf packages avail. AE, DC, DISC, MC, V.

RESTAURANT 🍴

Tyler's Cove

In Hammock Shops, US 17; tel 803/237-4848. **Regional American.** This casual eatery, built from pieces of old plantation homes and bricks and beams from old boats, specializes in fresh local seafood, pasta, and steaks. Typical Low Country–accented entrees include seafood strudel (shrimp, scallops, and crabmeat baked in phyllo dough with lobster sauce and vegetables in angel-hair pasta with sun-dried tomato and olive oil), and Carolina pork tenderloin (served au jus, with applesauce and garlic mashed potatoes). There's a terrace with a mesquite grill and (occasional) entertainment. **FYI:** Reservations accepted. Guitar/singer. Children's menu. **Open:** Lunch daily 11:30am–3pm; dinner daily 5:30–9pm; brunch Sun 11:30am–2:30pm. **Prices:** Main courses $11–$25. AE, DC, DISC, MC, V. 🔲

Pendleton

Located southwest of Greenville, the town features many authentically maintained mansions built by Low Country planters who journeyed north to escape malaria outbreaks.

INN 🏨

🔲🔲🔲 Liberty Hall Inn

621 S Mechanic St, 29670; tel 864/646-7500 or toll free 800/643-7944; fax 864/646-7500. ½ mi from Historic Square. 4 acres. Built in 1840, this 150-room home is part of one of the largest historic districts on the National Register of Historic Places. The wide wraparound porch is filled with rocking chairs, and there's a wooden deck looking over the grounds. **Rooms:** 10 rms. CI 3pm/CO 11am. No smoking. Individually decorated rooms feature high ceilings, heart-pine floorboards, and antique furnishings. There are no closets—small bathrooms have been built into the former closet space. **Amenities:** 🔲 🔲 A/C, cable TV. Complimentary wine in each room. **Services:** Afternoon tea and wine/sherry served. Linen changed every third night of multinight stay. Infant cribs must be rented in advance. **Facilities:** 🔲 1 restaurant (dinner only; see "Restaurants" below), lawn games. Small garden, wooden lawn chairs, horseshoes. **Rates**

(CP): $62 S; $72 D. Extra person $15. Children under age 10 stay free. Higher rates for special events/hols. Parking: Outdoor, free. Rates vary according to bed size. Minimum stay during special events. AE, CB, DC, DISC, MC, V.

RESTAURANT

★ Liberty Hall Inn Restaurant

621 S Mechanic St; tel 864/646-7500. ½ mi from Historic Square. **Southern.** Located on the first floor of a 150-year-old bed-and-breakfast. The two dining rooms feature pine floors, high ceilings, Victorian antiques, and displays of local crafts; dining is also available on the veranda or in the garden. Appetizers include shiitake and vidalia tart, and alligator cakes with ginger-peach sauce; praline trout, pecan bobwhite quail, and Brie-stuffed veal chops are typical entrees. There's a respectable wine list, and all desserts are homemade. **FYI:** Reservations accepted. No smoking. **Open:** Mon–Sat 5:30–9pm. **Prices:** Main courses $12–$17. AE, CB, DC, DISC, MC, V. ●■

Rock Hill

This small town 20 miles southwest of Charlotte, NC, is the home of Winthrop University. **Information:** York County Convention & Visitors Bureau, 201 E Main St, PO Box 11377, Rock Hill, 29731 (tel 803/329-5200).

HOTEL

Hampton Inn

2111 Taber Dr, 29730; tel 803/325-1100 or toll free 800/HAMPTON; fax 803/325-1100. A standard Hampton Inn, located near restaurants and a movie theater. **Rooms:** 162 rms and stes. CI 2pm/CO 11am. Nonsmoking rms avail. Exceptionally clean and orderly rooms look brand new. **Amenities:** A/C, cable TV. Some units w/whirlpools. **Services:** **Facilities:** Sauna, washer/dryer. **Rates (CP):** $51 S or D; $65 ste. Extra person $5. Children under age 16 stay free. Parking: Outdoor, free. AE, CB, DC, DISC, MC, V.

MOTELS

Comfort Inn

875 Riverview Rd, 29730; tel 803/329-2171 or toll free 800/221-2222; fax 803/329-2171. I-77 at exit 97. A basic motel, convenient to the interstate. **Rooms:** 101 rms. CI 1pm/CO noon. Nonsmoking rms avail. **Amenities:** A/C, cable TV, refrig. **Services:** **Facilities:** Playground, washer/dryer. **Rates (CP):** $35 S; $42 D. Extra person $5. Children under age 18 stay free. Parking: Outdoor, free. AE, CB, DC, DISC, MC, V.

UNRATED Holiday Inn

2690 N Cherry Rd, 29730; tel 803/329-1122 or toll free 800/465-4329; fax 803/329-1072. Charming, with an ap-pealing exterior and a large, well-appointed lobby. **Rooms:** 126 rms and stes. CI 3pm/CO noon. Nonsmoking rms avail. **Amenities:** A/C, cable TV, dataport, voice mail. 1 unit w/whirlpool. **Services:** **Facilities:** 1 restaurant (bkfst and dinner only), 1 bar (w/entertainment), washer/dryer. **Rates:** $55 S or D; $95–$139 ste. Extra person $5. Children under age 12 stay free. Parking: Outdoor, free. AE, CB, DC, DISC, JCB, MC, V.

Howard Johnson Lodge

2625 Cherry Rd, 29730; tel 803/329-3121 or toll free 800/446-4656; fax 803/366-1043. Basic, but comfortable budget accommodations. The inviting lobby has a big-screen TV and shelves full of books and magazines. **Rooms:** 140 rms and stes. CI 2pm/CO noon. Nonsmoking rms avail. **Amenities:** A/C, cable TV. All units w/terraces. **Services:** **Facilities:** **Rates:** $48–$54 S or D; $70 ste. Extra person $6. Children under age 16 stay free. Parking: Outdoor, free. AE, CB, DC, DISC, MC, V.

RESTAURANT

Shell Inn Fish Camp

Porter Rd; tel 803/324-3823. ½ mi from exit 72 off I-77. **Seafood/Steak.** Right off the interstate, Shell Inn is a classic example of a Carolina fish camp—the atmosphere is very down-home and family-friendly, and the fish is as fresh as can be. **FYI:** Reservations not accepted. Children's menu. No liquor license. **Open:** Wed–Thurs 4–9pm, Fri–Sat 4–10pm. **Prices:** Main courses $7–$15. No CC.

ATTRACTION

Museum of York County

4621 Mount Gallant Rd; tel 803/329-2121. This modern structure holds the world's largest collection of mounted hooved African mammals, as well as art galleries, a planetarium, and the new Vernon Grant Gallery, which features works by the artist who created Kellogg's Snap, Crackle, and Pop characters. The museum store sells Catawba pottery, and the planetarium offers free shows on weekends. Picnic facilities are available, and the entire complex is accessible to visitors with disabilities. **Open:** Tues 9am–9pm, Wed–Sat 9am–5pm, Sun 1–5pm. Closed some hols. $

Santee

Santee is a Native American word meaning "the rivers." Nearby Santee Cooper Lakes area covers 171,000 acres.

LODGE

Cabins at Santee State Park

251 State Park Rd, PO Box 79, 29142; tel 803/854-2408. Exit 98 off I-95. A great alternative to tent camping, especially for families. Although the cabins are nestled in a rustic, idyllic setting—10 of them are perched on piers over Lake

Monroe—they offer many modern conveniences. **Rooms:** 30 cottages/villas. CI 4pm/CO 10am. All cabins sleep six and have kitchens. **Amenities:** ⬛ A/C, cable TV, refrig. No phone. **Services:** 🛎 Children's program, babysitting. Boats are available for rent but you must provide your own motor. During the summer, there are free activities for the children. **Facilities:** ⚠ 🏊2 🎾 ⟋ 1 restaurant, 1 beach (lake shore), playground, washer/dryer. **Rates:** Peak (June–Aug) $55–$58 cottage/villa. Children under age 18 stay free. Min stay peak. Lower rates off-season. Parking: Outdoor, $2/day. One week minimum stay during the summer is required. MC, V.

ATTRACTION 🎭

Santee Cooper Lakes

US 301; tel 803/854-2131 or toll free 800/227-8510. Lake Marion and Lake Moultrie (known collectively as the Santee Cooper Lakes) cover more than 171,000 acres. Fishers note: Three world-record and eight state-record catches have been recorded here, and anglers flock to try their luck with the striped, largemouth, hybrid, and white bass, the catfish, and other assorted panfish that stock these waters. The lakes are rimmed with fish camps, marinas, campgrounds, and modern motels. You don't have to be an angler to enjoy this beautiful region: There are numerous golf courses, tennis courts, and wildlife sanctuaries too.

Spartanburg

Founded in 1785, this Upcountry city produces everything from textiles to peaches. Its international flavor is a result of the many immigrants seeking jobs generated by the city's industrial development. Roebuck, a suburb to the south of Spartanburg, is the site of "Festifall at Walnut Grove," with an encampment, a historical reenactment, and working artisans. **Information:** Spartanburg Convention & Visitors Bureau, 105 N Pine St, PO Box 1636, Spartanburg, 29304 (tel 864/594-5050).

HOTELS 🏨

☰☰☰ Courtyard by Marriott

110 Mobile Dr, 29303; tel 864/585-2400 or toll free 800/321-2211; fax 864/585-8121. Exit 72 off I-85. Standard Marriott, catering to the business traveler. **Rooms:** 108 rms and stes. Executive level. CI 4pm/CO noon. Nonsmoking rms avail. **Amenities:** 🔒 ⬦ A/C, cable TV w/movies. Some units w/terraces. **Services:** 🛏 🛎 **Facilities:** 🖼 🍴 🎾 ⟋ 1 restaurant (bkfst only; see "Restaurants" below), 1 bar, whirlpool. Nice patio/pool area, with a pebbled walkway and gazebo. **Rates:** $57–$77 S; $69–$84 ste. Extra person $10. Children under age 18 stay free. Parking: Outdoor, free. Reduced weekend rates. AE, DC, DISC, MC, V.

☰☰☰ Quality Hotel & Conference Center

7136 Asheville Hwy, 29303; tel 864/503-0780 or toll free 800/221-2222. Exit 72C off I-85. Well-maintained, six-story hotel. A good place to hold large meetings. **Rooms:** 143 rms and stes. Executive level. CI 3pm/CO noon. Nonsmoking rms avail. Rooms are slightly larger than average. **Amenities:** 🔒 ⬦ A/C, satel TV w/movies, voice mail. 1 unit w/whirlpool. Some rooms have refrigerators; suites have whirlpool tubs, hair dryers, and coffeemakers. **Services:** ✕ 🛏 🛎 🚗 Car-rental desk. **Facilities:** 🖼 🎾 ⟋ 1 restaurant, 1 bar. Bar/lounge has wide-screen TV, along with music. **Rates:** $52 S; $58 D; $99–$130 ste. Extra person $5. Children under age 18 stay free. Parking: Outdoor, free. Honeymoon and other packages avail. AE, CB, DC, DISC, EC, ER, JCB, MC, V.

UNRATED Ramada Inn

1000 Hearon Circle, 29303; tel 864/578-7170 or toll free 800/272-6232; fax 864/578-4243. At jct I-85/US 176. Located near the University of South Carolina and easily accessible from I-85. Lobby area is slightly run down. **Rooms:** 139 rms and stes. CI 3pm/CO noon. Nonsmoking rms avail. **Amenities:** 🔒 ⬦ ⬛ A/C, cable TV. **Services:** ✕ 🛏 🛎 🚗 DJ and line dancing in lounge. **Facilities:** 🖼 🎾 ⟋ 1 restaurant, 1 bar. **Rates:** Peak (Sept–May) $56–$63 S or D; $69 ste. Extra person $7. Children under age 12 stay free. Lower rates off-season. Parking: Outdoor, free. Golf and bed-and-breakfast packages avail. AE, CB, DC, DISC, MC, V.

☰☰☰ Residence Inn by Marriott

9011 Fairforest Rd, PO Box 4156, 29305; tel 864/576-3333 or toll free 800/331-3131; fax 864/576-3333. Near jct I-26/I-85. Set up like a village of small houses with a pool/sports center in the center, it has a nice atmosphere for a chain hotel. Cozy lobby, with big-screen TV and fireplace. **Rooms:** 88 stes. CI 3pm/CO noon. Nonsmoking rms avail. Penthouse suites have a loft with an extra bed. **Amenities:** 🔒 ⬦ ⬛ A/C, cable TV w/movies, refrig, voice mail. All units w/terraces, some w/fireplaces. In-room baskets with coffee and popcorn. **Services:** 🛏 🛎 🚗 Babysitting. Hospitality staff offers Wed night cookouts in summer, grocery service, and evening socials (light meals, beer, wine) on weekday nights. **Facilities:** 🖼 🏐 🎾 ⟋ Basketball, volleyball, whirlpool, washer/dryer. Fitness room has standard equipment (stationary bike, free weights, stairstepper) as well as a supply of rackets, basketballs, and other sports equipment. **Rates (BB):** Peak (Aug) $90–$139 ste. Children under age 18 stay free. Lower rates off-season. Parking: Outdoor, free. Corporate rates avail. AE, DC, DISC, JCB, MC, V.

MOTEL

☰☰ Hampton Inn

4930 College Dr, 29301; tel 864/576-6080 or toll free 800/HAMPTON; fax 864/587-8901. Exit 69 off I-85. One of the nicer budget motels in the area. **Rooms:** 112 rms. CI 10am/CO noon. Nonsmoking rms avail. Average-quality rooms. **Amenities:** 🔒 ⬦ A/C, cable TV w/movies. Rooms accessed with key cards. **Services:** 🖼 🗺 **Facilities:** 📶 🔲15 ❤ Guests may use local fitness center. **Rates (CP):** $47 S; $53 D. Children under age 12 stay free. Parking: Outdoor, free. AE, CB, DC, DISC, MC, V.

RESTAURANTS 🍽

Courtyard Cafe

In Courtyard by Marriott, 110 Mobile Dr; tel 864/585-2400. **Continental.** Breakfast buffet includes yogurt, eggs, meats, hot and cold cereals, and fresh seasonal fruit. "Heart-healthy" and à la carte items available. **FYI:** Reservations not accepted. Children's menu. No liquor license. **Open:** Mon-Fri 6:30am–10:30am, Sat–Sun 7am–noon. **Prices:** Main courses $6. AE, DC, DISC, MC, V. ❤

Piccadilly Cafeteria

In Westgate Mall, 166 Westgate Mall; tel 864/574-2044. Off I-26. **Cafeteria.** The decor here is fairly institutional, but the staff is very friendly and accommodating. The menu (which changes daily) includes meat, over 20 different vegetables, bread, and a large variety of desserts. **FYI:** Reservations accepted. Children's menu. No liquor license. **Open:** Daily 11am–8:30pm. **Prices:** Main courses $5–$7; prix fixe $5. AE, CB, DC, DISC, MC, V. 🎮

ATTRACTIONS 🏛

Thomas Price House

1200 Oak View Farms Rd, Woodruff; tel 864/476-2483. Located 7 mi S via I-26 to exit 35, then west via signposted county roads 50 and 86. This imposing house was built in 1795 from bricks made right on the premises. They were laid in a distinctive Flemish bond, which—along with the inside end chimney and gambrel roof—gives the house a style seldom seen is these parts. Its builder was a gentleman farmer, but an enterprising one: He ran a general store and the post office and even had a license to feed and bed stagecoach travelers in his home, licensed as a "house of entertainment." Furnishings, while not the originals, are all authentic items of the period. **Open:** Apr–Oct, Tues–Sat 11am–5pm, Sun 2–5pm; Nov–Mar, Sun 2–5pm. $

Walnut Grove Plantation

1200 Otts Shoals Rd, Roebuck; tel 864/576-6452. Located 15 mi SW of Spartanburg. A superb example of a colonial plantation house—not the stately columned sort found in the Low Country of South Carolina, but a large, simple farmhouse typical of landowner's homes in this region. Built in 1765 on a land grant from King George III, the house itself is fascinating, with its authentic furnishings (and its separate kitchen filled with early-vintage gadgets). Outbuildings include a barn that holds a Conestoga-type wagon. **Open:** Apr–Oct, Tues–Sat 11am–5pm, Sun 2–5pm; Nov–Mar, Sun 2–5pm. Closed some hols. $$

Sumter

Seat of Sumter County in central South Carolina. Site of dark, swamp-water lake that is home to eight species of swans. The tiny town of Horatio, nearby, is a popular home base for golfers visiting the area's many courses. **Information:** Greater Sumter Chamber of Commerce, 32 E Calhoun St, PO Box 1229, Sumter, 29151 (tel 803/775-1231).

MOTELS 🏨

🛏🛏🛏 Holiday Inn

2390 Broad St, 29150; tel 803/469-9001 or toll free 800/HOLIDAY; fax 803/469-9070. This beautiful Holiday Inn attracts visitors with its lush landscaping and convenient location. **Rooms:** 124 rms. CI 3pm/CO noon. Nonsmoking rms avail. Rooms are clean and well decorated. **Amenities:** 🛏 🍴 📺 🍴 A/C, cable TV w/movies. **Services:** ✕ 🖼 🗺 Babysitting. Contra-dancing instructor in bar on weekends. **Facilities:** 📶 🔲200 ❤ 1 restaurant, 1 bar. **Rates (BB):** $64 S; $69 D. Extra person $5. Children under age 18 stay free. Parking: Outdoor, free. AE, DC, DISC, MC, V.

🛏🛏🛏 Ramada Inn

226 N Washington St, 29150; tel 803/775-2323 or toll free 800/45-SOUTH; fax 803/773-9500. An attractive and recently remodeled motel, near to downtown Sumter and lots of golf courses. **Rooms:** 125 rms. CI 3pm/CO noon. Nonsmoking rms avail. Request a front room. **Amenities:** 🛏 🍴 A/C, cable TV. **Services:** ✕ 🖼 🗺 🍴 **Facilities:** 📶 🔲100 ❤ 1 restaurant (see "Restaurants" below), 1 bar, washer/dryer. Restaurant and bar area with an all-glass wall overlooking well-kept pool. **Rates:** $45 S; $49 D. Extra person $6. Children under age 18 stay free. Parking: Outdoor, free. Golf and B&B packages avail. AE, CB, DC, DISC, MC, V.

🛏🛏 Traveler's Inn

Broad St Extension, PO Box 2731, 29151; tel 803/469-9210 or toll free 800/304-6389; fax 803/469-4306. Jct SC 378/SC 521. A clean and well-managed budget motel located on the town's main business strip. **Rooms:** 104 rms. CI 7am/CO 11am. Nonsmoking rms avail. **Amenities:** 🍴 A/C, cable TV. Some units w/whirlpools. Rooms have big TVs. **Services:** 🗺 🍴 $5 fee for pets. **Facilities:** 📶 ❤ **Rates:** Peak (Mem Day–Labor Day) $36–$61 S or D. Extra person $5. Children under age 12 stay free. Lower rates off-season. Parking: Outdoor, free. AE, DC, DISC, MC, V.

RESTAURANT 🍽

The Sunporch

In Ramada Inn, 226 N Washington St; tel 803/775-2323. **Continental.** Pleasant, soft decor, with lots of plants and flowers and a nice view of a pool area. Many locals come here for the breakfast buffet; other options are burgers, clam platter, and shrimp fettuccine. Carrot cake, lemon pie for dessert. **FYI:** Reservations accepted. Children's menu. **Open:**

Breakfast daily 6:30am–10:30pm; lunch daily 11:30am–1:30pm; dinner daily 6–10pm. **Prices:** Main courses $7–$14. AE, CB, DC, DISC, MC, V.

ATTRACTIONS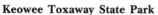

Sumter County Museum

122 N Washington St; tel 803/775-0908. A unique collection of artifacts housed in a beautifully restored Edwardian mansion surrounded by classically Southern formal gardens. The 1845 home contains a textile gallery, portraits of political leaders, a collection of historic toys and dolls, and gracious decorative arts and furnishings (mostly rococo revival and empire styles). Other buildings on the grounds include exhibits on Sumter's historical, cultural, and economic past. **Open:** Tues–Sat 10am–5pm, Sun 2–5pm. Closed some hols. **Free**

Lenoir Store

3240 Horatio Hagood Rd, Horatio; tel 803/499-4023. Located 20 mi NW of Sumter. This general store has been operated by the Lenoir family since 1765. Antique store implements (cheese cutter, tobacco cutter, coffee grinder) are still on display. **Open:** Mon–Sat 7am–7pm. Closed some hols. **Free**

Sunset

Located along the Cherokee Foothills Scenic Highway and near Lake Keowee, Sunset draws many vacationing families.

ATTRACTION

Keowee Toxaway State Park

108 Residence Dr; tel 864/868-2605. A 1,000-acre park nestled in the foothills of the Blue Ridge Mountains, near the site of Fort Prince George, an 18th-century British fort. The early British settlers in the area peacefully coexisted with their Cherokee neighbors until the 1790s, when settlers began driving the Cherokee off their land and into North Carolina. A museum in the park covers the history and culture of the Cherokee and displays arrowheads, pottery, and other artifacts. There are also camping facilities, a picnic area, hiking trails, and a meeting house that can accommodate up to 100 people. Lake Keowee offers boat launching ramps and an array of activities. **Open:** Apr–Oct, daily 9am–9pm; Nov–Mar, daily 9am–6pm. **Free**

Walterboro

The seat of Colleton County, west of Charleston. Once a major center of rice production, it is today a producer of lumber and cotton and a winter resort. **Information:** Walterboro-Colleton Chamber of Commerce, 109 Benson St, PO Box 426, Walterboro, 29488 (tel 803/549-9595).

MOTELS

Best Western Inn

1140 Sniders Hwy, PO Box 1085, 29488; tel 803/538-3600 or toll free 800/528-1234; fax 803/538-3600. Exit 53 off I-95. A basic motel near the highway, this place is perfect for the traveling family. **Rooms:** 114 rms. CI open/CO 11am. Nonsmoking rms avail. **Amenities:** A/C, cable TV w/movies. **Services:** **Facilities:** **Rates (CP):** $36 S; $43 D. Extra person $6. Children under age 18 stay free. Parking: Outdoor, free. AE, DC, DISC, MC, V.

Comfort Inn

1109 Sniders Hwy, 29488; tel 803/538-5403 or toll free 800/221-2222. Exit 53 off I-95/US 63. A standard, chain motel near I-95. **Rooms:** 106 rms and stes. Executive level. CI noon/CO noon. Nonsmoking rms avail. **Amenities:** A/C, cable TV. 1 unit w/minibar, 1 w/whirlpool. **Services:** **Facilities:** 1 bar. **Rates (CP):** Peak (Feb–Apr/Oct–Dec) $32–$50 S; $40–$70 D; $110–$115 ste. Extra person $6. Children under age 16 stay free. Lower rates off-season. Parking: Outdoor, free. AE, DISC, MC, V.

Holiday Inn

1120 Sniders Hwy, PO Box 889, 29488; tel 803/538-5473 or toll free 800/HOLIDAY; fax 538-5473. Exit 53 off I-95. An attractively laid-out establishment, where well-kept rooms surround interior courtyard with pool. Popular with families. **Rooms:** 172 rms. CI 2pm/CO noon. Nonsmoking rms avail. **Amenities:** A/C, cable TV w/movies. **Services:** **Facilities:** 1 restaurant. **Rates (BB):** $52 S or D. Extra person $5. Children under age 18 stay free. Parking: Outdoor, free. AE, CB, DC, DISC, JCB, MC, V.

TENNESSEE
Mountains and Melodies

"Tennessee—We're Playing Your Song." What an apt motto for a state that has nurtured the most important forms of American music: rock 'n' roll, the blues, soul, country. Although Mississippi was Elvis Presley's birthplace, "the King" is most close-ly associated with Memphis, since he recorded most of his classic records there and built his Graceland on the outskirts of town. The blues, called "the voice of the soul," sprang from the hard life of slaves laboring in the fields and came into its own on Memphis's Beale Street under the tutelage of such greats as W C Handy and B B King. What became known as soul music was practically invented by Memphis' Stax Records. Nashville—now known worldwide as Music City USA—helped popularize country music via the Grand Ole Opry, and is still the center of the multimillion dollar country music industry. Dolly Parton's roots in Pigeon Forge have brought numerous country music venues to the Smoky Mountains area of eastern Tennessee.

But Tennessee is also a state of superlative natural beauty. The nation's mightiest river—the Mississippi—forms its western border and the world's second-largest manmade lake (Kentucky Lake) is here. In fact, for a landlocked state, Tennessee has a lot of water—the Mississippi, Tennessee, and Cumberland Rivers; several Tennessee Valley Authority (TVA) lakes; and the white-water majesty of wild and scenic rivers such as the Ocoee (site of the white-water events of the 1996 Summer Olympics). The Smoky Mountains—with their steep-sided gorges, cool limestone caves, secluded valleys, and broad-shouldered plateaus—draw hundreds of thousands of nature lovers to the state each year.

Tennesseans are really neither Northerners nor Southerners. The state is a place where any resident or visitor can feel comfortable. Because of the TVA and other New Deal improvements, the once isolated pockets of Tennessee are now an integral part of its culture as well as a strong economic influence on the tourism industry. Maybe

Tennessee's lack of great wealth and comparative isolation accounts for the fact that almost everyone who visits this state feels welcome and comfortable here.

A Brief History

The Original Wild West Although paleo-Indians were living in the area as early as 9000 BC, Tennessee was long considered a wild frontier by Europeans and was explored and settled relatively late compared to the coastal colonies. Not only was the pass through the Cumberland Gap a difficult obstacle, the native Cherokee, Choctaw, and Chickasaw tribes were very protective of their territory. It was not until the Indian Treaty of Lochaber in 1770 and the Transylvania Purchase in 1775 that much of the land west of the Appalachians was opened to settlers. Fort Nashboro (eventually known as Nashville) was founded by 300 intrepid pioneers in April 1780, and statehood granted in 1796. In the early 19th century, Tennessee natives like frontiersman-legislator Davy Crockett and soldier-president Andrew Jackson personified the emerging state's populist political and social philosophy—one of the first clear breaks with the hold of the educated, landed gentry that had dominated the East Coast.

Caught in Between Tennessee's physical position between the North and South caused it to develop in its own unique way. Tennessee was clearly different from its neighbors in the Deep South that were dominated by a plantation economy. The state developed largely as an agglomeration of small farms, and the homogeneity of the Anglo-Saxon Protestant population remained almost intact because Tennessee wasn't touched by the waves of immigration into the coastal states. Slavery, however, was a significant factor in the state's economy due to the bustling shipping ports at Nashville and Memphis, and Tennessee seceded from the Union (the last state to do so) in June 1861. However, independent farmers and mountaineers in the eastern region remained loyal to the Union.

Bloody Battleground After Virginia, Tennessee saw the most intense fighting of the Civil War. Its many rivers served as Union invasion routes, and its status as a conflicted border state ensured that both sides would invest heavily in establishing control. One of the great encounters of the war was the battle of Shiloh, fought near the Mississippi state line. A less-than-clear-cut victory for the North, Shiloh was the scene of mass slaughter, with each side losing more than 10,000 men. The city of Chattanooga, vital to the Confederacy as the communications link between the East and the Mississippi River and valued by the Union as the key to loyal east Tennessee, was fought over in a bloody campaign during the fall of 1863. The city eventually fell into Union hands and remained so until the end of the war.

Recovery After the Civil War, Tennessee led the way in the New South's burgeoning economic and cultural growth. Nashville, home of Fisk University (one of the nation's first African American universities, founded in 1866) and Vanderbilt University (1873), became known as the "Athens of the South." Jacksonian democracy of entrepreneurial yeoman and vigorous Democratic politics characterized the western sections. The creation of the Tennessee Valley Authority (TVA) in 1933, considered one of America's major achievements in integrated regional economic development, helped lift thousands out of rural poverty and spurred a transition toward industry and tourism through the creation of multipurpose dams, reservoirs, and lakes.

Growing Pains Black and white Tennesseans continued to live almost entirely separate lives until the 1950s, when decades of protest and the slow accumulation of power led many African American residents to organize and work for an integrated state. Tragically, the struggle culminated in 1968 with the sanitation workers' strike that brought civil rights

---

Fun Facts

- Graceland, Elvis Presley's Memphis mansion, is the second-most-visited house in America. Only the White House has more visitors.
- The first modern miniature-golf course opened in 1929 near Chattanooga.
- Between 1784 and 1788, present-day eastern Tennessee was part of the State of Franklin, an independent government formed by settlers in the region after North Carolina ceded its western lands to the federal government.
- The Holiday Inn hotel chain was born in Memphis in 1952.
- The University of Tennessee at Knoxville, chartered in 1794 as Blount College, was the first nondenominational college in the United States.

leader Martin Luther King Jr to Memphis, the site of his assassination. Nevertheless, great strides have been made in the struggle for racial equality in the state—an effort that continues, as it does in many places throughout the country, to this day.

Toward the Future As the standard of living increased, a decades-long trend of greater emigration than immigration was finally broken in the 1960s. Today the state enjoys a varied manufacturing base, preeminence in the music industry, and a flourishing tourism trade. As a magnet for young musicians from around the country and a center for higher education, Tennessee is constantly infused with a youthful vigor that adds a healthy balance to the state's more traditional side.

A Closer Look

GEOGRAPHY

Tennessee is unusual among all the 50 states in that it is so long (432 miles east to west) and so squat (112 miles north to south). It stretches from the rugged peaks and broad valleys of the Appalachian Mountains on the eastern border with North Carolina, to the rolling hills and broad basins of Middle Tennessee, to the swampy alluvial plain of the Mississippi River, which forms the state's western border. Tennessee is home to three major rivers: the **Tennessee,** which flows southward in the east and northward in the west, drains to the east; the **Cumberland,** which drains the upper middle region; and the **Mississippi,** which drains a small portion of the west. Damming the mighty Tennessee and the Cumberland has created an impressive chain of lakes sometimes known as the Great Lakes of the South.

The eastern edge of the state is dominated by the towering peaks of the **Great Smoky Mountains.** The principal city in this region, Gatlinburg, was once a sleepy village but now is a touristy metropolis that merges almost imperceptibly with Pigeon Forge and Sevierville. Just west of the mountains is the **Great Appalachian Valley** of eastern Tennessee, a series of low ridges that vary from 30 to 60 miles wide.

DRIVING DISTANCES
Knoxville
111 mi W of Asheville, NC
112 mi NW of Chattanooga
177 mi E of Nashville
226 mi N of Atlanta, GA
385 mi NE of Memphis
Nashville
128 mi NW of Chattanooga
168 mi S of Louisville, KY
196 mi NW of Birmingham, AL
208 mi NE of Memphis
250 mi N of Atlanta
Memphis
138 mi NE to Little Rock, AR
208 mi SW of Nashville
212 mi N of Jackson, MS
246 mi NW of Birmingham, AL
385 mi SW of Knoxville

Running diagonally from southwest to northeast, the valley contains the vivacious modern cities of Chattanooga and Knoxville.

The **Cumberland Plateau,** in central Tennessee, has a generally flat and slightly undulating surface and is occasionally bisected by deep, sometimes wide river valleys. The cities of Clarksville, on the Cumberland River, and Waynesboro, on the Tennessee River, are located here. The **Nashville Basin** dominates the Interior Low Plateau—the largest of the state's regions. This 60-mile-wide basin runs north to south, its slightly rolling terrain punctuated by small hills known as knobs. The big city here, of course, is Nashville.

Nearly flat **western Tennessee,** which lies between the Tennessee and Mississippi Rivers, is laced with meandering, low-banked streams. Its rich river-bottom lands produce most of the state's cotton crop. Memphis, in the extreme southwestern corner of the state, lies within a narrow strip of floodplain and swamp along the Mississippi River.

CLIMATE

For the most part, Tennessee has a moderate climate, with cool (but not cold) winters and warm (but not hot) summers being the norm. Because Tennessee is so narrow, there is little temperature difference between the northern and southern regions. The rise in elevation from west to east, however, causes a significant drop in temperature in the mountains, where the climate is not unlike that of more northerly states. Snow, sometimes in significant amounts, falls in the eastern mountains.

WHAT TO PACK

Residents dress casually for the most part. You'll only need a dressy outfit if you plan to eat at a very expensive restaurant or take in a cultural performance. Otherwise, layered cottons in the summer and lightweight woolens in the winter will cover almost any occasion. Bring a sweater or jacket for cool evenings in the spring and fall. A coat may be necessary in the winter. In fact, in the higher elevations that experience snow, you may need a hat, boots, and gloves. Pack sturdy walking shoes for extensive sightseeing or strenuous hiking as well as long pants to protect against ticks.

TOURIST INFORMATION

For a copy of *Travel Tennessee: The Official Tennessee Vacation Guide,* contact the **Tennessee Department of Tourist Development,** PO Box 23170, Nashville, TN 37202-3170 (tel 615/741-2158). The state's home page (http://www.state.tn.us) contains general information about the state. To find out how to obtain tourist information for individual cities and parks in Tennessee, look under specific cities in the listings section of this book.

DRIVING RULES AND REGULATIONS

The maximum speed on interstates is 65 mph, 55 mph on major highways (unless otherwise posted). Tennessee law requires the use of seat belts for drivers and front seat passengers. All children under the age of four must be properly restrained in a child restraint device. The use of headlights is required during foggy conditions, and approved helmets are mandatory for motorcyclists. No open containers of alcoholic substances are permitted.

RENTING A CAR

All of the major national car rental companies have outlets in Tennessee. The minimum age to rent a car varies by company, so drivers between 21 and 25 should check ahead to make sure they qualify. Before you go, check your insurance or credit card to see if coverage extends to rental cars.

- **Alamo** (tel toll free 800/327-9633)
- **Avis** (tel 800/831-2847)
- **Budget** (tel 800/527-0700)
- **Dollar** (tel 800/800-4000)
- **Hertz** (tel 800/654-3131)
- **National** (tel 800/227-7368)
- **Thrifty** (tel 800/367-2277)

ESSENTIALS

Area Code: Tennessee has three area codes. In the western part of the state (including Memphis and Jackson), the area code is **901.** The central part of the state (including Nashville) uses the **615** area code. Beginning September 1, 1995, the eastern part of the state (including Chattanooga, Knoxville, and Bristol) began using the **423** area code.

AVG MONTHLY TEMPS (°F) & RAINFALL (IN)		
	Knoxville	Memphis
Jan	39/4.6	40/4.6
Feb	42/4.2	44/4.3
Mar	50/5.5	52/5.4
Apr	60/3.9	63/5.8
May	68/3.7	71/5.1
June	75/4.0	79/3.6
July	78/4.3	80/4.0
Aug	77/3.0	81/3.7
Sept	73/3.0	74/3.6
Oct	60/2.7	63/2.4
Nov	54/3.8	55/4.2
Dec	41/4.6	43/4.8

Emergencies: 911 is used statewide for summoning emergency aid. Motorists with a cellular phone can call *847 (THP) to be connected with a state trooper.

Liquor Laws: The legal drinking age is 21. Ten of Tennessee's 95 counties allow retail package store sales of alcoholic beverages. Four of these—Davidson (Nashville), Shelby (Memphis), Hamilton (Chattanooga), and Knox (Knoxville)—also allow the sale of liquor by the drink. Within the dry counties, some municipalities allow liquor sales; call the local chamber of commerce if in doubt.

Road Info: For information on the location of interstate construction, call the Tennessee Department of Transportation (tel toll free 800/858-6349).

Smoking: Smoking policies are set at the local level, and there is no uniform law pertaining to smoking in public places. Many restaurants, however, have elected to set aside nonsmoking areas.

Taxes: Tennessee's state sales tax is 6%, and counties may levy additional taxes of up to 2.7%.

Time Zone: Tennessee overlaps two time zones. The eastern part of the state (including Chattanooga and Knoxville) is in the Eastern time zone, while the remainder of the state is in the Central time zone. The entire state observes daylight saving time.

Best of the State

WHAT TO SEE AND DO

Below is a general overview of some of the top sights and attractions in Tennessee. To find out more detailed information, look under "Attractions" under individual cities in the listings portion of this book.

National Parks Foremost among national parks in the United States is the **Great Smoky Mountains National Park.** One of the largest protected land areas east of the Rockies, the park's 500,000 acres straddle the state border between Tennessee and North Carolina. Countless recreational opportunities are offered year-round, amid an enormous variety of plant and animal life. The **Big South Fork National River and Recreation Area,** accessed from Jamestown and Oneida, consists of 105,000 acres of scenic beauty and facilities for camping, hiking, and horseback riding. Mountain biking, swimming, fishing, hunting, canoeing, and white-water rafting are also popular here. At the **Cumberland Gap National Historical Park,** visitors can check out the pinnacle overlook, iron furnace, and pioneer settlement before getting their exercise along the 70 miles of hiking trails.

State Parks Unspoiled and natural, Tennessee's 50 state parks offer visitors year-round access to the splendor of the great outdoors. Deer, wild geese, and other types of wildlife are often sighted. Modern facilities include fully equipped marinas, resort inns, cabins, campgrounds, playgrounds, restaurants, and tennis courts. Eight of the parks boast golf courses and three have stables.

Natural Wonders Tennessee's size and geologic diversity make it among the richest Southern states in natural phenomena. For example, 13,000-acre **Reelfoot Lake,** in Tiptonville, was created by a series of earthquakes in 1811. The same geological upheavals have given the state many of its majestic mountains and fascinating caverns. The **Bell Witch Cave** in Adams is said to be haunted; the **Southport Saltpeter Cave** in Columbia is rich with various natural formations and Civil War history; **Raccoon Mountain Caverns** in Chattanooga are a crystal palace made of the most concentrated rock formations in the Southeast; **Wonder Cave** in Monteagle has been open since 1900 and is one of the oldest commercial caves in the country; **Tuckaleechee Caverns** in Townsend is noted for its onyx formations, high waterfalls, and large passageways. One of the most unusual caves anywhere is the **Lost Sea** in Sweetwater, where visitors can take a glass-bottom boat ride on a 4½-acre underground lake. Another spectacular and unexpected underground sight is **Ruby Falls** near Chattanooga, a 140-foot cascade located 1,120 feet below ground.

In the eastern part of the state, wild mountain rivers plunge over ledges and create spectacular waterfalls. Pikeville's **Fall Creek Falls** is one of the tallest (156 feet) waterfalls in the South. The unique **Virgin Falls,** near Sparta, are formed by an underground stream that emerges from a cave, drops 110 feet over a cliff, and then disappears back into the cave. Not all of Tennessee's waters are wild and uncontrolled; some of them have been noted for their purity and/or medicinal qualities. Historic **Beaty Springs,** near Jamestown, served as a source of fresh water for Native Americans and early pioneers. Today, its water is bottled and sold as Tennessee Branch Water. **Red Boiling Springs,** in the town of the same name near Lafayette, gave rise to a thriving mineral water health spa with two dozen hotels and boardinghouses at the turn of the century. You can test the healing waters yourself from several pumps around town. **Ebbing and Flowing Spring** in Rogersville flows regularly at 2-hour, 40-minute intervals. All that remains of an ancient stone monolith used in rituals by the Cherokee is the **Standing Stone Monument,** Monterey.

Manmade Wonders Tennesseans have long been at work striving to eclipse nature in the creation of awe-inspiring marvels. With 2,300 miles of shoreline, **Kentucky Lake** in northwest Tennessee is the second-largest manmade lake in the world. **Watts Bar Lake,** Spring City, is a major link in the nation's inland waterway system. The lock at the dam requires a lift of as much as 70 feet between the river and the lake. The route of the **Lookout Mountain Incline Railway** in Chattanooga has been called "America's Most Amazing Mile." (In some sections, the railway climbs at a 70° incline.) Built in the last century to celebrate Nashville's centennial, **The Parthenon** is the world's only full-size replica of the ancient temple in Athens. As spectacular as the building is, an even greater surprise is found inside: a 42-foot-tall statue of the goddess Athena. The world's oldest nuclear reactor, the **Graphite Reactor** at Oak Ridge, was built during World War II as part of the Manhattan Project. The skyline of downtown Memphis sports a 32-story glass-covered **Pyra-**

mid, modeled after the Egyptian pyramids of antiquity. The third-largest pyramid in the world, it serves as a venue for sports competitions.

Family Favorites With gigantic amusement parks such as Opryland USA, Dollywood, and Twitty City, some folks have called Tennessee one big theme park. There are also many less-obvious sites families will want to visit. It's practically a morning tradition in Memphis to go downtown and watch the **Peabody Ducks** descend the elevator, waddle across the red carpet, and hop into the fountain in the famous hotel's lobby. (After paddling around all day, the ducks go back upstairs in the afternoon.) Children's museums are on the rise in Tennessee. Housed in an old armory, the **Children's Museum of Memphis** is a hands-on discovery museum complete with a kid-size city. A flight simulator is the star attraction at the **Children's Discovery House** in Murfreesboro. Emphasis is on the Appalachian region and the city of Oak Ridge at the **Children's Museum of Oak Ridge. Libertyland** in Memphis offers 22 rides, including one of North America's oldest operating wooden roller coasters and a 1909 carousel, as well as live entertainment.

Tennessee's many major rivers and lakes provide a great atmosphere for a riverboat ride aboard an old-fashioned paddlewheeler. Some of the best are in Chattanooga, Nashville, and Memphis. There are even "water taxis" that whisk visitors back and forth between downtown Nashville and Opryland USA. Ride a monorail across the Mississippi River to **Mud Island** in Memphis, a 52-acre park and entertainment complex dedicated to life on the Big Muddy. Among the island's attractions are the **Mississippi River Museum,** a full-scale replica of an 1870 riverboat, the famous World War II B-17 bomber the *Mississippi Belle,* a detailed five-block-long scale model tracing the river's course, an amphitheater, and several restaurants.

Historic Buildings Tennessee has spawned three presidents: Andrew Jackson, Andrew Johnson, and James K Polk. The beautiful **Hermitage Home of Andrew Jackson,** near Nashville, sits on sweeping grounds that contain formal gardens, several original log cabins, other outbuildings, the tombs of Jackson and his wife Rachel, and a visitors center and museum. Guided tours include a visit to the nearby **Hermitage Church** and **Tulip Grove,** the home of Jackson's nephew. The **James K Polk Ancestral Home** in Columbia was built in 1816 and

is furnished with relics from Polk's White House years. Next door in the **Polk Sisters' House** are exhibits such as Mrs Polk's ball gown, jewels, the inaugural Bible, and memorabilia from the Mexican War. The **Andrew Johnson National Historic Site** in Greenville preserves two of the former president's homes, his tailor shop, and some of his personal belongings. There's also contains a visitors center and a National Cemetery.

Despite the amount of Civil War combat that took place in Tennessee, many significant antebellum buildings have survived. Built in 1828, the 2-story, 142-foot-long **Wynnewood** in Gallatin is the largest log structure ever constructed in Tennessee. Renowned as the "Queen of Tennessee Plantations," **Belle Meade Plantation** in Nashville was once an important stud farm. The site includes the mansion and outbuildings as well as a carriage collection housed in the former stables. A near-perfect example of Victorian architecture, **Glenmore Mansion** in Jefferson City is a T-shaped, 27-room mansion with five stories and an adjoining three-story section. The **Dickson-Williams Mansion** in Greeneville was known as the "Showplace of East Tennessee." It took six years to build (1815–1821) and is particularly noted for its three-story circular staircase. Both Union and Confederate armies commandeered it for use as a headquarters during the Civil War.

Civil War Sites Many significant Civil War battles were fought on Tennessee soil. **Shiloh National Military Park,** near Memphis, was the scene of one of the bloodiest battles of the war. The 4,000-acre park has a multimedia presentation describing the April 1862 battle, a 9½-mile self-guided auto tour, and a National Cemetery with over 3,500 grave sites. **Fort Donelson National Battlefield,** near Dover, was the site of the first major Union victory. The earthen fort, river batteries, outer earthworks, Dover Hotel, and National Cemetery are preserved. A six-mile self-guided auto route begins at the museum and interpretive center. Another 23,000 casualties fell during the battle on the site of what is now **Stones River National Battlefield** in Murfreesboro. The 400-acre park includes a National Cemetery and the oldest intact Civil War Memorial (erected in 1863). The **Chickamauga and Chattanooga National Military Park** straddles the Georgia/Tennessee border; the Chattanooga unit contains the site of "the Battle Above the Clouds," which took place on Lookout Mountain.

Museums Tennessee has museums dedicated to everything from beer and soda cans (**Museum of Beverage Containers and Advertising** in Goodlettsville) to tobacco (**Museum of Tobacco Art and History** in Nashville). Hunters and their dogs are honored at the **National Bird Dog Museum and Field Trial Hall of Fame** in Grand Junction (near Memphis), while the stately Tennessee Walking Horse is lauded at the **Tennessee Walking Horse Museum** in Shelbyville. The **Sequoyah Birthplace Museum** in Vonore tells the story of the inventor of the Cherokee alphabet. The **Museum of Appalachia** in Norris is considered to be the most authentic and complete replica of Appalachian pioneer life in the world. Collected on the 65-acre site are a total of 30 buildings and 250,000 artifacts. Mountain life is also portrayed and preserved at the **Folklife Center of the Smokies** at Cosby. The **National Civil Rights Museum,** located at the Lorraine Motel in Memphis, commemorates the site of Dr Martin Luther King Jr's 1968 assassination. Interpretive exhibits and audio-visual displays bring the civil rights struggle to life.

Music Attractions Tennessee has made an extraordinary contribution to America's musical heritage. First among all music shrines is **Graceland,** Elvis Presley's estate and burial place in Memphis. In addition to touring the mansion, you can see his automobile collection, two private jets, and tour bus. Fans of early rock 'n' roll will also want to check out Memphis's **Sun Studio,** where 1950s sessions launched the careers of the King as well as Jerry Lee Lewis, B B King, Muddy Waters, Roy Orbison, Johnny Cash, Carl Perkins, and others. (The tiny studio is still in operation today.) At the **Beale Street Historic District,** you can learn more about the birth of the blues by visiting the **W C Handy Museum** and then check out the state of modern blues music at any one of several nearby nightclubs. At **Loretta Lynn's Ranch** in Hurricane Mills, guests can tour the country music star's home and see memorabilia from her career and a reconstruction of her childhood home. Nashville is crammed with dozens of country music attractions but if you only have time to see one, go to the **Country Music Hall of Fame.** The complex, in the heart of Nashville's Music Row, contains rare artifacts and personal mementos from legendary performers as well as hot new stars. You can also take in a performance of the **Grand Ole Opry** at its present home near Opryland, or visit its old digs, the **Ryman Auditorium.**

Gardens Tennessee's moderate climate permits nature's beauty to flourish most of the year. Distinctive formal and informal plant collections include the **Cheekwood-Tennessee Botanical Gardens** in Nashville, the **Memphis Botanical Garden,** the **Reflection Riding driving tour** at the 300-acre Chattanooga Nature Center, and Chattanooga's **River Gallery Sculpture Garden.** The unique **Christus Gardens** in Gatlinburg combines blossoming displays with re-creations of Biblical scenes.

Parks & Zoos The **Memphis Zoo and Aquarium** is home to nearly 3,000 animals representing 400 species. (Among the newest exhibits are Cat Country, Animals of the Night, and Primate Canyon.) More than 1,000 exotic animals from around the world reside in a naturalistic environment at **Knoxville Zoological Gardens,** and the **Nashville Zoo** houses examples of several rare cat species (including snow leopards and white tigers). Animals indigenous to Tennessee are the highlight at Nashville's **Grassmere Wildlife Park** while Chattanooga's huge new state-of-the-art **Tennessee Aquarium** is devoted to freshwater fish and mammals.

Breweries, Distilleries & Wineries Think of Tennessee and liquid libations in the same breath and you may automatically think of bourbon and sour-mash whiskey. Oldest and foremost among distilleries is the **Jack Daniel's Distillery** in Lynchburg, where visitors may observe every step of the sour-mash whiskey art. You can also observe whiskey making at the **George A Dickel and Co Distillery** in Tullahoma. Tennessee's beer-brewing and wine-making industries are less well known but just as active. Among the breweries open to visitors are the **Coors Brewery** in Memphis and the **Bohannon Brewing Company** in Nashville. The state's premier wineries include **Cordova Cellars Winery and Vineyard** and **Laurel Hill Vineyard** in Memphis, **Twin Oaks Vineyard and Winery** in Shiloh, **Smoky Mountain Winery** in Gatlinburg, and **Mountain Valley Vineyards** in Pigeon Forge.

EVENTS AND FESTIVALS

- **Pigeon Forge Spring Kick-Off Parade,** Pigeon Forge. Floats and bands kick off the summer tourist season. Late April. Call toll free 800/251-9100.
- **Main Street Festival,** Franklin. Craftspeople, food, live entertainment, dancing. Late April. Call 615/790-7094.

- **Tennessee Renaissance Festival,** Triune. Medieval jousting, musicians, entertainers, food. Weekends in May. Call 615/320-9333.
- **Memphis in May,** Memphis. Barbecue cook-off, music, art exhibits, Beale Street Music Festival. Call 901/525-4611.
- **Summer Lights in Music City Festival,** Nashville. Music, art, dance, theater. Early June. Call 615/259-0900.
- **The Riverbend Festival,** Chattanooga. Sporting events, children's activities, fine arts, fireworks. Late June. Call 423/265-4112.
- **Old Time Fiddlers' Jamboree and Crafts Festival,** Smithville. Bluegrass music, clogging, buck dancing, folk singing, crafts, food. Late June or early July. Call 615/597-4163.
- **Jonesborough Days,** Jonesborough. Arts and crafts exhibitors, entertainment, music, clogging, tours, parade, fireworks. Early July. Call 423/753-5281.
- **Elvis Week,** Memphis. Dance party, memorabilia convention, candlelight vigil, laser show, 5K run. Mid-August. Call toll free 800/238-2000.
- **Appalachian Fair,** Gray. Country music entertainment, auto shows, livestock shows, midway. Late August. Call 423/477-3211.
- **Italian Street Fair,** Nashville. Food, rides, boutiques, entertainment, arts and crafts. Early September. Call 615/329-3033.

SPECTATOR SPORTS

Auto Racing For fast-paced motorsports, auto shows, and motorcycle races, check out the **Memphis Motorsports Park** (tel 901/358-7223). The **Nashville Motor Raceway** at the State Fairgrounds (tel 615/726-1818) attracts many top drivers during its April-to-October season. The high, banked curves of the **Bristol International Raceway** (tel 423/764-1161) make it one of the world's fastest half-mile tracks; it hosts two major NASCAR events as well as NASCAR's only night race.

Baseball Tennessee has no major league teams, but there are a plethora of minor league teams from which to choose. The **Memphis Chicks,** a class AA farm team for the Kansas City Royals, play at Tim McCarver Stadium (tel 901/272-1687). The **Nashville Sounds,** a AAA Chicago White Sox farm team, play at Herschel Greer Stadium (tel 615/242-4371). Among other teams are the **Chattanooga Lookouts** (tel 423/267-2208), who play at Engel Stadium; and

the **Knoxville Smokies** (tel 423/637-9494), who play at Bill Meyer Stadium.

Basketball The **University of Tennessee Volunteers** play at Thompson Boling Arena in Knoxville (tel 423/974-1212), while the **Vanderbilt University Commodores** (tel 615/322-4121) play at Memorial Gym in Nashville.

Boxing Professional boxing matches sanctioned by the World Boxing Federation are slugged out at the **Bristol Sports Arena** (tel 423/764-1161).

College Football The **University of Tennessee Volunteers** play at Neyland Stadium, Knoxville (tel 423/974-1212); and the **Vanderbilt University Commodores** (tel 615/322-4121) play at Vanderbilt Stadium, Nashville. The **Liberty Bowl Football Classic** post-season college game is held each year at the Liberty Memorial Stadium in Memphis (tel 901/795-7700).

Hockey The **Memphis Riverkings** of the Continental Hockey League play at the Mid-South Coliseum (tel 901/278-9009). The **Nashville Knights,** a farm team for the NHL's Pittsburgh Penguins, play at that city's Municipal Auditorium (tel 615/255-7825).

Equestrian Events Shelbyville is the home to one of the world's greatest walking horse shows: the **Tennessee Walking Horse National Celebration** (tel 615/684-5915). More than 2,000 horses participate each year.

Greyhound Racing The dogs run at **Southland Greyhound Park** (tel 501/735-3670) in West Memphis, AR, right across the Mississippi from Memphis proper. Nightly races and matinee races are held year-round.

ACTIVITIES A TO Z

Boating With dozens of TVA lakes and other major reservoirs, and hundreds of miles of navigable rivers (such as the Cumberland, Tennessee, and Mississippi), Tennessee offers thousands of acres of water surface for boating. Kentucky Lake, located near Paris, is 184 miles long and has more than 2,300 miles of shoreline. Center Hill, Cordell, Dale Hollow, Nickajack, Norris, Pickwick, and Watts Bar Lakes are popular for houseboating.

Fishing Tennessee's 19,000 miles of streams and thousands of smaller lakes are perfect for the weekend angler. The state is known for its abundance of catfish, a variety of bass species, crappie, bluegill, pickerel, walleye, and yellow perch. The world's record smallmouth bass was hooked in Tennessee, as was the world's record walleye and brown trout. Call the **Tennessee Wildlife Resources Agency** (tel 615/781-6500) for information on license requirements.

Golf   The only trouble with playing the challenging links in Tennessee is that the spectacular surrounding scenery may distract you from your game. The pleasant climate makes play possible year-round in most areas. The **Legends Club of Tennessee** (tel 615/791-8100) was ranked one of the state's top five courses by *Golf Week* magazine. Located in Franklin, just south of Nashville, the club features two 18-hole courses. Eight of Tennessee's state parks also operate well-maintained public courses; call 615/532-0446 for information on these courses.

Hang Gliding   Tennessee's tall mountains and broad valleys provide ideal launching and landing conditions for hang gliding. Chattanooga is a hotbed for the sport. The **Raccoon Mountain Adventure Park,** US 41 (tel 423/825-0444), features the nation's only hang-gliding simulator and offers programs for both the novice and the experienced glider. The Chattanooga-area **Lookout Mountain Flight Park** is actually just across the Georgia state border (tel toll free 800/688-LMFP). **Sequatchie Valley Soaring Supply** in Dunlap (tel 423/949-2301) is another source for instruction and practice.

Hiking   Tennessee's network of local, state, and national parks provides hundreds of miles of well-developed and -maintained hiking trails in all types of terrain and levels of difficulty. Trail maps can be obtained from the individual parks. Tennessee's section of the Appalachian Trail can accessed at Elizabethton. (For more information about the trail, contact the **Appalachian Trail Conference** in Asheville, NC, at 704/254-3708). There are nearly 400 miles of hiking trails in Great Smoky Mountains National Park, while 70 miles of trails—including the Daniel Boone Wilderness Trail—can be hiked in the Cumberland Gap National Historical Park. The scenic highlight of the 10-mile Piney River Trail at Spring City is a crossing of a 100-foot-high suspension bridge.

Horseback Riding   Horseback riding trips—lasting from an hour to overnight—are among the most popular outings in Tennessee. There are riding stables all over the state, but they are especially concentrated in the area around the Smokies. Just a few recommended stables you might want to contact for more information are: **McCarter's Stables** in

---

SELECTED PARKS & RECREATION AREAS

- **Great Smoky Mountains National Park,** 107 Park Headquarters Rd, Gatlinburg, TN 37738 (tel 423/436-1200)
- **Big South Fork National River and Recreation Area,** Rte 3, Box 401, Oneida, TN 37841 (tel 615/879-4890)
- **Obed National Wild and Scenic River,** Box 429, Wartburg, TN 37887 (tel 423/346-6294)
- **Shiloh National Military Park,** Box 67, Shiloh, TN 38376 (tel 901/689-5275)
- **Fort Donelson National Battlefield,** Box 434, Dover, TN 37058 (tel 615/232-5348)
- **Burgess Falls State Natural Area,** TN 135, Sparta, TN 38583 (tel 615/432-5312)
- **Chickasaw State Rustic Park,** TN 100, Jackson, TN (tel 901/989-5141)
- **David Crockett State Park,** US 64, Lawrenceburg, TN 38464 (tel 615/762-9408)
- **Davy Crockett Birthplace State Park,** US 11E, Limestone, TN 37681 (tel 423/257-2167)
- **Dunbar Cave State Natural Area,** TN 13, Clarksville, TN 37043 (tel 615/648-5526)
- **Fall Creek Falls State Resort Park,** TN 30, Pikeville, TN 37367 (tel 423/881-3297)
- **Fort Loudon State Historical Area,** US 411, Vonore, TN 37885 (tel 423/884-6217)
- **Natchez Trace State Resort Park,** off I-40, Wildersville, TN 38388 (tel 901/968-8176)
- **Nathan Bedford Forrest State Historical Area,** TN 191, Camden/Eva, TN 38333 (tel 901/584-6356)
- **Old Stone Fort State Archaeological Area,** US 41, Manchester, TN 37355 (tel 615/722-5073)
- **Paris Landing State Park,** US 79, Paris, TN 38242 (tel 901/644-7359)
- **Reelfoot Lake State Resort Park,** TN 21/78, Tiptonville, TN 38079 (tel 901/253-7756)
- **Roan Mountain State Resort Park,** TN 143, Roan Mountain, TN 37687 (tel 423/772-3303)
- **Sgt Alvin York's Gristmill and State Park,** US 127N, Pall Mall, TN 38577 (tel 615/879-4026)
- **Standing Stone State Rustic Park,** TN 52, Livingston, TN 38570 (tel 423/823-6347)
- **T O Fuller State Recreation Park,** US 61, 1500 Mitchell Rd W, Memphis, TN 38109 (tel 901/543-7581)

Gatlinburg (tel 423/436-5354); **Walden's Creek Horseback Riding** in Pigeon Forge (tel 423/429-0411); **Canyon Hills Riding Stables** in Sevierville (tel 423/428-3587); **Cades Cove Stables** (tel 423/448-6286) and **Davy Crockett Riding Stables** (tel 423/448-6411), both in Townsend.

Pack Trips The newest fad in hiking adventures is using friendly, placid llamas to carry the heavy stuff so you can conserve your energy for hiking. **Bentwood Farm Llamas** in Coker Creek (tel 423/261-2500) offers such trips to Cherokee National Forest and Coker Creek Falls; another option is the **Dunlap Rivendell Llama Farm** (tel 423/949-3868).

Sailing Sailing and yacht clubs dot the state's many mountain and flatland lakes. Sixty-mile-long **Fort Loudon Dam and Lake** is the home of a nationally recognized yacht club and the scene of colorful races every Sunday during the long sailing season. Call 423/986-3737 for more information.

Skiing The Great Smoky Mountains of east Tennessee are the site of a successful, though small, ski industry. **Ober Gatlinburg** (tel 423/436-5432) features two downhill slopes reached by a chair lift and a tram. Cross-country trails are maintained at **Roan Mountain State Park** (tel 423/772-3303) in the extreme northeastern corner of the state.

White-Water Rafting The state offers something for rafters and kayakers of every ability level. For beginners, **Elk River Canoe Rentals** in Kelso (tel 615/937-6886) and **Canoe the Sequatchie** in Dunlap (tel 423/949-4400) provide relaxing float trips. Numerous companies—such as **Hiwassee Outfitters** in Reliance (tel toll free 800/338-8133) and **Rapid Descent River Co** in Hartford (tel toll free 800/455-8808)—provide rental equipment and guided trips for more difficult rapids, like the famous Ocoee River (site of the 1996 Summer Olympics).

THE TENNESSEE RIVER VALLEY

Start	Chattanooga
Finish	Knoxville
Distance	130 miles
Time	2 days
Highlights	Civil War battlefield, Chattanooga Choo Choo, unusual rock formations, underground waterfall, caverns, museums, steepest incline railway in the country, gardens, freshwater aquarium, scenic railroad, Scopes Museum, locks and dams, hiking trails, historic homes, wineries, zoo, riverboat rides

A crescent-shaped wonder, the Tennessee River winds across four states, beginning where the Holston and French Broad Rivers merge at Knoxville and discharging into the Ohio River at Paducah, KY after having rolled across northern Alabama and a small corner of Mississippi along its 650-mile route. For most of its history, the river was hazardous or impractical for transportation. Places with names like the Narrows, the Suck, and the Boiling Pot testified to the river's dangers.

The Tennessee Valley Authority (TVA) was established by an act of Congress in 1933 to develop the entire Tennessee basin watershed—an area consisting of 40,000 square miles in seven states. Its comprehensive mission was to improve navigation, control flooding, combat erosion, generate power, enhance the residents' quality of life, and serve as a research center for water and soil management. In order to meet these directives, 10 massive dams and adjacent locks were built and the course of the river was modified. A pleasant side-benefit of this massive undertaking has been the development of numerous recreational facilities—including parks, boat launches, camping and picnicking facilities, and hiking trails—along the artificial lakes and the now-placid river. Along its course the Tennessee River also flows past historic sites, small towns, and bustling modern cities.

For additional information on lodgings, dining, and attractions in the region covered by the tour, look under specific cities in the listings portion of this chapter.

I-75 or I-24 give access to the first stop:

1. **Chattanooga,** a small city rich in Native American and Civil War history as well as in natural wonders. The surrounding region served as the last capital of the Cherokee Nation, and the name *Chattanooga* is believed to derive from the Cherokee word for "rock that comes to a point" (Lookout Mountain). Always an important crossroads, the area was traversed in ancient times by the Great Indian Warpath, a trail that stretched from Alabama to New York; another Native American trail ran diagonally from Manchester, TN, to St Augustine, FL.

A vital railroad junction during the Civil War, Chattanooga was also the gateway into Georgia and was, therefore, a pivotal city in the Union army's march to Atlanta. The major battle fought on Lookout Mountain, known as the Battle Above the Clouds, is commemorated at the **Chickamauga and Chattanooga National Military Park.** (The Chickamauga unit of the park is located in GA.) To understand how the battle progressed, begin with a stop at the **Battles for Chattanooga Museum,** 3742 Tennessee Ave, where a scale model of the area (including 5,000 miniature soldiers, 650 lights, and sound effects) re-creates the campaign for the city.

Next, experience "America's Most Amazing Mile" as you ride in the trolley-style railcars on the **Lookout Mountain Incline Railway,** 827 East Brow Rd, as it makes its mile-long, 72.7%-grade ascent to the summit of Lookout Mountain. (Not only is it the country's oldest incline railway, it is also the steepest.) Meanwhile, the **Point Park** unit of the Chickamauga and Chattanooga National Military Park encompasses a visitor center in which you can view James Walker's gigantic painting of the battle, several monuments, the Ochs Museum and Overlook, and the Bluff Trail.

Chattanooga contains several other sites that were significant to the Battle for Chattanooga. The **Cravens House Museum** on Lookout Mountain was the center of strenuous fighting. Union soldiers are buried at the **Chattanooga National Cemetery,** Holtzclaw and Bailey Ave. The National Park Service maintains several smaller sites: the **Orchard Knob Reservation,** Orchard Knob Ave at Third; **Missionary Ridge Reservation** and **Bragg Reservation,** both on Crest Rd; **Ohio Reservation; De-Long Reservation; Sherman Reservation;** and **Sig-**

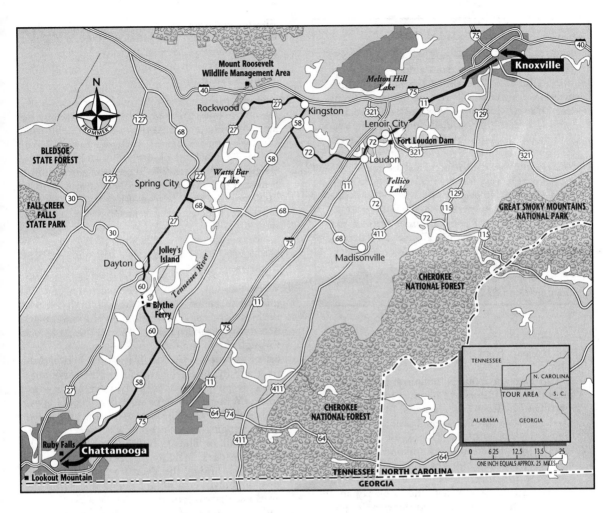

nal Mountain. The first Congressional Medals of Honor were awarded to Union soldiers; the history of the medal and other military events are described at the **National Medal of Honor Museum of Military History,** 400 Georgia Ave. At **Reflection Riding,** 400 Garden Rd, 354 acres that include Confederate trenches have been transformed into a botanical garden.

Now turn your attention to modern-day Chattanooga. Go downtown to the Tennessee River and stop at the **Welcome Center at Ross's Landing and Plaza** to see the multimedia presentation of Chattanooga history, *Marks on the Land.* Cross the square (through which a stream course representing the Tennessee River runs and imbedded art works and artifacts represent the history of the area) to the **Tennessee Aquarium,** One Broad St, the world's largest exhibit of freshwater fish and plant life. From Ross's Landing you can walk across the **Walnut Street Bridge,** a beautifully restored,

century-old steel-truss bridge believed to be the longest pedestrian bridge in the world, to the Audubon Society preserve at **McClellan Island Sanctuary.**

Visit the legendary **Chattanooga Choo Choo,** 1400 Market St, a complex of trains, shops, and restaurants built around the historic Beaux Arts **Terminal Station.** If you decide to spend the night, the complex's Holiday Inn offers standard hotel-style rooms as well as restored Victorian sleeper cars.

If you're a railroad buff, take time to visit the **Tennessee Valley Railroad,** 4119 Cromwell Rd. The largest operating historic railroad in the South conducts a 6½-mile round trip hourly between its two depots. If you are interested in getting out on the water to see Chattanooga from a different perspective, note that there are sightseeing, lunch, dinner, and moonlight cruises offered aboard the *Chattanooga Star* and the *Southern Belle,* both of

---

Take a Break

Diners at the **Chattanooga Choo Choo** (tel 423/266-5000) can choose from among several options. **Dinner in the Diner** serves up gourmet meals in an authentically restored railroad dining car. Entrees—including New York strip, rack of lamb in pecan crust, grilled salmon, pasta Provençal, and chicken roulade—range from $13 to $23 (by reservation only). The facility's **Gardens Restaurant** serves up a breakfast buffet; diners may choose from Monterey chicken, turkey pot pie, Cajun chicken pasta, or pit-smoked barbecue for lunch or dinner. Lunch portions average between $6 and $8, while dinner entrees are $10–$15. At the **Station House Restaurant**, patrons are served dinners of charbroiled chicken, filet mignon, baby back ribs, or golden fried jumbo shrimp by a singing wait staff. Entrees range between $12 and $19.

---

which depart from Ross's Landing (spring through fall).

Chattanooga abounds in natural geological formations. Most visitors to Chattanooga can't resist a stop at nearby **Rock City Gardens**, 1400 Patten Rd, Lookout Mountain, GA. (You'll probably have been seeing the SEE ROCK CITY signs for hundreds of miles.) Once the bottom of an inland sea, erosion, ice, wind, and earthquakes split and carved the sandstone into bizarre rock formations. Garnet and Frieda Carter, who owned the property in the 1920s, planted gardens around the rocky outcroppings and spectacular waterfall. They opened their gardens to the public and added overlooks, a swinging bridge, Fairyland Caverns, and Mother Goose Village. On a clear day you can see seven states from one of the overlooks.

At nearby **Ruby Falls**, Lookout Mountain Scenic Hwy, you can descend 1,120 feet into the ground to explore the fantastic stalagmites, stalactites, and other underground wonders culminating at the 145-foot subterranean waterfall. A forest of underground formations awaits on the Crystal Palace Tour at the **Raccoon Mountain Caverns**, 319 W Hills Dr. Snaking from the west through town and continuing east is the TVA's **Nickajack Lake**, a boating and fishing paradise with 192 miles of shoreline. The **Tennessee Riverpark** is a 20-mile walking, biking, and jogging path that stretches to **Chickamauga Lake and Dam.**

Take TN 58 north from Chattanooga to TN 60, which you will take north to:

2. **Blythe Ferry,** where you can cross toward the Meigs County shore and pass **Jolley's Island,** a 700-acre parcel of land where Sam Houston once lived.

Continue north on TN 60 to TN 30 and follow it 38 miles north to:

3. **Dayton,** forever remembered as the site of the famous Scopes "monkey trial," which pitted the aging William Jennings Bryan and defense attorney Clarence Darrow against each other in a debate about the teaching of evolution and the use of religion in public schools. The **Rhea County Courthouse,** 1475 Market St, has been restored to its 1925 appearance and converted into the **Scopes Museum,** which features memorabilia from the trial.

Return southeast on TN 30 to US 27, turn north for 17 miles toward Spring City, then east on TN 68 to the next stop:

4. **Watts Bar Lake.** With 72 miles of water and 783 miles of shoreline, the lake offers unlimited opportunities for water recreation and is particularly noted for its superb fishing. In order to pass boats through the 60-foot-wide by 360-foot-long lock, a lift of as much as 70 feet is required between the river and the lake. The **Watts Bar Nuclear Plant** is the only power plant in the country using water, coal, and nuclear power-generation technologies.

Nature lovers will be attracted to the hiking trails in the Stinging Fork Pocket Wilderness. The **Piney River Trail,** on Shut-In Gap Rd, is criss-crossed by several bridges, including a spectacular 100-foot suspension bridge; the **Twin Rocks Nature Trail,** also on Shut-In Gap Rd, includes a stop at a scenic overlook that towers above the Tennessee Valley and the Soak Creek and Piney River Gorges.

Return on TN 68 and turn north on US 27 to:

5. **Rockwood,** once a active mining town. The scenic overlook at the **Mount Roosevelt Wildlife Management Area** affords one of the best views in the state.

Continue on US 27 for 20 miles to:

6. **Kingston,** on the north end of Watts Bar Lake. The town's **Waterfront Park** provides good access to the lake and is the home of the Roane County boat races.

Take TN 58 south from Kingston, then TN 72 east for 10 miles to:

7. **Loudon,** a town with a focus on pre–Civil War history. After picking up self-guided walking tour brochures at 318 Angel Row, stop at the **Carmichael Inn,** Poplar St on the Courthouse Square, an 1810 log cabin that was once used as a stagecoach stop and today serves as a museum of antebellum local history. Now that the area surrounding

Loudon along the Tennessee River is becoming a center for winemaking, winery and vineyard tours are being offered by local producers. Both the **Loudon Valley Vineyards and Winery,** 525 Huff Ferry Rd, and the **Tennessee Valley Winery,** 15606 Hotchkiss Valley Rd, offer tours, tastings, and wine sales.

Follow TN 72 for 5 miles to:

8. **Lenoir City,** another important link on the Tennessee River. From the overlook at Fort Loudon, you can see the three uppermost TVA lakes: Fort Loudon, Watts Bar, and Tellico.

Turn southeast on US 321 and stay on for 5 miles. On the main channel of the river is the hydropower dam at **Fort Loudon Dam,** which you can visit by making prior arrangements. Also, there's an observatory/visitor center at **Melton Hill Dam and Lake** on the nearby Clinch River.

Return on US 321 to US 11 and take it 29 miles northeast to:

9. **Knoxville.** Located in the heart of the Southern Highlands, the city is surrounded by seven of the Tennessee Valley Authority's Great Lakes of the South. You might wish to begin your exploration of the town with a stop at the welcome center located in the **Sunsphere** at the World's Fair Park, a large golden orb that is a structural remnant of the 1982 World's Fair.

Knoxville is filled with beautiful antebellum structures. The earliest historic dwelling in Knoxville is **James White's Fort,** 205 East Hill Ave, constructed in 1786. The original "one-up, one-down" cabin housed a family of nine and served as an inn as well. Over the years, other structures were added, including a guest house, smokehouse, and loom house. The visitor center accommodates a small museum. Not far away is the **Blount Mansion,** 200 West Hill Ave. The first frame house built west of the Alleghenies, this mansion was the home of the territory's first governor. The interior furnishings are considered to be the finest collection of late-18th-century pieces in the area. Completed in 1797, the pink marble **Ramsey House,** 2614 Thorngrove Pike, was the first residence constructed of stone in Knox County. Among its outstanding architectural details are blue limestone quoins, keystone arches, and carvings under the dentilled cornices. Perched on a bluff overlooking a sweeping curve in the river, the **Armstrong-Locket House,** 2728 Kingston Pike, was called Crescent Bend because of its location. The cliff on which it sits has been transformed into a seven-tiered formal Italianate garden. Built in 1834, the restored mansion contains outstanding collections of American and English decorative arts, as well as English silver

from 1640 to 1820. **Marble Springs,** 1220 W Governor John Sevier Hwy, was the plantation home of Tennessee's first state governor. In addition to the house, you can tour six plantation buildings.

If you want to find out more general information about Knoxville's history, visit the **Frank H McClung Museum,** 1327 Circle Park Dr on the University of Tennessee campus. In addition to showcasing the state's geology, history, culture, and art, the museum also has prehistoric and Egyptian relics and exhibits. Military artifacts from the Revolutionary War through Desert Storm are displayed at the **Volunteer State Veterans Hall of Honor,** 4000 Chapman Hwy. Of particular interest are the items from the Mexican War. (It was Tennessee's very active participation in that war that won it its nickname: the Volunteer State.) In recognition of Tennessee's bitter division over the Civil War, both Confederate and Union artifacts are displayed. The Civil War is also interpreted through memorabilia and artifacts at **Confederate Memorial Hall,** 3148 Kingston Pike, a Victorian mansion occupied by Confederate Gen James Longstreet in 1863.

The natural and health sciences are the focus at the **East Tennessee Discovery Center,** 516 N Beaman St. In addition to the Akima Planetarium, the Kama Health Discovery, and the Discoverer Spacecraft, other highlights include the hands-on Cosmic Arcade, and the Kid Korner. Medical instruments and other memorabilia are the focus at the **Knoxville Academy of Medicine,** 422 Cumberland Ave. Visit the wild animals at the **Knoxville Zoological Gardens,** exit 392 off I-40, the parklike home of more than 1,000 rare animals including what is reputed to be the biggest collection of large cats in the country.

Take a Break

Located in a historic downtown warehouse and decked out in nautical decor to reflect its Maryland namesake, **Chesapeake's,** 500 Henley St (tel 423/673-3433), specializes in fresh seafood prepared using Eastern Shore recipes. Lunch entrees such as grilled salmon caesar salad or Thai pasta with peanut sauce cost $6 to $8, while dinner entrees (such as blue crab) range from $12 to $16. Maine lobster is priced by the pound. Steak and chicken dishes also available.

When the sun goes down, Knoxvillians really come out to play. Restaurants and nightspots abound around **World's Fair Park** and in the **Old**

City Historic District, the restored historic center of downtown where dance and concert clubs stay open until the wee hours. Known as the Music Crossroads of East Tennessee, the neighborhood offers jazz, classic rock, country, reggae, and other forms of popular music. Or, you may prefer to see the city from a leisurely dinner or moonlight cruise aboard the *Star of Knoxville* paddlewheeler, 300 Neyland Dr.

Knoxville is one of the gateways to **Great Smoky Mountains National Park,** which straddles the Tennessee/North Carolina border. To reach that area take US 441 southeast to Sevierville, Pigeon Forge, and Gatlinburg. From Knoxville you can take I-75 north into Kentucky, I-40/81 northeast into Virginia, or I-40 west to Nashville.

Tennessee Listings

Bristol

One of Tennessee's Tri-Cities (with Kingsport and Johnson City), with half of Bristol in Tennessee and half in Virginia. (The state line runs down the center of State Street.) Bristol International Raceway hosts many NASCAR events.

RESTAURANT 🍴

Athens Steak House
329 8th St; tel 423/652-2202. **American.** Upscale steak house that also offers a fine selection of seafood and Greek dishes. **FYI:** Reservations accepted. Children's menu. **Open:** Mon–Thurs 4–10pm, Fri–Sat 4–11pm. **Prices:** Main courses $8–$34. AE, DC, DISC, MC, V. ♥

ATTRACTION 🧳

Stacy Grayson Memorial at Steele Creek Park
Steele Creek Park Dr; tel 423/764-4023. A 2,300-acre city park with many of the recreational facilities of a more rural park. A 53-acre lake offers fishing, boating, and canoeing, while 25 miles of trails welcome hikers. The park's nature center even has a naturalist on staff. Golf, half-mile scenic train ride, lakeside pier, and paddleboats available Memorial Day–Labor Day. **Open:** Daily 9am–9pm. $

Caryville

Nearby Cove Lake State Park and Norris Reservoir draw many visitors (especially boaters) to this town in the northern section of the state.

MOTEL 🏨

≡≡ Holiday Inn
200 John McGee Blvd, PO Box 14, Rte 1, 37714; tel 423/562-8476 or toll free 800/640-9990; fax 423/562-8870. Exit 134 off I-75. Pleasant Holiday Inn offering beautiful views of the Cumberland Mountains. Located a mile from Cove Lake State Park. **Rooms:** 102 rms. CI noon/CO noon. Nonsmoking rms avail. **Amenities:** 📞 🍸 A/C, cable TV w/movies. Closed-captioned TV available in all rooms. **Services:** ✕ 🖨 🛎 🚭 **Facilities:** 🛗 🏊 ᴸ 1 restaurant, playground. **Rates**

(BB): Peak (June–Aug, Oct) $42–$49 S; $49–$65 D. Extra person $5. Children under age 20 stay free. Lower rates off-season. Parking: Outdoor, free. AE, CB, DC, DISC, JCB, MC, V.

RESTAURANT 🍴

Cove Lake Restaurant
In Cove Lake State Park, US 25W & I-65; tel 423/566-8848. Off I-75. **American.** Enjoy a wonderful view of the Cumberland Mountains while you dine on such specialties as veal parmesan, chopped sirloin, and catfish. **FYI:** Reservations not accepted. Children's menu. No liquor license. No smoking. **Open:** Sat–Thurs 11am–8pm, Fri–Sat 11am–9pm. **Prices:** Main courses $7–$9. MC, V. 🏔 🧺 ᴸ

ATTRACTION 🧳

Cove Lake State Park
US 25W; tel 423/566-9701. A 3,000-acre park situated in a picturesque valley and anchored by 210-acre Cove Lake. Not surprisingly, boating and fishing are popular, with bass, bluegill, and crappie the most common catches. The park also offers campsites, a year-round restaurant with a view of the lake, a swimming pool, and a picnic area with grills. **Open:** Daily 8am–sunset. **Free**

Chattanooga

Located in a mountainous region just north of the Georgia state line on the Tennessee River, this manufacturing, railroad, and tourism center is southeast Tennessee's largest metropolis. Historic Lookout Mountain lies to the southwest, and nearby are several Civil War battlefields. The University of Tennessee has a campus here. **Information:** Chattanooga Area Convention & Visitors Bureau, 1001 Market St, Chattanooga, 37402 (tel 423/756-8687).

HOTELS 🏨

≡≡≡ Chattanooga Choo Choo Holiday Inn
1400 Market St, 37402 (Downtown); tel 423/266-5000 or toll free 800/872-2529; fax 423/265-4635. Exit 178 off I-24. Originally built in 1909, and now listed on the National

Register of Historic Places, this converted railroad station contains gardens, fountains, old-fashioned shops, and a model railroad exhibit in addition to the hotel. The depot's Grand Dome, which presides over the hotel's 68 ft by 82 ft lobby, is lavishly beautiful in its prismatic colors. **Rooms:** 360 rms and stes; 48 cottages/villas. CI 3pm/CO 11am. Nonsmoking rms avail. Most rooms are standard, hotel-style rooms, but converted sleeper cars house 49 suites. **Amenities:** 🛁 🧖 A/C, cable TV w/movies. Some units w/terraces. **Services:** ✕ ☎ 🚗 🖨 🔌 **Facilities:** 🏋 🏞 🐎 🎾 ⚓ ⛵ 250 ⛳ 4 restaurants, 2 bars (1 w/entertainment), games rm. Hotel bar is in renovated Wabash Cannonball club car. **Rates:** Peak (May–Sept) $78–$95 S or D; $175 ste; $115 cottage/villa. Lower rates off-season. Parking: Outdoor, free. Family rates avail. AE, DC, DISC, MC, V.

⬛⬛⬛ Chattanooga Clarion Hotel

407 Chestnut St, 37402; tel 423/756-5150 or toll free 800/221-2222; fax 423/265-8708. 4th St exit off US 27. Located within walking distance of the Aquarium, the Creative Discovery Museum, and other downtown attractions, this chain hotel is a popular resting spot for families. **Rooms:** 205 rms and stes. CI 3pm/CO 11am. Nonsmoking rms avail. **Amenities:** 🛁 🧖 A/C, cable TV w/movies. **Services:** ✕ ☎ 🖨 🔌 Car-rental desk, babysitting. **Facilities:** 🏋 🐎 500 ⛳ 1 restaurant, 1 bar (w/entertainment), beauty salon. Guest privileges at nearby health club. **Rates:** Peak (May–Oct) $99 S or D; $199–$249 ste. Children under age 3 stay free. Min stay wknds and special events. Lower rates off-season. Parking: Outdoor, $1/day. Aquarium, Creative Discovery, and "Riverboats & Romance" packages avail. AE, CB, DC, DISC, MC, V.

⬛⬛ Guesthouse Inn

100 W 21st St, 37408 (Downtown); tel 423/265-3151 or toll free 800/828-4656; fax 423/265-3532. Exit 178 off I-24. Handsome and well-maintained. Located off of the same highway exit as the Chattanooga Choo-Choo, the Creative Discovery Center, and the Tennessee Aquarium. **Rooms:** 103 rms. CI 2pm/CO 11am. Nonsmoking rms avail. Rooms are clean and comfortable. **Amenities:** 🛁 A/C, cable TV w/movies. Some units w/terraces. **Services:** ✕ 🔌 🐕 **Facilities:** 🏋 50 ⛳ 1 restaurant, 1 bar (w/entertainment), washer/dryer. Large pool. **Rates:** Peak (June–Aug) $44–$54 S or D. Children under age 18 stay free. Lower rates off-season. Parking: Outdoor, free. AE, DC, DISC, MC, V.

⬛⬛⬛ Marriott at the Convention Center

2 Carter Plaza, 37402; tel 423/756-0002 or toll free 800/841-1674; fax 423/266-5147. MLK exit off US 27. A modern facility with direct access to the adjoining Chattanooga Convention Center. Located near major company headquarters and downtown attractions. **Rooms:** 343 rms and stes. Executive level. CI 4pm/CO noon. Nonsmoking rms avail. Views of Lookout Mountain or the city from every room. **Amenities:** 🛁 🧖 A/C, cable TV w/movies, dataport, voice mail. **Services:** ✕ ☎ 🆅🅿 🖨 🔌 **Facilities:** 🏋 🐎 400 ⛳ 2 restaurants (see

"Restaurants" below), 2 bars (w/entertainment), games rm, sauna, whirlpool. Hotel located on free shuttle route. **Rates:** Peak (June, Oct, Dec) $85–$105 S or D; $185 ste. Children under age 18 stay free. Min stay special events. Lower rates off-season. Parking: Indoor, $6/day. Marriott Two for Breakfast, Aquarium, Creative Discovery, Lookout Mountain, Discover Chattanooga, and honeymoon packages avail. AE, CB, DC, DISC, MC, V.

⬛⬛⬛ Radisson Read House Hotel and Suites

Martin Luther King Blvd & Broad St, PO Box 11165, 37401; tel 423/266-4121; fax 423/267-6447. Off US 27. Recognized as a National Historic Site and as a Historic Hotel of America. The third floor was utilized as a hospital for both North and South during the Civil War, and five US presidents have stayed here. Each of the 13 floors of the hotel showcase framed, museum-quality illustrations of various Civil War battles. **Rooms:** 237 rms and stes. Executive level. CI 3pm/CO noon. Nonsmoking rms avail. **Amenities:** 🛁 🧖 A/C, cable TV w/movies. **Services:** ✕ 🆅🅿 🚗 🖨 🔌 Babysitting. **Facilities:** 🏋 🐎 500 ⛳ 2 restaurants (see "Restaurants" below), 2 bars, beauty salon. **Rates:** Peak (June–Aug/Oct) $105 S or D; $115 ste. Children under age 17 stay free. Min stay special events. Lower rates off-season. Parking: Indoor/outdoor, $4/day. AE, CB, DC, DISC, JCB, MC, V.

MOTELS

⬛⬛⬛ Best Western Airport Inn

6650 Ringgold Rd, 37412; tel 423/894-1860 or toll free 800/528-1234; fax 423/894-1860 ext 300. Exit 1 off I-75. This beautifully decorated Best Western is convenient to downtown but not in the middle of the traffic. **Rooms:** 123 rms. CI 3pm/CO 11am. Nonsmoking rms avail. **Amenities:** 🛁 A/C, cable TV w/movies, dataport. Some units w/whirlpools. **Services:** ✕ 🚐 🔌 Babysitting. **Facilities:** 🏋 75 ⛳ The only indoor pool in this area. **Rates (CP):** Peak (Mar 15–Oct 15) $60–$100 S or D. Extra person $10. Children under age 18 stay free. Min stay special events. Lower rates off-season. Parking: Outdoor, free. Romantic, Aquarium, Lookout Mountain, "See Chattanooga," and school-group packages avail. AE, CB, DC, DISC, ER, JCB, MC, V.

⬛⬛⬛ Comfort Suites

7324 Shallowford Rd, 37421; tel 615/892-1500 or toll free 800/221-2222; fax 615/892-1500 ext 110. Exit 5 off I-75. This all-suite motel features large rooms with plenty of space to relax. **Rooms:** 62 stes. CI 2pm/CO 11am. Nonsmoking rms avail. Each room has a sofa sleeper. **Amenities:** 🛁 🧖 📺 🍽 A/C, satel TV w/movies, refrig. Some units w/whirlpools. Microwaves are standard in all rooms. **Services:** ✕ 🖨 🔌 **Facilities:** 🏋 🐎 40 ⛳ Whirlpool, washer/dryer. **Rates (CP):** Peak (June–Aug) $68–$78 ste. Extra person $5. Children under age 12 stay free. Lower rates off-season. Parking: Outdoor, free. AE, CB, DC, DISC, ER, JCB, MC, V.

Hampton Inn Airport
7013 Shallowford Rd, 37421; tel 423/855-0095 or toll free 800/426-7866; fax 423/855-0095. Exit 5 off I-75. Standard chain motel accommodations, located near shopping and restaurants. **Rooms:** 126 rms and stes. CI 3pm/CO 11am. Nonsmoking rms avail. **Amenities:** A/C, cable TV w/movies. **Services:** **Facilities:** 25 **Rates (CP):** Peak (June–Aug) $55–$69 S; $59–$78 D; $104 ste. Extra person $8–$10. Children under age 18 stay free. Lower rates off-season. Parking: Outdoor, free. Two guests stay for the price of one, four guests stay for the price of two. AE, CB, DC, DISC, MC, V.

Holiday Inn Lookout Mountain
3800 Cummings Hwy, 37419; tel 423/821-3531 or toll free 800/HOLIDAY; fax 423/821-8403. Exit 174 off I-24. Located near all of Chattanooga's major attractions, this is the only motel in Lookout Valley with a restaurant and bar. **Rooms:** 162 rms and stes. CI 1pm/CO 11am. Nonsmoking rms avail. **Amenities:** A/C, cable TV w/movies, dataport. **Services:** Bellman is on duty on weekends. **Facilities:** 80 1 restaurant, 1 bar (w/entertainment), basketball, volleyball, games rm, lawn games. **Rates:** Peak (July–Oct) $63 S or D; $83 ste. Extra person $7. Children under age 18 stay free. Lower rates off-season. Parking: Outdoor, free. Aquarium, Lookout Mountain, and Creative Discovery packages avail. AE, DC, DISC, MC, V.

Holiday Inn Southeast
6700 Ringgold Rd, 37412; tel 423/892-8100 or toll free 800/HOLIDAY; fax 423/499-5555. Exit 1 off I-75. Motel catering to the business traveler. **Rooms:** 231 rms. CI 3pm/CO 11am. Nonsmoking rms avail. **Amenities:** A/C, cable TV w/movies. Some units w/terraces. Complimentary morning coffee and copy of *USA Today*. **Services:** Babysitting. **Facilities:** 60 1 restaurant (bkfst and dinner only), 1 bar, games rm, playground, washer/dryer. Guests may have passes to nearby Gold's Gym. **Rates:** $52–$60 S; $58–$64 D. Extra person $6. Children under age 18 stay free. Parking: Outdoor, free. Aquarium and Lookout Mountain packages avail. AE, CB, DC, DISC, JCB, MC, V.

Quality Inn
2000 E 23rd St, 37404; tel 423/622-8353 or toll free 800/4-CHOICE; fax 423/622-0931. Exit 181 off I-24. Beautifully color-coordinated rooms, convenient location. **Rooms:** 154 rms and stes. CI 2pm/CO 11am. Nonsmoking rms avail. **Amenities:** A/C, cable TV w/movies. Some units w/whirlpools. **Services:** **Facilities:** 300 1 restaurant, 1 bar (w/entertainment). Restaurant open 24 hours a day. Pool and surrounding courtyard are very well kept. **Rates (CP):** Peak (June–Oct) $45–$72 S; $52–$87 D; $57 ste. Extra person $6. Children under age 16 stay free. Lower rates off-season. Parking: Outdoor, free. AE, CB, DC, DISC, MC, V.

Quality Inn South
6710 Ringgold Rd, 37412; tel 423/894-6820 or toll free 800/651-6767; fax 423/490-0824. Exit 1 off I-75. Standard, no-frills chain accommodations. **Rooms:** 129 rms and stes. CI 2pm/CO 11am. Nonsmoking rms avail. Good housekeeping standards in rooms. **Amenities:** A/C, cable TV w/movies. Some units w/whirlpools. **Services:** **Facilities:** 250 1 bar (w/entertainment). **Rates (CP):** Peak (May–Aug) $35–$125 S or D; $105–$125 ste. Extra person $5. Children under age 18 stay free. Lower rates off-season. Parking: Outdoor, free. AE, CB, DC, DISC, JCB, MC, V.

Ramada Inn South
6639 Capehart Lane, 37412; tel 423/894-6110 or toll free 800/2-RAMADA; fax 423/894-6110 ext 262. Exit 1 off I-75. This relaxing motel greets visitors with a beautiful lobby featuring a tremendous chandelier and elegant stairways. **Rooms:** 144 rms and stes. CI 3pm/CO noon. Nonsmoking rms avail. **Amenities:** A/C, satel TV w/movies, in-rm safe. Some units w/whirlpools. Mini suites feature coffeemakers, refrigerators, hair dryers, and sofa beds. **Services:** **Facilities:** 300 1 restaurant, 1 bar (w/entertainment), games rm. Patio lounge. **Rates:** Peak (Mar–Sept) $36–$68 S; $44–$74 D; $54–$115 ste. Extra person $6. Children under age 18 stay free. Lower rates off-season. Parking: Outdoor, free. AE, CB, DC, DISC, MC, V.

Ramada Limited
2361 Shallowford Village Dr, 37421; tel 423/855-2090 or toll free 800/2-RAMADA; fax 423/855-2090. Exit 5 off I-75. Comfortable accommodations within walking distance of restaurants. **Rooms:** 44 rms. CI 2pm/CO noon. Nonsmoking rms avail. A special honeymoon suite holds a heart-shaped tub and canopy bed. **Amenities:** A/C, cable TV w/movies, refrig, dataport. Some units w/whirlpools. All rooms have microwaves. **Services:** **Facilities:** Extra security measures—like cameras in parking areas, exterior walkways, and the lobby—give the guest a greater feeling of safety. **Rates (CP):** Peak (Jun–Aug) $40–$70 S; $50–$100 D. Extra person $6. Children under age 12 stay free. Lower rates off-season. Parking: Outdoor, free. AE, DC, DISC, MC, V.

Ramada Lookout Mountain
2100 S Market St, 37402; tel 423/265-0551 or toll free 800/2-RAMADA; fax 423/265-7946. Exit 178 off I-24. A two-story motel in a prime location near area attractions. Guests enter a spacious lobby featuring maroon leather couches. **Rooms:** 131 rms and stes. CI 2pm/CO 11am. Nonsmoking rms avail. Recently remodeled rooms with new linens and furnishings. **Amenities:** A/C, cable TV w/movies. Some units w/whirlpools. **Services:** **Facilities:** 1 restaurant, 1 bar (w/entertainment), washer/dryer. Karaoke offered nightly in the lounge. Pool is surrounded by a nice, grassy area with barbecue grills. **Rates (BB):** Peak (Apr–Aug)

$38–$68 S; $46–$76 D; $38–$76 ste. Extra person $4–$8. Children under age 18 stay free. Lower rates off-season. Parking: Outdoor, free. AE, CB, DC, DISC, JCB, MC, V.

▤ Scottish Inn

3210 S Broad St, 37408; tel 423/267-0414 or toll free 800/251-1962; fax 423/267-0414 ext 554. Exit 178 off I-24. An older lodging offering clean, comfortable rooms. **Rooms:** 130 rms. CI 11am/CO 11am. Nonsmoking rms avail. **Amenities:** 🛋 A/C, cable TV w/movies. **Services:** 🍽 **Facilities:** 🖼 & 1 restaurant (lunch and dinner only), 1 bar, games rm. **Rates:** $28–$30 S; $33–$36 D. Children under age 10 stay free. Parking: Outdoor, free. AE, CB, DC, DISC, MC, V.

RESTAURANTS 🍴

Big River Grille Brewing & Works

222 Broad St; tel 423/267-2739. **New American/American.** Full of life and energy. Four types of beers are brewed daily, as well as such specialty brews as blackberry ale. Menu is varied and extensive: everything from standard pub fare like shepherd's pie (made with beef and lamb, carrots, mushrooms, peas, and pearl onions and topped with garlic mashed potatoes and gravy) to angler's pasta (linguine with salmon, shrimp, and crawfish) and Jamaican jerk chicken breast with mango chutney sauce. Tasty floats feature home-brewed root beer. **FYI:** Reservations not accepted. Children's menu. **Open:** Daily 11am–11pm. **Prices:** Main courses $6–$12. AE, DC, DISC, MC, V. 👥 💟 &

Dinner in the Diner

In Chattanooga Choo Choo Holiday Inn, 1400 Market St (Downtown); tel 423/266-5000. **French.** Fine dining aboard an authentic train car. You might begin your meal with an appetizer such as wild mushroom tulip (sautéed exotic mushrooms in a phyllo-dough shell) and follow up with excellent soup, such as lobster bisque, or perhaps a diner car salad with goat cheese. For the main course, specialties such as grilled salmon, and pasta Provençal served on a bed of spinach fettuccini with tomato and basil laced with hollandaise sauce, are delicious options. Or perhaps you'd enjoy rack of lamb in pecan crust with cabernet sauvignon sauce. **FYI:** Reservations recommended. **Open:** Mon–Sat 6–10pm. **Prices:** Main courses $13–$20. AE, CB, DC, DISC, MC, V. 💟 ▤

The Gardens

In Chattanooga Choo Choo Holiday Inn, 1400 Market St (Downtown); tel 423/266-5000. **American.** This family-oriented restaurant offers individual breakfast entrees and an all-you-can-eat breakfast buffet. Lunch buffets are available Thurs, Fri, and Sat, while the lunch menu offers a variety of salads, sandwiches, and entrees such as Monterey chicken lasagna. The dinner menu combines traditional American and Southern cooking with specialties like Cajun chicken and shrimp jambalaya. **FYI:** Reservations accepted. Children's menu. **Open:** Peak (June–Aug/Oct) breakfast Mon–Sat 6:30–

11am, Sun 6:30–11:30am; lunch Mon–Wed 11am–3pm, Thurs–Sun 11am–5pm; dinner daily 5–10pm. **Prices:** Main courses $10–$15. AE, DISC, MC, V. ▤ 👥 &

Silver Diner

In Chattanooga Choo Choo Holiday Inn, 1400 Market St (Downtown); tel 423/266-5000. **American/Pizza.** Enjoy the fun and unique atmosphere of dining on an actual train, while munching on pizza, nachos, and stuffed baked potatoes. **FYI:** Reservations not accepted. No liquor license. **Open:** Peak (May–Sept) Sun–Thurs 11am–9pm, Fri–Sat 11am–11pm. **Prices:** Main courses $2–$15. AE, MC, V. 👥

Station House

In Chattanooga Choo Choo Holiday Inn, 1400 Market St (Downtown); tel 423/266-5000. **American.** The area of the train that once housed the baggage now serves as a steak house. A dinner show features singing waiters. The salad bar has lots of fresh shrimp. Closed on Sun in off-season. **FYI:** Reservations not accepted. Children's menu. **Open:** Peak (May–Sept) daily 6am–11pm. **Prices:** Main courses $9–$17. AE, CB, DC, DISC, MC, V. 👥 &

Steak at the Green Room

In Radisson Read House Hotel and Suites, 827 Broad St; tel 423/266-4121. **American.** Redecorated in 1995, this establishment still offers an elegant, fine dining experience. The menu consists of dishes such as smoked duckling with cherry sauce, rack of lamb, and choice prime rib. Corporate dining available. **FYI:** Reservations recommended. **Open:** Mon–Sat 5–11pm. **Prices:** Main courses $25–$40. AE, DISC, MC, V. 💟 ⓋⓅ &

Terrace

In Chattanooga Marriott at the Convention Center, 2 Carter Plaza; tel 423/756-0002. **American.** Offers relaxed, casual dining with a terrific view of the city. Popular appetizers include steamed mussels in a fresh herb and chardonnay sauce, penne with roasted vegetables, and lobster bisque. Entrees are just as varied and creative, with affordable selections like grilled pasta skillets with beef or chicken, garden lasagna, and New York strip. **FYI:** Reservations recommended. Children's menu. **Open:** Breakfast daily 6:30–11am; lunch daily 11am–2pm; dinner daily 6–11pm. **Prices:** Main courses $8–$17. AE, CB, DC, DISC, MC, V. 🏔 👥 ⓋⓅ &

212 Market

212 Market St; tel 423/265-1212. Across from the Aquarium. **New American/Continental.** Family-owned and -operated bistro serving elegant food in a casual, fun atmosphere. Atlantic salmon, eggplant parmesan, ravioli with fresh basil, mustard-coated rack of lamb with strawberry mint sauce, and other seasonally changing entrees. Special "healthy heart" meals available on request. Herbs are grown on premises, and a wide variety of baked goods from bread to desserts are prepared daily. **FYI:** Reservations accepted. Guitar/piano. Children's menu. **Open:** Lunch Mon–Fri 11am–3pm, Sat–

Sun 11:30am–3pm; dinner Mon–Thurs 5–9:30pm, Fri–Sat 5–10pm, Sun 5–9pm. **Prices:** Main courses $10–$22. AE, DC, DISC, MC, V.

ATTRACTIONS

Hunter Museum of Art
10 Bluff View; tel 423/267-0968. This museum's setting, in a turn-of-the-century classical revival mansion overlooking the Tennessee River, is as beautiful as what's displayed inside— one of the finest permanent collections of American paintings and photography in the Southeast. A nearby annex, built mostly underground so as not to compete aesthetically with the mansion, houses traveling exhibitions. **Open:** Tues–Sat 10am–4:30pm, Sun 1–4:30pm. Closed some hols. **$$**

Tennessee Aquarium
1 Broad St; tel 423/265-0695 or toll free 800/262-0695. America's first major institution devoted primarily to freshwater habitats is housed in a modern $45 million glass structure in downtown Chattanooga. Exhibits include a spectacular 60-foot canyon and two living forests, where over 7,000 animals swim, fly, and crawl in reproductions of their natural habitats. Special emphasis is given to river ecology in the "Rivers of the World" gallery. **Open:** Daily 10am–6pm. Closed some hols. **$$$**

Chattanooga Choo Choo Complex
1400 Market St; tel 423/266-5000. On March 5, 1880, the first passenger train connecting the north with the south traveled from Cincinnati to Chattanooga. The "Chattanooga Choo Choo" would become internationally famous more than 50 years later, when the Glenn Miller Orchestra recorded a catchy song about it. Today's 30-acre complex commemorating the glory days of the railroad is anchored by the renovated terminal station, now the lobby of a Holiday Inn. The station is also home to the restored Chattanooga Choo Choo engine, as well as the Chattanooga Southern Model Railroad, the largest HO gauge model railroad in the world, with over 3,000 feet of track and 100 freight cars. Retail shops and restaurants abound.

The **Downtown Arrow,** Chattanooga's only regularly scheduled passenger train, leaves from the Choo Choo every Saturday and Sunday afternoon for the Tennessee Valley Railroad Museum (call for information on schedules and ticket prices). **Open:** Daily 24 hours. **Free**

Lookout Mountain
Lookout Mountain. This 2,000-foot-tall mountain towers over Chattanooga and spreads across two states (Tennessee and Georgia). The site of a famous Civil War battle known as "the Battle Above the Clouds," Lookout Mountain is today one of the most widely known tourist complexes in the South. The amazing trolley cars of the **Lookout Mountain Incline Railway** (tel 423/821-4224) make three to four trips per hour up the steepest passenger railway in the world. (Some sections of the trip climb at a 72° angle!) The Lower Station (3917 St Elmo Ave) offers a food and gift shop, while the cloud-high Upper Station features a candy shop, ice cream parlor, and an observation deck (tel 423/821-7786). On a clear day, visitors can see Tennessee, Georgia, Alabama, and both Carolinas. The restored antebellum **Cravens House,** built in 1866 at the top of the mountain, is open for tours.

Also at the top of the mountain, visitors can explore the 14-acre **Rock City Gardens** (tel 706/820-2531), with its strange juxtaposition of natural rock formations and reconstructions of fairy tale scenes. During the summer, a free shuttle bus carries passengers from the Lookout Mountain observation deck to nearby Ruby Falls (see below). **Open:** Sept–May, daily 9am–6pm; June–Aug, daily 8:30am–10pm. Closed Dec 25. **$$$**

Ruby Falls
Lookout Mountain Scenic Hwy; tel 423/821-2544 or toll free 800/755-7105. One of America's most-visited underground waterfalls is located inside Lookout Mountain. Visitors board a high-speed elevator for a ride 20 stories below the ground, then walk through a half-mile-long cave in order to reach the falls. Guided tours depart every 15 minutes and take approximately one hour. Above ground, there's a lookout tower and Fun Forest playground for the kids. **Open:** June–Aug, daily 8am–9pm; Sept–Oct, Apr–Mar, daily 8am–8pm; Nov–Mar, daily 8am–6pm. Closed Dec 25. **$$$**

Audubon Acres
900 N Sanctuary Rd; tel 423/892-1499. This 130-acre floodplain and wildlife sanctuary, owned by the Chattanooga Audubon Society, features eight miles of hiking trails and nature walks. A cabin on the property is said to be the birthplace of 19th-century Cherokee naturalist Spring Frog, and has been restored to reflect his times and lifestyle. **Open:** Mon–Sat 9am–5pm, Sun 1–5pm. Closed some hols. **$**

Chickamauga and Chattanooga National Military Park
See Georgia

Clarksville

Tennessee's fifth-largest city and one of the fastest growing cities in the Southeast. The area has some of the state's richest farmland, and its vineyards produce premier Tennessee wines. **Information:** Clarksville-Montgomery County Tourist Commission, 180 Holiday Rd, Clarksville, 37040 (tel 615/648-0001).

HOTEL 🖼

☰☰☰ Quality Inn Downtown

803 N 2nd St, 37040; tel 615/645-9084 or toll free 800/221-2222; fax 615/645-9084 ext 340. A hotel built around a large atrium with pool. **Rooms:** 134 rms. CI 12:30pm/CO noon. Nonsmoking rms avail. All rooms face the atrium. **Amenities:** 🛏 🧊 A/C, cable TV w/movies. Dataports available in some rooms. **Services:** 🚗 🖨 🛎 📶 **Facilities:** 🏊 📶125 🔥 1 bar, games rm, sauna, whirlpool, playground, washer/dryer. **Rates (CP):** Peak (May 24–Sept 5) $40–$46 S or D. Extra person $6. Children under age 18 stay free. Lower rates off-season. Parking: Outdoor, free. AE, CB, DC, DISC, JCB, MC, V.

MOTELS

☰☰ Hampton Inn

190 Holiday Rd, 37040; tel 615/552-2255 or toll free 800/HAMPTON; fax 615/552-4871. Exit 4 off I-24. Tastefully decorated public areas, outdoor seating on the patio, and comfortable rooms make this a good choice. **Rooms:** 77 rms. CI noon/CO noon. Nonsmoking rms avail. **Amenities:** 🛏 🧊 A/C, cable TV. Some units w/whirlpools. Some rooms equipped with dataports, refrigerators, and microwaves. **Services:** 🖨 📶 **Facilities:** 🏊 🗄 📶15 🔥 Sauna, whirlpool, washer/dryer. **Rates (CP):** Peak (June–Aug) $45–$85 S; $49–$65 D. Children under age 18 stay free. Lower rates off-season. Parking: Outdoor, free. AE, CB, DC, DISC, MC, V.

☰☰☰ Holiday Inn

3095 Wilma Rudolph Blvd, 37040; tel 615/648-4848 or toll free 800/HOLIDAY; fax 615/648-4848. Exit 4 off I-24, at jct with US 79. An engaging Holiday Inn offering a large and beautifully landscaped lobby with plants and greenery. **Rooms:** 144 rms. CI 2pm/CO noon. Nonsmoking rms avail. **Amenities:** 🛏 🧊 A/C, cable TV w/movies. Some rooms equipped with refrigerator and stove. **Services:** ✕ 🚗 🖨 📶 📶 Limousine service available. **Facilities:** 🏊 🗄 📶250 🔥 1 restaurant, 1 bar, games rm, sauna, whirlpool, playground, washer/dryer. **Rates (BB):** $58–$63 S; $64–$69 D. Extra person $6. Children under age 18 stay free. Parking: Outdoor, free. AE, CB, DC, DISC, JCB, MC, V.

☰☰ Ramada Limited

3100 Wilma Rudolph Blvd, 37040; tel 615/552-0098 or toll free 800/2-RAMADA, 800/854-7854 in Canada; fax 615/645-3700. Exit 4 off I-24. Clean, comfortable accommodations. **Rooms:** 42 rms. CI open/CO noon. Nonsmoking rms avail. **Amenities:** 🛏 🧊 A/C, cable TV. Microwaves and refrigerators available in some rooms. **Services:** 📶 📶 **Facilities:** 🏊 🔥 Sauna, whirlpool. **Rates (CP):** Peak (May–Aug) $30–$55 S; $36–$60 D. Extra person $5. Children under age 16 stay free. Lower rates off-season. Parking: Outdoor, free. AE, DC, DISC, ER, MC, V.

INN

☰☰☰ Hachland Hill Inn

1601 Madison St, 37043; tel 615/647-4084; fax 615/552-3454. Exit 11 off I-24. 5 acres. There is a warm, homey atmosphere here. The main house, built in 1790, was Andrew Jackson's quarters during the construction of the Hermitage and today it is filled with antique furniture, tools, weapons, and quilts; the sitting room has a fireplace and a friendly dog. **Rooms:** 6 rms; 3 cottages/villas. CI 3pm/CO noon. Nonsmoking rms avail. The 200 year old honeymoon cottage is the oldest cabin in Montgomery County and has been featured in *Better Homes and Gardens*. The rooms in the main house are quaint and warmly decorated, often in a rustic fashion. **Amenities:** 🧊 A/C, cable TV. No phone. Some units w/fireplaces. **Services:** 🖨 📶 📶 Babysitting. **Facilities:** 📶350 1 restaurant, guest lounge. Restaurant is run by the inn owner, a local television personality and author of 17 cookbooks. Secured parking available. **Rates:** $45 S; $65 D; $45–$65 cottage/villa. Extra person $10. Parking: Outdoor, free. AE, MC, V.

ATTRACTION 🖼

Cumberland Riverwalk

Riverside Dr; tel 615/645-7476. Riverfront promenade in MacGregor Park, in the middle of Clarksville's historic River District, boasts picnic facilities, playground, flowering trees, scenic overlooks, and the docking point of the *Queen of Clarksville* riverboat. Recent additions include an amphitheater, a 10,000-seat concert stage, and a Cumberland River Interpretive Center with displays on the cultural, commercial, and geological history of the river. **Open:** Daily sunrise–midnight.

Cleveland

Nearby to Red Clay State Historical Area, the last capital of the Cherokee before their removal via the Trail of Tears. **Information:** Cleveland/Bradley Convention & Visitors Bureau, 2145 Keith St, PO Box 2275, Cleveland, 37320 (tel 423/472-6587).

MOTEL 🖼

☰☰ Ramada Inn Cleveland

US 64, PO Box 3896, 37311; tel 423/479-4531 or toll free 800/2-RAMADA; fax 423/339-1852. Exit 20 off I-75. Clean and comfortable accommodations. **Rooms:** 145 rms and stes. CI open/CO noon. Nonsmoking rms avail. **Amenities:** 🛏 🧊 A/C, satel TV w/movies. **Services:** ✕ 🖨 📶 📶 **Facilities:** 🏊 📶300 🔥 1 restaurant, playground. **Rates:** Peak (June–Aug) $46 S; $51 D; $65 ste. Extra person $6. Children under age 18 stay free. Lower rates off-season. Parking: Outdoor, free. Bed and breakfast packages avail; trucker and group rates avail. AE, DC, DISC, MC, V.

ATTRACTION 📷

L & N Depot Museum

Tennessee Ave, Etowah; tel 423/263-7840. Now a museum, this beautifully restored 15-room Victorian building was once the home of the L & N (Louisville & Nashville) Atlanta Division Headquarters. Its exhibits tell the story of the depot's vital role in the life of rural Tennessee in the 20th century—the early boom years, labor strikes, the Depression, and two world wars. There's also a railroad caboose, bandstand, picnic area, and gift shop on the grounds. **Open:** Tues–Sat 9am–4:30pm, Sun 1–4pm. Closed some hols. **Free**

Columbia

On the Duck River southwest of Nashville. First settled in 1807, Columbia was the boyhood home of James K Polk, the 11th US president. Site of The Athenaeum, an 1830s Gothic home that was transformed into the Athenaeum School for Young Ladies, renowned for its progressive curriculum. **Information:** Maury County Convention & Visitors Bureau, #9 Hunter-Matthews Building, Courthouse Sq, PO Box 1076, Columbia, 38402 (tel 615/381-7176).

MOTEL 🏨

🏨🏨🏨 Ramada Columbia

1208 US 31, 38402; tel 615/388-2720 or toll free 800/2-RAMADA; fax 615/388-2360. Southern-style hospitality, warmly decorated lobby. **Rooms:** 155 rms and stes. CI 2pm/CO noon. Nonsmoking rms avail. **Amenities:** 🛁 🐾 A/C, cable TV, dataport. Microwaves, refrigerators, and coffeemakers in some rooms. **Services:** ✗ 🖼 🕳 🕤 Car-rental desk, babysitting. Complimentary fruit and coffee in lobby. **Facilities:** 🏋️ 🔟 🔟 & 1 restaurant, 1 bar, washer/dryer. Guest privileges at local fitness center. **Rates:** Peak (May–Labor Day) $39–$52 S; $42–$58 D; $75–$85 ste. Extra person $5. Children under age 18 stay free. Lower rates off-season. Parking: Outdoor, free. AE, CB, DC, DISC, JCB, MC, V.

ATTRACTION 📷

James K Polk Ancestral Home

301 W 7th St; tel 615/388-2354. The 11th president of the United States grew up in this modest home, and he was living here when he began his legal and political career. The house is filled with antiques that belonged both to Polk's parents when they lived here and to Polk and his family during their time in the White House. In a separate building, there is an exhibit of political and Mexican War memorabilia. **Open:** Apr–Oct, Mon–Sat 9am–5pm, Sun 1–5pm; Nov–Mar, Mon–Sat 9am–4pm, Sun 1–5pm. Closed some hols. $

Cookeville

Located in north-central Tennessee and named for Maj Richard Cooke, who fought in the Mexican-American War. **Information:** Putnam Travel Development Council, 302 S Jefferson Ave, Cookeville, 38501 (tel 615/320-1222).

HOTELS 🏨

🏨🏨🏨 Holiday Inn

970 S Jefferson Ave, 38501; tel 615/526-7125 or toll free 800/HOLIDAY; fax 615/526-7125 ext 152. Exit 287 off I-40. Features a large Holidome filled with lush plants and trees. **Rooms:** 200 rms. CI noon/CO noon. Nonsmoking rms avail. **Amenities:** 🛁 🐾 A/C, satel TV w/movies, dataport. **Services:** ✗ 🚐 🖼 🕳 🕤 **Facilities:** 🏋️ 🔟 🔟 🖥️ & 1 restaurant, 1 bar (w/entertainment), games rm, whirlpool. **Rates (CP):** $64–$74 S or D. Extra person $10. Children under age 19 stay free. Parking: Outdoor, free. AE, CB, DC, DISC, JCB, MC, V.

🏨🏨 Howard Johnson Lodge

2021 E Spring St, 38506; tel 615/526-3333 or toll free 800/213-2016; fax 615/528-9036. Exit 290 off I-40. Standard chain accommodations featuring a nice sundeck area surrounding the pool. **Rooms:** 64 rms. CI 2pm/CO noon. Nonsmoking rms avail. **Amenities:** 🛁 🐾 A/C, cable TV, refrig. All units w/terraces, some w/whirlpools. **Services:** 🚐 🖼 🕳 🕤 VCR and movie rentals available. **Facilities:** 🏋️ & Basketball, whirlpool, playground, washer/dryer. **Rates (CP):** Peak (May 24–Sept 2) $32–$45 S; $36–$58 D. Extra person $5. Children under age 18 stay free. Lower rates off-season. Parking: Outdoor, free. AE, CB, DC, DISC, JCB, MC, V.

MOTELS

🏨 Days Inn Cookeville

1292 Bunker Hill Rd, 38501; tel 615/528-1511 or toll free 800/DAYS-INN; fax 615/528-1511 ext 100. Exit 287 off I-40. A basic, comfortable motel. **Rooms:** 97 rms. CI 1pm/CO 11am. Nonsmoking rms avail. **Amenities:** 🛁 A/C, cable TV. Some units w/whirlpools. Waterbeds and whirlpools in some rooms. **Services:** 🖼 🕳 🕤 **Facilities:** 🏋️ & Washer/dryer. **Rates (CP):** Peak (Apr 28–Sept) $40–$45 S; $45–$55 D. Extra person $5. Children under age 12 stay free. Lower rates off-season. Parking: Outdoor, free. AE, CB, DC, DISC, JCB, MC, V.

🏨🏨 Hampton Inn Cookeville

340 Interstate Dr, 38501; tel 615/520-1117 or toll free 800/HAMPTON; fax 615/520-8412. Exit 287 off I-40. Comfortable motel with tastefully decorated lobby. **Rooms:** 65 rms and stes. CI noon/CO 11am. Nonsmoking rms avail. **Amenities:** 🛁 🐾 A/C, cable TV, dataport. Some units w/whirlpools. Refrigerators and additional phones in some rooms. **Services:** 🚐 🖼 🕳 🕤 **Facilities:** 🏋️ 🔟 🔟 & Whirlpool, washer/dryer. Guest privileges at local health club. **Rates (CP):** Peak (May 15–Sept) $55–$60 S; $65–$70

D; $100–$110 ste. Children under age 18 stay free. Lower rates off-season. Parking: Outdoor, free. AE, CB, DC, DISC, MC, V.

RESTAURANT 🍴

Scarecrow Country Inn
644 Whitson Chapell Rd; tel 615/526-3431. Exit 290 off I-40. **Regional American/Southern.** A quaint restaurant housed in a building made from the logs of old cabins (some of the wood is over 150 years old). The interior is filled with antique china, silver, linens, and embroidered quilts. There are over a dozen magnificent stained-glass windows, and a courtyard with benches, lush greenery, flowers, and fish ponds. They are best known for their broccoli salad, fresh hickory-bark syrup, and country ham. **FYI:** Reservations recommended. Piano. Children's menu. Dress code. No liquor license. No smoking. **Open:** Peak (Dec) lunch Tues–Sat 11am–2pm; dinner Tues–Sat 5–9:30pm. **Prices:** Main courses $9–$18. MC, V. 🛢 ᴦ

ATTRACTION 🏛

Arda Lee's Hidden Hollow Park
1901 Mount Pleasant Rd; tel 615/526-4038. This 86-acre park has something for everyone: 11 picnic shelters surrounded by a scenic old mill house, waterfalls, and lakes; facilities for horseshoes, volleyball, fishing, and hiking; and a playground, petting zoo, and kiddie pool for the youngsters. **Open:** Daily 8:30am–10:30pm. $

Cumberland Gap National Historical Park (KY/TN/VA)

See Middlesboro, KY

Dayton

Dayton's courthouse was center of worldwide attention during the July 1925 Scopes "monkey trial." **Information:** Dayton Chamber of Commerce, 107 Main St, Dayton, 37321 (tel 423/775-0361).

ATTRACTION 🏛

Rhea County Scopes Trial Museum
1475 Market St; tel 423/775-7801. A small museum commemorating the famous 1925 "Scopes Monkey Trial," during which Dayton high school teacher John Scopes was found guilty of teaching the theory of evolution to his students. (The controversial case was dramatized in the film *Inherit the Wind.*) The basement courtroom where the trial was held is

still being used today and can be toured when court is not in session. **Open:** Mon–Thur 8am–4pm, Fri 8am–5:30pm. Closed some hols. **Free**

Dyersburg

The historic downtown of this northwestern Tennessee city centers around a traditional courthouse square. Host of annual Dogwood Festival and Dash. **Information:** Dyersburg/Dyer County Chamber of Commerce, 2455 Lake Rd, PO Box 747, Dyersburg, 38025 (tel 901/285-3433).

MOTELS 🏨

≡≡ Days Inn
2600 Lake Rd, 38024; tel 901/287-0888 or toll free 800/DAYS-INN; fax 901/287-0891. Standard chain accommodations. Sufficient for overnight stay. **Rooms:** 59 rms and stes. CI noon/CO 11am. Nonsmoking rms avail. **Amenities:** 🛎 ⌕ 🖵 ᴦ A/C, cable TV. Some rooms equipped with refrigerators and microwaves. **Services:** ☒ ⌑ **Facilities:** ⌂₁₅ ᴦ **Rates (CP):** Peak (June–Sept 15) $35–$39 S; $39–$43 D; $50 ste. Extra person $4. Children under age 17 stay free. Lower rates off-season. Parking: Outdoor, free. AE, DC, DISC, MC, V.

≡ Volunteer Inn
1004 TN 51 Bypass, 38024; tel 901/285-9730; fax 901/286-0463. This motel offers no frills, but the rooms are comfortable enough. **Rooms:** 60 rms. CI open/CO 11am. Nonsmoking rms avail. **Amenities:** 🛎 A/C, cable TV w/movies. 1 unit w/whirlpool. **Services:** ⌑ **Facilities:** ⌂₁ ⌂₂₀ Pool is unusually large for a chain motel. **Rates:** Peak (June–Aug) $32–$35 S; $37–$40 D. Extra person $6. Children under age 10 stay free. Lower rates off-season. Parking: Outdoor, free. AE, DC, DISC, MC, V.

Elizabethton

See also Bluff City

Located on the Watauga River in northeast Tennessee, in one of the earliest settled regions of the state. The Watauga Association—an early pioneer government—was organized here in 1772. Recreational lakes are in the surrounding area. Host to annual Covered Bridge celebration. **Information:** Elizabethton/Carter County Chamber of Commerce, 500 19E Bypass, PO Box 190, Elizabethton, 37644 (tel 423/547-3850).

MOTEL 🏨

≡≡ Comfort Inn
1519 19E Bypass, 37643; tel 423/542-4466 or toll free 800/221-2222; fax 423/542-6441. An exceptionally comfortable chain motel. The hallways are somewhat dark, but the cozy

lobby is hung with lace curtains, decorative rugs cover the floor, and plush, comfortable sofas are scattered throughout. The well-manicured grounds have an abundance of small bushes and flowers. **Rooms:** 58 rms and stes. CI 2pm/CO 11am. Nonsmoking rms avail. Rooms are airy and pleasant; nice for multinight stays. **Amenities:** 🛁 🏊 A/C, cable TV w/movies, dataport. Some units w/whirlpools. **Services:** ⌷ ◁ᑎ◁ᑄ Babysitting. **Facilities:** 🖼 🏊 ᵬ **Rates:** Peak (June–Oct) $40–$125 S or D; $100–$125 ste. Extra person $6. Children under age 18 stay free. Lower rates off-season. Parking: Outdoor, free. AE, CB, DC, DISC, ER, JCB, MC, V.

RESTAURANT 🍴

★ Ridgewood Restaurant
900 Elizabethton Hwy, Bluff City; tel 423/538-7543. Off Bristol. **Barbecue.** Known for serving up huge portions of great Tennessee-style barbecue. The decor is unpretentious, with Formica tables and vinyl chairs, but no one seems to mind the humble surroundings. **FYI:** Reservations not accepted. No liquor license. **Open:** Lunch Tues–Thurs 11:30am–3pm, Fri–Sat 11:30am–2:45pm, Sun 11:30am–2:45pm; dinner Tues–Thurs 3–7:30pm, Fri–Sat 4:30–8:30pm, Sun 4:30–7:30pm. **Prices:** Main courses $6–$11. No CC.

ATTRACTION 📷

Sycamore Shoals State Historic Area
US 321; tel 423/543-5808. Site of the first permanent colonial settlement (1772) west of the Blue Ridge Mountains. Today, this 47-acre park includes a reconstruction of the original Fort Watauga, a visitors center, a museum with a collection of 18th-century artifacts, and a theater which shows a half-hour film on the mountain men of the region. Picnic areas. **Open:** Mon–Sat 8am–4:30pm, Sun 1–4:30pm. Closed some hols. **Free**

Franklin

Located 19 miles south of Nashville, Franklin, with its historic downtown area, has been called one of the most charming cities of the South. An important Union victory was won here in 1864. The name was changed from Frankland to Franklin in honor of Benjamin Franklin. **Information:** Williamson County Chamber of Commerce, 109 2nd Ave S #107, PO Box 156, Franklin, 37065 (tel 615/794-1225).

ATTRACTIONS 📷

The Carter House
1140 Columbia Ave; tel 615/791-1861. The Carter House was built in 1830, only four years after Carnton Plantation (see below) was constructed, and during the Battle of Franklin it was commandeered as the Union Army command post. While the Carter family hid in the basement, their youngest

son, Todd, was killed in the battle. Tours of the restored home include a visit to an on-site museum offering many Civil War artifacts and a video presentation about the Battle of Franklin. **Open:** Nov–Mar, Mon–Sat 9am–4pm, Sun 1–4pm; Apr–Oct, Mon–Sat 9am–5pm, Sun 1–5pm. Closed some hols. **$$**

Carnton Plantation
1345 Carnton Lane; tel 615/794-0903. Built in 1826 by Randal McGavock, a former mayor of Nashville. The stately old home, with its seven square columns and porches that stretch the length of both floors in the front of the house, houses many original pieces of furniture and other antiques. During the Battle of Franklin in November 1864, this beautiful neoclassical antebellum mansion served as a Confederate hospital. Two years later, the McGavock family donated two acres of land to be used as a cemetery for Confederate soldiers who had died during the battle. There are more than 1,500 graves in the McGavock Confederate Cemetery, which makes this the largest privately owned Confederate cemetery. Carnton also hosts outdoor summer concerts by the Nashville Symphony. **Open:** Nov–Apr, Mon–Sat 9am–4pm, Sun 1–4pm; May–Oct, Mon–Sat 9am–5pm, Sun 1–5pm. Closed some hols. **$$**

Gatlinburg

See also Pigeon Forge, Sevierville

Framed by mile-high Mount LeConte and other peaks of the Smokies, Gatlinburg is the state's center for mountain arts and crafts and is one of its top tourist destinations. **Information:** Gatlinburg Convention Center, 234 Airport Rd, Gatlinburg, 37738 (tel 615/343-1475).

HOTELS 📷

⧸ Best Western Crossroads Motor Lodge
440 Parkway, PO Box 648, 37738; tel 423/436-5661 or toll free 800/225-2295. Next to Atrium Restaurant. Under the same ownership for 28 years, this is a comfortable place located conveniently on the parkway. **Rooms:** 78 rms, stes, and effic. CI 2pm/CO 11am. **Amenities:** 🛁 A/C, cable TV, refrig. Some units w/fireplaces, some w/whirlpools. Some rooms with wet bars and microwaves. **Services:** ⌷ Babysitting. **Facilities:** 🖼 ⛷ ᵬ Washer/dryer. **Rates:** Peak (June–Aug/Oct) $65–$84 S or D; $98–$130 ste; $130–$150 effic. Min stay wknds and special events. Lower rates off-season. Parking: Outdoor, free. Seventh night is free. Can have four guests in a room for the same rate. AE, CB, DC, DISC, MC, V.

⧸ Best Western Zoder's Inn
402 Parkway, PO Box 708, 37738; tel 423/436-5681 or toll free 800/528-1234; fax 423/436-6658. A family-owned facility with eight buildings situated along a mountain stream. A relaxing refuge in the middle of the Gatlinburg action.

Rooms: 90 rms, stes, and effic; 3 cottages/villas. CI 3pm/CO noon. Nonsmoking rms avail. **Amenities:** 🛏 ⓠ A/C, satel TV w/movies, refrig, VCR, voice mail, in-rm safe. Some units w/terraces, some w/fireplaces, some w/whirlpools. **Services:** ⬔ ⛛ Twice-daily maid svce, babysitting. Wine and cheese served 5–7pm; cookies and milk served 8–10pm. **Facilities:** ⚏ ⬚ 📺 ⛾ 🔲 ⅃. Basketball, games rm, racquetball, whirlpool, washer/dryer. Sun deck; outdoor area with grill. **Rates (CP):** Peak (Apr–Nov 15) $80 S or D; $108–$225 ste; $170 effic; $83–$135 cottage/villa. Min stay wknds and special events. Lower rates off-season. Parking: Outdoor, free. Off-season package avail. AE, CB, DC, DISC, JCB, MC, V.

☰☰ Comfort Inn Downtown

200 E Parkway, 37738; tel 423/436-5043 or toll free 800/933-8679; fax 423/436-5043. At US 321. Comfortable accommodations located in the heart of Gatlinburg. **Rooms:** 100 rms. CI 2pm/CO 11am. Nonsmoking rms avail. Specialty rooms with either king or water beds and hot tubs are available. **Amenities:** 🛏 A/C, cable TV w/movies. Some units w/fireplaces, some w/whirlpools. **Services:** ✕ ⛛ Free passes to Fun Mountain. **Facilities:** ⚏ 📺 🔲 ⅃. 1 restaurant (bkfst and lunch only), games rm, whirlpool, washer/dryer. **Rates:** Peak (June–Oct) $64–$82 S or D. Children under age 19 stay free. Min stay wknds and special events. Lower rates off-season. Parking: Outdoor, free. Honeymoon packages avail. AE, CB, DC, DISC, MC, V.

☰☰☰ Days Inn Glenstone Lodge

504 Airport Rd, PO Box 330, 37738; tel 423/436-9361 or toll free 800/362-9522; fax 423/436-6951. An upscale, comfortable lobby gives way to an indoor, two-level "lagoon" pool and another outdoor pool. **Rooms:** 216 rms and stes. CI 2pm/CO 11am. Nonsmoking rms avail. **Amenities:** 🛏 ⓠ A/C, cable TV w/movies, refrig, dataport. Some units w/terraces, some w/fireplaces. Closed-captioned TV available in all rooms. **Services:** ✕ ⬔ ⛛ Twice-daily maid svce. **Facilities:** ⚏ 📺 🔲 ⅃. 1 restaurant (bkfst and lunch only), whirlpool. The hotel loves catering to large groups. **Rates:** Peak (July–Oct) $65–$96 S or D; $85–$150 ste. Extra person $7. Children under age 13 stay free. Min stay special events. Lower rates off-season. Parking: Outdoor, free. AE, CB, DC, DISC, MC, V.

☰☰ The Edgewater Hotel

402 River Rd, PO Box 170, 37738; tel 423/436-4151 or toll free 800/423-9582, 800/423-4532 in TN; fax 423/436-6947. A peaceful mountain hideaway with great views from most of the rooms. **Rooms:** 205 rms and stes. CI 3pm/CO 11am. Nonsmoking rms avail. **Amenities:** 🛏 ⓠ A/C, satel TV w/movies. All units w/terraces, some w/fireplaces, some w/whirlpools. **Services:** ✕ ⬔ ⛛ **Facilities:** ⚏ 📺 🔲 ⅃. 1 restaurant (bkfst and dinner only; *see* "Restaurants" below), 1 bar (w/entertainment), whirlpool. Landscaped pool area with rock waterfalls. **Rates:** Peak (June–Oct) $94–$99 S or D; $139–$175 ste. Extra person $10. Children under age 16

stay free. Min stay wknds and special events. Lower rates off-season. Parking: Indoor/outdoor, free. CB, DC, DISC, MC, V.

☰ Greystone Lodge

559 Parkway, PO Box 408, 37738; tel 423/436-5621 or toll free 800/451-9202; fax 423/430-4471. Between lights 3 and 4. Basic hotel. **Rooms:** 257 rms and stes. CI 4pm/CO 11am. Nonsmoking rms avail. **Amenities:** 🛏 A/C, cable TV. All units w/terraces, some w/fireplaces, some w/whirlpools. Bring your own hangers from home—there may not be any in your room. **Services:** ⛛ **Facilities:** ⚏ 📺 🔲 ⅃. Washer/dryer. **Rates (CP):** Peak (May–Dec) $46–$94 S or D; $96–$144 ste. Extra person $8. Children under age 12 stay free. Min stay wknds and special events. Lower rates off-season. Parking: Outdoor, free. AE, CB, DC, DISC, JCB, MC, V.

☰☰☰ Holiday Inn Resort Complex

520 Airport Rd, 37738; tel 423/436-9201 or toll free 800/435-9201; fax 423/436-7974. Near Convention Center. Recreational activities are the strong point here. There's a creek with fishing, outdoor grills, and picnic tables for cooking and enjoying your catch, and there's also a Holidome for guests who would rather stay inside. Caters to families with young children. **Rooms:** 402 rms and stes. CI 3pm/CO 11am. Nonsmoking rms avail. **Amenities:** 🛏 ⓠ A/C, cable TV w/movies. **Services:** ✕ ⬔ ⛛ ⬡ Social director, children's program, babysitting. On staff are Uncle Polka and Aunt Dot, who plan daily activities for children. **Facilities:** ⚏ 📺 🔲 ⅃. 1 restaurant, 1 bar, games rm, sauna, whirlpool, washer/dryer. Adjacent city park has tennis courts, a playground, softball fields, and a large picnic area. **Rates:** Peak (May 15–Nov 15) $79–$109 S or D; $237–$327 ste. Extra person $6. Children under age 19 stay free. Min stay special events. Lower rates off-season. Parking: Outdoor, free. AE, CB, DC, DISC, MC, V.

☰☰☰ Homestead House

401 Parkway, PO Box 367, 37738; tel 423/436-6166 or toll free 800/233-4663; fax 423/436-2117. At Hemlock. The atmosphere here is warm and inviting, and the view of the mountains, while pretty all year, is spectacular in October. **Rooms:** 86 rms, stes, and effic. CI 2pm/CO 11am. Nonsmoking rms avail. All suites are two-bedroom suites; honeymoon suite includes a fireplace, whirlpool, and double balcony. **Amenities:** 🛏 ⓠ A/C, cable TV w/movies, refrig, VCR, CD/tape player. All units w/terraces, some w/fireplaces, some w/whirlpools. **Services:** ⛛ **Facilities:** ⚏ 📺 ⬚ 🔲 ⅃. Heated outdoor pool. **Rates (CP):** Peak (June–Aug/Oct) $74–$95 S or D; $160 ste; $64–$100 effic. Extra person $5. Min stay special events. Lower rates off-season. Parking: Outdoor, free. AARP discounts avail. AE, DISC, MC, V.

☰☰ Johnson's Inn

Baskin's Creek Rd, PO Box 392, 37738; tel 423/436-4881 or toll free 800/842-1930; fax 423/436-2582. This family-owned and -operated lodging is small enough to give individual attention to its guests. **Rooms:** 78 rms, stes, and effic. CI 2pm/CO 11am. Nonsmoking rms avail. Extra large rooms give families space to move around. **Amenities:** ☎ A/C, cable TV w/movies, refrig, VCR. Some units w/terraces, some w/fireplaces, some w/whirlpools. **Facilities:** ⚐ ⚐ ♿ Washer/dryer. **Rates:** Peak (June–Aug/Oct) $49–$64 S; $54–$69 D; $90–$115 ste; $59–$74 effic. Extra person $5. Children under age 7 stay free. Min stay special events. Lower rates off-season. Parking: Outdoor, free. DISC, MC, V.

≣≣≣ Park Vista Resort Hotel

Airport Rd at Cherokee Orchard Rd, PO Box 30, 37738; tel 423/436-9211 or toll free 800/421-7275; fax 423/436-5141. At light 8. Unusually elegant for the area. Common areas include an Oriental garden, a Southern-style gazebo, and a magnificent, open lobby with three glass elevators. **Rooms:** 312 rms and stes. CI 4pm/CO 11am. Nonsmoking rms avail. As the name suggests, many rooms have gorgeous views of the national park. **Amenities:** ☎ ⚐ A/C, cable TV w/movies, voice mail. All units w/terraces. **Services:** ✕ �📺 ⚐ ⚐ ⚐ **Facilities:** ⚐ ⚐ ⚐ ⚐ ♿ 1 restaurant (*see* "Restaurants" below), 1 bar (w/entertainment), games rm, whirlpool, washer/dryer. **Rates:** Peak (June–Nov) $65–$120 S or D; $150–$330 ste. Extra person $10. Children under age 17 stay free. Min stay special events. Lower rates off-season. Parking: Outdoor, free. AE, CB, DC, DISC, MC, V.

≣≣≣ River Terrace Resort

240 River Rd, PO Box 747, 37738; tel 423/436-5161 or toll free 800/251-2040; fax 423/436-7219. Convenient to shopping and trolley service, this facility offers facilities for seminars, conferences, retreats, tour groups, reunions, banquets, and weddings. Popular for family vacations, too. **Rooms:** 205 rms, stes, and effic. CI 4pm/CO 11am. Nonsmoking rms avail. Most rooms have views of mountains or river. **Amenities:** ☎ ⚐ A/C, cable TV. Some units w/terraces, some w/fireplaces, some w/whirlpools. **Services:** ✕ ⚐ ⚐ Babysitting. **Facilities:** ⚐ ⚐ ⚐ ♿ 1 restaurant (bkfst and lunch only), 1 bar, whirlpool. **Rates:** Peak (June–Aug/Oct) $74–$94 S or D; $129–$282 ste; $89–$109 effic. Extra person $6. Children under age 13 stay free. Lower rates off-season. Parking: Outdoor, free. AE, CB, DC, DISC, MC, V.

MOTELS

≣≣ Best Western Fabulous Chalet Inn

516 Sunset Dr, PO Box 11, 37738; tel 423/436-5151 or toll free 800/933-8675; fax 423/523-8363. Comfortable rooms and spectacular mountain views. **Rooms:** 80 rms, stes, and effic; 4 cottages/villas. CI 2pm/CO 11am. Nonsmoking rms avail. Some rooms have a view of the river; others are on the hillside. **Amenities:** ☎ ⚐ A/C, cable TV w/movies, refrig. Some units w/terraces, some w/fireplaces, some w/whirlpools. **Services:** ⚐ **Facilities:** ⚐ ⚐ Washer/dryer. **Rates (CP):** Peak (June–Dec) $69–$92 S or D; $87–$134 ste; $87 effic; $115–$124 cottage/villa. Extra person $5. Chil-

dren under age 12 stay free. Min stay special events. Lower rates off-season. Parking: Outdoor, free. Up to four people can stay in a room for no extra charge. AE, DC, DISC, MC, V.

≣≣ Best Western Twin Islands Motel

539 Parkway, PO Box 648, 37738; tel 423/436-5121 or toll free 800/223-9299; fax 423/436-6208. At light 3. Plenty of family fun in the heart of Gatlinburg, with a large playground and pool area set back from Gatlinburg's hustle and bustle. **Rooms:** 110 rms, stes, and effic; 4 cottages/villas. CI 1pm/CO 11am. **Amenities:** ☎ A/C, cable TV, refrig. Some units w/terraces, some w/fireplaces, some w/whirlpools. **Services:** ⚐ Security patrol. **Facilities:** ⚐ ⚐ ⚐ ♿ 1 restaurant, playground, washer/dryer. Pretty picnic area near the river. Guests receive 50% off admission to Ogle's Water Park. **Rates:** Peak (June–Aug/Oct) $69–$94 S or D; $135 ste; $98–$135 effic; $129 cottage/villa. Children under age 18 stay free. Min stay wknds and special events. Lower rates off-season. Parking: Outdoor, free. Up to four in a room. Ski and golf packages avail. AE, CB, DC, DISC, MC, V.

≣ Brookside Resort

463 E Parkway, 37738; tel 423/436-5611 or toll free 800/251-9597; fax 423/436-0039. On US 321. 3 acres. Located on the trolley route, this is perfect for a family stay because of its space and activities for children. **Rooms:** 227 rms, stes, and effic; 15 cottages/villas. CI 3pm/CO 11am. Some rooms overlook the river. Apartments (with up to three bedrooms) and cabins (with four bedrooms) available. **Amenities:** ☎ A/C, cable TV, refrig. Some units w/terraces, some w/fireplaces, some w/whirlpools. **Services:** ⚐ Babysitting. **Facilities:** ⚐ ⚐ ⚐ ⚐ ♿ Basketball, volleyball, whirlpool, playground, washer/dryer. **Rates:** Peak (May–Oct) $50–$110 S or D; $55–$135 ste; $55–$135 effic; $55–$135 cottage/villa. Extra person $5. Min stay wknds and special events. Lower rates off-season. Parking: Outdoor, free. AE, CB, DC, MC, V.

≣≣ Fairfield Inn

680 River Rd, 37738; tel 423/430-7200 or toll free 800/228-2800; fax 423/430-4343. Built in 1995, this motel offers some of Gatlinburg's most modern accommodations. **Rooms:** 54 rms and stes. CI 3pm/CO noon. Nonsmoking rms avail. Room balconies overlook the river. **Amenities:** ☎ ⚐ A/C, cable TV w/movies, dataport. All units w/terraces. **Services:** ⚐ **Facilities:** ⚐ ⚐ ⚐ ♿ **Rates (CP):** Peak (July–Oct) $80–$105 S or D; $85–$115 ste. Lower rates off-season. Parking: Outdoor, free. Golf packages avail for three nearby golf courses. Special rates for up to four people in a room. AE, DC, DISC, MC, V.

≣≣ Family Inn Suites Gatlinburg

218 Ski Mountain Rd, 37738; tel 423/436-3300 or toll free 800/468-6326; fax 423/436-3300. Near light 10. A comfortable, family-style facility, near the National Park and within walking distance of many restaurants and attractions. **Rooms:** 53 rms, stes, and effic. CI 2pm/CO 11am. Nonsmoking rms

avail. All rooms have shared balconies with river views. Rooms on third floor and higher have nice views of Mount LeConte. **Amenities:** 🛏 🕭 🍴 A/C, cable TV w/movies. All units w/terraces, some w/fireplaces, some w/whirlpools. **Services:** 🗲 **Facilities:** 🔧 🏊 [50] 🔥 Whirlpool. **Rates (CP):** Peak (June–Oct) $59–$99 S or D; $149–$199 ste; $149–$199 effic. Children under age 19 stay free. Min stay wknds and special events. Lower rates off-season. Parking: Outdoor, free. AE, CB, DC, DISC, JCB, MC, V.

▤▤ Gatlinburg Inn

755 Parkway, 37738; tel 423/436-5133. Run by fourth-generation innkeepers, who have kept all the inn's old ledgers. Early American hardrock maple rocking chairs on the porch and in the lobby take you back to a time when everyone stopped to smell the roses, and there is also a garden full of them here. It is claimed that the country music classic ''Rocky Top'' was written in Room 388. **Rooms:** 67 rms and stes. CI 6am/CO 11am. **Amenities:** 🛏 A/C, cable TV. All units w/terraces. Handmade quilts on the beds. **Services:** 🗲 **Facilities:** 🔧 🏊 🐾 Playground. Shuffleboard. **Rates:** $58–$78 S or D; $106–$184 ste. Extra person $10. Parking: Outdoor, free. Closed Nov–Apr. MC, V.

▤▤ Quality Inn at the Convention Center

938 Parkway, 37738; tel 423/436-5607 or toll free 800/933-8674. Standard chain motel with comfortable, clean rooms. Prime location. **Rooms:** 64 rms, stes, and effic. CI 2pm/CO 11am. Nonsmoking rms avail. Some rooms offer spectacular views of the mountains. **Amenities:** 🛏 A/C, cable TV w/movies, refrig. Some units w/terraces, some w/whirlpools. **Services:** 🗲 Babysitting. **Facilities:** 🔧 🏊 [50] 🔥 Washer/dryer. **Rates:** Peak (June–Oct) $67–$89 S or D; $109–$129 ste; $109–$129 effic. Children under age 18 stay free. Min stay wknds and special events. Lower rates off-season. Parking: Indoor/outdoor, free. AE, DC, DISC, MC, V.

▤▤ Quality Inn Smokyland

727 Parkway, 37738; tel 423/436-5191 or toll free 800/933-8671. Near light 7. Tastefully decorated accommodations in an excellent location make this a smart choice. **Rooms:** 40 rms. CI 2pm/CO 11am. Nonsmoking rms avail. **Amenities:** 🛏 🕭 🖭 A/C, cable TV w/movies. Some units w/terraces, some w/fireplaces. **Services:** 🗲 Babysitting. **Facilities:** 🔧 🏊 🔥 Parking may be difficult. **Rates:** Peak (May–Nov) $80–$88 S; $95–$105 D. Extra person $10. Children under age 18 stay free. Min stay wknds and special events. Lower rates off-season. Parking: Outdoor, free. Honeymoon package avail. AE, CB, DC, DISC, MC, V.

▤ Rainbow Motel

390 E Parkway, PO Box 1397, 37738; tel 423/436-5887 or toll free 800/422-8922. On US 321. No-frills place situated near the trolley line. **Rooms:** 49 rms and effic; 11 cottages/villas. CI 2pm/CO 11am. Nonsmoking rms avail. **Amenities:** 🛏 A/C, cable TV w/movies, refrig, VCR. Some units w/ter-races, some w/fireplaces, some w/whirlpools. **Services:** 🗲 **Facilities:** 🔧 🏊 **Rates:** Peak (June–Oct) $40–$65 S or D; $55–$80 effic; $95–$150 cottage/villa. Extra person $5. Min stay special events. Lower rates off-season. Parking: Outdoor, free. DISC, MC, V.

▤▤ Ramada Inn Four Seasons

756 Parkway, PO Box 528, 37738; tel 423/436-7881 or toll free 800/933-8678; fax 423/430-3029. Located in the very center of Gatlinburg. Balconies of the guest rooms overlook the Parkway. **Rooms:** 148 rms and stes. Executive level. CI 2pm/CO 11am. Nonsmoking rms avail. The new high-rise building has better rooms. **Amenities:** 🛏 A/C, cable TV w/movies. Some units w/terraces, some w/fireplaces, some w/whirlpools. Most rooms have refrigerators. **Services:** ✕ 🗲 🍽 **Facilities:** 🔧 🏊 [600] 🔥 1 restaurant, 1 bar, sauna, whirlpool, playground, washer/dryer. **Rates:** Peak (June–Oct) $56–$169 S or D; $89–$169 ste. Extra person $9. Min stay special events. Lower rates off-season. Parking: Outdoor, free. Room rates for up to four people. B&B, honeymoon packages avail. AE, CB, DC, DISC, ER, JCB, MC, V.

▤ River Edge Motor Lodge

665 River Rd, 37738; tel 423/436-9292 or toll free 800/544-2764. Basic motel, popular with families. Located near Ober Gatlinburg and within walking distance of shopping and restaurants. **Rooms:** 43 rms, stes, and effic. CI noon/CO 11am. Nonsmoking rms avail. Rooms are well-maintained. **Amenities:** 🛏 🖭 A/C, cable TV w/movies, refrig. All units w/terraces, some w/fireplaces, some w/whirlpools. **Services:** 🗲 Babysitting. **Facilities:** 🔧 🏊 The Gatlinburg trolley stops outside the front office. **Rates:** Peak (June–Nov) $55–$85 S or D; $90–$110 ste; $90–$110 effic. Extra person $5. Children under age 12 stay free. Min stay special events. Lower rates off-season. Parking: Outdoor, free. AE, CB, DC, DISC, MC, V.

▤▤ Rivermont MasterHost Motor Inn

293 Parkway, 37738; tel 423/436-5047 or toll free 800/624-2929, 800/634-2929 in TN. Near light 1. Located on the edge of town (so you don't have to battle Gatlinburg traffic), this motel features pleasant rooms with balconies overlooking the river. **Rooms:** 69 rms. CI 1pm/CO 11am. Nonsmoking rms avail. **Amenities:** 🛏 A/C, cable TV w/movies. All units w/terraces, some w/fireplaces, some w/whirlpools. **Services:** 🗲 On the trolley route. **Facilities:** 🔧 🏊 🔥 Whirlpool. **Rates (CP):** Peak (June–Aug/Oct) $45–$75 S or D. Children under age 18 stay free. Min stay wknds. Lower rates off-season. Parking: Outdoor, free. AE, DISC, MC, V.

▤ Riverside Motor Lodge

715 Parkway, 37738; tel 423/436-4194 or toll free 800/887-2323; fax 423/436-6460. Established in 1925, this classic five-story motel offers attractive rooms (with a hint of nostalgia) in the center of downtown Gatlinburg. **Rooms:** 81 rms. CI 2pm/CO 11am. **Amenities:** 🛏 🖭 A/C, cable TV. Some units w/terraces. **Services:** 🗲 **Facilities:** 🔧 🏊 [160]

Rates: Peak (June–Aug/Oct) $72 S; $79 D. Extra person $5. Children under age 17 stay free. Min stay special events. Lower rates off-season. Parking: Outdoor, free. AE, DISC, MC, V.

☰☰ Rocky Waters Motor Inn

333 Parkway, PO Box 230, 37738; tel 423/436-7861 or toll free 800/824-1111; fax 423/436-0241. At light 2. Housed in two buildings along the banks of the river, this charming place offers a relaxing atmosphere. **Rooms:** 100 rms, stes, and effic; 1 cottage/villa. CI 2pm/CO 11am. Nonsmoking rms avail. Rooms in one of the buildings have balconies overlooking the river. **Amenities:** 🛏 A/C, cable TV w/movies, refrig, VCR. Some units w/terraces, some w/fireplaces, some w/whirlpools. In-room hot tubs. **Services:** ⤵ Coffee available 24 hours. **Facilities:** 🖼 ⚞ ⛱ 💯 ⅙ Whirlpool, washer/dryer. Picnic area with grills and a rocking horse for kids. **Rates:** Peak (June–Aug/Oct) $76–$81 S or D; $86–$130 ste; $86 effic; $75–$100 cottage/villa. Extra person $5. Min stay wknds and special events. Lower rates off-season. Parking: Outdoor, free. AE, DC, DISC, MC, V.

☰☰ Travelodge

610 Airport Rd, 37738; tel 423/436-7851 or toll free 800/876-6888; fax 423/430-3580. Next to City Park. Clean and well-appointed, and great for nature lovers. The sound of the nearby river can be heard in most rooms. **Rooms:** 127 rms, stes, and effic. CI 2pm/CO 11am. Nonsmoking rms avail. **Amenities:** 🛏 📺 A/C, cable TV w/movies, refrig. Some units w/terraces, some w/fireplaces, some w/whirlpools. **Services:** ⤵ Babysitting. **Facilities:** 🖼 ⚞ ⛱250 ⅙ 1 restaurant, games rm, sauna, washer/dryer. Indoor pool with underwater "cave." Adjacent city park has facilities for tennis, basketball, and baseball. **Rates:** Peak (June–Oct) $57–$62 S or D; $94–$126 ste; $94–$126 effic. Extra person $6. Children under age 12 stay free. Min stay special events. Lower rates off-season. Parking: Outdoor, free. AE, CB, DC, DISC, JCB, MC, V.

INN

☰ Buckhorn Inn

2140 Tudor Mountain Rd, 37738; tel 423/436-4668; fax 423/436-5009. On US 321. 35 acres. A gem from the past with the welcoming comfort and security of going to Grandma's, this inn will be a pleasant surprise for its guests staying in Gatlinburg. Unsuitable for children under 6. **Rooms:** 6 rms; 6 cottages/villas. CI 3pm/CO 11am. No smoking. For a special treat request the tower. It is an individualized, two-level room in the old water tower. **Amenities:** ⚞ A/C, cable TV w/movies. No phone. Some units w/fireplaces. Room numbers four and five have showers without tubs. **Services:** 🚐 Coffee, tea, and soft drinks available at all times, and sack lunches available for hikers. **Facilities:** ⚞ ⛱25 1 restaurant (bkfst and dinner only), guest lounge. The inn has a wonderful ¾-mile nature trail. **Rates (BB):** Peak (Oct) $95–$120 S;

$105–$130 D; $125–$150 cottage/villa. Extra person $20. Min stay wknds and special events. Lower rates off-season. MAP rates avail. Parking: Outdoor, free. MC, V.

LODGE

☰ Le Conte Lodge

250 Apple Valley Rd, PO Box 350, 37738; tel 423/429-5704; fax 423/429-5705. Located atop beautiful, serene Mount Le Conte and known for its spectacular views and sunrises, this lodge is accessible to all of the foot trails leading to attractions on the mountain. **Rooms:** 10 cottages/villas. CI noon/CO 9:30am. Rooms are on the rustic side, with kerosene lanterns and heaters, double bunk beds, one chair per room, and an outdoor toilet. **Amenities:** A/C, cable TV. No phone. Some units w/fireplaces. **Services:** 🚶 Lunch can be arranged for stay-overs. **Rates (MAP):** $64 cottage/villa. Extra person $64. Closed Dec–Mar. No CC.

RESORT

☰☰ Bent Creek Golf Resort

3919 E Parkway, PO Box 1190, 37738; tel 423/436-2875 or toll free 800/251-9336; fax 423/436-3257. On US 321. Removed (20 minutes away) from the hectic downtown of Gatlinburg, this resort provides special care for the golf enthusiast. **Rooms:** 108 rms; 18 cottages/villas. CI 3pm/CO 11am. Nonsmoking rms avail. **Amenities:** 🛏 A/C, cable TV w/movies, refrig. All units w/terraces, some w/fireplaces, some w/whirlpools. **Services:** ✕ 🚐 🚶 ⤵ Social director, babysitting. **Facilities:** 🖼 ▶18 ⚞ ⛱2 ⛱300 ⅙ 1 restaurant, 1 bar, basketball, volleyball, playground. Gary Player–designed golf course, golf school, and many other services to golfers. **Rates:** Peak (June–Oct) $59–$109 S or D; $110–$130 cottage/villa. Extra person $10. Children under age 12 stay free. Lower rates off-season. Parking: Outdoor, free. Golf and honeymoon packages avail. AE, CB, DC, DISC, MC, V.

RESTAURANTS 🍴

Burning Bush Restaurant

11151 Parkway; tel 423/436-4669. **American.** The romantic ambience at this eatery capitalizes on the natural wonder of the Smokies. There are caged birds in the dining room, and the windows look out on bird and squirrel feeders. There's natural wood everywhere, and a large stone fireplace. The kitchen specializes in classic, simple dishes such as prime rib and roast duck. **FYI:** Reservations recommended. Children's menu. **Open:** Peak (May–Oct) breakfast daily 8am–2pm; lunch daily 11am–4pm; dinner Mon–Thurs 8am–9pm, Fri–Sat 8am–10pm. **Prices:** Main courses $13–$23. AE, CB, DC, DISC, MC, V. ♥ ⅙

Calhouns

1004 Parkway; tel 423/436-4100. Between lights 9 and 10. **American/Barbecue.** Calhoun's famous barbecued ribs are now available in Gatlinburg. All of their delicious soups, salads, sandwiches, and hamburgers—along with prime ribs, steaks, chicken, and seafood—are here. Fresh mountain trout is available, too. Homemade buttermilk biscuits and freshly baked corn bread are served with entrees, and generous slices of homemade desserts made from the finest ingredients are a perfect ending. Freshly brewed Cherokee Ale on draft, handcrafted in their own microbrewery, is available to quench your thirst. **FYI:** Reservations not accepted. Children's menu. **Open:** Mon–Thurs 11am–10:30pm, Fri–Sat 11am–11:30pm, Sun 11am–10pm. **Prices:** Main courses $7–$16. AE, CB, DC, DISC, MC, V.

Celebrations

In The Edgewater Hotel, 745 River Rd; tel 423/436-4151. **American.** A view of the river and the mountains provides a beautiful backdrop for such meals as mountain trout and prime rib. The bar and its live music is popular with both locals and tourists. **FYI:** Reservations accepted. Blues/country music/rock. Children's menu. **Open:** Breakfast daily 7am–11pm; dinner daily 5–10pm. **Prices:** Main courses $6–$13; prix fixe $7–$15. AE, CB, DC, DISC, MC, V.

Eleanor's Cafe

In Park Vista Resort Hotel, Airport Rd; tel 423/436-9211. **American.** Redecorated in 1995, this cafe offers a pleasant and relaxed atmosphere. The breakfast buffet includes made-to-order pancakes and waffles; the varied dinner menu offers salads, beef, pork, poultry, fish, seafood, and a vegetable plate. During high season, a seafood buffet is available Fri nights, while a prime rib buffet is offered Sat nights. **FYI:** Reservations accepted. Country music. Children's menu. **Open:** Breakfast daily 6:30–11:30am; lunch daily 11:30am–2pm; dinner daily 5–10pm. **Prices:** Main courses $10–$16; prix fixe $15–$16. AE, CB, DC, DISC, MC, V.

Ⓢ Ogle's Restaurant

516 Parkway; tel 423/436-4157. At light 3 next to Best Western Twin Islands Motel. **Regional American.** Open for 50 years, this down-home family-friendly buffet offers an unbelievable amount of food: roast beef, chicken, country-style ham, five vegetables, homemade mashed potatoes, an extensive salad bar, rolls and corn bread, nachos, and five delicious freshly prepared desserts. Customers receive discount coupon for Ogle's Water Park. Beautiful river views from the outdoor patio. **FYI:** Reservations recommended. Children's menu. No liquor license. **Open:** Daily 8am–9:30pm. Closed Dec–Mar. **Prices:** Prix fixe $9. AE, DC, DISC, MC, V.

Old Heidelberg Restaurant

148 Parkway; tel 423/430-3094. **American/German/Seafood.** German beer, German food, German music, and German fun for the whole family. Diners are treated to a stage show, and audience participation is encouraged. Ethnic specialties like sausages, schnitzel, jaeger (sautéed pork loin with mushrooms and onion gravy, served with homemade spaetzle) and sauerbraten (beef marinated in wine vinegar and served with German potato dumpling and red cabbage)

are available, as are steaks, seafood, and chicken. **FYI:** Reservations recommended. Children's menu. **Open:** Daily noon–11pm. **Prices:** Main courses $8–$20. AE, CB, DC, DISC, MC, V.

The Open Hearth

1138 Parkway; tel 423/436-5648. At light 10. **American.** Established in 1953, this has long been one of Gatlinburg's finest dining places. The menu relies on classic entrees: aged midwestern beef, fresh rainbow trout, fried chicken, baby back ribs, and fresh seafood. **FYI:** Reservations recommended. Country music/piano. Children's menu. **Open:** Sun–Thurs 5–10pm, Fri–Sat 5–11pm. **Prices:** Main courses $13–$30. AE, CB, DC, DISC, MC, V.

★ Pancake Pantry

628 Parkway; tel 423/436-4724. Near light 6. **American.** The most delectable smells fill this bright, lovely restaurant that offers 24 varieties of pancakes and 18 types of waffles, in addition to crepes, omelettes, bacon, ham, sausage, french toast, fruits, and juices. Old fashioned pancakes (buttermilk or whole wheat) can be served with light fluffy whipped butter and syrup or fruit compote and real fresh whipped cream. Gourmet sandwiches are available for lunch, including the Dutch Diplomat (a triple-decker on rye with ham, Swiss cheese, turkey, and lettuce, with cole slaw and homemade potato chips on the side). **FYI:** Reservations not accepted. Children's menu. No liquor license. **Open:** Peak (Apr–Oct) daily 7am–4pm. **Prices:** Lunch main courses $5–$8. No CC.

The Park Grill

1110 Parkway; tel 423/436-2300. At light 10. **American.** Unique decor and atmosphere reminiscent of a majestic national park lodge: the building is made of massive spruce tree logs and the waitstaff are dressed in park ranger attire. Guests may choose from three individually prepared entrees daily. The pan-fried Cherokee trout served with lemon, butter, capers, and Italian parsley is especially good. **FYI:** Reservations not accepted. Children's menu. **Open:** Daily 5–10pm. **Prices:** Main courses $13–$23. AE, CB, DC, DISC, MC, V.

★ The Peddler Steak House

820 River Rd; tel 423/436-5794. **American.** Long recognized by locals as one of Gatlinburg's finest, this steak house specializes in aged Western beef cooked over Tennessee hickory charcoal. Steaks are custom-cut at the diner's table; seafood and chicken also available. Salad and fruit bar, which comes with every entree, contains more than 40 garden fresh vegetables, fruits, and cheeses. **FYI:** Reservations not accepted. Children's menu. **Open:** Daily 5–10pm. **Prices:** Main courses $13–$23. AE, CB, DC, DISC, MC, V.

Ronnie Milsap Keyboard Cafe

812 Parkway; tel 423/430-1978. At light 8. **American.** Ronnie Milsap has had more chart-topping country hits than Elvis Presley. His cafe offers steaks, chicken, chops, catfish,

trout, fajitas, burgers, and lasagna—all in a fun atmosphere where the music never stops. **FYI:** Reservations not accepted. Country music/dancing. Children's menu. **Open:** Sun–Thurs 11am–10pm, Fri–Sat 11am–11pm. **Prices:** Main courses $7–$16. AE, DC, DISC, MC, V. ♿

Smoky Mountain Trout House

410 N Parkway; tel 423/436-5416. **American.** Freshest trout in Gatlinburg—caught live around 2pm and brought directly to the restaurant, where it is prepared to order. Superb clam chowder, trout fritters, and fresh homemade desserts such as coconut cream pie are good accompaniments. **FYI:** Reservations accepted. Children's menu. **Open:** Daily 5–10pm. Closed Jan–Mar. **Prices:** Main courses $10–$16. AE, CB, DC, DISC, MC, V. ▾

⑤ World Famous North of the Border Cafe and Cantina

705 E Parkway; tel 423/436-0444. Off US 321. **Mexican.** A 30-foot waterfall in the dining room and Old West meets Southwest decor provide a relaxing atmosphere for guests. Salsa is made fresh daily, and the fajitas are fabulous. The margarita pie is the most popular dessert. Celebrities like Dolly Parton, Bob Hope, Anthony Quinn, and Jack Klugman have all eaten here. **FYI:** Reservations not accepted. Country music/dancing/magician. Children's menu. **Open:** Peak (May–Dec) Sun–Thurs noon–10pm, Fri–Sat noon–11pm. **Prices:** Main courses $6–$15. AE, DC, DISC, MC, V. ▮ ▲ ▦ ♿

ATTRACTIONS 🏛

Ober Gatlinburg

1001 Parkway; tel 423/436-5423 or toll free 800/251-9202. This mountaintop, all-season recreation park and ski resort features indoor ice skating, bungee jumping, water rides, and a "dry" alpine slide, in addition to eight wintertime ski trails rated from beginner to advanced. For the little ones there's an amusement park, video arcade, and go-kart track. The two-mile aerial tramway ride up to the park is a thrill all its own. (Trams leave every 20 minutes, and the ride takes approximately 10 minutes. Please note that the tram is the only way to access Ober Gatlinburg.) **Open:** Mon–Thurs 10am–10pm, Fri–Sat 10am–11pm, Sun 10am–4pm. **$$$**

Guinness World Records Museum

631 Parkway, Baskins Square Mall; tel 423/436-9100. Hundreds of exhibits include memorabilia of famous Guinness record holders: Elvis, the Beatles, and Houdini. Self-guided tours. **Open:** Daily 10am–6pm. Closed Dec 25. **$$$**

Great Smoky Arts and Crafts Community

Glades Rd; tel 423/671-3600 ext 3504. This eight-mile loop (consisting of US 321, Buckhorn Rd, and Glades Rd) is home to over 80 shops selling traditional Smoky Mountain crafts. Pottery, candles, leather goods, paintings, baskets, handmade dolls, wall hangings, stained glass, and many more items are lovingly crafted by these skilled artisans. Drive around until a shop catches your eye, or catch the Arts and Crafts trolley at Gatlinburg City Hall. Trolleys leave every half-hour and one fare entitles you to ride all day. **Open:** Daily 9am–6pm. **Free**

Great Smoky Mountains National Park

For NC lodgings and dining, see Gatlinburg, Pigeon Forge, and Sevierville, TN; Balsam, Bryson City, Cherokee, Franklin, Maggie Valley, and Waynesville, NC

This 520,000-acre park, lying half in Tennessee and half in North Carolina, draws more visitors (almost 8½ million a year) than any other national park in the country. Within its limited compass—50 miles long and 15–19 miles wide—it contains all the glories of the Appalachians (the oldest mountain range in North America), with more than 20 peaks rising above 6,560 feet. Its deep forests, home to black bear, deer, and other wildlife, are often wreathed in the mist and tattered clouds that give it its name. Once the unapproachable realm of the Cherokee Nation, the Great Smoky Mountains park now offers the tourist magnificent landscapes (particularly from June to mid-July when the rhododendrons are in bloom) and spectacular scenic drives. The best views are undoubtedly those from **Newfound Gap** and **Clingman's Dome** (both in the Tennessee half).

Also in Tennessee, some 25 miles west of the Sugarlands entrance, is **Cade's Cove,** an outdoor museum of log cabins, a gristmill, and barns typical of those used by original mountain settlers.

Hiking and camping are best along the 70 miles of Appalachian Trail, following the ridge that forms the North Carolina–Tennessee border. Any of the entrance visitors centers can furnish details about campsites and shelters. Clear, rushing mountain streams abound with trout. Horseback riding is also popular, with more than 900 miles of marked horse and foot trails to explore, and saddle horses are available within the park—inquire at the visitors centers. For more information, contact the Superintendent, 107 Park Headquarters Rd, Gatlinburg, TN 37738 (tel 423/436-1200).

Greeneville

Established in 1781, it was the capital of the former State of Franklin (from 1785 to 1788) and the birthplace of President Andrew Johnson. Attractions include antebellum homes and historic sites. Home of Tusculum College, which was founded in 1794 and is the oldest college west of the Alleghenies. **Information:** Greene County Partnership, 115 Academy St, Greenville, 37743 (tel 423/638-4111).

MOTELS

Andrew Johnson Inn

2145 E Andrew Johnson Hwy, 37745; tel 423/638-8124 or toll free 800/545-8085; fax 423/638-8125. Acceptable for a less expensive overnight stay with an early checkout. **Rooms:** 44 rms. CI 10–11am/CO 11am. Nonsmoking rms avail. All rooms were renovated in 1995. **Amenities:** A/C, cable TV w/movies, dataport. Some units w/whirlpools. **Services:** Twice-daily maid svce. **Facilities:** **Rates:** $33 S; $36 D. Extra person $3. Children under age 10 stay free. Min stay special events. Parking: Outdoor, free. AE, CB, DC, DISC, MC, V.

Charray Inn

121 Serral Dr, 37745; tel 423/638-1331 or toll free 800/ 852-4682; fax 423/639-5289. This motel pays special attention to the needs of its guests. **Rooms:** 36 rms. CI noon/CO 11am. Nonsmoking rms avail. "Evergreen" rooms feature humidifiers and filtered water. **Amenities:** A/C, cable TV w/movies, refrig. **Services:** X **Facilities:** 1 restaurant (bkfst only). **Rates:** $38–$52 S; $42–$60 D. Extra person $4. Children under age 12 stay free. Min stay special events. Parking: Outdoor, free. AE, CB, DC, DISC, MC, V.

Holiday Inn

1790 E Andrew Johnson Hwy, 37743; tel 423/639-4185 or toll free 800/HOLIDAY; fax 423/639-7280. This recently renovated motel features an atrium with flowing streams and plants. **Rooms:** 90 rms. CI 2pm/CO noon. Nonsmoking rms avail. Renovated rooms feature 25" TV sets, hot tubs, and two phone lines. **Amenities:** A/C, cable TV, dataport. Some units w/terraces. **Services:** X **Facilities:** 1 restaurant, 1 bar. **Rates:** $41–$46 S or D. Extra person $7. Children under age 19 stay free. Min stay special events. Parking: Outdoor, free. B&B and wedding packages avail. AE, CB, DC, DISC, ER, JCB, MC, V.

ATTRACTION

Andrew Johnson National Historic Site

College and Depot Sts; tel 423/638-3551. Preserves several sites pertaining to the life of Johnson, Lincoln's successor to the presidency and the only president to be directly threatened with impeachment. Highlights include Johnson's tailor shop (now a visitors center), homestead, and gravesite and memorial. Daily tours offered. **Open:** Daily 9am–5pm. Closed some hols. $

Hendersonville

Just northeast of Nashville, the city is home to several country music stars. **Information:** Hendersonville Area Chamber of Commerce, 101 Wessington Place, PO Box 377, Hendersonville, 37077 (tel 615/824-2818).

ATTRACTIONS

House of Cash

700 Johnny Cash Pkwy; tel 615/824-5110. In addition to learning more about Cash ("the man in black"), his wife June Carter, and the famous Carter family, visitors to this museum can see a motorcycle that belonged to Buddy Holly, Buffalo Bill's Winchester rifle, Al Capone's chair, John Wayne's six-shooter, and many other interesting items. **Open:** Mon–Sat 9am–4:30pm. $$$

Twitty City

1 Music Village Blvd; tel 615/822-6650. Though Conway Twitty died in 1993, his home and 10 acres of manicured grounds are still a major Nashville-area attraction. Guided tours of Twitty's mansion include a visit to Conway's Showcase, a computerized display that traces the star's long music career. There are also live country music shows, retail shops, and museums highlighting Bill Monroe, Marty Robbins, and other stars in the Music Village USA complex. **Open:** Daily 9am–5pm. Closed some hols. $$$

Historic Rock Castle

139 Rock Castle Lane; tel 615/824-0502. Georgian-Federal home listed on the National Register of Historic Places. Daniel Smith—Tennessee pioneer, surveyor, Revolutionary War captain, US senator—lived here with his wife Sarah and their children. Built in 1784 from Tennessee limestone (hence its name), the house and its furnishings reflect a simple pioneer lifestyle informed by Smith's culture and good taste. Antiques (with some original Smith family pieces), family Bible, private letters, and Daniel Smith's extensive library. **Open:** Mon–Sat 10am–4pm, Sun 1–4pm. $

Henning

ATTRACTION

Alex Haley House and Museum

US 51; tel 901/738-2240. The small house where Haley, the Pulitzer Prize–winning author of *Roots,* lived as a boy is now a museum containing memorabilia and old portraits of the Haley family. Nearby is the family burial site, where Haley and many of his ancestors, including Chicken George (one of the most endearing characters in the TV miniseries), are buried. **Open:** Tues–Sat 10am–5pm, Sun 1–5pm. Closed some hols. $

Hurricane Mills

ATTRACTION

Loretta Lynn's Ranch

I-40; tel 615/296-7700. This huge ranch is well worth a stop, even if you're not familiar with the country-music icon's music. Popular recreational facilities include rental cabins, an

RV park, snack bars, swimming pool, and several craft and gift stores. Activities include canoeing, hiking fishing, hayrides, miniature golf, volleyball, horseshoes, and softball. If you are a fan of the singer, you may enjoy a visit to **Loretta's Gift Shop and Museum.** Between April and October, there are daily tours through Loretta and her husband Mooney's 100-year-old plantation home (to see how far the famous singer came in her life, you can visit a reconstruction of the home where she lived as a coal miner's daughter), and several times each summer Loretta gives concerts here at the ranch. **$$$$**

Jackson

Halfway between Memphis and Nashville, this little town was named for the seventh US president. Hometown and burial site of legendary railroading man Casey Jones, whose home is now a historic site and museum. **Information:** Jackson Area Chamber of Commerce, 197 Auditorium St, PO Box 1904, Jackson, 38302 (tel 901/423-2200).

HOTELS 🏨

≡≡≡ Comfort Inn Jackson

1963 US 45 Bypass, 38305; tel 901/668-4100 or toll free 800/228-5150; fax 901/664-6940. Exit 80A off I-40. Family-oriented; located next to Casey Jones Village. **Rooms:** 204 rms and stes. CI 4pm/CO noon. Nonsmoking rms avail. **Amenities:** 🛏 🔥 ☎ 🍴 A/C, cable TV. All units w/terraces. Many of the rooms have dataports, mini-refrigerators, and microwaves. **Services:** 🔼 🛎 **Facilities:** 🛗 🏊 🎱 300 🛗 Washer/dryer. **Rates (CP):** Peak (May–Oct) $47–$80 S; $54–$80 D; $80 ste. Extra person $5. Children under age 18 stay free. Lower rates off-season. Parking: Outdoor, free. AE, CB, DC, DISC, JCB, MC, V.

≡≡≡ Garden Plaza

1770 US 45 Bypass, 38305; tel 901/664-6900 or toll free 800/342-7336; fax 901/668-0474. Exit 80A off I-40. Comfortable, hospitable hotel with an open and airy lobby and glass-walled elevators. **Rooms:** 168 rms and stes. Executive level. CI 3pm/CO noon. Nonsmoking rms avail. Most rooms are well designed. **Amenities:** 🛏 🔥 A/C, cable TV w/movies, refrig, dataport. **Services:** ✗ 🔼 🛎 Babysitting. **Facilities:** 🛗 🏊 300 🛗 1 restaurant, 1 bar (w/entertainment), spa, whirlpool. **Rates:** Peak (June–Oct) $59–$69 S; $59–$79 D; $125 ste. Extra person $10. Children under age 18 stay free. Lower rates off-season. Parking: Outdoor, free. AE, CB, DC, DISC, MC, V.

≡≡≡ Holiday Inn

541 Carriage House Dr, 38305; tel 901/668-6000 or toll free 800/HOLIDAY; fax 901/668-9516. Exit 80A off I-40. Five-story, mostly-suites hotel built around a central atrium. Nice, spacious lobby. **Rooms:** 135 rms, stes, and effic. CI 2pm/CO noon. Nonsmoking rms avail. **Amenities:** 🛏 🔥 ☎ A/C, cable

TV, refrig, dataport. Some units w/terraces. Most rooms have microwaves. **Services:** ✗ 🔼 🛎 Masseur, children's program, babysitting. **Facilities:** 🛗 300 🛗 1 restaurant, 1 bar, games rm, beauty salon, washer/dryer. Guest privileges at local sports facility. **Rates:** $60 S or D; $78–$100 ste; $78–$100 effic. Extra person $6. Children under age 18 stay free. Parking: Outdoor, free. AE, CB, DC, DISC, JCB, MC, V.

≡≡≡ Sheraton Old English Inn

2267 N Highland Ave, 38305; tel 901/668-1571 or toll free 800/325-3535; fax 901/664-8070. Exit 82A off I-40. English Tudor–style architecture and decor in eastern Tennessee. The classy lobby is decorated with original and reproduction British antiques. **Rooms:** 103 rms and stes. Executive level. CI 3pm/CO noon. Nonsmoking rms avail. Rooms have armoires and desks with glass inlays. **Amenities:** 🛏 🔥 ☎ A/C, cable TV. Some units w/fireplaces, some w/whirlpools. **Services:** ✗ 🔼 🛎 Social director. **Facilities:** 🛗 300 🛗 1 restaurant (see "Restaurants" below), 1 bar (w/entertainment). Nicely landscaped pool area with bar and patio. Guest privileges to local fitness center. **Rates:** $68–$88 S; $74–$94 D; $88–$94 ste. Extra person $6. Children under age 18 stay free. Parking: Outdoor, free. AE, CB, DC, DISC, JCB, MC, V.

MOTELS

≡≡ Best Western Old Hickory Inn

1849 US 45 Bypass, 38305; tel 901/668-4222 or toll free 800/528-1234; fax 901/664-8536. Exit 80A off I-40. Well-maintained, comfortable accommodations. **Rooms:** 142 rms. CI noon/CO noon. Nonsmoking rms avail. Many rooms were recently renovated. **Amenities:** 🛏 🔥 A/C, cable TV. **Services:** ✗ 🔼 🛎 🐾 **Facilities:** 🛗 400 🛗 1 restaurant, 1 bar (w/entertainment), lawn games. Large pool area; picnic tables. **Rates:** Peak (May–Sept) $45 S; $49 D. Extra person $4. Children under age 12 stay free. Lower rates off-season. Parking: Outdoor, free. AE, CB, DC, DISC, MC, V.

≡≡ Comfort Inn

2600 Anderson Ave, Brownsville, 38012; tel 901/772-4082 or toll free 800/4-CHOICE; fax 901/772-4082. Exit 56 off I-40. Offers simple yet comfortable accommodations. **Rooms:** 52 rms and stes. CI 1:30pm/CO 11am. Nonsmoking rms avail. **Amenities:** 🛏 A/C, cable TV. **Services:** 🛎 **Facilities:** 🛗 45 🛗 Washer/dryer. **Rates (CP):** Peak (Mar–Sept) $40–$70 S; $50–$65 D; $65 ste. Extra person $5. Children under age 13 stay free. Lower rates off-season. Parking: Outdoor, free. AE, CB, DC, DISC, JCB, MC, V.

≡ Days Inn

2530 Anderson Ave, Brownsville, 38012; tel 901/772-3297 or toll free 800/329-7466; fax 901/772-3246. Exit 56 off I-40. A basic motel with nicely decorated rooms. **Rooms:** 43 rms. CI 1pm/CO 11am. Nonsmoking rms avail. **Amenities:** 🛏 A/C, cable TV. **Services:** 🛎 🐾 **Facilities:** 🛗 **Rates (CP):**

Peak (Mar–Sept) $40–$65 S; $50–$60 D. Extra person $5. Children under age 13 stay free. Lower rates off-season. Parking: Outdoor, free. AE, CB, DC, DISC, MC, V.

⊟⊟ Fairfield Inn

535 Wiley Parker Rd, 38305; tel 901/668-1400 or toll free 800/228-2800; fax 901/668-1400. Exit 80A off I-40. The first two floors of this three-story motel open to the outside, while there's an indoor entrance for the third floor. Popular with business travelers. **Rooms:** 105 rms. CI 3pm/CO noon. Nonsmoking rms avail. **Amenities:** 📺 ♨ A/C, satel TV w/movies. Some rooms feature dataports. **Services:** ⚐ ⚑ **Facilities:** 🏋 🏊 & **Rates (CP):** Peak (Apr–Aug) $39–$52 S; $45–$69 D. Extra person $7. Children under age 18 stay free. Lower rates off-season. Parking: Outdoor, free. AE, CB, DC, DISC, MC, V.

⊟ Quality Inn

2262 N Highland Ave, 38305; tel 901/668-1066 or toll free 800/221-2222. Exit 82A off I-40. A simple, basic stopover for budget travelers. **Rooms:** 88 rms. CI noon/CO noon. Nonsmoking rms avail. **Amenities:** 📺 A/C, cable TV. **Services:** ⚐ ⚑ **Facilities:** 🏋 & Washer/dryer. **Rates:** Peak (May–Sept) $30–$38 S; $40–$48 D. Extra person $6. Children under age 18 stay free. Lower rates off-season. Parking: Outdoor, free. AE, CB, DC, DISC, ER, JCB, MC, V.

RESTAURANTS 🍴

Oliver's

In Sheraton Old English Inn, 2267 N Highland Ave; tel 901/668-1571. Exit 82A off I-40. **International.** A quiet and cozy dining room serving classic cuisine, including prime rib, seafood, and pasta. The quality of the ingredients make this a standout. **FYI:** Reservations accepted. Guitar/piano/singer. **Open:** Breakfast daily 6–11am; lunch daily 11am–2pm; dinner daily 5–10pm. **Prices:** Main courses $5–$15. AE, CB, DC, DISC, MC, V. &

Suede's

2263 N Highland Ave; tel 901/664-1956. Exit 82A off I-40. **Southern.** Owned by legendary recording artist Carl Perkins, who wrote the classic "Blue Suede Shoes" and played with greats such as Elvis, Roy Orbison, and the Beatles. As you might expect, the dining room is full of photos and memorabilia, and a relaxed atmosphere predominates. The menu focuses on hearty regional favorites such as rib eye steak, ribs, and catfish. **FYI:** Reservations accepted. Children's menu. Beer and wine only. **Open:** Mon–Sat 11am–9pm, Sun 11am–2pm. **Prices:** Main courses $5–$14. AE, CB, DC, DISC, MC, V. &

ATTRACTION 📷

Casey Jones Home and Railroad Museum

US 45 Bypass, exit 80A; tel 901/668-1222. Amidst the turn-of-the-century buildings located in Casey Jones Village is the home of the famed engineer who became a hero by staying aboard his locomotive in an attempt to avoid a collision. The museum is filled with railroad memorabilia as well as period and personal furnishings. **Open:** Apr–Dec, daily 8am–8pm; Jan–Mar, daily 9am–5pm. Closed some hols. **$**

Jellico

Jellico, on Kentucky border, is located in a coal mining region in the mountainous eastern portion of the state.

MOTELS 🏨

⊟⊟ Best Western Holiday Plaza Motel

US 25 W, PO Box 177, 37762; tel 423/784-7241 or toll free 800/528-1234. Exit 160 off I-75. Humble cement-block motel with spectacular views of nearby Indian Mountain. Small lobby equipped with chairs and TV. **Rooms:** 50 rms. CI noon/CO 11am. Nonsmoking rms avail. **Amenities:** 📺 A/C, cable TV. **Services:** ⚑ ⚐ **Facilities:** 🏋 1 restaurant. **Rates (CP):** $26–$32 S; $36–$46 D. Extra person $5. Children under age 13 stay free. Parking: Outdoor, free. AE, CB, DC, DISC, MC, V.

⊟⊟⊟ Days Inn

US 25, PO Box 299, 37762; tel 423/784-7281 or toll free 800/325-2525; fax 423/784-4529. Exit 160 off I-75. Popular with families. There's also lots of outdoor play space for the kids. **Rooms:** 128 rms. CI noon/CO 11am. Nonsmoking rms avail. **Amenities:** 📺 📻 A/C, cable TV w/movies. **Services:** ⚑ ⚐ **Facilities:** 🏋 🏊 & 1 restaurant, playground. **Rates:** $38 S; $41 D. Extra person $4. Children under age 18 stay free. Parking: Outdoor, free. Family rates avail. AE, DC, DISC, MC, V.

⊟⊟ Jellico Motel

US 25W, PO Box 177, 37762; tel 423/784-7211 or toll free 800/251-9498. Exit 160 off I-75. A comfortable motel with a very welcoming atmosphere. Popular with vacationing families. **Rooms:** 92 rms. CI 2pm/CO 11am. Nonsmoking rms avail. **Amenities:** 📺 A/C, cable TV. **Services:** ⚑ ⚐ **Facilities:** 🏋 🏊 1 restaurant, basketball, playground. Large kiddie pool. **Rates:** $25 S; $34 D. Extra person $4. Children under age 12 stay free. Parking: Outdoor, free. AE, CB, DC, DISC, MC, V.

ATTRACTION 📷

Indian Mountain State Park

Indian Mountain Rd; tel 423/784-7958. This 200-acre park, built over the remains of an abandoned strip mine, is a wonderful example of land reclamation for public recreation. Boating, biking, picnicking, and hiking facilities are available here, along with a 50-site campground. **Open:** Daily 7am–9pm. **Free**

Johnson City

See also Jonesborough

Located 20 miles south of the Virginia border, this is an entry point for Cherokee National Forest and a center for lake recreation. It was first settled in the 1760s; today it is an important railroad center and livestock and dairy market. Site of Rocky Mount, a log cabin (built 1770) that served as the first capitol of the territory south of the Ohio River. East Tennessee State University is in Johnson City. **Information:** Johnson City Convention & Visitors Bureau, 603 E Market St, PO Box 180, Johnson City, 37605 (tel 423/461-8000).

HOTELS

Garden Plaza Hotel

211 Mockingbird Lane, 37604; tel 423/929-2000 or toll free 800/3-GARDEN; fax 423/929-2000. Off I-181. One of the area's nicest hotels, housed in a modern building with a large, glass-atrium lobby. **Rooms:** 187 rms and stes. CI 3pm/CO noon. Nonsmoking rms avail. Large TVs and wraparound windows give the guest lots to look at. **Amenities:** A/C, satel TV w/movies. **Services:** Twice-daily maid svce, masseur, babysitting. Discount tickets to the movie theater across the street. **Facilities:** 1 restaurant, 1 bar, sauna, whirlpool. Guests have free use of a nearby fitness center. **Rates:** $59–$83 S or D; $115 ste. Extra person $8. Children under age 12 stay free. Parking: Outdoor, free. AE, CB, DC, DISC, MC, V.

Holiday Inn

101 W Springbrook Dr, 37604; tel 423/282-4611 or toll free 800/HOLIDAY; fax 423/283-4869. Exit 35 off I-181. In keeping with the Sheraton reputation, this hotel is clean, attractive, and well maintained. **Rooms:** 205 rms and stes. CI 3pm/CO noon. Nonsmoking rms avail. **Amenities:** A/C, cable TV w/movies. **Services:** Social director, babysitting. **Facilities:** 1 restaurant (*see* "Restaurants" below), 1 bar (w/entertainment), sauna, whirlpool. **Rates:** Peak (June–Aug) $71–$77 S or D; $150–$260 ste. Extra person $10. Children under age 18 stay free. Lower rates off-season. Parking: Outdoor, free. AE, CB, DC, DISC, MC, V.

MOTELS

Days Inn

2312 Browns Mill Rd, 37601; tel 423/282-2211 or toll free 800/DAYS-INN; fax 423/282-6111. Exit 35B off I-181. A place that is showing its age. Fine for a night or two, but not for extended stays. **Rooms:** 102 rms and stes. CI 2pm/CO 11am. Nonsmoking rms avail. Rooms are in better shape than the public areas. **Amenities:** A/C, satel TV w/movies, dataport. Some units w/whirlpools. **Services:** Small pets only; $25 deposit required. **Facilities:** **Rates (CP):** Peak (May–Oct) $45 S or D; $85 ste. Extra person $5.

Children under age 18 stay free. Lower rates off-season. Parking: Outdoor, free. Corporate and trucker rates avail. AE, DC, DISC, MC, V.

Fairfield Inn

207 E Mountcastle Dr, 37601; tel 423/282-3335 or toll free 800/228-2800; fax 423/282-3335. Off I-181. Offers comfortable accommodations suitable for overnight stays. **Rooms:** 132 rms. CI open/CO noon. Nonsmoking rms avail. Rooms are dark-looking, but the furnishings are attractive. **Amenities:** A/C, satel TV w/movies. **Services:** **Facilities:** **Rates (CP):** Peak (Apr–Oct) $36–$41 S; $42–$48 D. Extra person $6. Children under age 18 stay free. Lower rates off-season. Parking: Outdoor, free. AE, DC, DISC, MC, V.

RESTAURANTS

Grady's American Grill

1914 N Roan St; tel 423/282-2722. Off I-181. **American.** A casual eatery housed in a beautiful brick building with high arched ceilings, black carved-wood chairs, and dark paisley tablecloths. The menu focuses on mesquite grilled chicken and steaks, but also offers an array of pasta, seafood, and salads. **FYI:** Reservations not accepted. Children's menu. **Open:** Sun–Thurs 11am–11pm, Fri–Sat 11am–midnight. **Prices:** Main courses $6–$20. AE, DC, DISC, MC, V.

Reflections

In Sheraton Plaza Hotel, 101 W Springbrook Dr; tel 423/282-4611. Off I-181. **American.** The formal burgundy-and-white dining room provides a fine setting for business or pleasure. The menu focuses on steaks. **FYI:** Reservations recommended. Children's menu. **Open:** Daily 6:30am–10:30pm. **Prices:** Main courses $9–$19. AE, CB, DC, DISC, MC, V.

ATTRACTIONS

Rocky Mount Historic Site

200 Hyder Hill Rd; tel 423/538-7396. Located 4 mi NE of Johnson City, on US 11E. This log house, built circa 1770, served as Gov William Blount's territorial capitol from 1790–1792. The main building, along with a log kitchen, slave cabin, barn, and blacksmith shop, have all been authentically restored and are decorated with period furnishings. Guides in period costumes conduct tours and perform craft demonstrations. **Open:** Mon–Sat 10am–5pm, Sun 2–6pm. Closed some hols. **$$**

Hands On! Regional Museum

315 E Main St; tel 423/928-6508 or 434-HAND. Interactive exhibits and programs in the sciences, arts, and humanities. Kids can learn about recycling in the discovery room, make a deposit or withdrawal of "Hands On!" money at the Kids' Bank, or mix a magical milkshake in the Science Lab.

Traveling exhibits and special events. **Open:** Tues–Fri 9am–5pm, Sat 10am–5pm, Sun 1–5pm. Closed Jan and some hols. **$$**

Jonesborough

Established in 1779, Tennessee's oldest town was once the capital of the unofficial State of Franklin. Today, a restored community featuring old-style frame and brick architecture and horse-drawn carriage rides affords a glimpse into history.

RESTAURANT

The Parson's Table

102 Woodrow Ave; tel 423/753-8002. **Continental.** Located in a former church, built in 1874; the interior atmosphere is flowery and intimate. The menu changes often but usually features Euro classics like shrimp vol-au-vent with lobster sauce and Gruyère cheese, and cherried breast of duck. **FYI:** Reservations recommended. BYO. No smoking. **Open:** Lunch Tues–Sun 11:30am–2pm; dinner Tues–Sun 5:30–10pm. **Prices:** Main courses $11–$23. AE, MC, V. ■

Kingsport

Located on the Holston River in the Cumberland Gap and encircled by mountains, this manufacturing city draws visitors to nearby Bays Mountain. Site of the annual Kingsport Fun Fest. **Information:** Kingsport Convention & Visitors Bureau, 151 E Main St, PO Box 1403, Kingsport, 37662 (tel 423/392-8818).

MOTELS

≡≡ Comfort Inn Kingsport

100 Indian Center Ct, 37660; tel 423/378-4418 or toll free 800/228-5150; fax 423/246-5249. A beautiful, clean motel with brand new furnishings. Good choice for an extended stay. **Rooms:** 122 rms and stes. CI 1pm/CO noon. Nonsmoking rms avail. Conservative color scheme and decor. **Amenities:** 🛁 A/C, satel TV w/movies, dataport. Some units w/whirlpools. **Services:** ✗ 🛁 🗘 ⬥ Babysitting. Meal plans available in conjunction with next-door Prime Sirloin restaurant. Small pets only, $8 charge. **Facilities:** 🏋 ⬛ 🏊 ⅕ 🔥 Sauna, whirlpool, washer/dryer. **Rates (CP):** Peak (Apr–Oct) $43–$50 S; $49–$75 D; $63 ste. Extra person $8. Children under age 18 stay free. Lower rates off-season. Parking: Outdoor, free. AE, CB, DC, DISC, EC, ER, JCB, MC, V.

≡≡ Ramada Inn

2005 La Mesa Dr, 37660; tel 423/245-0271 or toll free 800/2-RAMADA; fax 423/245-7992. Modest, tidy motel offering good, comfortable accommodations. Popular with families. **Rooms:** 195 rms. Executive level. CI noon/CO 2pm. Nonsmoking rms avail. Well-furnished, gaily decorated rooms. **Amenities:** 🛁 🖥 🏊 A/C, cable TV, dataport. **Services:** ✗ 🚐

🛁 🗘 Children's program, babysitting. **Facilities:** 🏋 ⬛ 🏊 ⅙ 1 restaurant, 1 bar. **Rates:** Peak (July–Oct) $75–$85 S; $85–$95 D. Extra person $6–10. Children under age 18 stay free. Lower rates off-season. Parking: Outdoor, free. AE, CB, DC, DISC, EC, ER, JCB, MC, V.

RESTAURANT

Skoby's Restaurant

1001 Konnarock Rd; tel 423/247-5629. **American.** A wonderful old-world restaurant, situated in an old brick building and featuring a dark dining room filled with hanging cheeses and breads, flickering antique-style lamps, and stained-glass lampshades. The upscale menu includes specialties such as chateaubriand-style filet mignon, Maine lobster, and maple-basted grilled fresh salmon. **FYI:** Reservations recommended. Children's menu. **Open:** Sun–Thurs 5–10pm, Fri–Sat 5–11pm. **Prices:** Main courses $5–$25. AE, DISC, MC, V. ■

ATTRACTION

Bays Mountain Park and Planetarium

853 Bays Mountain Park Rd; tel 423/229-9490. A 3,000-acre nature preserve with native wild animals in outdoor habitats, 25 miles of hiking trails, and a 44-acre lake. A modern visitors center houses a planetarium, several saltwater aquariums, and a variety of exhibits that range from natural history to space travel. Call for specific information on planetarium and natural history programs. **Open:** Mon–Fri 8:30am–5pm, Sat 8:30am–8pm, Sun 1–8pm. Closed some hols. **$**

Knoxville

Settled on the Tennessee River in 1825 and surrounded by mountains and lakes, Knoxville is the largest city of eastern Tennessee. It was the first capital of the state and the first planned city in the region; today it is the seat of the University of Tennessee at Knoxville and is headquarters of the Tennessee Valley Authority. Knoxville was site of the 1982 World's Fair. **Information:** Knoxville Convention & Visitors Bureau, 810 Clinch Ave, PO Box 15012, Knoxville, 37901 (tel 423/523-2316).

HOTELS

≡≡≡ Comfort Inn

7737 Kingston Pike, 37919; tel 423/690-0034 or toll free 800/221-2222; fax 423/690-8173. Across from West Town Mall. Standard chain hotel offering nice rooms directly across from West Town Mall and in the heart of West Knoxville business area. **Rooms:** 82 rms and stes. CI 3pm/CO noon. Nonsmoking rms avail. **Amenities:** 🛁 🏊 🖥 A/C, satel TV w/movies, dataport. Some units w/terraces. **Services:** 🛁 🗘 ⬥ Babysitting. The hotel provides free use of Court South health and exercise facility. **Facilities:** 🏋 ⬛ 🏊 ⅙ Spa, sauna, washer/dryer. **Rates (CP):** $59–$71 S; $65–$77 D;

$86–$104 ste. Extra person $5. Children under age 18 stay free. Parking: Outdoor, free. AE, CB, DC, DISC, JCB, MC, V.

UNRATED Holiday Inn Cedar Bluff
304 N Cedar Bluff Rd, 37923; tel 423/693-1011 or toll free 800/HOLIDAY; fax 423/694-0253. Exit 378 off I-40. A modern, recently renovated hotel. **Rooms:** 223 rms and stes. CI 3pm/CO 11am. Nonsmoking rms avail. **Amenities:** 🛅 🐕 A/C, cable TV w/movies, voice mail. **Services:** ✕ 🖼 ⌂ **Facilities:** 🔁 🎱 📦300 🔥 1 restaurant, 1 bar (w/entertainment), basketball, games rm, racquetball, sauna, whirlpool, washer/dryer. Children under 12 eat free in hotel restaurant. **Rates:** Peak (Sept–Jan) $85–$95 S; $90–$100 D; $125–$225 ste. Extra person $5. Children under age 18 stay free. Lower rates off-season. Parking: Outdoor, free. AE, CB, DC, DISC, JCB, MC, V.

🏨🏨 Holiday Inn Northwest
5335 Central Ave, 37912; tel 423/688-9110 or toll free 800/HOLIDAY; fax 423/687-8706. Exit 108 off I-75. Convenient to shopping, attractions, and many restaurants. Guests are welcomed into a large, relaxing lobby decorated in muted earth-tones and with lots of plants. **Rooms:** 109 rms. CI 2pm/CO noon. Nonsmoking rms avail. **Amenities:** 🛅 🐕 📧 A/C, cable TV w/movies. **Services:** ✕ 🖼 ⌂ **Facilities:** 🔁 📦250 🔥 1 restaurant, 1 bar, washer/dryer. **Rates (CP):** $64–$100 S or D. Extra person $8. Children under age 19 stay free. Min stay special events. Parking: Outdoor, free. AE, CB, DC, DISC, ER, JCB, MC, V.

🏨🏨🏨 Holiday Inn World's Fair
525 Henley St, 37902; tel 423/522-2800 or toll free 800/HOLIDAY; fax 423/523-0738. Located on the grounds of the World's Fair Park, near the Knoxville Art Museum, Fort Kidd, and the Tennessee Amphitheater. It features a huge playground for the kiddies. **Rooms:** 296 rms and stes. Executive level. CI 4pm/CO 11am. Nonsmoking rms avail. **Amenities:** 🛅 🐕 A/C, satel TV w/movies, dataport, voice mail. **Services:** ✕ 🖼 ⌂ Babysitting. **Facilities:** 🔁 🎱 📦8000 🔥 1 restaurant, 1 bar, sauna, whirlpool, washer/dryer. Guests have free use of the YMCA. **Rates:** $90–$100 S; $100–$110 D; $160–$170 ste. Extra person $10. Children under age 18 stay free. Min stay special events. Parking: Indoor/outdoor, free. AE, CB, DC, DISC, ER, JCB, MC, V.

🏨🏨 Howard Johnson North
118 Merchants Dr, 37912; tel 423/688-3141 or toll free 800/826-4360; fax 423/687-4645. Exit 108 off I-75. Average but comfortable chain hotel. **Rooms:** 213 rms and stes. CI 2pm/CO noon. Nonsmoking rms avail. **Amenities:** 🛅 📧 A/C, satel TV w/movies. Some units w/terraces. **Services:** ✕ 🖼 ⌂ ⌂ **Facilities:** 🔁 📦200 1 restaurant, 1 bar, games rm, whirlpool, washer/dryer. Indoor pool has a "mountain" slide. **Rates (CP):** $49–$75 S or D; $59–$69 ste. Extra person $7. Children under age 18 stay free. Parking: Outdoor, free. AE, CB, DC, DISC, MC, V.

🏨🏨🏨 Hyatt Regency Knoxville
500 Hill Ave SE, 37915 (Downtown); tel 423/637-1234 or toll free 800/233-1234; fax 423/546-4029. Comfortable accommodations just minutes away from the downtown business district, Knoxville Riverboat, and the University of Tennessee. **Rooms:** 387 rms and stes. Executive level. CI 3pm/CO noon. Nonsmoking rms avail. **Amenities:** 🛅 🐕 🍽 A/C, cable TV w/movies, dataport, voice mail. Some units w/terraces. **Services:** ✕ 🚍 🖼 ⌂ ⌂ Car-rental desk. **Facilities:** 🔁 🎱 📦3500 🖥 🔥 1 restaurant (see "Restaurants" below), 2 bars, volleyball, sauna, steam rm, beauty salon. **Rates:** $75–$140 S or D; $175–$300 ste. Extra person $20. Children under age 18 stay free. Min stay special events. Parking: Indoor/outdoor, free. Hyatt Business Plan available. AE, CB, DC, DISC, MC, V.

🏨🏨🏨 Knoxville Airport Hilton Inn
2001 Alcoa Hwy, 37701; tel 423/970-4300 or toll free 800/HILTONS; fax 423/984-7080. This hotel features a multilevel lobby with flags of the world overhead and a raised lounge. **Rooms:** 236 rms and stes. Executive level. CI 3pm/CO 1pm. Nonsmoking rms avail. **Amenities:** 🛅 🐕 📧 A/C, satel TV w/movies, voice mail. **Services:** ✕ 🚍 🖼 ⌂ Twice-daily maid svce, babysitting. **Facilities:** 🔁 🎱 📦275 🔥 1 restaurant, 2 bars, whirlpool. **Rates:** $69–$99 S; $69–$109 D; $190–$280 ste. Extra person $10. Children under age 19 stay free. Parking: Outdoor, free. AE, CB, DC, DISC, ER, JCB, MC, V.

🏨🏨🏨 Knoxville Hilton
501 W Church St, 37902 (Downtown); tel 423/523-2300 or toll free 800/HILTONS; fax 423/525-6532. A luxurious property offering an elegant lobby and very attentive service. **Rooms:** 318 rms and stes. Executive level. CI 3pm/CO noon. Nonsmoking rms avail. **Amenities:** 🛅 🐕 A/C, satel TV w/movies, voice mail. **Services:** ✕ 🚍 🖼 ⌂ Social director, babysitting. Free passes to YMCA across street. **Facilities:** 🔁 🎱 📦720 🔥 1 restaurant (see "Restaurants" below), 1 bar. **Rates:** Peak (Sept–Oct/May–June) $79–$118 S; $91–$130 D; $205–$250 ste. Extra person $10. Children under age 18 stay free. Min stay special events. Lower rates off-season. Parking: Indoor, free. Bounce Back Weekend and romance packages avail. AE, DC, DISC, MC, V.

🏨🏨 La Quinta Inn
5634 Merchants Center Blvd, 37912; tel 423/687-8989 or toll free 800/531-5900; fax 423/687-9351. Exit 108 off I-75. A standard chain hotel offering bare-bones accommodations. **Rooms:** 123 rms. CI 1pm/CO noon. Nonsmoking rms avail. King-size rooms equipped with dataports and recliners. **Amenities:** 🛅 🐕 A/C, cable TV w/movies. Some units w/terraces. **Services:** 🖼 ⌂ ⌂ **Facilities:** 🔁 📦90 🔥 Guests may use Court South Fitness Center across the street. **Rates (CP):** Peak (June–Sept) $51 S; $58 D. Extra person $7. Children under age 19 stay free. Lower rates off-season. Parking: Outdoor, free. Extended-stay discounts avail. AE, DC, DISC, MC, V.

≣≣ Quality Inn West

7621 Kingston Pike, 37919; tel 423/693-8111 or toll free 800/221-2222; fax 423/690-1031. Exit 380 off I-40. Located across from the West Town Mall, this hotel has an impressive lobby with a huge chandelier and several cozy sitting areas. **Rooms:** 162 rms and stes. CI 2pm/CO noon. Nonsmoking rms avail. **Amenities:** 🛅 ⓧ 🖭 A/C, cable TV w/movies. **Services:** ✗ 🖻 ⌂ 🕭 Babysitting. **Facilities:** 🛗 🚪 ⑤ ⅙ 1 restaurant (bkfst and dinner only), 1 bar (w/entertainment). **Rates:** $58 S; $68 D; $69–$160 ste. Extra person $10. Children under age 18 stay free. Parking: Outdoor, free. AE, CB, DC, DISC, ER, JCB, V.

≣≣≣ Radisson Hotel Knoxville

401 Summit Hill Dr, 37902 (Downtown); tel 423/522-2600 or toll free 800/333-3333; fax 423/523-7200. Exit 388 off I-40. Very attractive, 12-story Radisson. **Rooms:** 197 rms and stes. Executive level. CI 3pm/CO noon. Nonsmoking rms avail. **Amenities:** 🛅 ⓧ A/C, cable TV w/movies, dataport, voice mail. In-room fax machines and exercise bikes available. **Services:** ✗ 🆅🅿 🖻 ⌂ 🕭 Babysitting. **Facilities:** 🛗 🚪 ⑥⑤⓪ ⅙ 1 restaurant, 2 bars, whirlpool. Free use of local YMCA. **Rates:** $89–$109 S; $99–$119 S or D; $175–$275 ste. Extra person $10. Children under age 12 stay free. Min stay special events. Parking: Indoor, free. Romantic weekend packages avail. AE, CB, DC, DISC, JCB, MC, V.

MOTELS

≣≣ Comfort Inn

5334 Central Ave Pike, 37912; tel 423/688-1010 or toll free 800/221-2222; fax 423/688-1010. At exit 108 off I-75. Clean and comfortable rooms in a simple, two-story building. **Rooms:** 101 rms and stes. CI noon/CO noon. Nonsmoking rms avail. **Amenities:** 🛅 ⓧ 🖭 A/C, satel TV w/movies, dataport. **Services:** ⌂ 🕭 **Facilities:** 🛗 🚪 **Rates (CP):** $40–$60 S; $45–$65 D; $45–$70 ste. Extra person $5. Children under age 19 stay free. Parking: Outdoor, free. AE, CB, DC, DISC, JCB, MC, V.

≣≣ Days Inn East

5423 Ashville Hwy, 37914; tel 423/637-3511 or toll free 800/328-7266; fax 423/971-4445. Exit 394 off I-40. Attractive three-story motel with a bright white exterior and a comfortable, contemporary lobby with plush chairs, lush plants, and a small breakfast area. **Rooms:** 120 rms. CI 2pm/CO noon. Nonsmoking rms avail. **Amenities:** 🛅 A/C, cable TV w/movies. Some units w/whirlpools. Free local calls. **Services:** ⌂ **Facilities:** 🛗 🚪 Steam rm, whirlpool, washer/dryer. **Rates (CP):** Peak (June–Oct) $39–$69 S; $49–$69 D. Extra person $10. Children under age 19 stay free. Lower rates off-season. Parking: Outdoor, free. AE, CB, DC, DISC, JCB, MC, V.

UNRATED Fairfield Inn

126 Cusick Rd, Alcoa, 37701; tel 423/984-9350 or toll free 800/228-2800; fax 423/984-2823. Across from airport. Standard chain motel. **Rooms:** 91 rms and stes. CI 3pm/CO

noon. Nonsmoking rms avail. **Amenities:** 🛅 ⓧ A/C, cable TV w/movies, dataport. **Services:** 🚐 🖻 ⌂ **Facilities:** 🛗 🚪 ⅙ Washer/dryer. **Rates (CP):** $49–$99 S or D; $59–$109 ste. Extra person $7. Children under age 18 stay free. Lower rates off-season. Parking: Outdoor, free. AE, CB, DC, DISC, MC, V.

≣≣≣ Holiday Inn Knoxville West

1315 Kirby Road, 37909; tel 423/584-3911 or toll free 800/854-8315; fax 423/588-0920. Exit 383 off I-40. Decent, spacious accommodations. Suitable for business travelers. **Rooms:** 242 rms. Executive level. CI 2pm/CO 11am. Nonsmoking rms avail. King-size rooms are two feet wider than standard rooms. **Amenities:** 🛅 ⓧ A/C, satel TV w/movies, dataport, voice mail. Some units w/terraces. Executive-level rooms have complimentary continental breakfast, VCR, refrigerator, and microwave. **Services:** ✗ 🚐 ⌂ 🕭 Babysitting. **Facilities:** 🛗 🚪 ⑩⓪ 🖥 ⅙ 1 bar, spa, whirlpool, washer/dryer. Complimentary golf greens fees at nearby country club. Guest privileges at local health club. Comedy club on weekend nights. **Rates:** $71–$89 S; $75–$94 D. Extra person $5. Children under age 19 stay free. Parking: Outdoor, free. Bed-and-breakfast packages avail. AE, CB, DC, DISC, JCB, MC, V.

≣≣ La Quinta Motor Inn

258 Peters Rd N, 37923; tel 423/690-9777 or toll free 800/531-5900; fax 423/531-8304. Exit 378 off I-40. Standard La Quinta, with the chain's trademark Southwestern decor. **Rooms:** 130 rms. CI noon/CO noon. Nonsmoking rms avail. Rooms are spacious and well lit, and feature convenient working areas for business travelers. **Amenities:** 🛅 ⓧ A/C, satel TV w/movies, dataport. Mini-refrigerators available. **Services:** 🖻 ⌂ 🕭 **Facilities:** 🛗 ⑤⓪ ⅙ Washer/dryer. **Rates (CP):** $54–$61 S; $61–$68 D. Extra person $5. Children under age 18 stay free. Parking: Outdoor, free. AE, CB, DC, DISC, MC, V.

≣≣ Quality Inn Airport

2306 Alcoa Hwy, Alcoa, 37701; tel 423/970-3140 or toll free 800/221-2222; fax 423/970-3140. Very popular with families who prefer to stay in an out-of-the-way area while they visit the Smokies. (Gatlinburg is only 20 miles away.) **Rooms:** 53 rms. CI 2pm/CO 11am. Nonsmoking rms avail. **Amenities:** 🛅 A/C, satel TV w/movies, dataport. Every king room has a sofa sleeper. **Services:** 🚐 🖻 ⌂ 🕭 **Facilities:** 🛗 ⑦⑤ ⅙ Washer/dryer. Pool is surrounded by a wonderfully peaceful courtyard with trees, flowers, and lots of grass. **Rates (CP):** $50 S; $60 D. Extra person $5. Children under age 18 stay free. Parking: Outdoor, free. Park and Fly package avail. AE, DC, DISC, MC, V.

≣≣ Ramada Inn

1500 Cherry St, 37917; tel 423/546-7110 or toll free 800/2-RAMADA; fax 423/546-0954. Off I-40. Nice, quiet, comfortable rooms conveniently located near downtown Knoxville, minor-league baseball stadium, University of Tennessee, and the zoo. **Rooms:** 160 rms. CI 3pm/CO noon. Nonsmoking rms avail. **Amenities:** 🛏 🕰 A/C, satel TV w/movies. **Services:** 🛎 🧺 **Facilities:** 🏋 🔲 1 restaurant (bkfst and dinner only), washer/dryer. Free use of nearby fitness center. **Rates:** Peak (Sept–Nov) $64–$79 S; $74–$85 D. Extra person $5. Children under age 18 stay free. Lower rates off-season. Parking: Outdoor, free. AE, DC, DISC, MC, V.

🛏 Ramada Inn Knoxville

323 Cedar Bluff Rd, 37923; tel 423/693-7330 or toll free 800/2-RAMADA; fax 423/693-7383. Exit 378 off I-40. A modern, two-story property with a relaxing atmosphere. **Rooms:** 178 rms. CI 3pm/CO noon. Nonsmoking rms avail. **Amenities:** 🛏 🕰 A/C, cable TV w/movies. **Services:** ✗ 🖼 🛎 🧺 Pets under 20 lbs only. Free airport transportation during football season. **Facilities:** 🏋 🔲 🕰 1 restaurant, 1 bar (w/entertainment), whirlpool. Guests receive free use of nearby health club. **Rates:** Peak (Aug–Oct) $52 S; $62–$65 D. Extra person $7. Children under age 10 stay free. Lower rates off-season. Parking: Outdoor, free. AE, CB, DC, DISC, MC, V.

🛏 Super 8 Motel

503 Merchant Dr, 37912; tel 423/689-7666 or toll free 800/800-8000; fax 423/689-7666. Exit 108 off I-75. Nice, clean accommodations. Nothing fancy, but it's a good value. **Rooms:** 105 rms. CI 3pm/CO 11am. Nonsmoking rms avail. Some rooms have recliners. **Amenities:** 🛏 A/C, cable TV. **Services:** 🛎 **Facilities:** 🕰 Sauna, whirlpool. Ask about free passes to nearby Court Street Health Club. **Rates (CP):** $35–$40 S; $45–$60 D. Extra person $5. Children under age 13 stay free. Parking: Outdoor, free. AE, CB, DC, DISC, MC, V.

INN

🛏 Middleton House

800 W Hill Ave, 37902 (Downtown); tel 423/524-8100 or toll free 800/583-8100; fax 423/544-7514. W of Henley St. Conveniently located near the University of Tennessee. **Rooms:** 15 rms. CI 3pm/CO noon. No smoking. Rooms are inconveniently laid out: shower and toilet are on opposite sides of the room and the sink is in the middle. **Amenities:** 🛏 🕰 A/C, satel TV w/movies, dataport. 1 unit w/fireplace, some w/whirlpools. **Services:** 🖼 Wine/sherry served. **Facilities:** 1 restaurant (bkfst only), washer/dryer. **Rates (BB):** $54–$125 D. Extra person $10. Children under age 18 stay free. Min stay special events. Higher rates for special events/hols. Parking: Outdoor, free. AE, CB, DC, DISC, JCB, MC, V.

RESTAURANTS 🍴

★ Calhoun's

400 Neyland Dr; tel 423/673-3355. Exit 388A off I-40. **American/Barbecue.** Known for their award-winning baby back ribs, slowly smoked with Tennessee hickory and lightly basted with Calhoun's own barbecue sauce. Farm-raised catfish and hickory-smoked prime rib are additional menu highlights. Homemade desserts. **FYI:** Reservations not ac-

cepted. Children's menu. **Open:** Mon–Thurs 11am–10:30pm, Fri–Sat 11am–11pm, Sun 11am–10pm. **Prices:** Main courses $9–$19. AE, CB, DC, DISC, MC, V. ♿ 🕰

Copper Cellar/Cumberland Grill

1807 Cumberland Ave; tel 423/673-3411. **American.** A corporate-owned brewery that also offers a wide selection of fresh food. There's an intimate dining room downstairs and a more casual grill upstairs. Daily seafood specials, burgers, and prime rib are all popular, as is aged Western beef (slow roasted and sliced to order) served au jus with sour cream and horseradish. Other specialties include spinach artichoke dip (made with spinach, artichoke hearts, and two kinds of cheese) served hot with tortilla chips, sour cream, and salsa. Jack's famous cheesecake available in exotic flavors. **FYI:** Reservations recommended. Children's menu. **Open:** Mon–Sat 11am–11pm, Sun 11am–10pm. **Prices:** Main courses $5–$22. AE, CB, DC, DISC, MC, V. 🕰

Country Garden

In Hyatt Regency Knoxville, 500 Hill Ave SE (Downtown); tel 423/637-1234. **American.** Casual eatery, with a decor made up of street lights and umbrella-covered tables. They offer a varied menu, with specialties ranging from fajitas to the Rocky Top (shaved ham and turkey on English muffin topped with Swiss and cheddar cheese and bacon bits) to penne arrabbiata (with spicy tomato sauce and meatballs). **FYI:** Reservations recommended. Children's menu. **Open:** Sun–Thurs 6:30am–11pm, Fri–Sat 6:30am–midnight. **Prices:** Main courses $15–$19. AE, CB, DC, DISC, ER, MC, V. 🅅🅿 🕰

★ La Paz

8025A Kingston Pike; tel 423/690-5250. **Mexican.** Fun, laid-back atmosphere and very friendly service. The menu offers dishes like black and blue nachos (blue-corn chips with grilled chicken, black beans, and Monterey Jack cheese), fajitas (filled with chicken, steak, vegetable, or shrimp), and Santa Fe enchiladas (blue-corn tortillas layered with grilled chicken, Monterey Jack cheese, and green chile sauce). Many vegetarian options available. Margaritas are excellent. **FYI:** Reservations not accepted. **Open:** Daily 5–11pm. **Prices:** Main courses $5–$11. AE, DISC, MC, V. 🕰

Ⓢ Mandarin House

8111 Gleason Dr; tel 423/694-0350. Exit 380 off I-40. **Chinese.** For years this has been one of Knoxville's best buffets, offering a tremendous variety of traditional Chinese cuisine. Individual entrees are available also, such as General Tso's chicken; seafood combination plate (with fresh crab, shrimp, and scallops); and the Mandarin Deluxe (a combination of beef, shrimp, and chicken stir-fried with water chestnuts and bamboo shoots and sautéed with chef's special hot sauce). **FYI:** Reservations accepted. Dress code. **Open:** Sun–Thurs 11am–9:30pm, Fri–Sat 11am–10pm. **Prices:** Main courses $5–$14. AE, DC, DISC, MC, V. ♿ 🕰

🍴 **Orangery Restaurant**
5412 Kingston Pike; tel 423/588-2964. Off I-40. **Continental/French.** A romantic, old-world atmosphere, complete with pink-marble table tops and carved Chippendale chairs, complements the fine cuisine. Elegant specialties include crepes de Homard, lobster crepes in cognac cream and chervil, and sliced truffles in puff pastry. **FYI:** Reservations recommended. Piano. **Open:** Lunch Mon–Fri 11:30am–2:30pm; dinner Mon–Thurs 6–10pm, Fri–Sat 6–11pm. **Prices:** Main courses $16–$30; prix fixe $29–$55. AE, DC, MC, V. ♥ ▼ ♿

Regas Restaurant
318 Gay St; tel 423/637-9805. **Continental.** Opened 75 years ago by the Regas brothers, this local landmark has been offering fine dining in an elegant setting for decades. (Wendy's hamburger chain founder Dave Thomas started out here as a busboy.) They age their own beef (including their prime New York strip) and fresh seafood is flown in three times weekly. Classic desserts include strawberry shortcake and red velvet cake. **FYI:** Reservations recommended. Jazz. Children's menu. **Open:** Sun 11am–2:30pm, Mon–Fri 11am–10pm, Sat 5–10pm. **Prices:** Main courses $7–$48. AE, CB, DC, DISC, MC, V. ▼ ♿

Restaurant
In Knoxville Hilton, 501 W Church St; tel 423/523-2300. **American/Italian.** Elegant yet casual dining room overlooking the lobby of the Hilton; great for business or personal lunches and dinners. The chef's lunch special varies daily but is always a pleasant surprise. Filet mignon, shrimp scampi, and shrimp diablo are house favorites for dinner. **FYI:** Reservations accepted. Children's menu. **Open:** Breakfast daily 6–11am; lunch daily 11am–2pm; dinner daily 5–10pm. **Prices:** Main courses $12–$23. AE, CB, DC, DISC, MC, V. ♿

⭐ **Restaurant**
In Crosseyed Cricket, Exit 364 off I-40; tel 423/986-5435. **American.** Promise your family a fish dinner? Then take them out to catch it themselves. It's easy when the lake is stocked and the restaurant prepares your catch. Fishing poles, horseshoes, checkers, and paddle boats are available while you wait. Chicken and chuck steak are also offered. Delicious homemade desserts (including sugar-free ones). **FYI:** Reservations not accepted. Children's menu. No liquor license. No smoking. **Open:** Mon–Sat 5–9pm. Closed Dec–Jan. **Prices:** Main courses $3–$10. No CC. 👫

Tuscan II Ristorante
5200 Kingston Pike; tel 423/584-6755. **Continental/Italian.** The intimate dining room is decorated with lace curtains and flowers; lamp light and soft music complete the mood. Daily chef specialties include such culinary delights as veal pistachio (sautéed in a pistachio and sherry cream sauce), bistecca Gorgonzola (grilled strip steak served in creamy Gorgonzola sauce), pollo alla Sorrentino (breast of chicken topped with eggplant, mozzarella cheese, and tomato sauce), and zuppa di pesce (mixed seafood stew with shrimp, clams, mussels, calamari, herbs, and fresh tomato sauce). **FYI:** Reservations recommended. Dress code. **Open:** Lunch Mon–Fri 11am–2:30pm; dinner Sun–Thurs 5–10pm, Fri–Sat 5–11pm. **Prices:** Main courses $12–$24. AE, CB, DC, DISC, MC, V. ♥ ♿

ATTRACTIONS 🏛

Blount Museum
200 W Hill Ave; tel 423/525-2375. Now the only registered National Historic Landmark in Knoxville, this striking Colonial Revival house was once the home of William Blount, Governor of the Southwest Territory. During his distinguished career, Blount signed the US Constitution and was the first US senator from the new state of Tennessee. Visitors can tour the kitchen and the Governor's office, both of which are filled with authentic 19th-century furnishings. An adjacent visitors center offers an audiovisual display on the mansion's history and a museum shop selling a selection of period souvenirs. **Open:** Mar–Oct, Tues–Sat 9am–5pm, Sun 1–5pm; Nov–Feb, Tues–Fri 9am–5pm. Closed Dec 25 week. **$$**

Marble Springs
1220 W Gov John Sevier Hwy; tel 423/573-5508. John Sevier—Revolutionary War hero and future first Governor of the state of Tennessee—built this modest two-story log cabin on a land grant received after the War. The house was the Sevier family home during his tenure as governor, and the home is filled with period antiques and personal memorabilia. **Open:** Dec–Mar, Tues–Fri 1–5pm, Sat 10am–5pm, Sun 2–5pm; Apr–Nov, Tues–Sat 10am–5pm, Sun 2–5pm. Closed some hols. **$**

The Old City
123 S Central St; tel 423/523-2316. Historic downtown district featuring antique and specialty shops, restaurants offering ethnic cuisine from sushi to escargot, and nightly entertainment. **Open:** Daily 10am–1am. Closed Dec 25. **Free**

Knoxville Museum of Art
1050 World's Fair Park Dr; tel 423/525-6101. The KMA is much more than an art museum, although its collection of contemporary American artwork is impressive. The museum is perhaps most popular for its "extracurricular" activities, such as Alive After Five jazz on Friday nights and Sunday Afternoon in the Arts, with readings and chamber music. Guided tours, films, and lectures are available. **Open:** Tues–Thurs 10am–5pm, Fri 10am–9pm, Sat 10am–5pm, Sun 11:30am–5pm. Closed some hols. **Free**

Knoxville Zoological Park
Exit 392 off I-40 (Rutledge Pike S); tel 423/637-5331. Home to 1,100 animals including a rare red panda, polar bears, and penguins. The zoo is famous for its big cats, including a rarely seen white tiger. Miniature train ride; petting zoo. **Open:** Mon–Fri 9:30am–5pm, Sat–Sun 9:30am–6pm. Closed Dec 25. **$$$**

Knox County Regional Farmers' Market
Exit 8 off I-640; tel 423/524-3276. The region's largest indoor and outdoor market offers regionally produced crafts and prepared foods such as jams, jellies, farmmade ice cream, and baked goods, along with plenty of fresh seasonal produce. Monthly special events (concerts, magic shows, etc) add to the festive atmosphere. **Open:** Mon–Sat noon–6pm. Closed some hols. **Free**

Tennessee Riverboat Company
300 Neyland Dr; tel 423/525-STAR or toll free 800/509-BOAT. Narrated sightseeing cruises aboard an authentically restored 19th-century paddlewheeler take passengers from the site of the settlement of First Creek past old Cherokee encampments, and on to Looney Island. Gospel, bluegrass, jazz, brunch, and starlight theme cruises are also available. **Open:** Daily 9am–7pm. Closed Dec 25. **$$$$**

Lebanon

Located 31 miles east of Nashville, this is one of the state's oldest towns. Of interest is the courthouse square, antique district, and Fiddlers Grove pioneer village. **Information:** Lebanon–Wilson County Chamber of Commerce, 149 Public Sq, Lebanon, 37087 (tel 615/444-5503).

MOTELS 🏨

🎗🎗 Best Western Executive Inn of Lebanon
631 S Cumberland St, 37087; tel 615/444-0505 or toll free 800/528-1234; fax 615/449-8516. Exit 238 off I-40. This motel offers standard chain accommodations just off the highway. Fine for an overnight stay. **Rooms:** 124 rms. CI 2pm/CO 11am. Nonsmoking rms avail. **Amenities:** 🛏 📺 A/C, cable TV, dataport. Some units w/whirlpools. Refrigerators in some rooms. **Services:** 🛎 🍴 **Facilities:** 🏊 50 🔥 Games rm, sauna. Guests receive a voucher for Cracker Barrel restaurant next door. **Rates (BB):** Peak (May–Oct) $47–$80 S; $48–$80 D. Extra person $5. Children under age 12 stay free. Lower rates off-season. Parking: Outdoor, free. AE, CB, DC, DISC, JCB, MC, V.

🎗 Budget Host Inn
903 Murfreesboro Rd, 37087; tel 615/449-2900 or toll free 800/BUD-2498; fax 615/449-5809. Exit 238 off I-40. Basic, clean accommodations for budget travelers. **Rooms:** 120 rms. CI 11am/CO 11am. Nonsmoking rms avail. **Amenities:** 🛏 A/C, cable TV. Refrigerators in some rooms. **Services:** 🍴 **Facilities:** 🏊 🔥 **Rates (CP):** Peak (May 15–Sept 5) $40–$75 S or D. Extra person $4. Children under age 12 stay free. Lower rates off-season. Parking: Outdoor, free. AE, CB, DC, DISC, MC, V.

🎗🎗 Comfort Inn
892 S Cumberland St, 37087; tel 615/444-1001 or toll free 800/228-5150; fax 615/444-1001. Exit 238 off I-40. Comfortable chain accommodations. **Rooms:** 74 rms. CI noon/CO 11am. Nonsmoking rms avail. **Amenities:** 🛏 A/C, cable TV. 1 unit w/whirlpool. Refrigerators in some rooms. **Services:** 🛎 🍴 🐾 **Facilities:** 🏊 🏋 🔥 Sauna, washer/dryer. **Rates (CP):** Peak (May–Oct) $39–$43 S; $43–$59 D. Extra person $5. Children under age 18 stay free. Lower rates off-season. Parking: Outdoor, free. AE, CB, DC, DISC, ER, JCB, MC, V.

🎗🎗 Hampton Inn
704 S Cumberland St, 37087; tel 615/444-7400 or toll free 800/HAMPTON; fax 615/449-7969. Exit 238 off I-40. A standard Hampton Inn, with comfortable rooms and a courteous staff. **Rooms:** 87 rms and stes. CI 1pm/CO 11am. Nonsmoking rms avail. **Amenities:** 🛏 A/C, cable TV. Some units w/whirlpools. Some rooms have microwaves and refrigerators. **Services:** 🛎 🍴 🐾 **Facilities:** 🏊 🏋 50 🔥 Sauna, whirlpool, washer/dryer. **Rates (CP):** Peak (May 15–Sept 15) $45–$48 S; $51–$54 D; $85 ste. Children under age 18 stay free. Lower rates off-season. Parking: Outdoor, free. AE, CB, DC, DISC, MC, V.

Lynchburg

World-famous as the home of Jack Daniel's, the nation's oldest registered distillery. **Information:** Lynchburg–Moore County Chamber of Commerce, PO Box 421, Lynchburg, 37352 (tel 615/759-4111).

RESTAURANT 🍴

★ Miss Mary Bobo's Boarding House
Main St; tel 615/759-7394. **Regional American/Southern.** "Dinner" is served promptly at 1pm, and features home-grown vegetables, fried chicken, and a variety of meats, salads, and preserves—all accompanied by biscuits and corn bread. The benches on the front porch exude a down-home atmosphere to match the cuisine. **FYI:** Reservations recommended. No liquor license. No smoking. **Open:** Mon–Sat 1–3pm. **Prices:** Prix fixe $11. No CC. 🍴 📷 🔥

ATTRACTION 🏛

Jack Daniel's Distillery
TN 55; tel 615/759-4221. Founded in 1866, this is the oldest registered distillery in the United States and is on the National Register of Historic Places. Since the distillery is still active, guided tours allow visitors to see how Jack Daniel's whiskey is made and learn how it gets such a distinctive flavor. However, you will taste nary a dram of Mr Jack's water of life, since Moore County is "dry." **Open:** Daily 8am–4pm. Closed some hols. **Free**

Tennessee

Manchester

Located at the foot of the Cumberland Plateau, this was once a thriving cotton manufacturing town. **Information:** Manchester Area Chamber of Commerce, 110 E Main St, Manchester, 37355 (tel 615/728-7635).

MOTELS 🏨

▤▤ Comfort Inn
2314 Hillsboro Blvd, 37355; tel 615/728-0800 or toll free 800/228-5150; fax 615/728-0800. Exit 114 off I-24. Comfortable and homey property offering basic amenities. **Rooms:** 80 rms. CI 11am/CO 11am. Nonsmoking rms avail. **Amenities:** 🛁 A/C, cable TV. Some units w/whirlpools. Refrigerators in some rooms. **Services:** ✕ 🖾 🕭 Video rentals available. **Facilities:** 🖼 🔟 🕭 1 restaurant (dinner only), 1 bar, washer/dryer. **Rates (CP):** Peak (May–Sept 15) $30–$49 S; $49–$89 D. Extra person $5. Children under age 16 stay free. Lower rates off-season. Parking: Outdoor, free. AE, CB, DC, DISC, MC, V.

▤▤▤ Hampton Inn
33 Paradise St, 37355; tel 615/728-3300 or toll free 800/HAMPTON; fax 615/728-0159. Exit 110 off I-24. This recently remodeled property has an especially relaxing pool area with plants, benches, and tables. **Rooms:** 54 rms and stes. CI 11am/CO 11am. Nonsmoking rms avail. **Amenities:** 🛁 A/C, cable TV, dataport. Some units w/whirlpools. Microwaves and refrigerators in some rooms. **Services:** 🖾 🕭 🕭 **Facilities:** 🖼 🕭 Sauna, washer/dryer. **Rates (CP):** Peak (Apr–Nov) $40–$50 S; $50–$60 D; $70–$90 ste. Children under age 18 stay free. Lower rates off-season. Parking: Outdoor, free. AE, CB, DC, DISC, MC, V.

▤▤ Super 8 Motel
2430 Hillsboro Blvd, 37355; tel 615/728-9720 or toll free 800/800-8000; fax 615/728-9720. Exit 114 off I-24. A budget property with clean and comfortable accommodations. Guests are greeted with warm wood decor and a fireplace in the lobby. **Rooms:** 50 rms and stes. CI 11am/CO 11am. Nonsmoking rms avail. **Amenities:** 🛁 A/C, cable TV, dataport. Some units w/whirlpools. **Services:** 🖾 🕭 🕭 **Facilities:** 🖼 🕭 **Rates (CP):** Peak (May–Sept) $32–$38 S; $42–$52 D; $75 ste. Extra person $3. Children under age 12 stay free. Lower rates off-season. Parking: Outdoor, free. AE, CB, DC, DISC, MC, V.

Maryville

One of the lesser-known gateways to Great Smoky Mountains National Park. Former home of soldier and statesman Sam Houston. **Information:** Smoky Mountain Visitors Bureau, 201 S Washington St, Maryville, 37801 (tel 423/525-6834).

RESTAURANT 🍽

Mill House
4537 Old Walland Hwy; tel 423/982-5726. Off US 321. **Continental/Country dishes.** Fine dining in an authentic country manor, overlooking a pre–Civil War mill. Great prices. **FYI:** Reservations accepted. Children's menu. BYO. **Open:** Fri–Sat 5–10pm. **Prices:** Prix fixe $18. AE, CB, DC, MC, V. 🍴 🕭

McMinnville

The seat of Warren County in central Tennessee, it is on the old Native American war trace later used by Daniel Boone and other white explorers. **Information:** McMinnville–Warren County Chamber of Commerce, 110 S Court Sq, PO Box 574, McMinnville, 37110 (tel 615/473-6611).

ATTRACTION 🎟

Cumberland Caverns
1437 Cumberland Caverns Rd; tel 615/668-4396. America's second-largest cave. Guided tours take about 1½ hours and include breathtaking formations, pools, a waterfall, and the "God of the Mountain" underground sound and light show. Civil War–era saltpeter mines are also on display. Above ground, there's a picnic area and campground, and a gift shop. **Open:** May–Oct, daily 9am–5pm. Closed some hols. **$$$**

Memphis

Tennessee's largest city, Memphis was established by Andrew Jackson and others in 1819 on a bluff above the Mississippi River. It was a boomtown in the 19th century, due to its perfect location for transporting cotton from the Delta plantations, and remains an important commercial city and the largest spot-cotton market in the world. Most famous today as site of Elvis Presley's Graceland; downtown Beale Street is associated with blues musicians such as W C Handy. Memphis State University is here. **Information:** Memphis Convention & Visitors Bureau, 47 Union Ave, Memphis, 38103 (tel 901/543-5300).

PUBLIC TRANSPORTATION
The **Memphis Area Transit Authority (MATA)** operates citywide bus service. Stops are indicated by blue-and-white signs. Standard fare is $1.10; transfers cost 10¢. Exact change required. Summer discount passes are usually offered; call 901/722-7100 for information. The **Main Street Trolley** operates renovated 1920s trolley cars along the Main Street Mall; there are 20 stations on the route. Fare is 50¢ each way; all-day pass is $2. Exact change required.

HOTELS 🏨

☰☰☰ Adam's Mark

939 Ridge Lake Blvd, 38120 (East Memphis); tel 901/684-6664 or toll free 800/444-ADAM; fax 901/762-7411. A dramatic, futuristic-looking hotel. With its column of glass rising straight out of a semicircular pond, the Adam's Mark is impossible to miss. Popular for conferences and conventions. **Rooms:** 379 rms and stes. Executive level. CI 1pm/CO noon. Nonsmoking rms avail. Because the building is circular, most of the guest rooms are wedge-shaped. The slightly Asian decor is accented by rosewood-and-ivory armoires and rattan chairs. **Amenities:** 🔟 ☖ A/C, cable TV w/movies, dataport, voice mail. Some units w/minibars. **Services:** 🍽️ 🖅 VP 🚗 🛄 ↵ Masseur. **Facilities:** 🏋️ 🏊 1250 ⚖ 1 restaurant (*see* "Restaurants" below), 1 bar (w/entertainment). Bravo! Ristorante offers Italian cuisine served by opera-singing waiters. **Rates:** $115–$145 S; $125–$155 D; $125–$600 ste. Extra person $10. Children under age 18 stay free. Parking: Outdoor, free. AE, CB, DC, DISC, EC, ER, JCB, MC, V.

☰☰☰ Best Western Airport Hotel

2240 Democrat Rd, 38132; tel 901/332-1130 or toll free 800/528-1234; fax 901/398-5206. At Airways Blvd. While this hotel offers a wide range of executive suites, it also caters to travelers on a budget. **Rooms:** 380 rms and stes. Executive level. CI open/CO noon. Nonsmoking rms avail. Some rooms have air- and water-filtration systems. **Amenities:** 🔟 A/C, satel TV w/movies, dataport, voice mail. Some units w/whirlpools. **Services:** ✕ 🚗 🛄 ↵ Children's program. **Facilities:** 🏋️ 🏊 🏊 1400 🖥️ ⚖ 1 restaurant, 2 bars, games rm, spa, sauna. A 66-foot waterfall falls into the indoor pool. **Rates:** $55–$85 S; $60–$90 D; $175–$225 ste. Extra person $10. Children under age 18 stay free. Parking: Outdoor, free. AE, CB, DC, DISC, ER, JCB, MC, V.

☰☰ Comfort Inn Memphis East

5877 Poplar Ave, 38119; tel 901/767-6300 or toll free 800/645-0098; fax 901/767-0098. A good value for this upscale, business district. **Rooms:** 126 rms and stes. Executive level. CI 3pm/CO noon. Nonsmoking rms avail. **Amenities:** 🔟 ☖ A/C, cable TV. **Services:** ✕ 🚗 🛄 ↵ 🛎️ **Facilities:** 🏋️ 🏊 85 ⚖ 1 bar (w/entertainment). **Rates (CP):** $60–$80 S; $67–$85 D; $150 ste. Extra person $6. Children under age 12 stay free. Parking: Outdoor, free. AE, CB, DC, DISC, ER, MC, V.

☰☰☰ Courtyard by Marriott

1780 Nonconnah Blvd, 38132; tel 901/396-3600 or toll free 800/321-2211; fax 901/332-0706. Well maintained, and surprisingly quiet, too, considering its proximity to the airport. **Rooms:** 145 rms and stes. CI 4pm/CO noon. Nonsmoking rms avail. Many rooms offer outdoor patios with chairs facing the courtyard. **Amenities:** 🔟 ☖ 🖅 A/C, cable TV w/movies, dataport, voice mail. All units w/terraces. **Services:** ✕ 🚗 🛄 ↵ 🛎️ **Facilities:** 🏋️ 🏊 25 ⚖ 1

restaurant (bkfst and lunch only), spa, whirlpool. **Rates:** $74 S; $84 D; $88–$98 ste. Extra person $10. Parking: Outdoor, free. AE, CB, DC, DISC, MC, V.

☰☰☰ Days Inn Downtown

164 Union Ave, 38103 (Downtown); tel 901/527-4100 or toll free 800/329-7466; fax 901/525-1747. Downtown's most convenient budget lodging, attracting lots of young visitors. The lobby is unusually large. **Rooms:** 110 rms and stes. CI 3pm/CO noon. Nonsmoking rms avail. Rooms are on the small side. **Amenities:** 🔟 A/C, cable TV, in-rm safe. **Services:** ✕ VP 🚗 🛄 ↵ **Facilities:** 400 ⚖ Beauty salon. **Rates:** Peak (Mar–Nov 21) $45–$55 S; $55–$65 D; $225–$300 ste. Extra person $5. Children under age 18 stay free. Lower rates off-season. Parking: Indoor, $3/day. AE, CB, DC, DISC, MC, V.

☰☰☰ East Memphis Hilton

5069 Sanderlin Ave, 38117; tel 901/767-6666 or toll free 800/445-8667; fax 901/767-6666. Caters to a corporate clientele; located near a wide variety of restaurants. **Rooms:** 264 rms and stes. Executive level. CI 3pm/CO noon. Nonsmoking rms avail. Most rooms have two phones and large desks. **Amenities:** 🔟 ☖ A/C, cable TV w/movies, refrig. **Services:** ✕ 🖅 🚗 🛄 ↵ Babysitting. **Facilities:** 🏋️ 🏊 300 🖥️ ⚖ 1 restaurant, 1 bar, whirlpool, washer/dryer. Guest privileges at local fitness center. **Rates:** $105–$135 S; $115–$145 D; $149–$275 ste. Extra person $10. Children under age 18 stay free. Parking: Outdoor, free. AE, CB, DC, DISC, ER, MC, V.

☰☰☰ French Quarter Suites Hotel

2144 Madison Ave, 38104 (Midtown); tel 901/728-4000 or toll free 800/843-0353; fax 901/278-1262. A France-via-New Orleans ambience reigns at this elegant property. Wrought-iron accents, French Provençal furnishings are sprinkled throughout the beautiful atriumlike lobby. There's also a piano and a fountain. **Rooms:** 105 stes. CI 3pm/CO noon. Nonsmoking rms avail. Some rooms have half-canopied king-size beds; all have high ceilings and ceiling fans. Many rooms have French doors opening onto private balconies. **Amenities:** 🔟 ☖ 🖅 🍴 A/C, cable TV, refrig, dataport. Some units w/terraces, all w/whirlpools. **Services:** ✕ 🚗 🛄 ↵ Social director. **Facilities:** 🏋️ 🏊 100 ⚖ 1 restaurant (bkfst and dinner only), 1 bar (w/entertainment). **Rates (CP):** $105–$145 ste. Children under age 18 stay free. Parking: Outdoor, free. AE, CB, DC, DISC, EC, ER, JCB, MC, V.

☰☰ Hampton Inn Medical Center

1180 Union Ave, 38104 (Midtown); tel 901/276-1175 or toll free 800/447-4386; fax 901/276-4261. Located right in the heart of the Memphis Medical Center area. Reliable, comfortable accommodations. **Rooms:** 126 rms. Executive level. CI 3pm/CO 11am. Nonsmoking rms avail. **Amenities:** 🔟 A/C, cable TV w/movies, dataport. **Services:** 🛄 ↵ Babysitting. **Facilities:** 🏋️ 30 ⚖ **Rates (CP):** $48–$54 S; $56–$64 D. Extra person $6. Children under age 18 stay free. Parking: Outdoor, free. AE, CB, DC, DISC, MC, V.

≡≡ Hampton Inn Poplar

5320 Poplar Ave, 38119; tel 901/683-8500 or toll free 800/426-7866; fax 901/763-4970. Dependable accommodations, popular with business travelers and visitors to the University of Memphis. **Rooms:** 126 rms and stes. CI 2pm/CO noon. Nonsmoking rms avail. **Amenities:** 🛢 ⚬ A/C, cable TV, dataport. **Services:** 🖂 ⇦⇨ Babysitting. **Facilities:** 🛋 15 ⅙ Guests may use a nearby health club. **Rates (CP):** $61–$76 S; $64–$74 D; $82 ste. Extra person $10. Children under age 18 stay free. Parking: Outdoor, free. AE, CB, DC, DISC, MC, V.

≡≡ Hampton Inn Walnut Grove

33 Humphreys Center Dr, 38120; tel 901/747-3700 or toll free 800/HAMPTON; fax 901/747-3700. Roomy and comfortable. Located near Baptist East Hospital and less than 10 minutes from Shelby Farms. **Rooms:** 120 rms. CI 2pm/CO noon. Nonsmoking rms avail. **Amenities:** 🛢 ⚬ 🍴 A/C, cable TV, dataport. **Services:** 🖂⇦⇨ **Facilities:** 🛋 🖥 25 ⅙ **Rates (CP):** $56–$66 S; $64–$74 D. Extra person $8. Children under age 18 stay free. Parking: Outdoor, free. AE, CB, DC, DISC, MC, V.

≡≡≡ Holiday Inn Crowne Plaza

250 N Main St, 38103 (Downtown); tel 901/527-7300 or toll free 800/2-CROWNE; fax 901/526-1561. Located at the north end of downtown in a dramatic setting overlooking the Mississippi River, this sleek, modern hotel caters primarily to convention-goers. The elegant lobby features soaring ceilings, travertine marble floors, Oriental-motif carpets, and many intimate seating areas. **Rooms:** 392 rms and stes. Executive level. CI 3pm/CO noon. Nonsmoking rms avail. **Amenities:** 🛢 ⚬ 🖥 🍴 A/C, cable TV w/movies. **Services:** 🗙 🔑 VP 🖂 ⇦ Babysitting. **Facilities:** 🛋 🖥 500 ⬛ ⅙ 1 restaurant, 2 bars, sauna, whirlpool. Large pool has sundeck. **Rates:** Peak (Feb–Nov) $97–$125 S; $107–$135 D; $250–$350 ste. Extra person $10. Children under age 18 stay free. Lower rates off-season. Parking: Indoor/outdoor, $4/day. AE, CB, DC, DISC, MC, V.

≡≡≡ Holiday Inn Memphis East

5795 Poplar Ave, 38119; tel 901/682-7881 or toll free 800/HOLIDAY; fax 901/682-7881. A standard Holiday Inn, with a small and informal lobby. **Rooms:** 243 rms and stes. Executive level. CI 3pm/CO noon. Nonsmoking rms avail. **Amenities:** 🛢 ⚬ 🖥 🍴 A/C, satel TV w/movies, dataport. Some units w/whirlpools. **Services:** 🗙 🚐 🖂 ⇦⇨ **Facilities:** 🛋 🖥 250 ⅙ 1 restaurant, 1 bar, sauna, whirlpool, washer/dryer. **Rates:** $86–$100 S; $96–$110 D; $180–$360 ste. Extra person $10. Children under age 18 stay free. Parking: Outdoor, free. AE, CB, DC, DISC, JCB, MC, V.

≡≡≡ Holiday Inn Overton Square

1837 Union Ave, 38104 (Midtown); tel 901/278-4100 or toll free 800/HOLIDAY; fax 901/272-3810. Although this is one of the older Holiday Inns in town, its location near the nightclubs, museums, and Graceland make it a good choice for tourists. **Rooms:** 173 rms and stes. Executive level. CI 3pm/CO noon. Nonsmoking rms avail. **Amenities:** 🛢 ⚬ 🖥 A/C, cable TV w/movies. **Services:** 🗙 🚐 🖂 ⇦⇨ Babysitting. **Facilities:** 🛋 200 ⅙ 1 restaurant, 1 bar. Guests receive passes to a local fitness center. **Rates:** $65 S; $70 D; $85–$149 ste. Extra person $5. Children under age 18 stay free. Parking: Indoor, free. AE, CB, DC, DISC, MC, V.

≡≡≡ Homewood Suites

5811 Poplar Ave, 38119; tel 901/763-0500 or toll free 800/CALL-HOME; fax 901/763-0132. Attractive, spacious, all-suite hotel catering to guests on extended stays. The comfortable lobby has pine furnishings and lots of natural wood trim, and there's a central courtyard with a swimming pool and basketball court. **Rooms:** 140 stes. CI 3pm/CO noon. Nonsmoking rms avail. Full kitchen; large bathrooms with plenty of counter space. **Amenities:** 🛢 ⚬ 🖥 A/C, cable TV, refrig, dataport, VCR, voice mail. Some units w/fireplaces. All rooms include two TVs. **Services:** 🚐 🖂 ⇦⇨ Babysitting. **Facilities:** 🛋 🖥 20 ⬛ ⅙ Basketball, whirlpool, playground, washer/dryer. **Rates (CP):** $92–$149 ste. Parking: Outdoor, free. AE, DC, DISC, MC, V.

≡≡≡ Memphis Marriott

2625 Thousand Oaks Blvd, 38118; tel 901/362-6200 or toll free 800/627-3587; fax 901/362-7221. A luxury hotel located just down the street from the Mall of Memphis. The large lobby, with its travertine and red marble floor, overlooks a courtyard garden. **Rooms:** 324 rms and stes. Executive level. CI 3pm/CO noon. Nonsmoking rms avail. King rooms have large work desks and second phone by bed. **Amenities:** 🛢 ⚬ A/C, cable TV w/movies, dataport, voice mail. **Services:** 🗙 🔑 🚐 🖂 ⇦ Babysitting. **Facilities:** 🛋 🖥 1000 ⅙ 1 restaurant, 2 bars (1 w/entertainment), games rm, spa, sauna, whirlpool. Two concierge floors. **Rates:** $59–$129 S or D; $165–$275 ste. Children under age 18 stay free. Parking: Outdoor, free. Weekend "two-fer" rates avail. AE, CB, DC, DISC, EC, ER, JCB, MC, V.

≡≡≡≡ The Peabody Memphis

149 Union Ave, 38103 (Downtown); tel 901/529-4000 or toll free 800/PEABODY; fax 901/529-3600. A Memphis landmark, this historic hotel is most famous for its resident ducks, who parade through the lobby to their fountain every morning and evening like clockwork. The luxurious lobby features ornate, vaulted ceilings with exquisite stained glass, and there is a pianist for entertainment. **Rooms:** 468 rms and stes. Executive level. CI 4pm/CO 11am. Nonsmoking rms avail. Guest rooms convey an old-world elegance and are furnished with antique reproductions. The muted color scheme has a soothing effect. **Amenities:** 🛢 ⚬ 🍴 A/C, cable TV w/movies, dataport, voice mail. Some units w/whirlpools. Some rooms have fax machines. **Services:** 🍽 🔑 VP 🖂 ⇦ Masseur, babysitting. **Facilities:** 🛋 🖥 1600 ⅙ 4 restaurants (see "Restaurants" below), 2 bars (1 w/entertainment), spa, sauna, steam rm, whirlpool, beauty salon. The roof-top terrace is large and offers an excellent view of the Mississippi River. There is an authentic Art Deco skyway for supper club

dancing. Visitors will find everything they need (and want) in the several different gift shops on site. **Rates:** $130–$210 S; $160–$240 D; $495–$1,200 ste. Extra person $30. Parking: Outdoor, $5/day. AE, DC, DISC, ER, JCB, MC, V.

≣≣≣ Radisson Hotel Memphis

185 Union Ave, 38103 (Downtown); tel 901/528-1800 or toll free 800/333-3333; fax 901/526-3226. A posh, executive hotel built around the facade of a historic Memphis hostelry. The lobby is housed in a seven-story atrium with modern furnishings, a fountain, and live trees. **Rooms:** 280 rms and stes. CI 3pm/CO noon. Nonsmoking rms avail. Rooms are well designed and comfortably decorated. Corner rooms are more spacious (and more expensive) and have three walls of windows. **Amenities:** 🛎 🗗 A/C, cable TV w/movies, dataport, voice mail. **Services:** ✕ ⬛ VP ⬜ ↵ Babysitting. **Facilities:** 🔥 ➿ 400 🔥 1 restaurant (see "Restaurants" below), 1 bar, sauna, whirlpool. Ice cream parlor. **Rates:** $79–$99 S; $89–$109 D; $135–$220 ste. Extra person $10. Children under age 18 stay free. Parking: Indoor/outdoor, $4–$6/day. AE, CB, DC, DISC, ER, JCB, MC, V.

≣≣≣ Ramada Hotel Convention Center

160 Union Ave, 38103 (Downtown); tel 901/525-5491 or toll free 800/2-RAMADA; fax 901/525-5491 ext 2399. Comfortable accommodations. **Rooms:** 187 rms and stes. CI 2pm/CO noon. Nonsmoking rms avail. Eight rooms open out onto the pool/patio. **Amenities:** 🛎 🗗 🖥 A/C, cable TV w/movies, dataport. Some units w/terraces. **Services:** ✕ ⬛ ⬜ ↵ Twice-daily maid svce, babysitting. **Facilities:** 🔥 500 🔥 1 restaurant, 1 bar (w/entertainment). Guest privileges at local sports club. **Rates (CP):** Peak (Mar–Nov 15) $65–$95 S; $75–$105 D; $135–$175 ste. Extra person $10. Children under age 12 stay free. Lower rates off-season. Parking: Indoor, free. AE, CB, DC, DISC, JCB, MC, V.

≣≣≣ Residence Inn by Marriott

6141 Poplar Pike, 38119; tel 901/685-9595 or toll free 800/331-3131; fax 901/685-9595. Apartment-type accommodations; recommended for extended stays. **Rooms:** 105 stes. CI 4pm/CO noon. Nonsmoking rms avail. All rooms include a full kitchen. Two-bedroom suites have loft sleeping areas. **Amenities:** 🛎 🗗 🖥 A/C, cable TV, refrig, dataport, voice mail. All units w/terraces, some w/fireplaces, some w/whirlpools. **Services:** ✕ ⬜ ↵ 🎈 Children's program, babysitting. **Facilities:** 🔥 25 🔥 Whirlpool, washer/dryer. **Rates (CP):** Peak (Mar–Aug) $115–$149 ste. Lower rates off-season. Parking: Outdoor, free. Extended-stay discounts avail. AE, CB, DC, DISC, ER, MC, V.

≣≣≣ The Ridgeway Inn

5679 Poplar Ave, 38119; tel 901/766-4000 or toll free 800/822-3360; fax 901/763-1857. Operated by the same company that runs the prestigious Peabody, the Ridgeway offers sophisticated accommodations. Popular with business travelers. **Rooms:** 155 rms and stes. Executive level. CI 3pm/CO 11am. Nonsmoking rms avail. King rooms have desks and

sofas. **Amenities:** 🛎 🗗 A/C, satel TV w/movies, dataport. **Services:** ✕ ⬛ 🚗 ⬜ ↵ Babysitting. **Facilities:** 🔥 🛠 100 🔥 1 restaurant, 1 bar. Guest privileges at local fitness center. **Rates (BB):** $94–$124 S; $114–$134 D; $195–$350 ste. Extra person $10. Children under age 12 stay free. Parking: Outdoor, free. AE, CB, DC, DISC, ER, MC, V.

MOTELS

≣≣ Best Western Riverbluff Inn

340 W Illinois Ave, 38106; tel 901/948-9005 or toll free 800/345-2604; fax 901/946-5716. Older but well-kept, and perched on a grassy bluff overlooking the Mississippi River. **Rooms:** 100 rms and stes. CI 2pm/CO 11am. Nonsmoking rms avail. Rooms are larger than average and have lots of windows. **Amenities:** 🛎 A/C, cable TV. All units w/terraces. **Services:** 🚗 ↵ 🎈 **Facilities:** 🔥 275 1 restaurant, 1 bar (w/entertainment), games rm, washer/dryer. Rooftop restaurant. **Rates:** $49 S; $55 D; $125 ste. Extra person $5. Children under age 12 stay free. Parking: Outdoor, free. AE, CB, DC, DISC, MC, V.

≣≣ Country Suites by Carlson

4300 American Way, 38118; tel 901/366-9333 or toll free 800/456-4000; fax 901/366-7835. An all-suite motel, located near the Mall of Memphis. **Rooms:** 120 stes and effic. Executive level. CI 3pm/CO noon. Nonsmoking rms avail. **Amenities:** 🛎 🗗 🖥 A/C, cable TV w/movies, refrig, dataport, voice mail. **Services:** 🚗 ⬜ ↵ 🎈 Children's program, babysitting. **Facilities:** 🔥 65 🔥 Whirlpool, washer/dryer. Social hour Mon–Thurs. Complimentary use of local health facility. **Rates (CP):** Peak (Feb–Nov) $76–$86 ste; $66 effic. Children under age 18 stay free. Lower rates off-season. Parking: Outdoor, free. AE, CB, DC, DISC, JCB, MC, V.

≣≣ Days Inn at Graceland

3839 Elvis Presley Blvd, 38116 (East Memphis); tel 901/346-5500 or toll free 800/325-2525; fax 901/345-7452. Located just down the road from Graceland; as you might expect, the lobby is adorned with Elvis memorabilia. **Rooms:** 61 rms and stes. CI 2pm/CO 11am. Nonsmoking rms avail. **Amenities:** 🛎 🗗 A/C, cable TV. Some units w/whirlpools. **Services:** ⬜ ↵ 🎈 Elvis movies available for rent. **Facilities:** 🔥 10 🔥 Guitar-shaped pool. **Rates (CP):** Peak (Mar–Oct) $40–$55 S; $55–$67 D; $75 ste. Extra person $5. Children under age 12 stay free. Lower rates off-season. Parking: Outdoor, free. AE, CB, DC, DISC, MC, V.

≣ Red Roof Inn Medical Center

210 S Pauline St, 38104 (Midtown); tel 901/528-0650 or toll free 800/THE-ROOF; fax 901/528-0659. A no-frills three-story facility with no elevators. Nothing fancy, but fine for an overnight stay. **Rooms:** 120 rms. CI noon/CO noon. No smoking. **Amenities:** 🛎 A/C, satel TV, dataport. **Services:** ↵ 🎈 **Facilities:** 🔥 **Rates:** Peak (May–Aug) $34–$54 S; $45–$51 D. Extra person $6. Children under age 18 stay free. Lower rates off-season. Parking: Outdoor, free. AE, CB, DC, DISC, MC, V.

RESTAURANTS

The Arcade Restaurant
540 S Main St (Downtown); tel 901/526-5757. **American/ Greek.** Family-owned and -operated since 1919. The 1950s-style decor has been used in at least 10 films. The menu focuses on traditional American home cooked vittles, plus one Greek specialty each day. **FYI:** Reservations not accepted. Children's menu. **Open:** Daily 6:30am–9:30pm. **Prices:** Main courses $4–$12. DISC, MC, V. ■

Automatic Slim's Tonga Club
83 S 2nd St (Downtown); tel 901/525-7948. **Caribbean/ Southwestern.** Noted for its funky, eclectic atmosphere and creative decor: zebra-print upholstered banquettes, slag-glass wall sconces, colorfully upholstered bar stools, and tumbleweeds perched over the entrance. The menu picks up on the eclecticism. Popular dishes include Caribbean voodoo stew (with mussels, shrimp, whitefish, crab legs, and rice), Huachinanga (whole red snapper with tomato and onion), coconut-mango shrimp, and mesquite-grilled chicken salad. Vegetarian selections also available. **FYI:** Reservations recommended. Blues. **Open:** Lunch Mon–Fri 11am–2:30pm; dinner Mon–Sat 5–11pm. **Prices:** Main courses $10–$22. AE, MC, V. ♥ &

★ BB King's Blues Club
147 Beale St (Downtown); tel 901/524-5464. **Southern.** Diners here can enjoy classic Memphis blues performed by nationally known musicians while treating themselves to "comfort food" like fried catfish, fried chicken, ribs, and barbecue. There is a separate gift shop. **FYI:** Reservations accepted. Blues. **Open:** Peak (May–Aug) Mon–Thurs 11:30am–midnight, Fri–Sat 11:30am–2am. **Prices:** Main courses $7–$13. AE, CB, DC, DISC, MC, V. ♥ ♥ &

Bravo!
In Adam's Mark Hotel, 939 Ridge Lake Blvd (East Memphis); tel 901/684-6664. **Italian.** Most noted for its singing waiters and waitresses, this elegant eatery also serves up an extensive menu of Italian specialties. The wide array of pasta dishes (such as tagliatelle alla scaligera with prosciutto, peas, parmesan, and wild mushrooms) and the piccata of veal marsala are deservedly popular. Long wine list. **FYI:** Reservations recommended. Piano/singer. Children's menu. Dress code. **Open:** Daily 6:30am–midnight. **Prices:** Main courses $10–$19. AE, CB, DC, DISC, ER, MC, V. &

Cafe Samovar
83 Union Ave (Downtown); tel 901/529-9607. **Russian.** Owned and operated by Russian immigrants, this restaurant serves up delectable specialties such as veal and wild mushrooms in marsala sauce, baked salmon in a flaky pastry shell, and golubzi (cabbage leaves stuffed with sweet-and-sour ground beef). The dining room offers a fun and casual atmosphere, with lots of samovars, Russian dolls, and wall murals depicting Russian folk themes. **FYI:** Reservations

recommended. Singer. **Open:** Peak (May–Aug) lunch Mon–Fri 11am–2pm; dinner Tues–Sat 5–10pm. **Prices:** Main courses $9–$15. AE, DISC, MC, V. &

★ Chez Phillippe
In The Peabody Memphis Hotel, 149 Union Ave (Downtown); tel 901/529-4188. **French/International.** The classic French approach at this elegant spot is accented with a few Southern surprises. The dining room—with sparkling chandeliers, marble columns, and Louis XIV chairs—is full of French elegance. Diners can enjoy unusual creations like hush puppies stuffed with shrimp Provençal, and Maine lobster with marinated catfish, chive, and rosemary sauce. Traditional favorites include roasted rack of lamb with herbs and Roquefort-tomato sauce, and breaded lamb medallions with black olives and tomato sauce. **FYI:** Reservations recommended. Dress code. **Open:** Mon–Sat 6–10pm. **Prices:** Main courses $19–$25. AE, DC, DISC, MC, V. VP &

★ Corky's Bar-B-Q
5259 Poplar Ave; tel 901/685-9744. **Barbecue.** An informal joint serving up heaping plates of Memphis-style pulled pork shoulder, brisket, and chicken, served either "wet" (cooked in sauce) or "dry" (diner adds sauce after cooking). **FYI:** Reservations not accepted. Beer and wine only. **Open:** Sun–Thurs 11am–10pm, Fri–Sat 11am–10:30pm. **Prices:** Main courses $8–$12; prix fixe $8–$12. AE, CB, DC, DISC, MC, V. ▦ &

Landry's
263 Wagner Place (Downtown); tel 901/526-1966. **Seafood.** A spacious dining room and outdoor patio accompanying an excellent view of the Mississippi River. The menu is dominated by seafood—fried, broiled, baked, and sautéed. **FYI:** Reservations accepted. Children's menu. **Open:** Sun–Thurs 11am–10pm, Fri–Sat 11am–11pm. **Prices:** Main courses $10–$30. AE, DC, DISC, MC, V. ▲ &

Marena's
1545 Overton Park (Midtown); tel 901/278-9774. **Mediterranean.** Deep-blue walls, a stenciled ceiling, and dark-green table linens create a warm, almost medieval feeling. Two guitarists are featured nightly. The menu changes monthly, and draws on influences from 12 different Mediterranean countries. Diners can enjoy Algerian-style appetizers (onions stuffed with ground meat, rice, and spices; or a simple soup made with fish, potato, spice, herbs, and egg) and Spanish-style entrees such as fish with olive oil, lemon, garlic, and cilantro. **FYI:** Reservations recommended. Guitar. Beer and wine only. BYO. **Open:** Mon–Sat 6–9:30pm. Closed 1 week in spring/1 week in fall. **Prices:** Main courses $25–$30. AE, DISC, MC, V. &

★ Paulette's
2110 Madison Ave (Midtown); tel 901/726-5128. **Continental/Hungarian.** Modeled after a European country inn, Paulette's is popular with celebrities visiting Memphis and was featured in the movie *The Firm*. The original owners were

a Hungarian couple, and Hungarian dishes are still featured on the menu, like traditional gulyas with *uborka salata* (cucumber salad in sweet vinegar dressing). Vegetarian offerings include asparagus soufflé and broccoli fromage baked in phyllo dough. One of the rich desserts available is Kahluamocha pie made with pecan-coconut crust. **FYI:** Reservations accepted. Piano. Children's menu. **Open:** Sun–Thurs 11am–10pm, Fri–Sat 11am–11:30pm. **Prices:** Main courses $8–$20. AE, CB, DC, DISC, MC, V. &

The Pier

100 Wagner Place (Downtown); tel 901/526-7381. **Seafood.** Located in the historic Memphis cold storage warehouse; original warehouse equipment surrounds the dining areas, some of which offer exceptional views of the Mississippi River. The menu focuses on traditional dishes such as fresh-grilled seafood, lobster, and prime rib. **FYI:** Reservations accepted. Dress code. **Open:** Sun–Thurs 5–9:30pm, Fri–Sat 5–10pm. **Prices:** Main courses $14–$21. AE, DC, MC, V. 🖼 &

♥ Raji

712 W Brookhaven Circle (East Memphis); tel 901/685-8723. **French/Indian.** Raji's combines French cooking techniques with Indian seasoning to create a unique culinary fusion. The decor is simple yet elegant, with the food being the primary focus. Try such specialties as duck with coconut-ginger coulis and caramelized curry sauce; blue-crab salad with fresh mint, cilantro, and essence of lime in sauvignon blanc; and pan-seared yellow-fin tuna with mirepoix of cucumber and tamarind vinaigrette. Wine list rotates every two weeks. **FYI:** Reservations recommended. Dress code. Wine only. No smoking. **Open:** Tues–Sat 7–9:30pm. **Prices:** Main courses $50. AE, MC, V. &

★ Rendezvous

52 S 2nd St (Downtown); tel 901/523-2746. **Barbecue.** Lots of restaurants in Memphis boast that they serve the best barbecue in town, but this family-owned business probably wins the prize. A local institution since 1948, with a museumlike atmosphere filled with old bottles, tobacco boxes, and farm equipment, Rendezvous serves hickory-smoked pork ribs that are legendary. Barbecue beef is also available, as are nonbarbecue items such as skillet shrimp. **FYI:** Reservations not accepted. Beer and wine only. **Open:** Tues–Thurs 4:30–11:30pm, Fri–Sat noon–midnight. Closed July 2–18/Dec 30–Jan 8. **Prices:** Main courses $4–$10. AE, CB, DC, DISC, MC, V. 🖼 &

Sekisui of Japan

In Humphrey's Center, 50 Humphreys Blvd (East Memphis); tel 901/747-0001. **Japanese.** An elegant restaurant with a Japanese-style dining room where patrons sit on the floor. They also have a private party room and an exceptional VIP room. The menu offers a variety of traditional Japanese dishes: tempura, teriyaki, kushiyaki, and yakizakana. The sushi bar serves up octopus, conch, snapper, and flying fish

roe sushi. For something different for dessert, try the tempura ice cream. **FYI:** Reservations recommended. Karaoke. Children's menu. Additional location: 25 Belvedere (tel 725-0005). **Open:** Lunch Mon–Fri 11:30am–2pm; dinner Sun 5–9:30pm, Mon–Sat 5–10:30pm. **Prices:** Main courses $7–$15. AE, DC, DISC, MC, V. 🖼 ♥ &

Sun Studio Cafe

710 Union Ave (Downtown); tel 901/521-0664. **American/Southern.** The food here is simple, but the history is rich. Sun Studio—famous for being one of the birthplaces of rock-and-roll—is right next door, and photos of famous diner customers of the past cover the walls. Try the famous fried-banana pie or a '50s-style cheeseburger and milkshake. **FYI:** Reservations accepted. Beer and wine only. **Open:** Peak (May 29–Sept 4) daily 10am–6pm. **Prices:** Main courses $3–$5. AE, DISC, MC, V. 🖥

Veranda Restaurant

In Radisson Hotel Memphis, 185 Union Ave (Downtown); tel 901/528-1800. **Southern.** Offers an excellent lunch buffet Mon–Fri with a soup and salad bar. Try Southern specialties such as fried chicken and chicken and dumplings, as well their traditional meat loaf. **FYI:** Reservations accepted. Dress code. **Open:** Daily 6am–11pm. **Prices:** Main courses $17–$22. AE, CB, DC, DISC, MC, V. 🖼 VP

ATTRACTIONS 📷

TOP ATTRACTIONS

Elvis Presley's Graceland

3734 Elvis Presley Blvd; tel 901/332-3322 or toll free 800/238-2000. Purchased in the late 1950s for $100,000, Graceland today is more than the former home of one of rock 'n' roll's greats; it is Memphis's biggest attraction and resembles a small theme park in scope and design. Visitors are fed through the complex by guides who spout memorized descriptions of each of the public rooms in the mansion (the second floor, site of Elvis's bedroom, is off-limits). After touring the house, visitors are shepherded through Elvis's office, the trophy building containing all of Elvis's gold records and other awards, his racquetball building, and finally, Elvis's grave.

Then it's across Elvis Presley Blvd to Graceland Plaza, where visitors can catch a screening of *Walk a Mile in My Shoes* (a 22-minute video depicting highlights from Elvis's career) and visit the other Graceland attractions—Elvis's two personal jets (the *Lisa Marie* and the *Hound Dog II*), the Elvis Presley Automobile Museum (which includes Elvis's 1955 pink Cadillac, several Harley Davidson motorcycles—even the King's gasoline credit cards), and the Sincerely Elvis collection (a small exhibit of clothing, home movies, and other personal belongings).

The mansion tour is closed on Tuesdays from November through February, but the other attractions are open year-round. (The Platinum Tour ticket includes admission to all the attractions.) Advance reservations are not necessary but they are definitely recommended for visits in early January (Elvis's birthday) or mid-August (the anniversary of his death). **Open:** Mem Day–Labor Day, daily 8am–6pm; Labor Day–Mem Day, daily 9am–5pm. Closed some hols. **$$$$**

Historic Beale Street

Front St to 4th St. It was here in the clubs of Beale St that some of the most famous musicians in the blues world got their start—W C Handy, B B King, Furry Lewis, Rufus Thomas, Isaac Hayes, Alberta Hunter. Even today, Beale St continues to draw fans of the blues and of popular music in general. Nightclubs line Beale between Front and 4th Sts. The Orpheum Theater, once a vaudeville palace, now features Broadway road shows, while the New Daisy Theater presents performances by up-and-coming bands and once-famous performers. Historic markers up and down the street relate the area's colorful past, and two bronze statues commemorate the city's two most important musicians—W C Handy and Elvis Presley.

MUSEUMS

National Civil Rights Museum

450 Mulberry St; tel 901/521-9699. This enthralling museum located on the site of the Lorraine Motel, where Dr Martin Luther King Jr was assassinated on April 4, 1968, provides a comprehensive overview of the American civil rights movement of the 1950s and 1960s. Temporary displays, and objects such as a Montgomery, Alabama city bus like the one Rosa Parks rode in 1955, trace the history of the movement and its leaders. Call in advance for information on guided tours and special programs. **Open:** Mon and Wed–Sat 10am–5pm, Sun 1–5pm. Closed some hols. **$$**

Memphis Brooks Museum of Art

1934 Poplar Ave; tel 901/722-3500. The oldest art museum in Tennessee, the Brooks contains one of the largest art collections of any museum in the mid-South. With more than 7,000 pieces in the permanent collection, the Brooks frequently rotates works on display. The museum's emphasis is on European and American art of the 18th through the 20th centuries, with a very respectable collection of Italian Renaissance and baroque paintings and sculptures as well. Some of the museum's more important works include pieces by Auguste Rodin, Pierre Auguste Renoir, Thomas Hart Benton, and Frank Lloyd Wright. **Open:** Tues–Sat 10am–5pm, Sun 11:30am–5pm. Closed some hols. **$$$**

Dixon Gallery and Gardens

4339 Park Ave; tel 901/761-5250. The South's finest collection of French and American impressionist and post-impressionist artworks are the highlight of this small museum. The permanent collection includes works by Matisse, Renoir, Degas, Gauguin, and Cassatt. Twice a year, the museum's 17-acre gardens play host to the Memphis Symphony Orchestra. **Open:** Tues–Sat 10am–5pm, Sun 1–5pm. Closed some hols. **$$**

Memphis Pink Palace Museum

3050 Central Ave; tel 901/320-6320. "The Pink Palace" was the name locals gave to the ostentatious pink-marble mansion built by grocery-store magnate Clarence Saunders shortly after World War I. (It was Saunders who had revolutionized grocery shopping with the opening of the first Piggly Wiggly self-service market in 1916.) Unfortunately Saunders went bankrupt before he ever finished his "Pink Palace," and the building was acquired by the city of Memphis for use as a museum of cultural and natural history. In 1977 the museum moved into an adjoining modern annex, and today the original marble mansion is not open to the public.

Visitors can wander through a reproduction of the maze of aisles that constituted an original Piggly Wiggly. Other walk-through exhibits include a pre–Piggly Wiggly general store and an old-fashioned pharmacy with a soda fountain. Memphis is a major medical center and, not surprisingly, this museum has an extensive medical-history exhibit. On a lighter note, there's a hand-carved miniature circus that goes into animated action between 10:30 and 11am Monday–Saturday and from 2:30 to 3pm on Saturday and Sunday. **Open:** Daily, call for schedule. **$$$**

Pink Palace Planetarium

3050 Central Ave; tel 901/320-6320. Features frequently changing astronomy programs as well as rock 'n' roll laser shows. Not surprisingly, *Elvis: Legacy in Light* (offered every August) is the most popular. **Open:** Daily, call for schedule. Closed some hols. **$**

Union Planters IMAX Theater

3050 Central Ave; tel 901/320-6320. This brand-new theater boasts a screen that's four stories high and five stories wide, a multispeaker, 10,000-watt sound system, and visual images of unrivaled clarity. Only one of three theaters in the world to have a moveable screen, allowing for more extensive use of the facility. With 100 IMAX films currently available, the Union Planters IMAX promises a new film every 4–5 months. All films are prefaced by *Memphis . . . I Remember*, a multimedia presentation of the people, traditions, history, and landmarks of Memphis. **Open:** Daily, call for show times. Closed some hols. **$$$**

Center for Southern Folklore

130 Beale St; tel 901/525-3655. A small and rather informal museum, dedicated to the preservation and presentation of Southern life and culture. The emphasis is frequently on Memphis and the city's various musical traditions, from blues to jazz to soul to gospel. (One recent exhibit focused on early 1950s rockabilly.) Film screenings and tours of historic Beale St offered daily. Gift shop features handmade arts and crafts. **Open:** Mon–Thurs 10am–8pm, Fri–Sat 10am–10pm, Sun 11am–8pm. Closed Dec 25. **Free**

National Bird Dog Museum

505 TN 57 W, Grand Junction; tel 901/764-2058. Located 30 mi E of Memphis. Hundreds of exhibits here honor over 40 breeds of the hunter's best friend, including photographs,

etchings, prints, and sculptures of bird dogs; wildlife murals; hunting-dog trophies; historical objects and artifacts. The Field Trial Hall of Fame praises over 100 famous dogs and their owners, and there are displays devoted to the natural history of the area. **Open:** Tues–Fri 10am–2pm, Sat 10am–4pm, Sun 1–4pm. Closed some hols. **Free**

HISTORIC HOMES

Magevney House

198 Adams Ave; tel 901/526-4464. This diminutive, white clapboard cottage not far from the skyscrapers of downtown Memphis is one of the oldest buildings in the city. It was here that the first Catholic mass in Memphis was held. Purchased by Irish immigrant Eugene Magevney in 1839, the house is today furnished as it might have been in the 1850s. **Open:** Tues–Fri 10am–2pm, Sat 10am–4pm. Closed Jan–Feb and some hols. **Free**

Mallory-Neely House

652 Adams Ave; tel 901/523-1484. Listed on the National Register of Historic Places. The centerpiece of the Victorian Village Historic District, the Mallory-Neely House is an imposing Italianate mansion built in 1855. Remodeled shortly before 1900, the 3-story, 25-room home boasts elaborate plasterwork moldings, ornate ceiling paintings, and rooms full of original furnishings. Guided tours are given on the hour and half-hour. **Open:** Tues–Sat 10am–4pm, Sun 1–4pm. Closed Jan–Feb and some hols. **$$**

Woodruff-Fontaine House Museum

680 Adams Ave; tel 901/526-1469. Located adjacent to the Mallory-Neely House (see above), the Woodruff-Fontaine House displays an equally elaborate Victorian aesthetic, in this case influenced by French architectural styles. Built in 1870, the 16-room home has been fully restored and houses period furnishings. Mannequins throughout the house display the fashions of the late 19th century, including a collection of over two dozen vintage wedding gowns. **Open:** Mon–Sat 10am–3:30pm, Sun 1–3:30pm. Closed some hols. **$$**

W C Handy Home

Beale St at 4th St; tel 901/522-8300 or 527-2583. Handy's small wood-frame home was moved here a few years ago as part of the plan to revive Beale St. A visit will help you to learn more about Handy, his life, and his music. **Open:** Mon–Sat 10am–6pm, Sun 1–5pm. Closed some hols. **$**

PARKS AND GARDENS

Lichterman Nature Center

1680 Lynnfield; tel 901/767-7322. Visitors to this 65-acre wildlife sanctuary can stroll down woodland trails and view plants and animals in their natural habitat. There's even a sensory trail for the visually impaired. Picnicking facilities also available. **Open:** Tues–Sat 9:30am–5pm, Sun 1–5pm. Closed some hols. **$**

Memphis Botanic Garden

750 Cherry Rd, in Audubon Park; tel 901/685-1566. With 20 formal gardens covering 96 acres, visitors will most likely find something in bloom at almost any time of year, and even in winter the Japanese garden offers a tranquil setting for a quiet stroll. In April and May the Ketchum Memorial Iris Garden is in bloom, and during May, June, and September the Municipal Rose Garden is alive with color. Other popular spots include azalea and dogwood gardens, a cactus and herb garden, an organic vegetable garden, and a tropical conservatory. **Open:** Nov–Feb, Mon–Sat 9am–4:30pm, Sun 11am–4:30pm; Mar–Oct, Mon–Sat 9am–6pm, Sun 11am–6pm. **$**

Overton Park

Bounded by Poplar Ave, East Pkwy, North Pkwy, and McLean Blvd; tel 901/325-5759. This park, one of Memphis's largest, includes not only the Memphis Zoo and the Brooks Museum of Art, but also the Memphis College of Art, the Overton Park Municipal Golf Course, tennis courts, hiking and biking trails, and an open-air theater. Large, old shade trees make this a cool place to spend an afternoon in the summer, and the surrounding residential neighborhoods are some of the wealthiest in the city. **Open:** Daily sunrise–sunset. **Free**

Memphis Zoo and Aquarium

2000 Galloway Ave (Overton Park); tel 901/726-4775. Memphis's Egyptian namesake is evoked by the imposing and unusual entranceway to the Memphis Zoo. Built to resemble an ancient Egyptian temple, the zoo's entry is covered with traditional and contemporary hieroglyphics. Leading up to this grand entry is a wide pedestrian avenue flanked by statues of some of the animals that reside at the zoo. Once home to Volney, the famous MGM Studios lion, the Memphis zoo has recently remodeled its big-cat compound to provide a more naturalistic setting for its lions, snow leopards, and other big felines. In addition to the 2,800 animals in residence at the zoo, there is an area of children's carnival rides. **Open:** Apr–Sept, daily 9am–5pm; Oct–Mar, daily 9am–4:30pm. Closed some hols. **$$**

OTHER ATTRACTIONS

Sun Studio

706 Union Ave; tel 901/521-0664. In the early 1950s, Sun Studio owner and recording engineer Sam Phillips was the first to record such local artists as Elvis Presley, Jerry Lee Lewis, Roy Orbison, and Carl Perkins, who were creating a sound that would in a few years become known as rock 'n' roll. Over the years Phillips also helped start the recording careers of blues greats B B King and Howlin' Wolf, and country giant Johnny Cash. Sun Studio is still an active recording studio (now owned by Elvis Presley Enterprises), and for $49.95 anyone can rent 30 minutes of studio time. Next door is the Sun Studio Cafe, a 1950s-style diner that has long been a musicians' hangout. **Open:** Sept–May, daily 10:30am–5:30pm; June–Aug, daily 9:30am–6:30 pm. Closed some hols. **$$**

A Schwab

163 Beale St; tel 901/523-9782. Schwab's is as much a Memphis institution and tourist attraction as it is a place to shop. How many stores offer guided tours? Its battered wood floors and tables—little changed since the store opened in 1876—are covered with everything from plumbing supplies to religious paraphernalia. The offerings here are fascinating, even if you aren't in the market for a pair of spats or size 74 men's overalls. Some of the other merchandise on offer here includes 44 kinds of suspenders, a wall full of voodoo love potions and powders, and a kiosk of Elvis souvenirs. (In the early days of his career, Elvis bought his stage clothes here.) **Open:** Mon–Sat 9am–5pm. Closed some hols. **Free**

Mud Island

Mud Island Rd; tel 901/576-7241. This young island first appeared in 1900 and became permanent in 1913. Today, it is home to a 52-acre park that includes several attractions. **River Walk,** a five-block-long scale model of 900 miles of the Mississippi River, includes flowing water, street plans of cities and towns along the river, and informative panels on the river and its history. Eventually the "river" flows into the "Gulf of Mexico," which happens to be a huge public swimming pool with an unobstructed view of the Memphis skyline.

Over at the **Mississippi River Museum,** more than 10,000 years of river history are chronicled in several life-size reconstructions. The *Belle of the Bluffs* re-creates the front half of an 1870s steamboat; another evocative display features an ironclad Union gunboat under fire from a Confederate gun emplacement. World War II history buffs won't want to miss a visit to the *Memphis Belle,* one of the most famous B-17s that fought in that war. Meanwhile, top-name performers entertain on summer evenings at the **Mud Island Amphitheater.**

To reach Mud Island, you can drive by way of Auction Ave just north of the Pyramid, or take the monorail from Front St at Adams Ave. The monorail operates daily during the spring and summer months and on weekends only (or on concert evenings) in the autumn. **Open:** Grounds, daily 10am–5pm; museum, Tues–Sun 10am–5pm; swimming pool/beach, May–Aug, Tues–Sun 11am–5pm. **$$$**

The Pyramid

1 Auction St (Downtown); tel 901/521-9675. This 32-story stainless-steel pyramid is the third-largest pyramid in the world and is the most distinctive building in Memphis. As the city's main arena, it's where Memphis State University Tigers basketball games, rock concerts, and other large-scale performances are held. Tours available.

Adventure River Water Park

6880 Whitten Bend Cove; tel 901/382-9283. Family-friendly 25-acre aquatic park. Includes a wave pool, water slides, and a lazy river down which you can float. Proper swimwear required; no jeans or cutoffs. **Open:** Mem Day–Labor Day, call for hours. **$$$$**

Monteagle

See also Tracy City

Summer resort in south-central Tennessee. Home to several vineyards and wine cellars, as well as the University of the South.

INN 🏨

≣ ≣ ≣ **Adams-Edgeworth Inn**

23 Rappard, 37356; tel 615/924-4000; fax 615/924-3236. Exit 134 off I-24. 100 acres. Located in a quaint Queen Anne–style house, cloistered within an antique village. A wood-burning fireplace welcomes guests in the lobby area, and hundreds of original paintings and antiques gathered over three generations fill the house. **Rooms:** 14 rms and stes. CI 4pm/CO 11am. No smoking. Rooms are elegant, yet comfortably decorated. Beds have handmade mattresses. **Amenities:** 👜 🍴 A/C, cable TV, bathrobes. No phone. Some units w/terraces, some w/fireplaces. **Services:** VP 🚗 ↵ Babysitting. **Facilities:** 🏋 🛏 1 restaurant (bkfst and dinner only), lawn games, playground, washer/dryer. Small library with fireplace; seating galleries (with a phone) are found on each floor. Restaurant is administered by graduate of Culinary Institute of America and serves a five-course gourmet meal by candlelight. **Rates (BB):** Peak (June 15–Aug 15) $75–$150 D; $95–$175 ste. Extra person $25. Lower rates off-season. Higher rates for special events/hols. Parking: Outdoor, free. AE, MC, V.

REFRESHMENT STOP ☕

★ **Dutch Maid Bakery**

111 Main St, Tracy City; tel 615/592-3171. **Baked Goods.** Founded by a master chef from Switzerland, this bakery has been in continuous operation since 1902. It now specializes in fresh baked breads, pastries, and cheese. Secret family recipes are still used today by relatives of the original owner. **Open:** Daily 9am–6pm. DISC, MC, V.

ATTRACTIONS 🏛

South Cumberland State Park

US 41; tel 615/924-2980. This 12,000-acre park consists of seven separate areas spread out over three counties. The park visitors center, located between Tracy City and Monteagle on TN 56, offers maps, trail information, and directions to the various sections of the park. By far the largest is the 11,500-acre **Savage Gulf State Natural Area,** with over 50 miles of hiking trails and 10 primitive campgrounds. Other areas offer swimming, picnicking, hiking, camping, and spelunking. **Open:** Daily 8am–4:30pm. Closed Dec 25. **Free**

Wonder Cave

Foot of Monteagle Mountain on US 41, Pelham; tel 615/467-3060. Located 5 mi NW of Monteagle. Very little in this cave has changed since it was discovered in 1897. Tour guides use still use lanterns, since there's no electricity. Tours take approximately one hour, and cover the mysterious Mystic River, the Old Man Winter Room, and maybe even a few of the rare eyeless creatures who inhabit this underground world. **Open:** Mem Day–Labor Day, daily 9am–4pm. **$$$**

Monteagle Wine Cellars

Exit 134 off I-24; tel 615/924-2120 or toll free 800/556-WINE. This award-winning Southern winery produces 16 different varieties ranging from chardonnay to blackberry. Free tours and an on-site gift shop available. **Open:** June–Aug, Mon–Sat 8am–6pm, Sun noon–5pm; Sept–May, Mon–Sat 9am–5pm, Sun noon–5pm. Closed some hols. **Free**

Morristown

Located several miles south of Cherokee Lake and a short drive from the Smoky Mountains, this town attracts many vacationing families. Former home of Davy Crockett. **Information:** Morristown Area Chamber of Commerce, 825 W First N St, PO Box 9, Morristown, 37815 (tel 423/586-6382).

MOTELS

Holiday Inn

3230 W Andrew Johnson Hwy, 37814; tel 423/581-8700 or toll free 800/HOLIDAY; fax 423/581-7128. A simple yet attractive two-story motel. The exterior was renovated in 1995. **Rooms:** 118 rms. CI noon/CO noon. Nonsmoking rms avail. **Amenities:** A/C, cable TV w/movies, dataport. Executive rooms include a refrigerator and a VCR. **Services:** Facilities: 1 restaurant. Guests may have passes to a full-facility health club located three miles from the hotel. **Rates:** $49–$59 S. Extra person $5. Children under age 20 stay free. Parking: Outdoor, free. AE, CB, DC, DISC, JCB, MC, V.

Ramada Inn

5435 S Davy Crockett Pkwy, PO Box 190, 37815; tel 423/587-2400 or toll free 800/272-6232; fax 423/581-7344. Jct I-81/US 25E. Recently renovated, basic chain motel. **Rooms:** 112 rms. CI 3pm/CO noon. Nonsmoking rms avail. **Amenities:** A/C, cable TV. Some units w/terraces. **Services:** Twice-daily maid svce, babysitting. **Facilities:** 1 restaurant, games rm, playground. **Rates:** Peak (Apr–Dec) $50–$75 S; $55–$75 D. Extra person $5. Children under age 19 stay free. Min stay special events. Lower rates off-season. Parking: Outdoor, free. AE, CB, DC, DISC, JCB, MC, V.

Murfreesboro

Located on the West Fork of the Stone River, 33 miles southeast of Nashville. The state legislature met here from 1819 to 1825, although it was never officially named the state capital. A Civil War battle was fought here. Home to many antiques shops, the city is also the site of the International Grand Championship Walking Horse Show. **Information:** Rutherford County Chamber of Commerce, 302 S Front St, PO Box 864, Murfreesboro, 37133 (tel 615/893-6565).

HOTELS

Garden Plaza Hotel

1850 Old Fort Pkwy, 37129; tel 615/895-5555 or toll free 800/3-GARDEN; fax 615/895-5555 ext 165. Exit 78A off I-24. An airy and open atmosphere prevails at this attractive establishment, with an atrium lobby, glimmering glass elevators, and lush trees and plants filling the public areas. **Rooms:** 168 rms and stes. CI 3pm/CO noon. Nonsmoking rms avail. **Amenities:** A/C, satel TV w/movies, refrig, dataport. **Services:** Babysitting. **Facilities:** 1 restaurant, 1 bar, whirlpool. Complimentary passes to local fitness center. **Rates:** $59–$79 S or D; $99–$119 ste. Extra person $10. Children under age 18 stay free. Parking: Outdoor, free. AE, CB, DC, DISC, MC, V.

Holiday Inn

2227 Old Fort Pkwy, 37129; tel 615/896-2420 or toll free 800/HOLIDAY; fax 615/896-8738. Exit 78A off I-24. A four-story hotel with a Holidome filled with colorful plants, games, and recreational facilities. **Rooms:** 179 rms and stes. CI 2pm/CO noon. Nonsmoking rms avail. **Amenities:** A/C, cable TV w/movies, dataport. Some units w/terraces, some w/whirlpools. Hair dryers in some rooms. **Services:** **Facilities:** 2 restaurants, 1 bar (w/entertainment), games rm, sauna, whirlpool, washer/dryer. Guest privileges at local fitness club. **Rates:** $69 S or D; $85 ste. Parking: Outdoor, free. AE, DC, DISC, MC, V.

MOTELS

Hampton Inn Murfreesboro

2230 Old Fort Pkwy, 37129; tel 615/896-1172 or toll free 800/HAMPTON; fax 615/895-4277. Exit 78B off I-24. A clean and comfortable motel with tasteful decor. **Rooms:** 119 rms and stes. CI 2pm/CO noon. Nonsmoking rms avail. **Amenities:** A/C, cable TV, dataport. **Services:** **Facilities:** Guest privileges at local fitness center. **Rates (CP):** $49–$51 S; $54–$56 D; $55 ste. Children under age 18 stay free. Parking: Outdoor, free. AE, CB, DC, DISC, ER, MC, V.

Howard Johnson Inn

2424 S Church St, 37130; tel 615/896-5522 or toll free 800/I-GO-HOJO; fax 615/890-0024. Exit 81 off I-24. No-frills motel with basic amenities. **Rooms:** 77 rms and stes. CI 1pm/CO 11am. Nonsmoking rms avail. **Amenities:** A/C, cable TV. Some units w/whirlpools. Dataports, alarm clocks, radios, hair dryers, refrigerators, and microwaves are available in some rooms. **Services:** **Facilities:** 1 restaurant, washer/dryer. Large parking area for trucks and buses. Guest privileges at local fitness center. **Rates (CP):**

Peak (Mar–June, Sept) $39–$79 S; $44–$84 D; $55–$110 ste. Extra person $5. Children under age 18 stay free. Lower rates off-season. Parking: Outdoor, free. AE, CB, DC, DISC, MC, V.

≣≣≣ Quality Inn

118 Westgate Blvd, 37130; tel 615/848-9030 or toll free 800/228-5151; fax 615/896-3470. Exit 81 off I-24. This attractive place welcomes its guests with a tastefully decorated lobby. **Rooms:** 78 rms and stes. CI 1pm/CO 11am. Nonsmoking rms avail. **Amenities:** 🛅 🕭 A/C, cable TV w/movies, dataport. **Services:** 🖎 🗗 🗢 **Facilities:** 🛅 🛏️ ᵭ Guest privileges at local fitness center. **Rates (CP):** Peak (Mar, June–Labor Day) $44–$85 S; $49–$90 D; $55–$110 ste. Extra person $5. Children under age 18 stay free. Lower rates off-season. Parking: Outdoor, free. AE, CB, DC, DISC, MC, V.

≣≣≣ Ramada Limited

1855 S Church St, 37130; tel 615/896-5080 or toll free 800/2-RAMADA; fax 615/896-5080. Exit 81 off I-24. A cozy property featuring a well-decorated lobby and a spacious breakfast area with TV and couches. **Rooms:** 81 rms. CI 2pm/CO noon. Nonsmoking rms avail. **Amenities:** 🛅 🕭 A/C, cable TV. **Services:** 🗗 🗢 VCR and movie rentals available. **Facilities:** 🛅 🛏️ ᵭ Guest privileges at local fitness center. **Rates (CP):** Peak (Mar–Oct) $30–$65 S or D. Extra person $5. Children under age 18 stay free. Lower rates off-season. Parking: Outdoor, free. AE, CB, DC, DISC, MC, V.

≣≣ Travelodge

2025 S Church St, 37130; tel 615/896-2320 or toll free 800/578-7878; fax 615/893-0024. Exit 81 off I-24 at US 231. A well-located chain motel offering a variety of accommodations. **Rooms:** 101 rms. CI 1pm/CO 11am. Nonsmoking rms avail. **Amenities:** 🛅 🗐 A/C, satel TV. Some units w/whirlpools. Full-length mirrors and refrigerators in some rooms. **Services:** 🗗 **Facilities:** 🛅 🛏️ ᵭ Washer/dryer. **Rates (CP):** Peak (June/Aug–Labor Day) $40–$51 S or D. Extra person $5. Children under age 17 stay free. Lower rates off-season. Parking: Outdoor, free. AE, CB, DC, DISC, MC, V.

ATTRACTIONS 🖼️

Oaklands Historic House Museum

900 N Maney Ave; tel 615/893-0022. When the first Oaklands was completed in 1815, it was a simple 1½-story house. As the fortunes of the family who owned it increased, additions were made to the house. By the 1860s, Oaklands was the center of an elegant 1,500-acre plantation. Today, tours offer the visitor a glimpse into the antebellum world via period antiques and family furnishings. **Open:** Tues–Sat 10am–4pm, Sun 1–4pm. Closed some hols. **$**

Stones River National Battlefield

3501 Old Nashville Hwy; tel 615/893-9501. On New Year's Eve 1862, what would become the bloodiest Civil War battle west of the Appalachian Mountains began just north of Murfreesboro along the Stones River. Though by the end of the first day of fighting the Confederates thought they were assured a victory, Union reinforcements turned the tide against the rebels. By January 3, the Confederates were in retreat and 23,000 soldiers lay dead or dying on the battlefield. Today 351 acres of the battlefield are preserved. The site includes a national cemetery and the Hazen Brigade Monument, which was erected in 1863 and is the oldest Civil War memorial in the United States. In the visitors center, you can visit a museum full of artifacts and details of the battle and pick up a self-guided auto tour brochure. **Open:** Daily 8am–5pm. Closed Dec 25. **Free**

Nashville

See also Franklin, Hendersonville, Lebanon

World famous as "Music City USA," Nashville was the site of Grand Ole Opry broadcasts for more than 60 years and is still the center of the country music industry. Among its higher-educational institutions are Fisk University, Vanderbilt University, the University of Tennessee at Nashville, Tennessee State University, and Meharry Medical College. Just south of Nashville is the exclusive community of Brentwood, home to many country music stars. **Information:** Nashville Convention & Visitors Bureau, 161 4th Ave N, Nashville, 37219 (tel 615/259-4730)

PUBLIC TRANSPORTATION

The **Metropolitan Transit Authority (MTA)** provides extensive and efficient bus service. MTA bus stops are marked by a blue-and-white sign; express buses are marked with an "X" following the route number. Regular fare is $1.15; express bus fare is $1.45. Children under 4 ride free. A **RUSH card** (available from bus drivers) enables passengers to travel within the downtown area for just 25¢. The **Nashville Trolley Company** operates three popular tourist routes: downtown, Music Row (Mar–Oct only), and Music Valley (Mar–Oct only). Fare is 75¢. For transit information call 615/242-4433, or stop by the information center at Deaderick St and 5th Ave (Mon–Fri 7am–5pm, Sat 7am–3:30pm).

HOTELS 🏨

≣≣≣ AmeriSuites

220 Rudy's Circle, 37214 (Music Valley); tel 615/872-0422 or toll free 800/833-1516; fax 615/872-9283. Comfortable, roomy, all-suites hotel. Popular with families and those on extended stays. **Rooms:** 125 stes. CI 3pm/CO 11am. Nonsmoking rms avail. **Amenities:** 🛅 🕭 🗐 A/C, cable TV, refrig, dataport. VCRs available for rent. **Services:** ✕ 🚚 🖎 🗗 Free transportation to Opryland. **Facilities:** 🛅 🛏️ ᵭ Washer/dryer. **Rates (CP):** Peak (Apr–Nov) $98–$118 ste. Extra person $6. Children under age 18 stay free. Lower rates off-season. Parking: Outdoor, free. AE, DC, DISC, MC, V.

≣≣≣ Courtyard by Marriott Airport

2508 Elm Hill Pike, 37214 (Music Valley); tel 615/883-9500 or toll free 800/321-2211; fax 615/883-0172. A typical well-kept Courtyard. **Rooms:** 145 rms and stes. CI 4pm/CO noon. Nonsmoking rms avail. **Amenities:** 🛏 🚰 🖩 A/C, satel TV w/movies, dataport, voice mail. Some units w/terraces. **Services:** ✗ 🚐 🖼 🛎 Babysitting. **Facilities:** 🔥 🏋 🛏 ⅙ 1 restaurant (bkfst and lunch only), 1 bar, whirlpool, washer/dryer. **Rates:** Peak (Mar–Oct) $77–$87 S or D; $89–$99 ste. Extra person $10. Children under age 18 stay free. Lower rates off-season. Parking: Outdoor, free. AE, CB, DC, DISC, MC, V.

≣≣≣ Crowne Plaza Nashville

623 Union St, 37219 (The District); tel 615/259-2000 or toll free 800/447-9825; fax 615/742-6056. Located across the street from the State Capitol, this modern hotel has beautiful glass elevators and a large, open-atrium lobby with polished marble and dark-wood furniture. Popular with state politicians and convention-goers. **Rooms:** 477 rms and stes. Executive level. CI 3pm/CO noon. Nonsmoking rms avail. Northside rooms (facing the Capitol) have the best views. **Amenities:** 🛏 🚰 🖩 A/C, cable TV w/movies, dataport, voice mail. **Services:** ✗ 🖶 🆅🅿 🚐 🖼 🛎 Car-rental desk, babysitting. **Facilities:** 🔥 🏋 🛏 🖥 ⅙ 2 restaurants, 2 bars (1 w/entertainment), spa, sauna. Rooftop restaurant rotates for a 360° view of Nashville. **Rates:** Peak (Apr–May/Sept–Nov 15) $99–$169 S or D; $250–$600 ste. Children under age 18 stay free. Lower rates off-season. Parking: Indoor, $8/day. AE, CB, DC, DISC, MC, V.

≣≣≣ DoubleTree Guest Suites Nashville

2424 Atrium Way, 37214 (Music Valley); tel 615/889-8889 or toll free 800/222-8733; fax 615/883-7779. A luxurious, all-suite hotel. **Rooms:** 138 stes. CI 3pm/CO noon. Nonsmoking rms avail. **Amenities:** 🛏 🚰 🖩 🍽 A/C, cable TV w/movies, refrig, dataport. Some units w/terraces. Rooms stocked with complimentary coffee. **Services:** ✗ 🚐 🖼 🛎 Babysitting. **Facilities:** 🔥 🏋 🛏 ⅙ 1 restaurant, games rm, washer/dryer. **Rates:** Peak (Mar–Oct) $99–$165 ste. Extra person $20. Children under age 18 stay free. Lower rates off-season. Parking: Outdoor, free. AE, CB, DC, DISC, MC, V.

≣≣≣ DoubleTree Hotel Nashville

315 4th Ave N, 37219 (The District); tel 615/244-8200 or toll free 800/222-TREE; fax 615/747-4894. Near 2nd Ave. This recently renovated luxury hotel is hard to miss—it's the strikingly angular high-rise near Printer's Alley. **Rooms:** 337 rms and stes. Executive level. CI 3pm/CO noon. Nonsmoking rms avail. The rooms have mahogany furnishings inlaid with marble. **Amenities:** 🛏 🚰 A/C, cable TV w/movies. Some units w/whirlpools. Some rooms have dataports. **Services:** ✗ 🆅🅿 🚐 🛎 Babysitting. **Facilities:** 🔥 🏋 🛏 ⅙ 1 restaurant, sauna. **Rates:** Peak (Sept–Oct/Apr–June) $79–$139 S; $89–$149 D; $125–$239 ste. Extra person $10. Children under age 17 stay free. Lower rates off-season. Parking: Indoor, $8/day. AE, CB, DC, DISC, MC, V.

≣≣≣ Embassy Suites Nashville

10 Century Blvd, 37214 (Music Valley); tel 615/871-0033 or toll free 800/EMBASSY; fax 615/883-9245. An all-suite hotel featuring a relaxing lobby with many plants and hidden nooks for quiet conversation. Popular with families. **Rooms:** 296 stes. CI 4pm/CO noon. Nonsmoking rms avail. All units are two-room suites—large, ornately furnished, and designed for comfort and convenience with a couch, easy chairs, and a table for four. **Amenities:** 🛏 🚰 🖩 A/C, satel TV w/movies, refrig, dataport, voice mail. Some units w/terraces. **Services:** ✗ 🖶 🚐 🖼 🛎 🍴 Car-rental desk, babysitting. **Facilities:** 🔥 🏋 🛏 ⅙ 1 restaurant, 1 bar (w/entertainment), games rm, spa, sauna, whirlpool, washer/dryer. Guests receive complimentary passes for tennis at a local fitness center. **Rates (CP):** Peak (June–Aug) $119–$149 ste. Extra person $10. Children under age 17 stay free. Lower rates off-season. Parking: Outdoor, free. AE, CB, DC, DISC, JCB, MC, V.

≣≣≣ The Hermitage Hotel

231 6th Ave N, 37219 (The District); tel 615/244-3121 or toll free 800/251-1908; fax 615/254-6909. Nashville's first grand hotel (built in 1910), this downtown landmark greets every guest with an atmosphere of beaux arts elegance. A vaulted, stained-glass ceiling shines over a lobby luxuriously adorned with statues, beautiful floral arrangements, Persian carpets, and marbled columns. **Rooms:** 112 stes. CI 3pm/CO noon. Nonsmoking rms avail. Each unit is architecturally unique and has marbled bathroom floors. **Amenities:** 🛏 🚰 🍽 A/C, satel TV w/movies, refrig. **Services:** ✗ 🖶 🆅🅿 🚐 🖼 🛎 Babysitting. **Facilities:** 🛏 ⅙ 1 restaurant, 2 bars (1 w/entertainment). **Rates:** $139 ste. Extra person $10. Children under age 12 stay free. Parking: Indoor, $6/day. AE, CB, DC, DISC, MC, V.

≣≣ Holiday Inn Express Airport

1111 Airport Center Dr, 37214 (Music Valley); tel 615/883-1366 or toll free 800/HOLIDAY; fax 615/889-6867. Located off I-40. Despite its large size, this hotel has the cozy, comfortable look and feel of a lodge. The moose-antler chandeliers, exposed-beam roof, flagstone floor, and riverrock fireplace might have you thinking you're in a mountain resort. **Rooms:** 206 rms. CI 4pm/CO noon. Nonsmoking rms avail. Rooms have country-pine furniture and extra-roomy bathrooms. **Amenities:** 🛏 🚰 A/C, satel TV w/movies, dataport, voice mail. Some units w/terraces. **Services:** 🚐 🖼 🛎 **Facilities:** 🔥 🛏 ⅙ Guest privileges at local fitness center. **Rates (CP):** Peak (May–Oct) $55–$87 S or D. Extra person $8. Children under age 12 stay free. Lower rates off-season. Parking: Outdoor, free. AE, CB, DC, DISC, JCB, MC, V.

≣≣≣ Holiday Inn Select

2200 Elm Hill Pike, 37214 (Music Valley); tel 615/883-9770 or toll free 800/633-4427; fax 615/391-4521. Recently upgraded hotel geared toward business and family stays. **Rooms:** 387 rms and stes. CI 3pm/CO noon. Nonsmoking rms avail. **Amenities:** 🛏 🚰 🖩 🍽 A/C, satel TV w/movies, dataport, voice mail. Some units w/terraces. **Services:** ✗ ☎ 🚗 🖨 🗘 Car-rental desk. **Facilities:** 🎣 ⛳ 🏊 💻 ♿ 1 restaurant, 2 bars (1 w/entertainment), games rm, sauna, whirlpool, washer/dryer. **Rates:** Peak (Mar–Oct) $109–$159 S; $119–$159 D; $275 ste. Extra person $10. Children under age 18 stay free. Lower rates off-season. Parking: Outdoor, free. AE, CB, DC, DISC, JCB, MC, V.

🏨🏨🏨 Holiday Inn Vanderbilt

2613 West End Ave, 37203 (The West End); tel 615/327-4707 or toll free 800/777-5871; fax 615/327-8034. Large wooden doors lead into the lobby area of this hotel across the street from Centennial Park. With the Vanderbilt University football stadium right outside this hotel's back door, it's not surprising that this is a favorite with alumni and fans. **Rooms:** 301 rms and stes. CI 3pm/CO noon. Nonsmoking rms avail. Some parkside rooms have views of the Parthenon. **Amenities:** 🛁 🔺 📞 A/C, satel TV w/movies, dataport, voice mail. Some units w/terraces. **Services:** ✗ 🚗 🖨 🗘 🐾 Car-rental desk, babysitting. **Facilities:** 🎣 ⛳ 🍽 ♿ 1 restaurant, 1 bar (w/entertainment), washer/dryer. Large pool area with sundeck. **Rates (CP):** $79–$159 S or D; $160–$320 ste. Children under age 19 stay free. Parking: Outdoor, free. AE, CB, DC, DISC, JCB, MC, V.

🏨🏨🏨🏨 Loew's Vanderbilt Plaza Hotel

2100 West End Ave, 37203 (The West End); tel 615/320-1700 or toll free 800/336-3335; fax 615/320-5019. Full-service high-rise located across the street from Vanderbilt University. Popular site for conferences and conventions. The lobby features tapestries and large marble columns. **Rooms:** 338 rms and stes. Executive level. CI 3pm/CO noon. Nonsmoking rms avail. Rooms are furnished with antique reproductions. **Amenities:** 🛁 🔺 A/C, cable TV w/movies, dataport, voice mail. All units w/minibars, some w/fireplaces, some w/whirlpools. Some rooms equipped with fax machines; concierge-level rooms have coffeemakers and hair dryers. **Services:** ✗ 🚗 VP 🖨 🗘 🐾 Twice-daily maid svce, car-rental desk, masseur, children's program, babysitting. **Facilities:** ⛳ 🍽 💻 ♿ 2 restaurants, 2 bars (1 w/entertainment), beauty salon. **Rates:** $154 S; $174 D; $350–$650 ste. Extra person $20. Children under age 18 stay free. Parking: Indoor, $6–8/day. AE, CB, DC, DISC, JCB, MC, V.

🏨🏨 Marriott Residence Inn

2300 Elm Hill Pike, 37214 (Music Valley); tel 615/889-8600 or toll free 800/331-3131; fax 615/871-4970. More like an apartment complex than a standard hotel. All the rooms are suites and there's a centrally located sports court. **Rooms:** 168 stes. CI 4pm/CO noon. Nonsmoking rms avail. Some suites feature loft bedrooms. **Amenities:** 🛁 🔺 📞 A/C, cable TV, refrig, dataport. Some units w/terraces, some w/fireplaces. **Services:** 🖨 🗘 🐾 Grocery-shopping service. **Facilities:** 🎣 🏊 🍽 ♿ Basketball, volleyball, whirlpool,

washer/dryer. **Rates (CP):** Peak (May–Oct) $94–$144 ste. Lower rates off-season. Parking: Outdoor, free. AE, CB, DC, DISC, MC, V.

🏨🏨🏨 Nashville Airport Marriott

600 Marriott Dr, 37214 (Music Valley); tel 615/889-9300 or toll free 800/228-9290; fax 615/889-9315. Located on 17 wooded acres, this classy Marriott features a luxurious lobby with marble floors, spacious guest rooms, and lots of recreational facilities. **Rooms:** 399 rms and stes. Executive level. CI 4pm/CO noon. Nonsmoking rms avail. Patio rooms available upon request. **Amenities:** 🛁 🔺 📞 A/C, cable TV w/movies, dataport, voice mail. **Services:** ✗ 🚗 🖨 🗘 Babysitting. **Facilities:** 🎣 🏊 ⛳ 🍽 ♿ 1 restaurant, 1 bar, basketball, volleyball, games rm, lawn games, sauna, whirlpool, washer/dryer. **Rates:** $109–$129 S; $109–$140 D; $200–$300 ste. Children under age 18 stay free. Parking: Outdoor, free. AE, CB, DC, DISC, ER, JCB, MC, V.

🏨🏨🏨🏨 Opryland Hotel

2800 Opryland Dr, 37214 (Music Valley); tel 615/889-1000; fax 615/871-5728. Adjacent to Opryland Park and near the airport, this is one of the largest hotels in Nashville. It is designed as a series of atriums landscaped with bubbling brooks, plant conservatories, waterfalls, and elevated and ground-level paths. (The highlight is the Cascades atrium, with its 2½-acre glass roof and 40-foot waterfall.) Richly colorful and relaxing. **Rooms:** 2,870 rms and stes. CI 3pm/CO 11am. Nonsmoking rms avail. Rooms are exquisitely decorated with colonial American furnishings and tasteful floral wallpaper. **Amenities:** 🛁 🔺 A/C, cable TV w/movies, dataport, voice mail. Some units w/terraces, some w/fireplaces, some w/whirlpools. **Services:** 🍽 🚗 VP 🖨 🗘 Car-rental desk, masseur, babysitting. **Facilities:** 🎣 ▶18 ⛳ 🏊 💻 ♿ 7 restaurants, 5 bars (4 w/entertainment), games rm, spa, beauty salon. There are 22 separate gift shops, a revolving bar, a superbly landscaped pool area, and excellent exercise facilities. The Nashville Network's *Ralph Emery Show* broadcasts live from the hotel. **Rates:** $139–$219 S or D; $259–$2,000 ste. Extra person $15. Children under age 12 stay free. Parking: Outdoor, free. AE, CB, DC, DISC, MC, V.

🏨🏨 Quality Inn—Hall of Fame/Vanderbilt

1407 Division St, 37203 (Music Row); tel 615/242-1631 or toll free 800/228-5151; fax 615/244-9519. A standard chain hotel with a party atmosphere due to its location. The suites are a good deal for vacationing families. **Rooms:** 103 rms and stes. CI 3pm/CO noon. Nonsmoking rms avail. **Amenities:** 🛁 🔺 A/C, cable TV, in-rm safe. Some rooms have refrigerators. **Services:** 🖨 🗘 🐾 **Facilities:** 🎣 🏊 ♿ Washer/dryer. Lounge presents live country music most nights. **Rates (CP):** Peak (Apr–Oct) $44–$69 S; $48–$75 D; $59–$90 ste. Extra person $5. Children under age 18 stay free. Lower rates off-season. Parking: Outdoor, free. AE, CB, DC, DISC, EC, MC, V.

≣≣≣ Ramada Inn Across From Opryland

2401 Music Valley Dr, 37214 (Music Valley); tel 615/889-0800 or toll free 800/2-RAMADA; fax 615/883-1230. One of the more luxurious properties in the Opryland area. The slightly schizophrenic public spaces include a quaint colonial-style lobby and a sleek, modern atrium that contains the hotel's indoor pool. **Rooms:** 307 rms and stes. CI 3pm/CO 11am. Nonsmoking rms avail. Some rooms open onto the atrium. **Amenities:** 🛅 🍸 🖭 📶 A/C, cable TV w/movies. Some units w/whirlpools. **Services:** ✕ 🚐 🖼 ↩ Car-rental desk, babysitting. On-site travel agency. **Facilities:** 🛱 👘 300 ᐦ 1 restaurant, 2 bars (1 w/entertainment), games rm, sauna, steam rm, whirlpool. **Rates:** Peak (Mar–Nov) $72–$99 S or D; $160 ste. Extra person $8. Children under age 18 stay free. Lower rates off-season. Parking: Outdoor, free. AE, CB, DC, DISC, EC, ER, JCB, MC, V.

≣≣≣ Ramada Inn Airport—Briley Parkway

733 Briley Pkwy, 37217 (Music Valley); tel 615/361-5900 or toll free 800/2-RAMADA; fax 615/367-0339. Clean, comfortable 11-story property. One of the closest accommodations to the airport. **Rooms:** 200 rms and stes. CI 2pm/CO noon. Nonsmoking rms avail. **Amenities:** 🛅 A/C, cable TV w/movies. Some rooms have refrigerators and heat lamps. **Services:** ✕ 🚐 🖼 ↩ Car-rental desk. Complimentary Opryland shuttle. **Facilities:** 🛱 400 ᐦ 1 restaurant, 1 bar (w/entertainment), playground. Very large pool. **Rates:** Peak (Apr–Oct) $48–$71 S; $52–$67 D; $100 ste. Extra person $6. Children under age 18 stay free. Lower rates off-season. Parking: Outdoor, free. AE, CB, DC, DISC, MC, V.

≣≣≣ Regal Maxwell House

2025 MetroCenter Blvd, 37228; tel 615/259-4343 or toll free 800/457-4460; fax 615/259-4343 ext 1327. The original Maxwell House was in downtown Nashville, and it was there that President Theodore Roosevelt once commented that the hotel's coffee was "good to the last drop." Now located near Fountain Square Plaza, this new high-rise greets its guests with a large, elegant lobby and outside, glass elevators offering city views. **Rooms:** 289 rms and stes. Executive level. CI 3pm/CO noon. Nonsmoking rms avail. All rooms have lighted work stations, wooden headboards, wingback chairs, and TV set in armoire. **Amenities:** 🛅 🍸 A/C, satel TV w/movies, dataport, voice mail. Some rooms provide coffeemakers and full-length mirrors. **Services:** ✕ 🗝 🚐 🖼 ↩ Babysitting. Business services. **Facilities:** 🛱 🏋 🏊 👘 1000 ᐦ 2 restaurants, 2 bars, spa, sauna, steam rm, whirlpool. Rooftop restaurant provides a gorgeous view of Nashville skyline. Large whirlpool/spa area. **Rates:** $138 S; $153 D; $165–$350 ste. Extra person $15. Children under age 18 stay free. Parking: Outdoor, free. AE, CB, DC, DISC, JCB, MC, V.

≣≣≣≣ Renaissance Nashville Hotel

611 Commerce St, 37203 (The District); tel 615/255-8400 or toll free 800/HOTELS-1; fax 615/255-8202. Connected to the Nashville Convention Center, this luxurious downtown facility gets lots of business travelers but would make a pleasant vacation choice as well. **Rooms:** 673 rms and stes. Executive level. CI 3pm/CO noon. Nonsmoking rms avail. Spacious guest rooms feature wingback chairs and dark-wood furnishings. **Amenities:** 🛅 🍸 🖭 A/C, cable TV w/movies, dataport. 1 unit w/whirlpool. **Services:** 🍽 🗝 🆅🅿 🚐 🖼 ↩ 🕭 Car-rental desk, babysitting. Extensive business services available. **Facilities:** 🛱 👘 1500 ᐦ 2 restaurants, 2 bars (1 w/entertainment), sauna, whirlpool. **Rates:** $160–$180 S; $180–$200 D; $275–$1,000 ste. Extra person $20. Children under age 18 stay free. Parking: Indoor, $5/day. Golf packages avail. AE, CB, DC, DISC, ER, JCB, MC, V.

≣≣≣≣ Sheraton Music City

777 McGavock Pike, 37214 (Music Valley); tel 615/885-2200 or toll free 800/325-3535; fax 615/871-0926. Set amid 23 acres of beautifully landscaped grounds, this four-story hotel features a large lobby with a lion's-head fountain and marble floors. Popular with business travelers due to its location in a business park near the airport. **Rooms:** 412 rms and stes. Executive level. CI 3pm/CO 1pm. Nonsmoking rms avail. All rooms have large work desks, comfortable chairs, and plenty of closet space. **Amenities:** 🛅 🍸 🖭 A/C, satel TV w/movies, dataport, voice mail. All units w/terraces, some w/whirlpools. **Services:** 🍽 🗝 🆅🅿 🚐 🖼 ↩ 🕭 Car-rental desk, masseur, babysitting. Complimentary shuttles to Opryland. **Facilities:** 🛱 🏋 🏊2 👘 1100 🖥 ᐦ 1 restaurant, 2 bars (1 w/entertainment), spa, sauna, whirlpool, beauty salon. Meeting facilities range from an intimate conference room to a grand ballroom. **Rates:** Peak (Mar–Nov) $99–$133 S; $114–$148 D; $150–$600 ste. Extra person $15. Children under age 18 stay free. Lower rates off-season. Parking: Outdoor, free. AE, CB, DC, DISC, MC, V.

≣≣ The Spence Manor

11 Music Square E, Suite 601, 37203 (Music Row); tel 615/259-4400; fax 615/259-2148. Numerous recording professionals stay in this private hideaway, which is located near major music recording studios. **Rooms:** 45 stes. Executive level. CI open/CO 2pm. Large, comfortable rooms. **Amenities:** 🛅 🍸 🖭 A/C, cable TV, refrig, dataport, voice mail. Some units w/whirlpools. **Services:** ✕ 🖼 ↩ **Facilities:** 🛱 15 Large, guitar-shaped pool. **Rates:** $69–$300 ste. Extra person $10. Parking: Outdoor, free. AE, DISC, MC, V.

≣≣ Studio Plus at Nashville Airport

2511 Elm Hill Pike, 37214 (Music Valley); tel 615/871-9669 or toll free 800/646-8000; fax 615/231-6063. The perfect combination of apartmentlike privacy and hominess, hotel services, and economical rates. **Rooms:** 71 stes and effic. CI 3pm/CO 11am. **Amenities:** 🛅 🍸 🖭 A/C, cable TV, refrig, dataport. Private phone lines available. **Services:** 🖼 Mail delivery available for extended stays. **Facilities:** 🛱 👘 ᐦ Washer/dryer. **Rates:** Peak (Mar–Nov) $59–$69 ste; $49–$59 effic. Extra person $5. Children under age 12 stay free. Lower rates off-season. Parking: Outdoor, free. AE, CB, DC, DISC, MC, V.

Union Station Hotel

1001 Broadway, 37203 (The District); tel 615/726-1001 or toll free 800/331-2123; fax 615/248-3554. Housed in a renovated Romanesque Gothic–style train station built in 1900, this is one of Nashville's most elegant hotels. The enormous lobby boasts a stylish fountain, 65-foot barrel-vaulted ceilings of Tiffany stained glass, and bas-relief sculptures at each end. **Rooms:** 124 rms and stes. Executive level. CI 3pm/CO noon. Nonsmoking rms avail. Each room is architecturally unique. The gallery deluxe rooms have 22-foot ceilings and views of the lobby. **Amenities:** 🛏 🅰 A/C, cable TV w/movies, dataport, voice mail. **Services:** ✕ 🕭 VP 🚗 🖅 🍷 🍸 Twice-daily maid svce, children's program, babysitting. **Facilities:** 400 🖥 & 3 restaurants (see "Restaurants" below), 1 bar. **Rates:** Peak (Mar–Oct) $109–$129 S; $119–$149 D; $159–$220 ste. Extra person $10. Children under age 17 stay free. Lower rates off-season. Parking: Outdoor, $8/day. AE, CB, DC, DISC, MC, V.

Wyndham Garden Hotel

1112 Airport Center Dr, 37214 (Music Valley); tel 615/889-9090 or toll free 800/WYNDHAM; fax 615/885-1564. Located near the airport, this tastefully decorated hotel has many enjoyable spaces in the lobby and public areas. **Rooms:** 180 rms and stes. CI 3pm/CO noon. Nonsmoking rms avail. **Amenities:** 🛏 🅰 🖵 🍷 A/C, cable TV w/movies, voice mail. Many rooms have dataports. **Services:** ✕ 🚗 🖅 🍷 Business services. **Facilities:** 🛗 🖫 200 & 1 restaurant, 1 bar, whirlpool. Large indoor pool area. **Rates:** $74–$99 S; $84–$109 D; $109–$119 ste. Extra person $10. Children under age 18 stay free. Parking: Outdoor, free. AE, CB, DC, DISC, ER, JCB, MC, V.

MOTELS

Best Western Calumet Inn

701 Stewart's Ferry Pike, 37214 (Music Valley); tel 615/889-9199 or toll free 800/528-1234; fax 615/889-9617. Comfortable, clean accommodations located near the airport and all main attractions. **Rooms:** 80 rms and stes. CI 2pm/CO 11am. Nonsmoking rms avail. King suites have whirlpool tubs. **Amenities:** 🛏 A/C, cable TV, dataport. Some units w/whirlpools. Some rooms have microwaves and refrigerators. **Services:** 🖅 🍷 🍸 **Facilities:** 🛗 **Rates (CP):** Peak (May 24–Sept 2) $41–$90 S; $51–$100 D; $75–$150 ste. Extra person $10. Children under age 18 stay free. Lower rates off-season. Parking: Outdoor, free. AE, CB, DC, DISC, ER, MC, V.

Best Western Metro Inn

99 Spring St, 37207 (The District); tel 615/259-9160 or toll free 800/528-1234; fax 615/244-5871. Simple accommodations located near Second Street entertainment. **Rooms:** 140 rms. CI 3pm/CO 11am. Nonsmoking rms avail. **Amenities:** 🛏 A/C, satel TV. **Services:** 🍷 **Facilities:** 🛗 150 1 restaurant, games rm, washer/dryer. **Rates:** Peak (Apr–Oct) $42–$89 S;

$44–$89 D. Extra person $4. Children under age 12 stay free. Lower rates off-season. Parking: Outdoor, free. AE, CB, DC, DISC, MC, V.

Days Inn—Airport/Opryland Area

1 International Plaza, 37217 (Music Valley); tel 615/361-7666 or toll free 800/851-1962; fax 615/399-0283. Located within 10 minutes of both the airport and Opryland, this motel offers two floors of comfortable, family-friendly accommodations. **Rooms:** 227 rms and stes. Executive level. CI 3pm/CO noon. Nonsmoking rms avail. Many rooms face the large courtyard/pool area. **Amenities:** 🛏 🅰 A/C, satel TV w/movies. **Services:** ✕ 🚗 🖅 🍷 Babysitting. Housekeeping a bit spotty in some rooms. **Facilities:** 🛗 400 & 1 restaurant, 1 bar. **Rates:** Peak (May–Oct) $52–$68 S; $52–$72 D; $95–$125 ste. Extra person $6. Children under age 18 stay free. Lower rates off-season. Parking: Outdoor, free. AE, CB, DC, DISC, JCB, MC, V.

Days Inn Nashville East

3445 Percy Priest Dr, 37214 (Music Valley); tel 615/889-8881 or toll free 800/DAYS-INN; fax 615/889-8881. An aging but decent facility located near Percy Priest Lake and the airport. **Rooms:** 70 rms. CI 2pm/CO 11am. Nonsmoking rms avail. **Amenities:** 🛏 A/C, cable TV, dataport. Some units w/whirlpools. **Services:** 🍷 **Facilities:** 🛗 & **Rates (CP):** Peak (June–Aug) $54–$69 S; $63–$78 D. Extra person $5. Children under age 12 stay free. Lower rates off-season. Parking: Outdoor, free. AE, CB, DC, DISC, JCB, MC, V.

Days Inn—Vanderbilt/Music Row

1800 West End Ave, 37203 (The West End); tel 615/327-0922 or toll free 800/325-2525; fax 615/327-0102. Comfortable accommodations located near Music Row and downtown. **Rooms:** 151 rms. CI 3pm/CO noon. Nonsmoking rms avail. **Amenities:** 🛏 A/C, satel TV, in-rm safe. Some units w/whirlpools. **Services:** 🚗 🖅 🍷 Babysitting. **Facilities:** 🛗 50 & 1 restaurant (bkfst and dinner only). **Rates (BB):** Peak (June–Oct) $49–$65 S; $56–$85 D. Extra person $6. Children under age 18 stay free. Lower rates off-season. Parking: Indoor/outdoor, free. AE, CB, DC, DISC, JCB, MC, V.

Econo Lodge Opryland Area

2460 Music Valley Dr, 37214 (Music Valley); tel 615/889-0090 or toll free 800/553-2666; fax 615/889-0086. Simple accommodations less than a mile from Opryland. **Rooms:** 86 rms. CI 3pm/CO noon. Nonsmoking rms avail. Rooms are surprisingly large although the bathrooms are on the cramped side. **Amenities:** 🛏 🅰 A/C, satel TV. Some rooms with dataports. **Services:** 🍷 🍸 **Facilities:** 🛗 & Miniature-golf course next door. **Rates:** Peak (June–Oct) $62 S or D. Extra person $10. Children under age 18 stay free. Lower rates off-season. Parking: Outdoor, free. AE, CB, DC, DISC, MC, V.

Holiday Inn Express

2516 Music Valley Dr, 37214 (Music Valley); tel 615/889-0086 or toll free 800/HOLIDAY; fax 615/889-0086. Very basic, no-frills accommodations. **Rooms:** 121 rms. CI 3pm/CO noon. Nonsmoking rms avail. **Amenities:** 🛎 🖤 A/C, satel TV w/movies, dataport. Some rooms equipped with coffeemakers and/or hair dryers. **Services:** 🖾 🗋 🗇 **Facilities:** 🔄 🞄75🗆 ⅙ Small pool gets lots of traffic noise. **Rates (CP):** Peak (May 23–Sept 6) $71–$76 S or D. Extra person $6. Children under age 12 stay free. Lower rates off-season. Parking: Outdoor, free. AE, CB, DC, DISC, MC, V.

Holiday Inn Express

1414 Princeton Place, Hermitage, 37076; tel 615/871-4545 or toll free 800/HOLIDAY; fax 615/871-4545 ext 405. Standard chain accommodations approximately ten minutes from the airport. **Rooms:** 65 rms and stes. CI noon/CO 11am. Nonsmoking rms avail. **Amenities:** 🛎 🖤 🞄 A/C, cable TV, dataport. Some units w/whirlpools. **Services:** 🖾 🗋 Coffee available 24 hours. **Facilities:** 🔄 ⅙ Washer/dryer. **Rates (CP):** Peak (June–Oct) $60–$80 S; $65–$85 D; $125–$150 ste. Extra person $5. Children under age 18 stay free. Lower rates off-season. Parking: Outdoor, free. AE, CB, DC, DISC, ER, JCB, MC, V.

La Quinta Inn MetroCenter

2001 MetroCenter Blvd, 37228; tel 615/259-2130 or toll free 800/531-5900; fax 615/242-2650. A two-story motel with Southwestern-style architecture and decor. Small fountain in lobby. **Rooms:** 120 rms and stes. CI 3pm/CO noon. Nonsmoking rms avail. **Amenities:** 🛎 🖤 A/C, cable TV. **Services:** 🚐 🖾 🗋 🗇 **Facilities:** 🔄 🞄25🗆 ⅙ Washer/dryer. **Rates (CP):** Peak (May 15–Nov) $53–$60 S; $60–$67 D; $66–$73 ste. Extra person $7. Children under age 18 stay free. Lower rates off-season. Parking: Outdoor, free. AE, CB, DC, DISC, MC, V.

Red Roof Inn Nashville East

510 Claridge Dr, 37214 (Music Valley); tel 615/872-0735 or toll free 800/THE-ROOF; fax 615/871-4647. Basic, budget accommodations. Fine for I-40 travelers needing an overnight stop. **Rooms:** 120 rms. CI 4pm/CO 11am. Nonsmoking rms avail. Simple, clean rooms. **Amenities:** 🛎 A/C, satel TV, dataport. **Services:** 🚐 🗋 🗇 **Facilities:** ⅙ **Rates:** Peak (May–Aug) $36–$49 S; $36–$53 D. Extra person $6–8. Children under age 18 stay free. Lower rates off-season. Parking: Outdoor, free. AE, CB, DC, DISC, MC, V.

Shoney's Inn Nashville Music Row

1521 Demonbreun St, 37203 (Music Row); tel 615/255-9977 or toll free 800/222-2222; fax 615/242-6127. An antebellum-style building located near famous Music Row. The lobby walls are lined with autographed photos of country music stars who have stayed here. **Rooms:** 147 rms and stes. CI 3pm/CO noon. Nonsmoking rms avail. **Amenities:** 🛎 🖤A/C, satel TV. 1 unit w/whirlpool. **Services:** 🖾 🗋 🗇 Babysitting. Meals at nearby Shoney's restaurant can be billed to guest's room. **Facilities:** 🔄 🞄40🗆 ⅙ **Rates:** $65–$75 S; $75–$85 D; $89–$109 ste. Extra person $6. Children under age 18 stay free. Parking: Outdoor, free. AE, CB, DC, DISC, MC, V.

Super 8 Motel Nashville Airport

720 Royal Pkwy, 37214 (Music Valley); tel 615/889-8887 or toll free 800/800-8000; fax 615/885-7000. Simple accommodations located in a spiffy-looking brick building. Nothing fancy, but the rooms are clean and the beds are comfortable. **Rooms:** 105 rms and stes. CI 3pm/CO 11am. Nonsmoking rms avail. **Amenities:** 🛎 🖤 A/C, satel TV. Some units w/whirlpools. **Services:** 🚐 🗋 **Facilities:** 🔄 🔧 ⅙ Whirlpool. Newly built indoor pool. **Rates (CP):** Peak (Mar–Sept) $45–$70 S; $60–$80 D; $80–$100 ste. Extra person $7. Children under age 12 stay free. Lower rates off-season. Parking: Outdoor, free. AE, CB, DC, DISC, MC, V.

RESTAURANTS 🍴

Arthur's

In Union Station Hotel, 1001 Broadway (The District); tel 615/255-1494. **International.** One of the most elegant restaurants in the city. Tucked into its own room off the hotel's immense lobby, this restaurant breathes Southern gentility, with its huge plantation-style shutters, gilded plasterwork, 24-foot ceiling, and comfortable banquettes. The menu changes daily and is always given verbally, but you can count on such classic dishes as rack of lamb, chateaubriand, and tournedos of beef to make regular appearances. Fresh fish is flown in daily. There are 500–600 wines in a temperature-controlled storage facility, and flambéed desserts and coffee provide a great way to finish off the evening. **FYI:** Reservations recommended. Dress code. **Open:** Mon–Thurs 5:30–10pm, Fri–Sat 5:30–11pm, Sun 5:30–9pm. **Prices:** Prix fixe $49–$52. AE, CB, DC, DISC, MC, V. ❤ 🆅🅿 ⅙

Broadway Dinner Train

108 1st Ave S; tel 615/254-8000. **Continental.** Climb aboard antique train cars dating back to the 1940s and 1950s for a 2½-hour train ride along the historical Tennessee Central Railway. Five entrees are available, including the train's trademark hickory-smoked prime rib. The train boards promptly at 6:30. **FYI:** Reservations recommended. Guitar/singer. Dress code. **Open:** Thurs–Sat 6:30–9:30pm. **Prices:** Prix fixe $43. AE, CB, DC, DISC, MC, V. ❤

Cakewalk Restaurant

3001 West End Ave (The West End); tel 615/320-7778. **Eclectic.** Geometric cutouts on a curving faux-finished wall create an art deco effect at this bistro tucked into the back of a tiny shopping plaza. Menu selections range the globe, from the Pacific Rim to Spain to Asia. Chicken Kathmandu with tamarind-raisin sauce and curried vegetables, paella with spicy saffron rice, and catfish Clovis with black-eyed-pea salsa are some of the inventive choices. There's even a pastry chef on site, and the cakes here are locally famous. Winner of the *Wine Spectator* Award for 1994. **FYI:** Reservations recommended. **Open:** Lunch Sun–Fri 11am–3pm; dinner Sun–Thurs 5:30–10pm, Fri–Sat 5:30–11pm. **Prices:** Main courses $14–$20. AE, CB, DC, DISC, MC, V. &

⑤ Calypso Cafe
In Elliston Point Shopping Center, 2424 Elliston Place (The West End); tel 615/321-3878. **Caribbean.** A casual and colorful place located in a small shopping plaza, this cafe serves up Caribbean cuisine with an American flair. Low-fat vegetarian items and rotisserie chicken are popular with regular customers, as are the fresh Caribbean salads such as tropical chicken salad with pineapple and raisins, and black-bean salad topped with beef or chicken. **FYI:** Reservations not accepted. Children's menu. Beer and wine only. Additional locations: The Arcade between 5th & 6th Ave (tel 259-9631); 722 Thompson Lane (tel 297-6530). **Open:** Mon–Thurs 11am–9pm, Sat 11am–9pm, Fri 11am–10pm, Sun noon–8pm. **Prices:** Main courses $4–$6. AE, DISC, MC, V. &

⑤ Country Life Vegetarian Buffet
1917 Division St (The West End); tel 615/327-3695. **Vegetarian.** Formerly a health food store, this restaurant specializes in vegetarian food with some vegan (dairy-free) dishes. You can pile up your plate with such healthy and delicious offerings as fettuccine Alfredo, steamed broccoli, black-eyed-pea soup, and fruit salad. Meals are reasonably priced and based on weight, and all salad dressings are made fresh on the premises. **FYI:** Reservations not accepted. No liquor license. No smoking. **Open:** Mon–Thurs 11:30am–2:30pm, Fri 11:30am–2:15pm. Closed Dec 25–Dec 31. **Prices:** No CC. &

F Scott's
2210 Crestmoor Rd (Belle Meade); tel 615/269-5861. **New American/Regional American.** The unpretentious yet elegant art deco–style dining room features painted murals, black-and-white tile floors, and copies of paintings by Picasso, Renoir, and Chagall. Seasonal menu consistently offers a blend of Southwestern, Pacific Rim, and Southeastern cuisines: Andalusian gazpacho, escargots with vermouth and goat cheese, and grilled swordfish with roasted nuts and raisins are typical of the inventive options. The wine list offers over 650 choices and has received an Award of Excellence from *Wine Spectator*. **FYI:** Reservations accepted. Jazz/piano. Children's menu. Dress code. **Open:** Lunch Mon–Fri 11:30am–2pm; dinner Sun–Thurs 5:30–10pm, Fri–Sat 5:30–11pm; brunch Sun 11am–2pm. **Prices:** Main courses $13–$19. AE, CB, DC, DISC, MC, V. ⦿ VP &

The Gerst Haus
228 Woodland St (The District); tel 615/255-7133. **American/German.** This pub was opened by a German immigrant family at the turn of the century as a brewery. Today, they serve traditional German specialties—bratwurst, schnitzel, and sauerbraten—as well as American fare. German-style barbecue, too. **FYI:** Reservations not accepted. German

band. **Open:** Peak (May–Sept) Mon–Thurs 11am–9pm, Fri–Sat 11am–10pm, Sun 3–9pm. **Prices:** Main courses $8–$13. AE, MC, V.

Houston's
3000 West End Ave (The West End); tel 615/269-3481. **American.** Despite the fact that this is a new building, interior brick arches and exposed beams give the restaurant the feel of a renovated warehouse. The salads and burgers here are consistently voted the best in town, but they also do a good job on prime rib and barbecue, and the Hawaiian steak is among their most popular dishes. **FYI:** Reservations not accepted. Additional location: Poplar Ave, Memphis (tel 901/683-0915). **Open:** Sun–Mon 11am–10pm, Tues–Thurs 11am–10:30pm, Fri–Sat 11am–midnight. **Prices:** Main courses $5–$17. AE, MC, V. &

⑤ International Market and Restaurant
2010 Belmont Blvd (The West End); tel 615/297-4453. **Thai/Oriental.** For some Thai home-cooking (and Chinese, too), visit this small and simple 20-year-old restaurant in a residential neighborhood. Asian packaged snacks and grocery items are available in addition to hot dishes served cafeteria style. Pad Thai, kang kai (chicken curry), spicy chicken with garlic, and noodle soup are popular items. Any dish not on the menu will be cooked upon request. **FYI:** Reservations accepted. Beer and wine only. No smoking. **Open:** Daily 10:30am–9pm. **Prices:** Main courses $3–$5. AE, MC, V. &

Jamaica
1901 Broadway (The West End); tel 615/321-5191. **Caribbean/Seafood.** The colorful dining room features murals depicting typical Caribbean scenes (a marketplace, people fishing) and an aquarium full of tigerfish, eels, and other tropical fish. The owners frequently visit Jamaica and bring back authentic recipes; popular dishes such as chicken Marguerite, pasta de la Louisiane, and jerk chicken and pork are often available. **FYI:** Reservations accepted. Jazz. Children's menu. **Open:** Mon–Thurs 11am–11pm, Fri–Sat 11am–11:30pm. **Prices:** Main courses $8–$11. AE, CB, DC, DISC, MC, V. VP &

Jimmy Kelly's
217 Louise Ave (The West End); tel 615/329-4349. **Steak.** In its third generation of family proprietors, the restaurant is located in a refurbished Victorian mansion. Historic documents and pictures adorn the walls of the various dining rooms. There are two bars and porch seating as well. The kitchen turns out well-prepared traditional dishes such as chateaubriand in a burgundy-and-mushroom sauce and blackened catfish, and all their meat is cut in-house. The corn bread is among the best in the city. **FYI:** Reservations recommended. Children's menu. **Open:** Mon–Sat 5pm–midnight. **Prices:** Main courses $13–$25. AE, DC, MC, V. ▪ VP &

La Paz

3808 Cleghorn Ave (Belle Meade); tel 615/383-5200. **Mexican/Southwestern.** A big place that from the outside looks like the Alamo—there's even a cactus garden by the front door. Inside, you'll find rough-board floor and a partially rock wall that gives the interior an aged look that belies the restaurant's shopping-mall surroundings. California quesadillas with spinach and avocados, and a variety of pork and seafood dishes, are among the menu highlights. Tangy margaritas are available to wash it all down. **FYI:** Reservations not accepted. Guitar/singer. Children's menu. Additional location: 8025 Kingston Pike, Knoxville (tel 423/690-5250). **Open:** Mon–Thurs 11am–10pm, Fri 11am–11pm, Sat 11:30am–11pm, Sun 5–10pm. **Prices:** Main courses $8–$14. AE, CB, DC, DISC, MC, V. 🍴👍

Mario's

2005 Broadway (The West End); tel 615/327-3232. **Italian.** A family-owned trattoria specializing in Northern Italian food, Mario's offers elegant dining in a cozy atmosphere. Much of the restaurant's six hundred wines are on display in racks throughout the dining areas. Seafood, veal, pasta. **FYI:** Reservations recommended. Dress code. **Open:** Mon–Sat 5:30–10:30pm. Closed Dec 24–Dec 30. **Prices:** Main courses $16–$26. AE, CB, DC, DISC, MC, V. 👍

Mere Bulles

152 2nd Ave N (The District); tel 615/256-1946. **Continental.** This old Maxwell House Coffee warehouse has been renovated as the home of an extremely spacious and attractive eatery. A unique atmosphere prevails, with neon lighting, a rotating artwork collection, and live jazz. Enticing main courses—filet mignon with a red-pepper coulis, salmon grilled with a crust of herbs, and chicken sautéed with Jack Daniel's sauce—are complemented by a rotating wine list. **FYI:** Reservations recommended. Jazz/piano. Dress code. **Open:** Lunch Mon–Sat 11am–2pm; dinner Sun–Thurs 5:30–10pm, Fri–Sat 5:30–11pm; brunch Sun 11am–3pm. **Prices:** Main courses $15–$22. AE, DC, DISC, MC, V. 👍

Slice of Life Bakery and Restaurant

1811 Division St (The West End); tel 615/329-2525. **Natural Foods.** Around the corner from Music Row, this casual place has a light and natural feeling in the exposed brick, wood paneling, skylight, and wall of glass blocks. The menu offers healthy vegetarian specialties (stir fry, steamed vegetables, chili) as well as chicken, fish, and vegan macrobiotic meals. An off-premises bakery offers fresh-baked goods with no processed sugar, only fruit juices and other natural sweeteners. **FYI:** Reservations accepted. Guitar. Beer and wine only. No smoking. **Open:** Sun 8am–4pm, Mon 7am–4pm, Tues–Thurs 7am–9pm, Fri 7am–10pm, Sat 8am–10pm. **Prices:** Main courses $6–$13. AE, DC, DISC, MC, V. 👍👍

Sunset Grill

2001 Belcourt Ave (The West End); tel 615/386-FOOD. **New American/Regional American.** The revolving menu at this Hillsboro Village eatery highlights low-fat, high-flavor dishes, including hickory-smoked bucksnort trout and the beggar's purse (a phyllo pastry with crab, shrimp, and wild mushrooms), all cooked by a James Beard Award–winning chef. A *Wine Spectator* award-winning wine list includes over 300 labels, and the restaurant often hosts wine tastings. Neo-industrial style predominates in the black, gray, and white dining room. **FYI:** Reservations accepted. **Open:** Lunch Mon–Fri 11am–4:30pm; dinner Mon–Thurs 5–10pm, Fri–Sat 5pm–midnight. **Prices:** Main courses $7–$26. AE, CB, DC, DISC, MC, V. 🍴👍👍👍

The Wild Boar

2014 Broadway (The West End); tel 615/329-1313. **Continental.** Handsomely decorated in the spirit of a European hunting lodge with fine art dating back to the 14th century, the Wild Boar offers a high-dining experience. The wine list, which includes over 2,000 selections, was recently commended by *Wine Spectator* magazine as one of the best in the country. The frequently changing menu is always designed to complement the wine offerings. A sample entree might be bluefin tuna sushi and salmon tartare with flying fish caviar. The chef trained in France for 14 years. **FYI:** Reservations recommended. Piano. Jacket required. **Open:** Lunch Mon–Fri 11:30am–2pm; dinner Mon–Thurs 6–10pm, Fri–Sat 6–10:30pm. **Prices:** Main courses $20–$32; prix fixe $60. AE, CB, DC, DISC, MC, V. 🍷👍👍👍

ATTRACTIONS 🎟️

THEME PARK

Opryland USA

2802 Opryland Dr; tel 615/889-6611. Although this entertainment complex features popular music of all kinds—jazz, blues, folk, rock, gospel, musical comedy—country is the mainstay. Besides going from show to show, visitors can also spend the day on the white-knuckle roller coaster and log flume rides around the park. Restaurants and snack bars abound, and there are special shows and rides for little kids. Concerts by major country stars are staged daily at the **Chevrolet/GEO Celebrity Theater** (admission to these concerts is not included in the price of your park admission ticket).

Outside the front gates of the park are more attractions, including the new **Grand Ole Opry House,** the site of the live radio broadcasts of the famous country music show since 1974. This is also where you'll find the Star Walk, which commemorates stars and legends of country music. Three country music museums lie just outside the park—the Grand Ole Opry Museum, the Roy Acuff Museum (home of an informal Sunday morning worship service featuring gospel music), and the Minnie Pearl Museum.

The three-day Opryland USA Passport includes park admission, *General Jackson* showboat cruise, "Grand Ole Opry" matinee, Nashville city tour, ticket to a taping of the Nashville Network's *Nashville Now* TV show, and concert at

Opryland USA. **Open:** Mid-Mar–mid-May and mid-Sept–mid-Oct, Sat–Sun 10am–9pm; mid-May–mid-Sept, daily 10am–9pm. **$$$$**

MUSEUMS

Ryman Auditorium and Museum

116 5th Ave N; tel 615/254-1445. Originally built in 1892 as the Union Gospel Tabernacle by riverboat captain Tom Ryman, this building served as an evangelical hall for many years. However, by the early 1900s, the building's name had been changed to honor its builder and a stage had been added. That stage, over the years, saw the likes of Sarah Bernhardt, Enrico Caruso, Katherine Hepburn, Will Rogers, and Elvis Presley. However, it was not until 1943 that the "Grand Ole Opry" began broadcasting from the Ryman. In 1974 the "Grand Ole Opry" moved to a new theater at Opryland USA, and the Ryman, which had been listed on the National Register of Historic Places since 1971, became a shrine to country music. Visitors can sit in the old wooden church pews that were used for decades, have a look in the old dressing rooms, and take the stage themselves. **Open:** Daily 8:30am–4:30pm. Closed some hols. **$**

Country Music Hall of Fame and Museum

4 Music Sq E; tel 615/255-5333. Displays of classic and contemporary country music, as well as bluegrass, cowboy music (à la Roy Rogers), country swing, rockabilly, Cajun, and honky tonk. Among the exhibits here are a large display on the history of the "Grand Ole Opry," Elvis Presley's "solid-gold" Cadillac and his gold-leaf-covered baby-grand piano, and several cases full of costumes and clothing once worn by famous stars. Another section of the museum is devoted to country music in the movies and includes the black Trans Am from *Smokey and the Bandit,* the mechanical bull from *Urban Cowboy,* and a dress made by Loretta Lynn when she was 14 and worn by Sissy Spacek in *Coal Miner's Daughter.* Last but not least, the Hall of Fame Gallery contains plaques honoring each of the inductees. Ticket price also includes admission to Studio B, the historic RCA studio where the likes of Elvis, Chet Atkins, Charley Pride, and Eddy Arnold recorded some of their biggest hits. **Open:** Sun–Thurs 9am–5pm, Fri–Sat 8am–6pm. Closed some hols. **$$$**

Legends Hall of Fame

1520 Demonbreun St; tel 615/256-8311. Personal items and memorabilia from movie, TV, and music greats. Celebrity car and motorcycle collection, special salute to Elvis. Located on Nashville's Music Row. **Open:** Daily 8am–7pm. Closed some hols. **$$$**

Tennessee State Museum

5th Ave between Union and Deaderick Sts; tel 615/741-2692. Those desiring an understanding of Tennessee history can stop by this modern museum in the basement of the Tennessee Performing Arts Center. Collections include Native American artifacts from the Mississippian period, a time that well predates the arrival of the first whites in the

region, the so-called long hunters (named for their long hunting trips west of the Appalachian Mountains) who arrived in the 18th century. The most famous long hunter was Daniel Boone, and there's a pocket knife that belonged to the frontier legend on display here. Other displays focus on Presidents Andrew Jackson and James K Polk, as well as soldier/statesman Sam Houston, another Tennessean who went on to fame elsewhere.

There are numerous full-scale replicas of old structures and period rooms, such as a log cabin, a water-driven mill, a woodworking shop, and an 18th-century print shop and 1855 parlor. The lower level of the museum is devoted mostly to the Civil War and Reconstruction. One block west on Union St is the museum's Military Branch, which houses displays on Tennessee's military activity from the Spanish-American War through World War II. **Open:** Mon–Sat 10am–5pm, Sun 1–5pm. Closed some hols. **Free**

Cumberland Science Museum

800 Ridley Blvd; tel 615/862-5160. Interactive, child-friendly exhibits in areas such as technology, the environment, physics, and health. Demonstrations and special shows on weekends; Sudekum Planetarium. **Open:** June–Aug, Mon–Sat 9:30am–5pm, Sun 12:30–5:30pm. Closed Mon Sept–May and some hols. **$$$**

Van Vechten Gallery

1000 17th Ave (Fisk University); tel 615/329-8543. Part of famous photographer Alfred Stieglitz's art collection is housed in this small art museum on the Fisk University campus. The collection was donated by the photographer's widow, Georgia O'Keeffe, and contains not only photos by Stieglitz and paintings by O'Keeffe, but pieces by Picasso, Cézanne, Toulouse-Lautrec, Renoir, and Diego Rivera as well. Donation requested for admission. **Open:** Tues–Fri 10am–5pm, Sat–Sun 1–5pm.

Museum of Tobacco Art and History

8th Ave N and Harrison St; tel 615/271-2349. In this small museum operated by the United States Tobacco Manufacturing Company, you'll find an amazing array of antique pipes and snuff bottles from all over the world, as well as cigar-store Indians, tobacco tins, old tobacco advertisements, and Native American peace pipes. Informative displays illustrate the cultural and economic role of tobacco in the United States from pre-Columbian times to the present. **Open:** Mon–Sat 9am–4pm. Closed some hols. **Free**

Car Collectors Halls of Fame

1534 Demonbreun St; tel 615/255-6804. Though this antique and classic car museum located in the heart of Music Row advertises itself as having the cars of the country music stars, it also houses quite a few other beautiful old vehicles. Included here are a 1962 Lincoln Continental used by John F Kennedy, a Cadillac Eldorado that belonged to Elvis, and the original Batmobile from the TV series *Batman.* There are a total of about 45 cars on display at any given time. **Open:** Sept–May, daily 9am–5pm; June–Aug, daily 8am–10pm. Closed some hols. **$$**

HISTORIC HOMES

The Hermitage
Old Hickory Blvd, Hermitage; tel 615/889-2941. Andrew Jackson, the seventh president of the United States, built this "country house" in 1819 and enlarged it in 1834 after a fire. Today it is considered to be one of the finest Classical Revival buildings in the Deep South. Tours through the mansion and grounds are accompanied by recordings that describe each room and section of the grounds. In addition to the main house, you'll also visit the kitchen, smokehouse, garden, Jackson's tomb, an original log cabin, the spring house, and nearby the Old Hermitage Church and Tulip Grove mansion. **Open:** Daily 9am–5pm. Closed some hols. **$$$**

Belle Meade Plantation
5025 Harding Rd; tel 615/356-0501. Called the "Queen of Tennessee Plantations," the home was built in 1853 after the plantation had become famous as a stud farm. A long driveway cuts across the 30 acres of manicured lawns and leads uphill to the Greek Revival mansion, which is fronted by six columns and a wide veranda. Inside, the restored building has been furnished with elegant, 19th-century antiques. Also on the grounds are a large carriage house and stable that were built in 1890 and now house a large collection of antique carriages. A log cabin, smokehouse, and creamery are open to visitors as well. **Open:** Mon–Sat 9am–5pm, Sun 1–5pm. Closed some hols. **$$$**

Belmont Mansion
1900 Belmont Blvd; tel 615/269-9537. This pink-and-white Italianate villa was built in the 1850s by Adelicia Acklen, who was, at the time, one of the wealthiest women in the country. (She made her fortune smuggling cotton through the Union army blockade during the Civil War.) The tour of the mansion visits 15 rooms filled with period antiques, artwork, and marble statues. The grand salon is one of the most elegant and elaborate rooms ever built in an antebellum home. In the gardens surrounding the house is a large collection of 19th-century garden ornaments. **Open:** June–Aug, Mon–Sat 10am–4pm, Sun 2–5pm; Sept–May, Tues–Sat 10am–4pm. Closed some hols. **$$**

OTHER ATTRACTIONS

The Parthenon
Centennial Park, 1600 block of West End Ave; tel 615/862-8431. This full-size replica of the Parthenon in Athens, Greece, was the centerpiece of the Tennessee Centennial Exposition of 1897. However, the original structure was only meant to be temporary, and by 1921 the building, which had become a Nashville landmark, was in an advanced state of decay. In that year, the city undertook a reconstruction of

their Parthenon and by 1931 a new, permanent building stood in Centennial Park. The building now duplicates the floor plan of the original Parthenon.

Its two pairs of bronze doors, which weigh in at 7½ tons per door, are considered the largest matching bronze doors in the world. Inside, a 42-foot-tall statue (the largest piece of indoor sculpture in the country) of Athena Parthenos, the goddess of wisdom, warfare, and the arts, towers over spectators. Also of interest are the original plaster castings of the famous Elgin marbles—bas-reliefs that once decorated the pediment of the original Parthenon. Down in the basement galleries is an excellent collection of 19th- and 20th-century American art. **Open:** Tues–Sat 9am–4:30pm; also Apr–Sept, Sun 12:30–4:30pm. Closed some hols. **$$**

Grassmere Wildlife Park
3777 Nolensville Rd; tel 615/833-0632. Modern wildlife park, just south of downtown Nashville, that houses only animals that are indigenous to Tennessee. In the naturalistic habitats, visitors can see river otters, bison, elk, black bear, gray wolves, bald eagles, and cougars, as well as other smaller animals. **Open:** Mem Day–Labor Day, daily 10am–6pm; Labor Day–Mem Day, daily 10am–5pm. **$$**

Nashville Zoo
1710 Ridge Rd Circle, Joelton; tel 615/370-3333. Located 15 mi NW of downtown on I-24. Located on 150 acres of rolling hills near Nashville, this zoo has more than 800 residents representing 150 animal species. The naturalistic settings are home to a surprisingly wide variety of animals from around the world, including snow leopards, giraffes, tree frogs, llamas, lemurs, and white tigers. **Open:** May, daily 9am–5pm; June–Aug, daily 9am–6pm; Sept–Apr, daily 10am–5pm. **$$$**

Wave Country
Two Rivers Pkwy; tel 615/885-1092. Located about a mile from Opryland USA, this water park is popular with vacationing families. There's a huge wave pool and a whole bunch of water slides. **Open:** Mem Day–Labor Day, daily 10am–8pm. **$$**

Newport

Located on the bank of the French Broad River in eastern Tennessee. **Information:** Newport/Cocke County Chamber of Commerce, 433B Prospect Ave, Newport, 37821 (tel 423/623-7201).

MOTEL 🏨

📕📕 Holiday Inn
I-40 at US 32, PO Box 250, 37821; tel 423/623-8622 or toll free 800/HOLIDAY; fax 423/623-8622. This Holiday Inn caters to children and offers an extra-large pool and an adjacent game room. **Rooms:** 155 rms. CI open/CO noon. Nonsmoking rms avail. **Amenities:** 🛁 ⚹ A/C, satel TV

w/movies. Refrigerators are available upon request. **Services:** X △ ↵ ⬮ **Facilities:** �🔥 175 ⅊ 1 restaurant, 1 bar, games rm, whirlpool, washer/dryer. **Rates:** Peak (June–Aug, Oct) $63 S; $69 D. Extra person $6. Children under age 19 stay free. Lower rates off-season. Parking: Outdoor, free. AE, CB, DC, DISC, JCB, MC, V.

Normandy

This town on the Duck River is the site of the Tennessee Valley Authority's Normandy Dam and a major fish hatchery.

INN 🏨

⬮⬮⬮ Parish Patch Farm & Inn

625 Cortner Rd, 37360; tel 615/857-3017 or toll free 800/ 876-3017; fax 615/857-3017. Exit 97 off I-24. 330 acres. A peaceful retreat located on a working cattle and grain farm along the banks of the Duck River. **Rooms:** 15 rms and stes (2 w/shared bath); 2 cottages/villas. CI 2pm/CO 11am. Nonsmoking rms avail. Rooms are architecturally unique and feature walnut and cherry-wood furniture. **Amenities:** 🛏 ⌖ A/C, TV. Some units w/terraces, some w/fireplaces. **Services:** 🚐 ↵ ⬮ Babysitting. **Facilities:** 🔥 ⛰ ▨ 🎣 90 ⅊ 1 restaurant, 1 bar, games rm, lawn games, playground, washer/dryer, guest lounge w/TV. Lounge has a fireplace and games. Located near trout fishing, hiking, and six golf courses offering guest privileges. Restaurant is housed in a historic flour mill. **Rates (BB):** $62–$77 w/shared bath, $99 w/private bath; $124 ste; $149–$170 cottage/villa. Extra person $10. Children under age 4 stay free. Parking: Outdoor, free. DISC, MC, V.

Norris

A planned community, Norris was established at the time of the Tennessee Valley Authority's construction of the Norris Dam in 1933.

ATTRACTION 📷

Museum of Appalachia

TN 61; tel 423/494-7680. A remarkably authentic recreation of the culture of the hard-working mountain folk of southern Appalachia. This 65-acre complex includes dozens of authentic log structures plus a craft shop, auditorium, and the Appalachian Hall of Fame. The Display Building houses over 250,000 relics including furniture, primitive farm implements, and other household items from the pioneer past. Crafts demonstrations, music, barnyard animals, and seasonal events. $$$

Oak Ridge

Birthplace of the Atomic Age. Created in 1943 by the US government out of wilderness and farmland, Oak Ridge was the site of the Manhattan Project, which produced the first uranium bomb. The existence and purpose of the community was kept secret until 1945, but the city has since been turned over to its residents. Oak Ridge National Laboratory is here. **Information:** Oak Ridge Chamber of Commerce, 1400 Oak Ridge Tpk, Oak Ridge, 37830 (tel 423/483-1321).

HOTELS 🏨

⬮⬮⬮ Comfort Inn

433 S Rutgers Ave, 37830; tel 423/481-8200 or toll free 800/553-7830; fax 423/483-6142. At Illinois Ave. This award-winning hotel offers some beautiful scenery. **Rooms:** 122 rms and stes. CI 11am/CO noon. Nonsmoking rms avail. **Amenities:** 🛏 ⌖ A/C, cable TV w/movies, dataport, voice mail. **Services:** X 🚐 △ ↵ ⬮ **Facilities:** 🔥 100 ⅊ Washer/ dryer. Free passes to Paragon Health Club. **Rates (CP):** $59– $62 S; $66–$69 D; $69–$79 ste. Extra person $7. Children under age 13 stay free. Parking: Outdoor, free. Group rates avail. AE, DC, DISC, MC, V.

⬮⬮⬮ Garden Plaza Hotel

215 S Illinois Ave, 37830; tel 423/481-2468 or toll free 800/ 342-7336; fax 423/481-2474. Across from American Museum of Science and Energy. The staff at this full-service hotel is dedicated to making your stay a good one. **Rooms:** 168 rms and stes. CI 3pm/CO noon. Nonsmoking rms avail. Luxurious rooms have bay windows. **Amenities:** 🛏 ⌖ A/C, satel TV w/movies, refrig. TV/radio speakers in bathroom. Microwaves available upon request. **Services:** X △ ↵ ⬮ **Facilities:** 🔥 150 ⅊ 1 restaurant, 1 bar, whirlpool. Guest privileges at Paragon Athletic Center. Ezra's Restaurant offers free hors d'oeuvres during weekday happy hour (4:30– 7:30pm). **Rates:** $63–$85 S or D; $99 ste. Extra person $7. Children under age 17 stay free. Parking: Outdoor, free. AE, CB, DC, DISC, MC, V.

⬮⬮⬮ Hampton Inn

208 S Illinois Ave, 37830; tel 423/482-7889 or toll free 800/ 426-7866; fax 423/482-7889. Off I-40. A modern facility with comfortable accommodations and a very service-oriented staff. **Rooms:** 60 rms and stes. CI 2pm/CO 11am. Nonsmoking rms avail. **Amenities:** 🛏 ⌖ A/C, cable TV w/movies. Some units w/whirlpools. Excellent security; cameras on every floor as well as in the pool and parking areas. **Services:** △ ↵ Staff works hard to make sure guests feel as comfortable as possible. **Facilities:** 🔥 🎣 45 ⅊ Sauna, whirlpool, washer/dryer. **Rates (CP):** $59–$69 S; $69–$79 D; $75–$95 ste. Extra person $9. Children under age 19 stay free. Parking: Outdoor, free. AE, CB, DC, DISC, JCB, MC, V.

MOTEL

三三 Days Inn

206 S Illinois Ave, 37830; tel 423/483-5615 or toll free 800/ 329-7466; fax 423/483-5615. Off I-40. Popular with families due to its abundance of outdoor play space and its location near the American Museum of Science and Energy. **Rooms:** 80 rms and effic. CI noon/CO 11am. Nonsmoking rms avail. **Amenities:** 🛗 A/C, cable TV w/movies, refrig. **Services:** 🍴 🤿 **Facilities:** ⚡ 🔲 ᚼ Playground. **Rates (CP):** $47 S; $50 D; $50–$52 effic. Extra person $3. Children under age 18 stay free. Parking: Outdoor, free. AE, CB, DC, DISC, MC, V.

ATTRACTION 🖼

American Museum of Science and Energy

300 S Tulane Ave; tel 423/576-3200. Most of the first floor of this US Department of Energy museum is dedicated to Oak Ridge's role in the development of the atomic bomb. Other interactive exhibits include "The Age of the Automobile," "Earth's Energy Resources," and "The World of the Atom." Live demonstrations, lectures, and videos are scheduled throughout the day. **Open:** Daily 9am–5pm. Closed some hols. **Free**

Paris

Founded in 1821 and named in honor of the Marquis de Lafayette, the town has played up its name by erecting a replica of the Eiffel Tower. Its historic downtown boasts the oldest Tennessee courthouse still in use. **Information:** Paris–Henry County Chamber of Commerce, 2508 E Wood St, PO Box 8, Paris, 38242 (tel 901/642-3431).

MOTEL 🖼

三三三 Hampton Inn of Paris

1510 E Wood St, 38242; tel 901/642-2838 or toll free 800/ HAMPTON; fax 901/642-7556. Ranked the third-best Hampton Inn in the nation in 1994. **Rooms:** 61 rms and stes. CI 2pm/CO noon. Nonsmoking rms avail. Double sink vanities in all rooms make getting dressed more convenient. **Amenities:** 🛗 A/C, cable TV, dataport. Some units w/whirlpools. Some rooms have refrigerators. **Services:** 🚐 🍴 **Facilities:** ⚡ 🔲 ᚼ Outdoor electrical outlets for boats. **Rates (CP):** Peak (May 26–Sept 7) $41–$53 S or D; $59–$68 ste. Extra person $4. Children under age 18 stay free. Lower rates off-season. Parking: Outdoor, free. AE, CB, DC, DISC, MC, V.

Pigeon Forge

A popular resort town in the foothills of the Smoky Mountains and site of singer Dolly Parton's Dollywood. Together with Gatlinburg and Sevierville, hosts the Smoky Mountains Winterfest. **Information:** Pigeon Forge Convention & Visitors Bureau, 205 Pine Mountain Rd, PO Box 1278, Pigeon Forge, 37868 (tel 423/453-5700).

HOTELS 🖼

三三 Best Western Plaza Inn

3755 Parkway, PO Box 926, 37863; tel 423/453-5538 or toll free 800/232-5656; fax 423/453-2619. Near Dixie Stampede and Dollywood. Families love the spacious, comfortable rooms here. **Rooms:** 200 rms and stes. CI 2pm/CO 11am. Nonsmoking rms avail. **Amenities:** 🛗 A/C, satel TV w/movies, refrig. Some units w/terraces, some w/fireplaces, some w/whirlpools. **Services:** 🍴 Babysitting. **Facilities:** ⚡ 🔲 🔲 ᚼ Games rm, sauna, whirlpool. **Rates:** Peak (June–Aug/Oct) $69–$99 S or D; $125–$145 ste. Extra person $3. Min stay special events. Lower rates off-season. Parking: Outdoor, free. AE, CB, DC, DISC, MC, V.

三三 Budgetel Inn

2179 Parkway, 37863; tel 423/428-7305 or toll free 800/ 428-3438; fax 423/428-8977. A secluded spot, set back away from the hustle and bustle of Pigeon Forge. **Rooms:** 130 rms and stes. CI 2pm/CO noon. Nonsmoking rms avail. Some rooms offer a gorgeous view of the mountains. **Amenities:** 🛗 A/C, cable TV w/movies, dataport. **Services:** 🚐 🍴 🤿 **Facilities:** ⚡ 🔲 🔲 ᚼ Washer/dryer. **Rates (CP):** Peak (June–Oct) $29–$99 S or D; $39–$109 ste. Children under age 19 stay free. Min stay special events. Lower rates off-season. Parking: Outdoor, free. Group rates avail. AE, CB, DC, DISC, MC, V.

三三三 Country Inn & Suites

204 Sharon Dr, PO Box 187, 37863; tel 423/428-1194 or toll free 800/523-3919; fax 423/453-2564. You'll find fantastic rooms in this new hotel built in 1994, where resort professionals are dedicated to satisfying your every need. **Rooms:** 138 rms and stes. Executive level. CI 3pm/CO 11am. Nonsmoking rms avail. Celebration suites have a king bed and hot tub. Executive suites have a separate bedroom and a living room with whirlpool, fireplace, and sofa sleeper. Penthouses have two bedrooms and a living room with sofa sleeper. **Amenities:** 🛗 A/C, cable TV w/movies, refrig, dataport, voice mail. Some units w/fireplaces, some w/whirlpools. Free copies of *USA Today*, free local phone calls. **Services:** 🍴 Car-rental desk, babysitting. Coffee and cookies available 24 hours a day. **Facilities:** ⚡ 🔲 🔲 🔲 ᚼ 1 restaurant, whirlpool, washer/dryer. **Rates (CP):** Peak (June–Oct) $78–$128 S or D; $88–$168 ste. Extra person $6. Children under age 18 stay free. Min stay wknds and special events. Lower rates off-season. Parking: Outdoor, free. AE, DC, DISC, MC, V.

三三 Creek Stone Inn

4034 River Rd S, PO Box 187, 37868; tel 423/453-3557 or toll free 800/523-3919; fax 423/453-2564. Nature does the landscaping here, where all the rooms feature balconies with beautiful views of the river and the peaceful surroundings.

Rooms: 172 rms and stes. CI 3pm/CO 11am. Nonsmoking rms avail. All rooms are semidivided, with the bath between the two beds. **Amenities:** 📺 A/C, cable TV w/movies, refrig. All units w/terraces, some w/fireplaces, some w/whirlpools. **Services:** 🍽 Guests receive ten-percent discount on breakfast at nearby Pancake House. **Facilities:** 🛋 🏊 ♿ **Rates:** Peak (June–Aug/Oct–Nov) $62–$112 S or D; $82–$138 ste. Extra person $6. Children under age 18 stay free. Min stay wknds and special events. Lower rates off-season. Parking: Outdoor, free. AE, DC, DISC, MC, V.

⬛⬛⬛ Holiday Inn

3230 N Parkway, PO Box 1383, 37868; tel 423/428-2700 or toll free 800/555-2650; fax 423/428-2700. Off the Bluegrass Pkwy. A surprisingly nice Holiday Inn, with a luxurious lobby. **Rooms:** 208 rms and stes. Executive level. CI 3pm/CO 11am. Nonsmoking rms avail. **Amenities:** 📺 🏊 A/C, cable TV w/movies, dataport. Some units w/whirlpools. Special phones available for hard-of-hearing guests. **Services:** ✗ 🛏 🍽 🍹 **Facilities:** 🛋 🏊 🎾 🏊 ♿ 1 restaurant, games rm, sauna, whirlpool, beauty salon, washer/dryer. The waterfall at the end of the pool and the palms around it make for an inviting swimming area. Kids under 12 eat free in hotel restaurant. Specially designated security floor, with limited elevator access. **Rates:** Peak (Apr–Dec) $59–$99 S or D; $120 ste. Children under age 19 stay free. Min stay special events. Lower rates off-season. Parking: Outdoor, free. Bed-and-breakfast packages avail. AE, CB, DC, MC, V.

⬛⬛ Shular Inn

2708 Parkway, 37863; tel 423/453-2700 or toll free 800/451-2376; fax 423/428-0448. Near Ogle's Water Park. Engaging, family-oriented accommodations. **Rooms:** 201 rms, stes, and effic. Executive level. CI 3pm/CO 11am. Nonsmoking rms avail. Club-level rooms are larger and have two phones. **Amenities:** 📺 🏊 🖥 A/C, satel TV w/movies, refrig, dataport. Some units w/fireplaces, some w/whirlpools. **Services:** 🍽 Babysitting. **Facilities:** 🛋 🏊 ♿ Games rm, spa, sauna, whirlpool, washer/dryer. Pigeon Forge City Park is a mile away. **Rates (CP):** Peak (June–Oct) $99–$109 S or D; $109 ste; $275 effic. Children under age 18 stay free. Min stay special events. Lower rates off-season. Parking: Outdoor, free. AE, CB, DC, DISC, MC, V.

⬛⬛ Valley Forge Inn

2795 Parkway, 37863; tel 423/453-7770 or toll free 800/544-8740; fax 423/429-3816. Nice, well-appointed rooms right in the center of Pigeon Forge's attractions. **Rooms:** 172 rms, stes, and effic. CI 2pm/CO 11am. Nonsmoking rms avail. Family suites (with two or three bedrooms and kitchen) and honeymoon suite (with fireplace, whirlpool, and king-size bed) are available. **Amenities:** 📺 A/C, cable TV w/movies. Some units w/terraces, some w/fireplaces, some w/whirlpools. **Services:** 🍽 Babysitting. **Facilities:** 🛋 🛌 🏊 🏊 ♿ Washer/dryer. Lots of potted plants around the indoor pool. **Rates:** Peak (June–Oct) $49–$83 S or D; $59–

$185 ste; $59–$185 effic. Min stay wknds and special events. Lower rates off-season. Parking: Outdoor, free. Up to four people per room for the same rate. AE, DISC, MC, V.

MOTELS

⬛ Americana Inn

2825 Parkway, 37863; tel 423/428-0172. A simple no-frills motel popular with families. **Rooms:** 172 rms. CI noon/CO 11am. Nonsmoking rms avail. Room balconies overlook the parkway. **Amenities:** 📺 A/C, satel TV w/movies. **Services:** 🍽 **Facilities:** 🛋 🏊 1 restaurant (bkfst and lunch only), whirlpool. **Rates:** Peak (June–Oct) $45 S; $55 D. Children under age 18 stay free. Min stay special events. Lower rates off-season. Parking: Outdoor, free. DISC, MC, V.

⬛⬛ Best Western Toni Motel

3810 Parkway, 37863; tel 423/453-9058 or toll free 800/422-3232; fax 423/453-2621. Across the Parkway from the Dixie Stampede. Centrally located, no-frills accommodations. **Rooms:** 114 rms and stes. CI 2pm/CO 11am. Nonsmoking rms avail. **Amenities:** 📺 🏊 A/C, satel TV w/movies, refrig. Some units w/terraces, some w/fireplaces, some w/whirlpools. **Services:** 🍽 **Facilities:** 🛋 🏊 Whirlpool. **Rates (CP):** Peak (June–Aug/Oct) $65–$110 S or D; $89–$159 ste. Extra person $3. Children under age 19 stay free. Lower rates off-season. Parking: Outdoor, free. Up to four guests in a room. AE, CB, DC, DISC, MC, V.

⬛ Carriage House

2891 Parkway, PO Box 1406, 37868-1406; tel 423/453-5686 or toll free 800/453-5686. Across from Red Roof Mall. Popular with families, this conveniently located motel offers clean, basic rooms and lots of room for the kids to play. **Rooms:** 55 rms and effic; 1 cottage/villa. CI 1/CO 11am. Nonsmoking rms avail. Some rooms have balconies overlooking the river. **Amenities:** 📺 A/C, cable TV. Some units w/terraces. Microwaves and refrigerators available. **Services:** 🍽 **Facilities:** 🛋 🏊 ♿ Playground. Sheltered picnic area with an outdoor grill. Guests receive 10% discount at nearby Western Sizzler restaurant. **Rates:** Peak (June–Aug/Oct) $55–$99 S or D; $75–$85 effic; $125 cottage/villa. Extra person $5. Min stay wknds and special events. Lower rates off-season. Parking: Outdoor, free. Closed Jan–Mar. MC, V.

⬛⬛ Colonial House

3545 Parkway, 37862; tel 423/453-0717 or toll free 800/662-5444; fax 423/453-8412. Near the Old Mill. A nice three-story lodging—in the middle of everything. **Rooms:** 63 rms and effic; 1 cottage/villa. CI 11am/CO 11am. Nonsmoking rms avail. **Amenities:** 📺 A/C, satel TV w/movies, refrig. Some units w/terraces, some w/fireplaces, some w/whirlpools. **Services:** 🍽 **Facilities:** 🛋 🏊 1 restaurant. Very small children's pool. **Rates:** Peak (June–Aug/Oct) $58–$88 S or D; $78–$108 effic; $150–$350 cottage/villa. Children under age 19 stay free. Min stay special events. Lower rates off-season. Parking: Outdoor, free. Up to four people stay in one room for the same rate. AE, DISC, MC, V.

Discount Inns of America

3229 Parkway, 37868; tel 423/453-5568 or toll free 800/627-1727; fax 423/453-5568. Near light 6. Located near Magic World, this simple motel offers scrupulously clean and well-kept rooms. **Rooms:** 53 rms. CI 11am/CO 11am. Nonsmoking rms avail. **Amenities:** 🛏 A/C, cable TV w/movies. **Services:** 🍽 🛎 **Facilities:** 🚪 🕎 **Rates (CP):** Peak (June–Aug/Oct) $25–$100 S; $50–$135 D. Children under age 19 stay free. Min stay wknds and special events. Lower rates off-season. Parking: Outdoor, free. AE, DC, DISC, MC, V.

Howard Johnson Pigeon Forge

2826 Parkway, PO Box 1110, 37868; tel 423/453-9151 or toll free 800/453-6008; fax 423/428-4141. Next to Red Roof Mall. Standard chain motel. It stands out from the crowd with its pretty, artificial waterfall near the entrance. **Rooms:** 145 rms, stes, and effic. Executive level. CI 3pm/CO 11am. **Amenities:** 🛏 🕎 A/C, satel TV w/movies. Some units w/terraces, some w/whirlpools. **Services:** 🍽 **Facilities:** 🚪 🕎 🛗 Washer/dryer. **Rates:** Peak (June–Oct) $58–$82 S or D; $68–$88 ste; $90–$120 effic. Extra person $4. Children under age 12 stay free. Min stay special events. Lower rates off-season. Parking: Outdoor, free. AE, DC, DISC, JCB, MC, V.

McAfee Motor Inn

3756 Parkway, 37863; tel 423/453-3490 or toll free 800/925-4443; fax 423/429-5432. A no-frills facility offering nice, clean rooms—but not much else. **Rooms:.** CI 2pm/CO 11am. Nonsmoking rms avail. **Amenities:** 🛏 🕎 🖥 A/C, satel TV w/movies, refrig. Some units w/terraces, some w/fireplaces, some w/whirlpools. **Services:** 🍽 Babysitting. **Facilities:** 🚪 🕎 🛗 Whirlpool, washer/dryer. **Rates (CP):** Peak (June–Oct) $60–$95 S or D; $79–$119 ste; $79–$119 effic. Extra person $5. Children under age 5 stay free. Min stay special events. Lower rates off-season. Parking: Outdoor, free. AE, CB, DC, DISC, MC, V.

Ramada Inn

4025 Parkway, PO Box 220, 37863; tel 423/453-9081 or toll free 800/345-6799; fax 423/428-4230. Standard chain accommodations located in the heart of Pigeon Forge. **Rooms:** 131 rms. CI 2pm/CO noon. Nonsmoking rms avail. **Amenities:** 🛏 🕎 🖥 A/C, cable TV w/movies. Some units w/whirlpools. Some king rooms have refrigerators. **Services:** 🍽 **Facilities:** 🚪 🕎 🛗 🛗 1 restaurant (bkfst and dinner only), games rm, whirlpool, playground. **Rates (CP):** Peak (June–Aug/Oct) $59–$99 S or D. Extra person $9. Children under age 18 stay free. Min stay special events. Lower rates off-season. Parking: Outdoor, free. AE, CB, DC, DISC, MC, V.

Rodeway Mountain Skies Motel

4236 Parkway, 37863; tel 423/453-3530 or toll free 800/523-3919. Family-operated motel offering a clean place to stay near Dollywood and the Gatlinburg Golf Course. **Rooms:** 117 rms. CI 3pm/CO 11am. Nonsmoking rms avail. Forty choice rooms available with hand-held shower, large-number clock and phone, grab bars in tub, and alarm clock. **Amenities:** 🛏 A/C, cable TV w/movies, refrig. **Services:** 🍽 **Facilities:** 🚪 🕎 🛗 1 restaurant (bkfst only). **Rates (CP):** Peak (June–Aug/Oct) $36–$108 S or D. Extra person $6. Children under age 18 stay free. Min stay wknds and special events. Lower rates off-season. Parking: Outdoor, free. AE, CB, DC, DISC, MC, V.

Willow Brook Lodge

3035 Parkway, 37863; tel 423/453-5334 or toll free 800/765-1380. A fun, homey place for family gatherings and vacations. **Rooms:** 78 rms and stes. CI 2pm/CO 11am. Nonsmoking rms avail. **Amenities:** 🛏 🕎 A/C, satel TV w/movies, refrig. Some units w/terraces, some w/fireplaces, some w/whirlpools. **Services:** 🍽 **Facilities:** 🚪 🕎 🛗 Discount for adjacent Smoky Mountain Golf and ice cream shop. **Rates:** Peak (June–Aug/Oct) $58–$88 S or D; $110 ste. Extra person $5. Lower rates off-season. Parking: Outdoor, free. AE, CB, DISC, MC, V.

RESTAURANTS 🍴

Apple Tree Inn Restaurant

3215 Parkway; tel 423/453-4961. By light 6. **Regional American/American.** Named for the apple tree that grows in the middle of the dining room. Homestyle country cooking includes chicken and homemade dumplings, steaks (cut fresh daily), roast prime rib, and country ham. Homemade desserts include coconut pie. **FYI:** Reservations not accepted. Children's menu. No liquor license. **Open:** Daily 6:30am–10pm. Closed Dec–Mar 15. **Prices:** Main courses $6–$12. AE, MC, V. 🍴 🛗

Aunt Granny's Restaurant

In Dollywood, 700 Dollywood Lane; tel 423/428-9488. **Regional American.** Finding such a delicious, high-quality buffet in a family-fun park is unusual, but here it is: fried and baked barbecue chicken, catfish, ham, and a variety of vegetables, along with wonderful soups, salads, and fruit. Delicious, fresh rolls are served with every entree. **FYI:** Reservations not accepted. No liquor license. **Open:** Breakfast daily 8–10:30am; lunch daily 11am–4pm; dinner daily 4–9pm. Closed Jan–Apr 15. **Prices:** Prix fixe $7. AE, DC, DISC, MC. 🍴 🛗

The Old Hill Restaurant

2934 Middle Creek Rd; tel 423/429-3463. **Regional American.** Corn for the restaurant's special recipes is ground next door at a 150-year-old mill. Guests can relax by watching the ducks on the river outside while they wait for their fresh, homemade breads, corndrop biscuits, corn-bread muffins, and corn fritters. **FYI:** Reservations not accepted. Children's menu. No liquor license. **Open:** Breakfast Mon–Sat 8–11am, Sun 8am–noon; lunch Mon–Sat 11am–4pm; dinner Sun noon–9pm, Fri–Sat 4–10pm. **Prices:** Main courses $10–$15. AE, DC, DISC, MC, V. 🍴 🛗 🛗 🛗

Santo's

3270 Parkway; tel 423/428-5840. Near light 6. **American/Italian.** Family-owned and -operated trattoria offering such specialties as shrimp Milano (bay shrimp, fresh broccoli, mushrooms, green onions, and garlic in a classic white sauce served over linguine); chicken piccata (boneless chicken breast sautéed with capers, mushrooms, and lemon); and beef braciola (thinly sliced beef steak stuffed with cheeses, spicy Italian ham, bread crumbs, and spices). Vegetarian entrees also available. **FYI:** Reservations accepted. Piano. Children's menu. BYO. **Open:** Peak (June–Oct) Mon–Sat 11am–11pm. **Prices:** Main courses $7–$15. AE, DC, DISC, MC, V. 🖼️ &

REFRESHMENT STOP ☕

Garden Square Cafe

2470 Parkway; tel 423/453-6241. By Christmas Place. Nestled in a fascinating collection of shops, this place specializes in fudge—20 different varieties including tiger butter, chocolate cheesecake, chewy praline, and amaretto chocolate swirl, just to name a few. Ice cream (some of it sugar free), floats, shakes, banana splits, and frozen yogurt are also available. There's a model train and caged exotic birds out front. **Open:** Peak (June–Dec) daily 10am–10pm. Closed Jan, Feb. No CC. &

ATTRACTIONS 🏛️

Dollywood

1020 Dollywood Lane; tel 423/428-9488. Music and film star Dolly Parton is the guiding light of this theme park featuring rides, crafts, music, entertainment, and food. Among the rides are a "flooded mine," a log flume, and indoor and outdoor rollercoasters. Demonstrations of local culture and crafts—a unique aspect of the park—include lye-soap makers, carriage makers, blacksmiths, potters, and glass blowers. The Dolly Parton Museum chronicles her "rags to riches" career, there's a butterfly garden (butterflies are Parton's trademark), and up to 40 live shows a day can be seen at five theaters throughout the park. **Open:** Apr–Oct, daily, call for schedule. **$$$$**

Ogle's Water Park

2530 Parkway; tel 423/453-8741. A giant wave pool, 10 water slides, and a children's water play area make this a popular warm weather cool-off spot. **Open:** May, Sat–Sun 11am–6pm; Mem Day–Labor Day, daily 10am–8pm. **$$$$**

Flyaway

3106 Parkway; tel 423/453-7777. The only indoor skydiving simulator in the country creates the feeling of flight in a vertical wind tunnel. After a short orientation, visitors are given the opportunity to soar, swoop, and turn in the tunnel. **Open:** May–Oct, daily 10am–10pm. **$$$$**

Savannah

See also Shiloh National Military Park

Sevierville

Native Americans inhabited the caves here hundreds of years before white settlers arrived. Hometown of singer Dolly Parton; there's a statue of her on the courthouse lawn. **Information:** Sevierville Chamber of Commerce, 866 Winfield Dunn Pkwy, Sevierville, 37876 (tel 423/453-6566).

MOTELS 🏨

🚽🚽 Best Western Dumplin Valley Inn

3426 Winfield Dunn Pkwy, Kodak, 37767; tel 423/933-3467 or toll free 800/528-1234; fax 423/933-2515. Exit 407 off I-40. Offers clean, comfortable rooms away from the noise and traffic of the interstate. **Rooms:** 82 rms and effic. CI open/CO 11am. Nonsmoking rms avail. **Amenities:** 🛏️ A/C, cable TV w/movies. Some units w/terraces, some w/whirlpools. **Services:** 🚐 🐾 **Facilities:** 🏊 🍽️ & Washer/dryer. **Rates:** Peak (June–Oct) $38–$90 S; $40–$130 D; $110–$160 effic. Extra person $5. Children under age 12 stay free. Min stay special events. Lower rates off-season. Parking: Outdoor, free. Golf packages avail. AE, DC, DISC, MC, V.

🚽🚽 Comfort Inn

1850 Parkway, PO Box 1509, 37868; tel 423/428-1069 or toll free 800/233-3443; fax 423/429-0777. Near the Apple Barn. Award-winning property nestled in the foothills of the Smokies. **Rooms:** 111 rms and stes. CI 2pm/CO 11am. Nonsmoking rms avail. Suite-size rooms are very spacious and livable. **Amenities:** 🛏️ 🍴 A/C, cable TV w/movies, refrig. Some units w/terraces, some w/fireplaces, some w/whirlpools. **Services:** 🐾 **Facilities:** 🏊 🍽️ 🏊 & Whirlpool, washer/dryer. **Rates (CP):** Peak (June–Aug/Oct) $79–$129 S or D; $135–$175 ste. Children under age 18 stay free. Lower rates off-season. Parking: Outdoor, free. Room rates for up to four in one room. AE, CB, DC, DISC, JCB, MC, V.

🚽🚽🚽 Comfort Inn—Mountain View Suites

860 Winfield Dunn Pkwy, 37876; tel 423/428-5519 or toll free 800/441-0311; fax 423/428-6700. Exit 407 off I-40. Spacious suites allow room for weary travelers to kick back and relax. **Rooms:** 95 rms and stes. CI 2pm/CO 11am. Nonsmoking rms avail. **Amenities:** 🛏️ 🍴 📺 A/C, satel TV w/movies, refrig. Some units w/terraces, some w/fireplaces, some w/whirlpools. Each suite has two TVs. Microwaves available in some rooms. **Services:** 🐾 **Facilities:** 🏊 🏊 & Spa, whirlpool. **Rates (CP):** Peak (June–Oct) $59–$159 S or D; $59–$159 ste. Extra person $5. Children under age 18 stay free. Min stay special events. Lower rates off-season. Parking: Outdoor, free. Golf package avail. AE, CB, DC, DISC, V.

Days Inn of Sevierville

1841 Parkway, 37862; tel 423/428-3353 or toll free 800/329-7466; fax 423/428-7613. A new facility with spacious accommodations and excellent housekeeping standards. **Rooms:** 73 rms and stes. CI 1pm/CO 11am. Nonsmoking rms avail. Two-bedroom suites have two queen beds in each bedroom, full bath, whirlpool bath, refrigerator, and separate sitting room. **Amenities:** 🛁 ⌧ A/C, cable TV w/movies. Some units w/whirlpools. **Services:** ⌧ **Facilities:** 🛋 ⌧ ⌧ ⌧ **Rates (CP):** Peak (May–Oct) $38–$98 S or D; $78–$138 ste. Extra person $5. Children under age 17 stay free. Lower rates off-season. Parking: Outdoor, free. AE, CB, DC, DISC, MC, V.

Fairfield Inn

1650 Parkway, PO Box 1520, 37862; tel 423/429-8300 or toll free 800/228-2800; fax 423/429-0780. Opened in 1994. Excellent security, with cameras at all entrances. **Rooms:** 89 rms and stes. CI 2pm/CO noon. Nonsmoking rms avail. **Amenities:** 🛁 ⌧ A/C, cable TV w/movies. Some units w/terraces, some w/fireplaces, some w/whirlpools. **Services:** ⌧ **Facilities:** 🛋 ⌧ ⌧ ⌧ **Rates (CP):** Peak (June–Oct) $74–$99 S or D; $89–$110 ste. Extra person $5. Children under age 18 stay free. Min stay special events. Lower rates off-season. Parking: Outdoor, free. AE, DC, DISC, MC, V.

The Greenbrier Motel

711 Parkway, 37862; tel 423/453-4018 or toll free 800/572-5525. Family owned, offering pleasant, spotless rooms and personal attention. **Rooms:** 77 rms and effic. CI 11am/CO 11am. Nonsmoking rms avail. **Amenities:** 🛁 ⌧ A/C, cable TV w/movies, refrig, dataport. 1 unit w/terrace, some w/fireplaces, some w/whirlpools. **Services:** ⌧ Car-rental desk, babysitting. **Facilities:** 🛋 ⌧ ⌧ Playground, washer/dryer. **Rates:** Peak (June–Aug/Oct) $59–$120 S or D; $89 effic. Children under age 21 stay free. Min stay special events. Lower rates off-season. Parking: Outdoor, free. Golf packages avail. AE, DISC, MC, V.

Mountain Vista Lodge

1544 Parkway, 37862; tel 423/453-4066 or toll free 800/426-4066; fax 423/429-8133. Near Five Oaks Mall. Four-story motel with comfortable rooms, a large lobby, and well-manicured landscaping. **Rooms:** 58 rms. CI noon/CO 11am. Nonsmoking rms avail. Very noisy exhaust fans in bathrooms. **Amenities:** 🛁 A/C, cable TV. Some units w/terraces, some w/fireplaces, some w/whirlpools. **Services:** ⌧ ⌧ Tickets for Dollywood available. **Facilities:** 🛋 ⌧ ⌧ **Rates:** Peak (June–Aug/Oct) $79–$125 S or D. Children under age 19 stay free. Lower rates off-season. Parking: Outdoor, free. DISC, MC, V.

INN

Blue Mountain Mist Country Inn

1811 Pullen Rd, 37862; tel 423/428-2335 or toll free 800/497-2335; fax 423/453-1720. Off Jayelle Rd. 60 acres. Guests can enjoy Southern hospitality in a Victorian-style farmhouse with peaceful, relaxing views of the Smoky Mountains. **Rooms:** 12 rms and stes; 5 cottages/villas. CI 3pm/CO 11am. No smoking. Sugarlands room offers a whirlpool with a view of the mountains. Private cottages have bedside whirlpool, fireplace, TV with VCR, kitchenette, and private yard with grill and picnic table. **Amenities:** ⌧ A/C. No phone or TV. Some units w/whirlpools. **Services:** ⌧ ⌧ Afternoon tea served. Hot chocolate, coffee, and soft drinks available in the afternoons and evenings; delicious homemade dessert offered each evening. **Facilities:** ⌧ ⌧ ⌧ ⌧ 1 restaurant (bkfst only), guest lounge w/TV. Front porch has rocking chairs and a porch swing. **Rates (BB):** Peak (Apr–Dec) $79–$115 D; $95 ste; $125–$125 cottage/villa. Extra person $15. Min stay special events. Lower rates off-season. Parking: Outdoor, free. MC, V.

RESTAURANTS 🍴

Applewood Farmhouse Restaurant

240 Apple Valley Rd; tel 423/428-1222. **Regional American.** Located in the middle of an apple orchard, so the specialty here is not hard to guess: homemade apple fritters (some 10,000 are served daily in season), apple butter, and apple cider. There's also wonderful homemade vegetable soup, farmhouse Southern fried chicken, and homemade mashed potatoes and biscuits. Several dining rooms, including the Sideporch (where some of the tables have porch swings for seats). **FYI:** Reservations not accepted. Children's menu. No liquor license. **Open:** Sun–Thurs 8am–9pm, Fri–Sat 8am–10pm. **Prices:** Prix fixe $12–$17. AE, DC, DISC, MC, V. ⌧ ⌧

Five Oaks Beef and Seafood

1625 Parkway; tel 423/453-5994. **American.** Located in a green and white building, the Five Oaks offers relaxed fine dining in a country atmosphere. The chef cultivates herbs in his own garden on the grounds for use in his wonderful dishes. Caesar salad is prepared tableside, and cappuccino is available while you wait. Signature dishes include roasted rack of Colorado lamb served with whole grain mustard crust and fresh mint corelaise, and steak Diane with red wine shallot sauce, mushrooms, and parsley. The dessert menu stars mocha mousse cake and double-chocolate cheesecake. **FYI:** Reservations not accepted. Piano. Children's menu. BYO. No smoking. **Open:** Dinner Sun–Thurs 5–9pm, Fri–Sat 4:30–10pm. **Prices:** Main courses $11–$22. AE, CB, DC, DISC, MC, V. ⌧ ⌧ ⌧ ⌧

Josev's Restaurant

130 W Bruce St; tel 423/428-0737. **American.** Named after John Sevier (the first governor of Tennessee), this eatery offers casually elegant dining in a pleasant, unhurried atmosphere. House specialties include blackened chicken with pasta, beef Rossini, Bourbon Street rib eye steak, and fettuccine Alfredo. **FYI:** Reservations recommended. Children's

menu. BYO. **Open:** Lunch daily 11am–3pm; dinner Tues–Sat 4–9:30pm. **Prices:** Main courses $5–$20. AE, CB, DC, DISC, MC, V. ☑ ⅙

ATTRACTION 📷

Forbidden Caverns

455 Blowing Cave Rd; tel 423/453-5972. Originally, these caverns were home to early Native American tribes, who used flint from the caves to make arrowheads. From the 1920s to the 1940s, the cave was popular with moonshiners because of its hidden location and ready supply of water. Guided tours take approximately 55 minutes and feature towering natural chimneys, numerous grottos, and a crystal-clear underground stream, all enhanced by special lighting and stereophonic sound effects. Gift shop and refreshments available. **Open:** Apr–June 15 and Labor Day–Nov, daily 10am–5pm; June 15–Labor Day, daily 9am–6pm. $$$

Shelbyville

This central Tennessee city, situated on the Duck River in a farm and timber area, was one of the country's early planned cities, and many of its 19th-century structures remain. The area is a center for breeding the Tennessee walking horse; many farms and festivals are dedicated to the breed. **Information:** Shelbyville–Bedford County Chamber of Commerce, 100 N Cannon Blvd, Shelbyville, 37160 (tel 615/684-3482).

MOTEL 📷

≣≣ The Shelbyville Inn

317 N Cannon Blvd, 37160; tel 615/684-6050 or toll free 800/622-OINN; fax 615/684-2714. Off US 231. Basic accommodations near downtown Shelbyville. **Rooms:** 76 rms and stes. CI noon/CO noon. Nonsmoking rms avail. **Amenities:** 📷 A/C. **Services:** ✗ 🚐 🛄 🛎 Facilities: 🚹 🗐 ⅙ 1 restaurant, 1 bar (w/entertainment). **Rates:** Peak (May 23–25/Aug 29–Sept 7) $49 S; $55 D; $110 ste. Extra person $6. Children under age 18 stay free. Lower rates off-season. Parking: Outdoor, free. AE, CB, DC, DISC, JCB, MC, V.

ATTRACTION 📷

Tennessee Walking Horse Museum

Whitthorne St; tel 615/684-0314. The Tennessee walking horse, named for its unusual walking gait, is considered the world's premier breed of show horse, and it is here in the rolling hills of middle Tennessee that most of these horses are bred. Through the use of interactive videos, hands-on exhibits, and other displays, this museum presents the history of the breed. **Open:** Mon–Fri 9am–5pm. $

Shiloh

ATTRACTION 📷

Shiloh National Military Park

US 64E and TN 22S; tel 901/689-5275. Site of the first major land battle of the Civil War in April 1862. Northern troops under Gen Ulysses S Grant won out after confused and unusually bloody combat—24,000 men were reported dead, wounded, or missing. Films are shown at the military museum, and visitors can take a self-guided 10-mile automobile tour of the battlefield; stop by the visitors center for information or contact the Superintendent, PO Box 67, Shiloh, TN 38376. **Open:** June–Aug, daily 8am–6pm; Sept–May, daily 8am–5pm. Closed Dec 25. $

Sweetwater

Located 41 miles southwest of Knoxville. Site of the "Lost Sea," listed in the Guinness Book of World Records as the world's largest underground lake.

MOTELS 📷

≣≣ Comfort Inn West

249 US 68, PO Box 48, 37874; tel 423/337-3353 or toll free 800/228-5150. Exit 60 off I-75. Rooms new rooms make this a good choice for an off-the-interstate overnight stopover. **Rooms:** 54 rms. CI 11am/CO 11am. Nonsmoking rms avail. **Amenities:** 📷 🍴 A/C, cable TV w/movies, VCR. Some units w/whirlpools. **Services:** 🛄 🛎 **Facilities:** 🚹 Whirlpool. **Rates (CP):** $34–$65 S; $39–$65 D. Extra person $4. Children under age 18 stay free. Parking: Outdoor, free. AE, CB, DC, DISC, MC, V.

≣≣ Sweetwater Hotel and Convention Center

180 TN 68, 37874; tel 423/337-3511 or toll free 800/523-5727; fax 423/337-3511. Exit 60 off I-75. Oriented toward business clientele. **Rooms:** 135 rms and stes. CI noon/CO noon. Nonsmoking rms avail. Rooms are tastefully decorated. **Amenities:** 📷 A/C, cable TV w/movies. **Services:** ✗ 🚐 🛄 🛎 Airport transportation available with 3–5 day advance notice. **Facilities:** 🚹 🗐 ⅙ 1 restaurant, 1 bar, whirlpool. **Rates:** $36 S or D; $75 ste. Parking: Outdoor, free. AE, CB, DC, DISC, MC, V.

Tiptonville

Located along the New Madrid fault line, this small town just east of the Mississippi River is near unique, 13,000-acre Reelfoot Lake, created by a series of earthquakes in 1811. The lake is a prime watering area for the American bald eagle. **Information:** Reelfoot Area Chamber of Commerce, Rte 1, Box 140B, Tiptonville, 38079 (tel 901/253-8144).

ATTRACTION

Reelfoot Lake State Park

TN 213; tel 901/253-7756. This 280-acre park may be relatively small, but it has a big reputation with fishing aficionados: 25,000-acre Lake Reelfoot, the largest natural lake in the state, is home to crappie, bream, largemouth bass, and 53 other varieties of fish. Year-round camping, summertime scenic boat cruises. If you happen to come in the winter, ask at the visitors center about eagle tours. (A population of bald eagles winters here.) **Open:** Oct–May, daily 8am–sunset; June–Aug, daily 8am–10pm. **Free**

Townsend

A gateway to the Great Smoky Mountains National Park. Nearby Cades Cove is a re-created mountain community featuring log cabins and a gristmill. **Information:** Smoky Mountain Visitors Bureau, 7906 E Lamar Alexander Pkwy, Townsend, 37882 (tel 423/448-6134).

MOTELS

Best Western Valley View Lodge

7726 E Lamar Alexander Pkwy, PO Box 148, 37882-0275; tel 423/448-2237 or toll free 800/292-4844; fax 423/448-9957. On US 321. 15 acres. The exterior of this rather basic motel is a visual delight, with a large variety of flowers and other plants poking up along the walkways. **Rooms:** 94 rms, stes, and effic. CI 3pm/CO 11am. Nonsmoking rms avail. **Amenities:** A/C, cable TV w/movies, refrig. Some units w/terraces, some w/fireplaces, some w/whirlpools. All rooms have microwaves; Valley View Suites have fireplaces and whirlpools. **Services:** **Facilities:** Whirlpool, playground. **Rates (CP):** Peak (June–Oct) $53–$90 S or D; $71–$120 ste; $75 effic. Extra person $5. Children under age 12 stay free. Min stay special events. Lower rates off-season. Parking: Outdoor, free. AE, DC, DISC, MC, V.

Days Inn

7728 E Lamar Alexander Pkwy, PO Box 148, 37882; tel 423/448-9111 or toll free 800/615-9111; fax 423/448-6602. On US 321. A good option for visitors who want to relax and enjoy the quiet side of the Smokies. **Rooms:** 47 rms. CI 3pm/CO 11am. Nonsmoking rms avail. Newer, deluxe rooms have a balcony or terrace overlooking a beautiful garden. **Amenities:** A/C, cable TV w/movies, refrig. Some units w/terraces, 1 w/fireplace. Microwaves are in every room. **Services:** **Facilities:** Whirlpool, playground. Use of a nearby indoor pool available for guests. **Rates (CP):** Peak (June–Oct) $48–$89 S or D. Extra person $5. Children under age 18 stay free. Min stay wknds and special events. Lower rates off-season. Parking: Outdoor, free. AE, DISC, MC, V.

Family Inns of America Townsend

7239 E Lamar Alexander Pkwy, 37882; tel 423/448-9100 or toll free 800/332-8282; fax 423/448-6140. On US 321. A lovely, out of the way motel, with picnic tables by the river. **Rooms:** 39 rms, stes, and effic. CI 2pm/CO 11am. Nonsmoking rms avail. **Amenities:** A/C, cable TV, voice mail. Some units w/fireplaces, some w/whirlpools. **Services:** **Facilities:** **Rates (CP):** Peak (June–Oct) $29–$49 S; $39–$89 D; $109–$129 ste; $49–$99 effic. Extra person $10. Children under age 18 stay free. Lower rates off-season. Parking: Outdoor, free. Holiday packages avail. AE, DC, DISC, MC, V.

Hampton Inn

7824 E Lamar Alexander Pkwy, PO Box 28, 37882; tel 423/448-9000 or toll free 800/257-1932; fax 423/448-9000. On US 321. Well-maintained; built in 1991. The staff works hard to see that guests are taken care of. **Rooms:** 54 rms and stes. CI 3pm/CO 11am. Nonsmoking rms avail. Large suites are the size of two full rooms. **Amenities:** A/C, cable TV w/movies, refrig. Some units w/fireplaces, some w/whirlpools. **Services:** Free local phone calls. **Facilities:** **Rates (CP):** Peak (June–Oct) $68–$83 S or D; $115–$160 ste. Children under age 18 stay free. Lower rates off-season. Parking: Outdoor, free. AE, DC, DISC, MC, V.

RESTAURANTS

Creek Stone Inn

7016 E Lamar Alexander Pkwy; tel 423/448-1215. **American.** Outdoor dining on a fully screened porch is enhanced by the sounds from the nearby creek. For colder days, there's plenty of indoor seating around the fireplace. The menu highlights a variety of classic options: New York strip, catfish, chicken prepared in various ways, and broiled or pan-fried trout. **FYI:** Reservations accepted. Children's menu. BYO. **Open:** Peak (June–Oct) breakfast daily 8am–2pm; lunch daily 11am–9pm; dinner daily 5–9pm. Closed Jan–Mar. **Prices:** Main courses $9–$16. MC, V.

Hearth and Kettle

7767 E Lamar Alexander Pkwy; tel 423/448-6059. Off US 321. **American.** This family-oriented restaurant offers an all-you-can-eat seafood buffet on Fri and Sat nights, and an extensive children's menu at all times. Their specialty is chicken and dumplings. **FYI:** Reservations accepted. Children's menu. BYO. **Open:** Peak (June–Oct) daily 7am–9:30pm. **Prices:** Main courses $8–$18. DISC, MC, V.

Kinzel House

7002 E Lamar Alexander Pkwy; tel 423/448-9075. On US 321. **American.** Kinzel's offers a large menu with dishes ranging from country to gourmet cuisine. Homemade desserts and light-side menu choices are available. An all-you-can-eat buffet is available on Friday nights and Sunday afternoons, with three meats, vegetables, and a dessert bar. **FYI:** Reservations accepted. Children's menu. BYO. **Open:**

Peak (July–Oct) breakfast daily 8–11am; lunch daily 11am–3pm; dinner Sun–Thurs 3–9pm, Fri–Sat 3–10pm. Closed Jan–Mar. **Prices:** Main courses $9–$18. DISC, MC, V.

Timbers
8173 Lamar Alexander Pkwy; tel 423/448-6838. On US 321. **American.** One of the most popular restaurants in town, Timbers offers a prime rib special on Friday nights. The rib eye steak with a Jack Daniel's glaze is highly regarded, as is Timbers famous chicken. Carryout meals for the park are available. **FYI:** Reservations accepted. Children's menu. BYO. **Open:** Peak (May–Oct) breakfast Mon–Sat 7am–noon, Sun 7–11am; lunch daily 11am–4pm; dinner daily 4–10pm. Closed Nov–Feb. **Prices:** Main courses $9–$16. MC, V. 🍴&

Tullahoma

The abundance of limestone springs in the area (which were once thought to be a cure for malaria) make this small town an ideal location for distilling whisky. **Information:** Tullahoma Chamber of Commerce, 135 W Lincoln St, PO Box 1205, Tullahoma, 27288 (tel 615/455-5350).

ATTRACTION 🏛

George Dickel Distillery and Country Store
1950 Cascade Hollow Rd; tel 615/857-3124. Tour the distillery and learn about its history, see how whiskey is made, and then stop in at Miss Annie's General Store (open 8am–3pm Monday–Friday) to shop for souvenirs, gifts, and antiques. However, don't bother looking for bottles of George Dickel's finest for sale: Coffee County is "dry." **Open:** Mon–Fri 9am–3pm. Closed some hols. **Free**

Walland

An arts and crafts center in the heart of the eastern Tennessee mountains.

INN 🛏

UNRATED **The Inn at Blackberry Farm**
1417 W Millers Cove Rd, 37886; tel 423/984-9850; fax 423/983-5708. 2 mi off US 321. 1,100 acres. A luxurious inn with impeccable service and a spectacular mountain view. The grounds include ponds stocked with trout and bass. Perfect for a family stay. Unsuitable for children under 10. **Rooms:** 29 rms; 3 cottages/villas. CI 4pm/CO 1pm. Nonsmoking rms avail. Each room is named for a different type of Tennessee wildflower, and is individually decorated with English or American antiques. Feather mattresses, pillows, and comforters are used in all rooms (but can be removed for guests who are allergic). **Amenities:** 🛁 🍴 A/C, voice mail, bathrobes. No phone or TV. Some units w/terraces, 1 w/fireplace. **Services:** 🔑 VP 🚗 ⛴ 🛎 Twice-daily maid svce, babysitting. Saturday night bonfires. **Facilities:** 🏋 ⚠ 🚲 🎱 45 & Guest lounge

w/TV. **Rates (AP):** Peak (Oct) $275–$395 S; $375–$495 D; $795–$895 cottage/villa. Extra person $100–125. Children under age 6 stay free. Min stay wknds. Lower rates off-season. Parking: Outdoor, free. AE, MC, V.

Wartburg

On the edge of the Cumberland Mountains, this town is the headquarters of Obed Wild and Scenic River. Named for Wartburg, Germany.

ATTRACTION 🏛

Obed Wild and Scenic River National Park
208 N Maiden St; tel 426/346-6294. Few areas in the eastern United States are this rugged and remote. Over the centuries, the Obed and its tributaries have carved deep gorges, with dramatic cliffs rising as high as 500 feet above the water. Huge boulders, once part of the cliff face, now dot the Obed, creating obstacles to the rushing waters. Recreational facilities are purposefully limited, since the goal is to keep the river in as wild and natural a state as possible. There are no designated areas for swimming, hiking, or camping, but there are regions of the park that are traditionally used for those activities. (Those interested can ask at the visitors center in Wartburg; rangers there will also tell you where you can put in your canoe or kayak.)

Obed is one of the best and most difficult white-water rivers in the eastern United States, with ISRD ratings of II to IV. Rock climbers and mountain bikers, too, will find plenty of challenges in the area. **Open:** Park, daily 24 hours; visitor center, Mon–Fri 10am–noon and 2–4 pm, Sat–Sun 8–10am. Closed Dec 25. **Free**

Watts Bar Dam

Built by the Tennessee Valley Authority in 1932, the dam has provided this central Tennessee area with nearly 800 miles worth of shoreline and a host of other recreational opportunities.

RESORT 🏨

🏖 **Watts Bar Resort**
6767 Watts Bar Hwy, 37395; tel 426/365-9595 or toll free 800/365-9598. Off I-75 on TN 68. Quiet and peaceful, with 1950s decor. Well maintained. **Rooms:** 52 cottages/villas. CI 4:30pm/CO 1pm. Different sizes of cottages are available, offering homey accommodations for both large and small families. **Amenities:** A/C, TV. No phone. **Services:** 🛎 🔔 Pets allowed in spring and fall only. **Facilities:** 🏋 ⚠ 🚲 🎱 90 & 1 restaurant (see "Restaurants" below), basketball, playground. Public beach nearby. Table tennis. **Rates:** $30–

$86 cottage/villa. Min stay. Parking: Outdoor, free. Three-day minimum stay required for full kitchen cottages. Closed Nov–Mar. AE, DISC, MC, V.

RESTAURANT

Dining Room
In Watts Bar Resort, Rte 2; tel 423/365-9595. Off I-75. **American.** Large windows forming one corner of this spacious dining room offer excellent views of the lake and nearby dam, while paintings by local artists adorn the walls. The menu changes frequently, but always includes family-style meals of steaks, chicken, pork chops, fish, fried chicken, or roast beef, with fresh vegetables on the side. Homemade desserts. **FYI:** Reservations recommended. Beer and wine only. **Open:** Mon–Sat 7:30am–8:30pm, Sun 7:30am–8pm. Closed Nov–Mar. **Prices:** Main courses $7–$12. AE, DISC, MC, V.

Wildersville

Located in the central part of the state near the Tennessee River, this small town is the site of Natchez Trace State Resort Park.

RESORT

Pin Oak Lodge
567 Pin Oak Lodge Lane, 38388; tel 901/968-8176; fax 901/968-6515. Exit 116 off I-40. 48,000 acres. Simple accommodations in a beautiful, peaceful woodland area. **Rooms:** 20 rms; 18 cottages/villas. CI 2pm/CO 11am. **Amenities:** A/C, TV. Some units w/fireplaces. Cabins equipped with small stoves, refrigerators, and cooking utensils. **Services:** **Facilities:** 1 restaurant, 1 beach (lake shore), basketball, volleyball, games rm, lawn games, playground. Two lakes, an archery range, firing range, and softball. Camping also available. **Rates:** Peak (Mar–Oct) $44 S; $56 D; $50–$60 cottage/villa. Extra person $6. Children under age 16 stay free. Lower rates off-season. Parking: Outdoor, free. Closed Dec 24–Jan 1. AE, DISC, MC, V.

Index

Listings are arranged alphabetically, followed by a code indicating the type of establishment, and then by city, state, and page number. The codes for type of establishment are defined as follows: (H) = Hotel, (M) = Motel, (I) = Inn, (L) = Lodge, (RE) = Resort, (R) = Restaurant, (RS) = Refreshment Stop, (A) = Attraction.

AMERICA ON WHEELS

Frommer's #1

THE COMPLETE GUIDE TO WORRY-FREE TRAVEL ON THE ROAD!

10% OFF TIME & MILEAGE

Terms and Conditions

- Offer includes 10% discount off all time and mileage charges on Cruise America or Cruise Canada vehicles only.

- Offer not available in conjunction with other discount offers or promotional rates.

- Excludes rental charges, deposits, sales tax, amd fuels.

- Normal rental conditions and customer qualification procedures apply.

- Members must reserve through Central Reservations only, at least one week in advance of pick up and mention membership affiliation at time of reservation.

  For reservations, call: 1-800-327-7799 US and Canada

- By acceptance and use of this offer, member agrees to the above conditions.

- Offer expires December 31, 1997.

Save 10%   **Save 10%**

Sleep Comfort Quality Clarion

CHOICE HOTELS
INTERNATIONAL

Rodeway   Econo Lodge   MainStay Suites

Offer expires December 31, 1997.

**Savings are subject to certain restrictions and availability.
Valid for flights on most airlines.**

Minimum Ticket Price	Save
$200.00	$25.00
$250.00	$50.00
$350.00	$75.00
$450.00	$100.00

TRAVEL DISCOUNTERS
DISCOUNTING THE WORLD OF TRAVEL

AMERICA ON WHEELS

Frommer's
1

THE COMPLETE GUIDE TO WORRY-FREE TRAVEL ON THE ROAD!

All reservations must be made by calling our toll free reservation system, Superline. Any reservation requiring a guarantee must be guaranteed with the corporate V.I.P. identification number and the individual traveler's major credit card. If a guaranteed reservation is made and subsequently neither used nor cancelled, the corporate traveler will be billed for the one night's room charge plus tax.

expires December 31, 1997

Terms and Conditions

1. Advance reservations required.
2. Coupon must be presented at check-in.
3. Coupon cannot be combined with any other special offers, discounted rates.
4. Subject to availability.
5. Valid through December 31, 1997.
6. No photo copies allowed.

Travelodge®

For reservations, call **1-800-578-7878** or your travel agent and ask for the 5CPN discount.

A M E R I C A   O N   W H E E L S

Frommer's #1

THE COMPLETE GUIDE TO WORRY-FREE TRAVEL ON THE ROAD!

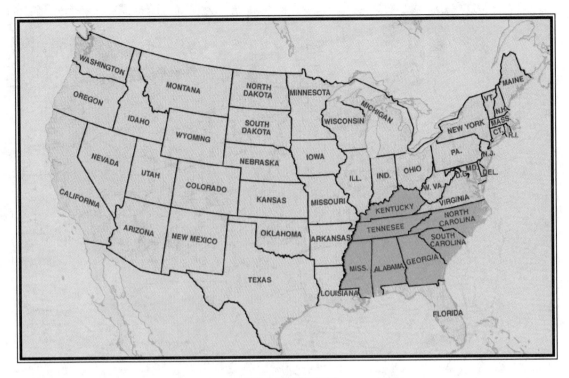

CONTENTS

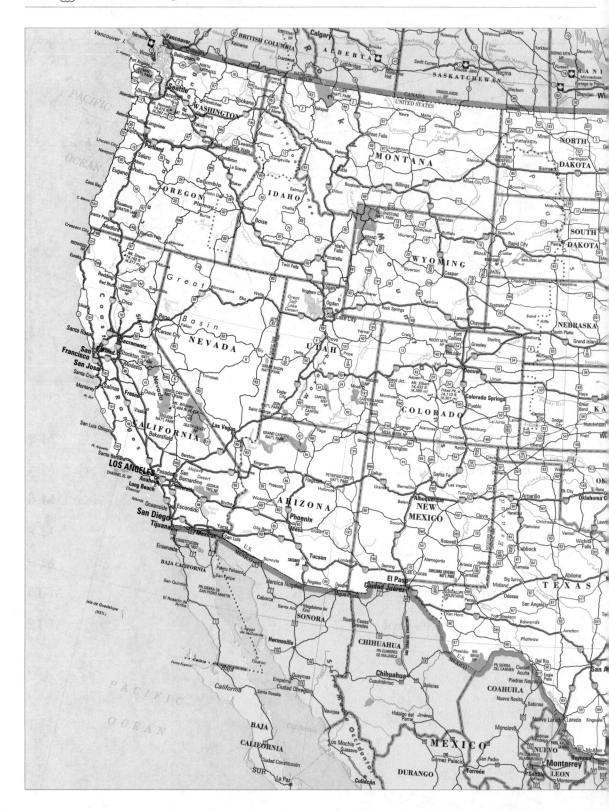

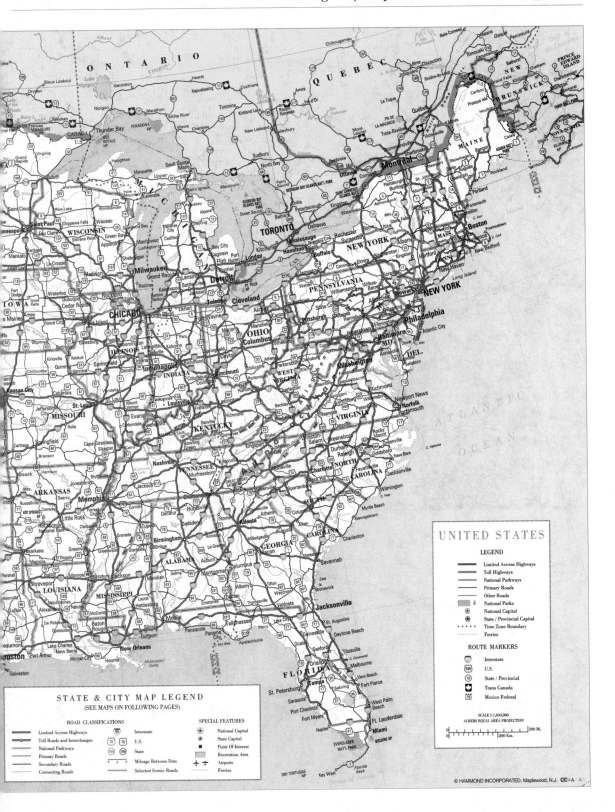

KENTUCKY
TENNESSEE
VA.
Middlesboro
Kingsport Bristol
Johnson City Elizabethton
Morristown
Greeneville
Knoxville
Sevierville
Gatlinburg
GREAT SMOKY MTS.
NAT'L PARK
Clingmans Dome 6,642
Maggie Valley
Cherokee Waynesville
Asheville
Mt. Mitchell 6,684
Black Mtn.
Hickory
Morganton
Bryson City
Sylva
Franklin
Brevard
Hendersonville
Shelby
Gastonia
Cleveland
Chattanooga
Charlotte
Rock Hill
Andrews
Murphy
Cashiers
Greenville
Spartanburg
Gaffney
TENN.
GEORGIA
Dalton
Blairsville
Clayton
Walhalla
Clemson
Anderson
Rome
Dahlonega
Clarkesville
Cornelia
Hartwell
Abbeville
Greenwood
Cartersville
Canton
Gainesville
Commerce
Jefferson
Athens
Augusta
Aiken
Marietta
ATLANTA
Decatur

CHEROKEE NATIONAL FOREST
Sevierville
Cosby
Pigeon Forge
Gatlinburg
PISGAH NAT'L FOR.
Alcoa
Maryville
Walland
Kinzel Springs
Townsend
Mt. Le Conte
Sugarlands Park H.Q.
Elkmont
Mt. Guyot
Mt. Sterling
GREAT SMOKY MOUNTAINS
Charlies Bunion
Cataloochee
Cades Cove
Clingmans Dome
Newfound Gap
Heintooga Overlook
Cove Creek Gap
NATIONAL PARK
Gregory Bald
Smokemont
Balsam Mountain
Oconaluftee Visitor Center
Deep Creek
CHEROKEE IND.
Waynesville
JOYCE KILMER MEM'L FOR.
Fontana Dam
Bryson City
Sylva
NANTAHALA NATIONAL FOREST
Robbinsville
To Franklin
SCALE OF MILES
0 5 10 15
HAMMOND INCORPORATED, Maplewood, N.J.

SOUTH CAROLINA
GEORGIA
Savannah

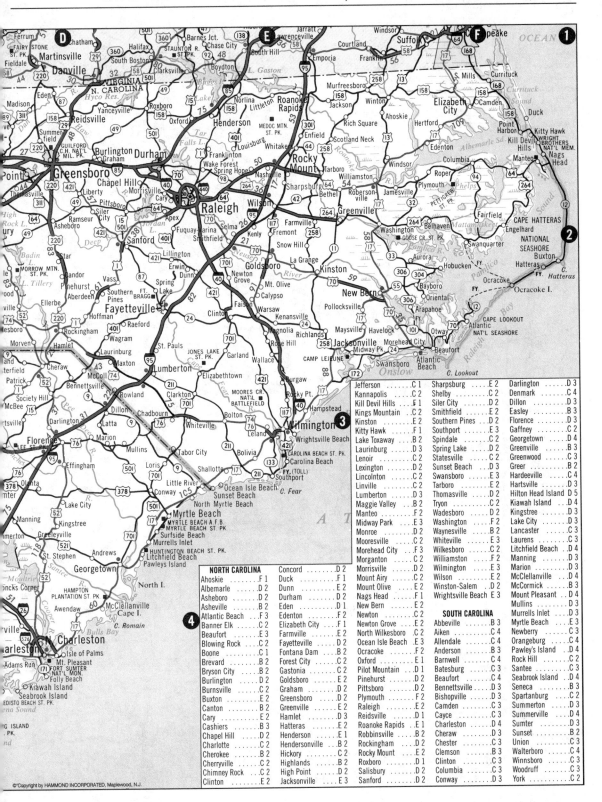

NORTH CAROLINA

Ahoskie	F 1	Concord	D 2	Jefferson	C 1	Sharpsburg
Albemarle	D 2	Duck	F 1	Kannapolis	C 2	Shelby
Asheboro	D 2	Dunn	E 2	Kill Devil Hills	F 1	Siler City
Asheville	B 2	Durham	D 2	Kings Mountain	C 2	Smithfield
Atlantic Beach	F 3	Eden	D 1	Kinston	E 2	Southern Pines
Banner Elk	C 2	Edenton	F 2	Kitty Hawk	F 1	Southport
Beaufort	E 3	Elizabeth City	F 1	Lake Toxaway	B 2	Spindale
Blowing Rock	C 2	Farmville	E 2	Laurinburg	D 3	Spring Lake
Boone	C 1	Fayetteville	D 2	Lenoir	C 2	Statesville
Brevard	B 2	Fontana Dam	B 2	Lexington	D 2	Sunset Beach
Bryson City	B 2	Forest City	C 2	Lincolnton	C 2	Swansboro
Burlington	D 2	Gastonia	C 2	Linville	C 2	Tarboro
Burnsville	C 2	Goldsboro	E 2	Lumberton	D 3	Thomasville
Buxton	E 2	Graham	D 2	Maggie Valley	B 2	Tryon
Canton	B 2	Greensboro	D 2	Manteo	F 2	Wadesboro
Cary	E 2	Greenville	E 2	Midway Park	E 3	Washington
Cashiers	B 3	Hamlet	D 3	Monroe	D 2	Waynesville
Chapel Hill	D 2	Hatteras	E 2	Mooresville	C 2	Whiteville
Charlotte	C 2	Henderson	E 1	Morehead City	F 3	Wilkesboro
Cherokee	B 2	Hendersonville	B 2	Morganton	C 2	Williamston
Cherryville	C 2	Hickory	C 2	Morrisville	D 2	Wilmington
Chimney Rock	B 2	Highlands	B 2	Mount Airy	C 1	Wilson
Clinton	E 2	High Point	D 2	Mount Olive	E 2	Winston-Salem
		Jacksonville	E 3	Nags Head	F 1	Wrightsville Beach
				New Bern	E 2	
				Newton	C 2	
				Newton Grove	E 2	
				North Wilkesboro	C 2	
				Ocean Isle Beach	E 3	
				Ocracoke	F 2	
				Oxford	E 1	
				Pilot Mountain	D 1	
				Pinehurst	D 2	
				Pittsboro	D 2	
				Plymouth	F 2	
				Raleigh	E 2	
				Reidsville	D 1	
				Roanoke Rapids	E 1	
				Robbinsville	B 2	
				Rockingham	D 2	
				Rocky Mount	E 2	
				Roxboro	D 1	
				Salisbury	D 2	
				Sanford	D 2	

Sharpsburg .... E 2
Shelby .... C 2
Siler City .... D 2
Smithfield .... E 2
Southern Pines .. D 2
Southport .... E 3
Spindale .... C 2
Spring Lake .... D 2
Statesville .... C 2
Sunset Beach .. D 3
Swansboro .... E 3
Tarboro .... E 2
Thomasville .... D 2
Tryon .... C 2
Wadesboro .... D 2
Washington .... F 2
Waynesville .... B 2
Whiteville .... E 3
Wilkesboro .... C 2
Williamston .... F 2
Wilmington .... E 3
Wilson .... E 2
Winston-Salem .. D 2
Wrightsville Beach E 3

SOUTH CAROLINA

Abbeville .... B 3
Aiken .... C 4
Allendale .... C 4
Anderson .... B 3
Barnwell .... C 4
Batesburg .... C 3
Beaufort .... C 4
Bennettsville .. D 3
Bishopville .... D 3
Camden .... C 3
Cayce .... C 3
Charleston .... D 4
Cheraw .... C 3
Chester .... C 3
Clemson .... B 3
Clinton .... C 3
Columbia .... C 3
Conway .... D 3

Darlington .... D 3
Denmark .... C 4
Dillon .... D 3
Easley .... B 3
Florence .... D 3
Gaffney .... C 2
Georgetown .... D 4
Greenville .... B 3
Greenwood .... C 3
Greer .... B 2
Hardeeville .... C 4
Hartsville .... D 3
Hilton Head Island D 5
Kiawah Island .. D 4
Kingstree .... D 3
Lake City .... D 3
Lancaster .... C 3
Laurens .... C 3
Litchfield Beach .. D 4
Manning .... D 3
Marion .... D 3
McClellanville .. D 4
McCormick .... B 3
Mount Pleasant .. D 4
Mullins .... D 3
Murrells Inlet .... D 3
Myrtle Beach .... E 3
Newberry .... C 3
Orangeburg .... C 4
Pawley's Island .. D 4
Rock Hill .... C 2
Santee .... C 3
Seabrook Island .. D 4
Seneca .... B 3
Spartanburg .... B 3
Summerton .... D 3
Summerville .... D 4
Sumter .... D 3
Sunset .... B 2
Union .... C 3
Walterboro .... C 4
Winnsboro .... C 3
Woodruff .... C 3
York .... C 2

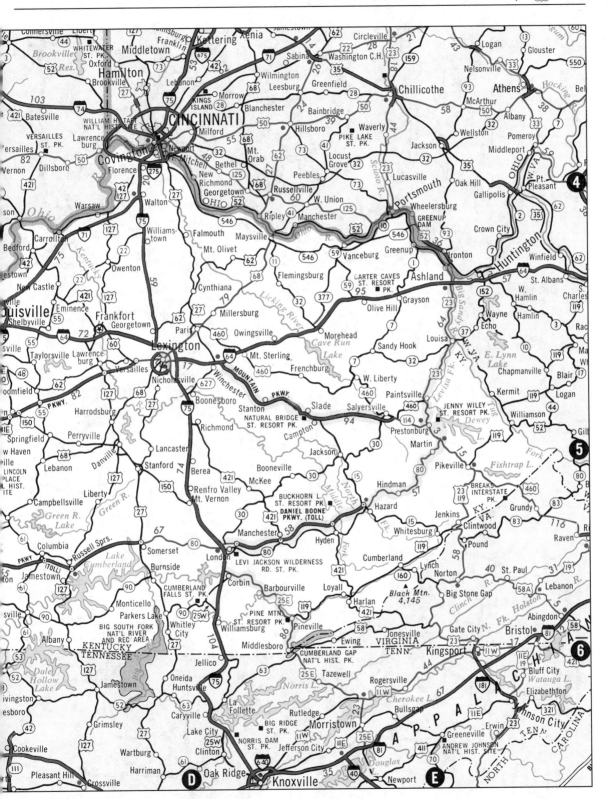

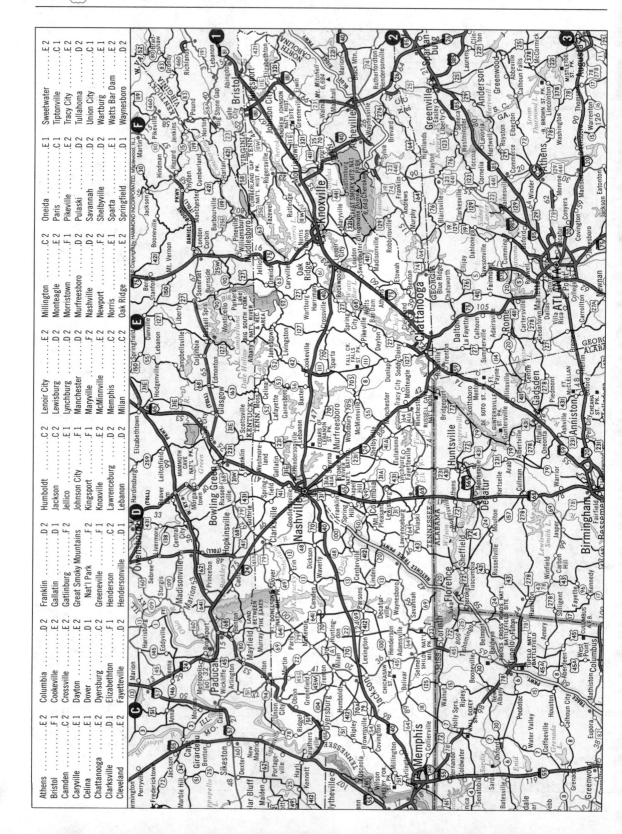

Adel	B 5	Atlanta	A 3	Brunswick	C 5	Douglas	B 5	Marietta	A 3
Albany	A 5	Augusta	C 4	Buford	B 3	Douglasville	A 3	Milledgeville	B 4
Alma	B 5	Bainbridge	A 5	Cairo	A 6	Dublin	B 4	Monroe	B 3
Americus	A 5	Barnesville	A 4	Calhoun	A 3	East Point	A 3	Montezuma	A 4
Andersonville	A 4	Baxley	B 5	Camilla	A 5	Eastman	B 5	Moultrie	B 5
Arco	C 5	Blakely	A 5	Carrollton	A 3	Eatonton	B 4	Nashville	B 5
Athens	B 3	Braselton	B 3	Cartersville	A 3	Elberton	B 3	Newnan	A 4
				Cedartown	A 3	Fitzgerald	B 5	Ocilla	B 5
				Chatsworth	A 3	Forest Park	A 3	Pelham	A 5
				Clarkesville	B 3	Forsyth	B 4	Perry	B 4
				Cochran	B 4	Fort Valley	A 4	Pine Mountain	A 4
				College Park	A 3	Gainesville	B 3	Plains	A 5
				Columbus	A 4	Garden City	C 5	Quitman	B 6
				Commerce	B 3	Greensboro	B 3	Rockmart	A 3
				Conyers	B 3	Griffin	A 4	Rome	A 3
				Cordele	B 5	Hamilton	A 4	Rossville	A 2
				Covington	B 3	Hartwell	B 3	Roswell	A 3
				Cuthbert	A 5	Hawkinsville	B 4	Saint Mary's	C 5
				Dahlonega	B 3	Hazlehurst	B 5	Saint Simons Island	C 5
				Dalton	A 3	Helen	B 3	Savannah	C 5
				Dawson	A 5	Hiawassee	B 2	Sea Island	C 5
				Decatur	A 3	Hogansville	A 4	Smyrna	A 3
				Donalsonville	A 5	Jekyll Island	C 5	Social Circle	B 3
						Jesup	C 5	Statesboro	C 4
						Kennesaw	A 3	Summerville	A 3
						LaFayette	A 3	Swainsboro	B 4
						LaGrange	A 4	Sylvania	C 4
						Lawrenceville	B 3	Sylvester	B 5
						Lincolnton	B 3	Thomaston	A 4
						Lumpkin	A 5	Thomasville	A 6
						Macon	B 4	Thomson	B 4
						Madison	B 3	Tifton	B 5
						Manchester	A 4	Toccoa	B 3
								Tybee Island	C 5
								Valdosta	B 6
								Vidalia	B 5
								Warm Springs	A 4
								Warner Robins	B 4
								Washington	B 3
								Watkinsville	B 3
								Waycross	B 5
								Waynesboro	C 4
								West Point	A 4
								Winder	B 3

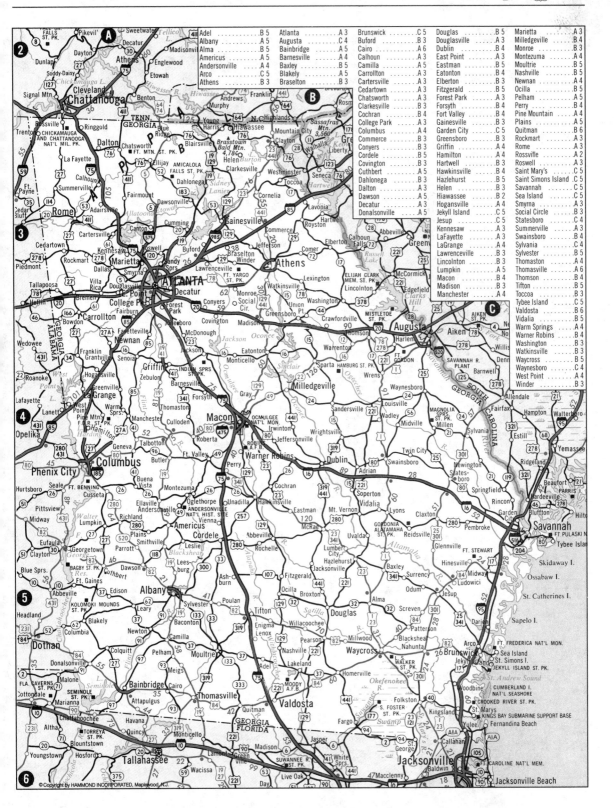

© Copyright by HAMMOND INCORPORATED, Maplewood, N.J.

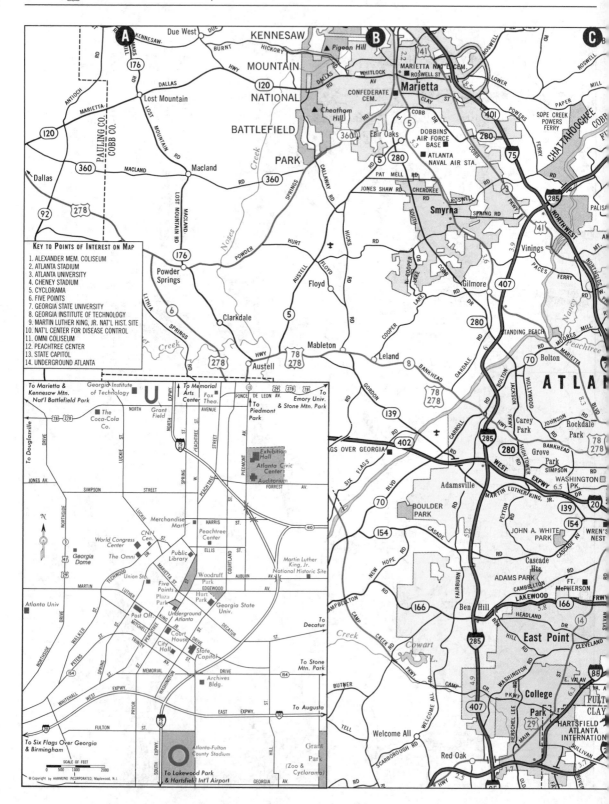

Key to Points of Interest on Map

1. ALEXANDER MEM. COLISEUM
2. ATLANTA STADIUM
3. ATLANTA UNIVERSITY
4. CHENEY STADIUM
5. CYCLORAMA
6. FIVE POINTS
7. GEORGIA STATE UNIVERSITY
8. GEORGIA INSTITUTE OF TECHNOLOGY
9. MARTIN LUTHER KING, JR. NAT'L HIST. SITE
10. NAT'L CENTER FOR DISEASE CONTROL
11. OMNI COLISEUM
12. PEACHTREE CENTER
13. STATE CAPITOL
14. UNDERGROUND ATLANTA

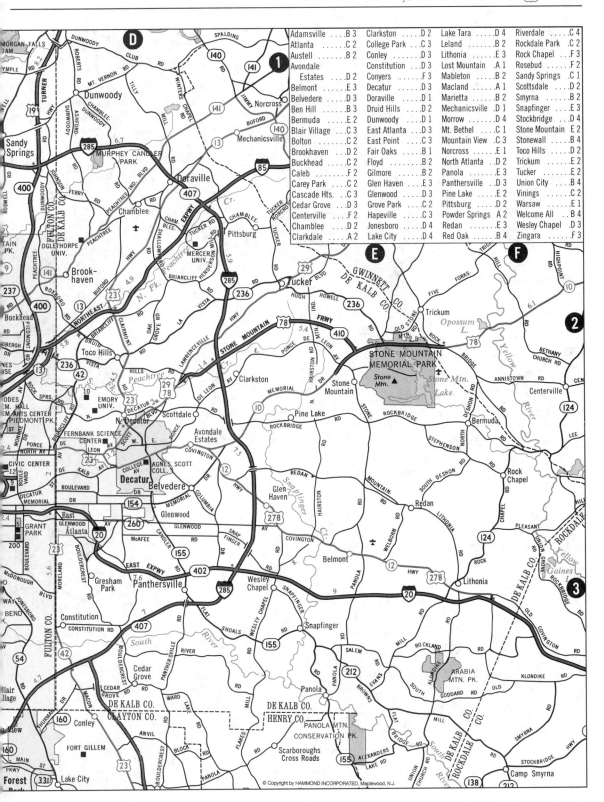

Adamsville	B 3	Clarkston	D 2	Lake Tara	D 4	Riverdale	C 4
Atlanta	C 2	College Park	C 3	Leland	B 2	Rockdale Park	C 2
Austell	B 2	Conley	D 3	Lithonia	E 3	Rock Chapel	F 3
Avondale		Constitution	D 3	Lost Mountain	A 1	Rosebud	F 2
Estates	D 2	Conyers	F 3	Mableton	B 2	Sandy Springs	C 1
Belmont	E 3	Decatur	D 3	Macland	A 1	Scottsdale	D 2
Belvedere	D 3	Doraville	D 1	Marietta	B 2	Smyrna	B 2
Ben Hill	B 3	Druid Hills	D 2	Mechanicsville	D 1	Snapfinger	E 3
Bermuda	E 2	Dunwoody	D 1	Morrow	D 4	Stockbridge	D 4
Blair Village	C 3	East Atlanta	D 3	Mt. Bethel	B 1	Stone Mountain	E 2
Bolton	C 2	East Point	C 3	Mountain View	C 3	Stonewall	B 4
Brookhaven	D 2	Fair Oaks	B 1	Norcross	E 1	Toco Hills	D 2
Buckhead	C 2	Floyd	B 2	North Atlanta	D 2	Trickum	E 2
Caleb	F 2	Gilmore	B 2	Panola	E 3	Tucker	E 2
Carey Park	C 2	Glen Haven	E 3	Panthersville	D 3	Union City	B 4
Cascade Hts.	C 3	Glenwood	D 3	Pine Lake	E 2	Vinings	C 2
Cedar Grove	D 3	Grove Park	C 2	Pittsburg	D 2	Warsaw	E 1
Centerville	F 2	Hapeville	C 3	Powder Springs	A 2	Welcome All	B 4
Chamblee	D 2	Jonesboro	D 4	Redan	E 3	Wesley Chapel	D 3
Clarkdale	A 2	Lake City	D 4	Red Oak	B 4	Zingara	F 3

© Copyright by HAMMOND INCORPORATED, Maplewood, N.J.

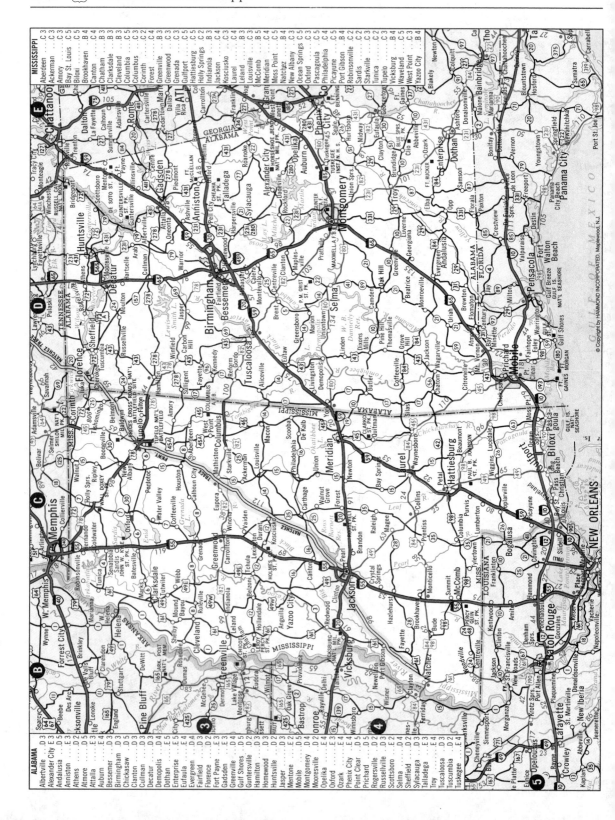